Committee on Health Insurance begins campaign to allow payment of clinical psychologists' services by health insurance plans without requiring medical supervision.

1969 California School of Professional Psychology founded.

APA begins publication of the journal, *Professiona[l]*

1970 Department
program au
psychologist
referral.

Classes begi
fessional Ps
dent clinical
in the Unite[d]

1971 Council for
logical Profe
advocacy gr
organized.

Journal of
published.

1972 Menninger
Education in

1973 Vail, Colorad

1974 National Re
viders in Psy

Federal gov
clinical psyc
ployees witl
referral.

APA establis
of Psycholog
First Inter-A
Psychology l

1977 All fifty U.S
licensing law

1980 Third editior
Smith, Glass,
fits of Psych[o]
Blue Shield h
Virginia succ
pay for clinical psychologists' services to people covered by their plans.

1981 APA publishes its revised *Ethical Principles of Psychologists*.

1983 Joint Commission for the Accreditation of Hospitals allows clinical psychologists to become members of hospital medical staffs.

1987 *DSM-III-R* published.
Conference on graduate education in psychology, Salt Lake City, Utah.

1988 American Psychological Society formed.

ht of
enu
ental

or a

Lt.
com-
1 at
com-
d to

ran-
pen-
oital

nce

ists
psy-
nts

resi-
han

ges
sts.

on

in
hat
to
in

2008 The U.S. House of Representatives passes legislation requiring mental health parity: *The Paul Wellstone Mental Health and Addiction Equity Act of 2007*.

Introduction to Clinical Psychology

SEVENTH EDITION

GEOFFREY P. KRAMER

West Shore Community College

DOUGLAS A. BERNSTEIN

University of South Florida

VICKY PHARES

University of South Florida

PEARSON

Prentice
Hall

Upper Saddle River, NJ 07458

Library of Congress Cataloging-in-Publication Data

Kramer, Geoffrey P.
  Introduction to clinical psychology / Geoffrey P. Kramer, Douglas A. Bernstein, Vicky Phares.—7th ed.
    p. cm.
  Includes bibliographical references and index.
  ISBN 0-13-172967-5 (alk. paper)
  1. Clinical psychology.   I. Bernstein, Douglas A.   II. Phares, Vicky.   III. Title.
  RC467.N54 2009
  616.89—dc22   2008015142

VP Editorial Director: Leah Jewell
Executive Editor: Jeff Marshall
Editorial Assistant: Aaron Talwar
Associate Managing Editor: Maureen Richardson
Production Liaison: Shelly Kupperman
Senior Operations Supervisor: Sherry Lewis
Director of Marketing: Brandy Dawson
Senior Marketing Manager: Kate Mitchell
Marketing Assistant: Jennifer Lang
AV Project Manager: Maria Piper
Associate Supplements Editor: Virginia Livsey
Director, Cover: Jayne Conte
Director, Image Resource Center: Melinda Patelli

Manager, Rights and Permissions: Zina Arabia
Manager, Visual Research: Beth Brenzel
Image Permissions Coordinator: Vickie Menanteaux
Manager, Cover Visual Research and Permissions:
  Karen Sanatar
Cover Researcher: Rita Wenning
Director, Cover Design: Jayne Conte
Cover Designer: Suzanne Behnke
Composition and Full-Service Project Management:
  TexTech International/Satishna Gokuldas
Printer/Binder: R.R. Donnelley & Sons
Cover Printer: R.R. Donnelley & Sons
Cover Image: Flickr Photos/Harold Davis

Credits and acknowledgments borrowed from other sources and reproduced, with permission, in this textbook appear on the appropriate page within text.

Pearson Education LTD., London
Pearson Education Singapore, Pte. Ltd
Pearson Education, Canada, Inc.
Pearson Education—Japan
Pearson Education Australia PTY, Limited

Pearson Education North Asia Ltd., Hong Kong
Pearson Educación de Mexico, S.A. de C.V.
Pearson Education Malaysia, Pte. Ltd.
Pearson Education, Upper Saddle River, New Jersey

PEARSON
Prentice
Hall

10 9 8 7 6 5 4 3 2 1

ISBN-13: 978-0-13-172967-4
ISBN-10:   0-13-172967-5

Contents

Preface   xi

Acknowledgments   xii

SECTION I: BASIC CONCEPTS

CHAPTER 1
What Is Clinical Psychology?   1

An Overview of Clinical Psychology   2

Clinical Psychologists at Work   10

Clinical Psychology in the 21st Century   22

Chapter Summary   28

CHAPTER 2
Clinical Psychology's Past and Present   30

The Roots of Clinical Psychology   30

Clinical Psychology Begins to Grow   42

The Major Approaches Develop   49

The Pros and Cons of Taking a Specific Approach   67

Clinical Psychology Today   69

Chapter Summary   70

SECTION II: ASSESSMENT

CHAPTER 3
Basic Features of Clinical Assessment 72

An Outline of the Assessment Process 73
The Goals of Clinical Assessment 78
Clinical Judgment and Decision Making 91
Other Factors Affecting Assessment Choices 100
Communicating Assessment Results 107
Ethical Considerations in Assessment 110
Chapter Summary 113

CHAPTER 4
Interviewing and Observation in Clinical Psychology 116

Clinical Interview Situations 117
Interview Structure 122
Stages in the Interview 129
Research on the Interview 138
Observational Assessment: Goals and Benefits 142
Observational Assessment: Approaches 144
Research on Observational Assessment 153
Chapter Summary 158

CHAPTER 5
Testing in Clinical Psychology 160

Basic Concepts in Psychological Testing 161
Tests of Intellectual Functioning 173
Tests of Attitudes, Interests, Preferences, and Values 182
Tests of Psychopathology and Personality 183
The Current Status of Psychological Testing 198
The Future of Psychological Testing 200
Chapter Summary 201

SECTION III: CLINICAL INTERVENTIONS

CHAPTER 6
Basic Features of Clinical Interventions   204

Overview of Clinical Interventions   204
The Participants in Psychotherapy   207
The Goals of Clinical Interventions   217
Ethical Guidelines for Clinical Interventions   221
Some Practical Aspects of Clinical Intervention   225
Chapter Summary   230

CHAPTER 7
Psychodynamic and Humanistic Psychotherapies   232

Psychoanalysis   232
Psychodynamic Psychotherapy   245
Humanistic Psychotherapy   252
Other Humanistic Approaches   262
Chapter Summary   267

CHAPTER 8
Behavioral and Cognitive-Behavioral Psychotherapies   269

Behavior Therapy   269
Cognitive Therapy   282
Cognitive-Behavior Therapy   292
The Current Status of Cognitive-Behavior Therapy   299
Chapter Summary   300

CHAPTER 9
Alternative Modes of Clinical Intervention   302

Group Therapy   302
Couples and Family Therapy   306
Community Psychology   315

Prevention   318

Self-Help   320

Really Alternative Approaches   323

Technological Innovations Influencing Psychological Treatment   325

Psychotherapy Integration   327

Chapter Summary   329

CHAPTER 10
Research on Clinical Intervention   331

Methods for Evaluating Psychotherapy   332

Practical Problems in Therapy Research   337

Effectiveness of Individual Psychological Treatments   341

Effectiveness of Alternative Modes of Intervention   352

Chapter Summary   355

SECTION IV: SOME CLINICAL SPECIALTIES

CHAPTER 11
Clinical Child Psychology   358

A Brief History of Clinical Child Psychology   359

Characteristics Unique to Clinical Child Psychology   362

Clinical Assessment of Children   371

Specific Childhood Disorders   377

Treatment and Prevention of Childhood Disorders   385

The Future of Clinical Child Psychology   392

Chapter Summary   394

CHAPTER 12
Health Psychology   397

What Is Health Psychology?   397

Risk Factors for Illness   406

Illness Prevention and Treatment Programs   410

A Health Psychology Case Example   414
Improving Adherence to Medical Treatment Regimens   416
Chapter Summary   418

CHAPTER 13
Clinical Neuropsychology   **421**

A Brief History of Neuropsychology   423
Basic Principles of Neuropsychology   426
Patterns of Neuropsychological Dysfunction   431
Neuropsychological Assessment   437
Neuropsychological Approaches to Psychopathology   440
The Current Status of Clinical Neuropsychology   444
Chapter Summary   445

CHAPTER 14
Forensic Psychology   **447**

The Scope of Forensic Psychology   448
Criminal Competence and Responsibility   449
Predicting Dangerousness   458
Assessing Psychological Status in Civil Trials   459
Psychological Autopsies and Criminal Profiling   462
Child Custody and Parental Fitness   465
Mental Health Experts in the Legal System   469
Chapter Summary   472

SECTION V: THE FUTURE OF CLINICAL PSYCHOLOGY AND YOUR POSSIBLE PLACE IN IT

CHAPTER 15
Professional Issues in Clinical Psychology   **475**

Professional Training   476
Professional Regulation   485
Professional Ethics   489

Professional Independence   498

Professional Multicultural Competence   504

The Future of Clinical Psychology   507

Chapter Summary   510

CHAPTER 16
Getting into Graduate School in Clinical Psychology   512

What Types of Graduate Programs Will Help Me Meet My Career Goals?   512

Am I Ready to Make the Commitment Required in Doctoral Programs
at This Time in My Life?   517

Are My Credentials Strong Enough for Graduate School in Clinical Psychology?   521

Given My Credentials, to What Type of Program Can I Realistically Aspire?   524

I Have Decided to Apply to Graduate School in Clinical Psychology.
What Should I Do First?   525

Should I Apply to a Master's Degree Program and Complete It Before I Apply
to a Doctoral Program?   526

If I Choose to Terminate My Training After Earning a Master's Degree, Will My
Opportunities for Doing Clinical Work Be Limited?   526

Application Procedures   527

Other Important Questions   546

Chapter Summary   548

References   551

Author Index   629

Subject Index   645

Preface

In the six previous editions of this book, we tried to accomplish three goals. First, we wanted a book that, while appropriate for graduate students, was written especially with sophisticated undergraduates in mind. Many undergraduate psychology majors express an interest in clinical psychology without having a clear understanding of what the field involves and requires. An even larger number of nonmajors also wish to know more about clinical psychology. We felt that both groups would benefit from a thorough survey of the field which does not go into all the details typically found in graduate study only texts.

Second, we wanted to present a scholarly portrayal of the history of clinical psychology, its scope, functions, and future that reviewed a full range of theoretical perspectives. For this reason, we have not allowed our preference for cognitive-behavioral theories to limit our presentation. Instead, we present psychodynamic, relational, humanistic/phenomenological, systems, group, and biological perspectives as well, and we have sought to do so in as neutral a manner as possible. We do champion the empirical research tradition of clinical psychology throughout the book because we believe it is a necessary and useful perspective for all clinicians to follow, regardless of their theoretical orientation.

Third, we wanted our book to be interesting and enjoyable to read. Because we like being clinical psychologists and because we enjoy teaching, we tried to create a book that communicates our enthusiasm for its content.

Though we are still guided by the above goals, we sought to make some significant changes in the seventh edition. For one thing, we emphasized clinical applications and decision-making much more than in the previous edition. To do so, we have included numerous case examples and scenarios in this edition. Because many of these examples present problems that have no easy answer, we have also emphasized ethical principles and professional codes of conduct that are critical for decision-making in clinical practice. We have also greatly expanded, through case examples and text discussion, our treatment of multicultural issues and multicultural competence in clinical psychology.

A second change was to expand the pedagogical features of the text. Each chapter, and each major section within each chapter, begins with a brief preview of the material to come. At the end of each section and at the end of each chapter is a summary of key facts and ideas. We have also included study questions at the end of each chapter. These questions can be used to orient students to the material within a chapter, as discussion questions in class, or as test questions. Another pedagogical feature is the significant increase in the number of tables, figures, and other displays. Not only do these features help add variety to the text, they also portray information in multiple ways, helping students learn through multiple modalities.

The chapter organization of the seventh edition is similar to that of the sixth, but there are changes here, too. We have significantly expanded the psychotherapy section by adding a complete chapter on behavioral and cognitive-behavioral therapy. So there is now an introductory chapter on basic features of clinical interventions (Chapter 6), as well as chapters on psychodynamic and humanistic psychotherapies (Chapter 7), behavioral and cognitive-behavioral psychotherapies (Chapter 8), alternative modes of psychotherapy (group, couples, family, systems, prevention, self-help, and the like; Chapter 9), and research on clinical intervention (Chapter 10). Specialty areas (e.g., clinical child psychology, health psychology, neuropsychology, forensic psychology) are still included, as is the chapter on professional issues. The ever-popular (getting into graduate school section, formerly an appendix, is now a full-fledged chapter.

The field of clinical psychology is changing rapidly. Accordingly, we have undertaken a comprehensive updating of research and other material in all chapters, reflected in hundreds of new references. Because information in the field changes daily, we have provided multiple Web sites at the end of each chapter so that students can check on the latest developments. Also, since our last edition, numerous changes have occurred in the health care delivery system, both in the United States and internationally. We have addressed these changes in some detail, including how managed care has continued to influence research and practice in clinical psychology. Finally, we have significantly expanded our coverage of multiculturalism in clinical psychology, a topic once regarded as being on the horizon, but now an essential component of clinical psychology training and practice. You will find discussion of diversity and multicultural concerns in virtually every chapter.

ACKNOWLEDGMENTS

We want to thank several people for their valuable contributions to this book. We wish to express our appreciation to Catherine Stoney for her help in updating the health psychology chapter, Joel Shenker for his help in updating the neuropsychology chapter, and to Elaine Cassel for her expertise in helping to update the chapter on forensic psychology. We would also like to thank Rachel Kramer for her comments on several chapter drafts and the Bills (White and Mueller) at the Mason-Lake Intermediate School District for their assistance with assessment materials.

Countless undergraduate and graduate students asked the questions, raised the issues, and argued the opposing positions that have found their way into the text; they are really the people who stimulated the creation of this book, and who continue to make us want to revise and update its content. We thank them all. We would also like to thank Jeff Marshall, our editor, at Pearson Prentice Hall for his help and patience in guiding the creation of this latest edition. Thanks also go to Satishna Gokuldas and the staff at TexTech International for professionally managing the production process. We are grateful to all those reviewers who provided their valuable input: Joel M. Martin, Butler University; Dorothy Mercer, Eastern Kentucky University; B. Jean Mandernach, University of Nebraska at Keamey; and John P. Garofalo, Washington State University at Vancouver.

Finally, we thank our families, loved ones, and friends for their support throughout this project. Your infinite patience and kind encouragement is a debt we can never repay.

GEOFFREY P. KRAMER

DOUGLAS A. BERNSTEIN

VICKY PHARES

CHAPTER 1
What Is Clinical Psychology?

Chapter Preview: In this chapter we introduce the field of clinical psychology. We first outline the requirements for becoming a clinical psychologist and discuss the profession's popularity. Next we describe how clinical psychology relates to other mental health professions. We describe the work activities of most clinical psychologists and the rewards of the profession, financial and otherwise. Finally, we introduce some of the key issues shaping the field today. These issues include how to (a) strike a balance between science and practice, (b) train new clinicians, (c) combine divergent theoretical approaches, and (d) adapt clinical practice to a changing health care environment.

A CLINICAL CASE

Bonnie, a 15-year-old European American girl in 9th grade, asked her parents to get her some help to deal with her fear and anxiety. They did so, and as part of the intake evaluation at her first appointment, Bonnie was interviewed by a clinical psychologist specializing in treatment of childhood anxiety disorders. At the beginning of the interview, Bonnie said her problem was that she would "get nervous about everything," particularly about things at school and doing anything new. When asked to give an example, Bonnie mentioned that her father wanted her to go to camp during the coming summer, but she did not want to because of her "nerves." It soon became clear that Bonnie's anxiety stemmed from a persistent fear of social situations in which she might be the focus of other people's attention. She said she felt very self-conscious in the local mall and constantly worried about what others might be thinking of her. She was also fearful of eating in public, using public restrooms, being in crowded places, and meeting new people. She almost always tried to avoid such situations. She experienced anxiety when talking to her teachers and was even more afraid of talking to store clerks and other unfamiliar adults. Bonnie would not even answer the telephone in her own home.

In most of these situations, Bonnie said that her fear and avoidance related to worry about possibly saying the wrong thing or not knowing what to say or do, which would lead others to think badly of her. Quite often, her fear in these situations became so intense that she experienced a full-blown panic attack, complete with rapid heart rate, chest pain, shortness of breath, hot flashes, sweating, trembling, dizziness, and difficulty swallowing.

To get a clearer picture of the nature of Bonnie's difficulties, the psychologist conducted a separate interview with Bonnie's parents. While confirming what their daughter had said, they reported that Bonnie's social anxiety was even more severe than she had described it (Based on Brown & Barlow, 2001, pp. 37–38.)

How can we best understand Bonnie's fears and anxieties? How did her problems develop, and what can be done to help her overcome them? These questions are important to Bonnie, her loved ones, and anyone interested in her condition, but they are especially important to clinical psychologists.

In this book you will learn how clinical psychologists address problems such as those faced by Bonnie. You will learn how clinicians assess and treat persons with psychological problems, how they conduct research into the causes and treatments for psychological disorders, and how they are trained. You will learn how clinical psychologists have become key providers of health care in the United States and in other countries, and how clinical psychology continues to evolve and adapt to the social, political, and cultural climate in which it is practiced.

AN OVERVIEW OF CLINICAL PSYCHOLOGY

Section Preview: Here we define clinical psychology and identify the essential requirements satisfied by its practitioners. We also discuss the continued appeal of clinical psychology, popular conceptions of clinical psychologists, and how clinical psychology overlaps with, and differs from, other mental health professions.

As its name implies, clinical psychology is a subfield of the larger discipline of psychology. Like all psychologists, clinical psychologists are interested in *behavior and mental processes*. Like some other psychologists, clinical psychologists generate research about human behavior, seek to apply the results of that research, and engage in individual assessment. Like the members of some other professions, clinical psychologists provide assistance to those who need help with psychological problems. It is difficult to capture in a sentence or two the ever-expanding scope and shifting directions of clinical psychology. Nevertheless, we can outline the central features of the discipline as well as its many variations.

Definition of Clinical Psychology

The "official" definition of clinical psychology adopted in 1991 by the American Psychological Association's Division of Clinical Psychology reads as follows: "The field of

Clinical Psychology involves research, teaching, and services relevant to the applications of principles, methods, and procedures for understanding, predicting, and alleviating intellectual, emotional, biological, psychological, social and behavioral maladjustment, disability and discomfort, applied to a wide range of client populations" (Resnick, 1991). A similar definition has been adopted by the Section on Clinical Psychology of the Canadian Psychological Association (Vallis & Howes, 1995).

The definition highlights *activities* in which clinical psychologists engage: research, teaching, consultation, assessment, treatment, and administration. It also highlights the overall *purpose* of engaging in those activities: to help alleviate and prevent psychological distress and dysfunction and to promote healthy physical, intellectual, emotional, and social development in persons of all ages. But there is much more to being a clinical psychologist than engaging in these activities and seeking these goals.

Personal Requirements to Be a Clinical Psychologist

Certain requirements for those wishing to be clinical psychologists have more to do with attitudes and character than with training and credentialing. Perhaps the most notable distinguishing feature of clinical psychologists has been called the *clinical attitude* or the *clinical approach* (Korchin, 1976), the tendency to combine knowledge from research on human behavior and mental processes with efforts at individual assessment in order to understand and help a particular person. The clinical attitude sets clinicians apart from other psychologists who search for general principles that apply to human behavior problems in general. Clinical psychologists are interested in research of this kind, but they also want to know how general principles shape lives, problems, and treatments on an individual level.

Because clinical psychology is both rigorously scientific and deeply personal, it requires that persons entering the field have a strong and compassionate interest in human beings. Directors of clinical training programs, the persons who make decisions about which applicants to admit to graduate study in clinical psychology, look for a number of characteristics in program applicants. Among them are an interest in people, honesty and integrity in dealing with others, and emotional stability (Johnson & Campbell, 2004). These traits are important in many jobs, but they are crucial in clinical psychology because clinicians regularly work in situations that can have significant and lasting personal and interpersonal consequences. Even those clinical researchers who don't themselves offer psychotherapy may still make decisions about matters of personal consequence to participants, so integrity, emotional stability, and sound judgment are required for them, too.

The potential impact that clinical psychologists can have helps explain why, when considering candidates for admission to graduate training in clinical psychology, many psychology departments tend to rank letters of recommendations, personal statements, and interviews as slightly more important than more standardized academic indicators such as grade point averages or Graduate Record Exam (GRE) scores (Norcross, Kohout, & Wicherski, 2005). Nevertheless, as noted in Chapter 16, "Getting into Graduate School in Clinical Psychology," those standardized academic admission requirements for clinical psychology programs are typically quite high.

Legal, Educational, and Ethical Requirements to Be a Clinical Psychologist

As one of the *core health care professions,* clinical psychology is a field that requires its practitioners to receive specific training. In addition to having a degree from an accredited institution, those who practice clinical psychology must be licensed or certified to do so by state and national agencies. In other words, clinical psychology, like medicine, pharmacy, law, and dentistry, for example, is a legally regulated profession. Here we consider the training and credentialing requirements for becoming a clinical psychologist (these topics are discussed in more detail in Chapter 15, "Professional Issues in Clinical Psychology").

In the United States, each state establishes the requirements for licensure in clinical psychology, awards licenses to those who qualify, and retains the power to penalize or revoke the licenses of those who violate licensing laws. Although the specific requirements vary somewhat among states, licensure laws for clinical psychology generally involve the following requirements:

- **Education:** graduation from a school or program approved by the licensing board and/or relevant professional organization. (For instance, the APA annually publishes a list of accredited clinical psychology programs and approved internship sites in its flagship journal, the *American Psychologist.*)
- **Experience:** some term of supervised practice in the field, often embodied in successful completion of an approved practicum, internship, or period of supervision.
- **Testing of Competence:** passing of a comprehensive examination, often called a *licensing board exam,* which may include both written and oral components. The written national licensing test is called the *Examination for Professional Practice in Psychology* (EPPP).
- **Good Character:** showing the physical, mental, and moral capability to engage in the competent practice of the profession, often denoted by recommendations by others and by the absence of ethical or legal violations.

(Adapted from Sales, Miller, & Hall, 2005b)

Legal requirements vary not only by state but also by levels of training. For instance, in most states a *full license* in clinical psychology involves the requirements just listed and allows one to practice independently, to "hang out a shingle." Fully licensed clinicians can rent or own their own offices, set fees, establish work hours, bill insurance companies or other third parties, and engage in a number of other activities characteristic of independent private practice. These privileges usually come after a trainee has (a) completed a doctoral-level degree that includes course work, research training, and an approved internship, (b) completed a certain number of hours of supervised practice (typically about 2000), and (c) passed a licensing board exam.

Doctoral-level degrees for fully licensed clinical psychologists are typically either the *PhD* or the *PsyD,* though they occasionally include others (e.g., the EdD, or Doctor of Education). The PhD and PsyD degrees both stress intensive clinical training in preparation for clinical practice, but they differ in the extent to which science and research are stressed. Later in this chapter and in subsequent chapters, we explain the differences in these two models of training and describe the debates about the advantages and disadvantages of each. For now, just be aware that the number of doctoral-level psychologists produced by the two models is approximately equal (Norcross, Castle, Sayette, & Mayne, 2004).

At the subdoctoral level, practitioners have titles such as *limited license psychologist, psychological assistant, mental health counselor,* and similar terms. Many states place limits on the practice of clinicians who are not fully licensed. An example would be requiring that the subdoctoral-level clinician always practices under the supervision of a fully licensed psychologist. To obtain a limited license, one usually needs a master's degree and a specific period of postgraduate supervised experience. Some states regulate the limited license much like they regulate the doctoral-level license, but other states provide less oversight, or no oversight, for subdoctoral practitioners (Sales, Miller, & Hall, 2005b). Of course, all practitioners should know the obligations, freedoms, and limitations that go with practice under their level of licensure and in their state.

Practitioners of clinical psychology should also know the *ethical codes* that guide practice: the American Psychological Association's *Ethical Principles of Psychologists and Code of Conduct* (2002b). Referred to hereafter as the *Ethics Code* for short, this publication was last revised in 2002. It offers guidance on a great many situations, especially the gray areas, that invariably come up in practice. For instance, consider the following:

- How much knowledge of or training in a new therapy technique is necessary before a therapist can begin to ethically offer it to clients?
- What kind of records should a therapist keep?
- With whom should those records be shared?
- If a potentially violent client reports seriously thinking of harming another person, what legal and ethical obligations (and liability) does the therapist have to report the danger?
- What restrictions, if any, should there be if a therapist and a client (or former client or relative of a former client) begin to develop romantic interests in each other?
- Can a clinical psychologist who has just read about an interesting new psychological test use it in the assessment of his or her next client?
- How should a clinical psychologist respond if asked to testify in divorce court on behalf of one of two spouses whom he or she treated in marital therapy?
- How should a clinical psychologist respond if a parent seeking custody of a child asks for a personal meeting, just before the psychologist is to conduct a court-ordered custody evaluation of a child?

These and hundreds of other situations like them confront clinicians every day. Familiarity with the Ethics Code, as well as with state and federal laws, is necessary for these psychologists to be effective and to avoid professional mistakes that could have serious consequences.

Most clinical psychologists hold professional licenses and provide psychotherapy treatment, but as suggested earlier, not all do. Rather than specialize in assessment and treatment, some choose to engage primarily in some combination of teaching, research, consulting, or administration, while doing little or no direct service delivery. But non-practicing clinical psychologists, too, are guided by specific codes and regulations governing their work. For instance, clinical researchers are subject to sections of the Ethics Code dealing with research in psychology, and their studies are overseen by *Institutional Review Boards,* which are established under federal guidelines to protect the rights and well-being of human participants in research.

The Popularity of Clinical Psychology

Clinical psychology is the largest subfield of psychology. Graduate programs in clinical psychology attract more applicants than do graduate programs in any other area of psychology, and far more doctoral-level degrees are awarded in clinical and related health care provider areas than in other areas of psychology (Norcross, Kohout, & Wicherski, 2005). The prominence of clinical psychology helps explain why the terms *psychologist* and *clinical psychologist* are practically synonymous in public discourse. Indeed, when members of the general public are asked what a psychologist does, they usually describe the activities of clinical psychologists (which irks some psychologists in other specialties who feel compelled to explain that they are "not that kind of psychologist").

The appeal of clinical psychology is also reflected in the composition of the American Psychological Association (APA), the largest organization of psychologists in the United States. The APA's 155,000 members list clinical psychology as their specialty by a margin of four to one over any other area (American Psychological Association, 2005). It is no wonder, then, that of the members of APA's 56 divisions, by far the largest number are affiliated with clinical psychology (see Figure 1.1).

The prominence of clinical psychology is all the more remarkable when you consider that it did not begin to grow rapidly until about 50 years ago (see Chapter 2, "Clinical Psychology's Past and Present"). Before then, very few psychologists were clinicians, and only a small minority of them practiced psychotherapy. With the proliferation of psychotherapy and other psychological treatments after World War II, clinical psychology grew rapidly, as did related mental health disciplines.

As clinical psychology has grown, it has captured the public interest. Indeed, portrayals of clinical psychologists and their distressed clients have become a mainstay of movies, television, and other media. This kind of popularity is a double-edged sword. On the one hand, accurate portrayals can contribute to the public's *mental health literacy*—accurate understanding of psychological disorders and their treatments (Jorm, 2000). On the other hand, inaccurate portrayals can decrease mental health literacy and create inaccurate, stereotyped views of the profession. Unfortunately, the latter outcome seems to be more common. Clinical psychologists are often portrayed as oracles, agents of social compliance, or wounded healers, and the techniques by which they help clients are seldom portrayed accurately (Orchowski, Spickard, & McNamara, 2006). Inaccurate portrayals might make for good drama, but they don't reveal what clinical psychology is really like (Grinfeld, 1998). We hope that this book does a much better job.

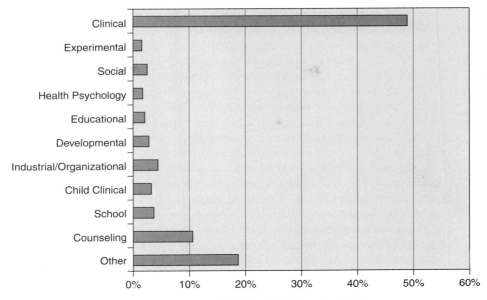

FIGURE 1.1 Major Fields of APA Members, 2005

Clinical Psychology and the Related Mental Health Professions

As noted earlier, clinical psychologists are considered *core mental health professionals.* Other professions in this category include counseling psychology, school psychology, social work, psychiatry, psychiatric nursing, and marriage and family therapy. Professionals in these fields are all recognized by governmental agencies and insurance companies as critical providers of mental health services. Like clinical psychology, each of these professions has national or international organizations, networks of accredited training programs, well-established research traditions, and specific licensing or certification requirements. Each group also has its own unique history and traditions. Practitioners from each group offer psychotherapeutic and mental health services in one form or another. How are clinical psychologists similar to, and different from, the other professionals?

Counseling Psychologists and School Psychologists. Counseling psychologists are generally the most similar to clinical psychologists in their training and in the types of services they offer. Counseling psychology programs are sometimes housed in psychology departments, but they are more often offered through education departments or other departments or divisions. Counseling psychologists can earn a PhD, PsyD, or EdD degree, all doctoral-level degrees but differing in emphasis (discussed later in this chapter and in Chapter 15). They are generally eligible for the same licensure, insurance reimbursement, and professional benefits as clinical psychologists, providing that they meet state requirements. Much of their course work and supervised training overlaps with that of clinical psychologists; practitioners are trained in psychopathology, interviewing, assessment, counseling and psychotherapy approaches research, and the like.

The differences between clinical psychology and counseling psychology are largely a matter of emphasis. Both are concerned with treatment and prevention of psychological disorders, but counseling psychologists deal also with normal transitions and adjustments that people may face. Counseling psychology was founded to promote personal, educational, vocational, and group adjustment (Counseling Psychology Division 17, 2006). Besides offering psychotherapy, counseling psychologists might, for instance, do career counseling or other forms of counseling related to life changes or developmental problems. Clinical psychology, on the other hand, was founded primarily to assess and treat persons with psychological disorders (see Chapter 2). Therefore, clinical psychologists focus more specifically on prevention, diagnosis, and treatment of psychological problems and on research related to these issues, and they generally deal with more severe pathology than counseling psychologists do. Despite these differences, there is considerable overlap between the professions.

School psychologists also have much in common with clinical and counseling psychologists: they generally share a scientist-practitioner model of training, move through similar internship and licensure requirements, conduct assessments, design interventions at the individual and system levels, and evaluate programs. The obvious difference is that school psychologists focus on interventions with children, adolescents, and their families in school and other educational settings. Despite the differences in emphasis, the similarities to clinical and counseling psychologists are greater than the differences (Cobb et al., 2004).

Social Workers.   As the nation's largest group of mental health service providers, social workers are employed in a variety of settings, including hospitals, businesses, community mental health centers, courts, schools, prisons, and family service agencies. Social workers provide direct services to clients or work to improve social conditions, or both. About half of the National Association of Social Workers members are engaged in direct clinical services, including various forms of therapy; the rest work in areas such as administration, public policy, research, and community organizing.

Social workers can earn a bachelors degree (Bachelor of Social Work, or BSW), masters degree (Master of Social Work, or MSW), or doctoral degree (Doctorate in Social Work, or DSW). As in clinical psychology, licensing and certification laws vary by state. Typically, the minimum degree required to provide psychotherapy services is an MSW (National Association of Social Workers, 2008). Social workers may be trained in various psychotherapy techniques, but as a general rule, they focus more on how social/situational variables, rather than intrapersonal and interpersonal variables, affect functioning. Social workers, like clinical psychologists, spend much of their time in direct client contact, helping clients cope with problems and navigate a world that has become complex and difficult because of those problems.

Psychiatrists.   Among the many specializations for physicians, psychiatry is the one that deals with the diagnosis, treatment, and prevention of mental disorders. Psychiatrists go beyond their basic MD degree to specialize in treating psychological disorders; they are specialists within the medical profession, just as are pediatricians (children), ophthal-mologists (eyes), and neurologists (brain and nervous system). Persons training to be psychiatrists typically complete a psychiatric residency in which they take course work in psychology and undergo supervision by qualified psychiatrists as they work with patients. This residency often occurs in a hospital setting and therefore generally involves exposure to more serious psychopathology, but it may also occur in outpatient settings. In addition to doing therapy, psychiatrists can prescribe medication and order or conduct other medical tests. Though psychiatrists generally have more medical training than clin-ical psychologists, clinical psychologists typically have more formal training in psycho-logical assessment and a broader exposure to a variety of approaches to psychology.

The historical distinction between psychiatrists and clinical psychologists has been understood as reflecting the difference between a more biological (psychiatrists) and a more psychological (clinical psychologists) view of the causes of mental disorders. Recent years, however, have seen increased collaboration between the professions. Much of the change can be attributed to the growing realization that psychological disorders are seldom *either* biological or psychological in origin but typically a complex inter-action of both. As a result, clinical psychologists are increasingly employed in medical settings, where their psychological and research expertise are valued. Psychiatrists and psychologists often work cooperatively on task forces devoted to issues of valid diag-noses and effective treatments (Hong & Leventhal, 2004). This is consistent with a broader shift toward psychology becoming a health profession rather than strictly a men-tal health profession (Belar et al., 2003).

Psychiatric Nurses. As specialists within the nursing profession, psychiatric nurses are trained in the care and treatment of persons with psychiatric disorders. They usually work in hospital settings and operate as part of a treatment team that is headed by a psychiatrist and includes one or more clinical psychologists. They may be trained in some forms of therapy, often those specific to the populations they encounter.

Marriage and Family Therapists (MFTs). MFTs are trained to treat psychological disorders as they occur within the context of marriages, couples, and families. MFTs earn masters or doctoral degrees within their profession and also have supervised clinical experience. Their training often emphasizes family systems models and psychotherapy techniques applicable to the populations they treat.

Paraprofessionals. Persons trained to assist in or supplement mental health servi-ces are called *paraprofessionals*. They are usually bachelor's-level or associate-level per-sonnel trained to administer a specific form of treatment to a specific population. Some come from disciplines that have some or all of the following indicators of professional quality: well-articulated standards of practice, national organizations that promote and oversee the profession, course offerings in colleges or universities, empirical research traditions and peer-reviewed journals. For instance, music therapy has a long history, a national organization (the American Music Therapy Association), educational and certifi-cation requirements (including internships), and a relatively large empirical literature suggesting the therapy's effectiveness when combined with other modes of therapy (Edwards, 2006).

Paraprofessionals generally work as part of a treatment team, and their activities are supervised by professionals. Other examples include recreation therapists, art therapists, acupuncturists, rehabilitation counselors, occupational therapists, case workers trained to conduct group sessions with teen drug users in residential facilities, and volunteers at telephone hot lines or other crisis intervention centers.

Other Specialists and Caregivers.   Mental health services are also offered by a variety of other *specialists* and *caregivers.* Some of these, such as health psychologists and rehabilitation psychologists, are trained within clinical psychology programs. Alternatively, persons who adopt certain specialties can attend graduate programs specifically devoted to that specialty (e.g., music therapy). Pastoral counselors typically get training in counseling from a faith-based perspective. For clients whose religious faith is central to their identity and outlook on life, the availability of a counselor who affirms this faith can be important. Indeed, for many persons, a rabbi, priest, minister, or other religious leader is the first person to consider when they need to talk about a distressing personal problem.

Others specialties, such as aromatherapy, reflexology, homeopathy, and spiritual healing techniques, have few or none of the indicators of professional quality that we have listed and might be described as further from the mainstream of mental health treatment. Often classified as *alternative treatments* or *alternative medicine,* many of these further-from-the-mainstream treatments combine somatic or sensual experiences with variants on psychological, social, or spiritual intervention. Some of these practices derive from ancient traditions; some are new inventions. Persons who practice alternative treatments often describe their work as falling within a *holistic* tradition that emphasizes the integration of mind, body, and spirit (Feltham, 2000).

Section Summary: Clinical psychology involves the application of principles, methods, and procedures to reduce or alleviate maladjustment, disability, and discomfort in a wide range of client populations. Its title and practices are regulated by professional organizations and by state licensing boards. Specific kinds of training are required for the different types of licensure, and certain personal traits, such as a clinical attitude, sound judgment, and emotional stability, are needed to practice the profession effectively. As one of the core mental health professions, clinical psychology overlaps with other mental health professions but is distinguished by psychological training that is both research oriented and practical. It remains the most popular specialty within psychology, one of the most popular majors among undergraduates, and a profession the practice of which is a source of considerable curiosity and interest in the public.

CLINICAL PSYCHOLOGISTS AT WORK

Section Preview: Here we describe the various professional activities of clinical psychologists and how clinicians distribute their work time among those activities. We also describe the various employment settings and general salary ranges of clinical psychologists.

The Activities of Clinical Psychologists

Let's consider in more detail some of the activities that clinical psychologists pursue, the variety of places in which they are employed, the array of clients and problems on which they focus their attention, and the rewards of the job. Not all clinicians are equally involved with all the activities we will describe, but our review should provide a better understanding of the wide range of options open to those who enter the field. It might also help explain why the field remains attractive to so many students.

About 95% of all clinical psychologists spend their working lives engaged in some combination of six activities: assessment, treatment, research, teaching (including supervision), consultation, and administration. Table 1.1 shows the results of surveys taken over the last few decades examining how clinical psychologists spend their time.

Assessment. Assessment involves collecting information about people: their behavior, problems, unique characteristics, abilities, and intellectual functioning. This information may be used to diagnose problematic behavior, to guide a client toward an optimal vocational choice, to facilitate selection of job candidates, to describe a client's personality characteristics, to select treatment techniques, to guide legal decisions regarding the commitment of individuals to institutions, to provide a more complete picture of a client's problems, to screen potential participants in psychological research projects, to establish pretreatment baseline levels of behavior against which to measure posttreatment improvement, and for literally hundreds of other purposes. Most clinical assessment instruments fall into one of three categories: tests, interviews, and observations. We cover each of these in detail in the chapters devoted to assessment.

Once an area of practice considered relatively stagnant, psychological assessment has undergone important changes. Clinicians now have an array of assessment options

TABLE 1.1

Percentage of Time Licensed Psychologists Spend in Professional Activities

Activity	Mean Percentage of Time				
	1973	1981	1986	1995	2003
Assessment	10	13	16	15	15
Psychotherapy	31	35	35	37	34
Research/writing	7	8	10	15	14
Teaching	14	12	14	9	10
Clinical supervision	8	8	11	7	6
Consultation	5	7	11	7	7
Administration	13	13	16	11	13

SOURCE: From "Clinical Psychologists Across the Years: The Practice of Clinical Psychology from 1960 to 2003," by J. C. Norcross, C. P. Karpiak, and S. O. Santoro, 2005, *Journal of Clinical Psychology,* 61, pp. 1467–1483. Copyright 2005 by Wiley Periodicals, Inc. Adapted with permission.

not formerly available to them. For instance, computers can administer assessment items, analyze results, and generate entire written reports. This supplementing or replacing of older, established paper-and-pencil interviews and tests might seem to diminish the need for extensive clinical training in assessment, but the opposite is true. With the proliferation of such tests, clinicians now must distinguish higher-quality computer-based assessments from lesser-quality ones, and they must pay careful attention to assure that computer-generated reports are accurate and appropriate for the assessment goals of each particular case. (We address computer-based assessment in more detail in Chapter 3, "Basic Features of Clinical Assessment," Chapter 4, "Interviewing and Observation in Clinical Psychology," and Chapter 5, "Testing in Clinical Psychology.")

Another frontier of psychological assessment is developing from research on a variety of biological factors associated with human functioning. During the last two decades, research focusing on genetic, neurochemical, hormonal, and neurological factors in the brain has led to the development of new neurobiological assessments. These changes, too, have the potential to greatly enhance the assessment efforts of clinicians, but as with computer-based assessment, they raise a number of procedural, practical, and ethical questions (Popma & Raine, 2006). For instance, if an insurance company is paying for a client's psychological assessment and treatment, should a clinician tell both the client and the insurance company that testing revealed genetic vulnerability not only to depression (the client's current problem) but also to a future or undiagnosed problem such as early-onset Alzheimer's disease?

Treatment.   Clinical psychologists offer treatments designed to help people better understand and solve distressing psychological problems. These interventions are known as psychotherapy, behavior modification, psychological counseling, or other terms, depending on the theoretical orientation of the clinician. Treatment sessions may include client or therapist monologues, painstaking construction of new behavioral skills, episodes of intense emotional drama, or many other activities that range from the highly structured to the utterly spontaneous. (Treatment is discussed in detail in Chapter 6, "Basic Features of Clinical Interventions," Chapter 7, "Psychodynamic and Humanistic Psychotherapies," Chapter 8, "Behavioral and Cognitive-Behavioral Psychotherapies," Chapter 9, "Alternative Modes of Clinical Intervention," and Chapter 10, "Research on Clinical Intervention.")

Individual psychotherapy has long been the single most frequent activity of clinicians (e.g., Norcross, Karpiak, & Santoro, 2005; Phelps, Eisman, & Kohout, 1998), but psychologists may also treat two or more clients together in couple, family, or group therapy. Sometimes, two or more clinicians work in therapy teams to help their clients. Treatment may be as brief as one session or may extend over several years. In whatever form it takes, psychotherapy has remained the activity that occupies the largest percentage of most clinicians' time (see Table 1.1).

The goals of treatment can range widely as well. They may be as limited as finding a specific solution to a particular problem or as ambitious as a complete analysis and reconstruction of a client's personality, or they may fall somewhere between these extremes. While most clinical psychologists design their treatments to reduce existing problems, some—known as community psychologists—focus instead on preventing psychological problems by altering the institutions, environmental stressors, or behavioral skills of people at risk for disorder (e.g., teenage parents) or of an entire community.

Treatment by a clinical psychologist may be conducted on an outpatient basis to clients living in the community or as one of the services offered to residents (inpatients) of hospitals or other mental health institutions. Therapy can be offered free of charge, for a fixed fee, as part of a prepaid health care plan, or on a sliding scale that is adjusted in light of the client's ability to pay. The clients one sees, the payment arrangements, and other factors are often strongly influenced by the setting, the clinician's training, and years of experience (Pingitore & Scheffler, 2005; also see Table 1.2).

The results of psychological treatments are usually positive, though in some cases the change may be small, nonexistent, or even negative (Lilienfeld, 2007). Of course, increasing the effectiveness of treatments offered to the public is a key goal of research.

Research. By training and by tradition, clinical psychologists are research oriented. For most of the first half of its existence, the field was strongly dominated by research rather than by application (see Chapter 2). Although that balance has changed, research continues to play a vital role in clinical psychology.

Research activity makes clinicians stand out among other helping professions, and we believe it is in this area that they may make their greatest contribution. In the realm of psychotherapy, for example, theory and practice were once based mainly on case study evidence, subjective impressions of treatment efficacy, and rather poorly designed research. This "prescientific" era (Paul, 1969a) in the history of psychotherapy research

TABLE 1.2						
Percentage of Clinicians Employed in Various Primary Work Settings						
Employment Site	**1960**	**1973**	**1981**	**1986**	**1995**	**2003**
Psychiatric hospital	15	8	8	9	5	4
General hospital	15	6	8	5	4	3
Outpatient clinic	15	5	5	4	4	4
Community mental health center	NR	8	6	5	4	2
Medical school	7	8	7	7	9	8
Private practice	17	23	31	35	40	39
University, psychology department	20	22	17	17	15	18
University, other department	NR	7	5	4	4	4
VA medical center	NR	NR	NR	NR	3	3
None	NR	1	1	4	1	0
Other	20	11	12	10	11	15

NOTE. NR, not reported.

SOURCE: From "Clinical Psychologists Across the Years: The Practice of Clinical Psychology from 1960 to 2003," by J. C. Norcross, C. P. Karpiak, and S. O. Santoro, 2005, *Journal of Clinical Psychology,* 61, pp. 1467–1483. Copyright 2005 by Wiley Periodicals, Inc. Adapted with permission.

has evolved into an "experimental" era in which the quality of research has improved greatly and the conclusions we can draw about the effects of therapy are much stronger (Lambert & Bergin, 1994). This development is due in large measure to the research of clinical psychologists.

The areas investigated by clinicians range widely, from neuropsychology, psychopharmacology, and health psychology to the causes of mental disorders in children and adults; from the diagnosis of those disorders to community interventions designed to prevent them; and from the evaluation of professional psychotherapy to the impact of nonprofessional helpers. A glance at a resource called *Psychological Abstracts,* which contains brief summaries of research in psychology, will document the diversity and intensity of clinical psychologists' involvement in research. Another journal, *Clinical Psychology Review,* includes longer reviews of topics germane to clinical psychology, while the *Journal of Consulting and Clinical Psychology, Psychological Assessment,* and the *Journal of Abnormal Psychology* publish many of the most influential research studies in clinical psychology.

Clinical research also varies greatly with respect to its setting and scope. Some studies are conducted in research laboratories, while others are conducted in the more natural, but less controllable, conditions outside the lab. Some projects are supported by governmental or private grants that pay for research assistants, computers and other costs, but a great deal of clinical research is performed by investigators whose budgets are limited and who depend on volunteer help and their own ability to obtain space, equipment, and participants.

Clinical psychology's tradition of research is reflected in graduate school admission criteria, which often emphasize applicants' grades in statistics or research methods over grades in abnormal psychology or personality theory. Many graduate departments in psychology in the United States regard research experience as among the three most important criteria for admission (Pate, 2001). Even though most clinical psychologists do not end up pursuing a research career—many never publish a single piece of research—most graduate programs in clinical psychology still devote a significant amount of time to training in empirical research. Why?

There are at least four reasons. First, it is important that all clinicians be able to critically evaluate published research so that they can determine which assessment procedures and therapeutic interventions are likely to be effective for their clients and which have not been empirically validated. Second, clinicians who work in academia must often supervise and evaluate research projects conducted by their students. Third, when psychologists who work in community mental health centers or other service agencies are asked to assist administrators in evaluating the effectiveness of the agency's programs, their research training can be very valuable. Finally, research training can help clinicians objectively evaluate the effectiveness of their own clinical work.

This last aspect of clinical research—systematically evaluating and documenting one's treatment outcomes—has become tremendously important in recent years. Tracking client change can signal the need to change treatment plans, but there are many other good reasons to systematically measure clinical outcomes (Hatfield & Ogles, 2004). Guidelines for how clinicians might keep records and track change are offered in a number of publications, one of which comes from APA's Board of Professional Affairs Committee on Professional Practice and Standards (COPPS). Revision of record-keeping guidelines was initiated in 2006 to stay consistent with current practices and to reflect changes in legal and regulatory environments (Association News, 2006).

In short, the ability to evaluate and conduct research has always been a hallmark of clinical psychology. The vast majority of clinical psychologists can assume that their research skills will be called upon sometime in their professional careers.

Teaching. A considerable portion of many clinical psychologists' time is spent in educational activities. Clinicians who hold full- or part-time academic positions typically teach undergraduate and graduate courses in areas such as personality, abnormal psychology, introductory clinical psychology, psychotherapy, behavior modification, interviewing, psychological testing, research design, and clinical assessment. They conduct specialized graduate seminars on advanced topics, and they supervise the work of graduate students who are learning assessment and therapy skills in practicum courses.

Supervising practica is a special kind of teaching that relies partly on empirical research evidence and partly on the instructor's clinical experience to enhance students' assessment and treatment skills. In most practica, each student sees one or more clients on a regular basis and, between sessions, meets with the supervisor to discuss the case (the client is aware of this arrangement, of course). Supervision may be one to one or part of a meeting with a small group of practicum students, all of whom agree to keep their discussions strictly confidential.

A good deal of clinical psychologists' teaching takes the form of research supervision. This kind of teaching begins when a student comes to the supervisor with a research topic and asks for advice and a list of relevant readings. In addition to providing the reading list, most research supervisors help the student frame appropriate research questions, apply basic principles of research design to address those questions, and introduce the student to the research skills relevant to the problem at hand.

Clinical psychologists also do a lot of teaching in the context of in-service (i.e., on-the-job) training of psychological, medical, or other interns, social workers, nurses, institutional aides, ministers, police officers, prison guards, teachers, administrators, business executives, day-care workers, lawyers, probation officers, and many other groups whose vocational skills might be enhanced by increased psychological sophistication. Clinicians even teach while doing therapy—particularly if they adopt a behavioral approach in which treatment includes helping people learn more adaptive ways of behaving (see Chapter 8). Finally, many full-time clinicians teach part time in colleges, universities, and professional schools. Working as an adjunct faculty member provides another source of income, but clinicians often teach because it offers an enjoyable way to share their professional expertise and to remain abreast of new developments in their field.

Consultation. Clinical psychologists often provide advice to organizations about a variety of problems. This activity, known as consultation, combines aspects of research, assessment, treatment, and teaching. Perhaps this combination of activities is why some clinicians find consultation satisfying and lucrative enough that they engage in it full time. Organizations that benefit from consultants' expertise range in size and scope from one-person medical or law practices to huge government agencies and multinational corporations. The consultant may also work with neighborhood associations, walk-in treatment centers, and many other community-based organizations. Consultants perform many kinds of tasks, including education (e.g., familiarizing staff with research relevant to their work), advice (e.g., about cases or programs), direct service (e.g., assessment, treatment, and evaluation), and reduction of intraorganizational conflict (e.g., eliminating sources of trouble by altering personnel assignments).

When consulting is *case* oriented, the clinician focuses attention on a particular client or organizational problem and either deals with it directly or offers advice on how it might best be handled. When consultation is *program* or *administration* oriented, the clinician focuses on those aspects of organizational function or structure that are causing trouble. For example, the consultant may suggest and develop new procedures for screening candidates for various jobs within an organization, set up criteria for identifying promotable personnel, or reduce staff turnover rates by increasing administrators' awareness of the psychological impact of their decisions on employees.

Administration. Many clinical psychologists find themselves engaged in the management or day-to-day running of organizations. Examples of the administrative posts held by clinical psychologists include head of a college or university psychology department, director of a graduate training program in clinical psychology, director of a student counseling center, head of a consulting firm or testing center, superintendent of a school system, chief psychologist at a hospital or clinic, director of a mental hospital, director of a community mental health center, manager of a government agency, and director of the psychology service at a Veterans Administration (VA) hospital.

Administration has become an increasingly popular professional activity for psychologists. Indeed, after psychotherapy, administration is close to teaching and assessment as the next most common activity (Norcross, Karpiak, & Santono, 2005). Administrative duties tend to become more common as clinicians move through their professional careers.

Distribution of Clinical Activities

Although some clinical psychologists spend their time at only one or two of the six activities we have described, most engage in more, and some perform all six. To many clinicians, the potential for distributing their time among several functions is one of the most attractive aspects of their field. Table 1.1 shows how licensed psychologists responded to questions about their allocation of time. Overall, the majority of clinicians identify themselves primarily as practitioners rather than as researchers or academicians, and more time is devoted to psychological treatment than to anything else.

However, the distribution of activities for clinical psychologists varies considerably by setting. A study commissioned by the American Psychological Association's Committee for the Advancement of Professional Practice (CAPP), which included 15,918 responses from practicing psychologists, found that psychologists in academic settings spend more professional time in teaching and research than in any other aspect of the profession, while those in private practice spend most of their time doing psychotherapy

The proportion of time that clinicians spend in activities such as therapy, assessment, research, teaching, consulting, or administration depends partly on their work settings.

and assessment (Phelps, Eisman, & Kohout, 1998). Psychologists in government and medical settings tend to distribute professional activities somewhat more evenly.

In other words, the way clinical psychologists spend their time is determined partly by the demands of the work settings they choose, partly by their training, and partly by their individual interests and expertise. But it is also influenced by larger social factors. For example, a clinician could not work in a Veterans Administration hospital today if federal legislation had not been passed in the 1940s creating such hospitals. (The role played by sociocultural forces in shaping clinical psychology is more fully detailed in Chapter 2.) Similarly, much of the research conducted by clinical psychologists today depends on grants from governmental agencies such as the National Institute of Mental Health, whose existence depends on continued congressional appropriations. Further, the clinical functions we have described are possible only because they are perceived by other professions—and the general public—as legitimate. If no one saw the clinician as capable of doing effective therapy, that function would soon disappear from the field.

In short, what clinicians do and where they do it has always depended—and always will depend—on the cultural values, political climate, and pressing needs of the society in which they function.

Diversity Among Clients

Changes in the U.S. population affect the work of clinical psychologists as well. By 2050, non-Hispanic whites are expected to be 50% of the U.S. population with ethnic minorities making up the other half. A greater proportion of Americans will have been born in other countries, or will have parents who were, than has been the case for decades. How does this diversity affect clinical psychology?

For one thing, persons from different backgrounds often have different ways of expressing psychological distress, so clinicians have become increasingly sensitive to cultural variations in symptoms (Hays & Iwamasa, 2006). Responses to treatments can also vary depending on clients' backgrounds. Even willingness to seek psychological help varies by cultural and ethnic background. Clinicians will therefore need additional training in order to provide culturally sensitive services to diverse groups (Hall, 2005). In numerous places throughout the remainder of this book, we describe how ethnic and cultural diversity affects clinical practice.

Diversity of Problems.   Within the limits imposed by their areas of expertise, clinical psychologists can work on almost any kind of human behavior problem. Which are the most common? The National Comorbidity Survey (1990–1992) and National Comorbidity Survey Replication (2001–2003) are among the largest studies to try to examine the general population prevalence and severity of psychological disorders. They show that anxiety disorders (e.g., panic disorders, social phobia), mood disorders (e.g., depression), impulse-control disorders (e.g., intermittent explosive disorder), and substance disorders (e.g., alcohol abuse, drug abuse) are among the most common. Yet only about half of those who receive treatment actually meet the criteria for a diagnosable mental disorder (Kessler, Demler, et al., 2005). The remainder have symptoms that do not quite fit the current diagnostic criteria (discussed in Chapter 3). Such problems include difficulties in interpersonal relationships, marital problems, school difficulties, psychosomatic and physical symptoms, job-related difficulties, and so on. The prevalence and types of problems for which people seek help have remained similar over the years, suggesting that the need for clinical psychologists has not declined, even though the cultural backgrounds of clients who experience those problems have become more diverse.

Not all clients who experience psychological disorders receive treatment. On this score, there is good news and bad news. The good news is that the number of persons seeking treatment is up from a decade ago. Part of this rise may be the result of increased public awareness about disorders and their effects (i.e., mental health literacy). Advertising of medications for psychological problems (e.g., depression, anxiety disorders, smoking and other problems of "craving" and impulse control, and sexual dysfunction) has helped legitimize some psychological disorders and made it more likely that troubled people seek treatment (Kancelbaum, Singer, & Wong, 2004). The bad news is that a significant proportion of those seeking treatment seek only minimally adequate medical treatment from their family doctor. Minimal treatment is often limited to medications; it does not include psychological treatment that could improve long-term outcomes. Many seek no treatment at all. According to one survey of more than 9,000 English-speaking respondents ages 18 and older, only 41% of persons with a disorder received some treatment within a 12-month period (Wang, Lane, et al., 2005). Other studies have similarly found that under half of those with a disorder receive treatment (Kessler, Demler, et al.,

2005). Undertreated populations include those who are poor, members of ethnic minorities, elderly, rural, and uninsured.

Employment Settings and Salaries for Clinical Psychologists

At one time, most clinical psychologists worked in a single type of facility: child clinics or guidance centers. Today, however, the settings in which clinicians function are much more diverse. You will find clinical psychologists in the following as well as many other settings:

college and university psychology departments

law schools

public and private medical and psychiatric hospitals

city, county, and private mental health clinics

community mental health centers

student health and counseling centers

medical schools

the military

university psychological clinics

child treatment centers

public and private schools

institutions for the mentally retarded

police departments

prisons

juvenile offender facilities

business and industrial firms

probation departmentss

rehabilitation centers for the handicapped

nursing homes and other geriatric facilities

orphanages

alcoholism treatment centers

health maintenance organizations (HMOs)

Table 1.2 lists the percentage of clinical psychologists employed in various settings during the last 40-plus years.

The financial rewards for employment as a clinical psychologist are significant. The median salary for a doctoral-level clinical psychologist with 10 years of experience and working in a direct human service position was approximately $73,000 per year in 2003. Of course, salary figures are dependent on economic conditions and historical eras. If salaries remained approximately the same but were adjusted for inflation at 3% per year, the median salary for our 10-year clinician in 2008 would be approximately $84,600 and in 2010 about $89,800. Table 1.3 presents the median as well as the 25th and 75th percentile salaries for clinical psychologists. It should give you an idea of salary ranges.

Employment settings also influence salaries, just as they influence the distribution of clinical activities and the diversity of clients whom a clinician sees. For instance, salaries at community mental health centers and public psychiatric hospitals tend to be lower than those at group psychological and psychological/medical practices. Clinical psychologists' salaries also differ by region of the country and by urban versus rural settings (see Table 1.4).

Faculty salaries for clinical psychologists at universities with doctoral degree-granting departments in 2006 ranged from about $55,000 for an assistant professor (less than 3 years experience) to about $92,800 for a full professor with up to 11 years of experience (Wicherski, Frincke, & Kohout, 2006). Of course, compensation for clinical

---

TABLE 1.3

Salaries of Licensed Doctoral-Level Clinical Psychologists in Direct Human Service Positions

Percentile	Years of Experience			
	2–4 years	**10–14 years**	**20–24 years**	**30+ years**
75%	70,000	88,000	120,000	120,000
Median	57,000	73,000	84,000	88,000
25%	50,000	60,000	65,000	68,500

SOURCE: From "Salaries in Psychology 2003: Report of the 2003 APA Salary Survey," by W. E. Pate II, J. L. Frincke, and J. L. Kohout, 2005. Adapted with permission. Accessed October 20, 2006, from http://research.apa.org/03salary/homepage.html/.

psychologists employed in academia varies considerably by institution. In general, salaries at masters degree–granting institutions and professional schools are typically lower than those at doctoral degree–granting institutions. Salary also varies by region of the country and other factors.

Not long ago, private practitioners of psychology earned substantially more than those employed in academic settings, but that gap has narrowed. The change is partly influenced by changes in the way health care is administered, a change we discuss later in this chapter. When adjusted for the 9- to 10-month academic year, salaries of clinical psychologists working in academic settings are now closer to the salaries earned by their private-practitioner colleagues.

TABLE 1.4

Median Salaries for Licensed Doctoral-Level Clinical Psychologists with 10 to 14 Years of Experience in Selected Settings

Employment Setting	Median Salary
Individual private practice	72,000
Group psychological practice	85,000
Medical-psychological group practice	88,000
VA hospital	82,000
Private general hospital	75,000
Public psychiatric hospital	62,000
Elementary/secondary school	83,000
Community mental health center	62,000

SOURCE: From "Salaries in Psychology 2003: Report of the 2003 APA Salary Survey," by W. E. Pate II, J. L. Frincke, and J. L. Kohout, 2005. Adapted with permission. Accessed October 20, 2006, from http://research.apa.org/03salary/homepage.html/.

The APA periodically surveys its members concerning salaries, demographics, practice concerns, and many other topics, and then makes the results public. Much of that information can be accessed at APA's Web site: http://www.apa.org (though some information is available only to APA members).

Diversity among Clinical Psychologists

The proportion of males and females within the field of psychology has changed considerably over the past half century. In 1950, women earned only 15% of the doctoral degrees awarded in psychology, but by 1999, they earned about 67% of them and made up approximately two-thirds of psychology graduate students (National Center for Education Statistics, 2000; Pate, 2001). Clinical psychology represents the largest portion of psychology graduate students, so the 2-to-1 ratio of women to men has appeared there as well. By 2004–2005, 70% of incoming doctoral-level graduate students in clinical psychology programs were female (Norcross, Castle, Sayette, & Mayne, 2004). This percentage is quite similar in both more practice-oriented and more research-oriented programs. Another recent survey of student gender distribution in clinical psychology programs showed that in European countries, too, women outnumber men, often by wide margins (Olos & Hoff, 2006).

Of course, there is a lag of several years between enrollment in a degree program and the attainment of senior status within a profession. As a result, there are still more men than women among senior clinical psychology faculty in colleges and universities and more men than women among the higher-salary private practitioners of clinical psychology. But at all levels, there is a clear trend toward greater representation of women.

Ethnic minorities currently make up just over 20% of the students accepted into clinical psychology doctoral programs in the United States (Norcross et al., 2004). African Americans represent the highest percentage of minorities in all psychology graduate programs, followed closely by persons of Hispanic and Asian origin; Native Americans represent about 1% (Pate, 2001). It is noteworthy that the proportion of minorities in *all* doctoral psychology programs has increased (see Figure 1.2). Many colleges and universities have specific recruitment plans for targeting persons of color, and many psychology departments have their own department-level strategies for recruiting minorities

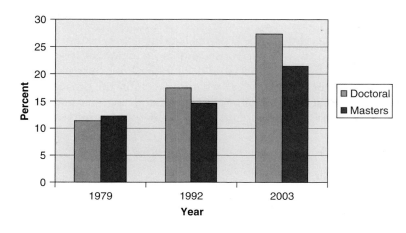

FIGURE 1.2 Percentage of Ethnic Minority First-Year Graduate Students in Psychology

(*Source:* J. C. Norcross, J. L. Kohout, & M. Wicherski (2005). Graduate study in psychology: 1971 to 2004. *American Psychologist, 60,* 959–975.)

(Kyle & Williams, 2000). Examples of such efforts include outreach programs to "feeder" undergraduate schools, financial assistance to minorities, brochures or other materials geared toward persons of color, and involvement of more persons of color in the recruitment and screening process. As is the case with gender trends, minority representation at the graduate school level is currently greater than minority representation at higher-status levels of the profession. But as minority students successfully work through the training pipeline, this traditional imbalance in the profession should begin to moderate.

Section Summary: Clinical psychologists spend most of their professional time engaged in assessment, psychotherapy, research, teaching, consultation, and administration. The activities in which they engage, and the clients they see, are strongly affected by employment settings, personal preferences, training, and broader social factors. Clinicians are employed in a variety of settings, including individual and group practices, hospitals of various types, community mental health centers, college and university psychology departments and medical schools, government agencies, private corporations, and others. In those settings, they see clients from a variety of cultural backgrounds and with a variety of problems. Clinicians' salaries vary by level of training, employment setting, and regional factors but are on par with many other professions with similar levels of training. Once dominated by white males, the field now has a higher percentage of women and ethnic minorities admitted to graduate school than in the past, so the demographics of the field should soon be in better balance.

CLINICAL PSYCHOLOGY IN THE 21ST CENTURY

Section Preview: Here we outline some of the more prominent issues shaping clinical psychology today. The first of these relates to the need to balance science and practice within the field. Other key issues concern how clinicians should be trained, how the traditionally separate "schools" or theoretical orientations within clinical psychology might be brought together, and how the practice of clinical psychology has been affected by the social and cultural environment, particularly by the way managed care has changed health care delivery.

Science and Practice

Some of the most lively discussions within clinical psychology involve the extent to which the field should reflect the concerns of its scientists and its practitioners. If scientists/researchers hold one viewpoint but practitioners hold another, whose view should prevail? There is a long history to this topic, and here we introduce only the broad outlines of the discussion and suggest some of its major implications. Later, especially in Chapters 2, 10, and 15, we detail the various positions and work through their implications for the field.

We have already noted that the official definition of clinical psychology incorporates both science and practice. The question is, *how* should science and practice be combined? This seemingly simple question goes well beyond mere philosophical or academic debate. It affects how clients are treated, how research is conducted, and how others view psychological interventions.

Evidence-Based Practice. Imagine, for instance, going to a physician who was unaware of, or who chose to disregard, the last several decades of medical research results and relied instead on intuition and folklore to decide what treatments to provide. If you wanted state-of-the-art treatment, you probably would not go back to that doctor. Basing professional practice on solid, up-to-date research is referred to as *evidence-based practice* (EBP). The need for evidence-based practice goes virtually unquestioned in medicine, but it has only recently become a central concern in fields such as mental health, education, and even architecture (Norcross, Beutler, & Levant, 2006a). The idea is that rather than rely on the best guesses of individuals or on "the way it's always been done," practitioners should use those diagnostic and therapeutic practices that the best scientific evidence finds most effective.

Clearly, evidence-based practice is an idea whose time has come, and no reasonable person doubts that clinical psychologists should base their practice on the results of high-quality scientific research. But, there is still no consensus on which research is of the highest quality, or what it shows, or exactly how it should guide practice. As yet, the APA has not clearly endorsed specific therapies or listed discredited therapies and made these judgments known to the public; indeed, different groups within the APA have different understandings of what evidence-based practice means.

There is some urgency in reaching consensus in the field on these issues, though. Already, some local and state agencies and some insurance providers have constructed lists of the psychotherapies for which they will provide reimbursement to patients (Norcross, Beutler, & Levant, 2006). They do so on the basis of *their* understanding of the research and of their needs, not on the basis of official positions taken by clinical psychologists. Many researchers and practitioners believe that clinical psychologists and their official organizations should be more active in listing which psychotherapies are most effective rather than having it done by corporations and government agencies. Presumably, clinical researchers and practitioners should have more expertise in these matters than persons working for insurance companies or state governments. Our own perspective, which we detail in Chapter 10, is that both empirical evidence and clinical experience are crucial for evaluating the usefulness of different psychological interventions. Clinical experience is invaluable as a starting point for generating hypotheses about what makes psychotherapy effective, but if certain therapy techniques underperform in repeated clinical trials, those techniques should be abandoned in favor of techniques that perform better.

Clinical Psychology Training. Decisions about the most desirable mix of science and practice also affect how students are trained in clinical psychology (and how textbooks such as this one are written!). There are two general models upon which clinical psychology training is based. Both are named after Colorado cities that hosted conferences where those models were developed. The *Boulder model* came out of clinical psychology's first major training conference, held in 1949 (Raimy, 1950). Often referred to as the *scientist-practitioner* model, the Boulder model recommended that clinical psychologists be proficient in research and professional practice, earn a PhD in psychology from a university-based graduate program, and complete a supervised, year-long internship.

In 1973, the National Conference on Levels and Patterns of Professional Training in Psychology was held at Vail, Colorado. The resulting *Vail model* recommended alternative training that placed proportionately less emphasis on scientific training and more on preparation for the delivery of clinical services (Korman, 1976). The Vail delegates also proposed that, when training emphasis is on the delivery and evaluation of professional services, the PsyD would be the appropriate degree. They suggested, too, that clinical psychology training programs could be housed not only in universities but also in medical schools or in free-standing schools of professional psychology (such as those in California, Illinois, and other states), and that these independent schools should have status equal to that of more traditional scientist-professional training venues. We discuss these models of clinical training in more detail in Chapter 15. For now, perhaps the most important thing to remember about the differences among the various types of clinical psychology training is that there is considerable variation across programs, regardless of the type of degree offered or the training model endorsed (Norcross et al., 2004).

Eclecticism and Integration

Most of the clinical psychologists engaged in practice, research, and teaching today were trained in programs that emphasized one main theoretical orientation, such as psychodynamic, cognitive-behavioral, humanistic, family/systems, and the like (Consoli & Jester, 2005). Is this the best way to organize clinical psychology training? Some have expressed concerns that a theory-based approach to clinical education has created such divisiveness within the field that those who have pledged allegiance to one orientation too often reflexively dismiss research and theory supporting other approaches (Gold & Strickler, 2006). This reaction is problematic because there is seldom a compelling empirical reason to adhere to only one theoretical approach; they all have their strengths and weaknesses. As a result, many clinical psychologists now favor *eclecticism,* an approach in which it is acceptable, and even desirable, to employ techniques from a variety of "schools" rather than sticking to just one.

Eclecticism is closely related to the idea of *psychotherapy integration,* the systematic combining of elements of various clinical psychology theories. In our view, it makes sense to combine approaches in reasonable ways rather than to strictly segregate them. If assessment and therapy techniques are tools, it is easy to see that possessing a wide range of tools, and knowledge of when and how to use them, makes for an effective psychotherapist. Indeed, most therapists now identify themselves as *eclectic* (Santoro, Kister, Karpiak, & Norcross, 2004), and there is now a journal—the *Journal of Psychotherapy Integration*—devoted to integrating various therapy approaches.

But integration and eclecticism are not as easy in practice as they are in theory. How should theories and practices be combined? Chapter 9 describes some of the answers to this question.

The Health Care Environment

Like all other professions, clinical psychology is shaped partly by the culture in which it operates. Popular beliefs and attitudes affect how mental health concerns are perceived, how problems are treated, and how treatment is funded.

Mental Health Parity. Psychological services are shaped by cultural attitudes. This is especially true when attitudes about psychological disorders and treatment are reflected in federal and state laws. Of particular concern to clinicians are laws affecting *mental health parity.* Parity laws require health insurers to provide the same level of coverage for mental illness as they do for physical illness. Parity has been the exception rather than the norm in U.S. health care. In other words, mental health problems have been regarded as less deserving than other health problems.

There seems to be little debate about whether health insurers should cover a range of physical illnesses—after all, that is what health insurers do. But should they also cover psychological disorders? A serious consideration of this question often reveals underlying beliefs about mental illness and the effectiveness of psychological treatments. Compare the following two cases:

Case 1 An employee of a medium-sized furniture manufacturer has a child who complains of an earache. The symptoms do not subside, and after a day, the parent calls the family doctor. The child is seen by a physician the next day, and the physician diagnoses an ear infection. The physician prescribes medication that initially appears effective, but upon follow-up after a week, the ear infection has returned. A second broad-spectrum antibiotic medication is tried, and the results are similar. After a final, unsuccessful round of antibiotics, the physician recommends surgery to insert drainage tubes in the child's ears to relieve the pressure and protect the child's hearing. This procedure is done, along with follow-up appointments. The employee's company-sponsored insurance plan pays for the treatment and the follow-up.

Case 2 An employee of a medium-sized furniture manufacturer has a child who has become reluctant to go to school. Over several days, the employee/parent is able to convince the child to go, but the child's reluctance grows. The child becomes increasingly withdrawn and despondent, cries easily, and takes less interest in activities at home that used to be enjoyable. The child has begun to show difficulties remembering and completing tasks. At times clinging and demanding, and at times agitated and restless, the child has two episodes of tantrums. After a discussion with teachers and the school counselor, the parent decides to seek professional help. The family physician, after examination, suggests childhood depression and possibly bipolar disorder (based also on family history) and recommends psychological assessment and intervention. The parent seeks help and initially is only able to have the child put on a waiting list. When finally seen a month later, the child is diagnosed with childhood bipolar disorder. A mental health team recommends carefully monitored medication and a series of psychological treatments with a child clinical psychologist. The employee's company-sponsored insurance plan pays for prescribed medications but not for psychological treatment.

What beliefs and attitudes about mental illness are at play here? The view that physical but not psychological disorders should be funded by insurance may reflect the belief that physical illnesses are visited upon persons without their consent, while psychological problems are largely created by families and by sufferers themselves. In short, people are seen as more responsible for their psychological problems than for their medical problems. This belief might have been easier to maintain a century ago when the most severe physical ailments were infectious diseases—smallpox, typhoid, diphtheria, for example—and when theories about the causes of mental illness did not incorporate interactions of biological, psychological, and social factors. But few people knowledgeable about psychological disorders today argue that persons simply choose to have a psychological problem. At the same time, many of today's most urgent physical problems—heart disease, obesity, diabetes, for example—are related to lifestyle choices that people make. In short, people probably do not choose to be psychologically ill any more, or any less, than they choose to be physically ill, but health coverage often suggests that they do.

The lack of parity laws is probably due to several factors: attitudes about mental illness, limited dissemination of evidence about the effectiveness and cost-effectiveness of psychological treatments, and the financial interests of certain stakeholders or constituents. In the United States in particular, the cost of insurance has risen sharply as health care costs have increased. Employers must pay increasingly higher prices for insurance plans to cover their employees. In shopping for a plan, an employer may favor one insurance company's lower-cost plan that excludes or limits mental health coverage over another company's that includes mental health coverage but costs more.

At the same time, employers are interested in keeping a healthy workforce. If mental health coverage is absent or limited, it could mean that employees will miss more work because of personal or family problems that go untreated. It might mean that employees have more relapses if initial mental health treatment were absent or inadequate. Employers, then, are caught in the middle; they want to save money on insurance costs, but they also want to limit the cost of having employees absent from work because of disorders that go untreated or undertreated. It all comes down to the issue of cost effectiveness—whether mental health treatment and prevention save money in the long run. As we discuss more fully in Chapter 10, they usually do.

Managed Care.   One aspect of society that is particularly important for clinical psychology in the United States involves the system of health care. Whereas clients once paid providers directly for services, now most health care, including mental health care, involves three parties: client, clinician, and an insurance company, HMO, or similar organization. When the third-party organization influences who provides service, which treatments are used, how long treatments last, how much providers are paid, what records are kept, and so on, it is called *managed care.* Managed care systems use business principles, not just clinicians' judgments, to make decisions about treatment.

As managed care systems in the United States have grown and exerted their influence over psychological treatments, clinicians have had to adapt. In one survey of independent practitioners, over half reported a decrease in salary and attributed it to the health care system (Williams, Kohout, & Wicherski, 2000). Managed care's influence helps explain why the salary discrepancy between private practice and other areas of clinical work is now smaller than it used to be. In another study, clinicians reported a culture clash between themselves and the managed care companies, complaining that they sometimes had to violate standards of care or ethical standards in order to be paid (Cohen, Marecek, & Gillham, 2006). No wonder, then, that in general, clinicians dislike managed care. In 2004, the Florida Psychological Association (with help from the APA's Practice Organization) joined in class action lawsuits against a number of national managed care companies. They argued that these companies manipulated diagnostic codes and performed other actions that resulted in reducing, delaying, or denying provider payments. By 2006, these suits had resulted in two settlements calling for financial reimbursement to providers and mandating changes in the procedures used by the managed care companies (Practice Directorate Staff, 2006).

Although the relationship between managed care and clinical psychology has sometimes been rocky, as it has between managed care and other health professions, it is not entirely negative (Bobbitt, 2006). One positive effect of managed care has been to stimulate research into which treatments are most effective for which problems. It is in the interest of clients, clinicians, *and* insurers to know which interventions have the most positive and lasting impact on health, because that information, correctly applied, will ultimately lower costs and improve client well-being. Managed care pressures are also partly responsible for the pressure on clinicians to more precisely measure the outcome of the treatments they provide.

Clinical psychologists are continuing to adapt, often changing services to better match those for which managed care systems will pay. This adaptability makes sense, but it can lead to problems if psychologists simply allow managed care personnel to make decisions about clinical practice. Those with the most training and expertise should be in the best position to provide empirical evidence about what works best and what should be reimbursed.

Prescription Privileges for Clinical Psychologists. A final aspect of the health care environment is the movement for clinical psychologists to be able to prescribe drugs. In 2002, New Mexico became the first state to pass legislation that permitted licensed psychologists with specialized training to prescribe psychotropic medications. In 2004, Louisiana followed, and other states are considering the change. There are several reasons that many think this trend will continue. One is the increasing public acceptance of medications for psychological problems, fueled in part by pervasive television and print advertising by drug companies. Another is that clinical psychologists deal extensively with persons taking certain medications. As a result, those psychologists are sometimes as knowledgeable, if not more so, about the effects of these drugs as the general practice physicians who referred the clients. Prescription privileges make sense also because psychologists see clients regularly, so they are often in a better position to monitor the effectiveness of the medications. There are also arguments against prescription privileges; we discuss the pros and cons in chapter 15.

Section Summary: Clinical psychology combines science and practice, but the appropriate mix of the two is a matter of a debate that has intensified as the need to establish clear evidence-based practices in clinical psychology has grown. That need comes both from within the profession and from outside organizations that fund and pay for clinical services. In light of changes within the profession and within the broader society, clinical psychologists continue to examine their training models, particularly the dominant models that lead to PhD and PsyD degrees. They have also had to think more carefully about ways to integrate and combine various approaches to psychotherapy and assessment, as it has become clear that the turf wars among adherents of different approaches do not benefit the profession. Managed care organizations have influenced clinical practice and will continue to do so. Cultural and legal factors affect the field as well, as exemplified by the fate of legislation requiring mental health parity and that permitting prescription privileges for clinicians.

CHAPTER SUMMARY

Clinical psychology is the largest single subfield within the larger discipline of psychology. It involves research, teaching, and other services designed to understand, predict, and alleviate maladjustment and disability. To become a licensed clinical psychologist, one must meet certain educational, legal, and personal qualifications. As one of the core mental health professions, clinical psychology is distinguished from other helping professions by the clinical attitude: the tendency to use the results of research on human behavior in general to assess, understand, and assist particular individuals. Clinicians deal with a wide range of clients from all age groups and focus on an even wider range of behavior problems, from anxiety, depression, and psychoses to occupational stress, mental retardation, and difficulties at school. The discipline is also distinguished by its emphasis on empirical research and by its diversity in training and practice.

That diversity can be seen in how clinicians distribute their time among six main functions: assessment, treatment, research, teaching, consultation, and administration. It can also be seen in the increasing diversity of the population in need of mental health care. Clinical psychologists are employed in many different settings, from university psychology departments and medical clinics to community mental health centers and prisons. Many are self-employed private practitioners.

Clinical psychology faces numerous challenges, not the least of which is that most people with psychological problems still do not receive treatment. Other factors shaping the discipline involve, among other issues, decisions about how science and practice should be combined, how training of new psychologists should be conducted, how the various theoretical approaches can be integrated, and how the current (and future) systems of health care delivery affect the practice of clinical psychology.

STUDY QUESTIONS

1. What are the general licensure or certification requirements to be a clinical psychologist?
2. What educational and degree options are available for someone who wants to go into clinical psychology?
3. What personal and ethical criteria are needed to be a good clinical psychologist?
4. How are clinical psychologists similar to and different from counseling psychologists, school psychologists, psychiatrists, social workers, and other mental health professionals?

5. How accurate are popular media portrayals of clinical psychology?
6. How do clinical psychologists spend most of their work time?
7. How does their work setting influence the way clinicians spend their time?
8. What are the salary ranges for clinical psychologists?
9. How have differing opinions about the balance of science and practice affected the way psychotherapists operate and how graduate schools educate?
10. What is the eclectic approach to psychopathology and treatment?
11. How might integration of different theoretical approaches be possible?
12. How does cultural diversity affect approaches to psychological treatment?
13. How has managed care affected clinical psychology research, training, and practice?
14. What is mental health parity?
15. Should specially trained clinical psychologists be able to prescribe certain kinds of drugs?

WEB SITES

- American Psychological Association (APA): http://www.apa.org
- Division 12 of the APA, the Society for Clinical Psychology: http://www.apa.org/divisions/div12/homepage.html
- Division 16 of the APA, School Psychology: http://www.apa.org/about/division/div16.html
- Association for Psychological Science: http://www.psychologicalscience.org
- Division 17 of the APA, the Society for Counseling Psychology: http://www.apa.org/about/division/div17.html
- American Psychiatric Association: http://www.psych.org
- National Association of Social Workers: http://www.socialworkers.org
- American Psychiatric Nurses Association: http://www.apna.org

CHAPTER 2
Clinical Psychology's Past and Present

Chapter Preview: In this chapter, we explain the events that gave birth to clinical psychology as a profession. We describe the slow but steady growth of the field during the first half of the 20th century, followed by the explosive growth that gave rise to the major approaches to clinical psychology. If you are already acquainted with psychodynamic, humanistic, behavioral, cognitive, systems, and biological approaches to personality, some of the chapter may be familiar, but we go beyond abstract theory to tell the story of how these approaches to clinical psychology came into being, and we outline how the different approaches might be applied to an individual case. (In subsequent chapters, we consider in detail the specific assessment and treatment tactics used by clinicians who adopt these approaches.) We end by describing certain themes that have been prevalent in clinical psychology's history and continue to affect the field today.

Anyone born in the United States after World War II might assume that the field of clinical psychology has always existed. However, clinical psychology did not emerge as a discipline until the beginning of the 20th century and did not begin rapid development until World War II ended. Between its beginning and its current form, the field of clinical psychology changed significantly (Benjamin, 2005; Resnick, 1997; Routh, 1994; Taylor, 2000). It was often a struggle for psychologists to become clinical psychologists.

THE ROOTS OF CLINICAL PSYCHOLOGY

Section Preview: Three sets of social and historical factors initially shaped clinical psychology and continue to influence it. These factors include (a) the use of scientific research methods—the empirical tradition, (b) the measurement of individual differences—the psychometric tradition, and (c) the classification and treatment of behavior disorders—the clinical tradition.

The roots of clinical psychology extend back to before the field of psychology was ever named, back to developments in philosophy, medicine, and several of the sciences. A few of these roots are especially important because they converged and created the field of clinical psychology, though only in embryonic form.

The Empirical Tradition

Historians typically mark the beginning of modern psychology as 1879, the year that Wilhelm Wundt established the first laboratory devoted to studying mental processes in Leipzig, Germany. Wundt was convinced that psychology—like biology, physics, and other sciences—should seek knowledge through the application of empirical research methods. He and others who came after him were determined to study human behavior by employing the two most powerful tools of science: observation and experimentation.

The founding of Wundt's laboratory was not the only beginning point for the new discipline. Others in physiology and medicine had been working on problems that were essentially psychological in nature. For instance, Johannes Müller and his student Herman Helmholtz identified and explored the neural pathways for vision and hearing, discoveries that addressed the question of how physical energy became mental experiences. Ernst Weber and Gustav Fechner showed that people's perceptual experiences changed in mathematically predictable ways as stimuli (e.g., weight or brightness) changed, suggesting that mind and body were fundamentally connected (Hunt, 1993). Still, Wundt is regarded as the founder of psychology because the advent of his laboratory so clearly proclaimed psychology as a science and because he trained many students who went on to establish psychology programs in European and U.S. universities.

One of Wundt's students was an American named Lightner Witmer. Following his graduation from the University of Pennsylvania in 1888, Witmer worked on his PhD in psychology with Wundt at the University of Leipzig. After completing his doctorate in 1892, Witmer was appointed director of the University of Pennsylvania psychology laboratory. In March 1896, a local schoolteacher named Margaret Maguire asked Witmer to help one of her students, Charles Gilman, whom she described as a "chronic bad speller." Once a schoolteacher himself, Witmer "took the case," thus becoming the first clinical psychologist and simultaneously beginning an enterprise that became the world's first psychological clinic (Benjamin, 2005; Routh, 1994).

Witmer's approach was to assess Charles's problem and then arrange for appropriate remedial procedures. His assessment showed that Charles had a visual impairment, as well as reading and memory problems that Witmer termed "visual verbal amnesia." Today, these difficulties would probably be diagnosed as a reading disorder. Witmer recommended intensive tutoring to help the boy recognize words without having to spell them first. This procedure successfully brought Charles to the point that he could read normally (McReynolds, 1987).

By 1900, three children a day were being served by a clinic staff that had grown to 11 members, and in 1907, Witmer set up a residential school for training retarded children. That same year, he founded and edited the first clinical journal, *The Psychological Clinic,* and wrote the lead article, which he titled simply "Clinical Psychology." By 1909, over 450 cases had been seen in Witmer's facilities. Under Witmer's influence, the University of Pennsylvania began offering formal courses in clinical psychology during the 1904 to 1905 academic year. Clinical psychology was on its way.

The initial reception for this new endeavor was not enthusiastic, however. In a talk at the 1896 meeting of the 4-year-old American Psychological Association, Witmer

Lightner Witmer (1867–1956)
(Courtesy of George Eastman House.
Reproduced by permission.)

described his new brand of psychology. His friend Joseph Collins recounted the scene as follows:

> [Witmer said] that clinical psychology is derived from the results of an examination of many human beings, one at a time, and that the analytic method of discriminating mental abilities and defects develops an ordered classification of observed behavior, by means of post-analytic generalizations. He put forth the claim that the psychological clinic is an institution for social and public service, for original research, and for the instruction of students in psychological orthogenics which includes vocational, educational, correctional, hygienic, industrial, and social guidance. The only reaction he got from his audience was a slight elevation of the eyebrows on the part of a few of the older members. (Quoted in Brotemarkle, 1947, p. 65)

This lead-balloon reception is understandable given the following four facts prevalent at the time: One, most psychologists considered themselves scientists and probably did not regard the role described by Witmer as appropriate for them. The first clinicians were trained as scientists in laboratories, so they tended to think about clinical problems in scientific terms and to use laboratory research methods in dealing with them. Two, even if they had considered his suggestions admirable, few psychologists were prepared by training or experience to perform the functions he proposed. Three, they were not about to jeopardize their identification as scientists, which was tenuous enough in those early years, by plunging their profession into what they felt were premature applications. Four, aside from any prevalent skeptical and conservative attitude, Witmer had an unfortunate talent for antagonizing his colleagues (Reisman, 1976, p. 46). The responses to Witmer's talk provided the first clues that conflicts would arise between psychology as a science and psychology as an applied profession, conflicts which remain to this day.

Although not everything Witmer did was to be equally influential, several aspects of his new clinic came to characterize subsequent clinical work for some time:

1. Most of his clients were children, a natural development since Witmer had been offering a course on child psychology, had published his first papers in the journal *Pediatrics,* and had attracted the attention of teachers concerned about their students.

2. His recommendations for helping clients were preceded by diagnostic assessment.

3. He did not work alone but in a team approach that saw members of various professions consulting and collaborating on cases.

4. He emphasized prevention of future problems through early diagnosis and remediation.

5. He emphasized that clinical psychology should be built on the principles being discovered in scientific psychology as a whole.

The last one in particular, that clinical practice should be built on solid scientific evidence, has remained a core of clinical psychology. It derives from the empirical tradition, given early expression by Wundt in Germany, and has been championed by countless psychologists in Europe and North America since. Although there remain heated debates about what constitutes the best scientific evidence (we review these issues in a later chapter), no responsible clinician denies that the practice of clinical psychology should be based on sound research. Following Witmer's lead, other empirically trained psychologists became interested in applying their knowledge to problems outside the laboratory. In the beginning, however, these first clinical psychologists remained closely tied to their laboratory science, just as Witmer was. Thus, the earliest history of clinical psychology, like the early history of psychology in general, is largely one of experimental psychology (Boring, 1950) (See Table 2.1).

Witmer got clinical psychology rolling, but he had little to do with steering it. He lost influence largely because he ignored developments that would later become central

TABLE 2.1

Landmarks of the Empirical Tradition in Clinical Psychology

Dates	Key Figures	Contributions
Mid-1800s	Müller, Helmholtz, Weber, Fechner	Studied sensory discrimination and perception; explored and measured nerve impulses; sought explanations of mental events in terms of physical processes
1879	Wundt	Established first laboratory designed specifically to study mental processes; trained many students who went on to establish psychology programs at universities in Europe and the United States
1896–1900	Witmer	Student of Wundt's; established the first psychology clinic and the first journal devoted to psychology clinics; founded clinical psychology in the United States

to the field. For instance, Witmer used psychological tests, but he largely ignored the development of new intelligence tests. This decision was costly because intelligence testing came to characterize applied psychology perhaps more than any other activity during the first half of the 20th century (Benjamin, 2005). Witmer also ignored early forms of adult psychotherapy—called *psychotherapeutics* at the time—that would come to dominate the field and virtually define psychology in the eyes of the public. Witmer remained active, of course, but mainly with functions and clients that have since become more strongly associated with school psychology, vocational counseling, speech therapy, and remedial education than with clinical psychology (Fagan, 1996).

His failure to keep pace with these developments led some to question whether Witmer should really be regarded as the founder of clinical psychology (Taylor, 2000). For instance, Raymond Cattell (1948) raised the question of whether we should consider "a challenge by a public school teacher regarding the case of a chronic bad speller" significant enough to be regarded as the beginning of clinical psychology (p. 3). But remember that, until this point, psychology had dealt with people only to study their behavior in general, not to become concerned about them as individuals. Witmer's decision was as unusual then as would be an attempt by a modern astronomer to determine the "best" orbit for the moon in order to alter its path. His conviction that psychology should "throw light upon the problems that confront humanity" (Witmer, 1897, p. 116), his commitment to empirical research, his promotion of psychological clinics, and his insistence that clinical psychologists receive strong scientific training helped define the field, then and now. In short, Witmer's contributions were significant, but they cannot account for the diversity and growth that clinical psychology experienced after him. For that, we must look to other sources.

The Psychometric Tradition

A second source from which clinical psychology developed was the practice of measuring people's physical and mental abilities. Because clinical psychology deals with the individual, it could not appear as a discipline until differences among human beings were identified and systematically measured.

The importance of measuring individual differences has been recognized for centuries. In his *Republic,* Plato suggested that prospective soldiers be tested for military ability before their acceptance in the army. In the sixth century B.C., Pythagoras selected members of his brotherhood on the basis of facial characteristics, intelligence, and emotionality, and 4,000 years ago, prospective government employees in China were given individual ability tests before being hired (DuBois, 1970; McReynolds, 1975).

Surprisingly, the earliest developments in the scientific measurement of individual differences came in the fields of astronomy and anatomy. The astronomical story began in 1796, when Nevil Maskelyne was Astronomer Royal at the Greenwich (England) Observatory. He recorded the moment at which various stars and planets crossed a certain point in the sky. His assistant, David Kinnebrook, made the same recordings, but Kinnebrook's recordings consistently differed from those of his boss by five- to eight-tenths of a second. Maskelyne assumed that his readings were correct and that Kinnebrook was in error. As a result, Kinnebrook lost his job.

This incident drew the attention of F. W. Bessel, an astronomer at the University of Konigsberg (Germany) observatory. Bessel wondered whether Kinnebrook's "error" might reflect something about the characteristics of various observers, and over the next several years, he compared his own observations with those of other experienced astronomers. Bessel found that discrepancies appeared regularly and that the size of the differences depended upon the person with whom he compared notes. The differences associated with each observer became known as the "personal equation," because they allowed calculations to be corrected for personal characteristics. Bessel's work led to later research by psychologists on the speed of and individual differences in reaction time.

A second source of interest in individual differences stemmed from the early 19th-century work of German anatomist Franz Gall and his pupil Johann Spurzheim. Gall thought he saw a relationship between his schoolmates' mental characteristics and the shapes of their heads. This notion later led Gall to espouse *phrenology* (see Figure 2.1),

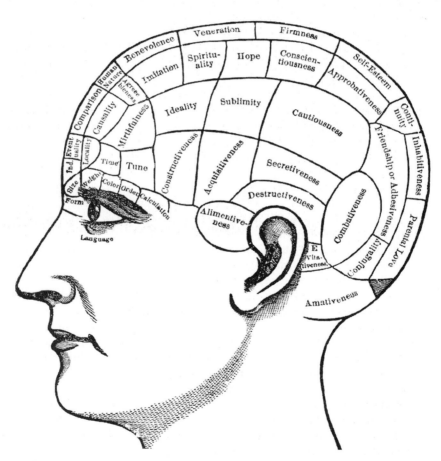

FIGURE 2.1   Phrenology, an Early Form of Psychological Testing, Involved the Practice of Assessing Personality by Reading Bumps or Variations in the Skull

an alleged science based on the assumptions that (1) each area of the brain is associated with a different faculty or function (e.g., self-esteem, language, or reverence); (2) the better developed each of these areas is, the more strongly that faculty or function is manifested in behavior; and (3) the pattern of over- or underdevelopment of each faculty is reflected in corresponding bumps or depressions in the skull. Gall traveled throughout Europe measuring the bumps on people's heads. He began with prisoners and mental patients whose behavioral characteristics seemed well established (he thought the "acquisitiveness" bump was especially strong among pickpockets). Later, under Spurzheim's influence, a map of the brain's 37 "powers" or "organs" was drawn, and phrenological measurements were made on more respectable segments of society. Many people actually paid to "have their head examined," after which they received a profile allegedly describing their mental makeup.

Although the brain does play a major role in controlling behavior, and though some of its areas are associated with certain functions such as vision, movement, and language, Gall's specific claims were recognized—even by the scientists of his day—as spectacularly wrong. Other efforts to relate people's physical characteristics to their mental or behavioral traits appeared in the late 19th-century work of Cesare Lombroso, an Italian psychiatrist whose theory of physiognomy correlated facial features with personality (Pettijohn, 1991).

A third source of interest in individual differences comes from Charles Darwin's momentous work, *Origin of Species,* published in 1859. In it, Darwin proposed two important ideas: that (1) variation of individual characteristics occurs within and between species (including humans), and (2) natural selection takes place in part on the basis of those characteristics. Darwin's cousin, Sir Francis Galton, was fascinated by these ideas, and he quickly applied Darwin's notions to the inheritance of individual differences—especially in mental abilities.

For example, Galton (1883) tried to distinguish high from low intelligence on the basis of individuals' ability to make fine discriminations between objects of differing weight and between varying intensities of heat, cold, and pain. He sought to measure individual differences in vividness of mental imagery; for this purpose, he invented the questionnaire. Galton's interests also extended to associative processes, so he developed the word-association test to explore this phenomenon. Eventually, Galton set up a laboratory in London where, for a small fee, anyone could take a battery of tests and receive a copy of the results. This facility, the world's first mental testing center, was included in the health exhibition in the 1884 International Exhibition (an early World's Fair). Galton's work began nearly 20 years before the official founding of psychology, but by the late 1880s, psychologists, too, were interested in measuring individual differences in mental functioning. The methods ultimately used in clinical assessment came not from measuring physical dimensions but from systematically collecting samples of behavior from large groups of people as they responded to standard sets of stimuli. These behavior sampling procedures came to be called mental tests.

A key figure in the mental testing movement was Alfred Binet, a French lawyer, scientist, and former student of Wilhem Wundt. Along with Henri Beaunis, Binet founded the first French psychology laboratory in 1895. Binet was especially interested in mental measurement, and he began to develop measures of complex mental ability in normal and "defective" children. His involvement in this testing grew out of the recognition that retarded children (who had been distinguished as a diagnostic group only as late as 1838) might be helped if they could be identified and given special educational attention. In 1896, Binet and his colleague Victor Henri described a battery of tests that measured not just "simple part processes," such as space judgment, motor skills, muscular effort, and memory, but also comprehension, attention, suggestibility, aesthetic appreciation, and moral values.

Binet's new intelligence test, the Binet-Simon scale, was introduced in the United States. Like Binet's earlier tests, this instrument was designed to measure complex mental processes, not the fixed mental structures with which Witmer was concerned. In spite of Binet's warning that it did not provide a wholly objective measure of intelligence, the Binet-Simon test gained wide attention. Henry H. Goddard of the Vineland (New Jersey) Training School heard about it while in Europe in 1908 and brought the Binet-Simon scale to the United States for assessing the intelligence of "feebleminded" children in the clinic he had set up 2 years earlier. The popularity of Goddard's translation of the Binet-Simon scale and Lewis Terman's 1916 revision of it (known as the Stanford-Binet) grew so rapidly in the United States that they overshadowed all other tests of intelligence, including those used by Witmer. The Binet scales provided a focus for clinical psychology's assessment function, which, until 1910, had been rather disorganized. All over the United States, new university psychological clinics (more than 20 of them by 1914) and institutions for the retarded began adopting the Binet approach while deemphasizing Witmer's "old-fashioned" methods.

The person usually credited with merging individual mental measurement with the new science of psychology is James McKeen Cattell, an American who completed his doctorate in Wundt's laboratory in Leipzig in 1886. Cattell was one of the first psychologists to appreciate the practical uses of tests in the selection and diagnosis of people. Cattell's experience in Wundt's laboratory taught him that "psychology cannot attain the certainty and exactness of the physical sciences unless it rests on a foundation of experiment and measurement" (Dennis, 1948, p. 347). Consequently, one of his first tasks was to construct a standard battery of mental tests for use by researchers interested in individual differences. He chose 10 tests that reflected the then-prevalent tendency to use sensorimotor functioning as an index of mental capacity, and he tested people's performance under varying conditions. He also collected less systematic information about people's dreams, diseases, preferences, recreational activities, and future plans (Shaffer & Lazarus, 1952).

Sensorimotor mental tests were adopted at universities, including Wisconsin, Clark, and Yale, but they were also criticized because of their low correlations with most other mental ability criteria (Reisman, 1976). By this time, however, an alternative approach to testing began to appear in several quarters. In 1891, Hugo Munsterberg, a psychologist at the University of Freiburg (Germany) who later came to Harvard, constructed a set of 14 tests to assess children's mental abilities. These tests went beyond the Galton-Cattell tasks to measure more complex functions such as reading, classifying objects, and performing mathematical operations.

Thus, by 1896, psychology was involved in measuring individual differences in mental functioning, and it hosted two overlapping approaches to the task: (1) the Galton-Cattell

TABLE 2.2		
Landmarks of the Psychometric Tradition in Clinical Psychology		
Dates	**Key Figures**	**Contributions**
Late 1700s–1880s	Bessell, Gall, Galton	Noted individual differences in recording observations; measured physical and physiological reactions to assess personality and mental functioning
1896	Binet	Developed a battery of tests to assess mental processes in children; administered tests to large numbers to develop norms
1890s–early 1900s	Goddard, Terman, Cattell	Helped to popularize Binet-style tests in the United States; founded a psychology laboratory in the United States that emphasized measurement

sensorimotor tests, aimed at assessing inherited, relatively fixed mental *structures,* and (2) the instruments of Binet and others, which emphasized complex mental *functions* that could be taught to some degree. Each approach was important to the development of clinical psychology, the former because it influenced Witmer and helped foster the appearance of the first psychological clinic, and the latter because it provided a mental test that was to give the new field its first clear identity.

Testing and measurement were also conducted by psychologists employed in mental hospitals. As early as 1890, psychologists undertook research to compare mental abilities of disturbed and normal individuals. Clinicians began to help psychiatrists diagnose and plan treatment for patients with brain damage and other problems. Indeed, after 1907, psychological examination of mental patients in some hospitals became routine. Similar assessments were done in prisons to assist staff members to identify disturbed convicts or plan rehabilitation programs. The tests available to psychologists working in mental hospitals were primarily tests of mental abilities, intelligence tests. It would be many years before psychological tests of personality and psychopathology were developed and became widespread (Benjamin, 2005) (See Table 2.2).

The employment of clinical psychologists in mental hospitals had two important effects. First, it widened psychologists' sphere of influence as they contributed to the assessment of persons with psychological problems. This influence increased as still more psychological tests were developed and deployed. Second, it promoted interaction between psychologists and psychiatrists. As practitioners of a medical specialty, psychiatrists had been attempting to categorize and treat forms of mental illness, especially severe mental illness, for many years. With their common interest in classification, assessment, and treatment of abnormal mental states, psychiatrists and psychologists would invariably influence each other. This cross-fertilization of ideas contributed to a third tradition that gave birth to clinical psychology—the clinical tradition.

The Clinical Tradition

From the beginning of recorded history, human beings have tried to explain behavior that is bizarre or apparently irrational. The earliest explanations of disordered behavior involved magical forces and supernatural agents. Persons who acted "crazy" were said to be possessed by demons or spirits, and treatment involved various forms of exorcism (including *trephining,* or boring small holes in the skull to provide evil spirits with an exit). In Greece, before Hippocrates, these ideas appeared in revised form: disordered behavior was attributed to the influence of one or more of the gods. Even in early monotheistic cultures, God was seen as a possible source of behavior problems. In the Old Testament, for example, we are told that "the Lord shall smite thee with madness, and blindness, and astonishment of heart" (Deuteronomy 28:28). Where supernatural approaches to behavior disorders were prevalent, philosophy and religion were dominant in explaining and dealing with them. (Although they are not prominent in Western cultures today, supernatural—and especially demonological—explanations remain influential in other cultures around the world and in some ethnic and religious subcultures in North America.)

Supernatural explanations of behavior disorders were still highly influential when, in about the fourth century B.C., the Greek physician Hippocrates suggested that these aberrations stem from natural causes. Hippocrates argued that behavior disorders, like other behaviors, are a function of the distribution of four bodily fluids, or humors: blood, black bile, yellow bile, and phlegm. This theory, generally acknowledged as the first medical model of disordered behavior, paved the way for the concept of *mental illness* and legitimized the involvement of the medical profession in its treatment. From Hippocrates until the fall of Rome in 476 A.D., physicians supported and reinforced a physical, or medical, model of behavior disorder.

In the Middle Ages, however, the medical model was swept away. The church became the primary social and legal institution in Europe, demonological explanations of behavior disorders regained prominence, and religious personnel again took over responsibility for dealing with cases of deviance. Ever resourceful, many physicians soon became priests. The church began treating the "insane" by exorcizing the spirits presumed to possess them.

Gradually, the treatment of deviant individuals took the form of confinement in newly established hospitals and asylums, such as London's St. Mary of Bethlehem (organized in 1547 and referred to by locals as "bedlam"). The hospital movement saved many lives, but it did not necessarily make them worth living. Even though many 18th-century scholars agreed that the insane were suffering from mental illness (not possession), the medical profession, which was now back in charge of the problem, had little to offer in the way of treatment. Feared and misunderstood by the general public—many undoubtedly still believed them to be possessed—the insane were little more than prisoners who lived under abominable conditions and received grossly inadequate care. Progressive doctors saw their mental illness as resulting from brain damage or, harking back to Hippocrates, an overabundance of blood, while less progressive doctors still viewed mental illness as reflecting character flaws.

These changing conceptions of mental illness led European and North American reformers of the 18th and early-19th centuries (Philippe Pinel, Benjamin Rush, William Tuke, & Dorothea Dix) to push for more humane living conditions and treatments in mental institutions. In France, Pinel ushered in this era of more humane treatment with the following comment: "It is my conviction that these mentally ill are intractable only because they are deprived of fresh air and liberty" (quoted in Ullmann & Krasner, 1975, p. 135).

In the United States and Great Britain, movements to improve the treatment of persons with severe disorders paralleled those in France. Benjamin Rush, often regarded as the father of American psychiatry (Schneck, 1975), was instrumental in changing the way institutionalized mental patients were treated in the United States. In Great Britain, William Tuke played a similar role. Both men were pivotal figures, with one foot in the past and one in the future. Rush, for instance, advocated the antiquated treatments of bloodletting and a tranquilizer chair for immobilization; Tuke favored the whirling chair and plunge baths. Yet both men also favored removing restraints (as Pinel had in France), both sought to study mental illness scientifically, and both argued that suffering persons were worthy of respect, kindness, and treatment.

Thus began a new awareness of the possibility that mental patients could be helped rather than simply hidden, and physicians assumed the responsibility for helping them. The role of physicians in treating mental disorders was further solidified when, later in the 19th century, syphilis was identified as the cause of general paresis, a deteriorative brain syndrome that had once been treated as a form of insanity.

Finding an organic cause for this mental disorder bolstered the view that all behavior disorders are organically based. The notion that there could be "no twisted thought without a twisted molecule" (Abood, 1960) triggered a psychiatric revolution in which doctors searched feverishly for organic causes of—and physical treatments for—all forms of mental illness (Zilboorg & Henry, 1941).

The conviction that mentally ill patients were suffering from diseases that could be treated led to the development of specialized mental hospitals. Dorothea Lynde Dix, a New England schoolteacher, was a key figure in their development. After visiting almshouses and local jails, she campaigned to improve conditions for the mentally ill, launched public information campaigns, lobbied legislative groups, and eventually played a role in founding more than 30 state institutions for the mentally ill (Schneck, 1975). Clifford Beers, a former mental patient, formed an organization that ultimately became the National Association for Mental Health. It worked to improve treatment of the mentally ill and to prevent psychological disorders.

Superintendents of several newly formed hospitals for the mentally ill—typically psychiatrists—formed the Association of Medical Superintendents of American Institutions for the Insane. At meetings, they discussed causes and treatments of mental illness. By 1892, the group was known as the American Medico-Psychological Association, and by 1921, it had become what it is today, the American Psychiatric Association (Schneck, 1975). Developments in psychiatry coincided with developments of this organization.

Among those developments were attempts to classify mental disorders. The pioneer here is Emil Kraepelin, a German psychiatrist who, over a 40-year period, wrote and revised the first formal classifications of psychological disorders. Kraepelin's career also included participation in the formation of the first state mental hygiene committee in the United States, attending Wundt's summer course in 1877 (2 years before Wundt established his laboratory), giving expert testimony in murder trials, screening soldiers in World War I, writing poetry, and studying Buddhism (Carlson, 1981). Kraepelin's main interest, however, was in a careful classification and description of the various forms of mental illness. Kraepelin's classification system is no longer used, but his approach—classifying mental illness in terms of observable symptoms—is still evident in the current system of classification, the *Diagnostic and Statistical Manual of Mental Disorders* (DSM).

Ironically, the revolution that viewed mental illness as disease also led to the idea that mental disorders might have *psychological* causes, too. In the mid-1800s, a French physician named Jean-Martin Charcot found that hypnosis could alleviate certain behavior disorders, particularly hysteria (today known as conversion disorder). Charcot's lectures, conducted at the same hospital where Pinel had worked, were well attended. Among the regulars were Alfred Binet, William James, Sigmund Freud, and a French neurologist named Pierre Janet. While Charcot favored explanations of hysteria based on neurological degeneration, Janet favored psychological explanations. He believed that some parts of the personality could become split off or *dissociated* from the conscious self and produce symptoms such as paralysis. He also noticed that dissociated aspects were often related to traumatic memories. He saw the physician's job as helping the person become aware of the dissociated aspects of the self, an awareness that would reduced the symptoms.

Janet's views anticipated those of Sigmund Freud, a young Viennese neurologist who, by 1896, had already proposed the first stage of a theory in which behavior disorders were seen not as the result of organic problems but as a consequence of the dynamic struggle of the human mind to satisfy instinctual (mainly sexual) desires while also coping with the rules and restrictions of the outside world. Dispute arose over whether Janet's or Freud's work came first, but there is little doubt that Freud did the most to develop the theory (Watson, 1978), and thus he became far better known than Janet.

Freud's theory brought a less-than-enthusiastic reaction, and his influence on clinical psychology was modest at first, both in Europe and in the United States. One doctor called Freud's ideas "a scientific fairy tale" (Krafft-Ebing, quoted in Reisman, 1976, p. 41). Nevertheless, those ideas grew to become a comprehensive theory of the dynamic nature of behavior and behavior disorder, and they ultimately redirected the entire course of the mental health professions, including clinical psychology. Much happened, however, between the introduction of Freud's ideas and their eventual dominance of clinical practice (See Table 2.3).

TABLE 2.3		
Landmarks of the Clinical Tradition in Clinical Psychology		
Dates	**Key Figures**	**Contributions**
1880–1890s	Kraepelin, Charcot, Janet, Hall	Classified psychological disorders; studied and treated patients with atypical neurological symptoms ("dissociations"); used case studies of pathology to reveal general principles about healthy and unhealthy workings of the mind
1890	James	Psychologist/physician who participated in both empirical and clinical traditions; introduced European psychology and psychiatry to U.S. audiences; wrote *The Principles of Psychology*, which some still regard as the most influential psychology book ever written
1895–1939	Freud	Advanced psychoanalytic view of personality and psychotherapy in numerous writings; his approach came to dominate psychiatry and clinical psychology in the United States during the first half of the 20th century

Section Summary: Although the seeds of clinical psychology were planted centuries ago by philosophers and by pioneers in the physical sciences, the roots of clinical psychology did not appear until the middle and late 1800s. The most prominent roots were the empirical research tradition that developed especially in Germany, the psychometric tradition that developed especially in Great Britain, and the clinical/therapeutic tradition that developed especially in France. Each of these traditions found expression in the United States, and in the U.S. melting pot tradition, eventually combined to form a new specialty in psychology. The three traditions provided a stable base for clinical psychology, much as three legs provide a stable base for a stool. Without any one of them, the discipline would have collapsed. With all three, it could grow and support future developments—which is exactly what happened.

CLINICAL PSYCHOLOGY BEGINS TO GROW

Section Preview: With its roots well established, clinical psychology began to grow during the first four decades of the 20th century. Opportunities for application expanded, initially in psychological testing and later in psychotherapy. Psychologists created professional organizations to support practitioners and establish guidelines for the discipline. Much of the accelerating growth of clinical psychology can be traced to societal needs made evident during and following World Wars I and II.

By the early 1900s, psychology departments had been established at many U.S. and European universities, and persons associated with these departments had begun to apply their discipline. There were 20 psychological clinics on university campuses by 1914 (Watson, 1953a). Many of them were created in the image of Witmer's clinic, but the emphasis gradually shifted from testing and treating children with academic difficulties to testing and treating children with other problems, and then to testing and treating adolescents and adults with problems.

Psychological Testing Expands

Because of its emphasis on careful measurement and standardized administration, psychological testing had the respect of many early empirical psychologists. Compared to psychotherapy, testing was considered a more rigorous, "hardheaded" application of psychology. And as psychologists were employed in mental hospitals, clinics, and specialized settings for the physically and mentally handicapped, their testing contributions were accepted by medical coworkers (usually psychiatrists). Those contributions often came during staff meetings to discuss individual cases (Benjamin, 2005).

During World War I, the need for "mental testers" became acute. When the United States entered the War, large numbers of military recruits had to be classified in terms of intellectual prowess and psychological stability. No techniques existed for such testing, so the Army asked Robert Yerkes (then president of the American Psychological Association) to head a committee of assessment-oriented experimental psychologists who were to develop appropriate measures. To measure mental abilities, the committee produced the Army Alpha and Army Beta intelligence tests (for group administration to literate and nonliterate adults respectively), and to help detect behavior disorders, it recommended Robert Woodworth's Psychoneurotic Inventory (discreetly retitled "personal data sheet";

Yerkes, 1921, in Dennis, 1948). By 1918, psychologists had conducted evaluations of nearly 2 million men.

For much of the first two decades of the 20th century, intelligence testing and psychological testing were synonymous. However, as psychologists found more employment opportunities in child guidance clinics, mental hospitals, and other adult facilities, it became clear that tests of intelligence were not enough. The foreword to Raymond Cattell's 1936 *A Guide to Mental Testing* described the situation:

> For some time there has been a lull in the progress of mental testing as a practical procedure. After the first wave of enthusiasm in the so-called Intelligence Tests, and their indiscriminate and often unintelligent application, this was bound to happen. It became evident that the results of these tests were influenced by factors other than intelligence, which seemed to elude measurement even if they were taken into account at all . . . The psychotherapist, faced with problems of behaviour dependent on forces much more instinctive than intellectual, found the estimation of mental endowment alone of only limited value, especially since variations in mental capacity were always complicated by disturbances of the personality. (Moodie, 1936, vii)

The need for measures of personality, interests, specific abilities, emotions, and traits led to the development of many new tests during the 1920s and 1930s. Clinicians developed many of these tests themselves, while adopting others from the psychoanalytically oriented psychiatrists of Europe. Some of the more familiar instruments of this period include Jung's Word Association Test (1919), the Rorschach Inkblot Test (1921), the Miller Analogies Test (1926), the Goodenough Draw-A-Man Test (1926), the Strong Vocational Interest Test (1927), the Thematic Apperception Test (TAT) (1935), the Bender-Gestalt Test (1938), and the Wechsler-Bellevue Intelligence Scale (1939). Testing was so popular during the first few decades of the 1900s that there were complaints from some quarters that professional meetings were being overrun with psychologists describing their newest mental tests (Benjamin, 1997, 2005). In fact, so many psychological tests appeared (over 500 by 1940) that a Mental Measurements Yearbook was needed to catalog them (Buros, 1938). As the testing role expanded, the distinction between assessment of intellectual abilities and mental illness grew increasingly difficult to maintain (Reisman, 1976). Some of the new personality tests, such as the Rorschach and the TAT, required complex interpretation, including consideration of clients' distorted perceptions, unconscious processes, psychological defenses, and so on. Discussing test results in these psychological terms gave psychologists and therapists (psychiatrists) a shared clinical language and brought clinical psychologists that much closer to the treatment role. For most clinicians of the day, treatment appeared a natural extension of the diagnostic and remedial services they were already providing. They were motivated to enter the treatment role because it expanded their professional identity beyond that of testing, allowed them to become involved with the "whole patient," and opened the door to better paying, more responsible jobs.

Clinicians Pursue Roles as Psychotherapists

Clinical psychologists added psychotherapy to their assessment role, but not without some opposition. Because psychology began as an academic, laboratory-based discipline, relatively few early psychologists sought to conduct psychotherapy with adults, and many, including Witmer, were quite skeptical about such activities (Benjamin, 2005; Taylor, 2000). Change occurred slowly as a natural outcome of at least three factors: (a) as already noted, psychological testing expanded to include measures of personality and psychopathology, (b) child guidance clinics, where clinical psychologists worked since the time of Witmer, broadened their client base to include treatment of social as well as educational maladjustment, and (c) psychologists of the early 20th century became eager to learn psychoanalysis, the dominant approach to psychotherapy among psychiatrists.

It was an English-born psychiatrist, William Healy, who founded the first child-guidance clinic in the United States in Chicago in 1909. Like Witmer, Healy worked with children, employed a team approach, and emphasized prevention, but otherwise his orientation was quite different. For one thing, instead of dealing mainly with learning disabilities or other educational difficulties, Healy focused on cases of child misbehavior that drew the attention of school authorities, the police, or the courts. Healy's clinic operated on the assumption that juvenile offenders suffered from mental illness that should be dealt with before it caused more serious problems. Second, the approach taken by the staff at Healy's Chicago clinic (first called the Juvenile Psychopathic Institute and later the Institute for Juvenile Research) was heavily influenced by Freud's psychoanalytic theories.

In the same year Healy opened his clinic, the psychoanalytic approach to clinical psychology received a huge boost in popularity when G. Stanley Hall, a psychologist, arranged for Sigmund Freud and two of his followers, Carl Jung and Sandor Ferenczi, to speak at a conference celebrating the 20th anniversary of Clark University in Worcester, Massachusetts. Freud's theories had been first introduced to American psychologists during the 1890s, mostly in journal reviews by William James and James Baldwin (Korchin, 1976; Taylor, 2000), psychologists with strong interests in the self, the ego, and "dissociated" states of consciousness such as trance, hypnosis, and unexplained memory loss. The United States was fertile ground for Freud's ideas, and the lectures helped "sell" psychoanalysis to American psychologists (Schneck, 1975).

The effect was gradual, however. Some U.S. psychologists remained skeptical (for instance, Witmer did not attend the conference; Routh, 1994). Nevertheless, by 1911, the first U.S. psychoanalytic association had formed (in New York), and over the next 20 years, psychiatrists and psychologists in increasing numbers identified themselves with Freud's theories (Watson, 1953a). To many it became clear that growth in clinical psychology would be in psychotherapy, and the foundations of psychotherapy would be in psychoanalysis. At the Clark University conference, William James said to Freud, "The future of psychology belongs to your work" (Jones, 1955, p. 27).

The influence of psychoanalytic treatment was gradual, too because few psychologists of the day engaged in any form of treatment. Indeed, even if early clinical psychologists had been interested in practicing psychoanalysis, training was difficult to obtain. University psychology departments, dominated by those trained in Wundt's empirical tradition, were reluctant to develop graduate programs in clinical psychology because their faculties questioned the appropriateness of "applied" psychology and worried about the cost of clinical training. Many also criticized the imprecise nature of Freud's concepts. With few exceptions, formal training in psychoanalysis was available only from psychoanalytic institutes and medical schools, and these were typically run by psychiatrists who were reluctant to admit

Sigmund Freud, seated at left, was introduced to an American audience in 1909, at a conference of psychologists held at Clark University, Worcester, Massachusetts.

psychologists (Abt, 1992; Schneck, 1975). Psychoanalytic treatment was therefore the province of psychiatrists, not psychologists, and for many years the psychiatric community sought to keep it that way. In 1917, for example, a New York psychiatric organization issued a report calling for an end to clinical psychologists' involvement in the diagnosis and treatment of persons with mental disorders (Benjamin, 2005). Even into the 1930s, there were few internships available for clinical psychologists who wanted to perform psychoanalytic psychotherapy. World War II created the conditions for psychoanalytic and other forms of psychotherapy to become a mainstay of clinical psychologists' activities, despite the objections of some psychiatrists.

As in World War I, there was great need for psychological assessment in World War II; many in the military experienced trauma and required treatment; families and communities were disrupted and required intervention. During the War, psychologists with clinical training were recruited in large numbers and worked shoulder to shoulder with psychiatrists and social workers (Korchin, 1976). Because of the great need, psychologists were often pressed into treatment functions, sometimes with minimal training. This "on-the-job" training—supported by the government and obtained via collaboration with psychiatrists, social workers, and persons in other related professions—helped clinical psychologists develop psychotherapeutic skills, most of which were based on the psychoanalytic model.

After the War, many psychologists sought to continue psychotherapy work. Fortunately for them, a series of initiatives dramatically affected their ability to do so. One of these was the Veteran's Administration's (VA) launching of a program to support training in the mental health disciplines in 1946. The VA made clinical internships available in VA hospitals and mental hygiene clinics. Prior to this program, internships for clinical psychologists—typically involving a full year of practical experience—had existed mainly in child guidance clinics and mental hospitals (Routh, 2000). With the VA's blessing, however, formal internship training became available for clinicians interested in being psychotherapists with adult clients.

A second initiative was the national effort to create community mental health clinics throughout the United States. Sponsored by the U.S. Public Health Services and the newly formed National Institute of Mental Health, the initiative was a broad response to concerns about mental health. It remains as one of the largest government-led mental health efforts. Some of these Community Mental Health (CMH) centers also established internships for psychologists in training, expanding the training opportunities for clinicians. By now, mental hospitals and psychiatric facilities, long the training ground for psychiatrists, had begun to open their doors to clinical psychologists, if only in small numbers (Abt, 1992).

Clinical psychologists now had training internships and job opportunities. Some universities and a few psychoanalytic institutes had created training programs for them. But there was no standard set of educational and training experiences that defined what a clinical psychologist was. These would come from professional organizations.

Clinicians Form Professional Organizations

Even though its settings, clients, and functions were expanding throughout the 1930s and into the 1940s, clinical psychology was not yet a recognized profession. At the beginning of World War II, there were still no official university training programs for clinicians. A few offered PhDs, some had MAs, most had BAs or less. To get a job as a clinical psychologist, all a person needed was a few courses in testing, abnormal psychology, and child development, along with an "interest in people."

In most professions, issues of training and qualification are first worked out in national and state professional organizations. Such organizations help provide guidelines for training and licensing, establish codes of conduct for practice, define professional boundaries, and in other ways support practitioners. Professionals need professional organizations.

Clinical psychologists did have an organization, the *American Psychological Association,* established in 1892, but it was dominated by researchers who had doubts about the wisdom of a clinical psychology profession. As more psychologists became interested in applying their knowledge beyond the laboratory, conflicts arose among APA members who wanted the discipline to be a pure science and those who wanted it to be an applied one (Benjamin, 1997).

Preoccupied with the scientific aspects of psychology, the APA had appointed committees on clinical training at various times during the 1920s and 1930s (and had even set up a short-lived clinical certification program), but its involvement was half-hearted. For example, in 1935 the APA Committee on Standards of Training in Clinical Psychology suggested that a PhD plus 1 year of supervised experience was necessary to become a clinical psychologist, but after issuing its report, the committee disbanded and little came of its efforts.

Those favoring an applied approach to psychology—mainly the practitioners of mental testing and psychotherapy—decided to form organizations that would be more

Leta Hollingworth was an influential figure in the early years of clinical psychology; she also anticipated variations in training models that would come about years later.

responsive to their concerns. The first such organization, the *American Association of Clinical Psychologists* (AACP), was cofounded in 1917 by Leta Hollingworth, a member of the Columbia University psychology faculty. Hollingworth was also the first to suggest a more practically oriented form of training for clinical psychologists (a PsyD) as an alternative to the research-based PhD; she also suggested a national examining board to identify and grant licenses to qualified clinicians (Benjamin, 2005; Donn, Routh, & Lunt, 2000). Although the AACP did not survive, it foreshadowed things to come.

During the 1920s, several statewide applied psychology organizations formed, the most prominent of which was the *New York Association of Consulting Psychologists,* which later became the *Association of Consulting Psychologists* (ACP). In 1933, the ACP established codes of ethics for practicing psychologists, and a few years later published the first journal for professional practitioners, the *Journal of Consulting Psychology.* After successful attempts to include more applied psychologists, this organization evolved into the *American Association for Applied Psychology* (AAAP). It contained divisions of consulting, clinical, educational, and industrial psychology and remained a viable alternative to the research-dominated APA, which seemed to have little interest in practice concerns.

As World War II approached, however, the American Psychological Association, long dominated by academic research interests, had begun to recognize that psychology was developing into an applied discipline. Members of APA, many of whom were now also members of alternative state and national professional psychology associations, decided to reorganize to make room for the practice concerns of the applied psychologists (Benjamin, 1997). By 1946, AAAP had dissolved and its members had returned to the

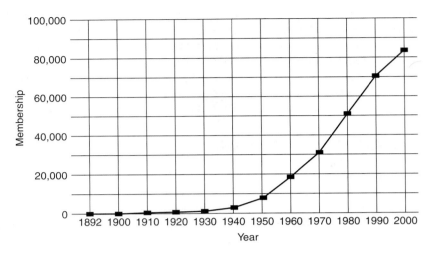

FIGURE 2.2   Total APA Membership, 1892–2000

(*Source*: American Psychological Association Archives (2006). Yearly Membership, American Psychological Association. Retrieved June 14, 2006, from http://www. apa.org/archives/yearlymembership.html.)

APA. When members affiliated with divisions of the reorganized APA, approximately twice as many chose to be in the division of clinical psychology (division 12) as chose to be in the second-most popular division (Benjamin, 1997). Figure 2.2 presents a history of APA membership.

Clinical psychology, firmly rooted and organized as a professional discipline by the mid-20th century, was poised for strong growth. Between the mid-1940s and the mid-1950s, a series of actions by APA and its members defined clinical psychology with a clarity that it had not known before. The most important of these actions included the following: beginning with Connecticut in 1945, states began passing certification laws for psychologists. A year later, the *American Board of Examiners in Professional Psychology* (ABPP) was established to certify that clinicians holding a PhD were qualified. The *American Psychologist,* the flagship journal of APA, was first published in 1946. Three years later, a conference was held in Boulder, Colorado, to discuss the various training models for clinical psychologists, and from this landmark *Boulder Conference* came the principal model of training for clinical psychologists in use today. In 1953, the APA published its first ethical guidelines for clinical psychologists. These and other events launched clinical psychology into a period of rapid expansion. We discuss them, and their impact, in more detail in later chapters.

Section Summary: By the early 1900s, psychology departments had been established at many U.S. and European universities, and persons associated with these departments had begun to apply their discipline. Psychological testing was the most accepted area of application, but clinical psychologists increasingly saw the value of treating psychological problems in adult clients. Unfortunately, they had difficulty finding training to do so. University programs were often dominated by faculty skeptical of psychotherapy, and psychiatrists, who practiced the most popular form of treatment and controlled training in it, were reluctant to grant expertise in psychotherapy to clinical psychologists. But the expanding need for treatment created by two world wars, combined with advances in testing and the establishment of strong professional organizations, eventually opened up the field of psychotherapy to clinical psychologists.

THE MAJOR APPROACHES DEVELOP

Section Preview: After World War II, clinical psychology grew rapidly. This section tells the stories of the more influential treatment approaches in modern clinical psychology—how they were formed, their basic assumptions, and how they are translated into clinical practice. Most students are somewhat familiar with these approaches because they remain central to modern psychology: psychodynamic, humanistic, behavioral, cognitive, systems, and biological. Each of these approaches is best thought of as a broad school of thought rather than a single theory. Our goal here is to describe the origins and assumptions of these broad approaches and to suggest their basic application to psychological problems. In subsequent chapters, we detail the variations of thought and technique within each approach and show how clinicians adopting these variations apply them to cases.

The Psychodynamic Approach

The psychodynamic approach is a collection of related approaches. At its historical core are Freud's psychoanalytic theories. Although others modified, discarded, or extended aspects of psychoanalysis, many of Freud's basic assumptions and psychotherapy techniques remain central to the psychodynamic approach.

Origins. The psychodynamic model is rooted in the work of neurologists and psychiatrists practicing in the French clinical tradition (e.g., Charcot, Breuer) and is given its fullest expression in the writings of Sigmund Freud. Beginning with his *Studies on Hysteria,* published with Breuer (1895), Freud wrote several books and papers over a 40-year period that changed the landscape of clinical psychology.

Like Breuer, Freud often saw patients with neurological symptoms for which no organic cause could be found. Some, for example, complained of paralysis that affected their entire hand but not their arm. Others suffered paralysis of the legs during the day but walked in their sleep. These patients were called *neurotics,* and Freud dealt with the most common type: those displaying hysterical (i.e., nonorganic) paralyses, amnesia, anesthesia, blindness, and speech loss. In Freud's day, treatment for hysteria included wet packs and baths or electrically generated heat. Freud believed that whatever success these methods had were caused by suggestion, so he began experimenting with techniques that maximized the benefits of suggestion, foremost among which was *hypnosis.*

Freud's use of hypnotic suggestion produced temporary results, and around 1890 he began to combine hypnosis with a new technique called the *cathartic method,* which he learned from Breuer, who had stumbled on this technique while attempting to relieve the hysterical symptoms of a patient known as Anna O. The symptoms, which included headaches, a severe cough, neck and arm paralyses, and other problems, began during her father's illness and intensified following his death. She began to display extremes of mood that went from agitation and hallucinations during the day to calm, trancelike states in the evenings. Breuer was struck by the fact that these "trances" resembled hypnosis.

Breuer discovered that if Anna were permitted, while in the hypnotic state, to recite the contents of all her hallucinations from the day, then she invariably would leave the trance state and enjoy a period of almost normal tranquility and lucidity during the following late night hours. Anna came to refer to the exercise of reciting her hallucinations as the "talking cure" or "chimney sweeping" (Fancher, 1973, p. 48).

This talking cure did not eliminate Anna's daytime disorders, however, and new symptoms began to appear. In attempting to cure one of these, an inability to drink liquids, Breuer made the discovery that would later start Freud on the road to psychoanalysis. During one of Anna's hypnotic states, she began describing to Breuer an Englishwoman whom she knew but did not especially like. The woman had a dog that Anna particularly despised. Anna described how on one occasion she entered the woman's room and observed the dog drinking water from a glass. When the event occurred, Anna was filled with strong feelings of disgust and loathing, but out of politeness she was unable to express them. As she recited this account to Breuer, she for the first time permitted herself the luxury of expressing fully and animatedly her negative feelings about the dog's drinking. When she emerged from the trance, she immediately asked for a glass of water, which she drank without the slightest difficulty (Fancher, 1973, p. 49).

Removal of Anna's fear of drinking was apparently brought about by her vivid recollection of a forgotten event while in a trance. It occurred to Breuer that other hysterical symptoms might be caused by forgotten memories and that their recall might cure them. He began hypnotizing Anna and asking her to remember everything she could about her symptoms. He discovered that every symptom could be traced to a traumatic or unpleasant situation for which all memory was absent in the waking state. Breuer found that whenever he could induce Anna to recall those unpleasant scenes and, more importantly, to *express the emotions* they had caused her to feel, the symptoms would disappear (Fancher, 1973, pp. 49–50; italics added).

Freud also found the cathartic method successful, but not all his patients could be hypnotized. To facilitate *conscious* recognition of emotional memories, Freud began asking his patients to relax with their eyes closed and to report whatever thoughts, feelings, or memories came to mind. Recall was often helped by having the patient lie on a couch. This procedure later became known as free association, a mainstay among the psychoanalytic techniques to be described later.

At first, Freud's nonhypnotic treatment of neurotic patients focused mainly on helping them remember important, usually unpleasant, memories and emotions that had been blocked from consciousness. For example, Freud saw evidence that many of his patients had suffered early sexual trauma, usually molestation by a parent or other relative, and he assumed that such events were the basis for most hysterical symptoms. By the turn of the century, however, he was convinced that this "seduction theory" was incorrect and that there were more important causal factors to be considered. For one thing, he found it hard to believe that the sexual abuse of children was as widespread as was suggested by his cases.

Freud also began to pay attention to dreams (his patients' and his own) and concluded that they represented the fulfillment of fantasies and wishes, many of which are socially unacceptable and thus appear—often in disguised form—only when defenses are relaxed during sleep. He suggested that, like dreams, hysterical symptoms could be based on unconscious wishes and fantasies, not just on memories of real events. Thus, a patient's "memory" of childhood seduction by a parent might actually be a *fantasy* or *wish* about such an encounter. The implications of this new theory altered Freud's approach to therapy as well. His *psychoanalytic* treatment of neurosis shifted from the recovery of memories to the broader illumination of the patient's unconscious.

Freud's psychodynamic theory was founded on the idea that human behavior is derived from the constant struggle between the individual's desire to satisfy inborn sexual and aggressive instincts and the need to respect the rules and realities imposed by the outside world (Funder, 2001). To Freud, then, the human mind is an arena where what the person *wants* to do (instincts, impulses) must be reconciled with the controlling requirements of what can or *should* be done (reason, social norms, morality). This conflict often leads to anxiety, against which the person tries to build defenses. If the anxiety gets too strong, or if the defenses become ineffective, a variety of psychological symptoms can appear.

In Freud's system, special mental structures are used to represent the competing mental forces (Freud offered these structures as hypothetical constructs but believed that neurology would some day confirm brain functions compatible with them). Unconscious instincts and primitive impulses make up the *id,* which is present at birth and contains all the psychic energy—or *libido*—available to motivate behavior. Id seeks to gratify its desires without delay, and therefore it is said to operate on the *pleasure principle* (i.e., "If it feels good, do it!"). As the newborn grows and the outside world imposes more limitations on direct id gratification, the *ego* begins to organize as an outgrowth of id around the age of 1 year and begins to find safe outlets for expression of instincts. Since ego adjusts to external demands, it operates on the *reality principle* (i.e., "If you are going to do it, at least do it quietly"). A third mental agency, *superego,* is another result of the socializing influence of reality. It contains all the teachings of family and culture regarding ethics, morals, and values, and according to Freud, these teachings are internalized to become the "ego ideal," or how one would like to be (i.e., "A good person would not do that!"). Superego also contains the conscience, which seeks to promote perfect, conforming, and socially acceptable behavior usually opposed by id.

Freud's three-part mental structure is constantly embroiled in anxiety-provoking internal conflicts. The ego's primary function is to protect against the anxiety that we would feel if we became aware of socially unacceptable id impulses or if we thought about violating the superego's rules (Funder, 2001). The ego attempts to keep these conflicts and their discomfort from reaching consciousness by employing a variety of *defense mechanisms,* usually at an unconscious level (denial, repression, suppression, reaction formation, projection, etc). In spite of constant efforts at repression, undesirable urges—much like an inflated balloon held under water—may sometimes threaten to surface. Although they may be at least temporarily successful, defense mechanisms waste a lot of psychic energy, and, under stress, they may fail. When they do, psychological symptoms are likely to develop (i.e., anxiety, paralysis, unrealistic fears).

Treatment in the psychoanalytic approach is aimed at unearthing the sources of the clients' symptoms. Freud compared his method with archeology: the therapist searches for deeper meaning, uncovering forgotten or repressed memories and unexpressed emotions that lie beneath the overt symptoms. With the therapist's help, the client gradually becomes aware of how historically rooted conflicts, pushed (not quite successfully) into the unconscious, have come to be expressed in current experience. This awareness, called *insight,* is a central goal in psychoanalytic treatment.

As the psychoanalytic approach developed, others expanded upon, challenged, and changed some of Freud's original concepts. We detail these variations on classical psychoanalysis in Chapter 7, "Psychodynamic and Humanistic Psychotherapies." For now, suffice it to say that later theorists expanded the role of the ego (i.e., beyond being a "referee" between the id and superego), placed more emphasis on social and cultural variables (i.e., less on sexual and aggressive impulses), and explored forms of psychodynamic treatment that were less restrictive than classical psychoanalysis (i.e., briefer in duration, greater flexibility in the therapists' role). Despite these modifications, however, all psychodynamic psychotherapies share certain basic assumptions (See Table 2.4).

The Humanistic Approach

The humanistic approach to psychotherapy developed as an alternative to the psychodynamic approach that dominated personality theory and clinical practice during the early 20th century. The humanistic approach views persons as creative, growthful beings who, if all goes well, consciously guide their own behavior toward realization of their fullest potential as unique individuals. When behavior disorders arise, they are usually seen as stemming from disturbances in awareness or restrictions on existence that can be eliminated through various therapeutic experiences (Fischer, 1989; Greenberg, Elliott, & Lietaer, 1994). Treatment approaches aimed at addressing and correcting these problems are also known as *phenomenological* or *experiential therapies.*

TABLE 2.4

Basic Concepts of the Psychoanalytic Approach

1. Human behavior is determined by impulses, desires, motives, and conflicts that are intrapsychic (within the mind) and often out of awareness.

2. Psychological problems typically occur because clients unsuccessfully defend against, and unconsciously replay, conflicts that were originally experienced in childhood relationships with family, peers, and authority figures.

3. Clinical assessment, treatment, and research should emphasize the aspects of intrapsychic activity that must be uncovered if behavior is to be understood and behavior problems are to be alleviated.

4. The goals of psychotherapy are to improve ego functioning and to help clients recognize and change the ways they inappropriately repeat the past.

Origins.   The roots of humanistic therapies are in the clinical tradition, but they also grow from the philosophical position of *phenomenology,* which states that behavior is determined by the perceptions and experiences of the behaving person. This theme is shared by existential philosophers such as Søren Kierkegaard and Jean-Paul Sartre, who emphasized that the meaning of life is not intrinsic but is constructed by the perceiver. The idea of individually construed reality was also emphasized by a group of German psychologists, including Koffka, Köhler, and Werthheimer, known as the Gestalt school. Phenomenology puts the client's perceptions and experiences at the center of therapy—what the client perceives, feels, and thinks in the here-and-now takes center stage. Childhood history buried in the unconscious may have played a formative role, but the client's current experiences of reality (including experiences of the self) are what matter most (See Figure 2.3).

Perhaps the most prominent advocate of humanistic psychology was Carl Rogers, a psychologist who was initially trained in psychoanalysis. Rogers received a PhD in clinical psychology from Columbia University in 1931, then worked at a child guidance clinic before moving to a series of positions at major universities. His first book, *Clinical Treatment of the Problem Child* (1939) reveals his early formulations of therapy, but his prolific writing thereafter fleshed out his approach. Rogers originally called his approach *nondirective* and later changed it to *client-centered* (Rogers, 1951), reflecting the essential importance of the client's construal of life.

Rogers assumed that people have an innate motive toward growth, which he called the *actualizing tendency:* "the directional trend which is evident in all organic and human life—the urge to expand, extend, develop, mature—the tendency to express and activate all the capacities of the organism" (Rogers, 1961, p. 351). Rogers saw all human behavior—from basic food-seeking to artistic creativity, from normal conversation to bizarre delusions—as a reflection of the individual's efforts at *self-actualization* in a uniquely perceived world.

FIGURE 2.3   What Is "Reality"? Your shifting perceptions of this fixed stimulus allow you to see it as either a young woman in a feathered hat or an old woman in a shawl

In Rogers's view, these efforts begin at birth. As the developing child begins to differentiate between the self and the rest of the world, there is a growing awareness of this self—a recognition of the "I" or "me." According to Rogers, all of a person's experiences, including "self" experiences, are evaluated as positive or negative, depending on whether they are consistent or inconsistent with the child's self-actualizing tendency. However, these evaluations are not made on the basis of direct or *organismic* feelings alone, as when a child evaluates the taste of candy as positive. They are also influenced by the judgments of other people. Thus, a young boy may end up negatively evaluating the experience of fondling his genitals (even though the direct feelings are positive) because his parents tell him that he is a bad boy to do so.

Rogers noted, however, that most people value the positive regard of others so highly that they will seek it even if it means thinking and acting in ways that are *incongruent* with organismic experience and the self-actualizing motive. This tendency is encouraged by what Rogers called *conditions of worth*—circumstances in which a person receives positive regard from others (and, ultimately, from the self) only for certain approved behaviors, attitudes, and beliefs. Conditions of worth are usually first created by parents, family, and other societal agents, but they are later maintained internally by the individual (note the similarity to Freud's concept of superego). People who face extreme or excessive conditions of worth are likely to be uncomfortable. If they behave primarily to please others, it may be at the expense of personal growth, as in the case of a woman who tries to fulfill the culturally encouraged role of employed mother despite genuine desires to be a full-time homemaker. On the other hand, people who display authentic feelings and behaviors that are discrepant with conditions of worth risk loss of the positive regard of others and the self.

Perhaps Rogers's most important contributions have been his emphasis on empathic listening on the part of the therapist and on the quality of the therapist–client relationship (Cain, 1990). He described the role of the therapist as follows:

> The therapist must lay aside his preoccupation with diagnosis and his diagnostic shrewdness, must discard his tendency to make professional evaluations, must cease his endeavors to formulate an accurate prognosis, must give up the temptation subtly to guide the individual and must concentrate on one purpose only: that of providing deep understanding and acceptance of the attitudes consciously held at this moment by the client as he explores step by step into the dangerous areas which he has been denying to consciousness. (Rogers, 1946, pp. 420–421)

This quote illustrates the similarities and differences between the psychodynamic and humanistic approaches. Both trace psychological problems to painful experiences that are prevented from fully entering consciousness. Unlike psychoanalysts, however, humanistic therapists do not look for deep historical roots of this problem. Rather, they attempt to help clients identify the phenomenal (here-and-now) experience of avoidance as they occur in perceptions, feelings, and thoughts. The idea is that if the therapist does this with compassion and empathy, the client can more accurately understand and accept the *self*.

The quote also makes evident contrasting views of the therapists' role. Psychoanalysis developed out of the medical/psychiatric profession, so it is natural that the therapist

TABLE 2.5
Basic Concepts of the Humanistic Approach

1. Humanistic psychologists view human nature as essentially positive and believe that their clients' lives can be understood only when viewed from the point of view of those clients.
2. Humanistic psychologists believe problems develop when a person tries to avoid experiencing emotions that are confusing or painful—such avoidance causes the person to become alienated from, and unaccepting of, his or her true self.
3. Therapists treat clients as responsible individuals who are experts on their own experiences and who must ultimately be the ones to make decisions about their lives.
4. Humanistic therapists view the therapeutic relationship as the primary vehicle by which therapy achieves its benefits—focusing on the immediate, moment-to-moment experiences in an atmosphere of honesty and acceptance is what helps clients perceive themselves more positively.

would conduct assessments, form diagnoses, and guide psychotherapy interactions in a manner not unlike physicians treating physical illnesses. Rogers, on the other hand, encouraged therapists to abandon the objective "doctor" role; he advised therapists to follow wherever clients lead them, to understand the client's perspective and communicate that understanding back to the client (See Table 2.5).

The Behavioral Approach

The behavioral approach to psychotherapy grew more from the empirical tradition in psychology than from the clinical or psychometric tradition. This orientation makes behavioral psychologists inclined to see the causes and treatment of disorders somewhat differently than psychodynamic or humanistic therapists do. In general, behaviorists are more inclined to focus on specific, learned behaviors and environmental conditions associated with those behaviors. They are also inclined to seek evidence of treatment outcomes that are objectively measurable. Although clinical observations are relevant, experimental findings form the basis of theory and application of behavior therapy.

Origins.   Groundwork for the emergence of behavior therapy occurred in the 1920s, when psychologists became interested in studying the role of conditioning and learning in the development of anxiety. For example, Ivan Pavlov observed *experimental neuroses* in his dogs after exposing them to electric shock or requiring them to make difficult sensory discriminations. The dogs' symptoms included agitation, barking, biting the equipment, and forgetting things they had previously learned. In the 1940s, Jules Masserman of Northwestern University studied the conditioning and deconditioning of experimental neuroses in cats.

The discovery of experimental neuroses in animals led to research on similar problems in humans. The most famous of these studies was a classic experiment in 1920 by John B. Watson and his graduate student, Rosalie Rayner. A 9-month-old infant, Albert B., was presented with several stimuli such as a white rat, a dog, a rabbit, a monkey, masks, and a burning newspaper. He showed no fear toward any of these objects, but he did become upset when a loud noise was sounded by striking a steel bar with a hammer. To see whether Albert's fear could be conditioned to a harmless object, Watson and Rayner associated the loud noise with a tame white rat. Albert was shown the rat, and as soon as he began to reach for it, the noise was sounded. After several pairings, the rat alone elicited a strong emotional reaction in the child. This conditioned fear also generalized to some extent to other, previously neutral, furry objects including a rabbit, a fur coat, Watson's own hair, and even a Santa Claus mask. Albert's fear persisted in less extreme form during assessments conducted over a 1-month period.

A few years later, Mary Cover Jones, another of Watson's students, investigated several techniques for *reducing* children's fears (Jones, 1924a, b). For example, she used social *imitation* to help a 3-year-old named Peter conquer his fear of rabbits. "Each day Peter and three other children were brought to the laboratory for a play period. The other children were selected carefully because of their entirely fearless attitude toward the rabbit" (Jones, 1924b, p. 310). The fearless examples set by the other children helped Peter become more comfortable with the rabbit, but his treatment was interrupted by a bout of scarlet fever, and his progress was jeopardized by a frightening encounter with a big dog. When treatment resumed, it included *direct conditioning,* a procedure in which Peter was fed his favorite food in a room with a caged rabbit. At each session, some of which were attended by Peter's fearless friends, the bunny was placed a little closer to him. This procedure eliminated Peter's fear of rabbits; Peter summed up the results of the treatment by announcing, "I like the rabbit."

The cases of Albert and Peter encouraged the application of conditioning principles to the treatment of fear and many other disorders; the 1920s and 1930s saw learning-based treatments for sexual disorders, substance abuse, and various anxiety-related conditions.

Mary Cover Jones helped pioneer the behavioral treatments of psychological disorders in children.

TABLE 2.6	
Basic Concepts of the Behavioral Approach	
1. Behavioral psychologists view human behavior as learned through conditioning and observation.	3. Behavior therapy focuses on changing variables that maintain situation-specific learned maladaptive responses.
2. Psychological problems are assumed to be learned and specific to situations or classes of situations.	4. Behavior therapy is derived from empirical research and stresses collection of data to evaluate treatment effectiveness.

The term *behavior therapy* first appeared in a 1953 paper that described the use of operant conditioning to improve the functioning of persons with chronic schizophrenia (Lindsley, Skinner, & Solomon, 1953). However, it was not until the late 1950s and early 1960s that behavior therapy began to achieve its status as a major treatment approach. It was then that treatment research in South Africa, England, and the United States by Joseph Wolpe, Stanley Rachman, Arnold Lazarus, Hans Eysenck, Knight Dunlap, Andrew Salter, and others began to attract widespread attention among clinicians. Their work, which laid the foundation for the behavioral treatment methods outlined in later sections was described in several influential books, including *Psychotherapy by Reciprocal Inhibition* (Wolpe, 1958), *Conditioning Techniques in Clinical Practice and Research* (Franks, 1964), *Case Studies in Behavior Modification* (Ullmann & Krasner, 1965), *Research in Behavior Modification* (Ullmann & Krasner, 1965), and *Behavior Therapy Techniques: A Guide to the Treatment of Neuroses* (Wolpe & Lazarus, 1966). B. F. Skinner's *Science and Human Behavior* (1953) provided a blueprint for the therapeutic use of operant conditioning (See Table 2.6).

The Cognitive Approach

Cognitively oriented researchers and therapists view certain cognitions, particularly thoughts about the self, as especially important in the development of disorders (Salovey & Singer, 1991). Because these thoughts are usually connected to emotions, they affect how persons feel about themselves and their relationships with others. Cognitive therapists attempt to modify maladaptive behavior by influencing a client's cognitions (beliefs, schemas, self-statements, and problem-solving strategies).

Origins.   The cognitive approach to clinical psychology grew from the more general "cognitive revolution" that has influenced all of psychology. This revolution can be traced to developments both inside and outside of psychology. The outside influences include advances in mathematics, biology, and artificial intelligence, and especially the development of the computer.

In 1948, Norbert Wiener, a professor of mathematics at MIT, published *Cybernetics: or Control and Communication in the Animal and the Machine.* Wiener was interested in the internal mechanisms of feedback and control, and his book helped popularize terms such as *input, output,* and *feedback.* Others, such as Alan Turing and Ludwig von Bertalanffy, were working on ways to understand internal routines that guided functional systems (Boeree, 2006). These efforts coincided with the development of the computer, the hardware that would make use of the feedback and control routines ("software") that humans developed.

Psychologists, too, began to speculate on how internal routines might explain normal and abnormal behavior. Of course, speculation about mental events was nothing new, but it should be remembered that serious consideration of mental experiences had been suppressed during the heyday of behaviorism within most of empirical psychology, especially in North America. But by the 1960s, the idea of mental structures had crept back into mainstream academic psychology in works of George Miller (memory, human factors), Noam Chomsky (language development), Jean Piaget (cognitive development in children), and others. Computer analogies and information processing language gave empirically oriented psychologists ways of talking about mental life that seemed less speculative than the concepts proposed by psychoanalysis or humanistic psychology.

Practicing clinicians also welcomed the expanded consideration of mental events. Behavioral clinicians had not adopted the concepts of psychoanalysis, preferring instead to remain closer to empirical psychology's emphasis on observable events and laboratory research. Yet it was inconvenient for behavioral clinicians to avoid references to the client's understanding of their conditions. The client's beliefs about the causes of events, called *attributions* or *appraisals,* seemed to play an important role in their problems.

George Kelly, a clinical psychologist, was arguably the first cognitive clinical psychologist (Reinecke & Freeman, 2003). He developed a theory based on the fundamental assumption that human behavior is determined by *personal constructs,* or ways of anticipating the world (Kelly, 1955). According to Kelly, individuals act in accord with their unique set of expectations about the consequences of behavior. In short, people's *constructs* about life comprise their reality and guide their behavior. For example, a person who sees knives as potentially dangerous would exercise caution when handling them. Because caution reflects an accurate anticipation of the consequences of carelessness and helps avoid accidents, the construct "sharp knives are dangerous" is validated. In Kelly's view, the major goal of human beings is not to satisfy their instincts or maximize their rewards but to validate their personal constructs and thus to make sense of the world as they perceive it. Like scientists who revel in discovering why and when a phenomenon occurs, people seek to understand and predict the phenomena in their lives.

According to Kelly's theory, disordered behavior results when a person develops inaccurate, oversimplified, or otherwise faulty constructs about social experiences. Much as a scientist will make incorrect predictions from faulty constructs, people are likely to behave inappropriately if their personal constructs do not allow them to anticipate and comprehend daily events. Thus, a man who construes everything in life as either "good" or "bad" is going to have problems, because not all events and people can be classified this way without distorting them. He may decide that all college students, political activists, and foreigners are bad and that all children, doctors, and clergy are good, but he will be wrong—at least part of the time. He will also be seen by others as close-minded, prejudiced, and a poor judge of character. His interpersonal relationships will likely be stormy.

Another influential figure in the cognitive approach was Albert Ellis (1962, 1973, 1993). The core principle of his *rational-emotive therapy* is evident in this quote:

> When a highly charged emotional Consequence (C) follows a significant Activating Event (A), A may seem to but actually does not cause C. Instead, emotional Consequences are largely created by B—the individual's Belief System. When, therefore, an undesirable Consequence occurs, such as severe anxiety, this can usually be quickly traced to the person's irrational Beliefs, and when these Beliefs are effectively Disputed (at point D), by challenging them rationally, the disturbed Consequences disappear and eventually cease to reoccur. (Ellis, 1973, p. 167)

According to Ellis, the therapist's task is to attack these irrational, unrealistic, self-defeating beliefs and to instruct clients in more rational or logical thinking patterns that will not upset them (Ellis, 1962; Ellis & Dryden, 1987; Ellis & Grieger, 1977). Unlike in psychoanalysis, where upsetting events are veiled from awareness, key thoughts leading to anxiety and dysfunction are often rather obvious in clients' statements (e.g., clients who believe that they are unlovable are likely to claim that "nobody likes me"; a belief that they cannot tolerate rejection and may break down emotionally is revealed by the comment, "I can't ask them for that—what if they say no?"). Ellis advocated use of strong, direct communication in order to persuade clients to give up the irrational ideas with which they indoctrinate themselves into misery. The cognitive therapist is active, challenging, demonstrative, and sometimes even abrasive.

Other versions of cognitive therapy, like the theories of Aaron Beck (1976), provided detailed accounts of how specific types of thoughts influence specific disorders, such as depression. They are all related to theories, such as those of Albert Bandura (1986) and Walter Mischel (1993), that describe the connections between cognitive activity and social behavior. We cover the contributions of these psychologists in Chapter 8, "Behavioral and Cognitive-Behavioral Psychotherapies" (See Table 2.7).

Cognitive theories share features with psychodynamic, humanistic, and behavioral approaches. For instance, certain cognitions can lead to anxiety and avoidance, as they

---

TABLE 2.7

Basic Concepts of the Cognitive Approach

1. Behavior develops not only from learned connections between stimuli and responses but also from how individuals *construe* or think about events.

2. Individuals develop their own idiosyncratic ways of understanding events that affect them, and those explanations affect how they feel and behave.

3. Psychological problems can develop when people's beliefs (assumptions, explanations, attributions) contribute to the things they most fear—for instance, when a depressed person's belief that she is not liked causes her to be uncommunicative which in turn causes others to see her as unapproachable (a faulty feedback loop).

4. Therapists engage clients in a rational examination of their beliefs, encouraging them to test their hypotheses, explore alternate beliefs, and practice applying alternate beliefs.

can in psychodynamic theory, but cognitive theorists look to conscious thoughts and emotions rather than to unconscious ones (Bandura, 2001). People's perceptions and beliefs about events determine how they behave, as in humanistic psychology, but cognitive psychologists focus especially on certain types of beliefs (self-referential beliefs, explanations for negative events). Cognitive therapists and behavior therapists also have much in common. Cognitively oriented therapists focus on learned connections between external events (stimuli) and behavior (responses), as behavior therapists do, but cognitive therapists add the mediating role of cognitions. Both use learning principles to help clients change: behavior therapists to change maladaptive behavior and cognitive therapists to change maladaptive thinking. In fact, the cognitive and behavioral approaches have so much in common that they have essentially merged, a development we discuss next.

The Cognitive-Behavioral Approach

Initially, the behavioral and cognitive approaches were conceptual adversaries: strict behaviorists abhorred "mentalism," and cognitive psychologists were convinced that strict behaviorism was too strict. But as early as the 1960s and 1970s, there were signs of a truce between the behavioral and cognitive camps (Mahoney, 1977). Behaviorally oriented therapists recognized the importance of cognitions in various disorders, and cognitively oriented therapists recognized the importance of translating cognitive change into behavior change. Albert Ellis, for instance, understood the importance of focusing on specific behaviors (in addition to irrational beliefs); he eventually changed the name of his treatment approach from rational-emotive therapy to *rational-emotive behavior therapy* (Ellis, 1993).

There were other reasons for combining behavioral and cognitive approaches to therapy. Both of them are focused on treating specific aspects of functioning, both had come from the empirical tradition in clinical psychology, and both emphasized well-controlled research to test their underlying theories, assessment techniques, and psychotherapy outcomes.

The result was that the two forms of therapy, originally distinct, are now typically taught and practiced together as *cognitive-behavioral therapy*, or *CBT*. Cognitive-behavioral therapy refers to a family of therapy techniques and approaches originally developed as either behavioral or cognitive. It now also includes refinements and integrations that were developed using both behavioral and cognitive principles (Reinecke & Freeman, 2003). That behavior therapy associations around the world have added the term cognitive to their names (Reinecke & Freeman, 2003) and that psychology textbooks now typically present the two systems together are testimony to the surging popularity of CBT (see Figure 2.4).

Group, Family, Marital, and Systems Approaches

During the latter half of the 20th century, many alternatives to the psychodynamic, humanistic, and cognitive-behavioral approaches developed. Many of these alternatives shared the view that people's behavior develops in, and is a reflection of, the relationship systems that they inhabit. These alternative approaches, which we call *group* or *systems*

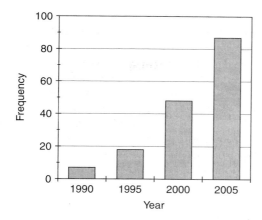

FIGURE 2.4 Frequency with which the Term *Cognitive-Behavioral Therapy* Appears in APA PsycINFO Journal Titles, 1990–2005

approaches, are quite diverse in terms of theoretical foundations and practice, but they all emphasize interventions directed toward a group or pair of interacting persons rather than toward an individual.

Group therapy was one of the first of the socially oriented therapies and was first practiced at the beginning of the 20th century in Boston by Joseph Pratt (Dies, 2003). Later, stimulated by the shortage of professional personnel around the time of World War II, group therapy became a practical answer to a surplus of clients (typically soldiers and veterans) and a shortage of clinicians. Group therapy grew in popularity especially in the 1960s and 1970s and has since progressed to the point that it is now regarded as a valuable intervention in its own right.

Every major approach to clinical psychology developed group treatments: there are analytic groups, client-centered and gestalt groups, and cognitive behavioral groups. As you might expect, groups are conducted somewhat differently depending on the approach employed. For instance, some psychodynamic theorists suggest that therapists should interpret collective, group-level conflicts and defenses rather than those of individual members (e.g., Bion, 1959). Behavioral and humanistically oriented clinicians found that their techniques were readily adaptable to multiclient interventions. For instance, behaviorists emphasized observable behaviors, social reinforcement, modeling, and other forms of overt learning that could be enhanced by a group context. Humanistically oriented therapists stressed attention to conscious experience and here-and-now communication. These techniques became central to most forms of group therapy and to other multiperson intervention. Groups also became popular with many nonprofessional self-help organizations (Gottlieb & Peters, 1991). Weight-control groups, assertiveness groups, consciousness-raising groups, and Alcoholics Anonymous are common examples.

Around the middle of the last century, *family therapy* developed as child clinical psychologists realized they could treat behavior problems more effectively if the parents were involved. Some therapists began to look at children's problems as symptoms of family dysfunctions rather than as the individual child's problem. In *Family Diagnosis: An Approach to the Preschool Child,* Ackerman and Sobel (1950) argued that the focus of diagnosis and treatment should be the family rather than the child. Also contributing to the rise of family therapy were works that examined how family communication patterns affected the development of schizophrenia (Bateson, Jackson, Haley, & Weakland, 1956) and works that studied how family interactions contributed to delinquency (Minuchin, Montalvo, Guerney, & Shumer, 1967). The focus was on the family as a system.

Closely allied with the family therapy movement was the marital therapy movement. The first marital therapists were often obstetricians, gynecologists, clergy, social workers, and educators. Conjoint marital therapy treatment (treating both partners at the same time) by clinical psychologists did not become commonplace until well into the 1970s. Initially, clinical work focused mostly on helping couples adjust to culturally accepted marital roles and giving advice about practical aspects of marriage such as sexuality and parenting (Gurman, 2003).

As psychologists became involved in marital conflicts, the theories supporting marital therapy expanded. Therapists like Jay Haley and Don Jackson of California's Mental Research Institute adopted many of the "family system" ideas from family therapy and applied them to marital therapy (Gurman, 2003). Predictably, humanistically oriented therapists developed marital therapy approaches (e.g., Satir, 1967), as did behaviorists (e.g., Stuart, 1969) and cognitive-behaviorists (e.g., Baucom & Epstein, 1990).

Many of the same factors that influenced the advancement of marital and family therapies contributed to the development of rehabilitation and prevention interventions. Many rehabilitation efforts included helping the client within the larger community. Preventive interventions often took the emphasis on community intervention a step further. For instance, drug use prevention efforts were designed to maximize the number of persons who avoided drugs and to "immunize" them against the influence of those who did use. We explore these alternative group, family, marital, and related systems therapies in Chapter 9, "Alternative Modes of Clinical Intervention" (See Table 2.8).

Biological Influences on Clinical Psychology

Various approaches to clinical psychology traditionally emphasize psychological variables such as unconscious conflicts, learned associations, and perceptions of the self, but few would disagree that disordered behavior can be most fully understood by also taking biological factors into account. Early psychiatrists in the clinical tradition took for granted that biological factors were involved in psychopathology, and more recently research in neuroscience, experimental psychopathology, behavioral genetics, and related areas has made clinicians aware that behavioral and mental processes rest on a foundation provided by

TABLE 2.8
Basic Concepts of the Group, Family, Marital, and Related Systems Approaches

1. Human behavior develops in, and is maintained by, social contexts.	3. Group, family, and marital therapists focus on and attempt to influence specific patterns of interaction and exchange that have significance for individuals in the system.
2. The interlocking system of roles, beliefs, behaviors, and feedback mechanisms can function well or poorly.	

each person's biological makeup. This makeup includes genetically inherited characteristics as well as the activity of the brain and other organs and systems that underlie all kinds of behavior, both normal and abnormal (Bernstein, Penner, Roy, & Clarke-Stewart, 2008).

Biological factors can influence mental disorders in various ways. Sometimes, the influence is direct, as when alcohol or other drugs cause intoxication, when degeneration of neurons in certain areas of the brain causes Alzheimer's disease, and when genetic abnormalities cause particular forms of mental retardation. Other disorders can result from more than one cause, only some of which involve biological factors. Such multiple pathways to disorder are suspected in the appearance of various subtypes of depressive disorders, anxiety disorders, schizophrenia, and personality disorders.

Clinicians also recognize that finding biological contributions to disorders does not automatically negate the value of psychological treatments. Thus, even if a child's hyperactivity is traced to a neurological defect, a solution might be provided by cognitive-behavioral therapy instead of, or in addition to, drugs. Clinicians are also becoming more interested in biological causes of mental disorders because it appears that those factors can often be modified by psychological interventions. You will see in Chapter 12, "Health Psychology," and Chapter 13, "Clinical Neuropsychology," for example, that researchers in health psychology and neuroscience are finding that the mind and body affect each other in ways we are just beginning to understand. In short, recognizing the importance of biological variables in psychopathology does not render traditional approaches to clinical psychology irrelevant; indeed, it deepens and expands their range of inquiry.

Clinical researchers today are focusing special attention on the diathesis-stress view of psychopathology in which biological factors are seen as one of three causal components. The first, known as a *diathesis,* is the presence of some kind of biological defect, usually a biochemical or anatomical problem in the brain, the autonomic nervous system, or the endocrine system. This defect or set of defects is often inherited but can also result from physical trauma, infection, or other disease processes. The second is known as *vulnerability* to developing a psychological disorder. People who carry certain diatheses are said to be at risk for or predisposed to developing the disorders with which those diatheses have been associated. The third causal component is the presence of *pathogenic (disease-causing) stressors.* If at-risk persons are exposed to such stressors, their predisposition for disorder may actually evolve into disorder. However, if those same at-risk individuals encounter less stressful environmental experiences, their predisposition may never express itself as a clinically significant disturbance.

The diathesis-stress view has been employed in the construction of a vulnerability model of schizophrenia that includes and integrates biological, psychological, and environmental causes (Cornblatt & Erlenmeyer-Kimling, 1985; Zubin & Spring, 1977). This model suggests that (a) vulnerability to schizophrenia is mainly biological; (b) different people have differing degrees of vulnerability; (c) vulnerability is transmitted partly through genetics and partly through neurodevelopmental abnormalities associated with prenatal risk factors, birth complications, and other problems (Barr, Mednick, & Munk-Jorgensen, 1990; DiLalla & Gottesman, 1995; Tyrka et al., 1995); and (d) psychological components, such as exposure to poor parenting or inadequate coping skills, may play a role in whether schizophrenia appears and in how severe it will be (Wearden, Tarrier, Barrowclough, Zastowny, & Rahill, 2000).

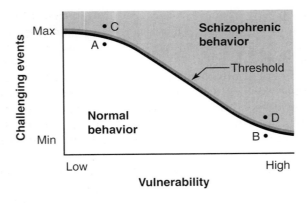

FIGURE 2.5 The Vulnerability Model of Schizophrenia. According to this model, a strong predisposition for schizophrenia and little environmental stress (point D), a weak predisposition and a lot of stress (point C), or any other sufficiently potent combination can lead a person to cross the threshold into schizophrenia

As shown in Figure 2.5, many different blendings of vulnerability and stress can lead to schizophrenia. And, in accordance with the diathesis-stress perspective, people vulnerable to schizophrenia will be especially likely to actually display it if they are exposed to environmental demands, family conflicts, and other stressors that elicit and maintain schizophrenic patterns of thought and action. Those same stressors would not be expected to lead to schizophrenia in people who are less vulnerable to it.

Numerous textbooks on abnormal psychology provide more detailed coverage of biological factors in mental disorders and of the use of diathesis-stress perspectives in explanatory theories. We address biological influences at various points throughout the remaining chapters.

Comparing Approaches: An Illustrative Case

How might the various treatment approaches be applied by clinical psychologists? Let's consider a case in point:

Anna B, a 17-year-old high school junior, was referred by her physician to a psychology clinic because of a suspected eating disorder and possible depression. She is underweight, has stopped menstruating, and complains of a sore throat along with other physical ailments. She also reports that she has difficulty sleeping. Her mother states that Anna's affluent, upper-middle-class family is loving and supportive and that Anna has seemed moody and depressed for the past several months. During an initial interview, Anna admitted that she had contemplated suicide and had been restricting her intake of food and occasionally inducing vomiting to avoid gaining weight. There are cut marks on her wrist, which Anna says she made on two occasions. She reports having two close friends with whom she talks intimately. Since a break-up with a boyfriend 4 months earlier, she has not been dating, but she is active in the school choir and hopes to pursue singing in college. Her grades in school, normally A's, have begun to slip to B's and one C, which deeply concerns her. Anna is reluctant to agree that she has an eating disorder, but she agrees that she may be depressed—she reports feeling constant pressure to succeed, has doubts about her ability to do so, and has begun to wonder if life is worth living that way.

Clinicians representing all theoretical approaches would consult with Anna's physician to insure that she had all necessary medical treatment, including any indicated medications. In states where it is permitted, some psychologists with special training might prescribe medications themselves, though still in collaboration with Anna's physician. Most psychologists would seek input and involvement of Anna's family as well, though the degree of family involvement sought and used in treatment could vary widely depending on how the clinician understands Anna's problems and their treatment. In short, clinicians from different approaches would likely focus on different causal explanations, diagnostic and assessment procedures, and treatment techniques. You might get some ideas about applying different approaches by examining Table 2.9.

Psychoanalytic therapists would likely speculate about unconscious conflicts that motivate Anna's behavior. They would use techniques designed to help Anna become aware of the anxiety-provoking conflicts she defends against, perhaps symbolically with self-starvation. They might also help her to understand how past and current relationships have contributed to these defenses.

Humanistic psychologists would likely focus on Anna's self-concept, on how she understands and experiences her symptoms, what they mean to her. They would help her to become more accepting of aspects of herself that she has likely become critical of—perhaps her desire to be perfect, to be in control, to be liked.

Behavioral psychologists might help Anna learn to recognize the situations in which she restricts her food intake and the situations present when she feels most depressed. They would help her examine her behavior in those situations as well as the potential rewards she might receive for those behaviors. They would probably help Anna develop a step-by-step plan for food intake that would maintain a weight she was comfortable with (and that was reasonable) and help her set up suitable ways to reward herself to maintain her gains. They may help Anna set up similar programs for behaviors related to her feelings of depression. They would also likely involve the family in these plans, as family members are a critical component of the situation in which the behavior occurs.

Cognitive clinicians would likely add to the behavioral approach by also exploring and challenging Anna's beliefs and assumptions, which would come out directly or indirectly in the course of talking with her (e.g., "I can't ever allow myself to fail," "My social worth depends on my appearance," "No one likes me"). Through practice, Anna might learn to recognize the situations in which she makes these statements to herself, and she might learn to counter them with more reasonable and adaptive self-statements.

Family therapists would likely focus on how family dynamics influence Anna's eating disorder and depression. Are there conflicts within the family that are overt or festering underground, unexpressed, and if so, are Anna's symptoms reactions to these broader problems she cannot fully understand or fix? How do other family members interact with Anna, and she with them? Can roles, expectations, or communication patterns be altered to relieve Anna or others in the family of burdens or help create more supportive relationships? Systems theorists, and likely therapists from the other orientations, would also help Anna to understand some of the cultural and gender issues that tend to make some achievement-oriented young women from affluent families feel such pressure.

A full treatment of the diagnostic and treatment stages of each approach is well beyond the scope of this chapter, but in subsequent chapters we cover therapeutic approaches in much more detail.

TABLE 2.9

Basic Assumptions of the Major Psychological Approaches to Psychotherapy

	Psychodynamic	Humanistic	Behavioral	Cognitive	Systems
View of Human Nature	Much of mental life is hidden from awareness and embroiled in conflict	Human nature is generally growth oriented; perception is reality	Human behavior is learned primarily via conditioning, reinforcement, and similar processes	Cognitions are learned and mediate between events (stimuli) and actions (responses)	Human behavior emanates from, and must be understood in, social contexts
Basic Causal Assumption about Pathology	Unconscious conflicts rooted in the past and unconsciously replayed in the present	Alienation from the true self caused by avoidance of threatening emotions	Learned maladaptive responses to situations	Learned maladaptive cognitions, particularly about the self	Dysfunctional systems
Focus of Therapeutic Intervention	Unconscious conflicts and historically based maladaptive patterns	Immediate experiences	Specific overt behaviors, their triggering antecedents, and their reinforcing consequences	Maladaptive cognitions (attributions, beliefs, etc.) that mediate between antecedents and consequences	Group, family roles, and interaction patterns
Role of the Therapist	"Archeologist": guide the client to an understanding of roots and current manifestations of intrapsychic conflicts	"Mirror": create a supportive emotional climate in which the client feels understood, accepted, and valued	"Coach": help the client identify, plan, and execute specific behavioral changes and the conditions for maintaining them	"Scientist": help the client learn to identify, challenge, and replace habitual maladaptive thoughts	"Social planner": help group members to make changes in roles, intergroup relations, and communication patterns

Section Summary: The foundations of psychodynamic and behavioral approaches to clinical psychology developed well before World War II, but after the war, when treatment became a central activity for clinicians, these approaches surged. Other approaches to treatment soon developed: humanistic, cognitive, group/systems, and hybrid approaches such as cognitive-behavioral. These "schools" dominated clinical psychology, shaping theory and practice during the field's most rapid period of development. They continue to exert strong influence today.

THE PROS AND CONS OF TAKING A SPECIFIC APPROACH

Section Preview: A single theoretical approach to clinical psychology can help to organize a vast amount of confusing information about human behavior. It can also help direct clinicians in their assessment and treatment activities. However, adopting a single approach can produce myopia and impede the development of the discipline, especially if clinicians are rigid or dogmatic in their championing of one approach.

An approach to clinical psychology provides clinicians with a framework to guide thinking and practice. It helps them narrow the vast range of variables to a few manageable ones. By doing so, clinicians can then more easily note relationships among those variables. They can propose and test explanations for how behavior develops and becomes problematic. Based on their explanations, clinicians can then develop assessment methods that efficiently provide data about the variables of interest, develop treatment techniques targeted for specific problems or persons, and conduct research to discover the level of effectiveness of those interventions. A clinician's approach guides all these activities.

Ironically, a specific approach to clinical psychology can act not only as a compass and guide but also as a set of blinders. As newer clinical approaches developed, they often defined themselves by their rejection of assumptions held dear by other approaches (e.g., behavioral approaches rejected unconscious and unobservable mental events in favor of observable behavior; humanistic approaches rejected deterministic assumptions of psychoanalysis and behaviorism in favor of self-determination in the here-and-now). Clinical training often compounds the perceived differences among approaches. Trained in graduate programs favoring one theoretical orientation, some therapists and researchers have championed their approaches over the others, more or less automatically.

Each specific approach tends to attract followers whose commitment to it ranges from healthy skepticism to fanatical zeal. Some clinicians allow their favorite approach to so completely organize their thinking about behavior that they become rigid and closed to new and potentially valuable ideas associated with other approaches. Gold and Strickler (2006) have suggested that adherents of the various psychotherapy approaches have exhibited "a powerful xenophobic fear and loathing that caused immediate and reflexive dismissal of approaches to psychotherapy that were different than one's own" (p. 3).

But there can also be healthy aspects to the "turf wars" among different approaches. As long as a discipline is guided by basic scientific practices, competing points of view stimulate research, and research advances theory and practice—it helps answer questions about causes of disorders and effectiveness of treatments. Fortunately, this has happened in clinical psychology. As we discuss more fully in Chapter 10, "Research on Clinical

Intervention," years of research show convincingly that no single approach has cornered the market on therapeutic effectiveness, and yet it is not accurate to say that all are equally effective. Each of the approaches we have discussed so far is effective with certain problems, certain clients, or in certain situations.

An approach is also like a region of the world that develops its own dialect. That dialect eases communication among those who share it; terms become a professional shorthand, making communication more efficient. But for those who do not share it, the dialect can obstruct discussions. Often, the exchange of ideas between persons espousing different approaches to clinical psychology is hampered by this kind of language barrier. Both parties think they are speaking clearly and comprehensibly when, in fact, their specialized terms and meanings keep them from fully understanding each other.

In short, their views become not just organized but fossilized in a way that makes objective evaluation and subsequent modification of professional practices unlikely. Clinicians who become overly dependent on a specific approach may continue to perform in strict accordance with its tenets even when empirical evidence suggests that change is in order. In other words, taking a consistent perspective can evolve from an asset to a liability if it produces such a narrow focus that other points of view are overlooked. When this happens, not only are clients poorly served but the profession is diminished.

Fortunately, most problems associated with taking a specific approach to clinical psychology can be reduced by (a) avoiding the overzealous commitment to it that fosters conceptual rigidity, behavioral inflexibility, and semantic narrowness, and (b) evaluating that approach according to rigorous scientific methods, and revising the approach when the data demand it. This is not to say that systematic use of a particular approach is not important; quite the opposite. However, understanding and appreciating other points of view can act as insurance against a narrow-mindedness that could be detrimental to clinicians and clients alike. We hope that the material in this chapter helps you remain open-minded.

How do clinicians choose their approach to clinical psychology? There are no universally agreed-upon criteria available to guide the choice; even the advice offered in this chapter about the value of scientifically testable approaches is based on the authors' personal biases, which, though shared by many, are biases nonetheless. Freudians might suggest that unconscious motivation influences clinicians' choices, behaviorists might argue that we tend to choose the approach modeled for us by our mentors, while humanistic psychologists might seek the answer in the perceived congruity between a particular approach and the self-concepts of its adherents. Perhaps the choice is made on the basis of "cognitive style" (Kaplan, 1964), emotional and personality characteristics (Poznanski & Mclennan, 2003), worldview (Murdock, Banta, Stromseth, Viene, & Brown, 1998), or just plain "personal preference" (Zubin, 1969). The orientation of a clinician's instructors during university training also plays a role, though not a definitive one (Poznanski & Mclennan, 2003).

The truth is that no one really knows exactly why particular clinicians choose particular approaches, but we do know what approaches they choose. Among clinicians expressing a specific choice, cognitive and cognitive-behavioral approaches are most often selected (Norcross, Karpiak, & Santoro, 2005). Psychodynamic approaches remain popular as well, though certainly not as popular as they were a few decades ago.

But not all clinicians make only one choice. When asked about their theoretical orientation, many clinicians say that they do not confine themselves to a single approach (Milan, Montgomery, & Rogers, 1994; Norcross, Hedges, & Castle, 2002). Instead, they tend to adopt aspects of two or more approaches that they find valuable and personally satisfying (Zook & Walton, 1989), a position described in Chapter 1 as *eclecticism.*

The ranks of the eclectic have grown in clinical psychology. Beginning in 1981 and at 10-year intervals since then, John Norcross and his colleagues have surveyed the American Psychological Association's Division of Psychotherapy (Division 29). In the 2001 survey of Division 29, "roughly one third of the responding psychologists self-identified as eclectic/integrative, one quarter identified themselves as psychoanalytic/psychodynamic, another quarter as cognitive or behavioral, and the remainder as subscribers to a variety of other psychotherapy systems" (Norcross et al., 2002, p. 98). Others' estimates of clinicians identifying themselves as eclectic range from near one third (Norcross et al., 2002; Norcross, Karg, & Prochaska, 1997) to two thirds or more (Hollanders & McLeod, 1999; Slife & Reber, 2001). Whatever the percentage, it is clear that eclecticism is a favored approach among practicing clinicians (Santoro, Kister, Karpiak, & Norcross, 2004).

Section Summary: There are a variety of approaches to clinical psychology. An approach is necessary for clinical psychologists to limit the number of variables they attend to and research. Yet an approach can do as much harm as good if clinicians become overzealous in their allegiances. Common sense and empirical research suggest that each major approach has contributed to clinical psychology. When viewed from the perspective of several decades, the three most noticeable trends in therapists' selection of approaches are (a) the decline in popularity of the psychodynamic approach from its dominance in the mid-20th century to its leveling off in the last two to three decades, (b) the increase in the percentage of clinicians selecting cognitive and cognitive-behavioral approaches, and (c) the increase in the percentage of clinicians favoring eclectic and integrative approaches.

CLINICAL PSYCHOLOGY TODAY

Section Preview: The history of clinical psychology reveals several key themes, the most prominent of which are (a) ongoing concerns about the balance of science and practice, (b) viewing theoretical diversity as a strength as well as a potential weakness, and (c) the impact of historical and cultural events that influence theory and practice.

A few themes emerge clearly from our review of clinical psychology's history. Perhaps the most evident one involves reliance on the twin pillars of science and practice within the profession. The blending of science and practice has always been a strength of the field but also a source of controversy and problems. Problems develop especially if clinicians become so invested in one set of activities that they become isolated from aspects of the field in which they seldom engage. For instance, if practitioners are insufficiently involved in research, they may fail to appreciate the value of systematic and carefully controlled studies. Conversely, if researchers, who often work in academic settings, are insufficiently involved in practice, they are in danger is losing sight of clinical realities that can affect day-do-day practice (Himelein & Putnam, 2001). Ideally, practice and research should inform each other.

A second theme is the diversity of theoretical perspectives within clinical psychology. This diversity can be a strength of the field but also a weakness. After decades that saw the emergence of new psychological theories and therapies, as well as numerous modifications to existing approaches, it has become obvious that some degree of integration is needed. Ideally, empirical evidence should guide how this is done. However, even when solid evidence is available and clinicians are open to evidence, there remain logistical problems for combining or selecting among approaches to clinical practice. Those diversity-based logistical problems affect how training is conducted and how services are delivered.

A third theme involves the sociocultural factors that are shaping the field of clinical psychology. These factors helped bring about the field in the first place, and they strongly influenced how the field developed. You can see this influence in the rise of empirical psychology in the field's beginning, the need for testing during World War I, and the need for treatment during and after World War II. Current sociocultural influences, such as increasing cultural diversity in the United States and the changing nature of health care (discussed in Chapter 1) are changing the ways in which clinical psychological services are offered and how clinicians are trained.

In short, clinical psychology has changed significantly since its post–World War II expansion. Some of today's most pressing issues have roots that extend all the way to the beginning of the field; other issues are the result of recent and unforeseen cultural changes. In order to maintain a healthy profession, clinical psychologists must recognize the lessons of the past and anticipate future change.

CHAPTER SUMMARY

Clinical psychology has grown rapidly since its birth in the late 19th and early 20th centuries. Although it began primarily as a laboratory-based research discipline, clinical psychology soon grew into an applied one, first in psychological testing and later in psychotherapy. World events, particularly the two world wars, were especially important in contributing to the development of the field.

Each of several theoretical approaches to clinical psychology that developed before and especially after World War II emphasizes different explanations of how behavior develops and becomes problematic. The psychodynamic approach is based on Sigmund Freud's psychoanalysis, which sees both normal and abnormal behavior as determined by intrapsychic processes, and conflicts among id, ego, and superego, that have roots in childhood. The humanistic approach sees behavior as determined primarily by unique perceptions of the world as experienced by humans who are responsible for themselves and capable of changing themselves. Clinicians taking this approach try to see the world through their clients' eyes and help them reach self-actualization by encouraging their awareness of genuine feelings, wishes, and goals. The behavioral approach focuses on measurable behavior, not inferred personality constructs, and emphasizes the principles of operant learning, classical conditioning, and observational learning in understanding the causes and treatments of problems. In recent years, the behavioral approach has blended with cognitive theories, which focus on habitual, learned ways of thinking about events. The combination, cognitive-behavioral, has become one of the most popular approaches in clinical psychology, particularly for those who favor a more focused, empirically based approach. Group, marital, family, and related systems approaches developed during the later half of the 20th century. What these approaches have in common is the recognition that interpersonal environments exert a powerful influence on behavior; treatments are therefore often built around changing some interpersonal system rather than changing a single individual.

Research in neuroscience and other areas has made clinicians from all approaches aware of the important role played by genetics, the nervous system, and other biological factors in behavior and behavior disorders. The value of integrating psychological and biological factors can be seen in diathesis-stress explanations of various forms of mental disorder and in the growth of fields such as health psychology and neuropsychology.

Although some approaches to clinical psychology are more popular than others, none has a monopoly on describing and explaining behavior. Many clinicians therefore adopt elements of more than one approach in their daily work. Just as the cultural environment affected clinical psychology's growth in the past, cultural factors continue to affect clinical psychology today. Among the most prominent recent trends is that toward psychotherapy integration and eclecticism, the need to determine, through empirical evidence, which forms of therapy are most effective, and the changing climate of health care delivery in the United States.

STUDY QUESTIONS

1. How did the field of clinical psychology come into being?

2. What are the empirical, psychometric, and clinical roots of clinical psychology?

3. What applications of clinical psychology developed during the first half of the 20th century?

4. How did historical events, especially the two world wars, influence the development of clinical psychology?

5. What major approaches to clinical psychology developed during the second half of the 20th century?

6. How do the major approaches to clinical psychology differ in their basic assumptions about causes of psychopathology and recommendations for treatment?

7. How might the different clinical approaches be applied to specific cases?

8. What are the pros and cons of taking a specific approach to clinical psychology?

9. What are the challenges and major areas of transition facing clinical psychology today?

WEB SITES

- APA's Society for the History of Psychology: http://www.apa.org/about/division/div26.html
- APA's Division 29, Psychotherapy: http://www.apa.org/about/division/div29.html
- The Association for Psychological Science: http://www.psychologicalscience.org
- A Web site for the Freud Museum in London, where Freud spent the last year of his life after fleeing Vienna from the Nazis in 1938: http://www.freud.org.uk

CHAPTER 3
Basic Features of Clinical Assessment

Chapter Preview: In this chapter we offer an overview of the clinical assessment process. We outline the range of assessment options available to clinicians, then detail the common goals of assessment: diagnosis, description, treatment planning, and prediction. We also introduce factors affecting a clinician's choices about how to conduct an assessment, including the purpose of the assessment, the clinician's theoretical views, the psychometric properties of assessment instruments, and other contextual factors. Because assessment involves combining data and drawing inferences, we discuss the use of clinical judgment, focusing especially on errors that clinicians should avoid. Assessments ultimately must be communicated to clients and third parties, so we conclude by discussing factors associated with reporting assessment results.

A CLINICAL CASE

Dr. T was asked to take the case of Jessie, a 17-year-old male whose school counselor had become concerned that Jessie was showing signs of depression and rebellion. In addition to missing school because of alleged illnesses (his counselor does not believe him), Jessie has frequently been belligerent with some of his teachers. Jessie's parents drove him to the appointment, but they declined to meet with the therapist, saying only that they wanted to know what was wrong with their son and that they wanted him to get whatever treatment the insurance would cover. In the intake interview, Jessie expressed a strong dislike of school, saying it was a waste of time. He said that no one understands him there, and most of his classmates only ignore him or make fun of him, especially when he "checks out" in class. Upon questioning, he described the "checking out" as going to sleep for a minute or two; twice this involved falling on the floor. He said that he had been prescribed medication for seizures, but he didn't always take it. In school, he was mostly silent and sullen and did not speak with classmates. Outside of school, he spent most of his time with a 20-year-old friend who worked as a dishwasher at a local diner. Last week, the two young men had been caught in possession of alcohol. He admitted that he had been depressed and that for at least the last 3 weeks had "no interest in anything." He said that during this time he had slept for longer periods, sometimes as much as 14 to 16 hours per day. He also claimed to have had "some pretty bizarre thoughts about leaving this life and living in another dimension." He also informed the therapist that his parents were in the process of getting a divorce.

How can the therapist best understand Jessie's problems? Which of the problems are the most pressing? What is his diagnosis? Is Jessie suicidal or otherwise dangerous? What role do the parents play in his difficulties? How can an effective treatment be designed? In order to answer these questions, the psychologist must conduct an assessment.

Assessment is the collection and synthesis of information to reach a judgment. Almost everyone engages in some type of assessment at one time or another. For example, whether we realize it or not, we collect, process, and interpret information about the background, attitudes, behaviors, and characteristics of the people we meet. Then, in light of our experiences, expectations, and sociocultural frame of reference, we form impressions that guide decisions to seek out some people and avoid others.

Clinical psychologists collect and process assessment information that is more formal and systematic than that available to nonprofessionals. As discussed in Chapter 2, "Clinical Psychology's Past and Present," before psychotherapy became a major role for clinicians, assessment was their most common applied activity. Assessment's relative popularity has declined since that time, but much of the decline has occurred because certain kinds of assessment, especially the Rorschach and related projective techniques, are taught and used less frequently than they once were. Other areas of assessment have more or less held their own (Clay, 2006a). Although no longer the dominant activity of clinical psychologists, assessment remains an important area for them. In this chapter, we consider what clinical psychologists have learned about the challenge of clinical assessment. In the following two chapters, we discuss specific types of assessments.

AN OUTLINE OF THE ASSESSMENT PROCESS

Section Preview: Assessment involves a series of steps, beginning with a problem or referral and ending with the psychologist's communicating the results of the assessment to appropriate parties. In between, the clinician must make a number of judgments, such as which instruments to use and how best to combine clinical assessment data into a clinical judgment. At each step, the clinician must engage in activities to insure that the most relevant data are gathered and analyzed.

Clinical assessment has been described in various ways (Tallent, 1992), but all of them portray it as a process of gathering information to solve a problem. All of them recognize that, to be most effective, assessment activities should be organized in a sequence of systematic, logically related steps driven by a goal. Most assessments follow the general sequence outlined in Figure 3.1.

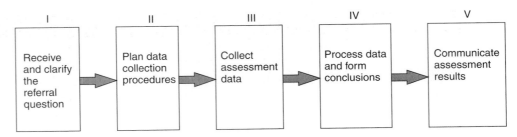

FIGURE 3.1   A Schematic View of the Clinical Assessment Process

Receiving and Clarifying the Referral Question

Two related questions must be answered before clinical assessment can begin (McReynolds, 1975): What do we want to know, and how best can we find out about it? Answers to the first question—what do we want to know?—depend on who requested the assessment and for what purpose. The person or agency requesting the psychological assessment is called the *referral source*, and the question or issue to be addressed in the assessment is called the *referral question*.

The referral question is very important because it shapes the clinician's choice of assessment instruments, interpretation of results, and communication of results (Shum, O'Gormon, & Myors, 2006). Clinicians must therefore understand the context of the referral and often must help referral sources clarify the purpose of the assessment (Groth-Marnat, 2003). In doing so, clinicians may need to educate others about what a psychological assessment can and cannot reveal. They may also need to educate them about the practical and ethical constraints involved in conducting assessments.

The referral question is the first step in shaping the ultimate goal of assessment, and the clearer the goal, the better the chance that a clinician can reach it. As you can see in Table 3.1, referral questions can be quite varied. Indeed, requests can range from educational assessments of children (Reynolds & Kamphaus, 2003) to diagnosis and treatment planning for specific disorders in adults (Brand, Armstrong, & Loewenstein, 2006) to assessments of psychological injuries in court cases (Koch, Douglas, Nicholls, & O'Neil, 2006) to predictions of suicide (Nisbet, 2006).

Planning Data Collection Procedures

Answers to the second question—how best can we find out what we need to know?—come into play after the referral question and the clinician's role have been clarified. With a clear goal in mind, the clinician can now begin planning methods to collect data.

There are four main sources of assessment data: interviews, behavioral observations, psychological tests, and case history data. The range of available choices from within this list is vast. To illustrate, consider the sheer number of things that can be asked about a person at several interrelated levels, from biological functioning to relationships

TABLE 3.1

Examples of Referral Questions from Various Sources

Source	Referral Question
Therapist	Would this person be a good candidate for group psychotherapy?
	How effective have I been in treating clients with anxiety disorders?
Physician or treatment team	What is the correct psychological diagnosis for this client?
	What cognitive and emotional limitations does this person have following her accident, and what strengths does she have to draw on during rehabilitation?
Client	What, if anything, should we do to salvage this marriage?
	Would I be good at this kind of job?
School	What is an appropriate educational placement for this child?
	How should we intervene to help this student better manage violent tendencies and problems in relationships with peers and teachers?
Parent	Is my child suffering from depression and in need of counseling?
	How can we help my child cope with the loss of his mother?
	My child becomes very emotional and refuses to go to school: what can I do?
Court	Does this person pose an imminent threat of danger to himself or others?
	Which custody arrangement is in the best interest of this child?
	Is this client mentally able to understand the criminal charges against him and to assist an attorney in mounting a legal defense?
	Has this person sustained psychological injuries that would be relevant to litigation?
Employer, government agency, or other third party	Is this person suffering from a mental illness that would qualify him to receive disability payments?
	What form of treatment would best help this person to resume productive employment, and for which types of employment would the person be best suited?

with other people (see Table 3.2). The enormous diversity of possible assessment data means that we can never learn all there is to know about a client.

Although the most important factor in the selection of assessment instruments is the referral question, other factors also affect the selection process. One of these is the quality of the assessment instrument or procedure. Interviews, behavioral observations, psychological tests, and life records vary in terms of their reliability, validity, standardization, and overall usefulness for particular purposes. Obviously, clinicians would be better off selecting assessment methods whose *psychometric properties* are the highest, but they might not always do so. For example, if one test had slightly lower (but still acceptable) reliability than another but provided more relevant information about a particular referral question, the clinician might select the one with slightly lesser reliability but greater relevance to assessment.

TABLE 3.2

A Case Study Guide

1. Identifying data, including name, sex, occupation, income (of self or family), marital status, address, date and place of birth, religion, education, cultural identity.

2. Reason for coming to the agency, expectations for service.

3. Present and recent situation, including dwelling place, principal settings, daily round of activities, number and kind of life changes over several months, impending changes.

4. Family constellation (family of origin), including descriptions of parents, siblings, other significant family figures, and respondent's role growing up.

5. Early recollections, descriptions of earliest clear happenings and the situation surrounding them.

6. Birth and development, including age of walking and talking, problems compared with other children, view of effects of early experiences.

7. Health and physical condition, including childhood and later diseases and injuries; current prescribed medications; current use of unprescribed drugs, cigarettes, or alcohol; comparison of own body with others; habits of eating and exercising.

8. Education and training, including subjects of special interest and achievement, out-of-school learning, areas of difficulty and pride, any cultural problems.

9. Work record, including reasons for changing jobs, attitudes toward work.

10. Recreation, interests, and pleasures, including volunteer work, reading, respondent's view of adequacy of self-expression and pleasures.

11. Sexual development, covering first awareness, kinds of sexual activities, and a view of adequacy of current sexual expressions.

12. Marital and family data, covering major events and what led to them, and comparison of present family with family of origin, ethnic or cultural factors.

13. Social supports, communication network, and social interests, including people talked with most frequently, people available for various kinds of help, amount and quality of interactions, sense of contribution to others, and interest in community.

14. Self-description, including strengths, weaknesses, ability to use imagery, creativity, values, and ideas.

15. Choices and turning points in life, a review of the respondent's most important decisions and changes, including the single most important happening.

16. Personal goals and view of the future, including what the subject would like to see happen next year and in 5 or 10 years and what is necessary for these events to happen, realism in time orientation, ability to set priorities.

17. Any further material the respondent may see as omitted from the history.

SOURCE: From *Assessment of Persons,* by N. D. Sundberg, 1977 (Englewood Cliffs, NJ: Prentice Hall), pp. 97–98. Reprinted by permission of Prentice Hall, Inc.

Clinicians must consider, too, the characteristics of clients when deciding on assessments, selecting instruments that are appropriate for each client in terms of reading level, length, and the like. Similarly, clinicians must explain to clients the procedures and purposes of the assessment, using language that clients can understand.

To plan assessments, then, the clinician must think broadly, weighing various features of assessment instruments against practical considerations of time, context, and usefulness to clients and other referral sources (Groth-Marnat, 2003; Matarazzo, 1990).

The clinician must also plan to combine and integrate the results of assessments into a narrative that serves a specific clinical purpose.

Collecting Assessment Data

Once the referral question has been clarified, the appropriate assessment methods have been selected, and the client's cooperation has been secured, the data-collection stage of assessment can begin. As noted earlier, clinical psychologists collect assessment data from four main sources: interviews, observations, tests, and historical records (case history data). These sources are so central to clinical assessment that we offer detailed coverage of them in the next two chapters.

The Value of Multiple Assessment Sources.   Clinical psychologists seldom rely on a single source of assessment data as they create a working image of a client. Instead, they use multiple assessment channels to cross-validate information about a wide variety of topics. Thus, hospital records may reveal that a patient has been there for 30 days, thus correcting the patient's self-reported estimate of 2 days. Indeed, the whole story of a client's problems is seldom clear until multiple assessment sources are tapped. One study showed, for example, that college students who described themselves as socially unassertive were observed to be capable of assertiveness, given the right conditions (Nietzel & Bernstein, 1976). It often takes multiple sources of assessment to separate those who cannot engage in certain behaviors from those who do not engage in them.

Another benefit of using multiple assessment sources appears when the clinician evaluates the effects of treatment. Suppose a couple enters therapy because they are considering divorce, and then, 3 months later, they do divorce. If the only outcome assessment employed in this case were "marital happiness," as expressed during interviews, the treatment might be seen as having worsened marital distress. However, observations, third-person reports, and life records might show that one or both partners find their newly divorced status liberating and that they are developing new interests and abilities. Table 3.2 shows a general case study guide that includes several different categories of information about clients that might be useful to a clinician. Clinicians would typically seek more information about the client in categories that are most relevant to the assessment goals.

Processing Data and Forming Conclusions

After assessment data are collected, the clinician must determine what those data mean. If the information is to be useful in reaching the clinician's assessment goals, it must be transformed from raw form into interpretations and conclusions that address a referral question. The processing task is formidable because it requires a mental leap from known data to what is assumed to be true on the basis of those data. In general, as the leap from data to assumption gets longer, inference becomes more vulnerable to error.

Consider this: A young boy is sitting on a lawn cutting an earthworm in half. It would be easy to infer from this observational data that the child is cruel and aggressive and that he might become dangerous later in life. These inferences would be off the mark, however, for "what the observer could not see was what the boy, who happened to have few friends, thought as he cut the worm in half:'There! Now you will have someone to play with'" (Goldfried & Sprafkin, 1974, p. 305). In short, elaborate inference, especially when based on minimal data, can be dangerous.

Processing assessment data is difficult also because information from various sources must be integrated. Unfortunately, there are few empirical guidelines for how best to combine data from interviews, tests, observations, and other sources to reach integrated conclusions. So in forming their conclusions, clinicians often must rely heavily on clinical judgment, a topic we describe in some detail later in this chapter.

Communicating Assessment Results

The final stage in the assessment process is the creation of an organized presentation of results called an *assessment report*. To be of greatest value, assessment reports must be clearly written and clearly related to the goal that prompted the assessment in the first place. If that goal was to classify the client's behavior into a diagnostic category, information relevant to diagnostic classification should be highlighted in the report. If assessment was aimed at determining a client's likely cooperativeness in and responsiveness to psychotherapy, the report should focus on those topics. These simple, self-evident prescriptions are sometimes ignored in assessment reports, especially when assessment goals were never explicitly stated or when clinicians do not fully understand what their assessment instruments can, and cannot, reveal about clients.

Section Summary: Assessment progresses in a series of steps that begin with a referral question. The referral question may come from a client, a third party, or the therapist, but the clinician must insure that the question is clear and can be addressed reasonably by the available assessment instruments. Once the referral question is clarified, planning for assessment begins. Planning involves selection of appropriate instruments—not a simple task given the number of factors affecting clinicians' choices—and preparation of the client. Data collection involves accumulating evidence from historical records, interviews, observations, and tests. Each of these sources has special strengths and limitations. In the data-processing stage, the accumulated data are analyzed and integrated into a coherent assessment. In the final stage, the clinician communicates conclusions and provides recommendations in ways that are clear and useful to the referral source.

THE GOALS OF CLINICAL ASSESSMENT

Section Preview: Most referral questions relate to diagnosis, description, treatment planning, or prediction. We first consider diagnostic classification, the labeling of psychological problems. Psychological diagnosis relies primarily on criteria described in the *Diagnostic and Statistical Manual of Mental Disorders* (DSM). Diagnosis alone seldom tells clinicians all they want to know about a client, so broader descriptions are also used to assess clients' strengths, weaknesses, and social connections. Diagnoses, descriptions, and other information can be used in designing treatments that are ideal for each client. Assessment also includes measuring the outcomes of treatment—an increasingly important activity in this era of accountability and evidence-based practice. Finally, clinicians sometimes conduct assessments to make prognoses or predictions, difficult judgments that can be improved if clinicians attend to the lessons provided by years of empirical research on the topic.

Diagnostic Classification

As discussed in Chapter 2, once clinical psychologists began working with adult clients during and after World War I, they came under the influence of medical personnel, particularly psychiatrists. As a result, they were often asked to perform clinical assessments for the purpose of diagnosing mental disorders in psychiatric patients, a process variously called diagnostic classification, psychodiagnosis, differential diagnosis, or diagnostic labeling. Today, diagnostic classification remains a significant part of clinical research and practice, especially among clinicians who work in psychiatric or other medically oriented settings.

Accurate psychodiagnosis is important for several reasons. First, proper treatment decisions often depend on knowing what, exactly, is wrong with a client (Vermande, van den Bercken, & De Bruyn, 1996). Second, research into the causes of psychological disorders requires reliable and valid identification of disorders and accurate differentiation of one disorder from another. Finally, classification allows clinicians to efficiently communicate with one another about disorders in a professional "shorthand" (Sartorius et al., 1996). Imagine, for example, how confusing it would be if medical patients who developed pharyngitis (a sore throat) because of A-beta-hemolytic *Streptococcus* (a bacterium) received a different diagnosis depending on which state or country they lived in. Fortunately, if you have this condition and are accurately assessed, you will be given the same diagnosis (strep throat) whether you are in New York, Peoria, Hong Kong, or Helsinki. That is because the World Health Organization's (WHO) *International Classification of Diseases* (ICD) provides common codes that identify each disease. In clinical psychology and psychiatry, the comparable system is the *Diagnostic and Statistical Manual of Mental Disorders,* or *DSM.*

A Brief History of the DSM. Various systems for classifying mental disorders had been used since the early 1900s, but classification of mental disorders became more formalized in 1952 when the American Psychiatric Association published the first *Diagnostic and Statistical Manual of Mental Disorders.* Known as DSM-I, it remained in use until 1968, when—to make the DSM more similar to the WHO's ICD—it was replaced by DSM-II.

DSM-I and DSM-II provided a uniform terminology for describing and diagnosing abnormal behavior, but they offered no clear rules to guide mental health professionals' diagnostic decisions. Some disorders were diagnosed on the basis of observable symptoms and some on inferred underlying causes. As a result, diagnoses sometimes varied considerably from one clinician to the next, making these diagnoses unreliable. Accordingly, when DSM-III appeared in 1980, it included a set of criteria for assigning each diagnostic label. These criteria—which referred mainly to specific symptoms and symptom durations, not inferred causes—were increased in number and specificity in DSM-III-R, which was published in 1987. Clients were to be diagnosed with a particular disorder only if they met a preestablished number of criteria from the full list of criteria associated with that disorder.

DSM-III and DSM-III-R also introduced *multiaxial* diagnoses, allowing clinicians to describe clients along different dimensions, or *axes,* providing a more complete picture of clients' problems and the factors affecting them. Any of 16 major mental disorders—the bulk of disorders in the DSM—were listed on Axis I, while various developmental problems and personality disorders appeared on Axis II. Using a separate axis helped distinguish disorders that had a more noticeable onset and course (Axis I disorders) from those that appeared to be present from birth or to be relatively more difficult to change. Axis II disorders were added also to ensure that they are not overlooked when an Axis I disorder is present.

Axis III provided a place to list physical disorders or conditions that might be related to a person's mental disorder. For example, it would be useful for a psychotherapist to note that a depressed person is also undergoing treatment for cancer. Axis IV provided a 6-point scale for rating the severity of recent psychosocial stressors that may have contributed to an Axis I or II disorder. Axis V listed the clinician's rating of the person's psychological, social, and occupational functioning during the past year.

In spite of the improvements they contained, DSM-III and DSM-III-R were criticized because (a) some of their diagnostic criteria were still too vague and open to biased use; (b) Axes II, IV, and V had measurement deficiencies; and (c) too little emphasis was placed on the construct validity of diagnoses (Bellack & Hersen, 1988; Kaplan, 1983; Millon & Klerman, 1986; Nathan, 1987; Vaillant, 1984). So in 1988, only a year after DSM-III-R appeared, the American Psychiatric Association established a task force to begin work on DSM-IV. The rush to develop a new edition of DSM was also spurred by the WHO's plan to publish the 10th edition of its ICD in 1993.

The DSM-IV and DSM-IV-TR.

DSM-IV planners organized numerous experts into 13 work groups, each of which followed a three-step procedure for studying a different set of disorders and how best to diagnose them (Widiger et al., 1991). Each group first reviewed all the clinical and empirical literature relevant to a given disorder and used their findings to guide initial suggestions for changes in diagnostic criteria for that disorder. When literature reviews failed to resolve issues, the work groups sought to conduct analyses on existing patient data sets. Another step involved asking clinicians to use diagnostic criteria in clinical settings with real clients. Conducted at more than 70 sites worldwide, these focused *field trials* examined issues such as how alternate wordings or alternate thresholds (cutoffs) affected reliability, prevalence rates, or concordance with the parallel diagnoses from ICD-10 (Nathan & Langenbucher, 1999). The DSM-IV, with its revised diagnostic criteria, was published in 1994.

Since the publication of DSM-IV, research on psychodiagnosis has expanded considerably. In order to accommodate the rapidly growing body of knowledge, the text of DSM-IV was revised in 2000. The *DSM-IV-Text Revision* (DSM-IV-TR) did *not* change the diagnostic criteria contained in DSM-IV, rather, it updated information about prevalence rates, onset, course, familial patterns, cultural, age, gender, and other related features (APA, 2000). The DSM-IV-TR also retains the multiaxial structure of DSM-III-R and DSM-IV (see Table 3.3).

The developers of DSM-IV and DSM-IV-TR sought to establish a classification system with a strong empirical base. They hoped to extend the improvements in reliability begun with DSM-III-R's use of observable criteria and to develop categories that might relate well to specific outcomes (predictive validity) or specific underlying neurological or genetic constellations (construct validity). The efforts to improve psychological

TABLE 3.3

Classification of Mental Disorders Using DSM-IV-TR

DSM-IV-TR retains the multiaxial system of classification and diagnosis first introduced in DSM-III, with some modifications in the earlier terminology and rating schemes used on the various axes.

Axis I: Major Mental Disorders

1. Disorders Usually First Diagnosed in Infancy, Childhood, or Adolescence (e.g., hyperactivity, severe conduct problems).

2. Delirium, Dementia, Amnesic, and Other Cognitive Disorders (problems caused by deterioration of the brain due to aging, drugs, or disease).

3. Mental Disorders Due to a General Medical Condition Not Elsewhere Classified.

4. Substance-Related Disorders (problems caused by alcohol, cocaine, or other drugs).

5. Schizophrenia and Other Psychotic Disorders (severe abnormalities in thinking, perception, emotion, motivation, or movement; often accompanied by hallucinations and/or delusions).

6. Mood Disorders (disturbances in mood, especially severe depression, overexcitement, or alternating periods of both).

7. Anxiety Disorders (e.g., specific or general fears, panic attacks, physical or mental rituals to control anxiety).

8. Somatoform Disorders (e.g., blindness, deafness, or paralysis that have no physical cause; preoccupation with physical health or illness).

9. Factitious Disorders (faking disorder for psychological reasons).

10. Dissociative Disorders (e.g., memory loss or identity fragmentation caused by psychological factors).

11. Sexual and Gender Identity Disorders (unsatisfactory sexual interactions, arousal prompted by problematic stimuli, or identification with the opposite gender).

12. Eating Disorders (self-starvation or binge eating followed by self-induced vomiting).

13. Sleep Disorders (severe problems caused by sleeping too little or too much).

14. Impulse Control Disorders Not Elsewhere Classified (e.g., compulsive gambling, stealing, or fire-setting).

15. Adjustment Disorders (failure to adjust to divorce or other stressors).

16. Other Disorders That May Be a Focus of Clinical Attention (e.g., noncompliance with treatment, problems caused by medication, or effects of physical or sexual abuse).

Axis II: Here, the diagnostician can list various forms of mental retardation and various personality disorders, such as paranoid, antisocial, narcissistic, avoidant, and dependent.

---

diagnoses have been extensively reviewed (Mineka, Watson, & Clark, 1998; Nathan & Langenbucher, 1999; Widiger & Sankis, 2000). How successful were they? Nathan and Langenbucher (1999) report that "DSM-IV's strong empirical base has yielded an instrument with good to excellent reliability and improved validity"(p. 79).

Consider the case of Jessie presented at the beginning of this chapter. A DSM-IV diagnosis for him is presented below. It is based on the information available in the vignette, but the clinician would also investigate further the extent of Jesse's substance use and the "pretty bizarre thoughts" that Jesse claimed to have had. Note the DSM also provides codes for problems that are the focus of clinical attention and yet do not fit the diagnostic categories of disorders. These include the parent–child relational problem, educational problems, and seizure disorder. Assuming that the clinician gathered enough assessment information to make a judgment on each axis, Jessie's diagnosis might look like this:

> Axis I: 296.22 Major Depressive Disorder, single episode, moderate, V61.20 Parent–Child Relational Problem
>
> Axis II: V71.09 No diagnosis on Axis II
>
> Axis III: 345.40 Epilepsy, partial with impairment of consciousness
>
> Axis IV: Problems with Primary Support Group: Family Conflict, Parental Divorce, Educational Problems: Discord with teachers and classmates
>
> Axis V: Global assessment of functioning (current): 55

Despite its improved empirical foundations, the DSM-IV diagnostic system has continued to draw criticism. For one thing, although many Axis I disorders show good to excellent reliability, disorders within the schizophrenic spectrum and some childhood and adolescence disorders do not. Axis II disorders, particularly the personality disorders, continue to show unacceptably low interrater reliability and test-retest reliability (Zanarini et al., 2000).

Critics especially question whether the either-or categorizations imposed by DSM-IV criteria are the best way to understand psychopathology. If individuals meet a certain number of criteria, they are said to "have" a disorder, while if they do not reach the cutoff, they do not "have" it. But psychological disorders can be present in varying degrees; there is no clear line between being depressed and nondepressed. Critics contend that diagnosis would better be considered as extremes along one or more underlying dimensions (Widiger & Trull, 2007).

Two other problems also argue against the validity of discrete categories for psychological disorders. One is the extensive comorbidity of psychological disorders. *Comorbidity* is the co-occurrence of two or more disorders within the same person. Comorbidity is frequent, especially among anxiety disorders, mood disorders, substance abuse disorders, and personality disorders (Watson, 2005). Many feel that high comorbidity undermines the hypothesis that the diagnoses represent distinct conditions (Kupfer, First, & Reiger, 2002; Widiger & Trull, 2007). A related problem is the frequency with which clinicians use the diagnostic label *not otherwise specified* (NOS). The NOS diagnosis is invoked frequently enough, especially with personality disorders (Axis II), that many believe the symptom clusters are neither as clear nor as distinct as the category list might lead one to believe (Verheul & Widiger, 2004).

DSM-III and DSM-IV sought to make diagnoses more reliable by focusing on observable symptoms but in so doing may have diverted focus away from the contexts, meaning, and causes of disorders (Bracha, 2006; Follette & Houts, 1996). For instance, some behaviorally oriented clinicians are concerned that DSM-IV classification ignores the context in which symptoms occur, thus providing no basis for understanding the meaning or purpose that the same behavior might have in different social circumstances. By failing to promote such an understanding, they argue, DSM-IV has done little to promote progress in discovering the psychological antecedents and consequences of many kinds of behavioral problems (Follette, 1996; Wulfert, Greenway, & Dougher, 1996).

Neurologically oriented clinicians and psychodynamically oriented clinicians share this concern. As the neurological circuitry associated with specific disorders (e.g., post-traumatic stress disorder) becomes better understood, it makes sense to incorporate that understanding into diagnostic schemes (Bracha, 2006). Psychodynamically oriented clinicians, too, have criticized DSM-IV's strong emphasis on observable symptoms. They are concerned that emphasis on assigning a diagnostic label may lead clinicians to assume that they understand a client because they can describe observable behaviors when in fact they may not understand what the client *subjectively* experiences in having the disorder (Packard, 2007).

Even the number of diagnoses in DSM has been criticized. In the first edition, DSM-I, there were 106 diagnoses; in DSM-IV, there are 365 (see Figure 3.2). This 300% increase in diagnostic categories over four decades is surprising and has led some to wonder if that many new disorders have been scientifically discovered and verified, or if the increase represents, to a significant extent, the expansion of the mental health field and its practitioners' need to identify and treat a variety of conditions (see Houts, 2004, for an interesting discussion).

Finally, critics have noted that the DSM excludes certain conditions. Each version of the DSM was developed on, and applies to, a North American population and does not include symptom clusters seen in other cultures around the world (Hall, 2005). Also missing from the DSM are the many types of problems that can be classified as *relational disorders*. These include marital conflict, parental discipline problems, neglect of children, sibling conflict, abuse, incest, and the like. These conditions produce considerable psychological suffering, but they are not to be found in the DSM (First, 2006). Should they be?

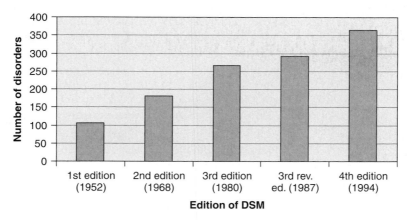

FIGURE 3.2   Number of Diagnoses in the Diagnostic and Statistical Manual of Mental Disorders (DSM) Across Editions

(*Source:* Houts, A. C. (2004). Discovery, invention, and the expansion of the modern *Diagnostic and Statistical Manuals of Mental Disorders*. In L. E. Beutler & M. L. Malik (Eds.), *Rethinking the DSM: A psychological perspective*. Washington, DC: American Psychological Association. Pp. 17–68).

Alternative Diagnostic Proposals and DSM-V. Clinicians and researchers concerned about these shortcomings in DSM-IV are increasingly interested in a revised diagnostic system (Beutler & Malik, 2002; First, 2006; Widiger & Trull, 2007). One alternative, called the *dimensional approach,* avoids the DSM's either-or dichotomy by measuring people on a select number of personality dimensions. Those dimensions might include extroversion, openness to experience, conscientiousness, emotional stability, and agreeableness (the "big five") or other traits measured by modern personality tests. This would allow persons to be described in terms of strengths and weaknesses, correcting what some see as an overemphasis on pathology in the current system. Efforts to employ the dimensional approach have focused especially on personality disorders, in which symptom overlap is greatest, but mood disorders, anxiety disorders, and schizophrenia have also received attention (Brown, Chorpita, & Barlow, 1998; Widiger & Trull, 2007). It is possible that dimensional approaches fit some disorders while categorical approaches will fit others. This is ultimately an empirical matter to be determined by analysis of the fit of each scheme with available data on specific disorders (Joiner & Schmidt, 2004).

Other diagnostic proposals call for describing psychopathology in terms of specific theories or contextual principles. For instance, Barron (1998) explored how diagnoses can be made more meaningful from the viewpoint of psychodynamic theory. Bornstein (2006) has similarly suggested that certain psychodynamic concepts such as ego strength, defense style, and mental representation of the self and others have considerable diagnostic utility, especially when applied to personality disorders.

One interesting development from the theory-based diagnosis camp has been the publication of an alternative diagnostic manual, the *Psychodynamic Diagnostic Manual* (PDM, 2006). This manual was developed by a task force whose members come from five major psychoanalytic groups. Although the developers of the PDM describe it as complementary to the DSM and ICD, its existence is nevertheless a commentary on the perceived shortcomings of the DSM. The PDM, designed to broaden the scope of diagnosis and give clinicians a fuller understanding of their clients (Packard, 2007), describes healthy and disordered functioning in adults and children. These descriptions are consistent with a dimensional rather than a categorical approach that focuses not just on observable symptoms but on patterns of relating, comprehending, expressing feelings, and coping. Like the DSM, the PDM uses a multiaxial system (Axis P profiles personality patterns and disorders; Axis M profiles mental functioning; Axis S profiles the subjective experiences of symptom patterns). A similar diagnostic manual, built around attempts to operationalize psychodynamic concepts, has been developed and used in Germany (Schneider et al., 2004).

Alternative diagnostic approaches based on positive psychology have also been developed. *The Handbook of Positive Psychology Assessment* (Lopez & Snyder, 2003) describes several approaches to assessment based on positive psychology. Similarly, the *Character Strengths and Virtues: A Classification and Handbook* (Peterson & Seligman, 2004) was designed to complement the DSM and to correct for its shortcomings. Along the same lines, Peterson's (2006) *Values in Action (VIA) Classification of Strengths: The un-DSM and the Real DSM* is a taxonomy of psychological strengths. Peterson and Seligman (2004) have even suggested that the "real" psychopathologies, the ones that "cut nature at the joints," might be better understood as the absence of the character strengths that they describe, not as the list of symptoms described by DSM (Duckworth, Steen, & Seligman, 2005).

Diagnostic proposals have come from other theoretical frameworks as well. Wulfert, Greenway, and Dougher (1996) offered a diagnostic approach consistent with behavioral principles. Sarbin (1997) advocated an approach that examines how disorders are affected by people's use of strategic self-narratives. Most of these alternatives are designed to expand the understanding of persons being diagnosed.

It is no wonder that the diagnostic classification enterprise continues to be a hotbed of controversy. After all, it attempts to differentiate a wide variety of complex, socioculturally defined disorders caused by multiple (often unknown) factors using a relatively small set of shorthand labels organized in a way that will help clinicians make the best possible decisions about their clients. No diagnostic system is likely to ever accomplish all these goals. So although various alternative approaches may each have their advantages, it is unlikely that any of them will replace the current categorical classification system. The categorical system is consistent with the medical model that dominates the health care industry, and it offers an efficient shorthand in which clinicians can communicate with each other. The challenge for competing diagnostic schemes will be to continue to improve reliability, validity, and utility while still maintaining an efficient system.

Toward that end, work on DSM-V has now begun. Preliminary efforts started several years ago, but formal activity began in 2006 with the appointment of the *DSM-V Task Force and Workgroups* (First, 2006). Publication of the DSM-V is expected in 2011, but given the number and complexity of the issues that must be addressed in this edition, it would not be surprising if its development takes somewhat longer.

Description

Diagnostic classification is not the only goal of assessment, nor should we expect any classification system to convey all that is meaningful or useful about a person suffering from a psychological disorder. As just noted, classification should be reliable and valid and serve as an efficient shorthand for communication among clinicians and researchers, but for many clinicians, diagnostic labels are not enough. They want to know more, and consequently, some alternative diagnostic proposals shade over into *descriptive assessment,* which these clinicians see as more important than diagnostic classification. It is worth noting that the multiaxial system in the DSM was meant to provide descriptive information about clients beyond the diagnosis, but even that cannot do the whole job. Accordingly, clinicians from a variety of orientations have sought to develop descriptive assessments.

Descriptive assessment by a cognitive-behavioral therapist, for instance, might focus on outlining factors such as antecedent conditions, environmental incentives and disincentives, alternative sources of reward, cognitive complexity, and attributional style. A psychodynamic therapist might focus descriptive assessment on ego strengths and weaknesses, cognitive functioning, defense mechanisms, quality of family and other relationships, and characteristics of the self (Gabbard, 2005). Of course, diagnostic classification and descriptive assessment can go hand in hand. Bertelsen (1999), for instance, suggests that clinical assessment should work at two separate levels: one concerned with diagnostic classification, the other concerned with evaluating multiple factors that influence the course of treatment.

Description-oriented assessment makes it easier for clinicians to pay attention to clients' assets and adaptive functions, not just to their weaknesses and problems. Accordingly, descriptive assessment data are used to provide pretreatment measures of clients' behavior, to guide treatment planning, and to evaluate changes in behavior after treatment. Descriptive assessment can also improve measurement in clinical research. For example, in an investigation of the relative value of two treatments for depression, assessments that describe clients' posttreatment behaviors (e.g., absenteeism, self-reported sadness, and depression test scores) are of greater value than diagnostic labels (e.g., depressive versus nondepressive).

Unfortunately, the movement toward broad description of persons may never dominate clinical assessment, especially in inpatient psychiatric settings and other managed-care facilities. The reason is time. As skyrocketing health care costs have increased economic pressures to limit hospital stays and to concentrate on short-term treatments, time-consuming and comprehensive patient evaluations are just too expensive. The degree to which descriptive approaches to assessment gain widespread usage will ultimately depend on their empirically demonstrated usefulness—the degree to which clinicians can perform assessments efficiently and use them to design better research and treatments.

Treatment Planning

Diagnostic and descriptive assessment can be used to plan treatments. In the simplest model, a diagnosis (e.g., depression) leads to a preferred treatment (e.g., cognitive-behavioral psychotherapy), just as a given medical illness (e.g., strep throat) might lead to a preferred treatment (e.g., antibiotic). Identifying ideal connections between diagnoses and psychotherapy methods has been a main goal of the empirically supported treatments movement (see our discussions in Chapter 1, "What Is Clinical Psychology," and Chapter 10, "Research on Clinical Intervention").

While efforts to match specific treatments with specific diagnoses has certainly improved the empirical base of psychotherapy, the enterprise has not worked out as cleanly in practice as many had hoped. As the previous discussion on diagnosis implies, symptoms of disorders overlap, and comorbidity is common, suggesting that at least some diagnostic categories are not discrete entities. It is difficult to argue that specific treatments work for specific diagnoses if the diagnoses themselves are indistinct. Further, the extensive research on psychotherapy effectiveness (discussed in Chapter 10) shows that treatments often have general and overlapping effects, some of which have more to do with characteristics of the persons involved than with the disorders to which they are applied (Beutler & Malik, 2002). Because of these problems, clinicians have sought to incorporate other factors into treatment-related assessment. The key is to identify which factors, apart from the diagnosis and the "brand" of psychotherapy, best predict how an intervention will work.

In short, treatment planning assessment goes beyond the basic medical-model question: *Which treatments work best for which disorders?* Instead, it addresses the more detailed question, famously stated by Gordon Paul (1967): "*What* treatment, *by whom,* is most effective for *this* individual with *that* specific problem, and under *which* set of circumstances?" (p. 44). We discuss treatment planning more in Chapter 6, "Basic Features of Clinical Interventions."

Treatment-related assessment can also include assessing how well treatment has worked. Indeed, clinicians in today's era of accountability are increasingly asked to provide ongoing evidence of their effectiveness. Such evidence requires ongoing assessment. As an example, consider a case illustration offered by Kazdin (2006).

> Gloria, a 39-year-old woman, was self-referred for depression. An initial assessment was conducted, and a treatment plan involving combined cognitive-behavioral and interpersonal therapy, administered on weekly visits, was devised. The therapist also had Gloria come about 20 minutes early each week and complete brief measures designed to track her progress. One measure was a rating on a series of statements developed collaboratively between Gloria and the therapist, which they called the G-Scale. Another was an abbreviated version of the Beck Depression Inventory (BDI; Beck, Steer, & Garbin, 1988), and the last was an abbreviated version of the Quality of Life Inventory (QOLI; Frish, 1998).
>
> Figure 3.3 represents the session-by-session changes in Gloria's scores over several weeks of treatment.

Prediction

A final goal of clinical assessment is to make predictions about human behavior. Such predictions might include prognosis (descriptions of how the symptoms of disorder might change with or without treatment), future performance (descriptions of how someone will perform in a given job or situation), or dangerousness (descriptions of the likelihood of someone behaving violently toward the self or others). In any of these predictions, clinicians must have valid (empirically based) information about the relationship between characteristics revealed by an assessment and the behavior being predicted. Without that, prediction is guesswork.

Prognosis.   Most often, prognosis refers to a prediction about the outcome of treatment, but it can also refer more generally to predictions about changes in symptoms without treatment or with certain circumstances (e.g., an auto accident results in some head injury and changes the prognosis for treatment of an anxiety disorder).

Considerable information about prognosis is already contained in DSM diagnoses. Included with many disorders in that text are results of long-term studies describing the course of a disorder as well as other information related to its typical onset, chronicity, which populations are most at risk, and the like. While the DSM does not provide specific prognostic statements, it is not difficult for clinicians (or students) to recognize that some disorders tend to be more debilitating than others, more chronic or prone to relapses, or more responsive to certain positive or negative life circumstances.

Clinicians can build upon the basic information in the DSM to improve prognostication. Information about the client's level of social support and subjective distress can

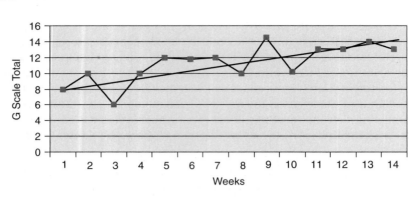

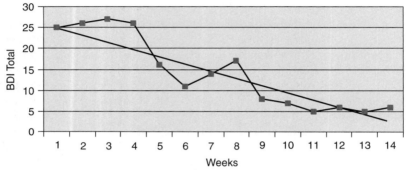

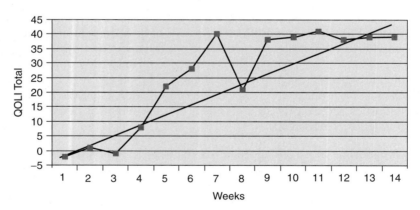

FIGURE 3.3 Assessment of Gloria's Psychotherapy Progress on Three Measures. (The first two weeks can be considered baseline measures. A linear regression line has been fitted to the data points on each graph.)

Note: G Scale is a scale developed by the client, Gloria, and the therapist; BDI is the Beck Depression Inventory (selected items), and QOLI is the Quality of Life Inventory.

(*Source:* Kazdin, A. E. (2006). Assessment and evaluation in clinical practice. In C. D. Goodheart, A. E. Kazdin, & R. J. Sternberg (Eds.), *Evidence Based Psychotherapy* (pp. 153–177). Washington, DC: American Psychological Association. Originally published in Kazdin, A. E. (2003). Research design in clinical psychology (4th ed., p. 322). Boston, MA: Allyn & Bacon.)

improve or worsen a prognosis (i.e., relatively high levels of support and moderate but not debilitating distress improve; relatively low levels of support and intense distress worsen). Factors relating to the client (e.g., impulsivity and coping style, resistance to direct guidance from the therapist), the setting (e.g., inpatient medical versus outpatient), or the "fit" between client and therapist (e.g., shared values or cultural background) can similarly influence outcomes. Of course, a prognosis based on these or any other factors should be informed by empirical research evidence that addresses the degree to which each factor has been shown to influence outcomes in similar cases.

Predicting Future Performance. Clinicians are sometimes asked by businesses, government agencies, police and fire departments, and the military to help them select people who are most likely to perform well in certain jobs. In such cases, the clinician must first collect and/or examine descriptive assessment results to provide data on which to base predictions and selections. This step is critical and often underappreciated by those who believe psychologists should be able to make predictions in any domain simply on the basis of general psychological training. In order to know how someone will perform in a given job or situation, psychologists must have empirical evidence about which characteristics reliably predict which performances. That means that for each job or domain, psychologists have to do their homework; they cannot rely on their assumptions or general clinical judgment. A classic example of how descriptive and predictive assessment can overlap was provided by Henry Murray's use of specialized tests, interviews, and observations to select soldiers who would be the most successful spies, saboteurs, and other behind-enemy-lines operatives during World War II (Office of Strategic Services, 1948). Murray's assessment program was so comprehensive that it took several days to complete and measured everything from intelligence to ability at planning murder.

Similar, though less extensive, prediction-oriented clinical assessment programs also appeared in large-scale postwar screening programs designed to select civilian and military employees (Institute of Personality Assessment and Research, 1970), graduate students in clinical psychology and psychiatry (Holt & Luborsky, 1958; Kelly & Fiske, 1951), and Peace Corps volunteers (Colmen, Kaplan, & Boulger, 1964). Because such assessment programs influence decisions affecting large numbers of people, they must be evaluated not only for their predictive validity but also for their impact on the people being assessed and on the organizations that utilize them.

Predicting Dangerousness. Predictions become especially harrowing when they involve life-or-death situations, such as "Will this client attempt suicide?" or "Is that client going to hurt someone if released from a mental hospital?" Predictions of dangerousness, long a part of clinical practice and research, are often called *forensic evaluations*. For instance, a clinician might be asked to evaluate whether an eighth grader who brings a handgun to school represents a continuing homicide risk and should be educated in a secure facility instead of in a regular school (Vincent, 2006). Clinical researchers might develop instruments designed to predict the likelihood that an adult sex offender will commit another offense if released (Langton et al., 2007). How accurate are such predictions?

In fact, clinical psychologists often find it difficult to predict dangerousness accurately (Borum, 1996; Hilton, Harris, & Rice, 2006; Monahan, 1988). One reason is that the

TABLE 3.4

Measuring the Accuracy of Clinical Predictions of Dangerousness

	Ultimate Outcome	
Clinician's Prediction	**Homicide**	**No Homicide**
Homicide	8 (true positives)	1,998 (false positives)
No homicide	2 (false negatives)	7,992 (true negatives)

base rate, or frequency with which dangerous acts are committed in any group of people, is usually very low. The following example shows why this is important. Assume that a clinician is 80% accurate in predicting homicidal behavior. Assume also that the base rate for homicide in the population the clinician examines is 10 murders per 10,000 people. The accuracy of predictions can be evaluated in terms of the pattern of four possible outcomes. If the clinician predicts dangerousness and the person indeed behaves dangerously, the outcome is called a *true positive.* If the clinician predicts that there is no danger, and the person does not behave dangerously, we have a *true negative* outcome. If the clinician predicts no danger, but the person does act dangerously, a *false negative* outcome occurs. Finally, when the clinician predicts dangerous behavior but dangerous acts do not occur, we call it a *false positive.* As indicated in Table 3.4, the clinician would correctly predict who 8 of the 10 murderers would be. However, if the clinician is 80% accurate, he would incorrectly categorize 20%, or 1,998, of the other 9,990 persons as potential murderers even though none of them would commit violence. So the 8 true positives must be viewed in light of the 1,998 false positives in which the clinician predicted homicides that did not occur.

In this example, then, the clinician's *positive predictive power* to identify murderers would be woefully low (less than 1% of predicted murderers would actually kill someone), while the accuracy of predicting nondangerousness, called *negative predictive power,* would be greater than 99.9%. To maximize true positives, then, the clinician could predict that no one will commit a murder, a prediction that would be correct 99.9% of the time. However, all the errors would be false negatives, and society usually believes that such mistakes (i.e., predicting that dangerous people are safe) are more serious than false positives (i.e., predicting that safe people are dangerous).

To err on the side of caution, then, clinicians tend to overpredict dangerousness. Of course, if there are no serious consequences to false positive errors, overprediction is not a problem. But typically, errors in either direction can have significant consequences. Imagine, for instance, trying to predict which young adults are likely to engage in school violence, a task that takes on special importance in the wake of the murderous rampages have taken place at Columbine High School, Virginia Tech and Northern Illinois Universities, and other places. School shootings are extremely low-base-rate events, so trying to identify at-risk individuals will inevitably result in many false positive errors. For every correctly identified killer, dozens or hundreds of other youths are at risk of being incorrectly stigmatized with the same label (Mulvey & Cauffman, 2001).

It is tempting to dismiss the effects of low base rates on prediction—after all, they are "only statistics"—and to cling to the belief that when push comes to shove, the "experts" will be able to accurately predict school violence, suicide, or other violent acts. But experts do not cling to such beliefs. They know that the base-rate statistics reflect how difficult it is for clinicians (and others) to predict dangerousness accurately. The American Psychiatric Association has taken the position that psychiatrists have no special knowledge or ability that allows them to accurately predict dangerous behavior (1983).

Of course, those who attempt to predict dangerousness do try to minimize false positives by following certain guidelines. For example, Cassel and Bernstein (2007) report that researchers seeking to improve prediction increasingly focus on combining assessment evidence from four domains: (a) the defendant's dispositional tendencies, such as anger or impulsiveness; (b) clinical factors, such as evidence of mental or personality disorders; (c) historical factors, especially a record of violence; and (d) contextual factors such as the strength of social support from family and friends (see also Gardner, Lidz, Mulvey, & Shaw, 1996; Monahan & Steadman, 1994; Zabow & Cohen, 1993).

Throughout the behavioral sciences, many researchers are involved in efforts to improve prediction of the dangerousness of mental patients and criminal offenders (e.g., Doyle & Dolan, 2006; Langton et al., 2007; Quinsey, Harris, Rice, & Cormier, 2006). Before attempting predictions, practicing clinicians must avail themselves of the best science and practices on those particular kinds of predictions. Indeed, clinicians are probably on safer ground when they make predictions about some level of risk (e.g., high, moderate, low) rather than about whether a particular individual will or won't commit a given act—and even then the prediction should be based on the best available empirical evidence about the ability of given signs to predict given outcomes.

Section Summary: Clinical assessment goals include diagnostic classification, description, treatment planning and evaluation, and prediction. Diagnosis is currently based on the DSM-IV-TR, though revisions to the DSM and alternative diagnostic systems are being considered to remedy perceived shortcomings of the current system. Description involves a fuller characterization of a client than is typically available from a diagnostic classification. Both diagnosis and description can be used to help plan treatments. Assessments can also be used to measure treatment effectiveness and to demonstrate it to others. Finally, clinicians are sometimes asked to make predictions about future behavior, including clients' dangerousness, often a difficult task.

CLINICAL JUDGMENT AND DECISION MAKING

Section Preview: Clinicians make judgments by combining information from different sources. In doing so, they can rely on empirically based methods of decision making or on clinical intuition. While clinical intuition is essential in many situations (e.g., spontaneous events that occur during the course of therapy), research shows that clinical psychologists have no special capacity for intuition: they are prone to the same kinds of error as are other human beings when relying on impressionistic thinking. Clinicians would be wise to incorporate empirically based, actuarial models into their judgments in situations when such models are available (e.g., prediction of dangerousness).

The mass media have long cast clinical psychologists as experts who can astutely translate obscure signs into accurate statements about a person's past, present, or future. As in the case of violence, some events are particularly difficult to predict. But whether a clinician is trying to judge the likelihood of a client attempting suicide, a stalker harming a victim, a child being abused by a parent, a brain-injured client succeeding in a new job, or a particular form of psychotherapy alleviating a sufferer's anxiety, all predictions involve clinical judgment.

Clinical Intuition

As our discussion of prediction of dangerousness suggests, empirical research does not support the idea that clinicians have special inferential capabilities. Donald Peterson made this point forcefully 40 years ago: "The idea that clinicians have or can develop some special kinds of antennae with which they can detect otherwise subliminal interpersonal stimuli and read from these the intrapsychic condition of another person is a myth which ought to be demolished" (Peterson, 1968a, p. 105). In fact, when clinical psychologists use an informal approach to assessment data processing (i.e., one based on subjective judgments about the meaning of assessment data), they are not significantly better than nonclinicians at making judgments.

A classic example of research on the clinician's alleged special inference abilities is provided by a study in which people were asked to infer the presence of brain damage on the basis of clients' responses to a psychological test (Goldberg, 1959). The test did not directly measure brain damage, but was widely used by clinicians who believed that it provided signs of brain damage for those who could interpret them. Half of the 30 clients actually had organic damage; the other half did not. The test results were judged by 4 PhD clinical psychologists with 4 to 9 years of experience with the test, 10 master's-level psychology trainees who had used the test for 1 to 4 years, and 8 secretaries with no psychology background or experience with the test. The inference to be drawn in this study was simply "organic" or "not organic," so the probability of being correct by chance in any given case was 50%. However, only 1 of the 4 PhD clinicians did better than chance. Indeed, they were no better than their students or their secretaries. More recent studies have obtained similar results (e.g., Gardner et al., 1996).

Other research shows that clinical psychologists also have no special memory capacity or other information-processing abilities. For example, numerous studies suggest that having larger amounts of assessment information may increase clinicians' confidence about their inferences, but it does not necessarily improve the accuracy of those inferences (Einhorn & Hogarth, 1978; Garb, 1984; Kleinmuntz, 1984; Rock, Bransford, Maisto, & Morey, 1987).

Why do clinicians not make better clinical judgments than other people, even after years of training and experience? Apparently, being human, clinicians are prone to the same cognitive habits and biases that can lead to error in anyone's information processing (MacDonald, 1996). For example, clinicians' judgments, like other humans' judgments, are more prone to error when they rely too heavily on experiences that are recent or remarkable enough to make them especially available to recall. The bias created by this *availability heuristic* can be seen, for example, when people are asked to judge which of the following is more common

7-letter English words ending in -*ing*   __ __ __ __ i n g or
7-letter English words with *n* in the sixth position   __ __ __ __ __ n __

People often choose the first option, simply because -*ing* words are much easier to bring to mind than words with *n* in the sixth position, but in fact, words in the latter category are more common. They include all -*ing* words, as well as all 7-letter words that end in *nt* (e.g., *payment*), or *ne* (e.g., *biplane*), and so on. The lesson here is that a more formal, less impressionistic, reasoning process is required to judge frequencies when the availability heuristic threatens judgment. If we trust our intuition or our gut instinct in such instances, we will be in error. In clinical situations, if some feature of a current case causes us to remember another highly memorable case, but if other features do not match, we may overvalue what comes most vividly to mind and misdiagnose (Garb, 1996).

Memorable clinical "folklore" can create *illusory correlations* (Chapman & Chapman, 1967) causing clinicians to draw false inferences from assessment data (Krol, DeBruyn, & van den Bercken, 1995; Lewis, 1991). Thus, some clinicians see paranoid tendencies in clients who draw large eyes on figure-drawing tests, even though there is no firm empirical evidence to support this association (Golding & Rorer, 1972).

Like the first impressions all people form, clinicians also tend to display an *anchoring bias* in which they establish their views of a client more on the basis of the first few pieces of assessment information than on any subsequent information (Tutin, 1993). Anchoring bias can also influence clinicians to let assessment information coming from certain sources (e.g., a parent's report of a child's behavior) outweigh any other information they receive (McCoy, 1976). The problem with anchoring bias is that we hold too firmly to first impressions and do not make sufficient adjustments when new data warrants doing so. If anchoring bias combines with *confirmation bias*—the tendency to interpret new information in line with existing beliefs—the clinician may ignore contradictory evidence or even distort it to fit initial impressions (Strohmer & Shivy, 1994).

Clinicians' judgments may also be prone to error because they misremember information or fail to get important information. Like other people, clinicians tend to remember their successes more clearly than their failures and so may remain wedded to incorrect inference tendencies (or invalid assessment methods) simply because they think of them as valid (Garb, 1989). Indeed, clinicians may not get enough *accurate feedback* about their successes and failures. Contrast clinicians who predict dangerousness with meteorologists who predict the weather. Meteorologists receive frequent, timely, and unambiguous feedback about their inferences; psychologists seldom do. These examples should help illustrate why assessment of treatment outcomes is important— not merely to prove to others that clinicians can be effective but to provide clinicians themselves with useful feedback that can lead to improved performance.

Various personal and cultural biases can also distort inferences (Rabinowitz, 1993). Some clinicians may more readily infer the presence of disorder, or certain kinds of disorder, in males than in females, or in people of a particular age, health status, or ethnic group (Atkinson et al., 1996; Coontz, Lidz, & Mulvey, 1994; Hickling, McKenzie, Mullen, & Murray, 1999; Hatala & Case, 2000; James & Haley, 1995). In one study of gender bias (Ford & Widiger, 1989), for example, psychologists were asked to diagnose a case report with clear signs of either antisocial personality disorder (APD; usually seen in males) or histrionic personality disorder (HPD; usually seen in females). Some of the psychologists in each group were told that the client was female, others were told that the client was male. The inference errors made by both male and female psychologists showed gender bias in that they were significantly more likely to miss the APD diagnosis if they thought the client was female and significantly more likely to miss the HPD diagnosis if they thought the client was male. Other studies have failed to find a robust overall bias in clinical judgments based on gender (e.g., Tomlinson-Clarke & Camilli, 1995), socioeconomic class, or ethnic minority status (Atkinson et al., 1996), but individual clinicians must nonetheless stay on guard against such bias. In short, there is little empirical evidence that justifies the granting of "expert" status to clinicians based on their clinical intuition (Wiggins, 1981).

Yet there are some clinicians whose inference accuracy appears superior to that of their colleagues and intelligent laypersons. Does this superiority reflect a stable ability (i.e., well-trained intuition or "automated expertise"), or is it more sporadic, depending on the client, situation, and judgment task involved? The answer is not yet clear; a person's inference ability may be a joint function of general skill as it interacts with situational variables (Bieri et al., 1966). Some studies show that trained clinicians are more accurate judges than laypersons *when they use well-validated psychological tests* (Garb, 1992), but this advantage is neither large nor frequent, and many other studies find no superiority for trained clinicians' judgments. The wise clinician does not simply assume his or her clinical expertise without solid and ongoing empirical evidence to back it up.

Clinical Versus Statistical Prediction. The sobering body of research that has challenged the image of clinicians as experts who can consistently predict future behavior has led some to question whether clinical predictions would be more accurate if they were based upon formal, statistical data-processing methods rather than on expert clinical judgment. There now exists a large body or research comparing clinical and statistical prediction head to head. *Statistical prediction* (also called *actuarial prediction* or *mechanical prediction*) involves inferences based on probability data and formal procedures for combining information, all usually derived from research. *Clinical prediction,* as we have seen, involves inferences based primarily on a practitioner's training, assumptions, and professional experiences. Which is better?

Clinicians have traditionally been divided on this question. Those who favor the informal, "clinical" approach see it as meaningful, organized, rich, deep, and genuine, and they see the formal "statistical" approach as artificial, trivial, superficial, and rigid. Proponents of formal, statistical inference praise it as objective, reliable, precise, and empirical, and they label the informal clinical approach as mystical, vague, unscientific, sloppy, and muddleheaded.

When clinicians interpret assessment data informally, make recommendations based on these interpretations, and do research on such activities, it is usually because they believe that they, and perhaps most members of their profession, are good at these tasks. Thus it came as a shock when Paul Meehl's 1954 review of 20 studies comparing formal versus informal inference methods found that, in all but one case, the accuracy of the statistical approach equaled or surpassed that of the clinical approach. Later, even the sole exception to this surprising conclusion was called a tie, and as additional research became available, the superiority of the statistical method of prediction was more firmly established (Dawes, Faust, & Meehl, 1989; Meehl, 1957, 1965; see Table 3.5).

TABLE 3.5

Summary of Outcomes of Studies Comparing Clinical and Statistical Prediction

Source	Number of Studies Reviewed	Variables Predicted	Outcome		
			Clinical Better	Statistical Better	Tie
Meehl (1954)[c]	20	Success in school or military; recidivism or parole violation; recovery from psychosis	1[a]	11	8
Meehl (1957)[c]	27	Same as above, plus personality description; therapy outcome	0	17	10
Meehl (1965)[c]	51	Same as above, plus response to shock treatment; diagnosis label; job success and satisfaction; medical diagnosis	1[b]	33	17
Grove et al. (2000)	136	Same as above, plus marital satisfaction; success on psychology internship; performance in medical school; and others	8	63	65
Ægisdóttir et al. (2006)	51	Brain impairment; personality; length of hospital stay; diagnosis; adjustment or prognosis; violence or offense; IQ; academic performance; if an MMPI profile was real or fictional; suicide attempt; sexual orientation	5	25	18

[a]Later called a tie.
[b]Later called a tie by Goldberg (1968).
[c]SOURCE: From *Personality and Prediction: Principles of Personality Assessment,* by J. S. Wiggins, 1973 (Reading, MA: Addison-Wesley). Reprinted by permission of Addison-Wesley.

In the years since Meehl's review, numerous published responses have appeared, many of which pointed out methodological defects in some of the studies that could have biased results in favor of statistical procedures. Frederick C. Thorne (1972, p. 44) put it this way: "The question must not be what naive judges do with inappropriate tasks under questionable conditions of comparability with actual clinical situations, but what the most sophisticated judges can do with appropriate methods under ideal conditions." Still, the furor over Meehl's conclusions could not negate the fact that inference based on subjective, clinical methods is not as accurate as it was assumed to be, even on many clinically relevant tasks (Dawes, 1994).

Consider, for example, a study that tried to specify the rules by which the very best clinical judges draw inferences from a particular personality test. In this study, a recognized expert at drawing inferences from the test was asked to "think aloud" while interpreting the test scores of 126 people (Kleinmuntz, 1963). The decision rules that emerged for designating these people as "adjusted" or "maladjusted" were then used to write a computer program that would formalize the process of interpreting the test. The study showed that an expert clinician's inference rules can be objectified and taught but that the best student may not be a human. The computer used the rules so perfectly and consistently with each new set of test scores that, in line with earlier data on formal versus informal inference, it did better at interpreting subsequent test scores than the clinician who had "taught" it (Kleinmuntz, 1969). Findings such as these are parallel with findings in economics: statistical programs often outperform expert investment professionals in selecting stocks.

Perhaps the strongest evidence comes from two recent meta-analyses comparing clinical and statistical prediction. Grove, Zald, Lebow, Snitz, and Nelson (2000) conducted a meta-analysis of 136 studies in which psychologists predicted criteria within their areas of expertise, including psychotherapy outcome, future criminal behavior, fitness for military service, marital satisfaction, psychiatric diagnoses, success on psychology internships, and several others. Other studies included in the meta-analysis examined counselors' judgments of clients' academic or job performance and physicians' judgments of patients' medical diagnoses and of students' performance in medical school. The results were consistent with previous studies: statistical/mechanical prediction outperformed clinical prediction overall, regardless of the type of judges, judges' experience, type of data being combined, or the design of the study. The advantage for statistical prediction was not large—roughly 10% on average—and in many studies mechanical and statistical prediction were essentially the same. In the small percentage of studies (6 to 16%) where clinical prediction outperformed mechanical prediction, the authors found no pattern of variables that reliably distinguished when or why clinical prediction was superior.

A very similar result was obtained by Ægisdóttir and colleagues (2006). They, too, found a larger effect size for statistical prediction, but, as in the previous study, the increase in accuracy with statistical judgment was not large, about 13%. In this study, the accuracy of clinical and statistical prediction varied by type of prediction, setting, type of statistical formula used, and amount of information available to clinicians and formulas. Statistical prediction more clearly outperformed when predictions involved dangerousness (see also Hilton, Harris, & Rice, 2006).

Based on years of research on the issue of statistical versus clinical prediction, the following conclusions seem reasonable:

- Statistical/actuarial prediction generally outperforms clinical prediction.
- The overall advantage for statistical prediction is modest, and occasionally clinical prediction does as well or slightly better, though not in any particular pattern of circumstances.
- The superiority of statistical prediction is most evident in predicting violence and other low-base-rate events.
- Practicing clinicians typically underutilize and undervalue actuarial prediction methods.

This last point is unfortunate but perhaps predictable. Clinicians find it discouraging to hear that their inferences are often inferior to mechanical decisions that can be arrived at by anyone who can read and has the relevant assessment data to plug into a formula. Clinicians often prefer cues based on their favored theories, assumptions, and experiences despite results indicating that predictive power is lower when using them (Odeh, Zeiss, & Huss, 2006).

Yet, if one takes a broader view, the generally superior performance of actuarial models, particularly for low-base-rate events such as violence, need not be seen as a sign of professional failure. A great deal of clinical experience and research typically goes into the development of useful actuarial models—we have always relied on research to separate the wheat from the chaff in clinicians' favored theories. Further, we don't denigrate meteorologists or stock brokers when they rely on statistical models and computer-generated forecasting. Sawyer (1966) notes, "The clinician may be able to contribute most not by direct prediction, but rather by providing, in objective form, judgments to be combined mechanically" (p. 193).

Nor do we distrust physicians who refer to computer databases to help them diagnose illnesses. Indeed, though some people are willing to accept intuitive, "from-the-hip" judgments from a doctor, we suspect that most appreciate the thoroughness and professionalism of physicians who take advantage of statistical information in reaching diagnoses. Finally, as Tony Ward (1999) and Howard Garb (2000) point out, there will always be an important role for clinicians in the inference process. There are many assessment and treatment tasks—such as describing symptoms, personality, or behavior; making causal inferences and treatment decisions; or simply deciding what to say next in a psychotherapy session—for which no statistical decision rules have been developed. These require clinical judgment, so clinicians need to possess a wide range of cognitive skills and the ability to apply various types of judgments appropriately.

Improving Clinical Judgment

The preceding discussion suggests that clinical psychologists should be familiar with the extensive research literature on clinical judgment and on clinical versus statistical prediction, and that they should be guided by it. Thorne (1972) suggested that "clinicians must become much more critical of the types of judgments they attempt to make, the selection of cues upon which judgments are based, and their modes of collecting and combining data" (p. 44). But there is considerable evidence that too few clinicians have appreciated the limits of clinical intuition. This makes clinical psychologists vulnerable to criticisms both within and from outside the profession (Faust & Ziskin, 1988; Tavris & Aronson, 2007). A number of proposals have been made to make clinical reasoning a more explicit, rather than implicit, part of training in the hopes of teaching health professions to avoid the more common sources of inference errors (Round, 1999). Although disagreement remains over exactly what assessment questions and roles clinicians should handle, the following conclusion still seems to apply: "Clinicians need not view themselves as second-rate IBM machines unless they choose to engage in activities that are more appropriately performed by such machines. In the realm of clinical observation and hypothesis formation, the IBM machine will never be more than a second-rate clinician" (Wiggins, 1973).

With this conclusion in mind, many clinicians and researchers now tend to focus on upgrading observational and other data-collection skills to optimize their value in the clinical assessment process. For example, clinical intuition has been recast as skill in observing a client's verbal and nonverbal behavior. Viewed this way, intuition can be developed, practiced, and improved (see Arkes, 1981; Dawes, 1986).

Computerized Assessment

The use of computers and computerized assessments, long a fixture of clinical research, has grown exponentially in clinical practice over the last few decades (Groth-Marnat, 2003). Psychological tests, structured interviews, questionnaires, and rating scales can all be administered via computer. Clinicians are also finding computers useful in presenting complex simulations, similar to realistic computer games, to clients for assessment and treatment purposes.

Computer-based assessments have obvious advantages. They can save time, reduce the cost of assessment, improve reliability, and eliminate bias that can arise from variability among different testers. They can also incorporate statistical information and complex decision processes that are difficult for humans to hold and combine in working memory. For example, computer-based assessment can remind clinicians to consider less obvious diagnoses even though a client's symptoms suggest a more obvious one (Garb, 2007). Computerized evaluations can also insure that clinicians remember to ask questions that are important but easy to forget.

Computerized assessments are not perfect, however (Lichtenberger, 2006). Some computer-based methods can be too mechanical and restrictive, as when a client's test score is blindly interpreted or when the computer generates a client's profile by "looking up" the characteristics of other people with similar profiles. In these instances, the testing is conducted less flexibly than would be the case with a live clinician. Imagine, for instance, if a clinician discovers, through observation or conversation, that a client is feeling groggy from pain medication while taking an intelligence test. The computer may never have found this out.

The usefulness of computerized assessment has remained controversial because assessments are often based on information that has not been demonstrated to make valid predictions and because they are sometimes based on information that is readily available through other means, such as history or observation (Garb, 2000; Lichtenberger, 2006). If computerized assessments interpret data not through empirically derived formulae but through decision rules distilled from clinicians' experiences and beliefs, these programs can offer little more than "automating clinical lore" (Wiggins, 1973). More than 400 software packages are available to clinicians, and the psychological reports derived from them can be quite detailed, but the programs that generate them vary considerably in sophistication and quality (Groth-Marnat, 2003).

There are also ethical issues associated with clinicians' use of computerized assessment. For instance, to what degree is a clinician responsible for the results, including judgment errors, that may arise from computer-generated reports? How much background knowledge, training, and practice should a clinician have in order to use a computer-based assessment? Computerized testing may make it easier for poorly trained testers to provide impressive-sounding assessment reports that they themselves may not fully understand and are not prepared to use in the most appropriate way.

Critics are also concerned that new discoveries about behavior are less likely to occur if clinicians become less involved in assessment data processing. Excluding the clinician from the data-processing role reduces the probability that rare behavioral events and relationships will be noticed, because actuarial tables and statistical formulae may not be sensitive to them. In short, some observers see relegation of clinicians to a data-collection role as decreasing the chances of future improvement of human data-processing skills (Matarazzo, 1986).

As criticisms like these focused attention on crucial computerized assessment issues, several steps were taken to improve and regulate computer-based testing and interpretation. There is now a special set of guidelines pertaining to computer testing (APA, 1986), and the APA's *Standards for Educational and Psychological Testing* (APA, 1985) includes several provisions about computerized testing. A journal called *Computers in Human Behavior* includes a section on computer software used to interpret psychological tests, and numerous journal articles on the pros and cons of computerized psychological assessment have appeared (e.g., Richard & Lauterbach, 2004). It seems likely that despite lingering concerns, computer-assisted clinical assessment will accelerate as more normative data are collected, as reliability and validity problems are addressed, and as administration of computerized tests becomes more flexible and interactive (Groth-Marnat, 2003).

Using Computers to Measure Treatment Effectiveness. Computers are also increasingly used in clinical practice to evaluate treatment outcomes. These systems attempt to document and measure change during treatments. For example, data from Figure 3.3 (showing Gloria's treatment changes) can be plugged into programs and combined with data from other clients. Systems have been developed that help clinicians evaluate treatment effectiveness in both inpatient and outpatient settings (Kinnaman, Farrell, & Bisconer, 2006; Marks, Cavanaugh & Gega, 2007). They can give clinicians systematic feedback about their performance, thus helping them to identify areas in which there is room for improvement. These systems also can be used to provide concrete evidence of treatment effectiveness to third-party payers or to other funding sources.

As computerized assessments proliferate in clinical psychology, it becomes increasingly important for clinicians to receive training in how to evaluate and use them (Lichtenberger, 2006; Schulenberg & Yutrzenka, 2004). We suggest the following recommendations for clinicians contemplating use of computerized assessments:

- Examine carefully the reliability and validity information available for assessments and favor those of higher quality; do not blindly accept packages because they appear useful or fit with a given theoretical bias.

- Select those assessments that generate focused and well-researched reports over ones that generate long, comprehensive reports; the former are likely to be more accurate.

- Use computerized assessments in the manner and for the purposes for which they were intended, and tell clients and/or referral sources which assessments were used; don't allow computerized assessment to substitute for clinical judgment, for example, by cutting and pasting from computer-generated assessments.

Section Summary: Clinicians are often asked to make inferences that go well beyond observable behavior. When clinicians rely on their beliefs about unobserved phenomena associated with behavior, or about presumed underlying mechanisms or psychic structures that cause behavior, their inferences can appear rich and insightful. However, those same inferences are also more prone to bias and inaccuracy. Years of research suggest that clinicians have no special capacity for intuition (or for predicting future behaviors such as violence). Therefore, clinicians should be especially aware of the limitations of clinical judgments and employ assessment instruments and decision-making procedures that have the best track records—doing so is the only reliable way to improve one's "clinical intuition." Although prediction is often a difficult task, accuracy can be improved if clinicians seek out the best available evidence and follow established ethical guidelines. Similar recommendations about empirical evidence and ethical guidelines apply to the use of computers in assessment.

OTHER FACTORS AFFECTING ASSESSMENT CHOICES

Section Preview: The assessment goal is the most important factor in determining a clinician's choice of assessment tools, but a number of other factors also affect selection. Among these are the psychometric properties of instruments, the clinicians' theoretical orientation and level of comfort with particular instruments, and the conditions under which the assessment takes place.

Most assessments can be conducted using more than one method, and it is often the case that no single instrument or combination of methods is clearly best. When a variety of different instruments might be used, or might be used in different ways, how should clinicians decide? An ideal strategy from our point of view is for clinicians to select instruments that are scientifically validated, that they are experienced in using, and that provide a level of detail appropriate to the contexts in which assessments will be used.

Psychometric Properties of Assessment Instruments

Clinicians' choices about assessment instruments should be influenced not only by the goals of assessment and availability of instruments but also by quality of the instruments. Instruments of higher quality are those that have been shown, in carefully conducted research, to be reliable, valid, and useful. We summarize information on several of the more popular ones in the next two chapters. Here we briefly consider the dimensions that determine an instrument's psychometric quality.

Reliability. *Reliability* refers to consistency in measurement or agreement among different raters. It can be evaluated in several ways. If the results of repeated measurements of the same client are very similar, the assessment procedures are said to have high *test-retest* reliability, analogous to a bathroom scale that shows the same weight when someone steps off and back on again.

Another way to evaluate reliability is to examine internal consistency. If data from one part of an assessment, such as odd-numbered test items, are similar to other parts, such as even-numbered items, that assessment is said to be *internally consistent.* This dimension has sometimes been called split-half reliability. Finally, *interrater* reliability is measured by comparing the conclusions drawn by different clinicians using a particular assessment system to diagnose, rate, or observe the same client. When clinicians judging the same set of assessment results arrive at significantly differing conclusions, interrater reliability is low. The more they agree, the higher the interrater reliability of the instrument.

Interrater reliability tends to be higher when clinicians make judgments about a diagnosis that has relatively clear diagnostic criteria (e.g., panic disorder). In such cases, they are all using the same interpretive rules. Interrater reliability tends to be lower when clinicians make judgments about a diagnosis with less precise criteria (e.g., antisocial personality disorder) and use unstructured interviews and projective tests—assessments with ambiguity in the possible meanings of information obtained.

What are the criteria for poor, good enough, and excellent reliability? It is important first to recognize that there is a degree of error in all psychological measurement; no assessment instrument is perfectly reliable. So most assessment manuals report reliability data that includes the *standard error of measurement* (SEM). The SEM uses the concept of standard deviation and allows clinicians to estimate and report a *confidence interval* for their assessment. For instance, if the SEM of an assessment instrument were 5 points, the clinician can report with 95% confidence (plus and minus one standard deviation) that the client's true score is within 5 points in either direction of the score obtained on the test. Obviously, the error of measurement would be lower and the reliability higher for measurement of concepts that are stable as opposed to unstable (such as trait versus state characteristics of persons) and for concepts that are precisely defined and measured.

To make the best use of reliability data, clinicians must examine the manuals and published research on specific assessment methods or instruments. They can also consult books that address assessment issues. These books often compile and summarize reliability data for various assessments. In Chapters 4 and 5, we present reliability information on a number of the more common assessment instruments that clinicians use.

Validity. The *validity* of an assessment method reflects the degree to which it measures what it is supposed to measure. Like reliability, validity can be evaluated in several ways. The *content* validity of an assessment method is determined by how well it taps all the relevant dimensions of its target. An interview-based assessment of depression that includes questions about sad feelings but not about their duration or cause would have low content validity. *Predictive* validity is measured by evaluating how well an assessment forecasts events, such as violent behavior or suicide attempts. When two assessment devices agree about the measurement of the same quality, they are said to have *concurrent* validity. Predictive and concurrent validity are subtypes of *criterion* validity, which measures how strongly an assessment result correlates with important independent criteria of interest.

Finally, there is *construct* validity (Cronbach & Meehl, 1955). To oversimplify somewhat, an assessment device has good construct validity when its results are shown to be systematically related to the construct it is supposed to be measuring. Psychologists evaluate construct validity by determining whether a test or other assessment method yields results that make sense in light of some theory about human behavior and mental processes. For example, scores on a measure of anxiety should increase under circumstances thought to increase anxiety (e.g., facing major surgery). If no change occurs, the measure's construct validity is suspect. Fully evaluating construct validity requires numerous studies and an elaborate set of statistical analyses (Campbell & Fiske, 1959).

Validity is related to reliability, because an assessment device cannot be any more valid than it is reliable. However, the validity of an instrument is not guaranteed just because the instrument is reliable. Consider a situation in which 50 people use their eyes to assess the gender of a man skilled in female impersonation. All 50 observers might agree on their judgment that the man is a female, but they would all be wrong. In this case, visual assessment had high interrater reliability but very poor criterion validity.

It is important to remember that reliability and validity are matters of degree, not all-or-none propositions. The question is always how much imprecision is tolerable in an assessment. For instance, if a bathroom scale varied by only a few ounces in test-retest procedures, we would likely consider the instrument reliable for our purposes, but if a postal scale varied by that much, we would consider it unreliable. How much error one tolerates depends on the goals and potential uses of the assessment, on the availability of alternative measurement instruments, and on practical constraints such as time and resources.

Remember, too, that the validity of an instrument must always be viewed in relation to the purposes for which the assessment instrument is to be used. For example, a test might be a valid measure of typing skill but an invalid measure of aggressiveness. Test validity can reasonably be assessed only when tests are used for the purposes for which they were designed. So clinicians should compare reliability and validity data only across tests designed for the same purpose—and select the better-performing instrument, all other considerations being equal.

Standardization.   When we say that a test or other assessment instrument is standardized, we mean that the designers of the test have given it to a large, representative sample of persons and analyzed the scores. Doing so gives the designers information about what the average score is in a population—the average mathematics score for 7-year-old children, for instance. It also gives information about the variance of scores on individual items or subtests. Without that information, there would be no way to determine whether a particular score on a test was average, below average, or above average.

Key considerations for a clinician are whether the size of the standardization sample was large enough and representative enough. If it wasn't clinicians should have limited confidence in a test. Another key consideration is whether the particular client being tested is similar enough to the sample on which that test was standardized. Suppose, for instance, a clinician suspects a client might have a somatoform disorder and wants to conduct a structured interview—a series of prescribed questions—to help make a diagnosis. However, the client is an immigrant from China. If the structured interview has not been validated on Chinese or other Asian populations, the client's responses might not be interpretable on the basis of the standardization of the test.

Bandwidth-Fidelity Issues.   Clinicians' assessment choices are further guided by their attempts to resolve the *bandwidth-fidelity* dilemma (Shannon & Weaver, 1949). Just as greater bandwidth is associated with lower fidelity in broadcasting, clinicians have found that, given limited time and resources, the more extensively they explore a client's behavior, the less intensive each aspect of that exploration becomes (and vice versa). The breadth of an assessment device is thus referred to as its *bandwidth* and the depth or exhaustiveness of the device as its *fidelity* (Cronbach & Glesser, 1964). This issue is also called the depth–breadth issue. If, during a 2-hour interview, for example, a clinician tries to cover a long list of questions, the result would be superficial information about a wide range of topics (broad bandwidth, low fidelity). If the time is spent exploring the client's early childhood memories, the result would be a lot of detailed information about only one part of the client's life (narrow bandwidth, high fidelity).

Accordingly, clinicians must seek assessment strategies and measurement tools that result in an optimum balance of bandwidth and fidelity. The questions, levels of inquiry, and assessment techniques that will be useful in identifying stress-resistant executives differ substantially from those that will help detect brain damage in a 4-year-old child.

The Assessment Context

The choices that clinicians make are dictated not only by the goals of their assessment enterprise, the quality of the instruments, and the time and resources available but also by the contexts, or settings, in which assessments are conducted. Common settings include general medical and psychiatric facilities, private or community psychological clinics, jails, prisons, forensic (legal) situations, schools and other educational institutions, and the like. Each type of setting influences the nature of the referral questions asked, the kinds of assessment instruments expected or preferred, and the style of reporting that is most appropriate or most often requested (Groth-Marnat, 2003). For instance, clinicians who are unfamiliar with legal settings may initially find it disconcerting to have their clinical judgments, and even their professional qualifications, challenged. The language used in legal contexts is also different from that used in psychological contexts, and it is incumbent on the clinician to translate psychological terms that may not be understood by non-psychologists into terms that those in the legal profession can understand. Similarly, educational settings bring with them their own preferred theories, terms, and methods of practice. So, as mentioned earlier, clinicians must not only clarify the referral question before conducting assessment, they must also select context-appropriate instruments and present their conclusions in ways that are the most useful to the referral source.

Clinicians' Experience and Theoretical Orientation

Clinical psychologists may tend to use, or avoid, particular assessment methods simply because those methods were either emphasized or criticized by faculty in their graduate training programs. Similarly, those who find certain measurement tactics tedious or unrewarding tend to seek answers to assessment questions through other procedures with which they are more comfortable. Ideally, a clinician's comfort with an instrument should not be the primary criteria for selection, but sometimes clinicians become comfortable—too comfortable, probably—with certain methods of assessments that are not optimal for the task. Such clinician-specific factors help explain why some assessment methods continue to be used by some clinicians even when research evidence fails to support their reliability or validity.

In recent years, a number of researchers have attempted to identify discredited assessment and treatment practices (e.g., Carroll, 2003; Lilienfeld, 2007; Lilienfeld, Lynn, & Lohr, 2003; Norcross, Koocher, & Garofalo, 2006). Although researchers use different methods to do this, they share a common goal: to identify ineffective or bogus assessment practices. We hope that as research converges on which are the truly ineffective ones, those practices will be entirely removed from training programs and clinicians will avoid them in practice.

The Assessment Outline. As just described, clinicians' differing theoretical orientations direct them to pursue certain questions and concerns; in effect, orientation provides an outline for assessment. Thus, psychodynamically oriented case study outlines tend to include questions about unconscious motives and fantasies, ego functions, early developmental periods, object relations, and character structure (e.g., Gabbard, 2005). Cognitive-behavioral case study outlines (e.g., Kanfer & Saslow, 1969) focus on clients' skills, habitual thought patterns, and the stimuli that precede and follow problematic behaviors. Humanistically oriented clinicians are less likely to follow a specific assessment outline; indeed, they are likely to see assessment as a collaborative process in which they seek to understand with each client how that client perceives the world (Fischer, 2001).

Ideally, a clinician's assessment outline will be broad enough to provide a general overview of the client yet focused enough to allow coverage of all the more specific questions that the clinician wishes to address. The outline guides production of the assessment report—the organized presentation of assessment results. Let's consider some sample assessment outlines representing various theoretical approaches to clinical psychology.

The following outline is suggested as a general guideline for clinical psychodynamic assessments (Gabbard, 2005, p. 89):

A Psychodynamic Assessment Outline

    I. Historical data
        A. Present illness with attention to associative linkages and Axis IV stressors
        B. Past history with emphasis on how the past is repeating itself in the present
            1. Developmental history
            2. Family history
            3. Cultural/religious background

   II. Mental status examination
        A. Orientation and perception
        B. Cognition
        C. Affect
        D. Action

  III. Projective psychological testing (if necessary)

  IV. Physical and neurological examination

   V. Psychodynamic diagnosis
        A. Descriptive DSM-IV diagnosis
        B. Interactions among Axes I–V
        C. Characteristics of the ego
            1. Strengths and weaknesses
            2. Defense mechanisms and conflicts
            3. Relationship to superego

    D. Quality of object relations
       1. Family relationships
       2. Transference-countertransference patterns
       3. Inferences about internal object relations
    E. Characteristics of the self
       1. Self-esteem and self-cohesiveness
       2. Self-continuity
       3. Self-boundaries
       4. Mind–body relationships
    F. Attachment patterns/mentalization capacity
    G. Psychodynamic formulation using above data

Following is an assessment outline representative of a cognitive-behavioral approach (adapted from Wright, Basco, & Thase, 2006):

A Cognitive-Behavioral Assessment Outline

   I. Patient name
  II. Diagnosis/symptoms
 III. Formative influences
  IV. Situational issues
   V. Biological, genetic, and medical factors
  VI. Strengths/assets
 VII. Treatment goals

In addition, a cognitive-behavioral assessment may focus on specific cognitions related to the client's difficulties. Wright, Basco, and Thase (2006) suggest that clinicians performing assessments use a worksheet. Table 3.6 illustrates a case conceptualization worksheet for Gina, a client with panic disorder, agoraphobia, and elevator phobia.

Humanistically Oriented Assessment

Humanistically oriented clinicians have suggested assessment alternatives that differ substantially from those of the cognitive-behavioral approach (e.g., Fischer, 2001; Fischer & Fischer, 1983). Some of them have argued against assessment on the grounds that such procedures are dehumanizing, take responsibility away from clients, and threaten the quality of clinician–client relations (Rogers, 1951). Other humanistic psychologists raise the possibility that assessment data collected through traditional means can be useful if they are processed in line with humanistic principles (Fischer, 1989). For example, test results can be viewed as clues to how a client looks at the world, and conducting those tests can provide opportunities for the clinician and client to build their relationship (Dana & Leech, 1974). Fischer, for instance, argues that assessments using standardized, empirically validated instruments can be both scientific and therapeutic when assessments are conducted interactively between therapist and client. She gives examples of discussing DSM-IV criteria and possible interpretations of MMPI-2 profiles with clients,

TABLE 3.6		
Cognitive-Behavioral Case Formulation Worksheet for Gina		
Event 1	**Event 2**	**Event 3**
Going to a crowded cafeteria	Thinking of riding in an elevator	Thinking of driving myself to work
Automatic Thoughts	**Automatic Thoughts**	**Automatic Thoughts**
"I'll drop my tray." "I'll faint." "I'll die."	"The elevator will fall." "It will be crowded." "I'll get stuck."	"I'll faint when I'm driving." "I'll have a wreck." "I'll kill someone on the highway."
Emotions	**Emotions**	**Emotions**
Anxiety, panic, sweating hands, fast breathing	Anxiety, tension, fast breathing	Anxiety, tension, sweating, fast breathing
Behaviors	**Behaviors**	**Behaviors**
Avoid the cafeteria or ask a friend to go along.	Take the stairs if possible.	Don't drive. Ask fiancé to drive.

Schemas: "I'm bound to be hurt"; "I'm the one who will be in an accident"; "The world is a very dangerous place"; "You must always protect yourself."

Working Hypothesis: (1) Gina has unrealistic fears of situations, underestimates her ability to control or manage these situations, and avoids the feared stimuli. (2) Her family background (e.g., illness and death, mother's tension and hypervigilance) contributed to the development of anxiety-ridden schemas and avoidance. (3) Current situational factors (new job and pressure to drive) may have played a role in triggering symptoms.

Treatment Plan: (1) Cognitive restructuring (e.g., examining the evidence, spotting cognitive errors, using thought records) to teach Gina that her fears are unrealistic and that she can learn to cope with her anxieties; (2) breathing training and imagery to provide tools for controlling anxiety; (3) graded exposure to feared stimuli (e.g., crowds, driving); (4) in vivo exposure for the elevator phobia; (5) modeling and coaching on ways to manage anxiety; and (6) later in therapy, focusing on revising maladaptive schemas.

Source: From *Learning Cognitive-Behavior Therapy*, by J. H. Wright, M. R. Basco, and M. E. Thase, 2006 (Washington, DC: American Psychiatric Association), pp. 54–55.

arguing that such collaboration not only provides additional data for assessments but avoids objectifying the client (Fischer, 2001; see also Finn, 1996).

Section Summary: The psychometric properties of various instruments—reliability, validity, and bandwidth (generality vs. specificity)—can affect a clinician's assessment choices. The contexts or settings in which assessments take place also affect which assessment methods are used and how results are communicated. Finally, the clinician's theoretical orientation and personal experiences with various instruments can affect choices. While theoretical approaches can be biasing if too rigidly held, they also provide useful guidelines for clinicians by directing data collection efforts toward discovery of selected, clinically relevant information.

COMMUNICATING ASSESSMENT RESULTS

Section Preview: Assessment results are communicated in an assessment report. Although it seems obvious, it is important to remember that reports should be clear, relevant to the goals of the assessment, and conveyed using language that will make them maximally useful to the consumers of the report.

If assessment results are to have maximal value, they must be presented in reports that are clear, relevant to the assessment goals, and useful to the intended consumer. Accordingly, clinicians must guard against problems that can make reports vague, irrelevant, and useless. Table 3.7 illustrates how an assessment outline—in this case, a cognitive-behavioral outline—is translated into an assessment report. Notice that it is sufficiently problem-oriented to be used with clients seeking help, while also reminding the assessor to consider broader and less problematic aspects of a person's life.

TABLE 3.7

An Assessment Report Based on a Cognitive-Behavioral Outline

Behavior During Interview and Physical Description

James is a clean-shaven, long-haired young man who appeared for the intake interview in well-coordinated college garb: jeans, wide belt, open shirt, and sandals. He came across as shy and soft-spoken, with occasional minor speech blocks. Although uneasy during most of the session, he nonetheless spoke freely and candidly.

Presenting Problem:

A. *Nature of problem:* Anxiety in public speaking situations and other situations in which he is being evaluated by others.

B. *Historical setting events:* James was born in France and arrived in this country 7 years ago, at which time he experienced both a social and language problem. His social contacts had been minimal until he entered college, at which time a socially aggressive friend of his helped him to break out of his shell. James describes his father as being an overly critical and perfectionistic person who would, on occasion, rip up James's homework if it fell short of the mark. The client's mother is pictured as a controlling, overly affectionate person who was always showing concern about his welfare. His younger brother, who has always been a good student, was continually thrown up to James by his parents as being far better than he.

C. *Current situational determinants:* Interaction with his parents, examinations, family gatherings, participation in classes, initial social contact.

D. *Relevant organismic variables:* The client appears to be approaching a number of situations with certain irrational expectations, primarily unrealistic strivings of perfection and an overwhelming desire to receive approval from others. He is not taking any medication at this time.

E. *Dimensions of problem:* The client's social and evaluative anxiety are longstanding and occur in a wide variety of day-to-day situations.

F. *Consequences of problem:* His chronic level of anxiety resulted in an ulcer operation at the age of 15. In addition, he has developed a skin rash on his hands and arms, apparently from excessive perspiration. He reports that his nervousness at one time caused him to stutter, but this appears to be less a problem in more recent years. His anxiety in examination situations has typically interfered with his ability to perform well.

Other Problems:

A. *Assertiveness.* Although obviously a shy and timid individual, James said that lack of assertiveness is no longer a problem with him. At one time in the past, his friends would take advantage of him, but he claims that this is no longer the case. This

TABLE 3.7

An Assessment Report Based on a Cognitive-Behavioral Outline (*Continued*)

should be followed up further, as it is unclear what he means by assertiveness.

B. *Forgetfulness:* The client reports that he frequently misses appointments, misplaces items, locks himself out of his room, and generally is absent-minded.

Personal Assets:

The client is fairly bright and comes across as a warm, friendly, and sensitive individual.

Targets for Modification:

Unrealistic self-statements in social-evaluative situations; possible behavioral deficits associated with unassertiveness; and forgetfulness.

Recommended Treatment:

It appears that relaxation training would be a good way to begin, especially in light of the client's high level of anxiety. Following this, the treatment should move along the lines of rational restructuring, and possibly behavior rehearsal. It is unclear as yet what would be the best strategy for dealing with forgetfulness.

Motivation for Treatment:

High.

Prognosis:

Very good.

Priority for Treatment:

High.

Expectancies:

On occasion, especially when going out on a date with a female, James would take half a sleeping pill to calm himself down. He wants to get away from this, and feels what he needs is to learn to cope with his anxieties by himself. It would appear that he will be very receptive to whatever treatment plan we finally decide on, especially if the emphasis is on self-control of anxiety.

Other Comments:

Considering the brief time available between now and the end of the semester, between-session homework assignments should be emphasized as playing a particularly important role in the behavior change process.

SOURCE: From *Clinical Behavior Therapy,* by M. R. Goldfried and G. C. Davison, 1976 (New York: Holt, Rinehart, and Winston), pp. 52–53. Copyright 1976 by Holt, Rinehart, and Winston. Reprinted by permission of Holt, Rinehart, and Winston.

Report Clarity

The first criterion for an assessment report is clarity. Without this basic attribute, relevance and usefulness cannot be evaluated. Lack of clarity in psychological reports is troublesome because misinterpretation of a report can lead to misguided decisions. Here is a case in point:

A young girl, mentally defective, was seen for testing by the psychologist, who reported to the social agency that the girl's test performance indicated moderate success and happiness for her in "doing things with her hands." Three months later, however, the social agency reported to the psychologist that the girl was not responding well. Although the social agency had followed the psychologist's recommendation, the girl was neither happy nor successful doing things with her hands. When the psychologist inquired what kinds of things, specifically, the girl had been given to do, he was told "We gave her music lessons— on the saxophone." (Hammond & Allen, 1953, p. v)

A related problem exists when the assessor uses jargon that may be meaningless to the reader. Consider the following excerpt from a report on a 36-year-old man:

> Test results emphasize a basically characterological problem with currently hysteroid defenses. Impairment of his ability to make adequate use of independent and creative fantasy, associated with emotional lability and naivete, are characteristic of him. Due to markedly passive-aggressive character make-up, in which the infantile dependency needs are continually warring with his hostile tendencies, it is not difficult to understand this current conflict over sexual expression. (Mischel, 1968, p. 105)

The writer may understand the client, but will the reader understand the writer? Anyone not well versed in psychoanalytic terminology would find such a report mystifying. Even professionals may not agree on the meaning of the terms employed. Factors such as excessive length (or cryptic brevity), excessively technical information (statistics or esoteric test scores), and lack of coherent organization also contribute to lack of clarity in assessment reports (Olive, 1972; Tallent & Reiss, 1959).

Relevance to Goals

Although far less common today than in the past, clinicians may still be asked for "psychologicals" (usually a standard test battery and interview) without being told why assessment is being done. Under such circumstances, the chances of writing a relevant report are minimal. Unfortunately, there are other cases in which a report's lack of relevance is due mainly to the clinician's failure to keep established assessment objectives in mind.

Usefulness of Reports

Finally, one must ask if an assessment report is useful. Does the information it contains add anything important to what we already know about the client? Reports that present clear, relevant information that is already available through other sources may appear useful but have little real value. Such reports tend to be written when the assessor has either failed to collect new information or has not made useful statements about new data. In the former case, the clinician may have employed techniques that have low incremental validity (Sechrest, 1963). For example, a clinician may use psychological tests to conclude that a client has strong hostile tendencies, but if police records show that the client repeatedly has been arrested for assault, this conclusion doesn't add much to the clinical picture. In other instances, the assessor's report may have limited usefulness because it says nothing beyond what would be expected on the basis of base-rate information, past experience, and common sense.

Consider the following edited version of a report written entirely on the basis of two pieces of information: (a) the client is a new admission to a Veterans Administration (VA) hospital, and (b) the case was to be discussed at a convention session entitled "A Case Study of Schizophrenia."

This veteran approached the testing situation with some reluctance. He was cooperative with the clinician but mildly evasive on some of the material. Both the tests and the past history suggest considerable inadequacy in interpersonal relations, particularly with members of his family. It is doubtful whether he has ever had very many close relationships with anyone. He has never been able to sink his roots deeply. He is immature, egocentric, and irritable, and often he misperceives the good intentions of the people around him. He tends to be basically passive and dependent, though there are occasional periods of resistance and rebellion against others. Vocationally, his adjustment has been very poor. Mostly he has drifted from one job to another. His interests are shallow, and he tends to have poor motivation for his work. Also, he has had a hard time keeping his jobs because of difficulty in getting along with fellow employees. Although he has had some relations with women, his sex life has been unsatisfactory to him. At present, he is mildly depressed. His intelligence is close to average, but he is functioning below his potential. Test results and case history suggest the diagnosis of schizophrenic reaction, chronic undifferentiated type. Prognosis for response to treatment appears to be poor. (Sundberg, Tyler, & Taplin, 1973, pp. 577–579)

In generating this impressive but utterly generic report, the clinician relied heavily on knowledge of VA hospital residents and familiarity with hospital procedures. For example, since the case was to be discussed at a meeting on schizophrenia, and since schizophrenia diagnoses are common for VA residents, it was easy to surmise the correct diagnosis. Also, because it fits the "average" VA resident, the report was likely to be at least partially accurate. This bogus document exemplifies a feature of assessment reports that reduces their usefulness: overgenerality, or the tendency to write in terms that are so ambiguous they can be true of almost anyone. Documents laden with overly general statements have been dubbed "Barnum reports" (in honor of P. T. Barnum's maxim that there is a sucker born every minute), "Aunt Fanny reports" (because the statements could also be true of "my aunt Fanny"), or "Madison Avenue reports" (given that they "sell" well) (Klopfer, 1983; Meehl, 1956; Tallent, 1992). Such overly general material has the dual disadvantages of spuriously increasing the impressiveness of a report while actually decreasing its usefulness.

Section Summary: While there is no universally "right" way to organize assessment data, the criteria of clarity, relevance, and usefulness may be more easily achieved by using an outline organized around the goals of assessment, the clinician's theoretical approach, and the assessment context. It is also worth repeating that the information sought in an outline, and the instruments used to gain that information, should be based on empirical research.

ETHICAL CONSIDERATIONS IN ASSESSMENT

Section Preview: A number of ethical issues confront clinicians who perform assessments, especially when they become embroiled in acrimonious divorce or child custody cases, when they help to determine whether clients are eligible for disability based on mental illness, or when they must decide what information to reveal about a client to third-party payers (e.g., insurance companies). Clinicians must know the limitations of the assessments they perform, and they must be clear in advance how those assessments are to be used. They should also be knowledgeable about how federal and state laws and the APA Ethical Principles of Psychologists and Code of Conduct govern their behavior.

The following scenario (from Pope & Vasquez, 1998) illustrates some of the many ethical problems faced by clinicians who conduct assessments:

A 17-year-old boy comes to your office and asks for a comprehensive psychological examination. He has been experiencing some headaches, anxiety, and depression. A high-school dropout, he has been married for a year and has a 1-year-old baby, but has left his wife and child and is again living with his parents. He works full time as an auto mechanic and has insurance that covers testing procedures. You complete the testing.

During the following year, you receive requests for information about the testing from

- The boy's physician, an internist.
- The boy's parents, who are concerned about his depression.
- The boy's employer, in connection with a worker's compensation claim filed by the boy.
- The attorney for the insurance company that is contesting the worker's compensation claim.
- The attorney for the boy's wife, who is suing for divorce and for custody of the baby.
- The boy's attorney, who is considering suing you for malpractice because he does not like the results of the tests.

Each of the requests asks for the full formal report, the original test data, and copies of each of the tests you administered (for example, instructions and all items for the MMPI-2).

How much information, if any, are you ethically or legally obligated to supply to each of these people? If you were to comply with any of these requests, which disclosures of information would require having the boy's prior written, informed consent?

The process of collecting, processing, and communicating assessment data obviously gives clinicians access to sensitive information that the client might not ordinarily reveal to others. This places a heavy responsibility on the assessor to use and report this privileged information in a fashion that safeguards the client's welfare and dignity and shows concern for (a) how psychological assessment data are being used, (b) who should have access to confidential material, and (c) the possibility that improper or irresponsible interpretation of assessment information will have negative consequences for clients.

With these concerns in mind, clinicians must first be sure that their inquiries do not constitute an unauthorized invasion of a client's privacy. In order to know what constitutes authorized and unauthorized disclosure of information, clinicians must be familiar with more than the details of individual cases. They must also wrestle with the problem of who may have access to assessment data if they do not maintain sole control over them. When test scores, conclusions, predictions, and other information are communicated in a report, they may be misused by persons who see the report but are not qualified to interpret it. In such cases, not only is the client's privacy invaded, but the assessment data may create harmful outcomes for the client. Minimizing these problems is a major concern of public officials, government agencies, citizens groups, and private individuals.

Perhaps the best way to insure that clinicians follow ethical assessment practices is for them to know the American Psychological Association's *Ethical Principles of Psychologists and Code of Conduct* (APA, 2002b), particularly Section 9, which deals with assessment. In addition, the APA offers guidelines for certain specialized assessment practices, such as the *Guidelines for Psychological Evaluations in Child Protection Matters* (APA, 1998). Psychologists should also know the *General Guidelines for Providers of Psychological Services* (APA, 1987) and *Standards for Educational and Psychological Testing* (APA, 1985). These guidelines reflect federal legislation, including the Equal Employment Opportunity Act (part of the Civil Rights Act of 1964), which prohibits discriminatory use of tests that have adverse impact on the selection of minority group job candidates, and the Civil Rights Act of 1991, which bans adjustment of test scores on the basis of race, color, religion, sex, or national origin (Sackett & Wilk, 1994). The guidelines must also be implemented in accordance with the regulations of the Individuals with Disabilities Education Act and the Americans with Disabilities Act.

The guidelines for assessors are often just that—guidelines; they do not clearly tell psychologists what they should or should not do. Ethical decision making often involves taking into account various federal, state, and local laws as well as professional codes and individual concerns. Clinicians faced with difficult decisions can also consult with colleagues and seek guidance from the American Psychological Association about the best course of action. Ethical problems and standards associated with clinical psychology are considered in greater detail in Chapter 15, "Professional Issues in Clinical Psychology."

Care should also be taken to assure that assessment goals are not socially or culturally biased such that certain clients (e.g., members of ethnic or racial minorities) are placed at a disadvantage (Malgady, 1996). For example, some psychological tests are alleged to be inappropriate for use with minority groups, leading to court decisions prohibiting their use for educational placement and other purposes (see Lambert, 1985, for discussion of the landmark *Larry P. v. Wilson Riles* case in California). When conducting assessments on clients from different cultures, clinicians must be knowledgeable about how sociocultural factors can affect diagnosis, assessment, and treatment (Lopez & Guarnaccia, 2000).

Core Competencies in Clinical Psychology Assessment

There are so many types of assessment that no clinician can be expected to have mastered them all. However, every clinical psychologist should possess a set of core competencies in assessment. While no single formal set of competencies is universally agreed upon, those suggested by professional organizations, employers, educational institutions, and clinical internship sites have many similarities (Krishnamurthy et al., 2004). We have drawn upon those to construct the following list. Some competencies relate to the empirical and theoretical foundations of assessment (e.g., an understanding of personality or cognitive variables that tests measure, an ability to judge reliability and validity), while others relate to the use of specific assessments (e.g., interview formats, intellectual tests, personality tests, diagnostic assessment). Of course, an understanding of diversity and ethical standards is also critical. Psychologists trained in assessment should be able to

- Understand the theoretical, empirical, and contextual bases of assessment.
- Evaluate the psychometric properties of assessment instruments.
- Successfully administer and interpret instruments designed to assess cognitive functioning, behavioral functioning, and personality.
- Conduct and interpret clinical interviews and behavioral observations.
- Formulate appropriate DSM-IV diagnoses.
- Recognize the limitations and appropriate uses of assessment instruments for special populations (cultural and linguistic groups, physically challenged, etc.).
- Integrate data from multiple assessment sources into empirically grounded conclusions.
- Effectively communicate the results of assessments to others in written and spoken reports.
- Understand and follow APA Ethics Code guidelines for assessment.

Section Summary: Numerous ethical concerns can accompany assessment, and to deal with these clinicians must be aware of professional guidelines, particularly the APA ethics code. They must also possess a set of core assessment competencies.

CHAPTER SUMMARY

Clinical assessment is the process of collecting information to be used as the basis for informed decisions by the assessor or by those to whom results are communicated. Interviews, tests, observations, and life records serve as the main sources of assessment data in clinical psychology. The clinical assessment process includes five stages: clarifying the referral, planning data collection, collecting data, processing data, and communicating results. The methods and levels of inquiry in assessment tend to follow a case study guide that is shaped by assessment goals, clinicians' theoretical preferences and experience, and contexts. Selection of assessment methods is also guided by research on their reliability (consistency) and validity (ability to measure what they are supposed to measure), and depth versus breadth.

The goals of clinical assessment tend to involve diagnostic classification, description, treatment planning, and prediction. Diagnostic classification normally employs DSM-IV-TR. Description involves broader assessments of clients' personalities by looking at person–environment interactions. Assessment for treatment planning involves collecting information about how clients might respond to various treatment approaches. Predictions often involve personnel selection but sometimes focus on a client's potential for violence or suicide.

Unfortunately, clinicians have no unique intuitive power or special information-processing capacity, so the quality of their judgments and decisions about clients can be threatened by the same cognitive biases and errors that affect all human beings. Indeed, research on clinical judgment suggests that in many situations, clinicians can make their greatest contribution to assessment as collectors of information that is then processed by computer-based statistical formulae.

Assessments are driven primarily by the assessment goals, but other factors can also influence how assessments are conducted. The reliability, validity, and generality of assessment instruments should play an important role in a clinician's selection. The clinician's theoretical orientation and prior experience with instruments affect assessment choices, too, as does the context in which assessments are made (i.e., legal, educational, psychiatric hospital, psychological clinic).

The results of clinical assessment are presented in an organized assessment report, which should be clear, relevant to assessment goals, and useful to the intended consumer. These reports often reflect the theoretical approach taken by each clinician, but they should be constructed in a way that is maximally useful to the referral source and consistent with ethical practices.

STUDY QUESTIONS

1. What core competencies in assessment should clinical psychologists possess?
2. What are the steps involved in a psychological assessment?
3. What are the most common data-collection techniques?
4. What are the general goals of assessment?
5. How do clinical psychologists make diagnoses?
6. What is the basic structure of the DSM-IV-R?
7. What are some criticisms of the DSM and alternate proposals for clinical diagnosis?
8. What has research revealed about clinical psychologists' abilities to predict future violence?
9. What are clinical judgment and clinical intuition, and how can they be improved?
10. How are computers used in psychological assessment?
11. Why are reliability, validity, and bandwidth important considerations in selecting assessment instruments?
12. How does a clinician's theoretical orientation influence assessment?
13. How does the clinical context or setting affect assessment data collection and reporting?
14. What are the basic requirements for a good psychological report?
15. How might clients' cultural or ethnic backgrounds affect the results of assessments?
16. What should clinicians do when assessments raise ethical concerns or dilemmas?

WEB SITES

- APA Rights and Responsibilities of Test Takers: http://www.apa.org/science/ttrr.html
- APA Report of the Task Force on Test User Qualifications: http://www.apa.org/science/tuq.pdf
- APA Strategies for Private Practitioners Coping With Subpoenas Compelling Testimony for Client Records or Test Data: http://www.apa.org/governance/reports/combinedannualreports.pdf

CHAPTER 4

Interviewing and Observation in Clinical Psychology

Chapter Preview: In this chapter, we describe a variety of interview and observation techniques. We begin with interviews, categorized first by their goals and then by their structure. We also address stages of the interview process and what research has revealed about the reliability and validity of interviews. We treat observations in much the same manner: discussing goals and types of observations as well as research on the strengths and limitations of observations. Throughout, we discuss how various factors—particularly interview/observation structure, client diversity, and clinician bias—can affect the results of interviews and observations.

Interviews and observations are the most widely employed tools in clinical psychology. They are central to clinical assessment and also play prominent roles in psychological treatment. Indeed, much of what we have to say in this chapter about interviews and observations also applies to treatment because treatment usually begins with—and is based on—the relationship established through the interview process.

In simplest terms, an interview is a conversation with a purpose or goal (Matarazzo, 1965). That interviews resemble other forms of conversation makes them a natural source of clinical information about clients, an easy means of communicating with them, and a convenient context for attempting to help them. Interviews are flexible, relatively inexpensive, and, perhaps most important, provide the clinician with simultaneous samples of clients' verbal and nonverbal behavior. These advantages make the interview useful in a variety of clinical situations.

This chapter does not attempt to teach you how to conduct specific types of interviews or observations; it offers instead an introduction to interviewing and observation as assessment data sources. Interview and observation techniques for various situations are detailed in a number of sources (e.g., Fine & Glasser, 1996; MacKinnon, Michels, & Buckley, 2006; Othmer & Othmer, 2002; Rogers, 2001; Shea, 1998; Sommers-Flanagan & Sommers-Flanagan, 1999; Turner, Hersen, & Heiser, 2003; Shipley & Wood, 1996), but learning how to use these techniques effectively requires more than reading (Bogels, 1994). Clinicians must also engage in carefully supervised interview practice as part of their professional training.

CLINICAL INTERVIEW SITUATIONS

Section Preview: There are interviews for a variety of clinical situations: intake interviews to establish the nature of someone's problem and assign a DSM diagnosis, orientation interviews to prepare a client for treatment or research, problem-referral interviews to address a specific referral question, termination or debriefing interviews to end treatment or research, and crisis intervention interviews to offer support through a crisis and to decide what, if any, intervention should be offered next. Although we address these situations separately, they often overlap in practice. A final situation we discuss involves cultural or ethnic differences between interviewer and interviewee and the importance of clinician sensitivity to cultural factors when interviewing.

Intake Interviews

The most common type of clinical interview occurs when a client first comes to the clinician because of some problem in living. *Intake interviews* are designed mainly to establish the nature of the problem. Often, the intake interviewer is asked for a classification or diagnosis of the problem in the form of a DSM-IV Axis I or Axis II label (e.g., Major Depressive Disorder), along with associated descriptions on the other axes. Clinicians may also use intake interviews to develop broader descriptions of clients and the environmental context in which their behavior occurs.

Information gathered in this situation may also help the clinician decide whether the client has come to the right place. If, on the basis of one or more intake interviews, the answer to the question is no, the clinician will refer the client to another professional or agency for alternative services. If further contact is seen as desirable, additional assessment or treatment sessions are scheduled. Most clinicians conduct their own intake interviews, but in some agencies and group practices, social workers or other personnel perform this function.

Some intake interviews are structured according to a sequence of important topics suggested by the case study outlines described in Chapter 3, "Basic Features of Clinical Assessment." Originally patterned after the question-and-answer format of medical history taking, many psychiatric interviews also include a *mental status examination* (MSE), a planned sequence of questions designed to assess a client's basic mental functioning in a number of important areas (see Table 4.1). The MSE is analogous to the physical examination that makes up part of the assessment of medical problems.

Intake interviews may also lay the groundwork for subsequent therapy efforts by establishing a productive working relationship and organizing the clinician's hypotheses about the origins and development of the client's problems (MacKinnon, Michels, & Buckley, 2006). The intake interview is important to successful treatment because almost half the clients who attend an intake interview fail to return for scheduled treatment (Baekeland & Lundwall, 1975; Morton, 1995). The clients' initial perception of their intake interviewer appears to affect this pattern. Clients are more likely to return for subsequent treatment after talking to an interviewer whom they feel treated them with warm friendliness as opposed to businesslike professionalism (Kokotovic & Tracey, 1987; Patterson, 1989; Tryon, 1990). Clients also rate interviews more positively when interviewers express correct understandings of the clients' partially or indirectly

TABLE 4.1

The Mental Status Examination

Here is a typical MSE topic outline (Siassi, 1984), followed by a short excerpt from an MSE interview:

I. **General appearance and behavior:** Client's level of activity, reaction to interviewer, grooming and clothing are assessed.

II. **Speech and thought:** Is client's speech coherent and understandable? Are delusions present?

III. **Consciousness:** Is the sensorium clear or clouded?

IV. **Mood and affect:** Is client depressed, anxious, restless? Is affect appropriate to situation?

V. **Perception:** Does client experience hallucinations, depersonalization?

VI. **Obsessions and compulsions:** Amount and quality of these behaviors are noted.

VII. **Orientation:** Is client aware of correct time, place, and personal identity?

VIII. **Memory:** What is condition of short- and long-term memory?

IX. **Attention and concentration:** Asking client to count backwards by 7s is a common strategy.

X. **Fund of general information:** Questions like "Who is the President?" or "What are some big cities in the United States?" are asked.

XI. **Intelligence:** Estimated from educational achievement, reasoning ability, and fund of information.

XII. **Insight and judgment:** Does client understand probable outcomes of behavior?

XIII. **Higher intellectual functioning:** What is the quality of client's form of thinking? Is client able to deal with abstraction?

CLINICIAN: Good morning. What is your name?

CLIENT: Randolph S.

CLINICIAN: Well, Mr. S, I would like to ask you some questions this morning. Is that all right?

CLIENT: Fine.

CLINICIAN: How long have you been here?

CLIENT: Since yesterday morning.

CLINICIAN: Why are you here?

CLIENT: I don't know. I think my wife called the police and here I am.

CLINICIAN: Well, what did you do to make her call the police?

CLIENT: I don't know.

CLINICIAN: What day is today?

CLIENT: Tuesday, the twelfth.

CLINICIAN: What year is it?

CLIENT: 1997.

CLINICIAN: What city are we in?

CLIENT: Chicago.

CLINICIAN: Who is the mayor of Chicago?

expressed concerns and emotions (Dimatteo & Taranta, 1976). Even nonverbal behavior during the intake interview, such as facial expressions of therapists and clients, can influence the subsequent therapeutic success (Rasting & Beutel, 2005).

Problem-Referral Interviews

Clinicians sometimes serve as diagnostic consultants to physicians, psychiatrists, courts, schools, employers, social service agencies, and other agencies. In these circumstances, the client is often referred in order to answer a specific question, such as *Is Mr. P. competent to stand trial? Is Jimmy G. mentally retarded?* or *Will such-and-such a custody arrange-ment with Ms. M. and Mr. O be in the best interest of this child?*

In these circumstances, the central goal of the interview is to address the referral question. For this reason, it is important that the referral question be stated clearly. Questions such as *Give me a profile on Mr. Q*, or *Will Ms. Y. make a good parent, or is she disturbed?* are too general or vague. And referral requests such as *Please test my child's IQ so I can prove to the schools that he should be in the gifted class* should raise red flags about the appropriateness of conducting the assessment without further clarification of the parent's motives and needs. As discussed in Chapter 3, the referral question, once clarified, determines the type of assessment conducted.

Orientation Interviews

People receiving psychological assessment or treatment often do not know what to expect, let alone what is expected of them. This is especially true if they have had no previous contact with mental health professionals. To make these new experiences less mysterious and more comfortable, many clinicians conduct special interviews (or reserve segments of interviews) to acquaint the client with the assessment, treatment, or research procedures to come (Prochaska & Norcross, 1994).

Such *orientation interviews* are beneficial in at least two ways. First, because the client is encouraged to ask questions and make comments, misconceptions that might obstruct subsequent treatment progress can be discussed and corrected. Second, orientation interviews can help clients understand upcoming assessment and treatment procedures and what their roles in these procedures will be (Couch, 1995). Thus, the clinician might point out that the clients who benefit most from treatment are those who are candid, cooperative, serious, and willing to work to solve their problems. Good orientation interviews, then, can help focus clinicians' efforts on those clients who are most willing to be full partners in the assessment or treatment enterprise.

Orientation interviews are also important for research participants. Although clinicians or researchers might not want to reveal every detail of the research design in order to avoid biasing participants, they are ethically required to assure that each participant understands the nature of the tasks to be performed and any risks associated with them. Research orientation interviews not only satisfy the requirement for informed consent, but they also help insure motivated cooperation from the participants, something especially important in long-term clinical trials and longitudinal research.

Termination and Debriefing Interviews

A different kind of orienting interview occurs when it is time to terminate a clinical relationship. For example, people who have just completed a series of assessment sessions involving extensive interviews, tests, and observations are understandably anxious to know "what the doctor found," how the information will be used, and who will have access to it. These concerns are particularly acute when the assessor has acted as consultant to a school or a court. A *termination interview* can help alleviate clients' anxiety about the assessment enterprise by explaining the procedures and protections involved in transmission of privileged information and by providing a summary and interpretation of the assessment results.

Termination interviews following clinical research are called *debriefings*. They include an explanation of the project in which the person has participated and a discussion of the procedures employed in it. Debriefings permit participants to ask questions and make comments about their research experiences. In accordance with the standards for ethical research established by the APA and other organizations, debriefing of participants is aimed at assuring that the research experience has done no harm and that the participant feels comfortable about it (see Chapter 15, "Professional Issues in Clinical Psychology."). Debriefing interviews can also benefit the clinical researcher by helping to clarify how participants perceived the experiment and whether factors outside the experimenter's control affected participants' behavior (Orne, 1962).

Termination interviews also occur when psychological treatment ends. When treatment has ended successfully, many loose ends must be tied up: There is gratitude to be expressed and accepted, reminders to be given about the handling of future problems, plans to be made for follow-up contacts, and reassurance given to clients about their ability to go it alone. Termination interviews help make the transition from treatment to posttreatment as smooth and productive as possible. When treatment ends unsuccessfully, such as when clients drop out, termination interviews can inform clinicians about the dynamics leading to drop-out and suggest ways to more effectively structure treatment (Hummelen, Wilberg, & Karterud, 2007).

Crisis Interviews

When people in crisis appear at clinical facilities or call a hotline, suicide prevention center, or other agency, interviewers do not have the luxury of scheduling a series of assessment and treatment sessions. Instead, they conduct *crisis interviews* in which they attempt to provide support, collect assessment data, and provide help, all in a very short time (Somers-Flanagan & Somers-Flanagan, 1995).

The interviewer must deal with the client in a calm and accepting fashion, ask relevant questions (e.g., "Have you ever tried to kill yourself?" "What kinds of pills do you have in the house?"), and work on the immediate problem directly or by putting the client in touch with other services. One or two well-handled interviews during a crisis may be the beginning and the end of contact with a client whose need for assistance was temporary and situation-specific. For others, the crisis interview leads to subsequent assessment and treatment sessions.

Ethnic and Cultural Issues in the Clinical Interview

As the U.S. population becomes increasingly diverse, the number of persons from different ethnic and cultural backgrounds seeking mental health treatment increases (Sue, 1999). However, cultural differences between clients and interviewers can be problematic, particularly when clients' cultural assumptions, values, and practices do not fit well with the assumptions, values, and practices of the mental health services offered.

Underutilization of Mental Health Care.   The importance of cultural factors is suggested by mental health utilization rates. Members of racial and ethnic minority groups generally receive less mental health care and lower-quality mental health care than the general population receives (Nevid, Rathus, & Green, 2006). Table 4.2 presents key reasons for this underutilization. Some of these relate to access to services while others relate to cultural norms and misunderstandings that can derail the interview process.

The concerns that many members of minority groups have about bias in the mental health system are not entirely unfounded. For instance, clinicians tend to diagnose African American and Hispanic clients with schizophrenia at higher rates than they diagnose that disorder among Caucasians (Aklin & Turner, 2006). At the same time, mood and anxiety disorders are diagnosed less often in African American children than in white children (Aklin & Turner, 2006). Such differences appear to be attributable to biases of clinicians more than to differences in objective criteria.

Cultural Sensitivity and Cultural Competence.   There can be several possible reasons that clinical interviewers might overdiagnose or underdiagnose psychological disorders among persons from different ethnic groups, but one of them is certainly lack of knowledge. If unaware of cultural variations, a clinician might misinterpret an African American client's reluctance to reveal symptoms as evidence of paranoid ideation rather than as caution or suspiciousness about the mental health system. A clinician might mistakenly assume that an Asian client's reluctance to disclose is evidence of resistance or lack of insight rather a cultural prohibition against immediate self-disclosure to strangers.

In Chapter 3, we introduced the idea of culture-bound syndromes—those that do not fit neatly into DSM-IV diagnoses. A specific example is *Ataque de nervios,* a syndrome that occurs largely among Hispanic groups and is characterized by anxiety and somatic

TABLE 4.2	
Reasons for Underutilization of Mental Health Care among Ethnic Minorities in the United States	
Failures of Access	Poverty leads to client being uninsured or underinsured
	Client lacks transportation
	Language barriers preclude communication (client and interviewer do not speak a common language)
Failures of Beliefs and Attitudes	Client does not know that mental health services are available
	Cultural norms prohibit expressing strong emotions to strangers or dictate that problems be discussed only with spiritual leaders, medical personnel (e.g., emergency room), or family members (e.g., trusted elders)
	Client fears that mental health workers will make him or her feel ashamed or stupid (e.g., because client did not understand procedures, remedies, or red tape)
	Based on a history of discrimination or oppression of one's people, client feels mistrust and fears being labeled, mistreated, or discriminated against

symptoms. Although it is similar to some DSM-IV diagnoses, it is not identical (Tolin, Robison, Gaztambide, Horowitz, & Blank, 2007). It is important that interviewers and therapists-in-training recognize cultural variations in the expression of distress. Misunderstanding of the meaning of spoken and body language seems to be an especially important problem. For instance, compared to Caucasians, Asian clients are more likely to express psychological complaints in terms of somatic symptoms such as nausea, faint vision, and vertigo (Hsu & Folstein, 1997). Such culture-specific symptoms may not be attributable to significantly higher rates of somatoform disorder among Asian people but rather to their cultural belief that it is more acceptable to use somatic terms to convey emotional distress.

Cultural values such as independence versus interdependence also can affect interviews. Among persons from Hispanic and Asian cultures, independence may not be as strongly valued as it is among Caucasian Westerners. Interdependence and family obligations may be assigned greater value instead. So interviewers who pursue questioning that seems to imply the value of emotional or psychological independence may unwittingly be alienating their interviewees who sense that the interviewer disapproves of one of their core values.

What should interviewers faced with possible cultural issues do? It is unrealistic for interviewers to be familiar with *all* the possible cultural variations in interview behavior (and discussion of these is also beyond the scope of this text), but it is possible for clinicians to have a reasonably thorough understanding of how interview conclusions can be distorted by ethnic and cultural misunderstandings. Interviewers can avoid bias by educating themselves about the more common cultural variations in interviewing behaviors and those related to the specific ethnic backgrounds of clients they interview. When confronted with situations that might involve cultural misunderstanding, interviewers should openly explore cultural concerns with the client, thereby conveying a sincere desire to understand, rather than just classify, the client. They should also consult with colleagues and, when possible, enlist the assistance of persons with more expertise in working with particular clients. Clinical interview training, too, should include analysis of the empirical literature on multicultural interviewing, supervised training in cross-cultural interviewing, and the use of assessment methods that have been empirically shown to reduce cultural bias. We address some of these instruments in the next section.

Section Summary: Clinical interviews are undertaken to establish the nature of someone's problem, assign a DSM diagnosis, prepare interviewees to participate in treatment or research, address a specific referral question, debrief after termination of treatment or research, and offer support and intervention in a crisis. Often, several of these goals are combined in an interview. As the U.S. population becomes more diverse, clinicians should be especially sensitive to how cultural or ethnic factors can bias interviews. Doing so involves both didactic education and supervised training.

INTERVIEW STRUCTURE

Section Preview: The most fundamental feature of clinical interviews is their structure: the degree to which the interviewer determines the content and course of the conversation. At one end of the structure continuum are *open-ended* or *nondirective interviews* in which the clinician does as little as possible to interfere with the natural flow of the client's speech and choice of topics. At the other end are *structured interviews,* which involve a carefully planned question-and-answer format. In between are many blends, usually called guided or *semistructured interviews.* While reliability and validity are higher with structured interviews, there are some disadvantages to them.

Several factors influence the degree of structure in an interview; among them are the theoretical orientation and personal preferences of the interviewer. In general, humanistic clinicians tend to establish the least interview structure. Psychodynamically oriented clinicians usually provide more, while cognitive-behavioral clinicians are likely to be the most verbally active and directive. Structure may also change during an interview—many interviewers begin in a nondirective way and become more structured as the interview continues. The interview situation also strongly affects the degree of structure. For instance, by their nature, crises demand more structure than might be desirable during a routine intake interview.

Nondirective Interviews

Consider first this segment from a nondirective intake interview.

> CLINICIAN: [Your relative] didn't go into much detail about what you wanted to talk about, so I wonder if you'd just start in at whatever you want to start in with, and tell me what kind of nervousness you have.
>
> CLIENT: Well, it's, uh, I think if I were to put it in, in a few words, it seems to be a, a, a complete lack of self-confidence in, and an extreme degree of self-consciousness. Now, I have always been a very self-conscious person. I mean ever, just about, since I was probably 14 years old the first I remember of it. But for a long time I've realized that I was sort of using people as crutches. I mean I, a lot of things I felt I couldn't do myself I did all right if someone was along.
>
> CLINICIAN: Um-hm.
>
> CLIENT: And it's just progressed to the point where I'm actually using the four walls of the house as an escape from reality. I mean I don't, I don't care to go out. I, I certainly can't go out alone. It's sort of a vicious circle. I find out I can't do it, and then I'm sure the next time I can't do it.
>
> CLINICIAN: Um-hm.
>
> CLIENT: And it just gets progressively worse. I think the first that I ever noticed it. . . . (Wallen, 1956, p. 146)

The client continued a narrative about the onset and duration of her problems, her occupation and marriage, her father's death, and other topics. Notice that the clinician hardly says a word, although as we shall see later, there are things he could have done to nondirectively encourage the client to talk had it been necessary. The nondirective interviewer uses direct questions sparingly and relies instead on responses designed to facilitate the client's talking about his or her concerns.

Semistructured Interviews

Compare this nondirective approach to the following semistructured interview in which an organized set of topics is explored in a way that gives the interviewer flexibility in wording questions, interpreting answers, and guiding decisions about what to address next.

> CLINICIAN: You say that you are very jealous a lot of the time and this upsets you a great deal.
>
> CLIENT: Well, I know it's stupid for me to feel that way, but I am hurt when I even think of Mike with another woman.
>
> CLINICIAN: You don't want to feel jealous, but you do.
>
> CLIENT: I know that's not the way a "liberated" woman should be.
>
> CLINICIAN: What is your idea of how a liberated woman should feel?
>
> CLIENT: I don't know. In many ways I feel I have changed so much in the last year. I really don't believe you have the right to own another person—and yet, when it happens to me, I feel really hurt. I'm such a hypocrite.
>
> CLINICIAN: You're unhappy because you are not responding the way you really would like to?
>
> CLIENT: I'm not the person I want to be.
>
> CLINICIAN: So there's really "double jeopardy." When Mike is with someone else, it really hurts you. And, when you feel jealous, you get down on yourself for being that way.
>
> CLIENT: Yes, I guess I lose both ways. (Morganstern & Tevlin, 1981, p. 86)

Notice the nondirective features in this excerpt—the clinician's responses conveyed an understanding of the client's experience and encouraged further talk but did not dictate what the client talked about by requesting specific information. However, the interviewer also placed limits on the topic by asking a specific question. The more specific questions the interviewer asks, the more structure he or she imposes on the interview.

Semistructured interviews have been developed for a variety of clinical purposes, most of them involving assessment of specific conditions or situations. For example, the *Crisis Intervention Semistructured Interview* was developed to help trained clinicians and novices interview clients in crisis situations. Information from the interview is used to provide a standardized method of arriving at intervention decisions (Kulic, 2005). A second example is the *Clinician Home-based Interview to Assess Function* (CHIF), a semistructured interview used to assess functioning in the elderly who show signs of dementia (Hendrie et al., 2006).

Structured Interviews

In structured interviews, the interviewer asks a series of specific questions phrased in a standardized fashion and presented in an established order. Consistent rules are also provided for coding or scoring the clients' answers or for using additional probes to elicit further scoreable responses. Thus, while structured interviews do not outlaw open-ended questions or prohibit interviewers from formulating their own questions to clarify ambiguous responses, they do provide detailed rules (sometimes called *decision trees* or *branching rules*) that tell the interviewer what to do in certain situations (e.g., "if the respondent answers no, skip to question 32; if the respondent answers yes, inquire as to how many times it happened and continue to the next question").

As an example of a structured interview, consider the *Structured Clinical Interview for DSM-IV Disorders* (SCID; Spitzer, Williams, Gibbon, & First, 1989). The purpose of this instrument is to elicit enough information about a client that a DSM diagnosis can be validly applied. To do so, the interviewer must ask questions that sample inclusion criteria for many disorders. Questions asked in the interview are organized into standard questions (required and routinely asked), branching questions (prescribed follow-ups to specific responses; e.g., "if yes . . ."), and optional probes.

Like the SCID, many structured interviews were designed to help clinicians arrive at psychiatric diagnoses by asking questions relevant to specific DSM diagnostic criteria. Examples are shown in Table 4.3, which lists some of the most widely used structured and semistructured interviews. Some, such as the SCID, have considerable bandwidth (breadth) but limited fidelity (depth). Others, such as the *Schedule of Affective Disorders and Schizophrenia,* are focused on one or a few disorders and have greater fidelity but limited bandwidth.

Structured interviews continue to be developed for tasks other than DSM diagnoses, such as planning and evaluating rehabilitation treatments (Ownsworth, McFarland, & Young, 2000; Rogers, Ustad, & Salekin, 1998), evaluating whether a criminal defendant is mentally competent to stand trial (DeClue, 2006), and assessing clients' personalities along the dimensions of the five-factor model (Stepp, Trull, Burr, Wolfenstein, & Vieth, 2006). For detailed coverage of structured interviews, see Rogers (2001).

Advantages and Disadvantages of Structured Interviews

In recent years, structured and semistructured interviews have been used increasingly in a variety of clinical situations (Rogers, 2001; Thienemann, 2004). This proliferation has occurred even though structured interviews eliminate much of the flexibility of open-ended interviews; they prescribe conversation topics and constrain client answers. So why are structured interviews so popular?

The answer comes largely from the fact that structured interviews provide a systematic way of assessing the variables that interviews are designed to explore. In other words, though they may not be as flexible, they are less prone to error. To understand why, you must understand the sources of error that can affect interviews. A classic paper by Ward, Beck, Mendelson, Mock, and Erbaugh (1962) helps categorize the sources of error in clinical interviewing.

One source of error, *patient variance,* occurs when the same patient provides different answers or displays different behaviors in response to the same questions asked by different clinicians. A second source of error, *information variance,* refers to differences in the way clinicians ask questions or make observations. For instance, if two clinicians do not ask questions the same way, they might receive different answers from a client.

TABLE 4.3

Structured Interviews Frequently Used in Clinical Psychology

Name of Interview	Reference	Purpose
Interviews for Axis I Disorders		
The Schedule for Affective Disorders & Schizophrenia (SADS)	Endicott & Spitzer (1978)	Semistructured interview for differential diagnosis of more than 20 categories of mental disorder
Diagnostic Interview Schedule (DIS-IV)	Robins, Cottler, Bucholz, & Compton (1995)	Extensive structured interview with several modules used in large-scale epidemiological studies; Chinese and Spanish versions available
Structured Clinical Interview for DSM-IV (SCID)	Spitzer, Williams, Gibbon, & First (1989)	Broad-scale differential diagnoses tied to DSM-IV criteria
Diagnostic Interview Schedule for Children, Revised (DISC-R)	Shaffer, Fisher, Lucas, Dulcan, & Schwab-Stone (2000)	Parallel formats for children and parents for making differential diagnoses of childhood disorders
Composite International Diagnostic Interview (CIDI-2)	World Health Organization— Alcohol, Drug, and Mental Health Administration (1997)	Many of the same items as the DIS but with modifications to improve cross-cultural use
Interviews for Axis II Disorders		
International Personality Disorder Examination (IPDE)	Loranger (1996)	Differential diagnoses among DSM III personality disorders; module available for DSM-IV
Structured Clinical Interview	First, Gibbon, Spitzer, Williams, & Benjamin (1997)	Semistructured interview for DSM-IV personality disorders; combined SCID and SCID-II are designed to provide a comprehensive diagnostic assessment interview
Specialized Interviews		
Psychopathy Checklist (PCL-R)	Hare (1991)	Semistructured interview consisting of structured questions and optional probes for evaluating antisocial functioning
Rogers Criminal Responsibility Assessment Scale (RCRAS)	Rogers, Wasyliw, & Cavanaugh (1984)	Assesses criminal responsibility against specific legal criteria
Structured Interview of Reported Symptoms (SIRS)	Rogers, Gillis, Dickens, & Bagby (1991)	Assesses malingering in clinical populations
Schedules for Clinical Assessment in Neuropsychiatry (SCAN)	World Health Organization (1994)	Used in national and international studies of the epidemiology of mental disorders; also in individual diagnoses
Cambridge Cognitive Examination (CAMDEX)	Roth et al. (1986)	Assesses cognitive dysfunctions such as memory loss and language problems

Consider these two questions: "Do you get anxious whenever you are in crowded places such as malls?" and "What situations seem to make you the most anxious?" Finally, there is *criterion variance,* which refers to disagreements that occur if clinicians apply different standards of judgment to the same set of client responses. For instance, different clinicians might use different cutoff points or inference rules for what a response means (e.g., what types of responses are sufficient to qualify as "substantially impaired"). Table 4.4 summarizes these sources of disagreement among clinicians in interview assessments. This table, compiled by Rogers (2001) and based on the work of Ward, Beck, Mendelson, Mock, and Erbaugh (1962), was designed to illustrate the importance of structured interviews in reducing unnecessary variability in assessment. It shows that much of clinicians' disagreement comes not from inconsistencies in client responses but from inconsistencies in clinicians' collection and use of those responses. While the percentages in this table are partly based on older versions of the DSM and may not be currently valid, the table nevertheless clearly illustrates the importance of having consistency across assessors—particularly in the ways they seek information and in the decision criteria they use.

Structured interviews are a mainstay in clinical research because they help reduce information variance and criterion variance. In addition, structured interviews have become almost indispensable in epidemiology, the study of how disorders and other behavior patterns are distributed in the population and of the factors that affect this distribution (Loranger, 1992; Wittchen, 1994). Indeed, many of the structured interviews used by clinicians in practice were originally developed for research purposes (again showing the interplay of science and practice in the field). The content of these interviews has been standardized, studied, and revised according to the results of research, so clinicians have some assurance that the interview will be comprehensive enough to reach specific assessment goals.

The increasing use of structured interviews by clinicians parallels other trends in the history of clinical assessment. As noted in Chapter 3, for example, using formal, statistical rules for combining assessment data is usually more effective than relying on clinicians' subjective judgments. Structured interviews are designed to make the data-collection process more consistent by standardizing how information is gathered. Empirically driven decision rules can also replace, or at least improve, clinicians' judgments.

TABLE 4.4	

Why Do Clinicians Disagree? Rogers's (2001) Distillation of Ward et al. (1962)

Percentage	Sources of Disagreement
32.5%	*Information variance:* Variations among clinicians in what questions are asked, which observations are made, and how the resulting information is organized.
62.5%	*Criterion variance:* Variations among clinicians in applying standards for what is clinically relevant (e.g., when does dysphoric mood qualify as depression) and when the diagnostic criteria are met.
5.0%	*Patient variance:* Variations within the same patient that result in substantial differences in clinical presentation and subsequent diagnosis.

SOURCE: From *Handbook of Diagnostic and Structured Interviewing,* by R. Rogers, 2001 (New York: Guilford), p. 5.

At the same time, however, there are limitations to structured interviews. Clinicians who depend too much on structured interviews risk becoming so "protocol bound" that they miss important information that the interview script did not explore. Further, the routine nature of structured interviews can alienate clients if the clinician fails to first establish rapport and to explain fully the rationale behind the use of the structured format. Clinicians must use their interaction skills inside and outside the structured interview to enhance rapport. Finally, structured interviews, like all other interviews, depend heavily on the memory, candor, and descriptive abilities of respondents. So while the reliability of clients' reports (or of different clinicians' inferences from those reports) might be excellent, the validity or meaning of structured interview data can be threatened if the client misunderstands questions, is not motivated to answer truthfully, or cannot recall relevant information.

Because both the questions and the inference rules of structured interviews are scripted, they can be conducted by professional clinicians, trained nonprofessionals, or even specially programmed computers (Groth-Marnat, 2003; Peters, Clark, & Carroll, 1998; Pilkonis et al., 1995; Reich, Cottler, McCallum, & Corwin, 1995). Researchers have also investigated whether structured and semistructured interviews can be effectively administered using (a) experienced interviewers with no formal clinical training (Brugha, Nienhuis, Bagchi, Smith, & Meltzer, 1999), (b) the telephone (Cacciola, Alterman, Rutheford, McKay, & May, 1999; Lyneham & Rapee, 2005), and (c) self-administered questionnaires (Erickson & Kaplan, 2000). Some are concerned that by permitting less well trained interviewers or automated administrations, the interview quality will be compromised. As yet, no statement about the general effectiveness of these techniques seems warranted, but there are indications. Lyneham and Rapee (2005) found that results from telephone administrations of the Anxiety Disorders Interview Schedule for Children for DSM-IV, a structured interview, showed good to excellent agreement with the same instrument administered face to face.

It is important to remember that structured interviews are most easily applied to clinical tasks that have well-defined decision-making criteria, such as diagnosis, but structured interviews do not exist for most face-to-face clinical contact hours, such as therapy interviews. Indeed, the unstructured interview remains the most common tool used by clinical psychologists on a day-to-day basis (Garb, 2007). So despite trends toward increasing the structure of many clinical interactions, clinicians still need a broad base of skills to manage the stages of all types of interviews.

Section Summary: Nondirective or open-ended interviews are those in which the clinician and client jointly determine the content and flow of the interview. At the other extreme are structured interviews, which involve a carefully planned question-and-answer format. In between are blends, usually called semistructured interviews. Structured and semistructured interviews have higher reliability and validity when the purpose of the interview involves judgments that have relatively clear-cut decision criteria, such as making a diagnosis. The disadvantages associated with structured interviews include the restrictions in the interview format that may result in failure to identify important content. If not handled appropriately by the clinician, the use of highly structured interviews can also inhibit rapport.

STAGES IN THE INTERVIEW

Section Preview: In the following sections, we examine techniques commonly employed by clinical psychologists during the beginning, middle, and end stages of interviews. Certain features, such as establishing and maintaining rapport, communicating the goals or purpose of the interview, demonstrating good listening skills, and providing emotional support, are common to most interviews. Others, such as whether to use a structured or unstructured format, for instance, depend on the goals of the interview. Both clinicians and clients must interpret verbal and nonverbal behavior during an interview, so it is important that clinicians are sensitive to various ways in which their communication can be misinterpreted. Sensitivity to differences of interpretation is especially important when clients come from cultural or ethnic backgrounds that differ from the interviewer's.

Interviews usually begin with efforts at making the client comfortable and ready to speak freely (stage 1), continue into a central information-gathering stage (stage 2), and end with summary statements, client questions, and, if appropriate, plans for additional assessment sessions (stage 3). Stage 2, generally the longest stage, can often be further subdivided into different stages or phases. Although not all clinical interviews are organized around a beginning–middle–end framework, the three-stage model offers a convenient guide for our discussion of typical clinical interviews. There is no single "right" way to conduct an interview, but certain strategies have proven valuable in practice and have thus been adopted by skilled clinicians representing every theoretical approach (Goldfried, 1980).

Stage 1: Beginning the Interview

In one sense, the interview begins prior to meeting the client with the clinician's processing of the referral. Sometimes, the clinician has only a client's general complaint, perhaps voiced to a secretary at the time of a self-referral. Other times, medical, school, court, or other mental health records may be available. Such information can help the clinician to decide whether specific interviewing or testing materials might be needed (e.g., structured interview or unstructured interview formats).

The Setting. Certain settings are especially conducive to building rapport for most clients. Except for clients whose cultural background might cause such surroundings to be threatening, interviews are best conducted in a comfortable, private office because most people find it easier to relax when they are physically comfortable. Also, privacy makes it easier to assure the client of the interview's confidential nature.

Several other office characteristics can aid rapport. A reassuring equality is established when two people sit a few feet apart on similar chairs of equal height. If the clinician sits in a massive, high-backed chair behind a huge desk placed 6 feet from the client's smaller, lower seat, rapport may be impaired. A desk cleared of other work, along with precautions to hold phone calls and prevent other intrusions, makes it clear that the clinician is fully attentive and sincerely interested in what the client has to say. Personal effects, such as pictures of family and favored vacation spots, add personal warmth. Interviewers should probably avoid decorations that make bold statements about views because these might alienate some clients (e.g., a big NRA poster or life-size cutout of Michael Moore). It is the client's self-expression, not the interviewer's, that should have priority. The list of rapport-building techniques could be extended almost indefinitely; the point is that from the beginning, the clinician should try to create a warm, comfortable environment that encourages the client to speak freely and honestly about whatever topics are relevant to the interview.

The Opening.   It is important that clinicians handle the first few minutes of initial interviews carefully. This early stage is important because clients may not be ready to talk candidly about personal matters yet, preferring instead to take a wait-and-see approach in which they carefully control what they say and don't say. If this reserved attitude prevails throughout the interview, the clinician is unlikely to gather very much valuable assessment information.

Accordingly, most clinicians see establishing rapport as their main task during the first part of initial interviews. Rapport can be built in several ways, many of which involve common sense and courtesy. A client's anxiety and uncertainty can be eased by demystifying the interview. Upon greeting, a warm smile, a friendly hello, an introduction (e.g., "I'm Doctor Jenkins"), and a handshake are excellent beginnings to an interview. Small talk about the weather or difficulty in finding the office also eases the client's transition into the interview. The skilled interviewer relaxes the client by appearing warm and approachable. But this informal rapport building should not go on so long that the interview loses its distinctive quality or the client begins to suspect that the interviewer might wish to avoid the topics that prompted the interview. The interviewer should get down to business within the first few minutes, thereby communicating that the client's time and possible problems are important. Skilled clinicians can establish remarkable rapport during the first stage of an initial interview, but even for them, the process continues into the second and third stages and into subsequent sessions as well.

Frame Setting and Transition.   Another task that typically accompanies the opening of an interview is called *frame setting*. The frame refers to the norms and expectations that surround an interview, consultation, or therapy session (Walter, Bundy, & Dornan, 2005). When clinicians set the frame, they explain to the client the basic ground rules for the interaction. For example, after introductions and a brief period of socially familiar small talk, the clinician might say something like the following (items in brackets would be replaced by mention of client's specific symptoms or complaints or with case-specific elaboration):

> We'll have an hour and a half to work together today. During that time, I hope we can talk about [the problems you've been having], maybe get a better handle on how and when these problems began, how they are affecting you now. My job is mostly to listen at this point, to try to understand [your situation]. As we continue, I might also ask you a set of questions and write some things down to study later. This information should help us understand and also develop a plan of action for [addressing your symptoms]. Our conversation is confidential—what we talk about stays in this room. The exceptions to this is [here the

interviewer might elaborate on limits of confidentiality such as if the client is an imminent threat of harm to himself or others, what information will go to third parties such as insurance companies or referral sources, etc.]. Please feel free to ask any questions you like; I'll do my best to answer them. If we don't complete all that we hope to today—that happens sometimes—we can continue during the next appointment.

Setting the frame clarifies time boundaries for the interview session, expresses an expectation about what will be covered and what basic roles the participants will take, and briefly introduces the idea of a structure. It also provides assurances of confidentiality as well as its limits and conveys information about the interviewer's commitment. Notice also the interviewer's use of "we," which is designed to enlist the interviewee as an ally in exploring the problem. This introduction of the frame could occur before or after discussion of the client's troubles has begun in earnest, but it should occur relatively early in the interview. Not all aspects of the frame need be introduced at once. Some topics might be discussed more fully later in the interview or during subsequent meetings as framework issues reemerge, as they frequently do in therapy (especially with clients diagnosed with particular disorders, such as borderline personality disorder for example).

In most cases, interviewers begin the transition into the second stage of the interview with nondirective, *open-ended* questions. Common examples are "So what brings you here today?" or "Would you like to tell me something about the problems you referred to on the phone?" A major advantage of this approach is that it allows a client to begin in his or her own way. An open-ended invitation to talk allows the client to ease into painful or embarrassing topics without feeling coerced and lets clients know that the clinician is ready to listen. Clients often begin with a "ticket of admission" problem that may not be the one of greatest concern to them. The real reason for the visit may appear only after they have "tested the water" with varying amounts of diversionary conversation.

Stage 2: The Middle of the Interview

Transition to the middle of an interview should be as smooth as possible. In the transition and frame setting, the therapist signals whether the therapist or the client will direct what the client talks about. These signals continue as the interview progresses. At one extreme are open-ended or nondirective techniques, and at the other are close-ended or directive techniques. As our previous discussion implies, directive techniques are used extensively in structured interviews. Accordingly, the following information refers mainly to clinical interviews that do not use structured instruments. Here are some ways in which the interviewer provides signals about who will lead the conversation.

Nondirective Techniques.   Open-ended questions are used whenever the clinician wishes to prompt clients to speak while exerting as little influence as possible over what they say. Classic remarks like "Tell me a bit more about that" and "How did you feel about that?" exemplify nondirective strategies. These strategies are supplemented by tactics designed to help clients express themselves fully and to enhance rapport by communicating the clinician's understanding and acceptance. The most general of these tactics is called *active listening,* which involves responding to the client's speech in ways that indicate understanding and encourage further elaboration. Active listening was represented in the clinician's "um-hms" in the nondirective interview excerpt presented earlier. Other signs of active listening include comments such as "I see," "I'm with you," "Right," or even just a nodding of the head.

A related nondirective strategy is called *paraphrasing* in which clinicians restate what their clients say in order to (a) show that they are listening closely and (b) give the clients a chance to correct the remark if it was misinterpreted. Carl Rogers called this strategy *reflection* and emphasized the importance of not only restating content but also highlighting client feelings. Consider these examples.

Example A
CLIENT: Sometimes, I could just kill my husband.
CLINICIAN: You would just like to get rid of him altogether.

Example B
CLIENT: Sometimes, I could just kill my husband.
CLINICIAN: He really upsets you sometimes.

Both are reflective responses, but notice that in example A, the clinician merely reworded the client's remark, and in example B, the clinician reflected the feeling contained in the remark. Most clients respond to paraphrasing by continuing to talk, usually along the same lines as before, often in greater detail. Paraphrasing often is preferable to direct questioning because such questioning tends to change or restrict the conversation, as illustrated in the following interaction.

CLIENT: What it comes down to is that life just doesn't seem worth living sometimes.
CLINICIAN: How often do you feel that way?
CLIENT: Oh, off and on.

There is a place for questions like this one, but unless the clinician knows enough about the general scope of a problem to start pinpointing specifics, interrupting with such questions is likely to limit, and even distort, the assessment picture. Clients who are hit with direct queries early in a nondirective interview may conclude that they should wait for the next question rather than spontaneously tell their story. For many clients, this experience can be frustrating and damaging to rapport. In effect, such behavior invokes the common *doctor–patient interview schema*: The doctor (psychologist) asks questions and the patient (interviewee) answers and then passively waits for the next question. While this format is appropriate for some situations, such as structured interviews, it is not as effective in drawing clients out and encouraging them to be active participants/ explorers in solving their own problems.

Paraphrasing can also be helpful when the clinician is confused about what a client has said. Consider the following:

CLIENT: I told my husband that I didn't want to live with him anymore, so he said "fine" and left. Well, when I got back, I found out that the son of a bitch kept all our furniture!

Most clinicians would have a hard time deciphering the sequence of events described here, but if they say "What?" the client might be put off or assume that the clinician is a dunce. Instead, a combination of paraphrase and request for clarification serves nicely:

> CLINICIAN: Okay, let's see if I've got this straight. You told your husband you didn't want to live with him, so he left. You later came back to your house from somewhere else and found he had taken the furniture. Is that right?

Ideally, the client will either confirm this interpretation or fill in the missing pieces. If not, the clinician may wish to use more direct questioning.

Directive Techniques. Most interviewers supplement nondirective tactics with more directive questions whose form, wording, and content are often the result of careful (though often on-the-spot) planning. Consider the following illustrative questions:

A. Do you feel better or worse when your husband is out of town?
B. How do you feel when your husband is out of town?

Example A offers a clear, but possibly irrelevant, two-choice situation. This is a version of the "Do you walk to work or carry your lunch?" question for which the most valid answer may be "Neither." Some clients are not assertive enough in an interview to ignore the choice, so they settle for one unsatisfactory response or the other. Unless there is a special reason for offering clients only a few response alternatives, skilled interviewers ask direct questions in a form, such as in example B, that gets at specific information but also leaves clients free to choose their own words.

Along the same lines, experienced clinicians also avoid asking questions that suggest their own answers. Notice the implications contained in this query: "You've suffered with this problem a long time?" Such questions communicate what the interviewer expects to hear, and some clients will oblige by biasing their response. "How long have you had this problem?" is a better alternative.

Combining Interview Tactics. Because interviews can be flexible, clinicians are usually free to combine the tactics we have described. They may facilitate the client's speech with open-ended requests, paraphrasing, prompts, and other active listening techniques, and then use more directive questions to "zoom in" on topics of special importance. However, directive procedures do not take over completely as interviews progress. They continue to be mixed with less directive tactics. An example of this blending is provided by the concept of *repeated scanning and focusing* in which interviewers first scan a topic nondirectively, then focus on it in more directive fashion:

> CLINICIAN: You mentioned that your family is back East. Could you tell me something about them?
> CLIENT: There's not much to tell. There's Dad, Mom, and the twins. They all seem to like it back there, so I guess they'll stay forever.
> CLINICIAN: What else can you say about them?

CLIENT: Well, Dad is a retired high school principal. Mom used to be strictly a housewife but, since us kids have grown, she's been working part time.

CLINICIAN: How did you get along with your folks when you lived at home?

CLIENT: Really fine. I've always thought they were great people and that's probably why they had so little trouble with me. Of course, now and then there would be a problem, but not often.

CLINICIAN: What kinds of problems were there?

The interviewer might go on to explore several specific issues about the client's relationship with both parents, then move on to another topic, again beginning with scanning procedures and later moving on to more direct questions. Clinicians can accomplish a lot by periodically summarizing their impressions. Consider the following example:

CLINICIAN: I know I asked you before, but are there any normal times when you are neither down nor high-strung?

CLIENT: You mean, when things just go easy and I don't feel driven or have to kick myself?

CLINICIAN: That's right, when things kind of fall in place and seem to run by themselves.

CLIENT: Yes, last year, I had a pretty good semester.

CLINICIAN: Do you feel good then for several months?

CLIENT: Usually not that long. Just a couple of months and I start down again.

CLINICIAN: Let me summarize. What you describe to me sounds as if you are on a roller coaster, going up and down. The downs seem to be more troublesome than the ups. But the deep downs rarely last longer than a few days. And there don't seem to be many straight stretches or periods when you feel normal.

CLIENT: That's it. That's exactly how I feel. (Othmer & Othmer, 2002, p. 61)

Maintaining Rapport. We have discussed several interview techniques that elicit information and also establish rapport in the beginning and middle stages of the interview. As you can see from Table 4.5, many of these are related to how clinicians understand their role in the interview, which in turn affects the interview behaviors that clinicians exhibit.

Stage 3: Closing the Interview

The last stage of an interview can provide valuable assessment data as well as an opportunity to enhance rapport. The interviewer may initiate the third stage with a statement like this:

We have been covering some very valuable information here, and I appreciate your willingness to tell me about it. I know our session hasn't been easy for you. Since we're running out of time for today, I thought we could look back over what we've covered and then give you a chance to ask *me* some questions.

TABLE 4.5

Strategies for Building and Maintaining Rapport

Put the patient and yourself at ease	Establish a comfortable setting, recognize and respond to signs of uneasiness in the client and in yourself; confront sources of tension with empathy, honesty, and patience
Find the suffering—show compassion	Get down to business, ask what is bothering the client, respond with reflective statements showing empathy
Assess insight—become an ally	Ask the client for his or her understanding of the history and meaning of problems; seek examples; ally yourself with the healthy part of the client (i.e., the part that observes his or her symptoms realistically), set therapeutic goals
Show expertise	Demonstrate knowledge of the client's problem or disorder, deal with his or her doubt, instill reasonable hope
Establish leadership	Set and maintain the frame: Explain the ground rules and conditions of the clinical contact; avoid overdoing it by becoming an authoritarian leader
Balance the interviewer roles	Be part empathic listener, part expert, and part authority, with liberal doses of the first and smaller, judicious applications of the other two roles
Balance the client roles	Regard the client (and help the client regard himself or herself) as an ordinary person, deserving of respect, and experiencing an illness or disorder; avoid enabling the role of sufferer (one whose core identity revolves around the client's disorder) or VIP (one whose problems entitle the client to privileged treatment, including 3:00 A.M. calls)

SOURCE: Adapted from *The Clinical Interview Using DSM-IV-TR (Vol. 1),* by E. Othmer and S. C. Othmer, 2003 (Washington, DC: American Psychiatric Publishing).

The clinician accomplishes several things here. First, the impending conclusion of the interview is signaled (frame setting). Second, the client is praised for cooperativeness and reassured that the clinician recognized how stressful the interview was (emotional support). Third, the suggested plan for the final minutes invites the client to ask questions or make comments that may be important but had not been put into words.

Sometimes, the last stage of an interview evokes clinically significant behavior or information. For example, suppose that a client said, "Oh gosh, look at the time. I have to hurry to my lawyer's office or I won't be able to find out until Monday whether I get custody of my son." Some clients wait until the end of the interview to reveal this kind of information because they want the clinician to know about it, but they had not yet been ready to discuss it. Others might just let such information slip out because the interview "feels" over and they let down the defenses they had been using earlier. Some simply don't want the interview to end. For these reasons, the clinician attaches as much importance to the final stage of the interview as to the stages that precede it. However, because the clinician is responsible for monitoring the boundaries—in this case, time constraints—a comment such as the following might be in order:

> You must be on pins and needles waiting to find out. That seems so important—custody of your son. We didn't talk about that today, but maybe next time we can, or we can make another appointment if you like. I hope things turn out well for you.

Through such a response, the therapist expresses empathy, points out in a nonpunitive way that the client omitted this information from discussion, and invites further discussion later.

Communication in the Interview

The fundamental objective in interview communication—as in all human communication—is to encode, transmit, and decode messages accurately. Speakers must encode what they want to convey into transmittable messages made up of words and gestures, which listeners must receive and decode (interpret) within their personal and cultural frame of reference. Lapses in both verbal and nonverbal communication can occur at many points in this process. To take just the simplest of examples, giving the "thumbs up" sign signals approval to people in the United States, but it says "up yours" in Australia.

Clinicians attempt to avoid the much more subtle communication problems that can plague interviews by maximizing the clarity of the messages they send to their clients and by clarifying the meaning of the messages received from them. Let's consider an example of poor clinical communication and then look at some ways to reduce the likelihood of such communication breakdowns. In the following hypothetical exchange, the speakers' thoughts are in parentheses:

> CLINICIAN: (I wonder what his teenage social life was like.) Tell me a little about the friends you had in high school.
>
> CLIENT: (I had dozens of social acquaintances but only one person who was a really close friend.) There was just one, a guy named Mike.
>
> CLINICIAN: (So he was pretty much of a loner.) How did you feel about that?
>
> CLIENT: (It was fine. I had a great time, went to lots of parties, had lots of dates, but knew I could always depend on Mike to talk with about really personal things.) I enjoyed it. Mike and I got along really well.
>
> CLINICIAN: (Not only was he a social isolate, he claims to have liked it that way. I wonder if he is being honest with himself about that.) Did you ever wish you had more friends?
>
> CLIENT: (For crying out loud, he makes it sound like it's a crime to have one really close friend. I think we've talked enough about this.) No.

In the preceding illustration, the clinician used *friend* to refer to casual as well as intimate acquaintances. Because this word had a different meaning for the client, it led to misunderstanding. The conversation could have gone on in this fruitless way for quite a while before the interviewer and the client straightened out their communication problem.

Although the client and clinician may technically be speaking the same language and thus assume they understand one another, the interviewer must be aware that educational, social, ethnic, cultural, economic, and religious factors can impair communication (Gureje, 2004; Karasz, 2005; Yutrzenka, 1995). For instance, what constitutes problem behavior in children can be quite different among different ethnic and cultural groups (Lopez & Guarnaccia, 2000). A complaint issued by a mother from one cultural group (e.g., "He is very often bad") might easily be misunderstood by an interviewer from another. Unless the clinician takes the client's background and frame of reference into account, and asks for clarification when verbal referents are unclear (e.g., "How many times per week does he behave this way?"), the interview will suffer.

Clients can become as confused as clinicians, but if they are reluctant to appear stupid or to question a person in authority, clients may not reveal their confusion. Some evidence on this point comes from a study conducted in a medical setting by Korsch and Negrete (1972). Their data showed that communication from doctors to patients' mothers in a pediatric clinic was obstructed by the use of medical terms and that client confusion and dissatisfaction often resulted. For example, a "lumbar puncture" (spinal tap) was sometimes assumed to be an operation for draining the child's lungs; "incubation period" was interpreted by one mother as the time during which her child had to be kept in bed.

Circumventing such problems in clinical interviews can be facilitated by attention to certain guidelines. Skilled interviewers avoid jargon, ask questions in a straightforward way ("What experiences have you had with masturbation?" not "Do you ever touch yourself?"), and request feedback from their client ("Is all this making sense to you?" or "Did I understand you correctly that . . . ?"). They also try to assure that their verbal behavior conveys patience, concern, and acceptance. Expressing impatience or being judgmental are not usually desirable.

Nonverbal Communication

As in all human communication, a constant stream of nonverbal behavior accompanies the clients' and interviewers' verbal behavior. Indeed, the nonverbal communication channel usually remains open even when the verbal channel shuts down. Since both members of an interview dyad are sending and receiving nonverbal messages, clinicians must be sensitive not only to incoming signals but also to those they transmit. Table 4.6 presents aspects of clients' nonverbal communication that tend to be of greatest interest to clinicians during interviews.

In addition to noting nonverbal client behaviors, clinicians look for inconsistencies between the verbal and nonverbal channels. The statement "I feel pretty good today" will be viewed differently if the client is on the verge of tears than if the client is showing a happy smile.

Interviewers also try to coordinate their own verbal and nonverbal behavior to convey unambiguous messages to their clients. A client will perceive the message to "take your time" in talking about a sensitive topic as more genuine if the clinician says it slowly and quietly than if it is accompanied by a glance at the clock. Similarly, friendly eye contact, some head nodding, an occasional smile, and an attentive posture lets the client know that the interviewer is listening closely. Overdoing it may backfire, however. A plastered-on smile, a continuously knitted brow, sidelong glances, and other theatrics are more likely to convey interviewer anxiety or inexperience than concern.

Clinicians differ as to what they think their clients' nonverbal behavior means. For example, a behaviorist's interpretation of increased respiration, perspiration, and fidgeting while a client talks about sex would probably be that emotional arousal is associated with that topic. Psychodynamic interviewers may infer more, postulating perhaps that

---

TABLE 4.6

Channels of Nonverbal Communications

---

1. Physical appearance—height, weight, grooming, style and condition of clothing, unusual characteristics, muscular development, hairstyle

2. Movements—gestures; repetitive arm, hand, head, leg, or foot motions; tics or other apparently involuntary movements; pacing; handling of cigarettes, matches, or other objects

3. Posture—slouching, rigidity, crossed or uncrossed arms or legs, head in hands

4. Eye contact—constant, fleeting, none

5. Facial expressions—smiles, frowns, grimaces, raised eyebrows

6. Emotional arousal—tears, wet eyes, sweating, dryness of lips, frequent swallowing, blushing or paling, voice or hand tremor, rapid respiration, frequent shifts in body position, startle reactions, inappropriate laughter

7. Speech variables—tone of voice, speed, slurring, lisp, stuttering, blocking, accent, clarity, style, sudden shifts or omissions

---

nonverbal behaviors (e.g., twirling a ring on a finger) are symbolic representations of sexual activity. Gestalt therapists might suspect that the client is avoiding awareness of unpleasant feelings associated with the belief that he or she is just "going round in circles." Alfred Adler interpreted where clients choose to sit: "One moves toward the desk; that is favorable. Another moves away; that is unfavorable" (Adler, 1933). Whatever they might infer from it, most clinicians believe that nonverbal behavior serves as a powerful communication channel and a valuable source of interview data.

In addition to concerns about aspects of interviewing that we have covered in this chapter, clinicians face many other interview-related challenges. Dealing with silences, how to address the client, handling personal questions from clients, note taking and recording, and confronting a client's inconsistencies are just a few of these. (If you are interested in a more detailed exploration of interviewing issues and techniques, consult the sources cited in the introduction of this chapter.)

Section Summary: Interview techniques commonly employed by clinical psychologists during the beginning, middle, and end stages of the interview include nondirective and directive communication. The former is particularly helpful early on in establishing rapport, while the latter, similar to that used in structured interviews, can help elicit and clarify specific areas the interviewer wishes to explore. Rapport can also be enhanced by a number of clinical behaviors such as compassionate and reflective responding, frame setting, and attention to verbal and nonverbal cues. It is important that clinicians are sensitive to various ways their communication can be misinterpreted, particularly when clients come from cultural or ethnic backgrounds different from their own.

RESEARCH ON THE INTERVIEW

Section Preview: As the primary tool of clinicians, interviews are often rich sources of data. They are also complex social interactions that can be interpreted in a variety of ways. Therefore, the reliability and validity of unstructured interviews suffers compared with the reliability and validity of more structured interviews.

Clinicians must remain aware of empirical research on the value of interviews as a source of assessment data and a format for therapy. Such awareness can point clinicians to areas where their own interviewing could be improved.

Early Studies of the Interview

Until 1942, when Carl Rogers published the first transcripts from phonographic recordings of therapy interviews, the exact nature of clinical interactions had been unknown. Research on the clinical interview grew rapidly thereafter. At first it focused on such issues as the effects of audio recording and the accuracy of clinicians' summaries compared to electrical recordings of the same interview (Covner, 1942; Snyder, 1945). After it was established that recording devices were not disruptive and that they provided the most complete account of an interview, research expanded in several new directions.

One of these directions involved efforts to describe relationships between interview characteristics, such as warmth and empathy, and outcome variables, such as rapport building and therapy effectiveness. Some studies focused on differences in interview tactics used by Rogerians and non-Rogerians (Porter, 1943; Seeman, 1949; Strupp, 1960), while others tried to define interview variables such as client resistance (Snyder, 1953). Still other investigators performed detailed analyses of the content of conversations as a means of better understanding the interview process (Auld & Murray, 1955). One team of researchers devoted years to the content analysis of the first five minutes of a single interview (Pittenger, Hockett, & Danehy, 1960).

To the surprise of no one, these investigations revealed that interviews were a rich source of information. To the surprise of many, they also revealed that open-ended interviews of clients can result in quite different information being obtained and different judgments being reached, depending on the clinician doing the interview. In other words, the significance of interview data is often in the eye of the beholder.

Reliability and Validity of Interview Data

In the context of interviews, reliability refers to the degree to which clients give the same information on different occasions or to different interviewers, while validity relates to the degree to which interview data or conclusions are accurate. The impact of these factors is of special interest to researchers trying to establish the value of interview data.

Reliability.   Researchers study the reliability of interviews by examining the consistency of clients' responses across repeated interview occasions. This procedure measures *test–retest reliability*. They also examine the degree to which different judges agree on the inferences (ratings, diagnoses, or personality trait descriptions) they draw from interviews with the same client, a procedure that measures *interrater reliability*.

One particularly useful research strategy is to have several clinicians view videotaped interviews and then make ratings or draw other inferences from the tapes. This approach has been widely used to establish the reliability of clinicians' judgments about DSM-IV diagnoses (Widiger, Frances, Pincus, Davis, & First, 1991); to evaluate the use of interpreters when conducting cross-cultural interviews (Wallin & Ahlström, 2006); and to assess, for example, clients' progress in therapy (Goins, Strauss, & Martin, 1995), the severity of Alzheimer's disease (Boothby, Mann, & Barker, 1995), the credibility of children's reports of sexual abuse (Anson, Golding, & Gully, 1993), and the quality of client–therapist alliances following intake interviews with immigrants (Shechtman & Tsegahun, 2004).

As you might expect, test–retest reliability tends to be highest when the interval between interviews is short and when adult clients are asked for innocuous information such as age and other demographic data (e.g., Ross, Stowe, Wodak, & Gold, 1995). Lower reliability coefficients tend to appear when test–retest intervals are longer, when clients are young children, and when interviewers explore sensitive topics such as illegal drug use, sexual practices, or traumatic experiences (Fallon & Schwab-Stone, 1994; Schwab-Stone, Fallon, & Briggs, 1994; Weiss, Najavits, Muenz, & Hufford, 1995).

Of course, it is sensitive information, rather than innocuous demographic information, that is often of greatest interest to clinicians. For this reason, structured interviews are often preferred for eliciting reliable information about more sensitive topics. Overall, the test–retest reliability of structured interviews tends to be 0.70 or higher, even when the most sensitive information is requested for diagnostic or other purposes (e.g., Cohen & Vinson, 1995; Grant et al., 1995; Jane, Pagan, Turkheimer, Fiedler, & Oltmanns, 2006; Segal, Hersen, & Van Hasselt, 1994). Conclusions about sensitive information tend to be less reliable in unstructured interviews (e.g., Rogers, 1995, 2001; Ruegg, Ekstrom, Dwight, & Golden, 1990; Steiner, Tebes, Sledge, & Walker, 1995). Interrater reliability is also higher for structured than for nonstructured interviews.

Reliability also depends on the population on which the instrument was standardized. In other words, an interview method having acceptable reliability with one group (e.g., English-speaking Caucasians) might not have acceptable reliability with another group (e.g., Spanish-speaking Hispanics). Researchers frequently study the degree to which specific instruments apply to diverse groups, so practicing clinicians should seek out this information when considering using interview formats or psychological tests with clients from different ethnic and cultural backgrounds. For instance, Grilo, Lorzano, and Elder (2005) have shown that a Spanish-language version of the Eating Disorder Examination Interview has comparable reliability across English-speaking and Spanish-speaking versions.

Validity. As stated in Chapter 3, validity is established in several ways, such as by including all of the relevant aspects of a target domain (content validity), by comparing interview results with other valid measures of the same concept (concurrent validity), or by an interview's ability to predict expected future outcomes (predictive validity). The latter two involve selecting an external criterion as the standard against which interview conclusions are measured. That external criterion is sometimes called the *gold standard* (Komiti et al., 2001).

When structured diagnostic interview outlines are first developed, they are often validated against the gold standard of clinical judgment (e.g., Zetin & Glenn, 1999).

Sometimes, however, it works the other way around: Clinical judgments are validated against the gold standard of established structured interviews (e.g., Komiti et al., 2001). How can we evaluate interviews if they are sometimes validated against clinical judgment and sometimes used as a standard for evaluating clinical judgment?

Data on predictive validity can help. Greater confidence in the value of any assessment tool is warranted when it can reliably predict certain outcomes. Thus, an interview designed to assess clients' responses to therapy can demonstrate predictive validity when it clearly distinguishes those who later drop out of therapy from those who do not. Validity is also enhanced when instruments correlate with several conceptually similar indices *(convergent validity)* or are uncorrelated with measures of conceptually different phenomena *(discriminant validity)*. For example, scores on a structured interview for hypochondriasis should not correlate highly with scores on measures of antisocial personality disorder.

Because there are so many kinds of interviews, no blanket statement about interview validity is warranted. As one distinguished researcher put it, "The interview has been used in so many different ways for various purposes, by individuals with varying skills, that it is a difficult matter to make a final judgment concerning its values" (Garfield, 1974, p. 90). However, in general, the interview formats that have the highest validity are those that are more structured and have been cross-validated using multiple indices, such as those in Table 4.3.

Finally, clinicians should not automatically assume that interviews shown to be valid with one population will be valid with another. Validity may be limited to the population sample on which the interview was based. Again, this is a concern especially when clinicians interview persons from different cultural and ethnic backgrounds. The cross-cultural validity of interviews is an empirical question in need of empirical research for each interview format and with various ethnic/cultural groups (e.g., Frank et al., 2005).

Error and Bias in the Interview

Clinicians should be attentive to factors that might threaten the validity of their interviews. The most obvious threats to interview validity occur if clients misremember or purposely distort information. The probability of error or distortion increases when clients are mentally retarded (e.g., Heal & Sigelman, 1995), suffer from various brain disorders (e.g., West, Bondy, & Hutchinson, 1991), or would prefer not to reveal the truth about their behavior problems, drug use, sexual behavior, criminal activity, or previous hospitalizations (e.g., Morrison, McCusker, Stoddard, & Bigelow, 1995; Williams, 1994). At the other extreme, clients motivated to appear mentally disturbed may give inaccurate interview responses aimed at creating the appearance of a mental disorder. Concern about such *malingering* led to the creation of special interview methods aimed at detecting it (Rogers, Gillis, Dickens, & Bagby, 1991; see Table 4.3). In short, the desire to present oneself in a particular light to a mental health professional—called *impression management* (Braginsky, Braginsky, & Ring, 1969)—can undermine the validity of interview data.

Especially worrisome is the possibility that personal biases might affect interviewers' perceptions and color their inferences and conclusions about what clients say during interviews. The role of such biases was noted nearly 70 years ago in a study showing that social workers' judgments of why "skid-row bums" had become destitute were related to the interviewers' personal agendas, not just to what respondents said (Rice, 1929). Thus, an antialcohol interviewer saw drinking as the cause of poverty, while a socialist interviewer concluded that interviewees' plights stemmed from capitalist-generated economic conditions. Similarly, as discussed in Chapter 2, "Clinical Psychology's Past and Present," psychoanalysts and behavior therapists tend to draw different causal conclusions about the behavior problems clients describe during interviews (Plous & Zimbardo, 1986). Indeed, interview-based psychodiagnoses, job interview decisions, and the outcome of medical school–admissions interviews may all be prejudiced by information that interviewers receive about interviewees before the interview (Dipboye, Stramler, & Fontenelle, 1984; Shaw, Martz, Lancaster, & Sade, 1995; Temerlin, 1968). This supports a point made in Chapter 3: that clinicians are like other human beings in their tendency to seek and recall information that confirms their preexisting biases.

Preconceptions about which disorders go with which client characteristics can also affect interviewers' interpretations of interview data. In one large-scale study, for example, medical and mental health professionals were more likely to diagnose depression in female than in male clients despite whether these clients' interview responses met standard criteria for defining depressive disorders (Potts, Burnam, & Wells, 1991). Other studies conducted in mental health, employment, and other settings have shown that interviewers' judgments can also be affected by clients' ethnicity, the clinician's theoretical orientation, or even the clinician's age (Pottick, Kirk, Hsieh, & Tian, 2007; Singer & Eder, 1989; Tomlinson & Cheatham, 1989). The impact of these factors can be reduced through training programs that sensitize interviewers to the potential effects of personal biases in interviews (Brown, 1990; Pottick, Kirk, Hsieh, & Tian, 2007; Sinacore-Guinn, 1995).

Section Summary: Research on the interview as an assessment tool does not justify all-encompassing conclusions, with the exception that structured interviews generally have higher reliability and validity than unstructured ones and that clinicians should not automatically assume that their interview impressions are valid. Clinicians should be aware of the limitations of interviews especially when working with persons from different backgrounds. Any tendency to view interviews as primarily an art form practiced by gifted clinicians and therefore exempt from scientifically rigorous examinations of reliability and validity will ultimately result in the loss of the interview's utility as an assessment tool.

OBSERVATIONAL ASSESSMENT: GOALS AND BENEFITS

Section Preview: Observations occur during interviews, so some of what needs to be said about observation has already been said. But there are also more formal observational assessment techniques that are different from interviews. These techniques can often provide information not otherwise available, especially information about situational determinants of behavior and ecological validity. Clinicians can observe client behaviors that occur naturally in real situations such as in hospitals, schools, homes, and other settings. They can also assess clients by developing contrived situations designed to elicit or assess particular kinds of responses.

The goals of observational assessment systems are to (a) collect information that is not available in other ways and/or (b) supplement other data as part of a multiple-assessment approach. For example, if a teacher and a pupil give different reports of why they fail to get along ("He's a brat," "She's mean"), a less-biased picture of the relationship will probably emerge from observations by neutral parties of relevant classroom interactions. In other instances, knowing what a person can or will do is so important that only observation can suffice. Thus, knowing that a mentally disturbed person feels better and wishes to leave the hospital may be less valuable than observing that person's ability to hold a job, use the bus system, and meet other demands of everyday life.

At one end of the spectrum are informal, anecdotal accounts of client behaviors occurring during tests or interviews. Clinicians who place greater emphasis on overt behavior have improved on informal observation methods in at least two ways. First, they developed more accurate and systematic methods for observing and quantifying behavior. Second, they demonstrated the feasibility of collecting observational data in situations beyond the testing or interview room. Together, these developments have made it possible for clinicians and researchers to observe scientifically a wide range of human behavior in a multitude of settings.

Advantages of Observational Assessment

Collecting observational data can be a difficult, time-consuming, and expensive procedure, and the problems associated with this type of assessment discourage many clinicians from attempting to use it (Mash & Foster, 2001). The environment of managed care, which often rewards more rapid and focused assessment techniques, also tacitly discourages clinicians from spending much time in observational assessment. Despite these obstacles, proponents of observational assessment argue that its benefits more than outweigh its difficulties, and they offer several reasons why observation is necessary if clinicians are to obtain a complete picture of their clients' functioning.

Supplementing Self-Reports.   Self-reports gathered from interviews and some tests may be inaccurate. It is very difficult for most people to provide objective and dispassionate reports on their own behavior, especially in relation to highly charged emotional events. It is questionable, for example, whether a distressed couple can accurately and objectively describe their own behavior in the relationship, especially behavior that occurs during arguments. Other clients, such as those with dementia, are sometimes unable to give accurate self-reports despite their best intentions to do so (Larner, 2005). Observational data are likely to provide much more valid information in these situations (Gottman & Levenson, 1992; Smallwood, Irvine, Coulter, & Connery, 2001).

In some cases, clients purposely distort their self-reports, usually by offering an overly positive portrayal of their behavior. Such distortions are particularly common in the self-reports of participants in smoking, drug, or alcohol treatment programs, which is the main reason such reports are often supplemented by family members' observations or by biological measures that can detect target substances. Intentional distortions on personality tests such as the MMPI-2 are so widely recognized that special indicators have been devised to detect when clients do not respond honestly (Berry, Baer, & Harris,

1991; Storm & Graham, 2000; see Chapter 5, "Testing in Clinical Psychology"). Observational assessment helps correct for self-report errors.

Highlighting Situational Determinants of Behavior.

Much of traditional assessment is guided by the assumption that responses to interviews and tests are adequate for understanding clients' personalities and problems because responses reflect general traits that control behavior. For clinicians adopting this view, observations are seen as *signs* of more fundamental, unobservable constructs. In contrast, clinicians who take a behavioral or cognitive-behavioral view tend to regard observational data as *samples* of behavior that help them understand important *person–situation interactions*. They are less likely to draw inferences about hypothesized personality characteristics or problems presumed to be stable across differing situations and over relatively long time periods. Conducting observation-driven functional analyses allows clinicians to avoid the relatively high levels of inference associated with sign-oriented testing and interviewing approaches. Observational procedures are designed to collect "just the facts," thereby minimizing the likelihood of drawing incorrect inferences about clients. Observational assessments allow the clinician to determine the circumstances under which problematic behaviors are most likely to occur, what situational stimuli tend to trigger the behaviors, and what reinforcing consequences in the situation serve to maintain the unwanted actions (Patterson, 1982). Traditional tests and interviews are not designed to accomplish this kind of functional analysis (Cairns & Green, 1979).

Enhancing Ecological Validity.

Because observations can occur in the physical and social environments where clients actually live, observational assessment can provide the clearest possible picture of people and their problems. Not only are these observations likely to be *ecologically valid,* they often provide situational details that help clinicians design treatment programs that can be most easily implemented in the home, school, or work environments. This custom-tailoring of interventions may increase the chances for treatment success. We return to the issue of ecological validity later in the chapter.

Section Summary: Observations of clients' behaviors is time consuming but has advantages. It can supplement or correct self-reports, reveal situational determinants of behavior, and establish ecological validity.

OBSERVATIONAL ASSESSMENT: APPROACHES

Section Preview: Observational assessments fall into two basic types: naturalistic and controlled. The former involves observing client behavior in the settings where they normally occur, such as homes, schools, hospitals, malls, airplanes, and the like. Controlled observations involve placing clients in purposely constructed situations that will elicit behaviors of clinical interest. Examples include simulations of airplanes, mock job interviews or other role-playing scenarios, and computer-generated virtual reality environments. In all observational assessments, clinicians must select specific behaviors to pay attention to and have a system to record observations. Ideally, the recording system will limit the biases and errors that can impair the accuracy of observations.

Observational methods have been defined as "the *selection, provocation, recording,* and *encoding* of behaviors" (Weick, 1968; italics added). This definition highlights the fundamental elements of nearly every type of observational system. The observer first *selects* people, classes of behavior, events, situations, or time periods to be the focus of attention. Second, a decision is made about whether to *provoke* (i.e., artificially bring about) behaviors and situations of interest or to wait for them to happen on their own. Third, plans are made to *record* observations using observer memory, record sheets, audio- or videotape, physiological monitoring systems, timers, counters, or other means. Finally, a system for *encoding* raw observations into usable form must be developed. Encoding is often the most difficult aspect of any observational procedure.

One way to organize the various methods of observation is in terms of the level of influence or control displayed by the observer. At one extreme is *naturalistic observation* whereby the assessor looks at behavior as it occurs in its natural context (e.g., at home or school). *Controlled* observation lies at the other extreme, as the clinician or researcher sets up a special situation in which to observe behavior. Between these extremes are approaches that blend elements of both to handle specific assessment needs, thus creating many subtypes of both naturalistic and controlled observation. In some assessment situations, observers may be *participants* who are visible to the clients being watched and who may even interact with them (as when parents record their child's behavior). *Nonparticipant* observers are not visible, although in most cases the clients are aware that observation is taking place. More comprehensive coverage of this material is available in a number of sources (e.g., Bellack & Hersen, 1998; Eid & Denier, 2005; Miller & Leffard, 2007; Haynes & O'Brien, 2000; Repp & Horner, 2000).

Naturalistic Observation

Natural settings, such as home, school, or work, provide a background that is realistic and relevant for understanding the client's behavior and the factors influencing that behavior. Additionally, naturalistic observation can be done in ways that are subtle enough to provide a picture of behavior that is not distorted by client self-consciousness or motivation to convey a particular impression to an interviewer. Naturalistic observation has been used to infer personality characteristics (Santostefano, 1962), intelligence (Lambert, Cox, & Hartsough, 1970), social goals (Brown, Odom, & Holcombe, 1996), and cognitive development (Schweinhart, McNair, Barnes, & Larner, 1993), but its primary focus has been on assessing the nature of, and changes in, problems that clinicians are asked to solve—everything from eating disorders, intrusive thoughts, maladaptive social interactions, and psychotic behavior to problems such as classroom disruptions and littering (Haynes, 1990).

Observation by Participant Observers. The classic case of naturalistic observation is the anthropological field study in which a scientist joins a tribe, subculture, or other social organization to observe its characteristics and the behavior of its members (e.g., Mead, 1928; Williams, 1967). In such cases, the observer is a participant in every sense of the term, and observations are usually recorded in anecdotal notes, which later appear as a detailed account called an *ethnography*.

In its early forms, naturalistic clinical observation required observers to make decisions and draw inferences about what certain behaviors mean and which behaviors should or should not be recorded. As a result, the interobserver reliability of naturalistic observation suffered. Lee Cronbach (1960, p. 535) summarized the problem well: "Observers interpret what they see. When they make an interpretation, they tend to overlook facts which do not fit the interpretation, and they may even invent facts needed to complete the event as interpreted." Figure 4.1 shows how observations of the same client can differ.

Attempts to improve anecdotal accounts in naturalistic clinical observation have taken many forms. To reduce unsystematic reporting of client behaviors, most modern observation schemes focus the observer's attention on specific behaviors. The frequency and intensity of these behaviors are then recorded on a checklist or rating scale. The more specific the observations to be made, the fewer judgment calls needed by the observer (for example, "physically striking another child with the hand" is more specific than "violence"). The observers are also trained to use these methods consistently so that interobserver reliability is as high as possible.

Unobtrusive Measures.   Another approach to naturalistic observation is to inspect the by-products of behavior. For example, school grades, arrest records, and court files have been used to evaluate the treatment of delinquent youth and adult offenders (Davidson, Redner, Blakely, Mitchell, & Emshoff, 1987; Rice, 1997); changes in academic grade point averages have served as indices of improvement in test anxiety (Allen, 1971). Life records, also called *institutional* or *product-of-behavior* measures (Haynes, 1990; Maisto & Maisto, 1983), are actually part of a broader observational approach, called *nonreactive* or *unobtrusive* measurement, that clinical psychologists and other behavioral scientists use to learn about people's behavior without altering it in the process (see Webb, Campbell, Schwartz, & Sechrest, 1966).

In clinical research, unobtrusive measures may be used to test theories about the causes of behavior problems. A creative use of unobtrusive measures in identifying the precursors of schizophrenia is seen in a study that took advantage of the fact that many families today make videotapes of their children as they grow (Walker, Grimes, Davis, & Smith, 1993). In this study, trained observers analyzed childhood videotapes of individuals who later became schizophrenic as well as of their same-sex siblings who did not. The results revealed that, long before they were diagnosed, the schizophrenics-to-be showed significantly more negative facial expressions than the other children (some of the differences appeared before the children were 4 years old).

In the following sections, we consider a set of naturalistic observation systems that, while not entirely unobtrusive, do allow for recording the frequency, intensity, duration, or form of specific categories of behaviors by persons who are both familiar to clients and in a position to observe them in a minimally intrusive way. In all observation, a key goal is to reduce observer bias (Haro et al., 2006).

Hospital and Clinic Observations.   Observations of hospitalized patients is an important component of their assessment. The Inpatient Multidimensional Psychiatric

Observer A: (2) Robert reads word by word, using finger to follow place. (4) Observes girl in box with much preoccupation. (5) During singing, he in general doesn't participate too actively. Interest is part of time centered elsewhere. Appears to respond most actively to sections of song involving action. Has tendency for seemingly meaningless movement. Twitching of fingers, aimless thrusts of arms.

Observer B: (2) Looked at camera upon entering (seemed perplexed and interested). Smiled at camera. (2) Reads (with apparent interest and with a fair degree of facility). (3) Active in roughhouse play with girls. (4) Upon being kicked (unintentionally) by one girl he responded (angrily). (5) Talked with girl sitting next to him between singing periods. Participated in singing (at times appeared enthusiastic). Didn't always sing with others. (6) Participated in a dispute in a game with others (appeared to stand up for his own rights). Aggressive behavior toward another boy. Turned pockets inside out while talking to teacher and other students. (7) Put on overshoes without assistance. Climbed to top of ladder rungs. Tried to get rung which was occupied by a girl but since she didn't give in, contented himself with another place.

Observer C: (1) Smiles into camera (curious). When groups break up, he makes nervous gestures, throws arm out into air. (2) Attention to reading lesson. Reads with serious look on his face, has to use line marker. (3) Chases girls, teases. (4) Girl kicks when he puts hand on her leg. Robert makes face at her. (5) Singing. Sits with mouth open, knocks knees together, scratches leg, puts fingers in mouth (seems to have several nervous habits, though not emotionally overwrought or self-conscious). (6) In a dispute over parchesi, he stands up for his rights. (7) Short dispute because he wants rung on jungle gym.

Observer D: (2) Uses guide to follow words, reads slowly, fairly forced and with careful formation of sounds (perhaps unsure of self and fearful of mistakes). (3) Perhaps slightly aggressive as evidenced by pushing younger child to side when moving from a position to another. Plays with other children with obvious enjoyment, smiles, runs, seems especially associated with girls. This is noticeable in games and in seating in singing. (5) Takes little interest in singing, fidgets, moves hands and legs (perhaps shy and nervous). Seems in song to be unfamiliar with words of main part, and shows disinterest by fidgeting and twisting around. Not until chorus is reached does he pick up interest. His special friend seems to be a particular girl, as he is always seated by her.

FIGURE 4.1 Four Observations of the Same Client. Notice the differing images and inferences generated by four observers who watched a 10-minute film, *This Is Robert,* which showed a boy in classroom and playground situations. (The observers were told to use parentheses to indicate inferences or interpretation. The numbers used refer to scenes in the film and were inserted to aid comparison.)

(*Source:* Excerpts from pages 534–535 from *Essentials of Psychological Testing,* 5th ed., by Lee J. Cronbach. Copyright 1949. Copyright 1984 by Harper & Row, Publishers, Inc. Copyright 1960, 1970, 1990 by Lee J. Cronbach.)

Scales, or IMPS (Lorr, McNair, & Klett, 1966), is an excellent example of a hospital observation system that can be used by ward staff. The IMPS contains 75 items, which are either rated by the observer on 5- or 9-point scales or responded to with a yes or no. These data are translated into scores on dimensions such as excitement, hostile belligerence, paranoid projection, grandiose expansiveness, disorientation, and conceptual disorganization. The scores can then be plotted as a profile describing the observed client.

A more recent example of such systems include the Routine Assessment of Patient Progress, or RAPP (Ehmann et al., 1995).

Hospitals and clinics are also excellent places to observe the developing skills of trainees who are learning to conduct interviews and other assessments. Psychologists-in-training, medical interns, and others who will eventually need to conduct these procedures can be observed by supervising faculty; this observation is a critical part of training. Just as with other observations, however, supervising faculty must have clear measures of the specific behaviors that they observe in order to provide useful and unbiased feedback to trainees (Holmboe, 2004).

School Observations.   The desire to observe children's behavior for clinical and educational purposes has spawned a number of systems for use in schools, playgrounds, and similar settings (Nock & Kurtz, 2005; Ollendick & Greene, 1990). Recording and coding systems designed by Sidney Bijou (Bijou, Peterson, & Ault, 1968) and Daniel O'Leary (O'Leary & Becker, 1967) use symbols to represent the behavior of children and the adults around them during time-sample observations. Like other observation systems of this type, the data gathered can be summarized in quantitative form. In this case, percentages can be calculated to summarize how much time a child spends on-task, out-of-seat, or talking to other children. Classroom observation may focus on a single child and those with whom the child interacts, or an observer can sequentially attend to and assess the behavior of several target children or even of a whole class (Milich & Fitzgerald, 1985). We have more to say about the observational assessment of children and the instruments designed for this purpose in Chapter 11, "Clinical Child Psychology."

Home Observations.   Observational assessment procedures are also available to measure clinically relevant behaviors in clients' homes. As was the case in other areas, early home-based clinical observations allowed much inference and rather unsystematic selection of target behaviors (e.g., Ackerman, 1958). More reliable home observation systems have now evolved. One of the first of these was designed by Gerald Patterson (Patterson, Ray, Shaw, & Cobb, 1969) for use in the homes of conduct-disordered children. After obtaining consent to do so, Patterson places trained observers in the client's living area for an hour or two on each of several days, usually just before dinner. The observers avoid interacting with the family and concentrate on using Patterson's Family Interaction Coding System to record the behavior of one member at a time as well as the family member with whom the person interacted. It is thus possible to record the target child's inappropriate behavior as well as the antecedents and consequences of this behavior (Patterson, 1982). More recently, Zaslow and colleagues (2006) collected observations of preschool children's behaviors and mothers' reports of their children's behaviors. They found that the observational measures did a better job than the mother's reports at predicting children's behaviors 4 years later.

Observations by Insiders.   The naturalistic observation systems we have described so far employ specially trained personnel as participant or nonparticipant observers. Because some researchers question whether these outsiders can do their job without inadvertently influencing the behavior they are to watch, observations are sometimes conducted by persons who are part of the client's day-to-day world. An example is the Child Behavior Checklist (Achenbach & Rescorla, 2001). The CBCL is one of several instruments popular among those interested in assessing behavior problems in children and adolescents. As its name implies, the instrument is a checklist completed by parents. Another example is the IMPS, discussed earlier, which relies on data collected by hospital nurses or other ward staff.

The use of insiders as observers of adult behavior for clinical purposes is less common but not unknown. For example, in helping clients quit smoking, a clinician may ask for corroborative reports of success or failure from family members or friends (e.g., Mermelstein, Lichtenstein, & McIntyre, 1983). Such reports may also be solicited as part of the assessment of alcoholism or drug use (e.g., Frank et al., 2005), sexual activity (e.g., Rosen & Kopel, 1977), marital interactions (Johnson, 2002; Jouriles & O'Leary, 1985), and other adult behaviors.

Self-Observation.   *Self-monitoring* requires clients to record the frequency, location, duration, or intensity of events such as exercise, headaches, pleasant thoughts, hair pulling, smoking, eating habits, stress, sleep disorders, anxiety disorders, health-promoting behaviors, or the like. Often, a client and therapist agree on target behaviors, and the client maintains a record or diary of when those behaviors occur, recording the instances, the conditions under which they occurred, and, often, thoughts associated with the instances. Unfortunately, self-monitoring for concerns such as drug use can involve underreporting or occasionally overreporting (Clark & Winters, 2002).

Controlled Observation

Because naturalistic observation usually takes place in an uncontrolled environment, unanticipated events can interfere with the assessment. For example, the client may move out of the observer's line of vision or might get help from someone else in dealing with a stressor. How would the client have reacted without help? Another limitation of naturalistic observation involves the long waits that sometimes must occur before low-probability events occur (e.g., a family argument).

One way of getting around some of the difficulties associated with naturalistic observation is to set up special circumstances under which clients can be observed as they react to planned, standardized events. This approach is usually called *controlled observation* because it allows clinicians to maintain control over the assessment stimuli in much the same way as they do when giving the psychological tests described in Chapter 5. Controlled observations are also known as *analog behavior observation* (ABO), *situation tests,* and *contrived observations.*

During World War II, military psychologists devised controlled observations for assessing personality traits as well as behavioral capabilities. In the Operational Stress Test, for example, would-be pilots were asked to manipulate the controls of an aircraft flight simulator. The candidates did not know that the tester was purposely trying to frustrate them by giving increasingly complicated instructions accompanied by negative feedback (e.g., "You're making too many errors"; Melton, 1947). During the test, the assessor rated the candidate's reaction to criticism and stress, and these ratings supplemented objective data on skill with the simulator.

The Office of Strategic Services Assessment Staff (OSS, later to become the CIA; 1948) used observational assessment to infer traits of initiative, dominance, cooperation, and group leadership among potential espionage agents and other special personnel. Candidates were assigned to build a 5-foot cube-shaped frame out of large wooden poles and blocks resembling a giant Tinker Toy set, and they were given two "assistants" (actually, psychologists) who called themselves Kippy and Buster. Kippy acted in a passive, sluggish manner. He did nothing at all unless specifically ordered to, but stood around, often getting in the way. Buster, on the other hand, was aggressive, forward in offering impractical suggestions, ready to express dissatisfaction, and quick to criticize what he suspected were the candidate's weakest points. It was their function to present the candidate with as many obstructions and annoyances as possible in 10 minutes. As it turned out, they succeeded in frustrating the candidates so thoroughly that the construction was never completed in the allotted time (OSS, 1948). Since World War II, milder versions of the OSS situational tests have been used for personnel selection.

Performance Measures. In current clinical and research settings, controlled observations take many forms. In some cases, the "control" consists of asking clients—usually couples, families, or parent–child pairs—to come to a clinic or laboratory and have a discussion or attempt to solve a problem. In controlled observations of performance, clinicians observe clients as they face a clinically relevant situation. For example, during marital therapy, a couple might be asked to discuss an area of conflict between them as the therapist records observations or videotapes the discussion for later analysis (Heyman, 2001). The eating style (amount, speed, preferences) of individuals in a weight loss program might be recorded during a meal or snack in a controlled setting (Spiegel, Wadden, & Foster, 1991). Alcoholic and nonalcoholic drinkers might be observed in specially constructed cocktail lounges or living rooms located in hospitals (Collins, Parks, & Marlatt, 1985).

Consider, for example the Specific Affect Coding System (SPAFF; Gottman & Krokoff, 1989), an observational coding system used to assess specific kinds of positive affect (affection, humor, interest, anticipation, excitement) and negative affective (anger/contempt, disgust, whining, sadness, fear/anxiety) in couples. Johnson (2002) compared data obtained from the SPAFF with another coding system and found that anger/contempt and humor/affection were the emotions most strongly correlated with marital satisfaction (sadness, fear, and anxiety were only weakly linked to marital adjustment). Clinicians can use results such as these to help couples who want to improve their marriage focus on improving specific kinds of interactions.

Role-Playing Tests. Psychologists sometimes create make-believe situations in which the client is asked to *role-play* his or her typical behavior. Role-playing has been advocated by clinicians for many years (e.g., Borgatta, 1995) and serves as the cornerstone for several group, psychodynamic, and humanistic treatments (e.g., Moreno, 1946; Perls, 1969). However, it was not until the late 1960s that role-playing became part of systematic clinical assessment. Since then, role-playing tests have become a standard ingredient in the observational assessment of children's social and safety skills (Harbeck, Peterson, & Starr, 1992), parent–child interactions (Carniero, Corboz-Warney, & Fivaz-Depeursinge, 2006; Jouriles & Farris, 1992), depressive behavior (Bellack, Hersen, & Himmelhoch, 1983), and the social competence and conversational skills of socially anxious or chronically mentally ill persons (Dilk & Bond, 1996; Norton & Hope, 2001). In most role-plays, the clients' or trainees' responses are videotaped and then rated by observers on any of dozens of criteria such as appropriateness of content, level of positive and refusal assertiveness, anxiety, latency to respond, response duration, speech dysfluencies, posture, eye contact, gaze, hand gestures, head movements, and voice volume.

For example, the Extended Interaction Test assesses the generality and robustness of clients' assertiveness skills by presenting a tape-recorded antagonist who makes a series of gradually escalating unreasonable requests and demands (McFall & Lillesand, 1971). Here is an excerpt from the test:

> Narrator: You are feeling really pressed for study time because you have an exam on Friday afternoon. Now, you are studying at your desk, when a close friend comes in and says, "Hi. Guess what. My parents just called and offered to pay for a plane ticket so I can fly home this weekend. Great, huh!? The only problem is, I'll have to skip my Friday morning class, and I hate to miss out on those notes; I'm barely making it in there as it is. Look, I know you aren't in that class, but it'd really be a big help if you'd go to the class Friday and take notes for me so I could go home. Would you do that for me?"
>
> If the participant refuses, the tape continues:
>
> "I guess it is kinda crazy to expect you to do it, but, gee, I've got so many things to do if I'm gonna get ready to leave, and I don't want to waste the time asking around. Come on, will you do it for me this once?"
>
> If the participant refuses, the tape continues:
>
> "Look, what're friends for if they don't help each other out of a bind? I'd do it for you if you asked. What do you say, will you?"
>
> If the participant refuses, the tape continues:
>
> "But I was counting on you to do it. I'd hate to have to call my folks back and tell them I'm not coming. Can't you spare just one hour to help me out?"
>
> If the participant refuses, the tape continues (sarcastically):
>
> "Now look, I don't want to impose on your precious time. Just tell me. Will you do it or do I have to call my folks back?"

Presumably, a person who withstands repeated requests is more assertive than one who gives in after an initial refusal.

Sometimes, clinicians or researchers use a *staged naturalistic event*. The idea is to look at behavior in a controlled setting that appears naturalistic to the client (Gottman, Markman, & Notarius, 1977). For example, unobtrusive role-playing tests have been used to measure social skills in psychiatric inpatients (Goldsmith & McFall, 1975). In these tests, the client is asked to meet and carry on a conversation with a stranger (actually an assistant to the clinician) who has been instructed to confront the client with three "critical moments": not catching the client's name, responding to a lunch invitation with an excuse that left open the possibility of lunch at another time, and saying "Tell me about yourself" at the first convenient pause in the conversation. Similar contrived situations—such as presenting prospective parents with a doll and instructing them to role play a situation or having parents respond to a videotaped incident of child misbehavior—have been used to assess parenting in clients (Carneiro, Carboz-Warney, & Fivaz-Depeursinge, 2006; Hawes & Dadds, 2006) and social behaviors among college students (Kern, 1982).

Of course, observations involving deception and possible invasion of privacy must be set up with care and with regard for clients' welfare and dignity. Proponents of unobtrusive controlled observation try to avoid its potential dangers and point out that its value may be limited to measuring specific behaviors (such as refusal) rather than more complex interactive social skills.

Physiological Measures.
Other performance tests measure physiological activity, such as heart rate, respiration, blood pressure, galvanic skin response, muscle tension, and brain functioning, that appears in relation to various stimuli. An early example was provided by a study of forehead muscle tension in a headache patient as she watched a film about headaches (Malmo, Shagass, & Davis, 1950). A classic example was Gordon Paul's (1966) use of measures of heart rate and sweating taken just before giving a talk to help identify speech-anxious clients. These measures were repeated following various anxiety-reduction treatments to aid in the evaluation of their effects (see also Nietzel, Bernstein, & Russell, 1988).

In recent years, clinical psychologists have increased their use of such physiological measures because they have become much more involved in studying insomnia, headache, chronic pain, sexual dysfunctions, gastrointestinal disorders, HIV/AIDS, diabetes, and many other disorders that have clear psychological components (see Chapter 12, "Health Psychology"). For instance, consider physiological measures in the assessment of sexual arousal and sexual dysfunctions. In one such performance-assessment system, male subjects listen to or watch tapes that present various types of erotic behavior involving appropriate and inappropriate sexual stimuli. While the tape is playing, a strain gauge attached to the participant's penis records changes in its circumference (called *phallometric measurement*). Greater erectile responses to the recorded material are assumed to signal higher levels of sexual arousal. Some studies have shown that, among child pornography offenders, those with higher levels of erectile response are also more likely to engage in pedophilia (Seto, Cantor, & Blanchard, 2006). Unfortunately, patterns of arousal to specific kinds of stimuli have not been identified for each of the various kinds of sex offenses (Blanchard & Barbaree, 2005; Looman & Marshall, 2005), but there is hope that this or other technology will eventually be able to do so.

With increased interest in the role of psychological factors in health and illness (see Chapter 12), the use of physiological recording devices in clinical assessment will likely continue to increase as well, especially now that many companies are able to market relatively inexpensive, portable devices—including virtual reality systems—that present stimuli and record responses.

Virtual Reality Assessment.
In *virtual reality assessment,* a client is exposed to a realistic simulation run by a computer. Sometimes, the client views a screen, but often the simulation is accomplished as clients wear a headset that provides visual, auditory, and sometimes tactile stimuli. This technology allows for the precise presentation and control of stimuli that appears three-dimensional; the experience is usually highly realistic for clients. During presentation, clinicians can obtain self-report measures, conduct behavioral observations, and

collect physiological measures or other assessment indices. The collection of such measures has helped establish the value of virtual reality both as an assessment tool and in the administration of treatments (Côtè & Bouchard, 2005; Gorman, 2006).

Concerns that assessments based on simulations or virtual reality may not carry over to real situations appear to be largely unfounded. Flight simulation training has long been an established and effective method of assessment and training among civilian and military pilots. Except perhaps for clients with autism, virtual reality assessments and treatment applications appear to transfer to real-world settings quite well (Standen & Brown, 2005). For example, Lew and his colleagues (2005) used a driving simulator to assess the long-term driving performance of clients who had suffered from traumatic brain injury. In this case, the virtual reality assessment was better at predicting future performance than was a (reality-based) road test.

Behavioral Avoidance Tests. Another popular performance measure in controlled observation is the behavioral avoidance test, or BAT, which is designed to assess overt anxiety in relation to specific objects and situations. In BATs, clients are confronted with a stimulus they fear while observers record the type and degree of avoidance displayed. Informal BATs were conducted with children as early as the 1920s (e.g., Jones, 1924a,b), but it was not until the early 1960s that systematic avoidance-testing procedures became a common form of controlled observational assessment.

In a study of systematic desensitization (see Chapter 8, "Behavioral and Cognitive-Behavioral Therapies") for snake phobia, Peter Lang and David Lazovik (1963) asked clients to enter a room containing a harmless caged snake and to approach, touch, and pick up the animal. Observers gave the clients avoidance scores based on whether they were able to look at, touch, or hold the snake. Many other fear stimuli, including rats, spiders, cockroaches, and dogs have been used in other versions of the BAT, and the "look–touch–hold" coding system for scoring responses has been replaced by more sophisticated measures. In BATs, too, virtual reality technology has made it possible to produce simulated environments to which clients react.

Section Summary: Observational assessment can be classified as naturalistic or controlled, though some observational techniques combine elements of both. Naturalistic observations of clients in schools, homes, clinics, and other settings provide ecological validity and can reveal valuable information about clients' responses to specific triggers. In some naturalistic observations, the clinician or researcher is unobtrusive and observes invisibly. In other situations, the clinician is a participant-observer. Controlled observations allow clinicians to target situations that elicit behaviors of greatest clinical interest. Certain techniques such as physiological measurements and virtual reality exposure continue to show promise as focused methods of observational assessment.

RESEARCH ON OBSERVATIONAL ASSESSMENT

Section Preview: Although they have face (ecological) validity, observational assessments do have limitations. Observers are more likely to disagree when they are not looking for the same sets of behaviors and coding them in the same way. It is therefore important for behavioral targets to be specified and coded/recorded clearly. As with interviews, reliability is also improved when there are clear inference rules on what recorded observations mean. Of particular concern in observational assessment are clinician biases, often unrecognized because observations seem to be so objective. Clinicians should cross-validate conclusions based on observations with those drawn from other assessment data. In clinical practice, formal observational assessments are frequently not done because of the time and effort required to conduct them; focused interviews and psychological tests are often preferred in today's health care environment.

Behaviorally oriented clinicians, the most enthusiastic proponents of observational assessment, have argued that observations provide the most accurate and relevant source of assessment data. Observations have even been likened to photographs in that they are thought to provide a clear and dispassionate view of human behavior. But as any photographer knows, a photograph is not just a rendering of a scene, but a combined product of scene elements, the photographer's choices about equipment and framing, and judgments made during the developing or editing process. Similarly, a number of factors can influence the reliability and validity of observational assessment.

Defining Observational Targets

A fundamental requirement for establishing both the reliability and validity of observational assessment is clarifying the target to be measured. Thus, decisions about what aspects of behavior to look for and code, and how these targets are defined, reflect the assessor's view of the presence and meaning of an observation. Consider assertiveness for instance. One clinician might assess assertiveness by observing clients' ability to refuse unreasonable requests, while another might focus on the direct expression of positive affect. This problem of definition may never be resolved to everyone's satisfaction, but evaluating the reliability and validity of an observational system begins with questions about what behavioral features are to be coded.

Reliability of Observational Assessment.
To what extent are observational assessments reliable? Test–retest reliability can be difficult to measure if clients' behaviors change substantially over time. For example, if couples show hostility and considerable anger when discussing a topic at one time but show much less of these emotions a week later, measures of hostility repeated on these two weeks may be considerably different (Heyman, 2001). Therefore, interrater reliability may be more important.

Two factors are especially important in interrater reliability: task complexity and rater training. Reducing *task complexity* often increases interrater reliability (e.g., reliability can be increased if the observer uses a 15-category rather than a 100-category coding system). *Observer training* can also affect reliability. If observers intend to record laughter, for instance, but are not given a definition of laughter, one observer might count belly laughs but not giggles, while another might include everything from smiles to violent guffaws. Finally, when people are first trained to use an observation system, they usually work hard during practice sessions and pay close attention to the task, partly because they are being evaluated. Later, when "real" data are being collected, the observers may become careless if they think no one is checking their reliability

(Taplin & Reid, 1973). Accordingly, supervision of persons doing observation and coding is sometimes necessary.

As with interviews, modern, empirically derived clinical observation assessment systems that use trained observers have higher reliability, sometimes with coefficients in excess of 0.80 and 0.90 (Ward & Naster, 1991; Zuardi, Loureiro, & Rodrigues, 1995). Less structured observations tend to have lower reliability.

Validity of Observational Assessment. At first glance, observation of behavior would appear to rank highest in validity among all clinical assessment approaches. Instead of hearing about behavior in interviews or speculating about behavior through tests, the clinician using observation can watch the "real thing."

To a certain extent, however, the directness or face validity of clinical observation has led to a deemphasis on measuring its validity in traditional terms (Cone, 1988). After all, if we observe aggression in a married couple, are we not assessing aggression, and is that not enough to establish the validity of our technique? The answer is yes only if we can show that (a) the behaviors coded (e.g., raised voices) constitute a satisfactory definition of aggression, (b) the data faithfully reflect the nature and degree of aggression occurring during observation, and (c) the clients' behaviors while under observation accurately represent their typical behavior in related, but unobserved, situations.

One way to assess the validity of observation is to ask about the extent to which the resulting conclusions correlate with conclusions drawn from other assessment methods. For example, does the ability to refuse unreasonable requests occur more often in people judged to be assertive by their peers? If so, then the peer judgment correlates with the observation, and we can say that the observation has shown convergent validity. The more an observation correlates with other data, such as interviews, physiological measures, self-reports, and others' appraisals, the greater the convergent validity of the observation.

If the observational assessment accurately predicts a future behavior, such as whether a client with a brain injury will be able to drive safely (e.g., Lew et al., 2005), we can say that the observational assessment has predictive validity. Not surprisingly, observations that involve clearly defined targets and sample repeated instances of behavior under realistic conditions tend to have higher predictive validity.

Representativeness of Observed Behavior. Clinicians using observational assessment must be concerned about the possibility that clients under observation will intentionally or unintentionally alter the behaviors that are of greatest clinical interest. The observation situation itself can exert an influence on client behavior through social cues, or *demand characteristics* (Orne, 1962), that suggest what actions are, or are not, appropriate and expected. Thus, if a clinician observes a couple in a setting that contains strong social cues about how the clients should behave (e.g., "We would like to measure just how much fighting you two actually do"), the observation may reveal a degree of conflict that is unusually high for that couple. For example, in a study designed to measure assertiveness, college students were asked to respond to tape-recorded social situations similar to those described earlier (Nietzel & Bernstein, 1976). The assertiveness of their responses was scored on a 5-point scale. All subjects heard the tape twice, under

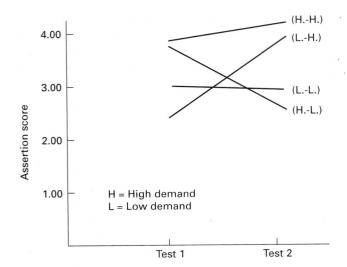

FIGURE 4.2 Situational Effects on Observed Assertiveness

(*Source:* M. T. Nietzel & D. A. Bernstein, 1976.)

either the same or differing demand situations. The "low-demand" situation asked participants for their "natural reactions," but in the "high-demand" situation, they were told to be "as assertive as you think the most assertive and forceful person could be." The results are summarized in Figure 4.2. Obviously, these instructions not only had an initial effect, but were capable of significantly altering participants' behavior from test to test. Other research on observational anxiety assessment has shown that the instructions given, the presence or absence of an experimenter, the characteristics of the physical setting, and other situational variables influence the amount of fear clients display during BATs (e.g., Bernstein, 1973; Bernstein & Nietzel, 1977).

Various strategies have been suggested to minimize situational bias in observational assessment (Bernstein & Nietzel, 1977; Borkovec & O'Brien, 1976), but the problem cannot be entirely eliminated. As long as the stimuli present when the client's behavior is being observed differ from those present when the client is not being observed, we cannot be sure that the behavior displayed during formal observation will generalize to other situations. The best clinicians can do is minimize any cues that might influence client behavior. Utterly naturalistic or unobtrusive observation is theoretically possible, but often not practical. Accordingly, clinicians will continue to rely on contrived, analog observations to assess some behavioral targets.

Observer Effects. Clinicians and researchers must attend to several issues relating to observer accuracy because the quality of observational data can be compromised by observer bias (Harris & Lahey, 1982). We have already discussed the variability of observer inferences when targets are not well defined or when observers with different coding schemes or theoretical orientations make inferences about the meaning of observations. In one study of this phenomenon, psychiatrists, psychologists, and graduate students listened to a taped interview in which an actor portrayed a well-adjusted man (Temerlin, 1968). When they listened under neutral conditions, 57% of the observers rated the man as healthy, while 43% called him neurotic. No one thought he was psychotic. However, ratings were biased if the tape was described as either that of a "perfectly healthy man" or a person who "looks neurotic but actually is psychotic." In the healthy-bias condition, 100% of the listeners rated the man as healthy, but in the psychotic-bias condition, an average of nearly 30% diagnosed the man as psychotic, and over 60% called him neurotic.

Trends in the Use of Observations Methods

As behavioral and cognitive approaches to assessment have merged over the past two decades, observational assessments have increasingly included client cognitions as targets. Of course, cognitions are inherently unobservable, but cognitive behavioral clinicians have "observed" cognitions by asking clients to *think aloud* at particular points during an observation. Sometimes, this *thought sampling* is prompted by a beeper or other device (Groth-Marnat, 2003). Clients might also be asked to report their thoughts at particular points in a videotape as a clinician replays it for them (Sanders & Dadds, 1992).

Naturalistic and informal observation remains a fundamental source of data for most clinicians, but the same cannot be said for many controlled observations. In 1984, only 20% of the Association for the Advancement of Behavior Therapy recommended the clinical use of controlled observational methods (Piotrowski & Keller, 1984), and more recent surveys continue to show that controlled or analog behavioral observations receive little attention in clinical practice and in graduate training programs (Mash & Foster, 2001). Researchers remain interested in developing and extending the use of systematic observational methods, but clinicians have not made these methods a staple of their practice.

Several reasons are offered for the decline in controlled clinical observation. The most prominent reasons relate to pragmatic concerns such as time and money. It takes considerable time and resources to undertake some of the observations we have described. There are situations to construct, coding systems to learn, observers to hire and train, and data to compile and encode. While these activities are standard activities for research clinicians in university-based clinics and training hospitals, they exceed the resources of most practicing clinicians. Some practitioners are also concerned that the content and presentation of controlled observational methods are not standardized in ways that, for example, many psychological tests are (Norton & Hope, 2001). Combine these concerns over the limited accessibility to, and lack of detailed information for, all but a few of the most popular observational techniques and it becomes clear why clinicians have not adopted them the way they have adopted more available and cost-effective psychological tests or structured interviews. Mash and Foster (2001, p. 13) conclude that "ABO [analog behavioral observation] has what may generously be described as a promising but disappointing track record as a method of clinical assessment."

Perhaps the biggest challenge still facing clinicians is to translate often cumbersome, expensive, and time-consuming procedures into a practical approach for collecting observational data that has clear utility in practice. Although some have made progress, there is no universally accepted procedure for behavioral observation (Miller & Leffard, 2007). Perhaps most importantly, the clinician or researcher must observe in a way that minimizes the influence of the various distorting factors we have discussed so that the data generated can have maximum value in an overall assessment plan.

Section Summary: While observational methods have ecological validity (they are real behaviors that occur in real situations), their concurrent and predictive validity often go unexamined. When they are examined, measures that are more explicitly defined and scored tend to have higher validity. Observations tend to be less reliable when the behavioral targets are not clearly specified and when different observers use different decision rules and therefore draw different conclusions from the same set of observations. Clinicians should be especially aware of their own potential biases in making observations, particularly inferring too much from single, limited observations. Clinicians can cross-validate conclusions based on observations with other conclusions from other assessment data. Although still a useful assessment tool, formal observational assessments are not used frequently in clinical practice because of the time and effort required to conduct them.

CHAPTER SUMMARY

Interviews are defined as conversations with a purpose, and in clinical situations, these purposes include client intake, problem referral, orientation, termination, crisis intervention, and observation. In nondirective interviews, the clinician interferes as little as possible with the client's speech, while structured interviews present planned inquiries in a fixed sequence. Semistructured interviews fall between these extremes.

Most interviews have a beginning, a middle, and an end. Intake and problem-identification interviews, for example, usually begin with efforts at making the client comfortable, enter an information-gathering middle stage, and end with a summary and discussion. Conducting each phase of an interview and moving smoothly from one to the next requires a combination of common sense, active listening skills, well-phrased questions, and tact. If interviews are to have maximum value, communication between client and interviewer must be as clear as possible in both verbal and nonverbal channels.

While the reliability of interviews, especially structured interviews, is generally good, it can depend on several variables, including how questions are phrased, the client's comfort with the interviewer, emotional state, memory skills, and motivation. Reliability and validity can both be threatened by interviewer errors or biases, especially those relating to preconceived views of clients with particular characteristics. Eliminating such errors and biases is a major challenge for clinicians.

Observational assessment systems are designed to collect information about clients that is not available in other ways or that corrects for biases inherent in other assessment methods (e.g., biases in self-reports from interviews). Observation can be conducted in naturalistic or controlled settings (or some blend of the two) by participant or nonparticipant observers. Sometimes, clients are asked to observe and record their own behavior, a procedure called self-monitoring.

Naturalistic observation systems have been developed for use in hospitals, schools, and homes. These systems have the advantage of realism and relevance, but they are expensive and time consuming and may be affected by uncontrollable situational factors. To minimize these problems, clinicians often use controlled observations—special circumstances under which clients can be observed as they react to standardized events—including role-played social interactions and performance tests of smoking, eating, drinking, or dealing with a feared object or situation.

During controlled observation, clinicians may monitor clients' physiological as well as overt responses.

While observation gets around some of the inference problems that reduce the reliability and validity of many interview and test procedures, it is not a perfect assessment tool. For one thing, data from observational assessments can be influenced by factors other than the behavior of clients. The reliability and validity of observational data depend on the precise definition of observation targets, training and monitoring of observers, efforts to guard against the effects of observer bias, reactivity in the observation process, and situational influences such as demand characteristics that might create unrepresentative samples of client behaviors.

STUDY QUESTIONS

1. What are the various types of interviews?
2. Which factors should clinicians consider when interviewing persons from diverse cultural or ethnic backgrounds?
3. How does the rate of health care utilization by minorities differ from that of the majority?
4. What are examples of nondirective interviewing techniques?
5. What are structured and semistructured interview formats, and what are examples of each?
6. What are advantages and disadvantages of structured interviews?
7. How can clinicians help clients to relax during initial stages of an interview?
8. What is frame setting, and what is its purpose?
9. What factors influence the reliability and validity of interviews?
10. What are the advantages and disadvantages of observational assessment?
11. What are the two main kinds of observational assessment?
12. What are virtual reality assessment and behavioral avoidance tests?
13. What factors influence the reliability and validity of observational assessment?
14. What trends have affected the clinical use of observational assessment?

WEB SITES

- World Health Organization Web site about the Composite International Diagnostic Interview (CIDI): http://www.hcp.med.harvard.edu/wmhcidi/about.php
- Centers for Disease Control Web site information on the Composite International Diagnostic Interview (CIDI): http://www.cdc.gov/nchs/data/nhanes/cidi_quex.pdf
- Diagnostic Interview Schedule for DSM-IV information: http://epi.wustl.edu/dis/dishisto.htm
- Structured Clinical Interview for DSM-IV information: http://epi.wustl.edu/dis/dishome.htm

CHAPTER 5
Testing in Clinical Psychology

Chapter Preview: In this chapter, we consider the nature of psychological tests, how tests are constructed, and how they are used by clinical psychologists. Most psychological tests can be categorized as measuring (a) intellectual abilities; (b) attitudes, interests, and values; or (c) aspects of personality, including psychopathology. Tests can also be categorized according to the kinds of responses requested—some ask for brief, easily scored responses (e.g., true or false) and some require longer, more difficult-to-score responses (e.g., stories, drawings). We describe several tests commonly used by clinicians and provide information about their psychometric properties and clinical utility. We end by examining recent developments in psychological testing.

The role of testing as an activity in clinical psychology has undergone large shifts in popularity over the years. Beginning in the 1930s and continuing through the mid-1960s, tests were touted as semi-magical pathways to the "truth" about intelligence, personality, and ability (Reisman, 1976). During those years, clinical psychology students were trained intensively in the use of tests. From the late 1960s through the 1970s, however, testing lost much of its appeal and was deemphasized as a training goal and professional activity for clinicians. The decline of testing during this time was brought about by (a) unflattering results of research on the reliability and validity of many tests; (b) awareness of the susceptibility of tests to various biases; (c) recognition that tests, particularly those assessing intelligence, may place members of certain minority groups at a disadvantage; (d) fear that the testing process may invade respondents' privacy; and (e) worry that tests are too easily misused or misinterpreted.

Within the last several years, testing has reversed its decline: it is now a regular part of most clinician's training and professional activities. This resurgence has occurred partly because new and better tests have been designed to address some of the concerns just mentioned. It has resulted, too, because today's educational and health care systems seem to require psychological tests. So as testing continues to evolve, it remains an important part of clinical psychology training, research, and practice.

BASIC CONCEPTS IN PSYCHOLOGICAL TESTING

Section Preview: Here we discuss the basic nature of tests and how they resemble and differ from other forms of assessment. We discuss methods of test construction and the basic requirements for a good test: adequate standardization, reliability, and validity. We also consider the need for test developers and users to avoid test bias. The section ends with some information about patterns of test usage among clinicians.

What Is a Test?

A test is a systematic procedure for observing and describing a person's behavior in a standard situation (Cronbach, 1970). Tests present a set of planned stimuli (inkblots or true–false questions, for example) and ask the client to respond in some way. The clinician then scores or interprets the client's responses using objective, empirically derived scoring rules. Usually, the clinician incorporates the test results into an overall assessment that may also include interviews and other sources of information (see Chapter 3, "Basic Features of Clinical Assessment").

Our description of tests highlights two of their most important features. First, tests are designed to be *objective* measures, just as a ruler is designed to be an objective measure of length. Although no test is perfectly objective, objectivity is the goal because tests are designed to measure the differences among clients, not clinicians. Second, our description highlights the importance of *standardization*. All persons taking the same test should be exposed to the same set of stimuli and evaluated with the same scoring criteria. For example, suppose that one 5-year-old taking an IQ test is asked, "What part of your body goes in your shoe?" and another is asked "How many quarters make two dollars?" If one child responded correctly and the other incorrectly, it would be very difficult to determine whether differences in their scores resulted from differences in their knowledge level or from difference in the test administration.

Domino and Domino (2006) have suggested the principles of objectivity and standardization allow us to view psychological tests with the same logic as that used to view experiments. In both, the idea is to eliminate extraneous variables so that results can be attributed to one source. If we are successful in an experiment, changes in the dependent variable can be attributed to changes in the independent variable, not extraneous variables. If we are successful in developing and using a test, its scores should reliably reflect characteristics of the client, not characteristics of test administration, scoring procedures, or clinicians.

So tests are like experiments, but they are also like the highly structured interviews discussed in Chapter 4, "Interviewing and Observation in Clinical Psychology," in that they ask clients to respond to specific stimuli presented in a predetermined sequence, and their responses are scored on the basis of explicit rules. Tests also share characteristics with observational assessments by providing an opportunity for the clinician to watch the client in the test situation. In some ways, however, tests are distinct from all other assessment techniques. For example,

1. Usually, a client's test responses can be quantitatively compared to statistical norms established by the responses of hundreds or thousands of other people who have taken the same test under standardized conditions. Standardization allows us to compare a particular 5-year-old's performance with the performance of the average 5-year-old.

2. A test can be administered in private, so observational assessment might not supplement test data.

3. Tests can be administered in groups as well as individually. The SAT and other college entrance examinations provide examples of how tests are used to assess large numbers of people at the same time.

What Do Tests Measure?

Tests provide measures of everything from A (anxiety) to Z (z-scores on achievement tests). In fact, there are so many tests that it takes special publications to list them all and review their reliability, validity, and utility. The best known and most authoritative of these is the *Mental Measurements Yearbook,* first published in 1938 (Buros, 1938) and updated frequently (Impara & Plake, 2003). This publication reviews over 2,200 standardized psychological tests. Of these, 286 tests are given full reviews, and the rest are given briefer reviews.

There are tests designed to be used with infants, children, adolescents, adults, senior citizens, students, soldiers, mental patients, office workers, job applicants, prisoners, and every other imaginable group (Impara & Plake, 2003). Some of these tests pose direct, specific questions ("Do you ever feel discouraged?"), while others ask for general reactions to less distinct stimuli ("Tell me what you see in this drawing"). Some have correct answers ("Is a chicken a mammal?), while others probe for opinions or preferences ("I enjoy looking at flowers: true or false?"). Some are presented in paper-and-pencil form, some are given orally. Some require verbal skill ("What does *analogy* mean?"), some ask the client to perform various nonverbal tasks ("Please trace the correct path through this puzzle maze"), and still others combine verbal, numerical, and performance items. Often, there are several different tests designed to measure the same characteristic.

One reason for the proliferation of tests is that testers are forever hoping to measure clinical constructs in ever more reliable, valid, and sophisticated ways. For example, one clinician may feel that a popular anxiety test does not really assess anxiety very well, and so the clinician creates a new, improved instrument. Other psychologists might be dissatisfied with both tests and soon come up with yet other devices. Another factor responsible for the increasing array of tests is that testers' interests are becoming more specific, thus prompting the development of special-purpose tests. In intelligence testing, for example, instruments are available for use with infants, the physically handicapped, and persons not fluent in English or from specific cultural backgrounds.

Despite their enormous variety, tests can be grouped into three general categories based on whether they seek to measure (a) *intellectual or cognitive abilities,* (b) *attitudes, interests, preferences, and values,* or (c) *personality characteristics* (see Table 5.1). The tests most commonly used by clinical psychologists in the United States and elsewhere are those of intellectual functioning and personality (Archer, Maruish, Imhof, & Piotrowski, 1991; Camara, Nathan, & Puente, 2000; Chan & Lee, 1995). These

TABLE 5.1

A Sampling of Tests Used by Clinical Psychologists

Cognition/Intellectual Functioning
Stanford-Binet V
Wechsler Adult Intelligence Scale (WAIS-III)
Wechsler Intelligence Scale for Children IV (WISC-IV)
Wechsler Preschool and Primary Scale of Intelligence (WPPSI-III)`
Kaufman Assessment Battery for Children (K-ABC-II)
Woodcock-Johnson Psychoeducational Battery III
Mini Mental Status Exam
Bender Visual Motor Gestalt Test

Personality
Cattell 16PF
California Psychological Inventory (CPI)
Myers-Briggs Type Indicator (MBTI)
NEO Personality Inventory-Revised (NEO-PI-R)
Internal-External Locus of Control (I-E)
Sentence Completion Tests
Projective Drawings (e.g., House-Tree-Person Test)

Emotional Functioning/Psychopathology
Minnesota Multiphasic Personality Inventory-2 (MMPI-2)
Millon Clinical Multiaxial Inventory (MCMI-III)
Psychological Screening Inventory (PSI)
Symptom Checklist 90-Revised
Beck Depression Inventory (BDI-II)
Hamilton Rating Scale for Depression
State-Trait Anxiety Inventory
Thematic Apperception Test (TAT)

Rorschach Inkblot Technique
Miller Hope Scale (MHS)
UCLA Loneliness Scale (ULS)
Hassles Scale

Attitudes, Interests, and Values
Strong Interest Inventory (SII)
Kuder Occupational Interest Survey (KOIS)
Rokeach Value Survey (RVS)
Study of Values (SoV)

Tests for Selected Populations
Child Development
Bayley Scales of Infant Development
Gesell Developmental Scales
Personality Inventory for Children (PIC)
Peabody Picture Vocabulary Test-Revised (PPVT-R)
Child Behavior Checklist (CBCL)
Marital/Family Disturbance
Dyadic Adjustment Scale
Family Environment Scale
Marital Satisfaction Inventory
Neurological Assessment/Aging
Halstead-Reitan Neuropsychological Test Battery
Luria-Nebraska Neuropsychological Battery
Wechsler Memory Scale

Forensic
Competency Screening Test
Georgia Court Competency Test
California F (fascism) Scale
Legal Attitudes Questionnaire (LAQ)

NOTE: Tests in this table are categorized according to their primary usage. However, some tests used in one category can also be used in another.

variables are especially relevant to most clinicians' treatment and research activities. Also, other people expect clinicians to offer advice on such things.

How Are Tests Constructed?

The seemingly odd items on some psychological tests, especially on certain personality tests, lead many people to wonder how psychologists come up with these things.

The answer is that they usually construct their tests using *analytic* or *empirical* approaches, though often they use a *sequential system* approach, which combines the two (Burisch, 1984).

Psychologists using the analytic approach, sometimes called the rational approach, begin by asking, What are the qualities I want to measure, and how do I define these qualities? They then build a test by creating items that answer these questions. In other words, a developer creates test materials or items by analyzing the content of a domain and matching questions that he or she believes (or that a theory says) tap that content.

To illustrate the simplest analytic approach, suppose that a clinician wanted to develop a test for identifying males and females. The first step would be to ask what kinds of test items are likely to be answered differently by members of the two sexes. The choice of items, then, will be shaped by what the clinician's knowledge, experience, and favorite theories say is different about the genders. If the clinician chooses to focus on variations in physical characteristics, and prefers a true–false format, the test might contain items such as the following:

1. I was born with a prostate gland.
2. I was born with a uterus.
3. I was born with a penis.
4. I was born with a vagina.

Suppose, however, that the clinician's interest in gender differences is not so much biological sex but rather the distribution of traits associated with being male or female. The clinician might develop items designed to tap unconscious processes associated with masculinity and femininity. Such a test might search for unconscious themes by asking clients to fill in incomplete sentences such as the following:

1. A dependent person is _____.
2. Strength is _____.
3. The trouble with most men is _____.
4. Most women are _____.

This example illustrates the importance of clearly defining the concept to be measured— a tester interested in gender is likely to construct very different instruments depending on whether the goal is to measure biological sex, gender identity, or gender-role stereotypes. In any case, items on an analytically constructed test will strongly reflect the tester's theory of what aspects of certain concepts should be tested, and how.

The main alternative to analytic test construction is the *empirical approach*. Here, instead of deciding ahead of time what test content should be used to measure a particular target, the tester lets the content "choose itself." Thus, in building a sex test, the clinician would amass a large number of self-report test items, performance tasks, inkblots, or other stimuli and then administer all of them to a large group of people *who have already been identified* as males or females using a biological criterion such as chromosome analysis. The clinician would then examine the entire group's responses to all these testing materials to see which items, tasks, or other stimuli were consistently answered differently by men and women.

Any test stimuli that reliably differentiated the sexes would be used to create the initial version of the sex test, *regardless of whether they have any obvious relationship to sex differences*. Thus, if many more males than females answered "true" to items like "I often have trouble sleeping" or "My shoes are too tight," those items would become part of the test. Empirically driven testers are usually willing to employ items that reliably discriminate among target groups even though the conceptual relevance of those items cannot always be explained clearly. *That* is why some tests contain such apparently odd items.

Several factors affect test developers' choice between analytic and empirical procedures. The analytic approach can be faster and less expensive because it does not require initial administration of many items to many people in order to settle on those that will comprise the test. These features make analytic procedures attractive to clinicians who do not have access to a large pool of test material and willing participants or who are forced by circumstances to develop a test on short notice. Analytic procedures also tend to be favored by clinicians evaluating a particular theory. Suppose that theory suggests that people differ in terms of "geekiness," but no test is available to measure it. To explore the geekiness dimension of personality, the researcher will need a test that taps what the theory says geekiness is. The test would also use measurement methods consistent with the theory. Development of a Geek Test would thus likely proceed on analytic grounds.

Clinicians who have time and other resources available often find the empirical approach more desirable, especially when attempting to make specific predictions about people. If the tester's task is to identify individuals likely to graduate from law school, for example, it makes sense to find out if students who graduate respond to specific test items in a way that is reliably different from those who fail or drop out. In short, the analytic method often results in items that appear sensible but may or may not work; the empirical approach often results in items that work but may or not appear sensible.

The *sequential system approach* to test construction combines aspects of the analytic and empirical techniques. The decision about which items to try is usually made on analytic grounds; some items are selected from existing tests, while others are those the clinician believes "ought" to be evaluated. Testers who choose initial test items analytically may then examine results statistically to determine which item responses are and which are not correlated with one another, which items are too easy or too difficult, and which items do and do not discriminate between people who differ on the characteristic of interest. Groups of correlated items are then identified as *scales,* which are thought to be relatively pure measures of certain dimensions of personality, mental ability, or the like (Maloney & Ward, 1976). Regardless of how a test is constructed initially, its value as an assessment instrument ultimately depends on empirical research demonstrating its reliability and validity (see Chapter 3).

Standardization and Score Interpretation. We have already mentioned that standardization refers to consistency in administration and scoring of a test. Ideally, tests are given in the same way to every person taking them, though this ideal can be taken too far. We know of a testing course in which the professor required that his student-examiners place certain stimulus materials for an IQ test directly in front of the client and exactly 7 inches from the edge of the table. He even walked around with a ruler during practice administrations to be sure this practice was followed. Exact consistency in administration is impossible, but clinicians try to maintain high levels of consistency.

In addition to consistency in administration, standardization can also refer to the sample on which the test was originally developed. To illustrate the importance of this sample, suppose that Amy, an 8-year-old, gets 14 out of 23 items correct on a memory test. Is that a high score? A low score? In order to know the answer, we must compare Amy's score with a large sample of scores from persons who are similar to her in age. If 1,000 8-year-olds took the test, and only the top 8% are able to get 14 or more answers correct, we know that Amy's score is a high one, at the 92nd percentile to be exact. In this example, the 1,000 children who took the test provide the *standardization sample* for the test. The scores obtained from this sample become the standard against which subsequent scores are compared. Their scores provide the main interpretive framework for all individual scores on the test.

The numbers that come from the standardization sample—means, variances, percentages, and so on—are called *norms*. These are the benchmarks that allow meaningful interpretation of a test performance. Every decade or so, major tests are *renormed*. This process can be complex and expensive because it involves identifying a large, representative sample of persons willing to take the test; finding examiners to give the test and report results; and compiling and analyzing all the data. The results of this renorming process are then usually published in the instruction manuals that accompany the tests. After giving a test, clinicians compare their client's scores with those contained in the manual. Most of the tests discussed in this chapter are norm-referenced tests.

Test scores can also be interpreted based on a *criterion* established by the tester rather than on a normative sample. For instance, to qualify as a pilot, candidates must meet a predetermined criterion, or level of proficiency; it is not enough simply to score, say, above the average set by other candidates (Domino & Domino, 2006). Finally, test scores can be interpreted not by comparing the test taker to others or to an external criterion but only to himself or herself. This process is often called *ipsative measurement*. For example, suppose a test asks clients to list their most important goals for the next year. Norms do not seem appropriate, and neither do criterion markers. However, it might be informative to compare the results of this test at the beginning of therapy and 6 months later. Ipsative measures are becoming increasingly important because they help clinicians measure the outcomes of treatment.

Avoiding Distortion in Test Scores

A multitude of factors can alter or distort the outcome of tests. A classic example is provided by a study in which college men who had just seen photographs of nude females gave more sex-related responses to the TAT when it was administered by a young, informally dressed male graduate student than when given by a man who was older and more formal (Mussen & Scodel, 1955). So the circumstances under which a test is given—anything from temperature extremes and outside noise to crowding and the presence of a stranger—can affect its results (Plante, Goldfarb, & Wadley, 1993). In one case, for example, a child's scores on repeated IQ tests went from 68 to 120 and back to 79 depending on whether or not a particular adult was in the testing room (Handler, 1974). While most variation is not this extreme, the case illustrates that establishing trust and avoiding distraction can affect the validity of certain kinds of tests (e.g., Grossarth, Eysenck, & Boyle, 1995).

Another source of distortion in test results is that some clients tend to respond in particular ways to most items, regardless of what the items are. This tendency has been called *response set* (Cronbach, 1946), *response style* (Jackson & Messick, 1958), and *response bias* (Berg, 1955). For example, clients exhibiting a *social desirability bias* will respond to test items in ways that are most socially acceptable, whether or not those responses reflect their true feelings or impulses (Edwards, 1957; Rychtarik, Tarnowski, & St. Lawrence, 1989). Clients have also been suspected of *acquiescent response styles* (Jackson & Messick, 1961), in which they tend to agree with virtually any self-descriptive test item. Defensive, deviant, and exaggerated styles have also been postulated (e.g., Isenhart & Silversmith, 1996). The significance of response styles in determining test scores has been hotly debated, partly because it is unclear whether response tendencies represent stable client characteristics (McCrae & Costa, 1983) or temporary behaviors dictated and reinforced by the testing circumstances (Linehan & Nielsen, 1983). Whatever the case, the client's point of view while taking a test cannot be ignored in evaluating a test.

It is impossible to eliminate all extraneous sources of variability in test scores, but test designers can minimize them by (a) developing clear, simple instructions for examiners and test takers, (b) extensively pilot-testing and studying response tendencies on items, (c) enlisting the participation of outside experts in test bias during test development, and (d) building indicators of response bias or deliberate distortion into the test so that these things can be identified if they occur. At the same time, those who give tests can reduce distortion by (a) clearly explaining the purposes of the test and answering any questions the client has, thereby enhancing rapport and client motivation; (b) paying careful attention to the circumstances under which testing takes place so that conditions are essentially the same for each client; and (c) noting and reporting (e.g., to referral sources) any circumstances in the testing that might compromise the validity of the test results.

Cultural Fairness and Bias in Psychological Tests

Suppose you are a clinician and find yourself in the following situation:

Mrs. P, a 37-year-old female immigrant from Vietnam, is referred to you as a new client. She speaks English reasonably well, and you conclude from the initial interview that she is probably suffering from depression, but it is difficult to determine the severity of the problem. She also voiced some vague somatic complaints, which you suspect indicate other problems, but, again, it is difficult to determine exactly what they might be. Her insurance company wants an accurate DSM diagnosis, as do you, and you would also like to have a better understanding of this client and her difficulties. To get a clearer picture, you decide to administer tests for psychological problems in general and depression in particular.

Will the client be able to understand the test items? Will she interpret the items in the same way as native English speakers would? Do the test norms apply to Vietnamese immigrants? This example introduces a broader question: To what extent do psychological tests adequately assess psychopathology, personality, intelligence, or other characteristics in diverse populations?

Concerns about the cultural fairness of tests appeared first and most prominently in relation to measures of intellectual abilities. Investigators consistently found that, on average, African Americans and Hispanics score lower than whites and Asians on standard intelligence tests. The controversy is not whether the lower scores occur but rather why they occur. Does the fact that different cultural or ethnic groups show different average scores on a test mean that the test is biased?

As Domino and Domino (2006) point out, test-related bias can result from factors occurring *before* the test, as when certain cultural and ethnic groups are disadvantaged by discrimination, lower-quality education, poverty, stereotyped portrayals, poor role models, and the like, or *during* the test itself, as when, for example, concepts or vocabulary used on the test are more familiar to clients from some cultural backgrounds than others. Either or both could be responsible for the observed gap in test results between cultural groups. Is there any way to detect which of these sources might explain the observed group differences in tests results?

There is, and the easiest to detect is test item bias. If test designers collect information about the gender and ethnic composition of the test's standardization sample, they can analyze responses to each test item. If, because of unfamiliarity with the item's vocabulary or other content, one group responds incorrectly significantly more often than other groups, developers can simply eliminate that item from the test. The courts have often used an "80%" or "four-fifths" rule to label an item as biased. That is, if there is a difference of 20% or more between the mean scores of majority and minority groups on a particular test item, that item is considered to be biased. Using such procedures during test development, most carefully designed and widely used psychological tests today have greatly reduced or eliminated culturally biased items. They have also addressed other biasing factors such as confusing instructions and cultural-specific testing materials.

What about cultural inequality as an explanation of intergroup score differences? Most persons familiar with test construction procedures view this factor as the best explanation of why certain minorities score differently, on average, on standardized tests when compared to majority group members (Domino & Domino, 2006). To illustrate the point, try this thought experiment: Imagine that researchers were able to construct culture-neutral intelligence tests in which minority and majority groups scored the same, on average. If you accepted *this* test as valid, you would have to argue that factors such as poverty, discrimination, and inferior educational opportunities have *no effect* on cognitive and academic test performance. To most people, that conclusion would make no sense. As Anne Anastasi (1988) put it,

> Tests are designed to show what an individual can do at a given point in time. They cannot tell us *why* he performs as he does. Tests cannot compensate for cultural deprivation by eliminating its effect from their scores. On the contrary, tests should *reveal* such effects, so that appropriate remedial steps can be taken. To conceal the effects of cultural disadvantages by trying to devise tests that are insensitive to such effects is equivalent to breaking a thermometer because it registers a body temperature of 101°. (p. 66)

In short, average test score differences between minority and majority groups are more likely the result of differences in cultural conditions than of bias in the tests. Further support for this comes from the fact that attempts to develop "culture-fair" tests have not been very successful. Such tests appear to be influenced just as much as, or more than, standard tests by cultural and environmental factors (Samuda, 1975), and their validity tends to be lower (Humphreys, 1988).

We are not arguing that test bias does not exist, only that test item bias is reasonably well controlled in more well-established and extensively studied tests. The same is not true for all tests—each test depends on the care with which standardization samples are chosen and the degree to which cross-cultural generalizability has been investigated and addressed.

Returning to the case of our 37-year-old client from Vietnam, a conscientious clinician would look for empirical evidence that supports the generalization of standard tests of personality and psychopathology to Asian populations. Were Asian American groups adequately represented in the standardization sample? Does the client have language or cultural background factors that could invalidate the test? Is there a validated version of these tests in the client's native language? Better still, the clinician might use the Vietnamese Depression Scale (Kinzie et al., 1982), a test developed specifically for persons from Mrs. P's background. The clinician would also be wise to seek out published material and advice from colleagues who could provide insight into how Mrs. P's background might affect her assessment and treatment (e.g., Hays & Iwamasa, 2006) and to engage Mrs. P in further discussion about her health beliefs, as these may differ from those commonly held by Westerners (Okazaki & Tanaka-Matsumi, 2006).

Many clinical researchers are now examining cross-cultural test use empirically on a case-by-case basis (Krull & Pierce, 1995). Their goal is to construct tests that will be valid for specific populations. For example, Jia-xi and Guo-peng (2006) recently investigated the validity and reliability of a Chinese version of the 16PF, a personality test. They found that the Chinese revision has good applicability, though the scale's internal consistency could be improved. The *International Test Consortium* (ITC) was formed to promote the study of the cross-cultural applications of tests (for an in-depth discussion of these and other efforts related to cross-cultural test use, see Hambleton, Merenda, & Spielberger, 2005).

Ethical Standards in Testing

Culturally sensitive assessment is one aspect of ethical testing practices. Testing raises many other ethical issues as well (Nagy, 2005). The following should give you an idea of some testing-related situations requiring ethical decisions. As you can see, these often relate to principles of confidentiality, privacy, informed consent, and social responsibility.

- If a clinician believes that the results of a test might be detrimental to a client, how should the clinician handle feedback to the client about the testing?
- If an adolescent (a minor) is tested, do the parents, the school, the courts, or others also have rights to the results of the test?
- If a researcher uses a test whose title might bias the way participants respond (e.g., the Test of Social Anxiety), what compromises, if any, in the principle of informed consent can ethically be taken?

- What third-party payers (e.g., an insurance company) have rights to know about the results of a client's test?
- The counseling center of a university bases certain student-guidance decisions on a test that has been discredited because of poor psychometric properties (i.e., it is unreliable or not valid). What responsibilities does a clinical psychologist faculty member have to dispute or report the counseling center's decisions?

The American Psychological Association has urged its members to reduce the possibility of ethical problems or abuse in testing by adhering to the *Standards for Educational and Psychological Tests* (1999), a document developed by the American Educational Research Association, the American Psychological Association, and the National Council on Measurement in Education. The APA's *Guidelines for Test User Qualifications* provides additional information for those considering the use of tests. The *Uniform Guidelines on Employee Selection Procedures* was developed by the Equal Employment Opportunity Commission (EEOC) to regulate the use of tests and other methods as selection techniques. Together, these documents guide test users and help insure that, when developed, evaluated, administered, interpreted, and published with due regard for scientific principles and the rights and welfare of clients, psychological tests can make a positive contribution to society (Robertson & Eyde, 1993). Table 5.2 lists the Ethics Code's general principles and provides examples of situations that might apply to each.

TABLE 5.2

Ethical Standards for Psychologists' Use of Tests

Principle	Example of Application
Competence	Clinicians should be experienced in the administration and interpretation of tests that they use to make decisions about a client.
Professional/scientific responsibility	Clinicians should be familiar with the research literature on a test, particularly its reliability, validity, appropriate uses, and limitations.
Integrity	Clinicians should use tests as intended and not make claims about tests or test results unless those claims are supported by empirical evidence.
Respect for rights and dignity	Clinicians should insure that a test genuinely applies to persons taking the test, such as persons from different cultures.
Concern for others' welfare	First, clinicians should do no harm in using tests with clients; they should recognize the potential for harm, especially if test results are inappropriately applied.
Social responsibility	Clinicians should not disseminate test materials or the protected content of tests to unauthorized personnel; they should take action to prevent the misuse of tests by others (e.g., colleagues, institutions).
Access to test materials	Ethical practice prohibits test developers and users from making public the contents of certain psychological tests (e.g., I.Q. tests); tests are commercially available only to qualified users.

While many tests are available from commercial vendors, other tests are developed by clinicians and published in professional journals. Sometimes, especially when the test is short, the test is published in full in a journal article, along with evidence of the test's psychometric properties. In either case, clinicians should contact the test's author to request the right to use the test and they are obligated to follow ethical principles in using them.

Patterns of Test Usage in Clinical Psychology

As noted earlier, testing continues to be a major focus of clinical psychology training, but patterns of specific test usage have evolved over the years. As you can see in Table 5.3, certain tests of intellectual functioning, personality, and psychopathology consistently receive attention. Clinicians prefer them, and training directors require that clinicians-in-training learn to use them (Belter & Piotrowski, 2001). At the same time, some tests, notably projective techniques, have declined in usage and are taught less often than they used to be.

Changes in test usage can be attributed to several factors. One is empirical evidence—tests that consistently show evidence of higher reliability and validity tend to rise to the top of the popularity list, while those that show less evidence tend to drift downward. The process of change may be slow, though, as test preferences among clinicians can

---

TABLE 5.3

Top 10 Psychological Tests

Test	Sundberg (1961) (N = 185)	Lubin, Wallis, & Paine (1971) (N = 251)	Lubin, Larsen, & Matarazzo (1984) (N = 221)	Watkins, Campbell, Nieberding & Hallmark (1995) (N = 412)	Camara, Nathan, & Puente (2000) (N = 120)
WAIS	6	1	1	1	1
MMPI	7.5	6	2	2	2
Bender-Gestalt Visual Motor Test	4	3.5	3	6	5
Rorschach	1	2	4	5	4
TAT	2.5	3.5	5	4	6
WISC	10	7	6	9	3
Peabody Picture Vocabulary Test	—	13	7.5	12	20
Sentence Completion Tests (All Kinds)	13.5	8.5	7.5	3	15
House-Tree-Person Test	12	9	9	7	8
Draw-A-Person Test	2.5	5	10	7	(not included)

NOTE: Numbers in the table represent rank, based on frequency of use, in each survey.

be influenced as much by clinical tradition as by empirical evidence (Norcross, Koocher, & Garofalo, 2006).

Test usage also changes because of social and contextual factors. Prominent among these is the influence of managed care. Insurance companies and other third-party providers are especially interested in efficiency. As a result, they are likely to favor quicker, more problem-focused assessment techniques over broad tests that give a full picture of the client (Piotrowski, Belter, & Keller, 1998). These companies want data showing that testing results can be used to select faster and more effective treatment. Their demands have stimulated research into how existing tests can be used to select treatment and into the development of new tests specifically designed for making treatment decisions.

To summarize our discussion of general features of tests, and to preview our discussion of specific tests in the following sections, we present Table 5.4. This table lists a variety of quality indicators of psychological tests. Discerning clinicians and researchers use such indicators in selecting the best tests for specific purposes.

In the next section, we summarize the tests that are most commonly used by clinical psychologists. Further information about these and other tests for individual and group administration to adults and children is available from the technical manuals associated with each test and from numerous other sources on psychological testing

TABLE 5.4

Criteria for Judging the Psychometric Quality of a Test

Criterion	What It Is
Norms	Measures of central tendency and variability for the test obtained from a large, representative standardization sample; these allow meaningful interpretation of scores.
Internal consistency reliability	A measure of reliability, usually accomplished by the split-half method.
Test-retest reliability	Similarity of results from repeat testings of the same persons.
Interrater reliability	Similarity of results when multiple raters independently score the same tests.
Content validity	Items on the test adequately sample all the important domains associated with the trait or ability being measured.
Construct validity	Results of the test correlate with other well-established measures of the same construct.
Generalization validity	The degree to which the test results remain valid across different segments of the population.
Clinical Utility	The degree to which test results clearly point to specific preferred treatments or can reliably measure changes that result from treatment.

SOURCE: Adapted from J. Hunsley and E. J. Mash, 2007.

(e.g., Domino & Domino, 2006; Gregory, 2006; Groth-Marnat, 2003; Impara & Plake, 2003; Kaplan & Saccuzzo, 2004; Kline, 2005).

Section Summary: Tests present clients with a series of stimuli in a planned sequence. If variables associated with the test construction, administration, and scoring are adequately controlled, differences in test performance should reflect real differences in the persons taking the test. Because eliminating bias is not easy, test developers must pay careful attention to how various groups of persons react to the items. Test users should be professionally qualified, understand what makes a high-quality test, and follow ethical principles in testing.

TESTS OF INTELLECTUAL FUNCTIONING

Section Preview: In this section, we outline how theorists have understood and measured intelligence. We then describe the variety of tests clinicians use to measure cognitive abilities. Some focus on a broad range of abilities and some on specific abilities. Prominent among the first are the Stanford-Binet scales and the Wechsler scales. Clinicians also use a variety of other tests to measure achievement and aptitude.

Theories of Intelligence

While everyone would agree that intelligence is a good thing to have, there is far less consensus about what it actually *is* (Furnham, 2000; Sternberg & Detterman, 1986). This state of affairs has generated the half-joking suggestion among clinicians that "intelligence is whatever intelligence tests measure." Indeed, the developers of most intelligence tests have initially proceeded on analytical grounds; each of the more than 200 assessment instruments they have produced reflects its creator's theoretical views about the essential nature of intelligence and about how best to measure intellectual functioning. A description of those theories is beyond the scope of this chapter (see Neisser et al. [1996] for a succinct review), but it is worth noting that various researchers have generally described intelligence in one of three ways, each of which is briefly described below.

General Intelligence Model (g).   One theory, often favored by those employing a mental testing, or *psychometric* approach to intelligence, describes intelligence as a *general* characteristic. Originally proposed by Spearman (1904), the notion of intelligence as a global, general ability has come to be referred to simply as *g*. While everyone has variations in their ability across different domains, *g* is presumed to be an underlying biological or psychological trait that influences all cognitive abilities. This view is supported by the observation that students who are exceptional in math, for instance, also tend to be good in English, biology, and many other areas. It fits also with the robust and well-established finding that test scores on a variety of cognitive tasks are positively correlated (van der Maas, 2006). The underlying factor common to the scores is presumed to be *g*.

Multiple Specific Intelligences Models.   Although researchers find that scores on a variety of cognitive tasks are correlated, the correlation is not always strong. As a result, some have argued that intelligence is better understood as a collection of relatively separate abilities. As many as 120 *specific* intellectual functions (called *s*'s) have been proposed, including abilities such as word fluency, short-term memory, and perceptual speed (Carroll, 1993; Domino & Domino, 2006).

One theory of multiple intelligence that has received considerable attention is Robert Sternberg's *triarchic theory* (Sternberg, 2004, 2006a). Sternberg argues that there are three basic kinds of intelligence—analytical, creative, and practical—and that conventional tests measure only the first kind well. Along with his colleagues, Sternberg has developed a test designed to measure all three (the *Sternberg Triarchic Abilities Test,* or *STAT*). This test is viewed favorably by many, but more research is needed to determine the test's validity and reliability (Santrock, 2008).

A second popular multiple intelligence approach is that of Howard Gardner, who lists eight intelligences or frames of mind: verbal, mathematical, spatial, bodily–kinesthetic, musical, intrapersonal, interpersonal, and naturalistic (Gardner, 1993, 2002). His theory has drawn considerable interest, especially in the field of education (Gardner, 1998).

Specific multiple intelligence theories propose that intelligence is better understood as a collection of separate abilities rather than as a single factor. It is noteworthy that both Sternberg's and especially Gardner's theories have expanded the term *intelligence* to include abilities that are not included in its traditional definition (e.g., kinesthetic athletic skill). Some see these theories as valuable; others argue that it overextends the definition of intelligence—not everything a person does should be considered a part of intelligence.

Hierarchical and Factor Analytic Models. A third view of intelligence might be considered a combination of the previous two. In this compromise view, separate and general cognitive abilities are related in a hierarchical fashion (see Figure 5.1). At the most elemental level are specific abilities such as vocabulary knowledge, visual pattern recognition, and the like (represented in Figure 5.1 as a1, a2, a3, b1, b2, etc.). Specific abilities are not entirely independent of each other: Certain ones correlate because they share a common factor (e.g., a good memory, verbal knowledge, rapid processing of visual information). The common factors are represented in Figure 5.1 as factors *a* through *d*. Finally, these higher-order factors are themselves correlated to some degree, and that correlation is represented by the common factor, *g,* that underlies them all.

Is there a way to evaluate these different views of intelligence? For instance, how do we know the degree to which specific abilities cluster together? *Factor analytic studies* measure the degree to which various measures are correlated. Carroll (1993) reviewed earlier work on intelligence by Cattell (1943) and Horn (1965), and then summarized 461 factor analytic studies of intelligence. From this work has emerged a hierarchical model that has, with some modifications, been adopted by most of the major intelligence test developers. As we review the various intelligence tests, note the similarities in the factors presumed to be measured by these widely used tests.

The Binet Scales

Alfred Binet was not the first person to develop a measure of intelligence, but his original test and the revisions based on it have been among the most influential means of assessing the mental ability of children. In its earliest form (1905), Binet's test consisted of

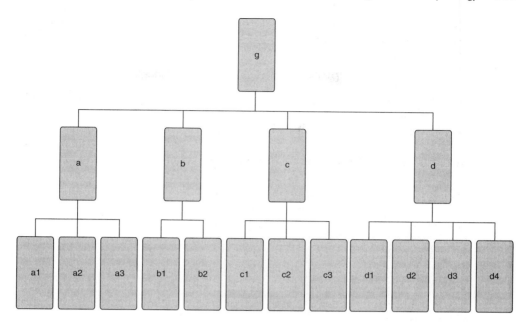

FIGURE 5.1 A Hierarchical Model of Intelligence

30 questions and tasks, including things like unwrapping a piece of candy, following a moving object with the eyes, comparing objects of differing weights, repeating numbers or sentences from memory, and recognizing familiar objects. The child's test score was simply the number of items passed. Beginning with a 1908 revision, the tasks in Binet's test were *age graded,* which means that they were arranged so that younger children were expected to pass only the earlier ones, while older children were expected to pass later ones as well.

The 1908 scale was brought to the United States by Henry Goddard and revised in 1916 by Lewis Terman, a Stanford University psychologist. Terman adopted an idea suggested by German psychologist William Stern for representing numerically the relationship between mental and chronological age: *Stanford-Binet* results were expressed as the *intelligence quotient* (or IQ) that results when mental age (MA) is divided by chronological age (CA) and multiplied by 100. Thus, a 6-year-old whose score on the Stanford-Binet yielded a mental age of 8 would have an IQ of 133 (8/6 × 100). Thus began the tradition of pegging the average IQ score at 100.

The most recent version of the Stanford-Binet, the SB5, was completed in 2003. As happens with all major test revisions, the SB5 went through a pilot phase before its final form was determined. The test was normed on a sample of 4,800 persons who were representative of the U.S. population and stratified on the variables of age, sex, race/ethnicity, geographic region, and socioeconomic level. By recording these variables in a large sample during pilot testing, the test developers could determine whether certain items

Alfred Binet is regarded as the father of intelligence testing.

were answered differently, on average, by persons from different ethnic groups or genders. During this phase, numerous items were pilot-tested and either kept or discarded (refer to our discussion of test construction earlier in this chapter). Of nearly 1,000 items considered, 293 were selected for the SB5 (Roid, 2003).

The SB5 is built around a hierarchical model of intelligence. Examiners can obtain a full-scale IQ score (a measure of *g*), as well as verbal and nonverbal IQ scores and individual subtest scores (each subtest has a mean of 10 and a standard deviation of 3). However, the subtests are now grouped into five factors representing the major domains of intellectual functioning (see Table 5.5). These factors are comparable to the midlevel factors in Figure 5.1 and were derived from factor analytic studies. In the SB5, those factors are labeled (1) Fluid Reasoning, (2) Knowledge, (3) Quantitative Reasoning, (4) Visual–Spatial Processing, and (5) Working Memory.

Research on the reliability of the fifth edition of the Stanford-Binet suggests that it has very high internal consistency, generally above 0.90. The test–retest reliability for the Full-Scale IQ was in the 0.93 to 0.95 range; for factor scores, the median was 0.88. A third measure of reliability, interscorer agreement, yielded a median correlation of 0.90 (Roid, 2003). These numbers suggest high levels of reliability.

One way to judge a test's validity is to compare its results with those obtained from other well-established measures of intelligence (i.e., criterion validity). Full-Scale IQ scores on the SB5 are similar to those obtained from other established intelligence tests, including the Wechsler scales (correlations are in the range of 0.78 to 0.84). The test is also able to discriminate among samples of gifted, retarded, and learning-disordered children (Roid, 2003). In short, the Stanford-Binet remains a highly reliable test widely used for testing of children, diagnosing mental retardation, and predicting and explaining academic achievement (Walsh & Betz, 2001).

TABLE 5.5

Items of the Type Included in the Stanford-Binet 5

Vocabulary: Define words like train, wrench, letter, error, and encourage.

Object Series/Matrices: Choose the right order in which a series of pictures was presented.

Absurdities: Identify the mistakes or "silly" aspects of pictures in which, for example, a man is shown using the wrong end of a rake or a girl is shown putting a piece of clothing on incorrectly.

Quantitative Reasoning: Determine which numbers come next in a series of numbers such as the following: 32, 26, 20, 14, ____, ____.

Memory for sentences: Correctly recall sentences that were presented.

Verbal Relations: Indicate how three objects or words are alike but different from a fourth. For example, how are dog, cat, and horse alike but different from boy.

Block Span: Separate blocks into rows coded with yellow and red stripes.

The Wechsler Scales

In the 1930s, David Wechsler, chief psychologist at New York's Bellevue Psychiatric Hospital, began developing an intelligence test specifically for adults. The result of his efforts, the *Wechsler-Bellevue (W-B) Intelligence Scale,* was published in 1939. This test differed in several ways from the Stanford-Binet, even though some W-B tasks were borrowed or adapted from it. First, the W-B was aimed at adults age 17 and older. Second, the W-B was a *point* scale in which the client received credit for each correct answer. With this method, IQ does not reflect the relationship between mental age and chronological age but compares the points earned by the client to those earned by persons of equal age in the standardization sample. Although an average IQ is still placed at 100, this method of calculating IQ has become standard for most tests.

Wechsler also developed comparable tests for children: the *Wechsler Intelligence Scale for Children* (WISC, often referred to phonetically as "the Wisk") and the *Wechsler Preschool and Primary Scale of Intelligence* (WPPSI, or "the Whipsee"). Each has gone through several revisions and become among the most frequently used tests of intelligence.

The WAIS. In 1955, Wechsler revised his adult test. This revision, called the *Wechsler Adult Intelligence Scale,* or WAIS, soon became the most popular adult intelligence test in the United States (see Table 5.3). The test was revised again in 1981 (WAIS-II) and most recently in 1997 (WAIS-III). As with previous versions of the test, items on the WAIS-III are arranged and presented in order of increasing difficulty within subtests. The clinician stops each subtest after a predetermined number of failures and then begins the next subtest. When the test is completed, the clinician can compute Full-Scale, Verbal, and Performance IQs by converting the client's point totals to standardized IQ scores with a mean of 100 and standard deviation of 15. Some examples of the types of items included on the WAIS-III are presented in Table 5.6.

The WAIS-III differs in some ways from its predecessors. It has an extended age range that allows computation of IQ scores through age 89. This was made possible by

TABLE 5.6

Items of the Type Included in the Wechsler Adult Intelligence Scale (WAIS-III)

Subtest	Simulated Items on the WAIS-III
Information	What does bread come from? What did Shakespeare do? What is the capital of France? What is the malleus malleficarum?
Comprehension	What should you do with a wallet found in the street? Why do foreign cars cost more than domestic cars? What does "the squeaky wheel gets the grease" mean?
Arithmetic	If you have four apples and give two away, how many do you have left? If four people can finish a job in six days, how many people would it take to do the job in two days?
Similarities	Identify similar aspects of pairs like hammer–screwdriver, portrait–short story, dog–flower.
Digit Symbol/ Coding	Copy designs that are associated with different numbers as quickly as possible.
Digit Span	Repeat in forward and reverse order two- to nine-digit numbers.
Vocabulary	Define chair, dime, lunch, paragraph, valley, asylum, modal, cutaneous.
Picture Completion	Find missing objects in increasingly complex pictures.
Block Design	Arrange blocks to match increasingly complex standard patterns.
Picture Arrangement	Place increasing numbers of pictures together to make increasingly complex stories.
Symbol Search	Visually scan and recognize a series of symbols.

the addition of new items more appropriate for older adults and by norming the test on a sample of 2,450 persons ages 16 to 89. The sample was also stratified according to age, gender, education, and geographic region.

One of the biggest changes on WAIS-III was the addition of four new index scores: Verbal Comprehension, Working Memory, Perceptual Organization, and Processing Speed. These are comparable to the midlevel factor scores in Figure 5.1. Each index score is obtained by combining scores on selected subtests. For instance, a score on Perceptual Organization is derived from subtest scores on Picture Completion, Block Design, and Object Assembly. The four index scores are derived from factor analytic studies (Saklofske, Hildebrand, & Gorsuch, 2000).

WISC and WPPSI. Appearing in 1949, the WISC was originally designed to be used for children ages 5 to 15. It had 12 subtests (6 verbal, 6 performance) of which only 10 were usually administered. The WPPSI was developed later, but still reached only the 4-year-old level (Wechsler, 1967). A revision of the further lowered the minimum age, its current, third edition covers the age range from 2.5 to 7 years.

The latest version of the WISC, the WISC-IV, covers ages 6 to 17 and retains the basic structure and format of its predecessors. However, the WISC-IV contains some significant changes. Three subtests were dropped (Picture Arrangement, Object Assembly, Mazes) and five others added (e.g., Picture Concepts, Letter-Number Sequencing, Matrix Reasoning, Word Reasoning, Cancellation). Developers also abandoned the Verbal IQ and Performance IQ measures, long a staple of Wechsler scoring. They retained the Full-Scale IQ and the four composite factor scores, or indexes, originally introduced in WISC-III. These composite scores are Verbal Comprehension, Perceptual Reasoning, Working Memory, and Processing Speed (Wechsler, 2003).

The Wechsler scales have strong psychometric properties. For instance, the WISC-IV, the most recently updated of the Wechsler family, was normed on a sample of 2,200 children ages 6 to 17. This sample matched the 2000 U.S. Census data in terms of the distribution of sex, race/ethnicity, parental education level, and geographic region. As with the recently revised SB5, inclusion of these and other variables allowed experts on cross-cultural research and intelligence testing to scour pilot-tested items for evidence of item bias. Individual items that were responded to differently by specific groups could be discarded in favor of items that did not show such group differences.

The reliability of each of the Wechsler scales is strong. The WAIS split-half reliabilities for Full-Scale, Verbal, and Performance IQ scores are 0.93 or above across all age ranges, and reliabilities for the index scores are nearly as high. For the WISC-IV, split-half reliabilities for the index and Full-Scale scores range from 0.92 to 0.97. WISC-IV scores are also extremely stable over time; test–retest reliabilities are in the high 0.80s to 0.90s range. Finally, the test's scoring has largely eliminated subjectivity; interscorer agreement ranges from 0.98 to 0.99 (Wechsler, 2003).

Validity studies show that the Wechsler tests correlate well with other established tests such as the Stanford-Binet. Also, as with the SB, factor analytic studies have been important in confirming that the composite index scores represent important constructs in the measurement of intelligence (Wechsler, 2003). There are appropriately strong correlations with criteria such as school grades, achievement test scores, and neuropsychological performance (Braden, 1995). Extensive discussion of standardization, reliability, and validity are provided by the technical manuals published for each test.

Interpreting Intelligence Test Scores. Using intelligence tests such as the WAIS, WISC, or SB, clinicians can obtain a multifaceted description of a person's cognitive strengths and weaknesses. They can also develop hypotheses about diagnoses, brain damage, impulsivity, or other personality characteristics by using the variability or "scatter" of subtest scores (Groth-Marnat, 2003, Ryan, Paolo, & Smith, 1992; Wechsler, 2003). For instance, Wechsler (2003) noted that children with ADHD, learning disorder or traumatic brain injury show relative weakness on measures of Processing Speed. However, others suggest that clinicians should use caution when making inferences on the basis of the pattern of subtest scores. Unequivocal diagnoses, they say, can rarely be made using the WAIS, SB, or WISC alone because the tests were not designed for neuropsychological assessment. Hunsley and Mash (2007) go further, arguing that the clinical usefulness of interscore comparisons has not been empirically established.

Other Intelligence Tests

Another individually administered intelligence test that has gained popularity in recent years is the *Kaufman Assessment Battery for Children* (Kaufman & Kaufman, 1983, 2004a). Suitable for children 3 to 18 years of age, the test is now in its second edition, the K-ABC-II. This test was based on research and theory in cognitive psychology and neuropsychology. It defines intelligence as the ability to solve new problems (an ability sometimes referred to as *fluid intelligence*) and also acquired knowledge of facts (which has been termed *crystallized intelligence*). As with the Binet and Wechsler tests, the Kaufman subtests (18 total, 10 core) are grouped into composite scores compatible with a hierarchical model of intelligence. The test's dual theoretical foundation yields two main (higher level) scores: one for Mental Processing and one for the combination of Mental Processing and Acquired Knowledge. With the K-ABC-II, the number of midlevel composite factor scores increases with age; there are three composite scores for children age 3, four for children ages 4 to 6, and five for children ages 7 and older. This arrangement is designed to reflect the increasing complexity of intelligence as children grow.

The standardization sample for the K-ABC-II consisted of 3,025 children who closely matched the U.S. Census on several demographic factors. Internal consistency reliabilities are in the 0.90s range, and test–retest coefficients are in the mid-0.80s to 0.90s. The developers of the K-ABC-II sought to produce a test free of cultural or ethnic bias. The test shows high correlations with the WISC, as well as appropriately strong correlations with criteria such as school grades, achievement test scores, and neuropsychological performance (Braden, 1995; Kaufman & Kaufman, 2004a). A brief version called the *Kaufman Brief Intelligence Test-2* (K-BIT-2) is designed to yield estimates for crystallized and fluid intelligence in about 20 minutes (Kaufman & Kaufman, 2004b).

Several other intelligence tests in use today assess intelligence without emphasis on verbal or vocalization skills. *The Peabody Picture Vocabulary Test–Revised,* the *Porteus Maze Test,* the *Leiter International Performance Scale,* and the *Raven's Progressive Matrices,* for example, allow clinicians to assess intellectual functioning in clients who are very young or have other characteristics that impair their ability at verbal tasks. These tests also provide a backup in cases in which the clinician suspects that a client's performance on a standard IQ test may have been hampered by anxiety, verbal deficits, cultural disadvantages, or other situational factors. Table 5.7 presents basic information for three popular intelligence tests.

Aptitude and Achievement Tests

Intelligence tests can be viewed as general mental ability instruments measuring both aptitude (the capacity to acquire knowledge or skill) and achievement (acquired knowledge or skill). However, there are a number of other tests designed to measure more specific mental abilities. Some aptitude tests are designed to predict success in an occupation or an educational program. They measure the accumulated effects of many different educational and living experiences and attempt to forecast performance on the basis of these effects. Achievement tests measure proficiency at certain tasks; that is, they measure how much people know or how well they can perform in specific areas.

TABLE 5.7

Three Popular Intelligence Tests at a Glance

Test	Age Ranges	Number of Core Subtests	Administration Time Estimates[1]	Primary Measures Obtained
Stanford–Binet Intelligence Scales (SB5), (Roid, 2003)	2 y–85 y+	10	45–75 min.	Full-scale IQ; Verbal IQ; Nonverbal IQ; five composite scales: Fluid Reasoning, Crystallized Knowledge, Quantitative Knowledge, Visual–Spatial Processing, Working Memory
Wechsler Intelligence Scale for Children–IV (WISC-IV) (Wechsler, 2003)	6 y 0 m–16 y 11 m	10	65–80 min.	Full-scale IQ; four composite scales (indexes): Verbal Comprehension, Perceptual Reasoning, Working Memory, Processing Speed
Kaufman Assessment Battery for Children–II (K-ABC-II) (Kaufman & Kaufman, 2004a)	3 y–18 y	7–11 (varies by age range)	25–75 min.	Mental Processing Index, Fluid-Crystallized Index; five composite scales: Sequential Processing, Simultaneous Processing, Learning Ability, Planning Ability, Knowledge

[1] Administration time estimates in publishers manuals may be on the conservative side. In practice, times are quite variable and depend on the examinee's age and full-scale IQ, the examiner's experience, and the setting (see Ryan, Glass, & Brown, 2007).

SOURCE: Roid (2003), Wechsler (2003), Kaufman & Kaufman (2004a).

The *Scholastic Aptitude Test* (now simply called the SAT), which is used to predict high school students' potential for college-level work, is familiar to most undergraduates. It yields verbal and quantitative scores, and its recent revision, the SAT-II, now includes scores for an essay in the English section. The specific content of the SAT is revised continuously. The questions change for each administration, and at any given time, some items are being piloted (and subsequently analyzed) for inclusion on a future test. Although the scoring scale stays the same, norms for the test are calculated on the basis of scores of the thousands of persons taking each particular version of the test.

Other popular aptitude or achievement tests include the *Woodcock-Johnson Cognitive Battery III* and its cousin, the *Woodcock-Johnson Achievement Battery III* (Woodcock, McGrew, & Mather, 2000). These batteries measure general intellectual ability and specific academic achievement in persons from 2 years old to over 90. The *Wide Range Achievement Test* (WRAT-3) is yet another well-known example (Wilkinson, 1993), as are the *Kaufman Test of Educational Achievement* (K-TEA-II) (Kaufman & Kaufman, 1985) and the *Wechsler Individual Achievement Test* (WIAT). Clinicians and (especially) school psychologists use these tests to assess aptitude and achievement, to help identify learning disorder and to develop educational plans for children and adults.

There are numerous other tests measuring achievement and aptitude. The more specific the ability or aptitude tested, the less familiar the test is likely to be. If you have never heard of the *Seashore Measures of Musical Talents* or the *Crawford Small Parts Dexterity Test,* it is probably because you have never had occasion to be tested on these very specialized abilities. Such ability testing is more often done by personnel officers and educational, vocational, and guidance counselors than by clinical psychologists.

Section Summary: The intelligence tests most commonly administered by clinical psychologists are the Stanford-Binet (SB5), the Wechsler Adult Intelligence Scale (WAIS-III), and the Wechsler Intelligence Scale for Children (WISC-IV). Each of these tests yields full-scale IQ scores (corresponding to g in a hierarchical model), composite factor scores (corresponding to midlevel factors), and specific subtests scores (corresponding to specific abilities). A number of other tests are used for assessing general intelligence and for specific aptitudes or levels of achievement. The more commonly used tests have been revised and renormed periodically, and have high levels of reliability and validity.

TESTS OF ATTITUDES, INTERESTS, PREFERENCES, AND VALUES

Clinical psychologists often find it useful to assess a person's attitudes, interests, preferences, and values. For example, before beginning to work with a distressed couple, the clinician may wish to get some idea about each partner's attitudes about marriage or other committed relationships. Similarly, it may be instructive for the clinician to know that the interests of a client who is in severe conflict about entering the medical profession are utterly unlike those of successful physicians. Finally, assessment of attitudes, interests, preferences, and values can encourage clients to engage in their own self-exploration with respect to career decisions (Holland, 1996).

We do not have room to describe all the many tests available, but among those commonly used to assess clients' preferences for various pursuits, occupations, academic subjects, and activities are the *Strong Interest Inventory* (SII) (Hansen & Campbell, 1985), the *Campbell Interest and Skill Survey* (CISS, 2008), of the *Kuder Occupational Interest Survey* (KOIS) (Zytowski, 2007), and the *Self-Directed Search* (SDS) (Holland, 1994).

Tests such as these are widely used by school counselors to help students select college majors and possible occupations. Most of them result in an interest profile that can be compared with composite profiles gathered from members of occupational groups such as biologists, engineers, army officers, carpenters, police, ministers, accountants, salespeople, lawyers, and the like. Originally designed as paper-and-pencil tests, most are available from their publishers online. For a fee, interested persons can take the test and, within minutes, receive a detailed report.

Instruments such as the *Study of Values* (SoV) (Allport, Vernon, & Lindzey, 1970) and the *Rokeach Value Survey* (RVS) are designed to measure values or generalized life orientations. Rokeach (2000) suggested that values are different from attitudes or interests in that values are fewer in number and more central to a person's belief system and psychological functioning. To measure values, the SoV asks the test taker to choose one option in each of 120 pairs of statements representing different values. Results show the relative strength of six basic interests: theoretical ("intellectual"), economic, aesthetic, social, political, and religious. In the RVS, people are asked to rank-order a set of 18 terminal values (e.g., health, social recognition, a comfortable life, a world at peace) and a set of 18 instrumental values (e.g., broad-minded, intellectual, obedient, courageous).

In general, reliability and validity of interest and values instruments is acceptable but not as high as those found with most of the cognitive measures we reviewed earlier. Assessing reliability or validity can be problematic with some of these instruments because they use rankings or forced choices, so when certain items are ranked high, others are necessarily ranked low. Also, test takers often don't have as much confidence in their rankings as they do in more focused items that can be objectively measured (e.g., an item ranked third in one testing might be ranked fifth or sixth 6 months later). Despite these psychometric limitations, the tests have relatively wide usage, perhaps because of their content validity and their ability to stimulate personal and career exploration.

TESTS OF PSYCHOPATHOLOGY AND PERSONALITY

Section Preview: People's attitudes, interests, preferences, and values can be seen as one aspect of their personalities, but the tests designed to measure them were not meant as measures of personality. In this section, we consider prominent examples of psychological tests designed specifically to assess various aspects of personality. Some focus on psychological abnormality; others are designed to measure aspects of normal functioning. We also distinguish between objective personality tests, which present clients with relatively simple, unambiguous items (e.g., true or false), and projective personality tests, which present clients with more ambiguous stimuli or tasks (e.g., inkblots or storytelling). We discuss the uses, strengths, and weaknesses of tests in both categories.

Personality can be defined as the pattern of behavioral and psychological characteristics by which a person can be compared and contrasted with other people. Some clinicians see personality as an organized collection of traits, while others see it in terms of dynamic relationships among intrapsychic forces, recurring patterns of learned behavior, or perceptions of the world. This theory-driven variation in how clinicians think about personality is reflected in a wide range of methods through which they have attempted to assess it. Indeed, more psychological tests are devoted to personality assessment than to any other clinical target.

There are two major types of personality tests: objective and projective. *Objective tests* present relatively clear, specific stimuli such as questions ("Have you ever wanted to run away from home?") or statements ("I am never depressed"), to which the client responds with direct answers, choices, or ratings. Most objective personality tests are of the paper-and-pencil variety and can be scored arithmetically, often by computers, much like the multiple-choice or true–false tests used in many college classes. Some objective tests focus on one aspect of personality, such as anxiety, dependency, or ego strength, while others provide a comprehensive overview of many personality dimensions.

Projective tests ask clients to respond to ambiguous or unstructured stimuli (such as inkblots, drawings, or incomplete sentences). Their responses tend to be complex verbal or graphic productions (e.g., descriptions, stories, drawings). These responses are then scored and interpreted by clinicians, often as a reflection of both conscious and unconscious aspects of personality structure and dynamics.

Objective Tests of Psychopathology

The first objective personality test developed by a psychologist was the *Personal Data Sheet* used during World War I to screen soldiers with psychological problems (Woodworth, 1920). It asked for yes-or-no answers to questions such as "Did you have a happy childhood?" "Does it make you uneasy to cross a bridge?" These items were selected because they reflected problems and symptoms reported at least twice as often by previously diagnosed "neurotics" as by "normals." No item was retained in the test if more than 25% of a normal sample answered it in an unfavorable manner. Item selection procedures such as these were a prelude to later, more sophisticated empirical test construction procedures (Butcher & Keller, 1984).

Minnesota Multiphasic Personality Inventory. Among the hundreds of objective personality measures that have appeared since the Personal Data Sheet, the most influential and widely used is the *Minnesota Multiphasic Personality Inventory* (MMPI). This test was first developed during the late 1930s at the University of Minnesota by Starke Hathaway (a psychologist) and J. C. McKinley (a psychiatrist) as an aid to psychiatric diagnosis of clinical patients. Hathaway and McKinley took about 1,000 items from older personality tests and other sources and converted them into statements to which clients could respond "true," "false," or "cannot say." More than half of these items were then presented to thousands of healthy people as well as to people already diagnosed with psychiatric disorders.

Certain response patterns appeared. When compared to people who had not been diagnosed with any disorder, members of various diagnostic groups showed statistically different responses to many items. For example, a particular group of items tended to be answered in the same way by depressed persons, while another group of items was answered in a particular way by persons diagnosed as schizophrenic. Eight of these item groups, or scales, were identified as being associated with a certain diagnostic category and as discriminating between normal and abnormal individuals. Later, two additional scales were identified as being responded to differently by males and females and by shy, introverted college students. Also included in the MMPI were four *validity scales*. These are groups of items designed to help detect various test-taking attitudes or response distortions. The finished test contained 567 items.

Although widely used (it has even been translated into American Sign Language; Brauer, 1993), the original MMPI eventually became outdated (Dahlstrom, 1992). Accordingly, an extensive revision of the MMPI began in 1982 and was completed in 1989. The revision effort focused on gathering new normative data from randomly selected samples of nondisordered adults and adolescents in seven U.S. states, as well as from several clinical populations. Twenty-six hundred people were included in the restandardization sample. Also, 154 items were evaluated for possible addition to the test. Table 5.8 shows

TABLE 5.8

MMPI-2 Scales and Simulated Items

Clinical Scales

1 or Hs (Hypochondriasis): Thirty-two items derived from patients showing abnormal concern with bodily functions, such as "I have chest pains several times a week" (answered True).

2 or D (Depression): Fifty-seven items derived from patients showing extreme pessimism, feelings of hopelessness, and slowing of thought and action, such as "I usually feel that life is interesting and worthwhile" (answered False).

3 or Hy (Conversion Hysteria): Sixty items from neurotic patients using physical or mental symptoms as a way of unconsciously avoiding difficult conflicts and responsibilities, such as "My heart frequently pounds so hard I can feel it" (answered True).

4 or Pd (Psychopathic Deviate): Fifty items from patients who show a repeated and flagrant disregard for social customs, an emotional shallowness, and an inability to learn from punishing experiences, such as "My activities and interests are often criticized by others" (answered True).

5 or Mf (Masculinity–Femininity): Fifty-six items from patients showing homoeroticism and items differentiating between men and woman, such as "I like to arrange flowers" (answered True, scored for femininity).

6 or Pa (Paranoia): Forty items from patients showing abnormal suspiciousness and delusions of grandeur or persecution, such as "There are evil people trying to influence my mind" (answered True).

7 or Pt (Psychasthenia): Forty-eight items based on neurotic patients showing obsessions, compulsions, abnormal fears, and guilt and indecisiveness, such as "I save nearly everything I buy, even after I have no use for it" (answered True).

8 or Sc (Schizophrenia): Seventy-eight items from patients showing bizarre or unusual thoughts or behavior, who are often withdrawn and experiencing delusions and hallucinations, such as "Things around me do not seem real" and "It makes me uncomfortable to have people close to me" (both answered True).

9 or Ma (Hypomania): Forty-six items from patients characterized by emotional excitement, overactivity, and flight of ideas, such as "At times I feel very 'high' or very 'low' for no apparent reasosn" (answered True).

0 or Si (Social Introversion): Sixty-nine items from persons showing shyness, little interest in people, and insecurity, such as "I have the time of my life at parties" (answered False).

Validity Scales

? (Cannot Say): Number of items left unanswered.

L (Lie): Fifteen items of overly good self-report, such as "I smile at everyone I meet" (answered True).

F (Frequency or Infrequency): Sixty items answered in the scored direction by 10% or less of normals, such as "There is an international plot against me" (answered True).

K (Correction): Thirty items reflecting defensiveness in admitting to problems, such as "I feel bad when others criticize me" (answered False).

VRIN (Variable Response Inconsistency): Ninety-eight items in pairs that would be expected to be answered in the same manner, such as "I have difficulty talking to people" and "I frequently cannot decide what to say to people" (one answered True, one False).

TRIN (True Response Inconsistency): Forty items in pairs that have opposite content, such that true answers to both would reflect inconsistency, such as "I feel tired and unmotivated most of the time" and "I feel energetic and enthusiastic most of the time" (both answered True).

F(b) (Fake Bad): Forty items, similar to the F Scale, designed to identify items that indicate problems but also have low endorsement frequency, such as "Both my legs occasionally become numb for no reason" (answered True).

the validity scales and clinical scales of the revised test, called the MMPI-2 (Butcher, Dahlstrom, Graham, Tellegen, & Kaemmer, 1989).

Among the major new developments contained in the MMPI-2, three are especially important:

1. There are 15 new content scales that allow supplementary assessment of personality factors not previously measurable with the basic clinical scales. These include scales for anxiety, obsessiveness, health concerns, cynicism, family problems, and others.

2. Some new validity scales have been added to supplement the ?, L, F, and K scales.

3. Scoring has been changed to equalize the clinical significance of similar scores on different scales. In the original MMPI, similar scores on different scales signified different levels of disturbance (Tellegen & Ben-Porath, 1992). In addition, the definition of a clinically significant score elevation has been lowered from 70 or higher on the MMPI to 65 or higher on the MMPI-2.

Paper-and-pencil administration of the MMPI-2 takes about 90 minutes for a person with average or above reading skills (the test is aimed at a sixth-grade reading level). Computer administration is usually somewhat faster. Interpretation of the test involves comparing a client's MMPI profile with those of other clients. This can be done *clinically* by recalling previous clients' patterns, or *statistically* by reference to books containing sample profiles and the characteristics of the people who produced them (e.g., Butcher & Williams, 1992; Dahlstrom, Lachar, & Dahlstrom, 1986; Dahlstrom, Welsh, & Dahlstrom, 1972; Graham, 1990). An example of an MMPI profile appears in Figure 5.2.

The most common method of scoring the MMPI uses the 2-code system, which refers to the client's two highest scores on clinical scales. For example, if those scores were on scales 4 and 9, the clinician would use codes 49 and 94. A 49/94 description in a book of sample profiles would likely include information about the person being impulsive, extraverted, and sensation-seeking; showing antisocial tendencies; and having an unstable family and work history. Sometimes information from additional scales can be used to modify the 2-code description. Hundreds of additional experimental scales have been constructed from the MMPI-2, many of which go well beyond the test's original diagnostic purposes.

For clinicians wishing to use the MMPI, there exists "a veritable flood of materials" (Domino & Domino, 2006, p. 177). The numerous interpretive and scoring manuals vary in quality, as do the computer programs designed to administer and generate MMPI-2 reports. Finger and Ones (1999) conducted a meta-analysis of studies comparing computer and standard administrations and found negligible to no differences between scores obtained in each manner. In other words, it appears that the MMPI can be administered by computer without seriously compromising results. Clinical interpretation of scores may be another matter—some manuals are better than others. New clinicians may be wise to stick with more established works for interpreting scores (e.g., Butcher, 1999, 2006; Butcher & Williams, 1992; Graham, 2000).

Shortened versions of the MMPI have also been developed. Called the "Mini-Mult" or "Midi-Mult," these abbreviated editions are less comprehensive and designed for quick classification and screening purposes (Stevens & Reilly, 1980). A shorter form developed

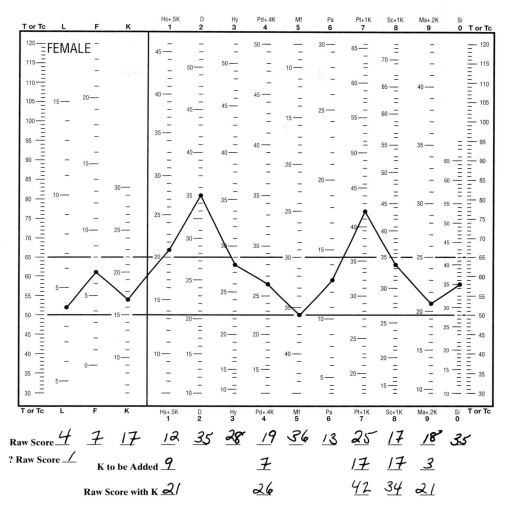

	T or Tc	L	F	K	Hs+.5K 1	D 2	Hy 3	Pd+.4K 4	Mf 5	Pa 6	Pt+1K 7	Sc+1K 8	Ma+.2K 9	Si 0
Raw Score		4	7	17	12	35	28	19	36	13	25	17	18	35
? Raw Score	1													
K to be Added					9			7			17	17	3	
Raw Score with K					21			26			42	34	21	

FIGURE 5.2 An MMPI-2 Profile

(*Source:* Minnesota Multiphasic Personality Inventory-2. Copyright by The Regents of the University of Minnesota 1942–1943 [renewed 1970], 1989. This Profile Form 1989.)

for adolescents, the MMPI-A, consists of 478 items, but it is still long enough to correlate highly with the MMPI and MMPI-2.

According to Walsh and Betz (2001), "There is little question that the Minnesota Multiphasic Personality Inventory (MMPI) is the most useful psychological test available in clinical and counseling settings for assessing the degree and nature of emotional upset" (p. 112). The test has spawned thousands of research reports, more than any other test. It has reasonably strong psychometric properties. For instance, test–retest reliability coefficients for the MMPI and MMPI-2 scales range from 0.60 to 0.90 (Pope, Butcher, & Seelen, 1993).

Researchers continue to investigate the extent to which the MMPI-2 can yield valid results when used with various ethnic and cultural groups. For instance, Chung, Weed, and Han (2006) examined the cross-cultural equivalence of the MMPI-2 in Korean bilinguals living in the United States. When participants took the test in both languages, the test–retest correlations were lower than same-language correlations except in a subsample of those proficient in English. Questions that contained more complicated English sentences or American idioms were especially problematic. Given findings such as these, clinicians should be cautious in generalizing the interpretation of MMPI-2 scores across cultural groups unless test validity with those groups has been studied (see also Butcher, 2004; Pace et al., 2006).

Millon Clinical Multiaxial Inventory (MCMI).   For assessing psychopathology, the main alternative to the MMPI is the Millon Clinical Multiaxial Inventory. At 175 items, it is shorter than the MMPI. The MCMI test was first published in 1982, revised in 1987, and revised again in 1997 (MCMI-III) (Millon, Millon, & Davis, 1997). The MCMI-III yields 28 scales, four of which are designed to assess the test's validity or to modify interpretation. The test is designed to link up with DSM diagnostic criteria, and its scales parallel diagnostic groups in the DSM-IV (e.g., anxiety, somatoform); 10 scales are devoted to personality patterns/disorders (e.g., avoidant, antisocial). Interpretation of the MCMI-III "requires considerable sophistication and knowledge related to psychopathology in general and personality disorders in particular" (Groth-Marnat, 2003, p. 323). As a result, its reliabilities tend to be somewhat lower than those associated with the MMPI. Nevertheless, the test remains one of the more popular in the clinical arsenal.

Tests Measuring Specific Aspects of Psychopathology.   Clinicians have also developed tests that assess more specific clinical targets. A prominent example is the *Beck Depression Inventory,* now in its second edition, the *BDI-II* (Beck, Steer, & Brown, 1996). At 21 items, the Beck is relatively easy to administer. Clients rate on a 0-to-3 scale the degree to which each item describes them. The test yields scores that are grouped from no or minimal depression (13 and below) to severe depression (29 and above). The factor structure of this test is reasonably clear, though some studies suggest it measures one factor (a general expression of depression), while others have found two (cognitive and somatic expressions of depression) (Ward, 2006). This test has wide clinical and research appeal, evidenced by the fact that over 1,000 research studies have used it (Groth-Marnat, 2003).

Other tests that focus on specific expressions of psychopathology include the *Fear Survey Schedule* (FSS). It is simply a list of objects, persons, and situations that the client rates in terms of fearsomeness. Different versions of this test contain from 50 to 122 items and use 1-to-5 or 1-to-7 scales for the fear ratings (e.g., Geer, 1965; Lawlis, 1971; Wolpe & Lang, 1969). The FSS-III has been translated into several languages (Abdel, 1994; Johnsen & Hugdahl, 1990) and there are special written and illustrated versions available for use with both cognitively unimpaired and retarded children (Fleisig, 1993; Gullone & King, 1992; Ramirez & Kratchowill, 1990). Others in this category include the *State-Trait*

Anxiety Inventory (Spielberger, Gorsuch, Lushene, Vagg, & Jacobs, 1983), the *Social Avoidance and Distress Scale* (Watson & Friend, 1969), the *Social Phobia and Anxiety Inventory* (SPAI) (Turner, Beidel, Dancu, & Stanley, 1989), the *PTSD Symptom Scale Self-Report* (PSS-SR) (Foa, Riggs, Dancu, & Rothbaum, 1993), and the *Bulimia Test-Revised* (BULIT-R) (Thelen, Farmer, Wonderlich, & Smith, 1991).

Objective Tests of Personality

Clinical psychologists are especially interested in assessing psychopathology, but they sometimes assess normal variations in personality, too. They may do so as part of clinical research and also to get a better idea of a client's strengths and weaknesses.

There are numerous tests designed to measure the dimensions of normal personality, each based on various theories of personality and/or on factor analytic research on personality. One of the first personality tests based on factor analytic research was the *Eysenck Personality Questionnaire* (Eysenck & Eysenck, 1975), which measured three basic personality factors: Psychoticism, Introversion–Extraversion, and Emotionality–Stability. Another was Tellegen's (1982) *Multidimensional Personality Questionnaire* (MPQ), which also measured three factors: Positive Emotionality, Negative Emotionality, and Constraint. Other, even broader, tests of normal personality used by clinicians are described in the next sections.

California Psychological Inventory (CPI). A prominent example of a broad-range, empirically constructed, objective personality test is the California Psychological Inventory. It was introduced in 1957 and revised in 1987 with updated content and reworded items (Gough, 1987). In contrast to the MMPI, MCMI, and other personality tests already described, the CPI was developed specifically for assessing personality in the "normal" population. About half of its 462 true–false items come from the MMPI, but CPI items are grouped into more diverse and positively oriented scales, including sociability, self-acceptance, responsibility, dominance, self-control, and others. There are also three validity scales that serve essentially the same purpose as those on the MMPI. The CPI's strengths include the representativeness of its standardization sample (13,000 males and females from all socioeconomic categories and all parts of the United States) and its relatively high reliability. The test has been used to predict delinquency, parole outcome, academic grades, and the likelihood of dropping out of high school (Anastasi & Urbina, 1997). Computerized scoring and interpretation services are available.

Sixteen Personality Factors Questionnaire (16PF). Raymond B. Cattell used both theory and factor analysis to identify 16 basic factors in personality, and created an instrument to measure them (Cattell, Eber, & Tatsuoka, 1970, 1992). For each of the 187 items on the 16PF, test takers select from among three choices (for example, "I would prefer to visit: a museum, a national park, or an art gallery"). Results reveal a person's score on each of the 16 factors, which include dimensions such as intelligence, ego strength, conservative–radical, and schizothymia–affectothymia (Cattell's terms for reserved-outgoing). With test–retest reliabilities near the 0.8 range and acceptable construct validity (Cattell, Eber, & Tatsuoka, 1970), the 16PF continues to be widely used.

Myers-Briggs Type Indicator (MBTI).   Another objective personality inventory is the *Myers-Briggs Type Indicator* (MBTI) (Myers & Briggs, 1943), an analytically derived test based on Jung's psychoanalytic personality-type classification system. The test's 126 forced-choice items are used to sort persons into 16 types based on combinations of four scales: Extraversion/Introversion (E or I), Sensation/Intuition (S or N), Thinking/Feeling (T or F), and Judging/Perceiving (J or P). Although the test results provide information about the strength of each dimension, the strength factor is sometimes overlooked in the interpretation and persons are simply labeled according to their four dominant dimensions (for example, ENTJ). The MBTI is an easily administered and scored test with acceptable split-half and test–retest reliabilities. Though the test has seen widespread use and correlates with other tests of personality and career interests (Myers & McCaulley, 1985), there are significant concerns about the validity of the MBTI (e.g., Domino & Domino, 2006).

NEO Personality Inventory–Revised (NEO-PI-R).   Another extremely popular personality test has developed out of the personality research program of Costa and McCrea (1980, 1985, 1992a). In its current revision, the NEO-PI-R, 243 items are used to measure the "big five" dimensions as well as six specific facets of each (Costa & McCrae, 1992a). The five dimensions include (1) *neuroticism* (a tendency to feel anxious, angry, and depressed in many situations), (2) *extraversion* (a tendency to be assertive, active, and to prefer to be with other people), (3) *openness* (a quality indicating active imagination, curiosity, and receptiveness to many experiences), (4) *agreeableness* (an orientation toward positive, sympathetic, helpful interactions with others), and (5) *conscientiousness* (a tendency to be reliable and persistent in pursuing goals).

The NEO-PI-R was developed as a comprehensive measure of nondisordered adult personality, but investigators have also used it to diagnose psychological disorders, predict progress in psychotherapy, and select optimal forms of treatment for some clients (Costa & McCrae, 1992b). These latter uses have been challenged by clinicians who are not convinced that instruments like the NEO-PI-R add clinically useful information beyond that provided by tests like the MMPI-2 (Ben-Porath & Waller, 1992). The test has good internal consistency and test–retest reliability (though not uniformly good for all scales) (McRea & Costa, 1987). It continues to be an extensively researched test whose clinical applications are not yet well developed.

Projective Personality Tests

Projective assessment goes back to the 1400s, when Leonardo da Vinci is said to have selected his pupils partly on the basis of the creativity they displayed while attempting to find shapes and patterns in ambiguous forms (Piotrowski, 1972). In the late 1800s, Binet adapted a parlor game called Blotto to assess "passive imagination" by asking children to tell what they saw in inkblots (Exner, 1976). Sir Frances Galton constructed a word-association test in 1879, and Carl Jung was using a similar test for clinical assessment by 1910. These informal projective techniques evolved into projective tests when their content was standardized such that each client was exposed to the same stimuli in the same way.

Projective tests in use today grew out of the psychodynamic approach to clinical psychology. Broadening Freud's notion that people "project," or attribute to others, the unacceptable aspects of their own personality, it was suggested that there is a "tendency of people to be influenced in the cognitive mediation of perceptual inputs by their needs, interests, and overall psychological organization" (Frank, 1939, quoted in Exner, 1976, p. 61). In other words, the *projective hypothesis* states that each individual's personality will determine, to a significant degree, how he or she interprets and responds to ambiguous stimuli. Tests that encourage clients to display this tendency are called *projective methods* (Frank, 1939). We have space here to consider only a few of the most prominent projective personality tests, but much more detailed coverage of such tests is available in standard references presented at the beginning of this chapter.

Rorschach Inkblot Test. One of the most widely known and frequently employed projective tests of personality is the *Rorschach Inkblot Test,* a set of 10 colored and black-and-white inkblots created by Swiss psychiatrist Hermann Rorschach between 1911 and 1921. When the test's manual (Rorschach, 1921) was published, only a few copies were printed. European test experts such as William Stern "denounced it as faulty, arbitrary, artificial, and incapable . . . of understanding human personality" (Reisman, 1976).

David Levy, an American psychiatrist studying in Switzerland in 1921, brought a copy of the test back to the United States and, in 1927, instructed a psychology trainee named Samuel Beck in its use. Beck published the first North American report involving the Rorschach, and in 1937, he provided a standardized procedure for administering and scoring the test. Another scoring manual appeared that same year (Klopfer & Kelley, 1937), and the Rorschach was on its way to popularity among North American psychologists who, until then, had no global test of personality available to them.

A number of variants on the Rorschach appeared later, the most notable of which is the *Holtzman Inkblot Test* (Holtzman, Thorpe, Swartz, & Herron, 1961), but none rivaled the popularity of the Rorschach. It became the most commonly used test among clinical psychologists from the 1930s through the 1960s. One prominent clinician noted that "it is hard to conceive of anyone in the field of clinical psychology reaching the postdoctoral level without being thoroughly well-versed in the Rorschach" (Harrower, 1965, p. 398). This is no longer the case. Relative to other tests such as the Wechsler or the MMPI, the Rorschach's popularity declined, but its use appears to have leveled off in the last several years (see Table 5.3).

The test itself is simple. The client is shown 10 cards, one at a time. Each card contains an inkblot similar to that shown in Figure 5.3, and the client is asked what she or he sees or what the blot could be. The tester records all responses verbatim and takes notes about response times, how the card was held (e.g., upside down, sideways) as responses occurred, noticeable emotional reactions, and other behaviors. After the last card is presented, the tester goes back through them and conducts an *inquiry* or systematic questioning of the client about the characteristics of each blot that prompted the responses.

The client's record of responses, or *protocol,* is later scored and interpreted using a special procedure. Scoring can be complex, but most systems code, at a minimum, the characteristics shown in Table 5.9. For instance, assume that a client responded to Figure 5.3 by saying, "It looks like a bat," and during subsequent inquiry, noted that "I saw the whole

FIGURE 5.3   Inkblot Similar to Those Used in the Rorschach

(*Source:* From Norman D. Sundberg, *Assessment of Persons,* Copyright 1977, p. 207.
Reprinted by permission of Prentice-Hall, Inc., Englewood Cliffs, New Jersey.)

blot as a bat because it is black and is just sort of bat shaped." Using one of the available scoring systems, these responses would probably be coded as WFC9 + AP, where W indicates that the whole blot was used (location); F means that the blot's form (F) was the main determinant of the response; and C9 means that achromatic color was also involved. The + shows that the form described corresponded well to the actual form of

TABLE 5.9	
Scoring Categories for the Rorschach Inkblot Technique	
Scoring Category	**Category Refers to**
Location	the area of the blot to which the client responds: the whole blot, a common detail, an unusual detail, white space, or some combination of these are location responses.
Determinants	the characteristic of the blot that influenced a response; they include form, color, shading, and "movement." While there is no movement in the blot itself, the respondent's perception of the blot as a moving object is scored in this category.
Content	subject matter perceived in the blot; content might include human figures, parts of human figures, animal figures, animal details, anatomical features, inanimate objects, art, clothing, clouds, blood, X-rays, sexual objects, and symbols.
Popularity	how often any particular response has been made by previous respondents.
Form Quality	the degree to which the specific content reported fits the blot.

the blot; A means that there was animal content in the response; and P indicates that bat is a popular response to this particular card.

That responses could be coded somewhat differently by different scoring systems and that each system tends to be used somewhat differently by individual clinicians led to some confusion (it also hurt interrater reliability, as you might imagine). This confusion led John Exner (1974, 1993, 2003; Exner & Erdberg, 2005) to propose what he called a *Comprehensive System* for scoring and interpreting the Rorschach. Using the Comprehensive System, the clinician records the overall number of responses (called *productivity*), categorizes the responses, records the frequency of responses in certain categories, and looks for recurring patterns of responses across cards. For example, because most people tend to use form more often than color in determining their responses, a high proportion of color-dominated determinants may be taken as evidence of weak emotional control. Numerous other response percentages, ratios, and relationships between and among categories are seen as significant (Exner, 2003, 2005). The clinician combines these various measures into a description of the client's psychodynamic functioning.

Thematic Apperception Test.   The *Thematic Apperception Test* (TAT) consists of 30 drawings of people, objects, and landscapes (see Figure 5.4). In most clinical applications, about 10 of these cards (one of them blank) are administered; the subset chosen is determined by the client's age and sex and by the clinician's interests. A separate set of cards depicting African Americans is also available. The examiner shows each picture and asks the client to make up a story about it, including what led up to the scene, what is now happening, and what is going to happen. The client is encouraged to say what the people in the drawings are thinking and feeling. For the blank card, the respondent is asked to imagine a drawing, describe it, and then construct a story about it. The TAT was designed in 1935 by Christiana D. Morgan and Henry Murray at the Harvard Psychological Clinic (Murray, 1938, 1943). It was based on the projective hypothesis and the assumption that, in telling a story, the client's needs and conflicts will be reflected in one of the story's characters (Lindzey, 1952).

Analysis of the TAT can focus on both the *content* and the *structure* of TAT stories. Content refers to what clients describe: the people, the feelings, the events, the outcomes. Structure refers to how clients tell their stories: their logic, organization, and use of language, the appearance of speech dysfluencies, the misunderstanding of instructions or stimuli in the drawings, and obvious emotional arousal. As with the Rorschach, however, there is more than one way to score and interpret clients' TAT responses. Those that use elaborate quantitative procedures for scoring TAT stories helped create TAT response norms to which clinicians can compare their clients' responses (Vane, 1981). Others make little use of formal scoring procedures, preferring instead to perform primarily qualitative analyses on the themes in the client's storytelling (Henry, 1956), while still others combine preliminary quantitative analysis with more subjective interpretation (Bellak, 1986; Ronan, Colavito, & Hammontree, 1993).

Most clinicians seem to prefer TAT scoring systems that are relatively unstructured. This tendency is illustrated by a TAT user's working notes about the following story told

FIGURE 5.4 Drawing of the Type Included in the TAT

(*Source:* Reprinted by permission of the publisher from Henry A. Murray, *Thematic Apperception Test,* Plate 12F, Cambridge, MA: Harvard University Press, copyright 1943 by the president and fellows of Harvard College. Copyright 1971 by Henry A. Murray.)

by a 25-year-old single man in response to a TAT card showing a young boy looking at a violin resting on a table in front of him:

> This child is sick in bed. He has been given sheet music to study, but instead of the music, he has come across a novel that interests him more than the music. It is probably an adventure story. He evidently does not fear the chance that his parents will find him thusly occupied as he seems quite at ease. He seems to be quite a studious type and perhaps regrets missing

school, but he seems quite occupied with the adventure in the story. Adventure has something to do with ocean or water. He is not too happy, though not too sad. His eyes are somewhat blank—coincidence of reading a book without any eyes or knowing what is in the book without reading it. He disregards the music and falls asleep reading the book.

Here are some of the clinician's interpretations of this response to the card:

> On the basis of this story alone, I feel certain that there is a schizophrenic process present, even though not necessarily a pure schizophrenia. Slightly pretentious, facade tone, helped along with basic fact of perverse refusal to acknowledge presence of violin, strongly suggests that he *does* see violin but consciously thinks that he's being "clever" or "original," or is out-tricking the examiner (whom he might see as trying to trick him) by ignoring it or seeing it as a book. That he is aware of it on some level is suggested by the fact that the basic theme, *p* Parental Imposed Task → *n* Auto Resis, passive Aggression, comes through. Consistent also is statement at the end: he *disregards* the music. Not a psychopath trying to act smart—too schizzy.
>
>   *Sick in bed as a child* may be an autobiographical theme. He's almost certainly "sick" (that is, psychotic) now, and so that may be enough explanation for it. But most psychotics don't [see the card this way]; therefore it becomes plausible that he may have had long illnesses as a child, cutting him off from other kids, and → to fantasy escape—dreams of travel and adventure. Sentence 3 may also describe his overt behavior: nonchalant, seemingly "at ease," really frightened underneath. Above are almost all hypotheses, to be confirmed or excluded by later stories. *Strong passivity* throughout—especially in outcome. Also suggestion of *flight* and *avoidance* of very passive sort—drastic enough to include denial of threatening aspects of reality. Nothing holds his interest long—not even adventure novel. Hero soon withdraws into his own fantasy, to conviction of knowing what's in book without reading it even though "took a chance" to read it, and finally withdraws into sleep. (Holt, 1978, pp. 166–167)

Other projective tests similar to the TAT include the *Rosenzweig Picture-Frustration Study* (Rosenzweig, 1949, 1977), which presents 24 cartoons showing one person frustrating another in some way (e.g., "I'm not going to invite you to my party"). The client's task is to say what the frustrated person's response would be. The cards of the *Children's Apperception Test* (CAT) (Bellak, 1992) depict animal characters rather than human beings; those of the *Roberts Apperception Test for Children* (RATC) (McArthur & Roberts, 1982) show children interacting with adults and other children.

Incomplete Sentence Tests. As their name implies, these tests ask clients to finish incomplete sentences. The projective assumption is that how the client does so reflects important personality characteristics. Originally used as a measure of intellect in the 19th century (Reisman, 1976), incomplete sentences began to be widely employed as projective stimuli in the 1940s; they remain among the more frequently used of all projective tests (Watkins, Campbell, Nieberding, & Hallmark, 1995).

The most popular version of sentence completion tests is the *Rotter Incomplete Sentences Blank* (Rotter & Rafferty, 1950). It contains 40 sentence stems such as "I like ___," "My father ___," and "I secretly ___." The client's response to each stem is compared to norms provided in the test manual and is then rated on a 7-point scale of adjustment–maladjustment based on how much the response deviates from those norms. Finally, ratings for all the sentences are summed to provide an overall adjustment score. These relatively objective scoring procedures are primarily associated with Rotter's test and a few other research-oriented sentence-completion instruments aimed at assessing specific aspects of personality (Lanyon & Lanyon, 1980).

Projective Drawings.
Other projective tests whose names describe their nature include the *Draw-a-Person* (DAP) test (Machover, 1949) and the *House-Tree-Person* (HTP) test (Buck, 1948). The client's drawings serve as a basis for the clinician's inferences about various aspects of the client's personality and also as a basis for discussion during an interview. Interpretive inferences are guided by projective assumptions that the inclusion, exclusion, and characteristics of each body part, along with the placement, symmetry, organization, size, and other features of the drawing, are indicative of the client's self-image, conflicts, and perceptions of the world (Machover, 1949).

Bender-Gestalt Test.
The *Bender Visual Motor Gestalt Test*, a figure-copying test designed to measure certain aspects of mental ability, particularly neuropsychological functioning, has remained one of the most popular psychological tests (Domino & Domino, 2006). Clients are shown geometric shapes on nine cards and asked to draw the shapes as accurately as possible. When used with children, the test is considered a measure of visual-motor development. Some clinicians also use the test as a projective personality measure, assuming that errors and distortions in the copied figures are indicators of a client's personality. Psychometric evidence supports the use of the Bender-Gestalt Test for rough neuropsychological screening and for visual-motor development, but less so for personality assessment (Domino & Domino, 2006).

Reliability and Validity of Projective Tests.
The Rorschach and other projective tests have generated considerable controversy. From the beginning, skeptics decried these tests for their weak psychometric properties and dependence on psychodynamic personality theory. Advocates championed them as instruments that can yield rich and detailed information about clients' personalities (Gabbard, 2005). How do they actually fare psychometrically?

When test–retest and interrater reliabilities have been calculated for Rorschach scores, results have varied considerably. For instance, Sultan, Andronkiof, Reveillere, and Lemmel (2006) found interrater reliabilities for some Rorschach variables "in the excellent range," but test–retest stability for variables commonly studied was "below expectations (median $r = 0.53$)" (p. 330). Using the Comprehensive System to score the Rorschach, advocates point to interrater reliability coefficients that average above 0.80 (Bornstein, Hill, Roginson, Cabrese, & Bowers, 1996; Exner, 2003; Exner & Erdberg, 2005; Parker, Hanson, & Hunsley, 1988). Indeed, Exner sought to use in the Comprehensive System only scores that had reliabilities of 0.85 or better. Such figures are comparable to reliabilities for the WAIS and MMPI. However, after reviewing meta-analytic evidence, Garb, Florio, and Grove (1998) concluded that the Rorschach was inferior to the MMPI in its psychometric support. Similarly, Spangler (1992) found certain scores on the TAT reliable, but Rossini and Moretti (1997) argue that the cumulative evidence does not support the test.

In short, the evidence for the reliability of projective techniques is mixed (Domino & Domino, 2006; Groth-Marnat, 2003; Hunsley & Mash, 2007).

Concerns about the validity of projective tests have focused on what the tests actually measure and what can be done with those measurements. For many years, clinicians used the Rorschach to help them make DSM diagnoses, but with the exception of diagnoses for schizophrenia, bipolar disorder, and one or two of the personality disorders, diagnoses based on the Rorschach have made a poor showing. Even clinicians with more training and expertise in projective testing are unable to make Rorschach-based diagnoses with acceptable levels of validity (Wood, Lilienfeld, Garb, & Nezworski, 2000). Empirical support has also failed to materialize for other traditional uses of projective tests, such as to predict dangerousness, predict response to treatment, or detect child sexual abuse.

Advocates of projective tests have backed away from claims that projective tests are valuable for predictive or diagnostic purposes. Weiner (2000), for instance, says that the Rorschach is an instrument designed to measure personality dynamics and that it makes little sense to use the test to classify someone according to a diagnostic system that changes from one revision to the next. There is similar ambiguity about what the TAT actually measures. It has been variously characterized as measuring drives, emotions, sentiments, complexes, conflicts, motivations, cognitions, emotions, and schemas (see Groth-Marnat, 2003; Murray, 1938, 1943; Teglasi, 2001).

Although projective tests have fared poorly in empirical studies as a rule, the scales derived from them are not uniformly inferior. One large-scale study shows that comparisons of validity coefficients for the Rorschach and TAT are not *consistently* lower than for other personality tests (Meyer et al., 2001). In their meta-analysis of projective techniques, Lilienfeld, Wood, and Garb (2000) identified a few indices that suggest validity (e.g., Thought Disorder Index from the Rorschach, the Overall Quality measure for projective drawings). Unfortunately, too few of the scales and indices from projective tests have such support. Hunsley and Mash argue that, taken as a whole, the use of the Rorschach, TAT, and projective drawings appears to have "outstripped its empirical evidence" (2007, p. 31).

Why don't clinicians abandon tests such as the DAP and the TAT, whose validity appears weakest (Boyle, 1995; Smith & Dumont, 1995)? Part of the answer is that many clinicians pay more attention to data that supports these tests than to damaging evidence about their validity. In this sense, the mixed data on projective techniques may be like a projective test itself: Clinicians see in them what they want to see. Indeed, some clinicians may view negative research findings about a test as irrelevant to that test's clinical value (Masling, 1992). One observer put it this way: "Published indexes of validity are but rough guides, for the psychologist must reach his own judgments of clinical validity and meaningfulness in each particular case" (Tallent, 1976, p. 14).

Indeed, certain clinicians are, for reasons not clearly understood, able to draw remarkably accurate inferences from test data. Almost every practitioner knows of at least one MMPI or Rorschach "ace" whose reputation shores up general confidence in particular tests. Most clinical psychologists are themselves reinforced for using even the least scientifically supported tests by the fact that, now and then, they make their own insightful inferences on the basis of test data. Clinicians remain loyal to projective tests, particularly because they believe that, regardless of what research results show, these measures offer special information about clients (Norcross, Koocher, & Garofalo, 2006). They may also find the tests useful for building rapport with clients (especially children) and for confirming what they might already suspect about a client on the basis of other assessment data.

Although projective instruments have remained among the most popular tests used by practicing clinicians, the Division of Clinical Psychology of the American Psychological Association recently excluded courses in the Rorschach from its recommendations for a model curriculum in assessment. Apparently, advocates of projective tests have not shown that these tests add sufficient reliable, valid, and clinically useful information to justify the time it takes to learn the often complicated scoring and interpretive systems.

Section Summary: Among tests of personality and psychopathology, the Minnesota Multiphasic Personality Inventory–2 is the most commonly used. It yields a client profile on a number of scales, revealing which ones, if any, are in the abnormal range. The Millon Clinical Multiphasic Inventory–II is a somewhat briefer alternative to the MMPI. A number of other tests attempt to measure specific problems; the Beck Depression Inventory is a common example. Several tests provide broader descriptions of normal personality traits. Among them are the California Personality Inventory and the NEO-PI-R. Projective tests such as the Rorschach and the Thematic Apperception Test are still widely used, though they are controversial. Advocates point to the rich and varied information available from such tests, while critics point to the tests' relatively weaker psychometric properties.

THE CURRENT STATUS OF PSYCHOLOGICAL TESTING

Section Preview: Here we take a broader look at psychological testing. First, in response to the well-known complaints about psychological tests, we discuss a study comparing the validity of psychological tests to that of medical tests. Next we discuss how the testing enterprise has developed, and we suggest near-term trends in psychological testing. Prominent among these is the need to focus more on how testing can be used to inform treatment selection and treatment evaluation.

Clinical psychologists are often the toughest critics of psychological tests. Even when a particular test meets acceptable psychometric standards, clinical psychologists are often the first to point out a test's shortcomings. The public, too, has learned to be critical of psychological and educational tests. By the time they have reached college, most students know that tests can be biased and that standardized tests often do a poor job of predicting their intended targets.

Of course, one beneficial effect of focusing attention on the shortcomings of tests has been to stimulate efforts to improve them (Glaser & Bond, 1981). As a result, we have seen ever more careful theorizing about the nature and structure of intelligence, mental abilities, attitudes, and personality. This has led in turn to broader conceptualizations of the construct validity of psychological tests. But testing remains controversial because, even given improvements, every test fails to some degree—none are perfect. But is perfect measurement the standard against which psychological tests should be judged? What makes a test "good enough" to justify its continued use?

The Validity of Psychological Testing Versus Medical Testing

Greg Meyer and his colleagues provided an interesting answer to these questions by considering the validity of psychological tests in comparison to the validity of medical tests (Meyer et al., 2001). Most people, psychologists included, have generally assumed that when it comes to accuracy, psychological tests probably lag well behind medical tests. Yet Meyer and his colleagues found otherwise. Their study was commissioned by the Psychological Assessment Work Group (PAWG), a group formed by the American Psychological Association's Board of Professional Affairs in 1996. Combining data from more than 125 meta-analyses examining test validity, they found that over a wide range of assessment procedures, the validity of psychological testing is indistinguishable from that of medical testing. Practitioners in both disciplines use tests whose results range from being basically uninformative for identifying a criterion to those that are highly informative (see Figure 5.5).

Obviously there is room for improvement in the validity of assessment instruments in both fields, but if the standard by which we judge the adequacy of psychological tests is the validity of medical tests, psychological tests fare reasonably well.

Clinical Utility and Evidence-Based Assessment

In the early years of clinical psychology, practitioners used tests mainly to make diagnostic classifications and to select persons for occupations or positions in the military. When treatment became a common application of clinical psychology after World War II, many tests had already been developed, and clinicians used them in much the same way as they always had. In effect, testing and psychotherapy developed on parallel, but separate, paths. Consequently, many authors have noted that "surprisingly little attention has been paid to the treatment utility of commonly used psychological instruments and methods" (Hunsley & Mash, 2007, p. 33). Few tests were developed specifically for making treatment decisions or for measuring treatment results.

Treatment utility (sometimes referred to more broadly as *clinical utility*) refers to the extent to which tests can be used to select specific treatments or to measure treatment outcomes. In an interesting study of treatment utility, Lima and colleagues (2005) asked numerous clients to take the MMPI prior to treatment. Half of the treating clinicians were informed about their clients' MMPI results, the other half were not. The researchers found no difference in treatment planning between the two groups of clinicians. Neither were there differences in the improvement ratings of clients or in the frequency of premature treatment terminations. Apparently, MMPI results had no effect on how therapists planned or conducted psychotherapy. Hunsley and Mash (2007) note that studies such as this one should alert us to the fact that the treatment utility of tests should be empirically assessed, not simply assumed.

Accordingly, they and others argue for testing that more clearly points to specific treatments. The best strategy for doing so may be the reverse of how testing and

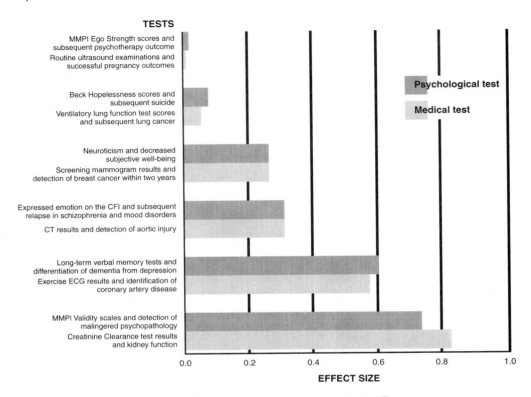

FIGURE 5.5 Sample Effect Sizes for Psychological and Medical Tests

(*Source:* Psychological Testing and Psychological Assessment, *American Psychologist,* February 2001, pp. 136–143, Table 2.)

psychotherapy developed historically. Rather than having tests already developed and adapted to treatment, researchers should identify the most important treatment variables and *then* develop tests specifically to measure those variables.

A few such tests have been developed. The *Outcome Questionnaire-45* (OQ-45) and the *Behavior and Symptom Identification Scale* (BASIS-32) are designed to measure treatment outcomes, and both have been shown to be sensitive to client changes over relatively short time periods. Both have also demonstrated convergent, divergent, and concurrent validity (Doerfler, Addis, & Moran, 2002; Ellsworth, Lambert, & Johnson, 2006). These instruments represent attempts to tie testing directly to treatment outcomes. They can also provide therapists with objective feedback about clients' progress.

THE FUTURE OF PSYCHOLOGICAL TESTING

The importance of psychological testing has waxed and waned. Tests continue to evolve. Here we offer (admittedly impressionistic) predictions about testing in the near future.

1. The tests that have survived decades of scrutiny (see Table 5.3) will continue to be used. Psychologists will continue to use the Wechsler scales, the Binet scales, and the MMPI. However, the "old standby" tests will not simply stand by; under continued empirical scrutiny and changes in the population, these tests will undergo periodic revisions, including renorming.

2. Tests that show unacceptably low levels of reliability, validity, and utility will see diminished use. Projective tests such as the Rorschach (whose materials have not evolved but whose scoring systems have) may never be entirely discredited because empirical evidence supports some scores derived from them and many clinicians continue to express confidence in these instruments. Slowly, however, these tests will be replaced.

3. Testing will continue to expand to include more cross-ethnic and international applications. As research yields information about administration and scoring modifications necessary for different cultural groups, more foreign-language versions of tests will be developed.

4. Computers will play an increasingly important role in assessment. This is a continuation of a trend toward computerizing many paper-and-pencil tests for easier administration and faster, more sophisticated scoring. But beyond that, the increased visual presentation capacities and physiological recording capacities of computers promise to make testing much more dynamic and realistic.

5. Testing designed to aid in treatment planning and treatment outcome measurement will flourish. In an age of accountability, when objective demonstrations of treatment outcomes are critical, such tests will become increasingly important and more of them will be developed.

Section Summary: Although psychological testing is often criticized, it is, in general, no less valid than testing in other areas of health care. Because testing developed largely independently from (and earlier than) psychotherapy, testing often does not inform treatment as much as it should. In the future, this shortcoming will likely be addressed, as will cross-cultural testing and quality issues.

CHAPTER SUMMARY

There are thousands of psychological tests available for use, and more are being developed all the time. Tests are developed using analytic (theoretical) and empirical procedures, often both. An empirical approach is needed to develop test norms, without which test score interpretation is difficult. Norms typically come from a large, representative standardization sample. Even with a representative sample, test developers and clinicians must be cautious to avoid bias that could occur if tests do not "fit" for persons from different backgrounds. Standards published by the APA and the federal government are designed to assure that tests are used with due regard for scientific principles and the rights and welfare of clients.

Tests commonly used by clinical researchers and practitioners can be categorized by what they measure: cognitive/intellectual abilities, interests/values, and personality/psychopathology.

Tests can also be categorized by how they measure. Those that constrain responses to simpler, unambiguous, and easily scored responses (e.g., true or false) are called objective tests. Those that allow complex verbal or graphic responses to ambiguous stimuli (e.g., an inkblot) are called projective tests.

Prominent objective tests of intellectual functioning (whose results are usually expressed as IQ scores) include the Stanford-Binet 5 and the Wechsler scales (e.g., WAIS-III, WISC-IV). The SAT and the Wide Range Achievement Test (WRAT) exemplify some of the general ability tests in use today. Attitudes, interests, preferences, and values are typically measured through tests such as the Strong Interest Inventory, the Self-Directed Search, the Study of Values, and the Rokeach Values Survey.

The most widely used test of personality/psychopathology in clinical settings is the Minnesota Multiphasic Personality Inventory (MMPI-2). The Millon Clinical Multiphasic Inventory (MCMI-II) is also commonly used in clinical settings. There are also many tests designed to measure specific areas of difficulty rather than personality broadly conceived. The Beck Depression Inventory (BDI) is a prominent example. Several tests are designed to measure normal personality: the California Psychological Inventory (CPI), the Personality Research Form (PRF), the Sixteen Personality Factor Questionnaire (16PF), and the NEO Personality Inventory (NEO-PI-R) are examples.

The Rorschach, the Thematic Apperception Test (TAT), sentence-completion tests, and the Draw-a-Person (DAP) test are projective instruments designed to measure aspects of personality and psychopathology. Once the most popular tests used by clinicians, they are used less often now because of concerns about their psychometric properties.

Today, the reliabilities and validities of the most commonly used objective tests are high for tests of intellectual functioning and adequate or better for most others. Relative to other instruments, the overall validity of projective personality tests remains marginal. The testing enterprise continues because tests can be useful and because clinical traditions and societal demands make it difficult to abandon this activity. At present, the overall validity of psychological tests is comparable to the overall validity of tests in other areas of health care, but there is wide variation in each field. With time, those tests that do a poorer job should be replaced, and tests that more clearly translate into treatment planning and evaluation will be more common.

STUDY QUESTIONS

1. How are psychological tests similar to, and different from, other forms of assessment?
2. What are standardization samples and test norms?
3. What are the main categories of tests used by clinical psychologists?
4. How are tests constructed using analytic and empirical procedures?
5. How can test developers determine if their test is biased against specific ethnic or cultural groups?
6. What ethical standards and guidelines should clinicians follow in using tests?
7. Which specific tests are most commonly used by clinical psychologists?
8. What are general, specific, and hierarchical models of intelligence?

9. What do intelligence tests used by clinical psychologists actually measure?

10. What is the Stanford-Binet 5, and what scores are derived from it?

11. What are the Wechsler scales, and what scores are derived from them?

12. What other tests of intelligence, achievement, and aptitude do clinicians commonly use?

13. What are the differences between objective and projective personality tests?

14. What is the Minnesota Multiphasic Personality Inventory, and what measures are derived from it?

15. What other tests do clinicians use to measure psychopathology or emotional distress?

16. What tests are commonly used to measure normal personality?

17. How are the Rorschach and the Thematic Apperception Test constructed and administered?

18. Why are projective tests controversial?

19. How do the validities of psychological tests compare with the validities of tests used in other areas of health care?

20. What do clinical utility and treatment utility mean, and why are they significant for testing?

WEB SITES

- APA Division 5: Evaluation, Measurement, and Statistics: http://www.apa.org/about/division/div5.html

- Buros Institute of Mental Measurements, publisher of the Mental Measurements Yearbook: http://www.unl.edu/buros/

- Searchable database of tests from Buros Institute of Mental Measurements: http://buros.unl.edu/buros/jsp/search.jsp

- Web site for the Stanford-Binet Intelligence Scales (SB5), fifth edition: http://www.riverpub.com/products/sb5/

- College Board, publishers of the SAT and other tests: http://www.collegeboard.com/testing/

- Web site for the MMPI-2: http://www.pearsonassessments.com/tests/mmpi_2.htm

CHAPTER 6

Basic Features of Clinical Interventions

Chapter Preview: In this chapter, we describe features common to most clinical interventions, focusing primarily on psychotherapy. We begin by examining what psychotherapy is and contrasting its characteristics with those portrayed in popular media. We describe what research tells us about clients and therapists and which of their characteristics influence therapy outcomes. Next, we examine the goals and basic processes involved in clinical interventions, as well as the professional and ethical codes that help guide practitioners in conducting treatment. Finally, we consider certain practical aspects of treatment such as fees, treatment duration, record keeping, treatment planning, and termination.

OVERVIEW OF CLINICAL INTERVENTIONS

Section Preview: Here we begin to define psychotherapy, first by way of a formal definition and then by way of popular portrayals, which are usually less than accurate. We reduce the hundreds of psychotherapy approaches to a handful based on shared assumptions and practices.

Clinical interventions occur when clinicians, acting in a professional capacity, attempt to change a client's behavior, thoughts, emotions, or social circumstances in a desirable direction. Intervention can take many forms, including individual and group psychotherapy, psychosocial rehabilitation, and prevention, but psychotherapy is the activity by which clinical psychologists are best known.

What Is Psychotherapy?

In a nutshell, psychotherapy is treatment offered by trained mental health professionals and administered within the confines of a professional relationship to help clients overcome psychological problems. While no definition of psychotherapy satisfies everyone, this one identifies psychotherapy's participants (clients and therapists), the basic framework (professional relationship), and the treatment's main goal (reduction of suffering).

The definition is, however, rather formal and probably not what comes to mind for most people when they hear the word *psychotherapy*.

Public (Mis)Perception of Psychotherapy. For many, the ready mental image for psychotherapy goes something like this:

> Two people are in a private office, sitting on comfortable chairs, and talking. Sometimes one of them, the client, is lying on a couch. The client talks about troubling events while the other, the therapist, asks probing questions or offers encouragement for the client to say more (e.g., "uh huh," "I see," "Tell me more about that," "And how did that make you feel?"). Over time, the therapist gradually directs the client to focus on emotionally painful events from childhood, events that had been buried in the unconscious. Once the client has fully remembered and discussed these, the client improves.

Unfortunately, the popular images of psychologists and other mental health professionals in movies and on television are often inaccurate. Although they may contain elements of truth, the portrayals are often caricatures or stereotypes (much like the popular images of police detectives, medical personnel, attorneys, and judges). In movies and on television, clinical psychologists and psychiatrists are frequently shown as professionals who fail to maintain appropriate professional boundaries, violate ethical codes, or shoot from the hip in treatment rather than conduct established and effective interventions (Orchowski, Spickard, & McNamara, 2006).

Treatments, too, are often inaccurately portrayed or oversimplified. This can occur because writers and filmmakers formed their impressions of therapy from watching previous media portrayals. That would explain why stereotyped versions of psychoanalysis are repeated with surprising regularity. Gabbard and Gabbard (1999) suggested that "if filmmakers have studied the history of the psychoanalytic movement, it would seem that they stopped reading Freud's work at this particular historical point. Most of the positive portrayals of psychotherapy revolve around the de-repression of a traumatic memory" (p. 28). Table 6.1 describes how psychotherapists are portrayed in five popular movies.

Even print media overgeneralize about psychotherapy. A recent *Newsweek* article (Begley, 2007) described efforts by psychologist Scott Lilienfeld and others to help distinguish ineffective or harmful psychological treatments from the effective ones (see Lilienfeld, 2007). But the magazine article's title, "Get Shrunk at Your Own Risk," implies that all psychotherapy may be risky (to "get shrunk" is slang for receiving psychotherapy treatment, just as "a shrink" is slang for a psychotherapist). It *is* true that clinical researchers have found that some forms of psychotherapy appear to cause more harm than good (e.g., the article mentions "stress debriefing" to prevent PTSD and using hypnosis to "discover" alternate personalities in persons diagnosed with dissociative identity disorder). It is also true that clinicians and the public would benefit from further efforts to identify ineffective or harmful "fringe" treatments. But the same can be said about medical treatment; researchers periodically discover that commonly used, FDA-approved medical treatments cause harm (for example, the drug Vioxx and hormone replacement therapy for postmenopausal women were both once routinely prescribed until researchers discovered the risks associated with them. However, a magazine headline that read "Get Medical Treatment at Your Own Risk" would probably be regarded as a gross overgeneralization.

TABLE 6.1	

Portrayals of Psychotherapists in Five Popular Movies

Movie	Portrayal
Analyze This	Billy Crystal plays a psychotherapist treating a mobster (played by Robert DeNiro). Although seeking to help, the therapist breaks confidentiality numerous times and allows his client to intimidate him.
Good Will Hunting	Robin Williams plays a psychotherapist treating a gifted but troubled young man (played by Matt Damon). The therapist is caring and helpful but at one point assaults and threatens his client and at another visits him at home, behaviors that most would consider well outside the bounds of professionalism.
Prince of Tides	Barbara Streisand plays a psychotherapist who becomes romantically involved with the brother of a suicidal client she is treating (her love interest is played by Nick Nolte), a clear violation of ethical conduct.
Prime	Meryl Streep portrays a psychotherapist providing supportive therapy to a young woman recovering from divorce (played by Uma Thurman). The client becomes romantically involved with a young man, and at first neither therapist nor client realize that the young man is actually the therapist's son. The therapist realizes it first but attempts to conceal the fact from her client, even as the client continues, over multiple sessions, to talk about her experiences in the relationship, including descriptions of sexual encounters. The therapist, no longer able to deny that her effectiveness is severely compromised, finally confesses.
As Good As It Gets	Psychotherapy portrayals play only a minor part in this movie about a challenging character with obsessive-compulsive disorder, played by Jack Nicholson. At one point, when Nicholson's character, Melvin Udall, barges into his therapist's office demanding to be seen, the therapist (played by Lawrence Kasdan) calmly but firmly explains to Mr. Udall that he needs to make an appointment—a positive portrayal of a therapist setting boundaries with a demanding and difficult client.

Common misconceptions and overgeneralizations about psychotherapy and psychotherapists can be explained partly by a lack of *mental health literacy*—people often don't know better. But inaccurate portrayals can have damaging effects. Not only can they mislead the public about the work of mental health professionals, they can also perpetuate stereotypes about the mentally ill and inhibit people from seeking available treatments that could help them.

So what is psychotherapy really like? Let's begin by considering the many kinds of psychotherapy that are available.

How Many Psychotherapy Approaches Are There?

Some investigators have identified as many as 400 "brand name" therapies (Feltham, 2000), and they literally run the gamut from A (Aikido) to Z (Zaraleya psychoenergetic technique) (Herink, 1980). However, there are important similarities among many of these variants, and many of the others are rarely used by, or even known to, most clinicians. Indeed, Gurman and Messer (2003) suggest that only about a dozen "essential" psychotherapies form the core of modern clinical practice. In short, no one knows exactly how many kinds of psychotherapy there are—the answer depends on how you group them. If arranged according to basic assumptions about personality development, the causes of disorders, and psychotherapy techniques, there are a handful of major approaches.

For example, in Chapter 2, "Clinical Psychology's Past and Present," we noted that five major schools or approaches came to dominate psychotherapy: psychodynamic, humanistic, behavioral, cognitive, and group/systems. To that list we now add alternative and integrative approaches, which include therapies that combine elements of older, more established approaches as well as treatment techniques that do not fit neatly into the other categories. The treatment methods within each major approach do differ from one another, and we point out many examples in Chapter 7, "Psychodynamic and Humanistic Psychotherapies," Chapter 8, "Behavioral and Cognitive-Behavioral Psychotherapies," and Chapter 9, "Alternative Modes of Clinical Intervention."

Section Summary: Psychotherapy refers to a variety of psychological treatments that mental health professionals provide to people suffering from various forms of psychopathology. Psychotherapy has captured the public imagination, but its features, methods, and effects are often misunderstood and misrepresented. Although there are numerous kinds of psychotherapy, most of them can be grouped into just a few categories, or approaches.

THE PARTICIPANTS IN PSYCHOTHERAPY

Section Preview: Here we discuss clients and therapists, focusing on characteristics of both that are important to successful treatment. We also describe the therapeutic relationship as an important component to treatment and end by describing the settings for clinical interventions.

Psychotherapy involves at least one client and one therapist, though it can involve more than one client at a time (e.g., couples therapy, group therapy) or more than one therapist at a time (e.g., co-therapists, therapeutic teams). Clients and therapists can vary in many ways: gender, age, racial or ethnic background, belief systems, personal strengths and weaknesses, communication styles, and so on. Let's first examine the problems and personality characteristics that clients bring to psychotherapy.

The Client

People seek psychological help for a variety of reasons. An unhappy marriage, a lack of self-confidence, a nagging fear, an identity crisis, depression, sexual problems, coping with injury or trauma, and insomnia are just a few of the things that motivate people to enter psychotherapy. In some persons, the disturbance is so great that day-to-day functioning is impaired, there is a risk of suicide or harm to others, and hospitalization may be necessary. In others, the disturbance may be less extreme but still very upsetting. The common essential feature is that the person's usual coping strategies—such as utilizing the support of friends and family or taking a vacation—are no longer sufficient to deal with the problems.

Client Problems and Treatment Utilization.   Mental disorders are found, with only minor variations, in all segments of U.S. society. Which disorders are the most common? When clients are given DSM diagnoses, anxiety disorders top the list, with mood disorders, impulse control disorders, and substance abuse disorders not far behind (National Institute of Mental Health, 2006). Disorders can occur at any point in life, but the more serious disorders usually start early—symptoms often appear by age 14. If untreated, these disorders are more likely to recur (Kessler, Berglund, Demler, Jin, & Walters, 2005).

Of course, not everyone who experiences psychological disorders seeks treatment. In fact, treatment utilization rates are relatively low. Figure 6.1 shows the number of clients per 100, in different demographic categories, who annually use nonhospital outpatient mental health services in the United States. For example, the National Comorbidity

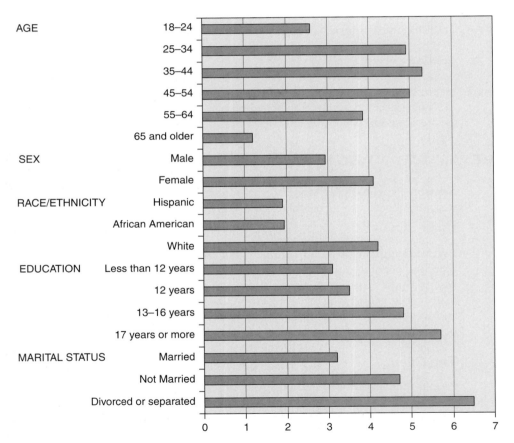

FIGURE 6.1   Annual Outpatient Psychotherapy Utilization Rates by Client Demographics (Number of Service Users Annually Per 100 Persons)

(*Source:* M. Olfson, S. C. Marcus, B. Druss, & H. A. Pincus, 2002. National trends in the use of outpatient psychotherapy. *American Journal of Psychiatry, 159,* 1912–1920.)

Survey Replication estimated the 12-month prevalence rates for anxiety disorders as 18%, and for any disorder it is 26% (Kessler, Berglund, Demler, Jin, & Walters, 2005). But it is easy to see that no group in Figure 6.1 approaches that rate of treatment-seeking. In short, in any given year, many persons with psychological disorders go untreated. Failure to obtain treatment is more common in minority and lower socioeconomic groups, as are earlier drop-out rates (Self, Oates, Pinnock-Hamilton, & Leach, 2005).

It is also common for persons with psychological problems to delay seeking treatment for many years. One study found that the median delay in seeking treatment for bipolar disorder, depression, and panic disorder were 6 years, 8 years, and 10 years respectively (Wang, Berglund, et al., 2005). As you can see from Figure 6.1, those seeking outpatient psychotherapy are more likely to be middle aged, educated, white, female, and divorced or separated.

Client Variables and Treatment Outcomes.   Among those who do seek treatment, the client's problem is perhaps the most obvious client-related characteristic. How important is the client's diagnosis in a therapist's selection of specific treatment methods and in the outcome of those treatments? Many clinicians and researchers have sought to match specific treatments to specific diagnoses, but the matching process has not resulted in dramatic gains in treatment effectiveness. Some researchers have even concluded that patient diagnosis has "largely failed as a basis for selecting among treatments" (Beutler & Harwood, 2000, p. 11). Clinicians and researchers have investigated many other client characteristics with an eye toward finding those that might predict successful treatment outcomes. Clients' sex, age, ethnicity, socioeconomic status, intelligence, religious attitudes, and dozens of other personality and demographic variables have been considered.

Of these, only a few show modest relationships with therapy outcome. For example, there is no strong evidence that the sex of the client is related to psychotherapy outcome (Garfield, 1994). And clients' age alone has only a negligible relationship to therapeutic outcome.

What about clients' personality and attitudes? Many therapists presume that a client's openness, along with certain other cognitive or emotional variables, affects treatment outcomes (Teasdale & Hill, 2006), and there is some support for this view. Orlinsky, Grawe, and Parks (1994) report that two client variables consistently show up as important in psychotherapy outcome research: *cooperation versus resistance* and *openness versus defensiveness.*

Conventional wisdom also holds that client motivation is directly related to therapeutic outcome. At one level, this is certainly true, in that clients who are more invested and try harder tend to do better. But some studies have found surprisingly weak relationships between client motivation and therapeutic outcomes (Garfield, 1994). These results might occur because only a minimal amount of motivation is actually needed for successful therapy or because motivation can change from one treatment session to the next, or even within sessions, and is therefore difficult to summarize in a single measure that can be related to outcome.

Other client characteristics are also being investigated in relation to therapy outcome. Knox, Goldberg, Woodhouse, and Hill (1999), for instance, studied clients' "internal representations" of their therapists, which they defined as how clients brought to awareness the image of their therapist (including the therapist's physical appearance, verbalizations, emotional tone, etc.) and found that these representations are indeed related to benefits in therapy. Beutler and Harwood (2000) and Messer (2006) also point to a client's *level of distress, expectations for treatment success,* and *coping style* (e.g., externalizing or internalizing) as important client dimensions. The importance of these variables has led Messer (2006) to note that "it is frequently more important to know what kind of patient has the disorder than what kind of disorder the patient has" (p. 39).

In short, clients vary on many dimensions. For purposes of treatment, a presenting problem and its diagnosis is often the first target of clinical attention. But other demographic and personality variables, some more traitlike (relatively permanent) and some more statelike (changeable), are also important. Identifying exactly which of the many client variables should be used in selecting the mode of treatment is an important, ongoing area of clinical research.

The Therapist

Therapists obviously differ in age, sex, ethnicity, personality, formal training, level of experience, and so on. Which therapist characteristics are essential and which are less important for successful therapy? As a general rule, broad demographic variables (e.g., age, sex, ethnicity, or socioeconomic status) play relatively insignificant roles in the overall effectiveness of therapy (Beulter, Machado, & Neufeldt, 1994).

Traits and Skills of Effective Therapists. Brem (2001), Inskipp (2000), Jennings and Skovholt (1999), and many others have suggested effective therapists possess a set of basic skills and traits. According to Inskipp, because psychotherapy is an interpersonal activity, psychotherapists must possess strong interpersonal skills, including those related to communication, relationship building, and self-monitoring.

Therapists who can recognize differences and intensities in clients' emotional experiences, and who also have a verbal repertoire capable of putting these shadings into words, are more likely to effectively communicate their understanding to their clients. In addition, therapists with these communication skills are more likely to help clients to learn a new psychological vocabulary and new ways of understanding their experiences. This learning can help clients make the behavioral, cognitive, and emotional changes that are the goals of therapy.

As we discuss shortly, the relationship that develops between therapist and client strongly affects therapy outcome. For this reason, a therapist's *relationship-building skills* are critical. Therapists need to communicate sincerity and to warmly support troubled clients without judging them, and at the same time, they must have the skill to remind clients of their capacity and responsibility for making beneficial changes in their lives. Clinicians often summarize these relationship qualities as *genuineness, empathy,* and *unconditional positive regard.* These are called *Rogerian* qualities because Carl Rogers claimed that they are the necessary and sufficient conditions for bringing about therapeutic change.

Finally, therapists need skills in self-awareness or self-management. As in any other line of work, the ability to monitor internal variables that might interfere with performance is important. *Self-monitoring skills* are seldom directly taught in clinical psychology programs, but these skills are learned indirectly as clinical training and supervision proceed.

Different approaches have different ways of developing self-monitoring skills. Psychoanalytically oriented therapists typically undergo analysis as the way to achieve self-monitoring skills. Cognitive or behaviorally oriented therapists are more likely to take an empirical approach, evaluating whether personal issues might be interfering when their interventions seem ineffective (see Burns, 1999, for an interesting discussion of this approach). Whatever the approach, a therapist needs some way to monitor his or her contributions to the therapy.

Certain attitudinal variables also appear to differentiate more effective therapists. Wicas and Mahan (1966) found effective therapists were more self-controlled and sympathetic than other therapists, while Jackson and Thompson (1971) found effective therapists to have more positive attitudes toward themselves and people in general. Jennings and Skovholt (1999) and Sullivan, Skovholdt, and Jennings (2005) used a peer-nomination procedure to select 10 master therapists and then attempted to determine what cognitive, emotional, and relational characteristics distinguished these therapists from those who are less effective. The characteristics of master therapists are presented in Table 6.2, along with a list developed by other researchers (Brems, 2001).

Broad skills such as communication, relationship building, and self-monitoring can be considered *macroskills*. They are needed regardless of the therapist's theoretical orientation. The importance of these skills can be illustrated by paraphrasing Messer (2006): It is frequently more important to know what kind of therapist is offering

---

TABLE 6.2

Characteristics of Effective Psychotherapists

Characteristics of Master Therapists (adapted from Jennings & Skovholt, 1999)	Selected Traits of Effective Mental Health Professionals (adapted from Brems, 2001)
Voracious learners	Self-esteem and competence
Draw heavily on accumulated experience	Willingness for introspection and self-reflection
Value cognitive complexity and ambiguity	Cognitive complexity and tolerance for ambiguity
Emotionally receptive	Cultural sensitivity and respect for others
Mentally healthy, mature, and attend to their own well-being	Personal mental health, self-respect, and appropriate use of power
Aware of how their emotional health impacts their work	Awareness and expression of personal style
Possess strong relationship skills	Empathy and capacity for intimacy
Believe in the working alliance	Good personal boundaries, ability to delay expression of affect
Experts at using their exceptional relational skills in therapy	Sense of ethics and professionalism

treatment than to know what kind of treatment the therapist offers. This is also a way of saying that effective psychotherapists are more similar to each other than their varying theoretical orientations might lead you to expect.

Therapists' Training and Experiences.

It seems obvious that therapists need advanced training, and research partially supports this view. For instance, Machado, Beulter, and Greenberg (1999) found that trained therapists could recognize others' emotions better than untrained novices could. Because emotion recognition is necessary for understanding another person and for expressing empathy with them, it qualifies as a critical psychotherapy skill. Therapists with more training and experience also tend to have lower client drop-out rates (Luborsky, 1989).

However, it is not clear exactly what kind of training and what level of experience are best. None of the core mental health professions, which include clinical psychology and psychiatry, for instance, can offer convincing evidence that they produce superior therapy results. Indeed, paraprofessionals who have only relatively brief and narrowly focused training sometimes produce results equal to those obtained by persons who have had long-term professional training. Taken as a whole, "research has consistently failed to demonstrate that therapists with more experience (i.e., years of experience working with patients) are more effective than therapists with less experience" (Leon, Martinovich, Lutz, & Lyons, 2005, p. 417).

This result is puzzling to many. Some suggest that methodological problems in the studies have obscured the importance of therapist training and experience (Leon et al., 2005). Perhaps one reason that level of experience does not clearly translate into improved outcomes is that therapists typically change the nature of their practice and the kinds of problems they encounter as they move through their careers. One survey (Pingitore & Sheffler, 2005) found that clinicians with less than 5 years of experience were more likely to work in public health and/or mental health settings than were those with more experience. Clinicians with more experience were more likely to be in private practice. Less-experienced psychologists also saw a greater percentage of clients with childhood disorders and substance abuse disorders, and they saw fewer clients per week (about 19 hours per week versus about 25 hours per week for clinicians with 11 to 20 years of experience). If clinicians are more likely to begin their careers in public, community mental health settings before moving into private practice, their clientele and their clients' typical problems change, too. If they take on tougher cases in later years, their success may be adversely affected, but not because experience doesn't help.

Challenges of Therapeutic Work.

Therapeutic work can be deeply rewarding. For those with a desire to help others, every day presents a new opportunity to make it easier for someone to improve and flourish. However, the work also has its challenges. Some are relatively minor irritations and frustrations, while other are major, causing the clinician to question his or her competence or character. Too often, therapists feel that their graduate training was inadequate in helping them to manage these emotions or to use them therapeutically (Pope, Kieth-Spiegel, & Tabachnick, 2006).

What difficulties do therapists most often face in their work? Schröder and Davis (2004) found that therapists' complaints clustered into three groups:

1. **Competency-related difficulties.** These were relatively transient difficulties resulting from situations in which therapists questioned whether they had the knowledge or skills to be effective in a given situation. For example, when a client being treated individually for depression wants to begin marital therapy with her alcoholic husband, the therapist wonders if he is qualified to treat substance abuse and marital problems in addition to the depression.

2. **Personality-based difficulties.** This category involved therapists questioning the degree to which their own enduring personal characteristics compromised their effectiveness. For example, therapists sometimes wonder if they are deficient in some of the traits listed in Table 6.2.

3. **Situational difficulties.** These resulted from characteristics of the therapists' client base or work situation. For instance, therapists who work with treatment-resistant violent sex offenders in a prison may have both competence and personal capacity but still find the work very difficult.

How do therapists prepare for and cope with these challenges? As noted earlier, personal therapy has been regarded as an important aspect of psychotherapy training for psychoanalysts and some other psychodynamically oriented therapists (Murdock, 2004). Although many programs do not specifically require it, surveys suggest that 70% to 90% of therapists have undergone personal therapy (Murdock, 2004; Norcross, Strausser-Kirkland, & Missar, 1988; Pope & Tabachnick, 2005). When Pope and Tabachnick asked a national sample of psychologists whether personal therapy should be required for licensing in clinical psychology, 54.4% said either "absolutely yes" or "probably," while 40.2% said "absolutely not" or "probably not" (the remainder endorsed "don't know"). It is not clear whether undergoing personal psychotherapy makes therapists more effective with clients, but the vast majority of clinicians believe that it does (Murdock, 2004). Incidentally, the problems therapists present when they go into therapy are much like the problems that other people face: depression, relationship and marital problems, self-esteem concerns, and anxiety.

The Therapeutic Relationship

In a sense, there is always a "third participant" in any therapeutic encounter: namely, the relationship that develops between client and therapist. From the moment they meet, each forms impressions, feelings, and cognitions about the other. As they move into extended interaction, these impressions begin to coalesce into a sense of what it is like to be with this other person. The therapeutic relationship, this third participant, is important because research consistently finds that it affects treatment outcomes (Crits-Christoph, Connolly-Gibbons, & Hearon, 2006).

The therapeutic relationship has many dimensions, but two of them are especially important: (a) the emotional bonds that develop between the therapist and client (liking, trust, etc.), and (b) the shared understanding of what is to be done (tasks) and what is to be achieved (goals). Together, these dimensions are often called the *therapeutic alliance* (see Bordin, 1979; Martin, Garske, & Davis, 2000).

Varying Views of the Therapeutic Alliance.

No one deserves more credit than Carl Rogers, the founder of client-centered therapy, for drawing attention to the therapeutic alliance. Rogers took the position that the client–therapist relationship is the crucible in which all the necessary and sufficient ingredients for therapeutic change are generated. In a departure from traditional views of therapy, Rogers saw the relationship itself, rather than the technique employed by the therapist, as the main curative factor in psychotherapy. According to Rogers (1951), "the words—of either client or [therapist]—are seen as having minimal importance compared with the present emotional relationship which exists between the two" (pp. 172–173).

Rogers believed that a positive therapeutic relationship develops because the therapist creates conditions known as acceptance, genuineness, and unconditional positive regard. Rogers did not stress the client's role in creating the therapeutic alliance; it was assumed that if the therapist offered the proper conditions, the relationship would typically develop and clients would benefit (Hovarth, 2000). Humanistically oriented therapists since Rogers have continued to share a similar view of the therapeutic relationship. To them, the alliance is not merely the context for treatment, it *is* the treatment.

Psychoanalysts and psychodynamically oriented clinicians also regard the alliance as critical but are less inclined to believe that the relationship itself is the main ingredient in therapy. According to Meissner (2006), the alliance is essentially a therapeutic pact—a shared understanding about the professional relationship and the kinds of interactions that take place within that pact. In a sense, the alliance provides the context for treatment, but therapeutic techniques are still critical.

Most behavioral and cognitive-behavioral therapists tend to view the therapy relationship as an important but not sufficient condition of therapy (Sweet, 1984). Most see the therapeutic alliance as a useful context in which more specific behavior-change techniques are introduced. In this sense, they are similar to psychoanalytic theorists—both view the relationship as the context for techniques—and different from the humanistically oriented therapists who view the relationship as a treatment in itself. Other behavioral therapists believe that the therapeutic relationship plays a larger role; they see it as the crucial element in bringing about beneficial change because it gives the therapist the opportunity to model new skills and reinforce improvements in the client's behavior (Follette, Naugle, & Callaghan, 1996). In their view, providing contingent reinforcement of clients' appropriate behavior as it occurs in the therapeutic relationship is one of the most powerful intervention tools therapists have (Kohlenberg & Tsai, 1991).

Research on the Therapeutic Alliance.

Landmark articles by Bordin (1979) and Luborsky (1976) were instrumental in operationally defining the therapeutic alliance. This, in turn, stimulated researchers to develop scales for measuring the concept. These scales include the *Working Alliance Inventory* (Hovarth & Greenberg, 1989), the *California Psychotherapy Alliance Scales* (Marmar, Gaston, Gallagher, & Thompson, 1989), the *Vanderbilt Psychotherapy Process Scale* (Suh, Strupp, & O'Malley, 1986), and the *Therapeutic Bond Scales* (Saunders, Howard, & Orlinsky, 1989). Some of them were designed with specific theoretical views of the alliance in mind (e.g., psychodynamic), while others aim to measure the alliance generally. Nevertheless, most of these scales are highly intercorrelated, which suggests that they measure essentially the same thing. They also have acceptable internal consistency and interrater reliability (Cecero, Fenton, Frankforter, Nich, & Carroll, 2001; Martin, Garske, & Davis, 2000).

Researchers have used these and other such scales in many studies on the influence of the alliance on therapy outcomes. Meta-analyses have generally found that the correlation between the nature of the therapeutic alliance and therapy outcomes is greater than the correlation between specific treatment techniques and outcomes (Crits-Christoph et al., 2006). These data support the view that the relationship that develops in therapy may be even more important than the particular techniques the therapist uses. We discuss this issue further in Chapter 10, "Research on Clinical Intervention."

Orlinsky and Howard (1986) found that the alliance is likely to flourish when both parties are capable of bringing three elements to the situation: role investment (the personal effort both parties devote to therapy), empathic resonance (the degree to which both parties are "on the same wavelength"), and mutual affirmation (the extent to which both parties care for each other's well-being). Still, questions about the therapeutic relationship remain: How does the alliance cause changes in clients? Does the nature of the relationship matter more for some disorders or types of therapy than for others? How well can the quality of the relationship be predicted? How can therapists be trained to improve the alliance? Questions such as these are currently under investigation (see Crits-Christoph et al., 2006).

The Settings for Psychotherapy

The settings for psychotherapy are most easily divided into two categories: *outpatient settings* and *inpatient settings*. The former includes therapists' offices, spaces in community centers or church basements, or anywhere else clients and therapists agree to meet. The latter includes facilities such as hospitals, prisons, or residential treatment centers, where patients reside for days, months, or rarely, years.

Outpatient Settings.   Therapists' offices are by far the most common setting for psychotherapy. The requirements for a therapist's office are minimal, but certain features are important. The first is privacy. Because of the emotional nature of therapy, clients have a right to expect that their communications remain between themselves and their therapists. For this reason, most therapists see clients in rooms that are soundproof, or nearly so. Arrangements should be made to hold calls and other interruptions during therapy sessions. Although it is advisable for offices to be private, to reassure both clients and therapists, they should not be too far removed from other people. Unfortunately, litigation brought by clients for actual or fabricated malpractice is a threat in this society (and one of the causes of skyrocketing malpractice insurance costs). And for therapists who work with potentially aggressive clients, it makes sense to have other persons not too far away from the office.

Comfortable places to sit are also essential. With adults, seating should place clients and therapists on approximately equal levels. Office decor should be inviting but relatively

A psychotherapist's office should be set up to maximize client comfort.

neutral. That is, therapists' should feel free to have their offices express their tastes and affections, but the decor should not be so exotic or so expressive of their personal lives as to make clients feel that they don't quite belong there. If the therapist works with children, the therapy space should have toys and furniture appropriate to the clients' ages. In short, office accommodations should be designed to maximize the treatment goals for the clients with whom a therapist works.

Of course, not all therapy takes place in an office. Group therapy is often conducted in larger spaces in office buildings, hospitals, community centers, senior centers, church basements, and the like. As with offices, therapists should try to structure the environment in way that maximizes therapeutic goals, though they may have less latitude to do so in rented or borrowed spaces.

Some types of treatment can even take place in public settings. For instance, a therapist treating a client with panic disorder might accompany the client to a mall so that the client can practice anxiety-management techniques learned in therapy. Similarly, therapists might ride with their elevator-phobic clients in an elevator to help them recognize symptoms, become more aware of cognitions, or practice breathing and relaxation exercises. Therapists may even take client groups on outings where they can practice social and other skills first learned in an office setting (also see Chapter 8).

Inpatient Settings. Inpatient therapy occurs in public, private, and VA hospitals, residential rehabilitation and treatment centers, prisons, jails, and many other settings. The requirements for therapy here are similar to those for inpatient settings—clients have a right to expect privacy and professional treatment. But there are important differences as well.

For example, in hospitals, the most common inpatient setting, clinicians are likely to be treating clients whose problems, such as schizophrenia or major depressive disorder, are particularly severe. Further, clinicians working within hospitals are often part of a treatment team that includes physicians, psychiatrists, social workers, and other personnel. Psychotherapists must therefore coordinate psychotherapy with other treatments, such as medication, physical therapy, or psychosocial rehabilitation.

Section Summary: Psychotherapy is a treatment offered by a trained professional to one or more clients who suffer from a psychological disorder or a social/emotional problem. The key participants in psychotherapy are clients and psychotherapists. Few of the characteristics of either appear to have a large impact on how successful psychotherapy is, but the relationship that develops between them does. Psychotherapy is conducted in both inpatient and outpatient settings.

THE GOALS OF CLINICAL INTERVENTIONS

Section Preview: The various approaches to psychotherapy differ in several ways, but they share common therapeutic goals. Those goals include (a) reducing emotional discomfort, (b) fostering insight, (c) encouraging catharsis or self-expression, (d) providing new information (education) (e) assigning extratherapy tasks (homework), and (f) developing faith, hope, and expectations for change.

Treatment approaches vary in a number of ways. They have different views of personality development and personality organization, different explanations for the causes of psychological problems. They also differ in terms of the changes they are designed to produce (Andrews, 1989; Messer & Winokur, 1980). For instance, behavioral therapists are likely to deal directly with the problem as the client initially presents it (along with other difficulties that might contribute to the primary complaint). For example, a mother who reports depression and fears that she will kill her children might be assigned a variety of "homework assignments" involving her relationship with her husband, disciplinary methods for her children, or the development of new, out-of-the-house activities for herself. By contrast, a psychoanalyst would explore the presumed underlying causes of the mother's depression; therapy might be aimed at helping the woman understand how her current symptoms relate to feelings of inadequacy as a mother because of failure to meet her own mother's rigid and unrealistic standards. Finally, a humanistic therapist might deal with the problem by helping the mother discover her potential for creating alternatives that would free her from the one-dimensional life in which she now feels trapped.

Despite their differences, most forms of clinical intervention have a number of common goals. While not every form of psychotherapy strives to maximize each goal, each of the following goals are sought to some degree in all forms of successful treatment.

Reducing Emotional Discomfort

Clients sometimes come to a therapist in such emotional anguish that it is difficult for them to participate actively in therapy. In such instances, the therapist will try to reduce the client's distress enough to allow the person to begin working on the problem. Therapists do not strive to eliminate all discomfort; in so doing, they might also eliminate the client's motivation for working toward more lasting change. The challenge is to diminish extreme distress without sapping the client's desire to deal with enduring problems.

A common method for reducing client discomfort is to use the therapeutic relationship to boost the client's emotional strength. Clients gain emotional stability and renewed confidence by knowing that the therapist is a personal ally, a buffer against the onslaughts of a hostile world. Some therapists offer direct reassurances such as "I know things seem hopeless right now, but I think you will be able to make some important changes in your life." In their study of master therapists, Sullivan, Skovholt, and Jennings (2005) found that the ability to provide a safe, collaborative, and supportive atmosphere was one of the key ways that master therapists understood the therapeutic alliance.

Fostering Insight

Insight into psychological problems was a chief objective for Freud, who described it as "re-education in overcoming internal resistances" (Freud, 1904, p. 73). While Freud was interested in a particular type of insight—into unconscious influences—most therapists aim for insight in the general sense of greater self-knowledge. Clients are expected to benefit from learning why they behave in certain ways, because such knowledge is presumed to contribute to the development of new behavior. The psychotherapist's rationale for fostering a client's insight is like the well-known value of studying history: knowing about the errors of the past helps to avoid repeating them.

Therapists of all theoretical persuasions seek to promote self-examination and self-knowledge in their clients, though they may go about it in different ways. Some clinicians focus on a specific type of content, such as dreams. Others try promoting insight by asking their clients to examine the implications of certain behaviors (e.g., "What relationship do you see between your troubles with your boss and the dislike you express for your father?"). Cognitive therapists help clients become more aware of the automatic and maladaptive ways in which they explain events, particularly negative events. Behavioral therapists stress the importance of helping the client understand how behavior is functionally related to past learning and current environmental factors.

A common technique for developing insight is for the therapist to *interpret* the client's behavior. The purpose of interpretation is not to convince clients that the therapist is right about the significance of some event but to motivate clients to carefully examine their own behavior and thoughts and draw new and more informed conclusions about them. Although interpretation remains a main technique for many psychotherapists, some clinicians caution against the dangers of interpretations that are too confrontive or challenging (Strupp, 1989). Particularly when working with very disturbed clients, therapists who minimize their use of interpretation in favor of being actively supportive, emotionally soothing, and directly reassuring tend to achieve the best outcomes. Conversely, less-disturbed clients benefit more from therapy experiences in which the therapist interprets connections between their behavior in therapy and their relationships outside of therapy (Jones, Cumming, & Horowitz, 1988).

Encouraging Catharsis

Clients are usually encouraged to express emotions freely in the protective presence of the therapist. This technique is known as *catharsis,* and it involves the release of pent-up emotions that the client has not acknowledged for a long time, if ever. The therapist encourages the client to give voice to those emotions, believing that through their release they will be eased. At the very least, catharsis may help the client become less frightened of certain emotions.

Although therapists have always been concerned with their clients' emotional experiences, empirical research on the value of emotion-focused techniques has been slow to accumulate. Research points to the value of emotion-focused interventions in at least five areas (Greenberg & Safran, 1989): (a) synthesizing or getting in touch with emotions so they can be understood and expressed in acceptable, even constructive ways; (b) intensifying certain emotions, often through nonverbal, expressive methods, so they can instigate useful behavior; (c) restructuring emotions by giving new information that allows emotions to be modified in desired directions; (d) evoking emotions so that thoughts and behaviors strongly and specifically bound up with these emotions can be reexamined; and (e) directly modifying those emotions that have become so maladaptive that the client's functioning is impaired.

Providing New Information (Education)

Psychotherapy is often educational. Certain areas of a client's adjustment may be plagued by misinformation, sexual functioning being a notable example, and therapists can often provide valuable information in these areas. Therapists are also educators in the sense that they provide new ways for the client to understand problems. As educators, part of a therapist's skill is in presenting information in ways the client can best understand. When clients understand how their disorders developed, are maintained, and can be overcome, they improve. Some therapists offer direct advice and information to their clients, adopting a teacherlike role. Others suggest reading material about a topic, a process known as *bibliotherapy* (Marx, Gyorky, Royalty, & Stern, 1992). Still others rely on less direct methods—a shrug of the shoulder or a skeptical facial expression—to suggest to clients that there are other ways of perceiving the world. New information gives clients an added perspective on their problems that makes them seem less unusual as well as more solvable.

Assigning Extratherapy Tasks (Homework)

Therapists often ask clients to perform tasks outside of therapy for the purpose of encouraging the transfer of positive changes to the "real world." A large percentage of therapists assign homework, and the practice appears to be increasing across many psychotherapy approaches (Kazantzis & Deane, 1999; Ronan & Kazantzis, 2006). Behavioral and cognitive-behavioral therapists have always been advocates of homework assignments, believing them to be an effective way to promote the generalization of new skills learned in the therapist's office (Nietzel, Guthrie, & Susman, 1991). Homework assignments are often made, too, by psychodynamically oriented practitioners, systems-oriented psychotherapists, and even client-centered therapists (Allen, 2006; Ronan & Kazantzis, 2006). Clients who complete homework assignments appear to fare better in therapy than those who do not (e.g., Burns & Spangler, 2000).

Developing Faith, Hope, and Expectations for Change

Of all the procedures common to all systems of therapy, raising clients' faith, hope, and expectations for change is the ingredient most frequently mentioned as a crucial contributor to therapeutic improvement. The curative power of positive expectations is not restricted to psychotherapy. It has been said, for example, that the history of medical treatment is largely the history of the placebo effect (Shapiro, 1971). Some therapy techniques may be particularly potent in raising expectations and creating placebo effects because they appear dramatic or high-tech or because they tap into ingrained cultural norms associated with the best ways to achieve personal change.

Clinicians are so accustomed to thinking about placebo effects in psychotherapy that many attribute much of psychotherapy's success to it rather than to specific techniques the therapist uses. Recognizing placebo effects in psychotherapy does not eliminate the importance of the specific techniques, nor does it eliminate the need to understand how specific techniques work differently. It does mean, however, that one important element (some might say the most important element) of any effective therapy is that it causes clients to believe that positive changes are attainable (Orlinsky, Grawe, & Parks, 1994).

Part art and part science, psychotherapy profits from the mystique that surrounds both fields. Clients often begin psychotherapy with the belief that they are about to engage in a unique, powerful experience conducted by an expert who can work miracles. The perceived potency of psychotherapy is further enhanced by the fact that clients usually enter it after having fretted for a long time about whether they really need treatment. By the time this internal debate is resolved, the client has a large emotional investment in making the most of a treatment that is regarded with a mixture of fear, hope, and relief.

For their part, therapists encourage clients' faith in the power of psychotherapy by providing assurance that they understand the problem and that, with hard work and commitment by both partners in the therapy relationship, desired changes are possible. The client's perception that "I have been heard and understood and can be helped" can be as important as the soothing effect that physicians create by displaying calm confidence in the face of a patient's mysterious physical symptoms. Most therapists bolster this perception by offering a theory-based *rationale* for why psychotherapy will be effective.

Having structured therapy to increase the client's motivation and expectations for success, the therapist attempts to ensure that the client actually does experience some success as soon as possible. This success might be minor at first—a limited insight after a simple interpretation by the therapist or the successful completion of a not-too-difficult homework assignment. Whatever the means, the objective is to bring about the kind of change the client expects. The cumulative impact of many small changes in the initial stages of therapy helps reinforce clients' confidence that they can control their lives and that their problems are understandable and solvable. As more positive expectancies are confirmed, they grow, and as clients believe that more meaningful changes can be attained, they pursue them with even greater determination, which in turn makes further success more likely (Howard, Lueger, Maling, & Martinovich, 1993). All the while, the therapist enhances the client's self-esteem by pointing out that the changes are the result of the client's own efforts (Bandura, 1982).

Section Summary: The different approaches to psychotherapy have similar goals. To varying degrees, they all try to reduce the client's suffering, help the client achieve insight, encourage the client's self-expression, educate the client, facilitate the transfer of in-session learning, and develop positive expectations.

ETHICAL GUIDELINES FOR CLINICAL INTERVENTIONS

Section Preview: Ethical guidelines help define and shape the therapeutic relationship. The APA provides primary guidelines in its Ethics code, and offers a number of other guidelines in publications designed to help practitioners who deal with more specialized situations and client populations.

The practice of psychotherapy is shaped by the therapist's commitment to ethical and professional guidelines. That commitment protects the client and insulates the relationship from the negative influence of outside forces, but ethical guidelines do much more than protect clients and therapists from legal hazards. Ethical principles are intimately tied to the clinician's day-to-day and even moment-to-moment decision making (Sperry, 2007). For example, consider the following examples: A depressed client calls a therapist at home and asks for an emergency therapy session that evening. Should she grant the request? A therapist considers presenting a case involving one of his clients (using a disguised name) at a convention. Should he do so? A 14-year-old client reports that her father occasionally strikes her 12-year-old brother and her mother, but she implores the therapist not to say anything about this during their next biweekly family therapy session. Should the therapist comply with the client's wish?

Each of these clinical situations involves ethical issues, and some involve balancing competing ethical issues (e.g., a duty of care against the requirement to maintain appropriate professional boundaries).

The APA Ethics Code

The main source of ethical guidelines for clinical psychologists is the *APA Ethical Principles of Psychologists and Code of Conduct* (APA Ethics Committee, 2002b). As the name implies, this work consists of two main sections: (a) General Principles and (b) Ethical Standards. There are five General Principles:

1. Beneficence and Nonmaleficence
2. Fidelity and Responsibility
3. Integrity
4. Justice
5. Respect for People's Rights and Dignity

There are 10 Ethical Standards, each of which is divided into sections and subsections, resulting in 151 ethical rules for psychologists. For instance, section 10 covers psychotherapy and has sections on issues such as informed consent, therapy involving couples or families, sexual intimacies with clients, and so on. Table 6.3 describes a number of clinical situations and shows the sections of the Ethics Code that apply.

Four ethical concerns are the most important to psychotherapists (Sperry, 2007). Sometimes called the "four horsemen" of professional ethics, they are confidentiality, competency, informed consent, and conflict of interest.

TABLE 6.3

Examples of Ethical Dilemmas That Therapists May Face

Situation Arousing Ethical Concerns	Applicable Sections of the APA Ethics Code
During therapy, a client says that he has been thinking about killing his girlfriend.	4.01 Maintaining confidentiality 4.02 Discussing the limits of confidentiality
A client who tested positive for HIV reveals to his therapist that he continues to have unprotected sex.	4.01 Maintaining confidentiality 4.02 Discussing the limits of confidentiality
During group therapy, a therapist learns that a group member has broken confidentiality by talking to friends about other group members.	10.03 Group therapy
The court has ordered a client to obtain treatment or face jail time, so the client enters treatment but is unwilling to commit to or invest in it.	3.07 Third-party requests for services
A therapist who has been treating a married couple is now called upon to be a witness for one party in a divorce proceeding.	10.02 Therapy involving couples or families
A therapist would like to present the case of a client at a seminar, but the client wants to remain anonymous.	4.07 Use of confidential information for didactic or other purposes
A therapist considers becoming romantically involved with the ex-husband of a client.	10.06 Sexual intimacies with relatives or significant others of current therapy clients/ patients
A therapist learns that a colleague has been using a controversial therapy that research suggests may produce more harm than good.	1.05 Reporting ethical violations 2.04 Bases for scientific and professional judgments

Confidentiality means that the therapist protects the client's privacy and, except in specific circumstances, does not reveal information that the client shares in therapy. (The special circumstances that require a breaching of confidentiality are described in the Ethics Code and discussed in more detail in Chapter 15, "Professional Issues in Clinical Psychology.") Confidentiality obligates clinicians to regard the welfare of their clients as their main priority. With very few exceptions, the therapist's commitment must be directed by a singular concern: *What is best for my client?*

Competency means that clinicians will be professionally responsible and practice only within their areas of expertise. They will maintain high standards of scientific and professional knowledge. Competence is difficult to measure, but it is based on a combination of education, training, experience, and credentialing. In practice, it means that clinicians will not engage in assessment or therapeutic practices unless they have appropriate education, training, and/or supervised experience to do so, nor will they conduct therapy with populations they are unfamiliar with (cultural competency). Competency is probably better thought of as a developmental process than as an either–or condition (i.e., competent or not competent). At its most extreme, the competency requirement protects consumers from blatant malpractice, but it is also designed to help motivate clinicians to engage in career-long training and education.

Informed consent obligates therapists to tell clients about the limits of confidentiality, about potential outcomes of treatment, and about anything else that might affect the clients' willingness to enter treatment. For instance, therapists conducting marital therapy typically inform clients that one possible outcome of the therapy is that the couple could decide to divorce.

Conflict of interest refers to the therapist's obligation to maintain therapeutic boundaries or a therapeutic "framework." As discussed in Chapter 4, the framework involves the set of expectations about the roles and interaction patterns that will occur within the therapeutic relationship. A conflict of interest occurs when the therapist's personal interests compete with the best interests of the client. Such conflicts might be minor, as when a therapist must decide whether venting his frustration at a client during a session is good for the client or simply self-indulgent. But conflicts of interest can also be major, such as when a therapist contemplates a sexual relationship with a client or a former client.

While the Ethics Codes instructs practitioners on what they should or should not do, it is important to note that the code cannot cover every situation that clinicians might face. In fact, as implied by the previous examples, clinical decisions often involve a balancing of ethical concerns. We discuss professional guidelines on the therapeutic relationship in more detail in Chapter 15. There are also a number of books on how ethics affects clinical practice; three that nicely show how ethical principles relate to clinical decision making are Nagy (2005), Pope and Vasquez (2005), and Sperry (2007). There are also several guidelines published by the APA for clinicians working in specific areas of practice. The following examples can be found on the APA's Web site; others appear as appendices in Pope and Vasquez's (2005) book.

- APA Guidelines for Child Custody Evaluations in Divorce Proceedings
- APA Guidelines for Psychological Practice with Older Adults
- APA Guidelines for Providers of Psychological Services to Ethnic, Linguistic, and Culturally Diverse Populations
- APA Guidelines for Psychotherapy with Lesbian, Gay, and Bisexual Clients
- APA Statement on Services by Telephone, Teleconferencing, and Internet

Ethics and the Therapist's Values

When clients struggle with value-related issues, therapists struggle as well, particularly if the therapist holds values that are different from those of the client. In fact, it is safe to say that every therapist is certain to have his or her cherished values challenged at some point. Some challenges appear relatively minor, such as having a teenage, court-referred client who finds professional wrestling the most exciting and meaningful thing in life; should the therapist try to convince him otherwise? Other challenges can be major, such as having a depressed client with terminal cancer contemplate suicide; should the therapist try to

TABLE 6.4		
Value-Laden Topics That Can Arise During Psychotherapy		
abortion	animal rights	assisted suicide
birth control choices	career choices	child abuse and neglect
criminal activity	death and dying	dietary choices
domestic violence	gang membership	gender roles
health care choices	marriage and cohabitation	medical ethics
politics	premarital sex	racism and sexism
religious beliefs	religious practices	sexual orientation
sexual practices	substance abuse	environmental practices
suicide	use of power in relationships	weight and weight loss

SOURCE: Based on Brems (2001), p. 46.

convince her not to kill herself? Table 6.4 lists a number of other value-laden topics that can come up in therapy.

There is no clear formula for deciding how to handle values conflicts in psychotherapy. Certainly the Ethics Code can apply, but exactly how it does so may not be clear in every case. Self-aware therapists must be clear about their own values and how those values can influence treatment, and when confronted with values conflicts, the therapists must make decisions. Should they set their values aside and follow the client's lead, explain to clients how their values are different, endeavor to change the client's perspective, endeavor to change their own perspective, discontinue working with the client, or adopt some other option? Most therapists find it very helpful to discuss the therapeutic and personal implications of values conflicts with supervisors or colleagues. Here again, the APA Ethics Code helps ground the discussion.

Section Summary: Clinical practice is guided by the APA Ethics Code, which provides general principles and specific standards in many areas, including psychotherapy. Standards most important to psychotherapy practice involve confidentiality, competency, informed consent, and conflict of interest. Although often thought of as useful only for avoiding malpractice or other hazards, the Ethics Code is an invaluable aid in many areas of clinical decision making, including situations in which a clinician's values conflict with those of their clients. A variety of other codes and guidelines exist to help clinicians navigate the ethical and personal dilemmas that inevitably occur in practice.

SOME PRACTICAL ASPECTS OF CLINICAL INTERVENTION

Section Preview: Here we address some practical questions and procedures that apply to all forms of psychotherapy. These include treatment duration, fees, record keeping, treatment planning, therapist self-disclosure, and termination.

There are numerous practical questions about psychotherapy: How long does psychotherapy last? How much does it cost? What records do therapists keep? Do therapists talk about themselves during psychotherapy? How do therapists decide what kind of treatment to use? Let's consider each of these questions now.

Treatment Duration and Fees

The duration of treatment can range from one session to several years, depending on the type and severity of the disorder, the motivation and other characteristics of the client, the skill and orientation of the therapist, and the availability of funding for treatment. Traditional psychoanalytic treatment often lasts for years, with clients being seen multiple times per week. Such treatment is relatively rare today, and most clients in individual psychotherapy are seen on a weekly basis (sometimes less, sometimes more) for sessions that average 45 to 55 minutes. Group sessions typically last 90 to 120 minutes.

Single-session fees charged by psychologists vary substantially, and summary data about fees are hard to come by. However, because clinics and private practitioners now advertise their fees and services on the Internet, it is easy to see that psychotherapy fees may differ considerably. One study of Colorado psychologists (Newlin, Adolph, & Kreber, 2004) found that the average fees for 45- to 50-minute psychotherapy sessions were $92.50 and $90.00 per session for male and female psychotherapists respectively. A variety of factors, including location (e.g., rural versus urban), clinicians' level of training, and funding sources affect fees. Further, psychologists or their employing agencies often provide free service or reduced payments for clients in need and accept lower payments from insurance companies who set reimbursement limits for particular assessments or services.

Record Keeping

Psychotherapists are ethically bound to keep good records of their services to clients. The *APA Record Keeping Guidelines* (APA, 1987) is the primary document outlining this obligation. As with most APA guidelines, they do not mandate exactly what records must be kept. Rather, they outline the basic content of records, control and retention of records, and disclosure of records. Psychologists should keep records of (a) their clients' identifying information, (b) dates and types of service, (c) fees, (d) assessment results, (e) treatment plans, and (f) consultations with others about clients. These should be presented at a level of detail that would allow another clinician to take over the case should circumstances require it. In short, good record keeping is designed to benefit clients, clinicians, and their institutions. Good records can also be valuable if clinicians are involved in legal proceedings, and reviewing records, especially records of effectiveness, can motivate clinicians to find ways to improve their services.

Case Formulation and Treatment Planning

In Chapter 3, we presented a general model for assessment, which begins when the clinician receives and clarifies the referral question and ends with the communication of assessment results (see Figure 3.1). Psychotherapy also begins with assessment, though it might not involve formal procedures such as structured interviews or psychological tests. Assessment for the purposes of treatment leads to the clinician's *case formulation,* a conceptualization of the client's problems. Case formulations (case study guides) may vary depending on the clinician's theoretical orientation (see Chapter 2), but the critical elements in any formulation are facts and impressions about the client that can be used in planning treatment. In short, *treatment planning* depends on case formulation, which in turn depends on assessment.

Three Approaches to Treatment Planning. Makover (2004) describes three approaches to treatment planning. The first approach is *therapist-based treatment,* but it could also be called orientation-based or theory-based treatment. In this approach, the therapist learns a basic theoretical orientation to psychotherapy (e.g., psychodynamic, behavioral, or whatever) and uses it for every client. Until about the 1950s, psychoanalysis was the dominant form of treatment. Gradually, other approaches emerged, each claiming to be more effective. Therapists and graduate training programs lined up behind one of these major "schools" of psychotherapy and (selectively) pointed to evidence demonstrating that outcomes with that approach were superior. Even today, many clinicians and graduate training programs still ascribe to one main approach to treatment. They acknowledge that clients are different, and their treatment plans vary in accord with those differences, but the treatments offered are still those under the umbrella of one theoretical approach.

Over time, many clinical practitioners and researchers became disenchanted with the therapist-based approach to treatment planning and adopted *diagnosis-based treatment,* in which the client's diagnosis, not the therapist's orientation, determines the mode of treatment. Modeled after medical treatment, this approach to treatment planning attempts to link specific diagnoses with the most effective treatment for that diagnosis (see our discussion of empirically supported treatments in Chapter 10). While most clinicians view diagnosis-based treatment as a more scientific approach to treatment selection than clinician-based treatment, it too has its detractors. As we discussed in Chapter 3, diagnosis is imprecise. Further, as mentioned earlier in this chapter, a great deal of research has shown that factors other than the client's diagnosis—such as the quality of the therapeutic alliance—are responsible for significant variations in treatment outcomes.

Outcome-based treatment is an attempt to base treatment planning on all the factors that can affect treatment outcome. Some of those factors are related to the client (e.g., diagnosis, personality traits), some to the therapist (e.g., orientation, techniques, personality traits), and some to situational or emergent qualities (e.g., treatment setting, therapeutic alliance).

An example of multifaceted, outcome-based treatment is the Systematic *Treatment Selection* (STS) designed by Beutler and Clarkin (1990) and subsequently refined (see Beutler & Groth-Marnat, 2003; Beutler & Harwood, 2000). Table 6.5 illustrates information that goes into this approach to treatment planning. The information can be obtained by interviews, observations, history, and tests. The idea is to fine-tune treatment procedures based on an understanding of all this information. STS has also led to the development of the Clinician's Rating Form-D (Fisher, Beutler, & Williams, 1999), which is designed to gather the assessment data needed for STS. In its computerized form, this

TABLE 6.5		
Information Sought in Systematic Treatment Selection		

Patient Predisposing Factors

Problem characteristics: symptoms, functional impairment, complexity/chronicity

Personality traits: coping style, defensive traits, subjective distress, self-esteem, assets and strengths

Environment: social support, social history, breadth of positive functioning

Treatment Context (Level of Care)

Setting: restrictiveness of care

Intensity: frequency and length of treatment

Mode: pharmacological, psychosocial, or both

Format: medication or psychosocial treatment class (i.e., individual, group, family, couple therapy)

Therapy Procedures and Therapist Relationship Qualities

Match of therapist and patient demographics and beliefs

Therapeutic actions: directiveness, insight versus skill and symptom focus, cathartic versus supportive, therapist skill and experience

Therapeutic alliance quality: collaboration and relationship strength

Fit of Patient and Therapy

Fit of functional impairment and complexity with setting, modality, format, and treatment intensity

Fit of coping style with insight orientation versus symptom/task focus of treatment

Fit of traitlike resistance to therapist directiveness

Fit of subjective distress with therapist support versus cathartic evocation

SOURCE: L. E. Beulter and G. Groth-Marnat (2003), p. 8.

instrument takes clients between 20 and 40 minutes to complete (Fisher, Beutler, & Williams, 1999).

Case Example.   The following is an abbreviated version of a case presented in Beutler and Groth-Marnat (2003). It illustrates some of the features of STS.

RW is a 22-year-old Mexican American woman. She has a history of panic attacks, associated with apparent agoraphobia, social phobias, and significant paranoid ideation. She carries a provisional diagnosis of undifferentiated schizophrenia (295.9) and social phobia (300.23). Her history ... suggests a good deal of social distrust and isolation, largely deriving from her initiation of a long-term but illicit relationship with a high school teacher while she was yet underage (pp. 80–81).

The clinician gathered background information on RW and administered several assessment tools, including the STS Client Rating Form and the Minnesota Multiphasic Personality Inventory-II. These revealed certain client characteristics that were relevant for treatment: a tendency toward externalizing, external fears and anticipation of being harmed, hypersensitivity to others' opinions and criticisms, resistance to authority and concerns about loss of control or autonomy, complex/chronic problems, and moderate levels of distress and adequate social support.

These characteristics in turn suggested long-term treatment that included psychoactive medications and therapy that was instructional, partially client-directed, and not highly charged or confrontational.

The externalizing tendencies suggest the need to focus on discrete symptoms and to utilize a concrete and structured approach that trains the patient in more effective thought and emotion management, effective interpersonal skills, and helps her to test out suspicions of others' motives and behaviors. The high levels of resistance led to the suggestion that self-directed treatments should supplement therapist activities to reduce the degree of confrontation (p. 81).

The STS is certainly neither the first nor the only approach to outcome-based treatment planning. In 1973 Lazarus suggested that clinicians should gather a range of information about a client when designing interventions. His approach, called *BASIC-ID* (Lazarus, 1973), encouraged clinicians to design treatments based on assessment of clients' **B**ehaviors, **A**ffects, **S**ensory experiences, **I**magery, **C**ognitions, **I**nterpersonal relationships, and need for **D**rugs.

An increasing number of investigators are working on treatment planning approaches, some of which conform to a particular theoretical approach and some of which attempt to be theory-neutral (e.g., Beutler & Harwood, 2000; Johnson, 2003; Jongsma & Peterson, 2003; Makover, 2004; Woody, Detweiler-Bedel, Teachman, & O'Hern, 2005).

Therapist Objectivity and Self-Disclosure

To what extent should the therapist disclose personal information to the client? Clients are expected to self-disclose—indeed, therapy would be impossible without it—but what about therapists? In many instances, therapists must decide whether to share personal information such as their emotional reactions, incidents from their own lives, and the like. Such sharing is called *therapist self-disclosure*. For example, should a therapist reveal to a client feelings of irritation, boredom, or sexual attraction? Should a therapist reveal that she is currently in mourning following a death in her family? Should a therapist discuss his former addiction, a past divorce, or related to his own psychotherapy?

There are potential benefits and risks in both disclosure and nondisclosure. Therapists who never self-disclose risk being perceived as aloof or more impersonal, which might damage the therapeutic relationship. Therapists who frequently self-disclose risk being perceived as impulsive, self-focused, or compromising the professional nature of the client–therapist relationship.

There is no firm rule about therapist self-disclosure, and practices vary depending on the therapist and his or her theoretical orientation. Traditional psychoanalytic therapists have advocated strict prohibitions against disclosing personal information. Modern psychodynamically oriented clinicians recognize that utter nondisclosure is an impossible ideal because therapists are always revealing something about themselves in their verbal and nonverbal behavior (Gabbard, 2005), so minimal self-disclosure is accepted. At the other extreme are some humanistically oriented therapists who favor considerable therapist disclosure; they regard doing otherwise as a lack of genuineness on the therapist's part. Therapists from other orientations fall somewhere in the middle on the acceptability of self-disclosure.

Ethical as well as theoretical guidelines may affect disclosure, too. Therapists must ask themselves (and sometimes make split-second decisions about) whether a disclosure is in the client's best interest. Certainly the intensity of the therapeutic relationship may tempt the therapist to discard a professional orientation in favor of more spontaneous reactions, including pity, frustration, hostility, boredom, or sexual attraction. Effective therapists try to stay alert to the ways in which their personal needs intrude upon therapy (i.e., through self-monitoring). The question that always applies is, Whose needs are most clearly being served by a therapist's disclosure?

Termination

Termination of psychotherapy can occur in two ways: with treatment completed or with treatment incomplete. The latter, sometimes called *attrition* or *premature termination,* occurs when the client, for whatever reason, decides to discontinue therapy before the treatment has finished.

Termination that occurs at the end of treatment is likely to bring mixed feelings to both client and clinician. On the one hand, the loss of a meaningful relationship is the most frequently mentioned negative factor for clients (Roe, Dekel, Harel, Fenning, & Fenning, 2006). Therapists, too, often experience a sense of loss. On the other hand, both client and therapist can reflect on their shared efforts and accomplishments. Clients typically experience termination as evidence of their independence and growth. After successful treatment, termination is a positive experience for both.

Section Summary: Practical considerations surrounding psychotherapy involve the setting of fees, decisions about the duration of treatment, and keeping of official records. Treatment planning is especially important because it sets the stage for how psychotherapy is conducted. If successfully conducted, the termination of psychotherapy and the aftereffects should be primarily positive for the client.

CHAPTER SUMMARY

Clinical intervention involves a deliberate attempt to make desirable changes in clients' behavior, thinking, and social interactions. Treatment is initiated when a client in need of help is seen by a therapist with special training. Therapists can include persons trained in clinical psychology, counseling psychology, psychiatry, psychiatric social work, psychiatric nursing, family counseling, or a variety of other paraprofessional and specialty areas.

The participants in psychotherapy—therapists and clients—bring individual strengths and weaknesses to the situation. Most clinicians agree that effective therapy is facilitated by the development of a supportive yet objective relationship, which in turn is fostered by certain therapist and client contributions. Effective therapists need advanced training and interpersonal skills in communication, relationship building, and self-monitoring. Characteristics described by Carl Rogers as genuineness, empathy, and unconditional positive regard are especially important in developing a strong therapeutic relationship. Client characteristics such as motivation and openness also contribute to the effectiveness of therapy, but the therapeutic alliance—the bond between therapist and client and their agreement on tasks and goals—remains one of the best predictors of therapeutic outcome.

Psychotherapy is most often conducted in an individual format in an outpatient setting. However, it is also conducted in inpatient settings. Each setting constitutes part of the environment or situation in which therapy takes place.

Although approaches to psychotherapy differ, they all attempt to accomplish a common set of goals (though to varying degrees): reduce suffering, achieve insight, encourage self-expression, educate the client, facilitate the transfer of in-session learning, and develop positive expectations.

Psychotherapy is guided by the APA Ethics Code. Standards most important to psychotherapy practice involve confidentiality, competency, informed consent, and conflict of interest. The Ethics Code is an invaluable aid in many areas of clinical decision making. A variety of other codes and guidelines exist to help navigate specific areas of clinical practice.

Psychological treatments involve a number of practical considerations: fees, decisions about the type and length of service, record keeping, and so on. One of the most important practical considerations involves treatment planning. Although this can be done in a variety of ways, we think that an approach based on psychotherapy outcome research is the most empirically and ethically defensible.

STUDY QUESTIONS

1. How accurate are media portrayals of psychotherapy and psychotherapists?
2. How many kinds of psychotherapy are there?
3. Which are the dominant approaches to psychotherapy?
4. What percentage of persons with psychological disorders seek psychotherapy?
5. What problems are most common among persons seeking psychotherapy?
6. What other client characteristics, besides diagnosis, appear to affect therapy outcomes?
7. What traits and skills do effective psychotherapists exhibit?
8. How is the therapist's training related to psychotherapy effectiveness?
9. What are the personal challenges of psychotherapeutic work for therapists?
10. How has the therapeutic relationship been understood?
11. What effect does the therapeutic relationship have on therapy outcomes?
12. What are the settings of psychotherapy?
13. What are the goals common to most forms of psychotherapy?
14. What are some of the ethical decisions that can confront psychotherapists?

15. What professional guidelines or standards do clinical psychologists use to help them make ethical decisions?

16. What are typical treatment durations and fees for psychotherapeutic services?

17. Why are psychotherapists ethically obligated to keep records?

18. What are commonly used approaches to treatment planning?

19. What positions have therapists taken on therapist self-disclosure?

WEB SITES

- APA Help Center: http://www.apahelpcenter.org
- National Institutes of Mental Health: http://www.nimh.nih.gov/nimhhome/index.cfm
- Centers for Disease Control and Prevention: http://www.cdc.gov
- Mayo Clinic description of psychotherapy: http://www.mayoclinic.com/health/psychotherapy/MH00009

CHAPTER 7

Psychodynamic and Humanistic Psychotherapies

Chapter Preview: In this and the next two chapters, we focus on specific approaches to psychotherapy. Our review begins with Freud's traditional psychoanalysis, which stresses the need for clients to develop insight into their primitive drives, unconscious conflicts, and patterns of relating. Next we cover other psychodynamic approaches that share some ideas with traditional psychoanalysis. We then describe the humanistic approaches, including person-centered therapy, Gestalt therapy, and existential and phenomenological treatments. All of these emphasize each client's unique way of experiencing the world. Psychodynamic and humanistic treatments can be considered *relational approaches* because they place strong emphasis on the role of the therapeutic relationship in treatment.

PSYCHOANALYSIS

Section Preview: Traditional psychoanalysis stresses the role of unconscious conflict stemming from early childhood relationships and of psychological defenses against anxiety. In therapy, it is assumed that clients will exhibit signs of these conflicts and defenses, such as by reacting to the therapist in ways that reflect relationships with parents and other significant figures from their pasts. By focusing on the transference of old relationship patterns onto the therapeutic relationship, the therapist can interpret the client's maladaptive behaviors and the unconscious causes that motivate them. These interpretations, in turn, help the client to develop insight into the historically grounded conflicts and patterns of behavior related to their symptoms.

Recall from Chapter 2, "Clinical Psychology's Past and Present," that neurologists in Europe (e.g., Charcot, Breuer) found that patients with medically unexplainable symptoms such as paralysis were sometimes cured by hypnotic suggestion. Sigmund Freud, a Viennese neurologist, took a special interest in these cases and used them as the basis for his lifelong study of psychological disorders and their treatments. Let's now consider Freud's approach to psychotherapy in more detail.

In developing *psychoanalysis,* Freud (1856–1939) became the founder of psychotherapy as we know it today, a one-on-one treatment involving frank discussion of a

Sigmund Freud (1856–1939).
(Courtesy of Historical Pictures Service,
Inc., Chicago, Illinois. Reprinted by
permission.)

client's thoughts and feelings. Although many more modern treatment approaches are now available, almost all of them reflect one or more of Freud's ideas, including his emphasis on (a) searching for relationships between a person's developmental history and current problems, (b) blockages or dissociations in self-awareness as causes of psychological problems, (c) talking as an approach to treatment, and (d) the therapeutic relationship as a curative factor.

Theoretical Foundations

Freud described mental life as occurring partly at the level of conscious awareness; partly at a preconscious level, which we can become aware of by shifting our attention; and partly at an unconscious level, which we cannot experience without the use of special therapy techniques. This continuum from unconscious, to preconscious, to conscious is called the *topographical model* of the mind, and it is fundamental to understanding Freud's views of personality.

Freud's Personality Theory and View of Psychopathology.   As discussed in Chapter 2, psychodynamic approaches are based on the proposition that mental life is best understood as an interaction among powerful competing forces within the person, some of which are conscious but most of which are unconscious. Those forces are represented in Freud's system as the id, ego, and superego. The *id* is the primitive source of instinctual drives, especially sexual/sensual and aggressive drives. Counterbalancing the

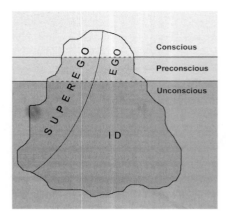

FIGURE 7.1   The Psychoanalytic Structural/Topographical Model of the Mind. Freud proposed that dynamic interaction among psychic structures occurred mostly subconsciously, outside one's awarness

id is the *superego,* the mental agency that incorporates norms from one's parents, family, and culture. The superego also contains the ego ideal, or how one would like to be. The id and the superego are often in conflict—the id seeks to discharge tension by expressing sexual or aggressive impulses, while the superego seeks to inhibit them or to prescribe more socially appropriate behavior. Refereeing this conflict is the *ego,* the part of the personality that tries to mediate between the demands of the id and superego while simultaneously recognizing and responding to external realities. The word *dynamic* refers to the tension-filled interaction among these forces. Together, these three agencies—id, ego, and superego—form a *structural model* of the mind (see Figure 7.1).

Freud proposed that dynamic conflict occurs continuously, as seen in many examples of conflicting urges. Imagine sitting through a boring class. One part of you wants to get up and leave, perhaps to do something more exciting. Another part of you urges you to stay and try to pay closer attention, reminding you that you need the class, need to be more mature, need to delay gratification, and the like. While you might be consciously aware of this particular conflict, Freud said that the most important and problematic psychic battles usually occur unconsciously, below the surface of awareness.

Defense Mechanisms.   Imagine a child who feels strong anger toward a parent but fears that expressing it would result in counteraggression (a realistic fear if the parent is sometimes verbally or physically abusive). This situation produces anxiety in the child because the child's angry id impulse continues to push for expression. According to psychoanalytic theory, a reasonable adaptation to this conflict would be for the child to adopt defense mechanisms that would help bind up the anxiety and keep it from repeatedly entering consciousness, where it might interfere with functioning. Defense mechanisms are essentially unconscious mental strategies or routines that the ego employs to ward off the anxiety produced by intrapsychic conflict (see Table 7.1).

While Sigmund Freud discussed defense mechanisms, it was his daughter, Anna, who most fully developed the idea. In her book, *Ego and the Mechanisms of Defense* (Freud, 1936/1966), she categorized and described defense mechanisms, stressing their role in

TABLE 7.1	
Defense Mechanisms	

Examples of Primitive Defenses	Description
Denial	Avoiding awareness of aspects of external reality that are difficult to face
Projection	Perceiving and reacting to unacceptable inner impulses as though they were outside the self, typically in another person
Splitting	Compartmentalizing experiences of the self and others so that contradictions in behavior, thought, or affect are not recognized
Dissociation	Disrupting one's sense of continuity in the areas of identity, memory, consciousness, or perception
Regression	Returning to an earlier phase of development or functioning
Examples of Higher-Level Defenses	
Identification	Internalizing the qualities of another person by becoming like him or her
Displacement	Shifting feelings associated with one idea, object, or person to another
Intellectualization	Using excessive and abstract ideation to avoid difficult feelings
Reaction Formation	Transforming an unacceptable impulse into its opposite
Examples of Mature Defenses	
Suppression	Consciously deciding not to attend to a particular feeling, state, or impulse
Humor	Finding the comic and/or ironic elements in difficult situations
Sublimation	Transforming socially or internally unacceptable impulses into socially acceptable expression

SOURCE: Adapted from G. O. Gabbard, 2005, pp. 35–37.

everyday life and in psychoanalytic treatment. Anna Freud also applied psychoanalytic concepts to developmental psychology, advancing theories of how psychological problems develop during childhood (Fonagy & Target, 2003).

Defense mechanisms are not always successful or adaptive. Someone who uses denial, repression, projection, or other defense mechanisms may temporarily reduce anxiety, but at the same time, he or she may distort reality and, over time, jeopardize interpersonal relationships. For instance, return to the child described earlier and imagine that person now grown up. It is not difficult to imagine this person as someone who has developed a habitual way of dealing with aggressive or hostile feelings. Instead of expressing anger when it occurs, he may mistakenly perceive signs of hostility in a relationship partner (an example of the defense mechanism called projection). He may become unable to remember important information (an example of dissociation). He may become extremely nice and solicitous (reaction formation). He might show any of

Anna Freud was instrumental in developing the concept of defense mechanisms.

a number of other behavior patterns, all of which are expressions of his attempts to deal with an anxiety-producing conflict. They are the surface disturbances that suggest some historically based emotional conflict lies beneath.

Transference and Countertransference. The psychoanalyst's job is to understand the origins and meaning of clients' symptoms and help clients do the same. Therapists are aided in this work by clients' tendency to repeat patterns of behavior, especially unconsciously motivated behavior. So if a client has developed a maladaptive pattern of relating to other people, characterized by the use of certain defense mechanisms and patterns of relating, those patterns will eventually show up in the way the client relates to the therapist. The client unconsciously brings a maladaptive pattern of relating into the therapy, a phenomenon called *transference*.

In Freud's theory, transference reactions are distortions in the client's reactions to the therapist. These distortions come about because the client's past relationships—especially early, significant past relationships such as those with one's parents—create a set of expectations and anticipatory reactions for future relationships. To put it another way, each new relationship is understood by reference to old relationships. For example, a client who is conflicted over aggressive impulses may begin to feel that the therapist is aggressive or punitive (i.e., inclined to punish any negative emotion expressed by the client). Assuming that the therapist is not truly being aggressive, the client's reactions are a demonstration of his or her habitual, internalized, and unconsciously motivated adaptations to relationship conflicts.

The more similar a new relationship is to an old one, the more likely it is that reactions based on the old relationship will occur. The psychotherapy relationship is one in which clients self-disclose intimate details of their mental life while therapists sit in a position of relative power. Emotionally, this situation is not unlike childhood. Therefore, clients are especially likely to replay their earlier emotional "scripts" in therapy. Psychoanalytic treatment is designed to reveal, analyze, and ultimately change those scripts.

Of course, clients are not the only ones whose current relationships are colored by those of the past. Therapists are affected by transference patterns, too. When therapists' reactions toward clients are based on the therapist's personal history and conflicts, those reactions are called *countertransference*. Countertransference can impair the progress of therapy if the therapist begins to distort the therapeutic interaction on the basis of his or her own conflicts and defenses. The inevitability of countertransference reactions is one reason psychoanalytically oriented clinicians believe that therapists themselves should undergo psychoanalysis as part of training. The more a therapist understands and has worked through his or her own conflicts, the less those conflicts will interfere with the treatment of clients.

Psychic Determinism.   In psychoanalysis, slips of the tongue and other unexpected verbal associations are presumed to be psychologically meaningful, as are mental images, failures of memory, and a variety of other experiences. If a client suddenly remembers something that seems trivial or unrelated to the topic of discussion during a therapy session (e.g., a family vacation taken when he was 6 years old, or his mother's blue dress), the therapist assumes that there is a reason this material "popped into" the client's head. By asking the client to elaborate, rather than ignoring the material, the therapist looks for clues that might reveal the unconscious connection. The idea that memories, impressions, or experiences that occur together in a client's mind are necessarily related and not random is called *psychic determinism*.

Resistance.   As psychoanalytic therapy progresses, the therapist and client often get closer to a client's core unconscious conflicts and emotions. The client may begin to experience increasing anxiety. He or she may consequently begin to "forget" appointments, experience panic, become overly intellectual and emotionally detached in discussing topics, or engage in other activities that appear to take the focus away from his or her conflicts. Psychoanalysts expect these or a variety of other *resistance* reactions as treatment focuses more intently on the client's core conflicts. As with transference, the manner in which the client resists is likely to be a reenactment of earlier patterns and therefore may be subject to analysis and interpretation (Gabbard, 2005).

Interpretation, Working Through, and Insight.   By offering both emotional support and judicious interpretations, the therapist helps the client understand and *work through* transference reactions and resistance. In so doing the client develops a new understanding of his or her problems, psychological makeup, and ways of relating to others.

Interpretation involves the analyst suggesting connections between patients' current experiences and their historically based conflicts. In simpler terms, interpretation is a way of pointing out how the past intrudes on the present. Interpretations can be based on material or reactions a client reveals in therapy or on reports of the client's experiences outside the therapy situation. Those that are based on in-session material often involve the transference—the client's reactions to the therapist. Optimal psychoanalytic interpretations are interpretations of transference reactions that can be related to the client's current difficulties outside of therapy (e.g., in a relationship) and also to historical forces in the client's past. Wolitzky (2003) describes it this way:

> The optimal interpretation, though not necessarily presented comprehensively at one time, would take the form of "what you are doing (feeling, thinking, fantasizing, etc.) with me now is what you also are doing with your current significant other (spouse, child, boss, etc.), and what you did with your father (and/or mother) for such and such reasons and motives and with such and such consequences. (p. 41)

If this explanation makes cognitive and emotional sense to the client (i.e., if it is accurate *and* the client is ready to process it), he or she may see a particular behavior pattern or problem in a new way. When this happens, it is called *insight*. In psychoanalysis, insight is the basic requirement for, and the beginning of, positive change.

Goals of Psychoanalysis

According to Freud, when patients understand the real, often unconscious, reasons they act in maladaptive ways and see that those reasons are no longer valid, they will not have to continue behaving in those ways. The process of self-understanding includes *intellectual* recognition of one's innermost wishes and conflicts, *emotional* involvement in discoveries about oneself, and the *systematic tracing* of how unconscious factors have determined past and present behaviors and affected relations with other people.

Thus, the main goals of psychoanalytic treatment are (a) intellectual and emotional *insight* into the underlying causes of the client's problems, (b) *working through* or fully exploring the implications of those insights, and (c) strengthening the ego's control over the id and the superego. Freud saw working through as particularly important because clients need to understand how pervasive their unconscious conflicts and defenses are if they are to be prevented from returning. Thus, it would do little good for a patient to know that she has unconscious feelings of anger toward her mother if she did not also see that she deals with women in the present as if they were her mother and that her problems in relation to these women are based on unconscious hostility and/or attempts to defend against it. Insight provides the outline of a patient's story; working through fills in the details.

Reaching the ambitious goals set by classical psychoanalysis involves dissecting and gradually reconstructing the patient's personality. This process requires a lot of time. In traditional psychoanalysis, three to five sessions each week are standard, and treatment can last for several years. With fees generally well in excess of $100 per hour, the process is expensive.

Case Example

Ellen, a 33-year-old female, sought psychotherapy after having a series of panic attacks over the last year and a half. She also stated that each day was a struggle and she felt little enjoyment of her life, so she had become concerned about depression. Finally, she said that she had questions about her marriage and herself.

At the time of referral, Ellen was employed as a sales representative for a large paper manufacturer, a position she had held for 4 years. She was married to Rick, a radiologist at the local hospital. They had no children but were contemplating them. This too was a source of discomfort, as she reported that she was more in favor of having children than Rick, who said that he was not ready.

Ellen reported having had one panic attack in college—at least she believes that is what it was—but no more until about a year and a half ago. At the time of that more recent incident, she had been attending an industry-related convention in a distant city. After mingling for a while at an evening social hour sponsored by her company, she returned to her room and lay on her hotel bed. While there she noticed her heart racing. It quickly escalated to a rapid, uncontrollable pounding. She had difficulty breathing and was sweating. At one point, she tried getting out of bed but had to lay back down for fear she would faint and fall, possibly injuring herself. By rolling sideways, she was able to reach the phone and call the front desk, and personnel there summoned an ambulance. By the time Ellen arrived at the hospital, her symptoms had subsided, but she still felt shaky and very anxious. After history taking and a number of tests at the hospital, she was given a provisional diagnosis of panic attack. Since that initial attack, she has had others: "some at home, two at work, one while shopping, and one while driving." She said, "They hit me out of the blue. They're terrible, terrifying . . . and embarrassing." She worried frequently about when the next attack might come.

Ellen's concerns about depression had arisen more gradually. During the last year or two, she reported, she had occasionally felt lost and unsure about what she was doing with her life. Despite that she was apparently valued at work—she had been promoted and given a raise twice in the last 2 years—Ellen often felt that there was no point to her daily activities there. These episodes of feeling down and unfulfilled had increased prior to her seeking treatment.

She was also not sure if she loved her husband or if he loved her. She regarded him as a good man, committed to his work, and reasonably pleasant to be around. But she feared that his interest in her had waned because he spent more time in activities with his friends (racquetball, cycling, poker) than ever before. Her satisfaction with their sexual relationship had diminished too. She found herself more inclined to avoid situations that might lead to sex.

Clinical Applications

History and Case Formulation.   As with most treatment, Ellen's psychoanalytic treatment begins with an assessment and case formulation by the therapist. Traditional psychoanalysts do not stress the use of structured assessment instruments. They may use them, especially to make differential diagnostic classifications, but psychoanalysts are more likely to rely on interview data and sometimes on projective tests to develop an understanding of the client. Assessment in psychoanalysis is an ongoing process that occurs over multiple sessions.

In Chapter 3, "Basic Features of Clinical Assessment," we presented a psychoanalytically oriented case study outline. The following would be especially important for psychoanalytic treatment of clients such as Ellen: (a) historical data such as family and developmental history (to identify information related to early conflicts or trauma); (b) mental status, level of distress, ego strengths and deficits, and "psychological mindedness" (to assess the client's intellectual and emotional ability to engage in psychoanalytic treatment); and (c) defense mechanisms, themes, or patterns of attachment difficulties in interpersonal relationships (to identify transference patterns).

> Ellen was the older of two children. When she was 12 years old, her father, a physician in a small town, divorced her mother and essentially abandoned the family. This was partly a relief, as there had been numerous fights in which Ellen's mother accused her husband of having affairs. But it also brought difficulties. Ellen's mother maintained a series of service-industry jobs and was barely able to keep the family out of poverty. The mother did not remarry but had a series of boyfriends, none of whom left any lasting impression on Ellen (or, apparently, her mother).
>
> Ellen's father was a particularly important figure in her childhood. A man she described as "dashing," he was outgoing and free-spirited at home. Particularly significant were Ellen's memories of him walking around the house in his underwear, pinching her, and teasing her about being ugly. This behavior continued as Ellen approached early adolescence. His pinching her on the buttocks or on her developing breasts brought her great embarrassment. She denied other forms of sexual abuse but reported strong anger about how his callous behaviors had hurt her self-esteem.
>
> In high school and college, Ellen had a few boyfriends. She said that she was attracted to the rebellious type, but these were often young men she felt to be her intellectual inferiors and the relationships typically did not last more than a few months. She met Rick when she was 27 (he was the same age) and felt that he was an interesting person and a more stable partner. His clear interest in her impressed her, and she agreed to marry him the following year.

Free Association.   After formalities of meeting times, payments, assessment procedures, and the like, are completed (important frame-setting procedures), psychoanalysis proper begins with the analyst explaining to the client that therapy requires following a single fundamental rule: The client should say everything that comes to mind without editing or censorship. This is *free association.* As noted earlier, free association evolved from Freud's search for a nonhypnotic way to help his patients recover memories and reveal intrapsychic associations. It is assumed that when the constraints of logic, social amenities, and other rules are removed, unconscious material will surface more easily.

Sometimes, the origins of unconscious conflict are clearly revealed, as when both client and therapist recognize a pattern that is both historical and current. Because of the operation of defense mechanisms, though, it is more common that the unconscious bases for clients' current problems are revealed only gradually and indirectly in the form of memories, feelings, wishes, and impressions arising through free association. It is the therapist's task to try to make sense of these emerging bits and pieces, some of which seem unrelated and even irrelevant. For example,

> During one session, Ellen related her reaction to a man she met at a company convention. "He was a jerk. I guess he thought he was hot stuff. I wondered if he was coming on to me, but I think he was like that with several women. Shameless. Greasy. I don't know why he bothered me so, I didn't even really get to know him." After a few moments of silence, Ellen reported, "I don't know why I just thought of this, but I remembered standing in our bathroom when I was growing up, holding my father's comb."

The fact that thoughts about meeting a man at a convention led to memories about holding her father's comb could have significance. In fact, psychoanalysts assume that it does. In Ellen's case, it could mean that characteristics of the man she met reminded her of her father (e.g., greasy black hair, inappropriately flirtatious with women). In therapy, the analyst may engage Ellen in a discussion of the possible connections. One way of doing so would be to encourage more free association around the man, the comb, and her father.

> Ellen's psychoanalyst formulated a tentative hypothesis about her problems. He assessed her depression as a secondary symptom arising gradually as she attempted, unsuccessfully, to cope with conflicts that affected her relationships. The analyst believed that her panic attacks were also related to concerns about intimacy, sexuality, and abandonment. Although secondary, the depression was the therapist's initial focus because he needed to determine its severity. After determining that Ellen was not suicidal, that she was motivated for treatment, and that she had sound intellect and adequate ego strength, the analyst and Ellen began a course of psychoanalysis.

The Role of the Therapist. During therapy sessions, traditional psychoanalysts maintain an "analytic incognito," revealing little about themselves during the course of psychotherapy. This orientation is aided by the office arrangements—the client lies on a couch and the therapist sits at its head, largely out of sight. In more recent variations of psychoanalytic approaches, chairs are substituted, but the therapist still maintains a relatively neutral attitude. The therapist's likes and dislikes, problems, hopes, and so on, remain unknown to the client. If clients ask personal questions, the therapist usually reminds them that the session is for their benefit and that while the exchange of personal information is appropriate in other circumstances, it does not benefit psychoanalysis. In other words, the therapist remains purposely opaque, much like a blank movie screen, so that clients can be free to *project* onto the therapist the attributes and motives that are unconsciously associated with parents and other important people in their lives. So at various times, the client may see the therapist as a loving caregiver, a vengeful father, a seductive mother, a jealous lover, or others. The therapist may also explore with the client, and perhaps interpret, the motives behind the client's desire to know more about the therapist. Doing so often reveals the client's own concerns, including transference-related concerns.

Of course, the ideal psychoanalyst is not coldly analytical and unresponsive. Psychoanalysts understand the importance of creating emotional safety in the therapeutic relationship, and so they are frequently empathic and reflective in their comments. They may use direct questions or encouraging phrases to help the client more deeply explore perceptions, emotions, motivations, and the like. The therapist's use of interpretation, when it occurs, can range from the suggestive (e.g., "I wonder if that seems familiar to you?") to the more direct statements that summarize patterns in current and historical conflicts.

Analysis of Everyday Behavior. Psychoanalysts are as attentive to clients' reports of activities outside of treatment as they are to what happens during treatment sessions. The analyst tries to maintain an "evenly divided" or "free-floating" attention to trivial as well as momentous events, to purposeful acts and accidental happenings, to body language as well as spoken language. Mistakes in speaking or writing (so-called "Freudian slips"), accidents, memory losses, and humor are seen as especially important sources of unconscious material.

Analysis of Dreams. Because unconscious material is believed to be closer to the surface in dreams than during waking consciousness, great importance is attached to them in psychoanalysis. The client's description of a dream—in which, say, she is running through the woods and suddenly falls into a lake—reveals its *manifest content* or obvious features. Manifest content often contains features associated with the dreamer's recent activities (called "day residue").

For psychoanalytic purposes, though, the most interesting aspect of dreams is their *latent content*: the unconscious ideas and impulses that appear in disguised form. The process of transforming unacceptable material into acceptable manifest content is called *dream work* (Freud, 1900), so most manifest dream content is viewed as being symbolic of something else—the specifics of which differ among people and among dreams. In spite of the popular belief that certain dream symbols (e.g., a snake) always mean the same thing (e.g., a penis), Freud believed dreams must be interpreted more flexibly.

A common analytic procedure is to ask the client to free associate to a dream's manifest content. In the process, unconscious material may be revealed. Frequently, a series of dreams is explored in analysis as a way of finding patterns of latent content and of not overemphasizing the importance of a single dream. In other words, dreams provide ideas for further probing more often than they provide final answers.

Analysis of Transference. When the patient–therapist relationship creates a miniature version of the causes of the client's problems, it is called the *transference neurosis* and becomes the central focus of analytic work. This reproduction of early unconscious conflicts allows the analyst to deal with important problems from the past as they occur in the present. Transference and transference neuroses must be handled with care as analysts try to decode the meaning of their clients' feelings toward them. If an analyst responded "normally" to a client's loving or hostile comments, the client would not learn much about what those comments reflect. Instead, the goal is to understand the meaning of the client's feelings for the therapist. If this can be done, the transference neurosis will be resolved and, with it, the client's main unconscious conflicts.

Because sensitive handling of the transference is thought so crucial to psychoanalysis, analysts are trained to be keenly alert to their own unconscious feelings, their *countertransference,* so that these feelings do not distort the analytic process. Training, supervision, and peer consultation are also used, as they are in other forms of therapy, to insure that the therapist consistently responds to the client in helpful ways.

Analysis of Resistance. Client behaviors that interfere with the analytic process are considered signs of resistance against achieving insight. Psychoanalysts try to help clients overcome resistance by pointing out its presence in obstructed free associations, distorted dream reports, missed appointments, lateness for treatment sessions,[1] avoidance of certain topics, failure to pay the therapist's bill, or a variety of other behaviors (Fine, 1971). Even clients' desire to address troubling symptoms rather than intrapsychic conflicts, or their request for evidence of the value of treatment, might be identified by psychoanalysts as an effort to divert attention from the unconscious causes of their problems.

As Ellen's analysis progressed, she explored her feelings about her childhood, especially her ambivalent feelings about her father and mother. On the one hand, she admired her father and longed to win his affection, but he seemed interested only in himself. On the other hand, Ellen felt rage at her father's selfishness and cruelty.

Being a "psychologically minded" person, Ellen was aware that her father's behavior toward her during her childhood had affected her self-concept and self-esteem. In adulthood, she therefore worked to convince herself that she was attractive and special. She reported that she did this partly by going through some "wild years" during and just after college. During this time, she exerted considerable effort to attract men, and she was typically successful, though with men that she was not that interested in or who were not that interested in her as a person.

Ellen and her therapist considered the possibility that her relationship patterns with men may have multiple causes and meanings (Freud called such situations "overdetermined"). Those patterns were a way to prove her father wrong (she was not ugly), but also they were a symbolic attempt to regain the affection that her father had never given (i.e., if she had been more attractive, more appealing, perhaps he would not have abandoned the family). A fear of abandonment pervaded her relationships.

In one particularly significant session, Ellen was exploring her feelings about her marriage. She discussed imagining herself leaving the relationship or having an affair. She recalled being at a convention and considering having a brief affair with a man who approached her there. Feeling tempted but overwhelmed by the impulse, she went to her hotel room to lie down briefly and consider the matter further. Moments later, a panic attack ensued. Several things seemed to connect in this session—sexual impulses, fears of loss, strivings for autonomy and self-esteem, and the feeling of panic.

---

[1]Some have jokingly suggested that you cannot win in analysis because you are dependent if you show up early, resistant if you show up late, and compulsive if you are right on time.

Making Analytic Interpretations. Analysts want clients to gain insight into unconscious conflicts, but they don't want to overwhelm them with potentially frightening material before they are ready to handle it. This is where analytic interpretation comes in. Through questions and comments about the client's behavior, free associations, dreams, and the like, the analyst guides the process of self-exploration. Thus, if the client shows resistance to seeing the potential meaning of some event, the therapist not only points out the resistance but also offers an interpretation of what is going on.

The interpretive process is tentative and continuous, a constant encouragement of clients to consider alternative views, to reject obvious explanations, to search for deeper meanings. As interpretations help clients understand and work through the transference, the therapeutic relationship changes. Clients not only see how defenses and unconscious conflicts caused problems, they learn to deal differently with the world, beginning with the therapist. They also learn that forces from their past no longer need to dictate their behavior in the present. Ideally, this emotional understanding will liberate the client to deal with life in a more realistic and satisfying manner than before.

As Ellen continued in psychoanalysis, she and the therapist began to feel that they better understood many of the complex emotional currents that defined Ellen's relationships. Ellen developed insight into her unconscious concern that her husband's activities "with the guys" foreshadowed his abandonment of the marriage, and she became less worried about his leaving. She recognized that her husband was fundamentally different from her "dashing" but uncommitted father.

Her panic attacks were less frequent but not entirely absent. Her relationship with her mother improved after they were able to have some candid conversations about her father (who had since died). Gradually, however, Ellen began to feel that her therapist was becoming less interested in working with her, though she did not verbalize these feelings.

After Ellen missed an appointment—she said that work required her attention—the therapist explored with Ellen whether her feelings about therapy had changed. She admitted that she had been thinking that maybe she had gone as far as she could go in therapy. Together, she and her analyst explored the possibility of termination. The analyst did not advise it, as he felt that they were working through some important material and talk of termination might be a form of resistance. However, he said that he would support her decision if she chose to terminate.

Ellen missed the next session—again, claiming work commitments. Days later, at the next session, she was cheerful and provocatively dressed but also reported that she had experienced another panic attack. When the therapist commented on her cheerful demeanor and manner of dress, Ellen became angry with him. She felt he did not appreciate her attempts to cheer herself up or to make their interaction more pleasant. She accused him of secretly wanting to terminate the relationship, of probably being bored and uninterested in her "case" any more.

This and the sessions that followed were especially productive because they represented opportunities to analyze Ellen's resistance (suggesting termination, missing appointments) as well as the transference. The therapist suggested that Ellen's feeling that she was about to be abandoned, that the therapist really did not care about her, were a reflection of how she had felt about her husband and about her father. Her attempts to prevent this abandonment by being more attractive, perhaps even seductive (but emotionally inauthentic), and then feeling angry, were also reflections of a historical pattern for her.

Over time, Ellen came to appreciate the repetitive unconscious conflicts that affected her most intimate relationships. In the ensuing sessions, she was able to more clearly differentiate the therapist from her father, as she had begun to do with her husband. Her marriage improved, as did her self-esteem and her relationship with her mother. Symptoms of depression diminished. Although the panic attacks did not disappear entirely, they became much less frequent. Ellen felt that she could now recognize the feelings and behavior patterns that went with her old scripts. This insight allowed her to try out other behaviors in her relationships. In short, by making unconscious conflicts conscious and then working through them in psychoanalysis, she was no longer compelled to repeat them. With insight, she developed greater ego control over her impulses and fears.

Our brief account of classic psychoanalysis techniques has left out many details and oversimplified others. More complete coverage of the approach is contained in numerous references (e.g., Freud, 1949; Kernberg, 1976; McWilliams, 2004; Menninger, 1958; Peterson, Cooper, & Gabbard, 2005; Ward, 2006).

Section Summary: Psychoanalysis, developed by Freud, rests on a description of personality that involves internal conflict among parts of the personality labeled as id, ego, and superego. When certain of these conflicts develop from early experiences, they are likely to become both habitual (they are repeated in later relationships) and unconscious (they are repeated automatically, without awareness of their origins or effects). Psychoanalysts use free association, dream analysis, and other techniques to understand how the client's past intrudes on the present. In therapy, they attempt to interpret or reveal to the client similarities in past relationships, current external relationships (e.g., with spouse or children), and especially in the therapy relationship itself (i.e., transference). As clients come to recognize and repeatedly work through these connections, they gain insight and become less impelled to repeat those patterns.

PSYCHODYNAMIC PSYCHOTHERAPY

Section Preview: Many theorists have advocated changes in Freudian psychoanalysis, ranging from minor alterations to wholesale rejection of certain fundamental principles. Most of today's psychodynamically oriented clinicians employ treatments that, although based on psychoanalysis, differ from it in that they involve (a) less emphasis on sexual and aggressive id impulses, (b) greater attention to adaptive functioning of the ego, (c) greater attention to the role of close relationships, and (d) flexibility in the degree to which therapists analyze and interpret versus offer empathy and emotional support.

Freud's theories attracted a broad following, but some theorists sought to change certain aspects of psychoanalytic theory while preserving others. Collectively, the therapies that share certain basic assumptions with psychoanalysis but significantly change others are called *psychodynamic psychotherapies*.

These variations were developed by like-minded theorists and practitioners who formed various schools or approaches (Pine, 1990; see Table 7.2). Space limitations prevent us from covering them all, but let's consider some of the most prominent versions of psychodynamic treatment.

Psychoanalytically Oriented Psychotherapy

Therapists whose psychoanalytic procedures depart only slightly from the guidelines set down by Freud are said to employ *psychoanalytically oriented psychotherapy*. For

TABLE 7.2

Variations on Psychoanalytic Theory and Practice

Approach	Theorists	Emphasis
Early Alternatives to Freudian Psychoanalysis		
Individual psychology	Alfred Adler	Striving to overcome feelings of inferiority; importance of social motives and social behavior
Analytical psychology	Carl Jung	Reconciliation of opposites (e.g., anima, animus) in personality, personality orientations of introversion and extroversion, personal and collective unconscious
Will therapy	Otto Rank	Client choice; therapist humanity rather than technical skill
More Recent Psychodynamic Alternatives		
Ego psychology	Anna Freud, Heinz Hartman, David Rapaport	Focus on adaptive ego functioning and establishment of firm identity and intimacy
Object relations theory	Melanie Klein, Otto Kernberg, David Winnicott, W. R. D. Fairbairn	Modifying mental representations of interpersonal relationships that come from early attachments
Self-psychology	Heinz Kohut	Closely related to object relations theory but stresses development of autonomous self
Interpersonal relations school	Harry Stack Sullivan, Clara Thompson	Interpersonal contexts of disorders and treatment
Relational and postmodern approaches	Steven Mitchell, Robert Stolorow, George Atwood	Strong emphasis on relationships with caretakers and exploration of the "intersubjective space" created jointly by client and therapist
Short-term psychodynamic approaches	Wilhelm Stekel, Hans Strupp	Coping strategies stressed over historical interpretation

SOURCES: Adapted from Curtis and Hirsch, 2003; Gabbard, 2005; Hergenhahn, 1994; Kutash, 1976; Prochaska and Norcross, 1999; Wolitzky, 2003.

example, during the 1930s and 1940s, Franz Alexander and his colleagues at the Chicago Psychoanalytic Institute questioned the belief that treatment must be intense, extended, and fundamentally similar in all cases (Alexander & French, 1946). They also sought to apply psychoanalysis to "nontraditional" clients such as the young and the severely disturbed.

In psychoanalytically oriented psychotherapy, not every patient is seen for the standard five sessions per week because daily sessions may foster too much dependence on the analyst or may become so routine that the patient pays too little attention to them. The frequency of sessions varies as circumstances dictate. Early in treatment, the patient may be seen every day; later, sessions may take place less often. Alexander even suggested that temporary interruptions in treatment could be beneficial by testing the patient's ability to live without therapy and reducing reliance on the therapist. He noted as well that, while some clients need lengthy psychoanalysis in order to fully explore and work through resistance, insights, and the transference, others—especially those whose problems are either relatively mild or especially severe—are candidates for less extensive treatment aimed at support rather than at the uncovering and reconstructing associated with classical analysis (for an example of this approach, see Davanloo, 1994).

Alfred Adler's Individual Psychology

Alfred Adler was an early follower of Freud who was the first to defect from the ranks of orthodox psychoanalysis. He deemphasized Freud's theory of instincts, infantile sexuality, and the role of the unconscious in determining behavior. His treatment methods focused on exploring and altering misconceptions (or maladaptive lifestyles, as he called them). So where a strict Freudian might see a teenage boy's vomiting before school each morning as a defense of some kind, the Adlerian analyst would view the problem as reflecting tension brought about by a misconception such as "I must do better than everyone else." And while the vomiting might be explored in Freudian analysis through free association, a therapist using Adler's individual analysis would discuss the symptom with the client as an illustration of a style of life driven by misconceptions that function to protect the client from perceived weaknesses. The youngster would then be helped to form more appropriate attitudes and given encouragement to change his style in a more adaptive direction.

In Adlerian analysis, client and therapist sit face to face in similar chairs. The feelings and reactions expressed toward the therapist (transference) are interpreted not as reflecting unconscious childhood conflicts but as the client's habitual style of dealing with people like the therapist. Similarly, Adlerians view resistance as a sample of how the client usually avoids unpleasant material, and dreams are interpreted not as symbolic wish fulfillment but as a "rehearsal" of how the client might deal with problems in the future. And where Freudians offer interpretations designed to promote insight into past causes of current problems, Adlerians interpret in order to promote insight into the patient's current lifestyle.

Adlerian therapists are more involved than Freudians are in advising and encouraging their clients to change. For example, once a client realizes that her dependence on her husband is part of her overall style of seeking protection (and thus controlling others), the therapist might point out several alternative ways she might start to change. Adlerians also use modeling, homework assignments, and other techniques to help patients become aware of their lifestyle and to prompt them to change. Many of these methods are similar to tactics employed in the behavioral and humanistic therapies described later.

Ego Psychology

While psychoanalytically oriented psychotherapists mainly revised Freud's procedures, another group of therapists known as *ego analysts* challenged some of his basic principles. They argued, for example, that Freud's preoccupation with sexual and aggressive instincts (the id) as the basis for behavior and behavior disorder is too narrow. Behavior, they said, is determined to a large extent by the ego, which can function not just to combat id impulses or to referee conflicts but also to promote learning and creativity. These ideas led analysts such as Heinz Hartmann (1958), David Rapaport (1951), Erik Erikson (1946), and Freud's daughter, Anna (1946), to use psychoanalytic techniques to explore patients' adaptive ego functions.

Ego-analytic techniques differ from classical analytic techniques in that therapists focus less on working through early childhood experiences and more on working through current problems. Therapists assess and attempt to bolster the client's *ego strengths,* which include reality testing, impulse control, judgment, and the use of more "mature" defense mechanisms such as sublimation. In ego psychology, the therapeutic relationship remains important, but less so for its distorting transferences than for its supportive and trusting functions.

Object Relations and Self-Psychology

Another prominent variation on psychoanalysis has emerged from object relations theory, a movement associated with a group of British analysts including W. R. D. Fairbairn (1952), Donald Winnicott (1965), Melanie Klein (1975), and Margaret Mahler (Mahler, Pine, & Bergman, 1975), as well as Otto Kernberg (1976) and Heinz Kohut (1977, 1983). While ego psychology expanded the role of the ego, object relations theory expanded the role of relationships, especially early relationships, in psychodynamic thought.

Object relations theories, and the therapies based on them, focus on the nature of interpersonal relationships that are built from very early infant—caregiver interactions (Blatt & Lerner, 1983; Eagle, 1984). Because these early relationships act as prototypes for later relationships, disruptions in them can have profound consequences later in life. Therapists working with psychotic or personality-disordered clients, for instance, might find that their client idealizes them at one point and demonizes them at another. With such clients, working through relationship concerns is expected to be especially difficult and time consuming.

Thus, in contrast to classical psychoanalysts, object relations theorists view the therapeutic relationship not as transference to be analyzed but as a "second chance" for the client to obtain in a close relationship the gratification that was absent during infancy. This emphasis on ego support, acceptance, and psychological "holding" of damaged selves has made object relations therapies among the most popular versions of psychoanalysis, largely because they allow a friendly, naturally human stance toward the therapeutic relationship, which many therapists prefer to traditional Freudian neutrality.

Kohut's *self-psychology* focuses more on the self or self-concept but, like object relations approaches, views the analyst's task as providing the type of empathic responding and nurturing that the client is assumed to have missed as an infant. The therapist's role in these approaches is similar to that taken in the humanistic/phenomenological therapies that we discuss later (Kahn, 1985).

Relational Psychodynamic Psychotherapy

The relational psychodynamic approaches blend several theories (Curtis & Hirsch, 2003; DeYoung, 2003), including elements from traditional psychoanalysis, ego psychology, object relations theory, self-psychology, Sullivan's interpersonal therapy, and humanistic, person-centered, and phenomenological approaches (described in the next section). As its name implies, relational psychodynamic theory stresses relationships with caretakers. Like object relations theorists, relational theorists stress the importance of early relationships as templates for later ones. They point out that relationships have an objective dimension (the events that actually happen) and a subjective dimension (the way the relationship is mentally represented, or perceived, by the persons involved). The latter plays an especially important role in relational psychodynamic theory and practice.

In contrast to Freud's intrapsychic approach, relational theorists adopt a strongly interpersonal approach. Harry Stack Sullivan, the father of the interpersonal perspective, played an important role in developing the relational approaches. Sullivan believed that therapists should use their observations of the client's current and past interpersonal relationships to clarify for them how their typical cognitions and behaviors interfere with successful living. However, Sullivan and later relational therapists cautioned against assuming that the therapist's view of the therapeutic relationship was objectively correct. Because the client and the therapist both work from their own subjective viewpoints, relational psychodynamic theorists believe that neither perception can be objectively validated.

The relational psychodynamic approach has achieved considerable popularity in the United States in the past decade (DeYoung, 2003; Wolitzky, 2003), partly because it is compatible with the broader intellectual trend variously called *intersubjectivism, constructivism,* or *postmodernism* (Neimeyer & Bridges, 2003). Central to this trend is the idea that no objective authority can judge whether one view of reality is "correct," but jointly constructed views are nevertheless highly meaningful. Accordingly, relational psychodynamic therapists view the shared conceptual and interpersonal understanding that develops between client and therapist as a psychological system in its own right, one worthy of analysis (Stolorow, 1993). For this reason, relational psychodynamic therapies are sometimes called "two-person theories" (Gabbard, 2000).

Short-Term Psychodynamic Psychotherapy

Until recently, few people associated short-term treatments with the psychodynamic approach, even though several of Freud's early treatments were brief (Levison & Strupp, 1999). *Short-term dynamic psychotherapy* approaches emphasize pragmatic goals that can be obtained in relatively few sessions, typically 20 or less. Therapists focus on helping clients cope with a current crisis or problem rather than on helping them work through early relationships or to reconstruct the personality.

Short-term dynamic therapists stress the formation a working therapeutic alliance as quickly as possible and then help clients adopt coping strategies within specific domains. They might focus on anxiety management or coping with a problem relationship at work. Because the pace of therapy is accelerated, therapists are more active than in other forms of psychodynamic therapy. They may use traditional techniques of psychoanalysis, but they also might assign homework, refer clients to self-help groups, or adopt other techniques not typically associated with psychodynamic treatment. There are several models for short-term dynamic therapy, some of which include manuals for treating specific disorders (Levison & Strupp, 1999). Interpersonal psychotherapy (IPT), a treatment typically used for persons with depressive disorders, is an example of a short-term dynamic treatment that has shown promising results (Klerman, Weissman, Rounsaville, & Chevron, 1984).

Common Features and Variations in Psychodynamic Therapies

A useful way of thinking about all the psychodynamic variations we have discussed is to categorize them along a continuum according to their similarity to psychoanalysis. At one end is psychoanalysis itself, and close to it is psychoanalytically oriented psychotherapy. At the other end are the relational and postmodern versions of psychodynamic psychotherapy. In between are treatments based on ego psychology, self-psychology, and interpersonal psychology. Although these variants seem different, and in some ways they are, remember that all of them share core beliefs about the psychological importance of (a) intrapsychic conflict (b) unconscious processes, (c) early relationships, (d) ego functioning, and (e) the client–therapist relationship. They differ largely in matters of emphasis and in how these concepts are best applied during treatment.

Another common feature of these variants is that the length of treatment is shorter than that of traditional psychoanalysis. Long-term psychodynamic psychotherapy lasts 6 months or longer and involves sessions usually lasting 45 to 50 minutes once or twice per week. Psychodynamic psychotherapy that is designed to be more supportive varies depending on the client's needs but can be as short as one 25-minute session once or twice per month or as frequent and long as long-term psychodynamic treatment (Gabbard, 2005).

The Supportive–Expressive Dimension. Contemporary psychodynamic psychotherapists seek to create an empathic and supportive atmosphere in which the client feels cared for and understood. Many believe that this atmosphere creates a *corrective emotional experience* for the client and is a healing factor independent of insight (Strupp, 1989; Strupp & Blinder, 1984). Psychodynamic psychotherapists can then practice interventions that range from the analytical ones advocated in psychoanalysis to the more supportive interventions stressed by interpersonal and relational approaches. Gabbard (2005) refers to these technique variations as the *supportive–expressive continuum.*

Therapists offering more supportive interventions typically seek to help clients with coping, stress reduction, and day-to-day functioning. In practice, these clinicians may be more active than they are in expressive therapy. For example, if a client has experienced a significant loss (e.g., the death of a child or spouse) or has very low frustration tolerance, the therapist might forego the goal of insight and engage in more empathic, encouraging, and supportive interventions. A client who is unhappy about an unsatisfying job might be encouraged to look for a better position, and the therapist's role will be supportive and educational. The idea is that the therapeutic relationship provides a stable context in which to form plans for progress that can be tested in real life.

How does a clinician decide whether to offer more supportive or more expressive interventions? Table 7.3 lists some of the factors that influence the clinician's decision.

The Current Status of Psychodynamic Psychotherapy

Classical psychoanalysis is practiced by only about 2% of clinicians (Bechtoldt, Norcross, Wyckoff, Pokrywa, & Campbell, 2001). However, psychodynamically oriented variations continue to be practiced by a large number of clinicians and taught as a dominant orientation by several graduate and professional schools. Psychodynamically oriented research publications are also easy to find. Indeed, along with cognitive-behavioral and eclectic approaches, the psychodynamic approach is among the three most popular in clinical psychology (Bechtoldt et al., 2001). So despite the tendency of some critics to dismiss all psychodynamic theory because certain aspects of Freud's theory have been discredited, the psychodynamic approach has evolved and remains a significant force in clinical psychology.

For more detailed coverage of psychodynamic psychotherapy, consult some of the excellent psychotherapy texts that are currently available (Corsini & Wedding, 2007;

TABLE 7.3

Indications for Expressive or Supportive Emphasis in Psychodynamic Psychotherapy

Expressive	Supportive
Strong motivation to understand	Significant ego defects of a chronic nature
Significant suffering	Severe life crisis
Ability to regress in the service of the ego	Low anxiety tolerance
Tolerance for frustration	Poor frustration tolerance
Capacity for insight (psychological mindedness)	Lack of psychological mindedness
Intact reality testing	Poor reality testing
Meaningful object relations	Severely impaired object relations
Good impulse control	Poor impulse control
Ability to sustain a job	Low intelligence
Capacity to think in terms of analogy and metaphor	Organically based cognitive dysfunction
Reflective responses to trial interpretations	Tenuous ability to form a therapeutic relationship

SOURCE: From *Psychodynamic Psychiatry in Clinical Practice*, 4th ed., by G. O. Gabbard, 2005 (Washington, DC: American Psychiatric Publishing), p. 115. Copyright 2005 by American Psychiatric Publishing. Adapted with permission.

DeYoung, 2003; Gabbard, 2005; Gurman & Messer, 2003; Kljenak, 2006; McWilliams, 2004; Murdock, 2004).

Section Summary: Psychoanalytic theory and practice has continued to develop beyond Freud's original formulations. Later psychoanalytic theorists moved away from his strong emphasis on id, sex, and aggression. They stressed the role of the ego as an adaptive, creative problem-solving agency. They also greatly expanded consideration of interpersonal relationships in the development of healthy personality, psychopathology, and psychotherapy. Many analytically oriented clinicians continue to analyze transference relationships with the aim of helping clients develop insight into their historically rooted maladaptive patterns. They do so with a view of the therapeutic relationship that differs from Freud's. Relational psychodynamic theorists, in particular, stress the subjective nature of all relationships, including the therapeutic one. This view requires that the process of interpretation and meaning-finding in therapy must be collaborative. Psychodynamic psychotherapists offer a wider range of interventions, from the highly expressive and analytical to the highly supportive.

HUMANISTIC PSYCHOTHERAPY

Section Preview: Here we describe humanistic approaches to psychotherapy, which emphasize conscious awareness rather than unconscious conflict. These approaches also stress the need for the therapist to seek to understand the experiential worlds of their clients and to communicate that understanding to clients as a way of creating a therapeutic atmosphere and the therapeutic relationship. The relationship itself is seen as the primary curative factor in the treatments offered by humanistic therapists.

Humanistic approaches to treatment stress the importance of clients focusing on their immediate, here-and-now experiences. Examples of these approaches include person-centered psychotherapy (Rogers, 1951), Gestalt therapy (Perls, 1969), existential therapy (May, 1981; Frankl, 1967), focusing-oriented psychotherapy (Gendlin, 1996), and several others.

As discussed in Chapter 2, humanistic psychotherapists view humans as creative, growthful beings who, if all goes well, consciously guide their own behavior toward realization of their fullest potential as unique individuals. When behavior disorders arise, they are usually seen as stemming from disturbances in awareness or restrictions on existence that can be eliminated through various therapeutic experiences (Fischer, 1989; Greenberg, Elliott, & Lietaer, 1994).

Several themes unify the goals and techniques associated with humanistic treatments. First, humanistic therapists assume that their clients' lives can be understood only from the viewpoint of those clients. Second, many humanistic therapists view human beings not as instinct-driven creatures but as naturally good people who are able to make choices about their lives and determine their own destinies. Third, humanistic therapists view the therapeutic relationship as the primary vehicle by which therapy achieves its benefits. It must be a relationship that guarantees honest, emotionally open, interpersonal experiences for both client and therapist. This implies that clients are regarded as equals;

therapists treat clients as responsible individuals who are experts on their own experiences and who must ultimately be the ones to make decisions about their lives. Finally, many humanistic therapists emphasize the importance of experiencing and exploring emotions that are confusing or painful.

Person-Centered Therapy

By far the most prominent of the humanistic approaches is the *person-centered psychotherapy* developed by Carl Rogers and introduced in Chapter 2. Rogers originally called his approach *client-centered therapy* but later changed the name as he expanded its applications. First trained in psychodynamic therapy methods in the late 1920s, Rogers eventually became uncomfortable with the idea of therapists as authority figures who searched relentlessly for unconscious conflicts. Rogers felt there had to be a better way to do clinical work, and an alternative began to take shape when he discovered a treatment approach advocated by Otto Rank, whose revision of Freud's ideas was mentioned in Table 7.2. To Rank, the client ". . . is a moving cause, containing constructive forces within, which constitute a will to health. The therapist guides the individual to self-understanding, self-acceptance. It is the therapist *as a human being* who is the remedy, not his technical skill. . . . The spontaneity and uniqueness of therapy lived in the present carry the patient toward health" (Meador & Rogers, 1973, p. 121; italics added).

Carl Rogers (1902–1987)
by John T. Wood.
(Courtesy of Carl Rogers.)

As Rogers began to incorporate these ideas about nonauthoritarianism and the value of a good human relationship into his therapy sessions, he came to believe that "it is the client who knows what hurts, what directions to go, what problems are crucial, what experiences have been deeply buried" (Rogers, 1961, pp. 11–12). He also began to see therapy as an "if . . . then" proposition: *If* the correct circumstances are created by the therapist, *then* the client—driven by an innate potential for growth—will spontaneously improve.

Rogers's Personality Theory and View of Psychopathology.

Rogers's person-centered theory proposes a developmental process leading to either more or less healthy personality functioning. Critical to this process is the concept of the self. The *self* represents the experiences the person recognizes as "me" (Murdock, 2004). It includes values, images, memories, behavior patterns, and, especially, current experiences. Two particularly important aspects of the self are the real self and the ideal self. Let's consider how they develop.

The Self and Conditions of Worth.

As children grow, they come to recognize their likes and dislikes, their abilities, emotional states, and the like. In short, their self-concept expands, but not in isolation; it develops in the context of relationships with others, especially parents. The child becomes aware that others regard certain of his or her self-experiences more highly than others.

According to Rogers, the ideal situation is one in which parents are successful at communicating their acceptance (if not approval) of all of the child's behavior and experiences. Rogers called such communication *unconditional positive regard* and considered it as a critical requirement for psychological growth. To the degree that parents communicate acceptance of their child's behavior and experiences, the child naturally incorporates those experiences into his or her *real self-concept*. The child comes to recognize these experiences as part of the self, and because others have valued them, the child values them, too.

However, when parents communicate disapproval or rejection of some of the child's behaviors and experiences, the child may experience love as conditional. This is especially likely to happen if the child feels that the parents' disapproval is of *him or her* rather than of *his or her behavior* (e.g., a parent who says, "You're so stupid!" communicates a different message from one who says, "I love you, but it makes me angry when you do that"). Rogers called this situation *conditions of worth* because the child comes to believe that acceptance, and indeed his or her worth as a person, depends on thinking and acting in certain ways. The more pronounced the conditions of worth, the more the child's real self-concept deviates from his or her *ideal self-concept*. The ideal self is not immediately experienced as "me" but as what the child believes he or she *should* be.

Incongruence.

The discrepancy between the real self and the ideal self is called *incongruence*. It is a matter of degree—no parent communicates unconditional positive regard for every behavior and experience a child has. But the more a person experiences his or her positive regard dependent upon acting and feeling in ways consistent with what other people value, the more the real self and the ideal self become separated (see

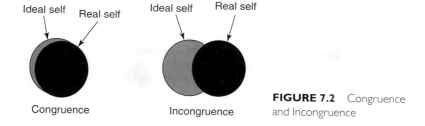

FIGURE 7.2   Congruence and Incongruence

Figure 7.2). In short, the conditions of worth force people to distort their real feelings or experiences. When it happens, symptoms of disorder may appear. Thus, if a person really wanted to be an artist but felt those feelings had to be ignored because of family pressure to become an accountant, depression might result. Growth would stop as the person's behavior (e.g., professing satisfaction with accounting) became increasingly discrepant, or incongruent, with real feelings. The distortions and lack of awareness that produce symptoms may not be entirely conscious, but neither are they inaccessible as the psychoanalytic approaches might suggest.

The Goals of Person-Centered Therapy

Person-centered therapists do not set treatment goals for their clients. Instead, clients are free to select their own goals (Bohart, 2003). From the therapist's point of view, though, a key aim of therapy is to make clients more authentically aware of their moment-to-moment experiences. The therapist promotes such awareness by providing an interpersonal relationship that the client can use to reduce incongruence and further personal growth. This growth-enhancing relationship can only appear, said Rogers, if the therapist experiences and expresses three interrelated attitudes: unconditional positive regard, empathy, and congruence.

Unconditional Positive Regard.   The therapeutic attitude Rogers called *unconditional positive regard* conveys that the therapist cares about the client, accepts the client, and trusts the client's ability to change. The ideal form of unconditional positive regard is *nonpossessive caring,* in which genuine positive feelings are expressed in a way that makes clients feel valued but still free to be themselves, not obligated to try to please the therapist. The therapist's *willingness to listen* is an important manifestation of unconditional positive regard. Patient, warm, and interested in what the client has to say, Rogerian therapists do not interrupt the client or change the subject or give other signs that they would rather be doing something else.

The "unconditional" aspect of unconditional positive regard is manifested in the therapist's willingness to accept clients as they are without judging them. Rogers believed that the experience of being prized as a human being, regardless of one's feelings or behaviors, can be a growth-enhancing experience for clients whose development has been hampered by conditions of worth and other evaluative pressures. Fortunately, expressing unconditional positive regard does not require *approving* of all the things a client says or does but merely *accepting* them as part of a person whom the therapist cares about. This ideal is illustrated in the following interaction:

> CLIENT: That was the semester my brother died and everything seemed to be going down the tubes. I knew how important it was to my parents that I get into medical school, but I also knew that my grades would be lousy that year unless I did something. To make a long story short, I bought a term paper and cheated on almost every exam that semester.
>
> THERAPIST: It was a really rough time for you.

Notice that the therapist focuses on the client's feelings in the situation, not on the ethics of the behavior. In other words, to express unconditional positive regard, the therapist must separate a client's worth *as a person* from the worth of the client's *behavior*.

The "positive" component of unconditional positive regard is reflected in the therapist's trust in the client's potential for growth and problem solving. Rogers believed that if clients perceive that their therapist lacks this trust, they will not develop the confidence they need to make changes. So, like other humanistic/experiential therapists, Rogerians try not to give advice, take responsibility for clients, or make decisions for them. Such restraint is sometimes difficult, especially when therapists feel that they know "what's best" for a client. However, the client must be allowed to make bad decisions or experience problems, even if they could have been averted by following the therapist's advice. Advice from a therapist might prevent one problem but could create others: the therapist would become a superior, the client would become more dependent, and, most important, both client and therapist would have less faith in the client's ability to deal independently with problems.

Empathy.   To understand a client's behavior and help the client understand it as well, the therapist must try to see the world as the client sees it. In Rogerian terms, this involves striving for accurate *empathy,* or *empathic understanding*. To illustrate, let's consider an excerpt from the beginning of a therapy session:

> CLIENT: I don't feel very normal, but I want to feel that way. . . . I thought I'd have something to talk about—then it all goes around in circles. I was trying to think what I was going to say. I tell you, I just can't make a decision; I don't know what I want. I've tried to reason this thing out logically—tried to figure out which things are important to me. I thought that there are maybe two things a man might do; he might get married and raise a family. But if he was just a bachelor, just making a living—that isn't very good. I find myself and my thoughts getting back to the days when I was a kid and I cry very easily. The dam would break through. I've been in the Army four and a half years. I had no problems then, no hopes, no wishes. My only thought was to get out when peace would come. My problems, now that I'm out, are as ever. I tell you, they go back to a long time before I was in the Army. I love children. When I was in the Philippines—I tell you, when I was young I swore I'd never forget my unhappy childhood—so when I saw these children in the Philippines, I treated them very nicely. I used to

give them ice cream cones and movies. It was just a period—I'd reverted back— and that awakened some emotions in me I thought I had long buried. (A pause. He seems very near tears.) (Rogers, 1951, pp. 32–33)

Many therapists would react to this client using what Rogers called an *external frame of reference.* They would observe the client from the outside and apply their values or psychological theories to what the client says (see the left side of Table 7.4). An empathic therapist, however, would try to adopt an internal frame of reference in an effort to understand what it must be like to be this client (see the right side of Table 7.4).

To communicate an empathic attitude to their clients, Rogerian therapists employ the active listening methods described in Chapter 4, "Interviewing and Observation in Clinical Psychology." Of particular value is *reflection,* which serves the dual purposes of (a) communicating the therapist's desire for emotional understanding and (b) making clients more aware of their own feelings. Reflection is one of the most misunderstood aspects of person-centered therapy because the therapist appears to be stating the obvious or merely repeating what the client has said. But reflection is more than repetition or paraphrasing. As suggested in Chapter 4, it involves distilling and "playing back" the client's feelings. For example, suppose a client says, "This has been such a bad day. I've had to keep myself from crying three or four times. I'm not even sure what's wrong!" The therapist's response could be externally oriented, such as "Well, what exactly happened?" but a more empathic comment might be "You really do feel bad. The tears just well up inside. And it sounds like it is scary to not even know why you feel this way."

TABLE 7.4

Some Therapist Thoughts That Reflect Internal versus External Frames of Reference

External	Internal
I wonder if I should get him started talking.	You're wanting to struggle toward normality, aren't you?
Is this inability to get underway a type of dependence?	It's really hard for you to get started.
Why this indecisiveness? What could be its cause?	Decision making just seems impossible for you.
What is meant by this focus on marriage and family?	You want marriage, but it doesn't seem to you to be much of a possibility.
The crying, the "dam," sounds as though there must be a great deal of regression.	You feel yourself brimming over with childish feelings.
He's a veteran. Could he have been a psychiatric case? I feel sorry for anybody who spent four and a half years in the service.	To you, the Army represented stagnation.
What is this interest in children? Identification? Vague homosexuality?	Being very nice to children somehow has meaning for you; but it was—and is—a disturbing experience for you.

SOURCE: From *Client-Centered Therapy,* by C. R. Rogers, 1951 (Boston: Houghton Mifflin), pp. 33–34. Copyright 1951 by Houghton Mifflin. Reprinted with permission.

At first glance, the clinician may seem to be a parrot, but look more closely. The client never *said* she felt bad; the therapist inferred it by taking the client's point of view. Similarly, the client never said her sadness frightened her—it was the clinician's ability to put himself in the client's shoes that led to this speculation. If the therapist's inferences are wrong, the client can correct them, but right or wrong, the clinician has let the client know that he wants to understand her experience rather than diagnose it.

Congruence.   Rogers also believed that the more genuine the therapist is in relating to clients, the more helpful the therapist will be. The therapist's feelings and actions, he said, should be *congruent,* or consistent, with one another. "This means that I need to be aware of my own feelings . . . [and willing] to express, in my words and my behavior, the various feelings and attitudes which exist in me" (Rogers, 1961, p. 33). According to Rogers, when the therapist is congruent, a real human relationship occurs in therapy.

To get an idea of how congruence promotes trust, think of a time when a close friend might have told you something that you did not want to hear, perhaps that you looked silly or were wrong about something. Once you know that a friend will say what he or she really feels even if it does not make you happy, it makes it easier to trust whatever else that friend might say. However, if you know that your friend can be incongruent, telling you what you want to hear instead of what he or she genuinely feels, your faith in that person's reactions ("You really look great.") is likely to be undermined.

Here is one way that congruence can be displayed in a therapist–client interaction:

CLIENT: I just feel so hopeless. Tell me what I'm doing wrong in my life.

THERAPIST: I guess when you are feeling this bad, it would be nice if someone could come along and tell you what is going wrong and how you can put everything right again. I wish I could do all that, but I can't. I don't think anyone else can either.

Notice the therapist's reflection of the client's feeling plus the direct expression of (a) a genuine wish to understand and solve the client's problems, and (b) an admission that she is not capable of such a feat.

The Nature of Change in Person-Centered Therapy.   Rogers argued that as clients experience empathy, unconditional positive regard, and congruence in a therapeutic relationship, they become more self-aware and self-accepting, more comfortable and less defensive in interpersonal relationships, less rigid in their thinking, more reliant on self-evaluation than on evaluations by others, and better able to function in a wide variety of roles (Rogers, 1951).

Carl Rogers was among the first to recognize the need for scientific research to substantiate the alleged value of any treatment technique, including his own. He was the first to record therapy sessions, and he conducted some of the first empirical research on the relationship between treatment outcome and therapist characteristics such as empathy and warmth (Rogers, 1942).

Case Example

The following case excerpts are taken from a person-centered therapy case presented by Murdock (2004, pp. 108–137).

> Richard is a 48-year-old Caucasian. He is a high school graduate and has worked as an insurance salesperson for the past 3 years. Prior to this period, he worked at the management level for a telecommunications company but left this job because he found it too stressful.
>
> Richard presents with depressed mood that affects his physical, social, and occupational functioning. He reports experiencing this depression for about the past 2 years. During this period, Richard characterizes himself as often fatigued, socially withdrawn, and ineffective at work. His income has dropped significantly during the last 2 years. Richard feels guilty for having to rely on his wife, Sandy, as the primary income provider. According to Richard, Sandy often expresses disapproval of him nonverbally, such as when she is writing checks for the monthly bills. The couple argues quite frequently about financial matters.
>
> Richard and Sandy have two adult children (Natalie and James) who have completed college within the past 5 years. Richard reports that both children currently earn more than his present income. This situation makes him feel inadequate. As a result, Richard feels emotionally distant from Natalie and James and sees them as closer to Sandy.
>
> Richard's social activities typically involve his wife and are work-related. He spends his spare time with his computer or reading. He reports having no close friends.
>
> During counseling sessions, Richard seems uncomfortable, has difficulty maintaining eye contact, laughs nervously during the shortest periods of silence, and comments on his discomfort with the lack of structure. Although he seems motivated to change, Richard seems to have difficulty discussing his situation.

Case Formulation. A person-centered therapist would not be inclined to seek Richard's personal or family history. Neither would the therapist be inclined to assign a DSM diagnosis unless perhaps insurance reimbursement required it. More important to the person-centered therapist is the client's internal perspective. The therapist would want to discover how Richard experienced his life, including, but not limited to, his symptoms.

> Daryl, Richard's person-centered therapist, begins with the assumption that Richard is inherently a positive, forward-moving individual.... Daryl approaches Richard as an equal and encourages him to determine the nature and content of the counseling relationship. He relies on Richard to provide the basic material of counseling. Even though this attitude seems somewhat surprising to Richard and tends to make him a little uncomfortable, Daryl persists in his gentle support of Richard's choices and decisions within the counseling session. In no way does Daryl assess, diagnose, or evaluate Richard....

Richard probably has a negative self-concept. He is able to recognize and reveal "negative" aspects of himself—he is socially withdrawn and ineffective at work. Because he unfavorably compares himself with his children, Richard feels inadequate. Very little in Richard's self-description seems positive, and Daryl also guesses that Richard's ideal self is so close to perfection as to be unobtainable by a human being.... Richard's need for positive regard is evident in his reactions to his wife Sandy's disapproval.... Daryl knows that Richard's self is conditional. His guilt and depression are likely the result of aspects of his experience that are inconsistent with his internalized conditions of worth. For example, Richard apparently holds the value that to be worthwhile, he should earn a certain amount of money—specifically that he should be the primary provider for his family. He is not fulfilling the conditions that men are strong and provide for their families....

At times Daryl finds himself wanting to mention to Richard something he is not sure Richard has recognized: feelings that Richard has denied or distorted. For instance, Daryl senses Richard's feelings of inadequacy around his role as a husband and provider. Richard becomes anxious if these feelings and their meaning start to surface. In the supportive atmosphere of their relationship, Daryl tries to help Richard move toward experiencing these feelings. He does not, however, push Richard into experiencing these feelings or in any way insist that Richard acknowledge them if Richard is not ready.

The Role of the Therapist. Daryl's primary responsibility as a therapist is to provide an atmosphere in which Richard can explore his thoughts and feelings about the things that trouble him. The therapist does this by being nondirective—he does not suggest topics, guide the conversation, or interpret Richard's behavior. Instead, the therapist listens empathically, responds reflectively, and models genuineness in his own behavior toward the client.

Empathy is shown in the degree to which the therapist communicates understanding of Richard's experiences, including emotions that he is not fully aware of. For example, when Richard reports that he "feels bad" whenever his wife balances the checkbook and says something such as, "Holy crap, Richard, we're barely squeaking by," the therapist may reply with something like the following:

THERAPIST: When you hear this, you feel negative emotions right away. I'm trying to get a better handle on what that feeling is like for you.

CLIENT: Well, like right away I feel myself tighten up. I know it's my fault. But I hate being reminded, you know. That doesn't help.

THERAPIST: So you feel yourself tighten or close up, then you get angry.

CLIENT: Well, kinda. I don't really *say* I'm angry. I don't know, I just feel bad all over again. It's my fault.

THERAPIST: So when your wife mentions the finances, you feel criticized by her *and* by yourself. You think of yourself as a loser. Another part of you becomes self-protective, and that part tells you that the criticism doesn't help, it only makes things worse.

CLIENT: Yeah, I guess I get all defensive. I'm a loser.

THERAPIST: You don't seem like a loser to me, Richard, and I think that if I felt criticized for being a loser on a regular basis, I'd want to protect myself too.

In these exchanges, the therapist worked to understand the client's feelings, including feelings that the client may not yet fully own. At one point, the therapist suggested Richard felt anger, but Richard's response suggested that this did not fit for him; rather, he felt "like a loser." The therapist later restated Richard's comment about "tightening up" as a self-protective impulse rather than anger. This may be a way of phrasing the experience that Richard can more easily own.

Daryl also demonstrated congruence in reporting his own feeling toward Richard. Congruence requires that the therapist be genuine and not try to maintain a facade of professionalism. However, this does *not* mean that therapists should just say whatever comes to mind, respond reflexively, or always "go with their gut." Nor does it mean that therapists should engage in confessional self-disclosure with the client. Rather, congruence means that therapists should recognize in themselves their genuine and persistent feelings toward their clients and that they may express those feelings to the clients in an appropriate way (Rogers, 1967).

As therapy provides an atmosphere of acceptance, warmth, and genuineness, clients become more accepting of their own experiences. For example, Richard begins to recognize the huge gap between what he thinks he should be and what he is. As he does so, he begins to take a more internal perspective on his emotions and reactions—evaluating them from within his own experiential system rather than from an external perspective. Reactions and behaviors that otherwise seemed irrational from an external perspective (and were the source of self-criticism) make more sense to him from an internal perspective. In short, irrational behavior is often rational from the client's perspective, and so person-centered therapists seek to expand the client's perspective rather than change the client's behavior. Bohart (2003, p. 131) calls the client's growing interest in exploring his internal perspective "mobilizing the client's critical intelligence." This mobilization allows the client to more fully experience emotions that were only vaguely experienced before.

The client's greater recognition and acceptance of internal experience allows him to try out new behaviors because the fear of failure has been reduced. So, for example, when Richard's wife complains about the family finances, Richard more clearly recognizes his automatic tendency to feel criticized, become emotionally defensive, and withdraw from the relationship. But his greater acceptance of himself means that he can tolerate these feelings more—they have less power over him. Because he is less self-defensive, he can try out new behaviors with reduced fear. For example, he may be able to imagine the possibility that Sandy is expressing concern for the family welfare rather than accusing him of being inadequate. Further, because therapy has provided a model for responding to others with empathy, Richard may be able to try out an empathetic response with her (e.g., "It's really frustrating. I'm worried about the money too"). Even if Richard discovered that Sandy really was criticizing him, he might be able to respond without withdrawing or counterattacking (e.g., "I know you're upset, but I'm trying, and criticism doesn't help me").

In short, the process of person-centered therapy is designed to develop a greater sense of self trust. As clients get better at listening to their feelings, they become less likely to misread them, become less self-critical, and their sense of efficacy develops (Bohart, 2003).

Section Summary: Carl Rogers's person-centered therapy is based on the idea that persons are basically good and oriented toward growth. His theory assumes that psychological problems develop when conditions of worth lead to incongruence (a divergence between the real self and the ideal self). In therapy, person-centered therapists take a nondirective approach, allowing the client to determine the problems discussed, how they are discussed, and what the goals of treatment should be. Therapists see their job as communicating empathy, unconditional positive regard, and congruence. It is this atmosphere, this genuine relationship, that is assumed to be the principal curative factor in treatment.

OTHER HUMANISTIC APPROACHES

Section Preview: Alternative humanistic therapies share with person-centered therapy the belief that awareness and acceptance of immediate emotional experiences is critical for mental health. They also share a strong emphasis on the therapeutic relationship as a curative factor in therapy. Some humanistic alternatives differ in that therapists are more directive. Others differ in the scope of the awareness sought collaboratively by client and therapist; some go beyond awareness of emotional experiences to include awareness of life's meaning and purpose.

Gestalt Therapy

After Rogers's person-centered approach, the Gestalt therapy approach developed by Frederick (Fritz) and Laura Perls is probably the best-known humanistic treatment. Like person-centered methods, Gestalt therapy aims at enhancing clients' awareness in order to free them to grow in their own consciously guided ways. More specifically, the Gestalt therapist seeks to reestablish clients' stalled growth processes by helping them (a) become aware of feelings they have disowned but that are a genuine part of them, and (b) recognize feelings and values they think are a genuine part of themselves but in fact are borrowed from other people.

One of the key differences between person-centered therapy and Gestalt therapy is that Gestalt therapists are much more active and dramatic than in person-centered treatment. Through a variety of therapeutic techniques, the client is encouraged to assimilate or "re-own" the genuine aspects of self that have been rejected and to reject the "phony" features that do not belong. Ideally, when clients assimilate and integrate all aspects of their personality (both the desirable and the undesirable), they start taking responsibility for themselves as they really are instead of being attached to and defensive of a partially phony, internally conflicted self-image.

Focus on the Here and Now. Gestalt therapists believe that therapeutic progress is made by keeping clients in contact with their feelings as they occur in the here and now. Perls expressed this belief in a conceptual equation where *now* = *experience* =

awareness = reality (Perls, 1970). Any attempt by the client to recount the past or antici- pate the future obstructs therapy goals. It is an escape from reality. So instead of reflect- ing (as a Rogerian might) the client's nostalgia for the past or thoughts about the future, a Gestalt therapist will point out the avoidance and insist that it be terminated.

Role-Playing. Through role-playing or part-taking, clients explore inner conflicts and experience the symptoms, interpersonal games, and psychological defenses they have developed to keep those conflicts—and various other aspects of their genuine selves—out of awareness. By asking clients to "become" their resistance to change, for example, Gestalt therapists help them toward an experiential awareness of what the resistance is doing for and to them.

Gestalt therapists also turn role-playing into extended "conversations" between var- ious parts of the client, including between the client's superego (what Perls called "top- dog") and the part that is suppressed by "shoulds" and "oughts" (the "underdog"). Using the *empty chair technique,* therapists encourage clients to "talk" to someone they imag- ine to be seated in a nearby chair. The person may be a parent, child, spouse, or even an internalized aspect of the self. The client is asked to talk to the imagined person and to express—perhaps for the first time—true feelings about him or her and about events or conflicts in which that person played a part. The client may even respond for the imag- ined person. Here is an example:

> CLIENT: My sister and I used to fight an awful lot when we were kids, but we seemed closer somehow then than we are now.
>
> THERAPIST: Can you put her in that chair and say this to your sister now?
>
> CLIENT: Okay. I feel so far away from you now, Rita. I want to have that feeling of being in a family again.

Clients may also be asked to clarify and release feelings toward significant people in their lives via the *unmailed letter technique*: They write—but do not send—a letter in which they express important but previously unspoken feelings. Role-played *reversals* also are used to enhance awareness of genuine feelings. So the client who conveys an image of cool self-sufficiency and denies feelings of tenderness toward others might be asked to play a warm, loving person. In the process, this client may get in touch with some feelings that have been suppressed for many years.

Frustrating the Client. Because it is not always this easy for clients to become aware of hidden feelings, Gestalt therapists use many other methods for self-exploration. To help clients give up their maladaptive interpersonal roles and games, for example, Perls deliberately set out to frustrate their efforts to relate to him as they normally would to others. During individual or group therapy, he put his clients on what he called the "hot seat," where all attention was focused on the client and where his or her symptoms, games, and resistances were pointed out and explored.

Suppose that a client begins a session by saying, "I've really been looking forward to having this session. I hope you can help me." Instead of reflecting this feeling or asking why the client feels this way, a Gestalt therapist would focus on the manipulative aspect of the statement, which seems to contain the message, "I expect you to help me without my having to do much." The therapist might say, "How do you think I could help you?" The client (perhaps taken aback) might respond, "Well, I was hoping you could help me understand why I'm so unhappy." From here, the therapist would continue to frustrate the client's attempt to get the therapist to take responsibility for solving the client's problems and, in the process, would help the client recognize how he avoids responsibility for improving. The therapist might also help the client recognize the unrealistic wish that the therapist would have a magic cure.

Use of Nonverbal Cues. Gestalt therapists pay special attention to what clients say and what they do, because the nonverbal channel often contradicts the client's words. For example, if a client says that she is nervous and clasps her hands, the therapist might wondered *what* the clasped hands meant. So instead of asking *why* the client clasped them, the therapist might ask her to repeat and exaggerate the hand clasp and to concentrate on the associated feelings. Once the client expressed these feelings, she would be asked to elaborate on them.

Existential and Other Humanistic Approaches

Rogers's and Perls's methods of treatment represent two prominent examples of humanistic therapies, but there are others, too, many of which blend Rogerian or Gestalt methods with principles from psychodynamic, behavioral, or existential psychology (Greenberg, Elliott, & Lietaer, 1994; Kahn, 1985; Maslow, 1968; May, 1969; May, Angel, & Ellenberger, 1958).

Existential Psychotherapies. Existential therapists help clients to explore fully what it means to be alive. These approaches are rooted in existential philosophy, which stresses the immense freedom that human beings have to make sense of their lives. Such freedom can be liberating, but it can also be frightening because it entails exploring questions about the meaning and purpose of one's life and assuming personal responsibility for the answer. In the process, one must confront the possible meaningless and finality of one's life. To cope with these questions, many people adopt meanings given to them by others (by parents, religious leaders, etc.). This external frame of reference can be comforting but may not last—at some point, people must fully face their freedom.

Existential approaches have a long history, but they developed especially among European thinkers following World Wars I and II. As you might expect, those humanistic therapists committed to European existential philosophies are less likely to argue that all clients naturally strive toward positive goals (Fischer, 1989). Instead, they view humans as having the capacity for extraordinary goodness, extraordinary cruelty, and everything in between.

As in person-centered psychotherapy, existential humanistic therapists try to understand the client's inner world, frames of reference, and flow of experiences. They do not try to formulate diagnoses or objective descriptions. The concept of personality has limited usefulness in existential therapies. Instead, existential humanistic therapists stress freedom, experiential reflection, and responsibility (Schneider, 2003). The client and therapist join in the client's very personal search for meaning.

One prominent existential psychotherapist, Rollo May (1981), regarded the therapeutic process as the client's struggle between freedom and the limits imposed by destiny (one's genetics, culture, and the like). Viktor Frankl (1963, 1965, 1967), founder of *logotherapy,* was oriented toward helping clients (a) take responsibility for their feelings and actions, and (b) find meaning and purpose in their lives. Frankl believed that people can feel a lack of meaning and purpose without displaying neurotic or psychotic behaviors. He saw his approach as applicable to anyone, whether they were officially suffering mental disorder or not.

The struggle with polar opposites is a recurring theme in existential psychotherapy: people have freedom and yet have limitations, the self is static and yet ever changing, people are isolated and yet related, existence feels meaningful and yet meaningless (Bugental & Sterling, 1995; Schneider, 2003). Accordingly, the struggle to resolve these opposites is a regular theme in existential treatment. Therapists use relationship-building and empathic responding, as in person-centered therapy, but they may also engage in analysis or interpretation, or they may use techniques from other approaches. In short, the focus is on the struggle for the meaning of existence, worked out one client at a time, but the method is eclectic or integrative. The therapy may be as brief as a few sessions but is more likely to extend into several months or even up to a few years (Bugental, 1995).

Postmodern Humanistic Approaches.   As discussed earlier in this chapter, *postmodernist* philosophies reject the idea of objective, absolute, or perceiver-independent truth. Also called *constructivist* or *intersubjective* approaches, these philosophies suggest that people live, psychologically speaking, not in an objective reality but in a reality of their subjective making. Accordingly, therapists adopting this view do not lead or direct or teach. Instead, they bring their own subjective realities to the treatment sessions and combine them with those of their clients' subjectivity. The model of therapist-as-expert is replaced by a model of therapist-as-collaborator.

Postmodern humanistic psychotherapy approaches share much with the psychodynamic postmodern and relational approaches and with the existential approaches. The emphasis in therapy is on helping clients "reauthor their life narratives or experiment with new constructions of the self and relationship that afford more hopeful possibilities for the future" (Neimeyer & Raskin, 2000, p. xi). All these approaches stress the subjective nature of perception for client *and* therapist, deemphasize categorization and diagnosis, and stress the importance of the therapeutic relationship as a curative factor.

Perhaps the main difference between the psychodynamic postmodern approaches and the humanistic ones is the allegiance to certain core theoretical principles: Psychodynamic theorists still think in terms of unconscious processes, personality structures, defenses, and repetition of past relationship patterns, while humanistic theorists think in terms of conscious decision making, personality process, alienation from the self, and lack of awareness.

The Current Status of Humanistic Psychotherapy

A relatively small percentage of clinical and counseling psychologists identify themselves as Rogerian or person-centered psychotherapists. However, if Gestalt, existential, and other humanistic approaches are combined with person-centered approaches, about 10% of clinical and counseling psychologists adopt this approach. Humanistic approaches are generally more popular in counseling psychology programs (11%) than in clinical psychology programs (5%). Indeed, only 1% of clinical psychologists identify themselves as Rogerian or Gestalt (Bechtoldt et al., 2001).

One criticism of humanistic psychotherapy revolves around its insistence on not "pathologizing" clients, as seeing even bizarre behavior as understandable from the client's point of view. If clients do not have a "problem," "deficit," "conflict," "illness," or "pathology," and if therapists do not have some conception of that problem that they believe is reasonably accurate (rather than merely their own invention), then what guides the therapist's behavior? Critics argue that humanistic therapists actually rely more on their assumptions about objective reality, personality structure, and psychopathology than they are willing to admit (Erwin, 1999). Indeed, these critics suggest that humanistic therapists try to guide clients toward certain conclusions and are therefore using some manner of interpretation; they are not entirely nondirective or intersubjective. Contemporary humanistic psychotherapists often concede that non-directionality is more a therapeutic attitude than anything else (see Brodley, 2006). But this attitude, they maintain, and the behaviors that stem from it, is what most helps clients.

Based on criticisms such as these and on the relatively fewer persons identifying themselves as humanistic, one might argue that person-centered, Gestalt, and related approaches have had limited impact on clinical psychotherapy practice. However, this is inaccurate. No approach to psychotherapy has done more than the person-centered approach to stress the unique nature of the therapeutic relationship. Research on the curative factors in psychotherapy (see Chapter 10, "Research on Clinical Intervention") has confirmed that attention to this relationship is warranted. The collaborative approach to psychotherapy advocated by Rogerians in particular and humanistic clinicians generally has gained many adherents in other approaches, especially the psychodynamic. But, as discussed in the next chapter, even behavioral and cognitive psychotherapists are increasingly attending to the quality of the therapeutic relationship. Finally, research documenting the effectiveness of certain techniques used by humanistic therapists (Greenberg, Elliott, & Lietaer, 1994) has led many therapists from other orientations to employ them. So humanistic treatment approaches still have an impact, but they have lost some of their unique identity as other approaches have adopted some of their concepts and practices.

Section Summary: Alternatives to person-centered psychotherapy include Gestalt therapy, existential therapy, and other approaches oriented toward fostering awareness. Gestalt therapists use a variety of techniques that are more directive and physically expressive than those used in person-centered therapy. Existential therapists work with clients to help them develop meaning in their lives. They use various techniques to help clients struggle with existential questions and take responsibility for their personal resolution. Postmodern humanistic approaches are similar to postmodern and relational psychodynamic approaches in that they view the therapeutic relationship as a collaboration between equals.

CHAPTER SUMMARY

Psychodynamic and humanistic psychotherapies share a strong emphasis on the importance of the therapeutic relationship. However, they differ in their assumptions about personality organization, psychopathology, and therapeutic technique.

In Freudian psychoanalysis, clients are helped to explore the unconscious wishes, fantasies, impulses, and conflicts that are presumed to lie at the root of their psychological problems. The goals of psychoanalytic treatment include insight into these underlying causes and then understanding, or working through, the implications of the insight. To get at unconscious material, much of which is based in infancy and childhood, Freud developed a number of treatment techniques, including free association and analysis of the meaning of dreams, of everyday behaviors, of resistance to treatment, and of transference appearing in the therapeutic relationship. Interpretations of the meaning of this material help move clients toward insight and understanding.

Other psychodynamically oriented therapists have developed variations on orthodox Freudian psychoanalysis. Among the most prominent of these methods are psychoanalytically oriented psychotherapy, ego analysis, object relations therapy, and Sullivan's interpersonal therapy. The interpersonal and object relations approaches have blended to form relational psychodynamic approaches. This approach remains fundamentally psychodynamic but shares with the humanistic approaches a belief in the subjective nature of all relationships. The psychodynamic variations tend to be briefer than classical psychoanalysis and to focus more on current problems than on childhood conflicts. They emphasize strengthening ego functions more than analyzing id impulses, more on actively repairing damage from inadequate early caregiver relationships than on gaining insight into them, and more on changing maladaptive interpersonal relationships than on delving into their unconscious origins.

Humanistic therapies are based on the assumption that people are inherently growthful and that their progress toward developing their potential will resume when problems that have impaired it are removed by the experience of a supportive therapeutic relationship. These problems are presumed to arise largely from socialization processes that prompt people to distort or suppress genuine feelings and wishes in order to please others, so therapy is aimed at creating a client–therapist relationship in which clients can become more aware and accepting of how they really think and feel.

Therapists using Carl Rogers's person-centered therapy create this relationship by using reflection and other active listening methods to convey empathy, unconditional positive regard, and congruence as they work with clients. The same goals of self-awareness and growth are sought in a more active and direct way through Perls's Gestalt therapy, whose methods include focusing on the present, having clients role-play suppressed or disowned aspects of the self, frustrating their efforts at resistance, attending to their nonverbal behavior, and having them engage in dialogues with imaginary versions of significant people in their lives. Existential humanistic approaches also stress the unique nature of the therapeutic relationship, but they stress helping clients recognize and deal with their most basic needs for meaning, purpose, and connection.

Relatively few clinical psychologists identify themselves as humanistic, person-centered, or existential. Nevertheless, some of the basic concepts of these approaches have been increasingly integrated into other more popular therapy approaches.

STUDY QUESTIONS

1. How did psychoanalysis develop?
2. What is the structural model of personality in psychoanalytic theory?
3. What is meant by psychic determinism?
4. What roles do anxiety and defense mechanisms play in the production of psychological problems?
5. What are transference and countertransference? How are they viewed by the various psychodynamic approaches?
6. How do psychodynamic psychotherapies attempt to help clients stop repeating the past?
7. What role do the following play in psychoanalysis: resistance, interpretation, and insight?
8. What major changes or variations in psychoanalytic thought have occurred after Freud?
9. How does the practice of contemporary psychodynamic therapists differ from the practice of psychoanalysts?
10. How do humanistic psychologists view personality and psychological problems?
11. What special role does the self have in humanistic psychotherapy?
12. What are unconditional positive regard, empathy, and congruence, and why are they important in person-centered psychotherapy?
13. What role does the therapeutic relationship play in person-centered and other humanistic psychotherapies?
14. How does Gestalt therapy differ from person-centered therapy?
15. What is the major focus of the existential humanistic psychotherapies?
16. Compared with other major approaches to psychotherapy, how prevalent are the humanistic approaches among practicing clinical and counseling psychologists?

WEB SITES

- APA Division 39, Psychoanalysis: http://www.apa.org/about/division/div39.html
- APA Division 39, Psychoanalysis, subdivision III: Women, gender, and psychoanalysis: http://www.section-three.org
- APA Division 39, Psychoanalysis, subdivision V: Psychoanalytic research society: http://www.sectionfive.org
- Web site of the Freud Museum, London, UK: http://www.freud.org.uk/index.html
- APA Division 32, Humanistic psychology: http://www.apa.org/about/division/div32.html
- Web pages devoted to Carl Rogers, created by his daughter, Nancy: http://www.nrogers.com/carlrogers.html
- Web site of the International Society of Existential Psychotherapy and Counseling: http://www.existentialpsychotherapy.net

CHAPTER 8
Behavioral and Cognitive-Behavioral Psychotherapies

Chapter Preview: Here we describe a family of approaches to psychotherapy that grew from learning theory and from cognitive psychology. Behavior therapists rely on techniques designed to identify maladaptive behavior and change it. Cognitive therapists view faulty reasoning as the main cause of many disorders, so cognitive therapy is designed to change how clients think about events and about themselves. Despite certain differences, the behavioral and cognitive approaches are highly compatible and are often combined into various forms of cognitive-behavior therapy, one of today's most popular approaches to psychotherapy.

BEHAVIOR THERAPY

Section Preview: Here we describe behavior therapy, which developed out of learning theories and research on learning. Applicable to numerous psychological problems, behavior therapy techniques are designed to help clients learn to change their problematic behaviors and/or the environmental circumstances that support those behaviors.

In Chapter 2, "Clinical Psychology's Past and Present," we described the origins of the behavioral approach to clinical psychology. You may recall Pavlov's conditioning of dogs, Watson's conditioning of fear in 9-month-old "Little Albert," and Mary Cover Jones's techniques for reducing children's conditioned fears. These were milestones in the development of learning theory, but they were also milestones in the development of psychological treatments based on learning theory. When behavioral treatments began to take shape in the 1950s and 1960s, they relied mainly on the principles of classical and operant conditioning. They have since expanded to encompass what psychologists in cognitive, social, and biological psychology have learned about how people think and feel (Viken & McFall, 1994).

Behavior therapy is not a single method but rather a large collection of techniques designed to address people's psychological problems. Included are systematic desensitization, exposure therapies, relaxation training, biofeedback, assertiveness training, operant conditioning and other reinforcement-based treatments, sensate focus for sexual dysfunction, "bell-and-pad conditioning" to prevent bed-wetting, and many others (Antony & Roemer, 2003). Some of these techniques, such as relaxation training, are applied in treatment programs for a wide variety of disorders: others, such as bell-and-pad conditioning for bed-wetting, were developed specifically for a particular type of problem. Behavioral techniques are used by theorists from a wide spectrum of clinical orientations to treat both children and adults.

Theoretical Foundations

The key assumption underlying behavioral approaches to therapy is that the behaviors seen in psychological problems develop through the same laws of learning that influence the development of other behaviors. So behaviorists see personality, problems in personality development, and most behavior disorders not as "things" that people have but as reflections of how the laws of learning have influenced particular people to behave in particular situations. Our understanding of these laws of learning has emerged from research on classical and operant conditioning as well as on observational learning.

Classical conditioning occurs when a neutral stimulus (such as a musical tone) comes just before another stimulus (such as a pin-prick) that automatically triggers a reflexive response (such as a startle reaction). If the two stimuli are paired often enough, the startle reaction begins to occur in response to the previously neutral musical tone. This learning process usually takes some time, though in some cases, such as when a small child is startled by a large barking dog, a classically conditioned fear response can occur very quickly and even become a phobia. *Operant conditioning* occurs when certain behaviors are strengthened or weakened by the rewards or punishments that follow those behaviors. For instance, a person who has had bad experiences at parties or other social situations will try to avoid such situations or leave them as soon as possible in order to reduce anxiety. These avoidance or escape behaviors are reinforced by the rewarding sense of relief and anxiety reduction that follows them. These behaviors thus become even more likely in the future, and over time the person may become socially crippled by fear, leading to all sorts of problems in dealing with group situations. But perhaps not in all group situations: the same socially anxious person who avoids parties might interact reasonably well with familiar coworkers. This phenomenon illustrates that the adaptive and maladaptive response patterns we learn can be associated with some situations but not others. When two situations are similar enough that they elicit the same response, *stimulus generalization* has occurred. Another way of saying this is that the person does not psychologically *discriminate* between the situations and instead responds to them as if they were the same. Thus, the child who was frightened by a large white dog may later react with fear to all large dogs, or maybe even to all dogs.

People learn many of their behaviors through direct experiences with classical conditioning and operant conditioning, but they also learn a lot by watching how others behave and what happens to them as a result. For example, the phenomena of *observational learning* and *vicarious conditioning* were demonstrated powerfully in Bandura and Ross's (1963) famous "Bobo doll" studies. In these studies, children who watched an adult being rewarded after behaving aggressively toward an inflatable "Bobo" doll were themselves significantly more aggressive when placed in a room with the doll than were children who saw nonaggressive behavior being modeled or saw an aggressive model being punished.

In short, according to the behavioral approach to personality and behavior disorder, normal and abnormal behavior can be explained by the same learning processes. The behavior therapist's task is to help clients learn how to modify problematic behaviors and/or learn new and more adaptive alternatives. As in most other approaches to therapy, the treatment process begins with assessment of the problem to be solved.

Assessment in Behavior Therapy.   Behavior therapy assessment is intended to identify a client's problematic behaviors, the environmental circumstances under which those behaviors occur, and the reinforcers and other consequences that maintain them. The behavioral assessment process does not typically employ projective personality tests, diagnostic labels, or other traditional methods. Instead, behavior therapists perform a *functional analysis* or a *functional assessment* (Nelson & Hayes, 1986), which examines four key areas: stimulus, organism, response, and consequence (abbreviated SORC). Table 8.1 illustrates the kinds of information that is typically included in such an assessment.

Notice that Table 8.1 includes assessment of cognitions and emotions as well as of observable behaviors. Behaviorally oriented clinicians who adopt a strict behavioral view of disorder do not focus much on cognitive variables, but those who prefer a more comprehensive view of the causes of behavior place greater emphasis on the assessment of those variables (Antony & Roemer, 2003). As described later, these cognitive and cognitive-behavior clinicians see their clients' learned patterns of thinking as important causes of normal and abnormal behavior, causes that must be examined carefully and, if maladaptive, changed.

Behavior therapists are especially likely to use objectively scored quantitative assessment methods such as structured interviews, objective psychological tests, and a variety of behavioral rating forms. These measures are used partly to establish the precise

---

TABLE 8.1

Areas Assessed in Functional Analysis of Behavior

Area Assessed	General Examples	Specific Examples for a Client Diagnosed with Bulimia (Binging/Purging Type)
Stimulus	Antecedent conditions and environmental triggers that elicit behavior	Watching television, watching commercials about food, selecting clothes to wear, walking by the refrigerator, smelling chocolate
Organism	Internal physiological responses, emotions, and cognitions	Sensation of hunger, anxiety, concern about weight, worry about being fat, anger over being deprived
Response	Overt behavior engaged in by the person	Avoidance of food for a period of minutes to about an hour, followed by binging
Consequences	What happens as a result of the behavior	Satiation, reduction of anxiety, increase in guilt

nature of a client's problems and also to establish an empirical baseline level of maladaptive responding. As therapy progresses, the same measures may be administered again in order to assess and document client progress (examples of such repeated assessment are shown in Figure 3.3 in Chapter 3, "Basic Features of Clinical Assessment," and in Figure 11.2 in Chapter 11, "Clinical Child Psychology"). Especially if required for insurance purposes, behavioral clinicians may assign a DSM diagnosis to their clients, but DSM diagnosis is generally not the focus of behavioral assessment.

Because behavioral treatments developed within an empirical tradition, there is a strong commitment to research among behavioral practitioners. Behavior therapists believe that therapy methods should be guided by the results of research on learning. They also place a high value on the evaluation of treatment techniques. Behavioral therapists are particularly likely to employ assessment instruments and treatment techniques whose efficacy has been established by the results of controlled research.

The Role of the Therapist. Behavior therapists recognize the importance of the therapeutic relationship, so they are empathic and supportive in response to clients' feelings of anxiety, shame, hopelessness, distress, or confusion. However, in contrast to humanistic therapists, behavior therapists believe that the client–therapist relationship merely provides the context in which specific techniques can operate to create change. Therapeutic benefits occur when clients make changes in their environments (e.g., by reducing exposure to triggers), internal responses (e.g., by learning relaxation to lower levels of arousal), and overt behaviors (e.g., by practicing conversational skills). Accordingly, behavior therapists focus on these factors in therapy. They also play an educational role, explaining the theory behind what they do in ways the client can understand. Ultimately, however, they hope to establish the client as collaborator in a systematic analysis of behavior and its consequences.

The Goals of Behavior Therapy

The primary goal of the behavior therapist is to help the client modify maladaptive overt behaviors as well as the cognitions, physical changes, and emotions that accompany those behaviors. Treatment can proceed without exploring early childhood experiences, unconscious processes, inner conflicts, or the like. In short, in behavior therapy, it is not critical to know how a maladaptive behavior disorder originated; it is enough to know how it is being maintained and how it can be changed.

Clinical Applications

Although it is built around a general learning model, behavior therapy is applied in a wide variety of treatment packages, each tailored to address particular sets of problematic behaviors. We do not have space to describe all the behavioral treatment techniques that can be combined in these packages, but in the following sections we introduce several of the most prominent and widely used examples.

Relaxation Training. One of the basic techniques behavior therapists use with anxious clients is *progressive relaxation training* (PRT) (Bernstein, Borkovec, & Hazlett-Stevens, 2000), an abbreviated version of a method pioneered by Edmund Jacobson in

1938 and popularized in the 1960s by Joseph Wolpe (1958). PRT involves tensing and then releasing various groups of muscles while focusing on the sensations of relaxation that follow. (You can get an idea of what the training feels like by clenching your fist for about 5 seconds and then abruptly releasing the tension.) By practicing, many clients can learn to relax themselves and lower their arousal level. As clients become better at relaxing, the process is shortened. Sometimes specific breathing exercises are included as well. This training is occasionally used by itself, but more often it is used in conjunction with other behavioral and cognitive techniques.

Systematic Desensitization.   The antianxiety treatment known as *systematic desensitization* (SD) was developed in 1958 by Joseph Wolpe, a South African psychiatrist. SD was based on research with cats that had been repeatedly shocked in a special cage. They resisted being put in that cage and refused to eat while there. Wolpe reasoned that if conditioned anxiety could inhibit eating, perhaps eating might inhibit conditioned anxiety through the principle of *reciprocal inhibition*. According to Wolpe (1958): "If a response antagonistic to anxiety can be made to occur in the presence of anxiety-evoking stimuli so that it is accompanied by a complete or partial suppression of the anxiety responses, the bond between these stimuli and the anxiety responses will be weakened" (p. 71). In fact, when he "counterconditioned" the cats' fear by hand-feeding them in cages that were placed closer and closer to where their anxiety had been learned, most animals showed greatly diminished emotional reactions when placed in the previously feared cage.

Applying these SD methods to persons who suffered phobias, Wolpe used progressive relaxation training instead of food to create responses that are incompatible with anxiety. Here is how SD is done: First, clients are taught progressive relaxation techniques. The next step is to create a *graduated hierarchy* of situations that the client finds increasingly anxiety-provoking. The content and ordering of these items (which are later to be imagined or experienced "live") are guided by the client so that each elicits just a bit more anxiety than the one before it (see Table 8.2). Too large an increase in arousal between items will make progress difficult, while too small an increase may lengthen treatment needlessly.

After relaxation training and hierarchy construction are complete, desensitization itself begins. In *imaginal desensitization,* the client relaxes and then visualizes the easiest item on the hierarchy. If the client can imagine the scene without anxiety for 10 seconds, the therapist describes the next one. If not, the client signals the anxiety and stops visualizing the scene. After regaining complete relaxation, the client again pictures the item for a shorter duration, then for gradually longer periods until it no longer creates distress. This sequence is continued until the client can handle all items in the hierarchy.

Ideally, reduction of anxiety to imagined scenes transfers to their real-life equivalents, but the client is also urged to seek out real-world counterparts of the visualized scenes in order to reinforce progress and to assess the generality of treatment effects. Completion of a hierarchy typically takes three to five sessions, though it is possible to finish a short hierarchy in a single meeting. Systematic desensitization can be very effective in the treatment of conditioned maladaptive anxiety. Indeed, Gordon Paul (1969b), a pioneer in research on SD, concluded that "for the first time in the history of psychological

TABLE 8.2

A Desensitization Hierarchy

In imaginal desensitization, the client relaxes while visualizing a series of increasingly frightening scenes. In *in vivo* desensitization, the client confronts real hierarchy items under controlled conditions. Here is an imaginal hierarchy used in the treatment of a 17-year-old woman who feared getting lice or other bugs in her hair. The numbers in parentheses indicate the session(s) of desensitization during which each item was presented.

1. Writing the words *bug* and *lice*. (1)
2. While reading in school, you notice a small bug on your book. (1)
3. While walking down the sidewalk, you notice a comb in the gutter. (1)
4. You are at home watching television when an ad concerning a dandruff-removing shampoo comes on. (2)
5. You are reading a *Reader's Digest* article that goes into detail concerning the catching and curing of a case of lice. (2)
6. You look at your desktop and notice several bobby pins and clips on it. (3)
7. You are in a department store, and the saleslady is fitting a hat on you. (3)
8. At a store, you are asked to try on a wig, and you comply. (3)
9. You are watching a movie, and they show a scene where people are being deloused. (4, 5, and 6)
10. At school, in hygiene class, the teacher lectures on lice and bugs in people's hair. (4 and 5)
11. A girl puts her scarf on your lap. (5)
12. In a public washroom, you touch the seat of a commode. (6)
13. You are in a beauty shop having your hair set. (6)
14. A girl sitting in front of you in school leans her head back on your books. (6 and 7)
15. While sitting at home with your sister, she tells you that she used someone else's comb today. (7 and 8)
16. While sitting in the local snack bar, a friend tells you of her experiences when she had a case of lice. (8 and 9)
17. You are combing your hair in the washroom when someone asks to borrow your comb. (9)
18. A stranger asks to use your comb and continues to ask why not when you say no. (9)
19. While you are standing looking at an ad in a store window, someone comes up beside you and puts his head near yours to see too. (10)
20. A stranger in the washroom at school hands you her comb and asks you to hold it for her. (10)
21. Your sister is fixing your hair when she drops the curlers on the floor, picks them up, and uses them in your hair. (11)
22. A stranger notices a tangle in your hair and tries to help you by combing it out with her comb. (11)

SOURCE: From "The Development of a Scale to Measure Fear," by J. H. Geer, 1965, *Behaviour Research and Therapy, 3,* pp. 45–53. Copyright 1965 by Elsevier Science. Adapted with permission.

treatments, a specific therapeutic package reliably produced measurable benefits for clients across a broad range of distressing problems in which anxiety was of fundamental importance" (p. 159). However, SD may be less successful in treating more general and complicated anxiety-related problems, such as panic disorder and obsessive-compulsive disorder. For these more complex problems, behavioral therapists have found that treatments involving directly exposing clients to feared stimuli may be the treatment of choice (Barlow & Wolfe, 1981; Farmer & Chapman, 2008.)

Virtual Reality Exposure. Desensitization appears especially effective when clients are exposed slowly and carefully to real (rather than imagined) items in their hierarchies (Chambless, 1990; McGlynn, Moore, Lawyer, & Karg, 1999). For example, in *in vivo* desensitization, clients use their relaxation skills, and the comforting presence of the therapist, to stay calm while actually confronting gradually more threatening versions of what they fear. However, exposing clients to real situations, such as heights, airline flights, or highway situations, can be difficult or expensive, and precise calibration of the desired level of exposure can be difficult to achieve. Computer-generated simulations of feared environments now offer a useful alternative. In *virtual reality (VR) exposure treatments,* clients can be exposed to carefully monitored levels of almost any stimulus situation. In one study, for instance, clients who feared heights wore a head-mounted VR helmet that gave them the impression of standing on bridges of gradually increasing heights, on outdoor balconies at higher and higher floors, and in a glass elevator as it slowly rose 49 stories (Rothbaum, Hodges, Kooper, & Opdyke, 1995).

The success of VR treatment of fear of heights is well established (Krijn, Emmelkamp, Olafsson, & Biemond, 2004; Rothbaum, 2006); it is also a promising and much less expensive alternative to live exposure treatments for fear of flying (Gorman, 2006). VR technology has also been helpful in the treatment of a variety of other anxiety disorders (Klein, 1999; Rothbaum, Hodges, Smith, Lee, & Price, 2000), and the range of its applications continues to expand. For instance, VR technology has recently been used to help persons with substance abuse problems reduce their responsiveness to external cues or triggers that lead to craving (Rothbaum, 2006). While the technology is promising, it is not without extra cost, so many clinicians are awaiting the results of controlled trials to see which applications of VR treatment achieve results that are superior to standard *in vivo* exposure treatments (Price & Anderson, 2007).

Exposure and Response Prevention Techniques. Like *in vivo* desensitization, *exposure treatments* entail direct exposure to frightening stimuli, but the idea here is not to prevent anxiety. Instead, exposure to feared stimuli is arranged so that anxiety occurs and continues until—because no harm comes to the client—it eventually disappears through the learning process known as *extinction.*

In a method called *flooding,* for example, clients who are crippled by fear of dirt or infection might be asked to spend long periods of time touching and holding a variety of everyday items that they are afraid might be "contaminated." While some therapists favor intense, prolonged exposures to items at the top of the client's anxiety hierarchy, others start with lower items before trying the most frightening ones (Barlow & Waddell, 1985). In either case, exposure times must be long enough—hours, if necessary—for anxiety to dissipate; exposure should not be terminated while the client is still anxious because the resulting anxiety reduction would reinforce avoidance behavior.

Exposure treatments are especially popular in cases of obsessive-compulsive disorder (in which clients experience *obsessions*—persistently intrusive and fearful thoughts—and engage in *compulsions,* which are repeated behavioral rituals designed to reduce or prevent anxiety stemming from their obsessions). In such cases, exposure is usually accompanied by *response prevention,* meaning that clients are not allowed to perform the rituals they normally use to reduce anxiety (Abramowitz, 1996; Lam & Steketee, 2001; see Table 8.3). The idea is that with continued exposure, but no response, the stimulus gradually becomes less anxiety provoking—in other words, the anxiety is gradually extinguished.

Exposure techniques are also used extensively with agoraphobia, a severe disorder involving fear of being away from home or some other safe place, or of being in a public place—such as a theater—from which escape might be difficult. Exposure treatments are also used for the panic attacks that often precede the development of agoraphobia, for binge craving in bulimia, and for other problems (see Hersen, 2002).

Social Skills Training.   Some psychological disorders may develop partly because people lack the social skills necessary for satisfying interpersonal relationships and other social reinforcers. If their skill deficits are severe, these people can become demoralized, anxious, angry, or alienated. Accordingly, behavioral therapists often include *social skills training* in the treatment of adult disorders such as schizophrenia, depression, anxiety, and a variety of childhood disorders, including delinquency, attention deficit hyperactivity disorder, autistic spectrum disorders, and even behavior problems resulting from fetal alcohol syndrome.

Social skills training encompasses many techniques, from teaching persons how to shake hands and make eye contact to ordering food in a restaurant and engaging in conversations. *Assertiveness training* is one of the most popular techniques, especially with adults whose inability to effectively express their needs and wishes leads to resentment, aggression, or depression. All too often, these people know what they would *like* to say and do in various social situations but, because of thoughts like "I have no right to make a fuss" or "He won't like me if I object," they suffer in silence. Assertiveness training is designed to (a) teach clients how to express themselves appropriately if they do not already have the skills to do so, and/or (b) eliminate cognitive obstacles to clear self-expression. They are also taught that *assertiveness is the appropriate expression of feeling in ways that do not infringe upon the rights of others* (Alberti & Emmons, 1974; Wolpe & Lazarus, 1966). Although initially focused on training in the "refusal skills" many clients need to ward off unreasonable requests, assertiveness training is now also aimed at promoting a broader range of social skills, including making conversation, engaging in interpersonal problem solving, and appropriately responding to emotional provocations (e.g., Tisdell & St. Lawrence, 1988).

Modeling.   As already noted, imitation—known in clinical psychology as modeling or observational learning—is a very important mechanism in the development of human behavior (Bandura, 1969). In fact, learning through modeling is usually more efficient than learning through direct reinforcement or punishment. (Imagine if everyone had to be hit by a car before knowing how to cross streets safely!) Observing the consequences of a model's behavior can also inhibit or disinhibit an observer's imitative behavior (e.g., we are unlikely to pet a dog that just bit someone, and we are more likely to cross against a red light after watching someone else do so).

Modeling has been used to treat many clinical problems, including social withdrawal among adults and children, obsessive-compulsive behaviors, unassertiveness, antisocial

TABLE 8.3

Exposure Treatment of Obsessive-Compulsive Disorder

Here is an excerpt from a treatment session in which a client's obsessions about contamination and resulting compulsive cleaning rituals are treated with exposure methods. Notice how the therapist guides and encourages the client to confront a frightening situation (a dead animal by the side of a road) and to stay in contact with it until anxiety begins to subside.

THERAPIST: (Outside the office.) There it is, behind the car. Let's go and touch the curb and street next to it. I won't insist that you touch it directly because it's a bit smelly, but I want you to step next to it and touch it with the sole of your shoe.

CLIENT: Yuck! It's really dead. It's gross!

T: Yeah, it is a bit gross, but it's also just a dead cat if you think about it plainly. What harm can it cause?

C: I don't know. Suppose I got germs on my hand?

T: What sort of germs?

C: Dead cat germs.

T: What kind are they?

C: I don't know. Just germs.

T: Like the bathroom germs that we've already handled?

C: SORT of. People don't go around touching dead cats.

T: They also don't go running home to shower or alcohol the inside of their car. It's time to get over this. Now, come on over and I'll do it first. (*Patient follows.*) OK. Touch the curb and the street, here's a stone you can carry with you and a piece of paper from under its tail. Go ahead, take it.

C: (*Looking quite uncomfortable.*) Ugh!

T: We'll both hold them. Now, touch it to your front and your skirt and your face and hair. Like this. That's good. What's your anxiety level?

C: Ick! Ninety-nine. I'd say 100 but it's just short of panic. If you weren't here, it'd be 100.

T: You know from past experience that this will be much easier in a while. Just stay with it and we'll wait here. You're doing fine.

C: (*A few minutes pass in which she looks very upset.*) Would you do this if it wasn't for me?

T: Yes, if this were my car and I dropped my keys here, I'd just pick them up and go on.

C: You wouldn't have to wash them?

T: No. Dead animals aren't delightful but they're part of the world we live in. What are the odds that we'll get ill from this?

C: Very small I guess . . . I feel a little bit better than at first. It's about 90 now.

T: Good! Just stay with it now.

The session continues for another 45 minutes or until anxiety decreases substantially. During this period, conversation focuses generally on the feared situation and the client's reactions to it. The therapist inquires about the client's anxiety level approximately every 10 minutes.

T: How do you feel now?

C: Well, it is easier, but I sure don't feel great.

T: Can you put a number on it?

C: About 55 or 60 I'd say.

T: You worked hard today. You must be tired. Let's stop now. I want you to take this stick and pebble with you so that you continue to be contaminated. You can keep them in your pocket and touch them frequently during the day. I want you to contaminate your office at work and your apartment with them. Touch them to everything around, including everything in the kitchen, chairs, your bed, and the clothes in your dresser. Oh, also, I'd like you to drive your car past this spot on your way to and from work. Can you do that?

C: I suppose so. The trouble is going home with all this dirt.

T: Why don't you call Ken and plan to get home after he does so he can be around to help you. Remember, you can always call me if you have any trouble.

C: Yeah. That's a good idea. I'll just leave work after he does. OK. See you tomorrow.

SOURCE: From "Obsessive-Compulsive Disorder," by G. Steketee & E. B. Foa, 1985, in D. H. Barlow (Ed.), *Clinical Handbook of Psychological Disorders: A Step-by-Step Treatment Manual* (New York: Guilford), pp. 69–144. Copyright 1985 by Guilford Press. Adapted with permission.

conduct, physical aggressiveness, and early infantile autism (Rosenthal & Steffek, 1991). In the tradition of Mary Cover Jones (1924b), it is also commonly used to treat fears. The simplest modeling approach involves having a client observe live or videotaped models fearlessly and successfully perform behaviors that the client avoids. For example, a dog-phobic client could observe a model interacting happily with a dog; a height-phobic client could watch someone calmly riding an escalator without experiencing any negative consequences. In a common variant on this basic modeling treatment, called *participant modeling,* the client first observes live models, then makes guided, gradual contact with the feared object or situation under controlled and protected circumstances.

Behavioral Rehearsal and Homework.

To help clients develop, solidify, and gain confidence in the new skills they are learning in behavior therapy, behavior therapists establish practice sessions and situations whose demands are minimal, thus maximizing the client's chances of early success. For instance, if a client is contemplating a behavioral task that seems complex or overwhelming, such as applying for a new job, the behavior therapist will help the client break the task into easier steps (e.g., making a phone call to inquire about openings, driving to pick up an application, filling out the first page of the application, etc.). With properly *graded task assignments,* the client's sense of mastery can grow.

These assignments can be carried out in the client's natural environment, but in cases where clients are not quite ready for "the real thing," the therapist will ask the client to rehearse the new behaviors in the therapy session. These practice sessions, in which client and therapist role-play various kinds of situations and interactions, can help clients fine-tune their approaches, anticipate reactions from others, prepare responses to various scenarios, and receive feedback from the therapist on how they are doing.

Aversion Therapy and Punishment.

Aversion therapy is a set of learning-based techniques in which painful or unpleasant stimuli are used to decrease the probability of unwanted behaviors such as drug abuse, alcoholism, overeating, smoking, and disturbing sexual practices. Following classical conditioning principles, most aversion methods pair a noxious stimulus such as electric shock with stimuli that normally elicit problematic behavior. So, for example, an alcoholic is exposed to a foul odor as he sits at a simulated bar, looking at a glass of scotch. Ideally, continued pairings should decrease the attractiveness of the eliciting stimuli until the unwanted behavior is reduced, if not eliminated. The same goal can be sought via the use of punishment in operant conditioning programs. Here, electric shock or some other aversive stimulus is delivered just after the client performs the problematic behavior (e.g., immediately after taking a drink of alcohol).

There is debate over several aspects of aversion and punishment methods. Some doubt whether the changes produced by these therapies are extensive, durable, and generalizable enough to justify the unpleasantness of the treatment. Critics also note that aversion therapy and punishment do not teach clients alternative behaviors that can replace their maladaptive ones. Finally, many therapists find it aversive to use aversion therapies and punishment because of (a) reluctance to intentionally inflict discomfort on clients, (b) worry over possible side effects such as generalized fear or aggressiveness, and (c) overuse of the procedures by therapists who might use them simply because they can bring about quick (but temporary) changes (Masters, Burish, Hollon, & Rimm, 1987). Accordingly, aversive therapy and punishment tend to be used as a last resort to control dangerous behavior (such as self-injury) that has not responded to less drastic methods, and even then, only as part of a broader treatment approach designed to promote more adaptive behavior.

There are numerous other behavioral techniques available for use with adults and children. Table 8.4 summarizes those we have discussed, along with some of the more commonly employed alternative techniques.

TABLE 8.4

A Sampling of Behavior Therapy Techniques

Technique	Description
Progressive relaxation training	Clients learn to lower arousal and reduce stress by progressively tensing and releasing specific muscle groups.
Systematic desensitization	Clients gradually substitute a new learned response (e.g., relaxation) for an old maladaptive response (e.g., fear of an object or situation) by moving stepwise through a hierarchy of situations involving the fear.
Exposure and response prevention	As clients are exposed for long periods to situations that they would normally avoid, the anxiety associated with those situations gradually extinguishes.
Virtual reality exposure	Realistic, computer-based simulations of troublesome situations provide less expensive and better calibrated exposures.
Social skills training	Clients with social skills deficits are trained in specific behaviors such as communication, dating, eating at a restaurant, and assertiveness.
Aversion conditioning and punishment	An aversive stimulus (e.g., shock, nausea) is associated with a stimulus (e.g., alcohol) that currently produces a pleasurable but problematic response (e.g., drunkenness). A problematic response, such as self-injury, is immediately followed by a shock or other unpleasant stimulus.
Shaping and graded task assignments	When behaviors to be learned are complex, clinicians break those behaviors down into simpler steps that can be successfully accomplished, gradually building to the complex behavioral goal.
Contingency contracting	A form of contingency management, contingency contracting involves a formal, often written agreement between client and therapist regarding the client's behaviors.
Behavioral rehearsal and homework	Clients agree to practice and record behaviors between sessions. The desired behavior(s) is often practiced during a therapy session before the client is given homework.
Response costs	This punishment contingency involves the loss of a reward or privilege following some undesirable behavior.
Token economies	Clients are reinforced with tokens that act as currency to purchase desired rewards (e.g., snacks, television time) when they perform designated behaviors.
Biofeedback	Clients are provided direct feedback of their recorded physiological responses (e.g., heart rate, blood pressure, muscle tension).

Case Example

Here is an example of how one team of therapists applied behavior therapy in the case of maladaptive behavior in a child and in the child's family (adapted from Wright, Basco, & Thase, 2006, pp. 138–140).

Bernice was a single mother with a 5-year-old boy, Ben, who could be difficult to manage at times. Bernice and her parents felt bad for Ben because his father had left them when Ben was just a toddler. So they doted on the child to try to compensate for his father's absence. Ben was quite smart and had figured out that if his mother would not give him what he wanted, his grandfather would. For example, Bernice told him, "No, you can't jump on the bed," but Ben begged, "Please, please, please," and began to cry. Bernice tried to stand firm, but she noticed later that her father would allow Ben to jump on his bed even though he knew that Bernice did not allow such behavior. In the past, Bernice would eventually give in to Ben's pleadings, but she had made efforts to set more consistent limits. She needed her father to do the same, but she did not know how to talk with him about it without hurting his feelings or putting him on the defensive. So she said nothing and allowed her son to continue to manipulate the situation and learn a double standard for behavior.

Bernice wanted to communicate with her father about enforcing rules with Ben, but she did not want to put additional strain on their relationship. The therapist's task was to help Bernice practice assertiveness. To do so, the therapist and Bernice first agreed upon a general goal. The therapist asked Bernice what she would ideally like to communicate, then helped her develop that into a clear statement. The process is one in which Bernice says what she would like to say, the therapist provides feedback on what message or messages come across in Bernice's statements, and then the statements are modified accordingly.

Bernice began with the statement, "Dad, I want to talk about Ben's habit of begging for things. You know how he can be. I don't think we should always give him what he wants." Although this statement describes part of the problem, it avoids telling her father directly that he is the one who needs to change his behavior. When she tried this approach in the past, her father responded with "Okay, honey. I agree." After working further on her communication skills, Bernice came up with a message that conveyed her main points: "Dad, I want to talk with you about my new strategy for handling Ben when he tries to get away with things we don't like him to do—for example, jumping on the bed. I want to say 'No' and stick with it even if he whines so that when he gets older, we have already set a precedent for following my instructions. But I need your help to make it work. Whenever you hear me set limits with Ben, I need you to back me up and treat him in the same way, even when you disagree with me or think I am being too hard on him. Are you willing to do that?"

The therapist encourages Bernice to begin and end her conversation with her father using positive or encouraging statements such as "I really appreciate your relationship with

Ben, and he does, too," "You do so much for us," "Thanks for agreeing to talk with me about this problem." The assertive part of the message is more likely to be favorably received if Bernice is able to communicate an overall appreciation of her father's positive contributions. She also wants her message to be seen as a request that she and her father work together for the child's (long-term) benefit rather than as an accusation that her father is doing a bad thing.

What if it doesn't go well? What if her father reacts defensively? There is always that possibility, so the therapist may ask Bernice to describe a worst-case scenario, a best-case scenario, and a most probable scenario. To help with confidence, they role-play the best-case scenario first, with the therapist role-playing the father. Afterwards, they role-play the other scenarios, allowing Bernice to develop responses for other reactions her father might have. Finally, the therapist elicits Bernice's predictions for the event. When both therapist and client agree that the communication is most likely to have the desired results, and the client is prepared for foreseeable contingencies, the client is ready to take the practiced behavior outside the therapy situation.

Bernice knew it was never a good idea to bring up difficult topics with her father when he was hungry or when he was in a hurry. She planned to talk with him after lunch on Saturday, when he would be most relaxed and when Ben would be taking a nap. If it went badly, she would apologize for upsetting him, thank him for being such a good grandfather, and suggest they talk about it again later.

Bernice's case illustrates several important features of behavior therapy: (a) the focus of therapy is on *specific problems* as opposed to, for instance, personality change or self-concept; (b) *thorough assessment* of problems and their contexts is required for each client; (c) therapists help clients primarily by facilitating *changes in behavior*; (d) behavior change recommendations are *carefully planned in collaboration with clients* to maximize the chances for success. Another feature perhaps not as evident from Bernice's case is that (e) behavior therapists *help clients generalize newly learned adaptive behaviors*. For instance, if Bernice learns to be appropriately assertive with her father about Ben, she will have a greater chance of using assertiveness skills with him, and with others, about other issues.

A number of sources provide much more detail about behavior therapy techniques (e.g., Antony & Roemer, 2003; Hersen, 2002; Miller, Rathus, Linehan, & Swenson, 2006; Murdock, 2004; Spiegler & Guveremont, 2004; Thorpe & Olson, 1997).

Section Summary: Behavior therapy developed around the middle of the last century as an application of learning principles to ameliorating psychological problems. Behavior therapists employ behavioral assessment and/or functional analysis to understand problematic behavior and the specific situations under which it occurs. They then employ a wide variety of learning-based treatments, some of which are widely applicable and some of which were developed to address specific disorders.

COGNITIVE THERAPY

Section Preview: Cognitive therapy relies on the assumption that cognitions mediate between environmental events, on one hand, and behavior and emotion on the other. First developed as a theory of depression, cognitive therapy has grown and been applied to many disorders. The key concept in cognitive therapy is that errors in thinking cause psychological distress. Cognitive therapists work to help clients identify, challenge, and replace those errors.

All therapeutic interventions involve thought processes, but the cognitive therapies are specifically directed toward identifying and changing clients' maladaptive cognitions. These cognitions may include a client's beliefs, causal explanations, expectations, schemas, self-statements, and problem-solving strategies.

Theoretical Foundations

We have seen that behavior therapists originally tended to focus primarily on modifying a client's overt behaviors and/or the environmental situations in which those behaviors occur. By the 1970s, however, many behaviorally oriented theorists had begun to stress the importance of cognitions and "self-statements" as mediators between environmental events and behaviors (Bandura, 1977; Beck, 1976; Ellis, 1973; Meichenbaum, 1977; Mischel, 1973). At around the same time, cognitive theorists in other areas of psychology were making significant contributions to our understanding of human memory, judgment, problem solving, and social interactions. It became clear that an understanding of psychological functioning that did not include cognitions was incomplete.

Cognitive theorists focused especially on how thoughts about the self can contribute to a number of psychological disorders (Murdock, 2004; Salovey & Singer, 1991). But unlike psychodynamic, humanistic, and strict behavioral theories of disorder, the cognitive approach did not develop as an effort to explain normal and abnormal personality development and structure. Accordingly, the cognitive approach has less to say about personality than some other theories do. However, the approach does identify some key concepts that form the basis for cognitive therapy methods (Reinecke & Freeman, 2003). These concepts include the following:

Cognitive Mediation. Perhaps the most basic notion in cognitive therapy is that normal and abnormal behavior is triggered by our cognitive interpretation of events, not by the events themselves. A cognitive model would suggest, then, that every event is followed by an appraisal—a cognitive response—that then shapes our emotional and behavioral responses to that event.

Imagine receiving an invitation to a party where you know there will be lots of strangers. What is your cognitive appraisal of this event? If your first thought is "Great. I'll be able to meet some new people," your emotional response is likely to be positive (anticipation, excitement), and your behavioral response will be to accept the invitation. But if your cognitive appraisal is "Hmm, I won't know a soul there; I'll probably feel awkward and won't know what to say," your emotional response is likely to be negative (e.g., dread, anxiety, shyness), and your behavioral response might be to make up an excuse

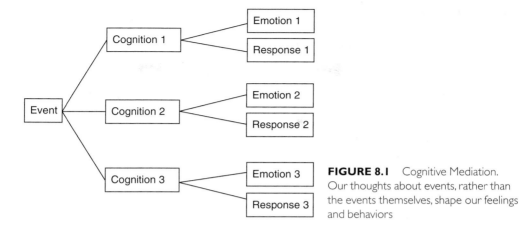

FIGURE 8.1 Cognitive Mediation. Our thoughts about events, rather than the events themselves, shape our feelings and behaviors

not to attend. In other words, the same event can produce drastically different reactions depending on what thoughts intervene (see Figure 8.1).

Schemas. With so many possible mediating thoughts available to us, what determines which ones we use? According to cognitive psychologists, our thoughts are guided by our *schemas,* also called *schematas,* the organized knowledge structures that influence how we perceive, interpret, and recall information. For instance, the first time a child goes to McDonalds, he or she may not know how to understand the event except at a very basic level (e.g., "mom takes me somewhere to eat"). However, after a few trips, the child will have constructed a fairly detailed understanding that involves knowledge of the setting and of the normal sequences of events and actions that take place there. In effect, the child has internalized a detailed set of beliefs and expectations about how things happen—a "going to McDonalds" schema. Schemas can be built around actions, objects, persons, and situations; they can be helpful guides in everyday life. They tell us that we can expect help from a police officer, that dark alleys can be dangerous, and that you can buy toothpaste at the supermarket. They can also create problems, as when schemas lead to inaccurate stereotypes about particular categories of people or things.

Schemas are of particular interest to cognitive therapists because they serve as filters that influence how persons perceive themselves and their relations to the world. Thus, a depressed person who always feels unworthy is likely to interpret new information in ways consistent with that schema. So, if someone mentions she is going to lunch and follows it with, "Would you like to come along?" the depressed person is likely to think, "She only asked because she feels sorry for me or because she feels socially obligated—she really doesn't want to have lunch with me." People who are guided by such a schemas are typically aware of the negative emotions they feel, but may not be fully aware of having engaged in negative schema-based thinking that led to that emotion. Why should this be?

The Role of Automatic Thoughts. The cognitive approach strongly emphasizes the habitual nature of some thoughts, including many maladaptive thoughts. Negative schema-driven thoughts can occur so quickly that we are not consciously aware of having them, let alone of being influenced by them. In this respect, the cognitive approach overlaps somewhat with the psychodynamic approach: Both propose that important mental events can take place without the client's conscious awareness. For cognitive therapists, however, these nonconscious cognitions are not deeply buried, nor are they made inaccessible by defense mechanisms. Instead, cognitive therapists view our maladaptive cognitions as learned habits that are near the surface and accessible by simple questioning and conversation. Accordingly, they use the term *automatic* rather than *unconscious* to describe clients' maladaptive and self-defeating cognitions.

The list of automatic self-defeating cognitions that characterize psychological problems is potentially endless. Table 8.5 presents some of the most common examples.

As cognitively oriented clinicians worked on identifying clients' automatic thoughts, they noted that persons with certain disorders were inclined to employ some cognitive distortions more than others. For instance, depressed persons have a habitual way of explaining the causes of events, particularly negative events. This is called a *negative attributional style*. Borrowing from theories in social and personality psychology (e.g., Heider, 1958; Weiner, 1974), Abramson, Seligman, and Teasdale (1978) proposed that depressed persons habitually explain negative events in a way that is most damaging to

TABLE 8.5	
A List of Automatic Self-Defeating Cognitions	
Cognitive Distortion	**Examples**
Dichotomous thinking	Others like me or they hate me.
	I'll either succeed or I'll be a miserable failure.
Personalization	The project's lack of success was my fault.
	When Jane said, "Some people aren't very funny," she was criticizing me.
Overgeneralization	Everyone thinks I'm a loser.
	I can't go anywhere without feeling terrified.
Catastrophizing	If this doesn't work, I won't be able to try anything like it again.
	My heart is beating fast—I must be having a heart attack.
Selective abstraction	It's been 4 days since Joe called me to play tennis; that means he's not interested in being friends any more.
	I got A's in other classes, but the C+ in history shows that I'm dumb.
Unrealistic expectations	Everyone needs to like me or I can't be happy.
	I should be perfect and not show weakness.
Core beliefs about the self	Bad things happen because I'm an unlovable and difficult person and I'll always be that way.
	I'm a fake and eventually I'll be found out.

SOURCES: M. A. Reinecke and A. Freeman (2003), pp. 224–271; J. H. Wright, M. R. Basco, and M. E. Thase (2006).

TABLE 8.6

Attributional Tendencies of Depressed Persons

Event	Internal, Stable, Global (Maladaptive) Attributions Characteristic of Depressed Persons	Examples of More Adaptive Attributions Characteristic of Nondepressed Persons
I was home this weekend and no one called me.	It's because of me, it's because I'm not likeable, and it will affect all my relationships.	People are busy right before the holidays (external attribution).
		I often work on weekends, and my friends know this, so they may have chosen not to call (unstable attribution).
		I have a few close friends, so some people like me (specific attribution).
I got a bad grade on a test.	I'm dumb and no good at things.	The test was unfairly difficult (external attribution).
		I didn't study for this test (unstable attribution).
		I'm not so hot in chemistry, but there are other subjects that I do well in (specific attribution).

their self-esteem and sense of hope. So when a negative event occurs, depressed persons are more likely than nondepressed persons to attribute the cause of the event to factors that are internal (i.e., something about them), stable (i.e., something relatively permanent), and global (something with widespread effects). This negative attributional style helps create the depression and contributes to its maintenance. Table 8.6 provides an example of negative attributions and more adaptive attributions.

The idea that characteristic clusters of cognitive errors are associated with specific disorders is called the *cognitive specificity hypothesis*. This hypothesis is an important element of cognitive therapy because it helps clinicians to conceptualize and assess disorders, develop treatment methods, and explain elements of the treatment to clients (Reinecke & Freeman, 2003).

Two pioneering forms of cognitive therapy, Aaron Beck's *cognitive therapy* and Albert Ellis's *rational-emotive behavior therapy*, illustrate the principles of cognitive therapy we have described. These theories were highly influential in shaping today's cognitive and cognitive-behavioral approaches to treatment.

Beck's Cognitive Therapy.   Aaron Beck's approach to the treatment of depression is based on the assumption that depression and other emotions are determined largely by the way people think about their experiences (Beck, Rush, Shaw, & Emery, 1979;

Aaron Beck (1921–), a founder of cognitive therapy, has published numerous works on cognitive therapy, trained many clinicians in cognitive techniques, and developed several widely used assessment scales.

Beck & Weishaar, 1995). Beck says that depressive symptoms result from logical errors and distortions that clients make about the events in their lives. For example, they draw conclusions about themselves on the basis of insufficient or irrelevant information, as when a woman believes she is worthless because she was not invited to a party. They also exaggerate the importance of trivial events, as when a man decides that his vintage record collection is ruined because one record has a scratch on it. And they minimize the significance of positive events, as when a student believes that a good test score was the result of luck, not intelligence or hard work.

Beck (1976) proposed that depressed individuals show a characteristic pattern of negative perceptions and conclusions about (a) themselves, (b) their world, and (c) their future. This *cognitive triad* was presumed to distinguish depressive thinking from nondepressive thinking. His version of cognitive therapy has also been applied to anxiety disorders, personality disorders, substance use disorders, and several other problems (Beck, Freeman, & Associates, 1990; Linehan, 1993, Miller, Rathus, Linehan, & Swenson, 2006).

Rational Emotive Behavior Therapy. Another influential and pioneering cognitive therapy is Albert Ellis's *rational-emotive behavior therapy,* or REBT (Ellis, 1995; 2001). As mentioned in Chapter 2, stated the core principles of REBT as follows:

When a highly charged emotional Consequence (C) follows a significant Activating Event (A), A may seem to but actually does not cause C. Instead, emotional Consequences are largely created by B—the individual's Belief System. When, therefore, an undesirable Consequence occurs, such as severe anxiety, this can usually be quickly traced to the person's irrational

Beliefs, and when these Beliefs are effectively Disputed (at point D), by challenging them rationally, the disturbed Consequences disappear and eventually cease to reoccur. (p. 167)

In short, Ellis proposed that psychological problems result not from external stress but from the irrational ideas people hold, which lead them to insist that their wishes must be met in order for them to be happy.

The therapist's task in REBT is to attack these irrational, unrealistic, self-defeating beliefs and to instruct clients in more rational or logical thinking patterns that will not upset them (Ellis, 1962; Ellis & Dryden, 1987). The REBT therapist is active, challenging, demonstrative, and often abrasive. Ellis advocated the use of strong, direct communication in order to persuade clients to give up the irrational ideas with which they indoctrinate themselves into misery. Here is an exchange that took place at the beginning of an initial REBT session between a therapist (T) and a young woman (C) who presented several problems, among them the abuse of alcohol.

C: *(After being asked what is wrong.)* ... my tendency is to say everything. I want to change everything; I'm depressed about everything; et cetera.

T: Give me a couple of things, for example.

C: What I'm depressed about? I, uh, don't know that I have any purpose in life. I don't know what I—what I am. And I don't know in what direction I'm going.

T: Yeah, but that's—so you're saying, "I'm ignorant!" *(Client nods.)* Well, what's so awful about being ignorant? It's too bad you're ignorant. It would be nicer if you weren't—if you had a purpose and knew where you were going. But just let's suppose the worst: For the rest of your life, you didn't have a purpose, and you stayed this way. Let's suppose that. Now why would you be so bad?

C: Because everyone should have a purpose!

T: Where did you get the "should"?

The REBT therapist's frontal assault on the client's irrational beliefs is not restricted to cognitive interventions. Role-playing, sensory-awareness exercises, desensitization, assertion training, and specific homework assignments are also employed in an attempt to provide behavioral complements to cognitive change.

Assessment in Cognitive Therapy. Assessment in cognitive therapy is similar to that in behavior therapy, but cognitive therapists are particularly interested in developing a detailed understanding of the chronicity, intensity, and extent of the client's automatic cognitive distortions. Accordingly, they, like behavior therapists, are likely to measure these behaviors at the beginning of therapy and throughout the course of treatment. Cognitive therapists use rating scales, self-reports, and standardized instruments (e.g., the Beck Depression Inventory) to do so.

Cognitive therapists also pay particular attention to assessing factors that will support or limit the client's ability to engage in the tasks required in cognitive therapy. These tasks include adopting a "thinking" attitude toward symptoms and emotional experiences, and tolerating the sometimes challenging, and even confrontational, approach adopted by therapists. Clients who are unable to take an objective, rational view of themselves and their experiences, at least occasionally, who are extremely pessimistic, or who are unable to take an active, responsible role in improving their lives may not be the best candidates for cognitive therapy (Wright, Basco, & Thase, 2006).

The Role of the Therapist. In Chapter 2 we characterized the role of the cognitive therapist as that of a "scientist" (see Table 2.9) who tries to help clients identify and alter the maladaptive and often automatic hypotheses, thoughts, and attributions they hold about themselves and their worlds. Their success in doing so depends in part on having a productive and collaborative therapeutic alliance. In order to foster this alliance, cognitive therapists are empathic and supportive in recognizing the distress associated with the client's emotional experiences, but they also make it clear that the client has an important role to play in treatment. So in addition to support and trust, the alliance is built on *education* about how maladaptive schemas, self-defeating beliefs, negative attributional styles, and other important cognitive factors create and maintain psychological disorders. This information is important because it helps clients to better understand the therapist's view of their problems, techniques used to address the problems, and expectations about the client's role in facilitating the process.

Once a satisfactory working alliance has been achieved and clients understand and accept the basic cognitive model, cognitive therapists work to engage clients in active examination of their own beliefs, focusing especially on the client's experiences and associated cognitive distortions. Wright, Basco, and Thase (2006) call this process *collaborative empiricism* in recognition of the fact that the therapist engages the client in a collaborative effort to assess the problem, determine goals, test hypotheses, develop tasks, and measure progress. As already noted, clients are often unaware of the cognitive distortions underlying some of their problems, so cognitive therapists use some of the interviewing techniques described in Chapter 4, "Interviewing and Observation in Clinical Psychology," to help clients become more aware of those distortions. As cognitive therapy continues, they also use role-playing, written exercises, self-assessment, and various other forms of homework.

The Goals of Cognitive Therapy

As implied by the theory underlying cognitive therapy, the cognitive therapist's goals in treatment are to (a) educate the client about the role of maladaptive thoughts in behavior and experience, (b) help clients learn to recognize when they engage in those thoughts, and (c) arm them with skills for challenging maladaptive thoughts and for replacing them with more accurate and adaptive ones. Perhaps the simplest formulation of cognitive therapy's goals is this: Identify, Refute, and Replace.

Clinical Applications

Psychoeducation. Early in therapy, the cognitive therapist begins educating the client about the role of cognitions in disorders. Education may involve mini-lectures on several topics: symptoms, realistic goal setting, behavioral activation, how thoughts affect feelings, the automatic nature of thoughts, strategies for challenging thoughts, and the like. The goal is not to deluge the client with information, so if your "teacher schema" calls to mind someone delivering a long, boring lecture, perhaps try invoking your "independent study project mentor" schema. Therapists seek to socialize clients into a way of thinking about their disorder so that they can quickly become a collaborator and eventually become self-sufficient in identifying, refuting, and replacing cognitive errors. In addition to discussion, the cognitive therapist might use diagrams or charts, recommend videotapes or books, or assign homework. Some therapists have begun to use computer-based multimedia programs to assist in therapy (Wright, Basco, & Thase, 2006).

This kind of "socialization" into treatment is important in all forms of therapy, but it can be especially crucial in cognitive therapy, because if clinicians do not thoroughly explain its rationale, they risk being perceived by their clients as accusatory or insufficiently supportive, and clients are less likely to comply with therapy recommendations (Reinecke & Freeman, 2003).

Socratic Questioning. Named after the philosopher Socrates, *Socratic questioning* is a style of discourse in which the therapist pursues a line of questioning until the client's fundamental beliefs and assumptions are laid bare and open to analysis. Judith Beck (Aaron's daughter) has identified six types of questions that are commonly asked by therapists and clients as cognitive therapy proceeds (J. S. Beck, 1995, p. 109):

1. What is the evidence?
2. Is there an alternative explanation?
3. What is the worst that could happen? Could you/I live with it? What is the best that could happen? What is the most realistic outcome?
4. What is the effect of your/my believing the automatic thought? What could be the effect of changing your/my thinking?
5. What should you/I do about it?
6. What would you/I tell _____ [e.g., a friend] if he or she was in the same situation?

Therapists use a number of variations on these questions, and they also model ways of thinking that provide rational alternative responses. They might also engage in deliberate exaggeration of a client's maladaptive beliefs (e.g., "I should never be late") so that the client can see the unreasonableness of such beliefs. Cognitive therapists commonly ask clients to quantify their statements by rating on a scale from 0 to 100, for example, some experience or emotion. So if a client states says that he is "the biggest loser in the world," the following exchange might take place:

> THERAPIST: Really? In the whole world?
> CLIENT: Practically. I feel like the biggest loser.
> T: Okay, I understand. You feel pretty incompetent compared with other people.
> C: Yeah.

> T: In your view, where would you say you fall on a scale of 0 to 100. Say that 0 is absolutely the biggest loser in the world, and 100 is the most competent person in the world. Where would you place yourself?
>
> C: Oh, I don't know, pretty low, maybe . . . 8.
>
> T: Can you think of people who would be near 0, what would they be like?
>
> C: No job, in jail, child molester, no friends, alcoholic, ignorant. . . .
>
> T: Okay, let's look at your situation. How far away from that 0 are you in reality?
>
> C: Well, I still have a job, a family, some friends. I'm not a child molester. . . .
>
> T: And what would someone, say, at about 20 be like? Or 50? Do you have anything in common with them?

In this example, the therapist has encouraged the client to be more explicit about his belief that he is a loser, to quantify it, and then uses Socratic questioning to encourage the client to examine the evidence for his belief. After a review of all the evidence, the client will likely decide to revise upward his evaluation of himself. The exercise is not intended to find the client's "true" standing on the scale but to show him how automatically he produces and accepts an exaggerated negative evaluation of himself. By pursuing exchanges such as this one, phrased in language that clients understand and paced so that they do not feel overwhelmed, clients and therapists in cognitive therapy are gradually able to uncover the clients' maladaptive beliefs about events and themselves.

Refuting and Replacing Maladaptive Thoughts.   The list of cognitive distortions in Table 8.5 presents a challenge for the cognitive therapist because clients are often quite tenacious in holding onto their self-defeating beliefs and attributions. Indeed, clients are like everyone else in seeking to preserve their core beliefs, even including beliefs about themselves that make them anxious, insecure, and unhappy. We discussed this pervasive human tendency, called *confirmation bias,* in Chapter 3 in the context of biasing factors in psychologists' clinical judgments. If you recall, the basic idea is that when it comes to core beliefs, we all tend to pay closer attention to evidence that support our beliefs than to evidence that undermines them.

To help clients overcome this tendency, cognitive therapists ask them to repeatedly practice challenging maladaptive beliefs. So depressed clients whose negative attributional style leads them to interpret events in the most negative way are pushed to consider alternate attributions. This *reattribution training* is illustrated in the following example of a 44-year-old client with an elderly mother living alone in the same town:

> THERAPIST: What went through your mind when your mother said she was unhappy?
>
> CLIENT: That it was my fault, that I don't do enough to help her.
>
> T: And what does that thought mean about you?
>
> C: That I should do more, that I'm . . . lazy . . . an uncaring person. I should take her out more. It's my fault she's unhappy.
>
> T: I understand that you feel concerned when your mother says she's having a bad day, and I understand your empathy for her. But do you think that you

caused her to have a bad day? Is there any other reason she might have a bad day?

C: Well, her arthritis has been bad lately.

T: Anything else?

C: It's getting close to the time my father died; she always goes through a bad time in February.

T: Okay, maybe you are the cause of her bad day, but it's also possible there could be other causes outside of you.

In this exchange, the therapist has encouraged the client to consider the internal versus external dimension of attributions (see also Table 8.6).

Decatastrophizing involves helping clients evaluate their catastrophic predictions. Used particularly with anxious and socially phobic clients, this approach is designed to help them see that there are gradations in discomfort and their most-feared scenarios may in fact be tolerable. For instance, if a socially phobic client fears that standing alone at a party would be the most humiliating thing imaginable, the therapist might ask her to imagine other things (such as standing there naked, or in a chicken suit) that would be more painful. The therapist might ask the client to gauge how long, in minutes and seconds, she thought she could tolerate standing alone. Exercises such as these help clients to recognize that their capacity to tolerate discomfort—an essential for overcoming their problem—is greater than they realized.

Thought Recording and Multicolumn Records.

As in behavior therapy, an important component of treatment is having the client engage in "homework" tasks between therapy sessions. One of the most common techniques for clients in cognitive therapy involves keeping written records of events that have emotional significance. Clients often begin with a *two-column thought record*. In one column, they record the event along with its date and time. In the adjacent column they record their automatic thoughts about the event. This procedure is designed to provide practice in recognizing automatic and often maladaptive cognitions.

Most clients can soon graduate to keeping *three-column records*. The client uses the third column to record emotional reactions and, sometimes, the intensity of those emotions. Eventually, *five-column records* are kept. The fourth column is used to record the name of the cognitive error they made in column two (e.g., overgeneralizing, catastrophizing, personalizing) and propose adaptive alternative behaviors and rational alternatives to the automatic thoughts recorded in column two. The fifth column is used to record the outcome of trying more adaptive thoughts and actions. Table 8.7 shows an example of one client's five-column record sheet.

Section Summary: Cognitive therapy is based on the idea that cognitions mediate between events and emotional experiences. Certain cognitions, called cognitive distortions, play key roles in creating and maintaining psychological disorders. The primary task of the cognitive therapist is to help clients learn to challenge these cognitive distortions and replace them with more adaptive modes of thinking, using techniques such as psychoeducation, Socratic dialogue, and thought records.

TABLE 8.7

A Client's Five-Column Thought Record

Event or Situation	Automatic Thoughts	Emotion (Intensity)	Rational Cognitive Alternatives	Outcome and Emotions
At work today, everyone left soon after I came into the lunchroom	Everybody hates me	Anger (70%)	Personalizing	I walked in the lunchroom and asked Joe if I could sit with him. He said yeah. I was anxious (70%) but tolerated it. I asked him about his daughter in college. I guess it went OK
			I came in at 12:40, so people probably had to get back to work	
			The two people who came in after me are best friends who only kinda know me, so maybe they had something to talk about	
			Tomorrow I'll consider sitting with someone when I walk in.	
	I'm not a likeable person	Sadness (95%)	Overgeneralizing	
			Only one person there seems to really hate me, and I guess it's his problem. I don't need everyone to like me. I have friends there	

COGNITIVE-BEHAVIOR THERAPY

Section Preview: Cognitive-behavior therapy (CBT) combines the theories and techniques of behavior therapy and cognitive therapy. A systematic and structured approach that stresses empirically tested methods, CBT has gained wide appeal.[1]

The behavioral and cognitive approaches have merged over the last several years, resulting in *cognitive-behavior therapy,* or (CBT). This merger occurred because behaviorally oriented clinicians recognized the importance of cognitions in various disorders, and

---

[1]In the psychology literature, the terms *cognitive-behavior therapy* and *cognitive-behavioral therapy* are used interchangeably. Although we lean toward the simpler form, we use the terms interchangeably as well.

cognitively oriented clinicians recognized the value of behavior therapy techniques that can help systematically translate cognitive changes into behavioral changes. But there are other reasons these two major approaches have combined.

Both behavioral and cognitive approaches come primarily from the empirical tradition in clinical psychology (see Chapter 2). As a result, many of the techniques used in both approaches were originally conceived and developed in research settings. Behavioral and cognitive clinicians therefore share a strong belief that clinicians should use methods that have been shown to be effective in carefully controlled research settings. Both approaches also emphasize ongoing collection of data during therapy to track therapeutic effectiveness. Both emphasize assessment of the client's current symptoms and the contexts in which they occur and deemphasize historical factors or global personality variables. Finally, the therapist's role is similar in both. Behavioral and cognitive therapists strive to be genuine and supportive, but they adopt an objective, educational stance toward the client and are quite directive—they aggressively pursue lines of questioning, assign tasks, challenge clients' assumptions, and the like.

Theoretical Foundations

The theoretical foundations of CBT are essentially those of the behavioral and cognitive approaches that we have already described. Most who adopt CBT think that the addition of cognitive principles and practices to the behaviorist theoretical framework (or vice versa) leads to a clear, persuasive, and evidence-based description of how normal and abnormal behavior develops and can be changed.

Clinical Applications

In practice, the combination of these two psychotherapy approaches means that cognitive-behavior therapists have at their disposal the full array of interventions that have been developed by behaviorally and cognitively oriented clinicians. How they use these interventions depends on their assessment of each client. As is true of both behavior therapists and cognitive therapists, clinicians who use CBT sometimes use formal, standardized tests, especially if they are required to assign diagnoses, but their therapy-related assessments entail behavioral rating scales, questionnaires, and client self-assessments.

Cognitive-behavior therapists tend to be quite explicit in the way they structure therapy sessions. Each session has an agenda, often a written one, and the sessions generally progress in relatively predictable ways as clients become familiar with the ideas and tasks of therapy. For example, Wright, Basco, and Thase (2006) suggest a structure for conducting the early phases of CBT treatment:

1. Greet patient.
2. Perform a symptom check.
3. Set agenda.
4. Review homework from previous session.
5. Conduct CBT work on issues from agenda.
6. Socialize to cognitive model. Teach basic CBT concepts and methods.

7. Develop new homework assignment.
8. Review key points, give and elicit feedback, and close session.

Examples of CBT work in the early part of therapy include identifying mood shifts, spotting automatic thoughts, making two- and three-column thought records, identifying cognitive errors, scheduling activities, and conducting behavioral activation. There is an emphasis in the beginning phases of CBT on demonstrating and teaching the basic cognitive model. Feedback is typically given and requested several times during the visit and at the end of the session. Some therapists prefer to set the agenda before performing a symptom check. Homework may be reviewed and/or assigned at multiple points in the session.

As therapy moves toward the middle phases, treatment might focus more on making five-column thought records, providing graded exposure to feared stimuli, and conducting beginning or midlevel work on changing schemas. Later phases of therapy might include identifying and modifying schemas, making five-column thought records, developing action plans to manage problems and/or practice revised schemas, completing exposure protocols, and preparing for termination Although most of the interventions used in CBT have been imported from behavioral and cognitive approaches to therapy, some have been developed specifically for use in CBT. Here we mention two such methods; more variations on and applications of CBT are being developed all the time.

Relapse Prevention. Alan Marlatt and Judith Gordon's *relapse prevention* treatment is a cognitive-behavioral intervention designed to help clients who are trying to overcome alcoholism or other substance use disorders (Marlatt & Gordon, 1985). Marlatt and Gordon believe that relapse is most likely when clients engage in thoughts (such as "I owe myself a drink") that lead to relapse. Once a relapse episode occurs, guilt and shame tend to generate a cascade of negative self-evaluations ("I've let my family down"; "I'm a complete failure") which increases the probability of continued drinking, an outcome known as the *abstinence violation effect* (Marlatt & Gordon, 1985).

The idea behind relapse prevention is to teach clients to monitor risky cognitions and to replace them with different thinking strategies. For example, instead of thinking about how good it would feel to drink, clients are taught to focus on how miserable it felt to be in jail after a drunk driving arrest. They are also taught to view a relapse episode not as an excuse to resume substance use but as a temporary setback whose recurrence can be prevented by working on better cognitive and behavioral self-control strategies. Relapse prevention techniques have now been adapted for use with other disorders and are a regular part of cognitive-behavior treatment, particularly in helping clients become better at recognizing the particular cognitions or schemas that appear to trigger their symptoms.

Dialectical Behavior Therapy. Pioneered by Marsha Linehan (Linehan, 1993; Linehan & Kehrer, 1993; Miller et al., 2006), *dialectical behavior therapy* or DBT, is a form of cognitive-behavior therapy often used to help clients who display the impulsive behavior, mood swings, fragile self-image, and stormy interpersonal relationships associated with borderline personality disorder. Many of these clients are adolescents who display multiple disorders; some present risks of suicide or aggressive acting out. DBT has also been applied to eating disorders such as bulimia nervosa (Safer, Telch, & Agras, 2001).

Initially, DBT helps these clients develop skill at containing their erratic behaviors, but after these "containment" goals have been reached, the therapist helps the client confront any traumatic experiences—such as physical or sexual abuse in childhood—that might have contributed to their current emotional difficulties. This phase of treatment concentrates on eliminating self-blame for these traumas, reducing posttraumatic stress symptoms, and resolving questions of who is to blame for the trauma. By consistently helping borderline clients see that almost all events can be thought about from varying perspectives, the dialectical therapist tries to encourage them to see the world in a more integrated or balanced way.

A Case Example

The following case of "Carlos," adapted from Gorenstein and Comer (2002, pp. 46–62), illustrates some of the ways in which the combination of behavioral and cognitive techniques can be applied to help a man suffering from depression and somatic concerns.

At the age of 39, Carlos, by now the successful part-owner of his family's plumbing supplies business and the proud father of four children, became increasingly preoccupied with his health. His cousin, who was about 15 years older than Carlos, had recently suffered a fatal heart attack. Carlos was saddened by the loss but didn't think much more of it at the time. However, within a few months, he started to worry about himself and ultimately became convinced that he might also have a heart condition. He began taking his pulse constantly and putting his hand to his chest to decide if his heartbeat was palpable, believing that a pounding heart could be the sign of a heart attack.

Eventually, Carlos went to see his doctor, even though he had just had a checkup a few months before. The doctor performed an electrocardiogram (EKG) in his office; the results were completely normal. Carlos left the doctor's office reassured in a factual sense; but somehow it didn't help his mood. "A heart attack is still possible," he thought to himself.

In the succeeding weeks, he could not get over the idea of disaster striking. On several nights he awoke with an overwhelming sense of despair and sobbed quietly to himself while his wife Sonia lay asleep next to him. At work, Carlos lost all interest in his usual activities and could barely focus his thoughts at times. At home, he just sat and moped. He looked at his children as if they were already orphans, and tears would come to his eyes.

Carlos decided to see his doctor again. This time, the physician told Carlos that his preoccupation with the idea of a heart attack was getting out of hand. "You're fine, my friend, so stop your worrying." As the doctor spoke, Carlos's eyes welled up with tears, and the doctor realized that his patient needed further help in dealing with his fears. The physician recommended that Carlos see a psychologist. . . .

Upon hearing Carlos's recital of his symptoms—feelings of despair, poor concentration, difficulty sleeping, loss of interest in usual activities, and tearfulness—the psychologist told Carlos that she believed he was suffering from depression and would benefit from psychological treatment. The psychologist also recommended that Carlos consult a psychiatrist who could advise him on the benefits of antidepressant medication.

Eventually, Carlos began treatment with Dr. Robert Walden, a psychologist who had in fact trained with Aaron Beck, a pioneer in the development of cognitive therapy, at Beck's Center for Cognitive Therapy in Philadelphia. Like other cognitive therapists and researchers, Dr. Walden explained and treated depression largely by focusing on a person's style of thinking. Although a disturbance in mood is the most obvious symptom in this disorder, research suggests that disturbances in cognition have an important—perhaps primary—role in the disorder.

Most of the first session of psychotherapy was devoted to a discussion of Carlos's current condition and the events leading up to it. In spite of his obvious distress, Carlos related the events of the past year in a coherent and organized fashion. At the same time, the desperation on his face was almost painful to observe, and his voice trembled with distress...

Dr. Walden spent the remaining 15 minutes of the session giving Carlos a brief overview of the cognitive theory of depression and the implied treatment.... The psychologist explained that a major part of therapy would be discovering those aspects of Carlos's thinking and behavior that were undermining his capacity to feel well, and then to help him develop alternative ways of thinking and behaving that would ultimately reduce his depression. To begin, the psychologist explained that Carlos would be asked to monitor his emotional reactions throughout the next week, recording all thoughts or events that produced distress (sadness, anger, anxiety, or whatever) and rating their intensity. In the next session, Dr. Walden explained, they would discuss these matters so as to bring out Carlos's thinking about them. In addition, the psychologist asked him to keep a diary of his activities.

At the next session, Dr. Walden reviewed the records Carlos had kept throughout the week of both his moods and his activities, and these provided the focus of discussion. A distressing thought that Carlos had written down several times each day pertained to the seriousness of his current condition, expressed in several forms: "I'm a basket case." "How did I get so sick?" "I can barely function." These thoughts seemed to arise spontaneously, particularly when Carlos was inactive.

Dr. Walden engaged Carlos in a type of Socratic dialogue that is typical of cognitive therapy.

DR. WALDEN: You say you are a "basket case" and can barely function. What leads you to those conclusions?

CARLOS: Well, I've been hospitalized. That's how bad it's been. I just can't believe it.

DR. WALDEN: I know we discussed it last time, but tell me again what led to that hospitalization.

CARLOS: I sort of got panicked when the medicine didn't help, and I stopped going to work or doing anything else. Dr. Hsu [the psychiatrist] figured that as long as I wasn't working, I might as well go into the hospital where I could try different drugs without having to manage all the side effects on my own. I also was pretty miserable at the time. I told Dr. Hsu that my family would be better off without me.

DR. WALDEN: Do you think they would be better off?

CARLOS: I don't know. I'm not doing them much good.

DR. WALDEN: What would life be like for them without you?

CARLOS: It would be terrible for them. I suppose saying they'd be better off without me is going too far. As bad off as I am, I'm still able to do a few things.

DR. WALDEN: What are you able to do? …

With continued discussion, the psychologist helped Carlos to recognize the various capabilities that he did have, and how, in practical terms, he wasn't as compromised as the terms "basket case" and "barely able to function" implied. Dr. Walden also pointed out that Carlos really didn't know the limits of his capabilities because he had deliberately reduced the demands on himself under the questionable assumption that "stress" would worsen his condition. The psychologist suggested that they start testing his assumption by having Carlos make a few simple additions to his activities. After some discussion, it was decided that each day Carlos would make a concerted effort to get up and leave for work at 8:00 A.M., the same time he used to leave before becoming depressed. Second, it was decided that Carlos would read a bedtime story to his two younger children each night; moreover, it was specified that he try hard to attend to the content of the story rather than allow his thoughts to drift into his own concerns. He was to note on his activity record his daily success in carrying out these two assignments.

Finally, Dr. Walden asked Carlos to continue to keep a record of his unpleasant emotions and the thoughts associated with them. This time, however, the client was also to try to produce alternative, more realistic thoughts by considering whether his initial thoughts truly reflected all the evidence. Furthermore, the more realistic thoughts were to be written down.

In subsequent sessions, Dr. Walden asked Carlos first about the behavioral assignments. The client responded that he had continued to read to the children each evening throughout the week and was doing so with a "clear head." On the other hand, he complained that for the rest of the evening, he would just sit around and mope, sometimes sitting in the living room chair for an hour or more worrying about his condition and his inability—or lack of desire—to do anything else, while the rest of the family went about their normal activities. Dr. Walden asked him about his negative thoughts during this period, and the client replied that it was "the same old thing," meaning thoughts about being a basket case and unable to function. The psychologist asked Carlos if he was able to refute such thoughts when they arose. The client replied that he was carrying out the exercise of weighing the evidence and forming alternative thoughts, but that within a few minutes the negative thoughts would return. Then he would carry out the exercise all over again. It was getting repetitive.

On hearing this, Dr. Walden reviewed with Carlos their earlier discussions about the objective extent of Carlos's disability. The client acknowledged that his characterization of his condition as being a basket case was exaggerated, but he seemed to have trouble holding on to this more accurate assessment and had to remind himself constantly that he was in fact functioning reasonably well, all things considered.

Dr. Walden felt that the next step was for Carlos to bring the force of behavior behind his reformulated thoughts. That is, it was time for Carlos to participate more fully in the family's evening routine. . . . A large portion of this session was therefore devoted to working out in detail the appropriate routine for Carlos to follow in the evening at home.

In the next session, Carlos reported that he had been able to follow the prescribed routine at home. He found that keeping his attention focused on the concrete tasks before him—reading the kids a story, asking them questions about school, doing some paperwork—had a way of reducing his pattern of depressive thinking. He told Dr. Walden he was pleased with his ability to do these things and he was even starting to enjoy some activities.

In subsequent sessions, Dr. Walden worked with Carlos to increase his activities at work. Carlos had increased his time at work to 6 hours per day but found himself feeling frequently depressed there. Apparently, he had severely cut down his activities at work under the assumption that stress could exacerbate his condition. As a result, he had a lot of dead time on his hands, which he would spend sitting at his desk, staring at his computer, and brooding over the extent of his disability and his rate of progress. . . .

Dr. Walden pointed out the inconsistency between Carlos's attempts to refute his negative thoughts and his actual behavior in the situation:

DR. WALDEN: It's good that you're challenging the incorrect idea that you're a basket case and can't function. But if you really know that such thinking is wrong, why are you still limiting your activities at work?

CARLOS: I guess I'm afraid that any increased stress might ruin my progress.

DR. WALDEN: What happened when you started taking on more responsibilities at home?

CARLOS: I got less wrapped up in my worries.

DR. WALDEN: What lesson does that seem to teach for the work situation?

CARLOS: That I should start doing more things. I'm not even doing the minimum. And I can't say that I ever had that much stress from work. I mean, I'm one of the owners. I set my own pace. I always put in a good day's work—at least I used to—but I never saw any point in going overboard.

DR. WALDEN: So, getting back to my original question about how to conduct yourself at work. . . .

CARLOS: I know, I know. It makes no sense at this point to be slacking off like I am.

In subsequent sessions, Carlos continued to perform behavioral and cognitive exercises that he and Dr. Walden agreed upon, and he continued to improve. Carlos had returned to full functioning and was in good spirits most of the time. He had even resumed going on overnight business trips. Accordingly, the therapy sessions themselves were now devoted to relapse prevention. The goal was to help Carlos understand the basic beliefs underlying much of his depressive thinking.

It was, for example, apparent that the client's most fundamental depressive belief was a so-called vulnerability to harm and illness schema—a belief that disaster is about to strike at any time and that the client is helpless to protect himself. This particular belief seems to be the basis of Carlos's original preoccupation with heart disease and his preoccupation later on with the prospect of a total mental breakdown.

Session time was spent reviewing the various negative thoughts that had arisen because of this belief. The goal was to improve Carlos's ability to recognize when the belief was active and to take it as a cue to confront the resulting negative thoughts.

Section Summary: CBT grew from the merger of the behavioral and cognitive approaches. Because these two approaches derive from the same empirical tradition in psychology, they share many similarities and are quite compatible. Cognitive-behavior therapists conduct carefully-planned therapy sessions employing both cognitive and behavioral treatment techniques.

THE CURRENT STATUS OF COGNITIVE-BEHAVIOR THERAPY

The behavioral and cognitive approaches have combined to such an extent that it is rare to find contemporary books or articles on behavior therapy that do not give serious consideration to cognition and equally rare to find works on cognitive therapy that do not stress behavior change. Conceptual distinctions between the two therapy approaches can still be made, but in practice the distinctions have virtually disappeared. Reinecke and Freeman (2003) point out that "Behavior therapy associations around the world have added the term 'cognitive' to their name, and the prestigious journal *Behavior Therapy* now carries the subtitle, 'An International Journal Devoted to the Application of Behavioral and Cognitive Sciences to Clinical Problems'" (p. 224).

As we mentioned in Chapter 2, CBTs have surged in popularity in the past several years. Articles and books on CBT have proliferated, and in surveys, an increasing number of clinical psychologists identify themselves as taking a cognitive-behavioral approach. For instance, in one survey, 38% of clinical psychologists endorsed cognitive and behavioral orientations (combined), while 24% endorsed psychoanalytic, psychodynamic, humanistic, Rogerian/client-centered, and interpersonal (combined) (Bechtoldt, Norcross, Wyckoff, Pokrywa, & Campbell, 2001). In short, the cognitive-behavioral approach to psychotherapy currently enjoys considerable popularity in training programs and in practice.

This popularity seems due not only to empirical evidence for the effectiveness of cognitive-behavioral techniques but also to their straightforward, problem-oriented approach. Most behavioral and cognitive interventions are designed around specific problem behaviors or cognitions, and so the translation from symptom to treatment is relatively clear. Further, the steps to be taken in behavioral and cognitive interventions are usually described in specific terms and in organized sequences. Compared to other approaches, especially psychodynamic and humanistic approaches, these "scripted" cognitive-behavioral interventions are far easier for trainees and practicing clinicians to learn.

Indeed, cognitive-behavioral interventions are also often taught and practiced via clearly written, highly structured procedure manuals, each of which is focused on a particular disorder. These manuals include information about the disorder, recommended assessment and recording instruments, outlines and protocols for conducting psychotherapy sessions, suggestions for client homework, and the like. Many of these manuals are so detailed as to specify the exact number of sessions usually required to reach certain goals and the tasks to be accomplished at each session. Some manuals even provide clinical trainees with practice or homework assignments, much as cognitive-behavioral clinicians do with their own clients.

Among the numerous cognitive-behavioral training manuals are those focused on the treatment of anorexia nervosa (Lock, Grange, Agras, & Dare, 2002), alcoholism (Wakefield, Williams, Yost, & Patterson, 1996), obsessive-compulsive disorder (March & Mulle, 1998), bipolar disorder (Ramirez-Basco & Rush, 2007), posttraumatic stress (Hickling & Blanchard, 2006), and dozens of others. Although many have criticized these manuals (see Chapter 10, "Research on Clinical Intervention"), there is no doubt that they provide a convenient way for clinicians to learn and deliver specific cognitive-behavioral interventions, most of which are based on well-controlled research studies.

For more information on the cognitive-behavioral approach to therapy, we recommend that you consult one of several textbooks on the subject (e.g., Dobson, 2002; Leahy, 2006; Ledley, Marx, & Heimberg, 2005; McMullin, 2000; Wright, Basco, & Thase, 2006).

CHAPTER SUMMARY

Behavioral and cognitive-behavioral therapies are based on the principles of learning and on research on cognitive psychology. Their treatment methods are aimed at directly modifying overt maladaptive behaviors as well as the maladaptive thinking patterns that accompany those behaviors. Behavioral methods include various kinds of systematic desensitization, exposure techniques, social skills training (including assertiveness training), behavioral rehearsal, several types of modeling, aversion therapy and punishment, contingency management, and biofeedback (among others).

Cognitive therapy methods were pioneered by Beck's cognitive therapy for depression and Ellis's rational-emotive behavior therapy. These methods, and those that followed, stressed the mediating role of cognitions in behavior, especially the influence of maladaptive cognitions. Such cognitions include dichotomous thinking, personalization, overgeneralization, catastrophizing, and unrealistic expectations (among others).

The cognitive therapist's primary task is to engage the client in identifying these cognitive errors, refuting them, and replacing them with more adaptive thoughts. This is done through the use of Socratic questioning and other directive techniques. As in behavior therapy, homework assignments play an important role—clients in cognitive therapy are often asked to maintain a record of events, of their automatic thoughts related to the event and themselves, and of their emotions. As they practice with cognitive techniques, clients become more adept at challenging and changing their problematic cognitions.

Cognitive-behavior therapy combines elements of behavior therapy and cognitive therapy whose theoretical and procedural approaches are highly compatible. This compatibility provides cognitive-behavior therapists with a wide array of possible interventions. Cognitive-behavior therapists stress empirical research, preferring interventions that have been validated by controlled studies. Currently, a large percentage of clinical psychologists identify themselves as cognitive-behavioral in orientation.

STUDY QUESTIONS

1. How do behavioral psychologists view personality organization?
2. What are classical conditioning, operant conditioning, observational learning?
3. What information and instruments are behavior therapists likely to favor?
4. How would you describe the role of the therapist in behavior therapy?
5. In what ways are the behavioral concept of stimulus generalization and the psychoanalytic concept of transference similar?
6. What is relaxation training, and what is it used for?
7. What is systematic desensitization, and how is it conducted?
8. Describe other techniques used by behavior therapists.
9. What does it mean to say that cognitions mediate between events and emotions?
10. What are cognitive distortions? Schemas? Give several examples.
11. How are automatic cognitive distortions similar to and different from unconscious processes in psychodynamic theory?
12. What are the main goals of cognitive therapy?
13. What is psychoeducation, and why do cognitive therapists consider it important?
14. What is Socratic questioning? For what purpose do cognitive therapists use it?
15. How do clients use the three-column and the five-column thought records to practice the principles of cognitive therapy?
16. How are cognitive-behavior therapy sessions typically structured?
17. What is relapse prevention, and how do cognitive therapists work with clients on it?
18. How would you describe the status of cognitive-behavioral psychotherapy in the United States today?

WEB SITES

- APA Behavior Analysis (Division 25): http://www.apa.org/about/division/div25.html
- International Association for Cognitive Therapy: http://www.academyofct.org
- Beck Institute for Cognitive Therapy and Research: http://www.beckinstititue.org
- Association for the Behavioral and Cognitive Therapies: http://www.aabt.org

CHAPTER 9
Alternative Modes of Clinical Intervention

Chapter Preview: This chapter provides an overview of alternatives to individual clinical treatment, including group, couples, and family therapy; community mental health programs; prevention efforts; and self-help. Also discussed here are new treatment modalities, such as those based on complementary/alternative medicine, spirituality, mindfulness, and a variety of new technologies.

The dominant therapy model of the early 20th century, psychodynamic psychotherapy, was originally designed for treating individual clients. Although some clinicians adapted psychoanalytic concepts to group therapy (Bion, 1959), most psychodynamic psychotherapists worked only in a one-on-one format. The behavioral and humanistic approaches that gained recognition during the mid-20th century were also originally designed for individuals. Since the middle of the last century, though, there has been a proliferation of therapy modes that involve more than one client at a time and that focus on relationships or relationship systems. Group therapy was the first of these socially oriented therapies, followed somewhat later by the advent of couples and family therapy. The 1960s saw the rise of the self-help movement and of community psychology, which emphasizes the value of treating disorders in local communities as well as of intervening in broader social systems to prevent the development or worsening of mental disorders.

These modes of intervention reflect trends in psychology that view individuals' behavior as a reflection of the relationship systems they inhabit. These approaches assume that psychological problems exist within social contexts; each emphasizes interventions built around these contexts (see Table 9.1).

GROUP THERAPY

Section Preview: This section provides an overview of group therapies and discusses their inner workings. In addition to covering traditional supportive and process-oriented groups, we discuss more recent advances in cognitive-behavioral group therapy and psychoeducational groups.

302

TABLE 9.1	
Socially Oriented Clinical Interventions	
Intervention Mode	**Emphasis**
Group therapy	Understand and alleviate disturbances in interpersonal relationships as revealed in a group setting.
Couples therapy	Help couples in intimate relationships to improve problem-solving and communication skills.
Family therapy	Change harmful family interaction patterns so that the family system functions better.
Community psychology	Create beneficial changes at a community or societal level to prevent disorders or to raise general levels of mental health.
Prevention	Head off the appearance of mental disorders by counteracting risk factors and strengthening protective factors.
Self-help	Encourage people to perform therapeutic functions for themselves, either in groups organized around a specific concern or individually through a course of study.

Group therapy was first practiced at the turn of the 20th century in Boston by Joseph Pratt. The increased use of group therapy was later stimulated by the shortage of professional personnel around the time of World War II (Klein, 1983). It grew in popularity especially in the 1960s and 1970s and has since progressed to the point that it is now regarded as a valuable intervention in its own right (Burlingame, MacKenzie, & Strauss, 2004).

Every major approach to clinical psychology offers group treatment. There are analytic groups, client-centered and gestalt groups, and behavioral groups. To varying degrees, most group therapists emphasize the importance of interpersonal relationships and assume that personal maladjustment involves difficulties in those relationships. Increasingly, evidence-based practices are being integrated into group therapy formats, with special focus on cognitive-behavioral groups for a number of problems (Bieling, McCabe, & Antony, 2006).

Therapeutic Factors in Group Therapy

Group therapies are meant to serve many clients at the same time, with the added benefit of providing support from other group members (Bieling et al., 2006). Indeed, group therapy is considered more than the simultaneous treatment of several individuals. Groups provide therapeutic opportunities that cannot be found in individual therapy, and group therapists must learn how to use those opportunities. We summarize these concepts below; a fuller discussion is contained in standard references on traditional group therapy (e.g., Corey, 2007; Yalom & Leszcz, 2005):

- **Sharing New Information.** New information is imparted from two sources in groups: The group leader may offer advice, and advice also comes from other members of the group who share their experiences. Often, feedback from several

Therapy groups can often include clients with a diverse array of concerns.

group members can have more impact on clients than feedback from a single therapist.

- **Instilling Hope.** Not only can confidence be instilled by the therapist, but group members can provide hope and can comment on positive changes that they see in other members.

- **Universality.** By showing that everyone struggles with problems in living, therapy groups help their members learn that they are not alone in their fears, low moods, or other difficulties. Learning about the universality of one's problems also soothes anxiety about "going crazy" or "losing control."

- **Altruism.** Groups give clients a chance to discover that they can help other people. Clinicians refer to the positive emotions that follow altruistic behavior as "feelings of self-worth," an outcome that is promoted by effective group therapy.

- **Interpersonal Learning.** A properly conducted therapy group is an ideal setting to learn new interpersonal skills. It presents repeated opportunities to practice fundamental social skills with various types of people and with immediate feedback on performance.

- **Group Cohesiveness.** Members of cohesive groups accept one another; they are willing to listen to and be influenced by the group. They participate in the group readily, feel secure in it, and are relatively immune to outside disruption of the group's progress. Cohesive groups also permit the expression of hostility, provided such conflicts do not violate the norms of the group. Cohesiveness is often regarded as the most important factor underlying the beneficial effects of group therapy (Yalom & Leszcz, 2005).

The Practice of Group Therapy

Therapy groups usually consist of 6 to 12 members. Some leaders of traditional groups believe that their groups should be *homogeneous,* consisting of members who are similar in age, sex, and type of problem. Others prefer to form groups that are *heterogeneous,* meaning that there is a mix of client types. Heterogeneous groups are easier to form. They also have the advantage of exposing members to a wider range of people and perspectives. The major advantage of homogeneous groups is that they facilitate a direct focus on the common problem that motivated each member to enter treatment. In practice, groups will invariably be homogeneous on some dimensions (e.g., diagnosis and problem severity) and heterogeneous on others (e.g., problem duration, personality characteristics, and coping style).

Group meetings usually last about 1 to 2 hours. They are longer than sessions of individual therapy, because it often takes more time for all of the clients in a group session to share their experiences and to process the information that is presented.

A Case Example of Group Therapy

Here is a brief description of the fifth session of therapy for a group of five women and three men, all in their late 20s and 30s and all unmarried or separated. The cognitive-behavioral orientation of the group's therapist is evident in that the members are asked to concentrate on helping each other improve their coping skills and interpersonal relationships (Rose & LeCroy, 1991, pp. 422–423).

As the group settled into places on the floor or on chairs, the therapist welcomed them and asked each member to review what he or she had done throughout the week to complete the assignment of the previous week. One at a time, members described their social achievements, their success in coping with anxiety, and the frequency with which they used the relaxation exercise. Several also related unusually stressful situations they had experienced during the week.

After each had summarized her or his experiences, amid a great deal of praise and support from group members for achievements, Delores volunteered to describe in some detail her situation in which her ever-present feelings of helplessness were intensified. Her supervisor at her office, she stated, was always giving her instructions on the least little thing. "It was as if she thought I was stupid and, frankly, I'm beginning to believe it." The other members inquired as to the nature of her job, which was quite complicated. They noted that she did receive good feedback from her peers, who often consulted with her on various problems. She also noted that in a previous job, no one gave her more than the briefest instructions, and she did fine. Charles wondered whether she couldn't conclude that there was a problem between her and her supervisor and not with her as a person. There was just no evidence that she was dumb in any way; in fact, she appeared to be uniquely qualified to do the job. The others agreed.

Delores said she guessed they were right, but she did not know what to do about it, and it was making her miserable. She had thought about quitting, but it was in other ways a good job; and besides, she added, "good jobs were hard to get these days."

> After careful questioning by the other clients in order to have a clear picture of what was going on, they provided her with a number of strategies she could employ to deal with the situation and suggested what she could specifically say to herself and to her supervisor. She evaluated and selected several from among these for practice in the group.

Cognitive-Behavioral Group Therapy

The cognitive-behavioral group therapy illustrated in this case example is one of the more common types of group therapy in use today (Bieling et al., 2006). Cognitive-behavioral groups are sometimes known as *psychoeducational groups* because they focus on learning and on sharing information rather than on group process. This approach to group therapy has been used effectively for a number of problems, including

- Depression and anxiety in adults (Oei & Browne, 2006)
- Trauma related to terrorism (Unger, Wattenberg, Foy, & Glynn, 2006)
- Alcohol abuse in college students (Michael, Curtin, Kirkley, Jones, & Harris, 2006)
- Chronic pain in adults (Thorn & Kuhajda, 2006)
- Obesity in adults (Radomile, 2000)
- Medication management for adults with chronic mental illness (Hayes et al., 2006)

Table 9.2 provides an outline of the cognitive-behavioral treatment procedure protocol for the first session of group treatment for clients suffering from a combination of depression and social phobia. More information on these procedures and other group therapy approaches is available from several sources (e.g. Bieling et al., 2006; Brabender, Fallon, & Smolar, 2004; Free, 2007; Gladding, 2007; Yalom & Leszcz, 2005).

Section Summary: Group therapy can be an effective and affordable modality of psychological treatment. There are a number of therapeutic factors in group therapy, including sharing new information, instilling hope, universality, altruism, interpersonal learning, and group cohesiveness. More recent forms of group therapy have included cognitive-behavioral group treatments and psychoeducational groups that focus on teaching clients new skills.

COUPLES AND FAMILY THERAPY

Section Preview: In addition to group treatment, therapy can focus on couples and families. This section reviews these therapies, which tend to focus on a disturbance within the relationship, such as conflict between spouses or difficult parent–child interactions.

In *couples therapy* and *family therapy*, the focus is on disturbed relationships rather than on individuals who happen to be in a relationship. Couples therapy used to be referred to as *marital therapy*, but the current term is more descriptive because it includes a wider array of heterosexual and homosexual couples, including spouses,

TABLE 9.2

Sample Treatment Protocol for First Session of a Group Cognitive-Behavioral Treatment for Comorbid Depression and Social Phobia

Session 1

1. Introduction of therapists and group members
2. Group "rules"
   a. Confidentiality
   b. Check-in and rating scales
   c. Homework
   d. Missing appointments
3. Introducing the CBT approach to depression and social phobia
   a. Behavioral interventions: Activation and exposure
   b. Cognitive interventions
4. Describing the biopsychosocial model of depression and social phobia, and introducing the five components:
   a. Behavior
   b. Thoughts

   c. Emotions
   d. Biology
   e. Environment
5. Overview of social phobia, including
   a. The nature of fear and social anxiety (e.g., occasional social anxiety is normal and has a survival function).
   b. Myths and misconceptions regarding fear and social anxiety
   c. The three components of fear (i.e., physical, cognitive, behavioral)
6. Homework: Complete biopsychosocial model and purchase companion manual

SOURCE: From *Cognitive-Behavioral Therapy in Groups,* by P. J. Bieling, R. E. McCabe, and M. M. Antony, 2006 (New York: Guilford Press), p. 382. Copyright 2006 by Guilford Press. Adapted with permission.

cohabitating partners, romantic partners who do not live together, and any other pair of individuals who consider themselves a couple. Couples therapy focuses on the dyad rather than the individual partners. Family therapy focuses on relationships involving one or more parents (or guardians) and their children. Because both couples and family therapy emphasize communication patterns within close relationships, therapists who work with couples often work with families and vice versa.

Prior to the 1950s, few therapists worked with couples or families (Harway, 2005). However, as other forms of social and multiclient intervention grew, so did family therapy. Since the 1970s, the number of couples and family therapists has increased 50-fold (American Association of Marriage and Family Therapy, 2001). Journals devoted to family psychology first appeared in the United States and Japan during the 1980s, and the Division of Family Psychology was founded within the American Psychological Association in 1985 (Kaslow, 2001). Courses in family psychology are now offered by many psychology, counseling, and social work graduate programs.

Diagnosis in Couples and Family Therapy

One challenge for couples and family therapists is how best to understand relationship difficulties. For individual clients, psychologists use a classification system, the *Diagnostic and Statistical Manual of Mental Disorders* (DSM) (or the *International Classification of Diseases,* or ICD), to better understand individual problems. But with couples and family therapy, the client is not so much an individual as a *relationship* or *system of relationships*. How should these relationships and systems be understood and diagnosed? Are there are identifiable patterns for dysfunctional relationships that might eventually point the way to effective intervention techniques?

The development of diagnostic categories for interpersonal conflicts has begun. The initial work in this area led to *V-Codes* for relational problems in *DSM-IV.* V-Codes are "Other Conditions That May Be a Focus of Clinical Attention" and include, for instance, Parent–child relational problem (V61.20), Partner relational problem (V61.10), and Sibling relational problem (V61.8). These V-Codes can be listed on Axis I in a DSM diagnosis, but most insurance companies do not reimburse for V-Codes. Some have suggested that disorders in relationships and relational processes should become formal diagnostic categories in the next edition of DSM (DSM-V; Beach & Kaslow, 2006). These categories might include, for example, relationship difficulties associated with partner conflict (Whisman & Uebelacker, 2006), relationship distress (Wamboldt & Reiss, 2006), and partner and child maltreatment (Heyman & Slep, 2006). Much research still needs to be done to establish the reliability, validity, and utility of relational diagnoses, but it appears that there is a great deal of interest in doing so (Beach, Wamboldt, Kaslow, Heyman, & Reiss, 2006; Lebow & Gordon, 2006).

Couples Therapy

Couples seek therapy for a variety of reasons (see Table 9.3), especially because of problems in affection and communication (Doss, Simpson, & Christensen, 2004). As illustrated in Figure 9.1, these problems tend to occur more frequently at particular stages of a marriage or other relationship, and it is during these stages that couples are most likely

TABLE 9.3

Reasons Couples Seek Treatment

Reason for Therapy	% of Couples Reporting Problem
Emotional affection (e.g., basic unhappiness, feeling alone)	57
Communication	57
Divorce/separation concerns	46
Improve relationship	46
Arguments/anger	44
Concerns about children	32
Sex/physical affection	28
Spouse critical/demanding	8
Spouse distant/withdrawn	8
Trust issues	8
Social activities/time together	8
Infidelity/flirting	6

Source: Adapted from B. D. Doss, L. E. Simpson, and A. Christensen (2004), .

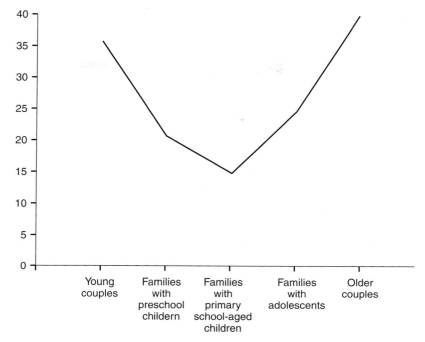

FIGURE 9.1   Marital Satisfaction Across the Lifespan

(*Source:* Carr, A. (2006). *The Handbook of Child and Adolescent Clinical Psychology: A Contextual Approach* (2nd ed.) (p. 60). New York: Routledge/Taylor & Francis Group.)

to enter treatment. Further, the problems and treatment targets dealt with in couples therapy are similar whether the couple is heterosexual or homosexual (Bigner & Wetchler, 2004). To provide a clearer picture of each partner's communication skills, therapists often ask the clients to complete self-reports on their communication skills before treatment begins (see Figure 9.2).

In most cases, couples therapy focuses mainly on relationship difficulties, but it can sometimes be combined with other methods designed to address other problems. For example, when depression, alcoholism, or severe anxiety disorders affect the quality, and even the existence, of a client's marriage or intimate relationship, some mental health experts recommend couples therapy—or at least the involvement of the client's partner—in the treatment of these disorders (Leonard & Eiden, 2006).

In many instances, the therapist sees both members of the couple at the same time, a procedure called *conjoint therapy.* In other cases, each partner is seen separately for some or all sessions. This is especially likely in *separation counseling,* when couples want help in ending a marriage or long-term relationship with a minimum of conflict over property and/or child custody.

The goals and techniques of couples therapy depend partly on the conflicts that are the most pressing for each couple and partly on the theoretical orientation of the therapist.

NAME: _____ DATE: _____

The aim of this form is to identify your strengths and weaknesses in communication and to select goals for improvement. Rate each of the skills below using this code:

 0 Very poor use of skill
 1 Unsatisfactory use of skill
 2 Satisfactory use of skill, but room for improvement
 3 Good use of skill
 N/A Not applicable

Skill	0	1	2	3	N/A
Specific descriptors					
Self-disclosure					
Clear expression of positives					
Assertive expression of negatives					
Attending to partner					
Minimal encouragers (e.g., nods, hm-mm)					
Reserving judgment					
Asking questions					
Summarizing content					
Paraphrasing feelings					
Positive suggestions					

Self-identified strengths in communication: _____

_____

Self-identified weakness in communication: _____

_____

FIGURE 9.2 Communication Skills Self-Evaluation Form

(Source: W. K. Halford, & E. N. Moore, (2002). Relationship education and the prevention of couple relationship problems. In A. S. Gurman & N. S. Jacobson (Eds.), *Clinical Handbook of Couple Therapy* (3rd ed.) (pp. 400–419). New York: Guilford Press.)

For example, therapists who prefer systemic interventions and who see couples as interpersonal systems rather than as two individuals would try to intervene at the level of the system (Weeks & Treat, 2001). Systemic therapists usually assume that there is circularity and interrelatedness in each individual's experience of the couple relationship. For example, the following statements alone could be seen as linear, but together they show the circularity of the couples' relationship from a systemic framework (Weeks & Treat, 2001; p. 28):

THERAPIST TO WIFE: Why do you get so angry?

WIFE: Because he always withdraws from me.

THERAPIST TO HUSBAND: Why do you withdraw?

HUSBAND: Because she is always so angry.

In contrast, a behaviorally oriented couples therapist would be likely to help with a couple's communication problems by teaching the partners to replace hostile, unconstructive criticism with comments that clearly express feelings and directly convey requests for the behaviors that each wants from the other. Cognitive-behavioral couples therapists work to help couples change the way they think about their relationship and modify the attributions they make about each other (Snyder, Castellani, & Shisman, 2006). Accordingly, the cognitive-behavioral therapist may teach each member of the couple to recognize, for example, that the other member's anger may reflect anxiety about the future of the relationship, not necessarily an effort to end it.

In general, most couples therapists tend to emphasize problem solving (Gurman & Jacobson, 2002). The touchstone of problem solving is teaching the couple how to communicate and negotiate more effectively with each other. Among the multiple tasks involved in building better communication are teaching the couple to accept mutual responsibility for working on problems, maintaining focus on current relationship problems rather than old grudges, fostering expression of preferences rather than demands for obedience, and negotiating compromises to problems the couple decide cannot be solved.

The following brief excerpt from a couples therapy session illustrates an attempt by the therapist (T) to help a wife (W) learn new ways of communicating some of her negative feelings to her husband:

T: I do think that what Pete is saying is an important point. There are things that are going to be different about you, and each of you is going to think the things you do maybe make more sense than the other person's, and that's probably going to be pretty much of a reality. You're not going to be able to change all those. You may not be able to change very many of them. And everybody is different. They have their own predilections to do things a certain way, and again what's coming through from you is sort of like damning those and saying those are wrong; they're silly, they don't make sense, I don't understand them or whatever. You may not understand them, but they are a reality of each of you. That's something you have to learn how to deal with in some way. Otherwise, you . . . the reason I'm stressing this is I think it plays a large part in your criticalness.

W: Well, I do find it difficult to cater to, I guess that's the word, cater to some idiosyncrasies that I find or think are totally foolish. I am intolerant. I am, and I find it very difficult. I find it almost impossible to do it agreeably and without coming on as "Oh, you're ridiculous."

T: I guess what would be helpful would be if you could come on honestly enough to say "I don't like them" or "It doesn't sit well with me" without having to add the additional value judgment of whether they're foolish or ridiculous or whatever. That's the part that hurts. It's when you damn him because of these things—that's gonna hurt. I'm sure from Pete's point of view they make sense for his total economy of functioning. There's some sense to why he does things the way he does, just as there is for why you do things the way you do. It's not that they're foolish. They make sense in terms of where you are, what you're struggling with, and what's the best way you can deal with right now. I'm not

> trying to say that means you have to like them, but when you come across and say "It's ridiculous or foolish"—that's the part that makes it hurt.
>
> W: Well, tell me again how to say it, because I find it hard to say anything except "That's really stupid—that's silly." I know you said it a minute ago, but I lost it.
>
> T: Well, anytime you can say it in terms of how it affects you and stay with it, like "It's hard—I find it hard to take," that doesn't say "I find you're an ass for wanting to do that such and such a way. It's just that, I find it hard to take—I get upset in this circumstance" or whatever. Stay with what your feelings are rather than trying to evaluate Pete. (Ables & Brandsma, 1977, pp. 92-94)

With two clients in the room, couples therapists must take care to avoid becoming *triangulated* by the couple—that is, for example, finding themselves in the middle of their clients' disagreements. Weeks and Treat (2001, pp. 4-8) offer a number of suggestions for preventing triangulation, including these:

- Don't take sides.
- Don't proceed until the problem(s) and goal(s) have been clarified.
- Don't discuss problems abstractly and nonconcretely.
- Don't discount problems, even small problems.
- Don't assume the partners in the couple will perceive the problem in the same way.
- Don't get hooked in the past.
- Don't allow the couple to take charge of the session.

Many of these same suggestions apply when therapists work with families.

Family Therapy

Just as couples therapy is aimed at changing a couple's relationship, family therapy aims to change patterns of family interaction so as to correct disturbances in those interactions (Sexton, Alexander, & Mease, 2004). Like couples therapy, family therapy arose from recognition that the problems of individual clients occur in social contexts and have social consequences. It was observed, for example, that clients who showed great improvement during individual therapy while hospitalized often relapsed when they returned to their families. This observation, along with other clinical insights and research, led to several theories that emphasized the family environment and parent–child interactions as causes of maladaptive behavior (Bateson, Jackson, Haley, & Weakland, 1956; Lidz & Lidz, 1949; Sullivan, 1953).

Family therapy often begins with a focus on a family member who is having particularly noticeable problems. Typically, this *identified client* is a male child whom the parents label as having an unmanageable behavior problem, or a girl who is withdrawn and sad. Soon, however, the therapist will try to reframe the identified problems in terms of disturbed family processes or faulty family communication, to encourage all family members to examine their own contributions to the problem, and to consider the positive changes that each member can make to solve them. As in couples therapy, a common goal of family therapy is improved communication and the elimination of coercion in the family system (Reid, Patterson, & Snyder, 2002).

As with individual, group, and couples therapy, there is no single agreed-upon technique for conducting family therapy. Rather, therapists can select from a wide variety of techniques. For example, those operating from a behavioral point of view try to teach family members alternative, noncoercive ways of communicating their needs. They teach parents to be firm and consistent in their child-discipline practices, encourage each family member to communicate clearly with the others, educate family members in behavior-exchange principles, discourage blaming of the identified client for all family problems, and help all members of the family to consider whether their expectations of other members are reasonable. These behavioral methods are also used in the *Ecological Family Intervention and Therapy* (EcoFIT) model, which conceptualizes families from a systemic, ecological perspective (Dishion & Stormshak, 2007).

As evidence-based practice becomes more prominent in all forms of therapy, family therapy, too, has tended to focus more closely on behavioral targets and methods. For example, *behavioral parent training* (Barkley, 1997), also known as *parent management training* (Kazdin, 2005a), has been used to effectively treat a number of externalizing behavior problems in children, such as oppositional defiant disorder and aggression. As in the following case example, behavioral parent training can be modified for use with younger adolescents as well (Weisz, 2004):

Sal is 13 years old, and he is a "bad dude." Sal is quick to anger and has been expelled from school a number of times for fighting, stealing, and yelling at teachers. Since preschool, his mother has felt that she could not control his behavior, and his father largely ignores the family while he spends most of his time watching television and drinking beer. Due to the repeated suspensions from school, Sal's mother finally tried to get help.

The therapy consisted of many components, including anger management and behavioral parent training. One of the key features of behavioral parent training is to document the child's problematic behavior objectively in order to target behaviors for improvement. Sal's mother comments to the therapist that she feels that Sal is disrespectful and disobedient, but she could not provide specific examples of behaviors that bothered her. Sal's mother also acknowledged that, other than complaining about Sal's behavior, she did little to try to stop him from acting out. Thus, the therapist worked with Sal's mother to identify problematic behaviors and to generate ideas of how to handle the behaviors more effectively. Most important is that the mother must identify just two or three behaviors to start modifying rather than trying to change everything at once (which often backfires on the family). In choosing behaviors to target for intervention, the therapist taught Sal's mother to: (a) be specific, (b) begin with problems you can see, (c) start with fairly neutral behaviors, (d) select behaviors that occur at least two or three times per day, and (e) say what replacement behaviors are needed (Weisz, 2004, pp. 302–302).

Sal's mother chose to target disobeying and disrespect (e.g., smirking, sighing, rolling his eyes). Because using a time-out procedure is not effective with older children, the mother and therapist developed a behavioral contract with Sal whereby there were no positive consequences for unwanted behaviors (e.g., he did not get his way when he complained about something) and there were clear positive consequences for desirable behavior. Based on a point-chart that was posted in the kitchen, Sal would earn points for adaptive behaviors (e.g., getting up on time, doing his chores, obeying his mother) and he would lose points for maladaptive behaviors (e.g., disobeying or disrespecting his mother). At the end of each day, Sal could cash in his points for things like watching television (if his homework was done), playing a computer game, and talking on the phone to his friends.

Both Sal and his mother embraced this program, and with relatively little upheaval, Sal's behavior began to improve rapidly. Since his behavior at school was also tied into the point-chart at home, behavioral improvements were seen both at school and at home (Weisz, 2004).

Interestingly, Sal's behavior improved even without the involvement of the father in treatment. Behavioral parent training can be effective with just one parent, but the effects are more long lasting when both mothers and fathers are involved in the treatment (Phares, Fields, & Binitie, 2006). Not all cases show such rapid improvement, especially when the clients are adolescents, but this one illustrates that behavioral parent training actually changes both the parent's and the child's behavior (Weisz, 2004).

Another form of family therapy is known as *parent–child interaction therapy* (PCIT). Originally developed by Sheila Eyberg (Eyberg & Matarazzo, 1980), this therapy is based on principles from attachment theory. The therapy allows therapists to work with both parents and children and directly coaches parents about how to interact with their child. PCIT has been found to be very effective with a number of types of problems, including oppositional defiant disorder (Brinkmeyer & Eyberg, 2003) and separation anxiety disorder (Choate, Pincus, Eyberg, & Barlow, 2005).

The Social Contexts of Couples and Family Therapy

Some of the most important challenges for couple and family therapists come from the changing *social contexts* in which couples and families live (see Figure 9.3). Families are invariably a part of a larger social context, and their functioning is partly dependent on that context. Consider that only about 64.2 % of children in the United States live in traditional nuclear families with married, heterosexual parents and one or more biological children (Hofferth, Stueve, Pleck, Bianchi, & Sayer, 2002). The rest are configured as multigenerational, multicultural units; foster families; blended families; gay or lesbian couples with children; or several people living together with no legal ties but with strong mutual commitments (Kaslow, 2004). To be effective in working with such a wide range of family constellations, therapists must understand the special problems each type of family faces and must guard against the influence of bias against family structures that differ from their own.

Our description of couples and family therapy techniques has been brief. Far more information about these techniques is available in a number of authoritative sources

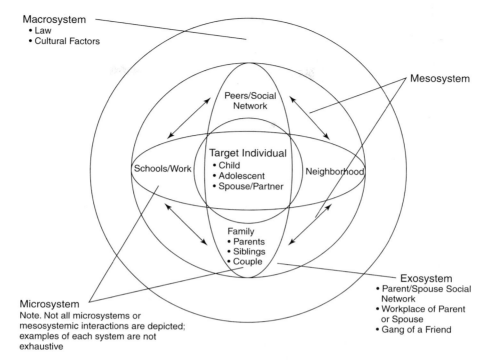

FIGURE 9.3 Couples and Families Exist Within a Larger System

(*Source:* M. S. Robbins, C. Mayorga, & J. Szapocznik, 2003, "The ecosystemic lens to understanding family functioning," In T. L. Sexton, G. Weeks, & M. S. Robbins (Eds.), *Handbook of Family Therapy,* p. 25. New York: Brunner Routledge.)

(e.g., Gurman & Jacobson, 2002; Harway, 2005; Lebow, 2005; Loveless & Holman, 2007a,b,c; McGoldrick, Giordano, & Garcia-Preto, 2005; Pinsof & Lebow, 2005).

Section Summary: Couples and family therapy are well-established treatment formats in clinical psychology. Couples therapy often deals with difficulties within the dyad (such as conflict between partners), whereas family therapy deals with problematic relationships in a larger family group. Therapists must be careful not to take sides when working with couples and families and need to remain neutral and open-minded in their role as a therapist.

COMMUNITY PSYCHOLOGY

Section Preview: This section covers community psychology, which deals with an even larger scope of problems than couples and family therapy: those that exist on the community level. The history of community psychology and the principles employed by community psychologists are discussed as well.

Despite the dominant status of individual, group, couples, and family therapy, not all clinical psychologists believe that these are the best modes of intervention for psychological problems. To produce truly meaningful improvements in individuals' lives, these critics say, psychologists must employ intervention strategies designed to maximize the "fit" between individuals and specific environments that are likely to promote their adjustment (Rappaport, 1977).

What Is Community Psychology?

One of the primary goals of community psychology is to help individuals adapt to and cope with their environment. Another is to understand the causes of disorders more broadly (e.g., that the cause of individual disorder can lie in larger problems in society, such as poverty), and when possible, to modify community-level causes before they have an opportunity to negatively influence individuals and groups. In short, community psychologists seek to apply psychological principles to (a) understanding individual and social problems, (b) preventing behavioral dysfunction, and (3) creating lasting social change.

Their efforts are based on the *ecological perspective,* which suggests that people's behavior develops out of their interactions with all aspects of their environment: physical, social, political, and economic. Accordingly, community psychologists argue that alleviating individual and social problems requires that we make changes in *both environmental settings and individual competencies.* Along with their emphasis on environmental factors in disorder, community psychologists also focus on the plight of the urban and rural poor and other groups whose problems (a) have tended to be underserved by traditional systems for therapy service delivery and (b) appear more social than psychological and thus require social rather than individual change.

A Brief History of Community Psychology

In the 1950s and 1960s, an array of influences came together to accelerate the development of community psychology. Some of the prominent factors that lead to the development of community psychology included disenchantment with the focus on psychodynamic approaches (Rappaport, 1977); skepticism about the reliability and validity of psychological diagnosis of disorders (Rosenhan, 1973) and about the benefits of traditional psychotherapy (Eysenck, 1952); shortages of mental health professionals to deliver individual treatment (Albee, 1959); sociopolitical turmoil over civil rights, gender equality, poverty, and the Vietnam War; and passage of the Community Mental Health Centers Act in 1962, which provided funds for the construction of comprehensive mental health centers.

Today, community psychology is in its fourth decade. It boasts its own division within the American Psychological Association, and there are several journals—including the *American Journal of Community Psychology,* the *Community Mental Health Journal,* and the *Journal of Community Psychology*—devoted to reporting the research and accomplishments of community psychologists. There are also a number of graduate training programs in community psychology, some of which are part of clinical psychology programs.

Principles and Methods of Community Psychology

Unlike traditional clinical psychologists, community psychologists often try to influence local citizens to become active in improving disorder-related conditions in their own communities. Among the other principles and methods that differentiate community psychology from traditional clinical psychology are:

- **Social-System Change.** In accordance with their ecological approach, community psychologists are often more interested in promoting social-system-level changes than in promoting person-oriented changes. Community psychologists emphasize indirect services that have no particular target client but are expected to achieve benefits because the social-system changes they produce radiate to intended target groups (Trickett, Barone, & Watts, 2000).

- **Promoting a "Psychological Sense of Community."** Community psychologists attempt to strengthen the ability of a community to plan and implement its own changes by promoting a psychological sense of community (Sarason, 1974). They encourage collective action by individuals with common needs or interests, and they seek to help these coalitions maintain their commitment to mutual problem solving.

- **Paraprofessionals.** Encouraging paraprofessionals (i.e., nonprofessionals) to provide behavior-change functions is a cornerstone of community psychology. Many of these helpers are known as *indigenous paraprofessionals* because they are drawn from the very groups that will receive their services. Indeed, their cultural rootedness in the to-be-served group is one of their fundamental assets.

- **Use of Activism.** Social activism is the use of power to accomplish social reform. This power may be economic, it may be political, or it may be the coercive power of civil disobedience, all of which have pros and cons. Advocates of activist tactics claim that professionals' willingness to provoke, agitate, and confront accounts for a large measure of their effectiveness in promoting change. Opponents of professional social action argue that such activity is incompatible with the objective empiricism that is the defining characteristic of a psychological scientist.

- **Use of Research as a Form of Intervention.** Research as intervention is exemplified by what is called *dissemination research*—experimentation designed to evaluate alternative methods of implementing programs that initial studies have shown to be successful. In the course of finding the most effective means of persuading other communities to adopt a given program, that program is, by necessity, adopted (Mayer & Davidson, 2000).

Despite its innovativeness and obvious good intentions, community psychology has evoked a number of concerns over the years, including concerns about who should make decisions for the community: members of the community or community psychologists. In general, community psychologists try to become integrated into local communities in order make sure that the changes they recommend are consistent with the wishes of the people who live there (Linney, 2000).

Section Summary: Community psychologists are concerned with the way the social environment influences individual well-being. Through principles of social-system change, promoting psychological sense of community, the use of paraprofessionals, political activism, and research, community psychologists attempt to improve the lives of large groups of individuals.

PREVENTION

Section Preview: This section provides an overview of efforts to prevent psychological disorders. These efforts are largely an outgrowth of community psychology. Examples of disorder prevention strategies include improving parenting skills, teaching social skills, changing environments, reducing stress, and increasing empowerment.

A central outgrowth of community psychology is prevention, which is now infused into the entire field of psychology. Decades ago, using principles borrowed from the field of public health, Gerald Caplan (1964) described three levels at which mental health problems can be prevented: tertiary, secondary, and primary. Later, the Institute of Medicine (1994) suggested other terminology (*indicated prevention interventions, selective mental health prevention,* and *universal mental health prevention,* respectively), which is becoming more common in the field. The following definitions refer to both systems of terminology:

- *Tertiary prevention (indicated prevention intervention)* seeks to lessen the severity of disorders and to reduce short-term and long-term consequences of mental health problems. One example of this type of prevention, *psychosocial rehabilitation,* teaches clients with severe psychopathology how to cope better with the effects of these problems and tries to help the client achieve the highest possible quality of life in the community in order to prevent further negative effects from the psychopathology (Hunter, 1995).
- *Secondary prevention (selective mental health prevention)* involves interventions for people who are at risk for developing a disorder. Effective secondary prevention requires knowledge of how risk factors culminate in specific disorders. It also usually requires assessment methods that are reliable and valid for detecting the initial signs of a disorder so that attempts can be made to intervene at the earliest possible point. Many secondary prevention programs attempt to increase protective factors for individuals who are at risk for the development of a disorder, a process which is likely to increase the *resilience* of individuals in the program (Fraser, 2004).
- *Primary prevention (universal mental health prevention)* involves avoiding the development of disorders by either modifying environments or strengthening individuals so that they are not susceptible to those disorders in the first place. Primary prevention programs seek to counteract risk factors and reinforce protective factors (Evans & Seligman, 2005).

These three types of prevention programs differ largely in terms of their target populations. For example, in order to prevent the recurrence of child abuse, a *tertiary* prevention program would identify parents who have abused their children in the past, then arrange for them to attend psychoeducational classes on more effective ways of dealing with children's behavior, along with child development classes, both of which would help them become more informed, competent parents. Anger management classes might be offered as well. A *secondary* prevention program would offer help to a population of parents who are identified as being at risk for abusing their children (e.g., parents who had been physically abused themselves) but who had not yet done so. These parents might be paired with a well-functioning parent in their community who could act as a source of support and helpful information about dealing effectively and nonviolently with children's behavior and misbehavior. *Primary* prevention efforts would involve the entire community population and might include a public-service campaign on radio, television, billboards, and in newspapers in which celebrities, prominent athletes, and other influential figures would discourage child abuse and direct people to get help for child-rearing problems.

The focus of prevention, which is now known as *prevention science,* has been influenced by the development of the National Institute of Mental Health's Prevention Intervention Research Centers (PIRCs), and by recommendations contained in the reports of two study groups sponsored by NIMH and the National Academy of Sciences' Institute of Medicine (Mrazek & Haggerty, 1994; NIMH, 1994). Many psychologists continue to pursue primary prevention programs consistent with the PIRC research model, which focused on multidisciplinary research to help prevent the development of psychopathology. Five examples of this type of research are improving parenting skills, teaching social skills, changing environments, reducing stress, and promoting empowerment.

Improving Parenting Skills. A number of primary prevention programs are aimed at improving parenting skills in order to reduce the incidence of family violence. Millions of children are victims of physical or sexual abuse or severe neglect or are witnesses to family violence every year. There is evidence that children reared in violent homes are more likely to become aggressive, abusive, or criminal adults themselves (Dodge, Coie, & Lynam, 2006). Prevention programs attempt to improve parenting skills, reduce the use of corporal punishment, and change parental attitudes (Kumpfer & Alvarado, 2003).

Teaching Social Skills. Another approach to primary prevention of mental disorder involves teaching children and adolescents the interpersonal skills crucial to later development and adjustment. For example, children lacking such skills tend to display, as early as kindergarten, a pattern of behavior that elevates their risk for later delinquency (Welsh & Farrington, 2007). However, there is evidence that if these children can be taught to use effective problem-solving strategies (Shure & Aberson, 2005), they can avoid developing the academic and social problems common in the backgrounds of conduct-disordered youngsters.

Changing Environments. A third approach to primary prevention entails making environments (such as homes, schools, and neighborhoods) more supportive of adaptive behavior. For example, programs such as Head Start that expand preschool opportunities and increase the commitment of parents and children to academic success have been shown to decrease antisocial behavior in the long run, even though this was not their original goal (Ripple & Zigler, 2003).

Reducing Stress. A fourth approach to primary prevention takes the form of reducing environmental stressors. For example, increasing the availability of affordable housing can reduce the frequency of household moves, a major stressor for poor families that has been linked to psychological maladjustment (Felner et al., 2000).

Promoting Empowerment. Finally, there are primary prevention programs designed to empower the powerless, to help those for whom old age, poverty, homelessness, ethnic minority status, physical disability, or other factors have left them without the ability or confidence to take control of their lives. *Empowerment* (Rappaport, 2002) is the development of a belief among formerly dependent and powerless individuals that they can master and control their lives. There is already some evidence that empowering minority-group parents to influence school policies or empowering neighborhoods to control crime can have long-term mental health benefits for the community as a whole (Zimmerman, 2000).

There are a number of other effective prevention programs in a number of different areas, including substance abuse, risky sexual behavior, delinquency, violence, and school failure (Nation et al., 2003). In short, the goal of prevention has now been fully integrated into the field of clinical psychology, with an especially heavy representation in the areas of pediatric and health psychology, including the prevention of HIV and AIDS (Earl & Albarracin, 2007; Fisher, Fisher, Bryan, & Misovich, 2002), cancer (Ellis et al., 2005), heart disease (Lisspers et al., 2005), and eating disorders (Franko et al., 2005). (We discuss several of these health care interventions in Chapter 12, "Health Psychology"). Moreover, prevention efforts in clinical and community psychology are consistent with and supportive of the growth of positive psychology (Duckworth, Steen, & Seligman, 2005), which focuses on the development of individual strengths and promotes individual well-being (Weisz, Sandler, Durlak, & Anton, 2005).

Section Summary: Preventive efforts have been integrated into nearly every aspect of clinical psychology. Tertiary prevention (also known as indicated prevention intervention) targets groups of individuals who have already experienced mental health problems, secondary prevention (selective mental health prevention) targets individuals who are at risk for the development of problems, and primary prevention (universal mental health prevention) targets the entire community, whether or not they are at risk for the development of mental health problems.

SELF-HELP

Section Preview: This section covers self-help efforts, which can be completed with or without the assistance of a trained professional. These efforts can be guided by self-help books as well as by face-to-face and Internet-based support groups.

Self-help programs have been around for decades, and their popularity seems to be on the rise. Surveys suggest that between 5% and 7% of U.S. adults have participated in a face-to-face self-help group within the past year, and it is estimated that 18% of all adults will attend a self-help group at some point in their lives (Norcross, 2006). Nearly 80% of individuals who use the Internet have sought information online for health-related problems, including mental health and relationship difficulties (Norcross, 2006).

If the popularity of an intervention is reflected in the number of books published about it, self-help would clearly be in first place. A recent search of the amazon.com book database yielded 58, 694 matches for "psychotherapy," but nearly three times that many 153,466 for "self-help." The growing popularity of self-help groups has led some to suggest that self-help interventions may soon rival all other forms of treatment (Barlow, Burlingame, Nebeker, & Anderson, 2000). For many persons, self-help is the prime source of psychological advice and treatment (Norcross, Santrock, Zuckerman, Sommer, & Campbell, 2003). Norcross (2000) has referred to the self-help movement as a "massive, systemic, and yet largely silent revolution" (p. 370).

The self-help movement has its roots in programs such as Alcoholics Anonymous (AA), one of the earliest such interventions. Self-help interventions are similar to psychological treatments in that they provide a structured way of understanding and dealing with a problem. Members assist one another by exchanging information, providing social support, and discussing mutual problems (Coleman, 2005).

With the development of electronic media, self-help groups are no longer restricted by geographical boundaries. Many online support groups now exist, most of them offering bulletin boards to which members post comments and replies (such interchanges are called "asynchronous communication"). One example from the clinical literature describes a therapist-facilitated online support group for Asian American men (Chang & Yeh, 2003). This online group provides information, guidance, and support to these men on issues related to race, culture, gender, and well-being.

As in this example, many self-help groups are not strictly "self-help," because they are conducted or supervised by professionals. In face-to-face groups, the professional might orient new members and act as a consultant to the group. In online groups, the professional might supervise the Web site design, suggest links to sources of information, and maintain the supportive milieu by encouraging communication, providing information, or trying to limit access by disruptive members.

Self-help interventions are not restricted to support groups. *Bibliotherapy*, that is, reading books about how to deal with psychological problems, is a large component of the self-help movement. A stroll or scroll through your local or online bookstore is all that is needed to get a sense of the prevalence of self-help books. Some of them, such as Burns's (1999) *Feeling Good: The New Mood Therapy*, are based on research in cognitive therapy or other treatment principles. Others were written by leading researchers who chose to disseminate scholarly material in a popular medium. A few examples in the latter category follow:

- Master Your Anxiety and Panic (Barlow & Craske, 2006)
- ADHD in Adults: What the Science Says (Barkley, Murphy, & Fisher, 2007)

- Overcoming Your Eating Disorder: A Cognitive-Behavioral Treatment for Bulimia Nervosa and Binge-Eating Workbook (Apple & Agras, 2007)
- Your Defiant Child: Eight Steps to Better Behavior (Barkley & Benton, 1998)
- Ten Lessons to Transform Your Marriage (Gottman & Gottman, 2006)
- Authentic Happiness: Using the New Positive Psychology to Realize Your Potential for Lasting Fulfillment (Seligman, 2004)

Although obviously designed for self-help, some of these books are employed by therapists as part of more extensive psychological treatment. One survey found that 82% of therapists recommend high-quality self-help materials to their clients (Norcross, 2006). Bookstore browsers should understand, though, that the vast majority of self-help books are not written by experts in the field and that their publication is no guarantee of their quality. Readers of these books should also recognize that some of the methods described might have proven effective in clinical settings but still need to be validated for use without the help of a trained therapist (Rosen, Glasgow, & Moore, 2003).

Indeed, many psychologists are concerned that some self-help books ignore or distort scientific findings in order to enhance sales. Publishers are typically more concerned with the potential sales of a book than with the empirical support for its recommendations. Accordingly, some self-help books carry a real danger of being misleading and even harmful.

With these considerations in mind, some psychologists have made efforts to help the public evaluate the numerous options of self-help. For example, John Norcross and his colleagues published the *Authoritative Guide to Self-Help Resources in Mental Health, Revised Edition* (Norcross, Santrock, Zuckerman, Sommer, & Campbell, 2003). This book reports the results of surveys of professionals on the value of individual self-help resources (books, groups, Internet sites, etc.) for various disorders. Unfortunately, there is no known resource that summarizes controlled outcome studies of popular self-help books, largely because such controlled studies are almost nonexistent (Rosen et al., 2003). Outcome studies do suggest that bibliotherapy (also known as *self-administered treatments*) can be effective for problems like depression, anxiety, and mild alcohol abuse, but not for smoking cessation or moderate to severe levels of alcohol abuse (Apodaca & Miller, 2003; Mains & Scogin, 2003).

Professionals' attitudes about self-help are mixed. Some are deeply committed to and involved in assisting the public through self-help ventures, while others are skeptical (Shepherd et al., 1999). The skeptics, in particular, point to the great many precautions that need to be taken before choosing self-help techniques (Rosen et al., 2003). Norcross (2006) argues that psychologists, and the general public, should think about self-help resources with an open mind but also with an eye toward identifying resources that are based on empirical evidence, not just the latest trends popularized in the media.

Section Summary: Support groups and self-help books (known as bibliotherapy) are used extensively throughout the United States. Many psychologists worry about people trying to treat themselves, so there is increasing awareness of the need to provide evidence-based material for use in self-help efforts.

REALLY ALTERNATIVE APPROACHES

Section Preview: This section covers recent developments in alternative treatment modalities and methods, including complementary/alternative medicine, spirituality, and mindfulness. Interest in these approaches is strong, but empirical support varies.

No chapter on alternative treatment approaches would be complete without some discussion of those that are furthest removed from traditional therapies.

Complementary/Alternative Medicine

Also known as *integrative techniques,* complementary/alternative medicine (CAM) includes herbology (use of over-the-counter herbs for improvement in well-being), chiropractic methods, massage therapy, nutrition (both healthier foods and vitamin supplements), applied kinesiology, and biofeedback (Bassman & Uellendahl, 2003). One study of over 3,000 adults in the United States (Honda & Jacobson, 2005) found that 54% had used some type of CAM technique in the past year.

The use of these methods in the hope of alleviating psychological disorders has increased significantly over the past decade. Kessler and his colleagues (2001) found that 56.7% of individuals with anxiety and 53.6% of individuals with depression were using CAM techniques to help with their symptoms. Among patients in traditional psychological treatment for these disorders, 65.9% with an anxiety disorder and 66.7% with a depressive disorder were also using CAM methods. Thus CAM techniques appear to be commonly used in the general population and even more common among people with mental health problems.

Although many CAM techniques have been around for centuries, researchers have only recently evaluated their effectiveness via controlled experiments. Some of these experiments indicate that some CAM techniques—many of which are used in conjunction with traditional psychological or medical treatments—can indeed be effective (Bassman & Uellendahl, 2003). Some of the more promising of these are the use of

- Omega-3 essential fatty acids to ameliorate symptoms of depression (Lake, 2007) and to lessen the likelihood of suicide attempts in people who have made previous attempts (Hallahan, Hibbeln, Davis, & Garland, 2007).
- Meditation for problems such as insomnia and other symptoms of stress (Walsh & Shapiro, 2006).
- Herbal therapies in conjunction with traditional treatment to reduce the side effects of chemotherapy in the treatment of prostate cancer (Auerbach, 2006).
- Techniques such as meditation, herbal remedies, massage, acupuncture, and prayer in dealing with pain and other physical symptoms associated with lung cancer (Wells et al., 2007).
- Multiple CAM techniques for dealing with stressors related to living with HIV or AIDS (Suarez & Reese, 2000).

Many other CAM techniques remain unevaluated, and those that do show promise must still be studied to determine which techniques are helpful for which difficulties.

We already know, though, that some CAM techniques, including a number of "new age" therapies, are not only ineffective but can actually be harmful (Lilienfeld, 2007). Two techniques in this category are recovered memory therapy (in which therapists try to "help" clients recall allegedly repressed experiences of past abuse) and rebirthing and reparenting therapy (in which therapists provide a new "birth experience" for clients by forcing them to spend hours working their way through confined spaces symbolic of the birth canal) (Lynn, Lock, Loftus, Krackow, & Lilienfeld, 2003). Singer and Nievod (2003) warn that although these therapies have been fully discredited, others like them (which also have no empirical support and often have harmful effects) seem to appear on the professional horizon frequently. Empirically oriented clinical psychologists remain open-minded about the possible usefulness of new treatments, including new CAM treatments, but they tend to stick to established interventions whose efficacy and effectiveness have been empirically supported and to demand the same support for innovative new methods before they adopt them.

More information on both promising and discredited CAM methods is available in a number of books (e.g., Lake, 2007), as well as in the *Physician's Desk Reference for Nonprescription Drugs, Dietary Supplements, and Herbs* (2007) and the *Journal of Alternative and Complementary Medicine*.

Spirituality

Traditionally, clinical psychologists and clinical researchers have not included spirituality and religiosity in the course of their professional work. For example, early measures of coping methods did not include space for clients to mention that they used prayer or other spiritual methods to deal with stressors, and even the current version of the *Ways of Coping* questionnaire (Folkman & Lazarus, 1988) lists only one religiously oriented option, namely, "I prayed." Yet survey research suggests that 90% to 95% of adults in the United States believe in God or some other higher power. Approximately 90% report that they pray, and about 69% of individuals say that they are members of a church, synagogue, mosque, or other place of worship (Miller & Thoresen, 2003).

As is true of politics or any other value-laden issue, most clinicians are reluctant to mention religion or spirituality during psychological treatment unless the clients bring it up as being an important part of their lives. Indeed, to do so might create relationship problems, especially for nonreligious clients who might start wondering if they are being subjected to some sort of conversion effort, or for gay or lesbian clients who might associate religion with intolerance of their sexual orientations (Yarhouse & Tan, 2005).

Clinicians' appreciation of religious issues in therapy is being enhanced by recent empirical research on the role of spirituality in individuals' lives. For example, the risk and resilience literature has reported that having a guiding faith and having a supportive faith-based community can serve as a protective factor for youth in harsh psychosocial environments (Wright & Masten, 2005). In adults, prayer and spirituality have been identified as effective mechanisms for coping with cancer (Zaza, Sellick, & Hillier, 2005), HIV and AIDS (Cotton et al., 2006), and stress related to cardiac surgery (Ai et al., 2007). And in general, the practice of prayer has been associated with higher quality of life and fewer physical and mental health problems (Bantha, Moskowitz, Acree, & Folkman, 2007).

Unfortunately, the same cannot be said for intercessory prayer, that is, when one person or group prays for a particular target person (Masters, Spielmans, & Goodson, 2006).

Although we expect that the separation between empirical psychological science and faith-based beliefs will continue, we also expect that more research on topics related to spirituality might give clinicians a broader understanding of religious clients' concerns (such as sin) as well as of their coping resources.

Mindfulness

The concept of mindfulness, which is in some ways related to spirituality and CAM methods, has received a great deal of attention in clinical psychology in recent years. Mindfulness is described as "intentionally bringing one's attention to the internal and external experiences occurring in the present moment" (Baer, 2003, p. 125). It is often taught to clients through meditation exercises designed to help them accept their own thoughts and feelings but also so that they can achieve a certain amount of detachment from those thoughts and feelings (Segal, Williams, & Teasdale, 2001). Mindfulness has been integrated into cognitive-behavioral treatments for depression (Hayes, Follette, & Linehan, 2004) and stress reduction (Bishop, 2007). Mindfulness is usually taught in a nonreligious context in therapy, but it has also been shown to be effective when taught within the context of a spiritual framework such as Buddhism (Ostafin et al., 2006).

More research is needed to establish a better operational definition of mindfulness (Bishop et al., 2004; Hayes & Shenk, 2004) and to identify the mechanisms through which mindfulness can facilitate treatment (Shapiro, Carlson, Astin, & Freedman, 2006), but it does appear to be a promising tool in some contexts and with some clients (Dimidjian & Linehan, 2003).

Section Summary: Alternative approaches, such as complementary/alternative medicine, spirituality, and mindfulness are all becoming more integrated into the traditional practices of clinical psychology. Largely because empirical research has supported their use, these practices are of great interest to clinical psychologists, especially those working within the health and pediatric fields. Care must be taken, however, to focus on methods that are evidence-based, since there are many alternative approaches that do not benefit clients' well-being.

TECHNOLOGICAL INNOVATIONS INFLUENCING PSYCHOLOGICAL TREATMENT

Section Preview: This section reviews both the difficulties and promises of new treatment technologies. We review some of the difficulties that have arisen out of online therapeutic activities and then discuss the ways in which computers have been able to help with psychological assessments and therapy.

Technological advances have changed everything over the past few decades, and the field of clinical psychology is no exception. As mentioned in previous chapters, technology, and especially the widespread use of the Internet, have led to innovations in assessment and treatment. They have also contributed to new types of problems.

Problems Caused by Technology

In one survey, therapists reported that a significant number of their nearly 1,500 adolescent and adult clients experienced a variety of Internet-related problems (Mitchell, Becker-Blease, & Finkelhor, 2005). For 61% of these clients, the problems had to do with disruptive overuse of the Internet; 20% of those clients reported spending more than 28 hours per week on Internet activities that were not related to work or to e-mail communications (see Figure 9.4).

The second most common problem (56% of clients, mainly men) was excessive use of the Internet to view pornography. The next most common problem (21% of clients) involved Internet activities that led, or threatened to lead, to marital infidelity. Of course, as the survey's authors acknowledged, many of these clients' problems may have occurred even without the Internet, but the results do highlight the fact that the pervasive availability of the Internet and its ability to create anonymous and potentially isolating communication around the clock can put some clients at added risk for problems that might not otherwise have occurred.

Technology as a Treatment Tool

The Internet can also help to solve clients' problems. In procedures collectively known as *e-health,* mental health professionals can assess, diagnose, and sometimes treat clients through remote contact via computer (Glueckauf, Pickett, Ketterson, Loomis, & Rozensky,

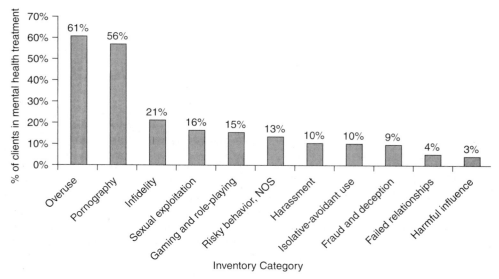

FIGURE 9.4 Percentage Endorsement of Different Problematic Internet Experiences

(*Source:* K. J. Mitchell, K. A. Becker-Blease, & D. Finkelhor, 2005, Inventory of problematic internet experiences encountered in clinical practice. *Professional Psychology: Research and Practice, 36,* 498–509.)

2003). These services are especially helpful in rural and other remote areas where many clients would not otherwise have access to a mental health professional.

We discussed the pros and cons of computer-based assessment in Chapter 3. Many of the same pros and cons are evident in the use of the Internet for psychological interventions. The Internet can be especially effective in delivering certain treatments, particularly those involving behavioral packages that target specific, discrete problems (Ritterband et al., 2003). In one randomized study of anxiety treatments, children who received some in-clinic meetings and some interventions delivered via the Internet showed improvement comparable to those who received in-clinic treatment alone (Spence, Holmes, March, & Lipp, 2006). A clinical psychologist is usually involved in Internet-based treatment programs, either through an initial face-to-face meeting or at least through regular phone calls or e-mails to assess the progress of treatment.

Internet interventions are unlikely to replace face-to-face interventions for most mental health difficulties (Ritterband et al., 2003), but the use of Internet-based psychological treatments is likely to continue to grow. As it does, clinicians will have to deal with a number of ethical issues in the delivery of online therapy (Rochlen, Zack, & Speyer, 2004; see our discussion of such issues in Chapter 15, "Professional Issues in Clinical Psychology").

Section Summary: Many problems have arisen from overreliance on computers and online activities, but through computer-based therapies known as e-health, the Internet also has potential as an effective treatment modality for some circumscribed problems with the use of evidence-based treatment packages.

PSYCHOTHERAPY INTEGRATION

Section Preview: This section reviews proposals for how therapists might use approaches from a number of different theoretical orientations. Although there is no consensus on exactly how integration should be accomplished, most in the field regard it as essential.

With all of the focus on different types of therapeutic orientation, it is important to understand that many therapists integrate the best practices across orientations in order to maximize their effectiveness with their clients. As mentioned in Chapter 1, "What Is Clinical Psychology?", *psychotherapy integration* is the process of combining elements of various clinical psychology theories in a systematic manner. Therapists as well as training directors in internships tend to appreciate at least some level of integration of therapies (Lampropoulos & Dixon, 2007).

As you have no doubt noticed, some of the therapies we have described are combinations of two or more "pure" approaches and thus represent at least partial integration. For example, relational psychodynamic approaches combine aspects of psychodynamic and humanistic theory and technique; cognitive-behavioral approaches combine . . . well, that one should be obvious. A number of other integrative therapies are gaining popularity, and their names alone suggest the combination of multiple influences: cognitive analytic therapy (Ryle, 2005), integrative problem-centered therapy (Pinsof, 2005), and cognitive-affective-relational-behavior therapy (Goldfried, 2006).

Integration is a good idea, but clinicians have not reached consensus about how to accomplish it. They have, however, at least agreed that there are four main models of psychotherapy integration (Strickler & Gold, 2006). In *technical integration,* clinicians select assessment and treatment methods from all those available in the field. So at various times, a clinician might use relaxation training, interpretation of transference, biofeedback, nondirective listening skills, and so forth. Ideally, selection would be based on research-demonstrated effectiveness and on the needs of the client. The technical integration approach might be thought of as a "cafeteria approach" in that clinicians select from a broad array of techniques. This approach, however, is not especially "integrative" in the sense that there is little attempt to resolve theoretical conflicts among the orientations that spawned the various techniques.

In contrast, *theoretical integration* proposes to resolve the real and apparent conflicts among the major psychological theories so that there is genuine theoretical integration in psychology. This is a desirable goal, but true theoretical integration has eluded the field of psychology from its beginning, so theoretical integration is probably the most difficult model of integration to achieve (Gold & Strickler, 2006).

The *common factors* approach seeks to identify the variables that are common to all (or most) effective treatments. It attempts to strip away much of the theoretical and technical arguments and instead identify the behaviors and characteristics that effective therapists across the spectrum have in common. These behaviors and characteristics then become the focus of training and practice.

Assimilative integration occurs when clinicians hold one primary theoretical orientation but use techniques from other approaches. This "mostly-this-but-some-of-that" approach is probably the closest to what clinicians actually do when they say they practice *eclecticism.* Most clinicians were trained in one theoretical orientation but have integrated into their practice some techniques from other approaches.

Graduate training programs have been slow to change from their tendency to teach one "brand name" theoretical orientation (Consoli & Jester, 2005). A few institutions have embraced integrative training models, and many have begun to adopt some degree of assimilative integration—teaching one main approach while occasionally training students in specific techniques from other approaches. Emphasizing one orientation has the advantage of theoretical coherence—students are taught to understand personality development and psychopathology using one relatively coherent approach (e.g., psychodynamic, cognitive-behavioral). At the same time, training students in specific methods, regardless of which orientation they come from (e.g., Rogerian listening and empathy skills, systematic desensitization, cognitive restructuring techniques) allows training and practice to evolve according to results of psychotherapy effectiveness research (which we discuss in Chapter 10).

Despite the slowness of changes in training and practice, the spirit of current times seems to favor increasing levels of integration (Stricker & Gold, 2006). Interested students are encouraged to explore sources such as the *Journal of Psychotherapy Integration, A Casebook of Psychotherapy Integration* (Stricker & Gold, 2006) or the *Handbook of Psychotherapy Integration* (Norcross & Goldfried, 2005).

CHAPTER SUMMARY

Psychological treatment can involve modes of intervention that focus on and attempt to use the social contexts in which individuals' problems are embedded. Interventions can be conducted with groups, couples, and families, using methods that combine those employed in individual psychotherapy with specialized techniques unique to these special formats. Group therapy seeks to change the way individuals interact in a wide range of interpersonal relationships, while couples therapy addresses these issues within the context of an intimate dyad. These approaches often rely on systems-theory approaches, so diagnosis and treatment are aimed at changing a system rather than changing individuals. Newer modalities apply cognitive-behavioral or behavioral principles to the group and family format.

Community psychology is a field that applies psychological principles to understanding individual and social problems and to creating beneficial social changes. Prevention is an outgrowth of community psychology, with a focus on preventing problems before they occur or trying to reduce any exacerbation of problems once they are evident.

Another offshoot of community psychology—self-help groups—has grown into a major therapeutic industry. Professionals' involvement in and attitudes toward the self-help movement are mixed, though it is clear that self-help is widely used.

Other alternative approaches to therapy include those offered by complementary medicine, spirituality, mindfulness, and the use of the Internet to assess and treat mental health problems.

STUDY QUESTIONS

1. What influences led to the growth of interventions that go beyond the individual?
2. When was group therapy first practiced, and by whom?
3. What are the primary therapeutic factors in group therapy?
4. Describe a common group therapy format (such as how many members are involved, what the therapists' role is, how long each session lasts, etc.).
5. How are psychoeducational and cognitive-behavioral therapy groups different from traditional process-oriented group therapies?
6. What are the most common reasons that couples seek treatment?
7. What are some important practices for therapists to keep in mind when working with groups, couples, and families?
8. Discuss the concept of an identified client in the context of family therapy (e.g., theoretical rationale for family therapy, understanding of how problems develop and are treated, etc.).
9. Discuss the use or nonuse of diagnosis within therapeutic work with couples and families.
10. What is community psychology, and how does it differ from other types of clinical psychology?
11. What are the principles and methods of community psychology?
12. What are the three types of prevention programs? Provide an illustrative example of each, along with pros and cons of each method.

13. Take a position either for or against self-help interventions and defend it.

14. Describe current examples of complementary/alternative medicine techniques that are used within clinical psychology. Provide any evidence that supports the use of those techniques.

15. What are the pros and cons of using computers and the Internet for assessment and treatment?

WEB SITES

- APA Division 49: Group Psychology and Group Psychotherapy: http://www.apa49.org
- APA Division 43: Family Psychology: http://www.apa.org/divisions/div43
- APA Division 27: Society for Community Research and Action: http://www.scra27.org
- Prevention programs that work, National Institutes of Health: http://www.oslc.org/Pubs/exper.html
- National Center for Complementary and Alternative Medicine: http://www.nccam.nih.gov

CHAPTER 10

Research on Clinical Intervention

Chapter Preview: This chapter provides an explanation of how we know what works in therapy. Methods of research to establish the usefulness of different therapies are discussed, as are the problems associated with each type of methodology. The overall findings of therapeutic efficacy and effectiveness are provided for traditional individual treatments as well as for alternative modes of intervention. The chapter closes with a discussion of the use of psychopharmacology in relation to psychological treatments.

A CLINICAL CASE

T.C. is a 26-year-old Chinese American male who is experiencing major depressive disorder, generalized anxiety disorder, and anger problems. He lives with his mother in a large city in the United States and is attending graduate school in a technology-related field.

T.C. is the youngest and "least successful" of three children. He was told by his parents that he resulted from an unwanted pregnancy that was almost aborted. There were many stressors in the family while T.C. was growing up, including financial hardship (due partially to the family owning a struggling grocery store), frequent fights between his parents, his father's gambling problem, and his mother's problem with hoarding items such as used containers. His older sisters were academically gifted, and they both graduated from prestigious universities, which made it all the more difficult when T.C. was not accepted into any colleges. It was at that point, during his senior year in high school, that T.C. experienced his first major depressive episode. He ended up graduating from high school and attending a community college and then transferred to a state university where he earned a bachelor of science degree in an engineering-related field. While T.C. was in college, his father's gambling problem intensified, and the family had to sell the grocery store, soon after which T.C.'s parents divorced. T.C. became increasingly depressed and had suicidal ideation, but no specific plan. He commented that he would kill himself if he could find a "fast, secure, and reliable" method.

T.C. sought treatment with Dr. Emily Liu, who is also Chinese American and who was in graduate school at the time. At the beginning of treatment, T.C. showed noticeably negative interpersonal characteristics, such as rolling his eyes at the therapist, sneering, and being sarcastic. On psychometrically sound assessment measures, he scored in the severe range of depression and in the moderate range of anxiety. He reported poor sleep quality and showed high levels of anger problems. On the positive side, he also showed many strengths, such as honesty, perseverance, and resilience.

T.C. was seen for 41 sessions. In addition to establishing a "no suicide" contract at the outset of treatment, Dr. Liu employed cognitive therapy, cognitive-behavioral case formulation, and cognitive–interpersonal cycle methodologies and also used her knowledge of multicultural techniques to overcome culture-specific challenges to treatment (e.g., T.C. expressed self-defeating thoughts, such as "Keep telling yourself that you are not good enough" and "Don't ever be satisfied with your accomplishments," which were consistent with his culture's values of humility and achievement but were also related to his depressive symptoms). In addition, T.C. received antidepressant medication from a psychiatrist.

By the end of the year-long therapy, T.C. showed decreased symptoms of depression, anxiety, and anger. He had made some improvements in his social skills, but those improvements were somewhat limited. He no longer had strong suicidal ideation. Dr. Liu completed her 1-year internship at the site and T.C. was transferred to another therapist to continue to work on improving his social skills and negative cognitions. (Liu, 2007)

This case illustrates the complicated histories that clients can bring to therapy. Luckily, T.C. found a therapist who employed the evidence-based practices described later in this chapter. Over the past few decades, no other area of clinical psychology has seen more intense research and debate than efforts to establish which psychological treatments work best. The idea is that clinicians should use only those therapies and assessment techniques that have been shown, through empirical research evidence, to work effectively. Those that do so are called *evidence-based therapies* and *evidence-based assessments,* which combined are known as *evidence-based practices*. Exactly what type of evidence is sufficient to show that a particular method is evidence-based? In this chapter, we explore some of the answers to this complicated question.

METHODS FOR EVALUATING PSYCHOTHERAPY

Section Preview: In this section, we review the most commonly used research designs for evaluating which forms of psychotherapy work best for which problems.

For a long time, the main question posed by clinical researchers about psychotherapy was *Is psychotherapy effective?* In trying to answer this question, they came to realize that it was too broad. Starting in the 1970s, therapy-outcome research began to be influenced by Gordon Paul's (1969a) more specific reformulation: "What treatment, by whom, is most effective for this individual with that specific problem, under which set of circumstances, and how does it come about?" (p. 44).

Alan Kazdin (1982) translated Paul's "ultimate question" into a list of outcome research goals, including (a) determining the efficacy of a specific treatment, (b) comparing the relative effectiveness of different treatments, and (c) assessing the specific components of treatment that are responsible for particular changes. Today, research on psychological treatments also seeks to (a) assess the durability of the benefits of particular treatments, (b) identify any negative side effects associated with a treatment, (c) determine how acceptable a treatment is to various kinds of clients, (d) map the cost-effectiveness of various treatments, and (e) discover whether a treatment's effects are clinically significant and socially meaningful (Goodheart, Kazdin, & Sternberg, 2006). In addition, there is keen interest in verifying that treatments that work in the research laboratory are also effective in clinical settings (Weisz, Jensen-Doss, & Hawley, 2006).

Designing Outcome Studies on Psychological Treatments

To reach all these goals, researchers must design and conduct their treatment outcome evaluations in such a way that the results can be interpreted unambiguously. Of all the research designs that can evaluate the presence of a cause–effect relationship between therapy and improvement, the most powerful is the controlled experiment (Greenhoot, 2005).

An experiment is an attempt to discover the causes of specific events by making systematic changes in certain factors and then observing changes that occur in other factors. The factors that researchers manipulate are called *independent variables*; the factors in which changes are observed are called *dependent variables*. In outcome research, the independent variable is usually the type of therapy that is given (e.g., cognitive-behavioral treatment versus nondirective therapy), and the dependent variable is the amount of change seen in clients (e.g., as measured by tests of depression or anxiety).

Most psychotherapy-outcome experiments employ either within-subjects or between-subjects research designs, both of which allow the researcher to examine the effects of varying treatment conditions (the independent variable) on clients' thinking and behavior (the dependent variables). In *between-subjects designs,* different groups of clients are exposed to differing treatments, and the amount and type of changes observed in each group are compared. In *within-subjects designs,* clients get a single kind of treatment, but the experimenter alters it in some way at various points and observes any changes in behavior that might occur.

Within-Subjects Research Designs

The within-subjects experimental design requires that the dependent variables (client behaviors) be measured on several occasions. The first of these observations usually takes place during a pretreatment, or baseline, period that provides a measure of the nature and intensity of a client's problematic behavior. Once baseline measures have established a stable picture, the intervention phase of the experiment begins. Here, the researcher manipulates the independent variable by introducing some form of treatment and watches the dependent variable for any changes from its baseline level. Several types of within-subjects experiments are used in clinical treatment research (Greenhoot, 2005), but the two most popular versions are the reversal design and the multiple-baseline design.

In the *reversal,* or *ABAB, design,* a no-treatment baseline period (A) is alternated with a treatment period (B). The lengths of the A and B phases are determined by many factors, but usually each phase continues until the client's behavior becomes relatively stable. The logic underlying this design suggests that if behavior changes reliably and substantially only during each treatment period, and returns toward the baseline each time treatment is discontinued, the researcher gains confidence that the treatment is responsible for the changes.

Figure 10.1 shows how an ABAB/reversal design was used to evaluate the treatment of a 4-year-old boy's excessive temper tantrums. During the intervention stage, when the mother employed brief "time-out" periods immediately after each temper tantrum, the frequency of temper tantrums decreased. When time out procedures were discontinued, the temper tantrums increased to a level that was even higher than the initial baseline. When time-out procedures were introduced again, the temper tantrums again decreased (Anderson & Kim, 2005).

Especially in situations that involve clinical or ethical concerns about interrupting treatment, researchers may prefer the *multiple-baseline design,* which allows them to evaluate the effect of an intervention without discontinuing it. Instead, the researcher

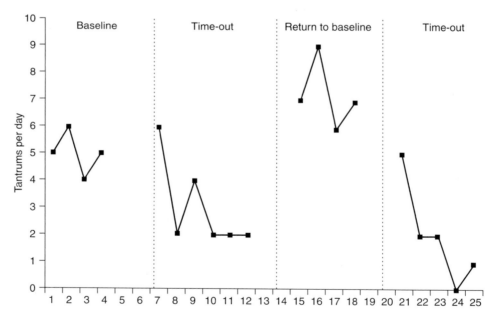

FIGURE 10.1   Frequency of Tantrums Emitted by a 4-year-old Boy

(*Source:* C. M. Anderson & C. Kim, 2005, "Evaluating Treatment Efficacy with Single-Case Designs," in M. C. Roberts & S. S. Ilardi, (Eds.), *Handbook of Research Methods in Clinical Psychology, p. 79.* Malden, MA: Blackwell Publishing.)

observes several problematic behaviors at once but applies treatment to only one of them. If the treatment has a specific causal effect, the only aspect of the client's behavior that should change is the one that was treated. The treatment is then applied to additional targets, one at a time, and the effect on each is observed. Confidence in the treatment's ability to cause specific effects on problematic behavior increases if each dependent measure changes when, and only when, treatment is applied to it. However, if behaviors change whether or not they were specifically targeted, the researcher can assume that the improvement may have been caused by some combination of treatment and more general factors, such as the passage of time or the client's positive expectations about treatment.

Figure 10.2 provides another example of how a multiple-baseline design can be used to evaluate treatment (Hegel & Ferguson, 2000). In this case, the client was a 28-year-old male who had sustained severe head injuries in a car accident 10 years earlier. He was now confined to a wheelchair, was unable to speak, and lived in a rehabilitation nursing facility. He had begun to make disruptive noises, and worse, was exhibiting increasing

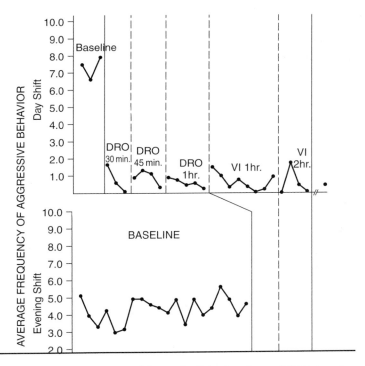

FIGURE 10.2   Mean Frequency of Aggressive Behaviors Across DRO Intervals and Between Daytime and Evening Nursing Shifts. DRO, Differential Reinforcement of Other Behavior; VI, Variable Interval

(*Source:* M. T. Hegel, & R. J. Ferguson, 2000, "Differential Reinforcement of Other Behavior (DRO) to Reduce Aggressive Behavior Following Traumatic Brain Injury." *Behavior Modification, 24,* 94–101.)

amounts of aggressive behaviors, such as kicking and grabbing people who walked near him. The treatment involved arranging for the day-shift staff to reward the client with food, his favorite music, or other reinforcers following any behavior that was not aggressive. The criterion for providing these rewards was gradually increased such that the client had to be nonaggressive for longer and longer periods. The evening staff was not trained in these techniques until well after the daytime treatment had begun. As shown in Figure 10.2, the client's aggressive behaviors decreased significantly with the day staff but remained relatively high in the evening until treatment was applied in the evening, too. Notice that the multiple-baseline design was able to confirm that the improvements that followed treatment were specific to the treatment itself, and not to client or staff expectancies or some other generalized factors or changes in the environment (Hegel & Ferguson, 2000).

As these examples show, within-subjects treatment research is usually conducted with a small number of clients, sometimes just one at a time. Indeed, single-subject, or $N = 1$, research is a popular treatment evaluation strategy because it permits the intensive study of clinical phenomena that are too rare to allow large-group designs (Morgan & Morgan, 2001).

Between-Subjects Research

The simplest example of a between-subjects experiment on therapy outcome is one in which the researcher manipulates an independent variable by giving treatment to one group of clients—the *experimental* group—and compares any observed changes to those seen in members of a *control* group, who received no treatment. Measures of the clients' problematic behavior (the dependent variable) are made for both groups before the study (the *pretest*), shortly after the treatment period ends (the *posttest*), and perhaps also at various posttreatment intervals (the *follow-up*).

It is important that clients be *randomly assigned* to experimental or control groups because, given a large enough number of clients, this procedure makes it likely that the treatment and control groups will be approximately equivalent in age, severity of disorder, socioeconomic status, and other important variables that might influence treatment outcome. If clients are not randomly assigned to conditions, any between-group differences in behavior seen at the end of the experiment might be attributed to differences that existed between groups before the experiment ever began.

Statistical comparisons between treatment and no-treatment groups is just a first step in therapy-outcome research. After all, even large and statistically significant differences between a treatment and a no-treatment group tells us only that giving treatment appears to be better than doing nothing. The simple treatment/no-treatment design cannot shed light on the more complex questions that therapy-outcome researchers want to address. In another common design, clients are randomly assigned to one of two treatments whose outcomes are then compared. For example, this type of design was used to compare the effects of motivational interviewing plus cognitive-behavioral therapy with interviewing alone in reducing alcohol abuse in gay men at high risk for HIV transmission (Morgenstern et al., 2007).

In addition, researchers want to know about whether treated clients' improvements were caused by specific therapeutic techniques, characteristics of the therapist, or the capacity of therapy to generate expectancy for improvement. One way of answering this question is to conduct *factorial experiments,* so named because they allow the researcher to examine the impact of various factors that might be responsible for observed changes in clients. In a typical factorial outcome study, one group of clients might receive a complete treatment package, while another gets only that part of treatment thought to be most important to its effectiveness. A third group might be exposed to procedures that are impressive enough to generate expectations for improvement but involve no formal treatment methods (a *placebo-control* condition). A *no-treatment* group might also be included to assess the impact of the mere passage of time. By comparing the changes seen in all four groups, the researcher can begin to determine whether the effects of the complete treatment package is better than no treatment, placebo effects, and a less extensive version of treatment. If yet another group of clients were to be given a completely different form of treatment, the researcher could also compare the first approach with that other treatment.

In a related research design called *dismantling,* researchers can take apart treatments that are known to work in order to identify their most helpful aspects (Lambert & Ogles, 2004). For example, if a treatment involves, say, relaxation training, education, and homework, a dismantling study would randomly assign some clients to get only the relaxation component, while others would get relaxation and education, and still others would get both of these plus the homework. This type of research design can help clinical scientists understand which aspects of the treatment are most crucial for clients' improvement in an attempt to streamline the treatment in the future (Lambert & Ogles, 2004).

Between-subjects research designs have been popular among therapy researchers because they allow manipulation of several independent variables simultaneously rather than sequentially, as required by within-subjects designs. Between-subjects designs are expensive, however. It usually takes many clients and a large research staff to recruit, organize, and treat groups of the size necessary for powerful statistical analyses of results (Greenhoot, 2005).

Section Summary: The most common within-subjects therapy-outcome research designs are the reversal design and multiple-baseline design. For between-subjects designs, the most basic design is to randomly assign clients to a treatment group or a control group and to measure the improvement of symptoms over time. In this example, the independent variable would be the treatment modality (i.e., treatment versus no treatment) and the dependent variable would be symptoms at the end of treatment.

PRACTICAL PROBLEMS IN THERAPY RESEARCH

Section Preview: In this section, we review threats to internal and external validity in single-subject designs, case-study research, randomized clinical trials, and laboratory analog studies.

Whether they employ within-subjects or between-subjects methods, therapy-outcome researchers' primary goal is to design experiments whose results have the highest possible levels of both internal and external validity. When they meet this goal, the researchers can be more confident that their studies can serve as useful guides for choosing treatments and charting progress in individual cases (Finger & Rand, 2005; Kendall, Holmbeck, & Verduin, 2004; Shadish, 2002).

Internal and External Validity

An experiment is said to have high *internal validity* if the design allows the researcher to assert that observed changes in dependent variable(s) were caused by manipulated independent variable(s), not by some unknown, unintended, or uncontrolled confounding factors. The researcher wants to be able to say, for example, that clients' reduced depression was caused by the cognitive therapy they received, not by the confidence they had in the treatment or by a television show they happened to see.

Experiments are high on *external validity* if their results are applicable, or generalizable, to clients, problems, and situations other than those included in the experiment. External validity does not always follow from internal validity. For example, a study evaluating systematic desensitization for claustrophobia might feature random assignment to groups and include all the control conditions necessary to conclude that desensitization was responsible for clients' improvement. However, suppose this internally valid design employed expert desensitization therapists who treated only European-American female college students with mild cases of claustrophobia. These restrictions on therapist and client variables might reduce the external validity of the study because the results may not apply to therapists in general, to clients from varying age or ethnic groups, or to clients who display more disabling phobias.

Most researchers agree that the best way to assess the outcome of psychological treatment is to conduct research on the treatments actually offered by clinicians to clinically disordered clients in real treatment settings. Unfortunately, most large-scale outcome studies are conducted in university research clinics, whereas most clinical services are delivered in the less controlled, and less controllable, world of community mental health centers, hospitals, private practice offices, and other settings. Accordingly, it is important to assure that treatments that are *efficacious* (i.e., work in large-scale studies run under controlled conditions) are also *effective* (i.e., are available and useful in the real world of clinical service delivery) (Kendall et al., 2004).

Dealing with Threats to Internal and External Validity

Clinical researchers use all their creativity and tenacity to conduct the best clinical research they can, and they try to eliminate as many threats to validity as possible. However, they recognize that because of fundamental differences between clinical and laboratory settings certain questions about psychological treatments cannot be answered with certainty outside a laboratory, while others cannot be answered with certainty inside a laboratory. In short, it is probably impossible to eliminate all threats to internal and external validity in therapy-outcome research. The best we can hope for is to reduce those threats to a bare minimum, as described below.

Single-Subject and Case-Study Research. As noted earlier, within-subjects designs help researchers conduct fine-grained analysis of the inner workings of therapy in real-world settings. A variant on this approach is the *case-study* model in which therapists evaluate their services in clinical settings by developing a specific treatment formulation for each client, then assessing the effects of the therapy for that client using techniques similar to those of single-subject research design (Edwards, Dattilio, & Bromley, 2004). Figure 10.3 illustrates case-study research in a clinical setting. The client was Rudy, a young boy whose crying and whining when asked to eat healthy food were ignored and his willingness to taste those foods was rewarded by extra play time or a taste of a preferred food (Anderson & Kim, 2005).

Clinical Trials.   Most federally funded research on treatment outcome currently focuses on *randomized clinical trials* (RCTs), whose internal validity benefits from homogeneous samples of clients and clinical problems, random assignment of clients to conditions, carefully monitored treatment regimes, and the like (Hollon, 2006). The results of RCTs are normally presented in accordance with the *Consolidated Standards of Reporting Trials* (CONSORT standards) (Khan, Khan, Leventhal, Krishnan, & Gorman, 2002). Researchers who follow these standards present flow charts portraying the progress of clients through each stage of the study, including screening, recruitment, random assignment, treatment, and follow-up.

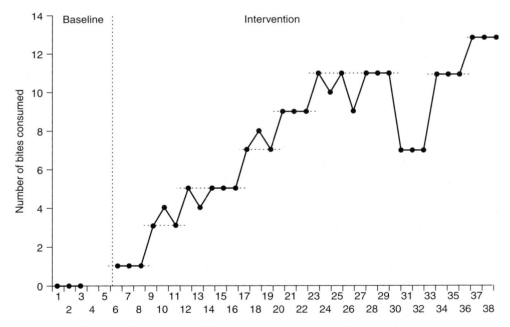

FIGURE 10.3   Number of Bites of Nonpreferred Foods Consumed During Baseline and Intervention. The criterion for reinforcement is indicated by the dashed line

(*Source:* C. M. Anderson & C. Kim, 2005, "Evaluating Treatment Efficacy with Single-Case Designs," in M. C. Roberts & S. S. Ilardi, (Eds.), *Handbook of Research Methods in Clinical Psychology,* p. 87. Malden, MA: Blackwell Publishing.)

Given the tight control seen in RCTs, there are often threats to the external validity, or generalizability, of their results. Some investigators have tried to address this concern by conducting cooperative outcome studies that combine the results of many different therapists' treatment of similar types of clients at several clinical centers. This type of study allows random assignment and other experimental procedures to be used to investigate psychotherapy as it is practiced in real clinical settings. A prime example of this strategy is the National Institute of Mental Health Collaborative Study on the treatment of depression (Solomon et al., 2005). Similar multisite studies are currently evaluating the treatment of other psychological problems.

Laboratory Analogs.   Another approach to maximizing both internal and external validity is to conduct *analog research,* which seeks to approximate clinical conditions in a controlled experimental setting. Its advantages include the ability to (a) control the client, therapist, and environmental variables that tend to fluctuate in unknown ways in clinical settings; (b) recruit (and even advertise for) a sufficient number of clients who display a particular problem and who meet other demographic criteria; (c) train therapists to conduct treatment(s) in specified ways; and (d) keep the number and length of treatment sessions constant for all clients.

The similarity between clinical and analog settings can be assessed along four dimensions. The first involves *client characteristics* and recruitment. The degree to which the results of an analog experiment can be generalized to a clinical population depends on the extent to which the participants are similar to clients who seek treatment.

The second dimension is the nature of the *target problem*. Certain target problems selected for analog studies, such as the fear of small animals or insects, may bear so little resemblance to the problems that most clients bring to clinics that they distort our understanding of the potency of therapeutic techniques.

A third dimension of interest relates to *therapist characteristics*. In many analog studies, the therapists are graduate students in clinical psychology who have far less experience in general, or with the particular treatment being evaluated, than the average practicing clinician. Therapists in analog studies, however, often have more specific training in the treatment of interest, including intense supervision and monitoring, than do therapists in the community.

Finally, clinical and analog studies can be compared in terms of the *treatment techniques* they employ. As noted, analog treatments can be standardized for all clients. This often means that therapists are given manuals that specify how a treatment should be conducted during the analog study (Chorpita, 2002; Henggeler & Schoenwald, 2002). In most clinics, however, therapists use methods tailored to the unique needs of each client. If manualizing treatment techniques simplify, alter, shorten, or otherwise change them in ways that do not fairly represent their use in clinical practice, the results of these analog methods may say little about the therapies they were designed to evaluate.

In general, clients seen in university-based analog studies differ from clients in real-world clinics in terms of showing lower rates of comorbidity and more stable backgrounds, but not in symptom severity (Southam-Gerow, Weisz, & Kendall, 2003). Therapists' training, access to supervision, and use of manualized, evidence-based treatments also vary between university-based analog studies and clinical work in the real world (Connor-Smith & Weisz, 2003). Thus, these are concerns that researchers must attend to when designing university-based analog studies and when considering how to transport the treatment into the real world.

Necessary Compromises in Therapy Research

Notice the dilemma inherent in any approach to designing valid research on psychological treatments: In order to exert the experimental control necessary to maximize internal validity, researchers may be forced to study clients, therapists, problems, treatments, and treatment settings that may not allow for high external validity. At the same time, if the researcher tries to maximize external validity by conducting research on real clients with real problems in community treatment settings, the resulting lack of experimental control may be lethal to internal validity. Given this dilemma, we must recognize that the results of well-controlled experiments can be used to draw only limited conclusions about therapies being conducted in clinical practice (Weisz, Jensen-Doss, & Hawley, 2006). At the same time, we must be wary of evaluative data coming from less well-controlled research in clinical settings. Indeed, any conclusions drawn from the results of any outcome study must be tempered by awareness of the compromises in research design and methods that were made in an effort to strike a reasonable balance between internal and external validity.

In short, answering Paul's (1969a) ultimate outcome question ("What treatment, by whom, is most effective for this individual, with that specific problem, under which set of circumstances, and how does it come about?") requires many researchers to conduct many different kinds of studies over many years. Let's now consider what researchers have discovered so far about the outcome of individual psychological treatments.

Section Summary: In providing maximally useful evaluations of treatment, clinical researchers must conduct studies that have high internal validity (i.e., reveal genuine cause–effect relationships) and high external validity (i.e., result in outcomes that apply or generalize to clients and problems seen in real-world clinical settings).

EFFECTIVENESS OF INDIVIDUAL PSYCHOLOGICAL TREATMENTS

Section Preview: This section reviews the long and controversial history of trying to establish which treatments work best for which problems. Included in the discussion are the use of box scores, meta-analytic studies, client satisfaction surveys, empirically supported treatments, evidence-based practices, and common or nonspecific factors.

The modern era of therapy-outcome research began in 1952 when Hans Eysenck, a British psychologist, reviewed several experiments and concluded that the recovery rate seen in patients who receive therapy is about the same as for those who do not. Eysenck argued that the rate of *spontaneous remission* (improvement without any special treatment) was 72% over 2 years compared to improvement rates of 44% for psychoanalysis and 64% for eclectic therapy (Eysenck, 1952). In later reviews, Eysenck (1966) evaluated more studies and, while persisting in his pessimism about the effectiveness of traditional therapy, claimed that behavior therapy produced superior outcomes.

Box Score Reviews

As you might imagine, Eysenck's conclusions sparked heated debate among clinicians. Many critics attacked his thoroughness, fairness, and his methods of statistical analysis. Others conducted their own reviews of the outcome literature and reached more optimistic conclusions about the effectiveness of psychotherapy. Indeed, most reviews from that time period have concluded that most forms of psychotherapy produce better outcomes than no treatment and that various types of therapy were equally effective with most clients (e.g., Lambert, Shapiro, & Bergin, 1986). But there were also reviews over the years that supported Eysenck's claim that (a) traditional psychotherapy shows results similar to no treatment, and (b) for several kinds of problems, behavior therapy is especially effective (e.g., Lambert & Bergin, 1994; Weisz, Donenberg, Han, & Weiss, 1995).

Among the many reasons for the discrepant, sometimes contradictory, results of therapy-outcome reviews is that different researchers have used differing standards in (a) selecting the outcome studies they survey, (b) evaluating the quality of these studies, (c) interpreting the magnitude of therapy effects, and (d) combining the results of many studies to reach their conclusions.

The traditional approach to summarizing outcome research has been the narrative, or *box score,* review. In a box score review, the researcher makes categorical judgments about whether each outcome study yielded positive or negative results and then tallies the number of positive and negative outcomes. Reviewers who use this method have been criticized (including by each other) for being subjective and unsystematic in the way they integrate research studies. Another problem with narrative reviews is that the sheer number of outcome studies makes it difficult for reviewers to weigh properly the merits and results of each study. Disagreements over these results made it clear that an alternative to box score analysis was needed, an alternative that would allow researchers to quantify and statistically summarize the effects of each outcome study, separately and in the aggregate.

Meta-Analytic Studies

One such alternative is *meta-analysis,* a quantitative technique that standardizes the outcomes of a large number of studies so they can be compared or combined (Hunter & Schmidt, 2004; Rosenthal & DiMatteo, 2001). The first application of meta-analysis to therapy research was done in 1977 by Mary Smith and Gene Glass, who concluded that, on the average, psychotherapy was very effective (Smith & Glass, 1977). They later conducted a much larger meta-analysis that encompassed 475 therapy-outcome studies (Smith, Glass, & Miller, 1980). In this monumental meta-analysis, therapeutic effectiveness was evaluated by computing effect sizes for all the treatments used in all the studies. An *effect size* was defined as the treatment group mean on a dependent measure minus the control group mean on the same measure divided by the standard deviation of the control group. Thus, an effect size indicates the average difference in outcome between treated and untreated groups in each study. There can be as many effect sizes for a treatment as there are measures on which that treatment is evaluated (Hedges & Olkin,

1982). Looking at effect sizes measured immediately after therapy ends, or in some cases, months after treatment, indicates how much better off the average treated client was compared with the average person in a no-treatment control group. In the Smith, Glass and Miller (1980) meta-analysis, the average treated client was found to be better off than 80% of untreated individuals. In the 1980s and 1990s, other research teams performed other meta-analyses using different statistical methods or differently selected sets of studies (e.g., Andrews & Harvey, 1981; Lambert & Bergin, 1994; Shapiro & Shapiro, 1982; Wampold et al., 1997), and these efforts continue today (Butler, Chapman, Forman, & Beck, 2006; Hetzel-Riggin, Brausch, & Montgomery, 2007; Malouff, Thorsteinsson, & Schutte, 2007; Spielmans, Pasek, & McFall, 2007; Vittengl, Clark, Dunn, & Jarrett, 2007). In general, these analyses have confirmed the conclusion that psychological treatment is an effective intervention for a wide variety of psychological disorders. As we shall see later, however, there are some differences among treatments in their usefulness with certain problems.

Client Satisfaction Surveys

The conclusions reached by most box score studies and meta-analyses are reflected in a survey conducted under the auspices of *Consumer Reports* (CR) magazine (Seligman, 1995). The survey asked about 4,100 respondents who had seen a mental health professional in the past 3 years to rate (a) the degree to which formal treatment had helped with the problem that led them to therapy, (b) how satisfied they were with the treatment they received, and (c) how they judged their "overall emotional state" after treatment. Their responses indicated that

- About 90% of clients felt better after treatment.
- There was no difference in the improvement of clients who had psychotherapy alone versus psychotherapy plus medication.
- No particular approach to psychotherapy was rated more highly than others.
- Although all types of professionals appeared to help their clients, greater improvements were associated with treatments by psychologists, psychiatrists, and social workers compared to family physicians or marriage counselors.

Follow-up research suggests that the rates of psychopathology in the *CR* survey sample are about the same as those found in the general population (Howard, Krause, Caburnay, Noel, & Saunders, 2001). However, a study that used the *CR* questionnaire in conjunction with other, more well-established measures of therapy outcome suggests that the results of the *CR* study were a bit too optimistic (Nielsen et al., 2004). For example, changes in positive emotions appeared to be overestimated when compared to other, more standardized measures. Still, the *CR* study and others like it suggest that most clients are indeed satisfied with the therapy they receive, no matter what type of therapy it is, and feel that they were helped by it.

Empirically Supported Treatments (ESTs)

Box score studies, meta-analyses, and client surveys suggest there are no significant differences in the *overall* outcomes of various types of treatment, but that doesn't mean that all treatments have the same effects for all clients with all problems. Accordingly, in 1993, APA Division 12 (now known as the Society of Clinical Psychology) convened a special task force to look more closely at the results of psychotherapy-outcome research to determine which specific treatment interventions were most strongly supported by empirical research as being effective for particular kinds of problems. This *Task Force on Promotion and Dissemination of Psychological Procedures* began by establishing a set of criteria for research designs capable of reaching reliable and valid conclusions about the effectiveness of clinical interventions. They then reviewed the massive therapy-outcome literature to determine what such studies said about the effects of various treatments. In 1995, the Task Force published a preliminary list of 25 treatments that high-quality empirical research identified as efficacious (Task Force, 1995). The list was updated in 1996 and again in 1998. The 1998 list included 71 treatments (Chambless et al., 1998). By 2001, the Task Force, along with seven other work groups using similar methods, had classified 108 treatments for adults and 37 for children as being either

- *Well-established/efficacious and specific* (i.e., supported by at least two rigorous randomized controlled trials in which treatment showed superiority to placebo-control conditions or another bona fide treatment, or by a large series of rigorous single-case experiments),
- *Probably efficacious/possibly efficacious* (i.e., supported by at least one rigorous randomized controlled trial in which treatment showed superiority to placebo-control conditions or another bona fide treatment, or by a small series of rigorous single-case experiments), or
- *Promising* (i.e., supported by studies whose research designs produced less convincing evidence than those in the first two categories (Chambless & Ollendick, 2001; see Table 10.1).

The 1995 report used the term *empirically validated* to describe those interventions that met the criteria of the Task Force. Many clinicians, however, believed that the term *validated* was too strong and contained unwanted connotations (e.g., that there was a final "answer" as to which treatments "worked"). Accordingly, in its next report, the Task Force referred to *empirically supported* treatments. Nevertheless, the terms *empirically validated* and *empirically supported* are often used interchangeably in the therapy-outcome literature.

Criticisms of EST Research. Regardless of which term is used, few efforts in the history of clinical psychology have generated as much controversy as have the attempts to use experimental research to identify treatments that work. Although many psychologists praised the work of the Task Force as the most comprehensive and systematic attempt yet to identify which of the more than 400 psychological treatments available are actually helpful, others criticized the effort on several grounds (Beutler, Kim, Davison, Karno, & Fisher, 1996; Silverman, 1996).

The most important of these relates to concern as to whether treatments shown to be effective in controlled settings generalize to clinical settings. As noted earlier, when a treatment produces outcomes for a given condition that are clearly superior to no

---

TABLE 10.1

Conclusions about Empirically Supported Treatments

The following conclusions can be drawn about the 108 treatments for adults and 37 for children identified as either well-established, probably efficacious, or promising (Chambless & Ollendick, 2001):

- Between 60% and 90% of the treatments on the list of ESTs are cognitive-behavioral in nature (Norcross, Beutler, & Levant, 2006b).

- Depression can be treated effectively by a number of different psychological treatments, such as cognitive-behavior therapy, cognitive therapy, interpersonal therapy, and brief dynamic therapies (Chambless & Ollendick, 2001).

- In a process known as *specificity* (in which a disorder is responsive to only one or two treatments), obsessive-compulsive disorder in adults was treated effectively by only one intervention: exposure plus response prevention (ERP).

- The ESTs tend to focus on skill building with attention to a specific problem and tend to be relatively brief (Norcross et al., 2006).

- Certain disorders, such as cocaine abuse, opiate dependence, and bipolar disorder, had no well-established treatments, but there are treatments that are considered probably efficacious at this time (Chambless & Ollendick, 2001).

- For children and adolescents, well-established and probably efficacious treatments for externalizing disorders (such as attention-deficit/hyperactivity disorder or conduct disorder) were likely to have a parent or family component (such as behavioral parent training with ADHD), whereas internalizing disorders (such as depression and anxiety) usually did not have a major parent or family component (Chambless & Ollendick, 2001).

---

treatment (or are equivalent to that achieved by an established treatment) under well-controlled conditions, it is said to have shown *efficacy*. But efficacy is not the same as *effectiveness* (Steele & Roberts, 2005b), which refers to how a treatment works in clinical settings.

Other criticisms had to do with the criteria used to select therapy-outcome studies for analysis. For instance, though the Task Force occasionally used research that classified client samples according to cutoff scores on diagnostic questionnaires (Chambless & Ollendick, 2001), many of these studies relied on *DSM diagnoses* to describe the client population. As we discussed in Chapter 3, "Basic Features of Clinical Assessment," some critics believe that DSM diagnostic classification may not be the best way to classify clients for therapy-outcome research. Further, clients often seek treatment for problems that are not disorders (e.g., they want to gain more joy from their life or they want to experience higher self-esteem) (Norcross et al., 2006).

Critics of EST research also pointed to evidence such as a meta-analysis of 27 studies that investigated the effects of "active ingredients" in therapy. In these dismantling studies, the effects of complete psychotherapy packages were compared with those same packages but with one theoretically important component added or subtracted (Ahn & Wampold, 2001). This analysis found no differences in the effect sizes of the various comparison packages, suggesting that the supposedly essential aspects of some treatments are not necessarily essential. In fact, in most therapy-outcome research, specific treatment techniques typically account for only a small proportion of therapy-outcome variance, while client, therapist, and other factors each account for equal or larger proportions of variance (Messer, 2001).

The *use of treatment manuals* in some of the psychotherapy research reviewed by the Task Force drew especially sharp criticism. Critics have complained that therapists rarely use such manuals in actual clinical practice (Beutler, 2002a). Indeed, one survey found that 23% of practicing psychologists said they had never even heard of treatment manuals (Addis & Krasnow, 2000). Others claim that manuals restrict therapists' ability to individualize treatment and lead to poorer outcomes for clients (Beutler, 2002a).

In general, then, critics contend that by controlling much of what influences therapy outcomes—nonspecific client, therapist, and relationship factors—EST research ignores, and thus fails to appreciate, the impact of these major influences on therapy effectiveness.

The Task Force did, in fact, have to make clear-cut decisions about what to include as support for a treatment and what not to include. In the end, members of the Task Force decided to favor studies with strong *internal validity*: studies in which the designs allowed for strong inferences about therapy effects based on unambiguously causal relationships between treatments and outcomes. To make stronger claims about the effects of specific treatments, the Task Force favored studies that sought to reduce therapist variability. In practice, this meant choosing studies in which therapists treated each client in substantially the same manner, typically by following relatively detailed treatment manuals (Chambless & Ollendick, 2001). There was also an attempt to control client variability, so studies that included treatment of only one specific disorder were favored over studies that included individuals with comorbid disorders.

Given its overriding concerns for internal validity and treatment specificity, the Task Force relied especially on studies using the randomized clinical trials described earlier, though they also used single-client designs when there were enough such studies available to establish generalizable patterns.

In our view, though it is far from perfect, we think that the work of the Task Force and other comparable review committees has done much to improve our understanding of the outcome of psychotherapy. The challenge for clinical scientists now is to combine

Treatment manuals are used frequently in clinical psychology.

research on EST methods with research on the common factors they share and to create a picture of psychotherapy effectiveness based on both sets of data (Messer, 2004; Westen & Bradley, 2005). So researchers are focusing not only on the long-term efficacy of psychotherapy—in naturalistic as well as laboratory settings—but also on the role of the therapeutic relationship in promoting that efficacy (Morrison, Bradley, & Westen, 2003; Nathan, Stuart, & Dolan, 2000; Wampold, Lichtenberg, & Waehler, 2005; Westen & Morrison, 2001). Ideally, their work will speed the development of evidence-based practice in clinical psychology (Levant, 2006; Messer, 2004), in which therapists are guided by clinically relevant as well as empirically supported research.

Evidence-Based Practice (EBP)

In 2005, the *APA 2005 Presidential Task Force on Evidence-Based Practice* proposed the following Policy Statement, which was officially adopted by the Council of Representatives of APA in August of 2005:

> Evidence-based practice in psychology (EBPP) is the integration of the best available research with clinical expertise in the context of patient characteristics, culture, and preferences. . . . The purpose of EBPP is to promote effective psychological practice and enhance public health by applying empirically supported principles of psychological assessment, case formulation, therapeutic relationship, and intervention. . . . (APA Presidential Task Force on Evidence-Based Practice, 2006, p. 273)

In general, the work of this evidence-based practice task force is an attempt to bring together researchers and clinicians in order to find the many ways that treatments can be shown to be effective in the real world. The policy statement delineates ideas on the best research evidence; clinical expertise; and patients' or clients' characteristics, values, and context.

There continues to be, however, a great divide between many empirical researchers (who cannot understand why clinicians are not jumping at the chance to use empirically supported treatments) and many clinicians (who cannot understand why researchers keep trying to force them to use treatment techniques with which they are not comfortable, especially because they feel that their own techniques already work). Some recent attempts to bridge this divide can be seen as

- Leaders in empirical research seek to find ways of transporting laboratory-based treatments to the clinic (Barlow, 2006; Weisz & Addis, 2006).
- Clinically oriented scholars and scientist-practitioners find ways to make evidence-based practices more palatable to practicing clinicians and easier to use on a day-to-day basis (Beutler, 2002a; Lebow, 2006). Their efforts are described as *implementation,* which is related to dissemination in that it refers to putting evidence-based techniques into practice in the real world (Gotham, 2006).
- Information about state-of-the-art treatments is disseminated to clinicians and clients. Examples of this effort can be found at two popular and well-respected

Web sites: www.therapyadvisor.com (which is funded by the National Institute of Mental Health) and www.effectivechildtherapy.com (which is maintained by the Society for Clinical Child and Adolescent Psychology–Division 53 of APA and funded by the John D. and Catherine T. MacArthur Foundation).

The need for these actions is clear from surveys of practicing clinicians. For example, one study found that, although some clinicians are fully aware of current research findings, the majority were not especially well informed (Boisvert & Faust, 2006). Further, clinicians who were not familiar with evidence-based practices tended to assume that these practices are less valuable than they really are in improving the quality of their clinical work (Boisvert & Faust, 2006). As can be seen in Table 10.2, the majority of practicing clinicians appear to rely far more heavily on their own experience than on empirical research findings or treatment manuals (Stewart & Chambless, 2007).

Admittedly, keeping up to date with all the empirical advances in clinical psychology takes time. One study estimated that it would take 627.5 hours each month to read all of the articles related to a particular clinical practice (Alper et al., 2004), so it is not hard to understand why practicing clinicians might be reluctant to try to master all the empirical knowledge pertinent to their area of specialization (Walker & London, 2007). Still, there are indications that clinicians are using and benefiting from various electronic information dissemination efforts. One study of therapyadvisor.com suggested that 60% of clinicians found the Web site to be helpful, that it increased their awareness of evidence-based practices, and that it increased their commitment to such practices (Riley et al., 2007). We hope that the rise of evidence-based practice will ultimately help researchers and clinicians to recognize that there are more commonalities than differences between them, and we are not alone in this hope (Southam-Gerow, Ringeisen, & Sherrill, 2006; Spring, 2007; Thorn, 2007). Ollendick and Davis (2004) pointed out that

---

TABLE 10.2

Sources Clinicians Use to Increase Therapy Skills and Effectiveness

Source	Mean	Standard Deviation
Past experiences with patients	5.62	1.08
Treatment materials informed by psychotherapy-outcome research findings	4.80	1.37
Treatment materials based on clinical case observations and theory	4.72	1.22
Discussions with colleagues	4.62	1.28
Popular books	2.96	1.19

NOTE: Higher numbers denote greater utilization.

SOURCE: From "Does psychotherapy research inform treatment decisions in private practice?", by R. E. Stewart & D. L. Chambless, 2007, *Journal of Clinical Psychology, 63,* 273. Copyright 2007 by *Journal of Clinical Psychology*. Used with permission.

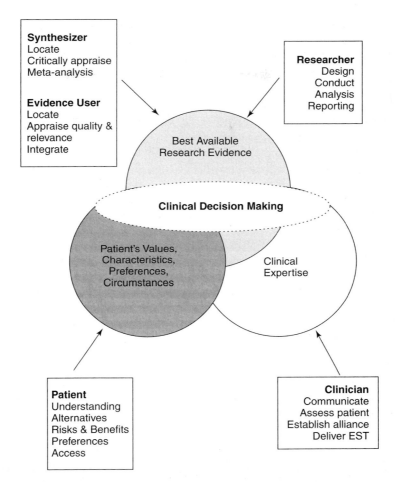

FIGURE 10.4 The Three Circles of Evidence-based Clinical Practice
(*Source:* B. Spring, 2007, "Evidence-Based Practice in Clinical Psychology:
What It Is, Why It Matters, What You Need to Know." *Journal of Clinical
Psychology, 63,* 611–631.)

clinical science and clinical practice depend on each other and that neither can work productively in isolation. Figure 10.4 shows a schematic model of the integration of clinical expertise, research evidence, and characteristics related to the client that, when combined, can lead to integrated clinical decision making (Spring, 2007).

Research on Common or Nonspecific Factors in Therapy

In Chapter 6, "Basic Features of Clinical Interventions," we introduced the notion that therapist characteristics, client characteristics, and the therapeutic relationship that forms between the client and therapist can be important factors in the outcome of psychotherapy. Here we summarize what researchers have found about how these variables operate to produce their effects.

Therapist Variables. What therapist characteristics or behaviors—apart from the therapist's adherence to a specific treatment method—predict positive therapy outcomes? In an attempt to answer this question, a Task Force on Empirically Supported Therapy Relationships was created by the APA Division of Psychotherapy (Division 29). After a thorough review and synthesis of the available research literature, the results were summarized in a book entitled *Psychotherapy Relationships That Work* (Norcross, 2002). The following therapist characteristics were found to be demonstrably effective:

- Strong therapeutic alliance with the client
- Higher levels of empathy
- Stronger goal consensus and collaboration with the client

The following factors were considered promising and probably effective:

- Positive regard toward the client
- Congruence and genuineness (see Chapter 6, "Basic Features of Clinical Interventions" and Chapter 7, "Psychodynamic and Humanistic Psychotherapies")
- Providing greater amounts of appropriate feedback
- Repair of alliance ruptures, if they occurred
- Self-disclosure, when appropriate
- Higher quality of relational interpretations

Overall, these factors were all associated with better outcomes for clients, regardless of what specific treatment technique or therapeutic orientation was used (Norcross, 2002). The Task Force also acknowledged that there is research evidence that supports customizing the therapy relationship to individual clients on the basis of characteristics or behaviors of the client. For example, clients who are not resistant to therapy tend to do better when there is a structured treatment provided by a more directive therapist, whereas clients who are more resistant to therapy appear to do better when the therapist is not too directive and when the therapist provides a treatment related to self-control (Norcross, 2002).

Client Variables. Although there is less consensus on which client variables are associated with better outcome, there are some indications about which client attitudes might be the most helpful in gaining benefits from treatment. As discussed in Chapter 6, from the limited studies that exist, the following conclusions about client characteristics that benefit psychotherapy can be drawn.

- Clients who are open and offer higher levels of disclosure and lower levels of resistance from the beginning of therapy tend to have better outcomes (Kahn, Achter, & Shambaugh, 2001).
- Clients with less severe psychological problems tend to do better in treatment than clients with more severe disorders (Clarkin & Levy, 2004).

- Clients who have strong expectations that the treatment will be successful tend to have better outcomes than those clients who do not expect success (Greenberg, Constantino, & Bruce, 2006).

Like therapist variables, client variables may interact with other factors to affect outcomes. For example, nondirective and paradoxical therapy techniques are more effective than directive ones for clients entering therapy with high levels of resistance, but directive treatments are more effective for clients with low levels of resistance (Beutler & Harwood, 2000).

Relationship Variables. In Chapter 6, we discussed various views of the therapeutic relationship and its measurement. Let's now consider the results of research investigating its influence on therapy outcome.

A large research literature on the *therapeutic alliance* now exists, with over 2,000 studies showing that better alliance and relationship factors between therapists and clients are associated with better treatment outcomes (Kazdin, 2005b). These findings have been well established in relation to both adults and children by meta-analyses (Hovarth & Symonds, 1991; Karver, Handelsman, Fields, & Bickman, 2006; Martin, Garske, & Davis, 2000) and literature reviews (Beutler et al., 2004; Shirk & Karver, 2006). These findings are also consistent with Norcross's (2002) conclusion that therapists who are better at developing a strong alliance with their clients are also better at helping those clients to benefit from therapy.

Tying together what we know about evidence-based practices and the importance of common factors such as good therapeutic relationships and high client expectations, it seems clear that both are important in offering therapy that works. Norcross (2002) put it this way: "Concurrent use of empirically supported relationships *and* empirically supported treatments tailored to the patient's disorder and characteristics is likely to generate the best outcomes" (p. 442). Of course, there is still a need to understand the mechanisms through which treatments work—both in terms of specific treatment techniques and also in terms of common factors across all treatments based on therapist, client, and relationship variables (Kazdin, 2007).

Section Summary: Although box scores and most meta-analytic studies showed equivalent results from various forms of treatment, the search for empirically supported treatments helped to identify treatments that were the most effective and efficacious for certain problems. This work has been combined with the search for common or nonspecific factors in order to identify overarching evidence-based practices.

EFFECTIVENESS OF ALTERNATIVE MODES OF INTERVENTION

Section Preview: This section summarizes therapeutic outcome studies of group, couples, and family therapy; preventive interventions; and self-help modalities. The effectiveness of psychopharmacology in relation to psychological treatments is also reviewed.

There is less research on the outcome of group, couple, and family therapies and self-help and preventive techniques than on individual therapies, but available results suggest that, in general, these alternative formats are associated with benefits that are at least equal to those of individual treatment.

Effectiveness of Group Therapy

Empirical evidence confirms that group therapy can be an effective form of treatment, especially when group members clearly understand how the group is run and what is expected of them (Forsyth & Corazzini, 2000). Certain group therapy interventions appear on lists of empirically supported treatments (e.g., supportive group therapy for schizophrenia; Chambless & Ollendick, 2001), and meta-analyses support the efficacy of group therapy for depression (McDermut, Miller, & Brown, 2001). Better outcomes are achieved when the group is cohesive, provides accurate feedback to members, and encourages interpersonal learning and supportive interactions.

Proponents of group therapy (e.g., Scheidlinger, 2000) contend that evidence of its effectiveness will lead to its increased use because of the cost savings for clients and insurance companies. And although the overall effectiveness of group therapy has tended to be less than that of individual therapy, that gap is beginning to close, partly as a result of the impact of cognitive-behavioral and psychoeducational treatment groups (Bieling, McCabe, & Antony, 2006).

Effectiveness of Couples Therapy

Compared with no-treatment control groups, almost all forms of marital therapy can produce significant improvements in couples' happiness and adjustment (Baucom, Epstein, & Gordon, 2000). However, the magnitude or clinical significance of these improvements is frequently disappointing. More than half of treated relationships remain distressed, and even among couples who show improvement, the changes are often not large enough to allow them to view their relationship as successful or happy (Christensen & Heavy, 1999). Further, the few available long-term follow-ups on the effects of successful marital therapy indicate that 30% to 40% of couples treated with behavioral marital techniques relapse into marital discord or divorce (Jacobson, Schmaling, & Holtzworth-Munroe, 1987; Snyder, Wills, & Grady-Fletcher, 1991). One review of research in this area (Christensen & Heavey, 1999) concluded that couples therapy usually produces positive effects lasting through a 6-month follow-up, but that most couples relapse to distressed states after 1 to 4 years.

More recent meta-analytic studies have painted a somewhat more positive picture, particularly of behavioral couples therapy. In one review of 30 studies, Shadish and Baldwin (2005) found that 72% of treated couples were better off at the end of treatment than were couples who did not receive treatment. Still, the need remains to find more effective couples therapy techniques and to identify the mechanisms in couples therapy that work best with different types of clients (Gottman & Ryan, 2005; Snyder, Castellani, & Whisman, 2006).

Effectiveness of Family Therapy

Families who complete a course of therapy together usually show significant improvements in communication patterns and in the behavior of the family member whose problems prompted therapy in the first place (Sexton, Alexander, & Mease, 2004). This outcome is typically reported in empirical research on family therapy for several kinds of identified client and family problems. Family therapies aimed at improving parental discipline techniques and at decreasing family members' criticism of, and emotional overinvolvement with, mentally ill relatives have proven particularly effective (Sexton et al., 2005).

Certain types of family therapy appear more successful than others. Behavioral and structural family therapies have received the strongest empirical support. Although research in this area too often focuses on nonclinical samples (Hawley, Bailey, & Pennick, 2000), the superiority of these approaches in well-controlled studies is still evident. As noted in Chapter 9, "Alternative Modes of Clinical Intervention," each of these approaches emphasizes pragmatic changes in the way families interact and go about solving problems. Treatments such as behavioral parent training or parent management training (Kazdin, 2005a) and parent–child interaction therapy (Brinkmeyer & Eyberg, 2003) are considered very effective evidence-based practices. Family-based treatments tend to be less effective for families from disadvantaged backgrounds (Lundahl, Risser, & Lovejoy, 2006), so more work is needed to find effective treatments for families from all socio-economic levels.

Effectiveness of Preventive Interventions

In Chapter 9, we described a number of prevention programs that grew out of the community psychology movement. Recall that prevention programs are often designed to modify social, economic, and environmental risk factors that lead to disorders or to strengthen positive qualities that can protect vulnerable individuals from developing disorders.

Large-scale, well-controlled studies have identified a number of effective prevention programs (Barrera & Sandler, 2006) such as the following:

- Preventing aggression by teaching adolescents anger management and social problem–solving skills as they make the transition from elementary to middle school (Lochman & Wells, 2004).
- Preventing HIV infection by addressing informational, motivational, and behavioral skills competence related to safe-sex methods among inner-city high school students (Fisher, Fisher, Bryan, & Misovich, 2002).
- Preventing cognitive and neurological deficits that result from lead poisoning by screening children to identify those who have been exposed to lead, such as in lead-based paint (Ripple & Zigler, 2003).
- Preventing substance abuse by children and adolescents by increasing parenting skills and strengthening healthy connections within families (Kumpfer & Alvarado, 2003).

To make such prevention programs even more effective, it is important that they take into account the cultural norms and traditions of the individuals who are targeted for help. By the year 2050, it is estimated that African Americans, Hispanic/Latino/Latina Americans, Asian Americans, and Native Americans will make up nearly 50% of the U.S. population. These demographic changes pose a fundamental challenge for prevention efforts because programs that work well in one cultural setting may not work well in another (Reppucci, Wollard, & Fried, 1999).

Effectiveness of Self-Help and Self-Help Groups

The effects of self-help groups are seldom evaluated empirically. Most self-help group members are simply convinced that their groups are valuable and thus see formal outcome research as unnecessary or even undesirable. Evaluation is further complicated because the goals of self-help groups are often hard to describe precisely. The few available outcome evaluations have produced mixed results (Barlow, Burlingame, Nebeker, & Anderson, 2000; Moos, Schaefer, Andrassy, & Moos, 2001), but it generally appears that active members value their involvement in the group and experience moderate improvements in some areas of their lives. It would be helpful if self-help groups were more receptive to empirical research so that clinicians could learn more about their beneficial effects and how they occur.

There has been somewhat more research on bibliotherapy (i.e., using books for self-help), but there is no empirically based listing of specific books that are most effective for particular problems (Rosen, Glasgow, & Moore, 2003). Some meta-analytic research suggests that self-help bibliotherapy appears more effective for problems such as anxiety, depression, and mild alcohol abuse than for chronic problems such as smoking and severe alcohol abuse (Apodaca & Miller, 2003; Mains & Scogin, 2003).

Effectiveness of Combining Psychotherapy and Medication Treatment

Combining medications and psychotherapy can be quite helpful and, in some cases, may be better than either approach alone (e.g., Hinshaw, 2006), but most studies have found that, for anxiety disorders and depression, at least, combined treatments do not greatly improve on what either treatment can achieve on its own (Hollon et al., 2005; Hollon, Stewart, & Strunk, 2006). Other studies have found that, for these disorders, psychotherapy can result in benefits that are greater and more enduring than drug treatments (e.g., Hollon et al., 2006; Figure 10.5 shows similar results in the treatment of binge eating).

Despite findings like these, many clients who might once have received psychotherapy alone are now getting drugs, or drugs and psychotherapy, even though they might have done just as well without the drugs. In addition, a number of surveys have found that most clients prefer a psychological intervention to a psychopharmacological intervention if they are given the choice (Hazlett-Stevens et al., 2002; Zoellner, Feeny, Cochran, & Pruitt, 2003). Thus, the increasing numbers of clients who are given only psychopharmacological options by their managed care companies may not be receiving the services they want or the ones that are most helpful for their problems.

Section Summary: Although many forms of alternative treatments are effective, the most effective group, couples, and family therapy as well as preventive interventions tend to utilize cognitive-behavioral or behavioral techniques. Unfortunately, little research exists to support the effectiveness of self-help methods, although many evidence-based practices are making their way to the popular market. The use of prescription drugs in the treatment of psychological disorders is very common, and can be effective in many cases, but it appears that there are some disorders for which psychological treatment is equal or superior to drug treatment.

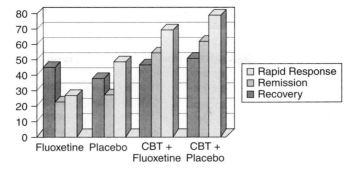

FIGURE 10.5   Here Are the Results of a Randomized Clinical Trial Comparing the Effects of Fluoxetine (Prozac), a Placebo Pill, Cognitive-Behavioral Treatment (CBT) Plus Fluoxetine, and CBT Plus a Placebo for Treating Binge Eating Disorder. Notice that the highest rates of recovery were associated with CBT with either real or placebo drugs. Rapid response and rates of remission and recovery across treatments: rapid response equals a 65% or greater reduction in frequency of binge eating episodes by the fourth treatment week; remission equals zero binges for the past month; recovery equals less than one binge weekly for the past month

(*Source:* C. M. Grilo, R. M. Masheb, & G. T. Wilson, 2006, "Rapid Response to Treatment for Binge Eating Disorder." *Journal of Consulting and Clinical Psychology, 74,* 602–613.)

CHAPTER SUMMARY

Evaluative research on clinical interventions has focused mainly on the effects of various forms of psychological treatment. The goals of this research are to answer questions about the efficacy of specific treatments, the relative effectiveness of different treatments, the components of treatment responsible for improvement, the durability of treatment benefits, and the clinical and social significance of different therapies.

The main method for establishing a causal relationship between therapy and improvement is the controlled experiment in which the researcher makes systematic changes in certain factors (called independent variables) and then observes changes occurring in other factors (called dependent variables). In psychotherapy outcome-research, the independent variable is usually the type of therapy given, and the dependent variable is the change seen in clients. Within-subjects experiments (including reversal, or ABAB, designs) manipulate a treatment variable and observe its effects on the same client(s) at different points in time. Between-subjects experiments randomly assign clients to different groups, each of which is exposed to differing treatments whose effects are compared.

Psychotherapy-outcome experiments should be designed with the highest level of both internal and external validity. If an experiment is high on internal validity, the researcher can be confident that observed changes in clients were actually caused by treatment, not by uncontrolled confounding factors. An experiment is high on external validity if its results are generalizable to clients, problems, and situations other than those included in the experiment. Unfortunately, in order to exert the experimental control necessary to maximize internal validity, researchers are usually forced to use clients, therapists, problems, treatments, and settings that may not be representative enough to allow for high external validity. External validity can be increased by studying real clients with real problems in real treatment settings, but the loss of experimental control in such studies may impair internal validity.

In spite of Hans Eysenck's claim that traditional psychotherapy is no more beneficial than receiving no treatment, most subsequent reviews, meta-analyses, and client surveys suggest that most forms of psychotherapy do produce better outcomes than no treatment.

Although the initial findings of box score reviews, meta-analyses, and surveys was that the various types of therapy were about equally effective, the movement to identify empirically supported treatments resulted in publication of lists of efficacious efficacious and possibly efficacious treatments, most of which were behavioral or cognitive-behavioral. Critics disputed the criteria used to determine ESTs, and they pointed to common or nonspecific factors, such as therapeutic alliance, that often account for a great deal of variance of treatment outcome. More recently, there has been a focus on evidence-based practices, which encompasses the use of evidence-based treatment techniques along with the use of strong relationship skills.

A much smaller body of outcome research exists for group, couples, and family therapy, though some interventions are noted to be quite efficacious and effective. A wide variety of programs designed to prevent mental disorders are promising, most of which attempt to intervene early in individuals' lives in order to alter many of the risk factors known to be associated with specific disorders. The combination of psychotherapy and drug treatment can be beneficial, but there are also many disorders that can be treated most effectively with psychological treatments alone.

STUDY QUESTIONS

1. Describe an example of a within-subjects research design, and discuss the pros and cons of this design.

2. Describe an example of a between-subjects research design, and make note of the independent and dependent variables.

3. What is internal validity, and why are clinical scientists concerned about threats to internal validity?

4. Discuss the importance of external validity, and list the major threats to external validity.

5. What are box scores, and why are they no longer used ?

6. Describe the process of meta-analysis, and discuss the strengths and weakness of this approach to investigating which treatments work.

7. What are the different research designs used to establish empirically supported treatments.

8. What are the major criticisms of the search for empirically supported treatments?

9. Is the process of identifying empirically supported treatments focused more on internal validity or external validity?

10. What is evidence-based practice?

11. What is dissemination, and why is it important?

12. Discuss the tensions between clinical researchers and therapists in relation to the definition and use of evidence for effective treatments.

13. List the therapist, client, and relationship variables that are related to positive therapeutic outcome.

14. Describe the effectiveness of alternative modes of treatment, including group, couples, and family therapy, prevention programs, and self-help programs.

15. What are the major findings from research on the combination of psychological treatment and drug treatment?

WEB SITES

- Therapies that work (funded by the National Institute of Mental Health): http://www.therapyadvsior.com
- Prevention programs that work, sponsored by the Substance Abuse and Mental Health Services Administration (SAMHSA): http://modelprograms.samhsa.gov
- Evidence-based behavioral practices (funded by NIH's Office of Behavioral and Social Sciences Research): http://www.EBBP.org
- Places to get popular self-help books as well as books on evidence-based practices:
- http://www.barnesandnoble.com
- http://www.amazon.com
- http://www.addALL.com

CHAPTER 11

Clinical Child Psychology

Chapter Preview: This chapter describes the field of clinical child psychology. We begin with a brief history of the field, then address the unique features of working with children and adolescents as opposed to adults. We describe risk factors that increase the probability of disorders in children, assessment, classification, treatment, and prevention of childhood psychopathology.

Let's assume that you are waiting tables at a fine-dining establishment, and after a father learns that you are a psychology major, he asks for your advice. He mentions that his daughter is acting like a bird more and more frequently. She has built herself a "nest" with boxes and blankets in her room, she often chirps rather than talks, and she insists on only eating things that look like worms (e.g., spaghetti, gummy worms). So, other than recommending that he pay his bill before you finish your shift, what is your advice?

Knowing the developmental level of a child will help us understand the child's behavior.

Before you run out to check the DSM-IV to explore a diagnosis like schizophrenia, it would be crucial to first ask the father the age of his daughter. Imagine this scenario with a 3-year-old and then imagine the scenario with a 13-year-old. With young children, imaginative play, such as pretending to be a cute animal for short periods of time, is very common and pretty adorable at that. With older children, however, a clinical child psychologist might want to conduct a full evaluation, including exploring the girl's ability to tell reality from fantasy, asking about family history of psychopathology, exploring whether there were any recent traumas such as abuse, and finding out about other aspects of psychosocial functioning such as academic achievement, peer relationships, and sibling relationships. Overall, the most important aspects to establish when considering children's behavior are their age and developmental level. Although most of the information in the previous chapters is relevant to clinical child psychology, you need additional information in order to understand how clinical child psychologists view the functioning of youth and treat problems that exist in children, adolescents, and their families.

A BRIEF HISTORY OF CLINICAL CHILD PSYCHOLOGY

Section Preview: This section highlights the ways that the history of clinical child psychology differs from the history of adult-oriented clinical psychology. Special attention is given to the diagnosis of children's problems.

The history of clinical child psychology reveals something of a paradox. On the one hand, clinical psychology has its roots in the assessment and treatment of childhood disorders (see Chapter 2, "Clinical Psychology's Past and Present"), but for much of the 20th century, behavior disorders in childhood were largely overlooked in favor of adult disorders (Rubinstein, 1948). Indeed, the study of childhood disorder was, for a long time, simply "a downward extension and extrapolation from the study of psychopathology in adults" (Garber, 1984, p. 30).

This adult-oriented perspective on childhood disorders reflects the history of the concept of childhood itself. Not that long ago, children were considered and treated as miniature adults. This "adultomorphic" view was reinforced by psychoanalytic and behavioral approaches to therapy, both of which tended to downplay the unique nature of childhood problems (Gelfand & Peterson, 1985). During the last three decades, this adult-oriented approach to children's behavior disorders has given way to a more child-centered approach. Clinical child psychologists are discovering that traditional adult-oriented methods of classification, assessment, and intervention may have limited relevance for childhood disorders. The changing approach to child clients appeared first in DSM-III, which included developmental considerations in the diagnostic criteria for childhood disorders. For example, the original DSM, published in 1952, did not have any disorders specific to childhood or adolescence. When DSM-II was published in 1968, there were a handful of disorders that were specific to children and adolescents (e.g., learning disturbances, hyperkinetic reaction, runaway reaction), but most diagnoses were still far more appropriate for adults rather than for youth.

Today, DSM-IV contains more than two dozen Axis I disorders specific to infants, children, and adolescents (see Table 11.1 for a partial list). In addition, since 1970, several

TABLE 11.1

Selected Diagnoses in DSM-IV That Can Be Used with Children and Adolescents

Disorders Usually First Diagnosed in Infancy, Childhood, or Adolescence

Mental Retardation (Coded on Axis II)

five levels of diagnoses (based on functioning)

Learning Disorders

reading disorder
mathematics disorder
disorder of written expression

Pervasive Developmental Disorders

autistic disorder
Asperger's disorder

Attention-Deficit and Disruptive Behavior Disorders

attention-deficit/hyperactivity disorder (3 types)
conduct disorder (2 types)
oppositional defiant disorder

Feeding and Eating Disorders of Infancy or Early Childhood

pica
rumination disorder
feeding disorder of infancy or early childhood

Elimination Disorders

encopresis
enuresis (3 types)

Other Disorders of Infancy, Childhood, or Adolescence

separation anxiety disorder
selective mutism
reactive attachment disorder of infancy or early childhood (2 types)

Other Clinical Disorders That Can Be Diagnosed in Childhood or Adolescence

Substance-Related Disorders

alcohol use disorders (2 types)
specific substance-related disorders (97 types)

Schizophrenia and Other Psychotic Disorders

schizophrenia (5 types)

Mood Disorders

major depressive disorder (2 types)
bipolar I disorder
bipolar II disorder

Anxiety Disorders

panic disorder (3 types)
specific phobia
social phobia
obsessive-compulsive disorder
posttraumatic stress disorder
generalized anxiety disorder

Eating Disorders

anorexia nervosa
bulimia nervosa

Impulse-Control Disorders Not Elsewhere Classified

intermittent explosive disorder
trichotillomania

Adjustment Disorders (6 types)

NOTE: Unless otherwise noted, all disorders are coded on Axis I. This list is not exhaustive.

SOURCE: *Diagnostic and Statistical Manual of Mental Disorders* (4th ed.): Text Revision (DSM-IV-TR). American Psychiatric Association, 2000 (Washington, DC: Author). Copyright 2000 by the American Psychiatric Association. Adapted with permission.

major new journals have appeared—such as the *Journal of Abnormal Child Psychology,* the *Journal of Clinical Child and Adolescent Psychology,* and *Development and Psychopathology*—devoted entirely to research on childhood behavior disorders. At the start of the new millennium, two new divisions of the APA devoted entirely to children's behavioral, learning, and medical problems were created: Division 53 (Society for Clinical Child and Adolescent Psychology) and Division 54 (Society for Pediatric Psychology). Finally, a relatively new field of study known as *developmental psychopathology* has evolved to study childhood disorders from a developmental perspective (Achenbach, 1982). Researchers working in this field focus on how various adaptive and maladaptive patterns of behavior are manifested during various stages of development (Kuperminc & Brookmeyer, 2006). Developmental psychopathologists also study how children develop competencies as well as disorders, and they try to learn about protective factors that prevent some children at risk for disorders from developing those disorders (Werner, 2005).

After so many years of neglect, why is so much attention being devoted to understanding and treating childhood psychopathology? First, psychopathology is relatively common in childhood; 14% to 22% of children are diagnosed with a behavioral, emotional, or learning disorder[1] (Mash & Dozois, 2003). Second, many childhood disorders (e.g., conduct disorders, learning disorders, autism) have lifelong consequences for the individual, the family, and society at large. Third, most adult disorders have their roots in childhood disorders, many of which go undiagnosed and untreated. One study found that fewer than 15% of children with a diagnosable psychiatric disorder had received any outpatient mental health services in the preceding year (Goodman et al., 1997). Fourth, by studying the risk factors, causes, and courses of childhood disorders, we may be better able to develop effective early intervention programs that prevent childhood problems from escalating into adult psychopathology. Finally, media attention devoted to some high-profile, child-related problems—school violence, the potential dangers of prescribing psychotropic medications for children, the increase in reported child abuse cases—has caused many individuals to reevaluate the mental health status of children and has led to the development of a number of national task forces, a Surgeon General's report on children's mental health (U.S. Public Health Service, 2000), and White House conferences devoted to understanding and ameliorating childhood mental health problems. Thus, the field of clinical child psychology has grown and is now a well-established specialty within clinical psychology.

Section Summary: Historically, children were seen as miniature adults, but more recently, increased professional and cultural focus on the special characteristics of children has raised has raised awareness of children's psychological development. The field of clinical child psychology has grown from this focus, especially that related to childhood psychopathology. Clinical child psychology is now an integral part of the field of clinical psychology.

CHARACTERISTICS UNIQUE TO CLINICAL CHILD PSYCHOLOGY

Section Preview: Here we review a number of characteristics unique to clinical child psychology, including the referral process, confidentiality, the context of children's behavior, developmental considerations, parent–child interactions, risk factors, and protective factors.

Referral Processes

When adults feel distressed, they can seek professional help, but children must depend on parents, teachers, or other significant people in their lives to determine whether they need the help of a mental health professional. On rare occasions, children are able to find the help they need on their own (e.g., hanging around the office of the guidance counselor at school and finally asking for help), but mostly children rely on their parents and other adults in order to gain access to mental health services. Conversely, children may be referred to a mental health professional for reasons that have more to do with parental or

---

[1]The terms *learning disability* and *learning disorder* are used interchangeably in the literature. To be consistent with DSM, we typically use the latter.

family problems than with the child's emotional or behavioral characteristics (McGoldrick, Giordano, & Garcia-Preto, 2005).

Confidentiality

Beginning at the point of referral, working with children is also different from working with adults because of issues related to confidentiality. Clinicians who work with adults know that they cannot share the information about their client with anyone else except in cases involving suicidal or homicidal intent or abuse of a child or an elderly, incapacitated person. But what about when the client is a child or an adolescent? Officially, parents or legal guardians are responsible for youth, so the legal commitment to confidentiality does not restrict clinicians from disclosing client information to parents or guardians (Knapp & VandeCreek, 2006). Of course, working with a young person, especially an adolescent, without being able to promise to keep information secret from the parents will often make the adolescent wary of sharing any information with the therapist. Most often, therapists set ground rules with parents and child or adolescent clients at the outset of treatment. The therapist might say, for example, that all information the adolescent client discloses will be kept private (i.e., not even disclosed to the parents) unless doing so would be potentially harmful to the client or someone else. As discussed in Chapter 3, "Basic Features of Clinical Assessment," Chapter 5, "Testing in Clinical Psychology," and Chapter 6, "Basic Features of Clinical Interventions," therapists are guided by the APA Ethics Code in setting these ground rules.

Contexts of Behavior

When working with children, it is important to consider the context of their behavior. A child's relationship to his or her environment is quite different from an adult's. For example, adults usually have some amount of control over where they live, what type of job they have, when they go to bed and wake up, with whom they spend their time, what they eat, and how they run their lives. Children and adolescents, for the most part, have less control over these things, and sometimes no control. Especially with younger children, the decisions that their parents make for them are the ones with which they must live (e.g., daycare or school settings, activities, food choices, daily routines, access to other children as potential friends). Thus, most clinical work and research has to consider the limited power that children have to structure or change their environments.

Developmental Considerations

As illustrated in the case of the girl who was acting like a bird, knowing a child's age and developmental level are crucial to understanding the child's behavior. For one thing, clinicians must evaluate the appropriateness or inappropriateness of a child's behavior relative to developmental norms in the child's culture. The following list provides a few examples of behaviors considered appropriate at certain developmental stages but less appropriate at other stages (reviewed in Carr, 2006; Phares, 2008):

- Children aged 2 to 4 years tend to fear imaginary creatures and the dark; children aged 5 to 7 years tend to fear natural disasters (such as fire, flood, thunder), injury, and animals; children aged 8 to 11 tend to fear poor academic and athletic performance; and adolescents aged 12 to 18 tend to fear peer rejection.

- Until the age of 5, some children still wet the bed on occasion. By the age of 5, most children have learned how to control their urge to urinate, with most children first learning to control their bladder functions during the day and then developing control while they sleep.
- Over 50% of boys aged 4 to 5 show excessive demands for attention, and nearly 60% of them show disobedience at home.
- For children between the ages of 6 and 18, nearly 40% of boys and 25% of girls are reported by their parents to have difficulty concentrating.
- The majority of adolescent girls experience poor body image, a phenomenon known as *normative discontent*.
- Over half of adolescent girls and boys reported that they had tried alcohol by the age of 16.

In fact, most symptoms of childhood disorders tend to be seen in a notable proportion of the population of children at some point in their lives. With the exception of symptoms associated with autism, mental retardation, and other severe disorders, the appropriateness of children's behavior must be evaluated in light of the developmental stage they are in at the time (Achenbach & Rescorla, 2006). Thus, a clinician working with children needs a strong background in normal developmental psychology in addition to training in abnormal child psychology.

Parent–Child Interaction Patterns

Many of the advances in understanding and treating childhood behavior disorders that have occurred in the last three decades have been made by theorists who take a *reciprocal* or *bidirectional* view of parent–child interactions (i.e., the child's temperament and behavior influence the parents' behavior, and parental tolerance and responses alter the child's behavior). An example of this perspective and how it has advanced our understanding of children's behavior problems can be seen in Patterson's (1976, 1982) coercion-escalation hypothesis of aggressive behavior. Patterson's detailed observations in the homes of nonaggressive and aggressive children showed that in both kinds of homes, parents' behavior alters the probability of certain child responses, just as the children's behavior alters the likelihood of certain parental responses (Patterson, Ray, Shaw, & Cobb, 1969). However, Patterson also saw important differences in the family interactions of nonaggressive versus aggressive children. For example, aggressive children were twice as likely as nonaggressive children to persist in their aversive behavior following parental punishment (Patterson, 1976). Rather than seeing this pattern as reflecting parents' ineffective punishment tactics or children's insensitivity to the consequences of their behavior, Patterson looked at how parents and children "teach" each other to adopt and rely on coercive, aversive control tactics that can lead to childhood aggressiveness. Here is a simple case example:

Suppose that Mrs. Jones has just picked up her 3-year-old son, Billy, from day care and they are now at the grocery store, buying food for dinner. As they pass a freezer case, Billy asks for an ice cream bar, but Mrs. Jones says, "No, you'll spoil your dinner." Billy responds by throwing a temper tantrum, which creates a problem for Mrs. Jones because she needs to finish her shopping, and besides, it is embarrassing to have her child acting out-of-control in public. Mrs. Jones solves the problem by giving Billy an ice cream bar, but with the admonition that this is the last time he will get one this close to dinner. Billy's tantrum stops immediately, and the shopping proceeds.

What do Billy and his mother learn from this interaction? First, Billy learns that if he throws a temper tantrum when his mom says no, he can get his way (tantrum-throwing is positively reinforced). At the same time, Mrs. Jones is reinforced for acceding to Billy's demands—especially when he throws a tantrum in public—because doing so terminates his aversive and humiliating behavior. The principles of operant conditioning outlined in Chapter 8, "Behavioral and Cognitive-Behavioral Psychotherapies," suggest that both Billy and his mother will behave in similar ways when confronted with similar situations in the future. Billy will throw tantrums, and Mrs. Jones, despite her best intentions to the contrary, will give in to them. Indeed, not giving in will probably cause Billy to escalate the intensity of his tantrum—perhaps including physical aggression or damage to property—until Mrs. Jones feels she has no choice but to give him what he wants. This family dyad has fallen into what Patterson (1982) called the *reinforcement trap:* each obtains a short-term benefit at the expense of undesirable long-term consequences. As Billy becomes harder to manage, his parents may resort to more aversive methods to control him.

Patterson's work on understanding children's aggressive behavior from the perspective of reciprocal interactions between parents and children has led to the development of a systematic and widely employed behavioral intervention program for dealing with such problems (Reid, Patterson, & Snyder, 2002). The program focuses on changing the parents' interactions with their children to decrease the occurrence of coercive exchanges. Overall, the treatments that are consistent with this conceptualization of aggressive and antisocial behavior are very effective (Reid et al., 2002).

Risk Factors

Clinicians studying developmental psychopathology have identified a number of *risk factors* for the development of emotional/behavioral problems. Risk factors are characteristics within the child, family, community, culture, or society that are associated with heightened risk that the child will develop some type of emotional/behavioral problem or psychopathology (Fraser, Kirby, & Smokowski, 2004; reviewed in Phares, 2008). Let's consider a few of the more salient of these risk factors.

Temperament. Children whose temperament in infancy was described as difficult have a higher probability of showing problematic behavior throughout their lives, including conduct problems, stormy peer relationships, and academic difficulties when they enter first grade (Calkins & Degnan, 2006), increased behavior problems at the age of 15 (Rothbart & Bates, 2006), challenging personality traits at the age of 26 (Caspi et al., 2003), and a greater likelihood of generalized anxiety disorder by the age of 32 (Moffitt et al., 2007). Given that infant temperament is considered to be largely genetically determined (Calkins & Degnan, 2006), these findings suggest that some childhood behavioral problems are partly a function of the child's innate biological characteristics. There are, however, numerous environmental factors (such as living in a safe and stable family and neighborhood) that can increase or decrease the risks posed by difficult temperament (Calkins & Degnan, 2006).

Interparental Conflict. When parents argue, children lose; decades of research on children's functioning in the context of interparental conflict has revealed this to be true. Parents' verbal arguments and fighting are associated with increased emotional/behavioral problems in children and adolescents, especially externalizing problems (Cummings, Goeke-Morey, & Papp, 2004; Lee, Beauregard, & Bax, 2005). When parents exchange high levels of negative communication and low levels of positive communication, children tend to blame themselves for their parents' conflict (Fosco & Grych, 2007). When children are put in the middle of their parents' conflicts, a process known as *triangulation,* the effects of those conflicts are even worse (Grych, Raynor, & Fosco, 2004). In fact, evidence suggests that children are better off if their parents divorce, assuming that the interparental conflict then decreases significantly, in comparison with children who remain in intact but highly conflicted families (Hetherington & Stanley-Hagan, 1999; Kelly, 2000).

What about research showing that children who had experienced a parental divorce are much more likely to show emotional/behavioral problems than children who had not experienced a parental divorce (Hetherington, Bridges, & Insabella, 1998)? That pattern does appear, but more recent research has clarified that those group differences tend to be due to other factors, such as continuing interparental conflict and post-divorce financial problems, rather than to the divorce itself (Hetherington & Elmore, 2003). Overall, it appears that what goes on in children's families (e.g., levels of interparental conflict and family functioning) are more important for children's well-being than whether they live with both parents or only one of them (Kelly, 2000).

Physical Abuse. Most of us think of child abuse in terms of parental aggression that leaves broken bones, head injuries, and permanent physical scars. But even some forms of harsh disciplinary actions by parents (such as spanking with a belt) can be considered child physical abuse (Wekerle & Wolfe, 2003). In fact, in most states, one of the operational definitions of child abuse is an action that leaves a mark of injury on the child's skin.

National estimates suggest that between 5% and 26% of youth in the United States are physically abused each year (Children's Defense Fund, 2005; DiLillo, Perry, & Fortier, 2006). Physical abuse is associated with a whole host of problems in children, such as conduct disorder, oppositional defiant disorder, aggression, depression, anxiety disorders, poor social competence, and poor academic performance (DiLillo et al., 2006).

Given the ramifications of physical abuse, it is not surprising to find that the estimates of physical abuse from clinical populations of children are much higher than the 5% to 26% range. One study in Los Angeles found that 46.9% of children receiving services at a community mental health center were victims of abuse (Lau & Weisz, 2003).

Sexual Abuse.   Sexual abuse can also be devastating to children and adolescents. Although there are many definitions of child sexual abuse, most of them focus on sexual exploitation of children by a perpetrator who is older and who has more power than the child (Mannarino & Cohen, 2006). Not all sexual abuse involves sexual intercourse or other forms of sexual contact; it can also include things like exposure to pornography or other sexual material.

It is extraordinarily difficult to get accurate estimates of the prevalence of sexual abuse. Documented cases suggest that approximately 3.2% of girls and 0.6% of boys are sexually abused, but other studies suggest much higher rates. For example, retrospective research in which adolescents and young adults are asked to report on previous sexual abuse (whether or not it was ever reported to a child protective agency) suggest that between 12% and 35% of girls and between 4% and 9% of boys have been abused sexually (Putnam, 2003). Even these figures may be underestimates. Although the media tends to focus on child sexual abuse that is perpetrated by strangers (as in the case of many child abductions), it is estimated that more than 90% of child sexual abuse cases involve a perpetrator who is a family member or who is known to the family, such as a neighbor, caretaker, or family friend (Berliner & Elliott, 2002).

The negative ramifications of child sexual abuse depend somewhat on the nature of the abuse. For example, children are more psychologically harmed by sexual abuse when (a) it was prolonged, (b) the perpetrator was a father or father figure, (c) there was more intrusive sexual contact, such as intercourse, (d) there was coercion or physical force or threats, and (e) the child's report of abuse was not believed (Mannarino & Cohen, 2006; Noll, Trickett, & Putnam, 2003). Sexual abuse is associated with higher risk of depression, a greater risk for suicide attempts, poor coping, and relationship problems in adulthood (Mannarino & Cohen, 2006; Noll et al., 2003; Testa, VanZile-Tamsen, & Livingston, 2005). Overall, sexual abuse can have significant damaging and long-lasting effects on children, particularly those who have less psychological resiliency or fewer protective factors, which we discuss later.

Poverty.   Living in poverty is correlated with a host of problems, including housing instability (Adam, 2004); chaotic family environments (Evans, Gonnella, Marcynyszyn, Gentile, & Salpekar, 2005); exposure to maladaptive peer networks (Leventhal & Brooks-Gunn, 2003), poorer water quality, fewer parks, and more community violence (Evans, 2004). In other words, poverty tends to expose children to several risk factors for behavior disorders.

About 29.2% of all U.S. children under the age of 18 are growing up in an impoverished environment (Urban Institute, 2004). The percentage varies greatly depending on ethnicity; it is 54.5% for Hispanic/Latino/Latina children, 44.4% for African American children, and 21.4% for Caucasian American children (Urban Institute, 2004). These numbers include children growing up in urban, inner-city areas and children growing up in

Children's harsh surroundings can have a significant impact on their well-being.

impoverished rural areas (Evans, 2004). Growing up in poverty is associated with a number of problems, most of which fall into the externalizing range of behaviors, such as aggression, conduct disorder, and oppositional defiant disorder (Conger & Donnellan, 2007; Grant et al., 2004; Kiser, 2007; Wadsworth & Berger, 2006).

Table 11.2 lists other risk factors for behavior/emotional problems in children. Given the large number of these risk factors, it is not surprising that many children are exposed to at least one of them. For example, data from the National Longitudinal Study of Adolescent Health (Parra, DuBois, & Sher, 2006) showed that among 11th graders, 43% were exposed to some type of socioeconomic disadvantage (e.g., poverty, inadequate housing, single-parent family), 21% were exposed to interparental conflict, abuse, inadequate schools, and 4% were exposed to parental psychopathology. Only about one-third (32%) of the youth were seen to be at low risk.

Protective Factors

Although risk factors can increase the likelihood of problems in children's lives, it is important to recognize that there are also *protective factors* that can lessen or eliminate the ramifications of negative situations (Wright & Masten, 2005). Like risk factors, protective factors can exist within the child, family, community, culture, or society (see Table 11.3).

Overall, these protective factors have been well established through research and are relevant for children of all ages and developmental levels (Wright & Masten, 2005).

TABLE 11.2

Risk Factors for the Development of Psychological Problems in Children

Examples of Risk Factors within the Child

Difficult temperament
Inadequate coping mechanisms
Limited problem-solving skills

Examples of Risk Factors within the Family

Parental psychopathology
Interparental conflict
Harsh parenting
Child physical abuse
Child sexual abuse
Psychological maltreatment
Neglect

Examples of Risk Factors within the Community

Poverty
Inadequate schools
Violent neighborhoods
Inadequate opportunities for gainful employment

Examples of Risk Factors within the Culture and in Society

Culture of violence
Racial discrimination

Figure 11.1 illustrates the process of *resilience* whereby children exposed to one or more risk factors (such as parental psychopathology) can still show positive outcomes when they are also exposed to protective factors (Seifer, 2003).

Section Summary: Working with children requires that psychologists understand the many different contexts that affect children's behavior. Because clinical child psychologists usually must interact with parents in order to gain access to children and to help them, parental factors are particularly important. Many children are exposed to risk factors that include biological forces (e.g., through predispositions toward certain temperaments), familial forces (e.g., parent–child interactions, parental psychopathology, interparental conflict, abuse), and social forces (e.g., poverty and violent environments). Protective factors can decrease the likelihood that children will develop psychopathology in the face of harsh forces in their environments.

TABLE 11.3

Protective Factors That Help Reduce the Risk of Psychological Problems in Children

Examples of Protective Factors within the Child

Social and adaptable temperament

Good cognitive abilities and problem-solving skills

Effective emotional and behavioral regulation strategies

Positive view of self, such as self-confidence and high self-esteem

Positive outlook on life, such as feeling hopeful about the future

Having characteristics that are valued by others, such as talents and a sense of humor

Examples of Protective Factors within the Family

Stable and supportive home environment

Low level of parental discord

Close relationship to responsive caregiver

Authoritative parenting style (high on warmth, structure/monitoring, and expectations)

Positive sibling relationships

Supportive connections with extended family members

Faith and religious affiliations

Parents involved in child's education

Socioeconomic advantages

Postsecondary education of parent

Examples of Protective Factors within the Community

Connections to caring adult mentors and prosocial peers

High neighborhood quality, such as safety, low level of community violence, affordable housing, access to recreational centers, and clean air and water

Effective schools, featuring well-trained well-trained and well-compensated teachers, after-school programs, school recreation resources (sports, music, art)

Employment opportunities for parents and teens

Good public health care

Access to emergency services (police, fire, medical)

Examples of Protective Factors within the Culture

Value and resources directed at education

Protective child policies, such as child labor laws, child health, and welfare

Prevention of and protection from oppression or political violence

Low acceptance of physical violence

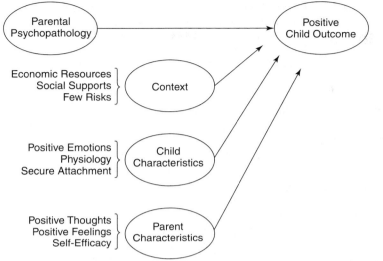

FIGURE 11.1   Resilience Processes in Young Children of Mentally Ill Parents

(*Source:* R. Seifer, 2003, "Young Children with Mentally Ill Parents: Resilient Developmental Systems," in S. S. Luthar (Ed.), *Resilience and Vulnerability: Adaptation in the Context of Childhood Adversities,* p. 43. New York: Cambridge University Press.)

CLINICAL ASSESSMENT OF CHILDREN

Section Preview: Clinical child assessment utilizes many techniques to ascertain the strengths and limitations of children who are experiencing difficulties. Common assessment techniques include behavior rating scales, clinical interviews, intellectual and achievement testing, behavioral observations, and measures to assess family and peer functioning.

For both children and adults, the assessment process is designed to serve a number of purposes, including arriving at a diagnosis, making treatment recommendations, offering information about long-term prognosis, and evaluating the progress of therapy. In conducting assessments with children, clinical child psychologists must be especially aware of developmental and contextual factors. Child assessments tend to be more comprehensive than adult assessments; information must be gathered from multiple sources reflecting the child's major life domains, including school, family, and peer group (Kamphaus & Frick, 2005).

Clinicians pay careful attention to information supplied by parents and teachers during interviews and on behavior rating scales. Children's emotional and behavioral states depend heavily on the nature of their family life, so assessment often includes exploration of the child's behavior within the family (e.g., observations of parent–child interactions), as well as exploration of parental functioning (e.g., parental depression, interparental conflict).

Because most child referrals pertain in some fashion to school-based problems, the clinical assessment of children routinely includes an evaluation of school performance, including intelligence and achievement testing as well as actual school behavior. Thus, a standard assessment battery for children includes behavior rating scales from multiple informants, clinical interviews, intelligence and achievement testing, structured observations, and an evaluation of family and peer functioning.

Behavior Rating Scales

Behavior rating scales have become a standard part of almost all child assessment batteries. The rating scales generally consist of a list of child behavior problems (e.g., fidgets, easily distracted, shy and withdrawn). The parent or teacher rates each behavior according to how often the behavior occurs. Behavior rating scales differ in their coverage, with some focusing on specific disorders (e.g., the *Child Depression Inventory;* Kovacs, 1992) whereas others cover most areas of child behavior problems (e.g., the *Child Behavior Checklist* (CBCL); Achenbach & Rescorla, 2001). Because they are inexpensive, easy to administer, and usually reliable and valid, behavior rating scales are routinely used in childhood assessment batteries.

Figure 11.2 shows an example of a mother's report on the CBCL of her 11-year-old son, Wesley, who was referred for missing school excessively because of asthma and

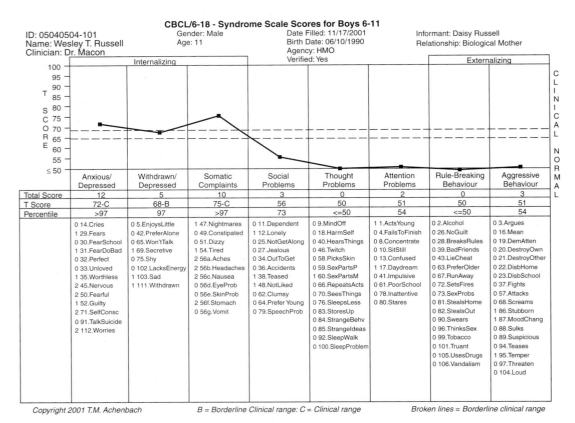

FIGURE 11.2   Syndrome Profile from CBCL Completed for Wesley Russell by His Mother

(Source: Manual for the Achenbach System of Empirically Based Assessment (ASEBA) School-Age Forms and Profiles, by T. M. Achenbach and L. A. Rescorla, 2001 (Burlington, VT: University of Vermont, Research Center for Children, Youth, and Families). Copyright 2001 by University of Vermont. P. 65. All names are fictitious.)

headaches (Achenbach & Rescorla, 2001). The profile shows that, compared to other boys his age, Wesley showed clinically elevated levels of anxious/depressed, withdrawn/depressed, and somatic complaints. The CBCL is an example of an empirically derived measure that is used extensively in clinical practice and there are also parallel measures for teachers and youth to complete.

The most frequently used behavior rating scales show high test–retest reliability and good validity (Kamphaus & Frick, 2005). For example, the measures from the Achenbach System of Empirically Based Assessment (ASEBA) have strong psychometric properties. Similarly, scores on the Conners (1998) *Parent Rating Scale* and *Teacher Rating Scale* can differentiate children with attention-deficit hyperactivity disorder (ADHD) from children with other behavior problems, and can distinguish children with ADHD on medication from those on placebo. Taken together, parent, teacher, and adolescent self-reports can provide reliable, valid, economical, and useful information on children's functioning.

Clinical Interviews

In a survey of clinical child and adolescent psychologists, 71.0% reported that conducting a clinical interview was the most important aspect of their clinical assessment procedures (Cashel, 2002). As they do in adult assessments, child clinicians can use unstructured or structured clinical interviews; most clinicians use both (see Chapter 4, "Interviewing and Observation in Clinical Psychology," for a discussion of these interview types).

During unstructured interviews, the clinician usually meets with the parents, and depending on the child's age and cognitive maturity, with the child as well. When interviewing the parents, the clinician has the following goals in mind: (a) establish rapport, (b) obtain specific details about the child's problem, (c) chart the course of the problem, (d) gather a developmental history of the child, and (e) explore family factors that may exacerbate the child's problem.

Unstructured interviews with referred children can offer valuable information about them and the environments in which their problems occur (Sattler & Hoge, 2006; Welsh & Bierman, 2003). The goals of child interviews often differ from those described for the parent interview and include the following: (a) establish rapport; (b) evaluate the child's understanding of the problem that led to referral; (c) evaluate the child's explanations of problematic behavior; (d) obtain a description of the fear, sadness, anxiety, anger, or low self-esteem associated with problems such as childhood depression and anxiety disorders; and (e) observe the child during the interview.

As valuable as unstructured child and parent interviews can be, many clinicians and most clinical researchers use structured clinical interviews to aid in making diagnostic decisions. Structured diagnostic interviews, such as the Diagnostic Interview Schedule for Children (DISC) (Shaffer, Fisher, Lucas, Dulcan, & Schwab-Stone, 2000) can be given to parents as well as children. They have the advantage of providing diagnostic information in a relatively reliable and valid manner. The concern with structured interviews is that they are often very long (e.g., 1 1/2 to 2 hours) and do not usually enhance the clinician's rapport with the child or parent. For these reasons, many clinicians opt for semistructured interviews, which combine the clinical sensitivity of the unstructured interview with the diagnostic reliability of structured interviews. One example of a semistructured interview is the Semistructured Clinical Interview for Children and Adolescents (McConaughy & Achenbach, 2001).

Intelligence and Achievement Tests

Poor school performance, most often in the first year of elementary school, accounts for a large number of child referrals for mental health services. Indeed, behavior problems and academic difficulties are related in complex and reciprocal ways in which behavior problems can impair academic functioning and academic difficulties can worsen behavior problems.

It was once the case that in order for children with behavior or academic difficulties to receive the school support services (e.g., tutoring, special placement) to which they are legally entitled, they had to have received a diagnosis based on standardized and individualized intelligence and achievement testing. Today, this standardized testing is just one part of a more comprehensive assessment.

The most common intellectual assessment in use today with children is the Wechsler Intelligence Scale for Children-Fourth Edition (WISC-IV) (Wechsler, 2003). As described in Chapter 5, the WISC-IV can be used with children aged 6 to 17 years, and yields a full-scale IQ score, four composite (index) scores (verbal comprehension, perceptual reasoning, working memory, and processing speed), and individual subtest scores. The most commonly used measure of academic achievement in the United States is the Woodcock-Johnson Psycho-Educational Battery–Third Edition (WJ-III) (Woodcock, McGrew, & Mather, 2000), also introduced in Chapter 5. The WJ-III is used to measure knowledge that children have acquired in the educational and school environment. Children in different grade levels are assessed on different topics, but the main characteristics assessed at all ages are broad reading, broad mathematics, and written expression.

Projective Tests

Among the projective personality tests used with children and adolescents are the Rorschach inkblot test (Rorschach, 1942), the Children's Apperception Test (CAT) (Bellak, 1954), which is the child version of the Thematic Apperception Test (TAT), drawing techniques such as the Draw-a-Person technique (Koppitz, 1968) and the House-Tree-Person technique (Buck, 1948), and incomplete sentence blanks (Rotter, Lah, & Rafferty, 1992).

As described in Chapter 5, the use of projective testing is controversial, and this is especially true in relation to the assessment of children. Test–retest and interrater reliabilities for these tests are often unacceptably low, especially among child samples (Hunsley, Lee, & Wood, 2003; Wood, Nezworski, Lilienfeld, & Garb, 2003). In addition, there is no evidence for the incremental validity of projective tests. In other words, even if they did allow valid inferences about children (e.g., that signs of aggression on the CAT predicted aggressive behavior), it is usually the case that this same information is already available through interviews, observations, or other simpler and more reliable and valid means (Hunsley et al., 2003).

Nearly three decades ago, one investigator summarized our knowledge in this way: projective tests with children "sometimes . . . tell us poorly something we already know" (Gittelman, 1980, p. 434). This summary remains true today. Nevertheless, some clinicians continue to use such tests, often citing their usefulness for quasi-diagnostic or descriptive purposes (e.g., to get an idea of how the child perceives himself or herself within the family). Other clinicians, however, remain concerned about the poor psychometric properties of these tests and the potential for bias or error that stems from those properties.

Behavioral Observations

Behavioral observations are an integral part of the assessment of childhood disorders. Children's problems usually occur in the home or school, so observations in these settings give clinicians the opportunity to validate, or get new perspectives on, reports made by parents and teachers through rating scales and interviews.

It is rare these days that clinicians conduct home observations, but they do often set up opportunities to observe parent–child interactions in the clinic office (e.g., Brinkmeyer & Eyberg, 2003). School observation systems focus primarily on classroom behavior, although playground behavior also may be monitored (Winsor, 2003). Classroom observations often concentrate on behaviors associated with ADHD, including off-task behavior, being disruptive or out-of-seat, and being noncompliant (Winsor, 2003). Observations can also be used to track the behavioral results after a child begins medication (Brown, Carpenter, & Simerly, 2005); (see Figure 11.3).

Family Interaction Measures

A thorough child assessment involves examining the child in the family context. This process is typically accomplished with observations of parent–child interactions in the clinic

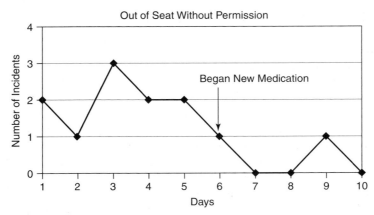

FIGURE 11.3 Examples of Data Collected Using Behavioral Observation

(*Source:* R. T. Brown, L. A. Carpenter, & E. Simerly, 2005, *Mental Health Medications for Children: A Primer,* p. 89. New York: Guilford.)

and on occasion with home observations. Assessment of the family context usually goes beyond simple observations and may include the following areas (Kamphaus & Frick, 2005): (a) family history of psychopathology, (b) parental psychopathology, (c) marital relationship and interparental conflict, (d) child-rearing methods and disciplinary patterns, and (e) stress and perceived support.

Sometimes child clinicians have to work hard at explaining why they need to gather this information. Parents may want to talk only about the child's problems and assume that if their parenting behaviors are being assessed, they are being blamed for the child's problems. Child clinicians must take care not to be pejorative or to blame the parents for the child's behavior. They need to explain the nature of a thorough evaluation diplomatically but frankly, stressing that the purpose of assessment is not to assign blame. Most parents eventually understand why these aspects of the assessment are important.

Peer Interaction Measures

Clinicians are interested in children's peer relations because many social skills (e.g., sharing, taking turns, cooperating) are learned best through peer interactions, and because disturbed peer relations are one of the strongest predictors of later behavioral and psychological problems (Collins & Steinberg, 2006). In an assessment procedure known as peer sociometrics, children evaluate their classmates or playmates by answering two simple questions: "Whom do you like?" and "Whom don't you like?" The answers to these questions allow any child in a group to be assigned two scores: a popularity index, which is the total number of classmates who indicate that they like the child, and a rejection index, which is the total number of classmates who dislike the child.

Although peer sociometric data are quite reliable and valid, collecting these data can be difficult, and there are concerns that—especially at school—the use of sociometry risks stigmatizing rejected children. Accordingly, some clinicians prefer to assess a child's social interactions via teacher ratings or by asking the child for self-reports on social anxiety, loneliness, and social goals (Mpofu, Carney, & Lambert, 2006).

Because of constraints on time and funding, many clinicians must choose only some of the assessment techniques we have described and select those that are most relevant to the referral question. Ideally, clinicians choose measures that are both broad (i.e., measure a range of behaviors) and specific (i.e., assess certain referral symptoms in depth), use multiple informants (e.g., mother, father, teacher, and child), use various methodologies (e.g., behavior ratings and observations), and select assessment techniques that are known to be reliable and valid for the type of child being evaluated. On the basis of such comprehensive assessments, child clinicians should be able to establish diagnoses, provide a clear picture of the level of emotional/behavioral problems displayed by each child, and gain a reasonably thorough understanding of the environmental and contextual factors that surround the child's behavior.

Section Summary: Assessing children and adolescents is often more complex than assessing adults because a youth's behavior is often more dependent on the contexts in which they are embedded. During assessment, a wide range of characteristics must be assessed, including behavior, emotions, cognitions, intellectual and achievement functioning, and family and peer functioning. Different informants (such as mothers, fathers, teachers, peers, and children themselves) often do not see the child's behavior in a similar manner, but integrating the divergent views from multiple informants is important in order to provide a comprehensive understanding of the child's behavior and to provide the most relevant recommendations for intervention, if needed.

SPECIFIC CHILDHOOD DISORDERS

Section Preview: This section reviews selected childhood disorders, beginning with the classification of childhood disorders as clinically derived or empirically derived. A review of all childhood diagnoses is beyond the purview of this chapter, but we describe the symptoms, prevalence, and associated features of attention deficit hyperactivity disorder, oppositional defiant disorder, conduct disorder, major depressive disorder, anxiety disorders, autism, and pediatric problems.

Classification of Childhood Disorders

The classification of childhood disorders has developed somewhat differently from that of adult disorders, although both have the same objectives. Adult disorders have been classified mainly into *clinically derived* diagnostic categories. Clinically derived systems rely on the judgments of experts, who use their clinical and research experience to determine diagnostic criteria. The pros and cons of this approach for the DSM, were discussed in Chapter 3; here we only note that these points also relate to diagnoses for children.

As we suggested earlier, the revisions of the DSM system have improved over the years, especially for diagnosing adult disorders, but the DSM system is still of more limited use with children. One improvement in the current diagnostic system has been its greater breadth of coverage of childhood disorders; DSM-IV contains more than four times as many childhood categories as DSM-II did. A major goal of the planning committee of DSM-IV was to introduce a developmental framework to the classification of the childhood disorders.

Unfortunately, the only consistent developmental data offered are age of onset and course of disorders. Further, DSM-IV diagnostic criteria are not adjusted to reflect developmental differences. For example, DSM-IV offers no guidelines for diagnosing the presence of attention problems in children of differing ages. In addition, for several disorders (e.g., depression, generalized anxiety) the clinician is instructed to use the adult criteria, somehow adjusting them to reflect how the symptoms may manifest themselves in childhood. Similarly, the DSM-IV offers the same diagnostic criteria for boys and girls, even though there is evidence that for some problems (e.g., aggression), the disorders may be manifested differently for the two sexes. Finally, recent editions of the DSM offer too little coverage of disorders seen in infancy and early childhood, so many child clinicians use a separate diagnostic system known as *Diagnostic Classification of Mental Health and Developmental Disorders of Infancy and Early Childhood,* Revised Edition (Zero to Three, 2005). It would be ideal, however, to bring disorders at all developmental levels under the umbrella of the DSM system.

Another difficulty in diagnosing children with the DSM has to do with *comorbidity,* the co-occurrence of two or more disorders within the same person. Comorbidity is common in adult clinical populations, and it is the rule rather than the exception in child clinical populations (Oland & Shaw, 2005; Wolff & Ollendick, 2006). For example, between 65% and 90% of adolescents referred for conduct disorder also met criteria for ADHD (Frick, 1998), and 83% of the children referred to an anxiety disorder clinic met criteria for an anxiety disorder and at least one other disorder (Verduin & Kendall, 2003). These high rates of comorbidity have led to questions about the usefulness of the DSM-IV for children and adolescents (Jensen, 2003).

Finally, test–retest and interrater reliabilities of DSM diagnoses are much lower for children than for adults, especially in relation to problems such as depression and alcohol abuse (American Psychiatric Association, 1998). Nevertheless, DSM-IV remains the single-most-used diagnostic categorization system for children and adolescents in the United States (Mash & Dozois, 2003).

In contrast to the clinical approach that characterizes DSM, empirically derived systems rely on statistical analyses of large amounts of data to determine the symptoms that make up a diagnostic category. The empirical approach to the diagnosis of childhood psychopathology is embodied in the work of Dr. Thomas Achenbach (1978; Achenbach & Edelbrock, 1979, 1981), who developed rating scales for assessing more than 100 of the most common problems of childhood. He asked thousands of parents and teachers to complete these rating scales in relation to both referred and nonreferred boys and girls ranging in age from 4 to 18. Although the results differed somewhat depending on the child's age and sex, several factors emerged that reflect a variety of childhood behavioral problems. Figure 11.2 showed a sample profile of child who was rated on the CBCL, and Table 11.4 delineates the broadband and narrowband factors on the CBCL, with sample item content (Achenbach & Rescorla, 2001).

Note that the broadband factors of *externalizing* problems and *internalizing* problems are used routinely to conceptualize children's behavior. These conceptualizations have been around for decades (Achenbach & Edelbrock, 1978), and their usefulness continues into the present day (Achenbach & Rescorla, 2007). The externalizing factor refers to acting-out behavior—such as hyperactivity, aggression, and delinquency—that is aversive to others in the child's environment. The internalizing factor refers to problems in which the child experiences depression, anxiety, somatic problems, and other significant discomfort that may not be evident, let alone disturbing, to others. These two broad factors offer a reliable and valid way of differentiating childhood behavioral problems. Although the broadband factors of externalizing and internalizing problems continue to be helpful in conceptualizing the behavior of youth, most clinicians and researchers also look specifically at narrowband factors (such as anxious/depressed or aggressive).

Some clinicians are interested in finding ways to combine the clinical and empirical approaches to diagnosis, and their concerns parallel those who are working on revising

TABLE 11.4

Narrowband and Broadband Factors and Sample Items from the CBCL

Internalizing		Externalizing
Anxious/Depressed	**Social Problems**	**Rule-Breaking Behavior**
feels worthless	lonely	breaks rules
fears	jealous	steals items from home
talks of suicide	not liked by peers	runs away
Withdrawn/Depressed	**Thought Problems**	**Aggressive Behavior**
prefers to be alone	hears or sees things	is mean to others
sad	has strange behavior	destroys own things
lacks energy	has strange ideas	attacks others
Somatic Complaints	**Attention Problems**	
tired	fails to finish tasks	
stomachaches	confused	
constipation	inattentive	

adult diagnoses. For example, a number of researchers have completed empirical tests to see how the CBCL maps onto DSM-IV diagnoses (Achenbach, Dumenci, & Rescorla, 2003; Krol, DeBruyn, Coolen, & vanAarle, 2006). Others are interested in making the next edition of DSM (DSM-V) more dimensional and more empirically based (Achenbach et al., 2003; Hankin, Fraley, Lahey, & Waldman, 2005). Finally, many are interested in adding to DSM-V relational diagnoses, such as troubled parent–child relationship or maltreatment (Beach, Wamboldt, Kaslow, Heyman, & Reiss, 2006; Heyman & Slep, 2006).

In the following sections, we offer descriptions of a variety of childhood disorders that clinical child psychologists often encounter in their assessment and treatment activities. These include attention deficit hyperactivity disorder, oppositional defiant disorder, conduct disorder, major depressive disorder, anxiety disorders, autism, and pediatric health problems. Our descriptions are necessarily brief, but you can learn more about these disorders in a number of textbooks on abnormal child behavior (Mash & Wolfe, 2007; Phares, 2008; Wenar & Kerig, 2006; Wicks-Nelson & Israel, 2006).

Attention-Deficit Hyperactivity Disorder

The core features of ADHD are inattention, impulsivity, and overactivity. The attention problems consist primarily of children having difficulty sustaining their focus; they fail to finish school assignments, and they do not stay on task in the classroom (American Psychiatric Association, 2000). Impulsivity refers to the fact that these children act before they think and that they have difficulty waiting to take turns, they interrupt others, and are impatient. Children with ADHD exhibit overactivity in both gross motor movements (e.g., running around the room, standing on chairs), and fine motor movements, (e.g., fidgeting and squirming, restlessness, and playing with objects).

ADHD is considered one of the most common childhood behavior disorders, affecting approximately 3% to 7% of school-age children (American Psychiatric Association, 2000). Although this figure represents, on average, only one child per classroom, it is enough to seriously disrupt the learning environment, as any schoolteacher will confirm. ADHD primarily affects boys (the boy-to-girl ratio ranges from 4:1 to 10:1), and although it appears prior to first grade, the problems it creates are intensified by the demands of the school environment. Approximately one-half to two-thirds of children with ADHD continue to experience ADHD into adulthood (Barkley, 2006).

Oppositional Defiant Disorder and Conduct Disorder

Oppositional defiant disorder (ODD) and conduct disorder (CD) are referred to as *disruptive disorders*. ODD is considered less severe than CD, and many children who display ODD during preschool and younger childhood go on to develop CD in adolescence. ODD is characterized by developmentally inappropriate levels of opposition and defiance toward a parent, caretaker, or teacher. Other characteristics of ODD include negative attitude, quick temper, recurrent anger, and deliberate annoyance of others. Prevalence rates of ODD range from 2% to 16%, and the disorder is more common in boys than girls before puberty but is seen about equally often in both sexes after puberty (American Psychiatric Association, 2000).

Conduct disorder is diagnosed when there is a persistent pattern of violating the rights of others and violating social norms. Examples of CD symptoms include bullying others, initiating physical fights, being physically cruel to other individuals or to animals, forcing sexual activity on an unwilling individual, deliberately setting fires, destroying others' property, being truant from school, and running away. Substance use and abuse is also evident in youth diagnosed with CD, but it is not part of the formal criteria (American Psychiatric Association, 2000). CD is more common in boys (with a prevalence rate that ranges from 6% to 16%) than in girls (with a prevalence rate from 2% to 9%).

Major Depressive Disorder

Childhood depression is similar to adult depression in terms of its emotional, cognitive, behavioral, and physical manifestations, but the specific symptom picture may differ depending on the child's developmental stage (Garber & Carter, 2006). Indeed, there is considerable debate over the fact that DSM-IV lists the same criteria for diagnosing depression in both children and adults. Regardless of age, major depressive disorder is diagnosed if the client experiences at least two weeks of sadness, lethargy, disturbances in energy, disturbed sleeping and eating patterns, possible suicidal ideation, and impairment

Depression is more common in girls after puberty.

in social, educational, vocational, or other functioning. In contrast to adults, younger children often show temper tantrums and irritability rather than sad affect (American Psychiatric Association, 2000).

Prevalence rates for depression in childhood and adolescents are often reported to be 2% to 5%, with the lowest rates in the younger years, and rates of 7% and higher in samples of adolescents (Hankin & Abela, 2005). Before puberty, depression is approximately equal in boys and girls. After puberty and throughout adulthood, girls and women are much more likely to experience depression, reflected in at least a 2:1 female-to-male ratio.

Anxiety Disorders

Like adults, children and adolescents can be diagnosed with a number of anxiety disorders, including specific phobia, social phobia, obsessive-compulsive disorder, generalized anxiety disorder, and posttraumatic stress disorder. Because separation anxiety disorder is listed in DSM's section on "Disorders Usually First Diagnosed in Infancy, Childhood, or Adolescence," it is highlighted here.

Separation anxiety disorder is diagnosed when children show developmentally inappropriate and extreme distress when separated from their primary caregiver, usually a parent. It is developmentally normal for infants and toddlers to show distress when separated from their caregiver, so separation anxiety disorder is only considered as a diagnosis when children are quite a bit older than 18 months and when they are terribly distressed when separated from their parent. The symptoms, which must last for at least four weeks, include distress upon separation, concern about future separation, worry about losing the parent permanently, reluctance to be alone, and nightmares about separating from the parent.

Separation anxiety disorder occurs in approximately 4% of the population of youth, with higher rates in younger children than in adolescents (American Psychiatric Association, 2000). Girls are more likely than boys to experience separation anxiety disorder.

Autistic Disorder

The pervasive developmental disorder known as autistic disorder is one of the most unusual and baffling disorders seen in childhood. It is unusual because of the symptom picture it presents and baffling because no adequate theory has been proposed to account for these symptoms (Siegel & Ficcaglia, 2006).

Children with autistic disorder have severe problems in social functioning and language development, and display a variety of unusual and inappropriate behaviors. The social difficulties seen in these children vary, but in many cases they are completely indifferent to others. They do not seek interactions with others, and even as infants they avoid making eye contact, resist physical contact, and show little or no emotion. They do not play with other children, do not imitate the behavior of others, and do not engage in pretend play.

Approximately half of children with autistic disorder do not develop normal, useful language, and those who do, speak in an unusual manner, occasionally using language for noncommunicative purposes. For example, they may engage in *echolalia,* in which they repeat whatever they hear. Also, their speech sounds differ from that of other children, often being flat and lacking inflection, somewhat like computer-generated language.

The unusual behavior exhibited by children with autistic disorder often involves abnormally under- or overreactivity to environmental events. Thus, they may be oblivious to the comings and goings of other individuals but may be hypersensitive to the rustling of paper. They may engage in unusual, repetitive behaviors that appear to serve a self-stimulatory purpose (such as repeatedly flapping their hands or hitting themselves). In addition, children with autistic disorder may gaze at spinning objects (e.g., fans) for long periods of time or constantly twirl a bowl or a piece of string.

Autistic disorder is presumed to be present at birth, although it may not become evident until around the age of 2, when the child still has not begun using language. Fortunately, it is a relatively rare disorder, occurring only in approximately 30 to 60 children per every 10,000 (0.3% to 0.6% prevalence; Maughan, Iervolino, & Collishaw, 2005). These rates are higher than the 5 cases per 10,000 (0.05%) rate reported some years ago in DSM-IV (American Psychiatric Association, 2000), but the difference appears to be due to improved assessment methods, greater awareness for referral, and better access to evaluation and treatment (Gernsbacher, Dawson, & Goldsmith, 2005). There is some confusion in the public mind between autism and another pervasive developmental disorder called Asperger's disorder (also known as Asperger's syndrome). In fact, though, Asperger's disorder is slightly more common and less debilitating. Like autistic disorder, Asperger's disorder is characterized by significant impairments in social interactions (e.g., lack of appropriate eye contact, not having friends, not reciprocating in interactions) and unusual behavior, interests, and activities that are restricted, repetitive, and stereotyped (such as being preoccupied with reading maps, maintaining inflexible patterns of behavior, and being preoccupied with parts of objects) (American Psychiatric Association, 2000). Unlike children diagnosed with autistic disorder, however, children with Asperger's disorder are able to develop language, though they use it in an unusual manner. Also unlike children with autistic disorder, children with Asperger's disorder appear to desire social interaction; they are just not very good at it.

Pediatric Health Problems

Increasingly, clinical child psychologists have been involved in helping understand and treat mental health problems that are related to physical illness in children and adolescents (see Chapter 12, "Health Psychology"). Known as *pediatric psychologists,* these professionals are usually trained as clinical psychologists and receive specialized training in pediatric health problems during graduate school, on internship, and/or on a postdoctoral fellowship. Pediatric psychologists deal with mental health problems associated with a wide array of physical conditions, including the following (Roberts, 2003): (a) pediatric asthma, (b) cystic fibrosis, (c) childhood diabetes, (d) sickle cell disease and hemophilia, (e) pediatric oncology (cancer), (f) HIV/AIDS in children and adolescents, (g) pediatric abdominal disorders, (h) childhood obesity, and others.

Pediatric psychologists are able to treat the mental health problems related to physical illness, but they are also committed to the prevention of such problems and the promotion of health (Peterson, Reach, & Grabe, 2003). They often work in hospitals as part of interdisciplinary teams that include pediatricians, medical specialists, pediatric nurses, and social workers. More information on pediatric psychology is available from APA Division 54 (Society for Pediatric Psychology).

A Clinical Case

The disorders we have described might seem abstract and categorical, but the real children encountered by clinical child psychologists present problems that do not always fit neatly into diagnostic categories and for whom clinical assessment data are not always clear. Consider the case of "Megan," for example (Weisz, 2004):

> Megan is 13 years old, and she is miserable. She alternates between seeming depressed and seeming furious with the world. Her grades have plummeted, enough so that a teacher contacted her parents to express concern. Megan is withdrawn and sullen at home and resents it when her parents try to help her with homework. Recently, she told her mother, "When I'm at home, I feel like a prisoner. All I ever do is work." She lives with her mother, father, and younger sister.
>
> Megan's interactions away from home are not much better. She wears black clothes and black lipstick constantly and no longer has any friends. She has recently gained a lot of weight (largely due to late-night snacking), and she skips gym class because she does not want her peers to see how "fat" she is. She is embarrassed by her appearance and feels that her life is "hopeless."
>
> Although Megan has always seemed to be a bit of a pessimist, this most recent bout of depression started when she was not invited to a social event that a number of her

friends were having. She became increasingly withdrawn from her friends and in a fit of sobbing, informed her mother that "no one likes me anymore. I'm an outcast."

Although she has not voiced any suicidal ideation directly, Megan has become fascinated by famous people who committed suicide. Her family is worried sick about Megan, and her little sister even asked recently "What's wrong with Megan?"

Given their concerns, Megan's parents take her to a local child psychologist, who uses a wide array of assessment techniques to confirm the diagnosis of depression. The therapist initiates cognitive-behavioral treatment for depression, which can be provided in individual or group sessions. Since Megan is showing negative cognitions, vegetative signs, and family and social stressors, a comprehensive CBT program was selected.

Through therapy, Megan learns to identify her feelings, to understand where they develop, and to identify the consequences of different emotions. The therapist also helps Megan to identify cognitions (i.e., thoughts) that are associated with feeling bad. Figure 11.4 shows the type of cognitive restructuring form that Megan used to understand

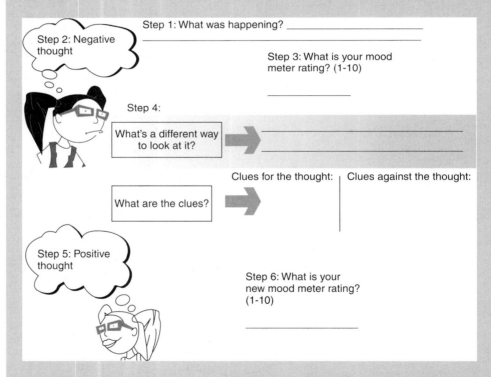

FIGURE 11.4   Cognitive Restructuring Form

(*Source:* K. D. Stark, J. Hargrave, J. Sander, G. Custer, S. Schnoebelen, J. Simpson, & J. Molnar, 2006, "Treatment of Childhood Depression: The ACTION Treatment Program," in P. C. Kendall (Ed.), *Child and Adolescent Therapy,* 3rd ed., p. 204. New York: Guilford.)

the connections between her thoughts and her feelings (Stark et al., 2006). The therapist also helps Megan to identify activities that used to be rewarding to her (e.g., listening to music, reading novels, going to a movie). Megan is helped to see that she can increase these pleasurable activities in order to help elevate her mood. Megan decides that she will "reward" herself with 30-minutes of music each day that she follows a healthy eating and exercise plan.

The therapist also includes Megan's parents in the treatment. Not only do the parents become informed about the skills that Megan has been learning, but they are also invited to engage in these behaviors themselves. For example, Megan and her parents used problem-solving skills to think of ways to help Megan join the family for dinner. Together they generated a number of possible solutions and chose one to try that they all believed would work.

Over the course of treatment, Megan's symptoms of depression decrease and her positive interactions with her family and peers increase. Although no one believes that Megan is "cured" forever, she feels that it is easier to talk with her parents and to use her problem-solving skills in situations that she finds challenging. Likewise, her parents have implemented their new problem-solving skills in order to help their relationship with Megan. Megan and her parents seem to have a renewed sense of hope for the future (Weisz, 2004).

Section Summary: Clinically derived classification systems and empirically derived systems are used with children as well as adults. The primary example of a clinically derived system is the DSM, and the most common example of an empirically derived system for children is the ASEBA. Among the many types of disorders in children, ADHD, ODD, and CD are considered examples of externalizing disorders, largely because the behavioral manifestations are external to the child (thereby more noticeable to others, such as parents and teachers). Depressive disorder and anxiety disorders are considered internalizing disorders because the experience is largely within the child's own subjective experience, and mild forms of these disorders are not necessarily noticeable to others. Pervasive developmental disorders, such as autistic disorder and Asperger's disorder, tend to severely affect affect the child and the family. Clinical child psychologists also work with emotional/behavioral difficulties associated with asthma and other pediatric health problems.

TREATMENT AND PREVENTION OF CHILDHOOD DISORDERS

Section Preview: Depending on the emotional/behavioral problems exhibited, a number of therapies are used with children and adolescents, including psychodynamic, behavioral, cognitive-behavioral, and psychopharmacological interventions. Research on the effectiveness of these interventions is summarized in this section, along with the growing evidence on the importance of the therapeutic alliance between therapists and their child clients. Given the potentially devastating long-term consequences of childhood disorders, a great deal of interest in clinical child psychology is focused on the prevention of childhood disorders.

The treatment of childhood disorders differs in important ways from clinical interventions for adults. As is the case with assessment, child therapy poses a special challenge for clinicians because children do not refer themselves for help, and thus, their contact with a therapist requires parental motivation and cooperation. The significance of these and related issues becomes apparent in the following review of the major forms of therapy for childhood disorders.

Psychodynamic and Humanistic Therapy

Children are usually not considered appropriate candidates for traditional psychoanalytic therapies (Russ, 2006). Instead, psychodynamically oriented therapists tend to adopt variations on usual analytical procedures—such as using play rather than free association as the main communication medium between client and therapist. Various forms of psychodynamically oriented play therapy focus on helping children become aware of and resolve inner conflicts without relying heavily on the verbal skills required in adult treatment (Reddy, Files-Hall, & Schaefer, 2005).

Play therapy was designed to allow children to express their inner concerns through play, such as through the voices they give to puppets and dolls and through their interactions with other materials, such as modeling clay. All the while, the therapist creates an accepting and empathic atmosphere in which children can feel secure enough to explore their feelings (Axline, 1976). Traditional psychoanalysts tend to interpret the child's verbal and nonverbal behavior during play as revealing unconscious motivation and conflicts, whereas object-relations therapists are more likely to see it as indicative of the quality of a child's attachment to caregivers (see Chapter 7, "Psychodynamic and Humanistic Psychotherapies"). Therapists who adopt a client-centered therapy approach are also likely to use play as a method for helping children explore their feelings and their problems.

Behavioral Therapy

Various forms of behavioral therapy, especially operant procedures, had been the most frequently employed interventions for childhood problems during the early part of the last three decades. As described in Chapter 8, this approach is characterized by several notable features:

1. An emphasis on the principles of learning as the basis of behavior disorder and treatment.
2. A focus on observable situational determinants of behavior (e.g., rewards and punishments, instead of inferred intrapsychic problems).
3. Treating problems by altering observable stimuli that control behavior today, not by exploring hypothesized underlying problems from the past.
4. Using evidence-based treatments and collecting objective, observable outcome data on treatment results (Houts, 2003).

Behavioral interventions often involve teaching parents and/or teachers to administer behavior-management procedures (Kazdin, 2005a). Parents and teachers are often in a better position than therapists to control the environmental antecedents and consequences that maintain problem behaviors in children at home and at school, and these adults spend many more hours with the child during the week than the therapist does.

Cognitive-Behavioral Interventions

As described in Chapter 8, cognitive-behavioral techniques deal with the child's cognitions (e.g., their expectations, thoughts) as well as with their overt behaviors (Kendall, 2006). Some of the adult cognitive-behavioral techniques discussed in Chapter 8 are used in the treatment of various child and adolescent disorders, but in all cases, those techniques are adjusted to make them more understandable to, and appropriate for, younger clients. The parents sometimes participate in the treatment, but most cognitive-behavioral techniques are completed solely with the child or adolescent (Kendall & Suveg, 2006).

Pharmacological Interventions

A number of stimulant drugs such as methylphenidate (Ritalin, Concerta, Metadate) and amphetamine (Adderall) are prescribed routinely for ADHD (Brown et al., 2005). As many as 6% of school-age children in the United States are currently taking these medications for behavioral or learning problems (Vitiello, 2001), an increase of 60% in the last decade. Hundreds of studies have shown that stimulant medication dramatically improves the behavior of children with ADHD (Brown et al., 2005). They remain seated longer, finish more academic work, give correct answers more often, and show improved social interactions with peers, parents, and teachers.

Nevertheless, controversy continues to surround the use of stimulant medication for ADHD children. For example, several lawsuits have claimed that stimulant medication is responsible for a variety of negative outcomes, including suicides and homicides. Other concerns about medicating children for ADHD and other emotional/behavioral problems include the following (Brown et al., 2005; Pathak, 2006):

- Adverse physical effects that, depending on the medication, can include lethargy, sedation, weight gain, restlessness, dry mouth, nausea, headache, dizziness, stunted growth, lowered blood pressure, heart problems, blurred vision, constipation, tics, seizures, or increased risk for suicide.

- Potential stigma associated with having to take a medication at school, where other children may learn about the child's use of medication.

- Changed attributions by children and their parents and teachers that lead to the presumption that the child cannot behave appropriately without the medication.

- Locating the focus of the problem as wholly within the child, while ignoring environmental factors (such as a chaotic home life or parental abuse).

- The illegal use of prescribed medication has increased dramatically among 12- to 14-year-olds, from an annual prevalence of 0.1% in 1992 to an annual prevalence of 2.8% in 1997 (NIDA Research Report, 2001).

Peter Breggin, a psychiatrist, is one of the strongest critics of prescribing drugs for children's emotional/behavioral problems. He has summarized his position in books such as *Talking Back to Ritalin: What Doctors Aren't Telling You about Stimulants for Children* (2001) and *The War against Children: How the Drugs, Programs, and Theories of the Psychiatric Establishment Are Threatening America's Children with a Medical "Cure" for Violence* (Breggin & Breggin, 1994). Of particular concern to Breggin is what he sees as the overuse of medication for behaviors that are not necessarily abnormal or that are only abnormal in particular cultures. He fears that we are trying to medicate the childhood out of children.

Indeed, a number of medications are contraindicated for children and adolescents or should be prescribed only with extreme caution (see Table 11.5; Brown et al., 2005; Richmond & Rosen, 2005). Given the pros and cons of using medication to treat children's emotional/behavioral problems, parents should discuss all treatment options before making a final decision about which is the best one for their child.

TABLE 11.5

Medications with Potentially Harmful Side Effects in Children and Adolescents

Medication	Use	Potential Side Effects
Amitriptyline/Elavil Etrafon Limbitrol Triavil	Depression	Can result in cardiac difficulties
Clomipramine/ Anafranil	Depression and obsessive-compulsive disorder	Associated with seizures as well as less severe side effects
Clozapine/Clozaril	Schizophrenia	Can cause a potentially fatal drop in bone marrow and white blood cell counts, and seizures
Desipramine/ Norpramin	Anxiety disorders, depression, ADHD	Has been associated with cardiac complications leading to death in rare cases
Imipramine/Tofranil	Anxiety disorders, depression, and ADHD	Has been associated with cardiac complications leading to death in rare cases
Nortriptyline/Aventyl		
Pamelor	ADHD	Can cause cardiac complications and low blood pressure, as well as less severe side effects
Pemoline/Cylert	ADHD	Has been associated with liver failure and other side effects

Sources: Adapted from R. T. Brown, L. A. Carpenter, E. & Simerly (2005); T. K. Richmond and D. S. Rosen (2005).

Effectiveness of Psychological Treatments for Childhood Disorders

The many meta-analyses and other outcome summaries of child therapy for external-izing and internalizing disorders (Chambless & Ollendick, 2001; Weisz, 2004; Weisz, Doss, & Hawley, 2005; Weisz, Sandler, Durlak, & Anton, 2005) have found effect sizes rang-ing from 0.7 to 0.8, which are comparable to those found in analyses of adult treatment studies. Further, these positive effects tend to persist for at least 6 months (Weisz, 2001).

The overall findings are that the most effective treatments for childhood disorders fall into the cognitive-behavioral category, with some behavioral techniques (especially those that include parents) also being identified as effective (Chambless & Ollendick, 2001; Kazdin & Weisz, 2003; Kendall, 2006). For example, the most efficacious treatment for childhood depression appears to be cognitive-behavioral therapy, with more promising effects for adolescents than for children (Garber & Carter, 2006). Similarly, the most effec-tive treatments for separation anxiety disorder are cognitive-behavioral treatment (Grover, Hughes, Bergman, & Kingery, 2006; Velting, Setzer, & Albano, 2004) and par-ent–child interaction therapy (PCIT) (Choate, Pincus, Eyberg, & Barlow, 2005). Behav-ioral parent training and cognitive-behavioral treatment are also successful with children and adolescents displaying antisocial behavior (either ODD or CD). As you might expect, behavioral parent training tends to be more effective with younger children, whereas cognitive-behavioral treatment tends to be more effective with adolescents (McCart, Priester, Davies, & Azen, 2006). Intensive behavioral techniques appear to offer promise in dealing with autistic disorder (reviewed in Lovaas & Smith, 2003), though many autis-tic children remain significantly impaired for their entire lives. Behavioral treatment and medication are both effective in improving the behavior of ADHD children across all major areas of functioning (Hoza et al., 2005; Jensen et al., 2005; Owens et al., 2003), and a growing literature suggests that a combination of medication and behavior modification may be the most effective treatment for these children (Barkley, 2006; Chronis, Jones, & Raggi, 2006). Overall then, for most disorders of childhood, cognitive-behavioral or behavioral techniques have received the most empirical support.

A review of 14 studies of more traditional psychodynamic and humanistic thera-pies found an effect size of 0.0 (Weisz, 2001), suggesting that these traditional "talking" therapies offer no documented benefits to child clients. This finding held even for stud-ies that averaged 60 or more individual therapy sessions with the child (Weiss, Catron, Harris, & Phung, 1999) or when the services offered to the families in the treatment group were more extensive (and more costly) than those services offered to the compar-ison families (Bickman, 1996). Nevertheless, child clinicians continue to employ these traditional therapies at surprisingly high rates (Weisz, 2001).

As in the adult therapy realm, a number of clinical researchers (e.g., Weisz & Addis, 2006) and scientist-practitioners (Lebow, 2006) are attempting to bring the science and practice of child treatment together so that clients can benefit from the combination of good science and good practice. Researchers are also increasing their efforts to dissemi-nate information about treatments that work for children and adolescents. For example, the Society for Clinical Child and Adolescent Psychology (Division 53 of APA) provides a Web site for professionals and parents: www.effectivechildtherapy.com.

The most effective treatments for most childhood problems involve cognitive-behavioral or behavioral methods.

Alliance in Therapy with Children

Clinical child researchers are interested not only in determining which treatments are best for which childhood and adolescent problems, but also in exploring common or nonspecific factors that operate to help make those treatments effective. As in adult psychotherapy, researchers want to know if the therapeutic alliance between therapists and their child clients (and with the children's parents) can help strengthen the effectiveness of treatment. This research has lagged behind similar research with adults, but a number of trends are already evident. For example, a strong therapeutic alliance between parents and therapists is associated with fewer canceled appointments, fewer instances of failing to appear for treatment appointments, and greater participation by the family in the therapy sessions (Hawley & Weisz, 2005).

Based on a meta-analysis of 49 treatment studies for child and adolescent emotional/behavioral problems, the following characteristics were found to be related to increased improvement in child and adolescent functioning (Karver et al., 2005):

- Therapeutic alliance with the parent
- Counselor interpersonal skills
- Therapist direct influence skills
- Child's willingness to participate in treatment
- Parent's willingness to participate in treatment
- Youth participation in treatment

- Parent participation in treatment
- Positive feelings toward the therapist

In short, a stronger alliance within youth treatment is associated with greater improvements in children's functioning. It may be, however, that therapeutic alliance is more meaningful in some treatments than in others. For example, one study of the treatment of troubled adolescents found that the therapeutic alliance was not influential in the effectiveness of cognitive-behavioral treatment but was strongly predictive of success in family therapy (Hogue, Dauber, Stambaugh, Cecero, & Liddle, 2006). Specifically, stronger alliance with family therapists was related to adolescents' decrease in drug use and externalizing behavior problems. This type of research into the specificity of alliance effects is likely to help clarify some of the debate about the importance of specific techniques versus strong relationship skills.

Prevention of Childhood Disorders

No discussion of the treatment of children's emotional/behavioral problems would be complete without a discussion of prevention. A great deal of work has been completed in trying to prevent disorders from occurring in children and adolescents (Weissberg, Kumpfer, & Seligman, 2003; Weisz et al., 2005). A number of effective strategies have been established through prevention programs, including the following:

- Increasing supportive teacher–student relationships in order to decrease childhood aggression (Hughes, Cavell, & Jackson, 1999).
- Improving parent–child attachment in order to prevent a myriad of emotional/behavioral problems (Van Zeijl et al., 2006).
- Using a television series to teach parents about positive parenting skills in order to increase compliance and decrease aggression in children (Sanders, Montgomery, & Brechman-Toussaint, 2000).
- Using cognitive-behavioral techniques to provide a primary prevention program to decrease the likelihood of anxiety problems in children (Barrett, Farrell, Ollendick, & Dadds, 2006).
- Educating parents and adolescents about interpersonal skills and cognitive strategies associated with the prevention of depression in adolescents (Shochet et al., 2001).
- Strengthening communication and parental monitoring in African American families in order to prevent adolescents' risky behavior, such as drinking alcohol, using illicit drugs, and having unprotected sex (Brody et al., 2006).
- Providing additional resources and extensive services to impoverished families and communities in order to prevent a whole host of emotional/behavioral problems in children and adolescents (Brotman et al., 2003).

Ironically, one of the most widely used prevention programs is also one of the least effective. The Drug Abuse Resistance Education (DARE) program is often run by law enforcement groups with the goal of demonstrating the negative consequences of alcohol and drug abuse (West & O'Neal, 2004). The program is used in all 50 states and in a large majority of school districts (West & O'Neal, 2004). Unfortunately, a wealth of well-controlled, long-term studies has shown that the DARE program is not effective in preventing the use of alcohol and drugs. Specifically, when comparing youth who did or did not participate in the DARE program, no differences were found in attitudes toward drugs, the use of drugs, or self-esteem (West & O'Neal, 2004). Other prevention programs, such as the Life Skills Training Program (Botvin & Griffin, 2004), have been shown to be effective in decreasing the likelihood that children will abuse substances, but unfortunately, those programs have not been adopted nearly as widely as the DARE program.

Another line of prevention-oriented research is related to the increasingly popular *positive psychology* movement (Duckworth, Steen, & Seligman, 2005). Specifically, many clinical child psychologists are interested in finding ways to increase *resilience* in children, that is, in finding ways to increase protective factors so as to decrease the likelihood of developing emotional/behavioral problems in children at risk for those problems (Goldstein & Brooks, 2005).

Section Summary: The most effective treatments for childhood disorders generally fall into the cognitive-behavioral and behavioral domains. Although drug treatments can help with some childhood disorders, they also have many drawbacks. There is growing evidence of the importance of the therapeutic alliance in working with children and their families. In addition to the focus on treating problems once they occur, many clinical child psychologists have dedicated their lives to finding ways to prevent childhood problems from ever occurring.

THE FUTURE OF CLINICAL CHILD PSYCHOLOGY

Section Preview: This section highlights three factors that are particularly relevant for the future of clinical child psychology: diversity and multiculturalism, increasing access to mental health care, and the rise of interdisciplinary research.

Although advances in clinical child psychology have lagged several decades behind developments in adult clinical psychology, the child field is catching up rapidly. In addition to the trends that have already been mentioned elsewhere in relation to clinical psychology in general (e.g., increasing focus on evidence-based assessment and treatment, dissemination of treatments that work so that they can be implemented in the community), a number of other trends are likely to characterize the future of clinical child psychology.

Diversity and Multiculturalism

Because most existing psychological treatments tend to be less effective for youth from single-parent homes, disadvantaged backgrounds, and ethnic minority backgrounds (Lundahl, Risser, & Lovejoy, 2006), researchers in clinical child psychology will be seeking to tailor psychological treatments in ways that make them more relevant for youth and families from a wide variety of backgrounds within the United States (Yasui & Dishion, 2007). For example, the Famlias Unidas program is a family-centered, ecologically and

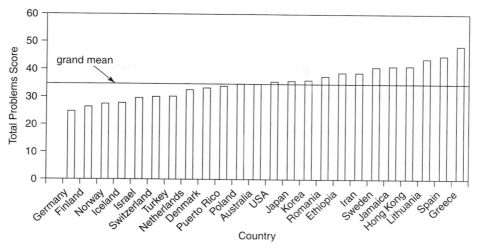

FIGURE 11.5 Youth Self-Report Total Problems Scores in 24 Countries ($N = 27,206$)

(*Source:* L. Rescorla, T. M. Achenbach, M. Y. Ivanova, L. Dumenci, F. Almqvist, N. Bilenberg, et al., 2007, "Epidemiological Comparisons of Problems and Positive Qualities Reported by Adolescents in 24 Countries." *Journal of Consulting and Clinical Psychology, 75*, 351–358.)

developmentally relevant intervention that works to reduce emotional/behavioral problems in Hispanic/Latino/Latina adolescents (Coatsworth, Pantin, & Szapocznik, 2002).

There will also be increasing interest in the commonalities and differences among children and adolescents in various countries around the world. For example, measures from the ASEBA have been translated into 74 languages and have been used in research in 67 different cultures, resulting in over 6,000 publications to date (Achenbach & Rescorla, 2007; Rescorla et al., 2007). These studies have already found that there are more similarities than differences in the psychological functioning and psychological problems of children and adolescents around the globe (Achenbach & Rescorla, 2007) (See Figure 11.5).

Access to Care

Many children, adolescents, and families do not have access to affordable mental health services (Storch & Crisp, 2004). This is particularly true for youth from racial/ethnic minority groups and from impoverished backgrounds (Steele & Roberts, 2005a). Accordingly, clinical child psychologists will be increasingly involved in efforts to make high-quality mental health care services more available to everyone (Steele & Roberts, 2005a). As with adults, however, these efforts will be complicated by disparities in health care funding across the United States, by reliance on managed care for both physical health and mental health needs, and by the limited funding provided to community mental health centers. One step in the right direction appears to be the delivery of evidence-based treatment programs in the school settings (Storch & Crisp, 2004). These programs make it possible for youngsters to be treated on a regular basis without the need to rely on (sometimes unmotivated) parents to make appointments and transport children to therapy sessions. On the other hand, when therapy is delivered at school, it may be more difficult to draw parents into the treatment process (Storch & Crisp, 2004). In addition, parents appear to prefer the idea of taking their child to a private psychologist rather than a psychologist who works in the school system (Raviv, Raviv, Propper, & Fink, 2003). Thus, alternative methods of delivery of services are still being sought.

Interdisciplinary Approaches to Research

As in clinical psychology generally, the field of clinical child psychology is moving toward an increasingly interdisciplinary view of children's functioning, with special attention to the many interconnections among biological/genetic, cognitive, social, behavioral, and environmental influences on children's functioning, problems, and well-being. For example, one volume in a three-volume book series called *Developmental Psychopathology* was dedicated solely to developmental neuroscience (Cicchetti & Cohen, 2006). Advances in genomics (McGuffin, 2004), genetics (Plomin & Kovas, 2005), behavioral genetics (Moffitt & Caspi, 2007), social neuroscience (Cacioppo, 2006), cognitive-affective neuroscience (Stein, 2006), and cortisol reactivity (Davies, Sturge-Apple, Cicchetti, & Cummings, 2007) have all converged toward interdisciplinary understandings of childhood psychopathology.

Section Summary: The field of clinical psychology is increasingly focused on the role of client diversity and on the impact of multiculturalism, and clinical child psychology is no exception. Efforts to increase access to mental health care, especially among impoverished and ethnic minority clients, will be of ever greater concern to clinical child psychologists, and research in the field will be characterized by the integration of various sciences (including biology, genomic studies, cognitive-affective neuroscience, and social neuroscience). The commitment to interdisciplinary research bodes well for improving our understanding of the development, maintenance, and treatment of childhood disorders.

CHAPTER SUMMARY

The longstanding focus of clinical psychologists on assessing and treating adults has changed over the last three decades to the point that clinical child psychologists have become a prominent subgroup in the field. Clinical psychologists have developed methods of classification, assessment, and intervention that are specialized for use with child and adolescent clients.

In dealing with these clients, clinical child psychologists pay special attention to referral issues, the context of behavior, developmental considerations, the nature of parent–child interactions, and the impact of childhood risk and protective factors.

Taking all these special considerations into account leads clinical child psychologists to ask assessment questions about child clients that they would usually not ask about adults and to use assessment methods (e.g., behavior rating scales, multiple informants during interviews, intelligence and achievement tests, and family and peer interaction measures) that are used less frequently with adult clients.

Unlike the clinically derived classification systems used with adults (which rely on the judgments of experts to determine diagnostic criteria), classification of childhood disorders has tended to emphasize empirically derived systems, which rely on statistical analyses of large amounts of data to determine the symptoms of given diagnostic categories. Empirically derived systems have identified two main types of childhood disorders: externalizing problems such as hyperactivity, aggression, and delinquency and internalizing problems such as depression, anxiety, and somatic problems. Other significant childhood problems include learning disorders and pervasive developmental disorders such as autistic disorder.

Treatment of child clients poses special challenges because children and parents often have different perspectives about a child's behavior and because their presence in therapy requires parental motivation and cooperation. Specialized forms of psychodynamic, behavioral, and cognitive-behavioral treatment have been developed for use with children, and some (such as operant and cognitive-behavioral approaches) have proven successful with a wide range of problems. Psychoactive medications are being used increasingly to treat childhood disorders, but there are great concerns about the side effects of many medications. Rather than dealing with childhood disorders after the damage has been done, clinical child psychologists would prefer early, comprehensive, and long-term interventions designed to prevent these disorders. Future directions in clinical child psychology include a greater emphasis on diversity, multiculturalism, making mental health services more accessible to clients, and interdisciplinary research that includes both biological and environmental factors in understanding the development and treatment of childhood disorders.

STUDY QUESTIONS

1. List the ways in which working clinically with children is different from working with adults.

2. How is the context of children's behavior taken into consideration in evaluating and treating childhood disorders?

3. Provide two examples of developmental issues to consider when working with troubled children.

4. What is infant temperament? How is it related to development over the life span?

5. What are some of the major risk factors linked to emotional/behavioral problems in youth?

6. Discuss the ramifications of childhood physical abuse and childhood sexual abuse.

7. What are protective factors, and how are they associated with children's behavior?

8. What are the pros and cons of using the following assessment techniques: behavior rating scales, unstructured interviews, behavioral observations, and family interaction measures?

9. Describe a thorough assessment protocol for a child who is experiencing academic and behavioral problems in school.

10. What is a clinically derived system of classification? What is an empirically derived system of classification? How are these two systems similar and different?

11. What are the major symptoms of the following disorders: ADHD, ODD, CD, major depressive disorder, separation anxiety disorder, autism, Asperger's disorder, and learning disorder?

12. What points from the research literature did the clinical case of "Billy" (the boy in the grocery store) illustrate?

13. List the principles involved in cognitive-behavioral treatment for children, and discuss the effectiveness of this treatment with children.

14. Describe the research findings related to alliance with children, adolescents, and families.

15. Describe a prevention program that works.

WEB SITES

- APA Division 53 Society for Clinical Child and Adolescent Psychology APA Division 54: http://www.clinicalchildpsychology.org
- Society of Pediatric Psychology: http://www.societyofpediatricpsychology.org/~division54/index.shtml
- List of effective child treatments from APA Division 53: http://www.effectivechildtherapy.com
- List of effective child treatments from New York University Child Study Center: http://www.aboutourkids.org
- Children's Defense Fund: http://www.childrensdefense.org

CHAPTER 12
Health Psychology

Chapter Preview: In this chapter, we describe how clinical psychologists work with medical professionals to treat disorders and to increase patients' adherence to medical treatment recommendations. We also describe how psychological factors contribute to disease, focusing on relationships among psychosocial variables (e.g., stress, cognitions) and physical functioning (e.g., nervous system activity, circulation, immune system functioning). Next we describe psychological risk factors and treatment interventions for illnesses such as cardiovascular disease, HIV/AIDS, chronic pain, and cancer.

In this chapter and the next, we discuss two specialized areas of clinical psychology—health psychology and neuropsychology—that illustrate how important it is for psychologists to study relationships between psychological and biological factors. We selected these areas because they have been some of clinical psychology's best "growth stocks" in the past 25 years. New research discoveries and expanding professional roles for clinicians have increasingly attracted psychologists to these areas.

WHAT IS HEALTH PSYCHOLOGY?

Section Preview: In this section, we present some of the theoretical foundations for health psychology. Health psychologists pay special attention to the role of stress on physical and mental health. They also consider how external stressors combine with internal variables such as coping strategies, cognitive habits, and perceived social support to affect vulnerability to illness.

Health psychology is a specialty that emerged in the 1970s and is devoted to studying "psychological influences on how people stay healthy, why they become ill, and how they respond when they do get ill" (Taylor, 1995, p. 3). This subfield has enjoyed such rapid growth over the last 25 years that it now has its own division in the APA (Division 38) and its own journal, *Health Psychology*. Health psychology research is also often published in the *Journal of Behavioral Medicine, Psychosomatic Medicine,* and the

Annals of Behavioral Medicine. Related professional organizations include the Society of Behavioral Medicine and the American Psychosomatic Society. Many clinical psychology training programs now include a "track" that specializes in the training of health psychologists, and some programs have developed health psychology as their major focus.

Health psychology is closely related to the larger field of *behavioral medicine,* which involves the integration of knowledge from the social/behavioral sciences (e.g., psychology, sociology, and anthropology), the biological sciences, and medicine into an interdisciplinary science focused on understanding and treating all types of medical disorders in the broadest possible ways. Health psychology and behavioral medicine follow a *biopsychosocial* model, which holds that physical illness is the result of biological, psychological, and social disruptions. They study how psychological conditions and behavioral processes are linked to illness and health.

Sir William Osler, a physician, is generally considered the father of modern behavioral medicine because he insisted that psychological and emotional factors must be considered in order to understand and treat various diseases. In 1910, Osler gave a lecture in which he suggested that many symptoms of heart disease "are brought on by anger, worry, or sudden shock." These ideas are remarkably similar to contemporary proposals about how key psychological factors may be linked to heart disease.

Osler's views were made more relevant by significant changes in the nature of illness in Western cultures during the 20th century. As recently as 100 years ago, most Americans died of acute infectious diseases such as pneumonia, typhoid fever, and tuberculosis. However, advances in education, sanitation, pharmaceuticals, and vaccination have all but eliminated these diseases, leaving chronic illnesses—heart disease and

Sir William Osler, the father of modern behavioral medicine.

cancer, for example—as the major threats to life (Blumenthal, 1994). These diseases are not only chronic in nature but also take years to develop. Further, the major risk factors for developing chronic illnesses include life-long health-damaging behaviors such as smoking, unhealthy eating, sedentary lifestyles, and alcohol abuse. Today, nearly half of all deaths that occur in the United States can be attributed to such risky behaviors (Mokdad, Marks, Stroup, & Gerberding, 2004). We now have evidence, for example, that behavioral and psychological factors contribute to the onset or severity of heart disease, ulcers, asthma, stomach disorders, cancer, arthritis, headaches, and hypertension. Reversing this trend will require increased awareness of the problem, changes in public policy, and most importantly, changes in individual health behaviors.

Physicians and other health professionals are becoming increasingly interested in the contributions of health psychologists. Indeed, emotional distress, sometimes as a result of difficulties in coping with an illness, is a factor in up to 60% of all physician office visits (Pallak, Cummings, Dorken, & Henke, 1995). Because physicians are seldom prepared to deal with these aspects of disease, prevention and treatment increasingly fall to persons in the health psychology field. In short, health psychology has grown because evidence strongly shows that it no longer makes sense to treat patients "from either the head up or the neck down" (Dornelas, 2001, p. 1261).

Several books provide more detailed discussions of the history and status of health psychology and behavioral medicine (e.g., Baum, Revenson, & Singer, 2001; Brannon & Feist, 2006; Sarafino, 2005; Straub, 2006; Taylor, 2005).

Stress, Coping, and Health

Stress is the negative emotional and physiological process that occurs as people try to adjust to or deal with environmental circumstances that disrupt, or threaten to disrupt, their daily functioning beyond their ability or perceived ability to cope (Taylor, 2005). The environmental circumstances that cause people to make adjustments are collectively called *stressors*. The physical, psychological, cognitive, and behavioral responses (such as increased heart rate, anger, and impulsiveness) that people display in the face of stressors are called *stress reactions*. Managing environmental stressors and one's own stress reactions is an ongoing challenge to health (see Figure 12.1).

Stress and the Nervous System

Physiological reactions to stress include a pattern of responses in the central and autonomic nervous systems that Hans Selye (1956) called the *general adaptation syndrome,* or GAS. The GAS begins with an *alarm reaction,* which is often called the fight-or-flight response because it helps us combat or escape stressors. The alarm reaction releases into the bloodstream a number of "stress hormones," including adrenal corticosteroids, catecholamines (e.g., adrenaline), and endogenous opiates (the body's natural painkillers). These hormones increase heart rate, blood pressure, and respiration, pupillary dilation, muscle tension, release of glucose reserves, and concentration of attention on the stressor. If the stressor persists, or if new ones occur in quick succession, alarm is followed by the *stage of resistance,* during which less dramatic but more continuous biochemical efforts to cope with stress can have harmful consequences. For example, prolonged release of

FIGURE 12.1 Stress Has Remained a Central Concern of Modern Life

(*Source: Time* magazine cover June 6, 1983; accessed at: http://www.time.com/time/covers/0,16641,19830606,00.html.)

stress hormones can create chronic high blood pressure, damage muscle tissue, and inhibit the body's ability to heal.

If stressors continue long enough, the *stage of exhaustion* appears as various organ systems begin to malfunction or break down. In the stage of exhaustion, people experience physical symptoms ranging from fatigue, weight loss, and indigestion to colds, heart disease, and other more serious problems.

Selye's model was an important contribution to the field of stress and disease research and in particular provided a framework for thinking about how stressors could contribute to physiological changes and, ultimately, disease processes. However, the model fails to account for the importance of cognitive, psychological, and perceptual factors in modifying how and which experiences would be experienced as stressors. In other words, the model does not allow for individual differences in the experience of stress. Thus, more comprehensive models that outline how stressors affect disease progression have been developed.

For example, Barbara Dohrenwend (1978) suggested a four-stage model of how stressors and stress reactions contribute to physical illness and/or psychological disorder. In the first stage, stressful life events occur, followed in the second stage by a set of physical and psychological stress reactions. In the third stage, these stress reactions are mediated by environmental and psychological factors that either amplify or reduce their intensity. Factors likely to reduce stress reactions include things like adequate financial resources, free time to deal with stressors, a full repertoire of effective coping skills, the help and support of friends and family, a strong sense of control over stressors, a tendency to be optimistic, and a view of stressors as challenges. Stress-amplifying factors include things like poverty, lack of social support, inadequate coping skills, pessimism, a sense of helplessness, and seeing stressors as terrifying threats. In stage four, the interaction of particular stressors, particular people, and particular circumstances results in physical and/or psychological problems that may be mild and temporary (some anxiety, a headache, or a few sleepless nights) or severe and persistent (e.g., an anxiety or mood disorder, or physical illness).

Stress and the Immune System

Another important effect of prolonged stress is suppression of the immune system, the body's first line of defense against disease-causing agents (Herbert & Cohen, 1993; Maier & Watkins, 1998). For example, chronic stressors (e.g., taking care of a seriously ill relative) have been shown to lower immune system functioning, and even brief stressors, such as final-exam periods, have been associated with a decline in the activity of immune system cells that fight viruses and tumors (Kiecolt-Glaser & Glaser, 1992). In one particularly interesting study of the relationship between stress and illness, researchers injected volunteer subjects with cold viruses or a placebo and then measured the amount of stress experienced by the volunteers over a given time period (Cohen, Tyrrell, & Smith, 1991). The results showed that the appearance of colds and other infections was correlated with the amount of stress the subjects experienced. Many researchers now suspect that *immunosuppression* is the basis for the association between stressors and increased risk for illnesses, including some forms of cancer (e.g., Cohen & Rabin, 1998).

The effects of stress on immune function can also be modified by procedures to reduce stress. A recent investigation of this phenomenon among married couples examined immune function and the ability of the body to heal minor wounds (Kiecolt-Glaser et al., 2005). On one day, couples were put under stress by discussing an area of marital discord; on another day, they were asked to provide social support to each other and given prompts on how to effectively do so. Measures of wound-healing capacity and other immune system activity were taken during both days. Wound-healing capacity was significantly lower after the couples engaged in a discussion of marital discord, and higher after couples provided social support to each other, and this difference was attributable to the changes in immune function.

This area of research, broadly called *psychoneuroimmunology,* is quite complex. For example, although stressors—especially prolonged stressors—can suppress immune function, short bouts of stress can actually enhance some portions of the immune system. These discrete bouts of stress appear to enhance the body's ability to respond to invasions of foreign substances (Atanackovic et al., 2006).

Measuring Stressors

To study the relationship between stress and illness, it is necessary to measure stress accurately, and health psychologists have tried to do so in several ways. One example is a questionnaire called the *Schedule of Recent Experiences* (SRE) (Amundson, Hart, & Holmes, 1986), which contains a list of 42 events involving health, family, personal, occupational, and financial matters. Respondents identify the events that have happened to them during the past 6, 12, 24, and 36 months, and then give each event a weight based on the amount of adjustment that was needed to deal with it (1, very little adjustment; 100, maximal adjustment). These weights are summed to give a *Life Change Unit Score.*

Many health psychologists believe that the most accurate assessment of stress comes not from evaluating environmental experiences but from assessing individual perceptions of stressors. Thus, some stress inventories query respondents about the frequency and intensity of perceptions of stress without linking these perceptions to actual events. Cohen's *Perceived Stress Scale* (PSS) is one such commonly used measure (Cohen, Kamarck, & Mermelstein, 1983).

The results of research with even the best stress assessment scales show that while there is undoubtedly a relationship between stress and illness, the strength of that relationship is relatively weak. In other words, even though people who are exposed to significant stressors are more likely overall to become ill than are those exposed to fewer stressors, most people who experience stressors do not become ill. This realization has led health psychologists to search for variables that might explain how people are protected from the potentially health-harming effects of stress. Among these variables are three particularly important *vulnerability* or *resistance factors* (Kessler, Price, & Wortman, 1985): adaptive coping strategies, stress-hardy personality characteristics, and social support.

Adaptive Coping Strategies

Coping refers to people's cognitive, emotional, and behavioral efforts at modifying, tolerating, or eliminating stressors that threaten them (Folkman & Lazarus, 1980). People vary in how they cope with stress. Some try to eliminate or otherwise deal with stressors directly; others attempt to change the way they think about stressors to make them less

TABLE 12.1

Ways of Coping

Problem-focused and emotion-focused coping are two major ways in which people deal with stressors.

Coping Skills	Example
Problem-focused coping	
Confronting	"I stood my ground and fought for what I wanted."
Seeking social support	"I talked to someone to find out more about the situation."
Planful problem solving	"I made a plan of action and I followed it."
Emotion-focused coping	
Self-controlling	"I tried to keep my feelings to myself."
Distancing	"I didn't let it get to me; I tried not to think about it too much."
Positive reappraisal	"I changed my mind about myself."
Accepting responsibility	"I realized I brought the problem on myself."
Escape/avoidance (wishful thinking)	"I wished that the situation would go away or somehow be over with."

SOURCE: From "Appraisal, Coping, Health Status, and Psychological Symptoms," by S. Folkman, R. S. Lazarus, R. J. Gruen, and A. DeLongis, 1986, *Journal of Personality and Social Psychology, 50,* 571–579. Copyright 1986. Adapted with permission.

upsetting; still others concentrate on managing the emotional reactions that stressors cause (Lazarus, 1993).

Richard Lazarus and Susan Folkman developed a *Ways of Coping* checklist consisting of 68 items that describe how 100 middle-aged adults said they coped with stressful events in their lives (Folkman & Lazarus, 1980). These items fall into two broad categories: *problem-focused* and *emotion-focused coping* (see Table 12.1). The 100 respondents reported on a total of 1,332 stressful episodes, and in 98% of them, said they used both coping methods. Their choice was not random, however. Problem-focused coping was favored for stressors related to work, while emotion-focused coping was used more often when the stressors involved health. Men tended to use problem-focused coping more often than women in certain situations, but men and women did not differ in their use of emotion-focused coping. Other researchers using different instruments have reached similar conclusions (Stone & Neale, 1984). The distinction between problem-focused and emotion-focused coping has been particularly useful, guiding research for the last two decades (Tennen, Affleck, Armeli, & Carney, 2000).

Stress-Hardy Personality Characteristics

Psychologists interested in positive psychology have examined a variety of personality and cognitive characteristics, including optimism (Peterson, 2000; Seligman, 2005; Seligman & Csikszentmihalyi, 2000), resilience (Fredrickson, 2001), faith and hope (see Myers, 2000), curiosity (Richman, Kubzansky, Maselko, & Kawachi, 2005), and adaptive defense mechanisms (Vaillant, 2000), all of which can contribute to adaptive coping.

In some cases, the health benefits of positive characteristics can be substantial. For example, a recent study measured both hope and curiosity in a large group of volunteers, and with their permission, tracked their health status as indicated by medical records. It turned out that those with higher hope and curiosity were less likely to develop high blood pressure, diabetes, and respiratory infections (Richman et al., 2005). Data such as these support the notion that positive emotional states may play a protective role with regard to health.

Other researchers in this area have investigated the role in physical and mental health of optimistic beliefs, including slightly overoptimistic distortions of reality ("positive illusions"). A review of literature in social psychology and related areas reveals, for example, that positively biased perceptions of reality are more common in people who are not depressed (Taylor, Kemeny, Reed, Bower, & Gruenewald, 2000). Healthy or mature defense mechanisms such as sublimation, altruism, suppression, and humor also appear to safeguard health and lessen the effects of some diseases (Vaillant, 2000).

The benefits of positive attitudes do have their limits, however. For example, it may not be a good idea simply to act happy when you're not. Efforts to inhibit or suppress negative emotions may have some short-term benefits but may be harmful to health in the long run (Salovey, Rothman, Detweiler, & Steward, 2000). One study found that rheumatoid arthritis sufferers who talked about stressful events more tended to have better outcomes than those who talked about it less (Kelley, Lumley, & Leisen, 1997). And James Pennebaker (1995) has shown that persons who write about stressful experiences over successive days have better health outcomes than those who do not. Other research has found that expressing thoughts and feelings about negative experiences can have a positive effect (Snowdon, Greiner, Kemper, Nanayakkara, & Mortimer, 1999; Snowdon, Greiner, & Markesbery, 2000). Findings such as these are consistent with evidence that disclosure of negative emotions (such as in psychotherapy) is related to positive physical health, while inhibition is generally not (Miller & Cohen, 2001).

Of course, certain questions about coping and positive psychology remain unanswered. One of these concerns the optimum balance of positive and negative expectations: Is it better to be optimistic or realistic? Optimism can often lead to self-deception and less-careful cognitive processing, but without a certain amount of optimism, people may be more vulnerable to stressors (see Schneider, 2001). Another question relates to how positive and negative experiences aggregate over time to affect health. Finally, we have yet to delineate clearly which features of maladaptive coping are deeply ingrained and therefore difficult to change through therapy (i.e., personality characteristics) and which are less deeply ingrained and are therefore teachable.

Social Support

Social support has been defined in many ways (Schradle & Dougher, 1985), but its essential element appears to be the experience of being cared for, loved, esteemed, and part of a network of communication and mutual obligation (Baumeister & Leary, 1995). Social support, then, involves more than the presence of others. It provides

Social support enhances psychological *and* physical health.

relationships in which emotional support, feedback, guidance, assistance, and values are exchanged.

Several studies have shown that the relationship between stress and illness is weaker among individuals who perceive high levels of social support in their lives (Brannon & Feist, 2006; Sarafino, 2005; Staub, 2006). One explanation is that social support acts as a *buffer* against stress. The buffer model claims that social support enables people who face intense stressors to neutralize those stressors' harmful effects. Social support also provides more opportunities for self-disclosure, and friends are likely to bolster efforts at constructive coping, thereby lessening the chances of self-defeating strategies such as excessive drinking (Myers, 2000; Thoits, 1986). In short, people's perception of social support can strengthen their belief that others care for and value them; it may also enhance their self-esteem and increase feelings of confidence about handling stress in the future.

Another view, sometimes termed the *direct-effect* model, holds that social support is helpful regardless of whether stressful events are experienced because there is a general health benefit to being embedded in supportive relationships (Baumeister & Leary, 1995). A third explanation for the apparent benefits of social support is that high levels of support, good health, and low levels of stress all reflect the influence of some underlying characteristic such as *social competence,* which has positive effects on many areas of functioning.

Of course, some combination of all three models may be operating. It does seem clear is that lack of social support, and particularly lack of emotional support, puts people at higher risk for both physical and psychological disorders (Cohen & Wills, 1985; Kessler, Price, & Wortman, 1985) and even premature death (House, Robbins, & Metzner, 1982).

Despite its general advantages, social support can carry some risks. For example, having a dense social support network entails increased exposure to large numbers of other people, which increases one's exposure to communicable diseases. Social ties can also create conflicts if others' helping efforts leave the recipient feeling guilty, overly indebted, or dependent. If a recipient is not able to reciprocate helping efforts, she or he may feel disadvantaged in future interactions with the donor. In other instances, potential helpers may behave in misguided ways (giving too much advice or becoming upset when their advice is not followed) that lead the recipient to feel invaded, incompetent, or rejected (Broman, 1993; Cohen, 2004, Malarkey, Kiecolt-Glaser, Pearl, & Glaser, 1994; Wortman & Lehman, 1985).

The complex nature of social support has led some researchers to propose that different aspects of social factors, including social support, the degree to which individuals are integrated into social networks, social conflicts, and sociability, can operate on health and illness positively or negatively and via varying pathways (Cohen, 2004; Cohen, Gottlieb, & Underwood, 2000).

Section Summary: Health psychologists are concerned with how psychological variables influence one's vulnerability to physical illness and recovery from physical illness. The field of health psychology has grown because more and more diseases are related to psychological factors. One of the most general of these factors is stress, which results from a combination of external events, physiological responses, and individuals' psychological interpretations. A number of psychological variables are important in the degree to which stress compromises health. Among these are coping style, personality characteristics, and perceived social support.

RISK FACTORS FOR ILLNESS

Section Preview: In this section, we examine risk factors for two of the most important illnesses that health psychologists study and help treat: chronic heart disease and HIV/AIDS.

Anything that increases a person's chances of developing an illness is called a *risk factor* for that illness. Some risk factors stem from biological and environmental conditions such as genetic defects or exposure to toxic chemicals (Stokols, 1992). Others come in the form of health-damaging patterns of behavior. For example, smoking, overeating, lack of exercise, and consumption of a high-fat, low-fiber diet have all been identified as risk factors for life-threatening illnesses (VandenBos, DeLeon, & Belar, 1991). Conversely, certain behaviors or lifestyles tend to promote health. For example, people who eat breakfast regularly, rarely snack between meals, exercise regularly, do not smoke, get 7 to 8 hours of sleep per night, and do not use alcohol excessively live an average of 11 years longer than people who practice none of these behaviors (Breslow, 1979).

Aggressiveness, anxiety, and depression, too, can act as psychological risk factors for illness by increasing physiological arousal, suppressing social support, and interfering with the pursuit of healthy lifestyles. The multifaceted influence of environmental, behavioral, and social risk factors is seen in several serious illnesses, including cardiovascular disease and HIV/AIDS.

Risk Factors for Cardiovascular Disease

About half of the deaths each year in North America result from cardiovascular diseases, which include coronary heart disease (CHD), high blood pressure, and stroke. That works out to more than 2,600 people per day, an average of one death every 33 seconds (Centers for Disease Control, 2001a). The list of predisposing risk factors for cardiovascular disease is long, and most of them are of direct relevance to health psychologists. They include family history, ethnicity, depression, anxiety, obesity, sedentary lifestyle, social isolation, hostility, and work-related stress (Schneiderman, Antoni, Saab, & Ironson, 2001). Let's first consider the role of stressors and other psychological factors in CHD.

The Role of Stressors.   Some of the first strong evidence for the role of stressors in cardiovascular disease came from research on monkeys' responses to various types of stress (Manuck, Kaplan, Adams, & Clarkson, 1988; Manuck, Kaplan, & Clarkson, 1983). Researchers wanted to know whether increases in cardiovascular and endocrine reactivity caused by stressors can, if repeated many times over several years, produce the kinds of changes in the heart or peripheral arteries seen in cardiovascular diseases. The answer appears to be yes; animals showing the greatest increase in heart rate in response to stressors also had significantly more plaque—a build-up of cholesterol and other fatty substances—in their coronary arteries than did animals whose reaction was less extreme. Such an increase in plaque formation makes it more difficult for blood to flow easily through the arteries of the body and is one underlying reason for clinical events like heart attack (lack of blood flow to the heart leading to tissue damage and sometimes death), angina (diminished blood flow leading to pain), and stroke (lack of blood flow to the brain).

As noted earlier, people, too, react to threatening stimuli and other stressors with increases in heart rate, as well as with pronounced changes in blood pressure, and secretion of epinephrine, norepinephrine, and other stress hormones (Anderson, 1989; Krantz & Manuck, 1984). In the short run, these changes are biologically adaptive because they provide the short-term increase in energy that is required to respond to many types of physical threats (the fight-or-flight response). Under optimal conditions, such changes in biological functioning return to normal soon after a stressor ends. However, if repeated stressors continually stimulate excessive cardiac activity, these normal biological changes may not be adaptive.

Demographic variables such as ethnicity and poverty are also related to the risk for cardiovascular diseases (Adler & Matthews, 1994), mainly because health-damaging behaviors tend to be inversely related to socioeconomic status (SES). Smoking, for example, is more common among less educated people, as is excessive drinking. Those with lower levels of education are less likely to work and, when they do work, are more likely to find themselves in higher-risk occupations and environments. Residents of poorer neighborhoods also display higher rates of obesity than do residents of higher income neighborhoods (Morland, Diez Roux, & Wing, 2006). Obesity, in turn, significantly increases people's risks for hypertension and coronary heart disease (e.g., Foster & Kendall, 1994).

On the other hand, CHD is about half as common among Chinese and Japanese Americans as among European or African Americans, while high blood pressure is about twice as common among African Americans as European Americans. Males, African Americans of both genders, and older people all suffer higher-than-average rates of heart disease *and* have higher-than-average blood pressure responses to certain stressors. Although the exact mechanisms explaining these differences is not yet clear, physical factors such as diet and cultural factors such as living in stressful environments are almost certainly important contributors.

Psychological Factors in CHD.   As noted earlier, the impact of stressors can be mediated by psychological factors, including whether we think about stressors as threats or challenges and whether we believe we can control them. People who feel helpless in the face of what they see as threats are likely to experience more intense physiological reactivity and emotional upset. On the other hand, those who view stressors as challenges, and feel confident about coping with them, may experience less reactivity and distress (Lazarus & Folkman, 1984).

The relationship between psychological factors and CHD can be complex, as in the case of the *Type-A behavior pattern* (Friedman & Rosenman, 1974). Type-A people are described as displaying (a) explosive, accelerated speech; (b) a heightened pace of living; (c) impatience with slowness; (d) attempts to perform more than one activity at a time; (e) preoccupation with self; (f) dissatisfaction with life; (g) evaluation of accomplishments in terms of numbers; (h) competitiveness; and (i) free-floating hostility (Matthews, 1982). In contrast to Type-A persons, Type-B persons are more relaxed and feel less time pressure. They appear less competitive, controlling, and hostile.

Early research suggested that Type-A behavior is an important risk factor for the development of CHD. For example, in the Western Collaborative Group Study (WCGS), 3,500 men between the ages of 39 and 59 were classified as Type A or Type B. Of 257 men who suffered heart attacks during the 8.5 year study, 178 (69%) of them were Type A's. In other words, Type A's were more than twice as likely to have had heart attacks as Type B's (Rosenman et al., 1975). The impact of Type A on CHD risk remained even after the researchers statistically controlled for several other risk factors, including family history of heart disease, high cholesterol, high blood pressure, and cigarette smoking.

The effects of Type-A on heart disease appears across genders and cultures. For example, one study compared the personality characteristics of 290 Japanese men and women who had suffered nonfatal heart attacks to those of 489 healthy control participants (Yoshimasu & Fukuoka Heart Study Group, 2001). The Type-A behavior pattern was significantly associated with risk, especially among Japanese women.

However, we now know that the relationship between Type-A behavior and CHD is more complex than was originally believed. For one thing, being a Type-A person does not mean that you are highly likely to suffer a heart attack or other form of CHD. Notice that even though Type A's in the WCGS were twice as likely as Type B's to develop CHD, the vast majority of Type A's never developed CHD. Careful reanalysis of the WCGS sample by other researchers suggests that not all aspects of Type-A behavior are risk factors for CHD (Cohen & Reed, 1985; Eaker, Abbott, & Kannel, 1989; Miller et al., 1991; Ragland & Brand, 1988). It appears that the most health-risky aspect of the Type-A pattern is *hostility*, a feature that not all Type A's display (Birks & Roger, 2000; Williams & Barefoot, 1988; Williams, 2001). Recent research has therefore focused less on the global Type-A pattern and more on hostility and other elements of personality or behavior that are more specifically associated with risk. It turns out that hostile individuals have significantly stronger physiological responses to stress than do less hostile individuals

(Rozanski, Blumenthal, & Kaplan, 1999). Specifically, they experience high levels of cardiovascular reactivity most notably in response to interpersonal stressors (Miller et al., 1998; Suls & Wang, 1993).

Depression also plays a role in CHD. Depression among patients with heart disease, and among those who have already had a myocardial infarction (commonly known as a heart attack), is as high as 20%, with an additional 27% showing some symptoms of depression (Burg & Abrams, 2001). After suffering a heart attack, those who are depressed tend to have poorer long-term outcomes, even after controlling for other factors (e.g., cardiac history). Depression also increases the risk of cardiovascular disease among initially healthy individuals (Rugulies, 2003; Wulsin & Singal, 2003). In fact, depression is a serious problem for many chronic illnesses (Zheng et al., 1997). Depression is also associated with lifestyle choices that are more likely to produce additional disease, so treatment of depression as part of an integrated treatment plan is critical.

Risk Factors for HIV/AIDS

It has been estimated that as many as 1 million people in the United States are infected with HIV, the virus that causes acquired immune deficiency syndrome (AIDS). As of 2000, over 770,000 cases of AIDS had been reported in the United States (Centers for Disease Control, 2001b), and although rates of infection are on the decline in the United States, 40,000 more Americans still become infected every year (Glynn & Rhodes, 2005). Homosexual males and intravenous drug users are at highest risk, but the incidence of HIV infection is increasing among low-income African-Americans and Hispanic-American adolescents, and via heterosexual contact. Up to a quarter of those infected in the United States do not know that they are HIV positive (Glynn & Rhodes, 2005). Sadly, the problem is even worse in other parts of the world. Globally, over 36 million persons, 47% of them women, are estimated to be living with HIV/AIDS, and 95% of the cases are in the developing countries of Africa and other third-world regions (Centers for Disease Control, 2001c).

Health psychologists have helped focus attention on the fact that most cases of AIDS can be prevented by avoiding several risky behavior patterns: (a) sexual activity without the use of condoms or other protective devices, (b) sexual contact with multiple partners and/or partners with an unknown sexual history, (c) heavy use of alcohol or other drugs that tend to impair judgment about the necessity of using condoms, and (d) for intravenous drug users, sharing injection needles. Stress is also a risk factor for AIDS (as it is for many other diseases) because it may distract attention from the need to avoid impulsive and health-damaging behaviors such as drug use or unprotected sex (e.g., Testa & Collins, 1997).

Section Summary: Health psychologists attempt to understand how combinations of risk factors produce specific diseases. Because they affect so many people, cardiovascular disease and HIV/AIDS have been of particular interest. Demographic variables play a significant role in cardiovascular diseases, but psychosocial factors such as perceived social support, hostility, and depression also contribute. Risks for HIV/AIDS are strongly related to behaviors associated with sexual activity and drug use.

ILLNESS PREVENTION AND TREATMENT PROGRAMS

Section Preview: In this section, we describe how health psychologists collaborate with physicians, health educators, and other professionals to develop programs for preventing and treating a variety of illnesses. The prevention programs are designed to reduce behavioral and psychological risk factors in specified populations, while treatment programs usually focus on helping medical patients, individually or in small groups, minimize or cope with the symptoms of their illnesses. We highlight health psychology interventions related to cardiovascular diseases, pain, cancer, and HIV/AIDS.

Cardiovascular Diseases

As noted earlier, many people who do not currently have CHD or hypertension are at risk for these diseases because of the health-damaging behaviors they engage in and because of certain cognitive and psychological factors. These people can benefit from preventive interventions designed to reduce their risk.

For example, several treatment programs have been developed to reduce Type-A behavior (Nunes, Frank, & Kornfeld, 1987; Thoresen & Powell, 1992). In the Recurrent Coronary Prevention Project, over 800 patients who had already suffered a heart attack received periodic counseling over a 3-year period (Friedman et al., 1986). For some, the counseling focused on the importance of changing diet, exercise, and smoking habits, and adherence to prescribed medications. Others received this counseling along with advice on how to reduce Type-A behavior. At the end of the 3-year program, only 7.2% of the patients who regularly attended the counseling-plus-Type A modification sessions had suffered another heart attack. The heart attack rate was 13.2% for those who had received counseling alone. Among the many techniques available, relaxation training (described in Chapter 8, "Behavioral and Cognitive-Behavioral Psychotherapies"), self-monitoring, and training in coping skills appear to have the largest effects on altering Type-A behavior. As noted earlier, much of the focus today is not on Type-A generally but on specific factors such as hostility or depression.

In another approach to preventing CHD, health psychologists have developed programs aimed at eliminating smoking and other harmful habits and at promoting regular exercise, low fat diets, and other healthy habits (e.g., Jeffery, 1988). Some of these programs focus on a specific risk factor, such as obesity; others address several risk factors at once. Workplace interventions have become popular because corporations believe these interventions reduce the cost of health care and because researchers find that health promotion programs based in work settings permit the control and investigation of several motivational and environmental variables (Glasgow & Terborg, 1988). Community-based and Internet-based interventions are also being tried, with some showing success in assisting patients with behavior change (Bull, Gaglio, Garth & Glasgow, 2005; Glasgow et al., 2006). A prominent example of multiple-component prevention programs was the Multiple Risk Factor Intervention Trial (MRFIT, 1982), which attempted to lower blood pressure, smoking, and blood cholesterol in thousands of high-risk individuals. Other prevention programs have been based in schools. For instance, the North Karelia, Finland project (Williams, Arnold, & Wynder, 1977) and the Minnesota Heart Health Program (Blackburn et al., 1984) focused on interventions with children and adolescents. Although the North Karelia project was able to demonstrate a 73% reduction in deaths due to coronary heart disease over a 25-year period (Puska, 1999), others have been less successful (Ebrahim, Beswick, Burke & Smith, 2006).

Pain

Pain may be the single most common physical symptom experienced by medical patients (Turk & Rudy, 1990), so pain management is an important objective in psychological interventions with many disorders. Health psychologists have focused their pain research and treatment on chronic pain conditions, headache, and rheumatoid arthritis (Keefe, Abernethy & Campbell, 2005). Their goals are to help patients to perceive less pain, to cope with the psychological distress associated with chronic pain conditions, to decrease impairment of day-to-day functioning, and to develop strategies for more effectively living with chronic pain.

For headache and chronic pain, biofeedback and relaxation training methods have a long record of success, and cognitive-behavioral techniques have also proved effective (e.g., Azar, 1996; Blanchard, 1992). Arthritis pain has generally been treated effectively via stress management and cognitive-behavioral therapy techniques (Young, 1992). These treatments also have some positive effects on the overall physical impairment associated

Health psychologists help clients to deal with chronic pain.

with arthritis. Clinicians working in health psychology also deal with *phantom pain,* which is sometimes experienced by individuals who have lost a limb. Phantom pain can be extremely difficult to treat, partly because we don't understand its origins. One apparently successful approach is described in a fascinating study using a behavioral treatment called graded motor imagery, in which patients imagine performing motor movements in their missing limb using visual cues provided by mirrors and other devices. Patients in this study experienced a significant reduction in phantom limb pain that had not responded to medications or other pain control methods (Moseley, 2006).

Cancer

Health psychologists have developed a number of interventions designed to address several aspects of cancer (Andersen, 1992; Baum, Reveson, & Singer, 2001). Their goal is to promote an improved quality of life for cancer patients by helping them to (a) understand and confront the disease more actively, (b) cope more effectively with disease-related stressors, and (c) develop emotionally supportive relationships in which they can disclose their fears and other emotions (Andersen, 1992). Behavioral techniques, such as relaxation training, hypnosis, stress management, and cognitive restructuring have proven especially useful. For example, one recent study showed that group therapy for breast cancer patients reduced stress and anxiety, improved perceptions of social support, resulted in decreased smoking and improved dietary habits, and may have improved biological markers of disease as well (Andersen et al., 2004).

Another aspect of health psychologists' work with cancer patients relates to the severe nausea and vomiting that often results from chemotherapy. After several chemotherapy treatments, some patients develop conditioned responses that cause them to become nauseated even before they receive the drugs. This reaction, known as *anticipatory nausea,* makes some of these patients want to discontinue what can be lifesaving treatment. Standard anti-emetic drugs have not proven very successful in reducing or preventing anticipatory nausea and vomiting, so attention has turned to the use of behaviorally oriented treatments such as relaxation training with guided imagery, systematic desensitization, progressive muscle relaxation, and biofeedback (Figueroa-Moseley et al., 2007; Redd et al., 1987).

A number of other psychological interventions, including educational programs and various kinds of supportive individual and group therapy, have been shown to improve the mental and physical well-being of some cancer patients (Andersen et al., 2004; Fawzy et al., 1995; Goodwin et al., 2001; Helgeson, Cohen, & Fritz, 1998).

HIV/AIDS

Health psychologists are working on AIDS prevention through programs designed to reduce the unprotected sexual contact and needle sharing that are known risk factors for HIV infection (e.g., Bowen & Trotter, 1995; Kalichman, Cherry, & Browne-Sperling, 1999; Taylor, 2005).

In one HIV/AIDS program aimed at African American teenagers at risk for HIV infection, participants were randomly assigned to either a single class on the basic facts

Health psychologists help cancer patients cope with their disease, including the side effects of medication, often by teaching progressive relaxation skills.

about HIV transmission and prevention or to an eight-session program combining the same basic information with behavioral skill training, role-playing, and group support for sexual abstinence, safer sex practices, and resisting pressure to engage in unsafe sex (St. Lawrence, Brasfield, Jefferson, Alleyne, & O'Bannon, 1995). Teenagers in the behavioral skills group decreased their rate of unprotected intercourse significantly more than those in the single-class group, and this difference was still evident a year later. Further, among those who had been sexually abstinent when the study began, 88.5% of the teens in the behavioral training program remained so during the follow-up, while only 69% of the one-session information group was still abstinent. Success has also been reported following similar programs aimed at adult African American women in inner cities (e.g., Kalichman, Rompa, & Coley, 1996). In another program, gay men participated in twelve group sessions of role-playing, behavioral rehearsal, and problem-solving techniques designed to promote condom use and other safe sex practices. Compared to a control group of gay men who did not receive training, program participants significantly increased their use of condoms, their resistance to sexual coercion, and their knowledge of AIDS risks (Kelly, St. Lawrence, Hood, & Brashfield, 1989).

With the help of health psychologists, many large U.S. cities have established AIDS education programs, clean needle exchanges, condom distributions, and publicity campaigns encouraging safe sex (Kelly & Murphy, 1992; Koester et al., 2007). There are also AIDS prevention programs in many other countries, including those of sub-Saharan Africa, Asia, and parts of the Caribbean where women's AIDS risks are increasing dramatically (Canning, 2006). A major goal of AIDS prevention programs in these countries is to empower women to (a) learn about HIV transmission, (b) take greater control of their sexual lives, (c) obtain protective devices such as female condoms or vaginal microbicides, and (d) become less economically dependent on men and therefore less subject to coerced or commercialized sex.

Another important area of research among health psychologists working with HIV/AIDS patients relates to the development of ways to improve these patients' coping skills and quality of life. In one program, 233 men and 99 women infected with HIV/AIDS were randomly assigned to either a five-session group intervention focused on practicing safer sex or a five-session health-maintenance support group (a standard-of-care comparison). The safer sex practices intervention included emphasis on information, motivation, and behavioral skills. At 6-month follow-up, participants in the safe-sex practices intervention engaged in significantly less unprotected intercourse and significantly more condom use (Kalichman et al., 2001). Other psychological interventions attempt to help patients cope with HIV/AIDS itself. One study of such interventions compared the effectiveness of various kinds of individual psychotherapy for treating depression among HIV-positive patients (Markowitz et al., 1998). In this study, cognitive-behavioral therapists focused on helping clients restructure their appraisals and replace irrational thoughts with more rational ones. Interpersonal therapists focused on mood and helped clients relate moods to environmental events and social roles. Supportive psychotherapy combined client-centered therapy with an educational component about depression. Yet another group received supportive psychotherapy plus imipramine, an antidepressant drug. Reductions in depression appeared in each therapy group, but reductions were significantly better for interpersonal therapy and for supportive psychotherapy plus medication.

Can psychotherapy with HIV-positive patients help to slow the development of full-blown AIDS? In one study on this question, 54 HIV-positive men were randomly assigned to a training program to enhance adherence to medication, while 76 others received the same training program plus a cognitive behavioral intervention (Antoni et al., 2006). The researchers wanted to know if the psychotherapy intervention might assist patients in adhering to and effectively coping with a complex medical treatment program and thereby improve the patients' immune function. Results indicated that, indeed, the 10-week cognitive behavior program plus medication adherence program was associated with improved immune function, whereas those in the adherence-only group showed no change.

Section Summary: Health psychologists apply their knowledge of risk factors by working to develop disease prevention and treatment programs. The prevention programs often take place in schools, workplaces, or other community settings. Treatment-related programs are typically designed to help patients cope with, and slow the progression of, their illnesses.

A HEALTH PSYCHOLOGY CASE EXAMPLE

Robert E. Feinstein and Marilyn Sommer Feinstein (2001) describe a case example that illustrates many of the conditions encountered by health psychologists. Perhaps the most prominent feature of their work with "Karen" was the co-occurrence of several problems that are of both medical and psychological concern.

Karen's case illustrates another important aspect of health psychology treatment, namely that therapists often must consider conducting interventions outside of the normally defined roles of clinical psychologists. Helping clients to increase exercise is one of these areas (Pollock, 2001). Such nontraditional interventions are indicated because

Karen, a 42-year-old woman, was married with two children (one a stepchild). When she came to the clinic for help with smoking cessation, she was 30 pounds overweight, drank excessively, and had high cholesterol and symptoms of depression. In some areas of her life, she functioned reasonably well, however.

Karen's therapists adopted a transtheoretical model (see Table 12.2) to design her treatment (Prochaska et al., 1994). This model is designed to assess a client's readiness and ability to inhibit certain behaviors (e.g., smoking) or perform others (e.g., exercise), and interventions are shaped accordingly.

The transtheoretical model is one of several models within health psychology that address cognitive factors involved in people's decision to change health-related behaviors (see Rothman, 2000). In this five-step model, the first three involve a person's cognitive readiness to change (Prochaska, DiClemente, & Norcross, 1992).

Karen's treatment planning began with a patient history, then empirical evidence about the health risk for items in that history were collected. Data on success rates for the various methods available to deal with the patient's various problems were also reviewed. These data provided an estimate of how easy or difficult change generally is. Karen and her therapists discussed her personal priorities for treatment and her hopes and expectations about its success. For instance, they considered Karen's motivation and expectations about change in light of the health threats she faced and her probability of achieving change. Through a process known as informed shared decision making, Karen and her therapists jointly developed an intervention plan.

Karen and her therapists decided to begin a program of once-a-week treatment sessions focused on her depression and lack of exercise. These targets were chosen because, given her history and current situation, efforts at dealing with them appeared to have the greatest chance of success.

TABLE 12.2

A Transtheoretical Model for Assessment and Intervention

Stage	Description
Precontemplation	The person does not perceive a health-related behavior as a problem and has not formed an intention to change.
Contemplation	The person is aware that a health-related behavior should be changed and is thinking about it.
Preparation	The person has formed a strong intention to change.
Action	The person is engaging in behavior change. (Relapse and backsliding are common at this stage.)
Maintenance	After behavior changes have begun, the person must continue performing and/or avoiding specified behaviors.

SOURCE: Based on J. O. Prochaska, W. F. Velicer, J. S. Rossi, M. G. Goldstein, et al., 1994.

of research evidence that exercise can be as effective as other, more traditional clinical interventions such as cognitive restructuring or emotional support. For instance, Babyak and colleagues (2000) found that exercise was at least as effective as antidepressant medication in reducing the symptoms of depression, and more effective in preventing remission.

IMPROVING ADHERENCE TO MEDICAL TREATMENT REGIMENS

Section Preview: In this section, we review a set of behaviors that are essential for health—adherence to medical treatment recommendations. Psychologists help to identify the causes of nonadherence; they also develop various interventions to improve adherence.

Psychological interventions aimed at disease prevention or symptom reduction often result in immediate improvements, but unfortunately, these changes may not be maintained long enough to promote a healthier life (Blanchard, 1994). Maintaining behavior change remains one of the most vexing problems in health psychology. For example, smoking cessation programs are usually followed by significant rates of abstinence, but more than 50% of smokers resume their habit within a year (Jason et al., 1995; Shiffman et al., 1996). A similar picture exists for the treatment of obesity. Although behavior modification appears to be the most effective psychological intervention for obesity, maintenance of weight loss and learning new eating habits are major difficulties for most people. So although most psychologically oriented weight-reduction interventions can achieve reductions of about 1 pound per week, it is difficult to maintain these reductions beyond 1 or 2 years (Brownell & Wadden, 1992). Similar difficulties are found even when patients try to alter their lifestyles after a heart attack. It would seem reasonable to assume that such a traumatic event might jolt people into permanent lifestyle changes, but as many as 50% of cardiac rehabilitation participants drop out of their programs within 1 year (Burke, Dunbar-Jacob, & Hill, 1997).

The effectiveness of medical treatment, too, depends not only on its being the correct treatment but also on the patient's continued cooperation with it. The extent to which patients adhere to medical advice and treatment regimens is called *compliance* or *adherence* (Rodin & Salovey, 1989). Research on the impact of adherence on medical outcomes makes it clear that adhering to treatment advice is important and that adherence can be affected by the severity and chronicity of the disease, patient age, and the type of treatment prescribed (DiMatteo, Giordani, Lepper & Croghan, 2002). Nonadherence in taking prescribed medication may occur in half or more of all patients, at least part of the time (Haynes, 1982). A survey among European adults demonstrated that 65% of them reported that they failed to complete their full prescribed dose of antibiotics; nearly all of these individuals reported that they did not take the full course of medication because they felt better (Branthwaite & Pechere, 1996). Nonadherence rates among parents who are providing medication for their children tend to be lower, but for some medications taken by adolescents, nonadherence rates can be as high as 80% (Rickert & Jay, 1995).

Indeed, adolescents may not take prescribed medications at all, may take it less frequently or more frequently than instructed, or they may ignore rules about the need to take medicine with food or not to consume alcohol while on medication. Nonadherence tends to be especially common in relation to treatments that are complicated, unpleasant, or involve substantial lifestyle changes. Health psychologists have been involved in efforts to understand the causes of nonadherence and in developing interventions to improve adherence.

Causes of Nonadherence

The chief cause of nonadherence appears to be miscommunication between physicians and patients. Patients frequently do not understand what physicians tell them about their illnesses or their treatments. As a result, they are confused about what they should do or they forget what they have been told. One study showed that 5 minutes after seeing their physician, general-practice patients had forgotten 50% of what the doctor had told them (Ley, Bradshaw, Eaves, & Walker, 1973).

The emotional aspects of patient–physician communication also are correlated with adherence. A common pattern of troubled communication involves patient antagonism toward the physician, accompanied by physician withdrawal from the patient. Adherence may also be reduced by the sheer complexity, inconvenience, or discomfort associated with some kinds of treatment. Finally, nonadherence with treatment may appear because patients do not have a good system for reminding themselves about what to do and when to do it.

A psychological theory called the *health belief model* (HBM) (Rosenstock, 1974) has been especially helpful in understanding the reasons for patient nonadherence (Becker & Maiman, 1975). According to the HBM, patients' adherence with treatment depends on factors such as (a) how susceptible to a given illness they perceive themselves to be and how severe the consequences of the illness are thought to be; (b) how effective and feasible versus how costly and difficult the prescribed treatment is perceived to be; (c) the influence of internal cues (physical symptoms) plus external cues (e.g., advice from friends) in triggering health behaviors; and (d) demographic and personality variables that modify the influences of the previous three factors.

Interventions to Improve Adherence

Attempts to improve adherence with treatment can be classified into three general approaches: (a) educating patients about the importance of adherence so that they will take a more active role in maintaining their own health, (b) modifying treatment plans to make adherence easier, and (c) using behavioral and cognitive-behavioral techniques such as self-monitoring, reminder cues, and other tools to increase patients' ability to adhere (Masur, 1981).

Education.   One direct and effective intervention for improving adherence with short-term treatments is to give patients clear, explicit, written instructions that supplement oral instructions about how treatment is to proceed. Educating physicians about the causes and management of nonadherence may also be beneficial. In one study

(Inui, Yourtee, & Williamson, 1976), physicians who had been educated about the HBM and ways to improve adherence had more adherent patients at a 6-month reassessment. Education can also counteract inaccurate or naive theories of illness that some clients may have.

Modification of Treatment Plans. A second strategy for increasing adherence is to reorganize treatment to make it easier for patients to follow treatment instructions. Examples include timing daily doses of medication to coincide with daily habits (e.g., taking pills right after brushing teeth), giving treatment in one or two injections rather than in several doses per day, packaging medicine in dosage strips or with pill calendars, and scheduling more frequent follow-up visits to supervise adherence. These procedures have shown promise (e.g., Boczkowski, Zeichner, & DeSanto, 1985), but many of them entail additional manufacturing costs and extra time from service providers, two characteristics that tend to limit their usefulness.

Behavior Modification. Health psychologists have used a number of behavioral techniques, including the use of postcard reminders, motivational interviewing, telephone calls, wristwatch alarms, and other environmental cues to prompt patients to take pills or perform other aspects of treatment plans (Rickert & Jay, 1995). They have also set up written *contingency contracts* (described in Chapter 8) between patient and physician that specify what behaviors the patient can perform in order to earn rewards (e.g., more conveniently timed office appointments). Such contracts encourage a more collaborative relationship between patient and physician and have been successful in improving adherence (Swain & Steckel, 1981).

Behavior modification procedures have also been used to reduce nonadherence motivated by the discomfort associated with medical procedures or treatments. The best-known illustration of these methods was described earlier in relation to behavioral treatments for the control of anticipatory nausea in cancer chemotherapy patients. Other examples include teaching children to use breathing exercises and distraction techniques to help them overcome fear of routine vaccinations (Blount et al., 1992), employing hypnosis to reduce pain in burn patients who are undergoing debridement procedures (Patterson, Everett, Burns, & Marvin, 1992), and using relaxation, systematic desensitization, and participant modeling to help fearful patients get the dental work they need but have been avoiding (e.g., Kleinknecht & Bernstein, 1978).

Section Summary: Health psychologists help design interventions, but they are also active in trying to find ways to encourage clients to adhere to treatment plans. This can be especially difficult if treatment is extended over weeks or months, which is the case with several of the illnesses described in this chapter. To enhance adherence, clinicians help health care providers modify treatments or communicate with clients; they help educate clients about factors related to adherence and nonadherence; and they employ a number of behavioral techniques.

CHAPTER SUMMARY

Health psychology is a specialty devoted to studying psychological influences on health, illness, and coping with health problems. It is closely related to the larger field of behavioral medicine, which involves the integration of knowledge from many disciplines in understanding and treating medical disorders. Both fields adopt a biopsychosocial model in which physical illness is viewed as involving biological, psychological, and social factors. Health psychologists seek to (a) understand how these factors interact to influence illness and health, (b) identify risk factors for sickness and protective factors for health, (c) promote healthy behaviors and prevent unhealthy ones, and (d) create interventions that contribute to medical treatment of illness.

Stress is the negative emotional and physiological process that occurs as people try to deal with environmental circumstances, called stressors, that disrupt or threaten to disrupt daily functioning. Stress reactions can be physical, psychological, and behavioral. Physical stress reactions include the general adaptation syndrome, which begins with an alarm reaction and, if stressors persist, continues into the stages of resistance and exhaustion. Prolonged stress can result in immunosuppression, impairment of the body's disease-fighting immune system. The impact of stressors tends to be lessened in people with better social support systems. Lack of social support increases risk for physical disorders.

Anything that increases the chances of developing an illness is called a risk factor for that illness. Behaviors associated with risk for coronary heart disease (CHD) and cancer include smoking, overeating, lack of exercise, and consumption of a high-fat diet. Stressors, hostility, and depression also appear to be a risk factor for CHD. Risk factors for HIV/AIDS include unprotected sexual activity and, for intravenous drug users, sharing injection needles.

Illness prevention programs in health psychology seek to reduce risk factors for cardiovascular disease, chronic pain, cancer, AIDS, and other diseases by working with individuals, groups, and whole communities to alter health-risky behaviors. Health psychologists often treat individuals with multiple health problems, and decisions must be made about which conditions have priority. Although many types of interventions are initially successful, long-term behavior change is difficult in some areas, particularly those involving strongly entrenched habits (e.g., smoking, substance abuse, overeating) and behavioral changes that must occur over a long period of time.

Health psychologists' efforts to improve patients' adherence to prescribed medical treatments include education about the importance of adherence, modifying treatment plans to make adherence easier, and using behavioral techniques to increase patients' ability to adhere.

STUDY QUESTIONS

1. What is health psychology?
2. How does stress affect the human nervous system?
3. How does stress affect the immune system?
4. How do health psychologists measure stress?
5. What are problem-focused and emotion-focused coping?
6. Which personality characteristics appear to help people cope with stressors?
7. How does social support affect the experience of stress?
8. What are risk factors for chronic heart disease?
9. What are risk factors for HIV/AIDS?
10. What psychological interventions have been attempted to prevent chronic heart disease?

11. What roles do health psychologists play in the prevention and treatment of chronic pain, cancer, and HIV/AIDS?

12. What are some of the causes of nonadherence to medical treatment?

13. What interventions have psychologists attempted to improve adherence to medical treatment?

WEB SITES

- Health Psychology Division of APA (Division 38): http://www.apa.org/about/division/div38.html
- Home page for the journal *Health Psychology:* http://www.apa.org/journals/hea/
- Health Psychology and Rehabilitation home Page: http://www.healthpsych.com

CHAPTER 13
Clinical Neuropsychology

Chapter Preview: Clinical neuropsychologists perform assessments and design interventions for persons who experience neurological dysfunction because of brain injury or illness. They also conduct research on both normal and abnormal brain functioning that has helped to shed light on psychological disorders such as depression and schizophrenia. Clinical neuropsychology is a relatively new and growing field, and its practitioners must understand brain–behavior relationships and be trained in a variety of assessment and intervention techniques unique to the field.

Muriel was driving her car when she was struck by another vehicle. She hit her head and lost consciousness, and a friend traveling with her was killed. She eventually made a full physical recovery, but she had some new problems. She would forget conversations, miss appointments, fail to meet deadlines, lose things, and ask the same questions again and again. How would you explain her new memory problem? You could consider several possibilities. For example, you might wonder if she is still upset about the accident, is mourning her lost friend, or perhaps feeling guilty about having survived. Such emotional turmoil could impair concentration and cause forgetfulness. But how could you know if, instead, brain damage was the cause of her memory loss? You might look at pictures of her brain structure with magnetic resonance imaging to spot areas of gross brain damage. But those pictures can't tell you if damage is fresh or old. Most important, you would still have to decide if the damage is relevant to Muriel's current problems. In other words, you would need to decide if the damaged regions are those which, when injured, could cause memory loss. Further complicating the picture is that brain damage on a microscopic or cellular level can impair psychological functioning but be invisible on an imaging scan. To help sort out all these possibilities, you need a way to assess Muriel psychologically, to test her mental abilities carefully. You must then use a detailed knowledge of psychology and brain function to decide if the pattern of findings suggests brain dysfunction, and if so, where it is. These are some of the tasks that neuropsychologists perform.

Neuropsychology is the field of study that seeks to understand how brain processes make human behavior and psychological functions possible (Heilman & Valenstein, 2003). Neuropsychologists are interested in a wide range of human abilities, including aspects of cognitive functioning (e.g., language, memory, attention, mathematical, and visuospatial skills), motor functioning (e.g., learned skilled movements, gross and fine motor skills), emotional functioning (e.g., motivation, understanding and expressing emotion, anxiety, depression, euphoria), social functioning (e.g., prejudice, social judgment, interpreting social information), and personality traits (e.g., extraversion, neuroticism). Neuropsychologists study how brain operations control such processes and how this control breaks down after brain dysfunction (e.g., stroke, infection, neurodegeneration) or psychological disorders (e.g., posttraumatic stress disorder, clinical depression, schizophrenia).

Clinical neuropsychologists become involved in the psychological and behavioral evaluation of individuals. By doing careful testing of a person's psychological functions, they can learn whether or not the person shows a pattern of impairments suggestive of brain damage, and if so, to what brain regions. Clinical neuropsychologists can also help quantify the severity of psychological deficits by comparing a person's performance to the average performance, or norms, established by the previous testing of many other people of similar educational and social backgrounds. The pattern of deficits identified by neuropsychological testing may even offer clues as to the cause of brain damage. Clinical neuropsychologists may help to clarify how a person's problems from brain damage are likely to affect that particular individual's ability to function socially, vocationally, and in other aspects of daily living. Finally, clinical neuropsychologists can help formulate a regimen for rehabilitation and recovery from the effects of brain damage.

Clinical neuropsychologists must use several kinds of knowledge and skills in their work. First, as with any clinical psychologist, they make use of the assessment skills described in Chapter 3, "Basic Features of Clinical Assessment," Chapter 4, "Interviewing and Observation in Clinical Psychology," and Chapter 5, "Testing in Clinical Psychology." Thus, neuropsychological assessments consider the entire person, including social and family background, personality dynamics, and emotional reactions to possible brain dysfunction. Second, clinical neuropsychologists must be able to use specialized assessment methods unique to neuropsychological assessment. Third, clinical neuropsychologists must have knowledge of the neurosciences, including neuroanatomy (the study of nervous system structures and the connections between them), neurophysiology (the study of the functioning of the nervous system and its parts, including the chemistry of nerve tissue and the relationship between the nervous system and endocrine functions), and neuropharmacology (the study of how drugs affect nervous system functioning). Fourth, clinical neuropsychologists must know about a wide range of human cognitive abilities, including language and perception, and about how those abilities develop and change over time (e.g., behavioral genetics and life-span psychology). Fifth, neuropsychologists must be able to distinguish behavioral and psychological problems caused by brain dysfunction from those caused by psychopathology in structurally intact brains. Finally, they should be able to design effective rehabilitative programs based on an in-depth understanding of clinical psychology.

A BRIEF HISTORY OF NEUROPSYCHOLOGY

Section Preview: Clinical neuropsychology's roots go back to debates in the 1800s about brain organization and function. As case examples and new assessment techniques resolved many of these debates, a clearer understanding of neurological function and dysfunction led to the development of neuropsychology as a specialty within clinical psychology.

Although neuropsychology includes topics that overlap with many areas of psychology, with experimental neuroscience, and with clinical neurology, it has grown into a distinct field with unique investigation methods and treatment approaches. To understand modern neuropsychology, it is important to understand how it developed.

Early Influences

Neuropsychology emerged as a separate field of study during the mid-20th century, but its roots are in two lines of 19th-century thinking about the relationship between specific behaviors and specific areas of the brain (Tyler & Malessa, 2000). One view came from anatomists Franz Gall and Johann Spurzheim, who advocated the concept of *localization of function*. According to this then-controversial view, different psychological functions were controlled by different brain areas. This view is largely accepted today, and Gall and Spurzheim would have been more revered figures for proposing it had they not framed their ideas within a larger theory called *phrenology*. Phrenologists reasoned that if certain functions were localized in certain brain areas, and that if a person used particular functions more than others, the corresponding brain region would get larger and raise a bump on the skull above it. As noted in Chapter 1, "What Is Clinical Psychology?" phrenology therefore claimed that individual differences in personality and intelligence could be assessed by the bumps and indentations on the surface of the skull. Phrenology was very popular with the public but disdained by most scientists because of the lack of evidence to support it. Once phrenology became discredited, the concept of localization of function was stained by association, so it too was seen as misguided (Zola-Morgan, 1995).

An alternative line of thinking about brain and behavior suggested that no particular brain area was more important than any other in the control of psychological function. Pierre Flourens, a widely respected scientist, argued for this view on the basis of careful experiments. For example, he surgically destroyed parts of animals' brains and then observed the behavioral consequences. He concluded that although there was some localization of cortical function, the regions within the cerebral hemispheres functioned more like a single unit than a collection of specialized parts. This view was later supported by the work of Karl Lashley, who emphasized the capacity of one area of the cortex to take over for the functions of a destroyed area, a capacity he called *equipotentiality*.

Eventually, work in behavioral neurology convincingly showed that different areas of the brain, especially in the cerebral cortex, do indeed underlie different specific psychological functions. The pendulum began to swing back toward a localization of function position due to the work of an esteemed French surgeon, Paul Broca (1861, 1865), who discovered that expressive language (e.g., speech) is controlled by a particular part of the brain. Broca had the opportunity to confirm, by autopsy, that a patient with a profound speech problem but otherwise normal intelligence had damage to one small area of cortex in the left frontal lobe. By 1863, he had collected a series of eight cases and had argued so convincingly for localization of function that this view seemed indisputable. Further support for localization of function came from the work of two Italian ophthalmologists: Antonio Quaglino, and Giambattista Borelli. In 1867, they published a paper describing a man who developed *prosopagnoisa,* the inability to recognize familiar faces, after bleeding in the brain damaged his right hemisphere. Findings such as these made it clear that particular psychological functions are especially dependent on specific brain areas.

Development of Neuropsychological Assessment Techniques

As part of their evaluation of people, clinical neuropsychologists use standardized tests that assess separate aspects of psychological function. As we described in Chapter 2, "Clinical Psychology's Past and Present," some of this testing tradition dates to the early 20th century, when French psychologist Alfred Binet had begun assessing children with brain damage. Tests such as his are usually associated with the beginning of modern intelligence testing (see Chapter 5), but they also laid the foundation for neuropsychological assessment. Many of the disorders commonly assessed today with neuropsychological techniques had been identified by Binet's time. These included *aphasia* (disordered language abilities), *apraxia* (impaired abilities to carry out learned purposeful movements), *agnosia* (disorders of perceptual recognition), and *amnesia* (disorders of memory). In Russia, the Psychoneurological Institute was formed in 1907 to study the behavioral effects of brain damage, and throughout the first decade of the 1900s, several people in the United States were using psychological tests to study how brain damage affects behavior.

One of these people was Ward Halstead, who in 1935 founded a neuropsychology laboratory at the University of Chicago. His major contribution was to observe persons with brain damage in natural settings. From these observations, he identified the key characteristics of behavior that should be assessed in any patient undergoing neuropsychological testing. After recording responses in many patients, Halstead compared their performance to control cases and identified 10 measures that could discriminate patients from controls (Reitan & Davison, 1974). His approach was to use a *test battery,* a set of several different tests designed to complement each other to assess all the key categories of psychological function (e.g., language, memory, visual recognition). Halstead's first graduate student, Ralph M. Reitan, started a neuropsychology laboratory in 1951 at the Indiana University Medical Center. Reitan revised Halstead's test battery and included the Wechsler Intelligence Scale and the Minnesota Multiphasic Personality Inventory (MMPI) in what came to be known as the *Halstead-Reitan Battery* (HRB). This battery is still widely used today.

Basic research in neuropsychology and advances in assessment methods grew dramatically following World War II, in part because of the need to assess many war-related cases of brain damage. A small number of prominent neuropsychologists developed and validated specific tests and test batteries (Jones & Butters, 1983), some of which were specifically designed to be used in special patient populations, such as people with traumatic brain injury. Others were aimed at assessing certain kinds of deficits, such as the loss of language function.

Split-Brain Research

Another important chapter in the history of neuropsychology is associated with the work of Roger Sperry and his colleagues at the California Institute of Technology (Sperry, 1961, 1982). They studied the psychological effects of cutting the *corpus callosum,* the band of nerve pathways that the brain's two hemispheres rely on to communicate directly with each other. This surgical procedure is performed in the hope that it will prevent the spread of epileptic seizures from one side of the brain to the other in certain cases where drug treatment fails. With the corpus callosum severed, there is no direct pathway between the hemispheres, so the activity of one cerebral hemisphere proceeds largely isolated from that of the other hemisphere. Although vast sections of brain tissue devoted to complex information processing are rendered incommunicado by this surgery, research methods in the 1940s detected no significant differences between normal people and so-called split-brain patients. Sperry (who won the Nobel Prize in 1981 for his work) and his associates devised new experimental procedures that could show that split brains were indeed different from intact ones and how they differ (e.g., Sperry, 1968).

Research on Normal Brains

Split-brain research, and the innovative testing techniques involved in it, stimulated an increase in studies of the organization of normal brains. Many of these studies used a *tachistoscope,* a device that displays visual stimuli for a very brief period of time. When the eyes are fixated on a central point in the visual field, stimuli briefly flashed to the left of the fixation point are seen only in the left visual field. Similarly, stimuli briefly flashed to the right of the fixation point appear only in the right visual field. Because of the way the eyes are "wired" to the brain, information from the left side of space is sent first to the right cerebral hemisphere and information from the right side goes first to the left hemisphere. The information from each side of space is then normally shared between hemispheres via their connections through the pathways provided by the corpus callosum.

Using tachistoscopic methods, experimenters directed the entry of visual stimuli into one hemisphere or the other and measured a person's accuracy of performance or reaction time in response. By measuring the relative accuracy of responses for the two visual fields, researchers have been able to document and confirm unique hemispheric superiorities for a wide variety of cognitive and perceptual tasks (Hellige, 2001).

Section Summary: Clinical neuropsychology emerged as a distinct discipline only a few decades ago, but its roots go back to earlier efforts to understand brain organization and function. Key efforts include (a) the finding that specific areas of the brain specialize in specific functions, (b) the development of tests and test batteries to measure intellectual functioning and identify specific areas of normal and abnormal brain function, (c) the discovery of disorders associated with disrupted communication between the brain's hemispheres, and (d) techniques (such as the tachistoscopic) that provided normative information about the functioning of normal brains.

BASIC PRINCIPLES OF NEUROPSYCHOLOGY

Section Preview: Here we provide some basic principles about how the brain works. Although various functions are compartmentalized, the various compartments or modules interact with each other in multiple ways. Each hemisphere has its specialties, but both hemispheres are involved in most tasks.

Certain principles of brain-behavior relationships are fundamental to neuropsychology. We review some of them here before describing how clinical neuropsychologists assess brain functioning in patients. In doing so, we refer often to the various regions of the brain presented in Figure 13.1.

Localization of Function

As already noted, the idea that specific parts of the brain are involved in specific behaviors and psychological functions became the prevailing view of scientists by the end of the 19th century (Tyler & Malessa, 2000), and this *localizationist* view is now widely

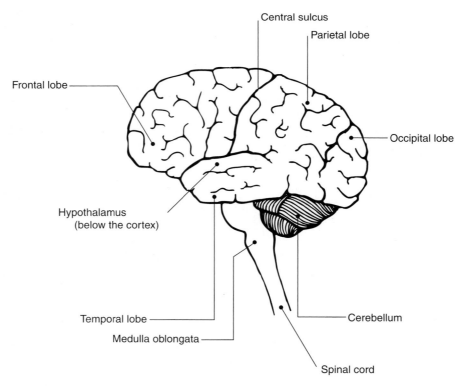

FIGURE 13.1 A Lateral View of the Human Cerebral Cortex and Other Brain Structures

accepted. What is less clear is just what it is that is being localized to a given brain region and how different brain regions interact.

Theorists who emphasize the interrelatedness of brain areas and who stress the holistic quality of brain functioning are sometimes known as *globalists*. John Hughlings Jackson, Karl Lashley, and Kurt Goldstein are three of the more influential globalists, but it was Alexander Luria who, more than any other scientist, proposed a theory of brain organization that emphasized its integration rather than its specificity (Glozman, 2007). Luria's theory was that the brain is organized into three functional systems: (a) a brain stem system for regulating a person's overall tone or waking state; (b) a system located in the posterior (back) portion of the cortex for obtaining, processing, and storing information received from the outside world; and (c) a system, located mainly in the anterior (front) portion of the cortex, for planning, regulating, and verifying mental operations. So like other globalists, Luria believed that the brain engaged in some specialized "division of labor," but he emphasized the importance of understanding how these different brain areas work together.

Modularity

Today, when neuropsychologists map the brain according to specific functions, they do so in a way that reflects both localizationist and globalist perspectives (Goldberg, 1995; Lezak, Howieson, & Loring, 2004). For example, the influential concept of *modularity* (Fodor, 1983) implies that the brain is divided into regions that are unique in how they receive information, process that information, and then send the processed information to other brain modules. Different brain areas are thus seen as different information-processing modules, something like the many different circuit boards contained in a vast, complex computer. According to the modular view, then, a complicated psychological function such as attention is not "controlled" by a single brain area. Rather, attentional functions are seen to rely on several different brain modules, each adding a different piece to the puzzle, working together in a network distributed widely across many brain regions (Mesulam, 1990). Since different aspects of attention will differently rely more on one brain module than another, it follows that damage to a single module would affect one aspect of attention more than another. It also follows that since a given module may provide a kind of information processing that several psychological functions may each rely on, damage to that particular brain module could have consequences for several different psychological functions if they are heavily dependent on the module in question. And because many different modules may be involved in the network of brain areas that attentional functions rely on, damage in many different brain areas can have some sort of affect on attention.

Levels of Interaction

Different modules interact with each other to produce a seamless sequence of behaviors. The modules are organized in a fashion that reflects both the structure and function of the brain. Thus, the brain can be seen as having several levels of organization, ranging from the global to the local. For example, the various areas identified in Figure 13.2 are associated with regions on either side of the central sulcus. These functions can be

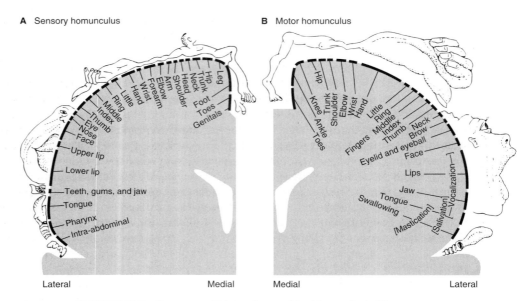

A Sensory homunculus

B Motor homunculus

Lateral   Medial   Medial   Lateral

FIGURE 13.2 Sensory and Motor Areas of the Human Brain. These maps show where on the human cortex sensory information is received (left) and where motor functions are controlled (right). note that areas of the body that are more sensitive to sensory information (such as the tip of the tongue or the fingers) are represented by more cortical area than areas that are less sensitive (such as the back of the head or the upper leg)

(*Source:* Kandel, Schwartz, and Jessell, 1991. Reprinted with the permission of Macmillan Publishing Company from *The Cerebral Cortex of Man* by Wilder Penfield and Theodore Rasmussen. Copyright 1950 Macmillan Publishing Company. Copyright renewed © 1978 Theodore Rasmussen.)

distinguished by whether they primarily process incoming information (sensory) or program outgoing behavior (motor). They can also be distinguished by modality (for example, whether they primarily process visual or auditory information). In general, brain regions behind the central sulcus are more involved in the reception of sensory information (e.g., touch, pressure, temperature, and body position), whereas brain regions in front of the central sulcus are more involved in programming motor output.

Lateralization of Function

As noted earlier, the cerebral cortex is divided into two hemispheres. The activity of each hemisphere is associated with somewhat different functions. At one time, this difference was described in terms of "cerebral dominance," because the left hemisphere was seen as the "dominant" or "major" one and the right as the "nondominant" or "minor" hemisphere. Over time, this distinction was found to be misleading. Work by Sperry and others showed that different aspects of psychological life may be more dependent on one side of the brain than the other, but in most cases both sides of the brain are involved, in some way, in most psychological functions. Thus, it is more appropriate to refer to a psychological function as being left or right "lateralized," but not "dominant."

Specialization of the Left Hemisphere.

In most right-handed people, the left hemisphere is specialized to handle speech and other aspects of linguistic processing, such as the ability to understand what others say. The ability to speak is very strongly left lateralized in most right-handed people so that the right hemisphere has little or no direct access to speech mechanisms. A similar brain organization is seen in left-handed people, but less consistently so (Strauss & Wada, 1983). Evidence that the left hemisphere is specialized for speech comes from a variety of sources. In addition to studies documenting language deficits in patients with left-hemisphere damage (Rasmussen & Milner, 1975), data from a number of neurosurgical procedures have provided comprehensive evidence for the left hemisphere's special language abilities. For example, before beginning a brain operation, neurosurgeons typically locate, and then try to avoid, regions of the brain that are crucial for language. They do this by electrically stimulating particular areas of the brain to disrupt the usual information processing mechanisms. If this renders the patient unable to speak when instructed to, then those areas may be important for language. Such explorations have shown that stimulation of the left hemisphere, but usually not the right, leads to disruptions in speech production and language processing. Furthermore, the disruptions are consistent with the general area of function subserved by the particular regions of the brain reviewed earlier. Thus, stimulation of the left temporal lobe disrupts verbal memory functions, whereas stimulation of the left frontal lobe disrupts speech production (because it involves complex motor sequences).

Another technique often used to investigate language lateralization involves injecting sodium amytal into the internal carotid artery (Wada & Rasmussen, 1960). This procedure temporarily puts one hemisphere "to sleep," during which time the neuropsychologist or neurologist can test the patient. When the left hemisphere is put to sleep, nearly all right-handed people lose their ability to speak (Milner, 1974; Wellmer et al., 2005). Split-brain research has also provided powerful evidence for left lateralization of language functions. For example, a patient with a severed corpus callosum might be asked to sit in front of a screen that makes it impossible to see objects placed in their hands. To identify the object, the patient must depend entirely on tactile information carried by sensory nerves extending from the hand to the brain. Like most nerve pathways, these sensory nerves cross over to opposite side of the brain before connecting to information processing areas in the cortex. As a result, information from the left hand initially arrives at the right parietal cortex, and information from the right hand arrives at the left parietal cortex. In a normal brain, the corpus callosum transfers this information to the opposite hemisphere in a split second. In split-brain patients, because the corpus callosum is severed, the only way their opposite hemisphere can obtain information about a touched object is if they look at it. What happens when the screen blocks the patient's view? Roger Sperry and his associates (e.g., Sperry, 1974) found that these patients have no difficulty naming objects being held in the right hand (which is connected to their left hemisphere), but when asked to name objects held in the left hand (which is connected to the right hemisphere), the patients could usually not do so. When they were asked to use their left hand to pick out a picture of the object, however, they could do so correctly every time. This finding proved that the right hemisphere "knew" what the object was but could not label it verbally. The obvious conclusion is that the right hemisphere was mute—it had insufficient access to speech mechanisms controlled by the left hemisphere.

Specialization of the Right Hemisphere.   Right-hemisphere function, too, plays an important role in language and communication, though it usually lacks direct access to the systems that allow people to speak. For example, people with right-hemisphere damage may have difficulty understanding the overall "point" of a paragraph, the plot of a story, or the punch line of a joke (Brownell, Potter, Bihrle, & Gardner, 1986; Lehman, 2003; Marini, Carlomagno, Caltagirone, & Nocentini, 2005). People with right-hemisphere damage also have difficulty understanding linguistic devices such as metaphors. So they might interpret statements like "I cried my eyes out" as if they were literally true (Gardner, Brownell, Wapner, & Michelow, 1983).

In addition to supporting these "supraordinate" levels of language communication, right-hemisphere function is important for social communication. For example, the prosody of language, or the "tone of voice," appears to stem largely from right-hemisphere function. *Aprosodia,* an interruption in normal prosody functions, occurs after right-hemisphere damage more often than after left-hemisphere damage (Schirmer, Alter, Kotz, & Friederici, 2001). A person with expressive aprosodia speaks in a monotone and sometimes must add a phrase such as "I am angry" to allow the listener to understand the intended emotional message. Those with receptive aprosodia, by contrast, may not pick up the sarcasm or anger in another person's voice, which can lead to some rather unfortunate social misinterpretations.

As Sperry and his colleagues showed, if given a nonverbal means of communication, the right hemisphere is able to perform at a level of intelligence equal to that of the left. Indeed, one of the greatest contributions of split-brain research has been to remove the right hemisphere's designation as the "minor" hemisphere and to demonstrate its capacity for high-level information processing. We now know that the right hemisphere is crucial for analyzing many types of spatial and nonverbal information, including the highly complex signals involved in social and emotional communication (Baird et al., 2006; Shamay-Tsoory, Tomer, Berger, Goldsher, & Aharon-Peretz, 2005). After all, only part of the most important information in a conversation is carried by the content of the utterances; a great deal of information is conveyed by *how* words are said. The right hemisphere is especially good at perceiving and decoding gestures, tone of voice, facial expressions, body language, and other nonverbal information, and then integrating them into a coherent message. Thus, right-hemisphere damage can cause sometimes dramatic dysfunctions in social communication (Blair & Cipolotti, 2000).

The difficulties patients with right-brain damage have in judging situations appropriately, in relating to others, and in accurately perceiving social cues is compounded by another problem—they are often unaware of their deficits. The inability to be aware of neurological problems is called *anosognosia* (Adair, Schwartz, & Barrett, 2003; Babinski, 1914). It occurs because of damage to the brain areas that allow one to self-monitor one's mental functioning and to know when things have gone wrong. Thus, even some people with severe paralysis caused by a right-hemisphere stroke do not appear to know that they cannot move all or part of their left sides (Heilman, Barrett, & Adair, 1998)! Anosognosia poses a serious obstacle to rehabilitation programs because remedial strategies are less likely to be effective if patients do not perceive that they have a problem (Andersson, Gundersen, & Finset, 1999).

Section Summary: Brain functions are localized in different regions, but those functions are not entirely compartmentalized. Brain regions, or modules, that specialize in certain functions often interact with other modules that may process information differently. The brain's modules are also connected in multiple levels. Because there are multiple connections and multiple layers of organization, damage to one area may result in impairment of certain aspects of a particular mental function (e.g., attention, visual perception) but not others. Damage to one or the other hemisphere often results in specific patterns of psychological or behavioral deficits.

PATTERNS OF NEUROPSYCHOLOGICAL DYSFUNCTION

Section Preview: Damage to specific parts of the brain are associated with particular kinds of psychological problems. Here we describe some behavioral manifestations of brain dysfunction, organized by the regions, or lobes, in which the damage occurred.

Occipital Lobe Dysfunction

Visual information is sent from the retina in each eye to the thalamus and then to the occipital lobes of the cerebral cortex. At each step along the way, this information is represented *topographically;* in other words, neighboring nerve cells respond to neighboring areas of the visual field. A similar arrangement for other types of specific sensory and motor information has given rise to the rather comical maps of the *homunculus* (literally, "little man") which display the relative size of cortical areas representing sensory information or motor output to and from various regions on the opposite side of the body (see Figure 13.2).

The most common problem caused by damage to the occipital lobe is blindness. Because about half of the retinal fibers coming from each eye cross over to the opposite side as they enter the brain, damage to one occipital lobe produces blindness in the opposite visual field. For example, damage to the right occipital lobe causes blindness in the left visual field. Usually, people with blindness due to occipital lobe damage say that they have no visual sensations in the affected visual field. But, neuropsychologists have shown that some of these people continue to process a certain amount of visual information. This phenomenon, called *blindsight,* can occur because some visual information processing occurs outside of the visual cortex (Stoerig, 2006), but without conscious awareness. So people with blindsight may duck when an object flies rapidly toward their head but not know why they have done so. Or, they may be able to guess the color of an object in front of them, though they are unaware of seeing the object.

Parietal Lobe Dysfunction

As suggested by the blindsight phenomenon, after visual information is received and processed in the occipital lobes, it is relayed to adjacent cortical areas in the posterior (back) superior (top) parts of the *parietal lobes*. These areas are classified as "association" cortex because they do not receive sensory information directly from sense organs, nor do they directly send movement commands to muscles; instead, they interact mainly with other cortical areas to combine and integrate information from multiple cortical modules.

Parietal association cortex is thus a meeting ground for visual, auditory, and sensory input, making it vital for creating a unified perception of the world. In particular, areas of the parietal lobes help create a map of our environment and the objects in it; they also perform an ongoing analysis of where objects are in our sensory world, and how they are moving. Because of this specialty, cortical parietal regions play a unique role in attention and awareness of spatial location (Ungerleider & Mishkin, 1982). Patients with damage to the parietal lobe on only one side of the brain often display an intriguing deficit called *hemineglect* in which they ignore the side of the body and the side of space opposite the damaged hemisphere (Heilman, Watson, & Valenstein, 2003). For example, people with damage in the right parietal region might not eat the food on the left side of their plates, forget to comb the hair on the left side of their heads, and neglect to button their left shirtsleeve. They might also ignore words on the left side of the page and fail to notice when a doctor or family member approaches from the left. They may even fail to notice the left side of scenes that they imagine in their head (Bisiach, Luzzatti, & Perani, 1979). Hemineglect can be so extreme in some patients that they may believe that parts of their bodies belong to other people. In an anecdote reported by neurologist Oliver Sacks (1990), a patient woke up in the middle of the night and tried to throw his leg out of bed because he thought that it belonged to an invading stranger. The hemineglect syndrome is most common after damage to regions of the right parietal lobe (probably because of the unique specialization of the right hemisphere for processing spatial information), but it can occur after damage to the left parietal lobe as well.

One way in which clinical neuropsychologists test for hemineglect is to ask a patient to draw a clock or a flower. People with hemineglect may draw all the numbers on the clock, or all the details of the flower, on one half of the paper and leave the other half blank. Other tests of hemineglect include tasks in which individuals try to cross out all of the letters or symbols on a page, or try to bisect a line in the middle. People with hemineglect may fail to cross out items on the neglected side, or they may bisect a line off-center, as if part of the neglected side of the line did not exist.

Another possible consequence of parietal lobe dysfunction, especially on the right side of the brain, is *simultanagnosia* (Coslett & Safran, 1991). Patients with this condition can see, but they have difficulty grouping seen items together in space. In essence, they can see the trees, but not the forest. Clinical neuropsychologists typically assess the presence of such parietal lobe deficits by using tests of visuospatial skills. For example, they present patients with "global–local" stimuli (Navon, 1983) such as the one shown in Figure 13.3.

Here is how one simultanagnosia patient responded when she looked at that figure (Shenker, 2005):

EXAMINER: What do you see?

PATIENT: I see T, T, T, T. . . . Do I keep going?

EXAMINER: Anything else?

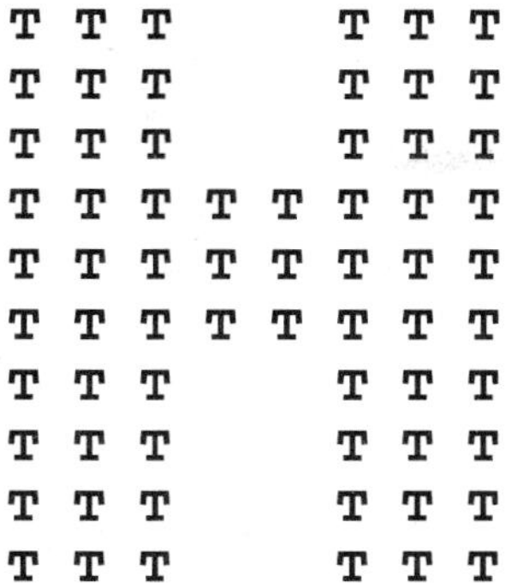

```
T  T  T        T  T  T
T  T  T        T  T  T
T  T  T        T  T  T
T  T  T  T  T  T  T  T
T  T  T  T  T  T  T  T
T  T  T  T  T  T  T  T
T  T  T        T  T  T
T  T  T        T  T  T
T  T  T        T  T  T
T  T  T        T  T  T
```

FIGURE 13.3 A "Global–Local" Stimulus for Testing Patients for Simultanagnosia

PATIENT: T, T, T, T . . . lots of T's.

EXAMINER: Are there any other letters?

PATIENT: No.

EXAMINER: Is there an H?

PATIENT: No, just T's.

EXAMINER: Is there a big letter?

PATIENT: No, I don't see one.

EXAMINER: Is there a big letter H?

PATIENT: No.

EXAMINER: Do the little letters together form the shape of a big letter H?

PATIENT: I don't see how.

EXAMINER: (Outlines the H with finger) Do you see how this is a big H?

PATIENT: I don't see an H.

Temporal Lobe Dysfunction

While incoming visual information is being integrated in the parietal lobes, that same information is also being analyzed in cortical areas of the *temporal lobe* (Ungerleider & Mishkin, 1982). This additional analysis, in cortical modules in the posterior and inferior (underneath) temporal lobes, allow a person to recognize the identity of seen objects. If these areas are damaged, the person could still see the objects, but might not be able to recognize what they are (Rubens & Benson, 1971). So when people with this problem, called visual *agnosia,* look at an apple, they might describe it as "a rounded smooth spherical object with a thin protrusion at the top" but be unable to name it, say what it is used for, where it can be found, and so on. Because visual agnosia is caused by problems that affect only visual pathways, these patients may instantly recognize and name objects if they are allowed to touch or smell them, for example. In other words, posterior inferior temporal lobe damage disrupts the ability to extract the identity of objects from visual sensations but does not destroy the more general understanding of what those objects are, nor does it impair the ability to recognize those objects via input from other sensory modalities. Some people with agnosia can be amazingly specific to particular dimensions of the visual world. For example, some patients lose the ability to recognize living things (e.g., a tree or a dog, an apple) yet retain the ability to recognize inanimate objects (e.g. a coffee cup, a book, a lamp). Such dissociations suggest that the brain honors a distinction between highly specific categories of knowledge (Farah, McMullen, & Meyer, 1991; Kurbat, 1997), a clinical observation that has prompted further study by cognitive scientists.

Certain areas of the temporal lobes also play roles in other psychological functions, such as the processing of auditory information. They are also involved in memory; indeed, the most dramatic effect of temporal lobe damage is the disruption of memory. For example, anterior (front) and medial (toward the inside) temporal lobe structures are critical for the ability to transfer information into long-term memory storage throughout the brain. So when medical conditions require surgery to remove the *hippocampus* from both medial temporal lobes, patients become unable to form new long-term memories (Scoville & Milner, 1957). Every event, no matter how often repeated, is perceived as if it is happening for the first time. These persons cannot recall previous conversations, nor can they remember the name of someone they met minutes earlier. Interestingly, their memory loss is most evident on a conscious level, because although these patients may not be *explicitly* aware of having seen a particular object in the past, their response to that object sometimes shows an *implicit* memory of having seen it. The implicit memory can be detected by improved performance after repeated practice with a puzzle task (Verfaellie & Keane, 1997) or by changes in heart rate or skin conduction in response to familiar stimuli (Gazzaniga, Fendrich, & Wessinger, 1994; Jacoby & Kelley, 1987; Milner & Rugg, 1992).

Other temporal lobe structures are important in attaching emotional or motivational significance to stimuli and events (McGaugh, 2006). People with *temporal lobe epilepsy,* for example, often display a collection of emotional traits, which some have termed the "temporal lobe personality" (Bear & Fedio, 1977). One of these traits is a tendency to see mundane events as imbued with personal emotional significance, a tendency that can lead to magical or sometimes paranoid thinking. Patients with temporal lobe epilepsy have also been described as "hypergraphic," which refers to their tendency to do a lot of writing and take a lot of notes, and they may be socially "sticky," meaning that it is difficult to end a conversation with them.

Clinical neuropsychologists often assess problems associated with temporal lobe pathology by using a variety of memory tests, such as *Benton's Visual Retention Test,* the *Wechsler Memory Scale,* and the *California Verbal Learning Test.* They also compare patients' memory for verbal material, reflective of left temporal lobe function, with their memory for visuospatial material, reflective of right temporal lobe function.

Frontal Lobe Dysfunction

Many areas in the brain's *frontal lobes* are involved in planning behavior. This kind of activity is sometimes called the *executive function* of the brain, because, like the work of a corporate executive, it entails organizing, supervising, sorting, strategizing, anticipating, planning, making judgments and decisions, engaging in self-regulation, assimilating new information, adapting to novel situations, and taking purposeful action (Miller & Cummings,

2006; Stuss & Alexander, 2000). As befits a position of such responsibility, the frontal lobes have lots of association cortex and receive input from almost all other parts of the brain. This input is necessary because making appropriate decisions about responses and actions requires taking into account as much current information as possible from the outside world and from the rest of the body. The frontal lobes can thus compare new information to previous information, assess its motivational and affective significance, and create appropriate sequences of responses.

No wonder, then, that damage to the frontal lobes can profoundly affect social and emotional functioning. A classic case is that of Phineas Gage (Neylan, 1999), a Vermont railroad worker who, in 1848, suffered frontal lobe damage when an explosion sent a steel rod into his skull, creating a hole through his frontal lobes (see Figure 13.4). He not only survived this trauma, but his speech, movements, and overall intelligence seemed unaffected. But his personality changed. Once a responsible, judicious, and socially adept fellow, he was now loud and profane and would blurt out inappropriate comments. He became irresponsible, made poor decisions, and did not follow through with plans, but he seemed oblivious to these changes (Harlow, 1848).

People with frontal lobe damage may show deficits in planning and organizing the various components of a cognitive task, but not with the components themselves. Eslinger and Damasio (1985) described a patient whose performance on multiple neuropsychological tests was unimpaired, yet he was unable to hold down a job, do household chores, or even decide what to do next. Despite wholly intact perceptual abilities and intellectual skills, he was unable to integrate all the information available to him and apply it to daily activities in an adaptive fashion. These individuals may also have problems performing goal-directed behavior. For example, when cooking a meal, they may fail to break the task

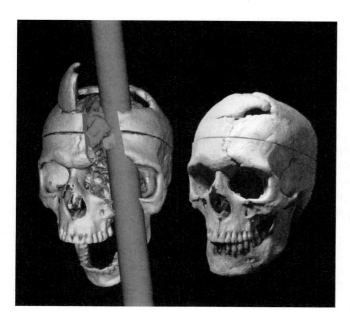

FIGURE 13.4   Based on Skull of Phineas P. Gage (right), a Digitally Remastered Image (left) Suggests the Route of Transit and Extent of Brain Damage When a 3 Foot 7 Inch Long, 1.25 Inch Diameter Rod Shot Through Gage's Head on September 13, 1848, on a Vermont Railroad

(*Source:* P. Ratiu & I.-F. Talos, 2004, "The Tale of Phineas Gage, Digitally Remastered," *New England Journal of Medicine, 351*, 23.)

TABLE 13.1

A Sampling of Neuropsychological Dysfunctions

Dysfunction	Prominent Symptom
Aphasia	Disordered language abilities
Apraxia	Impaired abilities to carry out learned purposeful movements
Agnosia	Disorders of perceptual recognition
Prosopagnosia	Inability to recognize faces
Amnesia	Disorders of memory
Aprosodia	An interruption in normal prosody (tone of voice) functions
Anosognosia	Inability to be aware of neurological problems
Hemineglect	Ignoring the side of the body and the side of space opposite the damaged hemisphere
Echolalia	Repeating the words someone else has just said
Akinetic mutism	Never moving or speaking
Blindsight	Having no conscious awareness of seeing and yet responding to moving stimuli as if it were seen
Simultanagnosia	Ability to see but difficulty grouping seen items together in space

---

down into its necessary steps, may misplan how to do each step, may mistime each step, or may not make proper adjustments—as when something starts to burn.

The problems in planning and organization created by frontal lobe damage can take curious forms. Some patients may *perseverate,* repeatedly saying or thinking or doing the same thing. It is often hard to steer the conversation onto a new topic with such people. Others simply imitate the words others say (*echolalia*) or the actions they see others do (*echopraxia*). Still other individuals display *abulia,* a reluctance to move, speak, or initiate interactions (Marin & Wilkosz, 2005). Abulic individuals appear withdrawn and unmotivated. In mild cases of abulia, patients show little variety in what they say or do. In extreme cases, they may display *akinetic mutism:* they literally never move or speak. Table 13.1 summarizes some of the many kinds of dysfunction that we have discussed.

It can be difficult to identify deficits in executive functioning using neuropsychological tests. The testing process usually includes tasks requiring a person to identify and act on temporal sequences, to plan and then revise strategies, or to solve problems whose demands change over time (Goldberg & Bougakov, 2005). Two tests commonly used to assess frontal lobe damage are the *Wisconsin Card Sorting Test* and the *Categories Test* from the HRB. Both tests use feedback from the examiner to tell patients whether they were right or wrong on each trial. This feedback is designed to signal when it is time to change unsuccessful strategies when matching or categorizing information. Patients with frontal lobe lesions will often perseverate in the same strategy even if it is unsuccessful.

Section Summary: A variety of disordered perception and behavior can occur in association with damage to various kinds of brain damage. Damage to the occipital lobe is likely to affect some aspects of vision; damage to the parietal lobe can affect attention or awareness of spatial location; damage to the temporal lobe can affect recognition, memory, or self-relevant processing; damage to the frontal lobe can affect impulse control, emotionality, and other executive functions.

NEUROPSYCHOLOGICAL ASSESSMENT

Section Preview: Clinical neuropsychologists' efforts to identify the symptoms and locations of brain damage and to plan rehabilitative interventions always begin with assessment. It can involve standardized batteries or individual tests specifically selected for individual patients. Because clinical neuropsychologists often work with physicians, they must be familiar with a wide range of medical and neurological assessment techniques.

One of the first steps clinical neuropsychologists take in dealing with patients is to assess their cognitive, emotional, or behavioral functioning. Assessment is designed to (a) establish the nature and severity of a patient's deficits, (b) determine the likelihood that the deficits stem from brain damage, (c) provide an educated guess as to where the damage might be located, and (d) identify the particular disease or the kind of damage responsible for the particular pattern of deficits seen. A deficit is defined as unusually poor task performance in comparison to the norms established by healthy, average people, or if possible, in comparison to the patient's own performance at an earlier time. In addition to using neuropsychological tests, a clinical neuropsychologist will conduct a thorough interview and examine the patient's medical records, including records of previous assessments. Information about *premorbid* (before the onset of the disorder) functioning, demographic, familial, linguistic, and educational history allows the clinician to place the current levels of functioning in a historical context. Repeated testing of the same person can yield information about how rapidly a difficulty is progressing or how general or specific the difficulty is.

Clinical neuropsychologists typically follow one of two approaches to assessment. The first is to use a predetermined, standardized battery of tests with all patients. As described earlier, these test batteries are comprehensive, and their standardization is useful for research. Further, because there is no need for expert judgments about what tests to use, these batteries can be administered by paraprofessionals. Test batteries can be inefficient, though, because they assess many functions that may not be impaired. Batteries may also become obsolete, because it is difficult to revise them to incorporate new and potentially improved tests.

The second approach to neuropsychological assessment is the *individualized method* in which an opening round of tests are routinely given to every patient, but the choice of other tests is based on the results of the first set and is tailored to answer the specific diagnostic questions of greatest interest. Individualized approaches allow in-depth assessment of particular problems, permit the use of new tests as they are developed, and focus more intensely on the specific difficulties that are most relevant for a given patient. One disadvantage of individualized approaches is that they require testers with the advanced training in neuropsychology necessary to know which diagnostic hypotheses to test and which tests will provide the information needed to confirm or disconfirm those hypotheses. Also, because different combinations of tests are used with different people, individualized testing data are less useful to researchers interested in making comparisons across patients.

Neuropsychological Test Batteries

The most widely used battery approach to neuropsychological assessment in the United States is the Halstead-Reitan Battery, or HRB (see Table 13.2 for a description of the tests making up the core of the HRB). It is suitable for persons aged 15 and older, but two other versions can be used for children aged 9 to 14 and for children between 5 and 8. Many examiners who use the HRB also administer a Wechsler Intelligence Scale, tests of memory, and personality tests such as the MMPI (e.g., Reitan & Wolfson, 1993). (The Wechsler tests and the MMPI are discussed in Chapter 5.)

The HRB evaluates four aspects of patients' performance. First, *level of performance* is assessed by comparing the patient's performance to that of normative groups; an impairment index is calculated according to the number of tests for which the patient's performance falls into a clinically deficient range. Second, *patterns of performance* are analyzed. Pattern analysis examines variations in performance on different components of a test; the most common example is the comparison of scores on verbal versus performance scores on a Wechsler Intelligence Scale. Third, emphasis is placed on *comparing right-side to left-side performance* and drawing inferences about hemispheric functioning

---

TABLE 13.2

The Halstead-Reitan Neurological Test Battery

Test Name	Test is Designed to Measure
Categories Test	mental efficiency, ability to derive a rule from experience, and ability to form abstract concepts
Tactual Performance Test	abilities such as motor speed, tactile and kinesthetic perception, and incidental memory
Seashore Rhythm Test	nonverbal auditory perception, attention, and concentration
Speech-Sounds Perception Test	language processing, verbal auditory perception, attention, and concentration
Finger Oscillation or Finger Tapping Test	motor speed
Trail-Making Test	speed, visual scanning, ability to use different sets, and dysexecutive function
Dynamometer or Strength of Grip Test	right- versus left-side comparison of physical strength
Sensory-Perceptual Exam	whether the patient can perceive sensory information separately and with standard variations in the location of the stimulation used
Tactile Perception Tests	tactile perception
Aphasia Screening Test	several aspects of language usage and recognition

when large differences appear. Fourth, *pathognomonic signs* are identified. These are deficits that are so strongly and specifically indicative of a disorder that their presence almost always establishes a diagnosis.

The HRB has shown good validity in discriminating patients with brain damage from healthy, undamaged people (Loring & Larrabee, 2006). It has also demonstrated good validity in detecting the lateralization and localization (Reitan, 1964) of brain damage, but it does a relatively poor job of discriminating between brain damage and serious psychological disorders such as schizophrenia (Jones & Butters, 1983).

Strong claims have been made for the value of another set of tests, the Luria-Nebraska battery, in discriminating patients with brain injury from patients with schizophrenia, but this battery has been severely criticized for flawed test construction, improper data analysis, inadequate standardization, and a distortion of Luria's original methods, which simply may not be translatable into items on a battery (see Lezak, Howieson, & Loring, 2004, for a review of these criticisms).

Individualized Approaches to Neuropsychological Testing

One of the most thorough and best-described individualized approaches is that of Muriel D. Lezak, a psychologist at the Oregon Health Sciences University and the Portland, Oregon, Veterans Administration Hospital. Lezak's strategy (Lezak, Howieson, & Loring, 2004) is to give all patients several standard tests that assess major functions in the auditory and visual receptive modalities as well as in the spoken, written, graphic, and constructional response modalities. Following this initial battery, which usually takes 2 to 3 hours, Lezak proceeds with "hypothesis testing," during which she shifts the focus of the assessment from one set of functions to another as the data indicate what abilities may be most impaired.

It is difficult to assess the validity of individualized approaches because they are tailored to each patient's needs and hence are not given in exactly the same form to sufficient numbers of patients to permit large-scale comparisons. And because individualized approaches depend much more than batteries do on the skill of the examiner using them, it becomes difficult to separate the validity of the tests from the clinical acumen of the examiner. Perhaps for these reasons, there is at least some judicial precedent for using only test battery approaches in court cases requiring testimony about a person's neuropsychological status (Bigler, 2007).

Despite their limitations, individualized approaches offer good construct validity and may be the best way to get the most personalized assessment of an individual patient. Individualized approaches usually reflect a better theoretical justification for the use of a particular test than does a typical neuropsychological battery. This difference is another example of the distinction between empirical and analytic approaches to test construction that we outlined in Chapter 5.

Section Summary: Clinical neuropsychologists use combinations of tests, called batteries, to assess a wide range of functioning in clients. The Halstead-Reitan Battery, consisting of 10 core tests, is one of the best known. An alternative, individualized approach involves clinicians giving a smaller group of tests initially and then selecting additional tests on the basis of the patient's performance.

NEUROPSYCHOLOGICAL APPROACHES TO PSYCHOPATHOLOGY

Section Preview: Neuropsychologists study the brain functioning of persons diagnosed with depression, schizophrenia, learning disorders, and other psychological disorders.

Research in neuropsychology has contributed to an understanding of psychological disorders, including depression and schizophrenia. Neuropsychological research has also expanded knowledge of several childhood problems, especially learning disorders.

Depression

Neuropsychologists have been interested in depression ever since Guido Gainotti (1972) documented in a systematic fashion that localized brain damage can produce emotional effects. For example, individuals with right-brain damage often show a rather cheerful, inappropriate, unconcerned reaction to their impairment and hospitalization. This "euphoric" or "indifference" reaction is often accompanied by anosognosia (unawareness of deficit). In contrast, individuals with left-brain damage often show a "catastrophic" reaction, which is characterized by tearfulness, despair, and other symptoms of depression. Subsequent studies confirmed that one-third to two-thirds of patients become depressed after experiencing damage to the left side of the brain (Starkstein & Robinson, 1988). These studies have also shown that the probability of depression rises with increasing proximity of the lesion to the front part of the brain. The closer the lesion is to the frontal pole of the left hemisphere, the more severe the depression.

To some degree, these emotional responses stem from the direct effects of losing certain areas of brain function, not simply because people are upset about being impaired. One reason for thinking so is that the degree of depression does not correlate with the severity of disability per se (e.g., Folstein, Maiberger, & McHugh, 1977). The asymmetry findings have been corroborated by EEG, PET, and fMRI measures of brain activity in the left versus the right hemispheres (e.g., Herrington et al., 2005). The left hemisphere in people who are clinically depressed is typically less active than the right; similarly, when people who are not clinically depressed are feeling sad, the left hemisphere is less active than the right hemisphere. These differences in brain activity are most evident over the frontal regions of the brain, confirming their importance for these emotional effects.

Tachistoscopic studies have also shown that when visual stimuli are projected to both hemispheres, the left hemisphere typically rates pictures as more positive than the right hemisphere—even though each hemisphere has seen exactly the same images (Heller, 1990). These results suggest that in the healthy brain, regions of the left hemisphere play some role in maintaining a positive perspective on things. It appears that negative mood states result when a lesion or other condition causes these left-side areas to be underactive relative to those in the right hemisphere.

Other studies have found that depression is associated with decreases in right posterior activity (Heller & Nitschke, 1997). People who are depressed show some of the same cognitive deficits displayed by patients with damage to parietal-temporal regions of the brain. They have difficulty with visuospatial information processing and show a number of attentional problems that are similar to patients with right-brain damage. These effects may be caused by the interrelationship of the frontal and posterior regions of the brain. Because frontal regions often inhibit activation in posterior regions, relatively greater activation in the right frontal region compared to the left may be producing too much inhibition of the right posterior regions.

These neuropsychological findings have implications not only for our understanding of depression but also for its diagnosis and treatment after brain damage (Mukherjee, Levin, & Heller, 2006). For example, it is important to consider the possibility that in addition to having problems with impaired language comprehension or expression, a patient with brain injury may also be depressed. Accordingly, neuropsychologists typically ask individuals and family members whether the individual is sleeping and eating normally and recovering as expected. If not, an underlying depression may be present and may require treatment with antidepressant medication and/or psychotherapy. Some people who are depressed, but have no apparent brain damage, also display deficits on neuropsychological assessment measures. Following successful treatment of the depression, these deficits are typically reduced.

Schizophrenia

Neuropsychologists have been deeply involved in studying brain functioning in people with schizophrenia. Early studies, most of which used tachistoscopic methods, suggested the possibility that schizophrenia is characterized by an overactivation of the brain's left hemisphere (Gur, 1978). Current studies continue to implicate the left hemisphere, but the picture is now more complicated.

Both structural (Sapara et al., 2007) and functional (Harrison et al., 2006) abnormalities have been demonstrated in the prefrontal cortex of schizophrenics. Studies measuring regional cerebral blood flow and glucose metabolism suggest that the left prefrontal region of persons with schizophrenia is abnormal because it is not activated during performance on assessments such as the Wisconsin Card Sort Test. In contrast, subcortical regions of the same hemisphere show a hyperactivation compared to controls (Rubin et al., 1991). Many researchers believe that the results of neuropsychological and brain imaging studies suggest that dysfunction of the prefrontal regions, particularly of the left hemisphere, is a fundamental characteristic of brain function in schizophrenia (Andreasen et al., 1986; Antonova, Sharma, Morris, & Kumari, 2004; Buschbaum et al., 1992; Carter, et al., 1998; Rubin et al., 1991).

These results are compatible with several observations regarding the symptoms of schizophrenia. Many individuals with schizophrenia display *negative symptoms,* which involve reductions in normal functioning, including "flat" affect, lack of initiative, lack of energy, absence of social engagement, and loss of spontaneity. These same losses are encountered in certain patients with structural lesions to prefrontal regions. Schizophrenia patients can also show *positive symptoms,* in the form of problematic additions to mental life, including nonlinear reasoning, delusions, hallucinations, intrusions into working memory, neologisms (new words), rhyming speech, and other odd language utterances. It is interesting to note that these problems can also be seen after some kind of damage to the specialized regions of the left hemisphere.

Some research suggests that disruptions of right-hemisphere processing may be involved as well, because the right hemisphere has been associated with affective and social functions that are impaired in schizophrenia (Mitchell & Crow, 2005). Other research has raised the possibility that disconnections between frontal and temporal, and perhaps other, brain regions may also be related to the pathology seen in schizophrenia patients (Brambilla et al., 2005; Meyer-Lindenberg et al., 2001). Unfortunately, however, a complete and integrated neuropsychological account of schizophrenia is still lacking.

Learning Disabilities

Given neuropsychologists' interest in cognitive abilities, it is not surprising that many of them focus their research, assessment, and intervention efforts on learning disabilities. Much of their work focuses on the role of behavioral, environmental, and social factors in these disorders, but they have discovered some fascinating biological correlates, too. Several neuropsychological studies have found, for example, that developmental dyslexia (disruptions in the ability to read) is usually related to dysfunction of the left hemisphere (Shaywitz & Shaywitz, 2005). Brain imaging studies show that variations in children's reading ability across both normal and dyslexic ranges correlate with microstructural variations in left-hemisphere nerve cell pathways (Niogi & McCandliss, 2006).

The results of postmortem examinations of people who were known to have had dyslexia also show that the structure of their left hemispheres differs from that of people without dyslexia. Researchers have also found evidence for misplaced brain cells, called *ectopias,* in the left hemisphere. Instead of migrating to their proper places during early stages of brain development, these cells appear to have "gotten lost," and some researchers suggest that ectopias can cause developmental delays and deficits in the functioning of the left hemisphere.

Assessments by pediatric clinical neuropsychologists can often help to delineate the specific difficulties in left-hemisphere functioning and help design remedial strategies. In fact, children who display school-related attentional difficulties (including attention deficit hyperactivity disorder), memory and language problems, and social and emotional problems (including depression and anxiety) are often referred to a pediatric clinical neuropsychologist. The clinician typically conducts a thorough examination and then consults with teachers and parents on how best to help the child.

Nonverbal Learning Disabilities

A different type of learning disability involves deficits in visuospatial and visuomotor skills, as well as in other abilities that depend on the right hemisphere. This syndrome of *nonverbal learning disability* was first described in the mid-1970s (Myklebust, 1975), but neuropsychological research has only recently been helping to delineate this disorder and communicate its significance to teachers and mental health professionals (McDonald, 2002). Children with nonverbal learning disabilities may have long escaped the notice of professionals because they are often talkative and show high levels of verbal intelligence. Consequently, they sound as though they should be more skillful in the nonverbal realm than they actually are. Children with nonverbal learning disabilities often have difficulty keeping up with other children on nonverbal tasks. They are slow to learn such skills as tying shoes, dressing, eating, and organizing their time and their environment. Because their difficulties are relatively subtle, they are likely to be labeled as having an emotional or behavioral problem, not a learning disability. Unfortunately, if these children are treated as "bad," "uncooperative," or "a problem" long enough, they may end up behaving accordingly. Thus early diagnosis and treatment of nonverbal learning disabilities is vital.

Nonverbal learning disabilities may result from right-hemisphere deficits early in childhood, which can dramatically interfere with normal development (Rourke, 1989). These difficulties inhibit a child from exploring the environment, learning the consequences of actions, and gaining essential experience in coordinated visuomotor skills. They can also interfere with the process of attachment between an infant and its caregivers, a process that depends on nonverbal skills. Because mother–infant interaction predicts the quality of attachment during the toddler phase, and because the quality of attachment predicts social adjustment in early and middle childhood, problems in right-brain functioning not only can create early motoric and cognitive difficulties but also can lead to abnormalities in social relationships that place the children at risk for emotional difficulties later in life.

Some of the social development difficulties seen in these children are probably related to their inability to meet the intense demands for nonverbal information processing in social situations. Overwhelmed by the task of integrating information about other children's facial information, tone of voice, physical activity, and verbal content, they fail to follow even simple exchanges. Over time, their lack of experience and interaction with other children can cause them to feel isolated, lonely, and depressed. It has even been suggested that nonverbal learning disability may be a risk factor for the development of schizophrenia.

In assessing the possible presence of nonverbal learning disabilities, pediatric clinical neuropsychologists look first for a discrepancy between Verbal and Performance IQ on the Wechsler Intelligence Scale for Children. Often, Verbal IQ will be average or well above average, and Performance IQ will be significantly lower. If the same pattern appears on other tests comparing verbal and visual-spatial/visual-motor skills, a nonverbal learning disability is likely to be diagnosed. Often, although not always, the pattern of poor performance on right-hemisphere tasks is accompanied by signs on the Halstead-Reitan Battery suggesting impaired right-hemisphere performance.

As with other learning disabilities, pediatric clinical neuropsychologists work to devise remedial programs for children with nonverbal learning disabilities. They encourage parents and teachers to take advantage of the children's verbal skills in ways that can help compensate for lack of understanding in nonverbal domains. They also recommend that these children receive individual attention from a learning disorders specialist or tutor; without this help, their academic achievement is likely to fall behind that of their classmates as the demands of school increase, as it often does with children with verbal learning problems. The children's impaired social skills can often be addressed by group therapy, social skills workshops, individual therapy, or facilitation of structured peer interactions or participation in after-school programs.

Section Summary: Depression appears to be associated with abnormal activity levels in the left frontal and right posterior brain regions. Schizophrenia appears to be associated with structural and functional abnormalities in the prefrontal cortex and regions of the right hemisphere. Left-hemisphere structure and function appears implicated in certain learning disorders. Findings such as these are important not only to help better understand persons diagnosed with these disorders but also to help alert clinical neuropsychologists that persons with damage to these regions may be at higher risks for other disorders.

THE CURRENT STATUS OF CLINICAL NEUROPSYCHOLOGY

The field of clinical neuropsychology has grown tremendously since the mid-20th century. In the late 1960s, the *International Neuropsychological Society* (INS) was founded; in the 1970s, clinical neuropsychology emerged as a distinctive professional specialty; and in 1980, the *Division of Clinical Neuropsychology* (Division 40) was formed within the American Psychological Association. Division 40 is now one of the largest divisions of the APA. In 1996, the APA designated clinical neuropsychology as a specialty (similar to clinical, counseling, or health psychology).

In September 1997, a group of specialists and educators meeting in Houston, Texas, developed guidelines for the training of clinical neuropsychologists. These guidelines specify core knowledge bases and skills. The core knowledge bases include (a) general psychology (including statistics and methodology, learning, cognition and perception, social psychology, biological bases of behavior, life span development, history, cultural and individual differences), (b) general clinical psychology (including psychopathology, psychometric theory, interviewing, assessment, intervention, and ethics), (c) foundations for the study of brain–behavior relationships (including neuroanatomy, neurological and related disorders and their etiology, pathology, course and treatment, nonneurological conditions affecting central nervous system functioning, neuroimaging and other neurodiagnostics, neurochemistry of behavior, and neuropsychology of behavior), and (d) foundations for the practice of clinical neuropsychology (specialized assessment, intervention, research design and analysis, ethics and practical implications of neuropsychological conditions). The core skills include (a) assessment, (b) treatment and intervention, (c) consultation, (d) research, and (e) teaching and supervision. Individuals acquire these skills and competencies in graduate school, internship, and postdoctoral residency. Individuals who have undergone the proper training and have had sufficient experience in the practice of clinical neuropsychology can apply to take the examination for diplomate status in clinical neuropsychology.

The Houston Conference guidelines suggest that specialization within clinical neuropsychology will become more common in the future. For instance, one of the most obvious trends in neuropsychological research and practice is an explosion in the use of functional magnetic resonance imaging (fMRI) and other high-tech brain-scanning techniques. Continued development and refinement of these techniques are likely, and they will become more accessible to researchers and clinicians. The growth of interest in fMRI and other measures of brain function has been accompanied by an increasing need for good neuropsychologists (Matarazzo, 1992). After all, if one wants to watch the activation of a brain region of interest, one must develop testing tasks that require information processing in that brain region (Miller et al., 2007). Neuropsychologists are in a perfect position to develop and use the tests that neuroscientists need to refine their exploration of brain functioning via imaging methods.

In addition to pursuing their assessment and diagnostic activities, neuropsychologists are also becoming more involved in designing effective interventions to help individual patients (Ponds & Hendriks, 2006; Winocur et al., 2007). Many of these neuropsychologists work in rehabilitation settings where their efforts to design and implement appropriate services for patients and patients' families take into account the cognitive, social and emotional consequences of brain damage as well as the long-term needs of people living with such damage. In short, neuropsychologists' contributions to providing patients with integrated and comprehensive diagnostic, assessment, and intervention plans will continue.

CHAPTER SUMMARY

The field of neuropsychology seeks to define the relationship between brain processes and human behavior and psychological functioning, including cognitive and motor abilities, emotional characteristics, personality traits, and mental disorders. Clinical neuropsychologists apply the results of neuropsychological research in their work with children and adults who have had brain trauma or injury or who are experiencing other problems related to brain impairment. Neuropsychology was not defined as a scientific field until the late 1940s, and clinical neuropsychology did not emerge as a distinctive professional specialty until the 1970s.

One of most important organizational principles underlying brain–behavior relationships is localization of function, which refers to the fact that different parts of the brain are involved in different skills or senses. Lateralization of function is another vital feature of the brain's organization that has important implications for behavior. In most right-handed people, the left hemisphere is particularly specialized to handle speech and other linguistic processing, including the ability to understand and produce spoken language. The right hemisphere is particularly specialized for analyzing spatial and other nonverbal information, including complex signals involved in social communication.

Clinical neuropsychologists use a variety of tools and one of two main approaches to assess patients' cognitive, emotional, or behavioral deficits, and to relate these deficits to specific impairments in brain functioning. In the battery approach, a standardized set of tests is given to all patients, while in the individualized approach, a set of tests is selected depending on the characteristics of each patient. The most widely used assessment battery is the Halstead-Reitan Neuropsychological Test Battery. It consists of ten specific tests and is usually combined with the MMPI and an IQ test. A prominent individualized approach has been developed by Muriel D. Lezak.

Today neuropsychology research is helping clinicians better understand a variety of psychological disorders, including depression, schizophrenia, and verbal and nonverbal learning disabilities.

APA's Division of Clinical Neuropsychology has defined the training and educational experiences necessary to become a clinical neuropsychologist and established criteria for demonstrating competence in this specialty.

STUDY QUESTIONS

1. What evidence helped decide debates in the 1800s about localization of function versus equipotentiality?

2. What were some early assessment techniques in clinical neuropsychology?

3. What did split-brain patients and research reveal about lateralization of functioning in the brain?

4. How do the functioning of modules within the brain show both localization and globalism?

5. Which functions appear to be most tied to the right side of the brain, and which to the left side?

6. What are the names and symptoms of some of the neurological dysfunctions clinical neuropsychologists see?

7. Which neurological dysfunctions are likely to be associated with damage to each of the lobes of the cortex?

8. What is the Halstead-Reitan Battery?

9. What is an individualized approach to neuropsychological assessment?

10. What neurological regions appear to be implicated in depression?

11. What neurological regions appear to be implicated in schizophrenia?

12. What professional organizations support clinical neuropsychology?

13. In what ways is clinical neuropsychology likely to continue to grow?

WEB SITES

- The International Neurological Society: http://www.the-ins.org
- APA Division of Clinical Neuropsychology (Division 40): http://www.apa.org/about/division/div40.html
- The American Academy of Clinical Neuropsychology (AACN): http://www.theaacn.org
- The American Board of Clinical Neuropsychology: http://www.theabcn.org

CHAPTER 14
Forensic Psychology

Chapter Preview: This chapter describes a number of ways that clinical psychologists contribute to the legal system and to legal decision making. Forensic psychologists contribute to decisions about whether a defendant is competent to stand trial, whether a defendant was insane at the time he or she committed a crime, and whether specific persons are a threat to others. Clinicians also become involved in civil actions such as determinations about the role of stress or the extent of psychological damages. While activities such as criminal profiling and psychological autopsies are infrequent, other activities such as evaluations in child custody and divorce proceedings are very common for forensic clinical psychologists.

In the fourth edition of this book, published in 1994, we predicted that forensic psychology—a specialty that applies psychological principles and knowledge to legal issues and proceedings—would be a "growth stock" for clinical psychologists. Our prediction was accurate. It is now clear that the demand for psychologists to contribute in various ways to the legal system has grown to the point that forensic psychology has become a major professional activity and a focal point of scholarship among clinical psychologists. Numerous signs indicate this growth surge. For example, the American Psychology-Law Society (Division 41 of the American Psychological Association) now lists almost 2,000 members and publishes its own journal, *Law and Human Behavior;* a newsletter, *American Psychology-Law Newsletter;* and a book series, *Perspectives in Law and Psychology.* In 1995, APA itself inaugurated publication of *Psychology, Public Policy, and Law,* another journal devoted to psychology and the law. There are several other journals devoted to legal issues, including *Behavioral Sciences and the Law, Law and Psychology Review, Journal of Forensic Neuropsychology, Journal of Forensic Psychology Practice,* and *Psychiatry, Psychology, and Law.* The popularity of the field is evident in the increasing number of graduate, and even undergraduate, concentrations in forensic psychology. Perhaps the most significant indication of the expansion of the field was the American Psychological Association's approval, in 2001, of forensic psychology as a specialty area of applied psychology, joining clinical, counseling, school, child, health, neuropsychology, and other practice areas.

THE SCOPE OF FORENSIC PSYCHOLOGY

Section Preview: Forensic psychologists apply psychological knowledge to a variety of legal contexts and legal decisions. They also research the effects of those decisions.

Forensic psychology (and forensic psychiatry) involves the application of mental health knowledge and expertise to the assessment and treatment of individuals who, in some way, are involved in the legal process or legal system (Weiner & Hess, 2006). The term *forensic* comes from the Latin word *forensis,* meaning "of the forum," where the law courts of ancient Rome were held.

Clinical psychologists working in the forensic area may be involved in addressing a wide range of legal issues, including whether (a) an individual is sufficiently mentally ill and potentially dangerous to justify involuntary hospitalization; (b) a person charged with a crime is mentally competent to stand trial; (c) a perpetrator of an illegal act was sane at the time of the offense; (d) a person suffered psychological harm as the result of an injury or trauma, and if so, how serious it is. Forensic psychologists might also be involved in questions relating to child custody, guardianship, and execution of wills. Clinical psychologists answer these and many other questions that arise in particular cases by applying the results of empirical research and the skills and techniques of their profession and offering their opinions during testimony at civil and criminal trials or other legal proceedings.

In this chapter, we illustrate the practice of forensic psychology by describing several areas: (a) competence to stand trial and take criminal responsibility; (b) predicting dangerousness of defendants; (c) psychological damages in civil trials; (d) competencies in civil (i.e., noncriminal) areas; (e) psychological autopsies and criminal profiling; and (f) child custody and parental fitness.

Our discussion covers the basic psycholegal questions experts must address in each area, examines the techniques clinicians typically use to evaluate these questions, and summarizes the empirical evidence and legal status associated with psychologists' activities in these areas. Remember, though, that our review of these five areas is merely an introduction to what is going on at the interface of psychology and law. Clinical psychologists play a variety of other roles in the legal system. Although we don't have the space to cover them in detail, let's consider them briefly.

Law enforcement psychology involves conducting research on the activities of law enforcement agencies and providing direct clinical services in support of these agencies (Super, 1999). A clinician working in this area might test candidates for police work to screen out those who are not psychologically fit (e.g., Gaines & Falkenberg, 1998), offer crisis intervention to police officers involved in violent encounters, consult with detectives about what kind of individual might have committed a certain type of crime, or help question witnesses in ways that enhance their recollections of crimes (e.g., Cassel, 2000; National Institute of Justice, 1999).

The *psychology of litigation* is concerned with the effects of various legal procedures used in civil or criminal trials. Clinicians working in this area may offer advice to attorneys about jury selection, study the factors that influence jury deliberations and verdicts such as eyewitness testimony (Loftus, 2003), and analyze the effects of specific portions of trials, such as opening statements, examination of witnesses, or closing arguments (Marcus, Lyons, & Guyton, 2000).

Correctional psychology is concerned primarily with the delivery of psychological services to individuals serving jail sentences after having been convicted of a crime (Schwartz, 2003). Most clinicians working as correctional psychologists are employed in prisons, penitentiaries, or juvenile facilities, but they may also operate out of a probation office or be part of a special community-based correctional program.

New research on the interface of psychology and law is constantly being published, and professional psychological services are continually expanding in the legal arena. You can review these advancements in the journals mentioned previously as well as in textbooks on law and psychology (e.g., Cassel & Bernstein, 2007; Monahan & Walker, 2006; Weiner & Hess, 2006; Wrightsman & Fulero, 2005).

Section Summary: Forensic psychologists are involved in a wide variety of research and practice activities. They contribute to cases in which defendants claim or appear to have mental illness; they provide evaluation and treatment services for law enforcement, corrections, and especially the courts; and they study the effects of these interventions as well as other aspects of legal decision making.

CRIMINAL COMPETENCE AND RESPONSIBILITY

Section Preview: The law requires that criminal defendants be competent to assist in their own defense. It also requires that, to be found guilty of a crime, a defendant must have understood that his or her behavior was wrong. Because these are psychological judgments, forensic psychologists are typically involved in decisions about criminal responsibility.

No area of law illustrates the controversies surrounding expert testimony as dramatically as the question of whether a defendant was insane while committing a crime. Proving insanity can result in a defendant's being acquitted, in which case the finding is not guilty by reason of insanity (NGRI). Alternately, the defendant can be found to be guilty but mentally ill (GBMI). If found GBMI, the defendant will be sentenced as any other convicted defendant but ordered to receive such mental health treatment as the correctional institution deems appropriate.

Courts allow defendants' mental conditions to be considered at trial because our society believes that it is immoral to punish people who, as a result of a mental disorder, either do not know that their actions are wrong or cannot control however, before a verdict is ever reached, courts must determine whether defendants are mentally competent to assist in their defense in court.

Criminal Competence

In 1996, John du Pont, the 58-year-old heir to the du Pont chemical fortune, drove up to a house on his vast Pennsylvania estate where he had allowed David Schultz, a world-class wrestler, to live while using the training facility du Pont had provided to the U.S. Olympic wrestling team. Du Pont approached Schultz, who was sitting in a car in the driveway, and killed him with three shots from a .44 magnum revolver. When du Pont appeared in court charged with first-degree murder, his attorneys claimed that he was not mentally competent to stand trial. This argument was supported by testimony from psychologists who had examined him as well as from many of du Pont's friends and acquaintances who recalled his recent odd behavior, including asking an acquaintance to check the billiard balls in his recreation room for the eavesdropping devices he claimed were embedded in them. This pretrial testimony convinced the judge that du Pont was suffering from a mental illness (paranoid schizophrenia), and he sent du Pont to a state hospital for treatment.

In the United States, it is not permissible to continue criminal proceedings against a defendant who is unable to understand the nature and purpose of those proceedings. Forensic psychologists assist in determining a defendant's competence to stand trial. The legal standard for *competence to stand trial* has not changed since the U.S. Supreme Court enunciated it in 1960: "The test will be whether [the defendant] has sufficient present ability to consult with his lawyer with a reasonable degree of rational understanding, and whether he has a rational as well as a factual understanding of the proceedings against him" (*Dusky v. Unites States*, 362 U.S. 402). In short, defendants must be able to understand the proceedings that are taking place and be able to assist their attorneys to prepare their defense.

Competence focuses on the defendant's "present ability" to proceed to adjudication and is to be distinguished from retrospective inquiries regarding criminal responsibility (such as the insanity defense), which focus on the defendant's mental state at the time of the offense. A defendant is considered competent unless and until the defendant convinces the judge otherwise. Defendants must be competent not only at the time of the trial but also at the time of sentencing and, if they received a death sentence, at the time of execution. Mental health experts, including clinical psychologists, are also asked to evaluate other kinds of competence in criminal defendants, including competence to confess to a crime, competence to waive the right to an attorney, competence to choose not to invoke the insanity defense, and competence to be sentenced and punished (perhaps by death).

The question of a defendant's competence can be raised by the prosecutor, the defense attorney, or the presiding judge at any point in the criminal process. It is estimated that between 25,000 and 39,000 competency evaluations per year are performed on criminal defendants in the United States (Poythress, Monahan, Bonnie, Otto, & Hoge, 2002). That works out to between 2% and 8% of felony defendants. With the increasing numbers of juveniles now being tried as adults for violent crimes, forensic psychologists are turning their attention to how cognitive immaturity affects the legal competence of juveniles (Cassel & Bernstein, 2007; Grisso et al., 2003).

Assessing Competence

If a question of competence is raised in a particular case, the judge will order a psychological evaluation. Most assessments take place at local community mental health centers, but

TABLE 14.1

Assessing Competence to Stand Trial

The assessment of a defendant's competence to participate in criminal proceedings usually begins with a mental status examination, a brief focused interview designed to evaluate the defendant's memory, mood, orientation, thinking, and ability to concentrate. The assessor usually then administers one or more specialized instruments, such as the Competency Screening Test (CST), the Competency Assessment Instrument (CAI), or the MacArthur Competence Assessment Tool–Criminal Adjudication (MacCAT-CA) (Hoge, Bonnie, Poythress, & Monahan, 1997).

The instruments are designed to determine the defendant's ability to

1. Understand the charges filed;
2. Understand the nature and range of possible criminal penalties if convicted;
3. Understand the adversarial nature of the legal process (prosecution versus defense);
4. Disclose to a defense attorney pertinent facts surrounding the alleged offense;
5. Relate to and communicate with the defense attorney;
6. Assist the defense attorney in planning a defense;
7. Realistically challenge the testimony of prosecution witnesses;
8. Behave appropriately in the courtroom;
9. Give relevant testimony in court; and
10. Engage in self-beneficial, as opposed to self-defeating, behaviors throughout the process. (Heilbrun & Collins, 1995).

if the defendant is suffering from a severe disorder such as major depression or schizophrenia, the evaluation may be performed at a state mental hospital or some other inpatient facility. In most states, psychiatrists, psychologists, and social workers are authorized to perform competency evaluations, and they often use special structured interviews to do so (see Table 14.1).

Although the burden of proving incompetence is only by a "preponderance of the evidence" (which is sometimes quantified as at least 51%), 70% to 90% of defendants referred for such evaluations are found competent. The more rigorous the evaluation, the more likely it is that the defendant will be found to be competent (Heilbrun & Collins, 1995), but most states have a very low threshold for competence. Here is an example of a case in which the question of competence to stand trial was raised (Wrightsman et al., 2002, p. 297):

Jamie Sullivan was a 24-four-year-old clerk charged with arson, burglary, and murder in connection with a fire he set at a small grocery store in Kentucky. Evidence in the case showed that, after closing time, Sullivan returned to the store where he worked and forced the night manager, Ricky Ford, to open the safe and hand over $800. Sullivan then locked Ford in a small office, doused the store with gasoline, and set it on fire. Ford was killed in the blaze. Police arrested Sullivan within hours at his grandmother's apartment on the basis of a lead from a motorist who saw Sullivan running from the scene.

If convicted on all charges, Jamie Sullivan could have faced the death penalty, but he was mentally retarded. He had dropped out of school in the eighth grade, and a psychologist's evaluation at that time reported his IQ to be 68. He could read and write only his name and a few simple phrases. He had a history of drug abuse and at age 15 had spent several months in a juvenile correctional camp after vandalizing five homes in his neighborhood. When he tried to enlist in the Army, he was turned down because of his limited intelligence and drug habit. Jamie's attorney believed that Sullivan's mental problems might render him incompetent to stand trial and therefore asked a psychologist to conduct an evaluation. The psychologist asked Jamie a series of questions about his upcoming trial, to which he gave the following answers:

QUESTION: What are you charged with?
ANSWER: Burning down that store and stealing from Ricky.
Q: Anything else?
A: They say I killed Ricky too.
Q: What could happen to you if a jury found you guilty?
A: Electric chair, but God will watch over me.
Q: What does the judge do at a trial?
A: He tells everybody what to do.
Q: If somebody told a lie about you in court, what would you do?
A: Get mad at him.
Q: Anything else?
A: Tell my lawyer the truth.
Q: What does your lawyer do if you have a trial?
A: Show the jury I'm innocent.
Q: How could he do that best?
A: Ask questions and have me tell them I wouldn't hurt Ricky. I liked Ricky.
Q: What does the prosecutor do in your trial?
A: Try to get me found guilty.
Q: Who decides if you are guilty or not?
A: That jury.

After interviewing and testing Sullivan, the psychologist found that his IQ was 65, which fell in the mentally retarded range, that he did not suffer any hallucinations or delusions, but that he expressed strong religious beliefs that "God watches over his children and won't let nothing happen to them." At a hearing to determine whether Jamie was competent to stand trial, the psychologist testified that the defendant was mentally retarded and consequently his understanding of the proceedings was not as accurate or thorough as it might otherwise be. However, the psychologist also testified that Sullivan did understand the charges against him as well as the general purpose and nature of his trial. The judge ruled that Jamie Sullivan was competent to stand trial. A jury convicted him on all the charges and sentenced him to life in prison.

What sort of person is usually judged to be incompetent? One large-scale study concluded that most people found incompetent are suffering from a severe mental disorder, such as schizophrenia (Poythress et al., 2002), but that is far from saying that everyone with a schizophrenia diagnosis is incompetent. Rather, people with a long history of schizophrenia or who are untreated are more likely to be incompetent to assist in their defense.

If a competency evaluation finds a defendant competent, the legal process resumes and the defendant faces trial. If the defendant is found incompetent, the picture becomes more complicated. For crimes that are not serious, the charges might be dropped, sometimes in exchange for requiring the defendant to receive treatment, usually psychotropic medication. If the charges are serious, the defendant usually is returned to an institution for treatment designed to restore competence, which, if successful, will result in the defendant ultimately standing trial. This is what happened in the case of John du Pont, who was tried and found guilty of murder. In most states, this mandatory treatment can last up to 6 months (4 months if the defendant is being tried under federal law), after which, if the person is still judged incompetent, the prosecutor may seek a civil commitment by showing that the defendant is a danger to self or others. In the case of a minor, nonviolent offense, the person might be released. Most incompetent defendants are restored to competency through psychotropic medications, at which time they are returned to jail to await trial.

Can a mentally ill defendant be forced to take medication solely to be made competent to stand trial? At least one federal court and several state courts have said yes. Consider the case of Russell Weston Jr., who, on July 24, 1998, stormed the U.S. Capitol building with a .38 caliber handgun. He was looking for the "Ruby Red Satellite System" that he claimed was spreading a deadly disease. During the attack, Weston shot and killed two police officers. Because of a history of schizophrenia and his manifestation of paranoid delusions at the time he was captured, he was sent to the federal prison medical facility in Butner, North Carolina, and evaluated for competency. In interviews with psychiatrists, who diagnosed him as suffering from paranoid schizophrenia, Weston expressed the delusion that the purpose of his trial would be to expose the threat of "cannibalism." When asked if he understood the nature of the death penalty that may be sought against him, he was nonchalant, saying that he could "wake up" whenever he wanted to. Indeed, he said he could "bring back" the victims at will. These statements, and others, indicated that he clearly did not understand the nature of the proceedings nor could he assist his attorneys in his defense.

The judge ordered that Weston receive psychotropic medications so that he could be tried. His attorneys objected to his being medicated because the prosecution might seek the death penalty. Legal wrangling over this issue was not resolved until December 2001, when the U.S. Supreme Court refused to hear the appeal of the court's medication order (Tucker, 2001). As of this writing, Weston remains hospitalized and on medication. It seems highly unlikely that he will ever be able to be tried, especially considering that he has been treated for years and has shown no improvement. The time limit on hospitalization for incompetent defendants does not apply to Weston since he has fought efforts to restore his competency.

The Insanity Defense

If Russell Weston ever is found competent to stand trial, he will no doubt plead not guilty by reason of insanity (NGRI). In order to understand the legal concept of insanity, it is necessary to understand more about criminal law and how crimes are punished.

A crime is an intentional act (or failure to act) that is a violation of criminal law and committed without a defense or excuse. But even acts that are prohibited by law generally will not rise to the level of criminal conduct unless the accused person possesses *mens rea,* the mental element of culpability. Mens rea literally means "guilty mind," or intent to do wrong.

Criminal defendants are presumed to have mens rea and to be legally responsible for the crimes with which they are charged. Therefore, if defendants plead NGRI, they must present evidence that they lacked the state of mind necessary to be held responsible for a crime. Because insanity is a legal term, not a psychological concept, it is defined by legal standards that have evolved over time.

These standards began to be formalized in 1843, when an Englishman named Daniel McNaughton tried to assassinate the British prime minister, Robert Peel. McNaughton suffered paranoid delusions that Peel was conspiring against him, so he waited outside the prime minister's house at Number 10 Downing Street, where he shot and killed Peel's secretary, whom he mistook for the prime minister. McNaughton was charged with murder but pleaded not guilty by reason of insanity, claiming that he did not know the difference between right and wrong. Nine medical experts testified that McNaughton was insane and, after hearing instructions from the judge, the jury did not even bother to leave the courtroom before deciding that McNaughton was not guilty by reason of insanity. This verdict infuriated the British public, and Queen Victoria was particularly upset because she herself had been the target of several assassination attempts. She demanded that Britain toughen its definition of insanity.

After extended debate in the House of Lords and among the nation's highest judges, a definition of insanity known as the *McNaughton rule* was enacted: ". . . to establish a defense on the grounds of insanity, it must be clearly proved that, at the time of committing the act, the accused was laboring under such a defect of reason, from disease of the mind, as not to know the nature and quality of the act he was doing or, if he did know it, that he did not know what he was doing (was) wrong" (quoted in Post, 1963, p. 113).

In the United States today, the criteria for insanity varies slightly among states. The federal system has its own rule as well, but generally all insanity laws require defendants to prove that, at the time of their crimes, they were suffering from a serious mental disease or defect and (a) lacked substantial capacity to appreciate the criminality or wrongfulness of their conduct or (b) were unable to conform their behavior to the requirements of law. In other words, the defendant has the burden of proving insanity.

Misperceptions of the Insanity Defense. At the time that John Hinckley used the insanity defense during his trial for the attempted assassination of President Ronald Reagan, press secretary James Brady, and three other people in 1982, the federal law under which Hinckley was tried did not require his lawyers prove that he was insane. Instead, it required the prosecution to prove that he was sane, a difficult task since Hinckley had

Daniel McNaughton, the man whose successful not guilty by reason of insanity plea in a 19th-century British murder case led to the legal definition of insanity that prevailed in most states for many years. His case also set the stage for controversy and continuing changes in the way courts deal with mentally ill people charged with crimes. (*Source:* The Bethlem Royal Hospital.)

a clear history of disordered behavior (Bonnie, Jeffries, & Low, 2000). After Hinckley was found NGRI, public pressure led to a revision of the federal law to require defendants to prove insanity, as is now the case in most state laws.

The uproar over the Hinckley verdict illustrates widespread dissatisfaction with the insanity plea, a dissatisfaction based mostly on misperceptions about the frequency of its use and about its outcomes. Many people believe that criminals routinely claim insanity to evade punishment. The fact is that insanity pleas occur in only 1 out of every 200 criminal cases and are successful in only 2 of every 1,000 cases. (Cassel & Bernstein, 2007). For each successful insanity plea, dozens are unsuccessful, including that of Jack Ruby, killer of Kennedy assassin Lee Harvey Oswald; Sirhan Sirhan, assassin of Robert Kennedy; and serial killers John Wayne Gacey, Jeffrey Dahmer, David Berkowitz (the "Son of Sam"), and Kenneth Bianchi (the "Hillside Strangler").

The typical defendant who is found not guilty by reason of insanity is similar to the typical defendant who is found incompetent to stand trial. This is not surprising, since most successful insanity pleas involve defendants who at one point were deemed incompetent to be tried. NGRI acquittees are generally seriously mentally ill, unemployed white males in their 20s and 30s, who have a history of hospitalization for mental illness and/or a history of arrest. Few have high school educations. Most are suffering from a serious disorder such as schizophrenia and have been charged with nonviolent crimes. However, even people diagnosed with schizophrenia or other delusional disorders may not convince a jury that they were legally insane at the time of the crime. Take the case of Andrea Yates, the Texas mother who drowned her five children in the bathtub of her Houston, Texas, home in 2001. She had a long history of serious mental illness, including schizophrenia and major depression, yet was found guilty. The jury found that, under Texas law, she knew what she was doing when she committed murder. She was sentenced to serve life in prison, but on appeal, she was retried and in 2006 was found NGRI and confined to a state mental hospital.

Do NGRI Acquittees Get Away with Murder?   Many people believe that NGRI acquittees walk free from the courtroom. But as Yates's case illustrates, only 1% of insanity acquittees are released without any restrictions, and a mere 4% are placed on conditional release; 95% are hospitalized (Steadman, 1993). In most states, the defendant's mental status is reviewed periodically. In accordance with the U.S. Supreme Court judgment in the case of *Foucha v. Louisiana*[1] (1992), defendants judged no longer mentally ill and not dangerous cannot be confined further. In fact, though, NGRI acquittees generally spend at least twice as long in state mental hospitals as they would have spent in prison had they been convicted (Rein, 2001; Steadman, 1993). It is no surprise then, that John Hinckley has been confined in St. Elizabeth's hospital in Washington, D.C., since 1982 and that, despite his annual efforts to be released, he is unlikely to get out for more than occasional supervised visits with his parents (Leonnig, 2006). McNaughton himself, whose case gave us the insanity defense, died after 20 years in a mental hospital.

The Role of Expert Witnesses in the Insanity Defense.   In federal courts and most states, expert witnesses are not allowed to give an opinion as to whether or not the defendant was "sane" or "insane" at the time of committing the offense. Sanity is a legal question that only the judge or jury can answer because there is no "insane" DSM-IV diagnosis. The expert witness can only testify as to the defendant's symptoms, behaviors, and diagnosis. Even before this restriction was codified in state and federal rules of criminal procedure, the American Psychiatric Association took the position that "[No] expert witness testifying with respect to the mental state or condition of a defendant in a criminal case may state an opinion or inference as to whether the defendant did or did not have the mental state or condition constituting an element of the crime charged or a defense thereto. Such ultimate issues are for the trier of fact alone" (APA, 1994).

According to the 1985 U.S. Supreme Court decision in *Ake v. Oklahoma*,[2] indigent (poor) defendants have the right to experts to assist in their insanity defense, but not to the expert of their choice. Absent a showing of some special circumstances or unusual disease or defect, indigents are evaluated by state or federal government–employed mental health professionals, most of whom are highly qualified and competent witnesses. Of course, a person who can afford more than one expert, or the most expensive expert, might mount a more impressive insanity defense than a less affluent defendant, but this economic reality applies to any kind of defense. Having more experts does not necessarily guarantee an insanity verdict, however; even uncontradicted mental health testimony does not always influence juries. Often jurors perceive psychology and psychiatry to be "soft sciences" that are too dependent on subjective interpretations to be used as the basis for decisions about a defendant's guilt or innocence (e.g., Faust & Ziskin, 1988; Rohde, 1999).

---

[1] 112 S. Ct. 1780(1992).
[2] 105 S. Ct. 977 (1985).

This view may change as forensic neuroscience makes its way into the courtroom. A new breed of brain experts is beginning to be recognized as experts who not only can explain how brain structure and function underlies human behavior but also can depict, with real-time, full-color imaging techniques, just what areas of the brain are responsible (Rosen, 2007; also see Chapter 13, "Clinical Neuropsychology"). Of course, jurors still must determine if brain malfunction releases someone from criminal liability, so the essence of the insanity issue has not changed.

Reforming the Insanity Defense

Two major changes have been made over the past 20 years that make it more difficult for mentally ill defendants to obtain the benefit of the insanity defense: Some states (Idaho, Utah, and Montana) have abolished the insanity plea altogether, while others have added the GBMI verdict mentioned earlier.

Guilty But Mentally Ill and Diminished Capacity Defenses.   For many decades, juries deliberating cases involving the insanity defense could only reach verdicts of guilty, not guilty, or not guilty by reason of insanity. Since 1976, however, 20 states have passed laws allowing juries to find defendants GBMI. This verdict option is available only for defendants who plead NGRI. A defendant found GBMI is usually sentenced to the same period of confinement as any other defendant convicted of the same crime. The order of sentence provides that the mentally ill defendant be treated in the correctional facility. However, such treatment is rarely adequate, if provided at all, because GBMI convicts have no guarantee of medical care beyond the minimal level required by law for other convicts (Slobogin, 1985; Steadman, 1993).

The intent of GBMI laws is to offer a compromise verdict that will decrease the number of defendants found NGRI. Indeed, research on verdicts indicates that when states allow both GBMI and NGRI, jurors usually require stronger proof of insanity before returning the NGRI verdict (Roberts, Sargent, & Chan, 1993) and render GBMI verdicts when they believe defendants may not have been sane enough to be held legally responsible for their actions but were culpable enough to warrant punishment (Sales & Shuman, 1996).

Some states have a defense in which a defendant can introduce evidence to show that at the time of a crime, he or she had a "diminished capacity" to know right from wrong or to control behavior. This defense is not designed to absolve the defendant of responsibility but to justify conviction on a lesser charge because of the defendant's incapacity to form meaningful premeditation. Former San Francisco County Supervisor Dan White, who in 1978 shot and wounded the city's mayor and killed another elected official, was found to have had a "diminished" capacity for murder based on the now famous "Twinkie defense." White claimed that his reasoning was clouded by eating too much junk food. The jury found him guilty of manslaughter instead of murder, and he was sentenced to 6 years in prison. In 1982, California abolished the diminished capacity defense.

Assessing Sanity

It is relatively straightforward to assess a defendant's competence, because it requires a determination of the defendant's present mental status. But assessing a defendant's mental condition during a criminal act that took place weeks, months, or even years earlier is a much tougher challenge for mental health professionals. To accomplish this task, a variety of methods are used, including a review of the defendant's family, educational, employment, and medical history; ascertaining if the defendant has a history of prior criminality or mental disorder and treatment; listening to the defendant's version of the crime; and administering a variety of psychological assessment instruments.

Assessments typically used include a structured interview as well as intelligence tests (usually either the Wechsler Adult Intelligence Scale or the Stanford-Binet Intelligence Scale), and several personality assessments such as the Minnesota Multiphasic Personality Inventory (MMPI-2), the Psychopathy Checklist–Revised (PCL-R), the Rorschach Inkblot Test, and the Thematic Apperception Test (TAT). Defendants whose history, observed behavior, or IQ test results suggest the possibility of brain dysfunctions may be given neurological tests like the Halstead-Reitan or Luria-Nebraska batteries. If there is a history of head trauma, brain injury, or recent change in personality or behavior, brain imaging procedures (such as an MRI and CT scan) may help determine if brain function or structure are compromised by disease or injury.(These various tests are discussed in more detail in Chapter 4, "Interviewing and Observation in Clinical Psychology," Chapter 5, "Testing in Clinical Psychology," and Chapter13 "Clinical Neuropsychology").

Although it is estimated that 20% to 25% of defendants attempt to malinger, or "fake," mental illness, assessment instruments and astute clinicians are very successful in detecting such deception (Schretlen, Wilkins, Van Gorp, & Bobholz, 1992). One famously identified malingerer was Kenneth Bianchi, the "Hillside Strangler," who murdered more than a dozen young women in California and Washington in the 1970s. Although four experts had diagnosed him as having multiple personality disorder (now known as dissociative identity disorder), a savvy prosecution expert detected that Bianchi was faking this condition. His cover blown, Bianchi abandoned his insanity plea and pled guilty to murder in exchange for the opportunity to escape the death penalty (Cassel & Bernstein, 2007).

Section Summary: Forensic psychologists help judges determine if defendants are competent to understand the charges against them and to assist in their legal defense. They also help judges and juries determine whether the insanity defense applies—whether, at the time of a crime, a mental disorder prevented defendants from understanding the wrongful nature of their behavior and from controlling their actions. Clinicians use a variety of psychological tests and other assessment data to arrive at their judgments, and then they present the information to judges and juries who make the final determination. Although used much less than is commonly thought, the insanity defense has remained controversial. Some states have abolished it; others have introduced alternatives such as the guilty but mentally ill verdict and allowed for claims of diminished capacity.

PREDICTING DANGEROUSNESS

Russell Weston Jr. had been suffering from paranoid schizophrenia long before his attack on the U.S. Capitol building. Two years earlier, Weston had been involuntarily committed to a Montana mental hospital because of his paranoid delusions and odd behavior, which included claims that President Clinton was his close friend and that he was being spied on by devices planted in television satellite dishes and cable boxes. Weston was released before the term of his court-ordered confinement ended because hospital officials deemed him to be no risk for violent behavior if he took his medications. That was a big "if," to be sure. But could psychologists have known in 1996 that Weston would kill people in 1998?

As we discussed in Chapter 3, "Basic Features of Clinical Assessment," clinical psychologists and other mental health professionals are often called upon by the courts to predict a person's potential for dangerous behavior. For example, psychologists might be asked to determine whether it is safe for someone charged with murder to be freed on bond pending trial or appeal, or whether a person found NGRI can be released from custody without posing a danger to self or society. In civil cases, psychologists might be asked to determine whether someone is likely to commit suicide and should therefore be placed in a mental hospital for his or her own protection.

ASSESSING PSYCHOLOGICAL STATUS IN CIVIL TRIALS

Section Preview: Forensic psychologists become involved in civil cases when there are allegations, such as in workers' compensation trials, that a person has suffered psychological harm. Clinicians may also help the courts determine whether someone has sufficient mental capacity to make important decisions, such as making a will or selling property.

Tort law provides a mechanism for individuals to seek redress for the harm they have suffered from the wrongful acts of another party. It thus differs from *criminal law* which—acting on behalf of society as a whole—prosecutes defendants for wrongful behavior and seeks to punish them in an attempt to maintain society's overall sense of justice. When plaintiffs in civil cases sue defendants for causing harm to them and/or to their property, the lawsuits are known as *tort actions*.

Assessing Psychological Damage in Tort Cases

Many kinds of behavior can constitute a tort. Slander and libel are torts, as are cases of medical malpractice, the manufacture of defective products resulting in a personal injury, and intentional or negligent behavior producing harm to another person. When clinical psychologists conduct assessments with civil plaintiffs, they typically perform an evaluation that, like most clinical assessments, includes a social history, a clinical interview, psychological testing, interviews with others, and a review of available records (see Chapters 3, 4, and 5). Based on these data, the clinician will reach a decision about what, if any, psychological problems the person might be suffering. This aspect of forensic evaluation is not much different from what a clinician might do with any client, whether or not the client is involved in a lawsuit.

The far more difficult additional question the clinician must answer is whether the psychological problems identified were caused by the tort, were aggravated by the tort, or existed prior to the tort. There is no established procedure for answering this question, so most clinicians try to locate all clinical records and other sources of data that might help establish the point in time at which any diagnosed disorder first appeared. When plaintiffs allege that they were targeted for harassment or some other intentional tort because the defendants knew they had a psychological problem that made them especially vulnerable, the clinician must take this prior condition into account in reaching conclusions about the effects of the tort. Sometimes people allege that a specific kind of mental harm resulted from a defendant's negligence.

Workers' Compensation Cases

When a worker is injured on the job, the law provides for the worker to be compensated, but it does so via a streamlined system that avoids the necessity of proving a tort. This system, known as *workers' compensation law,* is in place in all 50 states and in the federal government. In workers' compensation systems, employers contribute to a fund that provides workers' compensation insurance; they also waive their right to blame the worker or some other individual for the injury. For their part, workers give up their right to pursue a tort against their employers; the award they receive is determined by the type and duration of the injury and the amount of their salary at the time of the injury. Workers can seek compensation for (a) physical and psychological injuries sustained at work, (b) the cost of the treatment they receive for their injuries, (c) lost wages, and (d) the loss of future earning capacity.

Because psychological injuries or mental disorders arising from employment can be compensated, clinical psychologists are often asked to evaluate injured workers and render an opinion about the existence, cause, and implications of any mental disorders that might appear in a given case. Claims for mental disability usually arise in one of three ways.

First, a physical injury or job-related threatening event can cause a mental disorder and psychological disability. A common pattern seen in these *physical–mental* cases is that a worker sustains a serious physical injury—a broken back or severe burns, for example—that results in chronic pain. As the pain continues, the worker begins to experience psychological problems, usually depression and anxiety. These problems worsen until they become full-fledged mental disorders, resulting in further impairments in overall functioning.

The second work-related pathway to mental disability is for an individual to suffer a ~aumatic incident at work or to undergo a long period of continuous stress that leads to ~chological difficulties. The night clerk at a convenience store who is the victim of an ~ed robbery and subsequently develops posttraumatic stress disorder exemplifies such ~al–mental cases, as does the clerical worker who, after years of overwork and job ~e, experiences an anxiety disorder, perhaps even posttraumatic stress disorder.

~a third kind of case, known as *mental–physical,* work-related stress is blamed for ~ of a physical disorder such as high blood pressure. Many states have placed spe- ~ions on these types of claims, and psychologists are seldom asked to evaluate

~t years, the number of psychological claims arising in workers' compensa- ~has increased dramatically. In the 1980s, stress-related mental disorders ~st growing occupational disease category in the United States (Hersch & ~ with claims more than doubling from 1985 to 1990. Stress-related workers' compensation claims remain high in both public- and private-sector occupations (Macklin, Smith, & Dollard, 2006).

Civil Competencies

In our earlier discussion of competence to stand trial, we focused on the tasks required of defendants during the course of a criminal trial. However, the question of mental competence is raised in several noncriminal situations as well. We refer to these other situations as involving *civil competencies*.

Questions of civil competency focus on whether an individual has the capacity to understand information relevant to making a particular decision and then making an informed choice about what to do. For example, civil competency questions are commonly asked about whether a person is capable of managing personal financial affairs, making decisions about accepting or refusing medical or psychiatric treatment, or executing a will that directs how property should be distributed to heirs or other beneficiaries.

The legal standards used to define competence have evolved over many years, but scholars who have studied this issue agree that four abilities are essential to competent decision making (Appelbaum & Grisso, 1995). A competent individual is expected to be able to (a) understand basic information relevant to making a decision, (b) apply that information to a specific situation in order to anticipate the consequences of various choices that might be made, (c) use logical, rational thinking to evaluate the pros and cons of various strategies and decisions, and (d) communicate a personal decision or choice about the matter under consideration.

The specific abilities associated with each of these general criteria vary, depending on the decision the person must make. Deciding whether to have risky surgery demands different kinds of information and thinking processes than does deciding whether to leave one's estate to one's children versus a charitable organization.

Can persons with serious mental disorders make competent treatment decisions? Do their decision-making abilities differ from persons who do not suffer mental disorders? These questions have been the focus of the MacArthur Treatment Competence Study (Poythress et al., 2002), which has led to the development of a series of structured interview measures to assess the four basic abilities just discussed. Standardized interviews were conducted with three groups of patients—those with schizophrenia, major depression, or heart disease—and with groups of healthy persons from communities who were demographically matched to the patient groups (Grisso & Appelbaum, 1995). Only a minority of the persons in all of the groups showed significant impairments in decision making about various treatment options, and patients were capable of significantly better understanding when treatment information was presented to them gradually, one element at a time. However, the patients with schizophrenia and major depression tended to have a poorer understanding of treatment information and used less adequate reasoning in thinking about the consequences of the treatment than did the heart patients or community sample.

In 1990, the Supreme Court decision in *Cruzan v. Director, Missouri Department of Health*[3] recognized that states may allow patients to formalize their desire not to

---

[3]497 U.S. 261 (1990).

receive life-sustaining medical treatment should they become incapacitated or terminally ill. Accordingly, clinical psychologists and other mental health professionals may be called upon to determine a person's competence to make what are known as *advance medical directives*. The ethical and practical issues involved in determining patients' competence to make prospective end-of-life decisions are enormous; but the trend is to recognize that patients have a high degree of autonomy in accepting or rejecting a variety of treatments and health care provisions (Cantor, 1998; Rich, 1998). The state of Oregon, which has the only physician-assisted suicide law in the United States, requires psychological evaluations to rule out depression as a contributing factor in patients' decisions to end their lives.

Section Summary: When persons seek legal redress for psychological harm, they take tort action. Examples include claims for workers' compensation based on stress or claims of PTSD based on a traumatic experience. Clinicians gather evidence about the nature and extent of psychological harm using many of the same assessment procedures described in Chapters 3, 4, and 5. They also help courts to judge whether a person is mentally competent to make certain important decisions for themselves.

PSYCHOLOGICAL AUTOPSIES AND CRIMINAL PROFILING

Section Preview: Psychological autopsies are often done to help determine whether, for instance, a person's death resulted from suicide, accident, or homicide. Criminal profiling occurs when a crime has been committed but the identity of the person who committed it is unknown. Clinicians acting as profilers use psychological science to describe the most likely categories of suspects.

As already mentioned, most forensic assessments, like most other clinical assessments, include interviewing, observing, and testing living clients. Sometimes, though, clinicians may be called upon to give opinions about a deceased person's state of mind prior to death. In such cases, obviously, the clinician must conduct the evaluation without that person's participation. These postmortem psychological evaluations are known as *psychological autopsies* or equivocal death analyses (Ogloff & Otto, 1993).

Psychological Autopsies

The first psychological autopsies are believed to have been done in the 1950s, when a group of social scientists in Los Angeles began assisting the County Coroner's Office in determining whether suicide, murder, or accident was the most likely cause of death in certain equivocal cases. Since then, psychological autopsies have become commonplace, especially when insurance companies want to know whether their life insurance policyholder committed suicide, in which case death benefits could be denied. Psychological autopsies are also used (a) in workers' compensation cases when an employee's family claims that stressful working conditions or work-related trauma contributed to their relative's suicide or accidental death, (b) to decide whether a deceased individual had the mental capacity necessary to competently execute or modify a will, and (c) to support the argument made by criminal defendants that the person they allegedly killed died by suicide, not homicide.

There is no standard format for conducting psychological autopsies, but most clinicians rely heavily on documents and other life records that a person leaves behind, as well as on interviews with those who knew the decedent (Ebert, 1987). Some clinicians concentrate on evidence from the time just before the person's death. What was the person's mood? How was the person doing at work? Were there any pronounced changes in the person's behavior? Clinicians who take a psychodynamic approach look for evidence about family dynamics and personality traits appearing early in the person's life. As a child, how did the person interact with parents or other caregivers? What was the individual's approach to school? To competition with peers?

How valid are psychological autopsies—that is, do they accurately portray a person's state of mind at the time of death? There are certainly reasons to doubt their validity. For one thing, most of the assessment information comes "secondhand," because the person about whom inferences are to be made is not available for interviewing or testing. Further, as noted in Chapter 4, information obtained through third-party interviews may be distorted by memory lapses or by efforts to describe a person in an especially good, or bad, light. There is very little empirical research on the validity of psychological autopsies (Dattilio, 2006), partly because the decedent's "true" state of mind prior to death is unknown and thus cannot be compared to conclusions drawn later by clinicians. This problem may be partially solved if, in future studies, researchers were to assess how well reputed experts do when given psychological autopsy information about cases in which the cause of death appears ambiguous but is actually known. Studying the accuracy of these experts' conclusions, and the reasons behind them, may go a long way toward establishing the validity of psychological autopsies.

In the absence of better research evidence, judges have had mixed reactions to psychological autopsy evidence. In cases involving workers' compensation claims and questions of whether insurance benefits should be paid, the courts have usually admitted psychological autopsy testimony. They have been much more reluctant to do so in criminal cases and in cases involving the question of whether a person had the mental capacity to draft a will (Ogloff & Otto, 1993), because these cases may require psychologists to give testimony about the ultimate issue to be decided in a case. As noted earlier and discussed further later, that sort of testimony is usually not permitted.

Criminal Profiling

In some ways, psychological autopsies resemble a technique known as *criminal profiling*. In both cases, clinicians draw inferences about an individual's motives and state of mind on the basis of life records or other data a person has left behind. In psychological autopsies, however, the identity of the person being assessed is known, and the question is what they did, and why. In criminal profiling, the person's behavior is known, and the question is "who did it?"

One of the first examples of successful criminal profiling came in 1957, with the arrest of George Matesky, the so-called "Mad Bomber" of New York City. After trying for over a decade to identify the person responsible for more than 30 bombings in the

New York area, the police consulted Dr. James Brussel, a local psychiatrist. Brussel examined pictures of the bomb scenes and analyzed letters sent to police by the bomber. Based on these data, Brussel advised the police to look for a heavyset, middle-aged, Eastern European, Catholic man who was single and lived with a sibling or an aunt. Brussel also concluded that the man loved his mother and valued neatness. He even predicted that when the man was found, he would be wearing a buttoned double-breasted suit. When the police finally arrested Matesky, this profile turned out to be uncannily accurate, right down to the suit (Brussel, 1968).

Today, the major source of research and development on criminal profiling is the FBI's Behavioral Analysis Unit. This unit includes profilers who have training in behavioral science and who work with a very small number of psychologists and other mental health professionals who are involved in profiling activities. The unit analyzes about 1,000 cases a year (Homant & Kennedy, 1998) and has amassed large amounts of data on the backgrounds, family characteristics, current behaviors, and psychological traits of various types of criminal offenders (Douglas & Olshaker, 1995). The unit has concentrated on the study of violent offenders, especially those who commit bizarre or repeated crimes, including rape, arson, sexual homicides, and mass and serial murders. A key element of the unit's research is the interviewing of various types of known offenders in order to discover how each type selects and approaches their victims, how they react to their crimes, what demographic or family characteristics they share, and what personality features predominate among them. For example, as part of its study of mass and serial killers, the FBI conducted detailed interviews with many notorious killers, including Charles Manson, Richard Speck, and David Berkowitz.

One review of criminal profiling (Homant & Kennedy, 1998) concluded that different kinds of crime scenes can in fact be classified with reasonable reliability and that various kinds of crimes do correlate with certain offender characteristics. At the same time, research on profiling suggests several reasons for caution about its value. For one thing, in contrast to the "mad bomber" case, inaccurate profiles are quite common. Second, many of the evaluation studies have been conducted by FBI profilers themselves and have focused on a rather small number of cases. Finally, the concepts and approaches actually used by profilers have often not been objectively and systematically defined (Bartol & Bartol, 2008). In fact, a survey of 152 police psychologists found that 70% of them had serious questions about the validity of crime scene profiling (Bartol, 1996), and for good reason. Recall that, after a bomb exploded at the 1996 Olympics, Atlanta police almost immediately—and incorrectly, as it turned out—focused their suspicions on Richard Jewell, an Olympic Park security guard. Jewell was singled out because he fit an FBI profile for this kind of bombing; he is a white, single, middle-age male who craves the limelight, sometimes as a police "wannabe." In this case, the profile was wrong.

Section Summary: Psychological autopsies are assessments designed to determine the psychological causes behind a death when those causes are equivocal. Criminal profiling involves attempts to identify the psychological and demographic characteristics associated with people who commit particular types of crimes. Profiling is designed to focus police investigations and locate the guilty party. Although the practice is regarded as important by some, there is a lack of strong empirical evidence to support it.

CHILD CUSTODY AND PARENTAL FITNESS

Section Preview: Child custody cases involve more clinical psychologists than any other area of forensic work. Clinicians conduct evaluations of divorcing parents and their children to help the courts decide what courses of action are in the best interests of the children.

One of the fastest growing areas for clinicians in forensic psychology is the assessment of families in crisis.

Parental Fitness

Sometimes clinicians are asked to conduct evaluations of *parental fitness.* In these cases, the evaluator must determine if a parent's relationship with a child should be legally terminated and the child placed in permanent foster care or put up for adoption. The legal definition of parental unfitness varies among states (Azar & Benjet, 1994), but in general, the proponent of termination, usually the local or state department of child welfare, must prove that future contact between the parent and child is detrimental to the child's welfare. To prove parental unfitness in Virginia, for instance, a parent must (a) have abandoned the child for more than 6 months, (b) have been convicted of a murder or extreme physical harm to another child, (c) be physically or mentally unfit to care for the child in spite of all efforts of child welfare authorities to keep the child with the parent, or (d) have not remedied the situation that caused the child to first come in contact with child welfare workers (these latter cases typically involve physical or sexual child abuse, gross neglect of the child's physical or medical well-being, and parental drug or alcohol addiction). As in most other states, the proof must be "clear and convincing," which is quantified as a 75% likelihood.

Child Custody Disputes

More commonly, clinical psychologists' involvement in the legal aspects of family crises comes when parents are separating or divorcing. Here, the clinician is usually asked to conduct a *child custody evaluation* and to offer recommendations to help a court settle disputes over which parent can best meet the children's needs and which, therefore, should retain custody of them. The growth in these assessment activities is attributable, first, to the fact that with half of all marriages in the United States now ending in divorce, child custody issues arise in millions of families. One-third of U.S. children alive today will spend some time living in a stepfamily, and over half will spend time in a single-parent household (Arnold, 1998). Second, the preference for maternal custody that marked most of the 20th century gave way in the 1980s to gender-neutral laws that put parents on equal footing, in principle at least. Courts now routinely want to know about the parenting abilities of each parent before making a decision about custody (Liss & McKinley-Pace, 1999).

Most states permit two kinds of custodial arrangements: joint or sole custody. The law prefers joint custody, in large part because mental health experts have educated the courts about the fact that children's needs are best met when both parents are involved in their lives. But there are two categories of joint custody: legal and physical. Although parents may have joint legal custody, meaning they jointly make decisions about their children's welfare (such as those related to education and health care), generally one parent has sole physical custody; the other has visitation rights. Compared to sole legal custody, joint legal custody distributes the frequency of child contact more evenly between the two parents, leads to more interaction between the divorced parents (and generates more demands for cooperation concerning their children), and results in more variation in caregiving arrangements (Clingempeel & Repuccci, 1982).

Clinicians conduct custody evaluations under any of three sets of circumstances. In some cases, a judge appoints a clinician to conduct a custody evaluation that will be available to all the parties. In others, each party retains a different expert to conduct independent evaluations, and in still others, the two sides agree to share the cost of hiring one expert to conduct a single evaluation (Weissman, 1991). Most informed observers, including attorneys, prefer either the first or third option because they minimize the hostilities and adversarial pressures that usually arise when different experts are hired by each side (Keilin & Bloom, 1986).

Although the methods used in custody evaluations vary a great deal depending on the specific issues in each case, the American Psychological Association and the Association of Family and Conciliation Courts have published guidelines for conducting custody evaluations. Most evaluations include clinical and social histories, standardized testing of the parents and the children, observation of parent–child interactions, interviews with individuals who have had opportunities to observe family members, and a review of documents that might be relevant to the case, including medical records of children and parents.

A national survey of mental health professionals who conduct child custody evaluations found that these experts devoted an average of 30 hours to each custody evaluation (Ackerman & Ackerman, 1997). A substantial amount of this time is spent interviewing and observing the parties in various combinations. More than two-thirds of the respondents indicated that they conducted individual interviews with each parent and each child, observed each parent interacting (separately) with each child, and conducted formal psychological testing of the parents and the children. The MMPI was the test most often used with parents; intelligence tests and projective personality tests were the most common instruments used with the children (see Chapter 5). An increasing number of clinicians report using one or two instruments specifically designed for child custody evaluations: the Bricklin Perceptual Scales and the Ackerman-Schoendorf Scales for Parent Evaluation of Custody (ASPECT) (Nicholson, 1999).

The most common recommendation made by these experts was limited joint custody, in which parents share the decision making, but one parent maintains primary physical custody. Single-parent custody without visitation was the least recommended alternative. Do children adapt and function better when raised in joint custody or sole custody arrangements? One might expect it could go either way, because while joint custody allows the child to maintain close ties to both parents, sole custody simplifies custodial arrangements and minimizes children's confusion over where their home is. Indeed, most studies report either no major differences between children in the two types of custody or only somewhat better adjustment by joint-custody children (Bender, 1994; Crosbie-Burnett, 1991). However, consistent with the results of earlier research (Emery,

1982; Hetherington & Arasteh, 1988), Crosbie-Burnett (1991) found that continuing hostility and conflicts between the parents, regardless of the type of custody in force, was associated with poorer adjustment on the part of the children. It appears that the quality of the relationship between divorced parents is more important to the adjustment of their children than whether the children are raised in sole-custody or joint-custody arrangements (Hughes, 1996; Rodriguez & Arnold, 1998).

Many mental health professionals believe evaluations regarding child custody and parental fitness are among the most ethically challenging and clinically difficult of all forensic cases. For one thing, the emotional stakes are extremely high, and both parents are often willing to spare no expense or tactic in the battle over who will win custody. Associated with this conflict is the fact that the children are usually forced to live, for months if not years, in an emotional limbo in which they do not know with whom they will eventually live, where they will be going to school, or how often they will see each parent. Second, to conduct a thorough family assessment, the clinician must evaluate the children, both parents, and, when possible, other people who have observed the family's interaction. Often, not all parties agree to such evaluations or do so only under duress, a fact that often creates a lengthy and unfriendly assessment process. Third, to render an expert opinion, the clinician must possess a great deal of knowledge not only about the particular children and parents being evaluated but also about infant–parent attachment, child development, family systems, the effects of divorce on children, adult and childhood mental disorders, and several different kinds of testing (see Chapter 11, "Clinical Child Psychology").

Complicating the situation, too, are changes in traditional definitions of a "family." Increasing tolerance of variability in lifestyles has forced clinical psychologists and legal scholars to confront questions about whether parents' sexual orientation or ethnicity should have any bearing on custody and adoption decisions. For instance, the highest court in New Jersey has given gay men and lesbians the right to adopt children. This is not the case, however, in some other states.

Finally, child custody evaluations are usually highly adversarial processes in which one side challenges the procedures or opinions of any expert with whom it disagrees. Clinicians who conduct custody evaluations must therefore brace themselves for all sorts of attacks on their clinical methods, scholarly competence, personal character, and professional ethics. To guard against these, and to insure that evaluations are done competently and professionally, clinicians follow the APA Guidelines for Child Custody Evaluations in Divorce Proceedings (APA, 1994a) (see Table 14.2).

Custody Mediation

Because divorce is such a potent stressor for children and because protracted custody battles tend to leave a trail of emotionally battered family members in their wake, clinicians are devoting increasing attention to helping parents and children cope with these transitions or to finding alternatives to custody battles (Grych & Fincham, 1992; Kelly, 1991).

Custody mediation services are now often being used in lieu of adversarial court procedures. The job of the mediator is to try to help the parties agree on a resolution of their differences by providing a safe environment for communication and by helping

---

TABLE 14.2

Outline of the APA Guidelines for Child Custody Evaluations in Divorce Proceedings

---

I. Orienting Guidelines: Purpose of a Child Custody Evaluation
1. The primary purpose of the evaluation is to assess the best psychological interests of the child.
2. The child's interests and well-being are paramount.
3. The focus of the evaluation is on parenting capacity, the psychological and developmental needs of the child, and the resulting fit.

II. General Guidelines: Preparing for a Child Custody Evaluation
1. The role of the psychologist is that of a professional expert who strives to maintain an objective, impartial stance.
2. The psychologist gains specialized competence.
3. The psychologist is aware of personal and societal biases and engages in nondiscriminatory practice.
4. The psychologist avoids multiple relationships.

III. Procedural Guidelines: Conducting a Child Custody Evaluation

1. The scope of the evaluation is determined by the evaluator, based on the nature of the referral question.
2. The psychologist obtains informed consent from all adult participants and, as appropriate, informs child participants.
3. The psychologist informs participants about the limits of confidentiality and the disclosure of information.
4. The psychologist uses multiple methods of data gathering.
5. The psychologist neither overinterprets nor inappropriately interprets clinical or assessment data.
6. The psychologist does not give any opinion regarding the psychological functioning of any individual who has not been personally evaluated.
7. Recommendations, if any, are based on what is in the best psychological interests of the child.
8. The psychologist clarifies financial arrangements.
9. The psychologist maintains written records.

---

them to explore various options (Stahl, 1994). Psychologists can facilitate mediation by helping the parties emotionally accept the divorce, resolve disputes, and establish a stable co-parenting relationship (Melton et al., 1997). Indeed, a new role is evolving for psychologists in custody disputes. Some psychologists focus on the task of teaching divorced or separated parents how to co-parent their children. Known as *parenting coordinators,* these clinicians help clients address parenting issues by focusing on the developmental and emotional needs of the children and to resolve among themselves issues that otherwise would have to be decided by a judge in an adversarial setting (Bailey, 2005).

To assess the impact of mediated versus adversarial child custody procedures, Robert Emery and his colleagues conducted a study in which divorcing couples agreed to be randomly assigned to settle their custody disputes either through mediation or litigation. They found that while mediation greatly reduced the number of hearings and total amount of time required to reach a resolution, parents who mediated did not differ in terms of psychological adjustment from those who litigated. There was a consistent gender difference in satisfaction with the two methods, however. Fathers who went through mediation were much more likely to report feeling satisfied with the process than did fathers who litigated; mothers who went through mediation, on the other hand, were less likely to express satisfaction with its effects, and some measures showed better adjustment for mothers who litigated their dispute (Emery, Matthews, & Kitzmann, 1994; Emery, Matthews, & Wyer, 1991). There is little evidence showing that mediation, relative to litigation, has improved postdivorce adjustment of either parents or their children (Melton et al., 1997). Further, mediation may even be counterproductive or harmful when domestic violence or substance abuse has led to one partner having more power in the relationship (Liss & McKinley-Pace, 1999).

Section Summary: In child custody evaluations, clinicians provide the courts with evidence about the fitness of parents and about postdivorce arrangements that will most benefit the children involved. Clinicians' involvement in these legal actions is very common but can produce a number of practical and ethical dilemmas. Experienced clinicians rely on ethical codes and accepted practices to avoid pitfalls. Clinicians are also sometimes involved in conducting or arranging custody mediation, a procedure designed to reduce the number of divorce cases that end up in court.

MENTAL HEALTH EXPERTS IN THE LEGAL SYSTEM

Section Preview: Most of the forensic assessment practices we have described require clinicians to testify in court as expert witnesses on a wide range of issues. In doing so, they benefit from knowing how the legal system works and from using empirically validated practices.

Testifying as an expert witness is one of the most visible of clinical psychologists' forensic activities. Clinical psychologists (and psychiatrists) have testified in some of the most notorious criminal proceedings in recent U.S. history, including those of the Menendez brothers, O. J. Simpson, Jeffrey Dahmer, John Hinckley, Theodore Kaczynski, and Timothy McVeigh. By legal definition, an expert witness is someone with scientific, technical, or other specialized knowledge who may testify in the form of an opinion or otherwise if certain requirements are met:

1. An expert testifies at the discretion of the judge when the judge believes that the testimony will assist the court or the jury to understand evidence or determine the nature of a fact at issue.
2. The expert must be qualified by knowledge, skill, experience, training, or education to testify about a scientific, technical, or other specialized matter.
3. The expert's testimony must be based on reliable and accepted principles or methods within the expert's field.
4. The principles and methods used or referred to by the expert must be applicable to the facts or data in the case.

These standards are codified in Federal Rule of Evidence 702, Testimony by Experts, which reflects litigation in the 1990s concerning the reliability of scientific expert testimony

(*Daubert v. Merrell Dow Pharmaceuticals*,[4] 1993; *General Electric v. Joiner*,[5] 1997; and *Kumho v. Carmichael*,[6] 1999). Although the Federal Rule applies only to trials in federal court, the majority of states also apply its standards. Other states have differing requirements for the admissibility of expert testimony, but require, at the least, that the testimony be based on established and accepted scientific evidence (*Frye v. United States*,[7] 1923; Shuman & Sales, 1999). Table 14.3 describes many situations in which forensic clinical psychologists might testify.

Testimony of experts is limited by law to descriptions of parties' symptoms, behavior, and demeanor; explanation of the evaluation and assessment instruments used; and opinions about the party's mental status, including a diagnosis of mental disorder. Experts are *not* allowed to give an opinion as to whether or not a defendant is competent to stand trial or was sane at the time of an offense, whether a party was competent to make a will, which of two parents would make a better custodian of children, or any other opinion that goes to the ultimate issue before the court. As mentioned earlier, offering "ultimate opinion testimony" would be drawing a legal conclusion that usurps the prerogative of the judge and jury to apply the law to the facts and opinions given by the expert (Cassel & Bernstein, 2007).

Psychological and psychiatric expert testimony has, along with all other types of scientific expert evidence, grown rapidly in recent years. It is estimated that psychologists and psychiatrists testify in approximately 8% of all trials held in federal civil courts, and mental health witnesses participate in as many as a million cases each year (Shuman & Sales, 1999).

Expert testimony is frequent because, as shown in Table 14.3, there are many topics for psychologists to testify about. As scientists learn more about human behavior, attorneys are likely to find their research results helpful in court cases. The press usually focuses on testimony concerning criminal competence and responsibility, but testimony about these topics is actually relatively rare compared to those involving child custody, workers' compensation, tort, and discrimination cases.

Yet psychological expert testimony has often been criticized as lacking in reliability, validity, propriety, and usefulness. Former federal appellate judge David T. Bazelon, a supporter of legal rights for the mentally ill (1974), once complained that "in no case is it more difficult to elicit productive and reliable testimony than in cases that call on the knowledge and practice of psychiatry." This view was echoed by Warren Burger (1975), a former Chief Justice of the Supreme Court who chided experts for the "uncertainties of psychiatric diagnosis." Sharply worded critiques of psychologists' expert testimony can be found in several other sources (Bonnie & Slobogin, 1980; Ennis & Litwack, 1974; Morse, 1978), and one well-known guidebook is devoted entirely to the subject of how to cross-examine the expert testimony of psychologists (Ziskin & Faust, 1988).

Tightening the evidentiary standards, as Federal Rule 702 and case decisions have done, forces psychological experts to address some of the concerns lawyers, judges, and

---

[4]509 U.S. 579 (1993).
[5]522 U.S. 136 (1997).
[6]526 U.S. 137 (1999).
[7]293 F. 1013 (D.C. Cir. 1923).

TABLE 14.3

Topics for Expert Psychological Testimony

Expert witnesses from psychology testify about topics in criminal trials, civil litigation, and domestic disputes. If fact, expert testimony is given on these topics much more than on claims of insanity. Here are fourteen of the more common subjects of expert psychological testimony.

Topic of Testimony	Main Question Addressed in Testimony
1. Insanity	What is the relationship between the defendant's mental condition at the time of the alleged offense and the defendant's responsibility for the crime?
2. Criminal competency	Does the defendant have an adequate understanding of the legal proceeding in which he or she is involved?
3. Sentencing	What are the prospects for the defendant's rehabilitation? What deterrent effects do certain sentences have?
4. Eyewitness identification	What factors affect the accuracy of eyewitness identification?
5. Civil commitment	Does a mentally ill person present a danger, or threat of danger, such that hospitalization is necessary?
6. Psychological damages in civil cases	What psychological consequences has an individual suffered as a result of wrongful conduct? To what extent are the psychological problems attributable to a preexisting condition?
7. Negligence and product liability	How do environmental factors and human perceptual abilities affect an individual's use of a product?
8. Trademark litigation	Is a certain product name or trademark confusingly similar to that of a competitor?
9. Discrimination	What psychological evidence is there that equal treatment is being denied or that certain procedures and decisions discriminate against women and minorities in the schools or in the workplace?
10. Guardianship and conservatorship	Does an individual possess the necessary mental ability to make decisions concerning his or her health and general welfare?
11. Child custody	What psychological factors will affect the best interests of the child whose custody is in dispute?
12. Adoption and termination of parental rights	What psychological factors affect the best interests of a child whose parents' disabilities may render them unfit to raise and care for the child?
13. Professional malpractice	Did a mental health professional's conduct fail to meet the standard of care owed to the client?
14. Mitigating psychosocial factors in litigation	What are the effects of pornography, violence, spouse abuse, and the like on the behavior of litigants who claim that their conduct was affected by one of these influences?

appellate courts have had in the past (Smith, 1989), such as the fact that some of their opinions were not based entirely on valid research. Nevertheless, judges and juries still have to contend with the problems that arise when experts do a poor job of testifying and when attorneys who are not knowledgeable enough about psychology as a science fail to properly examine and cross-examine experts. These problems deprive judges and juries of the benefits of a well-presented and effectively challenged opinion; fact-finders cannot be enlightened by testimony they do not understand. Indeed, experts on expert testimony recommend that expert witnesses should take the role of teachers and try to present complex concepts in simple terms, using charts, videos, photographs, and models to help jurors visualize and comprehend the material (Sleek, 1998).

Another problem with psychological expert testimony is that juries are confused and frustrated when opposing sides present experts who directly contradict each other. Faced with this "battle of the experts," jurors tend to ignore them all and base their decision on nonexpert testimony (e.g., Brekke, Enko, Clavet, & Seelau, 1991). Several suggestions have been made that might reduce the overly adversarial nature of all kinds of scientific and technical expert testimony, including that of clinical psychologists. These include (a) limiting the number of experts each side may introduce to testify about a given topic, (b) requiring that the experts be chosen from an approved panel of individuals reputed to be objective and highly competent, and (c) allowing testimony only from experts who have been appointed by a judge, not those hired by opposing attorneys.

A number of scientific and professional organizations have come forward with proposals to aid the courts in finding skilled experts, an initiative supported by U.S. Supreme Court Justice Stephen Breyer (2000). The National Conference of Lawyers and Scientists, a joint committee of the American Association for the Advancement of Science and the Science and Technology Section of the American Bar Association, has developed a pilot project to test the feasibility of increased use of court-appointed experts in cases that present technical issues. The project will recruit a slate of candidates from science and professional organizations to serve as court-appointed experts in cases in which the judge decides that adversarial experts are unlikely to yield the information that is necessary for a well-reasoned resolution of the disputed issues. The project also is developing educational materials that will be helpful to scientists who are unfamiliar with the legal system (Breyer, 2000).

Section Summary: Forensic psychologists have testified in a number of high-profile cases. Because the testimony of experts sometimes conflicts, many jurors are skeptical about psychological evidence. The credibility of expert psychological witnesses increases when clinicians follow well-established protocols and provide evidence in clear language.

CHAPTER SUMMARY

Clinical psychologists are involved in forensic psychology, a specialty that applies mental health knowledge and expertise to questions about individuals involved in legal proceedings. The nature of forensic assessment depends on the questions being asked, but, like most clinical assessments, it often includes a social history, a clinical interview, psychological testing, a review of life records, and perhaps interviews with a variety of third parties.

Evaluating competence to stand trial requires assessment of whether defendants can understand the nature of their trial, participate in their defense, or consult with their attorneys. Most defendants referred for such evaluations are ultimately found competent. Defendants who plead not guilty by reason of insanity (NGRI) must present evidence that they lacked the state of mind necessary to be held responsible for a crime. Psychologists and other mental health experts evaluate these defendants to determine if they meet the legal definition of insanity. This definition has changed over time and can vary from one state to another, but the essence of the laws is that a defendant must be unable, because of a mental disease or defect, to understand the nature of a criminal act or to know that the act was wrong. A variety of reforms—including abolition of the insanity defense, further changes in the definition of insanity, and the advent of the guilty but mentally ill verdict—have been enacted in order to address public and political criticisms of the insanity defense.

Mental health professionals are called upon to assess the dangerousness of criminal defendants, a task that requires them to look into the future and predict which persons will reoffend.

Psychologists often testify in tort lawsuits, where plaintiffs seek compensatory and punitive damages for wrongful acts they claim caused them psychological harm. Their testimony concerns the nature, extent, and impact of that harm. Psychologists also conduct assessments designed to determine questions about civil competency, such as whether a person is mentally capable of making decisions about financial affairs, medical or psychiatric treatment, or disposition of assets in a will.

Clinicians involved in conducting psychological autopsies seek to determine the cause of a suspicious death, usually at the behest of courts and insurance companies, and often to rule out suicide. Psychologists with expertise in law enforcement may also be involved in criminal profiling, a practice that seeks to help find the perpetrator of especially heinous or serial crimes.

A growing area of forensic activity for clinical psychologists is assessing families in crisis. These psychologists offer opinions about the fitness of divorcing parents to retain custody of their children and whether joint custody, sole custody, or some other arrangement would be best for the children. Many clinicians are also involved in efforts to mediate, rather than litigate, custody battles. Some act as parenting coordinators who help divorced or separated parents agree on parenting issues.

While expert testimony by psychologists is common, critics doubt the reliability, validity, propriety, and usefulness of such testimony. A variety of reforms, including enactment of procedural rules that govern the type and limits of expert testimony and create registries of experts who will serve the court itself, not individual parties, may enhance the reputation of psychological expert testimony.

STUDY QUESTIONS

  1. In what ways do clinical psychologists become involved in legal proceedings?
  2. What is criminal competency?
  3. How do forensic psychologists assess criminal competency?
  4. What is the insanity defense, and how often is it used?
  5. How do forensic psychologists contribute to the determination of insanity?
  6. What variations of the insanity defense have different states used?
  7. What is a tort action?

8. In what ways do clinical psychologists become involved in assessing damages in tort actions?
9. What are psychological autopsies and criminal profiles; how do they differ?
10. How are clinical psychologists usually involved in child custody disputes?
11. What difficulties might clinicians face in conducting child custody and parental fitness assessments?
12. What APA guidelines help clinicians conduct ethically complex evaluations such as those involved in child custody and divorce proceedings?
13. What are some of the roles clinical psychologists assume when providing expert testimony?

WEB SITES

- APA's American Psychology Law Society (Division 41): http://www.apa.org/about/division/div41.html
- A description of the FBI's Behavioral Analysis Unit: http://www.fbi.gov/hq/isd/cirg/ncavc.htm#bau
- APA Guidelines for Child Custody Evaluations in Divorce Proceedings: http://www.apa.org/practice/childcustody.html

CHAPTER 15

Professional Issues in Clinical Psychology

Chapter Preview: This chapter describes professional issues within clinical psychology, including models for professional training, professional regulation, ethics, professional independence, and multicultural competence. Based on historical and current forces in the field, we also make predictions of where the field of clinical psychology is heading in the future.

As should be obvious from reading the previous 14 chapters, members in the field of clinical psychology take professional integrity very seriously. The field has changed significantly over the past 125 years, but the themes of helping people and furthering scientific understanding have remained intact for clinical psychologists worldwide.

The relatively recent changes in the field, including the increasing need for mental health services, the proliferation of the managed care system, the possibility of prescription privileges for psychologists, the focus on multiculturalism and diversity, and the intense focus and debate about evidence-based practice, all suggest that the field of clinical psychology has entered a new era. The discipline of clinical psychology looks very different than it did just 20 years ago, and it is expected to look different again in another 20 years.

The professionalization and current status of clinical psychology are our primary topics in this chapter. It is a story that has many subplots because the professionalization of clinical psychology involves several overlapping developments that have reshaped the identity of the field. We focus on five issues crucial to the struggle for professional recognition in clinical psychology:

1. *Professional training.* What training does one need to become a clinical psychologist, and what are the options for obtaining it?
2. *Professional regulation.* What are the mechanisms for insuring that a clinical psychologist possesses requisite skills and meets at least the minimum requirements to function professionally?
3. *Professional ethics.* What principles guide clinicians in determining the ethical standards for their profession? How is unethical behavior handled?

Training in clinical psychology involves learning in many venues, including the classroom, mental health clinic, research lab, and community.

4. *Professional independence.* What is the relationship between clinical psychology and other mental health professions?

5. *Professional multicultural competence.* How has the field changed with regard to diversity and the need for multicultural competence?

PROFESSIONAL TRAINING

Section Preview: In this section, we discuss the historical and current forces that have affected professional training in clinical psychology. These forces have included a number of national conferences on training, the development of the doctor of psychology (PsyD) degree, and the establishment of various training models.

You may recall from Chapter 2, "Clinical Psychology's Past and Present," that the first four decades of the 20th century saw little progress in the creation of advanced training for clinical psychologists. For clinicians of that period, experience was not only the best teacher, it was practically the only one. However, during the late 1940s, mental health and social needs brought about by World War II and the financial support provided by the Veterans Administration and the U.S. Public Health Service combined to offer clinical psychology a unique opportunity to establish its identity, expand its functions, and elevate its status. It was then that training became a central concern.

The psychologist most influential in the development of clinical training programs was Dr. David Shakow. Shakow chaired a Committee on Training in Clinical Psychology, with the task of formulating a recommended clinical training program. The committee prepared a report entitled "Recommended Graduate Training in Clinical Psychology," which APA accepted in September 1947 and published that same year in the premiere journal of the APA, the *American Psychologist.* The Shakow report set the pattern for clinical training and remains, with surprisingly few exceptions, a standard against which modern clinical programs can be evaluated. There were a great many recommendations in the Shakow report, but the three most important were that

1. A clinical psychologist should be trained first and foremost as a psychologist.
2. Clinical training should be as rigorous as that for nonclinical areas of psychology.
3. Preparation of the clinical psychologist should be broad and directed toward assessment, research, and therapy.

The Shakow report suggested a year-by-year curriculum to achieve these goals within four years.

Many of today's clinical training programs are informed by Shakow's prototype (see Table 15.1). However, it usually takes about 6, rather than 4, years to complete the entire training sequence for a PhD in clinical psychology (Norcross, Castle, Sayette, & Mayne, 2004), and the internship is now usually taken in the fifth or sixth year. The major reasons for the extra years are that most programs require a master's thesis (usually in the second year), some universities still retain requirements such as courses in a foreign language or full proficiency in statistics and research methods, and many clinical programs have added required courses on professional ethics as well as such specialty areas as human diversity, substance abuse, health psychology, clinical child psychology, sexual problems, and neuropsychological disorders.

The greatest impact of the Shakow report was that it prescribed that special mix of scientific and professional preparation that has typified most clinical training programs ever since. This recipe for training—described as the *scientist-professional model*—was officially endorsed at the first major training conference on clinical psychology, which was held in Boulder, Colorado, in 1949 (Raimy, 1950).

The Boulder Conference

The Boulder Conference on Training in Clinical Psychology was convened with the financial support of the Veterans Administration and the U.S. Public Health Service, which asked the APA to (a) name those universities that offered satisfactory training programs and (b) develop acceptable programs in universities that did not have them.

The Boulder participants accepted the recommendations of Shakow's committee for a scientist–professional model of training. Shakow's plan thus became known as the *Boulder model*.

Participants at the Boulder Conference further agreed that some mechanism was necessary for monitoring, evaluating, and officially accrediting clinical training programs and internship facilities. As a result, APA formed an Education and Training Board with a Committee on Accreditation, which was charged with these tasks. The most recent version of the APA criteria for accreditation was published in 2007 and is entitled, *Guidelines and Principles for Accreditation of Programs in Professional Psychology* (American Psychological Association, 2007b). These new standards apply to areas of "professional psychology," which include clinical, counseling, and school psychology.

TABLE 15.1

Sample Schedule for a PhD Program in Clinical Psychology

Although there are many variations in the curricula of APA-accredited clinical training programs, the schedule shown here approximates what students encounter in many of them.

Fall Semester	Spring Semester
First Year	
Psychological Statistics I	Psychological Statistics II
Clinical Assessment I:	Clinical Assessment II:
Cognitive/Intellectual/Achievement	Clinical and Psychopathology
Psychopathology–Foundations	Advanced Psychopathology
Practicum in Assessment	Practicum in Assessment
Professional Issues:	
Ethics, Cultural Diversity, and History and Systems of Psychology	Selected Core/Breadth Requirement (Social Psychology, Developmental Psychology, Learning, Physiological Psychology, Cognitive Psychology)
Second Year	
Evidence-Based Treatments I:	Evidence-Based Treatments II:
Interventions Practicum	Interventions Practicum
Selected Core/Breadth (choose one from list above)	Clinical Seminar (Advanced CBT, Behavior Therapy, Child and Family Therapy, Health Psychology, Addictions, Prevention, Dissemination, Group Therapy)
MA Research	MA Research
Third Year	
Psychotherapy Practicum	Psychotherapy Practicum
Clinical Seminar (choose one from list above)	Advanced Nonclinical Seminar
Advanced Clinical Research Seminar (Family Research, Psychopathology Research, Research in Psychotherapy)	Clinical or Nonclinical Research Seminar
Advanced Clinical Seminar	

A written qualifying examination is to be taken during the third year of graduate work, but no later than the beginning of the fourth year. Only those students who have completed their masters thesis are permitted to register for the qualifying examination.

Fall Semester	Spring Semester
Fourth Year	
Clinical or Nonclinical Research Seminar	Same as Fall Semester
Advanced Research Methods	
Research on Dissertation	
Fifth Year	
APA-Accredited Internship	

A Case Study of a Scientist-Practitioner in Action. Dr. Florence Kaslow (2008) has written or edited 30 books and has written more than 180 articles and chapters, largely focused on family functioning, relationship problems, and international issues such as treating Holocaust survivors. She has conducted workshops in over 50 countries, including presentations on psychotherapy, couples and family therapy, psychopathology, international and multicultural psychology and family issues, and family business consultation. She is the epitome of a scientist–practitioner in that she is an involved scholar–scientist and an active clinician—valuing both and remaining involved in both. Dr. Kaslow earned her doctorate from Bryn Mawr College in Pennsylvania in 1969 at a time when there were few women leading the field of psychology. At the time that she was in graduate school, her daughter, Nadine, was 7 years old and her son, Howard, was 4 years old. The children recall her as a "school girl" from 9:00 A.M. to 3:00 P.M. and then a "mommy" from 3:00 P.M. to 9:00 P.M. They also recall hearing typing late into the night after they were in bed and sometimes well into the morning while Dr. Kaslow was completing her dissertation. In case you don't know, typewriters were a lot louder than computer keyboards. After graduating, Dr. Kaslow joined the faculty of Hahnemann Medical University in Philadelphia, where she taught, conducted research, served in administrative roles, and saw clients. She was a Professor in the Department of Mental Health Sciences and chair of the Forensic Psychiatry/Psychology section as well as co-director of the PhD/JD program, which she initiated.

Dr. Kaslow's work has had a significant impact on the field of clinical psychology, largely because she can speak the same "language" as both clinicians and researchers. Dr. Kaslow currently runs the Florida Couples and Family Institute in Palm Beach Gardens, Florida where she continues to practice and write about families, family business, and family research. For example, she is one of the leaders in the movement to have relational diagnoses (discussed in Chapter 3) included in the next revision of the DSM (Beach & Kaslow, 2006). She has affected clinical psychology not only through her own work, but also by helping to interest her daughter in the field. Dr. Nadine Kaslow is a Professor on the faculty at the Emory University School of Medicine and is a leader in the field of clinical and family psycholoyg. When Nadine became president of APA Division 43 (Family Psychology) in 2002, it was the first time that a mother–daughter team had ever served as president for the same division of APA. Florence had served as president of Division 43 in 1987. Both Drs.Kaslow serve as impeccable role models for students who wish to integrate science and practice in clinical psychology.

Currently, clinical training sites are visited by an APA accreditation team about every 5 years; the longest permissible interval between site visits is 7 years. The results of accreditation site visits are published each year in the *American Psychologist* and can also be found online at the Web site of the APA Committee on Accreditation (http://www.apa.org/ed/accreditation/). As of December of 2006, there were 372 APA-accredited doctoral programs, 231 (62%) of which were in clinical psychology, with the remainder in counseling psychology (72; 19%), school psychology (58; 16%), and combined programs (11; 3%). Note that almost 50% of the programs in clinical psychology have been accredited since 1980 (McFall, 2006). In addition to these accredited programs, there are many doctoral training programs that operate without APA accreditation, either because the program has not requested a site visit or because approval has not been granted after an accreditation visit (see Chapter 16, "Getting into Graduate School in Clinical Psychology," for information about the importance of APA accreditation).

The Boulder model remains the pivot point for discussions of clinical psychology training today. However, since its birth in 1949, some clinicians have expressed discontent with it. Accordingly, they explored a number of alternatives in subsequent conferences such as the 1955 *Stanford Conference* (Strother, 1956), the 1958 *Miami Conference* (Roe et al., 1959), and the 1965 *Chicago Conference*. However, the National Conference on Levels and Patterns of Professional Training in Psychology, held in 1973 in Vail, Colorado, had the greatest impact.

The Vail Conference

Supported by a grant from the National Institute of Mental Health (NIMH), the *Vail Conference* brought together representatives from a wide range of psychological specialties and training orientations, and included graduate students and psychologists from various ethnic minority groups. The conference officially recognized professional training as an acceptable model for programs that defined their mission as the preparation of students for the delivery of clinical services. These "unambiguously professional" programs were to be given status equal to their more traditional scientist–professional counterparts.

One of the most controversial of the Vail recommendations was that persons trained at the master's level should be considered professional psychologists. The MA proposal was short-lived. In the APA voted that the title of *psychologist* should be reserved for those who have completed a doctoral training program. This policy remains in effect today, but it has come under intense attack as the number of MA psychology graduates continues to grow and as many states begin to allow master's-level clinicians to practice independently. Currently, master's-level clinical, counseling, and school psychology programs accept more applicants than doctoral-level programs do, and three times as many students graduate with master's degrees as graduate with PhDs (Morgan & Korschgen, 2006).

The Salt Lake City Conference

The 6th national conference on graduate education in psychology was held in July, 1987, at the University of Utah in Salt Lake City. The conference was convened for several reasons, but the primary issues revolved around the need to evaluate several changes that had taken place in the training of professional psychologists since the Vail conference. There was also a desire to reduce growing tensions between scientists and practitioners over numerous training and organizational issues. There were 67 resolutions passed at the conference, and perhaps the most salient for current training is that in graduate programs seeking accreditation, graduate students must be trained in a core of psychological knowledge that should include research design and methods; statistics; ethics; assessment; history and systems of psychology; biological, social, and cognitive-affective bases of behavior; and individual differences (see also Bickman, 1987, and a special issue of the *American Psychologist,* December 1987).

Clinical Psychology Training Today

What does training in clinical psychology look like after six national training conferences; several smaller conferences; countless hours of discussion, debate, and argument among clinicians, educators, and students; and, most recently, a lengthy process of revising the accreditation guidelines of APA? There is no easy answer to that question, but we can provide a general summary.

The scientist–practitioner model has proven to be a tough competitor and is still "the champ" in terms of the number of programs professing it as their training philosophy (see Belar, 2000; Peterson & Park, 2005). Many programs that favor the scientist–practitioner model, however, are struggling to find the best way to train clinical psychologists so that their practical skills are well integrated with a solid foundation of scientific knowledge.

Partly in reaction to the continued disconnect between science and practice, Richard McFall (1991) wrote a "Manifesto for a Science of Clinical Psychology," which highlighted the need for all practice to be research based. He argued that "scientific clinical psychology is the only legitimate and acceptable form of clinical psychology" (p. 76). Three years later, in 1994, McFall and other empirically oriented clinical psychologists formed the Academy of Psychological Clinical Science (APCS). Consistent with its empirical research focus, the Academy is housed within the Association for Psychological Science (APS) rather than the more practice-oriented APA. The Academy, which is made up of graduate training programs committed to clinical science, was created in response to concerns that recent developments in health care reform and licensure and accreditation requirements threaten to erode the role of science and empirical research in the education of clinical psychologists. As of 2008, the Academy had 45 doctoral programs and 9 internship sites as members (see the APCS Web address listed at the end of this chapter).

Academy programs are committed to training students in interventions and assessment techniques based on research evidence (see Chapter 10, "Research on Clinical Intervention"). Although nearly all of the programs are APA-accredited, the Academy is exploring the possibility of developing its own accreditation system. The Academy and its member programs play critical roles in moving the field of clinical psychology toward a more evidence-based orientation.

Training programs with different philosophies about how to train clinicians have also been created in the past few decades. These programs envision clinicians mainly as health care or human-services professionals and tend to deemphasize empirical research. Such programs are often housed in professional schools of psychology rather than in universities, and they usually offer the PsyD degree rather than the PhD.

Professional Schools and the Doctor of Psychology (PsyD) Degree

In Chapter 2, we noted that proposals to emphasize practice and deemphasize research in clinical psychology training appeared as early as 1917. However, it was 1951 before the first U.S. professional school of psychology, at Adelphi University, was begun; the first freestanding, non–university-based professional school of psychology was established as the California School of Professional Psychology (CSPP), which opened campuses in Los Angeles and San Francisco in 1970 (Benjamin, 2005).

Norcross, Kohout, and Wicherski (2005) argued that "*the* pivotal trend in graduate education in psychology over the past three decades is the emergence of PsyD training" (p. 974). Unlike Boulder model programs, PsyD programs provide training that concentrates on professional skills and clinical services. The emphasis is on the skills necessary for the delivery of a range of assessment, intervention, and consultation services. In most PsyD programs, a master's thesis is not required, nor is a research-oriented dissertation, although most do require a written, doctoral-level report of some type.

The number of APA-accredited PsyD programs continues to grow. As of 2006, there were 58 of them (APA, 2006). Their settings vary considerably, with 27% housed within university departments of psychology, 38% housed within university-based professional schools, 33% located in freestanding non–university-based schools, and 2% housed in other settings (Norcross et al., 2004). Norcross and colleagues (2004) found that freestanding programs enrolled more students than university professional school programs, which in turn enrolled more students than university department programs. Freestanding programs and university professional schools provided less financial aid than university-based departments of psychology. In contrast, PhD programs enrolled fewer students than PsyD programs and provided a greater percentage of students with financial aid. PsyD programs have a higher acceptance rate (41%) when compared with PhD programs that place equal emphasis on research and practice (17% acceptance) and when compared with PhD programs that mainly emphasize research (11% acceptance) (Norcross et al., 2004). There are differences, too, in selection criteria. Compared to PhD programs, PsyD programs tend to admit students with lower mean GPA and GRE scores (McFall, 2006; Templer, 2005).

Although there continue to be significantly more APA-accredited PhD programs in clinical psychology (173 versus 58), the larger class sizes in PsyD programs and professional schools leads to an interesting phenomenon with regard to the number of psychologists who graduate. Approximately 2,400 doctoral degrees in clinical psychology are earned each year, and approximately 42% of those graduating students have earned a PsyD degree (Mayne, Norcross, & Sayette, 2006). Regarding primary employment settings in psychology, PsyD graduates are more likely than PhD graduates to be employed in independent practice, managed care, and other health service settings (American Psychological Association, 2007a).

How do the two degrees compare otherwise? Norcross and colleagues (2004) found that there is a great deal of heterogeneity among PsyD training programs. It is therefore difficult to make sweeping statements about PsyD training programs generally. However, there are a number of troubling features associated with freestanding PsyD programs that are not as prevalent in university-based PsyD programs, including higher acceptance rates and lower admission criteria. Templer and Tomeo (2000) found that graduates of freestanding, non–university-based programs scored more poorly than graduates of university-based professional schools on the Examination for Professional Practice in Psychology (the licensing exam described later in this chapter). In short, it appears that the location of the training program (university-based or freestanding) as well as the training model espoused (Boulder model or other) may be more important indicators than whether the terminal degree is the PsyD or the PhD.

Training Models within Clinical Psychology

As discussed earlier, various models of training have emerged from conferences such as those held in Boulder and Vail. Currently, there are three predominant training models within clinical psychology (Cherry, Messenger, & Jacoby, 2000):

- *The clinical scientist model,* which grew out of the Academy of Psychological Clinical Science approach and places heavy emphasis on scientific research (more common in university settings).
- *The scientist–practitioner model,* which follows the Boulder model and provides for approximately equal emphasis on research and application to practice (common in traditional PhD programs and in some professional schools).
- *The practitioner–scholar model,* which follows the Vail model and stresses human-services delivery and places proportionately less emphasis on scientific training (common in professional schools and many PsyD programs).

Cherry and colleagues (2000) evaluated the training in these programs and, as expected, they found that graduates of the practitioner–scholar model spent the least time in clinical research, while graduates of clinical scientist programs spent the most time in that activity. These findings raise concerns among those who fear that professional school programs do not offer sufficient training in clinical research.

On the other hand, advocates of the professional school approach have their own concerns about research-oriented training programs. One survey found, for example, that only 51% of clinical faculty in PhD training programs reported current involvement in clinical practice, although the majority of them (74%) held a permanent or provisional license to practice clinical psychology; and an additional 5% reported that they had been licensed at some point in the past (Himelein & Putnam, 2001). So practice-oriented clinicians fear that research-oriented programs offer too little appreciation of, or training in, the realities of clinical practice.

It is important to note that when practice-oriented or research-oriented clinicians do not conform to the Boulder model's scientist–practitioner ideal, it is not always because they reject it—indeed, most think the scientist–practitioner model is a good one (Peterson, 2000). Rather, clinical psychologists often fail to integrate science and practice in their day-to-day work because the incentive systems operating in their work environments do not support it. For instance, university psychology departments seldom offer support or incentives for clinical faculty who wish to work with clients in a part-time private practice or in a nonprofit clinical setting (Himelein & Putnam, 2001), and it is increasingly difficult for clinical psychologists without postdoctoral experience to become licensed while holding an academic position (DiLillo, DeGue, Cohen, & Morgan, 2006). Conversely, few independent practice clinicians have the resources to conduct the kind of research that is published in scholarly journals (Himelein & Putnam, 2001). These differing reward structures can reinforce attitudes and behaviors that further split the field into practitioners and researchers. But as Belar (2000) points out, this is a problem with implementation, not a problem with the Boulder model itself. It sometimes seems, then, that the Boulder model is a good idea that has yet to be fully implemented—even after nearly 60 years (Stricker, 2000).

Evaluating Clinical Psychology Training

Unfortunately, we know relatively little about the comparative clinical effectiveness of graduates from the various training models. Most of the research comparing different training models focuses on the time students or professionals spend in various activities, where they are employed, how much they publish, or how they view the training they received. There is scant information about whether different training models ultimately lead to different outcomes in treating clients. This is unfortunate, but as suggested by meta-analytic and other studies of psychotherapy outcome (see Chapter 10), we would not be surprised if specific training models account for relatively small proportions of the variance in some arenas of clinical performance. Does this mean that there are no important differences across models or that it is impossible to evaluate them? We think the answer to both questions is no.

Our view is that clinical training programs can be evaluated in light of whether they produce clinicians who are competent at performing the professional functions that their work demands. This kind of technical competence is not enough, however. We believe that the single most important goal in training competent clinical psychologists is to teach them to choose and evaluate services in light of research evidence. We think that training programs should emphasize the teaching of those clinical services that have been supported by empirical evidence; they should not offer training in services or roles that have failed to gain research support. We also believe that if clinical training moves too far from its foundation in psychological science and concentrates only on teaching therapy techniques, assessment methods, and other professional skills, the clinical psychologist of the 21st century will become a narrowly specialized practitioner for whom research is of only passing interest. If that happens, clinical psychology will become a poorer science and, ultimately, a weaker profession.

The various models of training and the criteria for gaining, or retaining, APA-accreditation continue to be a point of discussion among scholars in the field. For more information on the pros and cons of professional and Boulder model training, read the special issue of the *American Psychologist* (February, 2000) on the Boulder Conference. There are several other excellent sources available, too (e.g., Kenkel, DeLeon, Albino, & Porter, 2003; Mayne et al., 2006; McFall, 2006; Norcross et al., 2004; Peterson, 2003).

Section Summary: Clinical psychologists have long debated the best way to train members of their discipline. The most influential national conferences have been the Boulder conference (which focused on the scientist–practitioner training model) and the Vail conference (which highlighted the need for professional psychologists and the PsyD degree). The PsyD degree is now well established; there is a great deal of heterogeneity in programs offering this degree. In terms of programs that are more research oriented, the Academy of Psychological Clinical Science is dedicated to using empirical methods to enhance psychological practice. Despite the sometimes vigorous debates about the advantages and disadvantages of different training models, little is known about how graduates from various programs differ in their effectiveness in treating clients.

PROFESSIONAL REGULATION

Section Preview: This section highlights the reasons for certification and licensure and delineates the process to establish both. ABPP certification is also described.

One major responsibility of any health care or human-services profession is to establish standards of competence that members of the profession must meet before they are authorized to practice. The primary purpose of such *professional regulation* is to protect the public from unauthorized or incompetent practice of psychology by impostors, untrained persons, or psychologists who are unable to function at a minimum level of competence. Caveat emptor ("let the buyer beware") is an inadequate protection when buyers such as mental health consumers are not sufficiently informed about what they should be aware of in the services they are seeking. Accordingly, clinical psychology has developed an active system of professional regulation that continues to evolve.

Certification and Licensure

The most important type of regulations are state laws that establish requirements for the practice of psychology and/or restrict the use of the term *psychologist* to persons with certain qualifications. This legislative regulation comes in two kinds of statutes: certification and licensure.

Certification laws restrict use of the title *psychologist* to people who have met requirements specified in the law. Certification protects only the title of psychologist; it does not regulate the practice of psychology. *Licensure* is a more restrictive type of statute. Licensing laws define the practice of psychology by specifying the services that a psychologist is authorized to offer to the public. The requirements for licensure are usually more comprehensive than for certification. To distinguish between certification and licensure, remember the following rule of thumb: Certification laws dictate who can be called a psychologist, while licensing laws dictate both the title and the activities allowed by psychologists.

Licensing laws are administered by *state boards of psychology,* which are charged by legislatures to regulate the practice of psychology in each state. State boards of psychology have two major functions:

- determining the standards for admission to the profession and administering procedures for the selection and examination of candidates, and

- regulating professional practice and conducting disciplinary proceedings involving alleged violators of professional standards.

Today, all 50 states, the District of Columbia, and all Canadian provinces have certification or licensure laws. Many states combine their certification and licensure laws into one statute.

The steps involved in becoming licensed differ somewhat from place to place, but there is enough uniformity in the procedures of most U.S. states to offer a rough sketch of how the aspiring clinical psychologist would approach this task (see Table 15.2).

Currently, the *Association of State and Provincial Psychology Boards* (ASPPB) coordinates the activities of the state boards of psychology and brings about uniformity in standards and procedures. ASPPB has developed a Code of Conduct for psychologists that consists of rules of professional behavior, and it also developed a standardized, objective test for use by state boards in examining candidates for licensure. First released in 1964 and revised frequently since then, this *Examination for Professional Practice in Psychology* (EPPP) is sometimes called the *multistate* or *national exam* because all jurisdictions can use it as a part of their examination procedure. A person must meet the requirements for licensure to take the examination, which is available throughout the year at various computer vendor sites (www.asppb.org).

Candidates' graduate training programs and clinical internship experiences are also evaluated as part of their eligibility for licensure. A number of states, such as Florida, Oklahoma, and Utah, now allow only graduates of APA-accredited doctoral programs to obtain licensure, so a student's choice of a graduate training program may influence his or her ability to obtain a license to practice clinical psychology (see Chapter 16).

After completing the doctoral degree, psychology graduates in most states must complete postdoctoral supervised activities in order to be eligible for licensure. These postdoctoral activities can include direct clinical practice, research, teaching, consulting, and the like, but in most states the work must be closely supervised by a licensed psychologist. Postdoctoral positions can be APA-accredited (Kaslow & Echols, 2006), but many psychologists receive postdoctoral training within the context of their first job. A review of the licensing laws across the United States shows that all the states except Alabama and Washington require some type of postdoctoral supervision of professional experience: Most require between 1,500 and 2,000 hours of such experience although Washington, DC and Michigan require as many as 4,000 hours (DiLillo et al., 2006).

In most states, psychologists are required to keep their license or certificate up to date by paying a periodic renewal fee and by documenting involvement in *continuing education* (CE). The amount of continuing education hours varies across the United States, with a range of 20 to 40 hours required per 2-year licensing cycle (Wright, 2005).

Because licensing laws vary among states, there is little *reciprocity* from state to state, meaning that someone licensed as a psychologist in one state cannot automatically transfer licensure to another. The issue of whether reciprocity

TABLE 15.2

So You Want to Be a Licensed Psychologist?

Imagine you have just completed a doctoral program in clinical psychology and are now interested in becoming a licensed clinical psychologist. What steps would you have to take? The following hurdles will be encountered in many states. First, you must ask that the state board of psychology review your credentials to determine your eligibility for examination. Their decision is based on several criteria:

1. *Administrative Requirements.* You must have reached a certain age, be a U.S. citizen, and have been a resident in the state for some minimum period. Not too much can be done about these requirements; you either meet them or you do not. One bit of advice: Don't commit any felonies, engage in treason, or libel your governor. These activities are judged to be indicative of poor moral character and may leave you plenty of time to fantasize about licensure while in prison.

2. *Education.* Most states require a doctoral degree in psychology from an accredited university. In most states, accreditation refers to accreditation of the university by a recognized accrediting agency, but many states have begun to require that you graduate from an APA-accredited program. Official graduate and undergraduate transcripts are required.

3. *Experience.* This usually amounts to one, or more commonly two, years of supervised professional experience in a setting approved by the board. Some of the experience must be postdoctoral; letters of reference will be required from your supervisor(s). If, after scrutinizing your credentials, the board finds that you are eligible for examination, you will be invited to take an examination. Here is what to expect:

Examination Fee.   There is a charge for the examination and for having the state board review your credentials. As of 2008, the Examination for Professional Practice in Psychology (EPPP) examination cost $515, and the state board fees ranged from $50 in Illinois to $985 in Florida, with most falling into the range of $200 to $300 (DiLillo, DeGue, Cohen, & Morgan, 2006).

The Examination.   Many states use the EPPP national examination that contains about 200 objective items covering general psychology, methodology, applications of psychology, and professional conduct and ethics. Because many candidates want to practice a specialty like clinical, school, or industrial psychology, state boards sometimes provide specialized state tests in these areas or related to state laws and regulations. You may also be required to take an oral examination given by the board in which any material relevant to psychology may be covered. If you pass—congratulations!!! Now you have to pay an annual fee to retain your license, attend continuing education courses, and pay for malpractice insurance. No really, congratulations!!

Reexamination.   If you fail any part of the examination, you will be given another chance to take that portion. Most boards feel that twice is enough, however; so if you fail the second time, it might be wise to reconsider the advantages of the family business.

should be expanded continues to be debated (Hall & Boucher, 2003; Jonason, DeMers, Vaughn, & Reaves, 2003; Merrill, 2003; Rehm & DeMers, 2006).

Licensed psychologists who have at least 5 years of professional experience, who have no professional disciplinary actions filed against them, and who meet certain other requirements can apply for a Certificate of Professional Qualification in Psychology through ASPPB. This certificate can be useful in seeking licensure in a state other than the one in which the person was originally licensed (Robinson & Habben, 2003). Similarly, seeking certification through the National Health Service Providers in Psychology or obtaining diplomate status through the American Board of Professional Psychology (ABPP; see next section) may give practicing psychologists more mobility across state lines (Robinson & Habben, 2003).

ABPP Certification

Another type of professional regulation is certification by the American Board of Professional Psychology (ABPP). ABPP was founded in 1947 as a national organization that certifies the professional competence of psychologists. Its certification is signified by the award of a diploma in one of 13 specialty-specific areas:

Child and adolescent
Clinical
Clinical health
Clinical neuropsychology
Cognitive and behavioral
Counseling
Family
Forensic
Group
Organizational and business
Psychoanalysis
Rehabilitation
School

Although it carries no special legal authority, an ABPP diploma is considered more prestigious than licensure. While licensure signifies a *minimal* level of competence (and is required before seeking diplomate status), diplomate status is an endorsement of professional expertise, an indication that the person possesses a masterful knowledge of some specialty field. Accordingly, requirements for the ABPP diploma are more rigorous than for licensure. Depending on the specialty-specific area, multiple years of experience are a prerequisite to even take the ABPP examination, which is conducted by a group of diplomates who observe the candidate dealing directly with clinical situations (e.g., giving a test or interacting with a therapy client) and who conduct an oral examination that includes the following related topics: professional knowledge, assessment competence, intervention competence, interpersonal competence with clients, ethical and legal standards and behavior, commitment to the specialty and awareness of current issues, and competence in supervision and consultation (Finch, Simon, & Nezu, 2006). More information about ABPP diplomate status can be found at http://www.abpp.org, a Web site that also provides a searchable Directory of Specialists for individuals interested in finding an ABPP professional in their geographic location.

Section Summary: In order to protect the public from untrained professionals, states and other regulating bodies have developed certification and licensing laws regarding the practice of psychology. In most states, certification refers to the right to call oneself a psychologist and licensure refers to the activities that clinicians are allowed to perform. Whereas certification and licensure confirm a minimum set of training criteria, the ABPP provides confirmation of excellent skills in the area of clinical practice.

PROFESSIONAL ETHICS

Section Preview: In several previous chapters, we discussed the APA *Ethical Principles of Psychologists and Code of Conduct,* or Ethics Code (American Psychological Association, 2002b). Here we describe how the Ethics Code is organized, how standards are implemented, and how ethical violations are reviewed and acted upon. We also discuss malpractice and malpractice litigation.

Ethical Standards of the American Psychological Association

The Ethical Principles of the APA consist of a Preamble, General Principles, and a large number of specific Ethical Standards. The Preamble and General Principles (see Table 15.3), are not enforceable rules; they are statements of the aspirations of psychologists to attain their highest ideals, and they provide guidance to psychologists who are evaluating what would be ethically desirable behavior in certain situations. In contrast, the Ethical Standards themselves are enforceable. They apply to members of APA and may be used by other organizations, such as state boards of psychology and courts, to judge and sanction the behavior of a psychologist, whether or not the psychologist is an APA member.

These Ethical Standards are organized under the following headings:

1. *Resolving Ethical Issues.* This first section contains standards about how psychologists are to resolve ethical questions or complaints.

2. *Competence.* This section states that psychologists must be trained in their specific area of expertise and that they must continue to keep current in their field in order to maintain competence. This section also addresses the issue of when psychologists have personal problems or conflicts that limit their ability to practice in a competent manner.

3. *Human Relations.* These ethical standards deal with such topics as preventing unfair discrimination, sexual or other harassment, multiple relationships, conflict of interest, providing informed consent, and avoiding termination of clinical services when it is not in the best interest of the client.

4. *Privacy and Confidentiality.* These rules cover psychologists' obligations to protect their clients' rights to confidentiality and privacy.

5. *Advertising and Other Public Statements.* Standards that control the way psychologists publicize their services and their professional credentials are presented under this category.

TABLE 15.3

Ethical Principles of Psychologists and Code of Conduct: Preamble and General Principles

---

Preamble

Psychologists are committed to increasing scientific and professional knowledge of behavior and people's understanding of themselves and others and to the use of such knowledge to improve the condition of individuals, organizations, and society. Psychologists respect and protect civil and human rights and the central importance of freedom of inquiry and expression in research, teaching, and publication. They strive to help the public in developing informed judgments and choices concerning human behavior. In doing so, they perform many roles, such as researcher, educator, diagnostician, therapist, supervisor, consultant, administrator, social interventionist, and expert witness. The Ethics Code provides a common set of principles and standards upon which psychologists build their professional and scientific work.

This Ethics Code is intended to provide specific standards to cover most situations encountered by psychologists. It has as its goals the welfare and protection of individuals and groups with whom psychologist work and the education of members, students, and the public regarding ethical standards of the discipline.

The development of a dynamic set of ethical standards for psychologists' work-related conduct requires a personal commitment and lifelong effort to act ethically; to encourage ethical behavior by students, supervisees, employees, and colleagues; and to consult with others concerning ethical problems.

General Principles

This section consists of General Principles. General Principles, as opposed to Ethical Standards, are aspirational in nature. Their intent is to guide and inspire psychologists toward the very highest ethical ideals of the profession. General Principles, in contrast to Ethical Standards, do not represent obligations and should not form the basis for imposing sanctions. Relying upon General Principles for either of these reasons distorts both their meaning and purpose.

Principle A: Beneficence and Nonmaleficence. Psychologists strive to benefit those with whom they work and take care to do no harm. In their pro-

fessional actions, psychologists seek to safeguard the welfare and rights of those with whom they interact professionally and other affected persons, and the welfare of animal subjects of research. When conflicts occur among psychologists' obligations or concerns, they attempt to resolve these conflicts in a responsible fashion that avoids or minimizes harm. Because psychologists' scientific and professional judgments and actions may affect the lives of others, they are alert to and guard against personal, financial, social, organizational, or political factors that might lead to misuse of their influence. Psychologists strive to be aware of the possible effect of their own physical and mental health on their ability to help those with whom they work.

Principle B: Fidelity and Responsibility. Psychologists establish relationships of trust with those with whom they work. They are aware of their professional and scientific responsibilities to society and to the specific communities in which they work. Psychologists uphold professional standards of conduct, clarify their professional roles and obligations, accept appropriate responsibility for their behavior, and seek to manage conflicts of interest that could lead to exploitation or harm. Psychologists consult with, refer to, or cooperate with other professionals and institutions to the extent needed to serve the best interests of those with whom they work. They are concerned about the ethical compliance of their colleagues' scientific and professional conduct. Psychologists strive to contribute a portion of their professional time for little or no compensation or personal advantage.

Principle C: Integrity. Psychologists seek to promote accuracy, honesty, and truthfulness in the science, teaching, and practice of psychology. In these activities psychologists do not steal, cheat, or engage in fraud, subterfuge, or intentional misrepresentation of fact. Psychologists strive to keep their promises and to avoid unwise or unclear commitments. In situations in which deception may be ethically justifiable to maximize benefits and minimize harm, psychologists have a serious obligation to consider the need for, the possible consequences of, and their responsibility to correct any resulting

TABLE 15.3 (Continued)

Ethical Principles of Psychologists and Code of Conduct: Preamble and General Principles

mistrust or other harmful effects that arise from the use of such techniques.

Principle D: Justice. Psychologists recognize that fairness and justice entitle all persons to access to and benefit from the contributions of psychology and to equal quality in the processes, procedures, and services being conducted by psychologists. Psychologists exercise reasonable judgment and take precautions to ensure that their potential biases, the boundaries of their competence, and the limitations of their expertise do not lead to or condone unjust practices.

Principle E: Respect for People's Rights and Dignity. Psychologists respect the dignity and worth of all people, and the rights of individuals to privacy, confidentiality, and self-determination. Psychologists are aware that special safeguards may be necessary to protect the rights and welfare of persons or communities whose vulnerabilities impair autonomous decision making. Psychologists are aware of and respect cultural, individual, and role differences, including those based on age, gender, gender identity, race, ethnicity, culture, national origin, religion, sexual orientation, disability, language, and socioeconomic status, and consider these factors when working with members of such groups. Psychologists try to eliminate the effect on their work of biases based on these factors, and they do not knowingly participate in or condone activities of others based upon such prejudices.

SOURCE: American Psychological Association, 2002b, pp. 3–4.

6. *Record Keeping and Fees.* This section provides guidance on documenting professional work, maintaining and disposing of confidential records, fees, referrals, and other financial arrangements.

7. *Education and Training.* This section contains several ethical standards that control psychologists' conduct as they teach and supervise students.

8. *Research and Publication.* Standards that control researchers' activities are included in this section, such as receiving approval from the Institutional Review Board before conducting research, obtaining voluntary informed consent from human research participants, debriefing participants, providing publication credit for coauthors, sharing research data, and conducting reviews of scholarly work.

9. *Assessment.* Rules pertaining to the use and interpretation of tests are listed.

10. *Therapy.* Rules about the structuring, conduct, and termination of therapy are identified here. Specific standards prohibit psychologists from having sexual intimacies with current clients or relatives and significant others of current clients and from accepting persons as clients if they have had previous sexual intimacies with them. Furthermore, psychologists should not have sexual intimacies with former therapy clients for at least 2 years after the termination of therapy, and even then only if the psychologist can demonstrate that no exploitation of the client has occurred.

Implementation of Ethical Standards

Most psychologists take great pains to deal with complex and ethically ambiguous situations in accordance with the highest standards of professional conduct. But because many situations involve moral and cultural questions and do not match exactly the terminology used in the APA Ethics Code, there is often no clear course of action, no right answer.

Consider, for example, the following examples of situations in which the therapist is in both a professional and a nonprofessional role with the client. Multiple relationships are considered unethical because they can harm the therapeutic relationship and they can ultimately harm the client. Do you think that is true in these cases?

> A therapist has been seeing a 45-year-old male for over a year for issues of stress and anxiety. The client recently lost his job as an office administrator because the company went bankrupt, and he is looking for work. At the same time, the therapist is in need of an office assistant/records clerk, and she has had a hard time finding someone who meets her high standards. She knows that the client received rave reviews as an office assistant. She hires him to be her records clerk and continues to see him professionally.
>
> A therapist is seeing a 38-year-old female client who has endured the painful break-up of a long-term relationship. The client mentions that she loves dogs and that she finds great comfort in their company. The therapist happens to be an avid dog lover as well, and she raises and breeds Rottweilers as a hobby. The therapist mentions that she has a new litter of Rottweilers that are ready for new homes, and the client purchases one of them from the therapist.
>
> A cognitive-behavioral therapist in a small town is the only one who specializes in treating clients with anxiety disorders. A 63-year-old male calls this therapist for help with severe agoraphobia, but he has a limited income, no insurance, and he can pay for only one session. In a brief discussion of the client's situation, the therapist learns that the client is an expert carpenter. The therapist offers to treat the client in exchange for carpentry services. The client accepts the offer and builds a set of bookshelves in the den of the therapist's home. (Adapted from Bersoff, 2003.)

How do psychologists manage such ethical problems? They begin with awareness of acceptable and unacceptable practices within their area. Proper informed consent procedures, release of information forms, and case documentation are also important risk-management procedures (Kennedy, Vandehey, Norman, & Diekhoff, 2003). Professionals can also consult books such as the following:

- Boundaries in Psychotherapy: Ethical and Clinical Explorations (Zur, 2007)
- Ethical Conflicts in Psychology, Third Edition (Bersoff, 2003)
- Ethical Practice in Forensic Psychology: A Systematic Model for Decision Making (Bush, Connell, & Denney, 2006)
- Ethics in HIV-Related Psychotherapy: Clinical Decision Making in Complex Cases (Anderson & Barret, 2001)
- Ethics in Plain English: An Illustrative Casebook for Psychologists, Second Edition (Nagy, 2005)
- Ethics in Research with Human Participants (Sales & Folkman, 2000)
- Practical Ethics for Psychologists: A Positive Approach (Knapp & VandeCreek, 2005)

Professionals can also consult professional journals, which periodically publish articles about ethics (APA Committee on Professional Practice and Standards, 2003; Berman, 2006; Kennedy et al., 2003). Consultation with colleagues and professional organizations is often done, too, as long as confidentiality can be maintained. Finally, many malpractice insurance companies provide consultation to clinician-policyholders who seek clarification on ethical and legal issues. Although these efforts do not provide immunity for psychologists from malpractice suits or other legal actions, they do reflect a conscientious effort to do the right thing, and documentation of such efforts is likely to be looked upon favorably by professional organizations and courts.

Dealing with Ethical Violations

When, as fallible human beings, psychologists behave in an ethically questionable manner, they are subject to censure by local, state, and national organizations whose task it is to deal with violations of ethical practice. Clients or other individuals who believe that a psychologist has been involved in wrongdoing can file a formal complaint with APA and/or with the state licensing board. Fortunately, the number of such complaints against clinical psychologists is relatively small. One recent national survey of state licensing boards (Van Horne, 2004) found that only 2% of licensed psychologists had ever had a complaint filed against them, and only 20% of these complaints were deemed serious enough to result in disciplinary action against the psychologist involved. And for 2006, the APA Ethics Committee reported only 85 cases in which a formal ethics complaint led to an investigation by the Committee. Given that the membership of APA exceeds 150,000, the number of active ethics violation cases is small indeed.

Once a complaint of unethical behavior is brought against an APA member and the appropriate committee has decided that the conduct in question was in fact unethical, the question of punishment must be decided. The most severe APA sanction is to dismiss the offender from the association and to inform the membership of this action. Unethical conduct can also cause psychologists to have their professional licenses taken away by the board of psychology in the state where they practice. Other actions can include censure, censure with probation, or a decision that no cause for action is warranted. Later, we discuss legal and financial sanctions associated with malpractice litigation.

About half of the cases that the APA Ethics Committee investigated during 2006 dealt with psychologists who had lost their license in the state where they practiced. The most common reasons for the loss of state licenses were related to psychologists' sexual misconduct with clients. The remaining cases involved conviction of a felony, insurance/fee problems, nonsexual dual relations, inappropriate professional practice in a child custody evaluation, working outside of one's competence area, inappropriate response to a clinical crisis, violation of confidentiality, or failure to uphold standards of the profession (APA, Ethics Committee, 2007c).

In terms of complaints to state boards of psychology, sexual misconduct remains a concern, but many other complaints at the state level deal with professional practice in high-risk areas, such as custody evaluations, acrimonious divorces, supervision, evaluations for a third party (such as for an insurance claim), or with high-risk clients, such as those who are suicidal, violent, known to be litigious, or who report that they have

TABLE 15.4

Reported Disciplinary Actions Against Psychologists in the United States, August 1983–November 2005*

Reason for Disciplinary Action	Percent Disciplined
Sexual/dual relationship with patient	30.3
Unprofessional/unethical/negligent practice	29.6
Conviction of crimes	9.3
Fraudulent acts	6.1
Improper/inadequate recordkeeping	5.4
Failure to comply with continuing education requirements	4.7
Breach of confidentiality	4.5
Inadequate or improper supervision	4.3
Impairment	4.0
Fraud in application for licensure	1.8

*$N = 2,858$

Source: Adapted from K. S. Pope and M. J. T. Vasquez, 2007.

recovered memories from previous sexual abuse (Thomas, 2005). Table 15.4 shows the reasons for disciplinary action against psychologists by state boards of psychology (Pope & Vasquez, 2007).

Other Ethical Standards

In addition to the APA *Ethical Principles of Psychologists and Code of Conduct,* a number of other ethical codes and guidelines are in place. Clinical psychologists are responsible for knowing about other standards that govern their research and psychological services. As mentioned in previous chapters, numerous guidelines must be followed in conducting research, performing assessments and psychotherapy, and when working with various groups of clients. Specialty guidelines in particular have proliferated. Examples include *Guidelines for Psychotherapy with Lesbian, Gay, & Bisexual Clients* (APA, 2000a), *Guidelines for Psychological Practice with Older Adults* (2004), and *Guidelines on Multicultural Education, Training, Research, Practice, and Organizational Change for Psychologists* (2003). The American Psychological Association has also published *Criteria for Evaluating Treatment Guidelines* (APA, 2002a), which should be of help to clinical psychologists in sorting through all the numerous guidelines.

Therapists, especially those in medical settings or those who bill insurance companies for their services, have to follow additional rules and regulations. The *Health Insurance Portability and Accountability Act* (HIPAA) was established by the Department of Health and Human Services in order to protect the confidentiality of information about clients and to deal with other issues regarding insurance reimbursement (Benefield, Ashkanazi, & Rozensky, 2006; Munsey, 2006a). Therapists who bill insurance companies also must register for a National Provider Identifier, which is another component of the HIPAA regulations (Munsey, 2007a).

Regulation through State Laws

The APA's ethical principles are usually consistent with state laws, but not always, so it is usually best for the psychologist to follow the more stringent of the two (Committee on Professional Practice of Psychology, 2003). For example, whereas the APA ethical standards allow consensual sexual contact between therapists and their former clients two years after termination of the therapeutic relationship (as long as no harm will be done to the client as a result), many states forbid any sexual contact between therapists and their former clients, ever. Psychologists who live in a state that forbids such contact in perpetuity would be well-advised to follow the state law rather than to presume that the less stringent APA ethical code would apply. State laws may also mandate particular actions by clinical psychologists in other areas, including *duty to warn*.

Duty to Warn.   Therapists must normally keep clients' information confidential, but should a therapist break confidentiality if clients reveal that they plan to harm someone? This was the question raised in the case of *Tarasoff vs. Regents of the University of California* (reviewed in Ewing & McCann, 2006), and the answer has turned out to be yes, at least in some states. Here are the facts of the case.

In 1969, Prosenjit Poddar was a student at the University of California–Berkeley, and he sought therapy through the student mental health services center. During a therapy session, Mr. Poddar told his psychotherapist, Dr. Lawrence Moore, that he intended to kill a young woman, Tatiana Tarasoff, who had apparently rejected his attempts at romantic involvement. The therapist informed his superior, Dr. Harvey Powelson, of this threat. The campus police were called and were also asked, in writing, to confine the client. They did so briefly, but then released him after concluding that he was rational, and they believed his promise that he would stay away from the Tarasoff's home. He did not do so. After terminating his relationship with his therapist, Mr. Poddar killed Ms. Tarasoff. He was later convicted of murder. No one had warned the woman or her parents of the threat. In fact, Dr. Powelson had asked the police to return Dr. Moore's letter and ordered that all copies of the letter and Dr. Moore's therapy notes be destroyed.

Ms. Tarasoff's parents sued the University of California–Berkeley, the psychologists involved in the case, and the campus police to recover damages for the murder of their daughter. Ultimately, the Supreme Court of California found in favor of the parents. Through this ruling, Ms. Tarasoff's parents helped to change mental health laws throughout the United States (Ewing & McCann, 2006).

In reaching its decision, the court weighed the importance of confidential therapy relationships against society's interest in protecting itself from dangerous persons. The balance was struck in favor of society's protection. "The protective privilege ends where the public peril begins."

The *Tarasoff* decision on therapists' *duty to warn* the potential victims of clients whom the therapist believes, or should believe, are dangerous has been implemented in California and some other U.S. states, but it is not legally binding in all states—a fact that even many psychologists misunderstand. About a third of the states have passed laws that specify the conditions under which a therapist is liable for failing to take precautions to protect third parties from the dangerous acts of the therapist's clients. But state laws can change, and they sometimes do (Meyer & Weaver, 2006), so therapists are responsible for keeping up to date about their state requirements regarding protection of third parties.

The analogy between potentially dangerous clients and potentially contagious patients is particularly apt for psychotherapists who see clients with HIV. With such clients, what are the limits of confidentiality? Do clients present a risk to others? Do Tarasoff principles apply? The case law on these questions is mixed; a review of relevant cases revealed that courts favored maintaining confidentiality in roughly half of the cases and favored at least limited disclosure in the other half (Anderson & Barret, 2001). Obviously, therapists dealing with clients who are HIV-positive or have AIDS must consider the foreseeability of harm, the identifiability of potential victims, ethical guidelines, and state or federal laws when evaluating possible courses of action (Meyer & Weaver, 2006).

Regulation through Malpractice Litigation. Civil lawsuits brought by clients who allege they have been harmed by the malpractice of professionals constitute another form of regulating clinical psychologists. If a jury agrees with the client's claim, the clinician may be ordered to pay the client monetary damages to compensate for the harm. To prove a claim of professional malpractice, four elements must be established:

1. A special professional relationship (i.e., service in exchange for a fee) had to exist between the client/plaintiff and the therapist.
2. The clinician was negligent in treating the client. Negligence involves a violation of the standard of care, defined as the treatment that a reasonable practitioner facing circumstances similar to those of the plaintiff's case would be expected to give.
3. The client suffered harm.
4. The therapist's negligence must be the cause of the harm suffered by the client.

Estimates are that only 1% to 2% of clinicians will ever be sued for malpractice during their professional careers (Baerger, 2001). This figure is much lower than for medical specialists in obstetrics, emergency medicine, surgery, or radiology (Mello, Studdert, & Brennan, 2003), but the number of malpractice charges against clinical psychologists has increased recently, and so has the cost of malpractice insurance. Many of these cases are settled out of court, and when they do go to trial, the large majority are won by clinicians (Baerger, 2001).

The most common complaint in malpractice lawsuits has been the failure to prevent a client's suicide (Scott & Resnick, 2006). Families of deceased clients often receive the largest financial settlements for successful cases of this kind (Gross, 2005; Scott & Resnick, 2006). Another common basis for malpractice claims involves charges that a psychologist engaged in sexual intimacies with a current or recently terminated client. Since the ethical codes of all mental health professions strictly forbid such behavior, and since there is empirical evidence that sexual contact between therapist and client is usually harmful to the client (Disch, 2006), plaintiffs who prove such contact can win large malpractice awards.

In another area of litigious action against psychologists, a few large malpractice verdicts have been returned in cases in which therapists are accused of influencing clients to falsely recall allegedly *repressed memories* of physical or sexual abuse in childhood. Here is one case example:

Gary Ramona—once a highly paid executive in the California wine industry—sued family counselor Marche Isabella and psychiatrist Richard Rose for planting false memories of trauma in his daughter, Holly, when she was their 19-year-old patient. Ramona claimed that the therapists told Holly that her bulimia and depression were caused by having been repeatedly raped by him when she was a child. They also told her that the memory of this molestation was so traumatic that she had repressed it for years. According to Ramona, Dr. Rose then gave Holly sodium amytal (a so-called truth serum) to confirm her "recovered memory." Finally, Isabella was said to have told Holly's mother that up to 80% of all bulimics had been sexually abused (a statement for which there is no scientific support).

At the trial, the therapists claimed that Holly suffered flashbacks of what seemed to be real sexual abuse. She also became increasingly depressed and bulimic after reporting these frightening images. Holly's mother, Stephanie, who divorced her husband after Holly's allegations came to light, testified that she suspected her husband had abused Holly and listed several pieces of supposedly corroborating evidence. Gary Ramona denied ever sexually abusing his daughter.

Dr. Elizabeth Loftus, a leading critic of aggressive memory therapy, testified that therapists often either suggest the idea of trauma to their clients or are too uncritical in accepting the validity of trauma reports that occur spontaneously. It appeared that Holly's memory had been so distorted by her therapists that she no longer knew what the truth was.

The jury decided that Holly's therapists had planted false memories in her and, in May 1994, awarded damages to Gary Ramona in the amount of $500,000. Since then, according to the False Memory Syndrome Foundation, a group devoted to uncovering abuses associated with memory recovery therapy, the number of "false memory" cases against therapists has grown.

There are a number of things that clinical psychologists and other mental health professionals can do to decrease their risk of being named in a malpractice lawsuit. The first and most obvious suggestion is that they act with the highest level of professional integrity and that they do not knowingly violate any ethical standards or laws governing mental health treatment (see Kennedy et al., 2003).

Section Summary: The APA ethical standards are used to set the highest standards of integrity in the field of psychology. The ethical standards are implemented largely through training, self-monitoring, and professional monitoring. Ethical violations that are reported to APA largely focus on the loss of license at the state level. State boards of psychology most often administer disciplinary action against psychologists for sexual/dual relationships with clients and unprofessional/unethical/negligent practices. Legal regulations, such as the duty to warn, also are in place. Professional practice is also influenced by malpractice litigation, which arises most often over a therapist's failure to prevent a client's suicide.

PROFESSIONAL INDEPENDENCE

Section Preview: This section describes how clinical psychologists have sought the right to practice psychotherapy independently. Establishing that right has involved conflicts with other professions, especially psychiatry. It has also involved attempts to adapt to the changing economics of mental health service delivery. The controversy over clinicians' right to prescribe medication is also covered.

Clinical psychologists must consult and collaborate with many other professionals. They often work closely with educators, attorneys, religious leaders, social workers, nurses, physicians, and other psychologists. For the most part, psychology's interprofessional relationships are healthy, profitable, and characterized by goodwill. The most obvious sign of this harmony is the frequency of referrals made across groups.

Interprofessional relationships are not always cordial, however. As described in Chapter 2, clinical psychology's most persistent interprofessional problem has been its wary, often stormy, relationship with the medical profession. Early disputes revolved around the role of psychologists as diagnosticians and treatment providers. More recently, the squabbles have concentrated on psychologists' eligibility for reimbursement under prepaid mental health plans and psychologists' obtaining privileges to prescribe medication for their clients. Although these controversies are related, we look at them in separate sections that clarify the development of each.

The Economics of Mental Health Care

Having won the battles over licensure and recognition of psychology as an independent profession in the 1970s and 1980s, clinicians turned to struggles involving the economic aspects of mental health care. The initial focus of these struggles was whether psychologists should be eligible for reimbursement for their services by insurance companies. Physicians opposed psychologists' inclusion, claiming that it would be too costly to third-party payers and consumers. Physicians also argued that if psychologists were to be included, their services should be reimbursed only when they were treating clients referred and supervised by physicians. As a result, many major health insurance companies (such as Blue

Cross/Blue Shield) excluded psychologists from third-party payments except when billing under a physician's supervision.

As members of a profession that aspired to full autonomy, psychologists found this arrangement intolerable. As a result, psychologists began lobbying state legislatures to pass *freedom-of-choice* laws, which mandate that services rendered by qualified mental health professionals licensed to practice in a given state shall be reimbursed by insurance plans covering such services regardless of whether the provider is a physician. Physicians fought hard against such legislation, using the term *medical psychotherapy* to refer to the only services they believed should be reimbursable. This term was condemned by psychologists, who argued that there is nothing "medical" about psychotherapy. They also presented data to counter claims that including them as providers, or including coverage of mental health treatment by any provider, would be too costly for third-party payers. They pointed, for example, to a study showing that even *a single session of psychotherapy* reduced subsequent use of medical resources by 60% among the recipients and that there was about a 75% reduction in medical utilizations by patients receiving two to eight sessions of psychotherapy (Cummings, 1977; see also Olbrisch, 1977). Psychologists contended that, far from being economically disadvantageous, reimbursing for psychotherapy can be *cost effective* because it saves money that would otherwise be spent for more expensive medical services. This reduction, known as *medical offset,* has been replicated in larger studies (e.g., Holder & Blose, 1987) and more recently has become a rallying point for clinical psychologists who claim that psychotherapy is a highly effective and efficient addition to the health care system (Crane & Law, 2002; Levant House, May, & Smith, 2006; Zuvekas & Meyerhoefer, 2006).

Over the years, psychologists have succeeded in having freedom-of-choice laws enacted in most U.S. states. By 1983, 40 states covering 90% of the U.S. population had passed legislation that provided free choice of licensed psychologists as reimbursable providers of mental health services (Lambert, 1985). Additional legislation at the federal level promoted recognition of psychologists as independent clinicians. The Rehabilitation Act of 1973 (PL 93-112) provided *parity* (i.e., equal coverage) for psychologists and physicians alike in both assessment and treatment services. Services provided by clinical psychologists are now reimbursable under both the Federal Employee Health Benefits Act (PL 93-363) and the Federal Work Injuries Compensation Program (PL 94-212). Licensed psychologists are also recognized as *independent providers* by CHAMPUS (Civilian Health and Medical Program of the Uniformed Services), a federal program covering several million beneficiaries in all 50 states and the District of Columbia. In 1996, the Mental Health Parity Act was established as a federal law in order to prevent insurance companies from providing lesser coverage for mental health as opposed to physical health services. This federal law is expected to be extended when it comes up for renewal (Munsey, 2007a).

For four decades, psychologists have fought for legislative changes that would make it possible for them to be directly reimbursed for their services under Medicaid (a shared federal/state program for the medically needy) and Medicare (a federal program for elderly and disabled clients). Physicians have strenuously lobbied against such amendments, repeating the refrain that including psychologists would be too costly and that psychologists are not qualified to diagnose and treat many mental disorders without the supervision of a physician.

However, the tide has now turned. With respect to Medicare, an amendment allowing psychologists to be included and reimbursed as direct providers has now been signed into law. Psychologists have been less successful in obtaining coverage for their services under Medicaid (Munsey, 2007a). This is partly because individual states are free to determine their own criteria for Medicaid recipient eligibility and to control which services are covered at what cost. Many states are concerned about excessive use of mental health services and so have limited the kinds of treatment they reimburse through this program.

Managed Care and Changing Health Care Systems. As noted in previous chapters, changes begun in the 1990s in the delivery, financing, and organization of health care—including mental health care—have strongly affected clinical psychology. Several forces have given rise to these changes. First, the costs of health care in the United States have skyrocketed and now account for approximately 16% of the U.S. gross domestic product (Munsey, 2007a). The United States spends a higher percentage of its GDP on health care than does any other country, but it lags behind many other developed nations in the quality of that care as measured by a variety of indices. For instance, it is an irony of the United States health system that it has many of the most advanced medical facilities and specialists in the world and yet one of the highest rates of infant mortality among the developed nations (Berk, 2002). One likely reason is that the focus of health care in the United States has been mainly on acute care, surgical procedures, and hospitalization—a focus that favors expensive medical procedures and medical specialization (Reed, Levant, Stout, Murphy, & Phelps, 2001). Accordingly, prevention, early intervention, and less acute medical and psychological conditions have received less attention.

Changes that have occurred in the U.S. health care system over the last decade have been largely driven by efforts to contain these high costs. With these changes have come numerous challenges to the practice of clinical psychology. In particular, psychologists have been forced to recognize that (a) the nature, quality, and availability of health care is often determined by health care economics; and (b) changes in health care financing could nullify all the victories psychologists have won in freedom-of-choice legislation battles.

Perhaps the most dramatic changes to clinical practice have come about because of health care reform known as managed care. *Managed care* developed under the assumption that fee-for-service health care (which dominated medical and psychological care in previous decades) provides incentives for escalating costs, whereas prepaid comprehensive plans that provide financial oversight of services could control or reduce costs (Reed et al., 2001). A managed care system develops methods of allocating health services to a group of people in order to provide the most appropriate care while still containing the overall cost of these services.

Managed care can be organized in several different ways, including, for example, as employee assistance programs (EAPs), health maintenance organizations (HMOs), preferred provider organizations (PPOs), integrated delivery systems (IDSs), and independent practice associations (IPAs). In general, these organizations provide specific packages of health care services to subscribers for a fixed, prepaid price.

Mental health care in the United States has been increasingly offered in the context of one of these managed behavioral health care plans. By one estimate, approximately

75% of persons with health care insurance are covered under some type of managed mental health program (see Sanchez & Turner, 2003). How have mental health services been affected by managed care?

One of the first and most noticeable effects was the *reduction in spending for mental health services*. By one estimate, reimbursement for mental health services decreased during the 1990s by 670%, a far larger reduction than any other area of health care (Reed et al., 2001). Managed care companies found that they could save money by denying payment for the kind of expensive, long-term psychotherapy that a fee-for-service system had encouraged. They could also save money by denying services for any therapeutic procedures that did not have clearly documented benefits (most of the time, benefits were assessed over short time periods; see our discussion of this topic in Chapter 10).

Managed care has also exerted increasing control over the types and length of treatments through a system known as *utilization review*. In this system, a case manager working for a managed care company may make decisions about the appropriateness of treatment. The case manager, who more than likely is not a mental health professional, determines whether the managed care company will pay for particular treatments and, if so, for how many sessions. As discussed in Chapter 10, other forms of utilization review are now being considered, such as requiring therapists to provide data on their effectiveness.

As you might imagine, the advent of managed care has caused great concern among mental health professionals. Some of their most serious criticisms are that managed care systems (a) are more interested in cutting costs and raising profits than in assuring excellent heath care, (b) result in many clients receiving too little treatment, (c) threaten the confidentiality of therapy by requiring that too much information about clients be included in the utilization review, (d) allow untrained personnel to conduct the utilization reviews, (e) collect inadequate data on the outcomes of their treatments, and (f) exclude from the system clients who have preexisting disorders. So while most clinicians welcome incentives that encourage the use of the most effective and efficient treatments available (Bobbitt, 2006), they oppose incentives that put profits before quality of treatment and that are determined by case managers who do not have expertise in the nature and treatment of mental disorders.

As mentioned in Chapter 10, there are signs that these concerns are beginning to change the way managed care operates. Research evidence is mounting that there can be substantial long-term costs associated with not treating or undertreating psychological disorders, particularly chronic disorders or those that are most likely to be accompanied by depression or addiction. As managed care companies digest this information, they may be more willing to forsake short-term gains for long-term profitability. The growing number of therapies that have been supported strongly by empirical evidence (see Chapter 10) has also begun to influence managed care companies' decisions.

Although it is unclear what the future of managed care will bring, a number of trends are evident, including increased use of self-help interventions for clients; increased coverage of mental health services within an easily accessible location, such as through schools, medical clinics, daycare centers, and workplaces; and an increased focus on the improvement of quality of services (Clarke, Lynch, Spofford, & DeBar, 2006). A number of observers also speculate that the increased focus on mental health services provided in primary care facilities may lead to a greater integration of medical and psychological practice in the future (Kiesler, 2000).

Prescription Privileges

As some aspects of medical and psychological practices have become more integrated, clinical psychologists and the medical profession remain at odds over a *prescription privileges* movement. This movement would allow specially trained clinical psychologists to prescribe psychotropic medication as well as offer psychotherapy.

Why should clinical psychologists have this *prescriptive authority*? Advocates of that authority point to several reasons. For one thing, surveys indicate that 98% of psychologists have referred a client to a psychiatrist or physician for psychotropic medication; 75% of psychologists make such referrals on a monthly basis; and approximately one out of three clients of psychologists are taking psychotropic medication (Meyers, 2006a). Thus, medication already is a frequent consideration in many clinical psychologists' practice. In addition, the knowledge necessary to competently and safely prescribe medication can apparently be learned in a relatively brief period and without a full medical education. Finally, many psychologists are worried about clients' inability to gain access to psychiatrists and qualified primary care physicians, especially in rural or other geographically isolated regions. In 1996, the APA Council of Representatives voted in support of seeking prescriptive authority for clinical psychologists. An APA Ad Hoc Task Force on Psychopharmacology suggested that most of the training necessary for obtaining prescription privileges could be conducted at the postdoctoral level. The Council

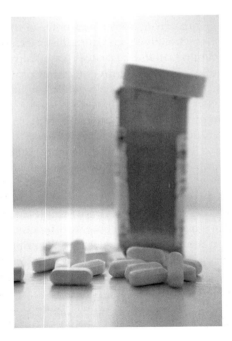

There are mixed opinions as to whether clinical psychologists should seek prescription privileges.

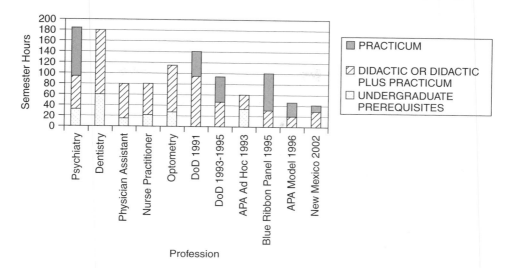

FIGURE 15.1 Comparison of Semester Hour Medical Training by Professions with Prescriptive Authority in all or Most States and Proposal for Medical Training for Psychologists in Order to Obtain Such Authority. Note that training guidelines have not yet been finalized.

(*Source:* E. M. Heiby, P. H. DeLeon, & T. Anderson, 2004, "A Debate on Prescription Privileges for Psychologists." *Professional Psychology: Research and Practice, 35*(4), 336–344.)

also recommended model legislation to be introduced in states where psychologists are seeking prescriptive authority, as well as a model postdoctoral curriculum (covering neurosciences, pharmacology, physiology, physical and laboratory assessments, and clinical pharmacotherapeutics) to be used in training prescribers (Cullen & Newman, 1997).

The medical profession is not the only faction opposed to these plans. The idea of psychologists prescribing drugs is a controversial one within psychology, too. A number of psychology journals have devoted special issues to the topic of prescription privileges (e.g., *Clinical Psychology: Science and Practice,* 2002, Volume 9, Issue 3; *Journal of Clinical Psychology,* 2002, Volume 58, Issue 6; *Professional Psychology: Research and Practice,* 2004, Volume 35, Issue 4), and although many psychologists support prescription privileges for properly trained clinicians (Robiner et al., 2002), the debate is far from settled. Some in psychology agree that prescription privileges make sense for psychologists, but they are worried, too, that existing training for this activity might not be adequate (see Figure 15.1). In particular, they say that training psychologists to prescribe medication could become a health hazard, largely because of inadequate training of psychologists in the medical and physical sciences (e.g., Robiner et al., 2002). Some argue that psychologists who want to prescribe medication should complete formal medical training, such as obtaining training as a nurse psychologist. But others are concerned that this move would lead to an increasingly intense focus on the medical and biomedical aspects of behavior, behavior disorder, and treatment, with a consequent loss of clinical psychology's traditional focus on important psychosocial, environmental, cognitive, and behavioral factors in explaining and treating disorders (Levine & Schmelkin, 2006). They say that "if you give someone a hammer, then everything looks like a nail," meaning that if psychologists have prescriptive authority, then every client's problems might seem to require drug treatment rather than psychotherapy. As of this writing, New Mexico and Louisiana are the only states to have passed laws allowing clinical psychologists to pre-scribe medications after proper training (Holloway, 2004; Stambor, 2006). However, sev-eral other states have launched initiatives or introduced bills to grant the authority, including Missouri in 2008 (APApractice.org, 2008; Munsey, 2006a).

Would clinical psychologists apply for prescriptive authority if it were available? It is uncertain. One survey suggests that clinical interns and training directors who favor prescriptive authority would seek prescriptive authority if it were available (Fagan et al., 2004), but another survey found that only 5% of nurse psychologists actually chose to seek prescriptive authority and were prescribing medications (Wiggins & Wedding, 2004). If the same pattern were to hold among clinical psychologists who have the option for prescriptive authority, only a minority might take advantage of the opportu-nity. Whether or not prescriptive privileges are gained by psychologists throughout the United States, most professionals agree that psychologists should proceed cautiously as they consider this important new option in their training and in their practice.

Section Summary: The fields of clinical psychology and psychiatry have battled over the right to provide psychotherapy, the right for comparable coverage of mental health services as for medical services, and the right to be reimbursed for services through managed care companies. The current battle has to do with the fight by clinical psychologists to obtain prescriptive author-ity. Psychiatrists as well as many psychologists are against the idea of psychologists being able to do so, even though two states have already passed laws granting prescription privileges to spe-cially trained psychologists.

PROFESSIONAL MULTICULTURAL COMPETENCE

Section Preview: Clinicians are becoming increasingly aware of how race, ethnicity, gender, and many other types of client diversity can affect clinical practice and outcomes. This section reviews attempts to enhance clinicians' multicultural competence.

As mentioned in Chapter 1, "What Is Clinical Psychology?" the population of the United States is more diverse than it has ever been, and it is becoming more so. Caucasian Americans still make up the majority of individuals within the United States (69.4%), but other racial/ethnic groups have increased over the past decade. Individuals from a Hispanic/Latino/Latina background represent 12.6% of the population, African American individuals represent 12.2%, Asian Americans represent 3.8%, and others (such as Native American Indians, multiracial individuals, and individuals from other racial/ethnic back-grounds) represent 2.0% of the U.S. population (Maton, Kohout, Wicherski, Leary, & Vinokurov, 2006). The field of clinical psychology is responding to these changes in sev-eral ways.

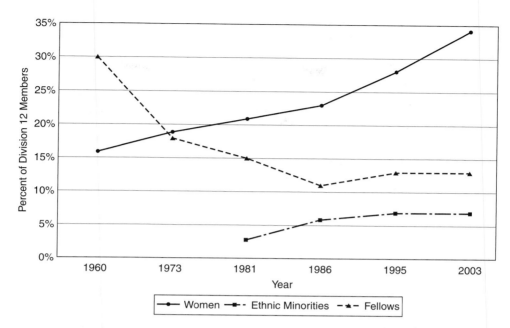

FIGURE 15.2 Percentage of Women, Racial/Ethnic Minorities, and Fellows by Year
(*Source:* J. C. Norcross, C. P. Karpiak, & S. O. Santoro, 2005, "Clinical psychologists
across the years: The division of clinical psychology from 1960 to 2003." *Journal of
Clinical Psychology, 61,* 1467–1483.)

One involves attempts to increase diversity within the ranks of professionals. Consider gender; clinical psychology was once a male-dominated profession, but it is less so now. The percentage of women in APA Division 12 (Society for Clinical Psychology) has increased over the last 40 years to reach approximately 35% (see Figure 15.2). The number of women entering clinical psychology graduate training has increased even more dramatically; women now substantially outnumber men (see Figure 1.4 in Chapter 1). In terms of ethnic diversity, the filed of clinical psychology remains dominated by Caucasian Americans (Maton, Kohout, Wicherski, Leary, & Vinokurov, 2006). As can be seen in Figure 15.2, the number of clinicians in Division 12 who are members of racial/ethnic minorities has increased, but it remains relatively low, having grown from 3% in 1981 to only 7% in 2003 (Norcross, Karpiak, & Santoro, 2005). This figure is likely to increase further, though, as graduate training programs in clinical psychology continue their efforts to recruit, train, and retain students from diverse backgrounds (Rogers & Molina, 2006).

Regardless of their own gender or ethnicity, practicing clinicians are being encouraged to increase their awareness of racial/ethnic/cultural diversity and to improve their skills in working with diverse client populations. As we have suggested in previous chapters, growing evidence indicates that psychological treatments and assessments sometimes must be altered in order to be most effective for clients from particular racial/ethnic minority groups (Miranda et al., 2005). Clinical training programs are recognizing the need to train graduate students to deal competently with issues of diversity and multiculturalism. There is also a growing awareness that diversity does not begin and end with gender and race/ethnicity. Clinicians are paying increasing attention to adjusting clinical practice to meet the needs of clients who are poor (Krous & Nauta, 2005; Smith, 2005), who are from various religious and spiritual backgrounds (Ali, Liu, & Humedian, 2004; Hathaway, Scott, & Garver, 2004), who are from countries other than the United States (Swierc & Routh, 2003), who have physical challenges (Williams & Abeles, 2004), and who are HIV-positive (Stepleman, Hann, Santos, & House, 2006). Psychologists also need to be sensitive to their clients' sexual orientation (Biaggio, Orchard, Larson, Petrino, & Mihara, 2003) and to develop competence in working with same-sex couples, for example (Riggle & Rostosky, 2005). Concern about all of these issues, and the need for training in diversity, led to the development of the APA's *Multicultural Guidelines: Education, Research, and Practice* (American Psychological Association, 2003). The guidelines are as follows:

1. Psychologists are encouraged to recognize that, as cultural beings, they may hold attitudes and beliefs that can detrimentally influence their perceptions of and interactions with individuals who are ethnically and racially different from themselves.

2. Psychologists are encouraged to recognize the importance of multicultural sensitivity/responsiveness to, knowledge of, and understanding about ethnically and racially different individuals.

3. As educators, psychologists are encouraged to employ the constructs of multiculturalism and diversity in psychological education.

4. Culturally sensitive psychological researchers are encouraged to recognize the importance of conducting culture-centered and ethical psychological research among persons from ethnic, linguistic, and racial minority backgrounds.

5. Psychologists are encouraged to apply culturally appropriate skills in clinical and other applied psychological practices.

6. Psychologists are encouraged to use organizational change processes to support culturally informed organizational (policy) development and practices.

Many of these guidelines can be conceptualized by the construct of *openness to the other,* which reflects individuals' ability to remain open to ideas, concepts, thoughts, feelings, and perspectives of others who are different from themselves (Fowers & Davidov, 2006). It is all part of efforts in the field of clinical psychology to improve the educational, research, and practice standards of psychologists with attention toward multicultural competence. More information on these efforts is contained in sources such as the *Encyclopedia of Multicultural Psychology* (Jackson, 2006) and *Addressing Cultural Complexities in Practice: Assessment, Diagnosis, and Therapy,* Second Edition (Hays, 2007).

Section Summary: The field of clinical psychology is still not as racially or ethnically diverse as it should be, and efforts are underway to correct this problem. Attention has also been focused in recent years on increasing multicultural competence in training, clinical work, and research, but much more needs to be done. Although much of the work on multicultural competence deals with racial/ethnic diversity, there is also attention paid to other types of diversity, such as sexual orientation, religious background, physical abilities, and country of origin.

THE FUTURE OF CLINICAL PSYCHOLOGY

Section Preview: This section highlights a number of trends that we think will occur in the not-too-distant future. Included in this discussion are changes in professional specialization, training, positive psychology, technological advances, dissemination of effective clinical methodology, and interdisciplinary science.

We have already discussed some future directions in clinical psychology, such as its increased emphasis on evidence-based practice, the possibility of prescriptive authority for psychologists, and the increasing emphasis on multicultural competence in teaching, research, and practice, but there are other changes on the horizon, too. Let's consider a few of the most important.

Professional Specialization

Specialization is increasing in clinical psychology. Members of the APA have debated whether to consider accrediting programs within clinical specialties other than school or counseling psychology (e.g., clinical child, neuropsychology, health psychology, forensic psychology), but that issue has yet to be settled.

There is also interest in increasing mental health services and empirical research with underserved populations, such as the chronically mentally ill, rural populations, substance abusers, and older patients. NIMH has directed training grant funds toward these "underserved groups." Services to these and other diverse cultural and ethnic groups will probably continue to increase.

Training

Controversy will likely continue over the question of how clinical psychologists should be trained. Differences among the philosophy and training agendas of doctoral training programs based on the clinical scientist, scientist–practitioner, and practitioner–scholar models show no signs of rapid resolution. We expect that some disconnect between PhD and PsyD training programs will continue, but we hope that this gap will lessen as programs focus on what is in the best interests of their students and the public in general. In order to do this, and to allow their students to be competitive in the job market, all training programs will need to focus on evidence-based practices (Lambert & Ogles, 2004), multicultural competence (Handelsman, Gottlieb, & Knapp, 2005), and the establishment of competence in practice, teaching, and research (Kaslow et al., 2004). McFall (2006) argued that clinical psychology training programs must not allow themselves to become narrowly focused vocational schools, but rather that they need to train students to have a variety of empirical skills that can be applied in a variety of settings.

Positive Psychology

The *positive psychology* movement, which focuses on understanding and promoting personal growth and human potential (Diener, Tamir, & Scollon, 2006), will play an increasingly important role in clinical psychology (Duckworth, Steen, & Seligman, 2005). It will appear in research on personal growth after a traumatic event or major illness (such as surviving breast cancer; Zoellner & Maercker, 2006), on *resilience* (i.e., the ability to adapt to and overcome challenges such as poverty, racism, abuse; Newman, 2005), and of course on preventing psychological problems before they occur (Ingram, 2005). Other aspects of the positive psychology movement will be seen in efforts to decrease the stigma that is still sometimes associated with receiving mental health services and to help clients function as best they can while living with severe psychological disorders (Corrigan, 2004; Hinshaw, 2007).

Technology

As in all other areas of 21st century culture, technology will play an increasing role in clinical training, research, and practice. For example, more undergraduate clinical psychology courses will be offered online (Rudestam, 2004). And although there are currently prohibitions against APA-accredited programs being taught solely online, significant components of graduate training will be provided through distance learning technology (Murphy, Levant, Hall, & Glueckauf, 2007).

Similarly, clinicians will also continue to make use of telephones and computers in the delivery of mental health services. Often referred to as *telehealth* or *e-health,* providing services via the phone or the Internet can be especially helpful for individuals in rural areas or other remote locations (Schopp, Johnstone, & Reid-Arndt, 2005). Technological innovation such as virtual reality–assisted treatments, computer-based assessment, and neuroimaging also expand the possibilities of clinical services. Although we need more outcome studies on the effectiveness of training and services provided through technology, it is clear that some types of educational and service delivery will continue to be provided through remote contacts (Ritterband et al., 2003).

Dissemination

At various points, we have stressed the importance of mental health literacy—public understanding about mental health issues. Perhaps the most important way to develop this literacy is to have clinicians and clinical researchers communicate with the public more often and more clearly. Known as *dissemination,* the sharing of information with other professionals and with the public is an important aspect of conducting research—especially outcome studies of psychological treatments.

Sommer (2006) argued that researchers should write parallel papers when they have important findings—one scholarly article for their colleagues that could be published in a professional journal and another article for the general public that could be published in a popular magazine. A number of APA presidents have encouraged the field to make psychology more accessible to the general public and to "make psychology a household word" (Levant, 2006). It appears that this trend to increase mental health literacy is gaining momentum and will continue in the future. We hope so; scholarly findings can be applied to the larger population more quickly if the points of dissemination are both at the professional and the public levels (see APA's Web site www.psychologymatters.org).

Interdisciplinary Science

A colleague of ours likes to compare the current bickering in the field of psychology (e.g., which training model is best, what "evidence" should be used to support evidence-based practices) with the bickering that blacksmiths must have had in the days just before auto-mobiles hit the scene (e.g., what is the best size and shape of the horseshoe, what is the best metal and color for the horseshoe). The point is that clinical psychology is only a small part of the scholarly world that is exploring ways to understand human behavior and that if we do not change with the times, we will go the way of the blacksmiths.

We predict that clinical psychology will become more integrated with other disciplines, such as genomics (McGuffin, 2004), genetics (Lemery & Doelger, 2005), behavioral genetics (Moffitt, 2005; Moffitt & Caspi, 2007), social neuroscience (Cacioppo, 2006; Norris & Cacioppo, 2007), cognitive-affective neuroscience (Stein, 2006), and developmental neuroscience (Cicchetti & Curtis, 2006). For example, a diverse group of scientists, including psychologists, have found that humans and nonhuman primates have what are known as *mirror neurons,* which facilitate learning behaviors by watching others and which allow the expression of empathy and feeling of emotions that others are experiencing at the time (Winerman, 2005). Mirror neuron systems are being explored in relation to a number of different types of psychopathology, including autistic disorder and other pervasive developmental disorders (Oberman & Ramachandran, 2007).

These types of interdisciplinary research projects will likely lead to other discoveries that any discipline alone might not discover. For this and other reasons, federal funding is increasingly supportive of *translational research,* in which the basic sciences are "translated" into applied practices. Increasingly, multidisciplinary teamwork is the only way to conduct research on certain topics.

A Final Word

As part of a special issue of the *Journal of Clinical Psychology* that focused on the future of clinical psychology Hayes, (2005; pp. 1056–1059) provided 11 rules for making the field more successful:

1. Be clear about your philosophical assumptions and be guided by them.
2. Define *psychology* clearly and stick to that definition.
3. There is nothing quite so practical as a good theory if it is broad enough.
4. Look for common core processes.
5. Include manipulable variables in your theories.
6. Be concerned with process, not just outcome.
7. Assemble packages from the bottom up and test their effectiveness early.
8. Involve the practitioner in research production.
9. Fit research to economic and political realities.
10. Develop a basic science capable of sustaining applied science.
11. Hold everything lightly, especially theories.

We believe that the vast majority of individuals within clinical psychology subscribe to these rules. Because they are talented and dedicated persons who sincerely wish to help others and to make a difference, we have a great deal of hope for the future of clinical psychology. We hope that this book plays a role in moving some of you to join in the creation of that future.

Section Summary: Specialized accreditation (e.g., clinical child, neuropsychology) is on the horizon, though some worry that it might weaken the field. Clinicians have debated how best to train new clinical psychologists in evidence-based practices, and those debates will continue. Clinicians will become more aware of the growing influence of positive psychology and of technological advances such as Web-based teaching, Web-based delivery of services, and computer-assisted assessment and treatment. To improve mental health literacy in the public (and help insure a receptive market), clinicians of the future will have to do a better job of dissemination—providing the public with usable information about evidence-based treatments and mental health services. Finally, clinical scientists of the future will need to work with scientists in fields such as biology, genetics, genomics, and other neurosciences.

CHAPTER SUMMARY

Five professional issues are of prime importance as clinical psychology continues to develop its scientific and professional identity in the 21st century. These issues involve training, regulation, ethics, independence, and the need for multicultural competence in relation to the profession of clinical psychology.

Since the late 1940s, clinical training programs have typically followed some version of the Boulder model, a scientist–practitioner curriculum that emphasizes psychology's scientific foundation more than the development of clinical service skills. Several training conferences since that time have reaffirmed the Boulder model, but training models that emphasize professional skills are also available now. Many of these are Doctor of Psychology (PsyD) programs and practice-oriented PhD programs offered in psychology departments or in freestanding schools of professional psychology.

Professional regulation of clinical psychologists comes in several forms, including (a) laws that establish criteria for who may use the title of "psychologist" (certification laws) and perform psychological services (licensing laws), (b) laws establishing therapists' duty to warn, and (c) lawsuits alleging clinical malpractice.

The code of ethics in psychology is unique because it was developed on the basis of psychologists' experiences with real ethical dilemmas. The current version, called "Ethical Principles of Psychologists and Code of Conduct," includes a Preamble, General Principles, and a large number of Ethical Standards covering a wide range of specific topics, from advertising services and testing to rules about confidentiality and sexual contact with clients.

The struggle of clinical psychology to gain and retain its status as a profession that is authorized to offer independent services has been long, difficult, and continuing. It first involved the right of clinicians to offer psychotherapy. Later, the issue was whether clinical psychologists could practice independently in hospitals and whether psychologists should be eligible for reimbursement under various public, private, and prepaid mental health insurance plans. While these rights are now reasonably well established in most states, some of them may be made irrelevant by the continuing growth of managed care systems whose provisions are making it increasingly difficult for clinical psychologists to function outside of HMOs, group medical practices, or other health-related organizations. There is growing interest in psychologists gaining prescriptive authority, but there are pros and cons to this venture.

Today, the field of clinical psychology has a greater commitment to understanding diversity, and there is a strong emphasis on developing multicultural competence. The field confronts the formidable challenge of shaping its training programs and service functions to meet needs of diverse client populations.

STUDY QUESTIONS

1. Discuss the different national conferences that led to changes in the training of clinical psychologists, and delineate how these conference changed the focus of training.

2. What are the differences in terms of qualifications and ultimate outcomes of students who enter PhD versus PsyD programs? What variables are important to consider in the heterogeneity of PsyD programs?

3. List the three primary models of training in clinical psychology currently. Discuss the pros and cons of these models.

4. What is the purpose of licensure, and how is licensure usually obtained?

5. What is an ABPP diploma, and why might it be important in the field of clinical psychology?

6. List four ethical principles and discuss their importance.

7. How are ethical violations dealt with when they arise?

8. What is duty to warn, and what is the case most associated with it?

9. What are the most common reasons for malpractice litigation against clinical psychologists?

10. What are the influences on the relationship between the fields of psychology and psychiatry historically? What is the biggest battleground currently?

11. How has managed care influenced the field of clinical psychology?

12. What are the pros and cons of gaining prescriptive authority for clinical psychologists?

13. Provide a rationale for why clinical psychology should be concerned about multicultural competence.

14. Of the primary points we discussed for the future of psychology, which do you think are the most promising for the enhancement of mental health of individuals around the world?

WEB SITES

- The Academy of Psychological Clinical Science (APCS): http://psych.arizona.edu/apcs/index.php
- APA Ethical Principles: http://www.apa.org/ethics/
- APA's Initiative to Make Psychology a Household Word: http://www.psychologymatters.org
- APA Division 42, Psychologists in Independent Practice: http://www.division42.org
- APA Division 55, American Society for the Advancement of Psychotherapy (ASAP): http://www.Division55.org
- American Board of Professional Psychology (ABPP): http://www.abpp.org

CHAPTER 16

Getting into Graduate School in Clinical Psychology

Chapter Preview: Students ask a number of questions when they are thinking of applying to graduate school in clinical psychology. In this chapter, we hope to answer some of those questions and to pose other questions that potential applicants need to consider. We begin by addressing questions related to deciding whether to apply to graduate school in clinical psychology: (a) In what type of program am I interested? (b) Am I ready to make the commitment required for a doctoral program in clinical psychology at this time in my life? (c) Are my credentials strong enough for admission to graduate school? (d) Given my credentials, to what type of program can I realistically aspire? Next we move into the logistics of applying to graduate school, addressing questions such as (a) How can I evaluate various programs? (b) What is involved in applying to a graduate program? and (c) What factors should I consider if I am accepted? In this chapter, we dispense with the Section Previews and Section Summaries, substituting instead a "frequently asked questions" format in which headings provide the questions and the paragraphs that follow provide the answers.

WHAT TYPES OF GRADUATE PROGRAMS WILL HELP ME MEET MY CAREER GOALS?

In thinking about life after college, the first questions you must ask yourself are, "What type of career do I want?" and "What types of graduate programs are available to meet my career goals?" There are many career options to consider within the field of clinical psychology. Note that APA provides a free brochure called "Psychology: Scientific Problems Solvers—Careers for the 21st Century," which can be accessed online at http://www.apa.org/students/brochure. There are many careers to consider, both within and outside of clinical psychology. Often your career preferences will help you decide the programs to which you will apply. Most students know about the possibility of being a clinician (psychotherapist) or a psychology professor. Below are some other possible careers in clinical psychology.

Administrator in a medical setting
Child therapist
Clinical neuropsychologist
Clinician in a university counseling center
Executive coach and consultant
Forensic psychologist
Gerontologist
Infant mental health specialist
Military psychologist
Public health educator
Researcher in a medical center
Researcher in a nonprofit research organization
Sport psychologist
Trial consultant

Research versus Clinical Emphasis?

All university-based graduate programs in clinical psychology provide training in research as well as in clinical functions, but there are differences in emphasis from one institution to another. It is worth your effort to learn each program's emphasis when you are gathering other information about the program. Subtle differences in a program's description (e.g., scientist–practitioner vs. clinical scientist; see Chapter 15, "Professional Issues in Clinical Psychology") may reveal a great deal about the program's training emphasis.

If your primary career interest is in researching issues of mental health, psychopathology, prevention, and treatment, then the PhD program in clinical is probably your best option. Such programs typically offer the most training in research and widest variety of clinical research options. Clinical researchers find careers in a variety of mental health settings, hospitals, medical schools, government, public, and private agencies. Research-oriented clinical PhD programs also provide training and supervision in clinical work, so graduates of these programs typically have the option of shifting into more clinical work so long as they have kept their licensure requirements up to date.

Certain nonclinical PhD psychology programs may also provide avenues to clinical research. Graduates of developmental psychology, personality psychology, experimental psychology, or social psychology doctoral programs sometimes conduct research with important clinical applications (e.g., childhood psychopathology, positive psychology). Programs that are strictly research oriented make this fact clear in their descriptive information and may even refrain from using "clinical psychology" as a program title. These nonclinical programs tend to attract fewer applicants than clinical programs do, and, though still quite competitive, may be less competitive than clinical programs. However, clinical research options may be more limited in these programs than in clinical PhD programs, and graduates of nonclinical programs will not be eligible for psychotherapy licensure or practice.

If your primary interest is in clinical work, especially therapy, then there are a number of options both inside and outside of clinical psychology, In Chapter 1, "What Is Clinical Psychology?" we described several mental health professions whose graduates do assessment, psychotherapy, or counseling. These include counseling psychologists, school psychologists, social workers, rehabilitation counselors, marriage and family therapists, psychiatrists, and psychiatric nurses. We do not have the space here to provide details about the graduate admission requirements for each of these fields, but for those interested, we hope that this chapter can help you to know what kinds of information to seek.

MA, PhD, or PsyD?

Many students seem to think that if they want to do clinical work, they must enter a PhD program in clinical psychology. In fact, approximately three times as many students get master's degrees in psychology as get the doctoral degree (Morgan & Korschgen, 2006). Many students who are considering clinical PhD programs probably could get their educational and employment needs met in an master's program or in other types of programs that offer training leading to careers in the mental health professions.

The growth of managed care systems has stimulated the job market at the master's-degree level for those seeking a career in direct service. Thus, the master's degree in clinical psychology is a more marketable degree than it had been in the past. Further, what was seen as the biggest drawback to the master's degree—the need for continual supervision from a licensed PhD psychologist—may be changing. The state of Kentucky, for example, allows master's-level psychologists to be licensed to work independently after they meet certain training and professional experience requirements. Other states, such as Florida, allow professionals with a master's degree in a mental health–related field (such as clinical or counseling psychology or rehabilitation counseling) to seek licensure as a Licensed Mental Health Counselor, which ultimately is an independent license. Thus, if you are interested in having a full-time clinical career and if you have limited interest in research training, then it may be wise for you to consider pursuing a master's degree in clinical psychology or a related field. It is reasonable to expect that a master's degree in clinical psychology will allow you to secure a full-time job providing mental health services (MacKain, Tedeschi, Durham, & Goldman, 2002).

There are, however, a number of limitations to the master's degree that would be avoided by earning a doctoral degree. In most states, if you want to be licensed as a psychologist (which means that you can actually use the term *psychologist* rather than another term like *counselor*), you have to have either a PhD or a PsyD. Income levels are typically lower for master's-level clinicians, and advancement opportunities are fewer. Certain career opportunities, such as being a professor in a college or university or being awarded program grants from granting agencies, are often unavailable to those without a doctorate. As Figure 16.1 shows, employment settings may be somewhat more restrictive for master's-level clinicians. Thus, the doctoral degree gives you more flexibility, which can be helpful given that your career interests will likely change somewhat over your lifespan.

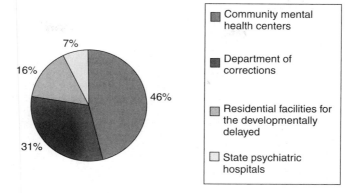

FIGURE 16.1 Work Settings of Individuals with a Master's Degree in Psychology, Based on a Study Was Conducted in North Carolina to See where Master's-Level Clinicians Worked in the State. Known as *Licensed Psychological Associates* (LPAs), master's-level clinicians can conduct therapy in the state of north carolina, but they have to receive supervision from a doctoral-level licensed psychologist. The distribution of settings in which these master's-level clinicians worked is based on information about 345 LPAs

At the doctoral level, you have the choice of PhD and PsyD programs. Traditionally, the PhD degree is considered the terminal degree in clinical psychology. As described in Chapter 15, PsyD programs place proportionately more emphasis on clinical training while reducing the emphasis on research. However, it is important to remember that PsyD programs vary considerably: Some follow the Boulder model and emphasize research as much as many PhD programs do, while others adopt the Vail model and emphasize research considerably less. Programs that deemphasize research still require that students acquire knowledge of statistics and research methods, but students are usually not required to conduct an empirically based thesis or dissertation. Figure 16.2 shows the distribution of how clinical psychologists view their professional roles.

As described in Chapter 15, a relatively recent development in the field is the rise in professional schools offering the PsyD degree. What is unique about these schools is that they often are not affiliated with a specific psychology department or with a university. Free-standing professional schools generally place the least emphasis on research training. These programs are attractive to some students because they so clearly emphasize practice over research and because they generally have considerably lower selection criteria than PhD clinical programs (see Table 16.1). However, some cautionary notes are necessary. First, because these programs are stand-alone institutions, they usually have to support themselves financially from student tuition. Thus, similar to medical schools and law schools, the tuition can be quite high with little financial assistance available. In contrast, most clinical PhD programs offer their students some financial support, including tuition remission and research

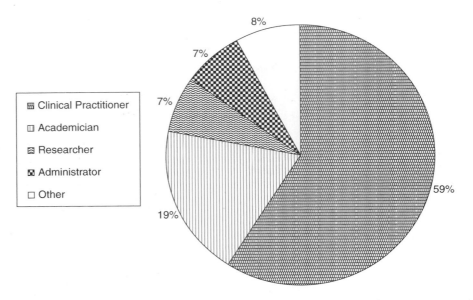

FIGURE 16.2 Professional Self-Views of Clinical Psychologists in 2003

(*Source:* J. C. Norcross, C. P. Karpiak, & S. O. Santoro, 2005, "Clinical psychologists across the Years: The division of clinical psychology from 1960 to 2003," *Journal of Clinical Psychology, 61,* 1467–1483.)

assistant (RA) or teaching assistant (TA) positions. Second, PsyD programs often need to accept large entering classes (e.g., as many as 100 students) in order to make the program succeed financially. Thus, students may not get the same individual attention that they would in a PhD program, where the entering class may be five to ten students. Finally, the relatively weaker research training in many of these programs means that graduates are less able to

TABLE 16.1

Average Acceptance Rates for APA-Accredited Clinical Psychology Programs

	Freestanding PsyD	University-based PsyD	Practice-oriented PhD	Equal-emphasis PhD	Research-oriented PhD
Number of applications	186	164	154	170	189
Number of acceptances	93	53	18	21	13
Acceptance rate	50%	41%	10%	10%	6%

Source: From *Insider's Guide to Graduate Programs in Clinical and Counseling Psychology,* 2006/2007 Edition, by T. J. Mayne, J. C. Norcross, and M. A. Sayette, 2006, p. 41 (New York: Guilford Press). Copyright 2006 by Guilford Press. Used with permission.

move into more research-oriented clinical positions or to combine research with their clinical work. These points are also made in Table 16.2, which presents myths and realities about getting into doctoral degree programs in clinical psychology.

AM I READY TO MAKE THE COMMITMENT REQUIRED IN DOCTORAL PROGRAMS AT THIS TIME IN MY LIFE?

After exploring the career options available with master's and PhD degrees, and after careful consideration of what you want to achieve, you have decided that a doctoral program in clinical psychology offers you the most career flexibility and the best chance to obtain your research and clinical goals. The next question you have to ask yourself is whether you are prepared to make the type of commitment required for such a program. A doctoral program in clinical psychology requires that you make major time, financial, academic, and emotional commitments.

Time Commitments

Typical weekly requirements in graduate school involve a full course load of academic work as well as a 20-hour-per-week job either as a TA, RA, or clinical trainee conducting supervised clinical work (such as completing assessments or conducting therapy). In addition, you will be expected to find time to make continual progress on your independent research toward completion of your thesis and dissertation. In more research-oriented programs, you will also be expected to publish and present your independent research as well as research with your major professor. Thus, it is not unusual for graduate students in clinical programs to work 60 hours or more per week, 12 months per year. Unlike college, summer is not a time for rest and relaxation for doctoral students. Ironically, many students as well as faculty look forward to summers so that they can actually get more work done.

On average, 5 to 7 years are needed to complete such a program, during which time you will be living on subsistence wages, at best. In addition, new licensing requirements almost guarantee that you will need to take a 1- to 2-year postdoctoral position after you graduate in order to obtain the necessary clinical supervision for licensure. Thus, it may take anywhere from 6 to 9 years after starting graduate school before you are ready to venture fully into the job market. Generally, the more research-oriented a program is, the longer it takes to complete the program.

Financial Commitments

Given the high cost of graduate education, the majority of graduate students in doctoral programs end up borrowing money. The debt they incur often varies according to the type of program attended. A survey conducted by the American Psychological Association found that 68% of recent psychology doctoral graduates had some type of debt after completing their degree (Bailey, 2006), with higher rates of debt from the more practice-oriented programs. The median loan debt for students who sought a research-related degree was $35,000, and the median debt for students in a practice-oriented area was

TABLE 16.2

Myths and Realities about Clinical Psychology Graduate Training

Topic	Myth	Reality
Graduate school acceptance rates	Anyone can get into a PsyD program, but it is very difficult to get into a PhD program.	Among APA-accredited programs, PsyD programs accept about 40% of applicants, some higher, some lower. PhD programs accept about 10% of applicants, some higher, some lower. PsyD programs typically enroll three to four times the number enrolled in PhD programs, but because there are more PhD programs, the number of PhDs and PsyDs awarded each year is about the same.
Financial assistance	You cannot get financial aid if you attend a PsyD program, but you can from a PhD program.	Over 60% of students in university-based PsyD programs received some financial aid, but only 26% of those attending freestanding clinical programs did. For financial assistance, university affiliation probably matters more than the type of degree offered.
Theoretical orientation of clinical faculty	Faculty in traditional PhD programs are mostly cognitive-behavioral, while those in PsyD programs are psychodynamic and humanistic.	A cognitive-behavioral orientation is the most frequently cited one in PhD and PsyD clinical programs. University-based graduate departments tend to have higher percentages of faculty endorsing a CBT perspective. The percentage of faculty endorsing humanistic orientations, though lower than CBT, is highest in freestanding schools.
Training in evidence-based practice	PsyD programs do not train students in empirically tested psychotherapies.	Most programs offer training in treatments that have been defined in manuals and found efficacious in at least two well-controlled randomized clinical studies, but few require both didactic and clinical supervision in them. Professional clinical psychology (PsyD) has the highest percentage of programs (67%) not requiring it.
Performance on national licensing board exam	PsyD students are not well prepared for the Examination for Professional Practice in Psychology (EPPP).	PsyD students score lower on average on the national licensing exam, but there is great variability. Higher exam scores are more reliably associated with smaller-sized clinical programs, better faculty-to-student ratios, and traditional (Boulder model) PhD curricula.

Source: J. C. Norcross, P. H. Castle, M. A. Sayette, & T. J. Mayne, 2004; M. M. Weissman, H. Verdell, M. J. Gameroff, S. E. Bledsoe, K. Betts, et al., 2006.

$70,000 (Munsey, 2007b). Some graduates of PsyD programs have run up debts approaching $100,000 (Mayne et al., 2006). Beginning salaries in clinical psychology are not so high that paying off these debts is easy; it often takes a few years.

Fortunately, many graduate programs offer income opportunities, usually in the form of assistantships or financial aid. Although funding has increased over the years, the median TA or RA stipends continue to be modest for a 20-hour-per-week position. The median graduate pay for either a TA or RA was $12,000 for the academic 9-month year of 2005/2006 (Munsey, 2007c). Many universities also offer fellowships and scholarships on a competitive basis. Fellowships and scholarships are usually given as outright grants to support and encourage students with outstanding academic and research potential (and there is no formal work requirement other than to do well in graduate school). Students can often find out about university-wide fellowships and scholarships by checking the Web site of the graduate school at the university. For example, it is not uncommon for programs to offer fellowships that will increase the diversity of the students accepted into the program. Many programs also provide some form of tuition remission. They may offer complete remission, meaning that the student pays no tuition at all, or they offer some portion of remission (e.g., 50%). Alternatively, the program may waive the out-of-state tuition and only require that the student pay in-state tuition, even if the student is coming from out of state.

Note that many programs, especially freestanding professional schools, do not offer funding to the large majority of students (Norcross, Castle, Sayette, & Mayne, 2004). One survey of APA-accredited clinical psychology doctoral programs found that approximately 6% of students entering a freestanding PsyD program were offered full financial aid, 57% of students who entered a PhD program with equal emphasis on research and practice were offered full financial aid, and 84% of students who entered a research-oriented PhD program received full funding (Norcross et al., 2004). Thus, the type of program you are seeking will likely have an impact on your pocketbook.

A relatively new program, called the National Institutes of Health (NIH) Loan Repayment Program, has added some much needed help for psychology graduates with student loan debt (Clay, 2006b). If graduates commit to working at least half time for 2 years in a research-oriented position (e.g., working on nonprofit or government-subsidized research in the areas of clinical, health, or pediatric psychology), they can receive up to $35,000 per year to repay their student loans. Students can apply for more than one year of this funding (Clay, 2006b). This federal program is competitive, so the funding is in no way guaranteed, but this program has helped a great many research-oriented students to decrease their debt while also adding to the research knowledge needed to help clients. Clinically oriented students also have an option to seek loan repayment through the National Health Service Corps (Clay, 2006b). Students who can commit to working for at least 2 years in an underserved area within the United States (such as an impoverished urban area or a rural area that has limited health care services) can apply to have up to $50,000 of their loans repaid. This program is also competitive, but successful applicants can reduce their debt significantly while also helping provide psychological services to individuals who might not otherwise have access to such services.

More information on the NIH Loan Repayment Program can be accessed at http://www.lrp.nih.gov and more information about the National Health Service Corp program can be found at http://www.nhsc.bhpr.hrsa.gov Both of these programs are funded by the federal government and can be modified during different budget years, so make sure to access the most up-to-date information when you are close to completing your graduate degree.

Academic and Emotional Commitments

In addition to the financial costs associated with doctoral programs in clinical psychology, you will be expected to make other commitments. For one thing, you will be asked to work harder than you have in previous academic endeavors. In addition, given the competitiveness of clinical psychology PhD programs, the majority of students have to move to attend a program, often uprooting themselves from their friends and family. This type of move is also likely to happen when students seek a 1-year full time internship toward the end of their graduate program.

The purpose of this admittedly sobering introduction is not to discourage you from applying to doctoral programs in clinical psychology. Rather, these issues are raised to help you prepare better for the initial decision-making process through which all potentials applicants should go before they spend the hundreds of dollars and numerous hours needed to apply successfully to graduate programs in clinical psychology.

Contrary to what you might have heard, your application to graduate school in clinical psychology will not be jeopardized if you decide to take some time off after completing your undergraduate studies (depending on what you do with your "time off"). If you decide to take time off before applying to graduate school, there are several things you can do to enhance your application. First, try to obtain a position in the field, either as a research assistant or as a mental health worker in a clinical setting. Both of these options will help document your commitment to the field as well as give you valuable experience and further insight in helping to decide your future. If you cannot obtain paid research or clinical positions, try to obtain a volunteer position in these areas. Second, if you are located near a university, consider taking one or more graduate courses. Once again, this will help document your commitment to the field and may help you decide whether graduate school is for you. Although your inclination may be to take clinically related courses, graduate admissions committees will probably be more impressed if you take (and do well in) graduate courses in nonclinical areas, such as statistics, research design, or psychology proseminars (e.g., learning or personality theory). In addition, you may receive credit for these latter courses when you enter a graduate program, whereas clinical programs often require that you repeat any clinically related courses you may have taken previously.

Having said all that, we also believe that perseverance and dedication to getting into a PhD program in clinical psychology will go a long way to helping you reach your goals. There is a relatively new construct being explored in social psychology called *grit* (Duckworth, Peterson, Matthews, & Kelly, 2007). Grit is defined as "perseverance and passion for long-term goals" (p. 1087), and it was found to predict educational attainment and grade point average. Grit was not significantly related to IQ, but it was related to conscientiousness. We bring up this construct to help you think about your own "grit" in seeking admission into a PhD program in clinical psychology.

TABLE 16.3
Recent PhD Graduates' Satisfaction with Their Current Job

Based on a large survey of students who graduated with a PhD in psychology in 2005, the following numbers reflect the percentage of recent graduates who were either satisfied or very satisfied with these characteristics in their current job:

Income/salary	63.4%
Benefits	73.4%
Opportunities for promotion	59.1%
Opportunities for personal development	76.0%
Opportunities for recognition	72.9%
Supervisor	74.7%
Coworkers	85.8%
Working conditions	80.4%

SOURCE: Data from Table 5c of the APA 2005 Doctorate Employment Survey (http://www.research.apa.org/des05tables.html).

We should also mention that for many of us, graduate school was an exciting and rewarding time. Despite the work load and relative poverty, there were riches in terms of learning, personal growth, and relationships with friends and colleagues. It is also heartening to know that graduates tend to be relatively satisfied with their jobs after they complete graduate school. As can be seen in Table 16.3, the majority of recent graduates were either satisfied or very satisfied with a number of aspects of their first full-time position after graduate school.

ARE MY CREDENTIALS STRONG ENOUGH FOR GRADUATE SCHOOL IN CLINICAL PSYCHOLOGY?

In order to evaluate your credentials objectively and to be aware of your strengths and weaknesses, it is important to understand the criteria employed by graduate admissions committees in clinical psychology. These include (a) the requisite course work and undergraduate experiences, especially research experience; (b) Graduate Record Exam (GRE) scores; (c) grade point average (GPA); and (d) letters of recommendation. Each graduate program may weigh these criteria differently, of course, and programs will examine other factors (e.g., personal statements, interviews) as well, but all of these criteria tend to be used, to some extent at least, by all doctoral clinical programs.

Undergraduate Coursework and Experience

Coursework. Your undergraduate department will have designed a graduate preparatory major to meet your course needs. It will probably include a core program of introductory psychology, statistics, and experimental psychology (including a laboratory). These are the minimum requirements for most graduate programs, regardless of specialization area. Note that a class in research methods has been identified as the most important class a student can take who is seeking training at the doctoral level in a clinical psychology PhD program (Mayne et al., 2006). For careers in clinically oriented fields, you also must consider taking courses like abnormal psychology, abnormal child psychology, behavior modification, clinical research methods, and other courses that are specific to your area of interest. If they are available, we encourage you to try to take small advanced seminars where you can learn about a topic in depth. Some programs also allow highly motivated undergraduate students, with strong grades, to take a graduate class as a non–degree-seeking student. All of these types of coursework activities should help you come to a better decision as to what type of career you wish to pursue, and they should help you score better on the GRE Subject Test in Psychology.

Research Experience.   In addition to standard course work, independent research such as an honors thesis and/or experience as a research assistant is very helpful, in general, and essential for PhD programs. As noted earlier, such research activity not only provides you with desirable experience but also allows faculty supervisors to observe your potential for scholarly endeavors and to include their evaluations and impressions in letters of recommendation.

There are many reasons you should gain research experience prior to applying to doctoral programs in clinical psychology. First, the PhD in clinical psychology is both a research degree and a clinical degree, and you may well spend as much, if not more, of your graduate training on research as on clinical work. Admissions committees want to ensure that applicants understand what is involved in research and that they enjoy participating in such activities. Second, working on several research projects will give you an excellent understanding of what research in graduate school will be like. It is not unusual for undergraduate students to sign up as research assistants because they know that the experience will help their application to graduate school, only to find that they love being involved in research. On the other hand, if you find that research is really not for you, then you may want to reconsider whether to apply to programs offering a PhD in clinical psychology, since much of your graduate training will focus on research activities. Third, as just noted, working with faculty on their research is an excellent way to obtain letters of recommendation that define more precisely your potential for graduate school. Fourth, working on research projects can help you decide which research areas you would (and would not) like to pursue in graduate school. This information, in turn, will help you apply to those psychology departments whose faculty are working in the areas of your greatest interest. Finally, research experience serves as an excellent basis for discussion with faculty during any faculty interviews that you might have. In fact, recent years have seen a trend in which an increasing number of interviewees for PhD programs have undertaken independent honors thesis or capstone research experiences. Thus, applicants who do not have such experiences are at a distinct disadvantage during the interview process, because they do not have the depth of knowledge of a specific research project that is associated with having undertaken an honors thesis study.

Clinical Experience.   If you think you want to be a clinician, but have never worked with a clinical population, then we encourage you to consider gaining some clinical experience. Often, structured programs (like working on a suicide or crisis hotline or working with a child advocacy group like the Guardian ad Litem program) will provide excellent training as well as close supervision for your volunteer work. Working with clients with psychological problems can be very demanding, and it is not for the faint of heart. We know of a number of professionals who had decided that they wanted to be a clinician but changed their mind after volunteering in a clinical facility. Others find that the experience confirms their beliefs that the work is both challenging and rewarding.

Although clinical experience can be valuable in helping students decide whether the mental health profession is the field for them, and in knowing which clinical areas (e.g., child, substance use) they are especially interested in, clinical experience appears not to be deemed especially important in the graduate selection process. This is especially true for PhD programs in clinical psychology. Other types of programs (e.g., master's, PsyD, or counseling psychology), which put more emphasis on clinical training, may value undergraduate clinical experience to a greater degree.

Extracurricular Activities.   Participation in extracurricular activities, including psychology clubs and honor societies such as Psi Chi, can help you learn about the field and come into contact with professionals from various specializations. Many psychology clubs or Psi Chi groups provide talks on different careers in psychology, how to prepare for the GREs, and how to apply to graduate school.

Graduate Record Exam (GRE) Scores

Most graduate schools use standardized tests to assist them in evaluating applicants. As already noted, the most common example is the GRE, including both the General Test and the Psychology Subject Test. Students often do not like to hear this, but performance on the GRE is an important predictor of success in graduate school and thus one of the most important selection criteria used by graduate admissions committees. A meta-analysis (Kuncel, Hezlett, & Ones, 2001) found that, across all disciplines, both GRE scores and undergraduate GPA were significant and powerful predictors of performance in graduate school, as measured by a variety of outcome measures (e.g., graduate GPA, publication citation counts, faculty ratings).

Students often ask what scores are necessary on the GREs to get past the initial screenings undertaken by admission committees. This is a difficult question to answer, for several reasons. First, programs vary considerably in the range of GRE scores they expect from their incoming students. Second, graduate programs often do not have strict cutoffs for the GRE scores but instead employ guidelines as to what they are looking for. For example, the minimally acceptable GRE scores reported by schools in the graduate guide books tend to be considerably below the median scores of the entering graduate classes (Morgan & Korschgen, 2006). In other words, if your GRE scores are just at or a little above the minimally acceptable scores reported by a school (e.g., an average of 500 per subtest), you probably will not be admitted to that program. If you wish to be admitted to an APA-accredited PhD clinical program, it would be ideal for you to average at least 600 on each of the GRE subtests in order to be a viable candidate for such programs (Mayne, Norcross, & Sayette, 2006). We discuss the GRE in more detail later in this chapter.

Grade Point Average

If the GRE is seen as a reliable and valid predictor of your overall ability, your GPA is seen as an excellent indicator of the effort you have exerted in college and your willingness to work up to or even beyond your predicted potential. Once again, it is impossible to offer absolute guidelines as to what PhD clinical programs are looking for when they examine an applicant's undergraduate GPA. Surveys of entering classes in PhD clinical programs suggest that a psychology GPA of 3.5 or 3.6 (on a 4-point scale) is necessary, at a minimum, to be a strong candidate for admission (Norcross et al., 1996). Thus, if you have obtained a somewhat marginal GPA, seriously consider repeating those courses in which you did poorly to improve your GPA. For example, if you earned a B– in undergraduate statistics, you would be well advised to retake the course to improve your grade. Otherwise, admission committees will be concerned about your ability to handle more difficult graduate statistics courses, where a B– is the minimally acceptable grade.

Letters of Recommendation

When reading letters of recommendation, admissions committee members tend to look for comments relating to the applicant's overall potential for graduate school, willingness to work hard, level of interpersonal skills, and likelihood of success in clinical work. Letter writers are not likely to learn these things about you through classroom contacts alone. Even if you received one of the top grades in the course, if that is the professor's only contact with you, there is not much he or she can write about you. Thus, it is crucial that you develop means of interacting with faculty outside the classroom. The best way to do this is to get involved as a paid or volunteer member of one or more faculty member's research groups. In addition, make a point of stopping by professors' offices to talk with them about class content that has intrigued you. Most professors welcome students stopping by to talk, especially if it does not concern complaining about a grade received or explaining why an assignment was missed. A good way to think about letters of recommendation is that, ideally, the professor should be able to write about your motivation, your conscientiousness, your ability to think intelligently about the subject material, your ability to take on independent responsibility, and your maturity, among other factors. You need to do whatever you can to give the professor enough samples of your behavior in these domains so that he or she can write a positive and knowledgeable letter about you.

GIVEN MY CREDENTIALS, TO WHAT TYPE OF PROGRAM CAN I REALISTICALLY ASPIRE?

One of the most difficult things you need to do when applying to graduate school is to be realistic about evaluating your credentials. Unfortunately, the credentials of many applicants are not strong enough to gain entry to PhD programs in clinical psychology.

PhD clinical programs routinely receive anywhere from 100 to 400 applications and these programs generally accept anywhere from five to ten students. Thus, these programs are extremely competitive, and shortcomings in any of the selection criteria described above can undermine your chances of receiving an offer of acceptance. Unless you have pursued other options as well, you may be setting yourself up for failure and disappointment.

Fortunately, several such options are available. For example, master's programs in clinical psychology usually have lower criteria for admission, in terms of expected GRE scores and GPA, than PhD programs. You might want to consider these programs either to earn a terminal master's degree or as the first step toward a PhD program. Counseling, school, or other psychology programs that offer clinical training also tend to be less competitive than PhD programs in clinical psychology. As noted earlier, students in these programs often receive as much applied training and experience as students in clinical psychology programs, and master's-level job openings, and even potential licensure, appear to be on the rise. Finally, nonclinical PhD programs in psychology (e.g., developmental, social) tend to attract fewer applicants and have lower admission criteria than do clinical programs. If you are committed to the field of psychology and want to remain in a research environment, you may find a nonclinical PhD program in psychology more rewarding than a mental health–related doctoral or master's program in another field.

In short, PhD programs in clinical psychology are not for everyone; they are highly competitive, they place great demands on their students, they take 5 to 7 years to complete, and they emphasize research training as much as, if not more than, clinical experience.

Having offered some guidelines to help you assess your credentials and aspirations and to determine whether you should apply to doctoral programs in clinical psychology, we now consider some more general issues that you must address before beginning the application process.

I HAVE DECIDED TO APPLY TO GRADUATE SCHOOL IN CLINICAL PSYCHOLOGY. WHAT SHOULD I DO FIRST?

In choosing graduate programs, you will want to make sure they provide the training and professional environment that will meet your needs. Therefore, you should clarify your personal goals, objectives, and plans. Are you most interested in research, balanced training in clinical practice and research, or primarily in clinical practice? Are you interested in doctoral-level or master's-level programs? Do you have an interest in a specific client population? These are but a few of the questions you should be asking yourself before the application process begins. You will not have definitive answers for all possible questions, but you will have some, and these will probably indicate what is most important to you in choosing a graduate program. In addition, the stronger your credentials, the more freedom you will have to use these factors in deciding to which programs to apply. Thus, students with a 3.5 GPA in psychology and an average of 550 on each GRE subtest will probably need to be concerned with getting into any PhD program they can, whereas students with a 4.0 GPA and 700 per GRE subtest probably have the luxury of identifying programs that are ideally suited for their needs in terms of relevant factors (e.g., faculty research interests, financial support offered, geographical location).

SHOULD I APPLY TO A MASTER'S DEGREE PROGRAM AND COMPLETE IT BEFORE I APPLY TO A DOCTORAL PROGRAM?

As noted earlier, there are various routes you can take to earn the doctorate in clinical psychology. Most PhD clinical programs are designed to prepare doctoral-level clinicians only. They may award the master's degree after a minimum number of credits and a master's thesis have been completed, but it is important to recognize that these departments accept applications for the doctoral degree only. If you earn a terminal masters degree and then wish to pursue a PhD or PsyD degree at a later point, that can be done, but if your ultimate goal is to gain admission into a PhD program in clinical psychology, then your best bet is to apply to those programs directly. If you are not sure that your qualifications are strong enough for admission into a PhD program, then you might consider applying to terminal master's programs as a back-up plan. Many graduates from these programs terminate their formal education at the master's level, but others go on to doctoral programs.

How does earning a master's degree affect your chances for admission to a doctoral program later on? The master's degree itself should neither hurt nor help your chances when applying to a PhD program in clinical psychology, but rather it is what you do with your time in the master's program that will be important for ultimate acceptance into a clinical PhD program. Graduate schools are interested in the best candidates they can find. If your credentials are excellent, your chances for being admitted to a doctoral program are good. Some students who feel they need to improve their credentials may find master's degree work helpful in achieving that goal, but doctoral admission committees consider all academic work when making their decision. A mediocre undergraduate academic record is not disregarded because it has been supplemented with a master's degree and good graduate school grades, but these graduate credentials can improve a student's chances for being seriously considered. If accepted into a master's program, you can use the time to strengthen your credentials, such as by studying for and retaking the GRE, excelling in your coursework in order to improve your grades, or getting more research experience.

IF I CHOOSE TO TERMINATE MY TRAINING AFTER EARNING A MASTER'S DEGREE, WILL MY OPPORTUNITIES FOR DOING CLINICAL WORK BE LIMITED?

Historically, the doctorate is considered the standard of the profession. You also need to consider that all U.S. states employ some form of licensing or certification for psychologists (see Chapter 15). Although requirements vary among states, an earned doctorate is a prerequisite in most of them. So while the growth of managed care systems has stimulated the job market at the master's degree level for those seeking a career in direct service, be certain that such jobs match your career expectations before deciding to prepare for clinical work by earning a master's degree. This is especially true if your ultimate goal is to have an independent clinical practice. Having said this, the recent change in the licensure law in Kentucky and other states suggests that the future for independent practice for master's-level clinicians may be more promising. Given the impact of managed care systems and the changes in the licensure laws, it is impossible to predict exactly how the job market for master's-level (and even PhD) clinical psychologists will look in 5 to 10 years.

APPLICATION PROCEDURES

It is now time to review the steps you must take to file admission applications for graduate programs in clinical psychology. There are a number of valuable resources available that can help in all stages of the application process.

How Do I Get Information about Graduate Schools and Identify "Good" Graduate Programs?

It is difficult to label graduate programs as "good" or "bad." The real question to be answered is whether a particular university, department, and program fits your needs. Part of the answer will lie in the "research" versus "clinical" emphasis of each program, and you can gather information about that by corresponding with current graduate students and faculty located there. You should also consider the size of the department and the program, whether there are faculty undertaking research in areas of interest to you, the student–faculty ratio, opportunities for a variety of practicum experiences, the size and location of the campus and the community, the type and extent of department resources, and the theoretical orientation(s) or approaches that may exist in or dominate the program.

There are a number of valuable resources available that can help in all stages of the application process. Some are listed in Table 16.4, but three books are highlighted here because they are extremely helpful to students during the application process. *Graduate Study in Psychology* (American Psychological Association, 2008) lists all master's and doctoral programs in the United States and Canada. The book delineates which programs are APA-accredited, but it also lists programs in other areas of psychology (industrial/organizational, behavioral neuroscience, cognitive, etc.). Thus, it can be used for students seeking graduate training in any area of psychology.

Similarly, *Getting In: A Step-by-Step Plan for Gaining Admission to Graduate School in Psychology,* 2nd ed. (American Psychological Association, 2007a) provides detailed information on the application process for graduate programs in any area of psychology. Many of the sections in the book focus on specific aspects of the application process (choosing which programs to apply to, preparing a resume, writing a personal statement, etc.), and there is an appendix with a timetable for the application process.

If you already know that you want to apply to a clinical or counseling doctoral program, then an extraordinary resource can be found in the *Insider's Guide to Graduate Programs in Clinical and Counseling Psychology 2008/2009 Edition* (Norcross, Sayette, & Mayne, 2008). This book focuses on the application process and also has a listing of every APA-accredited PhD and PsyD program in the United States and Canada, with helpful information about each program. Of particular interest to many applicants, each program is rated on a 1 to 7 scale (where 1 refers to a program that is fully clinically oriented, 4 refers to a program with equal emphasis on clinical and research skills, and

---

TABLE 16.4

Helpful Resources for Psychology Majors and Those Who Are Considering Applying to Graduate School

---

Although this is not an exhaustive list, many of these books have been extraordinarily helpful to students who are considering a career in psychology and who plan to apply to graduate school.

Majoring in Psychology and Considering Different Career Options

Career Paths in Psychology: Where Your Degree Can Take You, 2nd ed., by Robert J. Sternberg (Washington, DC: American Psychological Association, 2007)

Careers in Psychology: Opportunities in a Changing World, 2nd ed., by Tara L. Kuther and Robert D. Morgan (Belmont, CA: Thomson/Wadsworth, 2007)

Majoring in Psychology? Career Options for Psychology Undergraduates, 3rd ed., by Betsy L. Morgan and Ann J. Korschgen (Boston: Allyn and Bacon, 2006a)

Opportunities in Psychology Careers, by David E. Super and Charles Super (Chicago: VGM Career Books, 2001)

The Psychology Major's Handbook, 2nd ed., by Tara L. Kuther (Belmont, CA: Thomson/Wadsworth, 2006a)

What Can You Do with a Major in Psychology?, by Shelley O'Hara (New York: Cliffs Notes, 2005)

Your Career in Psychology: Clinical and Counseling Psychology, by Tara L. Kuther (Belmont, CA: Thomson/Wadsworth, 2006b)

Applying to Graduate School

Getting In: A Step-by-Step Plan for Gaining Admission to Graduate School in Psychology, 2nd ed., by the American, Psychological Association (Washington, DC: American Psychological Association, 2007a)

Graduate Study in Psychology, by the American, Psychological Association (Washington, DC: American Psychological Association, 2008)

Insider's Guide to Graduate Programs in Clinical and Counseling Psychology, 2008/2009 Edition, by John C. Norcross, Michael A. Sayette, and Tracy J. Mayne (New York: Guilford, 2008)

Surviving Graduate School and Beyond

The Compleat Academic: A Career Guide, 2nd ed., by John M. Darley, Mark P. Zanna, and Henry L. Roediger (Washington, DC: American Psychological Association, 2004)

Life after Graduate School in Psychology: Insider's Advice from New Psychologists, by Robert D. Morgan, Tara L. Kuther, and Corey J. Habben (New York: Psychology Press, 2005)

Negotiating Graduate School: A Guide for Graduate Students, 2nd ed., by Mark H. Rossman (Thousand Oaks, CA: Sage, 2002)

The Portable Mentor: Expert Guide to a Successful Career in Psychology, by Mitchell J. Prinstein and Marcus Patterson (New York: Kluwer Academic/Plenum Publishers, 2003).

Succeeding in Graduate School: The Career Guide for Psychology Students, by Steven Walfish and Allen K. Hess (Mahwah, NJ: Erlbaum, 2001)

---

7 refers to a program that is fully research oriented). This information is usually based on the report of the Director of Clinical Training, so the information can help students find programs that are consistent with their training needs and interests. Table 16.4 lists other helpful sources.

Information can also be accessed online. One valuable resource for gaining information about graduate schools and the application process is the APA Web site (http://www.apa.org), where students can find out about APA-accredited programs, careers in psychology, and salary information about various jobs within the field of psychology. Another valuable Web site, which provides links to specific programs, is: http://www.psychwww.com/resource/deptlist.htm.

The Council of University Directors of Clinical Psychology (CUDCP; http://www.am.org/cudcp/) also maintains a Web site that provides links to many clinical programs. Note that not all CUDCP programs are APA-accredited, so you must verify the accreditation status of a program through a resource other than this Web site. In an effort to help students learn more about programs as they decide where to apply, CUDCP has a voluntary program through which clinical programs list "full disclosure" of admissions and outcome data for their program on their Web site. This information is very useful to potential applicants, who can then compare programs directly on the same variables (e.g., number of applicants, number of accepted students, GRE and GPA averages for recently admitted students, number of graduate students who applied for and secured an internship, number of graduating students, average length of time it took for those students to graduate). If you are scanning different doctoral programs online, go to the clinical psychology Web page and look for this full disclosure data in a table format (which is often described as student data, student statistics, or admissions and outcome data).

As of January 2007, the American Psychological Association also requires all APA-accredited doctoral programs to provide the following information to applicants:

- Time it takes to complete the program.
- Cost of completing the program (e.g., tuition, fees, financial aid options, etc.).
- Success of graduate students in obtaining internships.
- Attrition (i.e., how many students enter the program and then drop out each year).
- Number and percentage of graduates from the program who have become licensed in the past decade (this requirement was mandated for the year 2008).

This information is meant to help students compare programs on the same variables so that they can make informed decisions when considering their options for graduate training (Munsey, 2007b).

There is also a wonderful resource posted on the Web site of the Society of Clinical Child and Adolescent Psychology (APA Division 53; http://www.clinicalchildpsychology.org). It is a helpful and student-friendly document written by Dr. Mitch Prinstein that gives advice to students who are interested in applying to graduate school in clinical child psychology. Much of the information is also relevant to students interested in other aspects of clinical psychology, so it is worth a look.

Finally, Fauber (2006) commented on the use of online message boards for students interested in clinical psychology. Sites such as *The Student Doctor Network* in clinical psychology receive a great deal of attention from prospective students. Students appear to use this type of message board as a source of information and as a source of support (Fauber, 2006). Given that the postings are mostly just other students' opinions, students may want to check more formal sites to confirm information that is crucial to their application (e.g., an application date or specific information about a professor), but it appears that message boards are yet another way that students can access up-to-date information from others going through the same process. In short, there is a wealth of information in printed material as well as online, so students should have access to plenty of resources during the arduous task of applying to graduate school.

Obviously, applying to graduate school is a major undertaking, not something to be done on the spur of the moment. Here is a list of the different tasks you must complete to successfully accomplish this undertaking:

1. Study for and take the GRE General and Subject tests at least once each.
2. Search the Web for programs to which to apply, and identify at least 10 to 15 appropriate programs.
3. Obtain information on these programs, and fill out the application and financial aid forms for each.
4. Arrange for your transcripts from all of your undergraduate institutions to be sent to each graduate program.
5. Arrange for your GRE scores to be sent to each program.
6. Identify three professors who are willing to write letters of recommendation for you, and get them the necessary forms and information about your undergraduate career at least one month prior to the first application deadline.
7. Write a personal statement and revise it as often as necessary based on feedback you have received from one or more faculty members.

Once you have done your "homework" and read these resources and sought information on the Web, you may want to talk with a trusted professor or two to see if they have any suggestions for you during the application process. In preparing for courses, doing research, and keeping current for clinical practice, most faculty members carefully review new ideas and research, attend professional meetings, and participate in continuing education workshops. This exposure to the field helps faculty members learn about various departments, programs, schools, training and research staff, the nature and theoretical orientations of different programs, recent changes in the direction of certain departments, and other pertinent information. Although it is not reasonable to expect faculty members to know about all or even most doctoral programs, they will be able to provide you with good information about many of them. In addition, the faculty may have personal contacts at schools that may help your application. A personal recommendation from a faculty member can be a valuable help in highlighting your credentials and increasing the attention your application receives.

Similarly, graduate students at your undergraduate institution may know a great deal about the application process—because many of them have just been through that process. If you have clinical psychology graduate students as teaching assistants or instructors, make sure to talk with them about the application process. They may have a great deal of information about programs that you are interested in because they may have also applied to and interviewed at those programs just a few years previously.

Professional journals and related publications are information sources that many applicants overlook. An excellent way to find programs that meet your needs is to use these sources to identify faculty who are studying topics that interest you. A thorough search of the literature—using PsycINFO, Google, or other online search engines—will very likely highlight faculty with whom you might like to study and indicate where they can be reached. The e-mail addresses of faculty with somewhat uncommon names can be easily identified through Google, but faculty with somewhat more common names may be a bit more difficult to track down with Google. PsycINFO usually lists e-mail addresses of faculty, but if that does not work, you can always track down a recent research article, which should definitely provide an e-mail address if the professor has one.

Overall, the use of these resources should help you gain a wealth of knowledge about the field of clinical psychology and what it takes to apply to graduate programs. The information may seem daunting at first, but the more you read, the more you will find overlap of information and opinions.

What Does American Psychological Association (APA) Accreditation of a Clinical Psychology Graduate Program Mean?

APA accreditation means the program has met a minimum standard of quality (see Chapter 15). Accreditation applies to educational institutions and programs, not to individuals. It does not guarantee jobs or licensure for individuals, though being a graduate of an accredited program greatly facilitates such achievement. It does speak to the manner and quality by which an educational institution or program conducts its business. It speaks to a sense of public trust, as well as professional quality (APA, 1996, p. ix).

Thus, graduating with a PhD from any accredited program is seen as a laudatory accomplishment, regardless of the school's apparent reputation. Further, many APA-approved internships will only accept applicants from APA-approved graduate programs. Thus, if you are thinking about a PhD in clinical psychology, there are many reasons to limit your search only to APA-approved programs.

A list of APA-accredited programs in clinical psychology is published each year in the December issue of the APA's main journal, *American Psychologist*. In addition, the APA accredits PhD programs in other areas, including counseling and school psychology, as well as a number of PsyD programs. In contrast, master's programs are not accredited by APA, making it more difficult to identify high-quality master's programs.

When Should I Apply, and What Kind of Timeline Should I Expect?

Specific timelines can be found in both *Getting In: A Step-by-Step Plan for Gaining Admission to Graduate School in Psychology,* 2nd ed. (American Psychological Association, 2007a) and *Insider's Guide to Graduate Programs in Clinical and Counseling Psychology* 2008/2009 Edition (Norcross, Sayette, & Mayne, 2008). Following one of these guidelines should help to make sure you are accomplishing all of the necessary tasks in a timely fashion.

In general, though, it is never too early to start. It is reasonable to start seeking information in June or July, a little over a year before your desired admission date (e.g., July for the fall admission 14 months later). Seeking information earlier than this can sometimes result in inaccurate information (e.g., admissions dates or requirements might change from year to year), although looking for programs that fit your needs can happen as early as you wish since programs and training philosophies do not change that rapidly.

Nearly all graduate programs have admissions information on their Web sites, which is clearly the preferred mode of information transmission on the part of the graduate programs. Most programs have application materials and all of the necessary information easily identified on their Web site, and many have a Frequently Asked Questions section that helps clarify the application process.

Although department application deadlines vary, most fall between December 1 and January 15. A few come earlier while others (mostly for master's degree programs or professional schools) run later. Some departments (primarily master's-level programs) that have later deadlines often select students as applications arrive for processing. If you apply to schools that use this "rolling admissions" plan, it is to your advantage to submit your application early in the process.

To How Many Programs Should I Apply?

Students often wonder how many schools they should apply to. It is difficult to identify a specific number of applications that is appropriate for all students. We are reminded of two cases: One student applied to six schools and was admitted to all of them, while another applied to 27 and was admitted to one. Since competition for admission to PhD programs is keen, the general rule is to apply to as many programs as you can reasonably afford. The larger the number of applications, the better your chances of being accepted.

It is our experience that even students with relatively strong credentials will want to apply to 10 to 15 programs to ensure at least one offer of acceptance and to increase their chances of receiving funding as well. Mayne and colleagues (2006) noted that, on average, students apply to 13 programs in clinical and counseling psychology. They further suggest that you apply to at least 10 to 12 programs, five of which you might consider "safe" schools where your credentials would be considered strong, five "ambitious" programs where your credentials might not be as strong as needed but at least you are in the ball park, and one or two "stretch" programs where your credentials are far below the average but perhaps where you have an especially good fit with the program (e.g., your area of expertise in the research or clinical domain).

As you gather information about potential graduate programs, you should also make a note of how many applications each program receives and how many applicants are admitted to the program. Even among excellent clinical doctoral programs, the number of admissions varies significantly (which then reflects on your chances of gaining acceptance into the program). For example, in 2006 for the PhD programs in clinical psychology, 126 students applied to the University of Illinois at Urbana–Champaign, while 608 students applied to Boston University. Both programs are excellent, both are accredited by the American Psychological Association and are members of the Academy of Psychological Clinical Science, both are heavily research oriented and well respected within the field—yet the numbers of applicants varied significantly. Although we know of no formal studies on this issue, it appears that programs in larger cities or programs in more desirable places to live (especially those with mild winters!) tend to receive more applications than comparable programs in smaller towns or in areas with harsher climates.

Thus, if your dream school is in a highly desirable city with perfect weather, you may want to consider looking into equally excellent programs in less popular places on the off chance that there are fewer applicants to the latter program.

Once you have decided on a final list of schools, ask yourself what you will do if you do not gain acceptance to any of them. If your credentials are somewhat marginal for doctoral programs, you may want to consider applying to a handful of master's programs as a back-up if you do not receive admission into any doctoral programs. Many well-respected psychologists have had to first complete a terminal master's program and then reapply to doctoral programs in clinical psychology in order to achieve their goal of the Ph.D. However, do not apply to programs that are really not acceptable to you. Such applications waste admission committee time, your time, and perhaps most importantly, your money.

How Much Will It Cost to Apply?

Applying to graduate school is an expensive process in terms of the time and effort involved as well as the money spent. Total GRE and other testing costs usually run somewhere close to $250. Departmental application fees usually vary from $20 to $50. Transcript costs (usually $5 to $10 each), additional test report fees (e.g., $15 for GRE scores to be sent to each school), postage, and photocopies can add up very quickly. Someone applying to 10 graduate programs can expect an average cost of $1,000 during the application process. Therefore, it is important to choose the programs you apply to with care and to realistically appraise your chances of receiving an offer. Note that if you are lucky enough to be invited for an interview, you will also need to cover your own travel costs in most cases.

If you are significantly financially strained, there may be ways for you to lighten the financial burden somewhat. For example, the Educational Testing Service offers a GRE Fee Reduction Voucher Program for students who receive financial aid at their university and who receive almost no money from their parents. Similarly, many universities have programs through which you can petition for a reduction or a waiver of the application fee—but these reductions and waivers do not come easily. Often, the financial hardship has to be documented thoroughly, and certain characteristics about the applicant (e.g., that he or she is from an underrepresented ethnic/minority group) must be evident in order to qualify the student for a reduced or waived fee. If money is a problem for you, make sure to look for these options—but do not count on them.

What Testing Is Involved in Applying to Graduate School?

The large majority of graduate schools require the GRE for admission, and most admissions committees weigh GRE scores heavily in their acceptance decisions (Norcross, Kohout, & Wicherski, 2005). We first review the contents of the GRE, discuss studying for it, and then discuss its role in the graduate school admissions process.

What is the GRE? The GRE consists of a general test and a subject test—in this case, the subject is psychology. The General Test is described in the *Graduate Record*

Examinations Information and Registration Bulletin (Educational Testing Service, 2007, p. 5; also see http://www.gre.org), as follows:

The General Test measures skills that have been developed over a long period of time and are not necessarily related to any particular field of study. The test is composed of Verbal Reasoning (V), Quantitative Reasoning (Q), and Analytical Writing (AW) sections. Typical testing time is listed below:

Verbal: 30-minute section (30 questions)

Quantitative: 45-minute section (28 questions)

Analytical Writing: two sections—one writing task per section:

Present Your Perspective on an Issue (45 minutes)

Analyze an Argument (30 minutes)

The subtests are further explained on the Web site as:

Verbal Reasoning—The skills measured include the test taker's ability to analyze and evaluate written material and synthesize information obtained from it; analyze relationships among component parts of sentences; recognize relationships between words and concepts

Quantitative Reasoning—The skills measured include the test taker's ability to understand basic concepts of arithmetic, algebra, geometry, and data analysis; reason quantitatively; solve problems in a quantitative setting

Analytical Writing—The skills measured include the test taker's ability to articulate complex ideas clearly and effectively; examine claims and accompanying evidence; support ideas with relevant reasons and examples; sustain a well-focused, coherent discussion; control the elements of standard written English

The Subject Test in Psychology, which is required by approximately two-thirds of doctoral programs in psychology, is described on the GRE Web site as follows:

Most editions of the test consist of approximately 205 multiple-choice questions. Each question in the test has five options from which the examinee is to select the one option that is the correct or best answer to the question . . . .

The questions in the Psychology Test are drawn from courses of study most commonly offered at the undergraduate level within the broadly defined field of psychology.

Questions may require recalling factual information, analyzing relationships, applying principles, drawing conclusions from data, evaluating a research design, and/or identifying a psychologist who has made a theoretical or research contribution to the field.

The Psychology Test yields two subscores in addition to the total score. Although the test offers only two subscores, there are questions in three content categories:

1. Experimental or natural science oriented (about 40% of the questions), including learning, language, memory, thinking, sensation and perception, physiological psychology, ethology, and comparative psychology. They contribute to the experimental psychology subscore and the total score.

2. Social or social science oriented (about 43% of the questions). These questions are distributed among the fields of clinical and abnormal, developmental, personality, and social psychology. They contribute to the social psychology subscore and the total score.

3. General (about 17% of the questions), including the history of psychology, applied psychology, measurement, research designs, and statistics. They contribute to the total score only.

The GRE General Test is given only by computer in the United States and Canada. The paper-based test is available only in countries where the computer-based testing system is not available. There are hundreds of official testing sites across the United States and Canada, and students can arrange to take the GRE General Test at a time that is convenient to them. With the computerized test, you can learn the results of the Verbal and Quantitative sections immediately after you have finished, and score reports are mailed to you and the schools you designate within 15 days. You can take the computer-based version of the test almost any day of the year, although you can take the test only once per calendar month.

Note that the computer-based testing for the General Test does not allow you to change your answer once it is entered. Thus, it is not possible to make a first pass through the test to answer "easy" questions and then go back and spend more time on those that take more thought. This restriction has tended to raise the anxiety level of some students because it forces them to change the way they have learned to take multiple-choice tests. For this reason, we suggest that you consider taking the practice computer-generated exams that are available from Educational Testing Services (ETS; http://www.ets.org).

The GRE Subject Test in Psychology can be taken only via the paper-based method, and it is offered only three times a year (usually in early October, early November, and mid-April). Because the GRE Subject Test is not currently available in a computer-based format, you must sign up to take it on one of the three standard testing dates. It takes approximately 6 weeks to receive the scores of paper-based tests, so the latest you can take the subject test is on a scheduled date that is at least 6 weeks before your earliest application deadline. For example, if December 1 is the first deadline for the schools to which you are applying, then only the October test date will meet that deadline. Also, it is important that you know the results of the GRE before you begin the application process so that your scores can help shape decisions about where to apply. Applying to certain graduate programs before you know what your GRE scores are can be a waste of time and money. Having scores at the 90th percentile makes it reasonable to apply to the most competitive schools, whereas scores at the 40th percentile require a more conservative strategy.

Should I Study for the GRE? You can, and should, study for the GRE! The GRE Web site describes the types of questions found on the general test, along with a number of strategies you can use in taking the computer-based test. A free full-length sample GRE general test, which includes instructions for evaluating your performance, is available from the GRE program at the Educational Testing Service. ETS also sells practice material, including GRE general tests and GRE subject tests actually administered in previous years. In addition, ETS now sells software that allows you to practice the computer version of the test and receive feedback on your performance. All of this material can help you become familiar with the types and forms of questions you are likely to encounter on the GRE, and it can also give you practice at pacing yourself during the actual examination.

You can also prepare for the GRE general test via test preparation courses (presented live or online by test preparation companies like Kaplan and Princeton Review) and with annually revised test preparation books. Because in-person and online courses can be quite expensive (with many in-person test preparation classes costing over $1,000), most students tend to use the test preparation books. These books usually provide a mathematics and vocabulary review, tips on test taking, and a set of sample test items, and many of them come with computer-based enhancement features. Some of the more frequently used "how to prepare" books are published by Barron's Educational Series, Arco Publishing Company, Kaplan, and Princeton Review. They are readily available at most bookstores (whether online or in the store).

Deciding on test preparation courses versus self-preparation is an individual decision. Some students do not have the time or inclination to design a disciplined preparation study schedule and, for them, the expense of test preparation courses is worth it because the courses provide needed structure. An alternative strategy is to do the self-preparation for the first time you take the test, and then if you are not satisfied with your scores, you can try the more formal test preparation courses. Whether you decide on a formal course or a do-it-yourself approach, it is important to prepare for the GRE General Test in some way. The stakes are rather high—whether you receive an offer to a PhD program and/or the type of financial aid you receive depend to a large degree on how well you do on the GRE tests.

As for the Subject Test in Psychology, remember that it covers all areas of the discipline. Names, theories, and definitions are likely to be covered on the test, as are basic concepts. No one is expected to know about every area, so if you have not been exposed to certain aspects of psychology, you will no doubt have trouble with some questions. You can prepare for the subject test in psychology by thoroughly reviewing a comprehensive introductory psychology textbook. In addition, books that present the history of psychology and/or systems and theories in psychology provide information that is particularly useful in preparing for the psychology subject test. As with the General GRE, there are also in-person, online, and printed materials that can help you prepare for the GRE subject test. If you are not a psychology major, then scoring well on the GRE subject test is especially important, since it may be the only way for you to show your knowledge of the field. Whether or not you are a psychology major, it is in your best interest to study for both the general and the subject GRE tests and to prepare extensively for these important exams.

Why is the GRE So Important to Admissions Committees?

Although there are many concerns about the use of the GRE, especially when trying to estimate the potential of students from ethnic/minority backgrounds (Vasquez & Jones, 2006), the test remains a central component in the admissions process of the majority of doctoral and master's programs in psychology.

In addition to the predictive validity of the GRE, there are other reasons these scores are valued by admissions committees. The GRE represents the only data for which direct comparisons can be made across all applicants. All students take exactly the same test, so performance is not influenced by differences in collegiate standards, as are letters of recommendation and college grades. A score of 600 on the verbal subtest for a student at the University of California–San Diego means the same as a 600 for someone at the University of Vermont. Thus, the GRE is widely viewed as providing a valid indicator of a student's potential for successful performance in graduate school. In addition, the GRE and undergraduate GPA together can serve as relatively objective screening instruments that help admission committees reduce several hundred applicants to a more manageable number. With this dramatically smaller pool of applicants, the admissions committee can then give much closer scrutiny to other, more qualitative and time-consuming selection criteria, such as the personal statement, letters of recommendation, and personal interview (Morgan & Korschgen, 2006).

Acceptable GRE scores, however, vary according to the type of program to which you are applying. For example, acceptance into a master's program will likely not require as high a GRE score as acceptance into a doctoral program. One survey found that students in master's programs averaged 1053 on the GRE (Verbal and Quantitative combined), whereas students in doctoral programs averaged 1183 (Norcross et al., 2005). Note, however, that this survey included all areas of psychology and also included both PsyD and PhD programs in the category of doctoral programs. There are indications that the GRE scores required for acceptance into university-based PhD programs in clinical psychology are much higher than 1183. A quick review of 13 clinical PhD programs from the Academy of Psychological Clinical Sciences (all of which are also APA-approved), showed that GRE scores were very competitive, with a mean average Verbal score of 625 and a mean average Quantitative score of 670, for a total average of 1295. GPA was also high in this group, with an average undergraduate GPA of 3.72 on a 4-point scale.

For students seeking more clinically oriented programs, it is difficult to estimate the average GRE scores of successful applicants in professional schools. In their study of APA-accredited PsyD programs in clinical psychology, Norcross and colleagues (2004) noted that only 12 out of 41 programs provided GRE information and only 13 out of 41 programs provided GPA information for their recently enrolled students. Thus, it is difficult to estimate the average GRE scores of students who are successful in gaining entrance into a PsyD program. The minimum GRE scores reported for PsyD programs are lower than in programs with equal emphasis on research and practice and lower than research-oriented PhD programs (Mayne et al., 2006). Note also that some freestanding, non–university-based PsyD programs do not require the GRE test as part of the admissions process.

Depending on the diversity-related rules and regulations of the university, scores on the GRE and other standardized quantitative tests are sometimes not given as much weight when evaluating applications from members of ethnic minority groups, international students, students with disabilities, and other "nontraditional" or disadvantaged students whose potential might not be captured fully by such tests. When GRE scores or other standardized tests are required by an admissions committee, everyone must submit them, but sometimes the scores are weighted differently depending on the other characteristics of the applicant.

How Important Is My Grade Point Average?

Your GPA is seen as an excellent indicator of the effort you have exerted in college and your willingness to work up to or even beyond your predicted potential. Thus, an outstanding undergraduate GPA may offset to some degree a less than desired GRE score. Conversely, outstanding GRE scores combined with a mediocre GPA could raise serious concerns about an applicant's motivation toward school. This is why the GRE and GPA make such excellent screening instruments—together they offer valid and objective measures of both academic potential and willingness to work hard.

Admissions committees look for several things when examining an applicant's college transcripts. Although your overall GPA is important, admissions committees often focus on your psychology GPA. They also want to make sure you are a serious student and that you did not just "blow off" your other courses because they may have been outside your major. However, the committees tend to be forgiving if you started off in another area of study (e.g., as a premed student) and did poorly in these courses. Second, the admissions committees look to see that you maintained or improved your GPA as you progressed through college rather than letting your GPA fall as you got closer to graduation. Often, you must submit the GPA for your last two years for this purpose. Admissions committees tend to be more forgiving of poorer grades early in your college career than they are of later poorer grades. They also may pay close attention to "less popular" required courses such as statistics and experimental methods.

Will I Need Letters of Recommendation for Graduate School Application? If So, How Many and from Whom?

Three letters of recommendation are required by most graduate programs in clinical psychology. At least two letters should be academic references—that is, from psychology faculty familiar with your academic ability. Ideally, at least one of the letters should be from a faculty member who has supervised you in research-related activities. If faculty from other disciplines can provide an additional picture of your academic achievement and potential for graduate study, feel free to ask them for letters.

A letter from someone who supervised a clinically related experience or relevant job generally is not given much weight by admissions committees. Similarly, letters from "important people" such as senators, governors, and religious leaders do not help your application. Generally, these say nothing more than "I have been asked to write . . ." and "please give this student full consideration." Such letters are likely to leave the impression that you feel incapable of "making it" on your own. Unless the writer is in a position to judge the candidate's potential as a graduate student, researcher, or a clinician, such "prestige" letters should not be submitted. Similarly, if you know a clinical psychologist socially but not through a formal mechanism (e.g., the psychologist is a friend of the family), then you should not ask him or her to write you a letter of recommendation. Although the psychologist knows what it takes to excel in graduate school, his or her judgment is not considered to be objective because of the personal and social relationships that exist between the psychologist, you, and your family. Most letters of recommendation include a statement as to how the letter writer knows the applicant, and admissions committees do not look kindly on letters that say things like "I have known the applicant for all of her life, and I have watched her grow from a timid toddler into a scintillating senior student."

What Should I Know about Asking for Letters of Recommendation?

When you approach a faculty member to ask if he or she is willing to write you a letter, it is likely that the faculty member will want you to provide information about yourself to update his or her memory of what role you served on the research project, what grade you got in the course, what honors you won, and other details. Information about your activities, accomplishments, and job experiences can supplement classroom contacts in a way that enhances the tone and thrust of a recommendation letter.

Here is a list of items you should provide to faculty who are writing letters of recommendation for you (Morgan & Korschgen, 2006, p. 106):

1. Your full name.
2. Major, minor, curriculum, and specialization.
3. A computation of the grade average in your major, in all college work, and in courses taken since the end of your sophomore year.
4. A transcript of your college courses and grades.
5. A list of the psychology laboratory courses you have had.
6. A current resume or curriculum vitae.
7. A description of other research experiences, including comments about the full extent of your participation (include a copy of any major research papers you wrote or contributed to).
8. A list of honor societies, clubs, and organizations to which you belong, along with comments on your participation (be sure to mention positions of responsibility you held).
9. A brief discussion of jobs you have held and volunteer work you have done. Some students carry heavy work loads while being enrolled as full-time students in order to pay for their education; this information should be included, too.
10. An outline of your personal and professional plans and goals.
11. Any other information that might be helpful to the person in writing your letter of recommendation.

Be sure to ask for letters and provide all appropriate recommendation information and other materials early, at least one month before the first application is due. Remember, faculty often write letters for many students; give them plenty of time to prepare yours. To reduce the possibility of error and to speed the process, you want to minimize the work the faculty has to do in putting the recommendation material together, thereby minimizing any errors that may occur. Therefore, (a) include a stamped, addressed envelope for each program for which a recommendation is to be sent, (b) when forms are included, be sure to type your name and other information that is not part of the formal recommendation in the appropriate spaces and attach the appropriate envelope to each form, and (c) include a list of all the schools—and their application deadlines—to which a recommendation letter is to be sent, indicating which schools have provided forms to be completed and which have not provided such forms and highlighting the specific program to which you are applying (e.g., master's program in counseling psychology, PhD program in clinical psychology)

Note that many universities are moving to self-contained applications, whereby the applicant has to collect all of the materials (including the letters of recommendation) and submit them in one packet. For these programs, you should provide your letter writers with a stamped envelope addressed to you, and you should ask them to sign the outside of the envelope once it is sealed. Make sure to type the professor's name on the return address area and note on the outside of the envelope which university the letter should be forwarded to once you receive it. If you have some of these self-contained applications in your list, it helps to make it clear to the professor which envelopes should be sent to the graduate program directly and which should be sent to you.

Some universities are even moving to a solely online application system, whereby the applicant submits the names and e-mail addresses for the letter writers and the graduate program contacts the letter writer directly in order to request a letter of recommendation. Even in these cases, you should provide your letter writer with all of the information above (except for the stamped envelope for the specific universities that have an online application system).

Will I Be Able to See My Letters of Recommendation?

Because of federal law, letters of reference are not confidential unless you waive your right to see them. We encourage you to consider waiving your right to see the letters because many admissions committee members feel that letter writers are more likely to provide candid evaluations when they know that the student will not see the letter. If you are concerned about what the letter might include, ask potential letter writers if they can write in support of your application, not just if they will write a letter of reference. Most faculty are more than willing to indicate whether they can write a favorable letter for you.

What Should I Write about in My Personal Statement?

Most applications require that you include some form of a personal statement, usually two to three pages in length. Good advice on writing a personal statement is provided in *Getting In: A Step-by-Step Plan for Gaining Admission to Graduate School in Psychology,* 2nd ed. (American Psychological Association, 2007a) and *Insider's Guide to Graduate Programs in Clinical and Counseling Psychology 2008/2009 Edition* (Norcross, Sayette, & Mayne, 2008). Generally, variations on the same personal statement can be used for all of your applications, but the essay should be revised to reflect how your research and clinical interests mesh with the particular faculty and program to which you are applying. Programs differ in how much weight they give to the personal statement, and what you write in the personal statement may not help your application a great deal, but it certainly can hurt your chances. Any grammatical or typographical errors can reflect negatively on your writing skills, your conscientiousness, and your attention to details. Therefore, it is absolutely imperative that you have someone else, preferably a faculty member, read your statement for coherence and writing style as well as to discover and correct any grammatical or typographical errors.

What should go into a personal statement? Contrary to its title, it should not be too personal. Think of the task as a professional statement rather than a personal statement. In other words, it is not an autobiography—do not bring up childhood experiences that may have shaped your life. Nor should the statement get into any personal problems that you or family members may have had, even if these experiences ultimately influenced your decision to apply to clinical psychology programs. Instead, the personal statement is your chance to convince the admissions committee that you are a good match for their graduate program. The fact that the committee is reading your personal statement means that you have already passed their initial screen and they feel your credentials are appropriate for their program. Thus, in writing your statement, you need to think about what graduate programs are looking for in their applicants, and then describe how you meet those criteria. As noted earlier, graduate programs generally are looking for students who are intellectually curious, highly motivated, hard working, and have a good familiarity with the science of psychology, especially as it relates to research experience. These are the factors that you should be addressing in some fashion in your personal statement. Bottoms and Nysse (1999) noted that a personal statement should cover four key components: (a) previous research experience, (b) current research interests, (c) other relevant experience, and (d) future career goals.

In the section on current research interests, make sure to include some brief discussion of how your interests coincide with ongoing research undertaken by the faculty in the program to which you are applying. Once students are accepted, many programs assign students to faculty for research mentoring, so it should be crystal clear how your interests match with those of one or more of the faculty in the program. It is quite common, and often expected, that students name faculty members in their personal statement to show with whom they would like to work. Listing up to about three faculty members with related interests is considered acceptable, but trying to list the entire clinical faculty makes you look unfocused and desperate. Ideally, the student will have already made contact with the faculty members to express interest in their work and to begin a dialogue that might help at the point of admissions decisions.

In the section on other relevant experience, you can include a brief discussion of any clinical volunteer work or extracurricular activities in which you have been involved. Having clinical experience may not be a very important criterion for admission, but it is helpful to know that you have some evidence of experience in "helping relationships." Similarly, a long list of extracurricular activities, such as being a member of Psi Chi, will not strengthen your application very much. However, it could help a lot if you served in a leadership role, which then also led to strong letters of support from faculty advisors and campus or community leaders. In general, clinical activities and extracurricular activities are not considered strongly in the admissions process except as they might indicate your involvement in psychology, your interpersonal skills, and your willingness to work hard.

Are Personal Interviews Required?

Once the applications have been reviewed by the admissions committee, it is common for strong candidates to be invited for an in-person interview. The large majority of programs require an interview and most prefer an in-person interview. Offers for interviews usually only come after the admissions committee has considerably narrowed down the number of applicants. Interviews are usually held on campus, which gives the candidate and the department a chance to size each other up. If you are invited to attend an interview, try to do so regardless of the inconvenience or expense involved. If departments have to choose between two equally qualified students, only one of whom interviewed in person, this individual will probably have the advantage. Graduate admissions committees take the lack of an interview as a possible sign that the applicant is not really interested in the program. All things being equal, admissions committees would rather offer acceptance to a student who is clearly interested in the program and who appears ready to attend the program rather than someone who expresses little interest in the program. If it is really financially or physically impossible for you to attend the interview, then you may want to show your motivation toward the program in other ways (e.g., request phone interviews with a number of faculty, contact a number of graduate students to begin a dialogue about the program, let the admissions committee know via e-mail that you remain very interested in their program). Of course, do not make yourself a pest, but use your judgment in finding a way to show that you are truly interested in the program.

Programs that require telephone interviews rather than in-person interviews are the exception rather than the rule. However, some programs conduct an initial screening interview on the phone to gauge the applicant's interest in and appropriateness for the program before actually inviting the candidate for an onsite interview. With this in mind, you might want to try a bit of strategy used by one successful applicant. Near his telephone at home, he kept information about each of the programs to which he had applied (e.g., faculty names, particular emphases and strengths) along with notes about his career interests and goals. He felt that if he received a call from a school to which he had applied, having this information handy would reduce his anxiety about the conversation and help him organize his responses so that his emphasis would be appropriate for each institution. This plan also assured that he would include all the points he wanted to make during a call and thus avoid regret over failing to mention something important. He did receive a call and his strategy worked.

The same strategy can be used when you are contacted by e-mail. Increasingly, graduate admissions committees deal with applicants solely electronically, so applicants should check their e-mail frequently throughout the application process. If you have a non–university-based e-mail address with a provocative name (e.g., sexything555), then you should definitely set up an e-mail account with a more formal address well before the application process begins. Also, double check any quotations or images that are sent automatically as part of your e-mail signature, since these sayings or images might not present you in the best light professionally.

Although social norms differ somewhat in the use of e-mail, your e-mail messages during the application in the application process should be very formal. Make sure to use proper grammar, punctuation, and spelling when communicating with a graduate program. Even contact with a graduate student assistant or secretary should be very formal, since these e-mails are often forwarded to the head of the admissions committee. Overall, each point of contact that you have with the university to which you have applied is another point where the admissions committee might make judgments about your professionalism.

While we are on the topic of technology, note that a number of admissions committees have now begun using the Web to seek additional information about applicants. For example, there are a number of programs that search sites like MySpace and FaceBook to see if they can find out anything about the applicants to their program. So, take a look at your postings, if you have them, and consider what an admissions committee would think about you after reviewing the posting (Behnke, 2007). Relatedly, once students are in a graduate program, their personal presentation of themselves on the Web may have professional repercussions. For example, graduate students who see clients should consider the ramifications of the possibility that their clients could conduct a Web search and possibly find personal or less-than-flattering information about their therapist. These points relate to many professional issues that were discussed in Chapter 15, but they also are relevant during the application and interview process.

If you did not take part in a face-to-face interview and if you were lucky enough to be admitted into the program, it is appropriate to visit the school and talk with department representatives and graduate students. Make an appointment well ahead of time by e-mailing the admissions coordinator or the director of clinical training and asking to meet with clinical psychology faculty and graduate students. Be prepared to outline briefly the nature of your questions, and have a number of alternative dates in mind before you contact them.

Often, students want to schedule interview appointments before they apply to a school or before they are admitted. Some departments, especially PsyD and master's programs, welcome early interviews. However, other departments have so many applicants that it is impossible to accommodate such requests. Usually, the information you gather through the methods mentioned earlier will be sufficient to help you decide whether or not to apply to a particular program. If the material you accessed is not sufficiently informative to give you a clear picture of a particular program, contact the department for additional details. Before doing so, though, be sure to carefully read the material you have on hand so that you do not ask about things that a department has already covered in its printed or online material. Once you are admitted, however, campus visits and interviews can help you to compare programs and make your "accept" or "reject" decisions.

How Do I Prepare for an Onsite Interview?

If you are invited for an interview by a program, this means that you are in their final, relatively small (e.g., 25 to 35) pool of applicants. Thus, you have a good chance of eventually receiving an offer from that program. You will want to optimize the impact of your interview, both in terms of the information you gather and the impression you make. To do so requires preparation and practice. There are several things you should do prior to your interview.

1. Gather and read as much information about the program as you can. Read and become familiar with everything the program has sent you, as well as any additional information you can get from the Web site. Nearly all graduate programs use their Web sites for recruitment purposes, so make sure to read everything on the clinical area Web site (including affiliated Web sites or attached documents, if they are provided).

2. Read and become familiar with several published articles by the faculty members with whom you are most interested in working. As you read these articles, make notes on topics that interest you and questions that the research raises.

3. Prepare yourself to talk at length about your own research experience. You should be able to describe the purposes of the research, the methodology, the primary results, and the lessons you have learned from this experience. It is a good strategy to prepare in advance a brief description of your research experience and to practice presenting this brief summary. Do not assume you can just show up at the interview and spontaneously describe your research in a coherent and knowledgeable fashion.

4. Plan ithe questions you will want to ask the faculty. The faculty will assume that you have such questions, and if you are not prepared, the interview will end early on a negative note. Try not to ask questions that can be answered by the written materials or information on the Web site (e.g., what courses will I take in my first year?). In addition, many of the "nuts-and-bolts" issues (e.g., financial support) are handled in group information sessions. Instead, in your faculty interview, you should ask substantive questions that better inform you about what it would be like to be a graduate student in this program. Thus, appropriate topics include the faculty member's mentoring style, the strengths and weaknesses of the program, graduate student–faculty relations, and the types of internships and jobs obtained by graduates from the program.

During the visit, you will want to spend some time talking with current graduate students in the program. Some programs offer to have their graduate students provide housing for you during the visit. It is a good strategy to take them up on this offer. It is an excellent opportunity for you to spend further time asking the graduate students about the program. You may want to ask them many of the same questions that you ask the faculty, especially those dealing with mentoring, student–faculty relations, and strengths and weaknesses of the program. A word of caution, however—it is very likely that the graduate students will offer feedback to the faculty regarding the applicants they have met. Therefore, do not let your guard down too much and do not say things that contradict what you told the faculty members. Further, if the students should happen to take you out on the town after the interview, be very careful about the amount of alcohol you may consume. Most faculty can recount instances in which an applicant's chances for admission were ruined by things said or done late at night with the graduate students.

During the interview, you will want to come across as poised, mature, motivated, thoughtful, and interpersonally skilled. Remember that clinical programs not only have to evaluate you in terms of your potential as a graduate student but also as someone who the faculty feel comfortable sending out into clinical settings. Obviously, applicants will differ in the degree to which they possess the aforementioned attributes. Nevertheless, there are at least two things you can do to maximize the positive impact you make during the interview: preparation and practice. In terms of preparation, make notes on everything of importance that you learn about a program, the articles you have read, the questions you want to ask, and anything else you can think of. The interview process can be quite stressful and our memory can fail us at inopportune times. Thus, for example, it is a good strategy to review your notes about a faculty member's research just before entering the interview. In terms of practice, a good strategy is to do one or more role-play interviews before going on the visit. This can be with a roommate or, better yet, with a faculty member at your home institution. Make the interview as realistic as possible. Dress appropriately, shake the person's hand, introduce yourself, and in all ways interact as if the interview were the real thing. If you can arrange to videotape your practice interview, all the better. Look at the videotape, get feedback from the practice interviewer, and consider doing another role-play interview, attempting to correct the problem areas. Given the importance of the interview in the final selection process, you want to do everything you can to ensure that you present yourself in the best possible light.

What Kind of Financial Aid Is Available for Graduate Study?

Most PhD programs in clinical psychology offer some form of financial aid to the students accepted into their program. PsyD- and master's-level programs are much less likely to do so. Financial aid comes in several forms: loans, fellowships, tuition remission, and work programs. The major source of financial aid for graduate students is the university in which they are enrolled, though aid may also be available through guaranteed loan programs (many of which are government sponsored) and national awards, which are competitive and have specific criteria for application. These awards are given directly to students for use at the school of their choice.

The availability of awards and loans changes regularly, so you should check with the financial aid officer at your college or at the institutions to which you are applying for current information. Because your financial support is most likely to come through the program to which you are admitted, the information you will receive with your application material is very important—read it carefully!

Loan programs exist on most campuses as a way of assisting students to invest in their own futures. These loans usually carry a low interest rate, and repayment begins only after the student leaves graduate school.

Fellowships and scholarships are given on many campuses as outright grants to support and encourage students with outstanding academic and research potential. These are few in number, and competition for them is fierce.

Assistantships come in two forms: research assistantships and teaching assistantships. As their names imply, both entail working at jobs that require the graduate student to assist faculty in research projects or in teaching responsibilities (e.g., as a discussion leader, laboratory instructor, or paper grader). Assistantships usually require 10 to 20 hours of work each week.

Some graduate programs receive grants from the federal government to provide *traineeships* in clinical psychology. As a result, there may be training grant funds available for a limited number of students at some institutions. Like fellowships, these are usually outright gifts, but they require that you carry a full academic load. They, too, are few in number, and there is keen competition for them.

Finally, many programs offer some form of tuition remission. They may offer complete remission, meaning that the student pays no tuition at all, or they offer some portion of remission (e.g., 50%). Alternatively, the program may waive the out-of-state tuition and only require that the student pay in-state tuition, even if the student is coming from out of state.

Not all types of aid are offered at all schools. Again, carefully read the financial aid information you receive to be sure you understand what is potentially available at each school you are considering. Further, tuition costs differ dramatically across schools. If the program does not guarantee tuition remission to its students, then you must factor the university's tuition costs into the equation when deciding to which schools to apply.

Are There Assistantships Available from Departments Other Than the One to Which I Have Applied?

Assistantships of various types may be available on a campus. If you are accepted to a clinical psychology program that offers little or no financial aid, it is well worth your time to check on the availability of assistantships in departments outside psychology. For example, administrators of campus residence halls may hire graduate students to serve as hall counselors. Further, departments offering large undergraduate courses may not have enough graduate students in their programs to fill the teaching assistantships available and thus may "import" assistants from related areas. Identify your skills and experiences and seek out jobs that fit them.

OTHER IMPORTANT QUESTIONS

Are There Any Last-Minute Things I Need to Do When Applying?

Once you have sent in your applications, check with each department to which you have applied to assure that your application is complete. Each year, some applications are not considered because students were unaware that their applications were incomplete. Some departments notify students when letters of reference or GRE scores are missing, but many do not. To eliminate this problem, be sure to enclose a stamped, self-addressed envelope or postcard for the department to use to verify that your application is complete, or check your submission status online if the school offers this service.

When I Am Admitted to a Program, How Long Will I Have to Make a Decision about Whether to Accept?

Most admissions offers are made with a specific deadline for when the student has to accept or reject the offer. For doctoral programs, offers of acceptance and financial aid must be given to applicants by April 1, and applicants must respond by April 15. Realistically, offers from competitive programs often are given well before the April 1st date, and many offers are made as early as February these days. In terms of how long students can hold an offer, the April 15th deadline was adopted by the APA Council of Graduate Departments of Psychology to protect students from being pressured to make decisions before having full information about their alternatives. Thus, graduate programs are not supposed to pressure students into making a decision before April 15 (American Psychological Association, 2008). Once you make a final decision, you should convey the information to all programs in which you are still being actively considered.

Graduate school can be enjoyable and rewarding.

Your acceptance decision is considered binding after the April 15th date, although professional courtesy suggests that the decision is binding even if it is made before April 15.

Ideally, applicants will have a rank order of programs after completing their interviews so that they can provide quick feedback to programs once they begin receiving offers. For example, students who are lucky enough to get an early offer from their top choice should quickly accept the offer and then also should withdraw their applications from the other programs. Similarly, if applicants receive an offer from their third choice, they could withdraw their applications from their fourth and lower choices but hold onto the acceptance at their third choice while they are waiting to hear from their first and second choices. Overall, if you have decided not to accept an offer, courtesy dictates that you inform the department of your decision as soon as possible. This courtesy will be appreciated by the department and may provide space for another student. If you do not receive an acceptance by April 1, you may be the one who appreciates an applicant turning down an offer quickly, since it may free up a space for you.

Will I Be Successful in Gaining Admission?

Obviously, we can't answer this question with certainty, but we hope the information and suggestions presented here are helpful to you. A careful examination of your own credentials and the advice of those who have experience with students applying to graduate school in clinical psychology will help you apply to appropriate programs and maximize your chances of admission. We wish you success!

CHAPTER SUMMARY

This chapter provided information on different career options for the helping professions and reviewed the requirements and procedures for applying to graduate training programs in clinical psychology. There are a number of paths that can lead to a career as a therapist, including earning a master's degree, PhD, or PsyD degree in clinical psychology, a master's or PhD degree in counseling psychology, an education specialist (EDS), EdD, or PhD degree in school psychology, a master's of social work degree, a master's degree in rehabilitation counseling, a medical degree in psychiatry or behavioral pediatrics, or a nursing degree in psychiatric nursing.

Depending on which career they are interested in pursuing, students can use coursework, research experiences, clinical experiences, and extracurricular activities to prepare for their career. Salaries vary across careers, with doctoral-level jobs paying more than master's-level positions.

There are a number of different training options in clinical psychology for students to consider, including whether to pursue a master's, PhD, or PsyD degree. If they are seeking a doctoral program, students are encouraged to seek only APA-accredited programs given potential limitations on licensure from unaccredited programs. In addition, students who are interested in high-level clinical scientist programs are encouraged to seek out programs that are members of the Academy of Psychological Clinical Science.

The reality of getting into graduate school is harsh, but students educated in the process of preparing for and applying to graduate programs should fare better than those who are not. There are significant personal and financial commitments required of persons attending doctoral programs, so students must evaluate their own motivation and goals.

If your motivation and energy are strong, then the components of the application process and the process itself should be manageable. The primary components of the application are GRE scores, GPA, letters of recommendation, and personal statements. The process of application is complex but relatively straightforward for students who can keep track of a lot of information. In general, carefulness and conscientiousness are encouraged throughout this process. Good luck!!

STUDY QUESTIONS

1. List the various degrees and career options that lead to the possibility of being a therapist.
2. How might research experience and clinical experience influence your professional life (in terms of career goals and admission to graduate school)?
3. What are the pros and cons of earning a master's versus a PhD in clinical psychology?
4. What are the pros and cons of earning a PhD versus a PsyD in clinical psychology?
5. Describe the APA accreditation process.
6. What is the primary emphasis of programs that are members of the Academy of Psychological Clinical Science?
7. Describe some of the personal costs that exist when in graduate school.
8. In terms of financial costs of graduate school, describe the differences between PhD and PsyD programs. What are the reasons for these differences?

9. Describe the content of the GRE General Test and discuss how the test is administered currently.

10. Describe the content of the GRE Subject Test and discuss how the test is administered currently.

11. What are the different types of GPA calculations that might be requested while applying to graduate programs?

12. What is the process to request letters of recommendation?

13. What should be included in your personal statement?

14. What are the ways to gather information about graduate programs and the application process?

15. What advice do we offer about how many applications to submit?

WEB SITES

- APA Committee on Accreditation (with a list of accredited programs): http://www.apa.org/ed/accreditation/
- Academy of Psychological Clinical Science (with a list of programs in the Academy): http://www.psych.arizona.edu/apcs
- APA Guide to Getting Into Graduate School: http://www.apa.org/ed/getin.html
- Graduate Record Exam from the Educational Testing Service: http://www.gre.org
- APA Site for Careers in Psychology: http://www.apa.org/students/student1.html

References

Abdel, K. A. M. (1994). Normative results on the Arabic Fear Survey Schedule III. *Journal of Behavior Therapy and Experimental Psychiatry, 25,* 61-67.

Ables, B. S., & Brandsma, J. M. (1977). *Therapy for couples.* San Francisco: Jossey-Bass.

Abood, L. G. (1960). A chemical approach to the problem of mental illness. In D. D. Jackson (Ed.), *The etiology of schizophrenia* (pp. 91-119). New York: Basic Books.

Abramowitz, J. S. (1996). Variants of exposure and response prevention in the treatment of obsessive-compulsive disorder: A meta-analysis. *Behavior Therapy, 27,* 583-600.

Abramson, L. Y., Seligman, M. E. P., & Teasdale, J. D. (1978). Learned helplessness in humans: Critique and reformulation. *Journal of Abnormal Psychology, 87,* 49-74.

Abt, L. E. (1992). Clinical psychology and the emergence of psychotherapy. *Professional Psychology: Research and Practice, 23,* 176-178.

Accredited. (2006). Accredited doctoral programs in professional psychology. *American Psychologist, 61,* 991-1005.

Achenbach, T. M. (1978). The Child Behavior Profile I: Boys aged 6-11. *Journal of Consulting and Clinical Psychology, 46,* 478-488.

Achenbach, T. M. (1982). *Developmental psychopathology* (2nd ed.). New York: Wiley.

Achenbach, T. M. (1994). Child Behavior Checklist and related instruments. In M. E. Maruish (Ed.), *The use of psychological testing for treatment planning and outcome assessment.* Hillsdale, NJ: Erlbaum.

Achenbach, T. M., Dumenci, L., & Rescorla, L. A. (2003). DSM-oriented and empirically based approaches to constructing scales from the same item pools. *Journal of Clinical Child and Adolescent Psychology, 32,* 328-340.

Achenbach, T. M., & Edelbrock, C. S. (1978). The classification of child psychopathology: A review and analysis of empirical efforts. *Psychological Bulletin, 85,* 1275-1301.

Achenbach, T. M., & Edelbrock, C. S. (1979). The Child Behavior Profile II: Boys aged 12-16 and girls aged 6-11. *Journal of Consulting and Clinical Psychology, 47,* 223-233.

Achenbach, T. M., & Edelbrock, C. S. (1981). Behavioral problems and competencies reported by parents of normal and disturbed children aged four to sixteen. Monographs of the Society for Research in Child Development, 46 (Serial No. 188).

Achenbach, T. M., McConaughy, S. H., & Howell, C. T. (1987). Child/adolescent behavioral and emotional problems: Implications of cross-informant correlations for situational specificity. *Psychological Bulletin, 101,* 213-232.

Achenbach, T. M., & Rescorla, L. A. (2001). *Manual for the Achenbach System of Empirically Based Assessment (ASEBA) school-age forms and profiles.* Burlington, VT: University of

Vermont, Research Center for Children, Youth, and Families.

Achenbach, T. M., & Rescorla, L. A. (2006). Developmental issues in assessment, taxonomy, and diagnosis of psychopathology: Life span and multicultural perspectives. In D. Cicchetti & D. J. Cohen (Eds.), *Developmental psychopathology, Vol. 1: Theory and method* (2nd ed., pp. 139–180). Hoboken, NJ: Wiley.

Achenbach, T. M., & Rescorla, L. A. (2007). *Multicultural understanding of child and adolescent psychopathology: Implications for mental health assessment.* New York: Guilford.

Ackerman, M. J., & Ackerman, M. (1997). Custody evaluation practices: A survey of experienced professionals (revisited). *Professional Psychology: Research and Practice, 28,* 137–145.

Ackerman, N., & Sobel, R. (1950). Family diagnosis: An approach to the preschool child. *American Journal of Orthopsychiatry, 20,* 744–753.

Ackerman, N. W. (1958). *The psychodynamics of family life.* New York: Basic Books.

Ackerman, S. J., & Hilsenroth, M. J. (2003). A review of therapist characteristics and techniques positively impacting the therapeutic alliance. *Clinical Psychology Review, 23,* 1–33.

Adair, J. C., Schwartz, R., L., & Barrett, A. M. (2003). Anosognosia. In K. M. Heilman & E. Valenstein (Eds.), *Clinical neuropsychology* (4th ed.). New York: Oxford.

Adam, E. K. (2004). Beyond quality: Parental and residential stability and children's adjustment. *Current Directions in Psychological Science, 13,* 210–213.

Addis, M. E., & Krasnow, A. D. (2000). A national survey of practicing psychologists' attitudes toward psychotherapy treatment manuals. *Journal of Consulting and Clinical Psychology, 68,* 331–339.

Adler, A. (1933). *Social interest: A challenge to mankind.* Vienna, Leipzig: Rolf Passer.

Adler, N. E., & Matthews, K. (1994). Health psychology: Why do some people get sick and some stay well. *Annual Review of Psychology, 45,* 229–259.

Ægisdóttir, S., White, M. J., Spengler, P. M., Maugrman, A. S., Anderson, L., Cook, R. S., et al. (2006). The meta-analysis of clinical judgment project: Fifty-six years of accumulated research on clinical versus statistical prediction. *Counseling Psychologist, 34,* 341–382.

Ahn, H., & Wampold, B. E. (2001). Where oh where are the specific ingredients? A meta-analysis of component studies in counseling and psychotherapy. *Journal of Counseling Psychology, 48,* 251–257.

Ai, A. L., Peterson, C., Tice, T. N., Huang, B., Rodgers, W., & Bolling, S. F. (2007). The influence of prayer coping on mental health among cardiac surgery patients: The role of optimism and acute distress. *Journal of Health Psychology, 12,* 580–596.

Aklin, W. M., & Turner, S. M. (2006). Toward understanding ethnic and cultural factors in the interviewing process. *Psychotherapy: Theory, Research Practice, Training, 43,* 50–64.

Albee, G. W. (1959). *Mental health manpower trends.* New York: Basic Books.

Alberti, R. E., & Emmons, M. L. (1974). *Your perfect right: A guide to assertive behavior.* San Luis Obispo, CA: Impact.

Alexander, F. M., & French, T. M. (1946). *Psychoanalytic therapy.* New York: Ronald Press.

Ali, S., Rasheed, Liu, W. M., & Humedian, M. (2004). Islam 101: Understanding the religion and therapy implications. *Professional Psychology: Research and Practice, 35,* 635–642.

Allen, D. M. (2006). Use of between-session homework in systems-oriented individual psychotherapy. *Journal of Psychotherapy Integration, 16,* 238–253.

Allen, G. J. (1971). The effectiveness of study counseling and desensitization in alleviating test anxiety in college students. *Journal of Abnormal Psychology, 77,* 282–289.

Alliger, G. M., Lilienfeld, S. O., & Mitchell, K. E. (1996). The susceptibility of overt and covert integrity tests to coaching and faking. *Psychological Science, 7,* 32–39.

Allport, G. W., Vernon, C. E., & Lindzey, G. (1970). *Study of values* (revised manual). Boston: Houghton-Mifflin.

Alper, B. S., Hand, J. A., Elliott, S. G., Kinkade, S., Hauan, M. J., Onion, D. K., et al. (2004). How much effort is needed to keep up with the literature relevant for primary care? *Journal of the Medical Library Association, 92,* 429–437.

American Association of Marriage and Family Therapy. (2001). *Who are marriage and family therapists?* Retrieved September 7, 2001, from http://www.aamft.org/faqs/whoare.htm.

American Psychiatric Association. (1952). *Diagnostic and statistical manual of mental disorders.* Washington, DC: Author.

American Psychiatric Association. (1968). *Diagnostic and statistical manual of mental disorders* (2nd ed.). Washington, DC: Author.

American Psychiatric Association. (1980). *Diagnostic and statistical manual of mental disorders* (3rd ed.). Washington, DC: Author.

American Psychiatric Association. (1983). *Statement on prediction of dangerousness.* Washington, DC: Author.

American Psychiatric Association. (1987). *Diagnostic and statistical manual of mental disorders* (3rd ed., revised.). Washington, DC: Author.

American Psychiatric Association. (1994). *Diagnostic and statistical manual of mental disorders* (4th ed.). Washington, DC: Author.

American Psychiatric Association. (1998). *DSM-IV sourcebook* (Vol. 4). Washington, DC: Author.

American Psychiatric Association. (2000). *Diagnostic and statistical manual of mental disorders (4th ed.): Text Revision (DSM-IV-TR).* Washington, DC: Author.

American Psychological Association. (1985). *Standards for educational and psychological tests.* Washington, DC: Author.

American Psychological Association. (1986). *Guidelines for computer-based tests and interpretations.* Washington, DC: Author.

American Psychological Association. (1987). *General guidelines for providers of psychological services.* Washington, DC: Author.

American Psychological Association. (1994a). Guidelines for child custody evaluations in divorce proceedings. *American Psychologist, 49,* 677–680.

American Psychological Association. (1994b). *Publication manual of the American Psychological Association* (4th ed.). Washington, DC: Author.

American Psychological Association. (1996). *Guidelines and principles for accreditation of programs in professional psychology/Accreditation operating procedures.* Washington, DC: Author.

American Psychological Association. (1998). *Guidelines for psychological evaluations in child protection matters.* Washington, DC: Author.

American Psychological Association. (2000a). *Guidelines for psychotherapy with lesbian, gay, & bisexual clients.* Washington, DC: Author.

American Psychological Association. (2000b). *Current major field of APA members by membership status* (Table 3). Retrieved December 13, 2001, from http://research.apa.org/member.

American Psychological Association. (2000c). *Criteria for evaluating treatment guidelines.* Washington, DC: Author.

American Psychological Association. (2001a). *Publication manual of the American Psychological Association* (5th ed.). Washington, DC: Author.

American Psychological Association. (2001b). Guidelines on test user qualifications. *American Psychologist, 56,* 1099–1113.

American Psychological Association. (2002a). Criteria for evaluating treatment guidelines. *American Psychologist, 57,* 1052–1059.

American Psychological Association. (2002b). *Ethical principles of psychologists and code of conduct.* Washington, DC: Author.

American Psychological Association. (2003). Guidelines on multicultural education, training, research, practice, and organizational change for psychologists. *American Psychologist, 58,* 377–402.

American Psychological Association. (2004). Guidelines for psychological practice with older adults. *American Psychologist, 59,* 236–260.

American Psychological Association Archives. (2006). Yearly membership, American Psychological Association. Retrieved June 14, 2006, from http://www.apa.org/archives/yearly-membership.html.

American Psychological Association. (2007a). *Getting in: A step-by-step plan for gaining admission to graduate school in psychology* (2nd ed.). Washington, DC: Author.

American Psychological Association. (2007b). *Guidelines and principles for accreditation of programs in professional psychology.* Washington, DC: Author.

American Psychological Association. (2007c). Report of the ethics committee, 2006. *American Psychologist, 62,* 504–511.

American Psychological Association. (2008). *Graduate study in psychology: 2008 edition.* Washington, DC: Author.

American Psychological Association Committee on Professional Practice and Standards. (2003). Legal issues in the professional practice of psychology. *Professional Psychology: Research and Practice, 34,* 595–600.

American Psychological Association Presidential Task Force on Evidence-Based Practice. (2006). Evidence-based practice in psychology. *American Psychologist, 61,* 271–285.

American Psychological Association Public Interest Directorate. (2001). *Guidelines for psychotherapy with lesbian, gay, and bisexual clients.* Retrieved December 13, 2001, from http://www.apa.org/pi/lgbc/guideline.html.

Amundson, M. E., Hart, C. A., & Holmes, T. H. (1986). *Manual for the schedule of recent experience.* Seattle: University of Washington Press.

Anastasi, A. (1988). *Psychological testing* (6th ed.). New York: Macmillan.

Anastasi, A. (1992). What counselors should know about the use and interpretation of psychological tests. *Journal of Counseling and Development, 70,* 610–615.

Anastasi, A., & Urbina, S. (1997). *Psychological testing* (7th ed.). Upper Saddle River, NJ: Prentice Hall.

Andersen, B. L. (1992). Psychological interventions for cancer patients to enhance the quality of life. *Journal of Consulting & Clinical Psychology, 60,* 552–568.

Andersen, B. L., Farrar, W. B., Golden-Kreutz, D. M., Glaser, R., Emery, C. F., Crespin, T. R., et al. (2004). Psychological, behavioral, and immune changes after a psychological intervention: A clinical trial. *Journal of Clinical Oncology, 22,* 3570–3580.

Anderson, C. M., & Kim, C. (2005). Evaluating treatment efficacy with single-case designs. In M. C. Roberts & S. S. Ilardi (Eds.), *Handbook of research methods in clinical psychology* (pp. 73–91). Malden, MA: Blackwell Publishing.

Anderson, J. R., & Barret, B. (2001). *Ethics in HIV-related psychotherapy: Clinical decision making in complex cases.* Washington, DC: American Psychological Association.

Anderson, N. B. (1989). Racial differences in stress-reduced cardiovascular reactivity and hypertension: Current status and substantive issues. *Psychological Bulletin, 105,* 89–105.

Andersson, S., Gundersen, P. M., & Finset, A. (1999). Emotional activation during therapeutic interaction in traumatic brain injury: Effect of apathy, self-awareness and implications for rehabilitation. *Brain Injury, 13*(6), 393–404.

Andreasen, N., Nasrullah, H., Dunn, V., Olson, S., Grove, W., Erhardt, J., et al. (1986). Structural abnormalities in the frontal system in schizophrenia. *Archives of General Psychiatry, 43,* 136–144.

Andrews, G., & Harvey, R. (1981). Does psychotherapy benefit the neurotic patient: A reanalysis of Smith, Glass, & Miller data. *Archives of General Psychiatry, 38,* 1203–1208.

Andrews, J. D. W. (1989). Integrating visions of reality: Interpersonal diagnosis and the existential vision. *American Psychologist, 44,* 803–817.

Anson, D. A., Golding, S. L., & Gully, K. J. (1993). Child sexual abuse allegations: Reliability of criteria-based content analysis. *Law and Human Behavior, 17,* 331–341.

Antoni, M. H., Carrico, A. W., Duran, R. E., Spitzer, S., Penedo, F., Ironson, G., et al. (2006). Randomized clinical trial of cognitive behavioral stress management on human immunodeficiency virus load in gay men treated with highly active antiretroviral therapy. *Psychosomatic Medicine, 68,* 143–151.

Antonova, E., Sharma, T., Morris, R., & Kumari, V. (2004). The relationship between brain structure and neurocognition in schizophrenia: A selective review. *Schizophrenia Research, 70* (2–3), 117–145.

Antony, M. M., & Roemer, E. (2003). Behavior therapy. In A. S. Gurman & S. B. Messer (Eds.),

Essential psychotherapies (2nd ed., pp. 182–223). New York: Guilford.

Antonuccio, D. O., Danton, W. G., & McClanahan, T. M. (2003). Psychology in the prescription era: Building a firewall between marketing and science. *American Psychologist, 58,* 1028–1043.

APApractice.org. (2008). Missouri gets a jump on prescriptive authority legislation. Retrieved February 22, 2008, from http://www.apapractice.org/apo/insider/newsfeed/practice_update_e-newsletter/january_16__2008.html#.

Apodaca, T. R., & Miller, W. R. (2003). A meta-analysis of the effectiveness of bibliotherapy for alcohol problems. *Journal of Clinical Psychology, 59,* 289–304.

Appelbaum, P. S., & Grisso, T. (1995). The MacArthur Treatment Competence Study. I: Mental illness and competence to consent to treatment. *Law and Human Behavior, 19,* 105–126.

Apple, R. F., & Agras, W. S. (2007). *Overcoming eating disorders: A cognitive-behavioral treatment for bulimia nervosa and binge-eating workbook.* New York: Oxford University Press.

Appleby, D. C., & Appleby, K. M. (2006). Kisses of death in the graduate school application process. *Teaching of Psychology, 33,* 19–24.

Archer, R. P., Maruish, M., Imhof, E. A., & Piotrowski, C. (1991). Psychological test usage with adolescent clients: 1990 survey findings. *Professional Psychology: Research and Practice, 22,* 247–252.

Arkes, H. A. (1981). Impediments to accurate clinical judgment and possible ways to minimize their impact. *Journal of Consulting and Clinical Psychology, 49,* 323–330.

Arnold, C. (1998). Children and families: A snapshot. Retrieved December 12, 2001, from http://www.clasp.org/pubs/familyformation/stepfamiliesfinal.BK!.htm.

Association News, No author indicated (2006). Submit comments on record-keeping guidelines. *Monitor on Psychology, 37,* 92.

Atanackovic, D., Schnee, B., Schuch, G., Faltz, C., Schulze, J., et al. (2006). Acute psychological stress alters the adaptive immune response: Stress-induced mobilization of effector T cells. *Journal of Neuroimmunology, 176,* 141–52.

Atkinson, D. R., Brown, M. T., Parham, T. A., Matthews, L. G., Landrum-Brown, J., & Kim, A. U. (1996). African American client skin tone and clinical judgments of African American and European American psychologists. *Professional Psychology: Research and Practice, 27,* 500–505.

Auerbach, L. (2006). Complementary and alternative medicine in the treatment of prostate cancer. *Journal of Men's Health and Gender, 3,* 397–403.

Auld, F., Jr., & Murray, E. J. (1955). Content-analysis studies of psychotherapy. *Psychological Bulletin, 52,* 377–395.

Axline, V. M. (1976). Play therapy procedures and results. In C. Schaefer (Ed.), *The therapeutic use of child's play.* New York: Jason Aronson.

Azar, B. (1996). Behavioral interventions are proven to reduce pain. *APA Monitor* (December), 22.

Azar, S. T., & Benjet, C. L. (1994). A cognitive perspective on ethnicity, race, and termination of parental rights. *Law and Human Behavior, 18,* 249–267.

Baare, W. F. C., van Oel, C. J., Hushoff, H. E., Schnack, H. G., Durston, S., Sitskoorn, M. M., & Kahn, R. S. (2001). Volumes of brain structures in twins discordant for schizophrenia. *Archives of General Psychiatry, 58,* 33–40.

Babinski, M. J. (1914). Contribiutions a l'etude des troubles mentaux dans l'hemiplegie organique cerebrale (anosognosie). *Review of Neurology, 12:* 845–847.

Babyak, M., Blumenthal, J. A., Herman, S., Khatri, P., Doraiswamy, M., Moore, M., et al. (2000). Exercise treatment for major depression: Maintenance of therapeutic benefit at 10 months. *Psychosomatic Medicine, 62,* 633–638.

Baekeland, F., & Lundwall, L. (1975). Dropping out of treatment: A critical review. *Psychological Bulletin, 82,* 738–783.

Baer, R. A. (2003). Mindfulness training as a clinical intervention: A conceptual and empirical review. *Clinical Psychology: Science and Practice, 10,* 125–143.

Baerger, D. R. (2001). Risk management with the suicidal patient: Lessons from case law.

Professional Psychology: Research and Practice, 32, 359–366.

Bailey, D. S. (2006). Student dept still on the rise. *GradPSYCH, 4,* 1.

Bailey, D. S. (2005, January). A niche that puts children first. *American Psychological Association Monitor* (p. 42). Retrieved March 15, 2007, from http://www.apa.org/monitor/jan05/niche.html.

Baird, A., Dewar, B. K., Critchley, H., Dolan, R., Shallice, T., & Cipolotti, L. (2006). Social and emotional functions in three patients with medial frontal lobe damage including the anterior cingulate cortex. *Cognitive Neuropsychiatry, 11*(4), 369–388.

Bandura, A. (1969). *Principles of behavior modification.* New York: Holt, Rinehart & Winston.

Bandura, A. (1977). Self-efficacy: Towards a unifying theory of behavior change. *Psychological Review, 84,* 191–215.

Bandura, A. (1982). Self-efficacy mechanism in human agency. *American Psychologist, 33,* 122–147.

Bandura, A. (1986). *Social foundations of thought and action: A social cognitive therapy.* Englewood Cliffs, NJ: Prentice Hall.

Bandura, A. (2001). Social cognitive theory: An agentic approach. *Annual Review of Psychology, 52,* 1–26.

Bandura, A., Ross, D., & Ross, S. A. (1963). Imitation of film-mediated aggressive models. *Journal of Abnormal and Social Psychology, 66,* 3–11.

Bantha, R., Moskowitz, J. T., Acree, M., & Folkman, S. (2007). Socioeconomic differences in the effects of prayer on physical symptoms and quality of life. *Journal of Health Psychology, 12,* 249–260.

Barkley, R. A., (1997). *Defiant children: A clinician's manual for assessment and parent training* (2nd ed.). New York: Guilford.

Barkley, R. A. (2006). *Attention-deficit hyperactivity disorder: A handbook for diagnosis and treatment* (3rd ed.). New York: Guilford.

Barkley, R. A., & Benton, C. M. (1998). *Your defiant child: Eight steps to better behavior.* New York: Guilford.

Barkley, R. A., Murphy, K. R., & Fischer, M. (2007). *ADHD in adults: What the science says.* New York: Guilford.

Barlow, D. H. (2006). Psychotherapy and psychological treatments: The future. *Clinical Psychology: Science and Practice, 13,* 216–220.

Barlow, D. H., & Craske, M. G. (2006). *Master your anxiety and panic.* New York: Oxford University Press.

Barlow, D. H., & Waddell, M. T. (1985). Agoraphobia. In D. H. Barlow (Ed.), *Clinical handbook of psychological disorders* (pp. 1–68). New York: Guilford.

Barlow, D. H., & Wolfe, B. (1981). Behavioral approaches to anxiety disorders: A report on the NIMH-SUNY, Albany, research conference. *Journal of Consulting and Clinical Psychology, 49,* 448–454.

Barlow, S. H., Burlingame, G. M., Nebeker, R. S., & Anderson, E. (2000). Meta-analysis of medical self-help groups. *International Journal of Group Psychotherapy, 50,* 53–69.

Barr, C., Mednick, S., & Munk-Jorgensen, P. (1990). Exposure to influenza epidemics during gestations and adult schizophrenia: A 40-year study. *Archives of General Psychiatry, 47,* 869–874.

Barrera, M., & Sandler, I. N. (2006). Prevention: A report of progress and momentum into the future. *Clinical Psychology: Science and Practice, 13,* 221–226.

Barrett, M. S., & Berman, J. S. (2001). Is psychotherapy more effective when therapists disclose information about themselves? *Journal of Consulting and Clinical Psychology, 69,* 597–603.

Barrett, P. M., Farrell, L. J., Ollendick, T. H., & Dadds, M. (2006). Long-term outcomes of an Australian universal prevention trial of anxiety and depression symptoms in children and youth: An evaluation of the Friends Program. *Journal of Clinical Child and Adolescent Psychology, 35,* 403–411.

Barrick, M. R., & Mount, M. K. (1996). Effects of impression management and self-deception on the predictive validity of personality constructs. *Journal of Applied Psychology, 81,* 261–272.

Barron, J. W. (Ed.). (1998). *Making diagnosis meaningful: Enhancing evaluation and treatment of psychological disorders.* Washington, DC: American Psychological Association.

Bartol, C. (1996). Police psychology: Then, now, and beyond. *Criminal Justice and Behavior, 23,* 70-89.

Bartol, C. R., & Bartol, A. M. (2008). *Criminal behavior: A psychosocial approach* (8th ed.). Upper Saddle River, NJ: Pearson Education, Inc.

Bassman, L. E., & Uellendahl, G. (2003). Complementary/alternative medicine: Ethical, professional, and practical challenges for psychologists. *Professional Psychology: Research and Practice, 34,* 264-270.

Bateson, C., Jackson, D. D., Haley, J., & Weakland, J. H. (1956). Toward a theory of schizophrenia. *Behavioral Science, 1,* 251-264.

Baucom, D. H., & Epstein, N. (1990). *Cognitive-behavioral marital therapy*. New York: Bruner/Mazel.

Baucom, D. H., Epstein, N., & Gordon, K. C. (2000). Marital therapy: Theory, practice, and empirical status. In C. R. Snyder & R. E. Ingram (Eds.), *Handbook of psychological change: Psychotherapy processes & practices for the 21st century* (pp. 280-308). Hoboken, NJ: Wiley.

Baum, A., & Posluszny, D. M. (1999). Health psychology: Mapping biobehavioral contributions to health and illness. *Annual Review of Psychology, 50,* 137-163.

Baum, A., Reveson, T. A., & Singer, J. E. (Eds.). (2001). *Handbook of health psychology*. Hillsdale, NJ: Erlbaum.

Baumeister, R. F., & Leary, M. R. (1995). The need to belong: Desire for interpersonal attachments as a fundamental human motivation. *Psychological Bulletin, 117,* 497-529.

Bazelon, D. (1974). Psychiatrists and the adversary process. *Scientific American, 230,* 18-23.

Beach, S. R. H., & Kaslow, N. J. (2006). Relational disorders and relational processes in diagnostic practice: Introduction to the special section. *Journal of Family Psychology, 20,* 353-355.

Beach, S. R. H., Wamboldt, M. Z., Kaslow, N. J., Heyman, R. E., & Reiss, D. (2006). Describing relationship problems in DSM-V: Toward better guidance for research and clinical practice. *Journal of Family Psychology, 20,* 359-368.

Bear, D. M., & Fedio, P. (1977). Quantitative analysis of interictal behavior in temporal lobe epilepsy. *Archives of Neurology, 34,* 454-467.

Bechtoldt, H., Norcross, J. C., Wyckoff, L., Pokrywa, M. L., & Campbell, L. F. (2001). Theoretical orientations and employment settings of clinical and counseling psychologists: A comparative study. *The Clinical Psychologist, 54,* 3-6.

Beck, A. T. (1976). *Cognitive therapy and the emotional disorders*. New York: International Universities Press.

Beck, A. T., Freeman, A., & Associates. (1990). *Cognitive therapy of personality disorders*. New York: Guilford.

Beck, A. T., Rush, A. J., Shaw, B. F., & Emery, G. (1979). *Cognitive therapy of depression*. New York: Guilford.

Beck, A. T., Steer, R. A., & Brown, G. K. (1996). *Beck Depression Inventory* (2nd ed.). San Antonio, TX: The Psychological Corporation.

Beck, A. T., Steer, R. A., & Garbin, M. G. (1988). Psychometric properties of the Beck Depression Inventory: Twenty-five years of evaluation. *Clinical Psychology Review, 8,* 77-100.

Beck, A. T., & Weishaar, M. E. (1995). Cognitive therapy. In R. J. Corsini & D. Wedding (Eds.), *Current psychotherapies* (5th ed., pp. 229-261). Itasca, IL: Peacock Publishers, Inc.

Beck, J. S. (1995). *Cognitive therapy: Basics and beyond*. New York: Guilford.

Becker, M. H. & Maiman, L. A. (1975). Sociobehavioral determinants of compliance with health and medical care recommendations. *Medical Care, 13,* 10-24.

Begley, S. (2007). Get "shrunk" at your own risk. *Newsweek* (June 18). Retrieved June 20, 2007, from http://www.newsweek.com/id/34105.

Behnke, S. (2007). Posting on the Internet: An opportunity for self (and other) reflection. *Monitor on Psychology, 38,* 60-61.

Belar, C. D. (2000). Scientist-practitioner =/= science + practice: Boulder is bolder. *American Psychologist, 55,* 249-250.

Belar, C. D., Brown, R. A., Hersch, L. E., Hornyak, L. M., Rozensky, R. H., et al. (2003). Self-assessment in clinical health psychology: A model for ethical expansion of practice. Prevention and treatment, 6, no pagination specified.

Bellack, A. S., & Hersen, M. (Eds.). (1988). *Behavioral assessment: A practical handbook* (3rd ed.). New York: Pergamon Press.

Bellack, A. S., & Hersen, M. (Eds.). (1998). *Behavioral assessment: A practical handbook* (4th ed.). Needham Heights, MA: Allyn & Bacon.

Bellack, A. S., Hersen, M., & Himmelhoch, J. M. (1983). A comparison of social skills training, pharmacotherapy and psychotherapy for depression. *Behaviour Research and Therapy, 21*, 101–107.

Bellak, L. (1954). *The Thematic Apperception Test and the Children's Apperception Test in clinical use.* New York: Grune & Stratton.

Bellak, L. (1986). *The Thematic Apperception Test, the Children's Apperception Test, and the Senior Apperception Technique in clinical use* (4th ed.). New York: Grune & Stratton.

Bellak, L. (1992). *The TAT, CAT, and SAT in clinical use* (5th ed.). Odessa, FL: Psychological Assessment Resources.

Belter, R. W., & Piotrowski, C. (2001). Current status of doctoral-level training in psychological testing. *Journal of Clinical Psychology, 57*, 717–726.

Bender, L. A. (1938). A visual motor Gestalt test and its clinical use. *American Orthopsychiatric Association Research Monograph,* No. 3.

Bender, W. N. (1994). Joint custody: The option of choice. *Journal of Divorce and Remarriage, 21*, 115–131.

Benefield, H., Ashkanazi, G., & Rozensky, R. H. (2006). Communication and records: HIPPA issues when working in health care settings. *Professional Psychology: Research and Practice, 37*, 273–277.

Benjamin, L. S. (1997). The origins of psychological species: A history of the beginnings of the divisions of the American Psychological Association. *American Psychologist, 52*, 725–732.

Benjamin, L. T. (2005). A history of clinical psychology as a profession in America (and a glimpse at the future). *Annual review of clinical psychology, 1*, 1–30.

Ben-Porath, Y. S., & Waller, N. G. (1992). "Normal" personality inventories in clinical assessment: General requirements and potential for using the NEO Personality Inventory. *Psychological Assessment, 4*, 14–19.

Berg, I. A. (1955). Response bias and personality: The deviation hypothesis. *Journal of Psychology, 40*, 61–71.

Berk, L. E. (2002). *Infants, children, and adolescents* (4th ed.). Boston: Allyn and Bacon.

Berliner, L., & Elliott, D. M. (2002). Sexual abuse of children. In J. E. B. Myers, L. Berliner, J. Briere, C. T. Hendrix, C. Jenny, & T. A. Reid (Eds.), *The APSAC handbook on child maltreatment* (pp. 55–78). Thousand Oaks, CA: Sage.

Berman, S. L. (2006). Risk management with suicidal patients. *Journal of Clinical Psychology, 62*, 171–184.

Bernstein, D. A. (1973). Behavioral fear assessment: Anxiety or artifact? In H. Adams & P. Unikel (Eds.). *Issues and trends in behavior therapy* (pp. 225–267). Springfield, IL: Charles C. Thomas.

Bernstein, D. A., & Nietzel, M. T. (1977). Demand characteristics in behavior modification: A natural history of a "nuisance." In M. Hersen, R. M. Eisler, & P. M. Miller (Eds.), *Progress in behavior modification* (Vol. 4, pp. 119–162). New York: Academic Press.

Bernstein, D. A., & Paul, G. L. (1971). Some comments on therapy analogue research with small animal "phobias." *Journal of Behavior Therapy and Experimental Psychiatry, 2*, 225–237.

Bernstein, D. A., Borkovec, T. D., & Hazlette-Stevens, H. (2000). *Progressive relaxation training: A manual for the helping professions* (2nd ed.). New York: Praeger.

Bernstein, D. A., Penner, L., Roy, E. J., & Clarke-Stewart, A. (2006). *Psychology* (7th ed.). Boston: Houghton Mifflin.

Bernstein, D. A., Penner, L., Roy, E. J., & Clarke-Stewart, A. (2008). *Psychology* (8th ed.). Boston: Houghton Mifflin.

Berry, D., Baer, R., & Harris, M. (1991). Detection of malingering on the MMPI: A meta-analysis. *Clinical Psychology Review, 11*, 585–598.

Bersoff, D. N. (2003). *Ethical conflicts in psychology* (3rd ed.). Washington, DC: American Psychological Association.

Bertelsen, A. (1999). Reflections on the clinical utility of the ICD-10 and DSM-IV classifications and their diagnostic criteria. *Australian & New Zealand Journal of Psychiatry, 32*, 166–173.

Beutler, L. E. (2002a). It isn't the size, but the fit. *Clinical Psychology: Science and Practice, 9*, 434–438.

Beutler, L. E. (2002b). Prescriptive authority: Editor's note on the special issue. *Journal of Clinical Psychology, 58,* 587–588.

Beutler, L. E., & Clarkin, J. F. (1990). *Systematic treatment selection: Toward targeted therapeutic interventions.* New York: Brunner/Mazel.

Beutler, L. E., & Groth-Marnat, G. (2003). *Integrative assessment of adult personality* (2nd ed.). New York: Guilford.

Beutler, L. E., & Harwood, T. M. (2000). *Prescriptive psychotherapy: A practical guide to systematic treatment selection.* New York: Oxford University Press.

Beutler, L. E., Kim, E. J., Davison, E., Karno, M., & Fisher, D. (1996). Research contributions to improving managed health care outcomes. *Psychotherapy, 33,* 197–206.

Beutler, L. E., Machado, P. P. P., & Neufeldt, S. A. (1994). Therapist variables. In A. Bergin & S. Garfield (Eds.), *Handbook of psychotherapy and behavior change* (4th ed.). New York: Wiley.

Beutler, L. E., & Malik, (2002). *Rethinking the DSM: A psychological perspective.* Washington, DC: American Psychological Association.

Beutler, L. E., Malik, M., Alimohamed, S., Harwood, T. M., Talebi, H., Noble, S., et al. (2004). Therapist variables. In M. J. Lambert (Ed.), *Bergin and Garfield's handbook of psychotherapy and behavior change* (5th ed., pp. 227–306). New York: Wiley.

Biaggio, M., Orchard, S., Larson, J., Petrino, K., & Mihara, R. (2003). Guidelines for gay/lesbian/bisexual-affirmative educational practices in graduate psychology programs. *Professional Psychology: Research and Practice, 34,* 548–554.

Bickman, L. (1987). Graduate education in psychology. *American Psychologist, 42,* 1041–1047.

Bickman, L. (1996). A continuum of care: More is not always better. *American Psychologist, 51,* 689–701.

Bieling, P. J., McCabe, R. E., & Antony, M. M. (2006). *Cognitive-behavioral therapy in groups.* New York: Guilford.

Bienefeld, D. (2005). *Psychodynamic theory for clinicians.* New York: Lippincott Williams & Wilkins.

Bieri, J., Atkins, A. L., Briar, S., Leaman, R. L., Miller, H., & Tripoldi, T. (1966). *Clinical and social judgment: The discrimination of behavioral information.* New York: Wiley.

Bigler, E. D. (2007). A motion to exclude and the "fixed" versus "flexible" battery in "forensic" neuropsychology: Challenges to the practice of clinical neuropsychology. *Archives of Clinical Neuropsychology, 22*(1), 45–51. E-pub Dec. 27, 2006.

Bigner, J. J., & Wetchler, J. L. (Eds.). (2004). *Relationship therapy with same-sex couples.* New York: Haworth Press.

Bijou, S. W., Peterson, R. F., & Ault, M. H. (1968). A method to integrate descriptive and experimental field studies at the level of data and empirical concepts. *Journal of Applied Behavior Analysis, 1,* 175–191.

Bion, W. R. (1959) *Experiences in groups.* New York: Basic Books.

Birks, Y., & Roger, D. (2000). Identifying components of type-A behavior: "Toxic" and "nontoxic" achieving. *Personality and Individual Differences, 28,* 1093–1105.

Bishop, S. R. (2007). What we really know about mindfulness-based stress reduction. In A. Monat, R. S. Lazarus, & G. Reevy (Eds.), *The Praeger handbook on stress and coping,* (Vol. 2, pp. 475–487). Westport, CT: Praeger Publishers/Greenwood Publishing.

Bishop, S. R., Lau, M., Shapiro, S., Carlson, L., Anderson, N. D., Carmody, J., et al. (2004). Mindfulness: A proposed operational definition. *Clinical Psychology: Science and Practice, 11,* 230–241.

Bisiach, E., Luzzatti, C., & Perani, D. (1979). Unilateral neglect, representational schema and consciousness. *Brain, 102*(3), 609–618.

Blackburn, H., Luepker, R. V., Kline, F. G., Bracht, N., Carlaw, R., Jacobs, B., et al. (1984). The Minnesota Heart Health Program: A research and demonstration project in cardiovascular disease prevention. In J. D. Matarazzo et al. (Eds.), *Behavioral health: A handbook of health enhancement and disease prevention* (pp. 1171–1178). New York: Wiley.

Blair, R. J. & Cipolotti, L. (2000). Impaired social response reversal. A case of 'acquired sociopathy'. *Brain, 123*(Pt. 6), 1122–1141.

Blanchard, E. B. (1992). Psychological treatment of benign headache disorders. *Journal of Consulting and Clinical Psychology, 60,* 537–551.

Blanchard, E. B. (1994). Behavioral medicine and health psychology. In A. E. Bergin & S. L. Garfield (Eds.), *Handbook of psychotherapy and behavior change* (pp. 701–733). New York: Wiley.

Blanchard, R., & Barbaree, H. E. (2005). The strength of sexual arousal as a function of the age of the sex offender: Comparisons among pedophiles, hebephiles, and teleiophiles. *Sexual Abuse: Journal of Research and Treatment, 12,* 441–456.

Blatt, S. J., & Lerner, H. (1983). Psychodynamic perspectives on personality theory. In M. Hersen, A. E. Kazdin, & A. S. Bellack (Eds.), *The clinical psychology handbook* (pp. 87–106). New York: Pergamon Press.

Blount, R. L., Bachanas, P. J., Powers, S. W., Cotter, M. C., Franklin, A., Chaplin, W., et al. (1992). Training children to cope and parents to coach them during routine immunizations: Effects on child, parent, and staff behavior. *Behavior Therapy, 23,* 689–705.

Blumenthal, S. J. (1994). Introductory remarks. In S. J. Blumenthal, K. Matthews, & S. M. Weiss (Eds.), *New research frontiers in behavioral medicine* (pp. 9–15). Washington, DC: National Institute of Mental Health.

Bobbitt, B. L. (2006). The importance of professional psychology: A view from managed care. *Professional Psychology: Research and Practice, 37,* 590–597.

Boczkowski, J. A., Zeichner, A., & DeSanto, N. (1985). Neuroleptic compliance among chronic schizophrenic outpatients: An intervention outcome report. *Journal of Consulting and Clinical Psychology, 53,* 666–671.

Boeree, C. G. (2006). Psychology: The cognitive movement. Retrieved June 18, 2006, from http://www.ship.edu/%7Ecgboeree/ai.html.

Bogels, S. M. (1994). A structured-training approach to teaching diagnostic interviewing. *Teaching of Psychology, 21,* 144–150.

Bohart, A. C. (2003). Person-centered psychotherapy and related experiential approaches. In A. S. Gurman & S. B. Messer (Eds.), *Essential psychotherapies* (2nd ed., pp. 107–148). New York: Guilford.

Boisvert, C. M., & Faust, D. (2006). Practicing psychologists' knowledge of general psychotherapy research findings: Implications for science-practice relations. *Professional Psychology: Research and Practice, 37,* 708–716.

Bonnie, R. J., Jeffries, J. C., Jr., & Low, P. W. (2000). *A case study in the insanity defense: The trial of John W. Hinckley, Jr.* (2nd ed.). New York: Foundation Press.

Bonnie, R., & Slobogin, C. (1980). The role of mental health professionals in the criminal process: The case for informed speculation. *Virginia Law Review, 66,* 427–522.

Boothby, H., Mann, A. H., & Barker, A. (1995). Factors determining interrater agreement with rating global change in dementia: The CIBIC-plus. *International Journal of Geriatric Psychiatry, 10,* 1037–1045.

Bordin, E. S. (1979). The generalizability of the psychoanalytic concept of the working alliance. *Psychotherapy: Theory, Research, and Practice, 16,* 252–260.

Borgata, L. (1995). Analysis of social interaction and sociometric perception. *Sociometry, 17,* 7–32.

Boring, E. G. (1950). *A history of experimental psychology* (2nd ed.). New York: Appleton-Century-Crofts.

Borkovec, T. D., & O'Brien, G. T. (1976). Methodological and target behavior issues in analogue therapy outcome research. In M. Hersen, R. M. Eisler, & P. M. Miller (Eds.), *Progress in behavior modification* (pp. 133–172). New York: Academic Press.

Bornstein, R. F., Hill, E. L., Roginson, K. J., Cabrese, C., & Bowers, K. S. (1996). Internal reliability of Rorschach Oral Dependency Scale scores. *Educational and Psychological Measurement, 56,* 130–38.

Borum, R. (1996). Improving the clinical practice of violence risk assessment. *American Psychologist, 51,* 945–956.

Bottoms, B. L., & Nysse, K. L. (1999, Fall). Applying to graduate school: Writing a compelling personal statement. *Eye on Psi Chi, 4,* 20–22.

Botvin, G. J., & Griffin, K. W. (2004). Life skills training: Empirical findings and future directions. *Journal of Primary Prevention, 25,* 211–232.

Bowen, A. M., & Trotter, R. T., II (1995). HIV risk in intravenous drug users and crack cocaine smokers: Predicting stage of change for condom use. *Journal of Consulting and Clinical Psychology, 63,* 238-248.

Boyle, G. J. (1995). Meyers-Briggs type indicator (MBTI): Some psychometric limitations. *Australian Psychologist, 30,* 71-74.

Brabender, V. A., Fallon, A. E., & Smolar, A. I. (2004). *Essentials of group therapy.* New York: Wiley.

Bracha, H. S. (2006). Human brain evolution and the "neuroevolutionary time-depth principle:" Implications for the reclassification of fear-circuitry-related traits in DSM-V and for studying resilience to warzone-related posttraumatic stress disorder. *Progress in Neuro-Psychopharmacology & Biological Psychiatry, 30,* 827-853.

Braden, J. P. (1995). Review of the Wechsler Intelligence Scale for Children (3rd ed.). In J. C. Conoley & J. C. Impara (Eds.), *Twelfth mental measurements yearbook.* Lincoln, NE: Buros Institute.

Braginsky, B. M., Braginsky, D. D., & Ring, K. (1969). *Methods of madness: The mental hospital as a last resort.* New York: Holt, Rinehart & Winston.

Braginsky, B. M., Grosse, M., & Ring, K. (1966). Controlling outcomes through impression management: An experimental study of the manipulative tactics of mental patients. *Journal of Consulting Psychology, 30,* 295-300.

Brambilla, P., Cerini, R., Gasparini, A., Versace, A., Andreone, N., Nose, N., et al. (2005). Investigation of corpus callosum in schizophrenia with diffusion imaging. *Schizophrenia Research, 79*(2-3), 201-210.

Brand, B. L., Armstrong, J. G. & Loewenstein, R. J. (2006). Psychological assessment of patients with dissociative identity disorder. *Psychiatric Clinics of North America, 29,* 145-168.

Brannon, L., & Feist, J. (2006). *Health psychology: An introduction to behavior and health.* Belmont, CA: Wadsworth.

Branthwaite, A., & Pechere, J. C. (1996). Pan-European survey of patients' attitudes to antibiotics and antibiotic use. *Journal of International Medical Research, 24,* 229-238.

Brauer, B. A. (1993). Adequacy of a translation of the MMPI into American Sign Language for use with deaf individuals: Linguistic equivalency issues. *Rehabilitation Psychology, 38,* 247-260.

Breggin, P. R. (2001). *Talking back to Ritalin: What doctors aren't telling you about stimulants for children.* Monroe, ME: Common Courage Press.

Breggin, P. R., & Breggin, G. R. (1994). *The war against children: How the drugs, programs, and theories of the psychiatric establishment are threatening America's children with a medical "cure" for violence.* New York: St. Martin's Press.

Brekke, J. S., & Long, J. D. (2000). Community-based psychosocial rehabilitation and prospective chance in functional, clinical, and subjective experience variables in schizophrenia. *Schizophrenia Bulletin, 26,* 667-678.

Brekke, N. J., Enko, P. J., Clavet, G., & Seelau, E. (1991). Of juries and court-appointed experts: The impact of nonadversarial expert testimony. *Law and Human Behavior, 15,* 451-477.

Brems, C. (2001). *Basic skills in psychotherapy and counseling.* Belmont, CA: Wadsworth.

Breslow, L. (1979). A positive strategy for the nation's health. *Journal of the American Medical Association, 242,* 2093-2094.

Breuer, J., & Freud, S. (1895/1955). *Studies on hysteria: Standard Edition* (Vol. 2). London: Hogarth Press.

Breyer, S. (2000, Summer). Science in the courtroom. *Issues in Science and Technology.* Retrieved December 8, 2001, from http://www.nap.edu/issues/16.4/breyer.htm.

Brinkmeyer, M. Y., & Eyberg, S. M. (2003). Parent-child interaction therapy for oppositional children. In A. E. Kazdin & J. R. Weisz (Eds.), *Evidence-based psychotherapies for children and adolescents* (pp. 204-223). New York: Guilford.

Broca, P. (1861). Remargues sur le siege de la faculte de la porle articulee, suives d'une observation d'aphemie (perte de parole). *Bulletin Societie Anatomie, 36,* 330-357.

Broca, P. (1865). Sur la faculté du langage articulé. *Bulletin Societe Anthropologie Paris, 6,* 337-393.

Brodley, B. T. (2006). Non-directivity in client-centered therapy. *Journal of Psychotherapy Integration, 16,* 140–161.

Brody, G. H., Murry, V. M., Gerrard, M., Gibbons, F. X., McNair, L., et al. (2006). The Strong African American Families Program: Prevention of youths' high-risk behavior and a test of a model of change. *Journal of Family Psychology, 20,* 1–11.

Broman, C. L. (1993). Social relationships and health-related behavior. *Journal of Behavioral Medicine, 16,* 335–350.

Brotemarkle, B. A. (1947). Fifty years of clinical psychology: Clinical psychology 1896–1946. *Journal of Consulting Psychology, 11,* 1–4.

Brotman, L. M., Klein, R. G., Kamboukos, D., Brown, E. J., Coard, S. I., & Sosinsky, L. S. (2003). Preventive intervention for urban, low-income preschoolers at familial risk for conduct problems: A randomized pilot study. *Journal of Clinical Child and Adolescent Psychology, 32,* 246–257.

Brown, L. S. (1990). Taking account of gender in the clinical assessment interview. *Professional Psychology: Research and Practice, 21,* 12–17.

Brown, L. S. (2005). Don't be a sheep: How this eldest daughter became a feminist therapist. *Journal of Clinical Psychology, 61,* 949–956.

Brown, R. T., Carpenter, L. A., & Simerly, E. (2005). *Mental health medications for children: A primer.* New York: Guilford.

Brown, T. A., & Barlow, D. H. (2001). *Casebook in abnormal psychology* (2nd ed.). Belmont, CA: Wadsworth.

Brown, T. T., Chorpita, B. F., & Barlow, B. F. (1998). Structural relationships among dimensions of the DSM-IV anxiety and mood disorders and dimensions of negative affect, positive affect, and autonomic arousal. *Journal of Abnormal Psychology, 107,* 179–192.

Brown, W. H., Odom, S. L., & Holcombe, A. (1996). Observational assessment of young children's social behavior with peers. *Early Childhood Research Quarterly, 11,* 19–40.

Brownell, H. H., Potter, H. H., Bihrle, A. M., & Gardner, H. (1986). Inference deficits in right brain-damaged patients. *Brain and Language, 27*(2), 310–321.

Brownell, K. D., & Wadden, T. A. (1992). Etiology and treatment of obesity: Understanding a serious, prevalent, and refractory disorder. *Journal of Consulting and Clinical Psychology, 60,* 505–517.

Brugha, T. S., Nienhuis, F., Bagchi, D., Smith, J., Meltzer, H. (1999). The survey form of SCAN: The feasibility of using experienced lay survey interviewers to administer a semi-structured systematic clinical assessment of psychotic and non-psychotic disorders. *Psychological Medicine, 29,* 703–711.

Brussel, J. A. (1968). *Casebook of a crime psychiatrist.* New York: Bernard Geis Associates.

Buck, J. N. (1948). The H-T-P technique: A qualitative and quantitative scoring manual. *Journal of Clinical Psychology, 4,* 319–396.

Bugental, D. B., & Grusec, J. E. (2006). Socialization processes. In N. Eisenberg (Ed.), *Handbook of child psychology* (6th ed., pp. 366–428). Hoboken, NJ: Wiley.

Bugental, J. F. T. (1995). Preliminary sketches for a short-term existential therapy. In K. J. Schneider & R. May (Eds.), *The psychology of existence: An integrative, clinical perspective* (pp. 261–264). New York: McGraw-Hill.

Bugental, J. F. T., & Sterling, M. (1995). Existential psychotherapy. In A. S. Gurman & S. B. Messer (Eds.), *Essential psychotherapies* (pp. 226–260). New York: Guilford.

Bull, S. S., Gaglio, B., Garth, M. H., & Glasgow, R. E. (2005). Harnessing the potential of the Internet to promote chronic illness self-management: Diabetes as an example of how well we are doing. *Chronic Illness, 1,* 143–155.

Burg, M. M., & Abrams, D. (2001). Depression in chronic medical illness: The case of coronary heart disease. *Journal of Clinical Psychology/In Session, 57,* 1323–1337.

Burger, W. E. (1975). Dissenting opinion in O'Connor v. Donaldson. *U.S. Law Week, 42,* 4929–4936.

Burisch, M. (1984). Approaches to personality inventory construction: A comparison of merits. *American Psychologist, 39,* 214–227.

Burke, L. E., Dunbar-Jacob, J. M., & Hill, M. N. (1997). Compliance with cardiovascular disease prevention strategies: A review of the research. *Annals of Behavioral Medicine, 19,* 239–263.

Burlingame, G. M., MacKenzie, K. R., & Strauss, B. (2004). Small-group treatment: Evidence for effectiveness and mechanisms of change. In M. J. Lambert (Ed.), *Bergin and Garfield's handbook of psychotherapy and behavior change* (5th ed. pp. 647–696). New York: Wiley.

Burns, D. D. (1999). *Feeling good: The new mood therapy, Vol. 1* (Rev. ed.). New York: Harper Collins.

Burns, D. D., & Spangler, D. L. (2000). Does psychotherapy homework lead to improvements in depression in cognitive-behavioral therapy or does improvement lead to increased homework compliance? *Journal of Consulting and Clinical Psychology, 68,* 46–56.

Buros, O. K. (Ed.). (1938). *The 1940 mental measurements yearbook.* Highland Park, NJ: Gryphon Press.

Buschbaum, M., Haier, R., Potkin, S., Nuechterlein, K., Bracha, H., Katz, M., et al. (1992). Frontostriatal disorder of cerebral metabolism in never-medicated schizophrenics. *Archives of General Psychiatry, 49,* 935–942.

Bush, S. S., Connell, M. A., & Denney, R. L. (2006). *Ethical practice in forensic psychology: A systematic model for decision making.* Washington, DC: American Psychological Association.

Butcher, J. N. (1999). *A beginner's guide to the MMPI-2.* Washington, DC: American Psychological Corporation.

Butcher, J. N. (2004). Personality assessment without borders: Adaptation of the MMPI-2 across cultures. *Journal of Personality Assessment, 83,* 90–104.

Butcher, J. N. (Ed.). (2006). *MMPI-2: A practitioner's guide.* Washington, DC: American Psychological Corporation.

Butcher, J. N., & Keller, L. S. (1984). Objective personality assessment. In G. Goldstein & M. Hersen (Eds.), *Handbook of psychological assessment* (pp. 307–331). New York: Pergamon Press.

Butcher, J. N., Dahlstrom, W. G., Graham, J. R., Tellegen, A., & Kaemmer, B. (1989). *Manual for administration and scoring of the MMPI-2.* Minneapolis: University of Minnesota Press.

Butcher, J. N., Perry, J. N., & Atlis, M. M. (2000). Validity and utility of computer-based test interpretation. *Psychological Assessment, 12,* 6–18.

Butcher, J. N., Perry, J., & Hahn, J. (2004). Computers in clinical assessment: Historical developments, present status, and future challenges. *Journal of Clinical Psychology, 60,* 331–345.

Butcher, J. N., & Williams, C. L. (1992). *Essentials of MMPI-2 and MMPI-A interpretation.* Minneapolis: University of Minnesota Press.

Butler, A. C., Chapman, J. E., Forman, E. M., & Beck, A. T. (2006). The empirical status of cognitive-behavioral therapy: A review of meta-analyses. *Clinical Psychology Review, 26,* 17–31.

Cacciola, J. S., Alterman, A. I., Rutheford, M. J., McKay, J. R., & May, D. J. (1999). Comparability of telephone and in-person Structured Clinical Interview for DSM-III-R (SCID) diagnoses. *Assessment, 6,* 235–242.

Cacioppo, J. T. (2006). Social neuroscience. *American Journal of Psychology, 119,* 664–668.

Cain, D. J. (1990). Celebration, reflection, and renewal: 50 years of client-centered therapy and beyond. *Person-Centered Review, 5,* 357–363.

Cairns, R. B., & Green, J. A. (1979). How to assess personality and social patterns: Observations or ratings? In B. Cairns (Ed.), *The analysis of social interactions: Methods, issues, and illustrations* (pp. 209–226). Hillsdale, NJ: Erlbaum.

Calkins, S. D., & Degnan, K. A. (2006). Temperament in early development. In R. T. Ammerman (Ed.), *Comprehensive handbook of personality and psychopathology* (Vol. 3, pp. 64–84). Hoboken, NJ: Wiley.

Camara, W. J., Nathan, J. S., & Puente, A. E. (2000). Psychological test usage: Implications in professional psychology. *Professional Psychology: Research and Practice, 31,* 141–154.

Campbell, D. T., & Fiske, D. W. (1959). Convergent and discriminant validation by the multitrait-multimethod matrix. *Psychological Bulletin, 56,* 81–105.

Canning, D. (2006). The economics of HIV/AIDS in low-income countries: the case for prevention. *Journal of Economic Perspectives, 20,* 121–42.

Cantor, N. L. (1998). Making advance directives meaningful. *Psychology, Public Policy, and Law, 4,* 629–652.

Caplan, G. (1964). *Principles of preventive psychiatry*. New York: Basic Books.

Carlson, E. T. (1981). Introduction. *Clinical psychiatry* [*Facsimile reproduction of the 1907 volume, History of Psychology Series,* R. I. Watson (Ed.)]. Delmar, NY: Scholars' Facsimiles & Reprints.

Carniero, C., Corboz-Warney, A., & Fivaz-Depeursinge, E. (2006). The prenatal Lausanne Trilogy Play: A new observational assessment tool of the prenatal co-parenting alliance. *Infant Mental Health Journal, 27,* 207-228.

Carr, A. (2006). *The handbook of child and adolescent clinical psychology: A contextual approach* (2nd ed.). New York: Routledge/Taylor and Francis Group.

Carroll, J. B. (1993). *Human cognitive abilities: A survey of factor-analytic studies*. Cambridge, UK: University of Cambridge Press.

Carroll, R. T. (2003). *The skeptic's dictionary*. Hoboken, NJ: Wiley.

Carter, C. S., Perlstein, W., Ganguli, R., Brar, J., Mintun, M., & Cohen, J. (1998). Functional hypofrontality and working memory dysfunction in schizophrenia. *American Journal of Psychiatry, 155,* 1285-1287.

Cashel, M. L. (2002). Child and adolescent psychological assessment: Current clinical practices and the impact of managed care. *Professional Psychology: Research and Practice, 33,* 446-453.

Caspi, A., & Silva, P. A. (1995). Temperamental qualities at age 3 predict personality traits in young adulthood: Longitudinal evidence from a birth cohort. *Child Development, 66,* 486-498.

Caspi, A., Harrington, H., Milne, B., Amell, J. W., Theodore, R. F., & Moffitt, T. E. (2003). Children's behavioral styles at age 3 are linked to their adult personality traits at age 26. *Journal of Personality, 71,* 495-513.

Cassel, E. (2000). Behavioral science research leads to Department of Justice Guidelines for eyewitness evidence. *Virginia Lawyer, 48,* 35-38.

Cassel, E. (2002, March 18). The Andrea Yates verdict and sentence: Did the jury do the right thing? *FindLaw's Writ*. Retrieved January 1, 2007, from http://writ.news. findlaw.com/commentary/

Cassel, E., & Bernstein, D. A. (2001). *Criminal Behavior*. Boston: Allyn & Bacon.

Cassel, E., & Bernstein, D. A. (2007). *Criminal behavior* (2nd ed.). Mahwah, NJ: Erlbaum.

Cattell, R. B. (1936). *A guide to mental testing*. London, UK: University of London Press, Ltd.

Cattell, R. B. (1943). The measurement of adult intelligence. *Psychological Bulletin, 40,* 153-193.

Cattell, R. B. (1948). The meaning of clinical psychology. In L. A. Pennington & I. A. Berg (Eds.), *An introduction to clinical psychology*. New York: The Roland Press.

Cattell, R. B., Eber, H. W., & Tatusoka, M. M. (1970). *Handbook for the Sixteen Personality Factor Questionnaire*. Champaign, IL: Institute for Personality and Ability Testing.

Cattell, R. B., Eber, H. W., & Tatusoka, M. M. (1992). *Handbook for the Sixteen Personality Factor Questionnaire (16PF)*. Champaign, IL: Institute for Personality and Ability Testing.

Cecero, J. J., Fenton, L. R., Frankforter, T. L., Nich, C., & Carroll, K. M. (2001). Focus on therapeutic alliance: The psychometric properties of six measures across three treatments. *Psychotherapy: Theory, Research, Practice, Training, 38,* 1-11.

Centers for Disease Control (2001a). About cardiovascular disease. Retrieved December 3, 2001 from http:// www.cdc.gov/nccdphp/cvd/aboutcardio.htm.

Centers for Disease Control (2001b). Basic statistics—Cumulative AIDS Cases. Retrieved December 3, 2001, from http://www.cdc.gov/hiv/stats/cumulati .htm.

Centers for Disease Control (2001c). Basic statistics—International Statistics. Retrieved December 3, 2001, from http://www.cdc.gov/hiv/stats/cumulati.htm.

Chambless, D. L. (1990). Spacing of exposure sessions in the treatment of agoraphobia and simple phobia. *Behavior Therapy, 21,* 217-229.

Chambless, D. L., & Ollendick, T. H. (2001). Empirically supported psychological treatments. *Annual Review of Psychology, 52,* 685-716.

Chambless, D. L., Baker, M., Baucom, D. H., Beutler, L. E., Calhoun, K. S., et al. (1998). Update on empirically validated therapies, II. *Clinical Psychologist, 51,* 3-16.

Chan, D. W., & Lee, H. B. (1995). Patterns of psychological test use in Hong Kong in 1993. *Professional Psychology: Research and Practice, 26,* 292-297.

Chang, T., & Yeh, C. J. (2003). Using online groups to provide support to Asian American men: Racial, cultural, gender, and treatment issues. *Professional Psychology: Research and Practice, 34,* 634-643.

Chapman, L. J., & Chapman, J. P. (1967). The genesis of popular but erroneous psychodiagnostic observations. *Journal of Abnormal Psychology, 72,* 193-204.

Cherry, D. K., Messenger, L. C., & Jacoby, A. M. (2000). An examination of training model outcomes in clinical psychology programs. *Professional Psychology: Research & Practice, 31,* 562-568.

Chess, S., & Thomas, A. (1986). *Temperament in clinical practice.* New York: Guilford.

Children's Defense Fund (2005). *Protect children not guns.* Washington, DC: Author.

Choate, M. L., Pincus, D. B., Eyberg, S. M., & Barlow, D. H. (2005). Parent-child interaction therapy for treatment of separation anxiety disorder in young children: A pilot study. *Cognitive and Behavioral Practice, 12,* 126-135.

Chorpita, B. F. (2002). Treatment manuals for the real world: Where do we build them? *Clinical Psychology: Science and Practice, 9,* 431-433.

Christensen, A., & Heavey, C. L. (1999). Interventions for couples. *Annual Review of Psychology, 50,* 165-190.

Chronis, A. M., Jones, H. A., & Raggi, V. L. (2006). Evidence-based psychosocial treatments for children and adolescents with attention-deficit/hyperactivity disorder. *Clinical Psychology Review, 26,* 486-502.

Chung, J. J., Weed, N. C., & Han, K. (2006). Evaluating cross-cultural equivalence of the Korean MMPI-2 via bilingual test-retest. *International Journal of Intercultural Relations, 30,* 531-543.

Cicchetti, D., & Cohen, D. J. (Eds.). (2006). *Developmental psychopathology, Vol. 2: Developmental neuroscience* (2nd ed.). Hoboken, NJ: Wiley.

Cicchetti, D., & Curtis, J. W. (2006). The developing brain and neuroplasticity: Implications for normality, psychopathology, and resilience. In D. Cicchetti & J. W. Curtis (Eds.), *Developmental psychopathology, Vol 2: Developmental neuroscience* (2nd ed., pp. 1-64). Hoboken, NJ: Wiley.

Clark, D. B., & Winters, K. C. (2002). Measuring risks and outcomes in substance use disorders prevention research. *Journal of Consulting and Clinical Psychology, 70,* 1207-1223.

Clarke, G., Lynch, F., Spofford, M., & DeBar, L. (2006). Trends influencing future delivery of mental health services in large healthcare systems. *Clinical Psychology: Science and Practice, 13,* 287-292.

Clarkin, J. F., & Levy, K. N. (2004). The influence of client variables of psychotherapy. In M. J. Lambert (Ed.), *Bergin and Garfield's handbook of psychotherapy and behavior change* (5th ed., pp. 194-226). New York: Wiley.

Clay, R. A. (2005). The changing face of psychology practice. *Monitor on Psychology, 35,* 48-50.

Clay, R. A. (2006a). Assessing assessment. *Monitor on Psychology,* January, 44-46.

Clay, R. A. (2006b). Loan repayment. *GradPSYCH, 4,* 1-3.

Clingempeel, W. G., & Reppucci, N. D. (1982). Joint custody after divorce: Major issues and goals for research. *Psychological Bulletin, 91,* 102-127.

Coatsworth, J. D., Pantin, H., & Szapocznik, J. (2002). Familias unidas: A family-centered ecodevelopmental intervention to reduce risk for problem behavior among Hispanic adolescents. *Clinical Child and Family Psychology Review, 5,* 113-132.

Cobb, H. C., Reeve, R. E., Shealy, C. N., Norcross, J. C., Schare, M. L., et al. (2004). Overlap among clinical, counseling, and school psychology: Implications for the profession and combined-integrated training. *Journal of Clinical Psychology, 60,* 939-955.

Cohen, B. B., & Vinson, D. C. (1995). Retrospective self-report of alcohol consumption: Test-retest reliability by telephone. *Alcoholism: Clinical and Experimental Research, 19,* 1156-1161.

Cohen, J., Marecek, J., & Gillham, J. (2006). Is three a crowd? Clients, clinicians, and managed care. *American Journal of Orthopsychiatry, 76,* 251-259.

Cohen, J. B., & Reed, D. (1985). Type A behavior and coronary heart disease among Japanese men in Hawaii. *Journal of Behavioral Medicine, 8,* 343-352.

Cohen, S. (2004). Social relationships and health. *American Psychologist, 59,* 676-684.

Cohen, S., Gottlieb, B., & Underwood, L. (2000). Social relationships and health. In S. Cohen, L. Underwood, & B. Gottlieb (Eds.), *Measuring and intervening in social support* (pp. 3-25). New York: Oxford University Press.

Cohen, S., Kamarck, T., & Mermelstein, R. (1983). A global measure of perceived stress. *Journal of Health and Social Behavior, 24,* 385-396.

Cohen, S., & Rabin, B. S. (1998). Psychological stress, immunity, and cancer. *Journal of the National Cancer Institute, 90,* 3-4.

Cohen, S., Tyrrell, D. A., & Smith, A. P. (1991). Psychological stress in humans and susceptibility to the common cold. *New England Journal of Medicine, 325,* 606-612.

Cohen, S., & Wills, T. A. (1985). Stress, social support, and the buffering hypothesis. *Psychological Bulletin, 98,* 310-357.

Coleman, P. (2005). Privilege and confidentiality in 12-step self-help programs: Believing the promises could be hazardous to an addict's freedom. *Journal of Legal Medicine, 26,* 435-474.

Collins, R. L., Parks, G. A., & Marlatt, G. A. (1985). Social determinants of alcohol consumption: The effects of social interactions and model status on the self-administration of alcohol. *Journal of Consulting and Clinical Psychology, 53,* 189-200.

Collins, W. A., & Steinberg, L. (2006). Adolescent development in interpersonal context. In N. Eisenberg (Ed.), *Handbook of child psychology* (6th ed., pp. 1003-1067). Hoboken, NJ: Wiley.

Colmen, J. G., Kaplan, S. J., & Boulger, J. R. (1964, August). *Selection and selecting research in the Peace Corps.* (Peace Corps Research Note No. 7).

Cone, J. D. (1988). Psychometric considerations and the multiple models of behavioral assessment. In A. S. Bellack & M. Hersen (Eds.), *Behavioral assessment: A practical handbook* (3rd ed., pp. 42-66). New York: Pergamon Press.

Conger, R. D., & Donnellan, M. B. (2007). An interactionist perspective on the socioeconomic context of human development. *Annual Review of Psychology, 58,* 175-199.

Conners, C. K. (1989). *Conners rating scales.* North Tonawanda, NY: Multi-Health Systems.

Conners, C. K. (1998). *Conners rating scales-revised.* Toronto: Multi-Health Systems.

Connor-Smith, J. K., & Weisz, J. R. (2003). Applying treatment outcome research in clinical practice: Techniques for adapting interventions to the real world. *Child Psychology and Psychiatry Review, 8,* 3-10.

Consoli, A. J., & Jester, C. M. (2005). Training in psychotherapy integration II: Further efforts. *Journal of Psychotherapy Integration, 15,* 355-357.

Coontz, P. D., Lidz, C. W., & Mulvey, E. P. (1994). Gender and the assessment of dangerousness in the psychiatric emergency room. *International Journal of Law and Psychiatry, 17,* 369-376.

Corey, G. (1999). *Theory and practice of group counseling.* Pacific Grove, CA: Wadsworth.

Corey, G. (2007). *Theory and practice of group counseling* (7th ed.). Belmont, CA: Thomson Brooks/Cole.

Cornblatt, B., & Erlenmeyer-Kimling, L. E. (1985). Global attentional deviance in children at risk for schizophrenia: Specificity and predictive validity. *Journal of Abnormal Psychology, 94,* 470-486.

Corrigan, P. (2004). How stigma interferes with mental health care. *American Psychologist, 59,* 614-625.

Corsini, R. J., & Wedding, D. (2007). *Current psychotherapies* (8th ed.). Belmont, CA: Wadsworth.

Coslett, H. B., & Saffran, E. (1991). Simultanagnosia: To see but not two see. *Brain, 114* (Pt. 4), 1523-1545.

Costa, P. T. Jr., & McCrea, R. R. (1980). Still stable after all these years: Personality as a key to some issues in adulthood and old age. In P. B. Baltes & O. G. Brim, Jr. (Eds.), *Life span development and behavior* (Vol. 3, pp. 65-102). New York: Academic Press.

Costa, P. T. Jr., & McCrae, R. R. (1985). *NEO-Personality Inventory manual.* Odessa, FL: Psychological Assessment Resources.

Costa, P. T. Jr., & McCrae, R. R. (1992a). *Manual for the Revised NEO Personality Inventory (NEO-PIR) and the NEO Five-Factor Inventory (BEO-FFI)*. Odessa, FL: Psychological Assessment Resources.

Costa, P. T. Jr., & McCrae, R. R. (1992b). Normal personality inventories in clinical assessment: General requirements and potential for using the NEO Personality Inventory. *Psychological Assessment, 4,* 5–13.

Côtè, S., & Bouchard, S. (2005). Documenting the efficacy of virtual reality exposure with psychophysiological and information processing measures. *Applied Psychophysiology and Biofeedback, 30,* 217–232.

Cotton, S., Puchalski, C. M., Sherman, S. N., Mrus, J. M., Peterman, A. H., et al. (2006). Spirituality and religion in patients with HIV/AIDS. *Journal of General Internal Medicine, 21 (Supplement 5),* 5–13.

Couch, R. D. (1995). Four steps for conducting a pregroup screening interview. *Journal for Specialists in Group Work, 20,* 18–25.

Counseling Psychology, Division 17. (2006). Home page of Division 17. Retrieved Oct. 22, 2006, from http://www.div17.org.

Covner, B. J. (1942). Studies in phonographic recordings. I: The use of phonographic recordings in counseling practice and research. *Journal of Consulting Psychology, 6,* 105–113.

Crane, D. R., & Law, D. D. (2002). Conducting medical offset research in a health maintenance organization: Challenges, opportunities, and insights. *Journal of Marital and Family Therapy, 28,* 15–19.

Crits-Christoph, P., Connolly-Gibbons, M. B., & Hearon, B. (2006). Does the alliance cause good outcome? Recommendations for future research on the alliance. *Psychotherapy: Theory, Research, Practice, Training, 43,* 280–285.

Cronbach, L. J. (1946). Response sets and test validity. *Educational and Psychological Measurement, 6,* 475–494.

Cronbach, L. J. (1960). *Essentials of psychological testing* (2nd ed.). New York: Harper & Row.

Cronbach, L. J. (1970). *Essentials of psychological testing* (3rd ed.). New York: Harper & Row.

Cronbach, L. J., & Glesser, G. C. (1964). *Psychological tests and personnel decisions.* Urbana: University of Illinois Press.

Cronbach, L. J., Glesser, G. C., Nanda, H., & Rajaratnam, N. (1972). *The dependability of behavioral measurements.* New York: Wiley.

Cronbach, L. J., & Meehl, P. E. (1955). Construct validity in psychology tests. *Psychological Bulletin, 52,* 281–302.

Crosbie-Burnett, M. (1991). Impact of joint versus sole custody and quality of co-parental relationship on adjustment of adolescents in remarried families. *Behavioral Sciences and the Law, 9,* 439–449.

Cullen, E. A., & Newman, R. (1997). In pursuit of prescription privileges. *Professional Psychology: Research and Practice, 28,* 101–106.

Cummings, E. M., Goeke-Morey, M. C., & Papp, L. M. (2004). Everyday marital conflict and child aggression. *Journal of Abnormal Child Psychology, 32,* 191–202.

Cummings, E. M., Goeke-Morey, M. C., & Raymond, J. (2004). Fathers in family context: Effects of marital quality and marital conflict. In M. E. Lamb (Ed.), *The role of the father in child development* (4th ed., pp. 196–221). Hoboken, NJ: Wiley.

Cummings, N. A. (1977). Prolonged (ideal) versus short-term (realistic) psychotherapy. *Professional Psychology, 8,* 491–501.

Curtis, R. C., & Hirsch, I. (2003). Relational approaches to psychoanalytic psychotherapy. In A. S. Gurman & S. B. Messer (Eds.). *Essential psychotherapies* (2nd ed., pp. 69–106). New York: Guilford.

Dahlstrom, W. G. (1992). The growth in acceptance of the MMPI. *Professional Psychology: Research and Practice, 23,* 345–348.

Dahlstrom, W. G., Lachar, D., & Dahlstrom, L. E. (1986). *MMPI patterns of American minorities.* Minneapolis: University of Minnesota Press.

Dahlstrom, W. G., Welsh, G. S., & Dahlstrom, L. E. (1972). *An MMPI handbook: Vol. 1. Clinical interpretation* (rev. ed.). Minneapolis: University of Minnesota Press.

Dahlstrom, W. G., Welsh, G. S., & Dahlstrom, L. E. (1975). *An MMPI handbook: Vol. 2. Research applications.* Minneapolis: University of Minnesota Press.

Dana, R. H., & Leech, S. (1974). Existential assessment. *Journal of Personality Assessment, 38,* 428–435.

Darley, J. M., Zanna, M. P., & Roediger, H. L. (Eds.). (2004). *The compleat academic: A career guide* (2nd ed.). Washington, DC: American Psychological Association.

Dattilio, F. M. (2006). Equivocal death psychological autopsies in cases of criminal homicide. *American Journal of Forensic Psychology, 24,* 5–22.

Davanloo, H. L. (1994). *Basic principles and techniques in short-term dynamic psychotherapy.* Northdale, NJ: Jason Aronson, Inc.

Davidson, W. S., Redner, R., Blakely, C., Mitchell, C. M., & Emshoff, J. G. (1987). Diversion of juvenile offenders: An experimental comparison. *Journal of Consulting and Clinical Psychology, 55,* 68–75.

Davies, P. T., Sturge-Apple, M. L., Cicchetti, D., & Cummings, E. M. (2007). The role of child adrenocortical functioning in pathways between interparental conflict and child maladjustment. *Developmental Psychology, 43,* 918–930.

Dawes, R. M. (1986). Representative thinking in clinical judgment. *Clinical Psychology Review, 6,* 425–442.

Dawes, R. M. (1994). *House of cards.* New York: The Free Press.

Dawes, R. M., Faust, D., & Meehl, P. E. (1989). Clinical versus actuarial judgment. *Science, 243,* 1668–1674.

DeClue, G. (2006). Review of Fitness Interview Test-Revised (FIT-R): A structured interview for assessing competency to stand trial. *Journal of Psychiatry & Law, 34,* 371–379.

DeLeon, P. H., Wedding, D., Wakefield, M. K., & VandenBos, G. R. (1992). Medicaid policy: Psychology's overlooked agenda. *Professional Psychology: Research and Practice, 23,* 96–107.

DeLosReyes, A., & Kazdin, A. E. (2005). Informant discrepancies in the assessment of childhood psychopathology: A critical review, theoretical framework, and recommendations for further study. *Psychological Bulletin, 131,* 483–509.

Dennis, W. (1948). *Readings in the history of psychology.* New York: Appleton-Century-Crofts.

DeYoung, P. A. (2003). *Relational psychotherapy: A primer.* New York: Burnner-Routledge.

Diener, C. I., & Dweck, C. S. (1978). An analysis of learned helplessness: Continuous changes in performance, strategy, and achievement cognitions following failure. *Journal of Personality and Social Psychology, 36,* 451–462.

Diener, E., Tamir, M., & Scollon, C. N. (2006). Happiness, life satisfaction, and fulfillment: The social psychology of subjective well-being. In P. A. M. & VanLange (Ed.), *Bridging social psychology: Benefits of transdisciplinary approaches* (pp. 319–324). Mahwah, NJ: Erlbaum.

Dies, R. (2003). Group Psychotherapies. In A. S. Gurman & S. B. Messer (Eds.). *Essential psychotherapies* (2nd ed., pp. 515–550). New York: Guilford.

DiLalla, D. L., & Gottesman, I. I. (1995). Normal personality characteristics in identical twins discordant for schizophrenia. *Journal of Abnormal Psychology, 104,* 490–499.

DiLillo, D., DeGue, S., Cohen, L. M., & Morgan, R. D. (2006). The path to licensure for academic psychologists: How tough is the road? *Professional Psychology: Research and Practice, 37,* 567–586.

DiLillo, D., Perry, A. R., & Fortier, M. (2006). Child physical abuse and neglect. In R. T. Ammerman (Ed.), *Comprehensive handbook of personality and psychopathology* (Vol. 3, pp. 367–387). Hoboken, NJ: Wiley.

Dilk, M. N., & Bond, G. R. (1996). Meta-analytic evaluation of skills training research for individuals with severe mental illness. *Journal of Consulting and Clinical Psychology, 64,* 1137–1146.

DiMatteo, R., Giordani, P. J., Lepper, H. S., & Croghan, T. W. (2002). Patient adherence and medical treatment outcomes: A meta-analysis. *Medical Care, 40,* 794–811.

Dimatteo, M. R., & Taranta, A. (1976). Nonverbal communication and physician-patient rapport: An empirical study. *Professional Psychology, 10,* 540–547.

Dimidjian, S., & Linehan, M. M. (2003). Defining an agenda for future research on the clinical application of mindfulness practice. *Clinical Psychology: Science and Practice, 10,* 166–171.

Dipboye, R. L., Stramler, C. S., & Fontenelle, G. A. (1984). The effects of the application on recall of information from the interview. *Academy of Management Journal, 27,* 561–575.

Disch, E. (2006). Sexual victimization and revictimization of women by professionals: Client experiences and implications for subsequent treatment. *Women and Therapy, 29,* 41–61.

Dishion, T. J., & Stormshak, E. A. (2007). Child and adolescent intervention groups. In T. J. Dishion & E. A. Stormshak (Eds.), *Intervening in children's lives: An ecological, family-centered approach to mental health care* (pp. 201–215). Washington, DC: American Psychological Association.

Division 17 Counseling Psychology. (2001). What is a Counseling Psychologist? Retrieved September 17, 2001, from http://www.div17.org/whatis.html.

Dobson, K. S. (Ed.), (2002). *Handbook of cognitive-behavioral therapies* (2nd ed.). New York: Guilford.

Dodge, K. A., Coie, J. D., & Lynam, D. (2006). Aggression and antisocial behavior in youth. In N. Eisenberg (Ed.), *Handbook of child psychology* (6th ed., pp. 719–788). Hoboken, NJ: Wiley.

Doefler, L. A., Addis, M. E., & Moran, P. W. (2002). Evaluating mental health outcomes in an inpatient setting: Convergent validity of the OQ-45 and BASIS-32. *Journal of Behavioral Health Services and Research, 29,* 394–403.

Dohrenwend, B. S. (1978). Social stress and community psychology. *American Journal of Community Psychology, 6,* 1–14.

Domino, G., & Domino, M. L. (2006). *Psychological testing* (2nd ed.). New York: Cambridge University Press.

Donn, J. E., Routh, D. K., & Lunt, I. T. I. (2000). From Leipzig to Luxembourg (via Boulder and Vail): A history of clinical psychology training in Europe and the United States. *Professional Psychology: Research and Practice, 31,* 423–428.

Dornelas, E. A. (2001) Introduction: Integrating health psychology into clinical practice. *Journal of Clinical Psychology/In Session, 57,* 1261–1262.

Doss, B. D., Simpson, L. E., & Christensen, A. (2004). Why do couples seek marital therapy? *Professional Psychology: Research and Practice, 35,* 608–614.

Douglas, J., & Olshaker, M. (1995). *Mind hunter: Inside the FBI's elite serial crime unit.* New York: Scribner's.

Doyle, M., & Dolan, M. (2006). Predicting community violence from patients discharged from mental health services. *British Journal of Psychiatry, 189,* 520–526.

DuBois, P. H. (1970). *A history of psychological testing.* Boston: Allyn & Bacon.

Duckworth, A. L., Peterson, C., Matthews, M. D., & Kelly, D. R. (2007). Grit: Perseverance and passion for long-term goals. *Journal of Personality and Social Psychology, 92,* 1087–1101.

Duckworth, A. L., Steen, T. A., & Seligman, M. E. P. (2005). Positive psychology in clinical practice. *Annual Review of Clinical Psychology, 1,* 629–651.

Duhig, A. M., Renk, K., Epstein, M. K., & Phares, V. (2000). Interparental agreement on internalizing, externalizing, and total behavior problems: A meta-analysis. *Clinical Psychology: Science and Practice, 7,* 435–453.

Eagle, M. N. (1984). *Recent developments in psychoanalysis: A critical evaluation.* Cambridge, MA: Harvard University Press.

Eaker, E. D., Abbott, R. D., Kannel, W. B. (1989). Frequency of uncomplicated angina pectoris in Type A compared with Type B persons (the Framingham study). *American Journal of Cardiology, 63,* 1042–1045.

Earl, A., & Albarracin, D. (2007). Nature, decay, and spiraling of the effects of fear-inducing arguments and HIV counseling and testing: A meta-analysis of the short-and long-term outcomes of HIV-prevention interventions. *Health Psychology, 26,* 496–506.

Ebert, B. W. (1987). Guide to conducting a psychological autopsy. *Professional Psychology: Research and Practice, 18,* 52–56.

Ebrahim, S., Beswick, A., Burke, M., & Davey-Smith, G. (2006). Multiple risk factor interventions for primary prevention of coronary heart disease. *Cochrane Database Syst Rev., 18,* CD001561.

Educational Testing Service (2007). *Graduate record examinations information and registration bulletin*. Princeton, NJ: Author.

Edwards, A. L. (1957). *The social desirability variable in personality assessment and research*. New York: Dryden.

Edwards, D. J. A., Dattilio, F. M., & Bromley, D. B. (2004). Developing evidence-based practice: The role of case-based research. *Professional Psychology: Research and Practice, 35,* 589–597.

Edwards, J. (2006). Music therapy in the treatment and management of mental disorders. *Irish Journal of Psychological Medicine, 23,* 33–35.

Ehmann, T. S., Higgs, E., Smith, G. N., Au, T., Altman, S., Llyod, D., & Honer, W. G. (1995). Routine assessment of patient progress: A multiformat, change-sensitive nurses instrument for assessing psychotic inpatients. *Comprehensive Psychiatry, 36,* 289–295.

Eid, M., & Diener, E. (Eds.). (2005). *Handbook of multimethod and measurement in psychology*. Washington, DC: American Psychological Association.

Einhorn, H. J., & Hogarth, R. M. (1978). Confidence in judgment: Persistence of the illusion of validity. *Psychological Review, 85,* 395–416.

Elias, M. (2007). Supporters renew push for mental health care. *USA Today*. Retrieved January 9, 2007, from http://www.usatoday.com/news/health/2007-01-07-mental-health-reform_x.htm.

Elias, Marilyn. (2004, May 3). 9/11 still haunts Pentagon workers, WTC rescuers. *USA Today*. Retrieved March 15, 2007, from http://www.usatoday.com/news/health/2004-05-03-sept11-ptsd_x.htm.

Ellis, A. (1962). *Reason and emotion in psychotherapy*. New York: Lyle Stuart.

Ellis, A. (1973). Rational-emotive therapy. In R. Corsini (Ed.), *Current psychotherapies* (pp. 167–206). Itasca, IL: F. E. Peacock.

Ellis, A. (1993). Changing rational-emotive therapy (RET) to rational-emotive behavior therapy (REBT). *The Behavior Therapist, 16,* 257–258.

Ellis, A. (1995). Rational emotive behavior therapy. In R. J. Corsini & D. Wedding (Eds.), *Current psychotherapies* (5th ed., pp. 162–196). Itasca, IL: Peacock Publishers, Inc.

Ellis, A. (2001). Reasons why rational emotive behavior therapy is relatively neglected in the professional and scientific literatures. *Journal of Rational-Emotive and Cognitive Behavior Therapy, 19,* 67–74.

Ellis, A., & Dryden, W. (1987). *The practice of rational-emotive therapy*. New York: Springer.

Ellis, A., & Grieger, R. (Eds.). (1977). *Handbook of rational-emotive therapy*. New York: Springer.

Ellis, P., Robinson, P., Ciliska, D., Armour, T., Brouwers, M., O'Brien, M. A., et al. (2005). A systematic review of studies evaluating diffusion and dissemination of selected cancer control interventions. *Health Psychology, 24,* 488–500.

Ellsworth, J. R., Lambert, M. J., & Johnson, J. (2006). A comparison of the Outcome Questionnaire-45 and Outcomes Questionnaire-30 in classification and prediction of treatment outcome. *Clinical Psychology and Psychotherapy, 13,* 380–391.

Emery, R. E. (1982). Interparental conflict and the children of discord and divorce. *Psychological Bulletin, 92,* 310–330.

Emery, R. E., Matthews, S. G., & Kitzmann, K. M. (1994). Child custody mediation and litigation: Parents' satisfaction and functioning one year after settlement. *Journal of Consulting and Clinical Psychology, 62,* 124–129.

Emery, R. E., Matthews, S. G., & Wyer, M. M. (1991). Child custody medication and litigation: Further evidence on the differing views of mothers and fathers. *Journal of Consulting and Clinical Psychology, 59,* 410–418.

Englemann, S. (1974). The effectiveness of direct verbal instruction on IQ performance and achievement in reading and arithmetic. In R. Ulrich, T. Stachnik, & J. Mabry (Eds.), *Control of human behavior* (Vol. 3, pp. 69–84). Glenview, IL: Scott, Foresman.

Ennis, B. J., & Litwack, T. R. (1974). Psychiatry and the presumption of expertise: Flipping coins in the courtroom. *California Law Review, 62,* 693–752.

Erickson, P. I., & Kaplan, C. P. (2000). Maximizing qualitative responses about smoking in structured interviews. *Qualitative Health Research, 10*, 829-840.

Erikson, E. H. (1946). *Ego development and historical change. The psychoanalytic study of the child* (Vol. 2, pp. 359-396). New York: International Universities Press.

Erwin, E. (1999). Constructivist epistemologies and therapies. *British Journal of Guidance and Counseling, 27*, 353-365.

Eslinger, P. J., & Damasio, A. R. (1985). Severe disturbance of higher cognition after bilateral frontal lobe ablation: Patient EVR. *Neurology, 35*, 1731-1741.

Evans, D. L., & Seligman, M. E. P. (2005). Introduction. In D. L. Evans, E. B. Foa, R. E. Gur, H. Hendin, C. P. O'Brien, M. E. P. Seligman & B. T. Walsh (Eds.), *Treating and preventing adolescent mental health disorders: What we know and what we don't know* (pp. xxv-xl). New York: Oxford University Press.

Evans, G. W. (2004). The environment of childhood poverty. *American Psychologist, 59*, 77-92.

Evans, G. W., Gonnella, C., Marcynyszyn, L. A., Gentile, L., & Salpekar, N. (2005). The role of chaos in poverty and children's socioemotional adjustment. *Psychological Science, 16*, 560-565.

Ewing, C. P., & McCann, J. T. (2006). *Minds on trial: Great cases in law and psychology*. New York: Oxford University Press.

Exner, J. E. (1974). *The Rorschach: A comprehensive system* (Vol. 1). New York: Grune & Stratton.

Exner, J. E. (1976). Projective techniques. In I. B. Weiner (Ed.), *Clinical methods in psychology* (pp. 61-121). New York: Wiley.

Exner, J. E. (1993). *The Rorschach: A comprehensive system: Vol. 1. Basic foundations* (3rd ed.). New York: Wiley.

Exner, J. E. Jr. (2003). *Basic foundations and principles of interpretation*. Hoboken, NJ: Wiley.

Exner, J. E. Jr., & Erdberg, P. (2005). *The Rorschach, advanced interpretation*. Hoboken, NJ: Wiley.

Eyberg, S. M., & Matarazzo, R. G. (1980). Training parents as therapists: A comparison between individual parent-child interactions training and parent group didactic training. *Journal of Clinical Psychology, 36*, 492-499.

Eysenck, H. J. (1952). The effects of psychotherapy: An evaluation. *Journal of Consulting Psychology, 16*, 319-324.

Eysenck, H. J. (1966). *The effects of psychotherapy*. New York: International Science Press.

Eysenck, H. J., & Eysenck, S. B. G. (1975). *Manual for Eysenck Personality Questionnaire*. San Diego, CA: Educational and Individual Testing Service.

Fagan, T. J., Ax, R. K., Resnick, R. J., Liss, M., Johnson, R. T., & Forbes, M. R. (2004). Attitudes among interns and directors of training: Who wants to prescribe, who doesn't, and why? *Professional Psychology: Research and Practice, 35*, 345-356.

Fagan, T. K. (1996). Witmer's contribution to school psychological services. *American Psychologist, 51*, 241-243.

Fairbairn, W. R. D. (1952). *Psychoanalytic studies of the personality*. London: Tavistock Publications/ Routledge & Kegan Paul.

Fallon, T., & Schwab-Stone, M. (1994). Determinants of reliability in psychiatric surveys of children aged 6-12. *Journal of Child Psychology and Psychiatry and Allied Disciplines, 35*, 1391-1408.

Fancher, R. E. (1973). *Psychoanalytic psychology: The development of Freud's thought*. New York: W. W. Norton.

Farah, M. J., McMullen, P. A., & Meyer, M. M. (1991). Can recognition of living things be selectively impaired? *Neuropsychologia, 29*(2), 185-193.

Fauber, R. L. (2006). Graduate admissions in clinical psychology: Observations on the present and thoughts on the future. *Clinical Psychology: Science and Practice, 13*, 227-234.

Faust, D., & Ziskin, J. (1988). The expert witness in psychology and psychiatry. *Science, 242*, 31-35.

Fawzy, F. I., Fawzy, N. W., Arndt, L. A., & Pasnau, R. O. (1995). Critical review of psychosocial interventions in cancer care. *Archives of General Psychiatry, 52*, 100-113.

Feinstein, R. E., & Feinstein, M. S. (2001). Psychotherapy for health and lifestyle change. *Journal of Clinical Psychology/In Session, 57*, 1263-1275.

Felner, R. D., Farber, S. S., & Primavera, J. (1983). Transitions and stressful life events: A model for primary prevention. In R. D. Felner, L. A. Jason, J. N. Moritsugu, & S. S. Farber (Eds.), *Preventive psychology: Theory, research, and prevention* (pp. 191–215). New York: Pergamon Press.

Felner, R. D., Felner, T. Y., & Silverman, M. M. (2000). Prevention in mental health and social intervention: Conceptual and methodological issues in the evolution of the science and practice of prevention. In J. Rappaport & E. Seidman (Eds.), *Handbook of community psychology* (pp. 9–42). Dordrecht, Netherlands: Kluwer Academic Publishers.

Feltham, C. (2000). What are counselling and psychotherapy? In C. Feltham & I. Horton (Eds.), *Handbook of counselling and psychotherapy*. London: Sage.

Figueroa-Moseley, C., Jean-Pierre, P., Roscoe, J. A., Ryan, J. L., Kohli, S., et al. (2007). Behavioral Interventions in Treating Anticipatory Nausea and Vomiting. *Journal of National Comprehensive Cancer Networks, 5,* 44–50.

Finch, A. J., Simon, N. P., & Nezu, C. M. (2006). The future of clinical psychology: Board certification. *Clinical Psychology: Science and Practice, 13,* 254–257.

Fine, R. (1971). *The healing of the mind: The technique of psychoanalytic psychotherapy*. New York: David McKay.

Fine, S., & Glasser, P. H. (1996). *The first helping interview: Engaging the client and building trust*. Thousand Oaks, CA: Sage.

Finger, M. S., & Ones, D. S. (1999). Psychometric equivalence of the computer and booklet forms of the MMPI: A meta-analysis. *Psychological Assessment, 11,* 58–66.

Finger, M. S., & Rand, K. L. (2005). Addressing validity concerns in clinical psychology research. In M. C. Roberts & S. S. Ilardi (Eds.), *Handbook of research methods in clinical psychology* (pp. 13–30). Malden, MA: Blackwell Publishing.

Finn, S. E. (1996). *Manual for using the MMPI-2 for a therapeutic intervention*. Minneapolis: University of Minnesota Press.

Finn, S. E. (2005). How psychological assessment taught me compassion and firmness. *Journal of Personality Assessment, 84,* 29–32.

First, M. B. (2006). Relational processes in the DSM-V revision process: Comment on the special section. *Journal of Family Psychology, 20,* 356–358.

Fischer, C. T. (1985). *Individualizing psychological assessment*. Monterey, CA: Brooks/Cole.

Fischer, C. T. (1989). A life-centered approach to psychodiagnostics: Attending to lifeworld, ambiguity, and possibility. *Person-Centered Review, 4,* 163–170.

Fischer, C. T. (2001). Psychological assessment: From objectification back to the life world. In B. D. Slife, R. N. Williams, & S. H. Barlow (Eds.), *Critical issues in psychotherapy* (pp. 29–44). Thousand Oaks, CA: Sage.

Fisher, C. T., & Fisher, W. F. (1983). Phenomenological-existential psychotherapy. In M. Hersen, A. E. Kazdin, & A. S. Bellack (Eds.), *The clinical psychology handbook* (pp. 489–505). New York: Pergamon Press.

Fisher, D. C., Beutler, L. E., & Williams, O. B. (1999). Making assessment relevant to treatment planning: The STS Clinician Rating Form. *Journal of Clinical Psychology, 55,* 825–842.

Fisher, J. D., Fisher, W. A., Bryan, A. D., & Misovich, S. J. (2002). Information-motivation-behavioral skills model-based HIV risk behavior change intervention for inner-city high school youth. *Health Psychology, 21,* 177–186.

Fleisig, W. E. (1993). The development of the Illustrated Fear Survey Schedule (IFSS) and an examination of its reliability and validity with children with mild mental retardation. *Dissertation Abstracts International, 54,* 1719.

Foa, E. B., Riggs, D., Dancu, C., & Rothbaum, R. (1993). Reliability and validity of a brief instrument for assessing post-traumatic stress disorder. *Journal of Traumatic Stress, 6,* 459–473.

Fodor, J. A. (1983). *Modularity of mind*. Cambridge, MA: MIT Press.

Folkman, S., & Lazarus, R. S. (1980). An analysis of coping in a middle-aged community sample. *Journal of Health and Social Behavior, 21,* 219–239.

Folkman, S., & Lazarus, R. S. (1988). *Manual for the ways of coping questionnaire*. Palo Alto, CA: Consulting Psychologists Press.

Follette, W. C. (1996). Introduction to the special section on the development of theoretically coherent alternatives to the DSM system. *Journal of Consulting and Clinical Psychology, 64,* 1117-1119.

Follette, W. C., & Houts, A. C. (1996). Models of scientific progress and the role of theory in taxonomy development: A case study of the DSM. *Journal of Consulting and Clinical Psychology, 64,* 1120-1132.

Follette, W. C., Naugle, A. E., & Callaghan, G. M. (1996). A radical behavioral understanding of the therapeutic relationship in effecting change. *Behavior Therapy, 27,* 623-642.

Folstein, M. F., Maiberger, P., & McHugh, P. R. (1977). Mood disorders as a specific complication of stroke. *Journal of Neurology, Neurosurgery & Psychiatry, 40,* 1018-1020.

Fonagy, P., & Target, M. (2003). *Psychoanalytic theories: Perspectives from developmental psychology.* New York: Brunner-Routledge.

Ford, M., & Widiger, T. (1989). Sex bias in the diagnosis of histrionic and antisocial personality disorders. *Journal of Consulting and Clinical Psychology, 57,* 301-305.

Forsyth, D. R., & Corazzini, J. G. (2000). Groups as change agents. In C. R. Snyder & R. E. Ingram (Eds.), *Handbook of psychological change* (pp. 309-336). New York: Wiley.

Fosco, G. M., & Grych, J. H. (2007). Emotional expression in the family as a context for children's appraisals of interparental conflict. *Journal of Family Psychology, 21,* 248-258.

Foster, G. D., & Kendall, P. C. (1994). The realistic treatment of obesity: Changing the scales of success. *Clinical Psychology Review, 14,* 701-736.

Fowers, B. J., & Davido, B. J. (2006). The virtue of multiculturalism: Personal transformation, character, and openness to the other. *American Psychologist, 61,* 581-594.

Frank, E., Shear, M. K., Rucci, P., Banti, S., Mauri, M., et al. (2005). Cross-cultural validity of the Structured Clinical Interview for Panic-Agoraphobic spectrum. *Social Psychiatry and Psychiatric Epidemiology, 40,* 283-290.

Frank, L. K. (1939). Projective methods for the study of personality. *Journal of Psychology, 8,* 343-389.

Frankl, V. (1963). *Man's search for meaning.* New York: Washington Square Press.

Frankl, V. (1965). *The doctor and the soul.* New York: Knopf.

Frankl, V. (1967). *Psychotherapy and existentialism: Selected papers on logotherapy.* New York: Washington Square Press.

Franko, D. L., Mintz, L. B., Villapiano, M., Green, T. C., Mainelli, D., Folensbee, L., et al. (2005). Food, mood, and attitude: Reducing risk for eating disorders in college women. *Health Psychology, 24,* 567-578.

Franks, C. M. (1964). *Conditioning techniques in clinical practice and research.* New York: Springer.

Fraser, M. W. (Ed.). (2004). *Risk and resilience in childhood: An ecological perspective* (2nd ed.). Washington, DC: National Association of Social Workers Press.

Fraser, M. W., Kirby, L. D., & Smokowski, P. R. (2004). Risk and resilience in childhood. In M. W. Fraser (Ed.) (2004). *Risk and resilience in childhood: An ecological perspective* (2nd ed., pp. 13-66). Washington, DC: National Association of Social Workers Press.

Fredrickson, B. L. (2001). The role of positive emotions in positive psychology: The broaden-and-build theory of positive emotions. *American Psychologist, 56,* 218-226.

Free, M. L. (2007). *Cognitive therapy in groups: Guidelines and resources for practice* (2nd ed.). Hoboken, NJ: Wiley.

Freud, A. (1936). The ego and the mechanisms of defense. In *The writings of Anna Freud* (Vol. 2, Revised Edition, 1966). New York: International Universities Press.

Freud, S. (1900). *The interpretation of dreams* (Avon Edition, 1965). New York: Avon Books.

Freud, S. (1901). *The psychopathology of everyday life.* New York: Macmillan.

Freud, S. (1904). On psychotherapy. Lecture delivered before the College of Physicians in Vienna. Reprinted in S. Freud, *Therapy and technique.* New York: Collier Books, 1963.

Freud, S. (1949). *An outline of psychoanalysis.* (J. Strachey, trans.). New York: W. W. Norton.

Freud, S. (1953/1964). *The standard edition of the complete psychological works of Sigmund Freud* (24 vols.). London: Hogarth Press.

Frick, P. J. (1998). Conduct disorders. In T. H. Ollendick & M. Hersen (Eds.), *Handbook of child psychopathology* (3rd ed., pp. 213–237). New York: Plenum.

Friedman, M., & Rosenman, R. H. (1974). *Type A behavior and your heart*. New York: Knopf.

Friedman, M., & Thoresen, C. (1986). Alteration of Type A behavior and its effect on cardiac recurrences in post-myocardial infarction patients: Summary results of the Recurrent Coronary Prevention Project. *American Heart Journal, 112,* 653–665.

Friedman, M., Thoresen, Gill, Ulmer, Powell, Price, Brown, Thompson, Labin, Breall, et al. (1986). Alteration of Type A behavior and its effect on cardiac recurrences in post-myocardial infarction patients: Summary results of the Recurrent Coronary Prevention Project. *American Heart Journal, 112,* 653–665.

Frish, M. B. (1998). Quality of life therapy and assessment in health care. *Clinical Psychology: Science and Practice, 5,* 19–40.

Funder, D. (2001). *The personality puzzle* (2nd ed.). New York: W. W. Norton.

Furman, W. (1980). Promoting appropriate social behavior: A developmental perspective. In B. Lahey & A. Kazdin (Eds.), *Advances in clinical child psychology* (Vol. 3, pp. 1–41). New York: Plenum Press.

Furnham, A. (2000). Thinking about intelligence. *The Psychologist. 13,* 510–515.

Gabbard, G. O. (2000). *Psychodynamic psychiatry in clinical practice* (3rd ed.). Washington, DC: American Psychiatric Press.

Gabbard, G. O. (2005). *Psychodynamic psychiatry in clinical practice* (4th ed.). Washington, DC: American Psychiatric Publishing.

Gabbard, K., & Gabbard, G. O. (1999). *Psychiatry and the cinema*. Washington, DC: American Psychiatric Press.

Gaines, L. K., & Falkenberg, S. (1998). An evaluation of the written selection test: Effectiveness and alternatives. *Journal of Criminal Justice, 26,* 175–183.

Gainotti, G. (1972). Emotional behavior and hemispheric side of lesion. *Cortex, 8,* 41–55.

Galton, F. (1883). *Inquiries into the human faculty and its development*. London: Macmillan.

Garb, H. N. (1984). The incremental validity of information used in personality assessment. *Clinical Psychology Review, 4,* 641–656.

Garb, H. N. (1989). Clinical judgment, clinical training, and professional experience. *Psychological Bulletin, 105,* 387–396.

Garb, H. N. (1992). The trained psychologist as expert witness. *Clinical Psychology Review, 12,* 451–468.

Garb, H. N. (1995). Sex bias and the diagnosis of borderline personality disorder. *Professional Psychology: Research and Practice, 26,* 526.

Garb, H. N. (1996). The representativeness and past-behavior heuristics in clinical judgment. *Professional Psychology: Theory and Practice, 27,* 272–277.

Garb, H. N. (2000). Computers will become increasingly important for psychological assessment: Not that there's anything wrong with that! *Psychological Assessment, 12,* 31–39.

Garb, H. N. (2007). Computer-administered interviews and rating scales. *Psychological Assessment, 19,* 4–13.

Garb, H. N., Florio, C. M., & Grove, W. M. (1998). The validity of the Rorschach and the Minnesota Multiphasic Personality Inventory: Results from meta-analyses. *Psychological Science, 9,* 402–404.

Garber, J. (1984). Classification of childhood psychopathology: A developmental perspective. *Child Development, 55,* 30–48.

Garber, J., & Carter, J. S. (2006). Major depression. In R. T. Ammerman (Ed.), *Comprehensive handbook of personality and psychopathology* (Vol. 3, pp. 165–216). Hoboken, NJ: Wiley.

Gardner, H. (1993). *Multiple intelligences*. New York: Basic Books.

Gardner, H. (1998). Multiple intelligences: Myths and messages. In A. Wolfolk (Ed.), *Readings in educational psychology* (2nd ed.). Boston: Allyn & Bacon.

Gardner, H. (2002). The pursuit of excellence through education. In M. Ferrari (Ed.), *Learning from extraordinary minds*. Mahwah, NJ: Erlbaum.

Gardner, H., Brownell, H. H., Wapner, W., & Michelow, D. (1983). Missing the point: The role of the right hemisphere in the processing of complex linguistic materials. In E. Perecman (Ed.), *Cognitive processing in the right hemisphere* (pp. 169-191). New York: Academic.

Gardner, W., Lidz, C. W., Mulvey, E. P., & Shaw, E. C. (1996). Clinical versus actuarial predictions of violence in patients with mental illnesses. *Journal of Consulting and Clinical Psychology, 64,* 602-609.

Garfield, S. L. (1974). *Clinical psychology: The study of personality and behavior.* Chicago: Aldine.

Garfield, S. L. (1994). Research on client variables in psychotherapy. In A. Bergin & S. Garfield (Eds.), *Handbook of psychotherapy and behavior change* (4th ed., pp. 190-228). New York: Wiley.

Gazzaniga, M. S., Fendrich, R., & Wessinger, C. M. (1994). Blindsight reconsidered. *Current Directions in Psychological Science, 3,* 93-95.

Geer, J. H. (1965). The development of a scale to measure fear. *Behaviour Research and Therapy, 3,* 45-53.

Gelfand, D. M., & Peterson, L. (1985). *Child development and psychopathology.* Beverly Hills, CA: Sage.

Gendlin, E. T. (1996). *Focusing-oriented psychotherapy: A manual of the experiential method.* New York: Guilford.

Gernsbacher, M. A., Dawson, M., & Goldsmith, H. H. (2005). Three reasons not to believe in an autism epidemic. *Current Directions in Psychological Science, 14,* 55-58.

Gittelman, R. (1980). The role of tests for differential diagnosis in child psychiatry. *Journal of the American Academy of Child Psychiatry, 19,* 413-438.

Gladding, S. (2007). *Groups: A counseling specialty.* Upper Saddle River, NJ: Prentice Hall.

Glaser, R., & Bond, L. (1981). Introduction to the special issue: Testing: Concepts, policy, practice, and research. *American Psychologist, 36,* 997-1000.

Glasgow, R. E., Nutting, P. A., Toobert, D. J., King, D. K., Strycker, L. A., Jex, M., et al. (2006). Effects of a brief computer-assisted diabetes self-management intervention on dietary, biological

and quality-of-life outcomes. *Chronic Illness, 2,* 27-38.

Glasgow, R. E., & Terborg, J. R. (1988). Occupational health promotion programs to reduce cardiovascular risk. *Journal of Consulting and Clinical Psychology, 56,* 365-373.

Glozman, J. M. (2007). A. R. Luria and the history of Russian neuropsychology. *Journal of the History of Neuroscience, 16,* (1-2), 168-180.

Glueckauf, R., Pickett, T. C., Ketterson, T. U., Loomis, J. S., & Rozensky, R. H. (2003). Preparation for the delivery of telehealth services: A self-study framework for expansion of practice. *Professional Psychology: Research and Practice, 34,* 159-163.

Glynn, M., & Rhodes, P. (2005). Estimated HIV prevalence in the US at the end of 2003. *National HIV Prevention Conference,* Atlanta, Georgia.

Goins, M. K., Strauss, G. D., & Martin, R. (1995). A change measure for psychodynamic psychotherapy outcome research. *Journal of Psychotherapy Practice and Research, 4,* 319-328.

Gold, J., & Strickler, G. (2006). Introduction: An overview of psychotherapy integration. In G. Strickler & J. Gold (Eds.), *A casebook of psychotherapy integration.* Washington, DC: American Psychological Association.

Goldberg, E. (1995). Rise and fall of modular orthodoxy. *Journal of Clinical and Experimental Neuropsychology, 17*(2), 193-208.

Goldberg, E. & Bougakov, D. (2005). Neuropsychologic assessment of frontal lobe dysfunction. *Psychiatric Clinics of North America, 28,* 567-580.

Goldberg, L. R. (1959). The effectiveness of clinicians' judgments: The diagnosis of organic brain damage from the Bender-Gestalt test. *Journal of Consulting Psychology, 23,* 25-33.

Goldberg, L. R. (1968). Simple models or simple processes? Some research on clinical judgments. *American Psychologist, 23,* 483-496.

Goldfried, M. R. (1980). Toward the delineation of therapeutic change principles. *American Psychologist, 35,* 991-999.

Goldfried, M. R. (2006). Cognitive-affective-relational-behavior therapy. In G. Stricker & J. Gold

(Eds.), *A casebook of psychotherapy integration* (pp. 153–164). Washington, DC: American Psychological Association.

Goldfried, M. R., & Sprafkin, J. N. (1974). *Behavioral personality assessment*. Morristown, NJ: General Learning Press.

Golding, S. L., & Rorer, L. G. (1972). Illusory correlation and subjective judgment. *Journal of Abnormal Psychology, 80,* 249–260.

Goldsmith, J. B., & McFall, R. M. (1975). Development and evaluation of an interpersonal skill-training program for psychiatric inpatients. *Journal of Abnormal Psychology, 84,* 51–58.

Goldstein, S., & Brooks, R. B. (2005). *Handbook of resilience in children*. New York: Kluwer Academic/ Plenum Publishers.

Goodheart, C. D., Kazdin, A. E., & Sternberg, R. J. (Eds.). (2006). *Evidence-based psychotherapy*. Washington, DC: American Psychological Association.

Goodman, S. H., Lahey, B. B., Fielding, B., Dulcan, M., Narrow, W., & Regier, D. (1997). Representativeness of clinical samples of youth with mental disorders: A preliminary population-based study. *Journal of Abnormal Psychology,* 3–14.

Goodwin, P. J., Leszcz, M., Ennis, M., Koopmans, J., Vincent, L., Guther, H., et al. (2001). The effect of group psychosocial support on survival in metastatic breast cancer. *The New England Journal of Medicine, 345,* 1719–1726.

Gorenstein, E. E., & Comer, R. J. (2002). *Case studies in abnormal psychology*. New York: Worth.

Gorman, J. M. (2006). Virtual reality: A real treatment option. *CNS Spectrums, 11,* 12–13.

Gotham, H. J. (2006). Advancing the implementation of evidence-based practices into clinical practice: How do we get there from here? *Professional Psychology: Research and Practice, 37,* 606–613.

Gottlieb, B. H., & Peters, L. (1991). A national demographic portrait of mutual aid group participants in Canada. *American Journal of Community Psychology, 19,* 651–666.

Gottman, J. M., & Gottman, J. S. (2006). *Ten lessons to transform your marriage*. New York: Crown Publishing Group.

Gottman, J. M., & Krokoff, L. J. (1989). Marital interaction and satisfaction: A longitudinal view. *Journal of Consulting and Clinical Psychology, 57,* 47–52.

Gottman, J. M., & Levenson, R. W. (1992). Marital processes predictive of later dissolution: Behavior, physiology, and health. *Journal of Personality and Social Psychology, 63,* 221–233.

Gottman, J. M., Markman, H. J., & Notarius, C. (1977). The topography of marital conflict: A sequential analysis of verbal and nonverbal behavior. *Journal of Marriage and the Family, 39,* 461–477.

Gottman, J. M., & Ryan, K. (2005). The mismeasure of therapy: Treatment outcomes in marital therapy research. In W. M. Pinsof & J. L. Lebow (Eds.), *Family psychology: The art of the science* (pp. 65–89). New York: Oxford University Press.

Gough, H. (1987). *California Psychological Inventory: Administrator's guide*. Palo Alto, CA: Consulting Psychologists Press.

Graham, J. R. (1990). *MMPI-2: Assessing personality and psychopathology*. New York: Oxford University Press.

Graham, J. R. (2000). *MMPI-2: Assessing personality and psychopathology* (3rd ed.). New York: Oxford University Press.

Grant, B. F., Harford, T. C., Dawson, D. D., Chou, P. S., & Pickering, R. (1995). The Alcohol Use Disorder and Associated Disabilities Interview Schedule (AUDADIS): Reliability of alcohol and drug modules in a general population sample. *Drug and Alcohol Dependence, 39,* 37–44.

Grant, K. E., Katz, B. N., Thomas, K. J., O'Koon, J. H., Meza, C. M., DiPasquale, A. M., et al. (2004). Psychological symptoms affecting low-income urban youth. *Journal of Adolescent Research, 19,* 613–634.

Grant, K. E., McCormick, A., Poindexter, L., Simpkins, T., Janda, C. M., Thomas, K. J., et al. (2005). Exposure to violence and parenting as mediators between poverty and psychological symptoms in urban African American adolescents. *Journal of Adolescence, 28,* 507–521.

Green, D. (2006). CPD: Why bother? In L. Golding & I. Gray (Eds.), *Continuing professional development for clinical psychologists: A practical handbook* (pp. 7-22). Leicester, England: British Psychological Society.

Greenberg, L. S., Elliot, R. K., & Lietaer, G. (1994). Research on experiential psychotherapies. In A. E. Bergin & S. L. Garfield (Eds.), *Handbook of psychotherapy and behavior change* (pp. 509-512). New York: Wiley.

Greenberg, L. S., & Safran, J. D. (1989). Emotion in psychotherapy. *American Psychologist, 44*, 19-29.

Greenberg, R. P., Constantino, M. J., & Bruce, N. (2006). Are patient expectations still relevant for psychotherapy process and outcome. *Clinical Psychology Review, 26*, 657-678.

Greenhoot, A. F. (2005). Design and analysis of experimental and quasi-experimental investigations. In M. C. Roberts & S. S. Ilardi (Eds.), *Handbook of research methods in clinical psychology* (pp. 92-114). Malden, MA: Blackwell Publishing.

Gregory, R. J. (2006). *Psychological testing: History, principles, and applications* (5th ed.). Boston: Allyn & Bacon.

Grilo, C. M., Lozano, C., & Elder, K. A. (2005). Interrater and test-retest reliability of the Spanish language version of the Eating Disorder Examination Interview: Clinical and research implications. *Journal of Psychiatric Practice, 11*, 231-240.

Grilo, C. M., Masheb, R. M., & Wilson, G. T. (2006). Rapid response to treatment for binge eating disorder. *Journal of Consulting and Clinical Psychology, 74*, 602-613.

Grinfeld, M. J. (1998). Psychiatry and mental illness: Are they mass media targets? Psychiatric Times, XV. Retrieved November, 14, 2006, from http://www.psychiatrictimes.com/p980301a.html.

Grisso, T., & Appelbaum, P. S. (1995). The MacArthur Treatment Competence Study. III: Abilities of patients to consent to psychiatric and medical treatments. *Law and Human Behavior, 19*, 149-174.

Grisso, T., Steinberg, L., Wollard, J., Cauffman, E., Scott, E., Graham, S., et al. (2003). Juveniles' competence to stand trial: A comparison of adolescents' and adults' capacities as trial defendants. *Law and Human Behavior 27*, 333-363.

Gross, B. (2005). Death throes: Professional liability after client suicide. *Annals of the American Psychotherapy Association, 8*, 34-35.

Gross, S. J. (1978). The myth of professional licensing. *American Psychologist, 33*, 1009-1016.

Grossarth, M. R., Eysenck, H. J., & Boyle, G. J. (1995). Method of test administration as a factor in test validity: The use of a personality questionnaire in the prediction of cancer and coronary heart disease. *Behaviour Research and Therapy, 33*, 705-710.

Groth-Marnat, G. (1999). *Handbook of psychological assessment* (3rd ed.). New York: Wiley.

Groth-Marnat, G. (2003). *Handbook of psychological assessment* (4th ed.). Hoboken, NJ: Wiley.

Grove, W. M., Zald, D. H., Lebow, B. S., Snitz, B. E., & Nelson, C. (2000). Clinical versus mechanical prediction: A meta-analysis. *Psychological Assessment, 12*, 19-30.

Grover, R. L., Hughes, A. A., Bergman, R. L., & Kingery, J. N. (2006). Treatment modifications based on childhood anxiety diagnosis: Demonstrating the flexibility in manualized treatment. *Journal of Cognitive Psychotherapy, 20*, 275-286.

Grych, J. H., & Fincham, F. D. (1992). Interventions for children of divorce: Toward greater integration of research and action. *Psychological Bulletin, 111*, 434-454.

Grych, J. H., Raynor, S. R., & Fosco, G. M. (2004). Family processes that shape the impact of interparental conflict on adolescents. *Development and Psychopathology, 16*, 649-665.

Gullone, E., & King, N. J. (1992). Psychometric evaluation of a revised fear survey schedule for children and adolescents. *Journal of Child Psychology and Psychiatry and Allied Disciplines, 33*, 987-998.

Gur, R. E. (1978). Left hemisphere dysfunction and the left hemisphere overactivation in schizophrenia. *Journal of Abnormal Psychology, 87*, 225-238.

Gur, R. E., Cowell, P. E., Latshaw, A., Turetsky, B. I., Grossman, R. I., Arnold, S. E., et al. (2000). Reduced dorsal and orbital prefrontal gray matter volumes in schizophrenia. *Archives of General Psychiatry, 57,* 761-768.

Gureje, O. (2004). What can we learn from cross-national study of somatic distress? Journal of *Psychosomatic Research, 56,* 409-412.

Gurman, A. S. (2003). Marital therapy. In A. S. Gurman & S. B. Messer (Eds.), *Essential Psychotherapies,* (2nd ed., pp 463-514). New York: Guilford.

Gurman, A. S., & Jacobson, N. S. (2002). *Clinical handbook of couple therapy* (3rd ed.). New York: Guilford.

Gurman, A. S., & Messer, S. B. (Eds.). (2003). *Essential psychotherapies* (2nd ed.). New York: Guildford.

Hall, G. C. N. (2005). Introduction to the special section on multicultural and community psychology: Clinical psychology in context. *Journal of Consulting and Clinical Psychology, 73,* 787-789.

Hall, G. C. N. (2006). Diversity in clinical psychology. *Clinical Psychology: Science and Practice, 13,* 258-262.

Hall, J. E., & Boucher, A. P. (2003). Professional mobility for psychologists: Multiple choices, multiple opportunities. *Professional Psychology: Research and Practice, 34,* 463-467.

Hall, J. E., Wexelbaum, S. F., & Boucher, A. P. (2007). Doctoral student awareness of licensure, credentialing, and professional organizations in psychology: The 2005 national register international survey. *Training and Education in Professional Psychology, 1,* 38-48.

Hallahan, B., Hibbeln, J. R., Davis, J. M., & Garland, M. R. (2007). Omega-3 fatty acid supplementation in patients with recurrent self-harm: Single-centre double-blind randomised controlled trial. *British Journal of Mental Science, 190,* 118-122.

Hambleton, R. K., Merenda, P. F., & Spielberger, C. D. (Eds.). (2005). *Adapting educational and psychological tests for cross-cultural assessment.* Mahwah, NJ: Erlbaum.

Hammond, K. R., & Allen, J. M. (1953). *Writing clinical reports.* Englewood Cliffs, NJ: Prentice-Hall.

Handelsman, M. M., Gottlieb, M. C., & Knapp, S. (2005). Training ethical psychologists: An acculturation model. *Professional Psychology: Research and Practice, 36,* 59-65.

Handler, L. (1974). Psychotherapy, assessment, and clinical research: Parallels and similarities. In A. I. Rabin (Ed.), *Clinical psychology: Issues of the seventies* (pp. 49-62). East Lansing: Michigan State University Press.

Hankin, B. L., & Abela, J. R. Z. (2005). Depression from childhood through adolescence and adulthood. In B. L. Hankin & J. R. Z. Abela (Eds.), *Development of psychopathology: A vulnerability-stress perspective* (pp. 245-288). Thousand Oaks, CA: Sage.

Hankin, B. L., Fraley, R. C., Lahey, B. B., & Waldman, I. D. (2005). Is depression best viewed as a continuum or discrete category? A taxometric analysis of childhood and adolescent depression in a population-based sample. *Journal of Abnormal Psychology, 114,* 96-110.

Hansen, J. C. (1984). Interest inventories. In G. Goldstein & M. Hersen (Eds.), *Handbook of psychological assessment* (pp. 157-177). New York: Pergamon Press.

Hansen, J. C., & Campbell, D. P. (1985). *Manual for the SVIB-SCII* (4th ed.). Palo Alto, CA: Consulting Psychologists Press.

Hanson, S. L., Kerkhoff, T. R., & Bush, S. S. (2004). *Health care ethics for psychologists: A casebook.* Washington, DC: American Psychological Association.

Harbeck, C., Peterson, L., & Starr, L. (1992). Previously abused child victims' response to a sexual abuse prevention program: A matter of measures. *Behavior Therapy, 23,* 375-388.

Harlow, J. M. (1848). Passage of an iron rod through the head. *Boston Medical and Surgical Journal, 39,* 389-393.

Haro, J. M., Kontodimas, S., Negrin, M. A., Ratcliffe, M., Saurez, D., & Windmeijer, F. (2006). Methodological aspects in the assessment of treatment effects in observational health outcomes studies. *Applied Health Economics and Health Policy, 5,* 11-25.

Harris, F. C., & Lahey, B. B. (1982). Recording system bias in direct observational methodology: A review. *Clinical Psychology Review, 2,* 539-556.

Harrison, B. J., Yucel, M., Shaw, M., Brewer, W. J., Nathan, P. J., Strother, S. C., et al. (2006). Dysfunction of dorsolateral prefrontal cortex in antipsychotic-naive schizophreniform psychosis. *Psychiatry Research, 148*, 23–31.

Harrower, M. R. (1965). Clinical psychologists at work. In B. B. Wolman (Ed.), *Handbook of clinical psychology* (pp. 1443–1458). New York: McGraw-Hill.

Hartmann, H. (1958). *Ego psychology and the problem of adaptation*. New York: International Universities Press.

Harway, M. (2005). *Handbook of couples therapy*. Hoboken, NJ: Wiley.

Hatala, R., & Case, S. M. (2000). Examining the influence of gender on medical students' decision making. *Journal of Women's Health & Gender-Based Medicine, 9*, 617–623.

Hatfield, D. R., & Ogles, B. M. (2004). The use of outcome measures by psychologists in clinical practice. *Professional Psychology: Research and Practice, 35*, 485–491.

Hathaway, S. R., & McKinley, J. C. (1967). *The Minnesota Multiphasic Personality Inventory manual*. New York: Psychological Corporation.

Hathaway, W. L., Scott, S. Y., & Garver, S. A. (2004). Assessing religious/spiritual functioning: A neglected domain in clinical practice? *Professional Psychology: Research and Practice, 35*, 97–104.

Hawes, D. J., & Dadds, M. R. (2006). Assessing parenting practices through parent-report and direct observation during parent-training. *Journal of Child and Family studies, 15*, 555–568.

Hawley, D. R., Bailey, C. E., & Pennick, K. A. (2000). A content analysis of research in family therapy journals. *Journal of Marital and Family Therapy, 26*, 9–16.

Hawley, K. M., & Weisz, J. R. (2005). Youth versus parent working alliance in usual clinical care: Distinctive associations with retention, satisfaction, and treatment outcome. *Journal of Clinical Child and Adolescent Psychology, 34*, 117–128.

Hayes, S. A., Hope, D. A., Terryberry-Spohr, L. S., Spaulding, W. D., VanDyke, M., Elting, D. T. et al. (2006). Discriminating between cognitive and supportive group therapies for chronic mental illness. *Journal of Nervous and Mental Disease, 194*, 603–609.

Hayes, S. C. (2005). Eleven rules for a more successful clinical psychology. *Journal of Clinical Psychology, 61*, 1055–1060.

Hayes, S. C., Follette, V. M., & Linehan, M. M. (Eds.). (2004). *Mindfulness and acceptance: Expanding the cognitive-behavioral tradition*. New York: Guilford.

Hayes, S. C., & Shenk, C. (2004). Operationaliing mindfulness without unnecessary attachments. *Clinical Psychology: Science and Practice, 11*, 249–254.

Haynes, R. B. (1982). Improving patient compliance: An empirical view. In R. B. Stuart (Ed.), *Adherence, compliance, and generalization in behavioral medicine* (pp. 56–78). New York: Brunner/Mazel.

Haynes, S. N. (1990). Behavioral assessment of adults. In G. Goldstein & M. Hersen (Eds.), *Handbook of psychological assessment* (2nd ed., pp. 423–463). New York: Pergamon Press.

Haynes, S. N., & O'Brien, W. O. (2000). *Principles of behavioral assessment: A functional approach to psychological assessment*. New York: Plenum/Kluwer Press.

Hays, P. A., & Iwamasa, G. Y. (Eds.). (2006). *Culturally responsive cognitive-behavioral therapy*. Washington, DC: American Psychological Association.

Hays, P. A. (2007). *Addressing cultural complexities in practice: Assessment, diagnosis, and therapy* (2nd ed.). Washington, DC: American Psychological Association.

Hazlett-Stevens, H., Craske, M. G., Roy-Birne, P. P., Sherbourne, C. D., Stein, M. B., & Bystritsky, A. (2002). Predictors of willingness to consider medication and psychosocial treatment for panic disorder in primary care patients. *General Hospital Psychiatry, 24*, 316–321.

Heal, L. W., & Sigelman, C. K. (1995). Response biases in interviews of individuals with limited mental ability. *Journal of Intellectual Disability Research, 39*, 331–340.

Hedges, L. V., & Olkin, L. (1982). Analyses, reanalyses, and meta-analysis. *Contemporary Education Review, 1*, 157–165.

Hegel, M. T., & Ferguson, R. J. (2000). Differential reinforcement of other behavior (DRO) to reduce aggressive behavior following traumatic brain injury. *Behavior Modification, 24,* 94–101.

Heidegger, M. (1968). *Being and time* (J. Macquarrie & E. Robinson, Trans.). New York: Harper & Row. (Original work published 1927)

Heider, F. (1958). *The psychology of interpersonal relations.* New York: Wiley.

Heilbrun, K., & Collins, S. (1995). Evaluations of trial competency and mental state at time of offense: Report characteristics. *Professional Psychology: Research & Practice, 26,* 61–67.

Heilman, K. M., Barrett, A. M., & Adair, J. C. (1998). Possible mechanisms of anosognosia: A defect in self-awareness. *Philosophical Transactions of the Royal Society of London: Series B. Biological Sciences, 353*(1377), 1903–1909.

Heilman, K. M., & Valenstein, E. (Eds.). (2003). *Clinical neuropsychology* (4th ed.). New York: Oxford University Press.

Heilman, K. M., Watson, R. T., & Valenstein, E. (2003). Neglect and related disorders. In K. M. Heilman & E. Valenstein (Eds.), *Clinical neuropsychology* (4th ed.). New York: Oxford University Press.

Helgeson, V. S., Cohen, S., & Fritz, H. (1998). Social ties and the onset and progression of cancer. In J. Holland (Ed.), *Psycho-oncology.* New York: Oxford University Press.

Heller, W. (1990). The neuropsychology of emotion: Developmental patterns and implications for psychopathology. In N. L. Stein, B. L. Leventhal, & T. Trabasso (Eds.), *Psychological and biological approaches to emotion* (pp. 167–211). Hillsdale, NJ: Erlbaum.

Heller, W., & Nitschke, J. B. (1997). Regional brain activity in emotion: A framework for understanding cognition in depression. *Cognition and Emotion, 11,* 637–661.

Hellige, J. B. (2001). *Hemispheric asymmetry: What's right and what's left.* Cambridge, MA: Harvard University Press.

Hendrie, H. C., Lane, K. A., Ogunniyi, A., Baiyewu, O., Gureje, O., Evans, R., et al. (2006). The development of a semi-structured home interview (CHIF) to directly assess function in cognitively impaired elderly people in two cultures. *International Psychogeriatrics, 18,* 653–666.

Henggeler, S. W., & Schoenwald, S. K. (2002). Treatment manuals: Necessary, but far from sufficient. *Clinical Psychology: Science and Practice, 9,* 419–420.

Henry, W. E. (1956). *The analysis of fantasy: The thematic apperception technique in the story of personality.* New York: Wiley.

Herbert, T. B., & Cohen, S. (1993). Stress and immunity in humans: A meta-analytic review. *Psychosomatic Medicine, 55,* 364–379.

Herink, R. (Ed.). (1980). *The psychotherapy handbook: The A to Z guide to more than 250 different therapies in use today.* New York: New American Library.

Herrington, J. D., Mohanty, A., Koven, N. S., Fisher, J. E., Stewart, J. L., Banich, M. T., et al. (2005). Emotion-modulated performance and activity in left dorsolateral prefrontal cortex. *Emotion, 5,* 200–207.

Hersch, P. D., & Alexander, R. W. (1990). MMPI profile patterns of emotional disability claimants. *Journal of Clinical Psychology, 46,* 795–799.

Hersen, M. (2002). *Clinical behavior therapy.* New York: Wiley.

Hetherington, E. M., & Arasteh, J. D. (Eds.). (1988). *Impact of divorce, single parenting, and stepparenting on children.* Hillsdale, NJ: Erlbaum.

Hetherington, E. M., Bridges, M., & Insabella, G. M. (1998). What matters? What does not? Five perspectives on the association between marital transitions and children's adjustment. *American Psychologist, 53,* 167–184.

Hetherington, E. M., & Elmore, A. M. (2003). Risk and resilience in children coping with their parents' divorce and remarriage. In S. S. Luthar (Ed.), *Resilience and vulnerability: Adaptation in the context of childhood adversities* (pp. 182–212). New York: Cambridge University Press.

Hetherington, E. M., & Stanley-Hagan, M. (1999). The adjustment of children with divorced parents: A risk and resiliency perspective. *Journal of Child Psychology and Psychiatry, 40,* 129–140.

Hetzel-Riggin, M. D., Brausch, A. M., & Montgomery, B. S. (2007). A meta-analytic investigation of therapy modality outcomes for sexually abused children and adolescents: An exploratory study. *Child Abuse and Neglect, 31,* 125–141.

Heyman, R. E. (2001). Observation of couple conflicts: Clinical assessment applications, stubborn truths, and shaky foundations. *Psychological Assessment, 13,* 5–35.

Heyman, R. E., & Slep, A. M. S. (2006). Creating and field-testing diagnostic criteria for partner and child maltreatment. *Journal of Family Psychology, 20,* 397–408.

Hickling, E. J., & Blanchard, E. B. (2006). *Overcoming the trauma of your motor vehicle accident: A cognitive-behavioral treatment program therapist guide.* London, UK: Oxford Press.

Hickling, F. W., McKenzie, K., Mullen, R., & Murray, R. (1999). A Jamaican psychiatrist evaluates diagnoses at a London psychiatric hospital. *British Journal of Psychiatry, 175,* 283–285.

Hilton, N. Z., Harris, G. T., & Rice, M. E. (2006). Sixty-six years of research on clinical versus actuarial prediction of violence. *Counseling Psychologist, 34,* 400–409.

Himelein, M. J., & Putnam, E. A. (2001). Work activities of academic clinical psychologists: Do they practice what they teach? *Professional Psychology: Research and Practice, 5,* 537–542.

Hinshaw, S. P. (2006). Treatment for children and adolescents with attention-deficit/hyperactivity disorder. In P. C. Kendall (Ed.), *Child and adolescent therapy: Cognitive-behavioral procedures* (3rd ed., pp. 82–113). New York: Guilford.

Hinshaw, S. P. (2007). *The mark of shame: Stigma of mental illness and an agenda for change.* New York: Oxford University Press.

Hofferth, S. L., Stueve, J. L., Pleck, J., Bianchi, S., & Sayer, L. (2002). The demography of fathers: What fathers do. In C. S. Tamis-LeMonda & N. Cabrera (Eds.), *Handbook of father involvement: Multidisciplinary perspectives* (pp. 63–90). Mahwah, NJ: Erlbaum.

Hoffman, P. J. (1960). The paramorphic representation of clinical judgment. *Psychological Bulletin, 57,* 116–131.

Hogue, A., Dauber, S., Stambaugh, L. F., Cecero, J. J., & Liddle, H. A. (2006). Early therapeutic alliance and treatment outcome in individual and family therapy for adolescent behavior problems. *Journal of Consulting and Clinical Psychology, 74,* 121–129.

Holder, H. D., & Blose, J. D. (1987). Changes in health care costs and utilization associated with mental health treatment. *Hospital and Community Psychiatry, 38,* 1070–1075.

Holland, J. L. (1994). *The self-directed search.* Odessa, FL: Psychological Assessment Resources.

Holland, J. L. (1996). Exploring careers with a typology. *American Psychologist, 51,* 397–406.

Holland, J. L., & Gottfredson, G. D. (1994). *Career attitudes and strategies inventory: An inventory for understanding adult careers.* Odessa, FL: Psychological Assessment Resources.

Hollanders, H. & McLeod, J. (1999). Theoretical orientation and reported practice: A survey of eclecticism among counselors in Britain. *British Journal of Guidance and Counseling, 27,* 405–414.

Hollon, S. D. (2006). Randomized clinical trials. In J. C. Norcross, L. E. Beutler, & R. F. Levant (Eds.), *Evidence-based practice in mental health* (pp. 96–105). Washington, DC: American Psychological Association.

Hollon, S. D., & Beck, A. T. (2004). Cognitive and cognitive behavioral therapies. In M. J. Lambert (Ed.), *Bergin and Garfield's handbook of psychotherapy and behavior change* (5th ed., pp. 447–492). New York: Wiley.

Hollon, S. D., DeRubeis, R. J., Shelton, R. C., Amsterdam, J. D., Salomon, R. M., O'Reardon, J. P., et al. (2005). Prevention of relapse following cognitive therapy versus medications in moderate to severe depression. *Archives of General Psychiatry, 62,* 417–422.

Hollon, S. D., Stewart, M. O., & Strunk, D. (2006). Enduring effects for cognitive behavior therapy in the treatment of depression and anxiety. *Annual Review of Psychology, 57,* 285–315.

Holloway, J. D. (2004). Louisiana grants psychologists prescriptive authority. *Monitor on Psychology, 35,* 20–21.

Holmboe, E. S. (2004). Faculty and the observation of trainees clinical skills: Problems and opportunities. *Academic Medicine. 79,* 16–22.

Holt, R. R. (1958). Formal aspects of the TAT: A neglected resource. *Journal of Projective Techniques, 22,* 163–172.

Holt, R. R. (1978). *Methods in clinical psychology: Projective assessment* (Vol. 1). New York: Plenum Press.

Holt, R. R., & Luborsky, L. (1958). *Personality patterns of psychiatrists: A study of methods for selecting residents* (Vol. 1). New York: Basic Books.

Holtzman, W. H., Thorpe, J. W., Swartz, J. D., & Herron, E. W. (1961). *Inkblot perception and personality: Holtzman Inkblot Technique.* Austin: University of Texas Press.

Holtzworth-Munroe, A., Meehan, J. C., Rehman, U., & Marshall, A. D. (2002). Intimate partner violence: An introduction for couple therapists. In A. S. Gurman & N. S. Jacobson (Eds.), *Clinical handbook of couple therapy* (3rd ed., pp. 441–465). New York: Guilford.

Homant, R., & Kennedy, D. B. (1998). Psychological aspects of crime scene profiling. *Criminal Justice and Behavior, 25,* 319–343.

Honda, K., & Jacobson, J. S. (2005). Use of complementary and alternative medicine among United States adults: The influences of personality, coping strategies, and social support. *Preventive Medicine, 40,* 46–53.

Horn, J. L. (1965). An empirical comparison of methods for estimating factor scores. *Educational and Psychological Measurement, 25,* 313–322.

House, J. S., Robbins, C., & Metzner, H. L. (1982). The association of social relationships and activities with mortality: Prospective evidence from the Tecumseh Community Health Study. *American Journal of Epidemiology, 116,* 123–140.

Houts, A. C. (2003). Behavioral treatment for enuresis. In A. E. Kazdin & J. R. Weisz (Eds.), *Evidence-based psychotherapies for children and adolescents* (pp. 389–406). New York: Guilford.

Houts, A. C. (2004). Discovery, invention, and the expansion of the modern Diagnostic and Statistical Manuals of Mental Disorders. In L. E. Beutler & M. L. Malik (Eds.), *Rethinking the DSM: A psychological perspective* (pp. 17–68). Washington, DC: American Psychological Association.

Hovarth, A. O. (2000). The therapeutic relationship: From transference to alliance. *Journal of Clinical Psychology/In Session: Psychotherapy in Practice, 56,* 163–173.

Hovarth, A. O., & Greenberg, L. S. (1989). Development and validation of the Working Alliance Inventory. *Journal of Counseling Psychology, 36,* 223–233.

Hovarth, A. O., & Symonds, B. D. (1991). Relation between working alliance and outcome in psychotherapy: A meta-analysis. *Journal of Counseling Psychology, 38,* 139–149.

Howard, K. I., Krause, M. S., Caburnay, C. A., Noel, S. B., & Saunders, S. M. (2001). Syzygy, science, and psychotherapy: The Consumer Reports study. *Journal of Clinical Psychology 57,* 865–874.

Howard, K. I., Lueger, R. J., Maling, M. S., & Martinovich, Z. (1993). A phase model of psychotherapy outcome: Causal mediation of change. *Journal of Consulting and Clinical Psychology, 61,* 678–685.

Hoza, B., Gerdes, A. C., Mrug, S., Hinshaw, S. P., Bukowski, W. M., Gold, J. A., et al. (2005). Peer-assessed outcomes in the multimodal treatment study of children with attention deficit hyperactivity disorder. *Journal of Clinical Child and Adolescent, 34,* 74–86.

Hsu, L. K., & Folstein, M. F. (1997). Somatoform disorders in Caucasian and Chinese Americans. *Journal of Nervous and Mental Disease, 185,* 382–387.

Hughes, J. N., Cavell, T. A., & Jackson, T. (1999). Influence of the teacher-student relationship on childhood conduct problems: A prospective study. *Journal of Clinical Child Psychology, 28,* 173–184.

Hughes, R., Jr. (1996). The effects of divorce on children. Retrieved December 13, 2001, from http://www.hec.ohio-state.edu/famlife/divorce/index.htm.

Hummelen, B., Wilberg, T., & Karterud, S. (2007). Interviews of female patients with borderline personality disorder who dropped out of group psychotherapy. *International Journal of Group Psychotherapy, 57,* 67–91.

Humphreys, L. G. (1988). Trends in levels of academic achievement of blacks and other minorities. *Intelligence, 12,* 231–260.

Hunsley, J., & Mash, E. J. (2007). Evidence-based assessment. *Annual Review of Clinical Psychology, 3,* 29–51.

Hunsley, J., Lee, C. M., & Wood, J. M. (2003). Controversy and questionable assessment techniques. In S. O. Lilienfeld, S. J. Lynn, & J. M. Lohr (Eds.), *Science and pseudoscience in clinical psychology* (pp. 39–76). New York: Guilford.

Hunt, M. (1993). *The story of psychology.* New York: Anchor Books.

Hunter, J. E., & Schmidt, F. L. (2004). *Methods of meta-analysis: Correcting error and bias in research findings* (2nd ed.). Thousand Oaks, CA: Sage Publications.

Hunter, R. H. (1995). Benefits of competency-based treatment programs. *American Psychologist, 50,* 509–513.

Impara, J. C., & Plake, B. S. (Eds.). (2003). *The fifteenth mental measurements yearbook.* Lincoln, NE: The Buros Institute of Mental Measurements.

Individuals with Disabilities Education Act (Public Law 105–17, 1997).

Ingram, R. E. (2005). Clinical training for the next millennium. *Journal of Clinical Psychology, 61,* 1155–1158.

Inskipp, F. (2000). Generic skills. In C. Feltham & I. Horton (Eds.), *Handbook of counselling and psychotherapy.* London: Sage Publications.

Institute of Medicine. (1994). *Reducing risk for mental disorders: Frontiers for prevention intervention research.* Washington, DC: National Academy Press.

Institute of Personality Assessment and Research. (1970). *Annual report: 1969–1970.* Berkeley: University of California.

Inui, T., Yourtee, E., & Williamson, J. (1976). Improved outcomes in hypertension after physician tutorials. *Annuals of Internal Medicine, 84,* 646–651.

Isenhart, C. E., & Silversmith, D. J. (1996). MMPI-2 response styles: Generalization to alcoholism assessment. *Psychology of Addictive Behaviors, 10,* 115–123.

Iwamasa, G. Y., Sorocco, K. H., & Koonce, D. A. (2002). Ethnicity and clinical psychology: A content analysis of the literature. *Clinical Psychology Review, 22,* 931–944.

Jackson, D. N. (1984). *Personality research form manual.* Port Huron, MI: Research Psychologists Press.

Jackson, D. N., & Messick, S. (1958). Content and style in personality assessment. *Psychological Bulletin, 55,* 243–252.

Jackson, D. N., & Messick, S. (1961). Acquiescence and desirability as response determinants on the MMPI. *Educational and Psychological Measurement, 21,* 771–790.

Jackson, M., & Thompson, C. L. (1971). Effective counselor: Characteristics and attitudes. *Journal of Counseling Psychology, 17,* 3–79.

Jackson, Y. (2006). *Encyclopedia of multicultural psychology.* Thousand Oaks, CA: Sage Publications.

Jacobson, N. S., Schmaling, K. B., & Holtzworth-Munroe, A. (1987). Component analysis of behavioral marital therapy: 2-year follow-up and prediction of relapse. *Journal of Marital and Family Therapy, 13,* 187–195.

Jacoby, L. L., & Kelley, C. M. (1987). Unconscious influences of memory for a prior event. *Personality and Social Psychology Bulletin, 13,* 314–336.

James, J. W., & Haley, W. E. (1995). Age and health bias in practicing clinical psychologists. *Psychology & Aging, 10,* 610–616.

Jane, S. J., Pagan, J. L., Turkheimer, E., Fiedler, E. R., & Oltmanns, T. F. (2006). The interrater reliability of the Structured Interview for the DSM-IV Personality. *Comprehensive Psychiatry, 47,* 368–375.

Jason, L. A., McMahon, S. D., Salina, D., Hedeker, D., Stockton, M., Dunson, K., & Kimball, P. (1995). Assessing a smoking cessation intervention involving groups, incentives, and self-help manuals. *Behavior Therapy, 26,* 393–408.

Jeffery, R. W. (1988). Dietary risk factors and their modification in cardiovascular disease. *Journal of Consulting and Clinical Psychology, 56,* 350–357.

Jennings, L., & Skovholt, T. M. (1999). The cognitive, emotional and relational characteristics of master therapists. *Journal of Counseling Psychology, 46,* 3–11.

Jensen, P. S. (2003). Comorbidity and child psychopathology: Recommendations for the next decade. *Journal of Abnormal Child Psychology, 31,* 293–300.

Jensen, P. S., Garcia, J. A., Glied, S., Crowe, M., Foster, M., Schlander, M., et al. (2005). Cost-effectiveness of ADHD treatments: Findings from the multimodal treatment study of children with ADHD. *American Journal of Psychiatry, 162,* 1628–1636.

Jia-xi, C., & Guo-peng, C. (2006). The validity and reliability research of 16PF 5th ed. in China. *Chinese Journal of Clinical Psychology, 14,* 13–46.

Johnsen, B. H., & Hugdahl, K. (1990). Fear questionnaires for simple phobias: Psychometric evaluations for a Norwegian sample. *Scandinavian Journal of Psychology, 31,* 42–48.

Johnson, B. W., & Campbell, C. D. (2004). Character and fitness requirements for professional psychologists: Training directors' perspectives. *Professional Psychology: Research and Practice, 35,* 405–411.

Johnson, M. D. (2002). The observation of specific affect in marital interactions: Psychometric properties of a coding system and a rating system. *Psychological Assessment, 14,* 423–438.

Johnson, S. (2003). *Therapist's guide to clinical intervention: The 1-2-3s of treatment planning.* New York: Academic Press.

Johnson, W. B., Porter, K., Campbell, C. D., & Kupko, E. N. (2005). Character and fitness requirements for professional psychologists: An examination of state licensing application forms. *Professional Psychology: Research and Practice, 36,* 654–662.

Johnston, C. (1995). The Rokeach Value Survey: Underlying structure and multidimensional scaling. *Journal of Psychology, 129,* 583–593.

Joiner, T. E., & Schmidt, N. B. (2004). Taxometrics can "do diagnostics right" (and it isn't quite as hard as you think). In L. E. Beutler & M. L. Malik (Eds.), *Rethinking the DSM: A psychological perspective* (pp. 107–120). Washington, DC: American psychological Association.

Jonason, K. R., DeMers, S. T., Vaughn, T. J., & Reaves, R. P. (2003). Professional mobility for psychologists is rapidly becoming a reality. *Professional Psychology: Research and Practice, 34,* 468–473.

Jones, B. P., & Butters, N. (1983). Neuropsychological assessment. In M. Hersen, A. E. Kazdin, & A. S. Bellack (Eds.), *The clinical psychology handbook* (pp. 377–396). New York: Pergamon Press.

Jones, E. E. (1955). *The life and work of Sigmund Freud* (Vol. 2). New York: Basic Books.

Jones, E. E. (1996). Introduction to the special section on attachment and psychopathology: Part I. *Journal of Consulting and Clinical Psychology, 64,* 5–7.

Jones, E. E., Cumming, J. D., & Horowitz, M. J. (1988). Another look at the nonspecific hypothesis of therapeutic effectiveness. *Journal of Consulting and Clinical Psychology, 56,* 48–55.

Jones, M. C. (1924a). The elimination of children's fears. *Journal of Experimental Psychology, 7,* 382–390.

Jones, M. C. (1924b). A laboratory study of fear: The case of Peter. *Pedagogical Seminary and Journal of Genetic Psychology, 31,* 308–315.

Jongsma, A. E., & Peterson, M. L. (2003). *The complete adult psychotherapy treatment planner* (3rd ed.). Hoboken, NJ: Wiley.

Jorm, A. F. (2000). Mental health literacy: Public knowledge and beliefs about mental disorders. *The British Journal of Psychiatry, 177,* 396–401.

Jouriles, E. N., & Farris, A. M. (1992). Effects of marital conflict on subsequent parent-child interactions. *Behavior Therapy, 23,* 355–374.

Jouriles, E. N., & O'Leary, K. D. (1985). Interspousal reliability of reports of marital violence.

Journal of Consulting and Clinical Psychology, 53, 419-421.

Kahn, E. (1985). Heinz Kohut and Carl Rogers: A timely comparison. *American Psychologist, 40,* 893-904.

Kahn, J. H., Achter, J. A., & Shambaugh, E. J. (2001). Client distress disclosure, characteristics at intake, and outcomes in brief counseling. *Journal of Counseling Psychology, 48,* 203-211.

Kalichman, S. C., Cherry, C., & Browne-Sperling, F. (1999). Effectiveness of a video-based motivational skills-building HIV risk-reduction intervention for inner-city African American men. *Journal of Consulting and Clinical Psychology, 67,* 959-966.

Kalichman, S. C., Rompa, D., & Coley, B. (1996). Experimental component analysis of a behavioral HIV-AIDS prevention for inner-city women. *Journal of Consulting and Clinical Psychology, 64,* 687-693.

Kalichman, S. C., Rompa, D., Cage, M., DiFonzo, K., Simpson, D. Austin, J., et al. (2001). Effectiveness of an intervention to reduce HIV transmission risks in HIV-positive people. *American Journal of Preventive Medicine, 21,* 84-92.

Kaminer, Y. (2005). Challenges and opportunities of group therapy for adolescent substance abuse: A critical review. *Addictive Behaviors, 30,* 1765-1774.

Kamphaus, R. W., & Frick, P. J. (2005). *Clinical assessment of child and adolescent personality and behavior* (2nd. ed.). New York: Springer.

Kancelbaum, B., Singer, B., & Wong, N. (2004). Therapy in America 2004. Psychology Today. Retrieved October 2, 2005, from http://cms.psychologytoday.com/pto/press_release_050404.html.

Kanfer, F. H., & Saslow, G. (1969). Behavioral diagnosis. In C. M. Franks (Ed.), *Behavior therapy: Appraisal and status* (pp. 210-215). New York: McGraw-Hill.

Kanner, L. (1943). Autistic disturbances of affective contact. *Nervous Child, 2,* 217-250.

Kaplan, A. (1964). *The conduct of inquiry.* San Francisco: Chander.

Kaplan, E. (1990). The process approach to neuropsychological assessment of psychiatric patients. *Journal of Neuropsychiatry and Clinical Neurosciences, 2,* 72-87.

Kaplan, M. (1983). A woman's view of DSM-III. *American Psychologist, 38,* 786-792.

Kaplan, R. M., & Saccuzzo, D. P. (2004). *Psychological testing: Principles, applications, and issues.* Belmont, CA: Thompson Wadsworth.

Karasz, A. (2005). Cultural differences in conceptual models of depression. *Social Science & Medicine, 60,* 1625-1635.

Karver, M. S. (2006). Determinants of multiple informant agreement on child and adolescent behavior. *Journal of Abnormal Child Psychology, 34,* 251-262.

Karver, M. S., Handelsman, J. B., Fields, S., & Bickman, L. (2005). Meta-analysis of therapeutic relationship variables in youth and family therapy: The evidence for different relationship variables in the child and adolescent treatment outcome literature. *Clinical Psychology Review, 26,* 50-65.

Kaslow, F. W. (2001). Families and family psychology at the millennium: Intersecting crossroads. *American Psychologist, 56,* 37-46.

Kaslow, F. W. (2004). *Family therapy around the world.* New York: Haworth Press.

Kaslow, F. W. (2005). Growing up everyone's trusted confidante: Why I really became a psychotherapist. *Journal of Clinical Psychology, 61,* 965-972.

Kaslow, N. J., Borden, K. A., Collins, F. L., Forrest, L., Illfelder-Kaye, J., Nelson, P. D., & Rallo, J. S. (2004). Competencies conference: Future directions in education and credentialing in professional psychology. *Journal of Clinical Psychology, 60,* 699-712.

Kaslow, N. J., & Echols, M. M. (2006). Postdoctoral training and requirements for licensure and certification. In T. J. Vaughn (Ed.), *Psychology licensure and certification: What students need to know* (pp. 85-95). Washington, DC: American Psychological Association.

Kaslow, N. J., & Rehm, L. P. (1985). Conceptualization, assessment, and treatment of depression in children. In P. H. Bornstein & A. E. Kazdin

(Eds.), *Handbook of clinical behavior therapy with children* (pp. 599-657). Homewood, IL: Dorsey Press.

Kaufman, A. S., & Kaufman, N. L. (1983). *KABC: Kaufman Assessment Battery for Children*. Circle Pines, MN: American Guidance Service.

Kaufman, A. S., & Kaufman, N. L. (1985). *Kaufman Test of Educational Achievement*. Circle Pines, MN: American Guidance Service.

Kaufman, A. S., & Kaufman, N. L. (1993). *Manual for the Kaufman Adolescent and Adult Intelligence Test (KAIT)*. Circle Pines, MN: American Guidance Service.

Kaufman, A. S., & Kaufman, N. L. (2004a). *KABC-II: Kaufman Assessment Battery for Children* (2nd ed.). Circle Pines, MN: AGS Publishing.

Kaufman, A. S., & Kaufman, N. L. (2004b). *KBIT-2: Kaufman Brief Intelligence Test-2* (2nd ed.). Upper Saddle River, NJ: Pearson Assessments.

Kavale, K. A., Holdnack, J. A., & Mostert, M. P. (2005). Responsiveness to intervention and the identification of specific learning disability: A critique and alternative proposal. *Learning Disability Quarterly, 28*, 2-16.

Kazantzis, N., & Deane, F. P. (1999). Psychologists' use of homework assignments in clinical practice. *Professional Psychology: Research and Practice, 30*, 581-585.

Kazdin, A. E. (1982). Single-case experimental designs. In P. C. Kendall & J. N. Butcher (Eds.), *Handbook of research methods in clinical psychology* (pp. 461-490). New York: Wiley.

Kazdin, A. E. (2005a). *Parent management training: Treatment for oppositional, aggressive, and antisocial behavior in children and adolescents*. New York: Oxford University Press.

Kazdin, A. E. (2005b). Treatment outcomes, common factors, and continued neglect of mechanisms of change. *Clinical Psychology: Science and Practice, 12*, 184-188.

Kazdin, A. E. (2006). Assessment and evaluation in clinical practice. In C. D. Goodhart, A. E. Kazdin, & R. J. Sternberg (Eds.), *Evidence-based psychotherapy* (pp. 153-177). Washington, DC: American Psychological Association.

Kazdin, A. E. (2007). Mediators and mechanisms of change in psychotherapy research. *Annual Review of Clinical Psychology, 3*, 1-27.

Kazdin, A. E., & Weisz, J. R. (Eds.). (2003). *Evidence-based psychotherapies for children and adolescents*. New York: Guilford.

Keefe, F. J., Abernethy, A. P., & Campbell, L. (2005). Psychological approaches to understanding and treating disease-related pain. *Annual Review of Psychology, 56*, 601-30.

Keijsers, G. P. J., Schaap, C. P. D. R., & Hoogduin, C. A. L. (2000). The impact of interpersonal patient and therapist behavior on outcome in cognitive-behavioral therapy: A review of empirical studies. *Behavior Modification, 24*, 264-297.

Keilin, W. G., & Bloom, L. J. (1986). Child custody evaluation practices: A survey of experienced professionals. *Professional Psychology: Research and Practice, 17*, 338-346.

Kelley, J. E., Lumley, M. A., & Leisen, J. C. C. (1997). Health effects of emotional disclosure in rheumatoid arthritis patients. *Health Psychology, 16*, 331-340.

Kelly, E. L., & Fiske, D. W. (1951). *The prediction of performance in clinical psychology*. Ann Arbor: University of Michigan Press.

Kelly, G. A. (1955). *The psychology of personal constructs*. New York: W. W. Norton.

Kelly, J. A., & Murphy, D. A. (1992). Psychological interventions with AIDS and HIV: Prevention and treatment. *Journal of Consulting and Clinical Psychology, 60*, 576-585.

Kelly, J. A., St. Lawrence, J. S., Hood, H. V., & Brashfield, T. L. (1989). Behavioral intervention to reduce AIDS risk activities. *Journal of Consulting and Clinical Psychology, 57*, 60-67.

Kelly, J. B. (1991). Parent interaction after divorce: Comparison of medicated and adversarial divorce processes. *Behavioral Sciences and the Law, 9*, 387-398.

Kelly, J. B. (2000). Children's adjustment in conflicted marriage and divorce: A decade review of research. *Journal of the American Academy of Child and Adolescent Psychiatry, 39*, 963-973.

Kendall, P. C. (Ed.). (2006). *Child and adolescent therapy* (3rd ed., pp. 243-294). New York: Guilford.

Kendall, P. C., Holmbeck, G., & Verduin, T. (2004). Methodology, design, and evaluation in psychotherapy research. In M. J. Lambert (Ed.), *Bergin and Garfield's handbook of psychotherapy and behavior change* (5th ed., pp. 16–43). New York: Wiley.

Kendall, P. C., & Suveg, C. (2006). Treating anxiety disorders in youth. In P. C. Kendall (Ed.), *Child and adolescent therapy* (3rd ed., pp. 243–294). New York: Guilford.

Kenkel, M. B., DeLeon, P. H., Albino, J. E. N., & Porter, N. (2003). Challenges to professional psychology education in the 21st century. *American Psychologist, 58,* 801–805.

Kennedy, P. F., Vandehey, M., Norman, W. B., & Diekhoff, G. M. (2003). Recommendations for risk-management practices. *Professional Psychology: Research and Practice, 34,* 309–311.

Kern, J. M. (1982). The comparative external and concurrent validity of three role-plays for assessing heterosocial performance. *Behavior Therapy, 13,* 666–680.

Kernberg, O. (1976). *Object relations, theory and clinical psychoanalysis*. New York: Jason Aronson.

Keisler, R. C., Berglund, P., Demler, O., Jin, R., & Walters, E. E. (2005). Lifetime prevalence and age-of-onset distributions of DSM-IV disorders in the National Comorbidity Survey Replication. *Archives of General Psychiatry, 62,* 593–602.

Keisler, R. C., Chiu, W. T., Demler, O., & Walters, E. E. (2005). Prevalence, severity, and comorbidity of 12-month DSM-IV disorders in the National Comorbidity Survey Replication. *Archives of General Psychiatry, 62,* 617–627

Keisler, R. C., Demler, O., Frank, R. G., Olfson, M., Pincus, H. A., et al. (2005). Prevalence and treatment of mental disorders 1990 to 2003. *New England Journal of Medicine, 352,* 2515–2523.

Keisler, R. C., Price, R. H., & Wortman, C. B. (1985). Social factors in psychopathology: Stress, social support, and coping processes. *Annual Review of Psychology, 36,* 531–572.

Keisler, R., Soukup, J., Davis, R., Foster, D., Wilkey, S., Van Rompay, M., & Eisenberg, D. (2001). The use of complementary and alternative therapies to treat anxiety and depression in the United States. *American Journal of Psychiatry, 158,* 289–294.

Khan, A., Khan, S. R., Leventhal, R. M., Krishnan, R. R., & Gorman, J. M. (2002). An application of the revised CONSORT standards to FDA summary reports of recently approved antidepressants and antipsychotics. *Biological Psychiatry, 52,* 62–67.

Kiecolt-Glaser, J. K., & Glaser, R. (1992). Psychoneuroimmunology: Can psychological interventions modulate immunity? *Journal of Consulting and Clinical Psychology, 60,* 569–575.

Kiecolt-Glaser, J. K., Loving, T. J., Stowell, J. R., Malarkey, W. B., Lemeshow, S., Dickinson, S. L., & Blaser, R. (2005). Hostile marital interactions, proinflammatory cytokine production, and wound healing. *Archives of General Psychiatry, 62,* 1377–1384.

Kiesler, C. A. (1985). Psychology and public policy. In E. M. Altmaier & M. E. Meyer (Eds.), *Applied specialization in psychology* (pp. 375–390). New York: Springer.

Kiesler, C. A. (2000). The next wave of change for psychotherapy and mental health in the health care revolution. *American Psychologist, 55,* 481–487.

Kinnaman, J. E. S., Farrell, A. D., & Bisconer, S. W. (2006). Evaluation of the Computerized Assessment System for Psychotherapy Evaluation and Research (CASPER) as a measure of treatment effectiveness with psychiatric inpatients. *Assessment, 13,* 154–167.

Kinzie, J. D., Manson, S. M., Vinh, D. H., Nguyen, T. T., Anh, B., Tolan, N. T., et al. (1982). Development and validation of a Vietnamese-language depression rating scale. *American Journal of Psychiatry, 139,* 1276–1281.

Kiser, L. J. (2007). Protecting children from the dangers of urban poverty. *Clinical Psychology Review, 27,* 211–225.

Klein, M. (1975). *The writings of Melanie Klein* (Vol. III). London: Hogarth Press.

Klein, R. A. (1999). Treating fear of flying with virtual reality exposure therapy. In L. VanderCreek & T. L. Jackson (Eds.), *Innovations in clinical practice: A sourcebook,* (Vol. 17). Sarasota, FL: Professional Resources Press.

Klein, R. H. (1983). Group treatment approaches. In M. Hersen, A. E. Kazdin, & A. S. Bellack (Eds.), *The clinical psychology handbook* (pp. 593–610). New York: Pergamon.

Kleinknecht, R. A., & Bernstein, D. A. (1978). Assessment of dental fear. *Behavior Therapy, 9,* 626–634.

Kleinmuntz, B. (1963). MMPI decision rules for the identification of college maladjustment: A digital computer approach. *Psychological Monographs, 77* (14, Whole No. 477).

Kleinmuntz, B. (1969). Personality test interpretation by computer and clinician. In J. N. Butcher (Ed.), *MMPI: Research developments and clinical applications* (pp. 97–104). New York: Wiley.

Kleinmuntz, B. (1984). The scientific study of clinical judgment in psychology and medicine. *Clinical Psychology Review, 4,* 111–126.

Klerman, G. L., Weissman, M. M., Rounsaville, B. J., & Chevron, E. S. (1984). *Interpersonal psychotherapy of depression.* New York: Basic Books.

Kline, T. J. B. (2005). *Psychological testing: A practical approach to design and evaluation.* Thousand Oaks, CA: Sage Publications.

Klopfer, B., & Kelley, D. M. (1937). The techniques of the Rorschach performance. *Rorschach Research Exchange, 2,* 1–14.

Klopfer, W. G. (1983). Writing psychological reports. In C. E. Walker (Ed.), *The handbook of clinical psychology* (Vol. 1, pp. 501–527). Homewood, IL: Dow Jones-Irwin.

Knapp, S. J., & VandeCreek, L. (2006). *Practical ethics for psychologists: A positive approach.* Washington, DC: American Psychological Association.

Knox, S., Goldberg, J. L., Woodhouse, S. S., & Hill, C. E. (1999). Clients' internal representations of their therapists. *Journal of Counseling Psychology, 46,* 244–256.

Koch, W. J., Douglas, K. S., Nicholls, T. L., & O'Neil, M. L. (2005). *Psychological injuries: Forensic assessment, treatment, and the law.* London: Oxford University Press.

Koester, K. A., Maiorana, A., Vernon, K., Myers, J., Rose, C. D., & Morin, S. (2007). Implementation of HIV prevention interventions with people living with HIV/AIDS in clinical settings: Challenges and lessons learned. *AIDS & Behavior.* [Epub ahead of print]

Kohlenberg, R. J., & Tsai, M. (1991). *Functional analytic psychotherapy: Creating intense and curative therapeutic relationships.* New York: Plenum.

Kohout, J., & Wicherski, M. (1999). 1997 Doctoral employment survey. Retrieved December 9, 2001, from http://research.apa.rg/des97contents.html.

Kohut, H. (1977). *The restoration of the self.* New York: International Universities Press.

Kohut, H. (1983). Selected problems of self-psychological theory. In J. D. Lichtenberg & S. Kaplan (Eds.), *Reflections on self psychology* (pp. 387–416). Hillsdale, NJ: Erlbaum.

Kokotovic, A. M., & Tracey, T. J. (1987). Premature termination at a university counseling center. *Journal of Counseling Psychology, 34,* 80–82.

Komiti, A. A., Jackson, H. J., Judd, F. K., Cockram, A. M., Kyrios, M., Yeatman, R., et al. (2001). A comparison of the Composite International Diagnostic Interview (CIDI-Auto) with clinical assessment in diagnosing mood and anxiety disorders. *Australian & New Zealand Journal of Psychiatry, 35,* 224–232.

Koppitz, E. M. (1968). *Psychological evaluation of children's human figure drawings.* New York: Grune & Stratton.

Korchin, S. J. (1976). *Modern clinical psychology: Principles of intervention in the clinic and community.* New York: Basic Books.

Korman, M. (Ed.). (1976). *Levels and patterns of professional training in psychology.* Washington, DC: American Psychological Association.

Korsch, B. M., & Negrete, V. F. (1972). Doctor-patient communication. *Scientific American, 227,* 66–74.

Kovacs, M. (1992). *The children's depression inventory (CDI).* North Tonawanda, NY: Multi-Health Systems.

Krantz, D. S., & Manuck, S. B. (1984). Acute psychophysiologic reactivity and risk of cardiovascular disease—A review and methodologic critique. *Psychological Bulletin, 96,* 435–464.

Krijn, M., Emmelkamp, P. M. G., Olafsson, R. P., & Biemond, R. (2004). Virtual reality exposure therapy of anxiety disorders: A review. *Clinical Psychology Review, 24,* 259–281.

Krishnamurthy, R., VandeCreek, L., Kaslow, N. J., Tazeau, Y. N., Miville, N. L. et al. (2004). Achieving competency in psychological assessment: Directions for education and training. *Journal of Clinical Psychology, 60,* 725–739.

Krol, N. P. C. M., De Bruyn, E. E. J., Coolen, J. C., & van Aarle, E. J. M. (2006). From CBCL to *DSM*: A comparison of two methods to screen for *DSM-IV* diagnoses using CBCL data. *Journal of Clinical Child and Adolescent Psychology, 35,* 127–135.

Krol, N., DeBruyn, E., & van den Bercken, J. (1995). Intuitive and empirical prototypes in childhood psychopathology. *Psychological Assessment, 7,* 533–537.

Krous, T. M. D., & Nauta, M. M. (2005). Values, motivations, and learning experiences of future professionals: Who wants to serve underserved populations? *Professional Psychology: Research and Practice, 36,* 688–694.

Krueger, R. F., Watson, D., & Barlow, D. H. (2005). Introduction to the special section: Toward a dimensionally based taxonomy of psychopathology. *Journal of Abnormal Psychology, 114,* 491–493.

Krull, C. D., & Pierce, W. D. (1995). IQ testing in America: A victim of its own success. *Alberta Journal of Educational Research, 41,* 349–354.

Kulic, K. R. (2005). The Crisis Intervention Semi-Structured Interview. *Brief Treatment and Crisis Intervention 5,* 143–157.

Kumpfer, K. L., & Alvarado, R. (2003). Family-strengthening approaches for the prevention of youth problem behaviors. *American Psychologist, 58,* 457–465.

Kuncel, N. R., Hezlett, S. A., & Ones, D. S. (2001). A comprehensive meta-analysis of the predictive validity of the Graduate Record Examinations: Implications for graduate student selection and performance. *Psychological Bulletin, 127,* 162–181.

Kuperminc, G. P., & Brookmeyer, K. A. (2006). Developmental psychopathology. In R. T. Ammerman (Ed.), *Comprehensive handbook of personality and psychopathology* (Vol. 3, pp. 100–113). Hoboken, NJ: Wiley.

Kupfer, D. J. (2005). Dimensional models for research and diagnosis: A current dilemma. *Journal of Abnormal Psychology, 114,* 557–559.

Kupfer, D. J., First, M. B., & Reiger, D. E. (2002). Introduction. In D. J. Kupfer, M. B. First, & D. E. Reiger (Eds.). *A research agenda for DSM-V* (pp. xv–xxiii). Washington, DC: American Psychiatric Association.

Kurbat, M. A. (1997). Can the recognition of living things really be selectively impaired? *Neuropsychologia, 35*(6), 813–827.

Kuther, T. L. (2006a). *The psychology major's handbook* (2nd ed.). Belmont, CA: Wadsworth.

Kuther, T. L. (2006b). *Your career in psychology: Clinical and counseling psychology.* Belmont, CA: Thomson/Wadsworth.

Kuther, T. L., & Morgan, R. D. (2007). *Careers in psychology: Opportunities in a changing world.* Belmont, CA: Thomson/Wadsworth.

Kyle, T. M. & Williams, S. (2000). Results of the 1998-1999 APA survey of graduate departments of psychology. Retrieved December 11, 2001, from http://research.apa.org.

Labette, L. A. (2006). Review of novel approaches to the diagnosis and treatment of posttraumatic stress disorder. *Annals of Clinical Psychiatry, 18,* 281.

Lake, J. (2007). Omega-3 essential fatty acids. In J. H. Lake & D. Spiegel (Eds.), *Complementary and alternative treatments in mental health care* (pp. 151–167). Washington, DC: American Psychiatric Publishing.

Lake, J. H., & Spiegel, D. (Eds.). (2007). *Complementary and alternative treatments in mental health care.* Washington, DC: American Psychiatric Publishing.

Lam, J. N., & Steketee, G. S. (2001). Reducing obsessions and compulsions through behavior therapy. *Psychoanalytic Inquiry, 21,* 157–182.

Lambert, D. (1985). *Political and economic determinants of mental health regulations.* Unpublished doctoral dissertation, Brandeis University.

Lambert, M. J., & Bergin, A. E. (1994). The effectiveness of psychotherapy. In A. E. Bergin & S. L. Garfield (Eds.), *Handbook of psychotherapy and behavior change* (pp. 143–189). New York: Wiley.

Lambert, M. J., & Ogles, B. M. (2004). The efficacy and effectiveness of psychotherapy. In M. J. Lambert (Ed.), *Bergin and Garfield's handbook of psychotherapy and behavior change* (5th ed., pp. 139–193). New York: Wiley.

Lambert, M. J., Garfield, S. L., & Bergin, A. E. (2004). Overview, trends, and future issues. In M. J. Lambert (Ed.), *Bergin and Garfield's handbook of psychotherapy and behavior change* (5th ed., pp. 805–821). New York: Wiley.

Lambert, M. J., Shapiro, D. A., & Bergin, A. E. (1986). The effectiveness of psychotherapy. In S. L. Garfield & A. E. Bergin (Eds.), *Handbook of psychotherapy and behavior change* (3rd ed., pp. 157–211). New York: Wiley.

Lambert, N. M., Cox, H. W., & Hartsough, C. S. (1970). The observability of intellectual functioning of first graders. *Psychology in the Schools,* 74–85.

Lampropoulos, G. K., & Dixon, D. N. (2007). Psychotherapy integration in internships and counseling psychology doctoral programs. *Journal of Psychotherapy Integration, 17,* 185–208.

Lang, P. J., & Lazovik, A. D. (1963). Experimental desensitization of a phobia. *Journal of Abnormal and Social Psychology, 66,* 519–525.

Langton, C. M., Barbaree, H. E., Seto, M. C., Peacock, E. J., Harkings, L., et al. (2007). Actuarial assessment of risk for reoffense among adult sex offenders: Evaluating the predictive accuracy of the Static-2002 and five other instruments. *Criminal Justice and Behavior, 34,* 37–59.

Lanyon, B. P., & Lanyon, R. I. (1980). *Incomplete sentences task: Manual.* Chicago: Stoelting.

Larner, A. J. (2005). "Who came with you?" A diagnostic observation in patients with memory problems. *Journal of Neurology, Neurosurgery, & Psychiatry, 76,* 1739.

Lau, A. S., & Weisz, J. R. (2003). Reported maltreatment among clinic-referred children: Implications for presenting problems, treatment attrition, and long-term outcomes. *Journal of*

the *American Academy of Child and Adolescent Psychiatry, 42,* 1327–1334.

Lawlis, G. F. (1971). Response styles of a patient population on the Fear Survey Schedule. *Behaviour Research and Therapy, 9,* 95–102.

Lazarus, A. A. (1973). Multimodel behavior therapy: Treating the "BASIC-ID." *Journal of Nervous and Mental Diseases, 156,* 404–411.

Lazarus, R. S. (1993). From psychological stress to the emotions: A history of changing outlooks. *Annual Review of Psychology, 44,* 1–21.

Lazarus, R. S., & Folkman, S. (1984). *Stress, appraisal, and coping.* New York: Springer.

Leahy, R. L. (Ed.). (2006). *Roadblocks in cognitive-behavioral therapy: Transforming challenges into opportunities for change.* New York: Guilford.

Leary, T. (1957). *Interpersonal diagnosis of personality. A functional theory and methodology for personality evaluation.* New York: Ronald Press.

Lebow, J. (2003). Integrative approaches to couple and family therapy. In T. L. Sexton, G. R. Weeks, & M. S. Robbins (Eds.), *Handbook of family therapy: The science and practice of working with families and couples* (pp. 201–225). New York: Brunner-Routledge.

Lebow, J. (2005). *Handbook of clinical family therapy.* Hoboken, NJ: Wiley.

Lebow, J. (2006). *Research for the psychotherapist: From science to practice.* New York: Routledge/ Taylor and Francis Group.

Lebow, J., & Gordon, K. C. (2006). You cannot choose what is not on the menu–Obstacles to and reasons for the inclusion of relational processes in the *DSM-V:* Comment on the special section. *Journal of Family Psychology, 20,* 432–437.

Ledley, D. R., Marx, B. P., & Heimberg, R. G. (2005). *Making cognitive-behavioral therapy work: Clinical process for new practitioners.* New York: Guilford.

Lee, C. M., Beauregard, C., & Bax, K. A. (2005). Child-related disagreements, verbal aggression, and children's internalizing and externalizing behavior problems. *Journal of Family Psychology, 19,* 237–245.

Lehman, B. M. (2003). Affective language and humor appreciation after right hemisphere brain damage. *Seminars in Speech and Language, 24,* 107–119.

Lemery, K. S., & Doelger, L. (2005). Genetic vulnerabilities to the development of psychopathology. In B. L. Hankin & J. R. Z. Abela (Eds.), *Development of psychopathology: A vulnerability-stress perspective* (pp. 161–198). Thousand Oaks, CA: Sage Publications.

Leon, S. C., Martinovich, Z., Lutz, W., & Lyons, J. S. (2005). The effect of therapist experience on psychotherapy outcomes. *Clinical Psychology & Psychotherapy, 12,* 417–426.

Leonard, K. E., & Eiden, R. D. (2007). Marital and family processes in the context of alcohol use and alcohol disorders. *Annual Review of Clinical Psychology, 3,* 285–310.

Leonnig, C. D. (2006, November 23). Hinckley's mother to be his sole escort. *The Washington Post,* p. B1.

Levant, R. F. (2006). Making psychology a household word. *American Psychologist, 61,* 383–395.

Levant, R. F., House, A. T., May, S., & Smith, R. (2006). Cost offset: Past, present, and future. *Psychological Services, 3,* 195–207.

Leventhal, T., & Brooks-Gunn, J. (2003). Children and youth in neighborhood contexts. *Current Directions in Psychological Science, 12,* 27–31.

Levine, E. S., & Schmelkin, L. P. (2006). The move to prescribe: A change in paradigm? *Professional Psychology: Research and Practice, 37,* 205–209.

Levison, H., & Strupp, H. H. (1999). Recommendations for the future of training in brief dynamic psychotherapy. *Journal of Clinical Psychology, 55,* 385–391.

Lew, H. L., Poole, J. H., Ha Lee, E., Jaffe, D. L., Huang, H., et al. (2005). Predictive validity of driving-simulator assessments following traumatic brain injury: A preliminary study. *Brain Injury, 19,* 177–188.

Lewis, G. (1991). Observer bias in the assessment of anxiety and depression. *Social Psychiatry and Psychiatric Epidemiology, 26,* 265–272.

Lewis, T. J., Lewis-Palmer, T., Newcomer, L., & Stichter, J. (2004). Applied behavior analysis and the education and treatment of students with emotional and behavioral disorders. In R. B. Rutherford, M. M. Quinn, & S. R. Mathur (Eds.), *Handbook of research in emotional and behavioral disorders* (pp. 523–545). New York: Guilford.

Ley, P., Bradshaw, P. W., Eaves, D. E., & Walker, C. M. (1973). A method for increasing patient recall of information presented to them. *Psychological Medicine, 3,* 217–220.

Lezak, M. D., Howieson, D. B., & Loring, D. W. (2004). *Neuropsychological assessment* (4th ed.). New York: Oxford University Press.

Lichtenberger, E. O. (2006). Computer utilization and clinical judgment in psychological assessment reports. *Journal of Clinical Psychology, 62,* 19–32.

Lidz, R. W., & Lidz, T. (1949). The family environment of schizophrenic patients. *American Journal of Psychiatry, 106,* 332–345.

Lilienfild, S. O. (2007). Psychological treatments that cause harm. *Perspectives on Psychological Science, 2,* 53–70.

Lilienfeld, S. O, Lynn, S. J., & Lohr, J. M. (Eds.). (2003). *Achieving the promise: Transforming mental health care in America. Final Report.* (DHHS Pub. No. SMA-03-3832). Rockville, MD: Department of Health and Human Services.

Lilienfeld, S. O., Wood, J. M., & Garb, H. N. (2000). The scientific status of projective techniques. *Psychological Science in the Public Interest, 1,* 27–66.

Lima, E. N., Stanley, S., Koboski, B., Reitzel, L. R., Richey, J. A., et al. (2005). The incremental validity of the MMPI-2: When does therapist access enhance treatment outcome? *Psychological Assessment, 17,* 462–468.

Lindsley, O. R., Skinner, B. F., & Solomon, H. C. (1953). *Study of psychotic behavior.* Studies in Behavior Therapy, Harvard Medical School, Department of Psychiatry, Metropolitan State Hospital, Waltham, MA, Office of Naval Research Contract N5-ori-07662, Status Report I, 1 June 1953-31 December 1953.

Lindzey, G. (1952). The thematic apperception test: Interpretive assumptions and related empirical evidence. *Psychological Bulletin, 49,* 1–25.

Linehan, M. M. (1993). *Cognitive-behavioral treatment of borderline personality disorder.* New York: Guilford.

Linehan, M. M., & Kehrer, C. A. (1993). Borderline personality disorder. In D. H. Barlow (Ed.), *Clinical handbook of psychological disorders* (pp. 396–441). New York: Guilford.

Linehan, M. M., & Nielsen, S. L. (1983). Social desirability: Its relevance to the measurement of hopelessness and suicidal behavior. *Journal of Consulting and Clinical Psychology, 51,* 141–143.

Linney, J. A. (2000). Assessing ecological constructs and community context. In J. Rappaport & E. Seidman (Eds.), *Handbook of community psychology* (pp. 647–668). New York: Kluwer Academic/ Plenum Publishers.

Liss, M. B., & McKinley-Pace, M. J. (1999). Best interests of the child: New twists on an old theme. In R. Roesch, S. D. Hart, & J. R. Ogloff (Eds.), *Psychology and the law: The state of the discipline* (pp. 339–372). New York: Kluwer Academic/Plenum.

Lisspers, J., Sundin, O., Ohman, A., Ofman-Bang, C., Ryden, L., & Nygren, A. (2005). Long-term effects of lifestyle behavior change in coronary artery disease: Effects on recurrent coronary events after percutaneous coronary intervention. *Health Psychology, 24,* 41–48.

Liu, E. T. (2007). Integrating cognitive-behavioral and cognitive-interpersonal case formulations: A case study of a Chinese American male. *Pragmatic Case Studies in Psychotherapy, 3,* 1–33.

Lochman, J. E., Powell, N. R., Whidby, J. M., & Fitzgerald, D. P. (2006). Aggressive children: Cognitive-behavioral assessment and treatment. In P. C. Kendall (Ed.), *Child and Adolescent therapy* (3rd ed., pp. 33–81). New York: Guilford.

Lochman, J. E., & Wells, K. C. (2004). The coping power program for preadolescent aggressive boys and their parents: Outcome effects at the 1-year- follow-up. *Journal of Consulting and Clinical Psychology, 72,* 571–578.

Lock, J., le Grange, D., Agras, W. S., & Dare, C. (2002). *Treatment manual for anorexia nervosa: A family-based approach.* New York: Guilford.

Locke, T. F., & Newcomb, M. D. (2003). Childhood maltreatment, parental alcohol/drug-related problems, and global parental dysfunction. *Professional Psychology: Research and Practice, 34,* 73–79.

Loftus, E. F. (2003). Make-believe memories. *American Psychologist, 58,* 867–873.

Loftus, E. F., & Davis, D. (2006). Recovered memories. *Annual Review of Clinical Psychology, 2,* 469–498.

Looman, J., & Marshall, W. L. (2005). Sexual arousal in rapists. *Criminal Justice and Behavior, 32,* 367–389.

Lopez, S., & Snyder, C. R. (Eds.). (2003). *Handbook of positive psychology assessment.* Washington, DC: American Psychological Association.

Lopez, S. R., & Guarnaccia, P. J. (2000). Cultural psychopathology: Uncovering the social world of mental illness. *Annual Review of Psychology, 51,* 571–598.

Lopez, S. R., Smith, A., & Wolkenstein, B. H. (1993). Gender bias in clinical judgment: An assessment of the analogue method's transparency and social desirability. *Sex Roles, 28,* 35–45.

Loranger, A. W. (1992). Are current self-report and interview measures adequate for epidemiological studies of personality disorders? *Journal of Personality Disorders, 6,* 313–325.

Loring, D. W., & Larrabee, G. J. (2006). Sensitivity of the Halstead and Wechsler Test batteries to brain damage: Evidence from Reitan's original validation sample. *Clinical Neuropsychology, 20,* 221–229.

Lorr, M., McNair, D. M., & Klett, C. J. (1966). *Inpatient Multidimensional Psychiatric Scale.* Palo Alto, CA: Consulting Psychologists Press.

Lovaas, O. I., & Smith, T. (2003). Early and intensive behavioral intervention in autism. In A. E. Kazdin & J. R. Weisz (Eds.), *Evidence-based psychotherapies for children and adolescents* (pp. 325–340). New York: Guilford.

Loveless, A. S., & Holman, T. B. (2007a). *The family in the new millennium (Vol. 1): The place of family in human society.* Westport, CT: Praeger.

Loveless, A. S., & Holman, T. B. (2007b). *The family in the new millennium (Vol. 2): Marriage and human dignity.* Westport, CT: Praeger.

Loveless, A. S., & Holman, T. B. (2007c). *The family in the new millennium (Vol. 3): Strengthening the family.* Westport, CT: Praeger.

Lowman, R. L. (2006). *The ethical practice of psychology in organizations* (2nd ed.). Washington, DC: American Psychological Association.

Luborsky, L. (1976). Helping alliances in psychotherapy. In J. Cleghhorn (Ed.), *Successful psychotherapy* (pp. 92–16). New York: Brunner/Mazel.

Luborsky, L. (1989). *Who will benefit from psychotherapy?* New York: Basic Books.

Lundahl, B., Risser, H. J., & Lovejoy, M. C. (2006). A meta-analysis of parent training: Moderators and follow-up effects. *Clinical Psychology Review, 26,* 86–104.

Lyneham, H. J., & Rapee, R. M. (2005). Agreement between telephone and in-person delivery of a structured interview for anxiety disorders in children. *Journal of the American Academy of Child and Adolescent Psychiatry, 44,* 274–282.

Lynn, S. J., Lock, T., Loftus, E. F., Krackow, E., & Lilienfeld, S. O. (2003). The remembrance of things past: Problematic memory recovery techniques in psychotherapy. In S. O. Lilienfeld, S. J. Lynn, & J. M. Lohr (Eds.), *Science and pseudoscience in clinical psychology* (pp. 205–239). New York: Guilford.

MacDonald, G. (1996). Inferences in therapy: Processes and hazards. *Professional Psychology: Research and Practice, 27,* 600–603.

Machado, P. P. P., Beutler, L. E., Greenberg, L. S. (1999). Emotion recognition in psychotherapy: Impact of therapist level of experience and emotional awareness. *Journal of Clinical Psychology, 55,* 39–57.

Machover, K. (1949). *Personality projection in the drawing of the human figure.* Springfield, IL: Charles C. Thomas.

MacKain, S. J., Tedeschi, R. G., Durham, T. W., & Goldman, V. J. (2002). So what *are* master's-level psychology practitioners doing? Surveys of employers and recent graduates in North Carolina. *Professional Psychology: Research and Practice, 33,* 408–412.

MacKinnon, R. A., Michels, R., & Buckley, P. J. (2006). *The psychiatric interview in clinical practice* (2nd ed.). Washington, DC: American Psychiatric Publishing.

Macklin, D. S., Smith, L. A., & Dollard, M. F. (2006). Public and private sector stress: Workers compensation, levels of distress and job satisfaction, and the demand-control-support model. *Australian Journal of Psychology, 58,* 130–143.

Mahler, M. S., Pine, F., & Bergman, A. (1975). *The psychological birth of the human infant.* New York: Basic Books.

Mahoney, M. J. (1977). Reflections on the cognitive-learning trend in psychotherapy. *American Psychologist, 32,* 5–13.

Maier, S. F., & Watkins, L. R. (1998). Cytokines for psychologists: Implications of bidirectional immune-to-brain communication for understanding behavior, mood, and cognition. *Psychological Review, 105,* 83–107.

Mains, J. A., & Scogin, F. R. (2003). The effectiveness of self-administered treatments: A practice-friendly review of the research. *Journal of Clinical Psychology, 59,* 237–246.

Maisto, S. A., & Maisto, C. A. (1983). Institutional measures of treatment outcome. In M. J. Lambert, E. R. Christensen, & S. S. DeJulio (Eds.), *The assessment of psychotherapy outcome* (pp. 603–625). New York: Wiley.

Makover, R. B. (2004). *Treatment planning for psychotherapists* (2nd ed.). Washington DC: American Psychiatric Publishing.

Malarkey, W. B., Kiecolt-Glaser, J. K., Pearl, D., & Glaser, R. (1994). Hostile behavior during marital conflict alters pituitary and adrenal hormones. *Psychosomatic Medicine, 56,* 41–51.

Malgady, R. G. (1996). The question of cultural bias in assessment and diagnosis of ethnic minority clients: Let's reject the null hypothesis. *Professional Psychology: Research and Practice, 27,* 73–77.

Malmo, R. B., Shagass, C., & Davis, F. H. (1950). Symptom specificity and bodily reactions during psychiatric interviews. *Psychosomatic Medicine, 12,* 362–376.

Maloney, M. P., & Ward, M. P. (1976). *Psychological assessment: A conceptual approach.* New York: Oxford University Press.

Malouff, J. M., Thorsteinsson, E. B., & Schutte, N. S. (2007). The efficacy of problem solving therapy in reducing mental and physical health problems: A meta-analysis. *Clinical Psychology Review, 27,* 46–57.

Mannarino, A. P., & Cohen, J. A. (2006). Child sexual abuse. In R. T. Ammerman (Ed.), *Comprehensive handbook of personality and psychopathology* (Vol. 3, pp. 388–402). Hoboken, NJ: Wiley.

Manuck, S. B., Kaplan, J. R., Adams, M. R., & Clarkson, T. B. (1988). Effects of stress and the sympathetic nervous system on coronary artery atheroslerosis in the cynomolgus macaque. *American Heart Journal, 116,* 328–333.

Manuck, S. B., Kaplan, J. R., & Clarkson, T. B. (1983). Behaviorally induced heart rate reactivity and atherosclerosis in cynomolgus monkeys. *Psychosomatic Medicine, 49,* 95–108.

March, J. S., & Mulle, K. (1998). *OCD in children and adolescents: A cognitive-behavioral treatment manual.* New York: Guilford.

Marcus, D. R., Lyons, P. M., & Guyton, M. R. (2000). Studying perceptions of juror influence in vivo: A social relations analysis. *Law and Human Behavior, 24,* 173–186.

Margolin, G., Mitchell, J., & Jacobson, N. (1988). Assessment of marital dysfunction. In A. S. Bellack & M. Hersen (Eds.), *Behavioral assessment: A practical handbook* (3rd ed., pp. 441–489). New York: Pergamon Press.

Marin, R. S., & Wilkosz, P. A. (2005). Disorders of diminished motivation. *Journal of Head Trauma Rehabilitation, 20,* 377–388.

Marini, A., Carlomagno, S., Caltagirone, C., & Nocentini. U. (2005). The role played by the right hemisphere in the organization of complex textual structures. *Brain and Language, 93,* 46–54.

Markowitz, J., Kocsis, M., Fishman, B., Spielman, L., Jacobsberg, L., & Francis, A. (1998). Treatment of depressive symptoms in Human Immunodeficiency Virus–positive patients. *Archives of General Psychiatry, 55,* 452–457.

Marks, I. M., Cavanaugh, K., & Gega, L. (2007). *Hands on help: Computer-aided psychotherapy.* New York: Maudsley Monographs Series.

Marlatt, G. A., & Gordon, J. R. (Eds.). (1985). *Relapse prevention maintenance strategies in the treatment of addictive behaviors.* New York: Guilford.

Marmar, C., Gaston, L., Gallagher, D., & Thompson, L. W. (1989). Alliance and outcome in late-life depression. *Journal of Nervous and Mental Disease, 177,* 464–472.

Martin, D. J., Garske, J. P., & Davis, K. M. (2000). Relation of the therapeutic alliance with outcome and other variables: A meta-analytic review. *Journal of Consulting and Clinical Psychology, 68,* 438–450.

Martsolf, D. S., & Draucker, C. B. (2005). Psychotherapy approaches for adult survivors of childhood sexual abuse: An integrative review of outcomes research. *Issues in Mental Health Nursing, 26,* 801–825.

Marx, J. A., Gyorky, Z. K., Royalty, G. M., & Stern, T. E. (1992). Use of self-help books in psychotherapy. *Professional Psychology: Research and Practice, 23,* 300–305.

Mash, E. J., & Dozois, D. J. A. (1996). Child psychopathology: A developmental-systems perspective. In E. J. Mash & R. A. Barkley (Eds.), *Child psychopathology* (pp. 3–60). New York: Guilford.

Mash, E. J., & Dozois, D. J. A. (2003). Child psychopathology: A developmental-systems perspective. In E. J. Mash & R. A. Barkley (Eds.), *Child psychopathology* (2nd ed., pp. 3–71). New York: Guilford.

Mash, E. J., & Foster, S. L. (2001). Exporting analogue behavioral observation from research to clinical practice: Useful or cost-defective? *Psychological Assessment, 13,* 86–98.

Mash, E. J., & Wolfe, D. A. (2006). *Abnormal child psychology* (3rd ed.). Belmont, CA: Wadsworth.

Masling, J. M. (1992). Assessment and the therapeutic narrative. *Journal of Training and Practice in Professional Psychology, 6,* 53–58.

Maslow, A. H. (1968). *Toward a psychology of being* (2nd ed.). New York: Van Nostrand Reinhold.

Maslow, A. H. (1971). *The farther reaches of human nature.* New York: Viking Press.

Masters, J. C., Burish, T. G., Hollon, S. D., & Rimm, D. C. (2007). *Behavior therapy: Techniques and empirical findings* (3rd ed.). San Diego: Harcourt, Brace, Jovanovich.

Masters, K. S., Spielmans, G. I., & Goodson, J. T. (2006). Are there demonstrable effects of distant intercessory prayer? A meta-analytic review. *Annals of Behavioral Medicine, 32,* 21-26.

Masur, F. T. (1981). Adherence to health care regimens. In C. K. Prokop & L. A. Bradley (Eds.), *Medical psychology: Contributions to behavioral medicine.* (pp. 442-470). New York: Academic Press.

Matarazzo, J. D. (1965). The interview. In B. B. Wolman (Ed.), *Handbook of clinical psychology* (pp. 403-450). New York: McGraw-Hill.

Matarazzo, J. D. (1986). Computerized clinical psychological test interpretations: Unvalidated plus all mean and no sigma. *American Psychologist, 41,* 14-24.

Matarazzo, J. D. (1990). Psychological assessment versus psychological testing: Validation from Binet to the school, clinic, and courtroom. *American Psychologist, 45,* 999-1017.

Matarazzo, J. D. (1992). Psychological testing and assessment in the 21st century. *American Psychologist, 47,* 1007-1018.

Maton, K. I., Kohout, J. L., Wicherski, M., Leary, G. E., & Vinokurov, A. (2006). Minority students of color and the psychology graduate pipeline: Disquieting and encouraging trends, 1989-2003. *American Psychologist, 61,* 117-131.

Matthews, K. A. (1982). Psychological perspectives on the Type A behavior pattern. *Psychological Bulletin, 91,* 293-323.

Maughan, B., Iervolino, A. C., & Collishaw, S. (2005). Time trends in child and adolescent mental disorders. *Current Opinion in Psychiatry, 18,* 381-385.

May, R. (1969). *Love and will.* New York: W. W. Norton.

May, R. (1981). *Freedom and destiny.* New York: Norton.

May, R., Angel, E., & Ellenberger, H. F. (Eds.). (1958). *Existence: A new dimension in psychiatry and psychology.* New York: Basic Books.

Mayer, J. P., & Davidson, W. S. (2000). Dissemination of innovation as social change. In J. Rappaport & E. Seidman (Eds.), *Handbook of community psychology* (pp. 421-443). New York: Kluwer Academic/ Plenum Publishers.

Mayne, T. J., Norcross, J. C., & Sayette, M. A. (2006). *Insider's guide to graduate programs in clinical and counseling psychology 2006/2007 ed.* New York: Guilford.

McArthur, D. S., & Roberts, G. E. (1982). *Roberts Apperception Test for Children: Manual.* Los Angeles: Western Psychological Services.

McCart, M. R., Priester, P. E., Davies, W. H., & Azen, R. (2006). Differential effectiveness of behavioral parent-training and cognitive-behavioral therapy for antisocial youth: A meta-analysis. *Journal of Abnormal Child Psychology, 34,* 527-543.

McConaughy, S. H. (2005). *Clinical interviews for children and adolescents: Assessment to intervention.* New York: Guilford.

McConaughy, S. H., & Achenbach, T. M. (2001). *Manual for the Semistructured Clinical Interview for Children and Adolescents* (2nd ed.). Burlington: University of Vermont, Center for Children, Youth, and Families.

McCoy, S. A. (1976). Clinical judgments of normal childhood behavior. *Journal of Consulting and Clinical Psychology, 44,* 710-714.

McCrae, R. R., & Costa, P. T. (1983). Social desirability scales: More substance than style. *Journal of Consulting and Clinical Psychology, 51,* 882-888.

McDermut, W., Miller, I. W., & Brown, R. A. (2001). The efficacy of group psychotherapy for depression: A meta-analysis and review of empirical research. *Clinical Psychology: Science and Practice, 8,* 98-116.

McDonald, B. C. (2002). Recent developments in the application of the nonverbal learning disabilities model. *Current Psychiatry Reports, 4,* 323-330.

McFall, R. M. (1991). Manifesto for a science of clinical psychology. *The Clinical Psychologist, 44,* 75-88.

McFall, R. M. (2006). Doctoral training in clinical psychology. *Annual Review of Clinical Psychology, 2,* 21-49.

McFall, R. M., & Lillesand, D. B. (1971). Behavior rehearsal with modeling and coaching in assertion training. *Journal of Abnormal Psychology, 77,* 313-323.

McGaugh, J. L. (2006). Make mild moments memorable: add a little arousal. *Trends in Cognitive Sciences, 10,* 345-347.

McGlynn, F. D., Moore, P. M., Lawyer, S., & Karg, R. (1999). Relaxation training inhibits fear and arousal during in vivo exposure to phobia-cue stimuli. *Journal of Behavior Therapy and Experimental Psychiatry, 30,* 155–168.

McGoldrick, M., Giordano, J., & Garcia-Preto, N. (2005). *Ethnicity and family therapy* (3rd ed.). New York: Guilford.

McGuffin, P. (2004). Behavioral genomics: Where molecular genetics is taking psychiatry and psychology. In L. DiLalla (Ed.), *Behavior genetics principles: Perspectives in development, personality, and psychopathology* (pp. 191–204). Washington, DC: American Psychological Association.

McMahon, T. J., & Luthar, S. S. (2006). Patterns and correlates of substance use among affluent, suburban high school students. *Journal of Clinical Child and Adolescent Psychology, 35,* 72–89.

McMullin, R. E. (2000). *The new handbook of cognitive therapy techniques.* New York: Norton.

McReynolds, P. (1975). Historical antecedents of personality assessment. In P. McReynolds (Ed.), *Advances in psychological assessment* (Vol. 3, pp. 477–532). San Francisco: Jossey-Bass.

McReynolds, P. (1987). Lightner Witmer: Little-known founder of clinical psychology. *American Psychologist, 42,* 849–858.

McWilliams, N. (2004). *Psychoanalytic psychotherapy: A practitioner's guide.* New York: Guilford.

Mead, M. (1928). *Coming of age in Samoa.* New York: Morrow.

Meador, B. D., & Rogers, C. R. (1973). Client-centered therapy. In R. Corsini (Ed.), *Current psychotherapies* (pp. 119–165). Itasca, IL: F. E. Peacock.

Meehl, P. E. (1954). *Clinical versus statistical prediction.* Minneapolis: University of Minnesota Press.

Meehl, P. E. (1956). Wanted—A good cookbook. *American Psychologist, 11,* 263–272.

Meehl, P. E. (1957). When shall we use our heads instead of the formula? *Journal of Consulting Psychology, 4,* 268–273.

Meehl, P. E. (1965). Seer over sign: The first good example. *Journal of Experimental Research in Personality, 1,* 27–32.

Meichenbaum, D. H. (1977). *Cognitive behavior modification.* New York: Norton.

Meissner, W. W. (2006). The therapeutic alliance—A proteus in disguise. *Psychotherapy: Theory, Research, Practice, Training, 43,* 264–270.

Mello, M. M., Studdert, D. M., & Brennan, T. A. (2003). The new medical malpractice crisis. *New England Journal of Medicine, 348,* 2281–2284.

Melton, A. W. (Ed.). (1947). *Apparatus tests.* Washington, DC: Government Printing Office.

Melton, G. B., Petrila, J., Poythress, N. G., & Slobogin, C. (1987). *Psychological evaluations for the courts.* New York: Guilford.

Melton, G. B., Petrila, J., Poythress, N. G., & Slobogin, C. (1997). *Psychological evaluations for the courts* (2nd ed.). New York: Guilford.

Menninger, K. (1958). *The theory of psychoanalytic technique.* New York: Basic Books.

Mermelstein, R., Lichtenstein, E., & McIntyre, K. (1983). Partner support and relapse in smoking-cessation programs. *Journal of Consulting and Clinical Psychology, 51,* 331–337.

Merrill, T. S. (2003). Licensure anachronisms: Is it time for a change? *Professional Psychology: Research and Practice, 34,* 459–462.

Messer, S. (2006). Patient values and preferences. In J. C. Norcross, L. E. Beutler, & R. F. Levant (Eds.). *Evidence-based practices in mental health* (pp. 31–40). Washington, DC: American Psychological Association.

Messer, S. B. (2001). Empirically supported treatments: What's a neobehaviorist to do? In B. D. Slife, R. N. Williams, & S. H. Barlow (Eds.), *Critical issues in psychotherapy.* Thousand Oaks, CA: Sage.

Messer, S. B. (2004). Evidence-based practice: Beyond empirically supported treatments. *Professional Psychology, 35,* 580–588.

Messer, S. B., & Winokur, M. (1980). Some limits to the integration of psychoanalytic and behavior therapy. *American Psychologist, 35,* 818–827.

Messick, S. (1995). Validity of psychological assessment: Validation of inferences from persons' responses and performances as scientific inquiry into score meaning. *American Psychologist, 50,* 741–749.

Mesulam, M. M. (1990). Large-scale neurocognitive networks and distributed processing for attention, language, and memory. *Annals of Neurology, 28,* 597–613.

Meyer, G. J., Finn, S. E., Eyde, L. D., Kay, G. G., Moreland, K. L., Dies, R. R., et al. (2001). Psychological testing and psychological assessment: A review of evidence and issues. *American Psychologist, 56,* 128–165.

Meyer, R. G., & Weaver, C. M. (2006). *Law and mental health: A case-based approach.* New York: Guilford.

Meyer-Lindenberg, A., Poline, J-B., Kohn, P. D., Holt, J. L., Egan, M. F., Weinberger, D. R., & Berman, K. F. (2001). Evidence for abnormal cortical functional connectivity during working memory in schizophrenia. *American Journal of Psychiatry, 158,* 1809–1817.

Meyers, L. (2006a). Psychologists and psychotropic medication. *Monitor on Psychology, 37,* 46–47.

Meyers, L. (2006b). Still a system in need of repairs. *Monitor on Psychology, 37,* 50–51.

Michael, K. D., Curtin, L., Kirkley, D. E., Jones, D. L., & Harris, R. (2006). Group-based motivational interviewing for alcohol use among college students: An exploratory study. *Professional Psychology: Research and Practice, 37,* 629–634.

Milan, M. A., Montgomery, R. W., & Rogers, E. G. (1994). Theoretical orientation revolution in clinical psychology: Fact or fiction? *Professional Psychology: Research and Practice, 25,* 398–402.

Milich, R., & Fitzgerald, G. (1985). Validation of inattention/overactivity and aggression ratings with classroom observations. *Journal of Consulting and Clinical Psychology, 53,* 139–140.

Miller, A. L., Rathus, J. H., Linehan, M. M., & Swenson, C. R. (2006). *Dialectical behavior therapy with suicidal adolescents.* New York: Guilford.

Miller, B. L., & Cummings, J. L. (2006). *The Human Frontal Lobes: Functions and Disorders* (2nd ed.). New York: Guilford.

Miller, G. A., Elbert, T., Sutton, B. P., & Heller, W. (2007). Innovative clinical assessment technologies: Challenges and opportunities in neuroimaging. *Psychological Assessment, 19,* 58–73.

Miller, G. E., & Cohen, S. (2001). Psychological interventions and the immune system: A meta-analytic review and critique. *Health Psychology, 20,* 47–63.

Miller, J. A., & Leffard, S. A. (2007). Behavioral assessment. In S. R. Smith & L. Handler (Eds.), *The clinical assessment of children and adolescents: A practitioner's handbook* (pp. 115–137). Mahwah, NJ: Erlbaum.

Miller, K. M. (1991). Use of psychological assessment and training in testing techniques in the UK. *Evaluacion Psicologica, 7,* 85–97.

Miller, S. B., Freise, M., Dolgoy, L., Sita, A., Lavoie, K., & Campbell, T. (1998). Hostility, sodium consumption, and cardiovascular response to interpersonal stress. *Psychosomatic Medicine, 60,* 71–77.

Miller, T. Q., Turner, C. W., Tindale, R. S., Posavac, E. J., & Dugoni, B. L. (1991). Reasons for the trend toward null findings in research on Type A behavior. *Psychological Bulletin, 110,* 469–485.

Miller, W. R., & DiPilato, M. (1983). Treatment of nightmares via relaxation and desensitization: A controlled evaluation. *Journal of Consulting and Clinical Psychology, 51,* 870–877.

Miller, W. R., & Thoresen, C. E. (2003). Spirituality, religion, and health: An emerging research field. *American Psychologist, 58,* 24–35.

Millon, J., Millon, C., & Davis, R. (1997). *Millon Clinical Multiaxial Inventory: III (MCMI-III) manual* (3rd ed.). Minneapolis, MN: National Computer Systems.

Millon, T., & Klerman, G. L. (Eds.). (1986). *Contemporary directions in psychopathology: Toward the DSM-IV.* New York: Guilford.

Milner, B. (1974). Hemispheric specialization: Scope and limits. In F. O. Schmitt & F. G. Worden (Eds.), *The neurosciences: Third study program* (pp. 75–89). Cambridge, MA: MIT Press.

Milner, D. A., & Rugg, M. D. (1992). *The neuropsychology of consciousness.* San Diego: Academic Press, Inc.

Mineka, S., Watson, D., & Clark, L. A. (1998). Comorbidity of anxiety and unipolar mood disorders. *Annual Review of Psychology, 49,* 377–412.

Minuchin, S., Montalvo, B., Guerney, B., & Shumer, E. (1967). *Families of the slums.* New York: Basic Books.

Miranda, J., Bernal, G., Lau, A., Kohn, L., Hwang, W., & LaFromboise, T. (2005). State of the science of psychosocial interventions for ethnic minorities. *Annual Review of Clinical Psychology, 1,* 113–142.

Mischel, W. (1968). *Personality and assessment.* New York: Wiley.

Mischel, W. (1973). Toward a cognitive social learning reconceptualization of personality. *Psychological Review, 80,* 252–283.

Mischel, W. (1986). *Introduction to personality* (4th ed.). New York: Holt, Rinehart & Winston.

Mischel, W. (1993). *Introduction to personality.* New York: Harcourt Brace.

Mitchell, K. J., Becker-Blease, K. A., & Finkelhor, D. (2005). Inventory of problematic internet experiences encountered in clinical practice. *Professional Psychology: Research and Practice, 36,* 498–509.

Mitchell, R. L., & Crow, T. J. (2005). Right hemisphere language functions and schizophrenia: The forgotten hemisphere? *Brain, 128* (Pt 5), 963–978.

Moffitt, T. E. (2005). The new look of behavioral genetics in developmental psychopathology: Gene-environment interplay in antisocial behaviors. *Psychological Bulletin, 131,* 533–554.

Moffitt, T. E., & Caspi, A. (2007). Evidence from behavioral genetics for environmental contributions to antisocial conduct. In J. E. Grusec & P. D. Hastings (Eds.), *Handbook of socialization: Theory and research* (pp. 96–123). New York: Guilford.

Moffitt, T. E., Caspi, A., Harrington, H., Milne, B. J., Melchior, M., Goldberg, D., & Poulton, R. (2007). Generalized anxiety disorder and depression: Childhood risk factors in a birth cohort followed to age 32. *Psychological Medicine, 37,* 441–452.

Mokdad, A. H., Marks, J. S., Stroup, D. F., & Gerberding, J. L. (2004). Actual causes of death in the United States, 2000. *Journal of the American Medical Association, 291,* 1238–1245.

Monahan, J. (1988). Risk assessment of violence among the mentally disordered: Generating useful knowledge. *International Journal of Law and Psychiatry, 11,* 249.

Monahan, J., & Steadman, H. J. (Eds.). (1994). *Violence and mental disorder: Developments in risk assessment.* Chicago: The University of Chicago Press.

Monahan, J., & Walker, L. (1990). *Social science in law: Cases and materials* (2nd ed.). Westbury, NY: Foundation Press.

Monahan, J., & Walker, L. (2006). *Social science in law* (6th ed.). Minneapolis, MN: Foundation Press.

Moodie, W. (1936). Forward. *A guide to mental testing* [au: R. B. Cattell]. London: University of London Press (vii–viii).

Moos, R., Schaefer, J., Andrassy, J., & Moos, B. (2001). Outpatient mental health care, self-help groups, and patients' one-year treatment outcomes. *Journal of Clinical Psychology, 57,* 273–287.

Moreno, J. (1946). *Psychodrama* (Vol. 1). New York: Beacon House.

Morgan, B. L., & Korschgen, A. J. (2006). *Majoring in psych? Career options for psychology undergraduates* (3rd ed.). Boston: Allyn and Bacon.

Morgan, D. L., & Morgan, R. K. (2001). Single-participant design: Bringing science to managed care. *American Psychologist, 56,* 119–127.

Morgan, R. D., Kuther, T. L., & Habben, C. J. (2005). *Life after graduate school in psychology: Insider's advice from new psychologists.* New York: Psychology Press.

Morgenstern, J., Irwin, T. W., Wainberg, M. L., Parsons, J. T., Muench, F., Bux, D. A., et al. (2007). A randomized controlled trail of goal choice interventions for alcohol use disorders among men who have sex with men. *Journal of Consulting and Clinical Psychology, 75,* 72–84.

Morganstern, K. P., & Tevlin, H. E. (1981). Behavioral interviewing. In M. Hersen & A. S. Bellack (Eds.), *Behavioral assessment: A practical handbook* (2nd ed., pp. 71–100). New York: Pergamon Press.

Morland, K., Diez Roux, A. V., & Wing, S. (2006). Supermarkets, other food stores, and obesity. *American Journal of Preventive Medicine, 30,* 333-339.

Morrison, C. S., McCusker, J., Stoddard, A. M., & Bigelow, C. (1995). The validity of behavioral data reported by injection drug users on a clinical risk assessment. *International Journal of the Addictions, 30,* 889-899.

Morrison, K. H., Bradley, R., & Westen, D. (2003). The external validity of controlled clinical trials of psychotherapy for depression and anxiety: A naturalistic study. *Psychology and Psychotherapy: Theory, Research, and Practice, 76,* 109-132.

Morse, S. J. (1978). Law and mental health professionals: The limits of expertise. *Professional Psychology, 9,* 389-399.

Morton, A. (1995). The enigma of non-attendance: A study of clients who do not turn up for their first appointment. *Therapeutic Communities: International Journal for Therapeutic and Supportive Organizations, 16,* 117-133.

Moseley G. L. (2006). Graded motor imagery for pathologic pain: A randomized controlled trial. *Neurology, 67,* 2129-2134.

Mpofu, E., Carney, J., & Lambert, M. C. (2006). Peer sociometric assessment. In M. Hersen (Ed.), *Clinician's handbook of child behavioral assessment* (pp. 233-263). San Diego: Elsevier Academic Press.

Mrazek, P. J., & Haggerty, R. J. (Eds.). (1994). *Reducing risks for mental disorders: Frontiers for preventive intervention research.* Washington, DC: National Academy Press.

Mukherjee, D., Levin, R. L., & Heller, W. (2006). The cognitive, emotional, and social sequelae of stroke: Psychological and ethical concerns in post-stroke adaptation. *Topics in Stroke Rehabilitation, 13,* 26-35.

Multiple Risk Factors Intervention Trial Research Group (MRFIT). (1982). Multiple risk factor intervention trial: Risk factor changes and mortality results. *Journal of the American Medical Association, 248,* 1465-1477.

Mulvey, E. P., & Cauffman, E. (2001). The inherent limits of predicting school violence. *American Psychologist, 56,* 797-802.

Munsey, C. (2006a). HIPAA enforcement rule issued. *Monitor on Psychology, 37,* 48.

Munsey, C. (2006b). RxP legislation made historic progress in Hawaii. *Monitor on Psychology, 37,* 42-44.

Munsey, C. (2007a). Health over health care. *Monitor on Psychology, 38,* 28-30.

Munsey, C. (2007b). New disclosure requirements help students compare psychology programs. *GradPSYCH, 5,* 1-2.

Murdock, N. L. (2004). *Theories of counseling and psychotherapy.* Upper Saddle River, NJ: Pearson.

Murdock, N. L., Banta, J., Stromseth, J., Viene, D., Brown, T. M. (1998). Joining the club: Factors related to choice of theoretical orientation. *Counselling Psychology Quarterly, 11,* 63-78.

Murphy, M. J., Levant, R. F., Hall, J. E., & Glueckauf, R. L. (2007). Distance education in professional training in psychology. *Professional Psychology: Research and Practice, 38,* 97-103.

Murray, H. A. (1938). *Explorations in personality.* Fair Lawn, NJ: Oxford University Press.

Murray, H. A. (1943). *Thematic Apperception Test.* Cambridge, MA: Harvard University Press.

Mussen, P. H., & Scodel, A. (1955). The effects of sexual stimulation under varying conditions on TAT sexual responsiveness. *Journal of Consulting Psychology, 19,* 90.

Myers, D. G. (2000). The funds, friends, and faith of happy people. *American Psychologist, 55,* 56-67.

Myers, I. B., & Briggs, K. C. (1943). *The Myers-Briggs type indicator.* Palo Alto, CA: Consulting Psychologists Press.

Myers, I. B., & McCaulley, M. H. (1985). *Manual: A guide to the development and use of the Myers-Briggs Type Indicator.* Palo Alto, CA: Consulting Psychologists Press.

Myklebust, H. R. (1975). Nonverbal learning disabilities: Assessment and intervention. In H. R. Myklebust (Ed.), *Progress in learning disabilities* (Vol. 3, pp. 85-121). New York: Grune & Stratton.

Naglieri, J. A., Drasgow, F., Schmit, M., Handler, L., Prifitera, A., Margolis, A., & Velasquez, R. (2004).

Psychological testing on the Internet: New problems, old issues. *American Psychologist, 59,* 150–162.

Nagy, T. F. (2005). *Ethics in plain English: An illustrative casebook for psychologists* (2nd ed.). Washington, DC: American Psychological Association.

Nathan, P. E. (1987). DSM-III-R and the behavior therapist. *Behavior Therapy, 10,* 203–205.

Nathan, P. E., & Langenbucher, J. W. (1999). Psychopathology: Description and classification. *Annual Review of Psychology, 50,* 79–107.

Nathan, P. E., Stuart, S. P., & Dolan, S. L. (2000). Research on psychotherapy efficacy and effectiveness: Between Scylla and Charybdis? *Psychological Bulletin, 126,* 964–981.

Nation, M., Crusto, C., Wandersman, A., Kumpfer, K. L., Seybolt, D., Morrissey-Kane, E., & Davino, K. (2003). What works in prevention: Principles of effective prevention programs. *American Psychologist, 58,* 449–456.

National Association of Social Workers. (2001). About NASW: NASW fact sheet. Retrieved September 17, 2001, from http://www.naswdc.org/about/naswfact.htm.

National Association of Social Workers. (2008). Choices: Careers in social work. Retrieved February 29, 2008, from http://www.socialworkers.org/pubs/choices/choices.htm.

National Center for Education Statistics. (2000). Digest of Education Statistics, 1999. Retrieved December 13, 2001, from http://nces.ed.gov/pubs2000/Digest99/d99t298.htm.

National Institute of Justice. (1999). *Eyewitness evidence: A guide for law enforcement.* Washington, DC: U.S. Department of Justice.

National Institute of Mental Health (2006). The numbers count: Mental disorders in America (2006 rev.). Retrieved August 8, 2006, from http://www.nimh.nih.gov.publicat/numbers.cfm.

Navon, D. (1983). How many trees does it take to make a forest? *Perception, 12,* 239–254.

Neimeyer, R. A., & Bridges, S. K. (2003). Postmodern approaches to psychotherapy. In A. S. Gurman & S. B. Messer (Eds.), *Essential Psychotherapies* (2nd ed., pp. 272–316). New York: Guilford.

Neimeyer, R. A., & Raskin, J. D. (Eds.). (2000). *Constructions of disorder: Meaning-making frameworks for psychotherapy.* Washington, DC: American Psychological Association.

Neisser, U., Boodoo, G., Bouchard, T. J., Boykin, A. W., Brody, N., Ceci, S. J., et al. (1996). Intelligence: Knowns and unknowns. *American Psychologist, 51,* 77–101.

Nelson, R. O., & Hayes, S. C. (1986). The nature of behavioral assessment. In R. O. Nelson & S. C. Hayes (Eds.), *Conceptual foundations of behavioral assessment* (pp. 3–41). New York: Guilford.

Nevid, J. S., Rathus, S. A., & Greene, B. (2006). *Abnormal psychology in a changing world.* Upper Saddle River, NJ: Prentice Hall.

Newlin, C. M., Adolph, J. L., & Kreber, L. A. (2004). Factors that influence fee setting by male and female psychologists. *Professional Psychology: Research and Practice, 35,* 548–552.

Newman, R. (2005). APA's resilience initiative. *Professional Psychology: Research and Practice, 36,* 227–229.

Neylan, T. C. (1999). Frontal lobe function: Mr. Phineas Gage's famous injury. *Journal of Neuropsychiatry and Clinical Neuroscience, 11,* 280.

Nicholson, R. A. (1999). Forensic assessment. In R. Roesch, S. D. Hart, & J. R. Ogloff (Eds.), *Psychology and law: The state of the discipline* (pp. 122–173). New York: Kluwer Academic/Plenum.

NIDA Research Report. (2001). *Prescription drugs: Abuse and addiction: NIH publication No. 01-4881,* Printed April, 2001 (Author).

Nielsen, S. L., Smart, D. W., Isakson, R. L., Worthen, V. E., Gregersen, A. T., & Lambert, M. J. (2004). The *Consumer Reports* effectiveness score: What did consumers report? *Journal of Counseling Psychology, 51,* 25–37.

Nietzel, M. T., & Bernstein, D. A. (1976). The effects of instructionally mediated demand upon the behavioral assessment of assertiveness. *Journal of Consulting and Clinical Psychology, 44,* 500.

Nietzel, M. T., Bernstein, D. A., & Russell, R. L. (1988). Assessment of anxiety and fear. In A. S. Bellack & M. Hersen (Eds.), *Behavioral*

Consulting and Clinical Psychology, 55, 391–395.

Reddy, L. A., Files-Hall, T. M., & Schaefer, C. E. (Eds.). (2005). *Empirically based play interventions for children*. Washington, DC: American Psychological Association.

Reddy, L. A., Springer, C., Files-Hall, T. M., Benisz, E. S., Hauch, Y., Braunstein, D., & Atamanoff, T. (2005). Child ADHD multimodal program: An empirically supported intervention for young children with ADHD. In L. A. Reddy, T. M. Files-Hall, & C. E. Schaefer (Eds.), *Empirically based play interventions for children* (pp. 145–167). Washington, DC: American Psychological Association.

Reed, G. M., Kemeny, M. E., Taylor, S. E., Wang, H. Y. J., & Visscher, B. R. (1994). "Realistic acceptance" as a predictor of decreased survival of gay men with AIDS. *Health Psychology, 13,* 299–307.

Reed, G. M., Levant, R. F., Stout, C. E., Murphy, M. J., & Phelps, R. (2001). Psychology in the current mental health marketplace. *Professional Psychology: Research and Practice, 1,* 65–70.

Rehm, L. P., & DeMers, S. T. (2006). Licensure. *Clinical Psychology: Science and Practice, 13,* 249–253.

Reich, W., Cottler, L., McCallum, K., & Corwin, D. (1995). Computerized interviews as a method of assessing psychopathology in children. *Comprehensive Psychiatry, 36,* 40–45.

Reid, J. B. B., Patterson, G. R., & Snyder, J. J. (2002). *Antisocial behavior in children and adolescents*. Washington, DC: American Psychological Association.

Rein, L. (2001, December 19). Crime panel assails Virginia insanity policy. *The Washington Post,* B1, B4.

Reinecke, M. A., & Freeman, A. (2003). Cognitive therapy. In A. S. Gurman & S. B. Messer (Eds.), *Essential Psychotherapies* (2nd ed., pp. 224–271). New York: Guilford.

Reisman, J. M. (1976). *A history of clinical psychology*. New York: Irvington.

Reitan, R. M. (1964). Psychological deficits resulting from cerebral lesions in man. In J. M. Warren & K. Akert (Eds.), *The frontal granular cortex and behavior*. New York: McGraw-Hill.

Reitan, R. M., & Davison, L. A. (Eds.). (1974). *Clinical neuropsychology: Current status and applications*. Washington, DC: V. H. Winston.

Reitan, R. M., & Wolfson, D. (1993). *The Halstead-Reitan Neuropsychological Test Battery: Theory and clinical interpretation*. Tucson, AZ: Neuropsychology Press.

Report of the Ethics Committee, 2000. (2000). *American Psychologist, 56,* 680–688.

Repp, A. C., & Horner, R. H. (2000). *Functional analysis of problem behavior: From effective assessment to effective support*. Belmont, CA: Wadsworth.

Reppucci, N. D., Wollard, J. L., & Fried, C. S. (1999). Social, community, and preventive interventions. *Annual Review of Psychology, 50,* 387–418.

Rescorla, L., Achenbach, T. M., Ivanova, M. Y., Dumenci, L., Almqvist, F., Bilenberg, N., et al. (2007). Epidemiological comparisons of problems and positive qualities reported by adolescents in 24 countries. *Journal of Consulting and Clinical Psychology, 75,* 351–358.

Resnick, J. H. (1991). Finally, a definition of clinical psychology: A message from the President, Division 12. *The Clinical Psychologist, 44,* 3–11.

Resnick, R. J. (1997). A brief history of practice—Expanded. *American Psychologist, 52,* 463–468.

Reynolds, C. R., & Kamphaus, R. W. (2003). *Handbook of psychological and educational assessment of children: Personality, behavior, and context* (2nd ed.). New York: Guilford.

Rice, M. E. (1997). Violent offender research and implications for the criminal justice system. *American Psychologist, 52,* 414–423.

Rice, S. A. (1929). Contagious bias in the interview: A methodological note. *American Journal of Sociology, 35,* 420–423.

Rich, B. A. (1998). Personhood, patienthood, and clinical practice: Reassessing advance directives. *Psychology, Public Policy, and Law, 4,* 610–628.

Richard, D. C. S., & Lauterbach, D. (2004). Computers in the training and practice of behavioral assessment. In S. N. Haynes & E. M. Heiby

(Eds.), *Comprehensive handbook of psychological assessment. Vol. 3: Behavioral assessment* (pp. 222–245). Hoboken, NJ: Wiley.

Richman, L. S., Kubzansky, L., Maselko, J., & Kawachi, I. (2005). Positive emotion and health: Going beyond the negative. *Health Psychology, 24,* 422–429.

Richmond, T. K., & Rosen, D. S. (2005). The treatment of adolescent depression in the era of the black box warning. *Current Opinion in Pediatrics, 17,* 466–472.

Richters, J. E. (1992). Depressed mothers as informants about their children: A critical review of the evidence for distortion. *Psychological Bulletin, 112,* 485–499.

Rickert, V., & Jay, S. (1995). The noncompliant adolescent. In S. Parker & B. Zuckerman (Eds.), *Behavioral and developmental pediatrics* (pp. 219–222). Boston: Little, Brown & Company.

Riggle, E. D. B., & Rostosky, S. S. (2005). For better or for worse: Psycholegal soft spots and advance planning for same-sex couples. *Professional Psychology: Research and Practice, 36,* 90–96.

Riley, W. T., Schumann, M. F., Forman-Hoffman, V. L., Mihm, P., Applegate, B. W., & Asif, O. (2007). Responses of practicing psychologists to a Web site developed to promote empirically supported treatments. *Professional Psychology: Research and Practice, 38,* 44–53.

Ripple, C. H., & Zigler, E. (2003). Research, policy, and the federal role in prevention initiatives for children. *American Psychologist, 58,* 482–490.

Ritterband, L. M., Gonder-Frederick, L. A., Cox, D. J., Clifton, A. D., West, R. W., & Borowitz, S. M. (2003). Internet interventions: In review, in use, and into the future. *Professional Psychology: Research and Practice, 34,* 527–534.

Roberts, C. F., Sargent, E. L., & Chan, A. S. (1993). Verdict selection processes in insanity cases: Juror construals and the effects of guilty but mental ill instructions. *Law and Human Behavior, 17,* 261–275.

Roberts, M. C. (Ed.). (2003). *Handbook of pediatric psychology* (3rd ed.). New York: Guilford.

Robertson, G. J., & Eyde, L. D. (1993). Improving test use in the United States: The development of an interdisciplinary casebook. *European Journal of Psychological Assessment, 9,* 137–146.

Robiner, W. N., Bearman, D. L., Berman, M., Grove, W. M., Colon, E., Mareck, S., & Armstrong, J. (2002). Prescriptive authority for psychologists: A looming health hazard? *Clinical Psychology: Science and Practice, 9,* 231–248.

Robinson, J. D., & Habben, C. J. (2003). The role of the American Board of Professional Psychology in professional mobility. *Professional Psychology: Research and Practice, 34,* 474–475.

Roche, K. M., Ensminger, M. E., Ialongo, N., Poduska, J. M., & Kellam, S. G. (2006). Early entries into adult roles: Associations with aggressive behavior from early adolescence into young adulthood. *Youth and Society, 38,* 236–261.

Rochlen, A. B., Zack, J. S., & Speyer, C. (2004). Online therapy: Review of relevant definitions, debates, and current empirical support. *Journal of Clinical Psychology, 60,* 269–283.

Rock, D. L., Bransford, J. D., Maisto, S. A., & Morey, L. (1987). The study of clinical judgment: An ecological approach. *Clinical Psychology Review, 7,* 645–661.

Rodin, J., & Salovey, P. (1989). Health psychology. *Annual Review of Psychology, 40,* 533–580.

Rodriguez, H., & Arnold, C. (1998). Children & divorce: A snapshot. Retrieved December 13, 2001, from http://www.clasp.org/pubs/familyformation/divfinal.htm.

Roe, A., Gustad, J. W., Moore, B. V., Ross, S., & Skodak, M. (Eds.). (1959). *Graduate education in psychology.* Washington, DC: American Psychological Association.

Roe, D., Dekel, R., Harel, G., Fenning, S., & Fenning, S. (2006). Clients' feelings during termination of psychodynamically oriented psychotherapy. *Bulletin of the Menninger Clinic, 70,* 68–81.

Rogers, C. R. (1939). *Clinical treatment of the problem child.* Boston: Houghton Mifflin.

Rogers, C. R. (1942). *Counseling and psychotherapy.* Boston: Houghton Mifflin.

Rogers, C. R. (1946). Significant aspects of client-centered therapy. *American Psychologist, 1,* 415–422.

Rogers, C. R. (1951). *Client-centered therapy.* Boston: Houghton Mifflin.

Rogers, C. R. (1961). *On becoming a person.* Boston: Houghton Mifflin.

Rogers, C. R. (1967/2003). *Client-centered therapy.* New York: Constable & Robinson.

Rogers, M. R., & Molina, L. E. (2006). Exemplary efforts in psychology to recruit and retain graduate students of color. *American Psychologist, 61,* 143–156.

Rogers, R. (1995). *Diagnostic and structured interviewing: A handbook for psychologists.* Odessa, FL: Psychological Assessment Resources, Inc.

Rogers, R. (2001). *Handbook of diagnostic and structured interviewing* (2nd ed.). New York: Guilford.

Rogers, R., Gillis, J. R., Dickens, S. E., & Bagby, R. M. (1991). Standardized assessment of malingering: Validation of the Structured Interview of Reported Symptoms. *Psychological Assessment, 3,* 89–96.

Rogers, R., Ustad, K. L., & Salekin, R. T. (1998). Convergent validity of the Personality Assessment Inventory: A study of emergency referrals in a correctional setting. *Assessment, 5,* 3–12.

Rohde, D. (1999, November 7). Juror and courts assailed in subway-killing mistrial. *New York Times,* 32.

Roid, G. H. (2003). *Stanford-Binet Intelligence Scales (fifth ed.) technical manual.* Itasca, IL: Riverside Publishing.

Rokeach, M. (2000). *Understanding human values.* New York: The Free Press.

Ronan, G. G., Colavito, V. A., & Hammontree, S. R. (1993). Personal problems-solving system for scoring TAT responses: Preliminary validity and reliability data. *Journal of Personality Assessment, 61,* 28–40.

Ronan, K. R., & Kazantzis, N. (2006). The use of between-session (homework) activities in psychotherapy: Conclusions from the Journal of Psychotherapy Integration Special Series. *Journal of Psychotherapy Integration, 16,* 254–259.

Rorschach, H. (1921). *Psychodynamics: A diagnostic test based on perception.* Oxford, England: Grune and Stratton.

Rorschach, H. (1942). *Psychodiagnostics: A diagnostic test based on perception.* Bern, Switzerland: Hans Huber (Original work published in 1921).

Rose, S. D., & LeCroy, C. W. (1991). Group methods. In F. H. Kanfer & A. P. Goldstein (Eds.), *Helping people change* (4th ed., pp. 422–453). New York: Pergamon Press.

Rosen, G. M., Glasgow, R. E., & Moore, T. E. (2003). Self-help therapy: The science and business of giving psychology away. In S. O. Lilienfeld, S. J. Lynn, & J. M. Lohr (Eds.), *Science and pseudoscience in clinical psychology* (pp. 399–424). New York: Guilford.

Rosen, J. (2007, March 11). The brain on the stand. *New York Times Magazine.* Retrieved March 11, 2007, at http://www.nytimes.com/2007/03/11/magazine/11Neurolaw.t.html?ref=magazine.

Rosen, R. C., & Kopel, S. A. (1977). Penile plethysmography and biofeedback in the treatment of a transvestite-exhibitionist. *Journal of Consulting and Clinical Psychology, 45,* 908–916.

Rosenhan, D. L. (1973). On being sane in insane places. *Science, 179,* 250–258.

Rosenman, R. H., Brand, R. J., Jenkins, D. D., Friedman, M., Straus, R., & Wurm, M. (1975). Coronary heart disease in the Western Collaborative Group Study: Final follow-up experience after 8 years. *Journal of the American Medical Association, 233,* 872–877.

Rosenstock, I. M. (1974). Historical origins of the health belief model. *Health Education Monographs, 2,* 328–335.

Rosenthal, R., & DiMatteo, M. R. (2001). Meta-analysis: Recent developments in quantitative methods for literature reviews. *Annual Review of Psychology, 52,* 59–82.

Rosenthal, T. L., & Steffek, B. D. (1991). Modeling methods. In F. H. Kanfer & A. P. Goldstein (Eds.), *Helping people change* (4th ed., pp. 70–121). New York: Pergamon Press.

Rosenzweig, S. (1949). Apperceptive norms for the Thematic Apperception Test. I. The problem of norms in projective methods. *Journal of Personality, 17,* 475–482.

Rosenzweig, S. (1977). *Manual for the Children's Form of the Rosenzweig Picture-Frustration (P-F) Study.* St. Louis: Rana House.

Ross, M. W., Stowe, A., Wodak, A., & Gold, J. (1995). Reliability of interview responses of injecting drug users. *Journal of Addictive Diseases, 14,* 1–2.

Rossini, E. D., & Moretti, R. J. (1997). Thematic Apperception Test interpretation: Practice recommendations from a survey of clinical psychology doctoral programs accredited by the American Psychological *Association. Professional Psychology: Research and Practice, 28,* 393–398.

Rothbart, M. K., & Bates, J. E. (2006). Temperament. In N. Eisenberg (Ed.), *Handbook of child psychology* (6th ed., pp. 99–166). Hoboken, NJ: Wiley.

Rothbaum, B. O. (2006). Virtual reality in the treatment of psychiatric disorders. *CNS Spectrums, 11,* 34.

Rothbaum, B. O., Foa, E. B., Hembree, E. (2006). *Reclaiming your life from a traumatic experience.* New York: Oxford University Press.

Rothbaum, B. O., Hodges, L. F., Kooper, R., & Opdyke, D. (1995). Effectiveness of computer-generated virtual reality graded exposure in treatment of agoraphobia. *American Journal of Psychiatry, 152,* 626–628.

Rothbaum, B. O., Hodges, L., Smith, S., Lee, J. H., & Price, L. (2000). A controlled study of virtual reality exposure therapy for the fear of flying. *Journal of Consulting and Clinical Psychology, 68,* 1020–1026.

Rotter, J. B., Lah, M. I., & Rafferty, J. E. (1992). *Manual: Rotter Incomplete Sentences Blank* (2nd ed.). Orlando, FL: Psychological Corporation.

Rotter, J. B., & Rafferty, J. E. (1950). *The Rotter Incomplete Sentences Test.* New York: Psychological Corporation.

Round, A. P. (1999). Teaching clinical reasoning— A preliminary controlled study. *Medical Education, 33,* 480–483.

Rourke, B. P. (1989). *Nonverbal learning disabilities: The syndrome and the model.* New York: Guilford.

Routh, D. K. (1994). *Clinical psychology since 1917: Science, practice, organization.* New York: Plenum.

Routh, D. K. (2000). Clinical psychology training: A history of ideas and practices prior to 1946. *American Psychologist, 55,* 236–241.

Rowe, R., Maughan, B., Pickles, A., Costello, E. J., & Angold, A. (2002). The relationship between DSM-IV oppositional defiant disorder and conduct disorder: Findings from the Great Smoky Mountains Study. *Journal of Child Psychology and Psychiatry, 43,* 365–373.

Rozanski, A., Blumenthal, J. A., & Kaplan, J. (1999). Impact of psychological factors on the pathogenesis of cardiovascular disease and implications for therapy. *Circulation, 99,* 2192–2217.

Rubens, A. B., & Benson, D. F. (1971). Associative visual agnosia. *Archives of Neurology, 24,* 304–316.

Rubin, R., Holm, S., Friberg, L., Videbech, P., Andersen, H. S., Bendsen, B. B., et al. (1991). Altered modulation of prefrontal and subcortical brain activity in newly diagnosed schizophrenia and schizophreniform disorder: A regional cerebral blood flow study. *Archives of General Psychiatry, 48,* 987–995.

Rubinstein, E. (1948). Childhood mental disease in American: A review of the literature before 1900. *American Journal of Orthopsychiatry, 18,* 314–321.

Rudestam, K. E. (2004). Distributed education and the role of online learning in training professional psychologists. *Professional Psychology: Research and Practice, 35,* 427–432.

Ruegg, R. G., Ekstrom, D. E., Dwight, L., & Golden, R. N. (1990). Introduction of a standardized report form improves the quality of mental status examination reports by psychiatric residents. *Academic Psychiatry, 14,* 157–163.

Rugulies, R. (2003). Depression as a predictor for the development of coronary heart disease: A systematic review and meta-analysis of the literature. *American Journal of Preventive Medicine, 23,* 51–61.

Russ, S. W. (2006). Psychodynamic treatments. In R. T. Ammerman (Ed.), *Comprehensive handbook of personality and psychopathology* (Vol. 3, pp. 425–437). Hoboken, NJ: Wiley.

Russell, E. W. (1998). In defense of the Halstead Reitan Battery: A critique of Lezak's review. *Archives of Clinical Neuropsychology, 13,* 365-381.

Ryan, J. J., Paolo, A. M., & Smith, A. J. (1992). Wechsler Adult Intelligence Scale—Revised intersubtest scatter in brain-damaged patients: A comparison with the standardization sample. *Psychological Assessment, 4,* 63-66.

Rychtarik, R. G., Tarnowski, K. J., & St. Lawrence, J. S. (1989). Impact of social desirability response sets on the self-report of marital adjustment in alcoholics. *Journal of Studies in Alcohol, 50,* 24-29.

Ryle, A. (2005). Cognitive analytic therapy. In J. C. Norcross, & M. R. Goldfried (Eds.), *Handbook of psychotherapy integration* (2nd ed., pp. 196-217). New York: Oxford Press.

Sackett, P. R., & Wilk, S. L. (1994). Within-group norming and other forms of score adjustment in preemployment testing. *American Psychologist, 49,* 929-954.

Sacks, O. (1985). *The man who mistook his wife for a hat.* New York: Summit Books.

Sacks, O. (1990). *A leg to stand on.* New York: Summit Books.

Safer, D. J., & Krager, J. M. (1994). The increased use of stimulant medication for hyperactive/inattentive students in secondary schools. *Pediatrics, 94,* 462-464.

Safer, D. L., Telch, C. F., & Agras, W. (2001). Dialectical behavior therapy for bulimia nervosa. *American Journal of Psychiatry, 158,* 632-634.

Saklofske, D. H., Hildebrand, D. K., & Gorsuch, R. L. (2000). Replication of the factor structure of the Wechsler Adult Intelligence Scale—Third Edition with a Canadian sample. *Psychological Assessment, 12,* 436-439.

Sales, B. D., & Folkman, S. (2000). *Ethics in research with human participants.* Washington, DC: American Psychological Association.

Sales, B. D., Miller, M. O., & Hall, S. R. (2005a). Legal credentialing and privileges to practice. In B. D. Sales, M. O. Miller, & S. R. Hall (Eds.), *Laws affecting clinical practice* (pp. 13-22). Washington, DC: American Psychological Association.

Sales, B. D., Miller, M. O., & Hall, S. R. (2005b). *Laws affecting clinical practice.* Washington, DC: American Psychological Association.

Sales, B. D., & Shuman, D. W. (1996). *Law, mental health, and mental disorder.* Pacific Grove, CA: Brooks/Cole.

Salovey, P., Rothman, A. J., Detweiler, J. B., & Steward, W. T. (2000). Emotional states and physical health. *American Psychologist, 55,* 110-121.

Salovey, P., & Singer, J. A. (1991). Cognitive behavior modification. In F. H. Kanfer & A. P. Goldstein (Eds.), *Helping people change* (4th ed., pp. 361-395). New York: Pergamon Press.

Samuda, R. J. (1975). *Psychological testing of American minorities: Issues and consequences.* New York: Dodd, Mead.

Sanchez, L. M., & Turner, S. M. (2003). Practicing psychology in the era of managed care: Implications for practice and training. *American Psychologist, 58,* 116-129.

Sanders, M. R., & Dadds, M. R. (1992). Children's and parents' cognitions about family interactions: An evaluation of video-mediated recall and thought listing procedures in assessment of conduct-disordered children. *Journal of Clinical Child Psychology, 21,* 371-379.

Sanders, M. R., Montgomery, D. T., & Brechman-Toussaint, M. L. (2000). The mass media and the prevention of child behavior problems: The evaluation of a television series to promote positive outcomes for parents and their children. *Journal of Child Psychology and Psychiatry, 41,* 939-948.

Santoro, S. O., Kister, K. M., Karpiak, C. P., & Norcross, J. C. (2004, April). *Clinical psychologists in the 2000s: A national study.* Paper presented at the annual meeting of the Eastern Psychological Association, Washington, DC.

Santostefano, S. (1962). Performance testing of personality. *Merrill-Palmer Quarterly, 8,* 83-97.

Santrock, J. W. (2008). *Educational psychology* (3rd ed.). Boston: McGraw Hill.

Sapara, A., Cooke, M., Fannon, D., Francis, A., Buchanan, R. W., Anilkumar, A. P., et al. (2007). Prefrontal cortex and insight in schizophrenia: A volumetric MRI study. *Schizophrenia Research, 89,* (1-3), 22-34. Epub Nov 13, 2006.

Sarafino, E. P. (2005). *Health psychology: Biopsychosocial interactions.* Hoboken, NJ: Wiley.

Sarason, S. B. (1974). *The psychological sense of community: Prospects for community psychology.* San Francisco: Jossey-Bass.

Sarbin, T. R. (1997). On the futility of psychiatric diagnostic manuals (DSMs) and the return of personal agency. *Applied Prevention Psychology, 6,* 233–243.

Sartorius, N., Kaelber, C. T., Cooper, J. E., Roper, M. T., et al. (1996). Progress toward achieving a common language in psychiatry: Results from the field trial of the clinical guidelines accompanying the WHO classification of mental and behavioral disorders in ICD-10. *Archives of General Psychiatry, 50,* 115–124.

Satir, V. (1967). *Conjoint family therapy* (rev. ed.). Palo Alto, CA: Science and Behavior Books.

Sattler, J. M., & Hoge, R. D. (2006). *Assessment of children: Behavioral, social and clinical foundations* (5th ed.). San Diego: Jerome M. Sattler, Publisher.

Saunders, S. M., Howard, K. I., & Orlinsky, D. E. (1989). The Therapeutic Bond Scales: Psychometric characteristics and relationship to treatment effectiveness. *Psychological Assessment, 1,* 323–330.

Sawyer, J. (1966). Measurement and prediction, clinical and statistical. *Psychological Bulletin, 66,* 178–200.

Scheidlinger, S. (2000). The group psychotherapy movement at the millennium: Some historical perspectives. *International Journal of Group Psychotherapy, 50,* 315–339.

Schirmer, A., Alter, K., Kotz, S. A., & Friederici, A. D. (2001). Lateralization of prosody during language production: A lesion study. *Brain and Language, 76,* 1–17.

Schneck, J. M. (1975). United States of America in J. G. Howells (Ed.), *World history of psychiatry.* New York: Brunner/Mazel, 432–475.

Schneider, K. J. (2003). Existential-humanistic psychotherapies. In A. S. Gurman & S. B. Messer (Eds.), *Essential psychotherapies* (2nd ed., pp. 149–181). New York: Guilford.

Schneider, S. L. (2001). In search of realistic optimism: Meaning, knowledge, and warm fuzziness. *American Psychologist, 56,* 250–263.

Schneider, W., Buchheim, P., Cierpka, M., Rainer, D. W., Freyberger, H. J., et al. (2004). Operationalized psychodynamic diagnostic: A new diagnostic approach in psychodynamic psychotherapy. In L. E. Beutler & M. L. Malik (Eds.), *Rethinking the DSM: A psychological perspective* (pp. 177–200). Washington, DC: American Psychological Association.

Schneiderman, N., Antoni, M. H., Saab, P. G., & Ironson, G. (2001). Health psychology: Psychosocial and biobehavioral aspects of chronic disease management. *Annual Review of Psychology, 52,* 555–580.

Schopp, L. H., Johnstone, B., & Reid-Arndt, S. (2005). Telehealth brain injury training for rural behavioral health generalists: Supporting and enhancing rural service delivery networks. *Professional Psychology: Research and Practice, 36,* 158–163.

Schradle, S. B., & Dougher, M. J. (1985). Social support as a mediator of stress. Theoretical and empirical issues. *Clinical Psychology Review, 5,* 641–662.

Schretlen, D., Wilkins, S. S., Van Gorp, W. G., & Bobholz, J. H. (1992). Cross-validation of a psychological test battery to detect faked insanity. *Psychological Assessment, 4,* 77–83.

Schröder, T. A., & Davis, J. D. (2004). Therapists' experience of difficulty in practice. *Psychotherapy Research, 14,* 328–245.

Schulenberg, S. E., & Yutzenka, B. A. (2004). Ethical issues in the use of computerized assessment. *Computers in Human Behavior, 20,* 477–490.

Schwab-Stone, M., Fallon, T., & Briggs, M. (1994). Reliability of diagnostic reporting for children aged 6–11 years: A test-retest study of the Diagnostic Interview Schedule for Children—Revised. *American Journal of Psychiatry, 151,* 1048–1054.

Schwartz, B. K., (Ed.). (2003). *Correctional psychology: Practice, programming, and administration.* Kingston, NJ: Civil Research Institute.

Schweinhart, L. J., McNair, S., Barnes, H., & Larner, M. (1993). Observing young children in action to assess their development: The High/Scope Child Observation Record study. *Educational and Psychological Measurement, 53,* 445–455.

Scott, C. L., & Resnick, P. J. (2006). Patient suicide and litigation. In R. I. Simon & R. E. Hales (Eds.), *The American Psychiatric Publishing textbook of suicide assessment and management* (pp. 527-544). Washington, DC: American Psychiatric Publishing.

Scoville, W. B., & Milner, B. (1957). Loss of recent memory after bilateral hippocampal lesions. *The Journal of Neurology, Neurosurgery, & Psychiatry, 20,* 11-21.

Sechrest, L. B. (1963). Incremental validity: A recommendation. *Educational and Psychological Measurement, 23,* 153-158.

Seeman, J. A. (1949). A study of the process of nondirective therapy. *Journal of Consulting Psychology, 13,* 157-168.

Segal, D. L., Hersen, M., & Van Hasselt, V. B. (1994). Reliability of the structured clinical interview for DSM-III-R: An evaluative review. *Comprehensive Psychiatry, 35,* 316-327.

Segal, Z. V., Williams, J. M. G., & Teasdale, J. D. (2002). *Mindfulness-based cognitive therapy for depression: A new approach to preventing relapse.* New York: Guilford.

Seifer, R. (2003). Young children with mentally ill parents: Resilient developmental systems. In S. S. Luthar (Ed.), *Resilience and vulnerability: Adaptation in the context of childhood adversities* (pp. 29-49). New York: Cambridge University Press.

Self, R., Oates, P., Pinnock-Hamilton, T., & Leach, C. (2005). The relationship between social deprivation and unilateral termination (attrition) from psychotherapy at various stages of the health care pathway. *Psychology and Psychotherapy: Theory, Research, and Practice, 78,* 95-111.

Seligman, M. E. P. (1995). The effectiveness of psychotherapy: The Consumer Reports study. *American Psychologist, 50,* 965-974.

Seligman, M. E. P. (2004). *Authentic happiness.* New York: Simon and Schuster.

Seligman, M. E. P., & Csikszentmihali, M. (2000). Positive psychology: An introduction. *American Psychologist, 55,* 5-14.

Seligman, M. E. P., Peterson, C., Kaslow, N. J., Tanenbaum, R. L., Alloy, L. B., & Abramson, L. Y. (1984). Explanatory style and depressive symptoms among school children. *Journal of Abnormal Psychology, 93,* 235-238.

Seligman, M. E. P., Steen, T. A., Park, N., Peterson, C. (2005). Positive psychology progress: Empirical validation of interventions. *American Psychologist, 60,* 410-421.

Selye, H. (1956). *The stress of life.* New York: McGraw-Hill.

Seto, M. C., Cantor, J. M., & Blanchard, R. (2006). Child pornography offenses are valid diagnostic indicators of pedophilia. *Journal of Abnormal Psychology, 115,* 610-615.

Sexton, T. L., Alexander, J. F., & Mease, A. L. (2004). Levels of evidence for the models and mechanisms of therapeutic change in family and couple therapy. In M. J. Lambert (Ed.), *Bergin and Garfield's handbook of psychotherapy and behavior change* (5th ed., pp. 590-646). New York: Wiley.

Shadish, W. R. (2002). Revisiting field experiments: Field notes for the future. *Psychological Methods, 7,* 3-18.

Shadish, W. R., & Baldwin, S. A. (2005). Effects of behavioral marital therapy: A meta-analysis of randomized controlled trials. *Journal of Consulting and Clinical Psychology, 73,* 6-14.

Shaffer, D., Fisher, P., Lucas, C. P., Dulcan, M. K., & Schwab-Stone, M. E. (2000). NIMH Diagnostic Interview Schedule for Children Version IV (NIMH DISC-IV): Description, differences from previous versions, and reliability of some common diagnoses. *Journal of the American Academy of Child and Adolescent Psychiatry, 39,* 28-38.

Shaffer, G. W., & Lazarus, R. S. (1952). *Fundamental concepts in clinical psychology.* New York: McGraw-Hill.

Shakow, D. (1942). The training of the clinical psychologist. *Journal of Consulting Psychology, 6,* 277-288.

Shakow, D. (1948). Clinical psychology: An evaluation. In L. G. Lowrey & V. Sloane (Eds.), *Orthopsychiatry, 1923-1948: Retrospect and prospect* (pp. 231-247). New York: American Orthopsychiatric Association.

Shakow, D. (1965). Seventeen years later: Clinical psychology in the light of the 1947 CTCP report. *American Psychologist, 20,* 353-362.

Shakow, D. (1968). Clinical psychology. In D. L. Sills (Ed.), *International encyclopedia of the social sciences* (pp. 513–518). London: Collier Macmillan.

Shakow, D. (1978). Clinical psychology seen some 50 years later. *American Psychologist, 33,* 148–158.

Shamay-Tsoory, S. G., Tomer, R., Berger, B. D., Goldsher, D., & Aharon-Peretz, J. (2005). Impaired "affective theory of mind" is associated with right ventromedial prefrontal damage. *Cognitive and Behavioral Neurology, 18,* 55–67.

Shannon, D., & Weaver, W. (1949). *The mathematical theory of communication.* Urbana: University of Illinois Press.

Shapiro, A. E., & Wiggins, J. G. (1994). A PsyD degree for every practitioner: Truth in labeling. *American Psychologist, 49,* 207–210.

Shapiro, A. K. (1971). Placebo effects in medicine, psychotherapy, and psychoanalysis. In A. E. Bergin & S. L. Garfield (Eds.), *Handbook of psychotherapy and behavior change: An empirical analysis* (pp. 439–473). New York: Wiley.

Shapiro, D. A., Firth-Cozens, J., & Stiles, W. B. (1998). The question of therapists' differential effectiveness: A Sheffield Psychotherapy Project addendum. *British Journal of Psychiatry, 154,* 383–385.

Shapiro, D. A., & Shapiro, D. (1982). Meta-analysis of comparative therapy outcome research: A critical appraisal. *Behavioral Psychotherapy, 10,* 4–25.

Shapiro, S. L., Carlson, L. E., Astin, J. A., & Freedman, B. (2006). Mechanisms of mindfulness. *Journal of Clinical Psychology, 62,* 373–386.

Shaw, D. L., Martz, D. M., Lancaster, C. J., & Sade, R. M. (1995). Influence of medical school applicants' demographic and cognitive characteristics on interviewers' ratings of noncognitive traits. *Academic Medicine, 70,* 532–536.

Shaywitz, S. E. & Shaywitz, B. A. (2005). Dyslexia (specific reading disability). *Biological Psychiatry, 57*(11), 1301–1309.

Shea, S. C. (1998). *Psychiatric interviewing: The art of understanding* (2nd ed.). Philadelphia: Saunders.

Shechtman, Z., & Tsegahun, I. (2004). Phototherapy to enhance self-disclosure and client-therapist alliance in an intake interview with Ethiopian immigrants to Israel. *Psychotherapy Research, 14,* 367–377.

Shenker, J. I. (April 2005). *When you only see trees, is there still a forest?* Paper presented at the American Academy of Neurology Annual Meeting, Miami Beach, FL.

Shepherd, M. D., Shoenberg, M., Slavich, S., Wituk, S., Warren, M., & Meissen, G. (1999). Continuum of professional involvement in self-help groups. *Journal of Community Psychology, 27,* 39–53.

Shiffman, S., Hickcox, M., Paty, J. A., Gnys, M., Kassel, J. D., & Richards, T. J. (1996). Progression from a smoking lapse to relapse: Prediction from abstinence violation effects, nicotine dependence, and lapse characteristics. *Journal of Consulting & Clinical Psychology, 64,* 993–1002.

Shipley, K. G., & Wood, J. M. (1996). *The elements of interviewing.* San Diego: Singular Publishing.

Shirk, S. R., & Karver, M. (2003). Prediction of treatment outcome from relationship variables in child and adolescent therapy: A meta-analytic review. *Journal of Consulting and Clinical Psychology, 71,* 452–464.

Shirk, S. R., & Karver, M. (2006). Process issues in cognitive-behavioral therapy for youth. In P. C. Kendall (Ed.), *Child and adolescent therapy* (3rd ed., pp. 465–491). New York: Guilford.

Shochet, I. M., Dadds, M. R., Holland, D., Whitefield, K., Harnett, P. H., & Osgarby, S. M. (2001). The efficacy of a universal school-based program to prevent adolescent depression. *Journal of Clinical Child Psychology, 30,* 303–315.

Shoham-Salomon, V. (1985). Are schizophrenics' behaviors schizophrenic? What medically versus psychosocially oriented therapists attribute to schizophrenic persons. *Journal of Abnormal Psychology, 94,* 443–453.

Shum, D., O-Gorman, J., & Myors, B. (2006). *Psychological testing and assessment.* New York: Oxford University Press.

Shuman, D. W., & Sales, B. D. (1999). The impact of *Daubert* and its progeny on the admissibility of behavioral and social science evidence. *Psychology, Public Policy, and Law, 5,* 3–15.

Shure, M. B., & Aberson, B. (2005). Enhancing the process of resilience through effective thinking. In S. Goldstein, & R. B. Brooks (Eds.), *Handbook of resilience in children* (pp. 373–394). New York: Kluwer Academic/Plenum Publishers.

Siegel, B., & Ficcaglia, M. (2006). Pervasive developmental disorders. In R. T. Ammerman (Ed.), *Comprehensive handbook of personality and psychopathology* (Vol. 3, pp. 254–271). Hoboken, NJ: Wiley.

Silverman, W. K. (1996). Cookbooks, manuals, and paint-by-number psychotherapy in the 90s. *Psychotherapy, 33,* 207–215.

Silverman, W. K., & Dick-Niederhauser, A. (2004). Separation anxiety disorder. In T. L. Morris & J. S. March (Eds.), *Anxiety disorders in children and adolescents* (2nd ed., pp. 164–188). New York: Guilford.

Sinacore-Guinn, G. A. (1995). The diagnostic window: Culture- and gender-sensitive diagnosis and training. *Counselor Education and Supervision, 35,* 18–31.

Singer, M. T., & Nievod, A. (2003). New age therapies. In S. O. Lilienfeld, S. J. Lynn, & J. M. Lohr (Eds.), *Science and pseudoscience in clinical psychology* (pp. 176–204). New York: Guilford.

Singer, M., & Eder, G. S. (1989). Effects of ethnicity, accent, and job status on selection decisions. *International Journal of Psychology, 24,* 13–34.

Skinner, B. F. (1953). *Science and human behavior.* New York: Macmillan.

Sleek, S. (1998, February). Jury tuned out the science in the Nichols trial. *APA Monitor,* 2.

Slife, B. D., & Reber, J. S. (2001). Eclecticism in psychotherapy: Is it really the best substitute for traditional theories? In B. D. Slife, R. N. Williams, & S. H. Barlow (Eds.), *Critical issues in psychotherapy* (pp. 213–234). Thousand Oaks, CA: Sage.

Slobogin, C. (1985). The guilty but mentally ill verdict: An idea whose time should not have come. *George Washington Law Review, 53,* 494–527.

Small, R. F., & Barnhill, L. R. (Eds.). (1998). *Practicing in the new mental health marketplace: Ethical, legal, and moral issues.* Washington, DC: American Psychological Association.

Smallwood, J., Irvine, E., Coulter, F., & Connery, H. (2001). Psychometric evaluation of a short observational tool for small scale research projects in dementia. *International Journal of Geriatric Psychiatry, 16,* 288–292.

Smith, D., & Dumont, F. (1995). A cautionary study: Unwarranted interpretations of the Draw-A-Person test. *Professional Psychology: Research and Practice, 26,* 298–303.

Smith, L. (2005). Psychotherapy, classism, and the poor: Conspicuous by their absence. *American Psychologist, 60,* 687–696.

Smith, M. L., & Glass, G. V. (1977). Meta-analysis of psychotherapy outcome studies. *American Psychologist, 32,* 752–777.

Smith, M. L., Glass, G. V., & Miller, T. I. (1980). *The benefits of psychotherapy.* Baltimore: Johns Hopkins University Press.

Smith, S. (1989). Mental health expert witnesses: Of science and crystal balls. *Behavioral Sciences and the Law, 7,* 145–180.

Snepp, F. P., & Peterson, D. R. (1988). Evaluative comparison of Psy.D. and Ph.D. students by clinical internship supervisors. *Professional Psychology: Research and Practice, 19,* 180–183.

Snowdon, D. A., Greiner, L. H., Kemper, S. J., Nanayakkara, N., & Mortimer, J. A. (1999). Linguistic ability in early life and longevity: Findings from the Nun Study. In J.-M. Robine, B. Forette, C. Franceschi, & M. Allard (Eds.), *The paradoxes of longevity* (pp. 103–113). Berlin: Springer-Verlag.

Snowdon, D. A., Greiner, L. H., & Markesbery, W. R. (2000). Linguistic ability in early life and the neuropathology of Alzheimer's disease and cerebrovascular disease: Findings from the Nun Study. *Annals of the New York Academy of Sciences, 903,* 34–38.

Snyder, D. K., Castellani, A. M., & Whisman, M. A. (2006). Current status and future directions in couple therapy. *Annual Review of Psychology, 57,* 317-344.

Snyder, D. K., Lachar, D., & Wills, R. M. (1988). Computer-based interpretation of the Marital Satisfaction Inventory: Use in treatment planning. *Journal of Marital and Family Therapy, 14,* 397-409.

Snyder, D. K., & Wills, R. M. (1989). Behavioral versus insight-oriented marital therapy: Effects on individual and interspousal functioning. *Journal of Consulting and Clinical Psychology, 57,* 39-46.

Snyder, D. K., Wills, R. M., & Grady-Fletcher, A. (1991). Long-term effectiveness of behavioral versus insight-oriented marital therapy: A 4-year follow-up study. *Journal of Consulting and Clinical Psychology, 59,* 138-141.

Snyder, W. V. (1945). An investigation of the nature of nondirective psychotherapy. *Journal of General Psychology, 33,* 193-232.

Snyder, W. V. (Ed.). (1953). *Group report of a program of research in psychotherapy.* State College: Department of Psychology, Pennsylvania State University.

Society of Clinical Psychology (Division 12). (2001). *Society of Clinical Psychology homepage.* Retrieved December 20, 2001, from http://www.apa.org/ divisions/div12/home-page.shtml.

Solomon, D. A., Leon, A. C., Mueller, T. I., Coryell, W., Teres, J. J., Posternak, M. A., et al. (2005). Tachyphylaxis in unipolar major depressive disorder. *Journal of Clinical Psychiatry, 66,* 283-290.

Somers-Flanagan, J., & Somers-Flanagan, R. (1995). Intake interviewing with suicidal patients: A systematic approach. *Professional Psychology: Research and Practice, 26,* 41-47.

Somers-Flanagan, R., & Somers-Flanagan, J. (1999). *Clinical interviewing* (2nd ed). Hoboken, NJ: Wiley.

Sommer, R. (2006). Dual dissemination: Writing for colleagues and the public. *American Psychologist, 61,* 955-958.

Southam-Gerow, M. A., Ringeisen, H. L., & Sherrill, J. T. (2006). Integrating interventions and services research: Progress and prospects. *Clinical Psychology: Science and Practice, 13,* 1-8.

Southam-Gerow, M. A., Weisz, J. R., & Kendall, P. C. (2003). Youth with anxiety disorders in research and service clinics: Examining client differences and similarities. *Journal of Clinical Child and Adolescent Psychology, 32,* 375-385.

Spangler, W. D. (1992). Validity of questionnaire and TAT measures of need for achievement: Two meta-analyses. *Psychological Bulletin, 112,* 140-154.

Spanos, N. P. (1994). Multiple identity enactments and multiple personality disorder. *Psychological Bulletin, 116,* 143-165.

Spearman, C. (1904). "General intelligence" objectively determined and measured. *American Journal of Psychology, 15,* 201-293.

Spence, S. H., Holmes, J. M., March, S., & Lipp, O. V. (2006). The feasibility and outcome of clinic plus internet delivery of cognitive-behavior therapy for childhood anxiety. *Journal of Consulting and Clinical Psychology, 74,* 614-621.

Sperry, L. (2007). *The ethical and professional practice of counseling and psychotherapy.* Upper Saddle River, NJ: Pearson.

Sperry, R. W. (1961). Cerebral organization and behavior. *Science, 133,* 1749-1757.

Sperry, R. W. (1968). Hemisphere deconnection and unity in conscious awareness. *American Psychologist, 23,* 723-733.

Sperry, R. W. (1974). Lateral specialization in the surgically separated hemispheres. In F. O. Schmitt & F. G. Worden (Eds.), *The neurosciences: Third study program* (pp. 5-20). Cambridge, MA: MIT Press.

Sperry, R. W. (1982). Some effects of disconnecting the cerebral hemispheres. *Science, 217,* 1223-1226.

Spiegel, T. A., Wadden, T. A., & Foster, G. D. (1991). Objective measurement of eating rate during behavioral treatment of obesity. *Behavior Therapy, 22,* 61-68.

Spiegler, M. D., & Guevremont, D. C. (1993). *Contemporary behavior therapy* (2nd ed.). Pacific Grove, CA: Brooks/Cole.

Spielberger, C. D., Gorsuch, R. L., Lushene, R., Vagg, P. R., & Jacobs, G. A. (1983). *Manual for the State-Trait Anxiety Inventory.* Palo Alto, CA: Consulting Psychologists Press.

Spielmans, G. I., Pasek, L. F., & McFall, J. P. (2007). What are the active ingredients in cognitive and behavioral psychotherapy for anxious and depressed children? A meta-analytic review. *Clinical Psychology Review, 27,* 642–654.

Spirito, A., & Esposito-Smythers, C. (2006). Addressing adolescent suicidal behavior: Cognitive-behavioral strategies. In P. C. Kendall (Ed.), *Child and adolescent therapy* (3rd ed., pp. 217–242). New York: Guilford.

Spitzer, R. L., Williams, J. B. W., Gibbon, M., & First, M. B. (1989). *Instruction manual for the Structured Clinical Interview for DSM-III-R (SCID).* Washington, DC: American Psychiatric Press.

Spring, B. (2007). Evidence-based practice in clinical psychology: What it is, why it matters, what you need to know. *Journal of Clinical Psychology, 63,* 611–631.

Sroufe, L. A., Egeland, B., Carlson, E. A., & Collins, W. A. (2005). *The development of the person: The Minnesota study of risk and adaptation from birth to adulthood.* New York: Guilford.

St. Lawrence, J. S., Brasfield, T. L., Jefferson, K. W., Alleyne, E., & O'Bannon, R. E., III (1995). Cognitive-behavioral intervention to reduce African American adolescents' risk for HIV infection. *Journal of Consulting & Clinical Psychology, 63,* 221–237.

Stahl, P. M. (1994). *Conducting child custody evaluations: A comprehensive guide.* Thousand Oaks, CA: Sage.

Stambor, Z. (2006). Psychology's prescribing pioneers. *Monitor on Psychology, July/August,* 30–32.

Standon, P. J., & Brown, D. J. (2005). Virtual reality in the rehabilitation of people with intellectual disabilities: Review. *CyberPsychology and Behavior, 8,* 272–282.

Stark, K. D., Hargrave, J., Sander, J., Custer, G., Schnoebelen, S., Simpson, J., & Molnar, J. (2006). Treatment of childhood depression: The ACTION treatment program. In P. C. Kendall (Ed.), *Child and adolescent therapy* (3rd ed., pp. 169–216). New York: Guilford.

Starkstein, S. E., & Robinson, R. G. (1988). Lateralized emotional response following stroke. In M. Kinsbourne (Ed.), *Cerebral hemisphere function in depression.* Washington, DC: American Psychiatric Press.

Staub, R. O. (2006). Health psychology: *A BioPsychoSocial approach.* New York: Worth.

Steadman, H. J. (1979). *Beating a rap? Defendants found incompetent to stand trial.* Chicago: University of Chicago Press.

Steadman, H. J. (1993). *Reforming the insanity defense: An evaluation of pre- and post-Hinckley reforms.* New York: Guilford.

Steele, R. G., & Roberts, M. C. (2005a). The future of mental health service delivery for children, adolescents, and families: An agenda for organization and research. In R. G. Steele & M. C. Roberts (Eds.), *Handbook of mental health services for children, adolescents, and families* (pp. 403–412). New York: Kluwer Academic/Plenum Publishers.

Steele, R. G., & Roberts, M. C. (2005b). Therapy and interventions research with children and adolescents. In M. C. Roberts & S. S. Ilardi (Eds.), *Handbook of research methods in clinical psychology* (pp. 307–326). Malden, MA: Blackwell Publishing.

Stein, B. D., Jaycox, L. H., Kataoka, S., Rhodes, H. J., & Vestal, K. D. (2003). Prevalence of child and adolescent exposure to community violence. *Clinical Child and Family Psychology Review, 6,* 247–264.

Stein, D. J. (2006). Advances in understanding the anxiety disorders: The cognitive-affective neuroscience of "false alarms." *Annals of Clinical Psychiatry, 18,* 173–182.

Steiner, J. L., Tebes, J. K., Sledge, W. H., & Walker, M. L. (1995). A comparison of the Structured Clinical Interview for DSM-III-R and clinical diagnoses. *Journal of Nervous and Mental Disease, 183,* 365–369.

Stepleman, L. M., Hann, G., Santos, M., & House, A. S. (2006). Reaching underserved HIV-positive individuals by using patient-centered psychological consultation. *Professional Psychology: Research and Practice, 37,* 75–82.

Stepp, S. D., Trull, T. J., Burr, R. M., Wolfenstein, M., & Vieth, A. Z. (2006). Incremental validity of the Structured Interview for the Five-Factor Model of Personality (SIFFM). *European Journal of Personality, 19,* 343–357.

Sternberg, R. J. (2004). Individual differences in cognitive development. In P. Smith & C. Hart (Eds.), *Blackwell handbook of cognitive development*. Malden, MA: Blackwell.

Sternberg, R. J. (2006a). *Cognitive psychology* (4th ed.). Belmont, CA: Wadsworth.

Sternberg, R. J. (2006b). Evidence-based practice: Gold standard, gold plated, or fool's gold? In C. D. Goodheart, A. E. Kazdin, & R. J. Sternberg (Eds.), *Evidence-based psychotherapy: Where practice and research meet* (pp. 261-271). Washington, DC: American Psychological Association.

Sternberg, R. J. (2007). *Career paths in psychology: Where your degree can take you* (2nd ed.). Washington, DC: American Psychological Association.

Sternberg, R. J., & Detterman, D. K. (Eds.). (1986). *What is intelligence? Contemporary viewpoints on its nature and definition*. Norwood, NJ: Ablex.

Stevens, M. R., & Reilly, R. R. (1980). MMPI short forms: A literature review. *Journal of Personality Assessment, 44*, 368-376.

Stewart, D. J., & Patterson, M. L. (1973). Eliciting effects of verbal and nonverbal cues on projective test responses. *Journal of Consulting and Clinical Psychology, 41*, 74-77.

Stewart, R. E., & Chambless, D. L. (2007). Does psychotherapy research inform treatment decisions in private practice? *Journal of Clinical Psychology, 63*, 267-281.

Stirman, S. W., & DeRubeis, R. J. (2006). Research patients and clinical trials are frequently representative of clinical practice. In J. C. Norcross, L. E. Beutler, & R. F. Levant (Eds.), *Evidence-based practice in mental health* (pp. 171-179). Washington, DC: American Psychological Association.

Stoerig, P. (2006). Blindsight, conscious vision, and the role of primary visual cortex. *Progress in Brain Research, 155*, 217-234.

Stokols, D. (1992). Establishing and maintaining healthy environments: Toward a social ecology of health promotion. *American Psychologist, 47*, 6-22.

Stolle, D. P., Wexler, D. B., & Winick, B. J. (Eds.). (2000). *Practicing Therapeutic Jurisprudence*. Durham: Carolina Academic Press.

Stolorow, R. D. (1993). An intersubjective view of the therapeutic process. *Bulletin of the Menninger Clinic, 57*, 450-458.

Stone, A. A., & Neale, J. M. (1984). New measures of daily coping: Developments and preliminary results. *Journal of Personality and Social Psychology, 46*, 892-906.

Stone, A. R., Frank, J. D., Nash, E. H., & Imber, S. D. (1961). An intensive five-year follow-up study of treated psychiatric outpatients. *Journal of Nervous and Mental Disease, 133*, 410-422.

Storch, E. A., & Crisp, H. L. (2004). Taking it to the schools: Transporting empirically supported treatments for childhood psychopathology to the school setting. *Clinical Child and Family Psychology Review, 7*, 191-193.

Storm, J., & Graham, J. R. (2000). Detection of coached general malingering on the MMPI-2. *Psychological Assessment, 12*, 158-165.

Strachey, J., & Freud, S. (2000). *The standard edition of the complete psychological works of Sigmund Freud*. New York: W. W. Norton.

Straub, R. O. (2006). *Health psychology: A biopsychosocial approach* (2nd ed.). New York: Worth Publishers.

Strauss, E., & Wada, J. (1983). Lateral preferences and cerebral speech dominance. *Cortex, 19*, 165-177.

Stricker, G. (2000). The scientist-practitioner model: Gandhi was right again. *American Psychologist, 55*, 253-254.

Stricker, G., & Gold, J. (Eds.). (2006). *A casebook of psychotherapy integration*. Washington, DC: American Psychological Association.

Strohmer, D. C., & Shivy, V. A. (1994). Bias in counselor hypothesis testing: Testing the robustness of counselor confirmatory bias. *Journal of Counseling and Development, 73*, 191-197.

Strother, C. R. (1956). *Psychology and mental health*. Washington, DC: American Psychological Association.

Strupp, H. H. (1960). Psychotherapists in action: Explorations of the therapist's contribution to the treatment process. New York: Grune & Stratton.

Strupp, H. H. (1989). Psychotherapy: Can the practitioner learn from the researcher? *American Psychologist, 44*, 717-724.

Strupp, H. H., & Blinder, J. L. (1984). *Psychotherapy in a new key:A guide to time-limited dynamic psychotherapy*. New York: Basic Books.

Stuart, R. B. (1969). Operant-interpersonal treatment of marital discord. *Journal of Consulting and Clinical Psychology, 33,* 675-682.

Stuart, R. B., & Lilienfeld, S. O. (2007). The evidence missing from evidence-based practice. *American Psychologist, 62,* 615-616.

Stuss, D. T. & Alexander, M. P. (2000). Executive functions and the frontal lobes: A conceptual view. *Psychological Research, 63* (3-4), 289-298.

Suarez, T., & Reese, F. L. (2000). Coping, psychological adjustment, and complementary and alternative medicine use in persons living with HIV and AIDS. *Psychology and Health, 15,* 635-649.

Suarez-Balcazar, Y., Durlak, J., & Smith, C. (1994). Multicultural training practices in community psychology programs. *American Journal of Community Psychology, 22,* 785-798.

Sue, D. W., & Sue, D. (1999). *Counseling the culturally different* (3rd ed.). New York: Wiley.

Sue, S. (1999). Science, ethnicity and bias: Where have we gone wrong? *American Psychologist, 54,* 1070-1077.

Sue, S., Fujino, D. C., Hu, L. T., Takeuchi, D. T., et al. (1991). Community mental health services for ethnic minority groups: A test of the cultural responsiveness hypothesis. *Journal of Consulting and Clinical Psychology, 59,* 533-540.

Suh, C. S., Strupp, H. H., & O'Malley, S. S. (1986). The Vanderbilt process measures: The Psychotherapy Process Scale (VPPS) and the Negative Indicators Scale (VNIS). In L. Greenberg & W. Pinsof (Eds.), *The psychotherapeutic process: A research handbook* (pp. 285-323). New York: Guilford.

Sullivan, H. S. (1953). *The interpersonal theory of psychiatry*. New York: W. W. Norton.

Sullivan, M. F., KSkovholt, T. M., & Jennings, L. (2005). Master therapists' construction of the therapeutic relationship. *Journal of Mental Health Counseling, 27,* 48-70.

Suls, J., & Wang, C. K. (1993). The relationship between trait hostility and cardiovascular reactivity: A quantitative review and analysis. *Psychophysiology, 30,* 1-12.

Sultan, S., Andronkiof, A., Reveillere, C., & Lemmel, G. (2006). A Rorschach stability study in a nonpatient adult sample. *Journal of Personality Assessment, 87,* 330-348.

Sundberg, N. D., Tyler, L. E., & Taplin, J. R. (1973). *Clinical psychology: Expanding horizons* (2nd ed.). Englewood Cliffs, NJ: Prentice-Hall.

Super, J. T. (1999). Forensic psychology and law enforcement. In A. K. Hess & I. B. Weiner (Eds.), *The handbook of forensic psychology* (2nd ed., pp. 409-439). New York: Wiley.

Swain, M. A., & Steckel, S. B. (1981). Influencing adherence among hypertensives. *Research Nursing and Health, 4,* 213-218.

Sweet, A. A. (1984). The therapeutic relationship in behavior therapy. *Clinical Psychology Review, 4,* 253-272.

Swierc, S. F., & Routh, D. K. (2003). Introduction to the special issues on international clinical psychology. *Journal of Clinical Psychology, 59,* 631-634.

Tallent, N. (1976). *Psychological report writing*. Englewood Cliffs, NJ: Prentice-Hall.

Tallent, N. (1992). *The practice of psychological assessment*. Englewood Cliffs, NJ: Prentice-Hall.

Tallent, N., & Reiss, W. J. (1959). Multidisciplinary views on the preparation of written psychological reports. *Journal of Clinical Psychology, 15,* 444-446.

Taplin, P. S., & Reid, J. B. (1973). Effects of instructional set and experimenter influence on observer reliability. *Child Development, 44,* 547-554.

Task Force on Promotion and Dissemination of Psychological Procedures (1995). Training in and dissemination of empirically validated psychological treatments: Report and recommendations. *Clinical Psychologist, 48,* 3-23.

Tavris, C., & Aronson, E. (2007). *Mistakes were made (but not by me)*. New York: Harcourt.

Taylor, E. (2000). Psychotherapeutics and the problematic origins of clinical psychology in America. *American Psychologist, 55,* 1029-1033.

Taylor, S. E. (1995). *Health psychology*. New York: McGraw-Hill.

Taylor, S. E. (1999). *Health psychology* (4th ed.). New York: McGraw-Hill.

Taylor, S. E. (2005). *Health psychology.* Boston: McGraw-Hill.

Taylor, S. E., Kemeny, M. E., Reed, G. M., Bower, J. E., & Gruenewald, T. L. (2000). Psychological resources, positive illusions, and health. *American Psychologist, 55,* 99-109.

Teasdale, A. C., & Hill, C. E. (2006). Preferences of therapists-in-training for client characteristics. *Psychotherapy: Theory, Research, Practice, Training, 43,* 111-118.

Teglasi, H. (2001). *Essentials of TAT and other storytelling techniques assessment.* Hoboken, NJ: Wiley.

Tellegen, A. (1982). *Brief manual for the Multidimensional Personality Questionnaire.* Unpublished manuscript, University of Minnesota.

Tellegen, A., & Ben-Porath, Y. S. (1992). The new uniform T scores for the MMPI-2: Rationale, derivation, and appraisal. *Psychological Assessment, 4,* 145-155.

Temerlin, M. K. (1968). Suggestion effects in psychiatric diagnosis. *Journal of Nervous and Mental Disease, 147,* 349-353.

Templer, D. I. (2005). Addendum to concerns about professional schools. *Psychological Reports, 97,* 117-118.

Templer, D. I., & Tomeo, M. E. (2000). Examination for professional practice in psychology subtest scores of professional and traditional clinical psychology program graduates. *Journal of Psychology: Interdisciplinary and Applied, 134,* 140-142.

Tennen, H., Affleck, G., Armeli, S., & Carney, M. A. (2000). A daily process approach to coping. *American Psychologist, 55,* 626-636.

Testa, M., & Collins, R. L. (1997). Alcohol and risky sexual behavior: Event-based analyses among a sample of high-risk women. *Psychology of Addictive Behaviors, 11,* 190-201.

Testa, M., VanZile-Tamsen, C., & Livingston, J. A. (2005). Childhood sexual abuse, relationship satisfaction, and sexual risk taking in a community sample of women. *Journal of Consulting and Clinical Psychology, 73,* 1116-1124.

Thelen, M. H., Farmer, J., Wonderlich, S., & Smith, M. (1991). A revision of the Bulimia Test: The BULIT-R. *Psychological Assessment, 3,* 119-124.

Thienemann, M. (2004). Introducing a structured interview into a clinical setting. *Journal of the American Academy of Child & Adolescent Psychiatry, 43,* 1057-1060.

Thoits, P. A. (1986). Social support as coping assistance. *Journal of Consulting and Clinical Psychology, 54,* 416-423.

Thomas, A., & Chess, S. (1977). *Temperament and development.* New York: Brunner/Mazel.

Thomas, A., Chess, S., & Birch, H. G. (1968). *Temperament and behavior disorders in children.* New York: New York University Press.

Thomas, J. T. (2005). Licensing board complaints: Minimizing the impact on the psychologist's defense and clinical practice. *Professional Psychology: Research and Practice, 36,* 426-433.

Thoresen, C. E., & Powell, L. H. (1992). Type A behavior pattern: New perspectives on theory, assessment, and intervention. *Journal of Consulting and Clinical Psychology, 60,* 595-604.

Thorn, B. E. (2007). Evidence-based practice in psychology. *Journal of Clinical Psychology, 63,* 607-609.

Thorn, B. E., & Kuhajda, M. C. (2006). Group cognitive therapy for chronic pain. *Journal of Clinical Psychology, 62,* 1355-1366.

Thorne, F. C. (1972). Clinical judgment. In R. H. Woody & J. D. Woody (Eds.), *Clinical assessment in counseling and psychotherapy* (pp. 30-85). Englewood Cliffs, NJ: Prentice-Hall.

Thorpe, G. L., & Olson, S. L., (1997). *Behavior therapy: Concepts, procedures, and applications* (2nd ed.). Boston: Allyn & Bacon.

Thunnissen, M., Remans, Y., & Trijsburg, W. (2006). Premature termination of short-term inpatient psychotherapy clients: Clients' perspectives on causes and effects. *Therapeutic Communities: International Journal for Therapeutic and Supportive Organizations, 27,* 265-273.

Tisdelle, D. A., & St. Lawrence, J. S. (1988). Adolescent interpersonal problem-solving skill training: Social validation and generalization. *Behavior Therapy, 19,* 171–182.

Tomlinson, S. M., & Cheatham, H. E. (1989). Effects of counselor intake judgments on service to Black students using a university counseling center. *Counseling Psychology Quarterly, 2,* 105–111.

Tomlinson-Clarke, S., & Camilli, G. (1995). An exploratory study of counselor judgments in multicultural research. *Journal of Multicultural Counseling and Development, 23,* 237–245.

Trickett, E. J., Barone, C., & Watts, R. (2000). Contextual influences in mental health consultation: Toward an ecological perspective on radiating change. In J. Rappaport & E. Seidman (Eds.), *Handbook of community psychology* (pp. 303–330). New York: Kluwer Academic/Plenum Publishers.

Tryon, G. S. (1990). Session depth and smoothness in relation to the concept of engagement in counseling. *Journal of Counseling Psychology, 37,* 248–253.

Tucker, N. (2001, December 11). High court passes on Capitol suspect. *The Washington Post,* B1.

Turk, D. C., & Rudy, T. E. (1990). Pain. In A. S. Bellack, M. Hersen, & A. E. Kazdin (Eds.), *International handbook of behavior modification and therapy* (2nd ed., pp. 399–413). New York: Plenum Press.

Turner, S. M., Beidel, D. C., Dancu, C. V., & Stanley, M. A. (1989). An empirically derived inventory to measure social fears and anxiety: The Social Phobia and Anxiety Inventory. *Psychological Assessment: Journal of Consulting and Clinical Psychology, 1,* 35–40.

Turner, S. M., Hersen, M., & Heiser, N. (2003). The interviewing process. In M. Hersen & S. M. Turner (Eds.), Diagnostic interviewing (3rd ed.). New York: Wiley and Sons.

Tutin, J. (1993). The persistence of initial beliefs in clinical judgment. *Journal of Social and Clinical Psychology, 12,* 319–335.

Tversky, A., & Kahneman, D. (1974). Judgment under uncertainty: Heuristics and biases. *Science, 185,* 1124–1131.

Tyler, K. L., & Malessa, R. (2000). The Goltz-Ferrier debates and the triumph of cerebral localizationalist theory. *Neurology, 55,* 1015–1024.

Tyrka, A. R., Cannon, T., Haslam, N., Mednick, S., Schulsinger, F., Schulsinger, H., & Parnas, J. (1995). The latent structure of schizotypy: I. Premorbid indicators of a taxon of individuals at risk for schizophrenia spectrum disorders. *Journal of Abnormal Psychology, 104,* 173–183.

U.S. Public Health Service. (2000). Report on the Surgeon General's Conference on Children's Mental Health: A National Action Agenda. Washington, DC: Author.

U.S. Surgeon General. (1999). *Mental health: A report of the surgeon general.* Rockville, MD: U.S. Department of Health and Human Services.

Ullmann, L. P., & Krasner, L. (Eds.). (1965). *Case studies in behavior modification.* New York: Holt, Rinehart & Winston.

Ullmann, L. P., & Krasner, L. (1975). *A psychological approach to abnormal behavior.* Englewood Cliffs, NJ: Prentice-Hall.

Unger, W. S., Wattenberg, M. S., Foy, D. W., & Glynn, S. M. (2006). Trauma-focus group therapy: An evidence-based group approach to trauma with adults. In L. A. Schein, H. I. Spitz, G. M. Burlingame, P. R. Muskin, & S. Vargo (Eds.), *Psychological effects of catastrophic disasters: Group approaches to treatment* (pp. 731–786). New York: Haworth Press.

Ungerleider, L. G., & Mishkin, M. (1982). Two cortical visual systems. In D. J. Ingle, M. A. Goodale, & R. J. W. Mansfield (Eds.), *Analysis of visual behavior.* Cambridge, MA: MIT Press.

Urban Institute (2004). Race, ethnicity, and economic well-being. *Snapshots of America's families, March 2004.* Washington, DC: Author.

Vaillant, G. E. (1977). *Adaptation to life.* Boston: Little, Brown.

Vaillant, G. E. (1984). The disadvantages of DSM-II outweigh its advantages. *American Journal of Psychiatry, 141,* 542–545.

Vaillant, G. E. (2000). Adaptive mental mechanisms: Their role in a positive psychology. *American Psychologist, 55,* 89–98.

Vallis, T. M., & Howes, J. L. (1995). The field of clinical psychology: Arriving at a definition. *Canadian Psychology, 37,* 120–127.

Van der Maas, H. L. J., Dolan, C. V., Grasman, R. P. P. P., Wicherts, J. M., et al. (2006). A dynamical model of general intelligence: The positive manifold of intelligence mutualism. *Psychological Review, 113,* 842–861.

Van Horne, B. A. (2004). Psychology licensing board disciplinary actions: The realities. *Professional Psychology: Research and Practice, 35,* 170–178.

VandenBos, G. R. (1993). U.S. mental health policy: Proactive evolution in the midst of health care reform. *American Psychologist, 48,* 283–290.

VandenBos, G. R., DeLeon, P. H., & Belar, C. D. (1991). How many psychological practitioners are needed? It's too early to know. *Professional Psychology: Research and Practice, 22,* 441–448.

Vane, J. R. (1981). The Thematic Apperception Test: A review. *Clinical Psychology Review, 1,* 319–336.

Van Zeijl, J., Mesman, J., Ijzendoorn, M. H. V., Bakermans-Kranenburg, M. J., Juffer, F., Stolk, M. N., Koot, H. M., & Alink, L. R. A. (2006). Attachment-based intervention for enhancing sensitive discipline in mothers of 1- to 3-year-old children at risk for externalizing behavior problems: A randomized controlled trial. *Journal of Consulting and Clinical Psychology, 74,* 994–1005.

Vasquez, M. J. T., & Jones, J. M. (2006). Increasing the number of psychologists of color: Public policy issues for affirmative diversity. *American Psychologist, 61,* 132–142.

Velting, O. N., Setzer, N. J., & Albano, A. M. (2004). Update on advances in assessment and cognitive-behavioral treatment of anxiety disorders in children and adolescents. *Professional Psychology: Research and Practice, 35,* 42–54.

Verduin, T. L., & Kendall, P. C. (2003). Differential occurrence of comorbidity within childhood anxiety disorders. *Journal of Clinical Child and Adolescent, 32,* 290–295.

Verfaellie, M., & Keane, M. M. (1997). The neural basis of aware and unaware forms of memory. *Seminars in Neurology, 17,* 153–61.

Verheul, R., & Widiger, T. A. (2004). A meta-analysis of the prevalence and usage of the personality disorder not otherwise specified (PDNOS) diagnosis. *Journal of Personality Disorders, 18,* 309–319.

Vermande, M. M., van den Bercken, J. H., & De Bruyn, E. E. (1996). Effects of diagnostic classification systems on clinical hypothesis generation. *Journal of Psychopathology and Behavioral Assessment, 18,* 49–70.

Viken, R. J., & McFall, R. M. (1994). Paradox lost: Implications of contemporary reinforcement theory for behavior therapy. *Current Directions in Psychological Science, 3,* 121–125.

Viliello, B. (2001). Psychopharmacology for young children: Clinical needs and research opportunities. *Pediatrics, 108,* 983–989.

Vincent, G. M. (2006). Psychopathy and violence risk assessment in youth. *Child and Adolescent Psychiatric Clinics of North America, 15,* 407–428.

Vittengl, J. R., Clark, L. A., Dunn, T. W., & Jarrett, R. B. (2007). Reducing relapse and recurrence in unipolar depression: A comparative meta-analysis of cognitive-behavioral therapy's effects. *Journal of Consulting and Clinical Psychology, 75,* 475–488.

Wada, J., & Rasmussen, T. (1960). Intracarotid injection of sodium amytal for the lateralization of cerebral speech dominance. *Journal of Neurosurgery, 17,* 266–282.

Wadsworth, M. E., & Berger, L. E. (2006). Adolescents coping with poverty-related family stress: Prospective predictors of coping and psychological symptoms. *Journal of Youth and Adolescence, 35,* 57–70.

Wakefield, P. J., Williams, R. E., Yost, E. B., & Patterson, K. M. (1996). *Couple therapy for alcoholism: A cognitive-behavioral treatment manual.* New York: Guilford.

Walker, B. B., & London, S. (2007). Novel tools and resources for evidence-based practice in psychology. *Journal of Clinical Psychology, 63,* 633–642.

Walker, E. F., Grimes, K. E., Davis, D. M., & Smith, A. J. (1993). Childhood precursors of schizophrenia: Facial expressions of emotion. *American Journal of Psychiatry, 150,* 1654–1660.

Wallace, B. A., & Shapiro, S. L. (2006). Mental balance and well-being: Building bridges between Buddhism and western psychology. *American Psychologist, 61,* 690–701.

Wallen, R. W. (1956). *Clinical psychology: The study of persons*. New York: McGraw-Hill.

Wallin, A., & Ahlström, G. (2006). Cross cultural interview studies using interpreters: Systematic literature review. *Journal of Advanced Nursing, 55,* 723-735.

Walsh, B. W., & Betz, N. E. (2001). *Tests and assessment* (4th ed.). Upper Saddle River, NJ: Prentice Hall.

Walsh, R., & Shapiro, S. L. (2006). The meeting of meditative disciplines and western psychology: A mutually enriching dialogue. *American Psychologist, 61,* 227-239.

Walter, A., Bundy, C., & Dornan, T. (2005). How should trainees be taught to open a clinical interview? *Medical Education, 39,* 492-496.

Wamboldt, M. A., & Reiss, D. (2006). Genetic strategies for clarifying a nosology of relational distress. *Journal of Family Psychology, 20,* 378-385.

Wampold, B. E. (2001). The great psychotherapy debate: Models, methods, and findings. Mahwah, NJ: Erlbaum.

Wampold, B. E., Lichtenberg, J. W., & Waehler, C. A. (2005). A broader perspective: Counseling psychology's emphasis on evidence. *Journal of Contemporary Psychotherapy, 35,* 27-38.

Wampold, B. E., Mondin, G. W., Moody, M., Stich, F., Benson, K., et al. (1997). A meta-analysis of outcome studies comparing bona fide psychotherapies: Empirically "all must have prizes." *Psychological Bulletin, 122,* 203-215.

Wang, P. S., Berglund, P., Olfson, M., Pincus, H. A., Wells, K. B., & Kessler, R. C. (2005). Twelve-month use of mental health services in the United States: Results from the National Comorbidity Survey Replication. *Archives of General Psychiatry, 62,* 603-613.

Wang, P. S., Lane, M., Olfson, M., Pincus, H. A., Wells, K. B., & Kessler, R. C. (2005). Twelve-month use of mental health services in the United States. *Archives of General Psychiatry, 62,* 629-640.

Ward, C. H., Beck, A. T., Mendelson, M., Mock, J. E., & Erbaugh, J. K. (1962). The psychiatric nomenclature. *Archives of General Psychiatry, 7,* 198-205.

Ward, J. C., & Naster, B. J. (1991). Reliability of an observational system used to monitor behavior in a mental health residential treatment unit. *Journal of Mental Health Administration, 18,* 64-68.

Ward, L. C. (2006). Comparison of facture structure models for the Beck Depression Inventory-II. *Psychological Assessment, 18,* 81-88.

Ward, T. (1999). Method, judgment, and clinical reasoning. *Behaviour Change, 16,* 4-9.

Watkins, L. E., Jr., Campbell, V. L., Nieberding, K., & Hallmark, R. (1995). Contemporary practice of psychological assessment by clinical psychologists. *Professional Psychology: Research and Practice, 26,* 54-60.

Watson, D. (2005). Rethinking the mood and anxiety disorders: A quantitative hierarchical ⌐ for DSM-V. *Journal of Abnormal P⌐ 114,* 522-536.

Watson, D., & Friend, R. (⌐   ⌐ent of social-evaluative anxie⌐ ⌐urnal of Consulting and Clinical Psych⌐ *33,* 448-457.

Watson, J. B. (1924). *Behavior.* New York: W. W. Norton.

Watson, J. B. (1930). *Behaviorism* (rev. ed.). New York: W. W. Norton.

Watson, R. I. (1953a). A brief history of clinical psychology. *Psychological Bulletin, 50,* 321-346.

Watson, R. I. (1953b). Measuring the effectiveness of psychotherapy: Problems for investigators. *Journal of Clinical Psychology, 8,* 60-64.

Watson, R. I. (1978). *The great psychologists* (2nd ed.). Philadelphia, PA: Lippincott.

Wearden, A. J., Tarrier, N., Barrowclough, C., Zastowny, T. R., & Rahill, A. A. (2000). A review of expressed emotion research in health care. *Clinical Psychology Review, 20,* 633-666.

Webb, E., Campbell, D. T., Schwartz, R. D., & Sechrest, L. B. (1966). *Unobtrusive measures: Nonreactive research in the social sciences.* Chicago: Rand-McNally.

Wechsler, D. (1967). *Manual for the WPPSI.* New York: Psychological Corporation.

Wechsler, D. (2003). *WISC-IV technical and interpretive manual.* San Antonio, TX: The Psychological Corporation.

Weeks, G. R., & Treat, S. R. (2001). *Couples in treatment: Techniques and approaches for effective practice* (2nd ed.). New York: Brunner-Routledge.

Weick, K. E. (1968). Systematic observational methods. In G. Lindzey & E. Aronson (Eds.), *Handbook of social psychology* (Vol. 2, 2nd ed., pp. 357–451). Reading, MA: Addison-Wesley.

Weiner, B. (Ed.). (1974). *Achievement motivation and attribution*. Morristown, NJ: General Learning Press.

Weiner, I. (2000). Using the Rorschach properly in practice and in research. *Journal of Clinical Psychology, 56*, 435–438.

Weiner, I. B., & Hess, A. K. (Eds.). (2006). *The handbook of forensic psychology* (3rd ed.). Hoboken, NJ: Wiley.

Weiss, B., Catron, T., Harris, V., & Phung, T. M. (1999). The effectiveness of child psychotherapy. *Journal of Consulting and Clinical Psychology, 67*, 82–94.

Weiss, R. D., Najavits, L. M., Muenz, L. R., & Hufford, C. (1995). Twelve-month test-retest reliability of the Structured Clinical Interview for DSM-III-R Personality Disorders in cocaine-dependent patients. *Comprehensive Psychiatry, 36*, 384–389.

Weissberg, R. P., Kumpfer, K. L., & Seligman, M. E. P. (2003). Prevention that works for children and youth: An introduction. *American Psychologist, 58*, 425–432.

Weissman, H. N. (1991). Child custody evaluations: Fair and unfair professional practices. *Behavioral Sciences and the Law, 9*, 469–476.

Weissman, M. M., Verdell, H., Gameroff, M. J., Bledsoe, S. E., Betts, K., et al. (2006). National survey of psychotherapy training in psychiatry, psychology, and social work. *Archives of General Psychiatry, 63*, 925–934.

Weisz, J. R. (July, 2001). Two traditions in psychotherapy with children and adolescents: The state of the evidence. Paper presented at the second biennial Niagara Conference on Evidence-based Treatments for childhood and adolescent mental health problems. Niagara-on-the-Lake.

Weisz, J. R. (2004). *Psychotherapy for children and adolescents: Evidence-based treatments and case examples*. New York: Cambridge University Press.

Weisz, J. R., & Addis, M. E. (2006). The research-practice tango and other choreographic challenges: Using and testing evidence-based psychotherapies in clinical care settings. In C. D. Goodheart, A. E. Kazdin, & R. J. Sternberg (Eds.), *Evidence-based psychotherapy: Where practice and research meet* (pp. 179–206). Washington, DC: American Psychological Association.

Weisz, J. R., Donenberg, G. R., Han, S. S., & Weiss, B. (1995). Bridging the gap between laboratory and clinic in child and adolescent psychotherapy. *Journal of Consulting and Clinical Psychology, 63*, 688–701.

Weisz, J. R., Doss, A. J., & Hawley, K. M. (2005). Youth psychotherapy outcome research: A review and critique of the evidence base. *Annual Review of Psychology, 56*, 337–363.

Weisz, J. R., Jensen-Doss, A., & Hawley, K. M. (2006). Evidence-based youth psychotherapies versus usual clinical care: A meta-analysis of direct comparisons. *American Psychologist, 61*, 671–689.

Weisz, J. R., McCarty, C. A., & Valeri, S. M. (2006). Effects of psychotherapy for depression in children and adolescents: A meta-analysis. *Psychological Bulletin, 132*, 132–149.

Weisz, J. R., Sandler, I. N., Durlak, J. A., & Anton, B. S. (2005). Promoting and protecting youth mental health through evidence-based prevention and treatment. *American Psychologist, 60*, 628–648.

Weisz, J. R., Sandler, I. N., Durlak, J. A., & Anton, B. S. (2006). A proposal to unite two different worlds of children's mental health. *American Psychologist, 61*, 644–645.

Wekerle, C., & Wolfe, D. A. (2003). Child maltreatment. In E. J. Mash & R. A. Barkley (Eds.), *Child psychopathology* (2nd ed., pp. 632–684). New York: Guilford.

Wellmer, J., Fernandez, G., Linke, D. B., Urbach, H., Elger, C. E., & Kurthen, M. (2005). Unilateral intracarotid amobarbital procedure for language lateralization *Epilepsia, 46*(11), 1764–1772.

Wells, M., Sarna, L., Cooley, M. E., Brown, J. K., Chernecky, C., Williams, R. D., et al. (2007). Use of complementary and alternative medicine therapies to control symptoms in women living with lung cancer. *Cancer Nursing, 30*, 45–55.

Welsh, B. C., & Farrington, D. P. (2007). Saving children from a life of crime: Toward a national strategy for early prevention. *Victims and Offenders, 2,* 1-20.

Welsh, J. A., & Bierman, K. L. (2003). Using the clinical interview to assess children's interpersonal reasoning and emotional understanding. In C. R. Reynolds & R. W. Kamphaus (Eds.), *Handbook of psychological and educational assessment of children: Personality, behavior, and context* (2nd ed., pp. 219-234). New York: Guilford.

Wenar, C., & Kerig, P. (2006). *Developmental psychopathology: From infancy through adolescence* (5th ed.). Boston: McGraw Hill.

Werner, E. E. (2005). What can we learn about resilience from large-scale longitudinal studies? In S. Goldstein & R. B. Brooks (Eds.), *Handbook of resilience in children* (pp. 91-105). New York: Kluwer Academic/Plenum Publishers.

West, M., Bondy, E., & Hutchinson, S. (1991). Interviewing institutionalized elders: Threats to validity. *Journal of Nursing Scholarship, 23,* 171-176.

West, S. L., & O'Neal, K. K. (2004). Project D.A.R.E outcome effectiveness revisited. *American Journal of Public Health, 94,* 1027-1029.

Westen, D. (1998). The scientific legacy of Sigmund Freud: Toward a psychodynamically informed psychological science. *Psychological Bulletin, 124,* 333-371.

Westen, D. (2006). Patients and treatments in clinical trials are not adequately representative of clinical practice. In J. C. Norcross, L. E. Beutler, & R. F. Levant (Eds.), *Evidence-based practice in mental health* (pp. 161-171). Washington, DC: American Psychological Association.

Westen, D., & Bradley, R. (2005). Empirically supported complexity: Rethinking evidence-based practice in psychotherapy. *Current Directions in Psychological Science, 14,* 266-271.

Westen, D., & Morrison, K. (2001). A multidimensional meta-analysis of treatments for depression, panic, and generalized anxiety disorder: An empirical examination of the status of empirically supported therapies. *Journal of Consulting and Clinical Psychology, 69,* 875-899.

Whisman, M. A., & Uebelacker, L. A. (2006). Impairment and distress associated with relations discord in a national sample of married or cohabiting adults. *Journal of Family Psychology, 20,* 369-377.

Wicas, E. A., & Mahan, T. W. (1966). Characteristics of counselors rated effective by supervisors and peers. *Counselor Education and Supervision, 6,* 50-56.

Wicherski, M., Frincke, J., & Kohout, J. (2006). 2005-2006 faculty salaries in graduate departments of psychology. American Psychological Association Research Office. Retrieved December, 28, 2006, from http://research.apa.org/facsals0506.pdf.

Wicks-Nelson, R., & Israel, A. C. (2006). *Behavior disorders of childhood* (6th ed.). Upper Saddle River, NJ: Pearson/Prentice Hall.

Widiger, T. A., Frances, A. J., Pincus, H. A., Davis, W. W., & First, M. B. (1991). Toward an empirical classification for the DSM-IV. *Journal of Abnormal Psychology, 100,* 280-288.

Widiger, T. A., & Sankis, L. M. (2000). Adult psychopathology: Issues and controversies. *Annual Review of Psychology, 51,* 377-404.

Widiger, T. A., & Trull, T. J. (2007). Plate tectonics in the classification of personality disorder: Shifting to a dimensional model. *American Psychologist, 62,* 71-83.

Wiggins, J. G. (1994). Would you want your child to be a psychologist? *American Psychologist, 49,* 485-492.

Wiggins, J. G., & Wedding, D. (2004). Prescribing, professional identity, and costs. *Professional Psychology: Research and Practice, 35,* 148-150.

Wiggins, J. S. (1973). Personality and prediction: Principles of personality assessment. Reading, MA: Addison-Wesley.

Wiggins, J. S. (1981). Clinical and statistical prediction: Where are we and where do we go from here? *Clinical Psychology Review, 1,* 3-18.

Wilkinson, G. S. (1993). *WRAT-3: Wide range achievement test administration manual.* Wilmington, DE: Wide Range, Inc.

Willams, R. B. (2001). Hostility and heart disease. *Advances in Mind-Body Medicine, 17,* 52-55.

Williams, C. L., Arnold, C. B., & Wynder, E. L. (1977). Primary prevention of chronic disease beginning in childhood: The Know Your Body Program: Design of study. *Preventive Medicine, 6,* 344-357.

Williams, C. R., & Abeles, N. (2004). Issues and implications of deaf culture in therapy. *Professional Psychology: Research and Practice, 35,* 643-648.

Williams, R. B., Jr., & Barefoot, J. C. (1988). Coronary-prone behavior: The emerging role of the hostility complex. In B. K. Houston & C. R. Snyder (Eds.), *Type A behavior pattern: Research, theory and intervention* (pp. 189-211). New York: Wiley.

Williams, S., Kohout, J. L., & Wicherski, M. (2000). Salary changes among independent psychologists by gender and experience. *Psychiatric Services, 51,* 1111.

Williams, T. R. (1967). *Field methods in the study of culture.* New York: Holt, Rinehart, & Winston.

Winerman, L. (2005). The mind's mirror. *Monitor on Psychology, 37,* 48-50.

Winnicott, D. W. (1965). *The maturational processes and the facilitating environment.* New York: International Universities Press.

Winocur. G., Craik, F. I., Levine, B., Robertson, I. H., Binns, M. A., Alexander, M., et al. (2007). Cognitive rehabilitation in the elderly: Overview and future directions. *Journal of the International Neuropsychology Society, 13,* 166-171.

Winsor, A. P. (2003). Direct behavioral observation for classrooms. In C. R. Reynolds & R. W. Kamphaus (Eds.), *Handbook of psychological and educational assessment of children: Personality, behavior, and context* (2nd ed., pp. 248-255). New York: Guilford.

Witmer, L. (1897). The organization of practical work in psychology. *Psychological Review, 4,* 116-117.

Wittchen, H. U. (1994). Reliability and validity studies of the WHO-Composite International Diagnostic Interview (CIDI): A critical review. *Journal of Psychiatric Research, 28,* 57-84.

Wolff, J. C., & Ollendick, T. H. (2006). The comorbidity of conduct problems and depression in childhood and adolescence. *Clinical Child and Family Psychology Review, 9,* 201-220.

Wolitzky, D. L. (2003). The theory and practice of traditional psychoanalytic treatment. In A. S. Gurman & S. B. Messer (Eds.), *Essential Psychotherapies* (2nd ed., pp. 244-68). New York: Guilford.

Wolpe, J. (1958). *Psychotherapy by reciprocal inhibition.* Stanford, CA: Stanford University Press.

Wolpe, J. (1982). *The practice of behavior therapy* (3rd ed.). New York: Pergamon Press.

Wolpe, J., & Lang, P. J. (1969). *Fear Survey Schedule.* San Diego: Educational and Industrial Testing Service.

Wolpe, J., & Lazarus, A. A. (1966). *Behavior therapy techniques: A guide to the treatment of neuroses.* New York: Pergamon Press.

Wood, J. M., Lilienfeld, S., Garb, H., & Nezworski, M. (2000). The Rorschach Test in clinical diagnoses: A critical review with a backward look at Garfield (1947). *Journal of Clinical Psychology, 56,* 395-430.

Wood, J. M., Nezworski, T., Lilienfeld, S. O., & Garb, H. N. (Eds.). (2003). *What's wrong with the Rorschach: Science confronts the controversial inkblot test.* San Francisco: Jossey-Bass.

Woodcock, R. W., McGrew, K. S., & Mather, N. (2000). *Woodcock-Johnson III.* Itasca, IL: Riverside Publishing.

Woodworth, R. S. (1920). *Personal data sheet.* Chicago: Stoelting.

Woody, S. R., Detweiler-Bedel, J., Teachman, B. A., & O'Hern, T. (2005). *Treatment planning for psychotherapy: Taking the guesswork out of clinical care.* New York: Guilford.

Wortman, C. B., & Lehman, D. R. (1985). Reactions to victims of life crises: Support attempts that fail. In I. G. Sarason & B. R. Sarason (Eds.), *Social support: Theory, research, and applications* (pp. 463-489). Dordrecht, The Netherlands: Martinus Nijhoff.

Wright, J. H., Basco, M. R., & Thase, M. E. (2006). *Learning cognitive-behavior therapy.* Washington, DC: American Psychiatric Association.

Wright, J. H., Wright, A. S., Albano, A. M., Basco, M. R., Goldsmith, L. J., Raffield, T., & Otto, M. W. (2005). Computer-assisted cognitive therapy for depression: Maintaining efficacy while reducing therapist time. *American Journal of Psychiatry, 162,* 1158-1164.

Wright, M. O., & Masten, A. S. (2005). Resilience processes in development: Fostering positive adaptation in the context of adversity. In S. Goldstein & R. B. Brooks (Eds.), *Handbook of resilience in children* (pp. 17-37). New York: Kluwer Academic/Plenum.

Wright, P. W. D., & Wright, P. D. (2005). *IDEA 2004*. Hartfield, VA: Harbor House Law Press.

Wright, R. H. (2005). The myth of continuing education: A look at some intended and (maybe) unintended consequences. In R. H. Wright & N. A. Cummings (Eds.), *Destructive trends in mental health: The well-intentioned path to harm* (pp. 143-151). New York: Routledge/Taylor and Francis Group.

Wrightsman, L. S., & Fulero, S. M. (2005). *Forensic psychology* (2nd ed.). Belmont, CA: Thomson-Wadsworth.

Wrightsman, L. S., Nietzel, M., Fortune, W., & Greene, E. (2002). *Psychology and the legal system* (5th ed.). Pacific Grove, CA: Brooks/Cole.

Wulfert, E., Greenway, D. E., & Dougher, M. J. (1996). A logical functional analysis of reinforcement-based disorders: Alcoholism and pedophilia. *Journal of Consulting and Clinical Psychology, 64,* 1140-1151.

Wulsin, L. R., & Singal, B. M. (2003). Do depressive symptoms increase the risk for the onset of coronary disease? A systematic quantitative review. *Psychosomatic Medicine, 65,* 201-210.

Yalom, I. D., & Leszcz, M. (2005). *The theory and practice of group psychotherapy*. New York: Basic Books.

Yarhouse, M. A., & Tan, E. S. N. (2005). Addressing religious conflicts in adolescents who experience sexual identity confusion. *Professional Psychology: Research and Practice, 36,* 530-536.

Yasui, M., & Dishion, T. J. (2007). The ethnic context of child and adolescent problem behavior: Implications for child and family interventions. *Clinical Child and Family Psychology, 10,* 137-179.

Yerkes, R. M. (1921). Psychological examining in the United States army. *Memoirs of the National Academy of Sciences. 15,* 1-890.

Ying, Y. (1989). Nonresponse on the Center for Epidemiological Studies depression scale in Chinese Americans. *International Journal of Social Psychiatry, 35,* 156-163.

Yoshimasu, K. (2001). Relation of type A behavior pattern and job-related psychosocial factors to nonfatal myocardial infarction: A case-control study of Japanese male workers and women. *Psychosomatic Medicine, 63,* 797-804.

Young, L. D. (1992). Psychological factors in rheumatoid arthritis. *Journal of Consulting and Clinical Psychology, 60,* 619-627.

Yutrzenka, B. A. (1995). Making a case for training in ethnic and cultural diversity in increasing treatment efficacy. *Journal of Consulting and Clinical Psychology, 63,* 197-206.

Zabow, T., & Cohen, A. (1993). South African psychiatrists' criteria for predicting dangerousness. *Medicine & Law, 12,* 417-430.

Zanarini, M. C., Skodol, A. E., Bender, D., Dolan, R., & Sanislow, C. (2000). The collaborative longitudinal personality disorders study: Reliability of axis I and II diagnoses. *Journal of Personality Disorders, 14,* 291-299.

Zaslow, M. J., Weinfeld, N. S., Gallagher, M., Hair, E. C., Ogawa, J. R. et al. (2006). Longitudinal prediction of child outcomes from differing measures of parenting in a low-income sample. *Developmental Psychology, 42,* 27-37.

Zaza, C., Sellick, S. M., & Hillier, L. M. (2005). Coping with cancer: What do patients do? *Journal of Psychosocial oncology, 23,* 55-73.

Zero to Three (2005). *Diagnostic classification of mental health and developmental disorders of infancy and early childhood: Revised Edition (DC: 0-3R)*. Washington, DC: Zero to Three Press.

Zetin, M., & Glenn, T. (1999). Development of a computerized psychiatric diagnostic interview for use by mental health and primary care clinicians. *CyberPsychology & Behavior, 2,* 223-233.

Zheng D, Macera CA, Croft JB, Giles WH, Davis D, Scott WK. (1997). Major depression and all-cause mortality among white adults in the United States. *Annals of Epidemiology, 7,* 213-218.

Zilboorg, G., & Henry, G. W. (1941). *A history of medical psychology*. New York: W. W. Norton.

Zimbardo, P. G. (2004). Does psychology make a significant difference in our lives? *American Psychologist, 59,* 339-351.

Zimmerman, M. A. (2000). Empowerment theory: Psychological, organizational and community levels of analysis. In J. Rappaport & E. Seidman (Eds.), *Handbook of community psychology* (pp. 42-63). New York: Kluwer Academic/Plenum Publishers.

Ziskin, J., & Faust, D. (1988). *Coping with psychiatric and psychological testimony* (4th ed., Vols. 1-3). Marina del Rey, CA: Law & Psychology Press.

Zoellner, L. A., Feeny, N. C., Cochran, B., & Pruitt, L. (2003). Treatment choice for PTSD. *Behaviour Research and Therapy, 41,* 879-886.

Zoellner, T., & Maercker, A. (2006). Posttraumatic growth in clinical psychology—A critical review and introduction of a two component model. *Clinical Psychology Review, 26,* 626-653.

Zola-Morgan, S. (1995). Localization of brain function: The legacy of Franz Joseph Gall (1758-1828). *Annual Review of Neuroscience, 18,* 359-383.

Zook, A., II, & Walton, J. M. (1989). Theoretical orientations and work settings of clinical and counseling psychologists: A current perspective. *Professional Psychology: Research and Practice, 20,* 23-31.

Zuardi, A. W., Loureiro, S. R., & Rodrigues, C. R. C. (1995). Reliability, validity, and factorial dimensions of the Interactive Observation Scale for Psychiatric Inpatients. *Acta Psychiatrica Scandinavica, 91,* 247-251.

Zubin, J. (1969). The role of models in clinical psychology. In L. L'Abate (Ed.), *Models of clinical psychology* (pp. 5-12). Atlanta: Georgia State College.

Zubin, J., & Spring, B. (1977). Vulnerability—A new view of schizophrenia. *Journal of Abnormal Psychology, 86,* 103-126.

Zur, O. (2007). *Boundaries in psychotherapy: Ethical and clinical explorations.* Washington, DC: American Psychological Association.

Zuvekas, S. H., & Meyerhoefer, C. D. (2006). Coverage for mental health treatment: Do the gaps still persist? *Journal of Mental Health Policy and Economics, 9,* 155-163.

Zytowski, D. G. (2007). Kuder Career Search with Person Match technical manual 1.1. Retrieved June 19, 2007, from http://www.kuder.com/publicweb/kcs_manual.aspx.

Author Index

A

Abbott, R.D., 408
Abela, J.R.Z., 381
Abeles, N., 506
Abernethy, A.P., 411
Aberson, B., 319
Ables, B.S., 312
Abood, L.G., 40
Abramowitz, J.S., 276
Abrams, D., 409
Abrahamson, L.Y., 284
Abt, L.E., 45, 46
Achenbach, T.M., 149, 361, 364, 372, 373, 374, 378, 379, 393
Achter, J.A., 350
Ackerman, M., 466
Ackerman, M.J., 466
Ackerman, N., 61
Ackerman, N.W., 148
Acree, M., 324
Adair, J.C., 430
Adam, E.K., 367
Adams, M.R., 407
Addis, M.E., 200, 346, 388, 390
Adler, A., 138
Adler, N.E., 407
Adolph, J.L., 225
Ægisdóttir, S., 95, 96
Affleck, G., 403
Agras, W., 295
Agras, W.S., 300, 322
Aharon-Peretz, J., 430
Ahlström, G., 140
Ahn, H., 345

Ai, A.L., 324
Aklin, W.M., 121
Albano, A.M., 389
Albarracin, D., 320
Albee, G.W., 316
Alberti, R.E., 276
Albino, J.E.N., 484
Alexander, F.M., 247
Alexander, J.F., 312, 352
Alexander, M.P., 435
Ali, S., 506
Allen, D.M., 219
Allen, G.J., 146
Allen, J.M., 108
Alleyne, E., 413
Allport, G.W., 182
Alper, B.S., 34
Alter, K., 430
Alterman, A.I., 128
Alvarado, R., 319, 353
American Association of Marriage and Family Therapy, 307
American Psychiatric Association, 79, 80, 91, 361, 378, 380, 381, 382, 383, 456, 467, 494
American Psychological Association, 20, 88, 99, 112, 225, 307, 444, 467, 480, 482, 493, 494, 506, 527, 528, 531, 540, 546
American Psychological Association Archives, 48, 482

American Psychological Association Committee on Professional Practice and Standards, 493
American Psychological Association Presidential Task Force on Evidence-Based Practice, 347
Amundson, M.E., 402
Anastasi, A., 168, 189
Andersen, B.L., 412
Anderson, C.M., 334, 339
Anderson, E., 321, 354
Anderson, J.R., 492, 496
Anderson, N.B., 407
Anderson, P., 275
Andersson, S., 431
Andrassy, J., 354
Andreasen, N., 441
Andrews, G., 343
Andrews, J.D.W., 217
Andronkiof, A., 196
Angel, E., 264
Anson, D.A., 140
Anton, B.S., 320, 389, 391
Antoni, M.H., 407, 414
Antonova, E., 441
Antony, M.M., 270, 271, 281, 303, 307, 352
APApractice.org, 504
Apodaca, T.R., 322, 354
Appelbaum, P.S., 461
Apple, R.F., 322
Arasteh, J.D., 467
Archer, R.P., 162

Arkes, H.A., 97
Armeli, S., 403
Armstrong, J.G., 74
Arnold, C., 465, 467
Arnold, C.B., 411
Aronson, E., 97
Ashkanazi, G., 495
Association News, 15
Astin, J.A., 325
Atanackovic, D., 402
Atkinson, D.R., 93, 94
Auerbach, L., 323
Auld, F., Jr., 139
Ault, M.H., 148
Axline, V.M., 387
Azar, B., 411
Azar, S.T., 465
Azen, R., 389

B

Babinski, M.J., 430
Babyak, M., 416
Baekeland, F., 117
Baer, R., 143
Baer, R.A., 325
Baerger, D.R., 496
Bagby, R.M., 126, 141
Bagchi, D., 128
Bailey, C.E., 353
Bailey, D.S., 468, 517
Baird, A., 430
Baldwin, S.A., 352
Bandura, A., 59, 60, 220, 270, 276, 282
Banta, J., 68
Bantha, R., 324
Barbaree, H.E., 152
Barefoot, J.C., 408
Barker, A., 140
Barkley, R.A., 313, 321, 322, 380, 390
Barlow, B.F., 84
Barlow, D.H., 2, 274, 275, 314, 321, 347, 389
Barlow, S.H., 321, 354
Barnes, H., 145
Barone, C., 317
Barr, C., 63
Barrera, M., 353
Barret, B., 492, 496
Barrett, A.M., 430
Barrett, P.M., 391
Barron, J.W., 84
Bartol, A.M., 464

Bartol, C.R., 464
Basco, M.R., 105, 280, 284, 288, 293, 300
Bassman, L.E., 323
Bates, J.E., 366
Bateson, C., 62, 312
Baucom, D.H., 62, 312
Baum, A., 399, 412
Baumeister, R.F., 404, 405
Bax, K.A., 366
Bazelon, D., 470
Beach, S.R.H., 308, 379, 479
Bear, D.M., 434
Beauregard, C., 366
Bechtoldt, H., 251, 266, 299
Beck, A.T., 59, 87, 125, 127, 188, 282, 285, 286, 289, 343
Beck, J.S., 289
Becker, W.C., 148
Becker-Blease, K.A., 326
Becker, M.H., 417
Begley, S., 205
Behnke, S., 543
Beidel, D.C., 189
Belar, C.D., 9, 406, 481, 484
Bellack, A.S., 80, 145, 151
Bellak, L., 193, 195, 374
Belter, R.W., 171
Bender, L.A., 43
Bender, W.N., 466
Benefield, H., 495
Benjamin, L.S., 43, 46, 48
Benjamin, L.T., 30, 31, 34, 38, 42, 43, 44, 45, 47, 482
Benjet, C.L., 465
Ben-Porath, Y.S., 186, 190
Benson, D.F., 433
Benton, C.M., 322
Berg, I.A., 167
Berger, B.D., 430
Berger, L.E., 368
Bergin, A.E., 14, 342, 343
Berglund, P., 209
Bergman, A., 248
Bergman, R.L., 389
Berk, L.E., 500
Berliner, L., 367
Bermand, S.L., 493
Bernstein, D.A., 63, 77, 91, 152, 155, 156, 272, 418, 449, 450, 455, 458, 470
Berry, D., 143
Bersoff, D.N., 492
Bertelsen, A., 85

Beswick, A., 411
Betz, N.E., 176, 187
Beutel, M.E., 118
Beutler, L.E., 23, 84, 86, 209, 210, 212, 227, 228, 344, 345, 346, 347, 351
Biaggio, M., 506
Bianchi, S., 314
Bickman, L., 389, 481
Bieling, P.J., 303, 306, 307, 352
Biemond, R., 275
Bieri, J., 94
Bierman, K.L., 373
Bigelow, C., 141
Bigner, J.J., 309
Bihrle, A.M., 430
Bijou, S.W., 148
Binitie, I., 314
Bion, W.R., 61, 302
Birks, Y., 408
Bisconer, S.W., 99
Bishop, S.R., 325
Bisiach, E., 432
Blackburn, H., 411
Blair, R.J., 430
Blakely, C., 146
Blanchard, E.B., 300, 411, 416
Blanchard, R., 152
Blatt, S.J., 248
Blinder, J.L., 250
Bloom, L.J., 466
Blose, J.D., 499
Blount, R.L., 418
Blumenthal, J.A., 409
Blumenthal, S.J., 399
Bobbitt, B.L., 27, 501
Bobholz, J.H., 458
Boczkowski, J.A., 418
Boeree, C.G., 58
Bogels, S.M., 116
Bohart, A.C., 255, 261, 262
Boisvert, C.M., 348
Bond, G.R., 151
Bond, L., 198
Bondy, E., 141
Bonnie, R.J., 450, 455, 470
Boothby, H., 140
Bordin, E.S., 214
Borgata, L., 150
Boring, E.G., 33
Borkovec, T.D., 156, 272
Bornstein, R.F., 196
Borum, R., 89
Bottoms, B.L., 541

Botvin, G.J., 392
Bouchard, S., 153
Boucher, A.P., 487
Bougakov, D., 436
Boulger, J.R., 89
Bowen, A.M., 412
Bower, J.E., 404
Bowers, K.S., 196
Boyle, G.J., 166, 197
Brabender, V.A., 306
Bracha, H.S., 82, 83
Braden, J.P., 179, 180
Bradley, R., 347
Bradshaw, P.W., 417
Braginsky, B.M., 141
Braginsky, D.D., 141
Brambilla, P., 442
Brand, B.L., 74
Brand, R.J., 408
Brandsma, J.M., 312
Brannon, L., 399, 405
Bransford, J.D., 92
Branthwaite, A., 416
Brasfield, T.L., 413
Brauer, B.A., 184
Brausch, A.M., 343
Brechman-Toussaint, M.L., 391
Breggin, G.R., 388
Breggin, P.R., 388
Brekke, N.J., 472
Brems, C., 211, 224
Brennan, T.A., 496
Breslow, L., 406
Breuer, J., 49
Breyer, S., 472
Bridges, M., 366
Bridges, S.K., 249
Briggs, K.C., 190
Briggs, M., 140
Brinkmeyer, M.Y., 314, 353, 375
Broca, P., 423
Brodley, B.T., 266
Brody, G.H., 391
Broman, C.L., 406
Bromley, D.B., 339
Brookmeyer, K.A., 361
Brooks, R.B., 392
Brooks-Gunn, J., 367
Brotemarkle, B.A., 32
Brotman, L.M., 391
Brown, G.K., 188
Brown, L.S., 142
Brown, R.A., 352
Brown, R.T., 375, 387, 388

Brown, T.A., 2
Brown, T.M., 68
Brown, T.T., 84
Brown, W.H., 145
Browne, A., 306
Brownell, H.H., 430
Brownell, K.D., 416
Browne-Sperling, F., 412
Bruce, N., 351
Brugha, T.S., 128
Brussel, J.A., 464
Bryan, A.D., 320, 353
Buck, J.N., 196, 374
Buckley, P.J., 116, 117
Bugental, J.F.T., 265
Bull, S.S., 410
Bundy, C., 130
Burg, M.M., 409
Burger, W.E., 470
Burisch, M., 164
Burish, T.G., 279
Burke, L.E., 416
Burke, M., 411
Burlingame, G.M., 303, 321, 354
Burnam, M.A., 142
Burns, D.D., 211, 219
Burns, G.L., 418
Buros, O.K., 43, 162
Burr, R.M., 125
Buschbaum, M., 441
Bush, S.S., 492
Butcher, J.N., 184, 186, 188
Butler, A.C., 343
Butters, N., 424, 439

C
Cabrese, C., 196
Caburnay, C.A., 343
Cacciola, J.S., 128
Cacioppo, J.T., 394, 509
Cain, D.J., 54
Cairns, R.B., 144
Calkins, S.D., 366
Callaghan, G.M., 214
Caltagirone, C., 430
Camara, W.J., 162, 171
Camilli, G., 94
Campbell, C.D., 3
Campbell, D.P., 182
Campbell, D.T., 101, 146
Campbell, L., 411
Campbell, L.F., 251, 299, 321, 322
Campbell, V.L., 171, 195
Canning, D., 413

Cantor, J.M., 152
Cantor, N.L., 462
Caplan, G., 318
Carlomagno, S., 430
Carlson, E.T., 40
Carlson, L.E., 325
Carney, J., 376
Carney, M.A., 403
Carniero, C., 151
Carpenter, L.A., 375
Carr, A., 309, 363
Carroll, F., 128
Carroll, J.B., 174
Carroll, K.M., 215
Carter, C.S., 441
Carter, J.S., 380, 389
Case, S.M., 93
Cashel, M.L., 373
Caspi, A., 366, 394, 509
Cassel, E., 91, 448, 449, 450, 455, 458, 470
Castellani, A.M., 311, 352
Castle, P.H., 5, 21, 24, 69, 477, 518, 519
Catron, T., 389
Cattell, R.B., 34, 43, 174, 189
Cauffman, E., 90
Cavanaugh, K., 99
Cavell, T.A., 391
Cecero, J.J., 215, 391
Centers for Disease Control, 407, 409
Chambless, D.L., 275, 344, 345, 346, 348, 352, 389
Chan, A.S., 457
Chan, D.W., 162
Chang, T., 321
Chapman, J.E., 343
Chapman, J.P., 93
Chapman, L.J., 93
Cheatham, H.E., 142
Cherry, C., 412
Cherry, D.K., 483
Chevron, E.S., 250
Children's Defense Fund, 366
Choate, M.L., 314, 389
Chorpita, B.F., 84, 340
Christensen, A., 308, 352
Chronis, A.M., 389
Chung, J.J., 188
Cicchetti, D., 394, 509
Cipolotti, L., 430
Clark, D., 128
Clark, D.B., 149

Clark, L.A., 81, 343
Clarke, G., 501
Clarke-Stewart, A., 63
Clarkin, J.F., 226, 350
Clarkson, T.B., 407
Clavet, G., 472
Clay, R.A., 73, 519
Clingempeel, W.G., 466
Coatsworth, J.D., 393
Cobb, H.C., 8
Cobb, J.A., 148, 364
Cochran, B., 354
Cohen, A., 91
Cohen, B.B., 140
Cohen, D.J., 394
Cohen, J., 27
Cohen, J.A., 367
Cohen, J.B., 408
Cohen, L.M., 484, 487
Cohen, S., 401, 404, 406, 412
Coie, J.D., 319
Colavito, V.A., 193
Coleman, P., 321
Coley, B., 413
Collins, R.L., 150, 409
Collins, S., 451
Collins, W.A., 376
Collishaw, S., 382
Colmen, J.G., 89
Comer, R.J., 295
Cone, J.D., 155
Conger, R.D., 368
Connell, M.A., 492
Conners, C.K., 373
Connery, H., 143
Connolly-Gibbons, M.B., 213
Connor-Smith, J.K., 341
Consoli, A.J., 24, 328
Constantino, M.J., 351
Coolen, J.C., 379
Coontz, P.D., 93
Cooper, A.M., 245
Corazzini, J.G., 352
Corboz-Warney, A., 151
Corey, G., 303
Cormier, C.A., 91
Cornblatt, B., 63
Corrigan, P., 508
Corsini, R.J., 251
Corwin, D., 128
Coslett, H.B., 432
Costa, P.T., 167
Costa, P.T., Jr., 190
Côté, S., 153

Cottler, L., 128
Cotton, S., 324
Couch, R.D., 119
Coulter, F., 143
Counseling Psychology,
  Division 7, 8
Covner, B.J., 139
Cox, H.W., 145
Crane, D.R., 499
Craske, M.G., 321
Crisp, H.L., 393, 394
Crits-Christoph, P., 213, 215
Croghan, T.W., 416
Cronbach, L.J., 101, 103, 146, 161, 167
Crosbie-Burnett, M., 466, 467
Crow, T.J., 442
Csikszentmihalyi, M., 403
Cullen, E.A., 503
Cumming, J.D., 218
Cummings, E.M., 366, 394
Cummings, J.L., 294, 435
Cummings, N.A., 399, 499
Curtin, L., 306
Curtis, J.W., 509
Curtis, R.C., 246, 249
Custer, G., 384

D
Dadds, M.R., 152, 157, 391
Dahlstrom, L.E., 186
Dahlstrom, W.G., 184, 186
Damasio, A.R., 435
Dana, R.H., 105
Dancu, C.V., 189
Danehy, J.J., 139
Dare, C., 300
Darley, J.M., 528
Dattilio, F.M., 339, 463
Dauber, S., 391
Davanloo, H.L., 247
Davey-Smith, G., 411
Davido, B.J., 506
Davidson, W.S., 146, 317
Davies, P.T., 394
Davies, W.H., 389
Davis, D.M., 146
Davis, F.H., 152
Davis, J.D., 213
Davis, J.M., 323
Davis, K.M., 214, 215, 351
Davis, R., 188
Davis, T.E., 348
Davis, W.W., 140

Davison, E., 344
Davison, L.A., 424
Dawes, R.M., 94, 95, 97
Dawson, M., 382
Deane, F.P., 219
DeBar, L., 501
De Bruyn, E.E., 79, 93
DeBruyn, E.E.J., 379
DeClue, G., 125
Degnan, K.A., 366
DeGue, S., 484, 487
Dekel, R., 229
DeLeon, P.H., 406, 484
DeMers, S.T., 487
Denney, R.L., 492
Dennis, W., 37, 43
DeSanto, N., 418
Detterman, D.K., 173
Detweiler, J.B., 404
Detweiler-Bedel, J., 228
DeYoung, P.A., 249, 252
Dickens, S.E., 126, 141
Diekhoff, G.M., 492
Diener, E., 145, 507
Dies, R., 61
Diez Roux, A.V., 407
DiLalla, D.L., 63
DiLillo, D., 366, 484, 486, 487
Dilk, M.N., 151
DiMatteo, M.R., 118, 342, 416
Dimidjian, S., 325
Dipboye, R.L., 142
Disch, E., 497
Dishion, T.J., 313, 392
Dixon, D.N., 327
Dobson, K.S., 300
Dodge, K.A., 319
Doelger, L., 509
Doerfler, L.A., 200
Dohrenwend, B.S., 401
Dolan, M., 91
Dolan, S.L., 347
Dollard, M.F., 461
Domino, G., 161, 166, 168, 173, 174, 186, 190, 196, 197
Domino, M.L., 161, 166, 168, 173, 174, 186, 190, 196, 197
Donenberg, G.R., 342
Donn, J.E., 47
Donnellan, M.B., 368
Dorken, H., 399
Dornan, T., 130
Dornelas, E.A., 399
Doss, A.J., 389, 391

Doss, B.D., 308
Dougher, M.J., 82, 85, 404
Douglas, J., 464
Douglas, K.S., 74
Doyle, M., 91
Dozois, D.J.A., 362, 378
Dryden, W., 59, 287
DuBois, D.L., 368
DuBois, P.H., 34
Duckworth, A.L., 85, 320, 392, 507, 520
Dulcan, M.K., 126, 373
Dumenci, L., 379
Dumont, F., 197
Dunbar-Jacob, J.M., 416
Dunn, T.W., 343
Durham, T.W., 514, 515
Durlak, J.A., 320, 389, 391
Dwight, L., 140

E
Eagle, M.N., 284
Eaker, E.D., 408
Earl, A., 320
Eaves, D.E., 417
Eber, H.W., 189
Ebert, B.W., 463
Ebrahim, S., 411
Echols, M.M., 486
Edelbrock, C.S., 378
Eder, G.S., 142
Educational Testing Service, 534
Edwards, A.L., 167
Edwards, D.J.A., 339
Edwards, J., 10
Ehmann, T.S., 148
Eid, M., 145
Eiden, R.D., 309
Einhorn, H.J., 92
Eisman, E.J., 12, 17
Ekstrom, D.E., 140
Elder, K.A., 140
Ellenberger, H.F., 264
Elliot, R.K., 52, 252, 264, 266
Elliott, D.M., 367
Ellis, A., 59, 60, 282, 286, 287
Ellis, P., 320
Ellsworth, J.R., 200
Elmore, A.M., 366
Emery, G., 285
Emery, R.E., 466, 469
Emmelkamp, P.M.G., 275
Emmons, M.L., 276
Emshoff, J.G., 146

Enko, P.J., 472
Ennis, B.J., 470
Epstein, N., 62, 312
Erbaugh, J.K., 125, 127
Erdberg, P., 193, 196
Erickson, P.I., 128
Erikson, E.H., 248
Erlenmeyer-Kimling, L.E., 63
Erwin, E., 266
Eslinger, P.J., 435
Evans, D.L., 318
Evans, G.W., 367, 368
Everett, J.J., 418
Ewing, C.P., 495
Exner, J.E., 190, 191, 193
Exner, J.E., Jr., 193, 196
Eyberg, S.M., 314, 353, 375, 389
Eyde, L.D., 170
Eysenck, H.J., 166, 189, 316, 341
Eysenck, S.B.G., 189

F
Fagan, T.J., 504
Fagan, T.K., 34
Fairbairn, W.R.D., 248
Falkenberg, S., 448
Fallon, A.E., 306
Fallon, T., 140
Fancher, R.E., 50
Farah, M.J., 434
Farmer, J., 189
Farrell, A.D., 99
Farrell, L.J., 391
Farrington, D.P., 319
Farris, A.M., 151
Fauber, R.L., 529
Faust, D., 94, 97, 348, 456, 470
Fawzy, F.I., 412
Fedio, P., 434
Feeny, N.C., 354
Feinstein, M.S., 414
Feinstein, R.E., 414
Feist, J., 399, 405
Felner, R.D., 320
Feltham, C., 10, 206
Fendrich, R., 434
Fenning, S., 229
Fenton, L.R., 215
Ferguson, R.J., 335, 336
Ficcaglia, M., 382
Fiedler, E.R., 140
Fields, S., 314
Figueroa-Moseley, C., 412
Files-Hall, T.M., 386

Finch, A.J., 488
Fincham, F.D., 467
Fine, R., 243
Fine, S., 116
Finger, M.S., 186, 338
Fink, A.S., 394
Finkelhor, D., 326
Finn, S.E., 106
Finset, A., 431
First, M.B., 82, 83, 84, 85, 125, 140
Fischer, C.T., 52, 104, 105, 106, 252, 264
Fischer, M., 321
Fischer, W.F., 105
Fisher, D.C., 227, 344
Fisher, J.D., 320, 353
Fisher, P., 126, 373
Fisher, W.A., 320, 353
Fiske, D.W., 89, 101
Fitzgerald, G., 148
Fivaz-Depeursinge, E., 151
Fleisig, W.E., 188
Florio, C.M., 196
Foa, E.B., 189
Fodor, J.A., 427
Folkman, S., 324, 402, 403, 408, 492
Follette, V.M., 325
Follette, W.C., 82, 214
Folstein, M.F., 122, 440
Fonagy, P., 235
Fontenelle, G.A., 142
Ford, M., 93
Forman, E.M., 343
Forsyth, D.R., 352
Fortier, M., 366
Fosco, G.M., 366
Foster, G.D., 150, 407
Foster, S.L., 143, 157
Fowers, B.J., 506
Foy, D.W., 306
Fraley, R.C., 379
Frances, A.J., 140
Frank, E., 141, 149
Frank, K.A., 410
Frank, L.K., 191
Frankforter, T.L., 215
Frankl, V., 252, 265
Franko, D.L., 320
Franks, C.M., 57
Fraser, M.W., 318, 365
Fredrickson, B.L., 403
Free, M.L., 306
Freedman, B., 325

Freeman, A., 60, 282, 284, 285, 286, 289, 299
French, T.M., 247
Freud, A., 234
Freud, S., 49, 218, 242, 245
Frick, P.J., 371, 373, 376, 378
Fried, C.S., 353
Friederici, A.D., 430
Friedman, M., 408, 410
Frincke, J., 19
Frish, M.B., 87
Fritz, H., 412
Fulero, S.M., 449
Funder, D., 51
Furnham, A., 173

G

Gabbard, G.O., 85, 104, 196, 205, 229, 235, 237, 245, 246, 249, 250, 251, 252
Gabbard, K., 205
Gaglio, B., 410
Gaines, L.K., 448
Gainotti, G., 440
Gallagher, D., 214
Galton, F., 36
Garb, H.N., 92, 93, 94, 97, 98, 128, 196, 197, 375
Garber, J., 359, 380, 389
Garbin, M.G., 87
Garcia-Preto, N., 315, 363
Gardner, H., 174, 430
Gardner, W., 91, 92
Garfield, S.L., 141, 209
Garland, M.R., 323
Garofalo, A., 23, 103, 172, 198
Garske, J.P., 214, 215, 351
Garth, M.H., 410
Garver, S.A., 506
Gaston, L., 214
Gazzaniga, M.S., 434
Geer, J.H., 185, 274
Gega, L., 99
Gelfand, D.M., 359
Gendlin, E.T., 252
Gentile, L., 367, 368
Gerberding, J.L., 399
Gernsbacher, M.A., 382
Gibbon, M., 125
Gillham, J., 27
Gillis, J.R., 126, 141
Giordani, P.J., 416
Giordano, J., 315, 363
Gittelman, R., 375

Gladding, S., 306
Glaser, R., 198, 406
Glasgow, R.E., 322, 354, 410
Glass, G.V., 342, 343
Glasser, P.H., 116
Glenn, T., 140
Glesser, G.C., 103
Glozman, J.M., 427
Glueckauf, R., 326
Glueckauf, R.L., 508
Glynn, M., 409
Glynn, S.M., 306
Goeke-Morey, M.C., 366
Goins, M.K., 140
Gold, J., 24, 67, 328
Goldberg, E., 427, 436
Goldberg, J.L., 209
Goldberg, L.R., 92, 95
Golden, R.N., 140
Goldfarb, L.P., 166
Goldfried, M.R., 78, 129, 328
Golding, S.L., 93, 140
Goldman, V.J., 514, 515
Goldsher, D., 430
Goldsmith, H.H., 382
Goldsmith, J.B., 151
Goldstein, S., 392
Gonnella, C., 367, 368
Goodheart, C.D., 88, 333
Goodman, S.H., 362
Goodson, J.T., 325
Goodwin, P.J., 412
Gordon, J.R., 294
Gorenstein, E.E., 295
Gorman, J.M., 153, 275, 339
Gorsuch, R.L., 178, 189
Gotham, H.J., 347
Gottesman, I.I., 63
Gottlieb, B., 406
Gottlieb, B.H., 61
Gottlieb, M.C., 507
Gottman, J.M., 143, 150, 151, 322, 352
Gottman, J.S., 322
Gough, H., 189
Grabe, S., 383
Grady-Fletcher, A., 352
Graham, J.R., 144, 186
Grant, B.F., 140
Grant, K.E., 368, 140
Greenberg, L.S., 52, 212, 214, 219, 252, 264, 266
Greenberg, R.P., 351
Greene, B., 121, 134

Greene, R., 148
Greenhoot, A.F., 333, 334, 337
Greenway, D.E., 82, 85
Gregory, R.J., 173
Greiner, L.H., 404
Grieger, R., 59
Griffin, K.W., 392
Grilo, C.M., 140, 355
Grimes, K.E., 146
Grinfeld, M.J., 6
Grisso, T., 450, 461
Gross, B., 497
Grossarth, M.R., 166
Groth-Marnat, G., 74, 76, 98, 99, 103, 128, 157, 173, 179, 186, 188, 197, 227
Grove, W.M., 95, 96, 196
Grover, R.L., 389
Gruenewald, T.L., 404
Grych, J.H., 366, 467
Guarnaccia, P.J., 112, 136
Guerney, B., 62
Gullone, E., 188
Gully, K.J., 140
Gundersen, P.M., 431
Guo-peng, C., 169
Gur, R.E., 441
Gureje, O., 136
Gurman, A.S., 162, 206, 252, 311, 315
Guthrie, P.R., 219
Guyton, M.R., 448
Gyorky, Z.K., 219

H

Habben, C.J., 488, 528
Haggerty, R.J., 319
Hahn, J., 188
Haley, J., 62, 312
Haley, W.E., 93
Hall, G.C.N., 18, 83
Hall, J.E., 487, 508
Hall, S.R., 4, 5
Hallahan, B., 323
Hallmark, R., 171, 195
Hambleton, R.K., 169
Hammond, K.R., 108
Hammontree, S.R., 193
Han, K., 188
Han, S.S., 342
Handelsman, M.M., 507
Handler, L., 166
Hankin, B.L., 379, 381

Hann, G., 506
Hansen, J.C., 182
Hanson, R.K., 196
Hanych, J.M., 524
Harbeck, C., 151
Harel, G., 229
Hargrave, J., 384
Harlow, J.M., 435
Haro, J.M., 146
Harris, F.C., 156
Harris, G.T., 89, 91, 96
Harris, M., 143
Harris, R., 306
Harris, V., 389
Harrison, B.J., 441
Harrower, M.R., 191
Hart, C.A., 402
Hartmann, H., 248
Hartsough, C.S., 145
Harvey, R., 343
Harway, M., 307, 315
Harwood, T.M., 209, 210, 226, 228, 351
Hatala, R., 93
Hatfield, D.R., 14
Hathaway, S.R., 184
Hathaway, W.L., 506
Hawes, D.J., 152
Hawley, D.R., 353
Hawley, K.M., 333, 341, 389, 390, 391
Hayes, S.A., 306
Hayes, S.C., 271, 325, 509
Haynes, R.B., 416
Haynes, S.N., 145, 146
Hays, P.A., 18, 506
Hazlett-Stevens, H., 272, 354
Heal, L.W., 141
Hearon, B., 213
Heavey, C.L., 352
Hedges, L.V., 342
Hedges, M., 69
Hegel, M.T., 335, 336
Heider, F., 284
Heilbrun, K., 451
Heilman, K.M., 422, 430, 432
Heimberg, R.G., 300
Heiser, N., 116
Helgeson, V.S., 412
Heller, W., 440, 441
Hellige, J.B., 425
Hendrie, H.C., 124
Hendriks, M., 445
Henggeler, S.W., 340

Henke, C.J., 399
Henry, G.W., 40
Henry, W.E., 193
Herbert, T.B., 401
Herink, R., 206
Herrington, J.D., 440
Herron, E.W., 191
Hersen, M., 80, 116, 140, 145, 151, 276, 281
Hess, A.K., 448, 449
Hetherington, E.M., 366, 467
Hetzel-Riggin, M.D., 343
Heyman, R.E., 150, 154, 308, 379
Hezlett, S.A., 523
Hibbeln, J.R., 323
Hickling, E.J., 300
Hickling, F.W., 93
Hildebrand, D.K., 178
Hill, C.E., 209
Hill, E.L., 196
Hill, M.N., 416
Hillier, L.M., 324
Hilton, N.Z., 89, 96
Himelein, M.J., 70, 483, 484
Himmelhoch, J.M., 151
Hinshaw, S.P., 354, 508
Hirsch, I., 246, 249
Hockett, C.F., 139
Hodges, L.F., 275
Hoff, E.H., 21
Hofferth, S.L., 314
Hogarth, R.M., 92
Hoge, R.D., 373
Hoge, S.K., 450
Hogue, A., 391
Holcombe, A., 145
Holder, H.D., 499
Holland, J.L., 182
Hollanders, H., 69
Hollon, S.D., 279, 354, 339
Holloway, J.D., 504
Holman, T.B., 315
Holmbeck, G., 338
Holmboe, E.S., 148
Holmes, J.M., 327
Holmes, T.H., 402
Holt, R.R., 89, 195
Holtzman, W.H., 191
Holtzworth-Munroe, A., 352
Homant, R., 464
Honda, K., 323
Hood, H.V., 413
Hope, D.A., 151, 157
Horn, J.L., 174

Horner, R.H., 145
Horowitz, M.J., 218
House, A.S., 506
House, A.T., 499
House, J.S., 405
Houts, A.C., 82, 83, 386
Hovarth, A.O., 214, 351
Howard, K.I., 215, 220, 343
Howes, J.L., 3
Howieson, D.B., 427, 439
Hoza, B., 389
Hsieh, D.K., 142
Hsu, L.K., 122
Hufford, C., 140, 342
Hugdahl, K., 188
Hughes, A.A., 389
Hughes, J.N., 391
Hughes, R., Jr., 467
Humedian, M., 506
Hummelen, B., 120
Humphreys, L.G., 169
Hunsley, J., 172, 179, 196, 197, 199, 374
Hunt, M., 31
Hunter, J.E., 342
Hunter, R.H., 318
Huss, M.T., 96
Hutchinson, S., 141

I

Iervolino, A.C., 382
Imhof, E.A., 162
Impara, J.C., 162, 173
Ingram, R.E., 508
Insabella, G.M., 366
Inskipp, F., 210
Institute of Medicine, 318
Institute of Personality
    Assessment and
    Research, 89
Inui, T., 418
Ironson, G., 407
Irvine, E., 143
Isenhart, C.E., 167
Israel, A.C., 379
Iwamasa, G.Y., 18

J

Jackson, D.D., 62, 312
Jackson, D.N., 167
Jackson, M., 211
Jackson, T., 391
Jackson, Y., 506
Jacobs, G.A., 189

Jacobson, J.S., 323
Jacobson, N.S., 311, 315, 352
Jacoby, A.M., 483
Jacoby, L.L., 434
James, J.W., 93
Jane, S.J., 140
Jarrett, R.B., 343
Jason, L.A., 416
Jay, S., 416, 418
Jefferson, K.W., 413
Jeffery, R.W., 410
Jeffries, J.C., Jr., 455
Jennings, L., 210, 211, 218
Jensen, P.S., 378, 389
Jensen-Doss, A., 333, 341
Jester, C.M., 328
Jia-xi, C., 169
Johnsen, B.H., 188
Johnson, B.W., 3
Johnson, J., 200
Johnson, M.D., 149, 150
Johnson, S., 228
Johnstone, B., 508
Joiner, T.E., 84
Jonason, K.R., 487
Jones, B.P., 424, 439
Jones, D.L., 306
Jones, E.E., 44, 218
Jones, H.A., 389
Jones, J.M., 536
Jones, M.C., 56, 153, 278
Jongsma, A.E., 228
Jorm, A.F., 6
Jouriles, E.N., 149, 151

K

Kaemmer, B., 186
Kahn, E., 249, 264
Kahn, J.H., 350
Kalichman, S.C., 412, 413, 414
Kamarck, T., 402
Kamphaus, R.W., 74, 371, 373, 376
Kancelbaum, B., 18
Kanfer, F.H., 104
Kannel, W.B., 408
Kaplan, A., 68, 89
Kaplan, C.P., 128
Kaplan, J.R., 407, 409
Kaplan, M., 80
Kaplan, R.M., 173
Kaplan, S.J., 89
Karasz, A., 136
Karg, R., 275

Karg, R.S., 69
Karno, M., 344
Karpiak, C.P., 11, 12, 13, 16, 24, 68, 69, 505, 516
Karterud, S., 120
Karver, M.S., 351, 390
Kaslow, F.W., 307, 314, 479
Kaslow, N.J., 308, 379, 479, 507
Kaufman, A.S., 180, 181
Kaufman, N.L., 180, 181
Kawachi, I., 404
Kazantzis, N., 219
Kazdin, A.E., 87, 88, 313, 333, 351, 387, 389
Keane, M.M., 434
Keefe, F.J., 411
Kehrer, C.A., 294
Keilin, W.G., 466
Keller, J.W., 157
Keller, L.S., 184
Kelley, C.M., 434
Kelley, D.M., 191
Kelley, J.E., 404
Kelly, D.R., 520
Kelly, E.L., 89
Kelly, G.A., 58
Kelly, J.A., 413
Kelly, J.B., 366, 467
Kemeny, M.E., 404
Kemper, S.J., 404
Kendall, P.C., 338, 340, 378, 387, 389, 407
Kenkel, M.B., 484
Kennedy, D.B., 464
Kennedy, P.F., 492, 493, 498
Kerig, P., 379
Kern, J.M., 152
Kernberg, O., 245, 248
Ketterson, T.U., 326
Khan, A., 339
Khan, S.R., 339
Kiecolt-Glaser, J.K., 401, 406
Kiesler, C.A., 502
Kieth-Spiegel, P., 212
Kim, C., 334, 339
Kim, E.J., 344
King, N.J., 188
Kingery, J.N., 389
Kinnaman, J.E.S., 99
Kinzie, J.D., 169
Kirby, L.D., 365
Kirk, S.A., 142
Kirkley, D.E., 306

Kiser, L.J., 368
Kister, K.M., 24, 69
Kitzmann, K.M., 469
Klein, M., 248
Klein, R.A., 275
Klein, R.H., 303
Kleinknecht, R.A., 418
Kleinmuntz, B., 92, 95, 96
Klerman, G.L., 80, 250
Klett, C.J., 147
Kline, T.J.B., 173
Klopfer, B., 191
Klopfer, W.G., 110
Knapp, S.J., 363, 507
Knox, S., 209
Koch, W.J., 74
Koester, K.A., 413
Kohlenberg, R.J., 214
Kohout, J.L., 3, 6, 12, 17, 19, 26, 482, 504, 505, 533
Kohut, H., 248
Kokotovic, A.M., 117
Komiti, A.A., 140, 141
Koocher, G.P., 23, 103, 172, 198
Kooper, R., 275
Kopel, S.A., 149
Koppitz, E.M., 374
Korchin, S.J., 3, 44, 45
Korman, M., 24
Kornfeld, S.D., 410
Korsch, B.M., 137
Korschgen, A.J., 480, 514, 523, 528, 537, 539
Kotz, S.A., 430
Kovacs, M., 372
Kovas, Y., 394
Krackow, E., 324
Krantz, D.S., 407
Krasner, L., 39, 57
Krasnow, A.D., 346
Kratchowill, T.R., 188
Krause, M.S., 343
Kreber, L.A., 225
Krijn, M., 275
Krishnamurthy, R., 113
Krishnan, R.R., 339
Krokoff, L.J., 150
Krol, N.P.C.M., 93, 379
Krous, T.M.D., 506
Krull, C.D., 169
Kubzansky, L., 404
Kuhajda, M.C., 306
Kulic, K.R., 124
Kumari, V., 441

Kumpfer, K.L., 319, 353, 391
Kuncel, N.R., 523
Kuperminc, G.P., 361
Kupfer, D.J., 82
Kurbat, M.A., 434
Kurtz, S.M.S., 148
Kuther, T.L., 528
Kyle, T.M., 22

L
Lachar, D., 186
Lah, M.I., 374
Lahey, B.B., 156, 379
Lake, J.H., 323, 324
Lam, J.N., 276
Lambert, D., 112, 499
Lambert, M.C., 376
Lambert, M.J., 14, 200, 337, 342, 343, 507
Lambert, N.M., 145
Lampropoulos, G.K., 327
Lancaster, C.J., 142
Lane, M., 18
Lang, P.J., 153, 188
Langenbucher, J.W., 80, 81
Langton, C.M., 89, 91
Lanyon, B.P., 196
Lanyon, R.I., 196
Larner, A.J., 143
Larner, M., 145
Larrabee, G.J., 439
Larson, J., 506
Lau, A.S., 367
Lauterbach, D., 99
Law, D.D., 499
Lawlis, G.F., 188
Lawyer, S., 275
Lazarus, A.A., 57, 228, 276
Lazarus, R.S., 37, 324, 402, 403
Lazovik, A.D., 153
Leach, C., 209
Leahy, R.L., 300
Leary, G.E., 504, 505
Leary, M.R., 404, 405
Lebow, B.S., 96
Lebow, J.L., 308, 315, 328, 347, 389
LeCroy, C.W., 305
Ledley, D.R., 300
Lee, C.M., 366, 374
Lee, H.B., 162
Lee, J.H., 275
Leech, S., 105
Leffard, S.A., 145, 157

le Grange, D., 300
Lehman, B.M., 430
Lehman, D.R., 406
Leisen, J.C.C., 404
Lemery, K.S., 509
Lemmel, G., 196
Leon, S.C., 212
Leonard, K.E., 309
Leonnig, C.D., 456
Lepper, H.S., 416
Lerner, H., 248
Leszcz, M., 304, 306
Levant, R.F., 23, 345, 347, 499, 500, 508
Levenson, R.W., 143
Leventhal, R.M., 339
Leventhal, T., 367
Levin, R.L., 441
Levine, E.S., 27, 504
Levison, H., 249, 250
Levy, K.N., 350
Lew, H.L., 155
Lewis, G., 93
Ley, P., 417
Lezak, M.D., 427, 439
Lichtenberg, J.W., 347
Lichtenberger, E.O., 98, 99
Lichtenstein, E., 149
Liddle, H.A., 391
Lidz, C.W., 92, 93
Lidz, R.W., 312
Lidz, T., 312
Lietaer, G., 52, 252, 264, 266
Lilienfeld, S.O., 13, 103, 197, 205, 324, 374
Lillesand, D.B., 151
Lima, E.N., 199
Lindsley, O.R., 57
Lindzey, G., 182, 193
Linehan, M.M., 167, 281, 286, 294, 325
Linney, J.A., 317
Lipp, O.V., 327
Liss, M.B., 465, 469
Lisspers, J., 320
Litwack, T.R., 470
Liu Rasheed, W.M., 506
Livingston, J.A., 367
Lochman, J.E., 353
Lock, J., 300
Lock, T., 324
Loewenstein, R.J., 74
Loftus, E.F., 324, 448
Lohr, J.M., 103

London, S., 348
Looman, J., 152
Loomis, J.S., 326
Lopez, S., 84
Lopez, S.R., 112, 136
Loranger, A.W., 127
Loring, D.W., 427, 439
Lorr, M., 147
Loureiro, S.R., 155
Lovaas, O.I., 389
Lovejoy, M.C., 353, 392
Loveless, A.S., 315
Low, P.W., 455
Lozano, C., 140
Luborsky, L., 89, 214
Lucas, C.P., 126, 373
Lueger, R.J., 220
Lumley, M.A., 404
Lundahl, B., 353, 392
Lundwall, L., 117
Lunt, I.T.I., 47
Lushene, R., 189
Lutz, W., 212
Luzzatti, C., 432
Lynam, D., 319
Lynch, F., 501
Lyneham, H.J., 128
Lynn, S.J., 103, 324
Lyons, J.S., 212
Lyons, P.M., 448

M
MacDonald, G., 92
Machado, P.P.P., 212
Machover, K., 196
MacKain, S.J., 514, 515
MacKenzie, K.R., 303
MacKinnon, R.A., 116, 117
Macklin, D.S., 461
Maercker, A., 508
Mahan, T.W., 211
Mahler, M.S., 248
Mahoney, M.J., 60
Maiberger, P., 440
Maier, S.F., 401
Maiman, L.A., 417
Mains, J.A., 322, 354
Maisto, C.A., 146
Maisto, S.A., 92, 146
Makover, R.B., 226
Malarkey, W.B., 406
Malessa, R., 423, 426
Malgady, R.G., 112
Malik, 84, 86

Maling, M.S., 220
Malmo, R.B., 152
Maloney, M.P., 165
Malouff, J.M., 343
Mann, A.H., 140
Mannarino, A.P., 367
Manuck, S.B., 407
March, S., 327
March, J.S., 300
Marcus, D.R., 448
Marcynyszyn, L.A., 367, 368
Marecek, J., 27
Marin, R.S., 436
Marini, A., 430
Markesbery, W.R., 404
Markman, H.J., 151
Markowitz, J., 414
Marks, I.M., 99
Marks, J.S., 399
Marlatt, G.A., 150, 294
Marmar, C., 214
Marshall, W.L., 152
Martin, D.J., 214, 215, 351
Martin, R., 140
Martinovich, Z., 212, 220
Martz, D.M., 142
Maruish, M., 162
Marvin, J.A., 418
Marx, B.P., 300
Marx, J.A., 219
Maselko, J., 404
Mash, E.J., 143, 157, 172, 179, 197,
    199, 362, 378
Masheb, R.M., 355
Masling, J.M., 197
Maslow, A.H., 264
Masten, A.S., 325, 368
Masters, J.C., 279
Masters, K.S., 325
Masur, F.T., 417
Matarazzo, J.D., 76, 99, 116,
    444
Matarazzo, R.G., 314
Mather, N., 181, 374
Maton, K.I., 504, 505
Matthews, K., 407
Matthews, K.A., 408
Matthews, M.D., 520
Matthews, S.G., 469
Maughan, B., 382
May, D.J., 128
May, R., 252, 264, 265
May, S., 499
Mayer, J.P., 317

Mayne, T.J., 5, 21, 24, 477, 482,
    484, 516, 518, 519, 522,
    524, 532, 537
McArthur, D.S., 195
McCabe, R.E., 303, 307,
    352
McCallum, K., 128
McCandliss, B.D., 442
McCann, J.T., 495
McCart, M.R., 389
McCaulley, M.H., 190
McConaughy, S.H., 374
McCoy, S.A., 93
McCrae, R.R., 167, 190
McCusker, J., 141
McDermut, W., 352
McDonald, B.C., 442
McFall, J.P., 343
McFall, R.M., 151, 269, 480, 481,
    482, 484, 507
McFarland, K., 125
McGaugh, J.L., 434
McGlynn, F.D., 275
McGoldrick, M., 315, 363
McGrew, K.S., 181, 374
McGuffin, P., 394, 509
McHugh, P.R., 440
McIntyre, K., 149
McKay, J.R., 128
McKenzie, K., 93
McKinley, J.C., 184
McKinley-Pace, M.J., 465, 469
Mclennan, J., 68
McLeod, J., 69
McMullen, P.A., 434
McMullin, R.E., 300
McNair, D.M., 147
McNair, S., 145
McNamara, J.R., 6, 205
McReynolds, P., 31, 34, 74
McWilliams, N., 245, 252
Mead, M., 146
Meador, B.D., 253
Mease, A.L., 312, 352
Mednick, S., 63
Meehl, P.E., 94, 95, 101, 110
Meichenbaum, D.H., 282
Meissner, W.W., 214
Mello, M.M., 496
Melton, A.W., 149
Melton, G.B., 468, 469
Meltzer, H., 128
Mendelson, M., 125, 127
Menninger, K., 245

Merenda, P.F., 169
Mermelstein, R., 149, 402
Merrill, T.S., 487
Messenger, L.C., 483
Messer, S.B., 206, 210, 211, 217,
    252, 346, 347
Messick, S., 167
Mesulam, M.M., 427
Metzner, H.L., 405
Meyer, G.J., 197, 199
Meyer, M.M., 434
Meyer, R.G., 496
Meyerhoefer, C.D., 499
Meyer-Lindenberg, A., 442
Meyers, L., 502
Michael, K.D., 306
Michelow, D., 430
Michels, R., 116, 117
Mihara, R., 506
Milan, M.A., 69
Milich, R., 148
Miller, A.L., 281, 286
Miller, B.L., 294, 435
Miller, G.A., 445
Miller, G.E., 404
Miller, I.W., 352
Miller, J.A., 145, 157
Miller, M.O., 4, 5
Miller, S.B., 408
Miller, T.I., 342, 343
Miller, T.Q., 409
Miller, W.R., 322, 324, 354
Millon, C., 188
Millon, J., 188
Millon, T., 80
Milner, B., 429, 434
Milner, D.A., 434
Mineka, S., 81
Minuchin, S., 62
Miranda, J., 505
Mischel, W., 59, 109, 282
Mishkin, M., 432, 433
Misovich, S.J., 320, 353
Missar, C.D., 213
Mitchell, C.M., 146
Mitchell, K.J., 326
Mitchell, R.L., 442
Mock, J.E., 125, 127
Moffitt, T.E., 366, 394, 509
Mokdad, A.H., 399
Molina, L.E., 505
Molnar, J., 384
Monahan, J., 89, 91, 449, 450
Montalvo, B., 62

Montgomery, B.S., 343
Montgomery, D.T., 391
Montgomery, R.W., 69
Moran, P.W., 200
Moodie, W., 43
Moore, P.M., 275
Moore, T.E., 322, 354
Moos, B., 354
Moos, R., 354
Moreno, J., 150
Moretti, R.J., 196
Morey, L., 92
Morgan, B.L., 480, 514, 523, 528,
    537, 539
Morgan, D.L., 336
Morgan, R.D., 484, 487, 528
Morgan, R.K., 336
Morgenstern, J., 336
Morganstern, K.P., 124
Morland, K., 407
Morris, R., 441
Morrison, C.S., 141
Morrison, K.H., 347
Morse, S.J., 470
Mortimer, J.A., 404
Morton, A., 117
Moseley, G.L., 412
Moskowitz, J.T., 324
Mpofu, E., 376
Mrazek, P.J., 319
Muenz, L.R., 140, 342
Mukherjee, D., 441
Mulle, K., 300
Mullen, R., 93
Multiple Risk Factors Intervention
    Trial Research Group
    (MRFIT), 410
Mulvey, E.P., 90, 92, 93
Munk-Jorgensen, P., 63
Munsey, C., 495, 499, 500, 504,
    519, 529
Murdock, N.L., 68, 213, 252, 254,
    259, 281, 282
Murphy, D.A., 413
Murphy, K.R., 321
Murphy, M.J., 500, 508
Murray, E.J., 139
Murray, H.A., 193, 194, 197
Murray, R., 93
Mussen, P.H., 166
Myers, D.G., 403, 405
Myers, I.B., 190
Myklebust, H.R., 442
Myors, B., 74

N
Nagy, T.F., 169, 223, 492
Najavits, L.M., 140, 342
Nanayakkara, N., 404
Naster, B.J., 155
Nathan, J.S., 162, 171
Nathan, P.E., 80, 81, 347
Nation, M., 320
National Association of Social
    Workers, 8
National Center for Education
    Statistics, 21
National Institute of Justice, 448
National Institute of Mental
    Health, 208
Naugle, A.E., 214
Nauta, M.M., 506
Navon, D., 432
Neale, J.M., 403
Nebeker, R.S., 321, 354
Negrete, V.F., 137
Neimeyer, R.A., 249, 265
Neisser, U., 173
Nelson, C., 96
Nelson, R.O., 271
Nevid, J.S., 121, 234
Newlin, C.M., 225
Newman, R., 503, 508
Neylan, T.C., 435
Nezu, C.M., 488
Nezworski, M., 197, 374
Nich, C., 215
Nicholls, T.L., 74
Nicholson, R.A., 466
NIDA Research Report, 388
Nieberding, K., 171, 195
Nielsen, S.L., 167, 343
Nienhuis, F., 128
Nietzel, M.T., 77, 152, 155,
    156, 219
Nievod, A., 324
NIMH Prevention Research
    Steering Committee, 319
Niogi, S.N., 442
Nisbet, R.J., 74
Nitschke, J.B., 440
Nocentini, U., 430
Nock, M.K., 148
Noel, S.B., 343
Noll, J.G., 367
Norcross, J.C., 3, 5, 6, 11, 12, 13,
    16, 21, 23, 24, 68, 69, 103,
    119, 172, 198, 213, 251,
    299, 321, 322, 328, 345,

350, 351, 477, 482, 484,
    505, 516, 518, 519, 524,
    533, 537
Norman, W.B., 492
Norris, C.J., 509
Norton, P.J., 151, 157
Notarius, C., 151
Nunes, E.V., 410
Nysse, K.L., 541

O
Oates, P., 209
O'Bannon, R.E., III, 413
Oberman, L.M., 509
O'Brien, G.T., 156
O'Brien, W.O., 145
Odeh, M.S., 96
Odom, S.L., 145
Oei, T.P.S., 306
Office of Strategic Services
    Assessment Staff, 150
Ogles, B.M., 14, 337, 507
Ogloff, J.R.P., 462, 463
O-Gorman, J., 74
O'Hern, T., 228
Okazaki, S., 169
Olafsson, R.P., 275
Oland, A.A., 378
Olbrisch, M.E., 499
O'Leary, K.D., 148, 149
Olive, H., 109
Olkin, L., 342
Ollendick, T.H., 148, 344, 345,
    346, 348, 352, 378,
    389, 391
Olos, L., 21
Olshaker, M., 464
Olson, S.L., 281
Oltmanns, T.F., 140
O'Malley, S.S., 214
O'Neal, K.K., 392
O'Neil, M.L., 74
Ones, D.S., 186, 523
Opdyke, D., 275
Orchard, S., 506
Orchowski, L.M., 6, 205
Orlinsky, D.E., 209, 215, 220
Orne, M.T., 120, 155
Ostafin, B.D., 325
Othmer, E.M., 116, 134, 135
Othmer, S.C., 116, 134, 135
Otto, R.K., 450, 462, 463
Owens, E.B., 389
Ownsworth, T.L., 125

P

Pace, T.M., 188
Packard, E., 83, 84
Pagan, J.L., 140
Pallak, M.S., 399
Pantin, H., 393
Paolo, A.M., 179
Papp, L.M., 366
Park, N., 481
Parker, K.C.H., 196
Parks, B.K., 209, 220
Parks, G.A., 150
Parra, G.R., 368
Pasek, L.F., 343
Pate, W.E., II., 14, 21
Pathak, S., 387
Patterson, C.H., 117
Patterson, D.R., 418
Patterson, G.R., 144, 148, 313, 364, 365
Patterson, K.M., 300
Paul, G.L., 13, 87, 152, 273
Pearl, D., 406
Pechere, J.C., 416
Pennebaker, J.W., 404
Penner, L., 63
Pennick, K.A., 353
Perani, D., 432
Perls, F.S., 150, 252, 263
Perry, A.R., 366
Perry, J., 188
Peters, L., 61, 128
Peterson, C., 84, 403, 481, 520
Peterson, D.R., 92, 228, 359, 403, 483, 484
Peterson, E.S., 245
Peterson, L., 151, 359, 383
Peterson, M.L., 228
Peterson, R.F., 148
Petrino, K., 506
Pettijohn, T.F., 36
Phares, V., 314, 363, 365, 379
Phelps, R., 12, 17, 500
Phung, T.M., 389
Physicians' Desk Reference, 324
Pickett, T.C., 326
Pierce, W.D., 169
Pilkonis, P.A., 128
Pincus, D.B., 314, 389
Pincus, H.A., 140
Pine, F., 246, 248
Pingitore, D., 13, 212
Pinnock-Hamilton, T., 209
Pinsof, W.M., 315, 328

Piotrowski, C., 157, 162, 171
Piotrowski, Z., 190
Pittenger, R.E., 139
Plake, B.S., 162, 173
Plante, T.G., 166
Pleck, J., 314
Plomin, R., 394
Plous, S., 142
Pokrywa, M.L., 251, 299
Pollock, K.M., 414
Ponds, R.W., 445
Pope, K.S., 111, 188, 212, 213, 223, 494
Popma, A., 12
Porter, E.H., Jr., 139
Porter, N., 484
Post, C.G., 454
Potter, H.H., 430
Pottick, K.J., 142
Potts, M.K., 142
Powell, L.H., 410
Poythress, N., 450, 453, 461
Poznanski, J.J., 68
Practice Directorate Staff, 27
Price, L., 275
Price, M., 275
Priester, P.E., 389
Prochaska, J.O., 69, 119, 415
Propper, A., 394
Pruitt, L., 35
Psychodynamic Diagnostic Manual Task Force, 84
Puente, A.E., 162, 171
Puska, P., 411
Putnam, E.A., 70, 483, 484
Putnam, F.W., 367

Q

Quinsey, V.L., 91

R

Rabin, B.S., 401
Rabinowitz, J., 93
Radomile, R.R., 306
Rafferty, J.E., 195, 374
Raggi, V.L., 389
Ragland, D.R., 408
Raimy, V.C., 23, 477
Raine, A., 12
Ramachandran, V.S., 509
Ramirez, S.Z., 188
Ramirez-Basco, M., 300
Rand, K.L., 338
Rapaport, D., 248

Rapee, R.M., 128
Rappaport, J., 316, 320
Raskin, J.D., 265
Rasmussen, T., 429
Rasting, M., 118
Rathus, J.H., 281, 286
Rathus, S.A., 121, 234
Raviv, A., 394
Ray, R.S., 148, 364
Raynor, S.R., 366
Reach, K., 383
Reaves, R.P., 487
Reber, J.S., 69
Redd, W.H., 412
Reddy, L.A., 386
Redner, R., 146
Reed, D., 408
Reed, G.M., 404, 500, 501
Reese, F.L., 323
Rehm, L.P., 487
Reich, W., 128
Reid, J.B.B., 155, 313, 365
Reid-Arndt, S., 508
Reiger, D.E., 82
Reilly, R.R., 186
Rein, L., 456
Reinecke, M.A., 60, 282, 284, 285, 289, 299
Reisman, J.M., 32, 37, 41, 43, 160, 191, 195
Reiss, D., 308, 379
Reiss, W.J., 109
Reitan, R.M., 424, 438, 439
Repp, A.C., 145
Reppucci, N.D., 353, 466
Rescorla, L.A., 364, 372, 373, 378, 379, 393
Resnick, J.H., 3
Resnick, P.J., 497
Resnick, R.J., 30
Reveillere, C., 196
Reveson, T.A., 399, 412
Reynolds, C.R., 74
Rhodes, P., 409
Rice, M.E., 89, 91, 96, 146
Rice, S.A., 142
Rich, B.A., 462
Richard, D.C.S., 99
Richman, L.S., 404
Richmond, T.K., 388
Rickert, V., 416, 418
Riggle, E.D.B., 506
Riggs, D., 189
Riley, W.T., 348

Rimm, D.C., 279
Ring, K., 141
Ringeisen, H.L., 348
Ripple, C.H., 320, 353
Risser, H.J., 353, 392
Ritterband, L.M., 327, 508
Robbins, C., 405
Roberts, C.F., 457
Roberts, G.E., 195
Roberts, M.C., 345, 383, 393
Robertson, G.J., 170
Robiner, W.N., 503
Robinson, J.D., 488
Robinson, R.G., 440
Rochlen, A.B., 327
Rock, D.L., 92
Rodin, J., 416
Rodrigues, C.R.C., 155
Rodriguez, H., 467
Roe, A., 480
Roe, D., 229
Roediger, H.L., 528
Roemer, E., 270, 271, 281
Roger, D., 408
Rogers, C.R., 53, 54, 105, 214,
    252, 253, 254, 257, 258,
    261
Rogers, E.G., 69
Rogers, M.R., 505
Rogers, R., 116, 125, 126, 127,
    140, 141
Roginson, K.J., 196
Rohde, D., 456
Roid, G.H., 176, 181
Rokeach, M., 182
Rompa, D., 413
Ronan, G.G., 193
Ronan, K.R., 219
Rorer, L.G., 93
Rorschach, H., 43, 191, 374
Rose, S.D., 305
Rosen, D.S., 388, 389
Rosen, G.M., 322, 354
Rosen, J., 457
Rosen, R.C., 149
Rosenhan, D.L., 316
Rosenman, R.H., 408
Rosenstock, I.M., 417
Rosenthal, R., 342
Rosenthal, T.L., 278
Rosenzweig, S., 195
Ross, D., 270
Ross, M.W., 140
Ross, S.A., 270

Rossini, E.D., 196
Rostosky, S.S., 506
Rothbart, M.K., 36
Rothbaum, B.O., 275
Rothbaum, R., 189
Rothman, A.J., 404
Rotter, J.B., 195, 374
Round, A.P., 97
Rounsaville, B.J., 250
Rourke, B.P., 443
Routh, D.K., 30, 31, 44, 46, 47,
    506
Roy, E.J., 63
Royalty, G.M., 219
Rozanski, A., 409
Rozensky, R.H., 326, 495
Rubens, A.B., 433
Rubin, R., 441
Rudestam, K.E., 508
Rudy, T.E., 411
Ruegg, R.G., 140
Rugg, M.D., 434
Rugulies, R., 409
Rush, A.J., 285
Rush, J.A., 300
Russ, S.W., 386
Russell, E.W., 439
Russell, R.L., 152
Rutheford, M.J., 128
Ryan, J.J., 179
Ryan, K., 353
Rychtarik, R.G., 167
Ryle, A., 328

S
Saab, P.G., 407
Saccuzzo, D.P., 173
Sackett, P.R., 112
Sacks, O., 432
Sade, R.M., 142
Safer, D.L., 295
Safran, J.D., 219
St. Lawrence, J.S., 167, 276, 413
Saklofske, D.H., 178
Salekin, R.T., 125
Sales, B.D., 4, 5, 457, 470, 492
Salovey, P., 57, 282, 404, 416
Salpekar, N., 367, 368
Samuda, R.J., 169
Sanchez, L.M., 501
Sander, J., 384
Sanders, M.R., 157, 391
Sandler, I.N., 320, 353, 389, 391
Sankis, L.M., 81

Santoro, S.O., 11, 12, 13, 16, 24,
    68, 69, 505, 516
Santos, M., 506
Santostefano, S., 145
Santrock, J.W., 174, 321, 322
Sapara, A., 441
Sarafino, E.P., 399
Sarason, S.B., 317
Sarbin, T.R., 85
Sargent, E.L., 457
Sartorius, N., 79
Saslow, G., 104
Satir, V., 62
Sattler, J.M., 373
Saunders, S.M., 215, 343
Sawyer, J., 97
Sayer, L., 314
Sayette, M.A., 5, 21, 24, 477, 482,
    516, 518, 519, 524, 537
Schaefer, C.E., 386
Schaefer, J., 354
Scheffler, R.M., 13, 212
Scheidlinger, S., 430
Schirmer, A., 430
Schmaling, K.B., 352
Schmelkin, L.P., 27, 504
Schmidt, F.L., 342
Schmidt, N.B., 84
Schneck, J.M., 40, 44, 45
Schneider, K.J., 264, 265
Schneider, S.L., 404
Schneider, W., 84
Schneiderman, N., 407
Schnoebelen, S., 384
Schoenwald, S.K., 340
Schopp, L.H., 508
Schradle, S.B., 404
Schretlen, D., 458
Schröder, T.A., 213
Schulenberg, S.E., 99
Schutte, N.S., 343
Schwab-Stone, M.E., 126, 140, 373
Schwartz, B.K., 449
Schwartz, R.D., 146
Schwartz, R.L., 430
Schweinhart, L.J., 145
Scodel, A., 166
Scogin, F.R., 322, 354
Scollon, C.N., 507
Scott, C.L., 497
Scott, S.Y., 506
Scoville, W.B., 434
Sechrest, L.B., 109, 146
Seelau, E., 472

Seelen, J., 188
Seeman, J.A., 139
Segal, D.L., 140
Segal, Z.V., 325
Seifer, R., 369, 371
Self, R., 209
Seligman, M.E.P., 84, 85, 284, 318,
 320, 322, 343, 391, 392,
 403, 507
Sellick, S.M., 324
Selye, H., 399
Seto, M.C., 152
Setzer, N.J., 389
Sexton, T.L., 312, 353
Shadish, W.R., 338, 352
Shaffer, D., 126, 373
Shaffer, G.W., 37
Shagass, C., 152
Shamay-Tsoory, S.G., 430
Shambaugh, E.J., 350
Shannon, D., 102
Shapiro, A.K., 220
Shapiro, D., 343
Shapiro, D.A., 342, 343
Shapiro, S.L., 323, 325
Sharma, T., 441
Shaw, B.F., 285
Shaw, D.A., 148, 364
Shaw, D.L., 142
Shaw, D.S., 378
Shaw, E.C., 92
Shaywitz, B.A., 442
Shaywitz, S.E., 442
Shea, S.C., 116
Shechtman, Z., 140
Shenk, C., 325
Shepherd, M.D., 322
Sher, K.J., 368
Sherrill, J.T., 348
Shiffman, S., 416
Shipley, K.G., 116
Shirk, S.R., 351
Shivy, V.A., 93
Shochet, I.M., 391
Shum, D., 74
Shuman, D.W., 457, 470
Shumer, E., 62
Shure, M.B., 319
Siegel, B., 382
Sigelman, C.K., 141
Silverman, M.M., 320
Silverman, W.K., 344
Silversmith, D.J., 167
Simerly, E., 375
Simon, N.P., 488

Simpson, J., 384
Simpson, L.E., 308
Sinacore-Guinn, G.A., 142
Singal, B.M., 409
Singer, B., 18
Singer, J.A., 57, 282
Singer, J.E., 399, 412
Singer, M., 142
Singer, M.T., 324
Skinner, B.F., 57
Skinner, B.F., 57
Skovholt, T.M., 210, 211, 218
Sledge, W.H., 140
Sleek, S., 472
Slep, A.M.S., 308, 379
Slife, B.D., 69
Slobogin, C., 457, 470
Smallwood, J., 143
Smith, A.J., 146, 179
Smith, A.P., 401
Smith, D., 197
Smith, J., 128
Smith, L., 506
Smith, L.A., 461
Smith, M., 189
Smith, M.L., 342, 343
Smith, R., 499
Smith, S., 275, 471
Smith, T., 390
Smokowski, P.R., 365
Smolar, A.I., 306
Snitz, B.E., 96
Snowdon, D.A., 404
Snyder, C.R., 84
Snyder, D.K., 311, 352
Snyder, J.J., 313, 365
Snyder, W.V., 139
Sobel, R., 61
Solomon, D.A., 340
Solomon, H.C., 57
Somers-Flanagan, J., 120
Somers-Flanagan, R., 120
Sommer, R., 321, 322, 508
Southam-Gerow, M.A., 340, 348
Spangler, D.L., 219
Spangler, W.D., 196
Spearman, C., 173
Spence, S.H., 327
Sperry, L., 221, 223
Sperry, R.W., 425, 429
Speyer, C., 327
Spickard, B.A., 6, 205
Spiegel, D., 324
Spiegel, T.A., 150
Spiegler, M.D., 281

Spielberger, C.D., 169, 189
Spielmans, G.I., 325, 343
Spitzer, R.L., 125
Spofford, M., 501
Sprafkin, J.N., 78
Spring, B., 63, 349
Stahl, P.M., 468
Stambaugh, L.F., 391
Stambor, Z., 504
Stanley, M.A., 189
Stanley-Hagan, M., 366
Stark, K.D., 384, 385
Starkstein, S.E., 440
Starr, L., 151
Staub, R.O., 405
Steadman, H.J., 91, 456, 457
Steckel, S.B., 418
Steele, R.G., 345, 393
Steen, T.A., 85, 320, 392, 507
Steer, R.A., 87, 188
Steffek, B.D., 278
Stein, D.J., 394, 509
Steinberg, L., 376
Steiner, J.L., 140
Steketee, G.S., 276
Stepleman, L.M., 506
Stepp, S.D., 125
Sterling, M., 265
Stern, T.E., 219
Sternberg, R.J., 88, 173, 174,
 333, 528
Stevens, M.R., 186
Steward, W.T., 404
Stewart, M.O., 354
Stewart, R.E., 348
Stoddard, A.M., 141
Stoerig, P., 431
Stokols, D., 406
Stolorow, R.D., 249
Stone, A.A., 403
Storch, E.A., 393, 394
Storm, J., 144
Stormshak, E.A., 313
Stout, C.E., 500
Stramler, C.S., 142
Straub, R.O., 399
Strauss, B., 303
Strauss, E., 429
Strauss, G.D., 140
Strausser-Kirkland, D., 213
Stricker, G., 328, 484
Stricker, G., 24, 67, 328
Strohmer, D.C., 93
Stromseth, J., 68
Strother, C.R., 480

Subject Index

A

Abstinence violation effect, 294
Abulia, 436
Academy of Psychological
	Clinical Science, 481, 483,
	485, 532, 537, 548-549
Achenbach System of Empirically
	Based Assessment
	(ASEBA), 373, 393
Active listening, 131-132
Actualizing tendency, 53
Actuarial prediction, 94
Ad Hoc Task Force on
	Psychopharmacology
	(APA), 502
Agnosia, 424, 433-434, 436
Akinetic mutism, 436
Alder's individual psychology,
	247-248
Alternative treatments/medicine,
	10, *See* Clinical
	interventions, alternative
	modes
American Association for
	Applied Psychology
	(AAAP), 47
American Association of Clinical
	Psychologists (AACP), 47
American Board of Examiners in
	Professional Psychology
	(ABEPP), 48
American Board of Professional
	Psychology (ABPP), 488
*American Journal of Community
	Psychology,* 316

American Psychological
	Association (APA), 4, 6, 46,
	112, 170, 221, 223, 347,
	477, 489-491, 494, 502,
	506, 529, 531
American Psychologist, 4, 48,
	476, 484, 531
Amnesia, 424, 436
Analog behavior observation
	(ABO), 157
Analog research, 340-341
Anchoring bias, in clinical
	judgment, 93
Annals of Behavioral Medicine,
	398
Anosognosia, 430-431, 436
Anticipatory nausea, 412
Anxiety disorders, in children,
	381-382
Aphasia, 424, 436
Approaches, basic concepts of
	behavioral, 57
	cognitive, 59
	group, family, marital, related
		systems, 62
	humanistic, 55
	psychoanalytic, 52
Apraxia, 424, 436
Aprosodia, 430, 436
Asperger's disorder,
	382-383
Assertiveness training, 276
Assessment, in clinical
	psychology, 72
	children, 371-377

clinical judgment and decision
	making, 91-100
	clinical intuition, 92-97
	computerized assessment,
		98-100
	improving, 97
clinicians' theoretical
	orientation, 103-105
collecting data
	multiple assessment
		sources, value of, 77
	sources of assessment data,
		74-75
communicating assessment
	results, 78, 107-110
	relevance to goals, 109
	report clarity, 108-109
	usefulness of reports,
		109-110
context, 103
ethical considerations,
	110-113
goals of, 78
	descriptive assessment,
		85-86
	diagnostic classification,
		79-85
	prediction, 87-91
	treatment planning, 86-87
humanistically oriented
	assessment, 105-106
process, 73-78
	case study guide, 76
	planning data collection
		procedures, 74-77

Assessment, in clinical
  psychology (*cont.*)
  referral question, receiving
    and clarifying, 74, 75
  processing data, 77–78
  psychometric properties,
    of instruments
    bandwidth-fidelity issues,
      102–103
    reliability, 100–101
    standardization, 102
    validity, 101
Assimilation integration, 328
Assistantships, 545, 546
Association of Consulting
  Psychologists (ACP), 47
Association of State and
  Provincial Psychology
  (ASPPB), 486
Asynchronous communication,
  321
Attention-deficit hyperactivity
  disorder (ADHD), 373,
  379–380, 388, 389
Attrition, 229
*Authoritative Guide to Self-Help
  Resources in Mental
  Health, Revised Edition,*
  322
Autistic disorder, 382–383, 389
Automatic thoughts, role of,
  283–285
Availability heuristic, 92, 93
Aversion therapy, 278–279

B
Bandwidth-fidelity, 102–103, 125
Beaunis, Henri, 36
Beck, Aaron, 59, 188
Beck Depression Inventory, 188
Beck's cognitive therapy, 285–286
Beers, Clifford, 40
Behavioral avoidance tests, 153
Behavioral parent training, 313,
  314, 353, 389
Behavioral therapy, to clinical
  psychology, 55–57, 269,
  386–387
  case example, 280–281
  clinical applications, 272–279
  aversion therapy and
    punishment, 278–279
  behavioral rehearsal and
    homework, 278

exposure and response
    prevention techniques,
    275–276
  modeling, 276–278
  relaxation training, 272–273
  social skills training, 276
  systematic desensitization,
    273–274
  virtual reality exposure, 275
  goals of, 272
  theoretical foundations,
    270–272
  assessment, 271–272
  therapist, role of, 272
Behavior and Symptom
  Identification Scale
  (BASIS-32), 200
Behavior rehearsal, 278, 279
Bender-Gestalt Test, 43, 196
Bender Visual Motor Gestalt Test,
  196
Bessel, F. W., 35, 38
Between-subject research
  designs, 333, 336–337
Bibliotherapy, 219, 321, 322, 354
Binet, Alfred, 36–37, 38, 41, 174
Binet-Simon scale, 37
Blindsight, 431, 436
Boulder Conference, 48,
  477–480, 484
Boulder model, 23
Box score reviews, 342
Buffer model, 405

C
California Psychological
  Inventory (CPI), 189
California Psychotherapy
  Alliance Scales, 214
Campbell Interest and Skill
  Inventory (CISI), 182
Cancer, prevention and treatment
  programs for, 412
Cardiovascular disease
  prevention and treatment
    programs, 410–411
  risk factors for, 406–409
Case formulation, 226, 239, 259
Cathartic method, 49–50
Cattell, James McKeen, 37, 38
*Character Strengths and Virtues:
  A Classification and
  Handbook,* 84
Charcot, Jean-Martin, 41

Child Behavior Checklist (CBCL),
  149, 372, 373, 379
Child custody evaluation,
  465–467
Child Depression Inventory, 372
Childhood depression, 380–381
Children's Apperception Test
  (CAT), 195, 374
Civil competencies, 461–462
Classical conditioning, 270
Client, in psychotherapy, 207–210
  problems and treatment
    utilization, 208–209
  variables and treatment
    outcomes, 209–210,
    350–351
Client-centered therapy, 53, 214,
  253, 386
Client satisfaction surveys, 343
Clinical attitude, 3
Clinical child psychology, 358
  characteristics, unique
  confidentiality, 363
  context of behavior, 363
  developmental
    considerations, 363–364
  parent–child interaction
    patterns, 364–365
  referral processes, 362–363
  childhood disorders,
    classification of, 377–379
  clinically derived systems,
    377–378
  empirically derived systems,
    378
  externalizing factors in, 378
  internalizing factors in, 378
  childhood disorders,
    prevention of, 391–392
  childhood disorders, specific
  anxiety disorders, 381–382
  attention-deficit
    hyperactivity disorder
    (ADHD), 379–380
  autistic disorder, 382–383
  childhood depression,
    380–381
  conduct disorder, 380
  oppositional defiant
    disorder, 380
  pediatric health problems,
    383
  childhood disorders, treatment
    of, 385–391

behavioral therapy, 386–387
cognitive-behavioral
    interventions, 387
psychodynamic therapy,
    386–387
psychological treatments,
    effectiveness of, 389–390
psychopharmacological
    interventions, 387–388
therapeutic alliance, 390–391
children, clinical assessment,
    371–377
behavioral observations, 375
behavior rating scales,
    372–373
clinical interviews, 373–374
family interaction measures,
    375–376
intelligence and
    achievement tests, 374
peer interaction measures,
    376
protective tests, 374–375
clinical case, 383–385
future of
care, access to, 393
diversity and
    multiculturalism, 392–393
research, interdisciplinary
    approaches to, 394
history of, 359–362
protective factors, 368–369, 370
risk factors, 369
interparental conflict, 366
physical abuse, 366–367
poverty and affluence,
    367–368
sexual abuse, 367
temperament, 365–366
Clinical interventions
ethical guidelines, 221–224
goals of, 217
assigning extratherapy tasks,
    219
developing faith, hope, and
    expectation for change,
    219–220
encouraging catharsis,
    218–219
fostering insight, 218
providing new information,
    219
reducing emotional
    discomfort, 217–218

practical aspects of, 224–229
psychotherapy
case formulation and
    treatment planning,
    226–228
definition of, 204
ethical concerns in, 221–223
kinds of approaches,
    206–207
participants in, 207–215
public misperception of,
    205–206
record keeping in, 225
settings for, 215–216
termination of, 229
therapist objectivity and
    self-disclosure, 228–229
treatment duration and fees,
    225
research on
effectiveness of alternative
    modes of intervention,
    351–355
effectiveness of individual
    psychotherapy, 341
methods for evaluating
    psychotherapy, 332–337
practical problems in,
    337–341
Clinical interventions, alternative
    modes
community psychology
definition of, 316
history of, 316
principles and methods of,
    317
complimentary/alternative
    medicine (CAM), 323–324
couples therapy, 306, 308–312
diagnosis in, 307–308
effectiveness of, 352
social contexts of, 314–315
family therapy, 61–62, 306,
    312–314
diagnosis in, 307–308
effectiveness of, 352–353
social context of, 314–315
group therapy, 302–306
case example, 305–306
cognitive-behavioral, 306
effectiveness of, 352
practice of, 305
therapeutic factors in,
    303–304

mindfulness, 325
self-help interventions,
    320–322, 354
spirituality, 324–325
Clinical intuition, 92–97
availability heuristic, 92, 93
clinical versus statistical
    prediction, 94–97
Clinical judgment and decision
    making, 91–100
clinical intuition, 92–97
computerized assessment,
    98–100
improving, 97
Clinical neuropsychology, 421
assessment, 437–439
individualized approaches,
    437, 439
test batteries, 437, 438–439
basic principles of
lateralization of function,
    428–431
levels of interaction,
    427–428
localization of function,
    426–427
modularity, 427
current status of, 444–445
dysfunction, patterns of
frontal lobe dysfunction,
    434–436
occipital lobe dysfunction,
    431
parietal lobe dysfunction,
    431–433
temporal lobe dysfunctions,
    433–434
history of
early influences, 423–424
neuropsychological
    assessment techniques,
    development of, 424–425
normal brains, research on,
    425
split-brain research, 425
neuropsychological
    approaches to
    psychopathology
depression, 440–441
learning disabilities, 442
nonverbal learning
    disabilities, 442–443
schizophrenia, 441–442
Clinical prediction, 94–97

Clinical psychologists
activities of
administration, 16
assessment, 11–12
consultation, 15–16
research, 13–15
teaching, 15
treatment, 12–13
clients and their problems,
17–18
clinical activities, distribution
of, 16–17
clinical attitude of, 3
diversity among, 21–22
educational requirements of,
4–5
employment settings and
salaries, 19–21
ethical codes of, 5–6, 98,
110–112
legal requirements of, 4
personal requirements of, 3
prescription privileges for, 27
from professional
organizations, 46–48
as psychotherapists, 43–46
Clinical psychology
approaches to
behavioral, 55–57
cognitive, 57–60
cognitive-behavioral, 60
comparison of, 64–66
family therapy, 61–62
group therapy, 60, 61
humanistic, 52–55
marital therapy, 62
pros and cons of taking
specific approach, 67–69
psychodynamic, 49–52
behavior and mental
processes, 2
biological influences on,
62–64
definition of, 2–3
expansion of, 42–48
full license in, 4
popularity of, 6
roots of, 30–42
clinical tradition, 38–42
empirical tradition, 31–34
psychometric tradition,
34–38
training, 23–24, 507
21st century, 22, 69

eclecticism and integration
in, 24
health care environment
and, 24–28
science and practice in,
22–24
during World Wars I and II,
42–48
Clinical Psychology Review, 14
Clinical scientist model, 483
*Clinical Treatment of the
Problem Child,* 53
Clinical utility, 199–200
Clinician Home-based Interview
to Assess Function
(CHIF), 124
Cognitive-behavioral group
therapy, 306
Cognitive-behavioral therapy
(CBT), 60, 292
case example, 295–299
clinical applications, 293–295
dialectical behavior therapy,
294–295
relapse prevention, 294
current status of, 299–300
theoretical foundations, 293
Cognitive mediation, 282–283
Cognitive restructuring, 384
Cognitive specificity hypothesis,
285
Cognitive therapy, 57–60
clinical applications
maladaptive thoughts,
refuting and replacing,
290–291
psychoeducation, 288–289
Socratic questioning,
289–290
thought recording and
multicolumn records,
291
goals of, 288
theoretical foundations,
282–288
assessment, 287–288
automatic thoughts, role of,
283–285
Beck's cognitive therapy,
285–286
cognitive mediation,
282–283
rational-emotive behavior
therapy, 286–287

schemas, 283
therapist, role of, 288
Collaborative empiricism, 288
Committee for the Advancement
of Professional Practice
(CAPP), 16
Committee on Standards of
Training in Clinical
Psychology (APA), 46–47
Common factors approach, 328
*Community Mental Health
Journal,* 316
Community psychology
definition of, 316
history of, 316
principles and methods of, 317
Comorbidity, of psychological
disorders, 82, 378
Competency, 112–113, 213,
222–223, 449–453,
461–462, 489, 504–506
Complimentary/alternative
medicine (CAM), 323–324
Computers in
assessment, 98–99
treatment, 99, 326–327
Computers in Human Behavior,
99
Concurrent validity, 101, 140
Conditions of worth, 54, 254, 255
Conduct disorder (CD), 380
Confidence interval, 101
Confidentiality, 222, 363, 489
Confirmation bias, 93, 290
Conflict of interest, 223
Congruence, 258, 261
Conjoint therapy, 309
Consolidated Standards of
Reporting Trials
(CONSORT) standards,
339
Construct validity, 101, 172, 198,
439
Consumer Reports (CR), 343
Content validity, 101, 140, 172
Contingency contracting, 279,
418
Controlled observation, 145,
149–153
behavioral avoidance tests,
153
performance measures, 150
physiological measures, 152
role-playing tests, 150–152

virtual reality assessment, 152–153
Convergent validity, 141, 155
Core health care professions, 7–10
Coping strategies, 402–403
Correctional psychology, 449
Corrective emotional experience, 250
Council of University Directors of Clinical Psychology (CUDCP), 529
Counseling psychologists, 7–8
Countertransference, 236, 237, 243
Couples therapy, 306, 308–312
  diagnosis in, 307–308
  effectiveness of, 352
  social contexts of, 314–315
Crawford Small Parts Dexterity Test, 182
Criminal competence, 449–450
Criminal profiling, 463–464
Crisis Intervention Semistructured Interview, 124
Crisis interviews, 120
Criteria for Evaluating Treatment Guidelines (APA), 494
Criterion validity, 101, 102, 176
Criterion variance, 127
Crystallized intelligence, 180
Cultural competence, 121–122, 504–506
Cultural fairness, 167–169
Cultural sensitivity, in clinical interviews, 121–122
Custody mediation, 467–469

D

Debriefing interviews, 120
Decatastrophizing, 291
Depression, neuropsychological approaches to, 440–441
Desensitization. *See* Systematic desensitization (SD)
Developmental considerations, 363–364
Developmental psychopathology, 361
Development and Psychopathology, 361
Diagnosis-based treatment, 226

Diagnostic and Statistical Manual of Mental Disorders (DSM), 40, 307, 377
  alternative diagnostic proposals and, 84–85
  children and adolescents, 360–361, 377–379
  DSM-IV and DSM-IV-TR, 80–83, 360–361, 377
  history of, 79–80
Dialectical behavior therapy (DBT), 294–295
Diathesis, 63, 64
Dimensional approach (diagnostic system), 84
Direct-effect model, 405
Discriminant validity, 141
Dismantling research design, 337
Dissemination, 317, 508
Diversity, 17–19, 21–22, 392–393, 504–506
Dix, Dorothea, L., 40
Draw-a-Person (DAP) test, 196, 374
Dream work, 242
Drug Abuse Resistance Education (DARE) program, 391–392

E

Echolalia, 382, 436
Eclecticism, 24
Ecological Family Intervention and Therapy (EcoFIT), 313
Ecological validity, 144
Ectopias, 442
Effect size, 342–343
Ego, 51, 104, 233, 234
Ego and the Mechanisms of Defense, 234
Ego psychology, 248
E-health, 326, 508
Ellis, Albert, 59, 286–287
Emotion-focused coping, 403
Empathy, 136, 210, 256–258, 260
Employment for Clinical Psychologists
  salaries, 19–20
  settings, 20, 482, 514–515
Empirically supported treatments (ESTs), 343–347

Empowerment, 320
Empty chair technique, 263
Equal Employment Opportunity Commission (EEOC), 170
Equipotentiality, 423
Ethical Principles of Psychologists and Code of Conduct (APA). *See* Ethics Code
Ethics Code, 5, 110–112, 170, 221–224, 489–495
Ethnicity/race, 17–18, 21–22, 120–122, 208–210, 367, 392–393, 504–506
Evidence-based practice (EBP), 23, 303, 313, 332, 347–349
Examination for Professional Practice in Psychology (EPPP), 4, 486, 487
Exhopraxia, 436
Existential psychotherapies, 264–265
Experiential therapies, 52
Experimental neuroses, 55
Expert testimony, 469–472
Exposure techniques, 275–276, 279
Extended Interaction Test, 151
External frame of reference, 257, 264
External validity, 338, 339, 341
  dealing with threats to clinical trials, 339–340
  laboratory analogs, 340–341
  single-subject and case-study research, 338–340
Externalizing problems, 378–379
Eysenck Personality Questionnaire, 189

F

Factor analytic studies, 174, 179
Factorial experiments, 337
False negative outcome, 90
False positive outcome, 90
Family Diagnosis: An Approach to the Preschool Child, 61
Family therapy, 61–62, 306, 312–314
  diagnosis in, 307–308
  effectiveness of, 352–353
  social context of, 314–315
Famlias Unidas program, 392–393

Fear Survey Schedule (FSS), 188
Fechner, Gustav, 31, 33
Federal Employee Health
    Benefits Act, 499
Federal Work Injuries
    Compensation Program,
    499
*Feeling Good: The New Mood
    Therapy,* 321
Fellowships, 519, 545
Flooding, 275
Fluid intelligence, 180
Forensic evaluations, 89
Forensic psychology, 447
    child custody disputes,
        465–467
    criminal competence and
        responsibility, 449–450
    assessing competence,
        450–453
    insanity defense, 454–458
    criminal profiling, 463–464
    custody mediation, 467–469
    dangerousness, predicting,
        458–459
    mental health experts in legal
        system, 469–472
    parental fitness, 465
    psychological autopsies,
        462–463
    psychological damages in civil
        trials
    civil competencies, 461–462
    tort cases, 459–460
    workers' compensation
        cases, 460–461
    scope of, 448–449
Frame setting, of interview,
    130–131
Free association, 50, 240–241,
    247
Freedom of choice laws, 499
Freud, Sigmund, 41, 44, 45, 49–52,
    232–234, 238
Frontal lobe dysfunction,
    434–436

G
Gall, Franz, 35, 38, 423
Galton, F., 36, 38
Gender bias, in clinical judgment,
    93–94
General adaptation syndrome
    (GAS), 399

*General Guidelines for
    Providers of
    Psychological Services*
    (APA), 112
General Intelligence Model, 173
Gestalt therapy, 262–264
*Getting In: A Step-by-Step Plan
    for Gaining Admission to
    Graduate School in
    Psychology,* 527, 531, 540
Goddard, Henry H., 37, 38
Gold standard, 140–141
Goodenough Draw-A-Man Test, 43
Graded motor imagery, 412
Graded task assignments, 278,
    279
Grade Point Average (GPA), 524,
    525, 537–538
Graduate Record Exam (GRE),
    523–524, 525, 533–537
Graduate schools, getting into
    acceptance decision, 546–547
    application procedures,
        527–546
    APA accreditation, 531
    application deadlines,
        531–532
    assistantships from
        departments, 546
    cost to apply, 533
    financial aid, 545–546
    grade point average, 537–538
    Graduate Record Exam,
        533–537
    letters of recommendation,
        538–540
    onsite interview, 543–545
    personal interview, 541–543
    personal statement,
        540–541
    resources, 527–531
    assessing credentials and
        aspirations, 524–525
    choosing graduate programs,
        512
    MA, PhD, or PsyD, 514–517
    research versus clinical
        emphasis, 513–514
    commitment and doctoral
        programs
    academic and emotional,
        520–521
    finance, 517–520
    time, 517

credentials needed for
    admission
    Grade point average, 524
    GRE scores, 523–524
    letters of recommendation,
        524
    undergraduate coursework
        and experience, 521–523
    master's degree programs and,
        526–527
*Graduate Study in
    Psychology,* 527
Grit, 520
Group therapy, 60, 61, 216,
    302–306
    case example, 305–306
    cognitive-behavioral, 306
    effectiveness of, 352
    practice of, 305
    therapeutic factors in,
        303–304
*Guidelines and Principles for
    Accreditation of
    Programs in Professional
    Psychology* (APA), 477
Guidelines for Child Custody
    Evaluations in Divorce
    Proceedings (APA), 467,
    468
*Guidelines for Psychological
    Evaluations in Child
    Protection Matters* (APA),
    112
Guidelines for Psychological
    Practice with Older
    Adults (APA), 494
Guidelines for Psychotherapy
    with Lesbian, Gay, &
    Bisexual Clients (APA),
    494
Guidelines for Test User
    Qualifications (APA), 170
Guidelines on Multicultural
    Education, Training,
    Research, Practice, and
    Organizational change for
    Psychologists (APA), 494
Guilty but mentally ill (GBMI),
    449, 457

H
Halstead, Ward, 424
Halstead-Reitan Battery (HRB),
    424, 438–439, 443

The Handbook of Positive Psychology Assessment, 84
Handbook of psychotherapy integration, 328
Health belief model (HBM), 417, 418
Health Insurance Portability and Accountability Act (HIPAA), 494
Health psychology
 case example, 414–416
 definition of, 397–399
 illness prevention and treatment programs
  for cancer, 412
  for cardiovascular diseases, 410–411
  for HIV/AIDS, 412–414
  for pain, 411–412
 improving adherence to medical treatment regimens, 416–418
  interventions, 417–418
  nonadherence, causes of, 417
 risk factors for illness
  cardiovascular disease, 406–409
  HIV/AIDS, 409
 stress, coping and health
  coping strategies, 402–403
  measuring stressors, 402
  social support, 404–406
  stress and immune system, 401–402
  stress and nervous system, 399–401
  stress-hardy personality characteristics, 403–404
Healy, William, 44
Helmholtz, Herman, 31, 33
Hemineglect, 432, 436
Henri, Victor, 37
Hierarchical and Factor Analytic Models, 174
HIV/AIDS
 prevention and treatment programs, 412–414
 risk factors for, 409
Hollingworth, Leta, 47
Holtzman Inkblot Test, 191
Home observations, 148, 375
House-Tree-Person (HTP) test, 196, 374

Humanistically oriented therapists, 61, 62, 104, 105, 214, 229
Humanistic psychotherapy, 52–55, 252
 current status of, 265–266
 existential psychotherapies, 264–265
 Gestalt therapy, 262–264
 person-centered therapy, 253–262
 postmodern humanistic approaches, 265
Hypnosis, 49–50

I

Id, 51, 233, 234
Ideal self-concept, 254
Illusionary correlations, 93
Imaginal desensitization, 273, 274
Immunosuppression, 401
Impression management, 141
Incomplete sentence tests, 195–196, 374
Incongruence, 254–255
Indicated prevention intervention, 318
Indigenous paraprofessionals, 317
Individual psychology, 247–248
Information variance, 125, 127
Informed consent, 223
Inpatient Multidimensional Psychiatric Scales (IMPS), 146–147, 149
Insanity defense, 454–458
 expert witnesses, role of, 456–457
 GBMI verdict and, 457
 misperceptions of, 454–456
 NGRI acquitees and, 456
Insider's Guide to Graduate Programs in Clinical and Counseling Psychology 2008/2009 Edition, 527, 531, 540
Insight, 52, 218, 237–238
Institutional Review Board (IRB), 6, 491
Intake interviews, 117–118
Intelligence, theories of
 General Intelligence Model, 173

Hierarchical and Factor Analytic Models, 174
Multiple Specific Intelligence Models, 173–174
Interdisciplinary, 383, 394, 398, 508–509
Internal validity, 338, 339, 341, 346
 dealing with threats to
  clinical trials, 339–340
  laboratory analogs, 340–341
  single-subject and case-study research, 338–340
Internalizing problems, 378–379
International Classification of Diseases (ICD), 79, 307
International Neuropsychological Society (INS), 444
International Test Consortium (ITC), 169
Internet, 326–327, 508
Interparental conflict, 366
Interpersonal psychotherapy (IPT), 249, 250
Interpretations of transference reactions, 237–238
Interrater reliability, 100–101, 139, 140, 154, 172, 378
Interviewing, in clinical psychology, 116
 clinical interview situations
  crisis interviews, 120
  ethnic and cultural issues, 120–122
  intake interviews, 117–118
  orientation interviews, 119
  problem-referral interviews, 118–119
  termination and debriefing interviews, 119–120
 communication in
  nonverbal, 137–138
  verbal, 136–137
 observational assessment
  approaches to, 144–153
  goals and benefits, 142–144
  research on, 153–158
 research on the interview, 138–142
  early studies of interview, 139
  interviewer error and bias, 141–142
  reliability and validity of data, 139–141

Interviewing, in clinical
psychology (*cont.*)
stages in, 129–136
structure, 122–128
nondirective interviews, 123
semistructured interviews,
124
structured interviews,
124–128
Interviews, in graduate school
admission, 541–545
Ipsative measurement, 166

J

James, Williams, 41
Janet, Pierre, 41
Jones, Mary Cover, 56, 269
*Journal of Abnormal Child
Psychology*, 361
Journal of Behavioral Medicine,
397
*Journal of Clinical Child and
Adolescent Psychology*,
361
*Journal of Community
Psychology*, 316
*Journal of Consulting and
Clinical Psychology*, 14
*Journal of Consulting
Psychology*, 47
*Journal of Psychotherapy
Integration*, 24, 328

K

Kaufman Assessment Battery for
Children, 180
Kaufman Brief Intelligence Test-2
(K-BIT-2), 180
Kaufman Test of Educational
Achievement (K-TEA-II),
181
Kelly, George, 58
Kraepelin, Emil, 40, 41
Kuder Occupational Interest
Survey (KOIS), 182

L

Latent content of dream, 242
Lateralization of brain function,
428–431
Law enforcement psychology, 448
Learning disorders, 360, 442
Leiter International Performance
Scale, 180

Letters of recommendation, 524,
538–540
Licensure, 4–5, 485–488
Life Skills Training Program, 392
Limited license psychologist, 5
Loan programs, 545
Localization of brain function,
423, 426–427
Lombroso, Cesare, 36

M

Major depressive disorder in
children, 380–381
Managed care, 26–27, 143, 172,
500–502
Manifest content of dream, 242
Marital therapy, 62, 306, 352
Marriage and family therapists, 9
Maskelyne, Nevil, 34
Masters degree, 5, 8, 20, 21, 480,
514–515, 525–527, 537
Mechanical prediction, 94
Medical offset, 499
Meehl, Paul, 94–95
Mental health literacy, 6
Mental health parity, 25–26
Mental Health Parity Act, 499
Mental illness, 39
*Mental Measurements
Yearbook*, 43, 162
Mental status examination
(MSE), 117, 118
Meta-analysis, 342–343
Miller Analogies Test, 43
Millon Clinical Multiaxial
Inventory (MCMI), 188
Mindfulness, 325
Minnesota Multiphasic
Personality Inventory
(MMPI), 184–188, 199, 466
Mirror neurons, 509
Modularity, 427
Müller, Johannes, 31, 33
Multicultural Guidelines:
Education, Research, and
Practice (APA), 506
Multiculturalism, 392, 504–506
Multidimensional Personality
Questionnaire (MPQ), 189
Multiple-baseline design,
334–336
Multiple Specific Intelligence
Models, 173–174
Munsterberg, Hugo, 37

Myers-Briggs Type Indicator
(MBTI), 190

N

National Academy of Sciences'
Institute of Medicine, 319
National Health Service Corps,
519
National Institute of Health
(NIH) Loan Repayment
Program, 519
National Institute of Mental
Health's Prevention
Intervention Research
Centers, 319
Naturalistic observations
home observation, 148
hospital observation, 146–148
observation by insiders,
148–149
by participant observers,
145–146
school observation, 148
self-observation, 149
unobtrusive measures, 146
Negative attributional style,
284–285, 290
Negative predictive power, 90
NEO Personality Inventory-
Revised (NEO-PI-R), 190
Neurotics, 49, 184
Newsweek, 205
New York Association of
Consulting Psychologists,
47
Nonadherence, 416–417, 418
Nondirective interviews, 123,
131–133
active listening, 131–132
paraphrasing, 132
Nonverbal communication, 97,
118, 137–138, 264
Nonverbal learning disabilities,
neuropsychological
approaches to, 442–443
Not guilty by reason of insanity
(NGRI), 449, 454, 455, 456
Not otherwise specified (NOS)
diagnosis, 82

O

Objective personality tests, 183
California Psychological
Inventory (CPI), 189

Myers-Briggs Type Indicator
(MBTI), 190
NEO Personality Inventory-
Revised (NEO-PI-R), 190
Sixteen Personality Factors
Questionnaire (16PF), 189
Object relations theory, 248
Observation, in clinical
psychology
controlled, 149–153
behavioral avoidance tests,
153
performance measures, 150
physiological measures, 152
role-playing tests, 150–152
virtual reality assessment,
152–153
naturalistic
home observation, 148
hospital observation,
146–148
observation by insiders,
148–149
by participant observers,
145–146
school observation, 148
self-observation, 149
unobtrusive measures, 146
research on, 153–158
observation methods, trends
in the use of, 157
observer effects, 156–157
reliability of assessment,
154–155
representativeness of
observed behavior,
155–156
validity of assessment, 155
Observational assessment,
142–158
Observational learning, 270–271,
276
Obsessive-compulsive disorder,
275, 277
Occipital lobe dysfunction, 431
Operant conditioning, 57, 270,
278, 365
Oppositional defiant disorder
(ODD), 380
Orientation interviews, 119
Osler, William Sir, 398
Outcome-based treatment, 226
Outcome Questionnaire-45
(OQ-45), 200

P
Pain, prevention and treatment
programs for, 411–412
Paraphrasing, 132, 211
Paraprofessionals, 9–10, 317
Parental fitness, 465
Parent–child interaction therapy
(PCIT), 314, 353, 389
Parent-child interactions, 364–365
Parent management training,
313, 353
Parent Rating Scale and Teacher
Rating Scale, 373
Parietal lobe dysfunction,
431–433
Participant modeling, 278
Pathogenic stressors, 63
Patient variance, 125, 127
Pavlov, Ivan, 55
Peabody Picture Vocabulary
Test-Revised, 180
Pediatric psychologists, 383
Perceived Stress Scale (PSS), 402
Personal constructs theory, 58
Personality
objective tests, 183, 189–190
projective tests, 184, 190–198
Personal statement, in graduate
school admission,
540–541
Person-centered therapy,
253–262, 266
case example, 259–262
congruence, 258
empathy, 256–258
nature of change in, 258
unconditional positive regard,
255–256
Person-situation interactions, 144
Phallometric measurement, 152
Phantom pain, 411–412
PhD degree, 4, 7, 23, 28, 47, 48,
477–478, 480–483, 507,
510, 513–519, 521–526,
531–532, 537
Phenomenological therapies,
52, 53
Phrenology, 35–36, 423
Physical abuse, 366–367
Play therapy, 386
Porteus Maze Test, 180
Positive predictive power, 90
Positive psychology, 84, 392, 404,
507–508

Postmodern humanistic
psychotherapy, 265
Poverty, 367
Practitioner–scholar model, 483
Prediction
clinical versus statistical,
94–97
of dangerousness, 89–91
of future performance, 89
prognosis, 87–89
Predictive validity, 101, 140, 141,
155
Premature termination, 229
Prescription privileges, 27,
502–504
Presidential Task Force on
Evidence-Based Practice
(APA), 347
Preventive intervention, 318–320
effectiveness of, 353
prevention strategies, 319–320
Primary prevention, of
psychological disorders,
318, 319
Problem-focused coping, 403
Problem-referral interviews,
118–119
Professional issues, in clinical
psychology, 475
future of clinical psychology,
507–509
dissemination, 508
interdisciplinary science,
508–509
positive psychology,
507–508
professional specialization,
507
technology, 508
training, 507
multicultural competence,
504–506
professional ethics
of American Psychological
Association, 489–491
ethical violations, 493–494
implementation of ethical
standards, 491–493
other standards, 494
regulation through state
laws, 495–498
professional independence
economics of mental health
care, 498–502

Professional issues, in clinical psychology (*cont.*)
prescription privileges, 502–504
regulation
ABPP certification, 488
certification and licensure, 485–488
training, 476–484
Boulder Conference, 477–480
clinical training today, 481
Doctor of Psychology (PsyD) degree, 482–483
evaluating clinical training, 484
professional schools, 482
Salt Lake City Conference, 480–481
training models, 483–484
Vail Conference, 480
Professional regulation of psychologists
ABPP certification, 488
certification and licensure, 485–488
through state laws, 495–498
duty to warn, 495–496
malpractice litigation, 496–498
Prognosis, 87–89
Progressive relaxation training (PRT), 272–273, 279
Projective personality tests, 184, 190–198, 374–375
Bender-Gestalt Test, 196
incomplete sentence tests, 195–196
projective drawings, 196
reliability and validity of, 196–198
Rorschach Inkblot Test, 191–193
Thematic Apperception Test (TAT), 193–195
Prosopagnosia, 424, 436
Protective factors, 368–371
Psychiatric nurses, 9
Psychiatrists, 8–9
Psychic determinism, 237
Psychoanalysis, 44–45, 232–245, 247, 248
basic concepts, 52
clinical applications

analytic interpretations, 244–245
dreams, analysis, 242
everyday behavior, analysis, 242
free association, 240–241
history and case formulation, 239–240
resistance, analysis, 243
therapist, role of, 241–242
transference, analysis, 242–243
goals of, 238–239
theoretical foundations
defense mechanisms, 234–236
Freud's personality theory, 233–234
interpretation, work through, and insight, 237–238
psychic determinism, 237
resistance, 237
transference and countertransference, 236–237
Psychoanalytically oriented psychotherapy, 246–247
Psychodynamic approach, to clinical psychology
Freudian psychoanalysis, 49–52
cathartic method, 49
defense mechanism, 51–52, 234–236
mental structure, 51
Psychodynamic Diagnostic Manual, 84
Psychodynamic psychotherapy, 245
Adler's individual psychology, 247–248
common features and variations in therapies, 250–251
current status of, 251–252
ego psychology, 248
object relations and self-psychology, 248
psychoanalytically oriented psychotherapy, 246–247
relational psychodynamic approaches, 249
short-term dynamic psychotherapy, 249–250

Psychoeducational groups, 306
Psychological Abstracts, 14
Psychological Assessment, 14
Psychological Assessment Work Group (PAWG), 199
Psychological autopsies, 462–463
The Psychological Clinic, 31
Psychology of litigation, 448
Psychometric properties, of assessment instruments
bandwidth-fidelity issues, 102–103
reliability, 100–101
standardization, 102
validity, 101
Psychoneuroimmunology, 402
Psychopathology tests, 183–190
Millon Clinical Multiaxial Inventory (MCMI), 188
Minnesota Multiphasic Personality Inventory (MMPI), 184–188, 199, 466
tests measuring specific aspects of, 188–189
Psychosomatic Medicine, 397
Psychotherapeutics, 34
Psychotherapy
case formulation and treatment planning, 226–228
definition of, 204
drug treatment and, 354
ethical concerns in
competency, 223–224
confidentiality, 222
conflict of interest, 223
informed consent, 223
integration, 24, 327–328
kinds of approaches, 206–207
participants in, 207–215
clients, 207–210, 350–351
therapeutic relationship, 213–215, 351
therapists, 210–213, 350
public misperception of, 205–206
record keeping in, 225
settings for, 215–216
inpatient settings, 216
outpatient settings, 215–216
termination of, 229
therapist objectivity and self-disclosure, 228–229

treatment duration and fees, 225

Psychotherapy integration, 24, 327–328

Psychotherapy Relationships That Work, 350

PsyD degree, 4, 7, 24, 28, 47, 476, 481–483, 485, 507, 514–519, 523, 526, 537

R

Rapport, building and maintaining, 134, 135

Rational-emotive behavior therapy (REBT), 59, 60, 286–287

Raven's Progressive Matrices, 180

Rayner, Rosalie, 55, 56

Real self-concept, 254

Reattribution training, 290–291

Reciprocal inhibition, 273

Record Keeping Guidelines (APA), 225

Referral question, 74, 75

Referral source, 74

Reflection strategy, 132, 257

Rehabilitation Act of 1973, 499

Reinforcement trap, 365

Relapse prevention treatment, 294

Relational psychodynamic psychotherapy, 249

Reliability, 100–101, 139–140, 154, 172, 196–198

Repeated scanning and focusing, 133

Research on clinical intervention
effectiveness of alternative modes of intervention, 351–355
effectiveness of individual psychotherapy, 341
box score reviews, 342
client satisfaction surveys, 343
common or nonspecific factors in therapy, 349–351
empirically supported treatments (ESTs), 343–347
evidence-based practice (EBT), 347–349
meta-analytic studies, 342–343

methods for evaluating psychotherapy, 332–337
between-subject designs, 333, 336–337
designing outcome studies, 333
within-subject designs, 333–336
practical problems in, 337–341
internal and external validity, 338–341
necessary compromises in research, 341

Resilience process, 318, 369, 371, 508

Resistance reactions, 237

Response prevention techniques, 275–276, 279

Reversal/ABAB design, 334

Risk factors, 365–368

Roberts Apperception Test for Children (RATC), 195

Rogers, Carl, 53–55
conditions of worth, 54, 254, 255
person-centered therapy, 253–262
qualities of therapist, 210
reflection strategy, 132
role of therapist, 54
self-actualization, 53–54
therapeutic relationship, 214

Rokeach Value Survey (RVS), 182, 183

Role-playing tests, 150–152

Rorschach Inkblot Test, 43, 191–193, 374

Rosenzweig Picture-Frustration Study, 195

Rotter Incomplete Sentences Blank, 195

Routine Assessment of Patient Progress (RAPP), 148

Rush, Benjamin, 40

S

Salaries, 19–21, 521, 529

Salt Lake City Conference, 480–481

Schedule of Affective Disorders and Schizophrenia, 125

Schedule of Recent Experiences (SRE), 402

Schizophrenia, neuropsychological approaches to, 441–442

Scholastic Aptitude Test (SAT), 181

School observations, 148, 375

School psychologists, 8

Scientist–practitioner model, 23, 481, 483

Seashore Measures of Musical Talents, 182

Secondary prevention, of psychological disorders, 318, 319

Selective mental health prevention, 318

Self-actualization, 53–54

Self-administered treatments, 322

Self-Directed Search (SDS), 182

Self-help groups, effectiveness of, 354

Self-help interventions, 320–322

Self-observation, 149

Self-psychology, 248, 249

Semistructured interviews, 124, 374

Separation counseling, 309

Sexual abuse, 367

Short-term dynamic psychotherapy, 249–250

Simultanagnosia, 432–433

Sixteen Personality Factors Questionnaire (16PF), 189

Social skills training, 276

Social workers, 8

Society of Clinical Child and Adolescent Psychology, 529

Socratic questioning, 289–290

Specific Affect Coding System (SPAFF), 150

Spirituality, 324–325

Split-brain research, 425, 429, 430

Split-half reliability, 100, 179

Spurzheim, Johann, 35, 423

Staged naturalistic event, 151

Standard error of measurement (SEM), 101

Standardization
of assessment instruments, 102
for KABC-II, 180
of psychological testing, 161, 165–166

...us for Educational and
Psychological Testing
(APA), 99, 112, 170
...anford-Binet fifth edition (SB5),
175–176
Statistical prediction, 94–97
Sternberg Triarchic Abilities Test
(STAT), 174
Stimulus generalization, 270
Stress, 320, 399
immune system and, 401–402
nervous system and, 399–401
alarm reactions, 399
stage of exhaustion, 400
stage of resistance, 399
Stressors, 63, 320, 399, 400, 401
coping strategies, 402–403
measuring, 402
role, in cardiovascular disease,
407–408
Stress reactions, 399, 401
Strong Interest Inventory (SII),
182
Strong Vocational Interest Test, 43
Structured Clinical Interview for
DSM-IV Disorders (SCID),
125, 126
Structured interviews, 124–128,
373
Study of Values (SoV), 182, 183
Superego, 51, 54, 234
Supportive–expressive
continuum, 250–251
Systematic desensitization (SD),
153, 273–274, 279
Systematic Treatment Selection
(STS), 226–228

T
Tachistoscope, 425, 440
Task Force on Promotion and
Dissemination of
Psychological Procedures,
344–347
Technical integration, 328
Technological innovations, in
psychological treatment,
325–327
Temperament, 365–366
Temporal lobe dysfunctions,
433–434
Terman, Lewis, 37, 38, 175
Termination interviews, 119–120

Tertiary prevention, of
psychological disorders,
318, 319
Testing, in clinical psychology,
160
cultural fairness and bias in,
167–169
current status of, 198–200
definition of, 161–162
ethical standards, 169–171
expansion of, 42–43
future of, 200–201
intellectual functioning, tests,
173–182
aptitude and achievement
tests, 180–182
Binet scales, 174–177
intelligence, theories of,
173–174
other intelligence tests, 180
Wechsler scales, 177–179
measurement of, 162–163
personality tests, 183–184,
190–198
psychological testing versus
medical testing, 199
psychopathology tests,
183–190
test construction procedures,
163–166
analytical approach, 164
empirical approach,
164–165
sequential system approach,
165
test of attitude, interests,
preferences, and values,
182–183
test scores, distortion in,
166–167
test usage, patterns of, 171–173
Test-retest reliability, 100, 139,
140, 154, 172, 373, 378
Thematic Apperception Test
(TAT), 43, 193–195, 374
Theoretical integration, 328
Therapeutic alliance, 351, 390
research on, 214–215
varying views of, 214
Therapeutic Bond Scales, 215
Therapist, in psychotherapy
challenges of therapeutic
work, 212–213

communication skills, 210
ethical concerns in, 221–223,
224
relationship-building skills, 210
self-disclosure, 228–229
self-monitoring skills, 211
training and experiences of,
212
variables, 350
Therapist-based treatment, 226
Tort actions, 459
Traineeships, 545
Transference, 236–237, 242–243
Transference neurosis, 242
Treatment planning, 86–87,
226–228
Treatment utility, 199
Triangulation, 312, 366
Triarchic theory, 174
True negative outcome, 90
True positive outcome, 90
Tuke, William, 40
Type-A behavior pattern, in
coronary heart disease,
408

U
Unconditional positive regard,
210, 254, 255–256, 258
Underutilization, of mental
health care, 121
Uniform Guidelines on Employee
Selection Procedure, 170
Universal mental health
prevention, 318
Unmailed letter technique, 263
Unstructured interviews, 128,
140, 373
Utility, 172, 199–200
Utilization review, 501

V
Vail Conference, 480
Vail model, 24
Validity, 101–102, 140–141, 155,
172, 196–199, 338
Values in Action (VIA)
Classification of
Strengths: The un-DSM
and the Real DSM, 84
Vanderbilt Psychotherapy
Process Scale, 214
Vicarious conditioning, 270

Virtual reality assessment, 152–153
Virtual reality (VR) exposure treatment, 152–153, 275, 279
Vulnerability model of schizophrenia, 63–64

W
Watson, John B., 55, 56
Weber, Ernst, 31, 33
Wechsler Adult Intelligence Scale (WAIS), 177–178, 179

Wechsler-Bellevue (W-B) Intelligence Scale, 43, 177
Wechsler Individual Achievement Test (WIAT), 181
Wechsler Intelligence Scale for Children (WISC), 177, 178–179, 374
Wechsler Preschool and Primary Scale of Intelligence (WPPSI), 177, 178–179
Wide Range Achievement Test (WRAT-3), 181
Wiener, Norbert, 57–58

Within-subject research designs, 333–336
Witmer, Lightner, 31–34
Woodcock-Johnson Cognitive Battery III, 181, 374
Word-association test (Galton), 36, 190
Word Association Test (Jung), 43
Workers' compensation law, 460
Working Alliance Inventory, 214
Wundt, Wilhelm, 31, 33

Y
Yerkes, Robert, 42